COLLINS
POCKET
ITALIAN
DICTIONARY

ITALIAN·ENGLISH   ENGLISH·ITALIAN

HarperCollins*Publishers*

First published in this edition 1990

© William Collins Sons & Co. Ltd. 1990

Latest reprint 1993

ISBN 0 00 433249 0 (vinyl)
ISBN 0 00 470309 X (hardback)

---

editors/redazione
Catherine E. Love   Michela Clari

assistant editor/segreteria di redazione
Anne Bradley

supplement/supplemento
Roy Simon
reproduced by kind permission of
Tayside Region Education Department

Printed in Great Britain by
HarperCollins Manufacturing, Glasgow

INTRODUCTION

Produced for today's learner and user of Italian, this is a dictionary adapted to the requirements of the 1990's.

The new colour format introduces a more user-friendly approach to word search, and a wealth of modern and idiomatic phrases not normally found in a volume this size.

In addition, the supplement contains a variety of entertaining ways to improve your dictionary skills, and to help you to get the most out of the bilingual dictionary.

We hope you will enjoy using it and that it will significantly enhance your language studies.

aggettivo	adj	adjective
abbreviazione	abbr	abbreviation
avverbio	adv	adverb
amministrazione	ADMIN	administration
aeronautica, viaggi aerei	AER	flying, air travel
aggettivo	ag	adjective
agricoltura	AGR	agriculture
amministrazione	AMM	administration
anatomia	ANAT	anatomy
architettura	ARCHIT	architecture
articolo definito	art def	definite article
articolo indefinito	art indef	indefinite article
attributivo	attrib	attributive
ausiliare	aus, aux	auxiliary
l'automobile	AUT	the motor car and motoring
avverbio	av	adverb
aeronautica, viaggi aerei	AVIAT	flying, air travel
biologia	BIOL	biology
botanica	BOT	botany
inglese della Gràn Bretagna	BRIT	British English
consonante	C	consonant
chimica	CHIM, CHEM	chemistry
commercio, finanza, banca	COMM	commerce, finance, banking
informatica	COMPUT	computers
comparativo	compar	comparative
congiunzione	cong, conj	conjunction
edilizia	CONSTR	building
sostantivo usato come aggettivo, non può essere usato né come attributo, né dopo il sostantivo qualificato	cpd	compound element: noun used as adjective and which cannot follow the noun it qualifies
cucina	CUC, CULIN	cookery
davanti a	dav	before
articolo definito	def art	definite article
determinativo: articolo, aggettivo dimostrativo o indefinito etc	det	determiner: article, demonstrative etc
diminutivo	dimin	diminutive
diritto	DIR	law
economia	ECON	economics
edilizia	EDIL	building
elettricità, elettronica	ELETTR, ELEC	electricity, electronics
esclamazione	escl, excl	exclamation

iv

ABBREVIAZIONI

ABBREVIATIONS

femminile	f	feminine
familiare (! da evitare)	fam(!)	colloquial usage (! particularly offensive)
ferrovia	FERR	railways
figurato	fig	figurative use
fisiologia	FISIOL	physiology
fotografia	FOT	photography
(verbo inglese) la cui particella è inseparabile dal verbo	fus	(phrasal verb) where the particle cannot be separated from main verb
nella maggior parte dei sensi; generalmente	gen	in most or all senses; generally
geografia, geologia	GEO	geography, geology
geometria	GEOM	geometry
impersonale	impers	impersonal
articolo indefinito	indef art	indefinite article
familiare (! da evitare)	inf(!)	colloquial usage (! particularly offensive)
infinito	infin	infinitive
informatica	INFORM	computers
insegnamento, sistema scolastico e universitario	INS	schooling, schools and universities
invariabile	inv	invariable
irregolare	irreg	irregular
grammatica, linguistica	LING	grammar, linguistics
maschile	m	masculine
matematica	MAT(H)	mathematics
termine medico, medicina	MED	medical term, medicine
il tempo, meteorologia	METEOR	the weather, meteorology
maschile o femminile, secondo il sesso	m/f	either masculine or feminine depending on sex
esercito, lingua militare	MIL	military matters
musica	MUS	music
sostantivo	n	noun
nautica	NAUT	sailing, navigation
numerale (aggettivo, sostantivo)	num	numeral adjective or noun
	o.s.	oneself
peggiorativo	peg, pej	derogatory, pejorative
fotografia	PHOT	photography
fisiologia	PHYSIOL	physiology
plurale	pl	plural
politica	POL	politics
participio passato	pp	past participle

v

ABBREVIAZIONI

ABBREVIATIONS

preposizione	prep	preposition
pronome	pron	pronoun
psicologia, psichiatria	PSIC, PSYCH	psychology, psychiatry
tempo passato	pt	past tense
qualcosa	qc	
qualcuno	qn	
religione, liturgia	REL	religions, church service
sostantivo	s	noun
	sb	somebody
insegnamento, sistema scolastico e universitario	SCOL	schooling, schools and universities
singolare	sg	singular
soggetto (grammaticale)	sog	(grammatical) subject
	sth	something
congiuntivo	sub	subjunctive
soggetto (grammaticale)	subj	(grammatical) subject
superlativo	superl	superlative
termine tecnico, tecnologia	TECN, TECH	technical term, technology
telecomunicazioni	TEL	telecommunications
tipografia	TIP	typography, printing
televisione	TV	television
tipografia	TYP	typography, printing
inglese degli Stati Uniti	US	American English
vocale	V	vowel
verbo	vb	verb
verbo o gruppo verbale con funzione intransitiva	vi	verb or phrasal verb used intransitively
verbo riflessivo	vr	reflexive verb
verbo o gruppo verbale con funzione transitiva	vt	verb or phrasal verb used transitively
zoologia	ZOOL	zoology
marchio registrato	®	registered trademark
introduce un'equivalenza culturale	≈	introduces a cultural equivalent

TRASCRIZIONE FONETICA

PHONETIC TRANSCRIPTION

CONSONANTS CONSONANTI

NB The pairing of some vowel sounds only indicates approximate equivalence/La messa in equivalenza di certi suoni indica solo una rassomiglianza approssimativa.

puppy	p	*padre*
baby	b	*bambino*
tent	t	*tutto*
daddy	d	*dado*
cork kiss chord	k	*cane che*
gag guess	g	*gola ghiro*
so rice kiss	s	*sano*
cousin buzz	z	*svago esame*
sheep sugar	ʃ	*scena*
pleasure beige	ʒ	
church	tʃ	*pece lanciare*
judge general	dʒ	*giro gioco*
farm raffle	f	*afa faro*
very rev	v	*vero bravo*
thin maths	θ	
that other	ð	
little ball	l	*letto ala*
	ʎ	*gli*
rat brat	r	*rete arco*
mummy comb	m	*ramo madre*
no ran	n	*no fumante*
	ɲ	*gnomo*
singing bank	ŋ	
hat reheat	h	
yet	j	*buio piacere*
wall bewail	w	*uomo guaio*
loch	x	

VOWELS VOCALI

NB **p, b, t, d, k, g** are not aspirated in Italian/sono seguiti da un'aspirazione in inglese.

heel bead	iː i	*vino idea*
hit pity	ɪ	
	e	*stella edera*
set tent	ɛ	*epoca eccetto*
apple bat	æ a	*mamma amore*
after car calm	ɑː	
fun cousin	ʌ	
over above	ə	
urn fern work	əː	
wash pot	ɔ	*rosa occhio*
born cork	ɔː	
	o	*ponte ognuno*
full soot	u	*utile zucca*
boon lewd	uː	

DIPHTHONGS DITTONGHI

ɪə	*beer tier*
ɛə	*tear fair there*
eɪ	*date plaice day*
aɪ	*life buy cry*
au	*owl foul now*
əu	*low no*
ɔɪ	*boil boy oily*
uə	*poor tour*

MISCELLANEOUS

VARIE

*per l'inglese: la "r" finale viene pronunciata se seguita da una vocale.
'precedes the stressed syllable/precede la sillaba accentata.

ITALIAN PRONUNCIATION

VOWELS

Where the vowel **e** or the vowel **o** appears in a stressed syllable it can be either open [ɛ], [ɔ] or closed [e], [o]. As the open or closed pronunciation of these vowels is subject to regional variation, the distinction is of little importance to the user of this dictionary. Phonetic transcription for headwords containing these vowels will therefore only appear where other pronunciation difficulties are present.

CONSONANTS

c before "e" or "i" is pronounced *tch*.

ch is pronounced like the "k" in "kit".

g before "e" or "i" is pronounced like the "j" in "jet".

gh is pronounced like the "g" in "get".

gl before "e" or "i" is normally pronounced like the "lli" in "million", and in a few cases only like the "gl" in "glove".

gn is pronounced like the "ny" in "canyon".

sc before "e" or "i" is pronounced *sh*.

z is pronounced like the "ts" in "stetson", or like the "d's" in "bird's-eye".

Headwords containing the above consonants and consonantal groups have been given full phonetic transcription in this dictionary.

NB All double written consonants in Italian are fully sounded: eg. the *tt* in "tutto" is pronounced as in "ha*t t*rick".

ITALIAN VERBS

1 Gerundio *2* Participio passato *3* Presente *4* Imperfetto *5* Passato remoto *6* Futuro *7* Condizionale *8* Congiuntivo presente *9* Congiuntivo passato *10* Imperativo

andare *3* vado, vai, va, andiamo, andate, vanno *6* andrò *etc* *8* vada *10* va'!, vada!, andate!, vadano!

apparire *3* apparso *3* appaio, appari *o* apparisci, appare *o* apparisce, appaiono *o* appariscono *5* apparvi *o* apparsi, apparisti, apparve *o* apparì *o* apparse, apparvero *o* apparirono *o* apparsero *8* appaia *o* apparisca

aprire *2* aperto *3* apro *5* aprii *o* apersi, apristi *8* apra

AVERE *3* ho, hai, ha, abbiamo, avete, hanno *5* ebbi, avesti, ebbe, avemmo, aveste, ebbero *6* avrò *etc* *8* abbia *10* abbi!, abbia!, abbiate!, abbiano!

bere *1* bevendo *2* bevuto *3* bevo *etc* *4* bevevo *etc* *8* beva *etc* *9* bevessi *etc*

cadere *5* caddi, cadesti *6* cadrò *etc*

cogliere *2* colto *3* colgo, colgono *5* colsi, cogliesti *8* colga

correre *2* corso *5* corsi, corresti

cuocere *2* cotto *3* cuocio, cociamo, cuociono *5* cossi, cocesti

dare *3* do, dai, dà, diamo, date, danno *5* diedi *o* detti, desti *6* darò *etc* *8* dia *etc* *9* dessi *etc* *10* da'!, dia!, date!, diano!

dire *1* dicendo *2* detto *3* dico, dici, dice, diciamo, dite, dicono *4* dicevo *etc* *5* dissi, dicesti *6* dirò *etc* *8* dica, diciamo, diciate, dicano *9* dicessi *etc* *10* di'!, dica!, dite!, dicano!

dolere *3* dolgo, duoli, duole, dolgono *5* dolsi, dolesti *6* dorrò *etc* *8* dolga

dovere *3* devo *o* debbo, devi, deve, dobbiamo, dovete, devono *o* debbono *6* dovrò *etc* *8* debba, dobbiamo, dobbiate, devano *o* debbano

ESSERE *2* stato *3* sono, sei, è, siamo, siete, sono *4* ero, eri, era, eravamo, eravate, erano *5* fui, fosti, fu, fummo, foste, furono *6* sarò *etc* *8* sia *etc* *9* fossi, fossi, fosse, fossimo, foste, fossero *10* sii!, sia!, siate!, siano!

fare *1* facendo *2* fatto *3* faccio, fai, fa, facciamo, fate, fanno *4* facevo *etc* *5* feci, facesti *6* farò *etc* *8* faccia *9* facessi *etc* *10* fa'!, faccia!, fate!, facciano!

FINIRE *1* finendo *2* finito *3* finisco, finisci, finisce, finiamo, finite, finiscono *4* finivo, finivi, finiva, finivamo, finivate, finivano *5* finii, finisti, finì, finimmo, finiste, finirono *6* finirò, finirai, finirà, finiremo, finirete, finiranno *7* finirei, finiresti, finirebbe, finiremmo, finireste, finirebbero *8* finisca, finisca, finisca, finiamo, finiate, finiscano *9* finissi, finissi, finisse, finissimo, finiste, finissero *10* finisci!, finisca!, finite!, finiscano!

giungere *2* giunto *5* giunsi, giungesti

leggere *2* letto *5* lessi, leggesti

mettere *2* messo *5* misi, mettesti

morire *2* morto *3* muoio, muori, muore, moriamo, morite, muoiono *6* morirò *o* morrò *etc* *8* muoia

muovere *2* mosso *5* mossi, movesti

nascere *2* nato *5* nacqui, nascesti

nuocere *2* nuociuto *3* nuoccio, nuoci, nuoce, nociamo *o* nuociamo, nuocete, nuocciono *4* nuocevo *etc* *5* nocqui, nuocesti *6* nuocerò *etc* *7* nuoccia

offrire *2* offerto *3* offro *5* offersi *o* offrii, offristi *8* offra

parere *2* parso *3* paio, paiamo, paiono *5* parvi *o* parsi, paresti *6* parrò *etc* *8* paia, paiamo, paiate, paiano

PARLARE *1* parlando *2* parlato *3* parlo, parli, parla, parliamo, parlate, parlano *4* parlavo, parlavi, parlava, parlavamo, parlavate, parlavano *5* parlai, parlasti, parlò, parlammo, parlaste, parlarono *6* parlerò, parlerai, parlerà, parleremo, parlerete, parleranno *7* parlerei, parleresti, parlerebbe, parleremmo, parlereste, parlerebbero *8* parli, parli, parli, parliamo, parliate, parlino *9* parlassi, parlassi, parlasse, parlassimo, parlaste, parlassero *10* parla!, parli!, parlate!, parlino!

piacere *2* piaciuto *3* piaccio, piacciamo, piacciono *5* piacqui, piacesti *8* piaccia *etc*

porre *1* ponendo *2* posto *3* pongo, poni, pone, poniamo, ponete, pongono *4* ponevo *etc* *5* posi, ponesti *6* porrò *etc* *8* ponga, poniamo, poniate, pongano *9* ponessi *etc*

potere *3* posso, puoi, può, possiamo, potete, possono *6* potrò *etc* *8* possa, possiamo, possiate, possano

prendere *2* preso *5* presi, prendesti

ridurre *1* riducendo *2* ridotto *3* riduco *etc* *4* riducevo *etc* *5* ridussi, riducesti *6* ridurrò *etc* *8* riduca *etc* *9* riducessi *etc*

riempire *1* riempiendo *3* riempio, riempi, riempie, riempiono

rimanere *2* rimasto *3* rimango, rimangono *5* rimasi, rimanesti *6* rimarrò *etc* *8* rimanga

rispondere *2* risposto *5* risposi, rispondesti

salire *3* salgo, sali, salgono *8* salga

sapere *3* so, sai, sa, sappiamo, sapete, sanno *5* seppi, sapesti *6* saprò *etc* *8* sappia *etc* *10* sappi!, sappia!, sappiate!, sappiano!

scrivere *2* scritto *5* scrissi, scrivesti

sedere *3* siedo, siedi, siede, siedono *8* sieda

spegnere *2* spento *3* spengo, spengono *5*

spensi, spegnesti 8 spenga

stare 2 stato 3 sto, stai, sta, stiamo, state, stanno 5 stetti, stesti 6 starò *etc* 8 stia *etc* 9 stessi *etc* 10 sta'!, stia!, state!, stiano!

tacere 2 taciuto 3 taccio, tacciono 5 tacqui, tacesti 8 taccia

tenere 3 tengo, tieni, tiene, tengono 5 tenni, tenesti 6 terrò *etc* 8 tenga

trarre 1 traendo 2 tratto 3 traggo, trai, trae, traiamo, traete, traggono 4 traevo *etc* 5 trassi, traesti 6 trarrò *etc* 8 tragga 9 traessi *etc*

udire 3 odo, odi, ode, odono 8 oda

uscire 3 esco, esci, esce, escono 8 esca

valere 2 valso 3 valgo, valgono 5 valsi, valesti 6 varrò *etc* 8 valga

vedere 2 visto *o* veduto 5 vidi, vedesti 6 vedrò *etc*

VENDERE 1 vendendo 2 venduto 3 vendo, vendi, vende, vendiamo, vendete, vendono 4 vendevo, vendevi, vendeva, vendevamo, vendevate, vendevano 5 vendei *o* vendetti, vendesti, vendé *o* vendette, vendemmo, vendeste, venderono *o* vendettero 6 venderò, venderai, venderà, venderemo, venderete, venderanno 7 venderei, venderesti, venderebbe, venderemmo, vendereste, venderebbero 8 venda, venda, venda, vendiamo, vendiate, vendano 9 vendessi, vendessi, vendesse, vendessimo, vendeste, vendessero 10 vendi!, venda!, vendete!, vendano!

venire 2 venuto 3 vengo, vieni, viene, vengono 5 venni, venisti 6 verrò *etc* 8 venga

vivere 2 vissuto 5 vissi, vivesti

volere 3 voglio, vuoi, vuole, vogliamo, volete, vogliono 5 volli, volesti 6 vorrò *etc* 8 voglia *etc* 10 vogli!, voglia!, vogliate!, vogliano!

VERBI INGLESI

present	pt	pp	present	pt	pp
arise	arose	arisen	find	found	found
awake	awoke	awaked	flee	fled	fled
be (am, is, are; being)	was, were	been	fling	flung	flung
			fly (flies)	flew	flown
bear	bore	born(e)	forbid	forbade	forbidden
beat	beat	beaten	forecast	forecast	forecast
become	became	become	forego	forewent	foregone
begin	began	begun	foresee	foresaw	foreseen
behold	beheld	beheld	foretell	foretold	foretold
bend	bent	bent	forget	forgot	forgotten
beseech	besought	besought	forgive	forgave	forgiven
beset	beset	beset	forsake	forsook	forsaken
bet	bet, betted	bet, betted	freeze	froze	frozen
bid	bid, bade	bid, bidden	get	got	got, (US) gotten
bind	bound	bound	give	gave	given
bite	bit	bitten	go (goes)	went	gone
bleed	bled	bled	grind	ground	ground
blow	blew	blown	grow	grew	grown
break	broke	broken	hang	hung, hanged	hung, hanged
breed	bred	bred	have (has; having)	had	had
bring	brought	brought			
build	built	built	hear	heard	heard
burn	burnt, burned	burnt, burned	hide	hid	hidden
burst	burst	burst	hit	hit	hit
buy	bought	bought	hold	held	held
can	could	(been able)	hurt	hurt	hurt
cast	cast	cast	keep	kept	kept
catch	caught	caught	kneel	knelt, kneeled	knelt, kneeled
choose	chose	chosen	know	knew	known
cling	clung	clung	lay	laid	laid
come	came	come	lead	led	led
cost	cost	cost	lean	leant, leaned	leant, leaned
creep	crept	crept	leap	leapt, leaped	leapt, leaped
cut	cut	cut	learn	learnt, learned	learnt, learned
deal	dealt	dealt	leave	left	left
dig	dug	dug	lend	lent	lent
do (3rd person; he/she/it does)	did	done	let	let	let
			lie (lying)	lay	lain
			light	lit, lighted	lit, lighted
draw	drew	drawn	lose	lost	lost
dream	dreamed, dreamt	dreamed, dreamt	make	made	made
			may	might	—
drink	drank	drunk	mean	meant	meant
drive	drove	driven	meet	met	met
dwell	dwelt	dwelt	mistake	mistook	mistaken
eat	ate	eaten	mow	mowed	mown, mowed
fall	fell	fallen	must	(had to)	(had to)
feed	fed	fed	pay	paid	paid
feel	felt	felt	put	put	put
fight	fought	fought	quit	quit, quitted	quit, quitted
			read	read	read

present	pt	pp	present	pt	pp
rid	rid	rid	split	split	split
ride	rode	ridden	spoil	spoiled, spoilt	spoiled, spoilt
ring	rang	rung	spread	spread	spread
rise	rose	risen	spring	sprang	sprung
run	ran	run	stand	stood	stood
saw	sawed	sawn	steal	stole	stolen
say	said	said	stick	stuck	stuck
see	saw	seen	sting	stung	stung
seek	sought	sought	stink	stank	stunk
sell	sold	sold	stride	strode	stridden
send	sent	sent	strike	struck	struck, stricken
set	set	set	strive	strove	striven
shake	shook	shaken	swear	swore	sworn
shall	should	—	sweep	swept	swept
shear	sheared	shorn, sheared	swell	swelled	swollen, swelled
shed	shed	shed	swim	swam	swum
shine	shone	shone	swing	swung	swung
shoot	shot	shot	take	took	taken
show	showed	shown	teach	taught	taught
shrink	shrank	shrunk	tear	tore	torn
shut	shut	shut	tell	told	told
sing	sang	sung	think	thought	thought
sink	sank	sunk	throw	threw	thrown
sit	sat	sat	thrust	thrust	thrust
slay	slew	slain	tread	trod	trodden
sleep	slept	slept	wake	woke, waked	woken, waked
slide	slid	slid	waylay	waylaid	waylaid
sling	slung	slung	wear	wore	worn
slit	slit	slit	weave	wove, weaved	woven, weaved
smell	smelt, smelled	smelt, smelled	wed	wedded, wed	wedded, wed
sow	sowed	sown, sowed	weep	wept	wept
speak	spoke	spoken	win	won	won
speed	sped, speeded	sped, speeded	wind	wound	wound
spell	spelt, spelled	spelt, spelled	withdraw	withdrew	withdrawn
spend	spent	spent	withhold	withheld	withheld
spill	spilt, spilled	spilt, spilled	withstand	withstood	withstood
spin	spun	spun	wring	wrung	wrung
spit	spat	spat	write	wrote	written

I NUMERI   # NUMBERS

uno(a)	1	one
due	2	two
tre	3	three
quattro	4	four
cinque	5	five
sei	6	six
sette	7	seven
otto	8	eight
nove	9	nine
dieci	10	ten
undici	11	eleven
dodici	12	twelve
tredici	13	thirteen
quattordici	14	fourteen
quindici	15	fifteen
sedici	16	sixteen
diciassette	17	seventeen
diciotto	18	eighteen
diciannove	19	nineteen
venti	20	twenty
ventuno	21	twenty-one
ventidue	22	twenty-two
ventitré	23	twenty-three
ventotto	28	twenty-eight
trenta	30	thirty
quaranta	40	forty
cinquanta	50	fifty
sessanta	60	sixty
settanta	70	seventy
ottanta	80	eighty
novanta	90	ninety
cento	100	a hundred, one hundred
cento uno	101	a hundred and one
duecento	200	two hundred
mille	1 000	a thousand, one thousand
milleduecentodue	1 202	one thousand two hundred and two
cinquemila	5 000	five thousand
un milione	1 000 000	a million, one million

primo(a), 1º	first, 1st
secondo(a), 2º	second, 2nd
terzo(a), 3º	third, 3rd
quarto(a)	fourth, 4th
quinto(a)	fifth, 5th
sesto(a)	sixth, 6th
settimo(a)	seventh
ottavo(a)	eighth
nono(a)	ninth
decimo(a)	tenth
undicesimo(a)	eleventh

I NUMERI

dodicesimo(a)
tredicesimo(a)
quattordicesimo(a)
quindicesimo(a)
sedicesimo(a)
diciassettesimo(a)
diciottesimo(a)
diciannovesimo(a)
ventesimo(a)
ventunesimo(a)
ventiduesimo(a)
ventitreesimo(a)
ventottesimo(a)
trentesimo(a)
centesimo(a)
centunesimo(a)
millesimo(a)
milionesimo(a)

Frazioni etc

mezzo
terzo
due terzi
quarto
quinto
zero virgola cinque, 0,5
tre virgola quattro, 3,4
dieci per cento
cento per cento

Esempi

abita al numero dieci
si trova nel capitolo sette, a pagina
  sette
abita al terzo piano
arrivò quarto
scala uno a venticinquemila

NUMBERS

twelfth
thirteenth
fourteenth
fifteenth
sixteenth
seventeenth
eighteenth
nineteenth
twentieth
twenty-first
twenty-second
twenty-third
twenty-eighth
thirtieth
hundredth
hundred-and-first
thousandth
millionth

Fractions etc

half
third
two thirds
quarter
fifth
(nought) point five, 0.5
three point four, 3.4
ten per cent
a hundred per cent

Examples

he lives at number 10
it's in chapter 7, on page 7

he lives on the 3rd floor
he came in 4th
scale 1:25,000

L'ORA	THE TIME
che ora è?, che ore sono?	*what time is it?*
è ..., sono ...	*it is ...*
mezzanotte	midnight, twelve pm
l'una (della mattina)	one o'clock (in the morning), one (am)
l'una e cinque	five past one
l'una e dieci	ten past one
l'una e un quarto, l'una e quindici	a quarter past one, one fifteen
l'una e venticinque	twenty-five past one, one twenty-five
l'una e mezzo *o* mezza, l'una e trenta	half-past one, one thirty
le due meno venticinque, l'una e trentacinque	twenty-five to two, one thirty-five
le due meno venti, l'una e quaranta	twenty to two, one forty
le due meno un quarto, l'una e quarantacinque	a quarter to two, one forty-five
le due meno dieci, l'una e cinquanta	ten to two, one fifty
mezzogiorno	twelve o'clock, midday, noon
l'una, le tredici	one o'clock (in the afternoon), one (pm)
le sette (di sera), le diciannove	seven o'clock (in the evening), seven (pm)
a che ora?	*at what time?*
a mezzanotte	at midnight
all'una, alle tredici	at one o'clock
fra venti minuti	in twenty minutes
venti minuti fa	twenty minutes ago

ITALIANO - INGLESE
ITALIAN - ENGLISH

A

a (*a+il* = **al**, *a+lo* = **allo**, *a+l'* = **all'**, *a+la* = **alla**, *a+i* = **ai**, *a+gli* = **agli**, *a+le* = **alle**) *prep* **1** (*stato in luogo*) at; (: *in*) in; **essere alla stazione** to be at the station; **essere ~ casa/~ scuola/~ Roma** to be at home/at school/in Rome; **è ~ 10 km da qui** it's 10 km from here, it's 10 km away
2 (*moto a luogo*) to; **andare ~ casa/~ scuola** to go home/to school
3 (*tempo*) at; (*epoca, stagione*) in; **alle cinque** at five (o'clock); **~ mezzanotte/ Natale** at midnight/Christmas; **al mattino** in the morning; **~ maggio/ primavera** in May/spring; **~ cinquant'anni** at fifty (years of age); **~ domani!** see you tomorrow!
4 (*complemento di termine*) to; **dare qc ~ qn** to give sth to sb
5 (*mezzo, modo*) with, by; **~ piedi/ cavallo** on foot/horseback; **fatto ~ mano** made by hand, handmade; **una barca ~ motore** a motorboat; **~ uno ~ uno** one by one; **all'italiana** the Italian way, in the Italian fashion
6 (*rapporto*) a, per; (: *con prezzi*) at; **prendo 500.000 lire al mese** I get 500,000 lire a *o* per month; **pagato ~ ore** paid by the hour; **vendere qc ~ 500 lire il chilo** to sell sth at 500 lire a *o* per kilo.

abbacchi'ato, a [abbak'kjato] *ag* downhearted, in low spirits.
abbagli'ante [abbaʎ'ʎante] *ag* dazzling; **~i** *smpl* (*AUT*): **accendere gli ~i** to put one's headlights on full (*BRIT*) *o* high (*US*) beam.
abbagli'are [abbaʎ'ʎare] *vt* to dazzle; (*illudere*) to delude; **ab'baglio** *sm* blunder; **prendere un abbaglio** to

blunder, make a blunder.
abbai'are *vi* to bark.
abba'ino *sm* dormer window; (*soffitta*) attic room.
abbando'nare *vt* to leave, abandon, desert; (*trascurare*) to neglect; (*rinunciare a*) to abandon, give up; **~rsi** *vr* to let o.s. go; **~rsi a** (*ricordi, vizio*) to give o.s. up to; **abban'dono** *sm* abandonment; neglect; (*SPORT*) withdrawal; (*fig*) abandon; **in abban- dono** (*edificio, giardino*) neglected.
abbas'sare *vt* to lower; (*radio*) to turn down; **~rsi** *vr* (*chinarsi*) to stoop; (*livello, sole*) to go down; (*fig: umiliarsi*) to demean o.s.; **~ i fari** (*AUT*) to dip *o* dim (*US*) one's lights.
ab'basso *escl*: **~ il re!** down with the king!
abbas'tanza [abbas'tantsa] *av* (*a sufficienza*) enough; (*alquanto*) quite, rather, fairly; **non è ~ furbo** he's not shrewd enough; **un vino ~ dolce** quite a sweet wine, a fairly sweet wine; **averne ~ di qn/qc** to have had enough of sb/sth.
ab'battere *vt* (*muro, casa*) to pull down; (*ostacolo*) to knock down; (*albero*) to fell; (: *sog: vento*) to bring down; (*bestie da macello*) to slaughter; (*cane, cavallo*) to destroy, put down; (*selvaggina, aereo*) to shoot down; (*fig: sog: malattia, disgrazia*) to lay low; **~rsi** *vr* (*avvilirsi*) to lose heart; **abbat'tuto, a** *ag* (*fig*) depressed.
abba'zia [abbat'tsia] *sf* abbey.
abbecc'dario [abbetʃe'darjo] *sm* primer.
abbel'lire *vt* to make beautiful; (*ornare*) to embellish.
abbeve'rare *vt* to water; **~rsi** *vr* to drink.
'abbia *etc vb vedi* **avere**.
abbicci [abbit'tʃi] *sm inv* alphabet;

(*sillabario*) primer; (*fig*) rudiments *pl*.

abbi'ente *ag* well-to-do, well-off.

abbi'etto, a *ag* = abietto.

abbiglia'mento [abbiʎʎa'mento] *sm* dress *no pl*; (*indumenti*) clothes *pl*; (*industria*) clothing industry.

abbigli'are [abbiʎ'ʎare] *vt* to dress up.

abbi'nare *vt*: ~ (**a**) to combine (with).

abbindo'lare *vt* (*fig*) to cheat, trick.

abbocca'mento *sm* talks *pl*, meeting.

abboc'care *vt* (*tubi, canali*) to connect, join up ♦ *vi* (*pesce*) to bite; (*tubi*) to join; ~ (**all'amo**) (*fig*) to swallow the bait.

abboc'cato, a *ag* (*vino*) sweetish.

abbona'mento *sm* subscription; (*alle ferrovie etc*) season ticket; **fare l'~** to take out a subscription (*o* season ticket).

abbo'narsi *vr*: ~ **a un giornale** to take out a subscription to a newspaper; ~ **al teatro/alle ferrovie** to take out a season ticket for the theatre/the train; **abbo'nato, a** *sm/f* subscriber; season-ticket holder.

abbon'dante *ag* abundant, plentiful; (*giacca*) roomy.

abbon'danza [abbon'dantsa] *sf* abundance; plenty.

abbon'dare *vi* to abound, be plentiful; ~ **in** *o* **di** to be full of, abound in.

abbor'dabile *ag* (*persona*) approach-able; (*prezzo*) reasonable.

abbor'dare *vt* (*nave*) to board; (*persona*) to approach; (*argomento*) to tackle; ~ **una curva** to take a bend.

abbotto'nare *vt* to button up, do up.

abboz'zare [abbot'tsare] *vt* to sketch, outline; (*SCULTURA*) to rough-hew; ~ **un sorriso** to give a hint of a smile; **ab'bozzo** *sm* sketch, outline; (*DIR*) draft.

abbracci'are [abbrat'tʃare] *vt* to embrace; (*persona*) to hug, embrace; (*professione*) to take up; (*contenere*) to include; ~**rsi** *vr* to hug *o* embrace (one another); **ab'braccio** *sm* hug, embrace.

abbreviazi'one [abbrevjat'tsjone] *sf* abbreviation.

abbron'zante [abbron'dzante] *ag*

tanning, sun *cpd*.

abbron'zare [abbron'dzare] *vt* (*pelle*) to tan; (*metalli*) to bronze; ~**rsi** *vr* to tan, get a tan; **abbronza'tura** *sf* tan, suntan.

abbrusto'lire *vt* (*pane*) to toast; (*caffè*) to roast.

abbru'tire *vt* to exhaust; to degrade.

abbu'ono *sm* (*COMM*) allowance, discount; (*SPORT*) handicap.

abdi'care *vi* to abdicate; ~ **a** to give up, renounce.

aberrazi'one [aberrat'tsjone] *sf* aberration.

a'bete *sm* fir (tree); ~ **rosso** spruce.

abi'etto, a *ag* despicable, abject.

'abile *ag* (*idoneo*): ~ (**a qc/a fare qc**) fit (for sth/to do sth); (*capace*) able; (*astuto*) clever; (*accorto*) skilful; ~ **al servizio militare** fit for military service; **abilità** *sf inv* ability; cleverness; skill.

abili'tato, a *ag* qualified; (*TEL*) which has an outside line; **abilitazi'one** *sf* qualification.

a'bisso *sm* abyss, gulf.

abi'tacolo *sm* (*AER*) cockpit; (*AUT*) inside; (: *di camion*) cab.

abi'tante *sm/f* inhabitant.

abi'tare *vt* to live in, dwell in ♦ *vi*: ~ **in campagna/a Roma** to live in the country/in Rome; ~ **abi'tato, a** *ag* inhabited; lived in ♦ *sm* (*anche: centro abitato*) built-up area; **abitazi'one** *sf* residence; house.

'abito *sm* dress *no pl*; (*da uomo*) suit; (*da donna*) dress; (*abitudine, disposizione, REL*) habit; ~**i** *smpl* (*vestiti*) clothes; **in ~ da sera** in evening dress.

abitu'ale *ag* usual, habitual; (*cliente*) regular.

abitu'are *vt*: ~ **qn a** to get sb used *o* accustomed to; ~**rsi a** to get used to, accustom o.s. to.

abitudi'nario, a *ag* of fixed habits ♦ *sm/f* regular customer.

abi'tudine *sf* habit; **aver l'~ di fare qc** to be in the habit of doing sth; **d'~** usually; **per ~** from *o* out of habit.

abo'lire *vt* to abolish; (*DIR*) to repeal.

abomi'nevole *ag* abominable.

abo'rigeno [abo'ridʒeno] *sm* aborigine.

abor'rire *vt* to abhor, detest.

abor'tire *vi* (*MED: accidentalmente*) to miscarry, have a miscarriage; (: *deliberatamente*) to have an abortion; (*fig*) to miscarry, fail; **a'borto** *sm* miscarriage; abortion; (*fig*) freak.

abrasi'one *sf* abrasion; **abra'sivo, a** *ag, sm* abrasive.

abro'gare *vt* to repeal, abrogate.

A'bruzzo *sm*: **l'~, gli ~i** the Abruzzi.

'abside *sf* apse.

a'bulico, a, ci, che *ag* lacking in will power.

abu'sare *vi*: **~ di** to abuse, misuse; (*alcool*) to take to excess; (*approfittare, violare*) to take advantage of; **a'buso** *sm* abuse, misuse; excessive use.

a.C. *av abbr* (= *avanti Cristo*) B.C.

'acca *sf* letter H; **non capire un'~** not to understand a thing.

acca'demia *sf* (*società*) learned society; (*scuola: d'arte, militare*) academy; **acca'demico, a, ci, che** *ag* academic ♦ *sm* academician.

acca'dere *vb impers* to happen, occur; **acca'duto** *sm*: **raccontare l'accaduto** to describe what has happened.

accalappi'are *vt* to catch; (*fig*) to trick, dupe.

accal'care *vt* to crowd, throng.

accal'darsi *vr* to grow hot.

accalo'rarsi *vr* (*fig*) to get excited.

accampa'mento *sm* camp.

accam'pare *vt* to encamp; (*fig*) to put forward, advance; **~rsi** *vr* to camp.

accani'mento *sm* fury; (*tenacia*) tenacity, perseverance.

acca'nirsi *vr* (*infierire*) to rage; (*ostinarsi*) to persist; **acca'nito, a** *ag* (*odio, gelosia*) fierce, bitter; (*lavoratore*) assiduous, dogged; (*fumatore*) inveterate.

ac'canto *av* near, nearby; **~ a** *prep* near, beside, close to.

accanto'nare *vt* (*problema*) to shelve; (*somma*) to set aside.

accapar'rare *vt* (*COMM*) to corner, buy up; (*versare una caparra*) to pay a deposit on; **~rsi qc** (*fig: simpatia, voti*) to secure sth (for o.s.).

accapigli'arsi [akkapiʎ'ʎarsi] *vr* to come to blows; (*fig*) to quarrel.

accappa'toio *sm* bathrobe.

accappo'nare *vi*: **far ~ la pelle a qn** (*fig*) to bring sb out in goosepimples.

accarez'zare [akkaret'tsare] *vt* to caress, stroke, fondle; (*fig*) to toy with.

acca'sarsi *vr* to set up house; to get married.

accasci'arsi [akkaʃ'ʃarsi] *vr* to collapse; (*fig*) to lose heart.

accat'tone, a *sm/f* beggar.

accaval'lare *vt* (*gambe*) to cross; **~rsi** *vr* (*sovrapporsi*) to overlap; (*addensarsi*) to gather.

acce'care [attʃe'kare] *vt* to blind ♦ *vi* to go blind.

ac'cedere [at'tʃedere] *vi*: **~ a** to enter; (*richiesta*) to grant, accede to.

accele'rare [attʃele'rare] *vt* to speed up ♦ *vi* (*AUT*) to accelerate; **~ il passo** to quicken one's pace; **accele'rato** *sm* (*FERR*) slow train; **accelera'tore** *sm* (*AUT*) accelerator; **accelerazi'one** *sf* acceleration.

ac'cendere [at'tʃendere] *vt* (*fuoco, sigaretta*) to light; (*luce, televisione*) to put o switch o turn on; (*AUT: motore*) to switch on; (*COMM: conto*) to open; (*fig: suscitare*) to inflame, stir up; **~rsi** *vr* (*luce*) to come o go on; (*legna*) to catch fire, ignite; **accen'dino** *sm*, **accendi'sigaro** *sm* (cigarette) lighter.

accen'nare [attʃen'nare] *vt* to indicate, point out; (*MUS*) to pick out the notes of; to hum ♦ *vi*: **~ a** (*fig: alludere a*) to hint at; (: *far atto di*) to make as if; **~ un saluto** (*con la mano*) to make as if to wave; (*col capo*) to half nod; **accenna a piovere** it looks as if it's going to rain.

ac'cenno [at'tʃenno] *sm* (*cenno*) sign; nod; (*allusione*) hint.

accensi'one [attʃen'sjone] *sf* (*vedi accendere*) lighting; switching on; opening; (*AUT*) ignition.

accen'tare [attʃen'tare] *vt* (*parlando*) to stress; (*scrivendo*) to accent.

ac'cento [at'tʃento] *sm* accent;

(*FONETICA*, *fig*) stress; (*inflessione*) tone (of voice).

accen'trare [attʃen'trare] *vt* to centralize.

accentu'are [attʃentu'are] *vt* to stress, emphasize; **~rsi** *vr* to become more noticeable.

accerchi'are [attʃer'kjare] *vt* to surround, encircle.

accerta'mento [attʃerta'mento] *sm* check; assessment.

accer'tare [attʃer'tare] *vt* to ascertain; (*verificare*) to check; (*reddito*) to assess; **~rsi** *vr*: **~rsi (di)** to make sure (of).

ac'ceso, a [at'tʃeso] *pp di* **accendere** ♦ *ag* lit; on; open; (*colore*) bright.

acces'sibile [attʃes'sibile] *ag* (*luogo*) accessible; (*persona*) approachable; (*prezzo*) reasonable; (*idea*): **~ a qn** within the reach of sb.

ac'cesso [at'tʃesso] *sm* (*anche INFORM*) access; (*MED*) attack, fit; (*impulso violento*) fit, outburst.

acces'sorio, a [attʃes'sɔrjo] *ag* secondary, of secondary importance; **~i** *smpl* accessories.

ac'cetta [at'tʃetta] *sf* hatchet.

accet'tabile [attʃet'tabile] *ag* acceptable.

accet'tare [attʃet'tare] *vt* to accept; **~ di fare qc** to agree to do sth; **accettazi'one** *sf* acceptance; (*locale di servizio pubblico*) reception; **accettazione bagagli** (*AER*) check-in (desk).

ac'cetto, a [at'tʃetto] *ag*: (**ben**) **~** welcome; (*persona*) well-liked.

accezi'one [attʃet'tsjone] *sf* meaning.

acchiap'pare [akkjap'pare] *vt* to catch.

acci'acco, chi [at'tʃakko] *sm* ailment.

acciaie'ria [attʃaje'ria] *sf* steelworks *sg*.

acci'aio [at'tʃajo] *sm* steel.

acciden'tale [attʃiden'tale] *ag* accidental.

acciden'tato, a [attʃiden'tato] *ag* (*terreno etc*) uneven.

acci'dente [attʃi'dɛnte] *sm* (*caso imprevisto*) accident; (*disgrazia*) mishap; **non si capisce un ~** it's as clear as mud; **~!** (*fam: per rabbia*) damn

(it)!; (: *per meraviglia*) good heavens!

accigli'ato, a [attʃiʎ'ʎato] *ag* frowning.

ac'cingersi [at'tʃindʒersi] *vr*: **~ a fare** to be about to do.

acciuf'fare [attʃuf'fare] *vt* to seize, catch.

acci'uga, ghe [at'tʃuga] *sf* anchovy.

accla'mare *vt* (*applaudire*) to applaud; (*eleggere*) to acclaim; **acclamazi'one** *sf* applause; acclamation.

acclima'tare *vt* to acclimatize; **~rsi** *vr* to become acclimatized.

ac'cludere *vt* to enclose; **ac'cluso, a** *pp di* **accludere** ♦ *ag* enclosed.

accocco'larsi *vr* to crouch.

accogli'ente [akkoʎ'ʎɛnte] *ag* welcoming, friendly; **accogli'enza** *sf* reception; welcome.

ac'cogliere [ak'kɔʎʎere] *vt* (*ricevere*) to receive; (*dare il benvenuto*) to welcome; (*approvare*) to agree to, accept; (*contenere*) to hold, accommodate.

accol'lato, a *ag* (*vestito*) high-necked.

accoltel'lare *vt* to knife, stab.

ac'colto, a *pp di* **accogliere**.

accoman'dita *sf* (*DIR*) limited partnership.

accomia'tare *vt* to dismiss; **~rsi** *vr*: **~rsi (da)** to take one's leave (of).

accomoda'mento *sm* agreement, settlement.

accomo'dante *ag* accommodating.

accomo'dare *vt* (*aggiustare*) to repair, mend; (*riordinare*) to tidy; (*conciliare*) to settle; **~rsi** *vr* (*sedersi*) to sit down; **s'accomodi!** (*venga avanti*) come in!; (: *si sieda*) take a seat!

accompagna'mento [akkompaɲ-ɲa'mento] *sm* (*MUS*) accompaniment.

accompa'gnare [akkompaɲ'ɲare] *vt* to accompany, come *o* go with; (*MUS*) to accompany; (*unire*) to couple; **~ la porta** to close the door gently.

accomu'nare *vt* to pool, share; (*avvicinare*) to unite.

acconcia'tura [akkontʃa'tura] *sf* hairstyle.

accondi'scendere [akkondiʃ'ʃɛndere] *vi*: **~ a** to agree *o* consent to; **accondi'sceso, a** *pp di* **accondiscendere**.

acconsen'tire *vi*: ~ (a) to agree *o* consent (to).

acconten'tare *vt* to satisfy; ~**rsi di** to be satisfied with, content o.s. with.

ac'conto *sm* part payment; **pagare una somma in** ~ to pay a sum of money as a deposit.

accoppia'mento *sm* coupling, pairing off; mating; (*TECN*) coupling.

accoppi'are *vt* to couple, pair off; (*BIOL*) to mate; ~**rsi** *vr* to pair off; to mate.

accorci'are [akkor'tʃare] *vt* to shorten; ~**rsi** *vr* to become shorter.

accor'dare *vt* to reconcile; (*colori*) to match; (*MUS*) to tune; (*LING*): ~ **qc con qc** to make sth agree with sth; (*DIR*) to grant; ~**rsi** *vr* to agree, come to an agreement; (*colori*) to match.

ac'cordo *sm* agreement; (*armonia*) harmony; (*MUS*) chord; **essere d'**~ to agree; **andare d'**~ to get on well together; **d'**~! all right!, agreed!

ac'corgersi [ak'kordʒersi] *vr*: ~ **di** to notice; (*fig*) to realize; **accorgi'mento** *sm* shrewdness *no pl*; (*espediente*) trick, device.

ac'correre *vi* to run up.

ac'corto, a *pp di* **accorgersi** ♦ *ag* shrewd; **stare** ~ to be on one's guard.

accos'tare *vt* (*avvicinare*): ~ **qc a** to bring sth near to, put sth near to; (*avvicinarsi a*) to approach; (*socchiudere: imposte*) to half-close; (*: porta*) to leave ajar ♦ *vi* (*NAUT*) to come alongside; ~**rsi a** to draw near, approach; (*fig*) to support.

accovacci'arsi [akkovat'tʃarsi] *vr* to crouch.

accoz'zaglia [akkot'tsaʎʎa] (*peg*) *sf* (*di idee, oggetti*) jumble, hotchpotch; (*di persone*) odd assortment.

accredi'tare *vt* (*notizia*) to confirm the truth of; (*COMM*) to credit; (*diplomatico*) to accredit; ~**rsi** *vr* (*fig*) to gain credit.

ac'crescere [ak'kreʃʃere] *vt* to increase; ~**rsi** *vr* to increase, grow; **accresci'tivo, a** *ag*, *sm* (*LING*) augmentative; **accresci'uto a** *pp di* **accrescere**.

accucci'arsi [akkut'tʃarsi] *vr* (*cane*) to lie down.

accu'dire *vt* (*anche*: *vi*: ~ *a*) to attend to.

accumu'lare *vt* to accumulate.

accura'tezza [akkura'tettsa] *sf* care; accuracy.

accu'rato, a *ag* (*diligente*) careful; (*preciso*) accurate.

ac'cusa *sf* accusation; (*DIR*) charge; **la pubblica** ~ the prosecution.

accu'sare *vt*: ~ **qn di qc** to accuse sb of sth; (*DIR*) to charge sb with sth; ~ **ricevuta di** (*COMM*) to acknowledge receipt of.

accu'sato, a *sm/f* accused; defendant.

accusa'tore, 'trice *sm/f* accuser ♦ *sm* (*DIR*) prosecutor.

a'cerbo, a [a'tʃerbo] *ag* bitter; (*frutta*) sour, unripe; (*persona*) immature.

'acero ['atʃero] *sm* maple.

a'cerrimo, a [a'tʃerrimo] *ag* very fierce.

a'ceto [a'tʃeto] *sm* vinegar.

ace'tone [atʃe'tone] *sm* nail varnish remover.

A.C.I. ['atʃi] *sigla m* (= *Automobile Club d'Italia*) ≈ A.A.

'acido, a ['atʃido] *ag* (*sapore*) acid, sour; (*CHIM*) acid ♦ *sm* (*CHIM*) acid.

'acino ['atʃino] *sm* berry; ~ **d'uva** grape.

'acne *sf* acne.

'acqua *sf* water; (*pioggia*) rain; ~**e** *sfpl* (*di mare, fiume etc*) waters; **fare** ~ (*NAUT*) to leak, take in water; ~ **in bocca!** mum's the word!; ~ **corrente** running water; ~ **dolce** fresh water; ~ **minerale** mineral water; ~ **potabile** drinking water; ~ **salata** salt water; ~ **tonica** tonic water.

acqua'forte (*pl* **acque'forti**) *sf* etching.

a'cquaio *sm* sink.

acqua'ragia [akkwa'radʒa] *sf* turpentine.

a'cquario *sm* aquarium; (*dello zodiaco*): **A**~ Aquarius.

acqua'santa *sf* holy water.

ac'quatico, a, ci, che *ag* aquatic; (*SPORT, SCIENZA*) water *cpd*.

acqua'vite *sf* brandy.

acquaz'zone   [akkwat'tsone]   *sm*

cloudburst, heavy shower.

acque'dotto *sm* aqueduct; waterworks *pl*, water system.

'acqueo, a *ag*: **vapore ~** water vapour.

acque'rello *sm* watercolour.

acquie'tare *vt* to appease; *(dolore)* to ease; **~rsi** *vr* to calm down.

acqui'rente *sm/f* purchaser, buyer.

acqui'sire *vt* to acquire.

acquis'tare *vt* to purchase, buy; *(fig)* to gain; **a'cquisto** *sm* purchase; **fare acquisti** to go shopping.

acqui'trino *sm* bog, marsh.

acquo'lina *sf*: **far venire l'~ in bocca a qn** to make sb's mouth water.

a'cquoso, a *ag* watery.

'acre *ag* acrid, pungent; *(fig)* harsh, biting.

a'crobata, i, e *sm/f* acrobat.

acu'ire *vt* to sharpen.

a'culeo *sm* (*ZOOL*) sting; (*BOT*) prickle.

a'cume *sm* acumen, perspicacity.

a'custica *sf* (*scienza*) acoustics *sg*; (*di una sala*) acoustics *pl*.

a'cuto, a *ag* (*appuntito*) sharp, pointed; (*suono, voce*) shrill, piercing; (*MAT, LING, MED*) acute; (*MUS*) high-pitched; (*fig: dolore, desiderio*) intense; (*: perspicace*) acute, keen.

ad (*dav V*) *prep* = **a**.

adagi'are [ada'dʒare] *vt* to lay *o* set down carefully; **~rsi** *vr* to lie down, stretch out.

a'dagio [a'dadʒo] *av* slowly ♦ *sm* (*MUS*) adagio; (*proverbio*) adage, saying.

adatta'mento *sm* adaptation.

adat'tare *vt* to adapt; (*sistemare*) to fit; **~rsi (a)** (*ambiente, tempi*) to adapt (to); (*essere adatto*) to be suitable (for).

a'datto, a *ag*: **~ (a)** suitable (for), right (for).

addebi'tare *vt*: **~ qc a qn** to debit sb with sth; (*fig: incolpare*) to blame sb for sth.

ad'debito *sm* (*COMM*) debit.

adden'sare *vt* to thicken; **~rsi** *vr* to thicken; (*nuvole*) to gather.

adden'tare *vt* to bite into.

adden'trarsi *vr*: **~ in** to penetrate, go into.

ad'dentro *av* (*fig*): **essere molto ~ in qc** to be well-versed in sth.

addestra'mento *sm* training.

addes'trare *vt* to train; **~rsi** *vr* to train; **~rsi in qc** to practise (*BRIT*) *o* practice (*US*) sth.

ad'detto, a *ag*: **~ a** (*persona*) assigned to; (*oggetto*) intended for ♦ *sm* employee; (*funzionario*) attaché; **~ commerciale/stampa** commercial/press attaché; **gli ~i ai lavori** authorized personnel; (*fig*) those in the know.

addì *av* (*AMM*): **~ 3 luglio 1978** on the 3rd of July 1978 (*BRIT*), on July 3rd 1978 (*US*).

addi'accio [ad'djattʃo] *sm* (*MIL*) bivouac; **dormire all'~** to sleep in the open.

addi'etro *av* (*indietro*) behind; (*nel passato, prima*) before, ago.

ad'dio *sm, escl* goodbye, farewell.

addirit'tura *av* (*veramente*) really, absolutely; (*perfino*) even; (*direttamente*) directly, right away.

ad'dirsi *vr*: **~ a** to suit, be suitable for.

addi'tare *vt* to point out; (*fig*) to expose.

addi'tivo *sm* additive.

addizio'nare [addittsjo'nare] *vt* (*MAT*) to add (up); **addizi'one** *sf* addition.

addob'bare *vt* to decorate; **ad'dobbo** *sm* decoration.

addol'cire [addol'tʃire] *vt* (*caffè etc*) to sweeten; (*acqua, fig: carattere*) to soften; **~rsi** *vr* (*fig*) to mellow, soften.

addolo'rare *vt* to pain, grieve; **~rsi (per)** to be distressed (by).

ad'dome *sm* abdomen.

addomesti'care *vt* to tame.

addormen'tare *vt* to put to sleep; **~rsi** *vr* to fall asleep, go to sleep.

addos'sare *vt* (*appoggiare*): **~ qc a qc** to lean sth against sth; (*fig*): **~ la colpa a qn** to lay the blame on sb; **~rsi qc** (*responsabilità etc*) to shoulder sth.

ad'dosso *av* (*sulla persona*) on; **mettersi ~ il cappotto** to put one's coat on; **non ho soldi ~** I don't have any money on me; ~ **a** (*sopra*) on; (*molto vicino*) right next to; **stare** ~ **a qn** (*fig*) to breathe down sb's neck; **dare** ~ **a qn** (*fig*) to attack sb.

ad'durre *vt* (*DIR*) to produce; (*citare*) to cite.

adegu'are *vt*: ~ **qc a** to adjust *o* relate sth to; **~rsi** *vr* to adapt; **adegu'ato, a** *ag* adequate; (*conveniente*) suitable; (*equo*) fair.

a'dempiere *vt* to fulfil, carry out.

adem'pire *vt* = **adempiere**.

ade'rente *ag* adhesive; (*vestito*) close-fitting ♦ *sm/f* follower; **ade'renza** *sf* adhesion; **aderenze** *sfpl* (*fig*) connections, contacts.

ade'rire *vi* (*stare attaccato*) to adhere, stick; ~ **a** to adhere to, stick to; (*fig: società, partito*) to join; (*: opinione*) to support; (*richiesta*) to agree to.

ades'care *vt* to lure, entice.

adesi'one *sf* adhesion; (*fig*) agreement, acceptance; **ade'sivo, a** *ag*, *sm* adhesive.

a'desso *av* (*ora*) now; (*or ora, poco fa*) just now; (*tra poco*) any moment now.

adia'cente [adja'tʃɛnte] *ag* adjacent.

adi'bire *vt* (*usare*): ~ **qc a** to turn sth into.

adi'rarsi *vr*: ~ (**con** *o* **contro qn per qc**) to get angry (with sb over sth).

a'dire *vt* (*DIR*): ~ **le vie legali** to take legal proceedings.

'adito *sm*: **dare** ~ **a** to give rise to.

adocchi'are [adok'kjare] *vt* (*scorgere*) to catch sight of; (*occhieggiare*) to eye.

adole'scente [adoleʃ'ʃɛnte] *ag*, *sm/f* adolescent; **adole'scenza** *sf* adolescence.

adope'rare *vt* to use; **~rsi** *vr* to strive; **~rsi per qn/qc** to do one's best for sb/sth.

ado'rare *vt* to adore; (*REL*) to adore, worship.

adot'tare *vt* to adopt; (*decisione, provvedimenti*) to pass; **adot'tivo, a** *ag* (*genitori*) adoptive; (*figlio, patria*) adopted; **adozi'one** *sf* adoption.

adri'atico, a, ci, che *ag* Adriatic ♦ *sm*: **l'A~, il mare A~** the Adriatic, the Adriatic Sea.

adu'lare *vt* to adulate, flatter.

adulte'rare *vt* to adulterate.

adul'terio *sm* adultery.

a'dulto, a *ag* adult; (*fig*) mature ♦ *sm* adult, grown-up.

adu'nanza [adu'nantsa] *sf* assembly, meeting.

adu'nare *vt* to assemble, gather; **~rsi** *vr* to assemble, gather; **adu'nata** *sf* (*MIL*) parade, muster.

a'dunco, a, chi, che *ag* hooked.

a'ereo, a *ag* air *cpd*; (*radice*) aerial ♦ *sm* aerial; (*aeroplano*) plane; ~ **a reazione** jet (plane); **ae'robica** *sf* aerobics *sg*; **aerodi'namica** *sf* aerodynamics *sg*; **aerodi'namico, a, ci, che** *ag* aerodynamic; (*affusolato*) streamlined; **aero'nautica** *sf* (*scienza*) aeronautics *sg*; **aeronautica militare** air force; **aero'plano** *sm* (aero)plane (*BRIT*), (air)plane (*US*); **aero'porto** *sm* airport; **aero'sol** *sm inv* aerosol.

'afa *sf* sultriness.

af'fabile *ag* affable.

affaccen'darsi [affattʃen'darsi] *vr*: ~ **intorno a qc** to busy o.s. with sth.

affacci'arsi [affat'tʃarsi] *vr*: ~ (**a**) to appear (at).

affa'mato, a *ag* starving; (*fig*): ~ (**di**) eager (for).

affan'nare *vt* to leave breathless; (*fig*) to worry; **~rsi** *vr*: **~rsi per qn/qc** to worry about sb/sth; **af'fanno** *sm* breathlessness; (*fig*) anxiety, worry; **affan'noso, a** *ag* (*respiro*) difficult; (*fig*) troubled, anxious.

af'fare *sm* (*faccenda*) matter, affair; (*COMM*) piece of business, (business) deal; (*occasione*) bargain; (*DIR*) case; (*fam: cosa*) thing; **~i** *smpl* (*COMM*) business *sg*; **Ministro degli A~i esteri** Foreign Secretary (*BRIT*), Secretary of State (*US*); **affa'rista, i** *sm* profiteer, unscrupulous businessman.

affasci'nante [affaʃʃi'nante] *ag* fascinating.

affasci'nare [affaʃʃi'nare] *vt* to bewitch; (*fig*) to charm, fascinate.

affati'care vt to tire; **~rsi** vr (durar fatica) to tire o.s. out.

af'fatto av completely; **non ... ~** not ... at all; **niente ~** not at all.

affer'mare vt (dichiarare) to maintain, affirm; **~rsi** vr to assert o.s., make one's name known; **affermazi'one** sf affirmation, assertion; (successo) achievement.

affer'rare vt to seize, grasp; (fig: idea) to grasp; **~rsi** vr: **~rsi a** to cling to.

affet'tare vt (tagliare a fette) to slice; (ostentare) to affect; **affet'tato, a** ag sliced; affected ♦ sm sliced cold meat.

affet'tivo, a ag emotional, affective.

af'fetto sm affection; **affettu'oso, a** ag affectionate.

affezio'narsi [affettsjo'narsi] vr: **~ a** to grow fond of.

affezi'one [affet'tsjone] sf (affetto) affection; (MED) ailment, disorder.

affian'care vt to place side by side; (MIL) to flank; (fig) to support; **~ qc a qc** to place sth next to o beside sth; **~rsi a qn** to stand beside sb.

affia'tarsi vr to get on well together.

affibbi'are vt (fig: dare) to give.

affida'mento sm (DIR: di bambino) custody; (fiducia): **fare ~ su qn** to rely on sb; **non dà nessun ~** he's not to be trusted.

affi'dare vt: **~ qc o qn a qn** to entrust sth o sb to sb; **~rsi** vr: **~rsi a** to place one's trust in.

affievo'lirsi vr to grow weak.

af'figgere [af'fiddʒere] vt to stick up, post up.

affi'lare vt to sharpen.

affili'are vt to affiliate; **~rsi** vr: **~rsi a** to become affiliated to.

affi'nare vt to sharpen.

affinché [affin'ke] cong in order that, so that.

af'fine ag similar; **affinità** sf inv affinity.

affio'rare vi to emerge.

affissi'one sf billposting.

af'fisso, a pp di **affiggere** ♦ sm bill, poster; (LING) affix.

affit'tare vt (dare in affitto) to let, rent (out); (prendere in affitto) to rent; **af'fitto** sm rent; (contratto) lease.

af'fliggere [af'fliddʒere] vt to torment; **~rsi** vr to grieve; **af'flitto, a** pp di **affliggere**; **aflizi'one** sf distress, torment.

afflosci'arsi [afflof'farsi] vr to go limp; (frutta) to go soft.

afflu'ente sm tributary; **afflu'enza** sf flow; (di persone) crowd.

afflu'ire vi to flow; (fig: merci, persone) to pour in; **af'flusso** sm influx.

affo'gare vt, vi to drown; **~rsi** vr to drown; (deliberatamente) to drown o.s.

affol'lare vt to crowd; **~rsi** vr to crowd; **affol'lato, a** ag crowded.

affon'dare vt to sink.

affran'care vt to free, liberate; (AMM) to redeem; (lettera) to stamp; (: meccanicamente) to frank (BRIT), meter (US); **~rsi** vr to free o.s.; **affranca'tura** sf (di francobollo) stamping; franking (BRIT), metering (US); (tassa di spedizione) postage.

af'franto, a ag (esausto) worn out; (abbattuto) overcome.

af'fresco, schi sm fresco.

affret'tare vt to quicken, speed up; **~rsi** vr to hurry; **~rsi a fare qc** to hurry o hasten to do sth.

affron'tare vt (pericolo etc) to face; (assalire: nemico) to confront; **~rsi** vr (reciproco) to come to blows.

af'fronto sm affront, insult.

affumi'care vt to fill with smoke; to blacken with smoke; (alimenti) to smoke.

affuso'lato, a ag tapering.

a'foso, a ag sultry, close.

'Africa sf: **l'~** Africa; **afri'cano, a** ag, smlf African.

afrodi'siaco, a, ci, che ag, sm aphrodisiac.

a'genda [a'dʒenda] sf diary.

a'gente [a'dʒente] sm agent; **~ di cambio** stockbroker; **~ di polizia** police officer; **agen'zia** sf agency; (succursale) branch; **agenzia di collocamento** employment agency; **agenzia immobiliare** estate agent's

(office) (BRIT), real estate office (US);
agenzia pubblicitaria/viaggi advertising/
travel agency.

agevo'lare [adʒevo'lare] vt to facilitate,
make easy.

a'gevole [a'dʒevole] ag easy; (strada)
smooth.

agganci'are [aggan'tʃare] vt to hook up;
(FERR) to couple.

ag'geggio [ad'dʒeddʒo] sm gadget, contraption.

agget'tivo [addʒet'tivo] sm adjective.

agghiacci'ante [aggjat'tʃante] ag (fig)
chilling.

agghin'darsi [aggin'darsi] vr to deck o.s.
out.

aggior'nare [addʒor'nare] vt (opera,
manuale) to bring up-to-date; (seduta
etc) to postpone; ~**rsi** vr to bring (o
keep) o.s. up-to-date; **aggior'nato, a** ag
up-to-date.

aggi'rare [addʒi'rare] vt to go round;
(fig: ingannare) to trick; ~**rsi** vr to
wander about; **il prezzo s'aggira sul
milione** the price is around the million
mark.

aggiudi'care [addʒudi'kare] vt to award;
(all'asta) to knock down; ~**rsi qc** to win
sth.

ag'giungere [ad'dʒundʒere] vt to add;
aggi'unta sf addition; **aggi'unto, a** pp
di **aggiungere** ♦ ag assistant cpd ♦ sm
assistant; **sindaco aggiunto** deputy
mayor.

aggius'tare   [addʒus'tare]   vt
(accomodare)   to   mend,   repair;
(riassettare) to adjust; (fig: lite) to
settle; ~**rsi** vr (arrangiarsi) to make
do; (con senso reciproco) to come to an
agreement.

agglome'rato sm (di rocce) con-
glomerate; (di legno) chipboard; ~
urbano built-up area.

aggrap'parsi vr: ~ a to cling to.

aggra'vare vt (aumentare) to increase; (appesantire: anche fig) to
weigh down, make heavy; (fig: pena)
to make worse; ~**rsi** vr (fig) to worsen,
become worse.

aggrazi'ato, a [aggrat'tsjato] ag grace-

ful.

aggre'dire vt to attack, assault.

aggre'gare vt: ~ **qn a qc** to admit sb
to sth; ~**rsi** vr to join; ~**rsi a** to join,
become a member of; **aggre'gato, a** ag
associated ♦ sm aggregate; **aggregato
urbano** built-up area.

aggressi'one sf aggression; (atto)
attack, assault.

aggres'sivo, a ag aggressive.

aggrot'tare vt: ~ **le sopracciglia** to
frown.

aggrovigli'are [aggroviʎ'ʎare]   vt   to
tangle; ~**rsi** vr (fig) to become
complicated.

agguan'tare vt to catch, seize.

aggu'ato sm trap; (imboscata)
ambush; **tendere un** ~ **a qn** to set a
trap for sb.

agguer'rito, a ag fierce.

agi'ato, a [a'dʒato] ag (vita) easy;
(persona) well-off, well-to-do.

'agile ['adʒile] ag agile, nimble; **agilità**
sf agility, nimbleness.

'agio ['adʒo] sm ease, comfort; **vivere
negli** ~**i** to live in comfort; **mettersi a
proprio** ~ to make o.s. at home o
comfortable.

a'gire [a'dʒire] vi to act; (esercitare
un'azione) to take effect; (TECN) to
work, function; ~ **contro qn** (DIR) to
take action against sb.

agi'tare [adʒi'tare] vt (bottiglia) to
shake; (mano, fazzoletto) to wave; (fig:
turbare) to disturb; (: incitare) to stir
(up); (: dibattere) to discuss; ~**rsi** vr
(mare) to be rough; (malato,
dormitore) to toss and turn; (bambino)
to fidget; (emozionarsi) to get upset;
(POL) to agitate; **agi'tato, a** ag rough;
restless; fidgety; upset, perturbed;
agitazi'one sf agitation; (POL) unrest,
agitation; **mettere in agitazione qn** to
upset o distress sb.

'agli ['aʎʎi] prep + det vedi **a**.

'aglio ['aʎʎo] sm garlic.

a'gnello [aɲ'ɲello] sm lamb.

'ago (pl **aghi**) sm needle.

ago'nia sf agony.

ago'nistico, a, ci, che ag athletic;

(*fig*) competitive.

agoniz'zare [agonid'dzare] *vi* to be dying.

agopun'tura *sf* acupuncture.

a'gosto *sm* August.

a'graria *sf* agriculture.

a'grario, a *ag* agrarian, agricultural; (*riforma*) land *cpd*.

a'gricolo, a *ag* agricultural, farm *cpd*; **agricol'tore** *sm* farmer; **agricol'tura** *sf* agriculture, farming.

agri'foglio [agri'fɔʎʎo] *sm* holly.

agrimen'sore *sm* land surveyor.

agritu'rismo *sm* farm holidays *pl*.

'agro, a *ag* sour, sharp; ~**dolce** *ag* bittersweet; (*salsa*) sweet and sour.

a'grume *sm* (*spesso al pl: pianta*) citrus; (: *frutto*) citrus fruit.

aguz'zare [agut'tsare] *vt* to sharpen; ~ **gli orecchi** to prick up one's ears.

a'guzzo, a [a'guttso] *ag* sharp.

'ai *prep* + *det vedi* **a**.

'Aia *sf*: **l'**~ the Hague.

'aia *sf* threshing-floor.

ai'rone *sm* heron.

aiu'ola *sf* flower bed.

aiu'tante *sm/f* assistant ♦ *sm* (*MIL*) adjutant; (*NAUT*) master-at-arms; ~ **di campo** aide-de-camp.

aiu'tare *vt* to help; ~ **qn (a fare)** to help sb (to do).

ai'uto *sm* help, assistance, aid; (*aiutante*) assistant; **venire in** ~ **di qn** to come to sb's aid; ~ **chirurgo** assistant surgeon.

aiz'zare [ait'tsare] *vt* to incite; ~ **i cani contro qn** to set the dogs on sb.

al *prep* + *det vedi* **a**.

'ala (*pl* **'ali**) *sf* wing; **fare** ~ to fall back, make way; ~ **destra/sinistra** (*SPORT*) right/left wing.

'alacre *ag* quick, brisk.

a'lano *sm* Great Dane.

a'lare *ag* wing *cpd*.

'alba *sf* dawn.

Alba'nia *sf*: **l'**~ Albania.

'albatro *sm* albatross.

albeggi'are [albed'dʒare] *vi*, *vb impers* to dawn.

albera'tura *sf* (*NAUT*) masts *pl*.

alberghi'ero, a [alber'gjɛro] *ag* hotel *cpd*.

al'bergo, ghi *sm* hotel; ~ **della gioventù** youth hostel.

'albero *sm* tree; (*NAUT*) mast; (*TECN*) shaft; ~ **genealogico** family tree; ~ **a gomiti** crankshaft; ~ **di Natale** Christmas tree; ~ **maestro** mainmast; ~ **di trasmissione** transmission shaft.

albi'cocca, che *sf* apricot; **albi'cocco, chi** *sm* apricot tree.

'albo *sm* (*registro*) register, roll; (*AMM*) notice board.

'album *sm* album; ~ **da disegno** sketch book.

al'bume *sm* albumen.

'alce ['altʃe] *sm* elk.

al'colico, a, ci, che *ag* alcoholic ♦ *sm* alcoholic drink.

alcoliz'zato, a [alcolid'dzato] *sm/f* alcoholic.

'alcool *sm* alcohol; **alco'olico** *etc* = **alcolico** *etc*.

al'cuno, a (*det: dav sm*: **alcun** +*C*, *V*, **alcuno** +*s impura, gn, pn, ps, x, z*; *dav sf*: **alcuna** +*C*, **alcun'** +*V*) *det* (*nessuno*): **non ...** ~ no, not any; ~**i, e** *det pl*, some, a few; **non c'è** ~**a fretta** there's no hurry, there isn't any hurry; **senza alcun riguardo** without any consideration ♦ *pron pl*: ~**i, e** some, a few.

aldilà *sm*: **l'**~ the after-life.

a'letta *sf* (*TECN*) fin; tab.

alfa'beto *sm* alphabet.

alfi'ere *sm* standard-bearer; (*MIL*) ensign; (*SCACCHI*) bishop.

al'fine *av* finally, in the end.

'alga, ghe *sf* seaweed *no pl*, alga.

'algebra ['aldʒebra] *sf* algebra.

Alge'ria [aldʒe'ria] *sf*: **l'**~ Algeria.

ali'ante *sm* (*AER*) glider.

'alibi *sm inv* alibi.

a'lice [a'litʃe] *sf* anchovy.

alie'nare *vt* (*DIR*) to alienate, transfer; (*rendere ostile*) to alienate; ~**rsi qn** to alienate sb; **alie'nato, a** *ag* alienated; transferred; (*fuor di senno*) insane ♦ *sm* lunatic, insane person; **alienazi'one** *sf* alienation; transfer; insanity.

ali'eno, a *ag* (*avverso*): ~ (**da**)

opposed (to), averse (to) ♦ *sm/f* alien.

alimen'tare *vt* to feed; (*TECN*) to feed; to supply; (*fig*) to sustain ♦ *ag* food *cpd*; **~i** *smpl* foodstuffs; (*anche*: *negozio di ~i*) grocer's shop; **alimentazi'one** *sf* feeding; supplying; sustaining; (*gli alimenti*) diet.

ali'mento *sm* food; **~i** *smpl* (*cibo*) food *sg*; (*DIR*) alimony.

a'liquota *sf* share; (*d'imposta*) rate.

alis'cafo *sm* hydrofoil.

'alito *sm* breath.

all. *abbr* (= *allegato*) encl.

'alla *prep* + *det vedi* **a**.

allacci'are [allat'tʃare] *vt* (*scarpe*) to tie, lace (up); (*cintura*) to do up, fasten; (*due località*) to link; (*luce, gas*) to connect; (*amicizia*) to form.

alla'gare *vt* to flood; **~rsi** *vr* to flood.

allar'gare *vt* to widen; (*vestito*) to let out; (*aprire*) to open; (*fig: dilatare*) to extend.

allar'mare *vt* to alarm.

al'larme *sm* alarm; **~ aereo** air-raid warning.

allar'mismo *sm* scaremongering.

allat'tare *vt* to feed.

'alle *prep* + *det vedi* **a**.

alle'anza [alle'antsa] *sf* alliance.

alle'arsi *vr* to form an alliance; **alle'ato, a** *ag* allied ♦ *sm/f* ally.

alle'gare *vt* (*accludere*) to enclose; (*DIR: citare*) to cite, adduce; (*denti*) to set on edge; **alle'gato, a** *ag* enclosed ♦ *sm* enclosure; **in allegato** enclosed.

allegge'rire [alleddʒe'rire] *vt* to lighten, make lighter; (*fig: sofferenza*) to alleviate, lessen; (: *lavoro, tasse*) to reduce.

alle'gria *sf* gaiety, cheerfulness.

al'legro, a *ag* cheerful, merry; (*un po' brillo*) merry, tipsy; (*vivace: colore*) bright ♦ *sm* (*MUS*) allegro.

allena'mento *sm* training.

alle'nare *vt* to train; **~rsi** *vr* to train; **allena'tore** *sm* (*SPORT*) trainer, coach.

allen'tare *vt* to slacken; (*disciplina*) to relax; **~rsi** *vr* to become slack; (*ingranaggio*) to work loose.

aller'gia, 'gie [aller'dʒia] *sf* allergy;

al'lergico, a, ci, che *ag* allergic.

alles'tire (*cena*) to prepare; (*esercito, nave*) to equip, fit out; (*spettacolo*) to stage.

allet'tare *vt* to lure, entice.

alleva'mento *sm* breeding, rearing; (*luogo*) stock farm.

alle'vare *vt* (*animale*) to breed, rear; (*bambino*) to bring up.

allevi'are *vt* to alleviate.

alli'bire *vi* to be astounded.

allibra'tore *sm* bookmaker.

allie'tare *vt* to cheer up, gladden.

alli'evo *sm* pupil; (*apprendista*) apprentice; (*MIL*) cadet.

alliga'tore *sm* alligator.

alline'are *vt* (*persone, cose*) to line up; (*TIP*) to align; (*fig: economia, salari*) to adjust, align; **~rsi** *vr* to line up; (*fig: a idee*): **~rsi a** to come into line with.

'allo *prep* + *det vedi* **a**.

al'locco, a, chi, che *sm* tawny owl ♦ *sm/f* oaf.

allocuzi'one [allokut'tsjone] *sf* address, solemn speech.

al'lodola *sf* (sky)lark.

alloggi'are [allod'dʒare] *vt* to accommodate ♦ *vi* to live; **al'loggio** *sm* lodging, accommodation (*BRIT*), accommodations (*US*); (*appartamento*) flat (*BRIT*), apartment (*US*).

allontana'mento *sm* removal; dismissal.

allonta'nare *vt* to send away, send off; (*impiegato*) to dismiss; (*pericolo*) to avert, remove; (*estraniare*) to alienate; **~rsi** *vr*: **~rsi (da)** to go away (from); (*estraniarsi*) to become estranged (from).

al'lora *av* (*in quel momento*) then ♦ *cong* (*in questo caso*) then; (*dunque*) well then, so; **la gente d'~** people then *o* in those days; **da ~ in poi** from then on.

allor'ché [allor'ke] *cong* (*formale*) when, as soon as.

al'loro *sm* laurel.

'alluce ['allutʃe] *sm* big toe.

alluci'nante [allutʃi'nante] *ag* awful; (*fam*) amazing.

allucinazi'one [allut∫inat'tsjone] *sf* hallucination.

al'ludere *vi*: ~ a to allude to, hint at.

allu'minio *sm* aluminium (*BRIT*), aluminum (*US*).

allun'gare *vt* to lengthen; (*distendere*) to prolong, extend; (*diluire*) to water down; ~**rsi** *vr* to lengthen; (*ragazzo*) to stretch, grow taller; (*sdraiarsi*) to lie down, stretch out.

allusi'one *sf* hint, allusion.

alluvi'one *sf* flood.

al'meno *av* at least ♦ *cong*: (*se*) ~ if only; (*se*) ~ **piovesse!** if only it would rain!

a'lone *sm* halo.

'Alpi *sfpl*: **le** ~ the Alps.

alpi'nismo *sm* mountaineering, climbing; **alpi'nista, i, e** *sm/f* mountaineer, climber.

al'pino, a *ag* Alpine; mountain *cpd*.

al'quanto *av* rather, a little; ~, **a** *det* a certain amount of, some ♦ *pron* a certain amount, some; ~**i, e** *det pl*, *pron pl* several, quite a few.

alt *escl* halt!, stop! ♦ *sm*: **dare l'**~ to call a halt.

alta'lena *sf* (*a funi*) swing; (*in bilico*, *anche fig*) seesaw.

al'tare *sm* altar.

alte'rare *vt* to alter, change; (*cibo*) to adulterate; (*registro*) to falsify; (*persona*) to irritate; ~**rsi** *vr* to alter; (*cibo*) to go bad; (*persona*) to lose one's temper.

al'terco, chi *sm* altercation, wrangle.

alter'nare *vt* to alternate; ~**rsi** *vr* to alternate; **alterna'tiva** *sf* alternative; **alterna'tivo, a** *ag* alternative; **alter'nato, a** *ag* alternate; (*ELETTR*) alternating; **alterna'tore** *sm* alternator.

al'terno, a *ag* alternate; **a giorni** ~**i** on alternate days, every other day.

al'tezza [al'tettsa] *sf* height; width, breadth; depth; pitch; (*GEO*) latitude; (*titolo*) highness; (*fig: nobiltà*) greatness; **essere all'**~ **di** to be on a level with; (*fig*) to be up to *o* equal to; **altez'zoso, a** *ag* haughty.

al'ticcio, a, ci, ce [al'tittʃo] *ag* tipsy.

altipi'ano *sm* = **altopiano**.

alti'tudine *sf* altitude.

'alto, a *ag* high; (*persona*) tall; (*tessuto*) wide, broad; (*sonno, acque*) deep; (*suono*) high(-pitched); (*GEO*) upper; (: *settentrionale*) northern ♦ *sm* top (part) ♦ *av* high; (*parlare*) aloud, loudly; **il palazzo è** ~ **20 metri** the building is 20 metres high; **ad** ~**a voce** aloud; **a notte** ~**a** in the dead of night; **in** ~ up, upwards; at the top; **dall'**~ **in** *o* **al basso** up and down; **degli** ~**i e bassi** (*fig*) ups and downs; ~**a fedeltà** high fidelity, hi-fi; ~**a moda** haute couture.

alto'forno *sm* blast furnace.

altolo'cato, a *ag* of high rank.

altopar'lante *sm* loudspeaker.

altopi'ano (*pl* **altipiani**) *sm* plateau, upland plain.

altret'tanto, a *ag, pron* as much; (*pl*) as many ♦ *av* equally; **tanti auguri!** — **grazie,** ~ all the best! — thank you, the same to you.

'altri *pron inv* (*qualcuno*) somebody; (: *in espressioni negative*) anybody; (*un'altra persona*) another (person).

altri'menti *av* otherwise.

───────────────
PAROLA CHIAVE
───────────────

'altro, a *det* **1** (*diverso*) other, different; **questa è un'**~**a cosa** that's another *o* a different thing

2 (*supplementare*) other; **prendi un** ~ **cioccolatino** have another chocolate; **hai avuto** ~**e notizie?** have you had any more *o* any other news?

3 (*nel tempo*): **l'**~ **giorno** the other day; **l'altr'anno** last year; **l'**~ **ieri** the day before yesterday; **domani l'**~ the day after tomorrow; **quest'**~ **mese** next month

4: **d'**~**a parte** on the other hand

♦ *pron* **1** (*persona, cosa diversa o supplementare*): **un** ~, **un'**~**a** another (one); **lo farà un** ~ someone else will do it; ~**i, e others; **gli** ~**i** (*la gente*) others, other people; **l'uno e l'**~ both (of them); **aiutarsi l'un l'**~ to help one another; **da un giorno all'**~ from day to

day; (*nel giro di 24 ore*) from one day to the next; (*da un momento all'altro*) any day now
2 (*sostantivato: solo maschile*) something else; (*: in espressioni interrogative*) anything else; **non ho ~ da dire** I have nothing else *o* I don't have anything else to say; **più che ~** above all; **se non ~** at least; **tra l'~** among other things; **ci mancherebbe ~!** that's all we need!; **non faccio ~ che lavorare** I do nothing but work; **contento? — ~ che!** are you pleased? — and how!; *vedi* **senza; noialtri; voialtri; tutto.**

al'tronde *av:* **d'~** on the other hand.
al'trove *av* elsewhere, somewhere else.
al'trui *ag inv* other people's ♦ *sm:* **l'~** other people's belongings *pl.*
altru'ista, i, e *ag* altruistic.
al'tura *sf* (*rialto*) height, high ground; (*alto mare*) open sea; **pesca d'~** deep-sea fishing.
a'lunno, a *sm/f* pupil.
alve'are *sm* hive.
'alveo *sm* riverbed.
al'zare [al'tsare] *vt* to raise, lift; (*issare*) to hoist; (*costruire*) to build, erect; **~rsi** *vr* to rise; (*dal letto*) to get up; (*crescere*) to grow tall (*o* taller); **~ le spalle** to shrug one's shoulders; **~rsi in piedi** to stand up, get to one's feet; **al'zata** *sf* lifting, raising; **un'alzata di spalle** a shrug.
a'mabile *ag* lovable; (*vino*) sweet.
a'maca, che *sf* hammock.
amalga'mare *vt* to amalgamate.
a'mante *ag:* **~ di** (*musica etc*) fond of ♦ *sm/f* lover/mistress.
a'mare *vt* to love; (*amico, musica, sport*) to like.
amareggi'ato, a [amared'dʒato] *ag* upset, saddened.
ama'rena *sf* sour black cherry.
ama'rezza [ama'rettsa] *sf* bitterness.
a'maro, a *ag* bitter ♦ *sm* bitterness; (*liquore*) bitters *pl.*
ambasci'ata [ambaʃ'ʃata] *sf* embassy; (*messaggio*) message; **ambascia'tore, 'trice** *sm/f* ambassador/ambassadress.

ambe'due *ag inv:* **~ i ragazzi** both boys ♦ *pron inv* both.
ambien'tare *vt* to acclimatize; (*romanzo, film*) to set; **~rsi** *vr* to get used to one's surroundings.
ambi'ente *sm* environment; (*fig: insieme di persone*) milieu; (*stanza*) room.
am'biguo, a *ag* ambiguous; (*persona*) shady.
am'bire *vt* (*anche: vi: ~ a*) to aspire to.
'ambito *sm* sphere, field.
ambizi'one [ambit'tsjone] *sf* ambition; **ambizi'oso, a** *ag* ambitious.
'ambo *ag inv* both.
'ambra *sf* amber; **~ grigia** ambergris.
ambu'lante *ag* travelling, itinerant.
ambu'lanza [ambu'lantsa] *sf* ambulance.
ambula'torio *sm* (*studio medico*) surgery.
amenità *sf inv* pleasantness *no pl.*
a'meno, a *ag* pleasant; (*strano*) funny, strange; (*spiritoso*) amusing.
A'merica *sf:* **l'~** America; **l'~ latina** Latin America; **ameri'cano, a** *ag, sm/f* American.
ami'anto *sm* asbestos.
a'mica *sf vedi* **amico.**
ami'chevole [ami'kevole] *ag* friendly.
ami'cizia [ami'tʃittsja] *sf* friendship; **~e** *sfpl* (*amici*) friends.
a'mico, a, ci, che *sm/f* friend; (*amante*) boyfriend/girlfriend; **~ del cuore** *o* **intimo** bosom friend.
'amido *sm* starch.
ammac'care *vt* (*pentola*) to dent; (*persona*) to bruise; **~rsi** *vr* to bruise.
ammaes'trare *vt* (*animale*) to train; (*persona*) to teach.
ammai'nare *vt* to lower, haul down.
amma'larsi *vr* to fall ill; **amma'lato, a** *ag* ill, sick ♦ *sm/f* sick person; (*paziente*) patient.
ammali'are *vt* (*fig*) to enchant, charm.
am'manco, chi *sm* (ECON) deficit.
ammanet'tare *vt* to handcuff.
ammas'sare *vt* (*ammucchiare*) to amass; (*raccogliere*) to gather together; **~rsi** *vr* to pile up; to gather;

am'masso *sm* mass; *(mucchio)* pile, heap; *(ECON)* stockpile.

ammat'tire *vi* to go mad.

ammaz'zare [ammat'tsare] *vt* to kill; **~rsi** *vr* *(uccidersi)* to kill o.s.; *(rimanere ucciso)* to be killed; **~rsi di lavoro** to work o.s. to death.

am'menda *sf* amends *pl*; *(DIR, SPORT)* fine; **fare ~ di qc** to make amends for sth.

am'messo, a *pp di* **ammettere** ♦ *cong:* **~ che** supposing that.

am'mettere *vt* to admit; *(riconoscere: fatto)* to acknowledge, admit; *(permettere)* to allow, accept; *(supporre)* to suppose.

ammez'zato [ammed'dzato] *sm* *(anche: piano ~)* mezzanine, entresol.

ammic'care *vi:* **~ (a)** to wink (at).

amminis'trare *vt* to run, manage; *(REL, DIR)* to administer; **amministra'tivo, a** *ag* administrative; **amministra'tore** *sm* administrator; *(di condominio)* flats manager; **amministratore delegato** managing director; **amministrazi'one** *sf* management; administration.

ammiragli'ato [ammiraʎ'ʎato] *sm* admiralty.

ammi'raglio [ammi'raʎʎo] *sm* admiral.

ammi'rare *vt* to admire; **ammira'tore, 'trice** *sm/f* admirer; **ammirazi'one** *sf* admiration.

ammis'sibile *ag* admissible, acceptable.

ammissi'one *sf* admission; *(approvazione)* acknowledgment.

ammobili'are *vt* to furnish.

am'modo *av* properly ♦ *ag inv* respectable, nice.

am'mollo *sm:* **lasciare in ~** to leave to soak.

ammo'niaca *sf* ammonia.

ammoni'mento *sm* warning; admonishment.

ammo'nire *vt* *(avvertire)* to warn; *(rimproverare)* to admonish; *(DIR)* to caution.

ammon'tare *vi:* **~ a** to amount to ♦ *sm* (total) amount.

ammorbi'dente *sm* fabric conditioner.

ammorbi'dire *vt* to soften.

ammortiz'zare [ammortid'dzare] *vt* *(ECON)* to pay off, amortize; *(: spese d'impianto)* to write off; *(AUT, TECN)* to absorb, deaden; **ammortizza'tore** *sm* *(AUT, TECN)* shock-absorber.

ammucchi'are [ammuk'kjare] *vt* to pile up, accumulate; **~rsi** *vr* to pile up, accumulate.

ammuf'fire *vi* to go mouldy *(BRIT)* o moldy *(US)*.

ammutina'mento *sm* mutiny.

ammuti'narsi *vr* to mutiny.

ammuto'lire *vi* to be struck dumb.

amnis'tia *sf* amnesty.

'amo *sm* *(PESCA)* hook; *(fig)* bait.

a'modo *av* = **ammodo**.

a'more *sm* love; **~i** *smpl* love affairs; **il tuo bambino è un ~** your baby's a darling; **fare l'~** o **all'~** to make love; **per ~** o **per forza** by hook or by crook; **amor proprio** self-esteem, pride; **amo'revole** *ag* loving, affectionate.

a'morfo, a *ag* amorphous; *(fig: persona)* lifeless.

amo'roso, a *ag* *(affettuoso)* loving, affectionate; *(d'amore: sguardo)* amorous; *(: poesia, relazione)* love *cpd*.

ampi'ezza [am'pjettsa] *sf* width, breadth; spaciousness; *(fig: importanza)* scale, size.

'ampio, a *ag* wide, broad; *(spazioso)* spacious; *(abbondante: vestito)* loose; *(: gonna)* full; *(: spiegazione)* ample, full.

am'plesso *sm* *(eufemismo)* embrace.

ampli'are *vt* *(ingrandire)* to enlarge; *(allargare)* to widen.

amplifi'care *vt* to amplify; *(magnificare)* to extol; **amplifica'tore** *sm* *(TECN, MUS)* amplifier.

am'polla *sf* *(vasetto)* cruet.

ampu'tare *vt* *(MED)* to amputate.

anabbagli'ante [anabbaʎ'ʎante] *ag* *(AUT)* dipped *(BRIT)*, dimmed *(US)*; **~i** *smpl* dipped *(BRIT)* o dimmed *(US)* headlights.

a'nagrafe *sf* *(registro)* register of births, marriages and deaths; *(ufficio)* registration office.

analfa'beta, i, e *ag, sm/f* illiterate.

anal'gesico, a, ci, che [anal'dʒɛziko] *ag, sm* analgesic.

a'nalisi *sf inv* analysis; (*MED: esame*) test; ~ **grammaticale** parsing; **ana'lista, i, e** *sm/f* analyst; (*PSIC*) (psycho)analyst.

analiz'zare [analid'dzare] *vt* to analyse; (*MED*) to test.

analo'gia, 'gie [analo'dʒia] *sf* analogy.

a'nalogo, a, ghi, ghe *ag* analogous.

'ananas *sm inv* pineapple.

anar'chia [anar'kia] *sf* anarchy; **a'narchico, a, ci, che** *ag* anarchic(al) ♦ *sm/f* anarchist.

'ANAS *sigla f* (= *Azienda Nazionale Autonoma delle Strade*) national roads department.

anato'mia *sf* anatomy; **ana'tomico, a, ci, che** *ag* anatomical; (*sedile*) contoured.

'anatra *sf* duck.

'anca, che *sf* (*ANAT*) hip; (*ZOOL*) haunch.

'anche ['anke] *cong* (*inoltre, pure*) also, too; (*perfino*) even; **vengo anch'io** I'm coming too; ~ **se** even if.

an'cora *av* still; (*di nuovo*) again; (*di più*) some more; (*persino*): ~ **più forte** even stronger; **non** ~ not yet; ~ **una volta** once more, once again; ~ **un po'** a little more; (*di tempo*) a little longer.

'ancora² *sf* anchor; **gettare/levare l'**~ to cast/weigh anchor; **anco'raggio** *sm* anchorage; **anco'rare** *vt* to anchor; **ancorarsi** *vr* to anchor.

anda'mento *sm* progress, movement; course; state.

an'dante *ag* (*corrente*) current; (*di poco pregio*) cheap, second-rate ♦ *sm* (*MUS*) andante.

an'dare *sm*: **a lungo** ~ in the long run ♦ *vi* to go; (*essere adatto*): ~ **a** to suit; (*piacere*): **il suo comportamento non mi va** I don't like the way he behaves; **ti va di andare al cinema?** do you feel like going to the cinema?; **andarsene** to go away; **questa camicia va lavata** this shirt needs a wash *o* should be washed;

~ **a cavallo** to ride; ~ **in macchina/ aereo** to go by car/plane; ~ **a fare qc** to go and do sth; ~ **a pescare/sciare** to go fishing/skiing; ~ **a male** to go bad; **come va?** (*lavoro, progetto*) how are things?; **come va? — bene, grazie!** how are you? — fine, thanks!; **va fatto entro oggi** it's got to be done today; **ne va della nostra vita** our lives are at stake; **an'data** *sf* going; (*viaggio*) outward journey; **biglietto di sola andata** single (*BRIT*) *o* one-way ticket; **biglietto di andata e ritorno** return (*BRIT*) *o* round-trip (*US*) ticket; **anda'tura** *sf* (*modo di andare*) walk, gait; (*SPORT*) pace; (*NAUT*) tack.

an'dazzo [an'dattso] (*peg*) *sm*: **prendere un brutto** ~ to take a turn for the worse.

andirivi'eni *sm inv* coming and going.

'andito *sm* corridor, passage.

an'drone *sm* entrance hall.

a'neddoto *sm* anecdote.

ane'lare *vi*: ~ **a** (*fig*) to long for, yearn for.

a'nelito *sm* (*fig*): ~ **di** longing *o* yearning for.

a'nello *sm* ring; (*di catena*) link.

a'nemico, a, ci, che *ag* anaemic.

a'nemone *sm* anemone.

aneste'sia *sf* anaesthesia; **anes'tetico, a, ci, che** *ag, sm* anaesthetic.

anfite'atro *sm* amphitheatre.

an'fratto *sm* ravine.

an'gelico, a, ci, che [an'dʒɛliko] *ag* angelic(al).

'angelo ['andʒelo] *sm* angel; ~ **custode** guardian angel.

anghe'ria [ange'ria] *sf* vexation.

an'gina [an'dʒina] *sf* tonsillitis; ~ **pectoris** angina.

angli'cano, a *ag* Anglican.

angli'cismo [angli'tʃizmo] *sm* anglicism.

anglo'sassone *ag* Anglo-Saxon.

ango'lare *ag* angular.

angolazi'one [angolat'tsjone] *sf* (*FOT etc*, *fig*) angle.

'angolo *sm* corner; (*MAT*) angle.

an'goscia, sce [an'gɔʃʃa] *sf* deep anxiety, anguish *no pl*; **angosci'oso, a**

ag (*d'angoscia*) anguished; (*che dà angoscia*) distressing, painful.

angu'illa *sf* eel.

an'guria *sf* watermelon.

an'gustia *sf* (*ansia*) anguish, distress; (*povertà*) poverty, want.

angusti'are *vt* to distress; ~**rsi** *vr*: ~**rsi** (**per**) to worry (about).

an'gusto, a *ag* (*stretto*) narrow; (*fig*) mean, petty.

'anice ['anitʃe] *sm* (*CUC*) aniseed; (*BOT*) anise.

a'nidride *sf* (*CHIM*): ~ **carbonica/ solforosa** carbon/sulphur dioxide.

'anima *sf* soul; (*abitante*) inhabitant; **non c'era** ~ **viva** there wasn't a living soul.

ani'male *sm*, *ag* animal.

ani'mare *vt* to give life to, liven up; (*incoraggiare*) to encourage; ~**rsi** *vr* to become animated, come to life; **ani'mato, a** *ag* animate; (*vivace*) lively, animated; (: *strada*) busy; **anima'tore, 'trice** *sm/f* guiding spirit; (*CINEMA*) animator; (*di festa*) life and soul; **animazi'one** *sf* liveliness; (*di strada*) bustle; (*CINEMA*) animation; **animazione teatrale** amateur dramatics.

'animo *sm* (*mente*) mind; (*cuore*) heart; (*coraggio*) courage; (*disposizione*) character, disposition; **avere in** ~ **di fare qc** to intend *o* have a mind to do sth; **perdersi d'**~ to lose heart.

'anitra *sf* = **anatra**.

anna'cquare *vt* to water down, dilute.

annaffi'are *vt* to water; **annaffia'toio** *sm* watering can.

an'nali *smpl* annals.

annas'pare *vi* to flounder.

an'nata *sf* year; (*importo annuo*) annual amount; **vino d'**~ vintage wine.

annebbi'are *vt* (*fig*) to cloud; ~**rsi** *vr* to become foggy; (*vista*) to become dim.

annega'mento *sm* drowning.

anne'gare *vt*, *vi* to drown; ~**rsi** *vr* (*accidentalmente*) to drown; (*deliberatamente*) to drown o.s.

anne'rire *vt* to blacken ♦ *vi* to become black.

an'nesso, a *pp di* **annettere** ♦ *ag* attached; (*POL*) annexed; ... **e tutti gli** ~**i e connessi** and so on and so forth.

an'nettere *vt* (*POL*) to annex; (*accludere*) to attach.

annichi'lare [anniki'lare] *vt* to annihilate.

annichi'lire [anniki'lire] *vt* = **annichilare**.

anni'darsi *vr* to nest.

annienta'mento *sm* annihilation, destruction.

annien'tare *vt* to annihilate, destroy.

anniver'sario *sm* anniversary.

'anno *sm* year.

anno'dare *vt* to knot, tie; (*fig: rapporto*) to form.

annoi'are *vt* to bore; (*seccare*) to annoy; ~**rsi** *vr* to be bored; to be annoyed.

anno'tare *vt* (*registrare*) to note, note down; (*commentare*) to annotate; **annotazi'one** *sf* note; annotation.

annove'rare *vt* to number.

annu'ale *ag* annual.

annu'ario *sm* yearbook.

annu'ire *vi* to nod; (*acconsentire*) to agree.

annul'lare *vt* to annihilate, destroy; (*contratto, francobollo*) to cancel; (*matrimonio*) to annul; (*sentenza*) to quash; (*risultati*) to declare void.

annunci'are [annun'tʃare] *vt* to announce; (*dar segni rivelatori*) to herald; **annuncia'tore, 'trice** *sm/f* (*RADIO, TV*) announcer; **l'Annunciazi'one** *sf* the Annunciation.

an'nuncio [an'nuntʃo] *sm* announcement; (*fig*) sign; ~ **pubblicitario** advertisement; ~**i economici** classified advertisements, small ads.

'annuo, a *ag* annual, yearly.

annu'sare *vt* to sniff, smell; ~ **tabacco** to take snuff.

'ano *sm* anus.

anoma'lia *sf* anomaly.

a'nomalo, a *ag* anomalous.

a'nonimo, a *ag* anonymous ♦ *sm*

(*autore*) anonymous writer (*o painter etc*); **società** ~**a** (*COMM*) joint stock company.

anor'male *ag* abnormal ♦ *sm/f* subnormal person; (*eufemismo*) homosexual.

ANSA *sigla f* (= *Agenzia Nazionale Stampa Associata*) press agency.

'ansa *sf* (*manico*) handle; (*di fiume*) bend, loop.

'ansia *sf* anxiety.

ansietà *sf* = ansia.

ansi'mare *vi* to pant.

ansi'oso, a *ag* anxious.

'anta *sf* (*di finestra*) shutter; (*di armadio*) door.

antago'nismo *sm* antagonism.

an'tartico, a, ci, che *ag* Antarctic ♦ *sm*: l'A~ the Antarctic.

antece'dente [antetʃe'dɛnte] *ag* preceding, previous.

ante'fatto *sm* previous events *pl*; previous history.

antegu'erra *sm* pre-war period.

ante'nato *sm* ancestor, forefather.

an'tenna *sf* (*RADIO*, *TV*) aerial; (*ZOOL*) antenna, feeler; (*NAUT*) yard.

ante'prima *sf* preview.

anteri'ore *ag* (*ruota*, *zampa*) front; (*fatti*) previous, preceding.

antia'ereo, a *ag* anti-aircraft.

antia'tomico, a, ci, che *ag* antinuclear; **rifugio** ~ fallout shelter.

antibi'otico, a, ci, che *ag*, *sm* antibiotic.

anti'camera *sf* anteroom; **fare** ~ to wait (for an audience).

antichità [antiki'ta] *sf inv* antiquity; (*oggetto*) antique.

antici'pare [antitʃi'pare] *vt* (*consegna*, *visita*) to bring forward, anticipate; (*somma di denaro*) to pay in advance; (*notizia*) to disclose ♦ *vi* to be ahead of time; **anticipazi'one** *sf* anticipation; (*di notizia*) advance information; (*somma di denaro*) advance; **an'ticipo** *sm* anticipation; (*di denaro*) advance; **in anticipo** early, in advance.

an'tico, a, chi, che *ag* (*quadro*, *mobili*) antique; (*dell'antichità*) ancient; **all'**~**a** old-fashioned.

anticoncezio'nale [antikontʃettsjo'nale] *sm* contraceptive.

anticonfor'mista, i, e *ag*, *sm/f* nonconformist.

anti'corpo *sm* antibody.

anti'furto *sm* (*anche: sistema* ~) antitheft device.

An'tille *sfpl*: le ~ the West Indies.

antin'cendio [antin'tʃɛndjo] *ag inv* fire cpd.

antio'rario [antio'rarjo] *ag*: **in senso** ~ anticlockwise.

anti'pasto *sm* hors d'œuvre.

antipa'tia *sf* antipathy, dislike; **anti'patico, a, ci, che** *ag* unpleasant, disagreeable.

antiquari'ato *sm* antique trade; **un oggetto d'**~ an antique.

anti'quario *sm* antique dealer.

anti'quato, a *ag* antiquated, old-fashioned.

antise'mita, i, e *ag* anti-Semitic.

anti'settico, a, ci, che *ag*, *sm* antiseptic.

antista'minico, a, ci, che *ag*, *sm* antihistamine.

antolo'gia, 'gie [antolo'dʒia] *sf* anthology.

anu'lare *ag* ring cpd ♦ *sm* third finger.

'anzi ['antsi] *av* (*invece*) on the contrary; (*o meglio*) or rather, or better still.

anzianità [antsjani'ta] *sf* old age; (*AMM*) seniority.

anzi'ano, a [an'tsjano] *ag* old; (*AMM*) senior ♦ *sm/f* old person; senior member.

anziché [antsi'ke] *cong* rather than.

anzi'tutto [antsi'tutto] *av* first of all.

apa'tia *sf* apathy, indifference.

'ape *sf* bee.

aperi'tivo *sm* apéritif.

a'perto, a *pp di* **aprire** ♦ *ag* open; **all'**~ in the open (air).

aper'tura *sf* opening; (*ampiezza*) width, spread; (*POL*) approach; (*FOT*) aperture; ~ **alare** wing span.

'apice ['apitʃe] *sm* apex; (*fig*) height.

apicol'tore *sm* beekeeper.

ap'nea *sf*: **immergersi in** ~ to dive without breathing apparatus.

a'polide *ag* stateless.

apoples'sia *sf* (*MED*) apoplexy.

a'postolo *sm* apostle.

a'postrofo *sm* apostrophe.

appa'gare *vt* to satisfy; ~**rsi** *vr*: ~**rsi di** to be satisfied with.

ap'palto *sm* (*COMM*) contract; **dare/ prendere in** ~ **un lavoro** to let out/ undertake a job on contract.

appan'nare *vt* (*vetro*) to mist; (*metallo*) to tarnish; (*vista*) to dim; ~**rsi** *vr* to mist over; to tarnish; to grow dim.

appa'rato *sm* equipment, machinery; (*ANAT*) apparatus; ~ **scenico** (*TEATRO*) props *pl*.

apparecchi'are [apparek'kjare] *vt* to prepare; (*tavola*) to set ♦ *vi* to set the table; **apparecchia'tura** *sf* equipment; (*macchina*) machine, device.

appa'recchio [appa'rekkjo] *sm* piece of apparatus, device; (*aeroplano*) aircraft *inv*; ~ **televisivo/telefonico** television set/telephone.

appa'rente *ag* apparent; **appa'renza** *sf* appearance; **in** *o* **all'apparenza** apparently, to all appearances.

appa'rire *vi* to appear; (*sembrare*) to seem, appear; **appari'scente** *ag* (*colore*) garish, gaudy; (*bellezza*) striking.

apparta'mento *sm* flat (*BRIT*), apartment (*US*).

appar'tarsi *vr* to withdraw; **appar'tato, a** *ag* (*luogo*) secluded.

apparte'nere *vi*: ~ **a** to belong to.

appassio'nare *vt* to thrill; (*commuovere*) to move; ~**rsi a qc** to take a great interest in sth; to be deeply moved by sth; **appassio'nato, a** *ag* passionate; (*entusiasta*): **appassionato (di)** keen (on).

appas'sire *vi* to wither.

appel'larsi *vr* (*ricorrere*): ~ **a** to appeal to; (*DIR*): ~ **contro** to appeal against; **ap'pello** *sm* roll-call; (*implorazione*, *DIR*) appeal; **fare appello a** to appeal to.

ap'pena *av* (*a stento*) hardly, scarcely; (*solamente*, *da poco*) just ♦ *cong* as soon as; (**non**) ~ **furono arrivati** ... as soon as they had arrived ...; ~ ... **che** *o* **quando** no sooner ... than.

ap'pendere *vt* to hang (up).

appen'dice [appen'ditʃe] *sf* appendix; **romanzo d'**~ popular serial.

appendi'cite [appendi'tʃite] *sf* appendicitis.

Appen'nini *smpl*: **gli** ~ the Apennines.

appesan'tire *vt* to make heavy; ~**rsi** *vr* to grow stout.

ap'peso, a *pp di* **appendere**.

appe'tito *sm* appetite; **appeti'toso, a** *ag* appetising; (*fig*) attractive, desirable.

appia'nare *vt* to level; (*fig*) to smooth away, iron out.

appiat'tire *vt* to flatten; ~**rsi** *vr* to become flatter; (*farsi piatto*) to flatten o.s.; ~**rsi al suolo** to lie flat on the ground.

appic'care *vt*: ~ **il fuoco a** to set fire to, set on fire.

appicci'care [appittʃi'kare] *vt* to stick; (*fig*): ~ **qc a qn** to palm sth off on sb; ~**rsi** *vr* to stick; (*fig: persona*) to cling.

appi'eno *av* fully.

appigli'arsi [appiʎ'ʎarsi] *vr*: ~ **a** (*afferrarsi*) to take hold of; (*fig*) to cling to; **ap'piglio** *sm* hold; (*fig*) pretext.

appiso'larsi *vr* to doze off.

applau'dire *vt*, *vi* to applaud; **ap'plauso** *sm* applause.

appli'care *vt* to apply; (*regolamento*) to enforce; ~**rsi** *vr* to apply o.s.; **applicazi'one** *sf* application; enforcement.

appoggi'are [appod'dʒare] *vt* (*mettere contro*): ~ **qc a** to lean *o* rest sth against sth; (*fig: sostenere*) to support; ~**rsi** *vr*: ~**rsi a** to lean against; (*fig*) to rely upon; **ap'poggio** *sm* support.

appollai'arsi *vr* (*anche fig*) to perch.

ap'porre *vt* to affix.

appor'tare *vt* to bring.

apposita'mente *av* specially; (*apposta*) on purpose.

ap'posito, a *ag* appropriate.

apposta 19 architetto

ap'posta *av* on purpose, deliberately.
appos'tare *vt* to lie in wait for; **~rsi** *vr* to lie in wait.
ap'prendere *vt* (*imparare*) to learn; (*comprendere*) to grasp.
appren'dista, i, e *sm/f* apprentice.
apprensi'one *sf* apprehension; **appren'sivo, a** *ag* apprehensive.
ap'presso *av* (*accanto, vicino*) close by, near; (*dietro*) behind; (*dopo, più tardi*) after, later ♦ *ag inv* (*dopo*): **il giorno ~** the next day; **~ a** (*vicino a*) near, close to.
appres'tare *vt* to prepare, get ready; **~rsi** *vr*: **~rsi a fare qc** to prepare *o* get ready to do sth.
ap'pretto *sm* starch.
apprez'zabile [apprettsabile] *ag* noteworthy, significant.
apprezza'mento [apprettsa'mento] *sm* appreciation; (*giudizio*) opinion.
apprez'zare [appret'tsare] *vt* to appreciate.
ap'proccio [ap'prɔttʃo] *sm* approach.
appro'dare *vi* (*NAUT*) to land; (*fig*): **non ~ a nulla** to come to nothing; **ap'prodo** *sm* landing; (*luogo*) landing-place.
approfit'tare *vi*: **~ di** to make the most of, profit by.
approfon'dire *vt* to deepen; (*fig*) to study in depth.
appropri'ato, a *ag* appropriate.
approssi'marsi *vr*: **~ a** to approach.
approssima'tivo, a *ag* approximate, rough; (*impreciso*) inexact, imprecise.
appro'vare *vt* (*condotta, azione*) to approve of; (*candidato*) to pass; (*progetto di legge*) to approve; **approvazi'one** *sf* approval.
approvvigio'nare [approvvidʒo'nare] *vt* to supply; **~rsi** *vr* to lay in provisions, stock up; **~ qn di qc** to supply sb with sth.
appunta'mento *sm* appointment; (*amoroso*) date; **darsi ~** to arrange to meet (one another).
appun'tato *sm* (*CARABINIERI*) corporal.
ap'punto *sm* note; (*rimprovero*) reproach ♦ *av* (*proprio*) exactly, just; **per**

l'~!, ~! exactly!
appu'rare *vt* to check, verify.
apribot'tiglie [apribot'tiʎʎe] *sm inv* bottleopener.
a'prile *sm* April.
a'prire *vt* to open; (*via, cadavere*) to open up; (*gas, luce, acqua*) to turn on ♦ *vi* to open; **~rsi** *vr* to open; **~rsi a qn** to confide in sb, open one's heart to sb.
apris'catole *sm inv* tin (*BRIT*) *o* can opener.
a'quario *sm* = **acquario**.
'aquila *sf* (*ZOOL*) eagle; (*fig*) genius.
aqui'lone *sm* (*giocattolo*) kite; (*vento*) North wind.
A'rabia 'Saudita *sf*: **l'~** Saudi Arabia.
'arabo, a *ag, sm/f* Arab ♦ *sm* (*LING*) Arabic.
a'rachide [a'rakide] *sf* peanut.
ara'gosta *sf* crayfish; lobster.
a'raldica *sf* heraldry.
a'rancia, ce [a'rantʃa] *sf* orange; **aranci'ata** *sf* orangeade; **a'rancio** *sm* (*BOT*) orange tree; (*colore*) orange ♦ *ag inv* (*colore*) orange; **aranci'one** *ag inv*: **(color) arancione** bright orange.
a'rare *vt* to plough (*BRIT*), plow (*US*).
a'ratro *sm* plough (*BRIT*), plow (*US*).
a'razzo [a'rattso] *sm* tapestry.
arbi'trare *vt* (*SPORT*) to referee; to umpire; (*DIR*) to arbitrate.
arbi'trario, a *ag* arbitrary.
ar'bitrio *sm* will; (*abuso, sopruso*) arbitrary act.
'arbitro *sm* arbiter, judge; (*DIR*) arbitrator; (*SPORT*) referee; (*: TENNIS, CRICKET*) umpire.
ar'busto *sm* shrub.
'arca, che *sf* (*sarcofago*) sarcophagus; **l'~ di Noè** Noah's ark.
ar'cangelo [ar'kandʒelo] *sm* archangel.
ar'cano, a *ag* arcane, mysterious.
ar'cata *sf* (*ARCHIT, ANAT*) arch; (*ordine di archi*) arcade.
archeolo'gia [arkeolo'dʒia] *sf* arch(a)eology; **arche'ologo, a, gi, ghe** *sm/f* arch(a)eologist.
ar'chetto [ar'ketto] *sm* (*MUS*) bow.
archi'tetto [arki'tetto] *sm* architect; **architet'tura** *sf* architecture.

ar'chivio [ar'kivjo] *sm* archives *pl*; (*IN-FORM*) file.
arci'ere [ar'tʃɛre] *sm* archer.
ar'cigno, a [ar'tʃiɲɲo] *ag* grim, severe.
arci'vescovo [artʃi'veskovo] *sm* arch-bishop.
'arco *sm* (*arma*, *MUS*) bow; (*ARCHIT*) arch; (*MAT*) arc.
arcoba'leno *sm* rainbow.
arcu'ato, a *ag* curved, bent; **dalle gambe ~e** bow-legged.
ar'dente *ag* burning; (*fig*) burning, ardent.
'ardere *vt, vi* to burn.
ar'desia *sf* slate.
ar'dire *vi* to dare ♦ *sm* daring; **ar'dito, a** *ag* brave, daring, bold; (*sfacciato*) bold.
ar'dore *sm* blazing heat; (*fig*) ardour, fervour.
'arduo, a *ag* arduous, difficult.
'area *sf* area; (*EDIL*) land, ground.
a'rena *sf* arena; (*per corride*) bullring; (*sabbia*) sand.
are'narsi *vr* to run aground.
areo'plano *sm* = **aeroplano**.
'argano *sm* winch.
argente'ria [ardʒente'ria] *sf* silverware, silver.
argenti'ere [ardʒen'tjɛre] *sm* silver-smith.
Argen'tina [ardʒen'tina] *sf*: **l'~** Argentina; **argen'tino, a** *ag*, *sm/f* Argentinian.
ar'gento [ar'dʒɛnto] *sm* silver; **~ vivo** quicksilver.
ar'gilla [ar'dʒilla] *sf* clay.
'argine ['ardʒine] *sm* embankment, bank; (*diga*) dyke, dike.
argomen'tare *vi* to argue.
argo'mento *sm* argument; (*motivo*) motive; (*materia*, *tema*) subject.
argu'ire *vt* to deduce.
ar'guto, a *ag* sharp, quick-witted; **ar'guzia** *sf* wit; (*battuta*) witty remark.
'aria *sf* air; (*espressione*, *aspetto*) air, look; (*MUS: melodia*) tune; (: *di opera*) aria; **mandare all'~ qc** to ruin *o* upset sth; **all'~ aperta** in the open (air).
'arido, a *ag* arid.

arieggi'are [arjed'dʒare] *vt* (*cambiare aria*) to air; (*imitare*) to imitate.
ari'ete *sm* ram; (*MIL*) battering ram; (*dello zodiaco*): **A~** Aries.
a'ringa, ghe *sf* herring *inv*.
'arista *sf* (*CUC*) chine of pork.
aristo'cratico, a, ci, che *ag* aris-tocratic.
arit'metica *sf* arithmetic.
arlec'chino [arlek'kino] *sm* harlequin.
'arma, i *sf* weapon, arm; (*parte dell'esercito*) arm; **chiamare alle ~i** to call up (*BRIT*), draft (*US*); **sotto le ~i** in the army (*o* forces); **alle ~i!** to arms!; **~ da fuoco** firearm.
ar'madio *sm* cupboard; (*per abiti*) wardrobe.
armamen'tario *sm* equipment, instru-ments *pl*.
arma'mento *sm* (*MIL*) armament; (: *materiale*) arms *pl*, weapons *pl*; (*NAUT*) fitting out; manning.
ar'mare *vt* to arm; (*arma da fuoco*) to cock; (*NAUT: nave*) to rig, fit out; to man; (*EDIL: volta, galleria*) to prop up, shore up; **~rsi** *vr* to arm o.s.; (*MIL*) to take up arms; **ar'mata** *sf* (*MIL*) army; (*NAUT*) fleet; **arma'tore** *sm* shipowner; **arma'tura** *sf* (*struttura di sostegno*) framework; (*impalcatura*) scaffolding; (*STORIA*) armour *no pl*, suit of armour.
armeggi'are [armed'dʒare] *vi*: **~** (*intorno a qc*) to mess about (with sth).
armis'tizio [armis'tittsjo] *sm* armistice.
armo'nia *sf* harmony; **ar'monica, che** *sf* (*MUS*) harmonica; **ar'monico, a, ci, che** *ag* harmonic; (*fig*) harmonious **armoni'oso, a** *ag* harmonious.
armoniz'zare [armonid'dzare] *vt* to harmonize; (*colori, abiti*) to match ♦ *vi* to be in harmony; to match.
ar'nese *sm* tool, implement; (*oggetto indeterminato*) thing, contraption; **male in ~** (*malvestito*) badly dressed; (*di salute malferma*) in poor health; (*di condizioni economiche*) down-at heel.
'arnia *sf* hive.
a'roma, i *sm* aroma; fragrance; **~i** *smpl* (*CUC*) herbs and spices; **aro'matico, a, ci, che** *ag* aromatic;

(*cibo*) spicy.

'**arpa** *sf* (*MUS*) harp.

ar'peggio [ar'pɛddʒo] *sm* (*MUS*) arpeggio.

ar'pia *sf* (*anche fig*) harpy.

arpi'one *sm* (*gancio*) hook; (*cardine*) hinge; (*PESCA*) harpoon.

arrabat'tarsi *vr* to do all one can, strive.

arrabbi'are *vi* (*cane*) to be affected with rabies; ~**rsi** *vr* (*essere preso dall'ira*) to get angry, fly into a rage; **arrabbi'ato, a** *ag* rabid, with rabies; furious, angry.

arraf'fare *vt* to snatch, seize; (*sottrarre*) to pinch.

arrampi'carsi *vr* to climb (up).

arran'care *vi* to limp, hobble.

arran'giare [arran'dʒare] *vt* to arrange; ~**rsi** *vr* to manage, do the best one can.

arre'care *vt* to bring; (*causare*) to cause.

arreda'mento *sm* (*studio*) interior design; (*mobili etc*) furnishings *pl*.

arre'dare *vt* to furnish; **arreda'tore 'trice** *sm/f* interior designer; **ar'redo** *sm* fittings *pl*, furnishings *pl*.

ar'rendersi *vr* to surrender.

arres'tare *vt* (*fermare*) to stop, halt; (*catturare*) to arrest; ~**rsi** *vr* (*fermarsi*) to stop; **ar'resto** *sm* (*cessazione*) stopping; (*fermata*) stop; (*cattura, MED*) arrest; **subire un arresto** to come to a stop *o* standstill; **mettere agli arresti** to place under arrest; **arresti domiciliari** house arrest *sg*.

arre'trare *vt, vi* to withdraw; **arre'trato, a** *ag* (*lavoro*) behind schedule; (*paese, bambino*) backward; (*numero di giornale*) back *cpd*; **arretrati** *smpl* arrears.

arric'chire [arrik'kire] *vt* to enrich; ~**rsi** *vr* to become rich.

arricci'are [arrit'tʃare] *vt* to curl; ~ **il naso** to turn up one's nose.

ar'ringa, ghe *sf* harangue; (*DIR*) address by counsel.

arrischi'are [arris'kjare] *vt* to risk; ~**rsi** *vr* to venture, dare; **arrischi'ato, a** *ag*

risky; (*temerario*) reckless, rash.

arri'vare *vi* to arrive; (*accadere*) to happen, occur; ~ **a** (*livello, grado etc*) to reach; **lui arriva a Roma alle 7** he gets to *o* arrives at Rome at 7; **non ci arrivo** I can't reach it; (*fig: non capisco*) I can't understand it.

arrive'derci [arrive'dertʃi] *escl* goodbye!

arrive'derla *escl* (*forma di cortesia*) goodbye!

arri'vista, i, e *sm/f* go-getter.

ar'rivo *sm* arrival; (*SPORT*) finish, finishing line.

arro'gante *ag* arrogant.

arro'lare *vb* = **arruolare**.

arros'sire *vi* (*per vergogna, timidezza*) to blush, flush; (*per gioia, rabbia*) to flush.

arros'tire *vt* to roast; (*pane*) to toast; (*ai ferri*) to grill.

ar'rosto *sm, ag inv* roast.

arro'tare *vt* to sharpen; (*investire con un veicolo*) to run over.

arroto'lare *vt* to roll up.

arroton'dare *vt* (*forma, oggetto*) to round; (*stipendio*) to add to; (*somma*) to round off.

arrovel'larsi *vr:* ~ (**il cervello**) to rack one's brains.

arruf'fare *vt* to ruffle; (*fili*) to tangle; (*fig: questione*) to confuse.

arruggi'nire [arruddʒi'nire] *vt* to rust; ~**rsi** *vr* to rust; (*fig*) to become rusty.

arruo'lare *vt* (*MIL*) to enlist; ~**rsi** *vr* to enlist, join up.

arse'nale *sm* (*MIL*) arsenal; (*cantiere navale*) dockyard.

'**arso, a** *pp di* **ardere ♦** *ag* (*bruciato*) burnt; (*arido*) dry; **ar'sura** *sf* (*calore opprimente*) burning heat; (*siccità*) drought.

'**arte** *sf* art; (*abilità*) skill.

arte'fatto, a *ag* (*cibo*) adulterated; (*fig: modi*) artificial.

ar'tefice [ar'tefitʃe] *sm/f* craftsman/woman; (*autore*) author.

ar'teria *sf* artery.

'**artico, a, ci, che** *ag* Arctic.

artico'lare *ag* (*ANAT*) of the joints, articular ♦ *vt* to articulate;

(*suddividere*) to divide, split up; **articolazi'one** *sf* articulation; (*ANAT*, *TECN*) joint.

ar'ticolo *sm* article; ~ **di fondo** (*STAMPA*) leader, leading article.

'Artide *sm*: **l'**~ the Arctic.

artifici'ale [artifi'tʃale] *ag* artificial.

arti'ficio [arti'fitʃo] *sm* (*espediente*) trick, artifice; (*ricerca di effetto*) artificiality.

artigia'nato [artidʒa'nato] *sm* craftsmanship; craftsmen *pl*.

artigi'ano, a [arti'dʒano] *sm/f* craftsman/woman.

artiglie'ria [artiʎʎe'ria] *sf* artillery.

ar'tiglio [ar'tiʎʎo] *sm* claw; (*di rapaci*) talon.

ar'tista, i, e *sm/f* artist; **ar'tistico, a, ci, che** *ag* artistic.

'arto *sm* (*ANAT*) limb.

ar'trite *sf* (*MED*) arthritis.

ar'trosi *sf* osteoarthritis.

ar'zillo, a [ar'dzillo] *ag* lively, sprightly.

a'scella [aʃ'ʃɛlla] *sf* (*ANAT*) armpit.

ascen'dente [aʃʃen'dɛnte] *sm* ancestor; (*fig*) ascendancy; (*ASTR*) ascendant.

ascensi'one [aʃʃen'sjone] *sf* (*ALPINISMO*) ascent; (*REL*): **l'A**~ the Ascension.

ascen'sore [aʃʃen'sore] *sm* lift.

a'scesa [aʃ'ʃesa] *sf* ascent; (*al trono*) accession.

a'scesso [aʃ'ʃɛsso] *sm* (*MED*) abscess.

'ascia ['aʃʃa] (*pl* **'asce**) *sf* axe.

asciugaca'pelli [aʃʃugaka'pelli] *sm* hair-drier.

asciuga'mano [aʃʃuga'mano] *sm* towel.

asciu'gare [aʃʃu'gare] *vt* to dry; ~**rsi** *vr* to dry o.s.; (*diventare asciutto*) to dry.

asci'utto, a [aʃ'ʃutto] *ag* dry; (*fig: magro*) lean; (: *burbero*) curt; **restare a bocca** ~**a** (*fig*) to be disappointed.

ascol'tare *vt* to listen to; **ascolta'tore, 'trice** *sm/f* listener; **as'colto** *sm*: **essere o stare in ascolto** to be listening; **dare o prestare ascolto (a)** to pay attention (to).

as'falto *sm* asphalt.

asfissi'are *vt* to suffocate, asphyxiate; (*fig*) to bore to tears.

'Asia *sf*: **l'**~ Asia; **asi'atico, a, ci, che**

ag, sm/f Asiatic, Asian.

a'silo *sm* refuge, sanctuary; ~ **(d'infanzia)** nursery(-school); ~ **nido** crèche; ~ **politico** political asylum.

'asino *sm* donkey, ass.

'asma *sf* asthma.

'asola *sf* buttonhole.

as'parago, gi *sm* asparagus *no pl*.

aspet'tare *vt* to wait for; (*anche COMM*) to await; (*aspettarsi*) to expect ♦ *vi* to wait; ~**rsi** *vr* to expect; ~ **un bambino** to be expecting (a baby); **questo non me l'aspettavo** I wasn't expecting this; **aspetta'tiva** *sf* wait; expectation; **inferiore all'aspettativa** worse than expected; **essere in aspettativa** (*AMM*) to be on leave of absence.

as'petto *sm* (*apparenza*) aspect, appearance, look; (*punto di vista*) point of view; **di bell'**~ good-looking.

aspi'rante *ag* (*attore etc*) aspiring ♦ *sm/f* candidate, applicant.

aspira'polvere *sm inv* vacuum cleaner.

aspi'rare *vt* (*respirare*) to breathe in, inhale; (*sog: apparecchi*) to suck (up) ♦ *vi*: ~ **a** to aspire to; **aspira'tore** *sm* extractor fan.

aspi'rina *sf* aspirin.

aspor'tare *vt* (*anche MED*) to remove, take away.

'aspro, a *ag* (*sapore*) sour, tart; (*odore*) acrid, pungent; (*voce, clima, fig*) harsh; (*superficie*) rough; (*paesaggio*) rugged.

assaggi'are [assad'dʒare] *vt* to taste.

as'sai *av* (*molto*) a lot, much; (: *con ag*) very; (*a suffficienza*) enough ♦ *ag inv* (*quantità*) a lot of, much; (*numero*) a lot of, many; ~ **contento** very pleased.

assa'lire *vt* to attack, assail.

as'salto *sm* attack, assault.

assassi'nare *vt* to murder; to assassinate; (*fig*) to ruin; **assas'sinio** *sm* murder; assassination; **assas'sino, a** *ag* murderous ♦ *sm/f* murderer; assassin.

'asse *sm* (*TECN*) axle; (*MAT*) axis ♦ *sf* board; ~ *sf* **da stiro** ironing board.

assedi'are vt to besiege; **as'sedio** sm siege.

asse'gnare [asseɲ'ɲare] vt to assign, allot; (*premio*) to award.

as'segno [as'seɲɲo] sm allowance; (*anche*: ~ *bancario*) cheque (*BRIT*), check (*US*); **contro** ~ cash on delivery; ~ **circolare** bank draft; ~ **sbarrato** crossed cheque; ~ **di viaggio** traveller's cheque; ~ **a vuoto** dud cheque; ~**i familiari** ≈ child benefit *no pl*.

assem'blea sf assembly.

assen'nato, a ag sensible.

as'senso sm assent, consent.

as'sente ag absent; (*fig*) faraway, vacant; **as'senza** sf absence.

asses'sore sm (*POL*) councillor.

assesta'mento sm (*sistemazione*) arrangement; (*EDIL*, *GEOL*) settlement.

asses'tare vt (*mettere in ordine*) to put in order, arrange; ~**rsi** vr to settle in; ~ **un colpo a qn** to deal sb a blow.

asse'tato, a ag thirsty, parched.

as'setto sm order, arrangement; (*NAUT*, *AER*) trim; **in** ~ **di guerra** on a war footing.

assicu'rare vt (*accertare*) to ensure; (*infondere certezza*) to assure; (*fermare*, *legare*) to make fast, secure; (*fare un contratto di assicurazione*) to insure; ~**rsi** vr (*accertarsi*): ~**rsi (di)** to make sure (of); (*contro il furto etc*): ~**rsi (contro)** to insure o.s. (against); **assicu'rata** sf (*anche*: *lettera assicurata*) registered letter; **assicu'rato, a** ag insured; **assicurazi'one** sf assurance; insurance.

assidera'mento sm exposure.

assi'eme av (*insieme*) together; ~ **a** (together) with.

assil'lare vt to pester, torment.

as'sillo sm (*fig*) worrying thought.

as'sise sfpl (*DIR*) assizes; **Corte** sf **d'A~** Court of Assizes, ≈ Crown Court (*BRIT*).

assis'tente sm/f assistant; ~ **sociale** social worker; ~ **di volo** (*AER*) steward/stewardess.

assis'tenza [assis'tɛntsa] sf assistance; ~ **ospedaliera** free hospital treatment;

~ **sanitaria** health service; ~ **sociale** welfare services *pl*.

as'sistere vt (*aiutare*) to assist, help; (*curare*) to treat ♦ vi: ~ **(a qc)** (*essere presente*) to be present (at sth), to attend (sth).

'asso sm ace; **piantare qn in** ~ to leave sb in the lurch.

associ'are [asso'tʃare] vt to associate; (*rendere partecipe*): ~ **qn a** (*affari*) to take sb into partnership in; (*partito*) to make sb a member of; ~**rsi** vr to enter into partnership; ~**rsi a** to become a member of, join; (*dolori*, *gioie*) to share in; ~ **qn alle carceri** to take sb to prison.

associazi'one [assotʃat'tsjone] sf association; (*COMM*) association, society; ~ **a o per delinquere** (*DIR*) criminal association.

asso'dato, a ag well-founded.

assogget'tare [assoddʒet'tare] vt to subject, subjugate.

asso'lato, a ag sunny.

assol'dare vt to recruit.

as'solto, a pp di **assolvere**.

assoluta'mente av absolutely.

asso'luto, a ag absolute.

assoluzi'one [assolut'tsjone] sf (*DIR*) acquittal; (*REL*) absolution.

as'solvere vt (*DIR*) to acquit; (*REL*) to absolve; (*adempiere*) to carry out, perform.

assomigli'are [assomiʎ'ʎare] vi: ~ **a** to resemble, look like.

asson'nato, a ag sleepy.

asso'pirsi vr to doze off.

assor'bente ag absorbent ♦ sm: ~ **igienico** sanitary towel; ~ **interno** tampon.

assor'bire vt to absorb; (*fig: far proprio*) to assimilate.

assor'dare vt to deafen.

assorti'mento sm assortment.

assor'tito, a ag assorted; matched, matching.

as'sorto, a ag absorbed, engrossed.

assottigli'are [assottiʎ'ʎare] vt to make thin, to thin; (*aguzzare*) to sharpen; (*ridurre*) to reduce; ~**rsi** vr to grow

thin; *(fig: ridursi)* to be reduced.
assue'fare *vt* to accustom; **~rsi a** to get used to, accustom o.s. to.
as'sumere *vt (impiegato)* to take on, engage; *(responsabilità)* to assume, take upon o.s.; *(contegno, espressione)* to assume, put on; *(droga)* to consume; **as'sunto, a** *pp di* **assumere ♦** *sm (tesi)* proposition.
assurdità *sf inv* absurdity; **dire delle ~** to talk nonsense.
as'surdo, a *ag* absurd.
'asta *sf* pole; *(modo di vendita)* auction.
astante'ria *sf* casualty department.
aste'nersi *vr*: **~ (da)** to abstain (from), refrain (from); *(POL)* to abstain (from).
aste'risco, schi *sm* asterisk.
'astice ['astitʃe] *sm* lobster.
asti'nenza [asti'nɛntsa] *sf* abstinence; **essere in crisi di ~** to suffer from withdrawal symptoms.
'astio *sm* rancour, resentment.
as'tratto, a *ag* abstract.
'astro *sm* star.
'astro... *prefisso*: **astrolo'gia** [astrolo'dʒia] *sf* astrology; **as'trologo, a, ghi, ghe** *sm/f* astrologer; **astro'nauta, i, e** *sm/f* astronaut; **astro'nave** *sf* space ship; **astrono'mia** *sf* astronomy; **astro'nomico, a, ci, che** *ag* astronomic(al).
as'tuccio [as'tuttʃo] *sm* case, box, holder.
as'tuto, a *ag* astute, cunning, shrewd; **as'tuzia** *sf* astuteness, shrewdness; *(azione)* trick.
A'tene *sf* Athens.
ate'neo *sm* university.
'ateo, a *ag, sm/f* atheist.
at'lante *sm* atlas.
at'lantico, a, ci, che *ag* Atlantic **♦** *sm*: **l'A~, l'Oceano A~** the Atlantic, the Atlantic Ocean.
at'leta, i, e *sm/f* athlete; **at'letica** *sf* athletics *sg*; **atletica leggera** track and field events *pl*; **atletica pesante** weightlifting and wrestling.
atmos'fera *sf* atmosphere.

a'tomico, a, ci, che *ag* atomic; *(nucleare)* atomic, atom *cpd*, nuclear.
'atomo *sm* atom.
'atrio *sm* entrance hall, lobby.
a'troce [a'trotʃe] *ag (che provoca orrore)* dreadful; *(terribile)* atrocious.
attacca'mento *sm (fig)* attachment, affection.
attacca'panni *sm* hook, peg; *(mobile)* hall stand.
attac'care *vt (unire)* to attach; *(cucendo)* to sew on; *(far aderire)* to stick (on); *(appendere)* to hang (up); *(assalire: anche fig)* to attack; *(iniziare)* to begin, start; *(fig: contagiare)* to pass on **♦** *vi* to stick, adhere; **~rsi** *vr* to stick, adhere; *(trasmettersi per contagio)* to be contagious; *(afferrarsi)*: **~rsi (a)** to cling (to); *(fig: affezionarsi)*: **~rsi (a)** to become attached (to); **~ discorso** to start a conversation; **at'tacco, chi** *sm (azione offensiva: anche fig)* attack; *(MED)* attack, fit; *(SCI)* binding; *(ELETTR)* socket.
atteggia'mento [atteddʒa'mento] *sm* attitude.
atteggi'arsi [atted'dʒarsi] *vr*: **~ a** to pose as.
attem'pato, a *ag* elderly.
at'tendere *vt* to wait for, await **♦** *vi*: **~ a** to attend to.
atten'dibile *ag (storia)* credible; *(testimone)* reliable.
atte'nersi *vr*: **~ a** to keep *o* stick to.
atten'tare *vi*: **~ a** to make an attempt on; **atten'tato** *sm* attack; **attentato alla vita di qn** attempt on sb's life.
at'tento, a *ag* attentive; *(accurato)* careful, thorough; **stare ~ a qc** to pay attention to sth **♦** *escl* be careful!
attenu'ante *sf (DIR)* extenuating circumstance.
attenu'are *vt* to attenuate; *(dolore, rumore)* to lessen, deaden; *(pena, tasse)* to alleviate; **~rsi** *vr* to ease, abate.
attenzi'one [atten'tsjone] *sf* attention **♦** *escl* watch out!, be careful!
atter'raggio [atter'raddʒo] *sm* landing.

atter'rare vt to bring down ♦ vi to land.
atter'rire vt to terrify.
at'tesa sf waiting; (tempo trascorso aspettando) wait; **essere in attesa di qc** to be waiting for sth.
at'teso, a pp di **attendere**.
attes'tato sm certificate.
'attico, ci sm attic.
at'tiguo, a ag adjacent, adjoining.
attil'lato, a ag (vestito) close-fitting, tight; (persona) dressed up.
'attimo sm moment; **in un ~** in a moment.
atti'nente ag: **~ a** relating to, concerning.
atti'rare vt to attract.
atti'tudine sf (disposizione) aptitude; (atteggiamento) attitude.
atti'vare vt to activate; (far funzionare) to set going, start.
attività sf inv activity; (COMM) assets pl.
at'tivo, a ag active; (COMM) profit-making, credit cpd ♦ sm (COMM) assets pl; **in ~** in credit.
attiz'zare [attit'tsare] vt (fuoco) to poke.
'atto sm act; (azione, gesto) action, act, deed; (DIR: documento) deed, document; **~i** smpl (di congressi etc) proceedings; **mettere in ~** to put into action; **fare ~ di fare qc** to make as if to do sth.
at'tonito, a ag dumbfounded, astonished.
attorcigli'are [attortʃiʎ'ʎare] vt to twist; **~rsi** vr to twist.
at'tore, 'trice sm/f actor/actress.
at'torno av round, around, about; **~ a** round, around, about.
at'tracco, chi sm (NAUT) docking no pl; berth.
attra'ente ag attractive.
at'trarre vt to attract; **attrat'tiva** sf (fig: fascino) attraction, charm; **at'tratto, a** pp di **attrarre**.
attraversa'mento sm: **~ pedonale** pedestrian crossing.
attraver'sare vt to cross; (città, bosco, fig: periodo) to go through; (sog: fiume) to run through.

attra'verso prep through; (da una parte all'altra) across.
attrazi'one [attrat'tsjone] sf attraction.
attrez'zare [attret'tsare] vt to equip; (NAUT) to rig; **attrezza'tura** sf equipment no pl; rigging; **at'trezzo** sm tool, instrument; (SPORT) piece of equipment.
attribu'ire vt: **~ qc a qn** (assegnare) to give o award sth to sb; (quadro etc) to attribute sth to sb; **attri'buto** sm attribute.
at'trice [at'tritʃe] sf vedi **attore**.
at'trito sm (anche fig) friction.
attu'ale ag (presente) present; (di attualità) topical; (che è in atto) actual; **attualità** sf inv topicality; (avvenimento) current event; **attual'mente** av at the moment, at present.
attu'are vt to carry out; **~rsi** vr to be realized.
attu'tire vt to deaden, reduce.
au'dace [au'datʃe] ag audacious, daring, bold; (provocante) provocative; (sfacciato) impudent, bold; **au'dacia** sf audacity, daring; boldness; provocativeness; impudence.
audiovi'sivo, a ag audiovisual.
audizi'one [audit'tsjone] sf hearing; (MUS) audition.
'auge ['audʒe] sf: **in ~** popular.
augu'rare vt to wish; **~rsi qc** to hope for sth.
au'gurio sm (presagio) omen; (voto di benessere etc) (good) wish; **essere di buon/cattivo ~** to be of good omen/be ominous; **fare gli ~i a qn** to give sb one's best wishes; **tanti ~i!** all the best!
'aula sf (scolastica) classroom; (universitaria) lecture theatre; (di edificio pubblico) hall.
aumen'tare vt, vi to increase; **au'mento** sm increase.
au'reola sf halo.
au'rora sf dawn.
ausili'are ag, sm, sm/f auxiliary.
aus'picio [aus'pitʃo] sm omen; (protezione) patronage; **sotto gli ~i di**

under the auspices of.

aus'tero, a *ag* austere.

Aus'tralia *sf*: l'~ Australia; australi'ano, a *ag*, *sm/f* Australian.

'Austria *sf*: l'~ Austria; aus'triaco, a, ci, che *ag*, *sm/f* Austrian.

au'tentico, a, ci, che *ag* (*quadro, firma*) authentic, genuine; (*fatto*) true, genuine.

au'tista, i *sm* driver.

'auto *sf inv* car.

autoade'sivo, a *ag* self-adhesive ♦ *sm* sticker.

autobiogra'fia *sf* autobiography.

auto'botte *sf* tanker.

'autobus *sm inv* bus.

auto'carro *sm* lorry (*BRIT*), truck.

autocorri'era *sf* coach, bus.

au'tografo, a *ag*, *sm* autograph.

auto'linea *sf* bus company.

au'toma, i *sm* automaton.

auto'matico, a, ci, che *ag* automatic ♦ *sm* (*bottone*) snap fastener; (*fucile*) automatic.

automazi'one [automat'tsjone] *sf* automation.

auto'mezzo [auto'meddzo] *sm* motor vehicle.

auto'mobile *sf* (motor) car.

autono'mia *sf* autonomy; (*di volo*) range.

au'tonomo, a *ag* autonomous, independent.

autop'sia *sf* post-mortem (examination), autopsy.

auto'radio *sf inv* (*apparecchio*) car radio; (*autoveicolo*) radio car.

au'tore, 'trice *sm/f* author.

auto'revole *ag* authoritative; (*persona*) influential.

autori'messa *sf* garage.

autorità *sf inv* authority.

autoriz'zare [autorid'dzare] *vt* (*permettere*) to authorize; (*giustificare*) to allow, sanction; autorizzazi'one *sf* authorization.

autoscu'ola *sf* driving school.

autos'top *sm* hitchhiking; autostop'pista, i, e *sm/f* hitchhiker.

autos'trada *sf* motorway (*BRIT*), high-

way (*US*).

auto'treno *sm* articulated lorry (*BRIT*), semi (trailer) (*US*).

autove'icolo *sm* motor vehicle.

autovet'tura *sf* (motor) car.

au'tunno *sm* autumn.

avam'braccio [avam'brattʃo] (*pl* (*f*) -cia) *sm* forearm.

avangu'ardia *sf* vanguard.

a'vanti *av* (*stato in luogo*) in front; (*moto: andare, venire*) forward; (*tempo: prima*) before ♦ *prep* (*luogo*): ~ a before, in front of; (*tempo*): ~ Cristo before Christ ♦ *escl* (*entrate*) come (*o go*) in!; (*MIL*) forward!; (*coraggio*) come on! ♦ *sm inv* (*SPORT*) forward; ~ e indietro backwards and forwards; andare ~ to go forward; (*continuare*) to go on; (*precedere*) to go (on) ahead; (*orologio*) to be fast; essere ~ negli studi to be well advanced with one's studies.

avanza'mento [avantsa'mento] *sm* progress; promotion.

avan'zare [avan'tsare] *vt* (*spostare in avanti*) to move forward, advance; (*domanda*) to put forward; (*promuovere*) to promote; (*essere creditore*): ~ qc da qn to be owed sth by sb ♦ *vi* (*andare avanti*) to move forward, advance; (*fig: progredire*) to make progress; (*essere d'avanzo*) to be left, remain; avan'zata *sf* (*MIL*) advance; a'vanzo *sm* (*residuo*) remains *pl*, left-overs *pl*; (*MAT*) remainder; (*COMM*) surplus; averne d'avanzo di qc to have more than enough of sth; avanzo di galera (*fig*) jailbird.

ava'ria *sf* (*guasto*) damage; (*: meccanico*) breakdown.

a'varo, a *ag* avaricious, miserly ♦ *sm* miser.

a'vena *sf* oats *pl*.

PAROLA CHIAVE
---

a'vere *sm* (*COMM*) credit; gli ~i (*ricchezze*) wealth *sg*

♦ *vt* 1 (*possedere*) to have; ha due bambini/una bella casa she has (got)

two children/a lovely house; **ha i capelli lunghi** he has (got) long hair; **non ho da mangiare/bere** I've (got) nothing to eat/drink, I don't have anything to eat/drink
2 (*indossare*) to wear, have on; **aveva una maglietta rossa** he was wearing *o* he had on a red tee-shirt; **ha gli occhiali** he wears *o* has glasses
3 (*ricevere*) to get; **hai avuto l'assegno?** did you get *o* have you had the cheque?
4 (*età, dimensione*) to be; **ha 9 anni** he is 9 (years old); **la stanza ha 3 metri di lunghezza** the room is 3 metres in length; *vedi* **fame**; **paura** *etc*
5 (*tempo*): **quanti ne abbiamo oggi?** what's the date today?; **ne hai per molto?** will you be long?
6 (*fraseologia*): **avercela con qn** to be angry with sb; **cos'hai?** what's wrong *o* what's the matter (with you)?; **non ha niente a che vedere** *o* **fare con me** it's got nothing to do with me
♦ *vb aus* **1** to have; **aver bevuto/mangiato** to have drunk/eaten
2 (+*da* +*infinito*): ~ **da fare qc** to have to do sth; **non hai che da chiederlo** you only have to ask him.

'**avi** *smpl* ancestors, forefathers.
aviazi'one [avjat'tsjone] *sf* aviation; (*MIL*) air force.
avidità *sf* eagerness; greed.
'**avido, a** *ag* eager; (*peg*) greedy.
avo'cado *sm* avocado.
a'vorio *sm* ivory.
Avv. *abbr* = **avvocato.**
avvalla'mento *sm* sinking *no pl*; (*effetto*) depression.
avvalo'rare *vt* to confirm.
avvam'pare *vi* (*incendio*) to flare up.
avvantaggi'are [avvantad'dʒare] *vt* to favour; ~**rsi** *vr*: ~**rsi negli affari/sui concorrenti** to get ahead in business/of one's competitors.
avvele'nare *vt* to poison.
avve'nente *ag* attractive, charming.
avveni'mento *sm* event.
avve'nire *vi*, *vb impers* to happen,

occur ♦ *sm* future.
avven'tarsi *vr*: ~ **su** *o* **contro qn/qc** to hurl o.s. *o* rush at sb/sth.
avven'tato, a *ag* rash, reckless.
avven'tizio, a [avven'tittsjo] *ag* (*impiegato*) temporary; (*guadagno*) casual.
av'vento *sm* advent, coming; (*REL*): **l'A~** Advent.
avven'tore *sm* (regular) customer.
avven'tura *sf* adventure; (*amorosa*) affair.
avventu'rarsi *vr* to venture.
avventu'roso, a *ag* adventurous.
avve'rarsi *vr* to come true.
av'verbio *sm* adverb.
avver'sario, a *ag* opposing ♦ *sm* opponent, adversary.
av'verso, a *ag* (*contrario*) contrary; (*sfavorevole*) unfavourable.
avver'tenza [avver'tentsa] *sf* (*ammonimento*) warning; (*cautela*) care; (*premessa*) foreword; ~**e** *sfpl* (*istruzioni per l'uso*) instructions.
avverti'mento *sm* warning.
avver'tire *vt* (*avvisare*) to warn; (*rendere consapevole*) to inform, notify; (*percepire*) to feel.
av'vezzo, a [av'vettso] *ag*: ~ **a** used to.
avvia'mento *sm* (*atto*) starting; (*effetto*) starting; (*AUT*) starting; (: *dispositivo*) starter; (*COMM*) goodwill.
avvi'are *vt* (*mettere sul cammino*) to direct; (*impresa, trattative*) to begin, start; (*motore*) to start; ~**rsi** *vr* to set off, set out.
avvicen'darsi [avvitʃen'darsi] *vr* to alternate.
avvici'nare [avvitʃi'nare] *vt* to bring near; (*trattare con: persona*) to approach; ~**rsi** *vr*: ~**rsi (a qn/qc)** to approach (sb/sth), draw near (to sb/sth).
avvi'lire *vt* (*umiliare*) to humiliate; (*degradare*) to disgrace; (*scoraggiare*) to dishearten, discourage; ~**rsi** *vr* (*abbattersi*) to lose heart.
avvilup'pare *vt* (*avvolgere*) to wrap up; (*ingarbugliare*) to entangle.
avvinaz'zato, a [avvinat'tsato] *ag* drunk.

av'vincere [av'vintʃere] *vt* to charm, enthral.

avvinghi'are [avvin'gjare] *vt* to clasp; **~rsi** *vr*: **~rsi a** to cling to.

avvi'sare *vt* (*far sapere*) to inform; (*mettere in guardia*) to warn; **av'viso** *sm* warning; (*annuncio*) announcement; (: *affisso*) notice; (*inserzione pubblicitaria*) advertisement; **a mio avviso** in my opinion.

avvis'tare *vt* to sight.

avvi'tare *vt* to screw down (*o* in).

avviz'zire [avvit'tsire] *vi* to wither.

avvo'cato, 'essa *sm/f* (*DIR*) barrister (*BRIT*), lawyer; (*fig*) defender, advocate.

av'volgere [av'voldʒere] *vt* to roll up; (*avviluppare*) to wrap up; **~rsi** *vr* (*avvilupparsi*) to wrap o.s. up; **avvol'gibile** *sm* roller blind (*BRIT*), blind.

avvol'toio *sm* vulture.

azi'enda [ad'dzjɛnda] *sf* business, firm, concern; **~ agricola** farm.

azio'nare [attsjo'nare] *vt* to activate.

azi'one [at'tsjone] *sf* action; (*COMM*) share; **azio'nista, i, e** *sm/f* (*COMM*) shareholder.

a'zoto [ad'dzɔto] *sm* nitrogen.

azzan'nare [attsan'nare] *vt* to sink one's teeth into.

azzar'darsi [addzar'darsi] *vr*: **~ a fare** to dare (to) do; **azzar'dato, a** *ag* (*impresa*) risky; (*risposta*) rash.

az'zardo [ad'dzardo] *sm* risk.

azzec'care [attsek'kare] *vt* (*risposta etc*) to get right.

azzuf'farsi [attsuf'farsi] *vr* to come to blows.

az'zurro, a [ad'dzurro] *ag* blue ♦ *sm* (*colore*) blue; **gli ~i** (*SPORT*) the Italian national team.

B

bab'beo *sm* simpleton.

'babbo *sm* (*fam*) dad, daddy; **B~ natale** Father Christmas.

bab'buccia, ce [bab'buttʃa] *sf* slipper;

(*per neonati*) bootee.

ba'bordo *sm* (*NAUT*) port side.

ba'cato, a *ag* worm-eaten, rotten.

'bacca, che *sf* berry.

baccalà *sm* dried salted cod; (*fig: peg*) dummy.

bac'cano *sm* din, clamour.

bac'cello [bat'tʃɛllo] *sm* pod.

bac'chetta [bak'ketta] *sf* (*verga*) stick, rod; (*di direttore d'orchestra*) baton; (*di tamburo*) drumstick; **~ magica** magic wand.

baci'are [ba'tʃare] *vt* to kiss; **~rsi** *vr* to kiss (one another).

baci'nella [batʃi'nɛlla] *sf* basin.

ba'cino [ba'tʃino] *sm* basin; (*MINERALOGIA*) field, bed; (*ANAT*) pelvis; (*NAUT*) dock.

'bacio ['batʃo] *sm* kiss.

'baco, chi *sm* worm; **~ da seta** silkworm.

ba'dare *vi* (*fare attenzione*) to take care, be careful; (*occuparsi di*): **~ a** to look after, take care of; (*dar ascolto*): **~ a** to pay attention to; **bada ai fatti tuoi!** mind your own business!

ba'dia *sf* abbey.

ba'dile *sm* shovel.

'baffi *smpl* moustache *sg*; (*di animale*) whiskers; **ridere sotto i ~** to laugh up one's sleeve; **leccarsi i ~** to lick one's lips.

ba'gagli [ba'gaλλi] *smpl* luggage *sg*.

bagagli'aio [bagaλ'λajo] *sm* luggage van (*BRIT*) *o* car (*US*); (*AUT*) boot (*BRIT*), trunk (*US*).

bagli'ore [baλ'λore] *sm* flash, dazzling light; **un ~ di speranza** a ray of hope.

ba'gnante [baɲ'ɲante] *sm/f* bather.

ba'gnare [baɲ'ɲare] *vt* to wet; (*inzuppare*) to soak; (*innaffiare*) to water; (*sog: fiume*) to flow through; (: *mare*) to wash, bathe; **~rsi** *vr* (*al mare*) to go swimming *o* bathing; (*in vasca*) to have a bath.

ba'gnato, a [baɲ'ɲato] *ag* wet.

ba'gnino [baɲ'ɲino] *sm* lifeguard.

'bagno ['baɲɲo] *sm* bath; (*locale*) bathroom; **~i** *smpl* (*stabilimento*) baths; **fare il ~** to have a bath; (*nel mare*) to go swimming *o* bathing; **fare il ~ a qn** to give sb a bath; **mettere a ~** to soak; **~ schiuma** bubble bath.

bagnoma'ria [baɲɲoma'ria] *sm*: **cuocere a ~** to cook in a double saucepan.

'baia *sf* bay.

baio'netta *sf* bayonet.

balaus'trata *sf* balustrade.

balbet'tare *vi* to stutter, stammer; (*bimbo*) to babble ♦ *vt* to stammer out.

balbuzi'ente [balbut'tsjɛnte] *ag* stuttering, stammering.

bal'cone *sm* balcony.

baldac'chino [baldak'kino] *sm* canopy.

bal'danza [bal'dantsa] *sf* self-confidence, boldness.

'baldo, a *ag* bold, daring.

bal'doria *sf*: **fare ~** to have a riotous time.

ba'lena *sf* whale.

bale'nare *vb impers*: **balena** there's lightning ♦ *vi* to flash; **mi balenò un'idea** an idea flashed through my mind; **ba'leno** *sm* flash of lightning; **in un baleno** in a flash.

ba'lestra *sf* crossbow.

ba'lia *sf*: **in ~ di** at the mercy of.

'balla *sf* (*di merci*) bale; (*fandonia*) (tall) story.

bal'lare *vt, vi* to dance; **bal'lata** *sf* ballad.

balle'rina *sf* dancer; ballet dancer; (*scarpa*) ballet shoe.

balle'rino *sm* dancer; ballet dancer.

bal'letto *sm* ballet.

'ballo *sm* dance; (*azione*) dancing *no pl*; **essere in ~** (*fig: persona*) to be involved; (*: cosa*) to be at stake.

ballot'taggio [ballot'taddʒo] *sm* (*POL*) second ballot.

balne'are *ag* seaside *cpd*; (*stagione*) bathing.

ba'locco, chi *sm* toy.

ba'lordo, a *ag* stupid, senseless.

'balsamo *sm* (*aroma*) balsam; (*lenimento, fig*) balm.

'Baltico *sm*: **il (mar) ~** the Baltic (Sea).

balu'ardo *sm* bulwark.

'balza ['baltsa] *sf* (*dirupo*) crag; (*di stoffa*) frill.

bal'zare [bal'tsare] *vi* to bounce; (*lanciarsi*) to jump, leap; **'balzo** *sm* bounce; jump, leap; (*del terreno*) crag.

bam'bagia [bam'badʒa] *sf* (*ovatta*) cotton wool (*BRIT*), absorbent cotton (*US*); (*cascame*) cotton waste.

bam'bina *ag, sf vedi* **bambino**.

bambi'naia *sf* nanny, nurse(maid).

bam'bino, a *sm/f* child.

bam'boccio [bam'bɔttʃo] *sm* plump child; (*pupazzo*) rag doll.

'bambola *sf* doll.

bambù *sm* bamboo.

ba'nale *ag* banal, commonplace.

ba'nana *sf* banana; **ba'nano** *sm* banana tree.

'banca, che *sf* bank; **~ dei dati** data bank.

banca'rella *sf* stall.

ban'cario, a *ag* banking, bank *cpd* ♦ *sm* bank clerk.

banca'rotta *sf* bankruptcy; **fare ~** to go bankrupt.

ban'chetto [ban'ketto] *sm* banquet.

banchi'ere [ban'kjere] *sm* banker.

ban'china [ban'kina] *sf* (*di porto*) quay; (*per pedoni, ciclisti*) path; (*di stazione*) platform; **~ cedevole** (*AUT*) soft verge (*BRIT*) *o* shoulder (*US*).

'banco, chi *sm* bench; (*di negozio*) counter; (*di mercato*) stall; (*di officina*) (work-)bench; (*GEO, banca*) bank; **~ di corallo** coral reef; **~ degli imputati** dock; **~ di prova** (*fig*) testing ground; **~ dei testimoni** witness box.

'Bancomat ® *sm inv* automated banking; (*tessera*) cash card.

banco'nota *sf* banknote.

'banda *sf* band; (*di stoffa*) band, stripe; (*lato, parte*) side; **~ perforata** punch tape.

banderu'ola *sf* (*METEOR*) weathercock, weathervane.

bandi'era *sf* flag, banner.

ban'dire *vt* to proclaim; (*esiliare*) to exile; (*fig*) to dispense with.

ban'dito *sm* outlaw, bandit.

bandi'tore *sm* (*di aste*) auctioneer.

'**bando** *sm* proclamation; (*esilio*) exile, banishment; ~ **alle chiacchiere!** that's enough talk!

'**bandolo** *sm*: **il** ~ **della matassa** (*fig*) the key to the problem.

bar *sm inv* bar.

'**bara** *sf* coffin.

ba'**racca, che** *sf* shed, hut; (*peg*) hovel; **mandare avanti la** ~ to keep things going.

bara'**onda** *sf* hubbub, bustle.

ba'**rare** *vi* to cheat.

ba'**ratro** *sm* abyss.

barat'**tare** *vt*: ~ **qc con** to barter sth for, swap sth for; **ba'ratto** *sm* barter.

ba'**rattolo** *sm* (*di latta*) tin; (*di vetro*) jar; (*di coccio*) pot.

'**barba** *sf* beard; **farsi la** ~ to shave; **farla in** ~ **a qn** (*fig*) to do sth to sb's face; **che** ~! what a bore!

barbabi'**etola** *sf* beetroot (*BRIT*), beet (*US*); ~ **da zucchero** sugar beet.

bar'**barico, a, ci, che** *ag* barbarian; barbaric.

'**barbaro, a** *ag* barbarous; ~**i** *smpl* barbarians.

barbi'**ere** *sm* barber.

bar'**bone** *sm* (*cane*) poodle; (*vagabondo*) tramp.

bar'**buto, a** *ag* bearded.

'**barca, che** *sf* boat; ~ **a remi** rowing boat; **barcai'olo** *sm* boatman.

barcol'**lare** *vi* to stagger.

bar'**cone** *sm* (*per ponti di barche*) pontoon.

ba'**rella** *sf* (*lettiga*) stretcher.

ba'**rile** *sm* barrel, cask.

ba'**rista, i, e** *sm/f* barman/maid; bar owner.

ba'**ritono** *sm* baritone.

bar'**lume** *sm* glimmer, gleam.

ba'**rocco, a, chi, che** *ag, sm* baroque.

ba'**rometro** *sm* barometer.

ba'**rone** *sm* baron; **baro'nessa** *sf* baroness.

'**barra** *sf* bar; (*NAUT*) helm; (*linea grafica*) line, stroke.

barri'**care** *vt* to barricade; **barri'cata** *sf* barricade.

barri'**era** *sf* barrier; (*GEO*) reef.

ba'**ruffa** *sf* scuffle.

barzel'**letta** [bardzel'letta] *sf* joke, funny story.

ba'**sare** *vt* to base, found; ~**rsi** *vr*: ~**rsi su** (*sog: fatti, prove*) to be based *o* founded on; (*: persona*) to base one's arguments on.

'**basco, a, schi, sche** *ag* Basque ♦ *sm* (*copricapo*) beret.

'**base** *sf* base; (*fig: fondamento*) basis; (*POL*) rank and file; **di** ~ basic; **in** ~ **a** on the basis of, according to; **a** ~ **di caffè** coffee-based.

ba'**setta** *sf* sideburn.

ba'**silica, che** *sf* basilica.

ba'**silico** *sm* basil.

bassi'**fondi** *smpl* (*fig*) dregs.

'**basso, a** *ag* low; (*di statura*) short; (*meridionale*) southern ♦ *sm* bottom, lower part; (*MUS*) bass; **la** ~**a Italia** southern Italy.

bassorili'**evo** *sm* bas-relief.

'**basta** *escl* (that's) enough!, that will do!

bas'**tardo, a** *ag* (*animale, pianta*) hybrid, crossbreed; (*persona*) illegitimate, bastard (*peg*) ♦ *sm/f* illegitimate child, bastard (*peg*).

bas'**tare** *vi, vb impers* to be enough, be sufficient; ~ **a qn** to be enough for sb; **basta chiedere** *o* **che chieda a un vigile** you have only to *o* need only ask a policeman.

basti'**mento** *sm* ship, vessel.

basto'**nare** *vt* to beat, thrash.

baston'**cino** [baston'tʃino] *sm* (*SCI*) ski pole.

bas'**tone** *sm* stick; ~ **da passeggio** walking stick.

bat'**taglia** [bat'taʎʎa] *sf* battle; fight.

bat'**taglio** [bat'taʎʎo] *sm* (*di campana*) clapper; (*di porta*) knocker.

battagli'**one** [battaʎ'ʎone] *sm* battalion.

bat'**tello** *sm* boat.

bat'**tente** *sm* (*imposta: di porta*) wing, flap; (*: di finestra*) shutter; (*batacchio: di porta*) knocker; (*: di orologio*) hammer; **chiudere i** ~**i** (*fig*) to shut up shop.

'**battere** *vt* to beat; (*grano*) to thresh;

(*percorrere*) to scour ♦ *vi* (*bussare*) to knock; (*urtare*): ~ **contro** to hit *o* strike against; (*pioggia, sole*) to beat down; (*cuore*) to beat; (*TENNIS*) to serve; ~**rsi** *vr* to fight; ~ **le mani** to clap; ~ **i piedi** to stamp one's feet; ~ **su un argomento** to hammer home an argument; ~ **a macchina** to type; ~ **bandiera italiana** to fly the Italian flag; ~ **in testa** (*AUT*) to knock; **in un batter d'occhio** in the twinkling of an eye.
bat'teri *smpl* bacteria.
batte'ria *sf* battery; (*MUS*) drums *pl*.
bat'tesimo *sm* baptism; christening.
battez'zare [batted'dzare] *vt* to baptize; to christen.
batticu'ore *sm* palpitations *pl*.
batti'mano *sm* applause.
batti'panni *sm inv* carpet-beater.
battis'tero *sm* baptistry.
battis'trada *sm inv* (*di pneumatico*) tread; (*di gara*) pacemaker.
battitap'peto *sm* vacuum cleaner.
'battito *sm* beat, throb; ~ **cardiaco** heartbeat; ~ **della pioggia/dell'orologio** beating of the rain/ticking of the clock.
bat'tuta *sf* blow; (*di macchina da scrivere*) stroke; (*MUS*) bar; beat; (*TEATRO*) cue; (*frase spiritosa*) witty remark; (*di caccia*) beating; (*POLIZIA*) combing, scouring; (*TENNIS*) service.
ba'ule *sm* trunk; (*AUT*) boot (*BRIT*), trunk (*US*).
'bava *sf* (*di animale*) slaver, slobber; (*di lumaca*) slime; (*di vento*) breath.
bava'glino [bavaʎ'ʎino] *sm* bib.
ba'vaglio [ba'vaʎʎo] *sm* gag.
'bavero *sm* collar.
ba'zar [bad'dzar] *sm inv* bazaar.
baz'zecola [bad'dzekola] *sf* trifle.
bazzi'care [battsi'kare] *vt* to frequent ♦ *vi*: ~ **in/con** to frequent.
be'ato, a *ag* blessed; (*fig*) happy; ~ **te!** lucky you!
bec'caccia, ce [bek'kattʃa] *sf* woodcock.
bec'care *vt* to peck; (*fig: raffreddore*) to pick up, catch; ~**rsi** *vr* (*fig*) to squabble.
becchegi'are [bekked'dʒare] *vi* to pitch.

bec'chino [bek'kino] *sm* gravedigger.
'becco, chi *sm* beak, bill; (*di caffettiera etc*) spout; lip.
Be'fana *sf* old woman who, according to legend, brings children their presents at the Epiphany; (*Epifania*) Epiphany; (*donna brutta*): b~ hag, witch.
'beffa *sf* practical joke; **farsi ~e di qn** to make a fool of sb; **bef'fardo, a** *ag* scornful, mocking; **bef'fare** *vt* (*anche*: *beffarsi di*) to make a fool of, mock.
'bega, ghe *sf* quarrel.
'begli ['beʎʎi] *ag vedi* **bello**.
'bei *ag vedi* **bello**.
bel *ag vedi* **bello**.
be'lare *vi* to bleat.
'belga, gi, ghe *ag*, *sm/f* Belgian.
'Belgio ['beldʒo] *sm*: **il ~** Belgium.
bel'lezza [bel'lettsa] *sf* beauty.
'bella *sf* (*SPORT*) decider; *vedi anche* **bello**.

'bello, a (*ag: dav sm* **bel** +*C*, **bell'** +*V*, **bello** +*s impura, gn, pn, ps, x, z, pl* **bei** +*C*, **begli** +*s impura etc o V*) *ag* **1** (*oggetto, donna, paesaggio*) beautiful, lovely; (*uomo*) handsome; (*tempo*) beautiful, fine, lovely; **le belle arti** fine arts
2 (*quantità*): **una ~a cifra** a considerable sum of money; **un bel niente** absolutely nothing
3 (*rafforzativo*): **è una truffa ~a e buona!** it's a real fraud!; **è bell'e finito** it's already finished
♦ *sm* **1** (*bellezza*) beauty; (*tempo*) fine weather
2: **adesso viene il ~** now comes the best bit; **sul più ~** at the crucial point; **cosa fai di ~?** are you doing anything interesting?
♦ *av*: **fa ~** the weather is fine, it's fine.

'belva *sf* wild animal.
belve'dere *sm inv* panoramic viewpoint.
benché [ben'ke] *cong* although.
'benda *sf* bandage; (*per gli occhi*) blindfold; **ben'dare** *vt* to bandage; to

blindfold.

'**bene** *av* well; (*completamente*, *affatto*): **è ben difficile** it's very difficult ♦ *ag inv*: **gente ~** well-to-do people ♦ *sm* good; **~i** *smpl* (*averi*) property *sg*, estate *sg*; **io sto ~/poco ~** I'm well/not very well; **va ~** all right; **volere un ~ dell'anima a qn** to love sb very much; **un uomo per ~** a respectable man; **fare ~** to do the right thing; **fare ~ a** (*salute*) to be good for; **fare del ~ a qn** to do sb a good turn; **~i di consumo** consumer goods.

bene'**detto, a** *pp di* **benedire** ♦ *ag* blessed, holy.

bene'**dire** *vt* to bless; to consecrate; **benedizi'one** *sf* blessing.

benedu'**cato, a** *ag* well-mannered.

benefi'**cenza** [benefi'tʃentsa] *sf* charity.

bene'**ficio** [bene'fitʃo] *sm* benefit; **con ~ d'inventario** (*fig*) with reservations.

be'**nefico, a, ci, che** *ag* beneficial; charitable.

beneme'**renza** [beneme'rɛntsa] *sf* merit.

bene'**merito, a** *ag* meritorious.

be'**nessere** *sm* well-being.

benes'**tante** *ag* well-to-do.

benes'**tare** *sm* consent, approval.

be'**nevolo, a** *ag* benevolent.

be'**nigno, a** [be'niɲɲo] *ag* kind, kindly; (*critica etc*) favourable; (*MED*) benign.

benin'**teso** *av* of course.

ben**sì** *cong* but (rather).

benve'**nuto, a** *ag*, *sm* welcome; **dare il ~ a qn** to welcome sb.

ben'**zina** [ben'dzina] *sf* petrol (*BRIT*), gas (*US*); **fare ~** to get petrol (*BRIT*) *o* gas (*US*); **benzi'naio** *sm* petrol (*BRIT*) *o* gas (*US*) pump attendant.

'**bere** *vt* to drink; **darla a ~ a qn** (*fig*) to fool sb.

ber'**lina** *sf* (*AUT*) saloon (car) (*BRIT*), sedan (*US*).

Ber'**lino** *sf* Berlin.

ber'**noccolo** *sm* bump; (*inclinazione*) flair.

ber'**retto** *sm* cap.

bersagli'**are** [bersaʎ'ʎare] *vt* to shoot at; (*colpire ripetutamente*, *fig*) to bombard; **bersagliato dalla sfortuna**

dogged by ill fortune.

ber'**saglio** [ber'saʎʎo] *sm* target.

bes'**temmia** *sf* curse; (*REL*) blasphemy.

bestemmi'**are** *vi* to curse, swear; to blaspheme ♦ *vt* to curse, swear at; to blaspheme.

'**bestia** *sf* animal; **andare in ~** (*fig*) to fly into a rage; **besti'ale** *ag* beastly; animal *cpd*; (*fam*): **fa un freddo bestiale** it's bitterly cold; **besti'ame** *sm* livestock; (*bovino*) cattle *pl*.

be'**ttola** (*peg*) *sf* dive.

be'**tulla** *sf* birch.

be'**vanda** *sf* drink, beverage.

bevi'**tore, 'trice** *sm/f* drinker.

be'**vuta** *sf* drink.

be'**vuto, a** *pp di* **bere**.

bi'**ada** *sf* fodder.

bianche'**ria** [bjanke'ria] *sf* linen; **~ intima** underwear; **~ da donna** ladies' underwear, lingerie.

bi'**anco, a, chi, che** *ag* white; (*non scritto*) blank ♦ *sm* white; (*intonaco*) whitewash ♦ *sm/f* white, white man/woman; **in ~** (*foglio*, *assegno*) blank; (*notte*) sleepless; **in ~ e nero** (*TV*, *FOT*) black and white; **mangiare in ~** to follow a bland diet; **pesce in ~** boiled fish; **andare in ~** (*non riuscire*) to fail; **~ dell'uovo** egg-white.

biasi'**mare** *vt* to disapprove of, censure; **bi'asimo** *sm* disapproval, censure.

'**bibbia** *sf* bible.

bibe'**ron** *sm inv* feeding bottle.

'**bibita** *sf* (soft) drink.

biblio'**teca, che** *sf* library; (*mobile*) bookcase; **bibliote'cario, a** *sm/f* librarian.

bicarbo'**nato** *sm*: **~ (di sodio)** bicarbonate (of soda).

bicchi'**ere** [bik'kjɛre] *sm* glass.

bici'**cletta** [bitʃi'kletta] *sf* bicycle; **andare in ~** to cycle.

bi**dé** *sm inv* bidet.

bi'**dello, a** *sm/f* (*INS*) janitor.

bi'**done** *sm* drum, can; (*anche: ~ dell'immondizia*) (dust)bin; (*fam*: *truffa*) swindle; **fare un ~ a qn** (*fam*)

to let sb down; to cheat sb.
bien'nale *ag* biennial.
bi'ennio *sm* period of two years.
bi'etola *sf* beet.
bifor'carsi *vr* to fork; **biforcazi'one** *sf*
fork.
bighello'nare [bigello'nare] *vi* to loaf
(about).
bigiotte'ria [bidʒotte'ria] *sf* costume
jewellery; (*negozio*) jeweller's (*selling
only costume jewellery*).
bigli'ardo [biʎ'ʎardo] *sm* = **biliardo**.
bigliette'ria [biʎʎette'ria] *sf* (*di
stazione*) ticket office; booking office;
(*di teatro*) box office.
bigli'etto [biʎ'ʎetto] *sm* (*per viaggi,
spettacoli etc*) ticket; (*cartoncino*)
card; (*anche: ~ di banca*) (bank)note;
~ **d'auguri/da visita** greetings/visiting
card; ~ **d'andata e ritorno** return (ticket), round-trip ticket (*US*).
bignè [biɲ'ɲe] *sm inv* cream puff.
bigo'dino *sm* roller, curler.
bi'gotto, a *ag* over-pious ♦ *sm/f* church
fiend.
bi'lancia, ce [bi'lantʃa] *sf* (*pesa*) scales
pl; (*: di precisione*) balance; (*dello
zodiaco*): B~ Libra; ~ **commerciale/dei
pagamenti** balance of trade/payments;
bilanci'are *vt* (*pesare*) to weigh; (*: fig*)
to weigh up; (*pareggiare*) to balance.
bi'lancio [bi'lantʃo] *sm* (*COMM*)
balance(-sheet); (*statale*) budget; **fare
il ~ di** (*fig*) to assess; ~ **consuntivo**
(*final*) balance; ~ **preventivo** budget.
'bile *sf* bile; (*fig*) rage, anger.
bili'ardo *sm* billiards *sg*; billiard table.
'bilico, chi *sm*: **essere in** ~ to be
balanced; (*fig*) to be undecided; **tenere
qn in** ~ (*fig*) to keep sb in suspense.
bi'lingue *ag* bilingual.
bili'one *sm* (*mille milioni*) thousand
million; (*milione di milioni*) billion
(*BRIT*), trillion (*US*).
'bimbo, a *sm/f* little boy/girl.
bimen'sile *ag* fortnightly.
bimes'trale *ag* two-monthly,
bimonthly.
bi'nario, a *ag* (*sistema*) binary ♦ *sm*
(railway) track *o* line; (*piattaforma*)

platform; ~ **morto** dead-end track.
bi'nocolo *sm* binoculars *pl*.
bio... *prefisso*: **bio'chimica** [bio'kimika]
sf biochemistry; **biodegra'dabile** *ag*
biodegradable; **biogra'fia** *sf* biography;
biolo'gia *sf* biology; **bio'logico, a, ci,
che** *ag* biological.
bi'ondo, a *ag* blond, fair.
bir'bante *sm* rogue, rascal.
biri'chino, a [biri'kino] *ag* mischievous
♦ *sm/f* scamp, little rascal.
bi'rillo *sm* skittle (*BRIT*), pin (*US*); ~**i**
smpl (*gioco*) skittles *sg* (*BRIT*), bowling
(*US*).
'biro ® *sf inv* biro ®.
'birra *sf* beer; **a tutta** ~ (*fig*) at top
speed; **birre'ria** *sf* ≈ bierkeller.
bis *escl, sm inv* encore.
bisbigli'are [bisbiʎ'ʎare] *vt, vi* to
whisper.
'bisca, sche *sf* gambling-house.
'biscia, sce [bi'ʃʃa] *sf* snake; ~ **d'acqua**
grass snake.
bis'cotto *sm* biscuit.
bises'tile *ag*: **anno** ~ leap year.
bis'lungo, a, ghi, ghe *ag* oblong.
bis'nonno, a *sm/f* great grandfather/
grandmother.
biso'gnare [bizoɲ'ɲare] *vb impers*: **bisogna che tu parta/lo faccia** you'll have to
go/do it; **bisogna parlargli** we'll (*o* I'll)
have to talk to him.
bi'sogno [bi'zoɲɲo] *sm* need; ~**i** *smpl*:
fare i propri ~**i** to relieve o.s.; **avere** ~
di qc/di fare qc to need sth/to do sth; **al**
~, **in caso di** ~ if need be; **biso'gnoso,
a** *ag* needy, poor; **bisognoso di** in need
of, needing.
bis'tecca, che *sf* steak, beefsteak.
bisticci'are [bistit'tʃare] *vi* to quarrel,
bicker; ~**rsi** *vr* to quarrel, bicker;
bis'ticcio *sm* quarrel, squabble; (*gioco
di parole*) pun.
'bisturi *sm* scalpel.
bi'sunto, a *ag* very greasy.
'bitter *sm inv* bitters *pl*.
bi'vacco, chi *sm* bivouac.
'bivio *sm* fork; (*fig*) dilemma.

'**bizza** ['biddza] *sf* tantrum; **fare le** ~**e** (*bambino*) to be naughty.

biz'zarro, a [bid'dzarro] *ag* bizarre, strange.

biz'zeffe [bid'dzɛffe]: **a** ~ *av* in plenty, galore.

blan'dire *vt* to soothe; to flatter.

'**blando, a** *ag* mild, gentle.

bla'sone *sm* coat of arms.

blate'rare *vi* to chatter, blether.

blin'dato, a *ag* armoured.

bloc'care *vt* to block; (*isolare*) to isolate, cut off; (*porto*) to blockade; (*prezzi, beni*) to freeze; (*meccanismo*) to jam; ~**rsi** *vr* (*motore*) to stall; (*freni, porta*) to jam, stick; (*ascensore*) to stop, get stuck.

'**blocco, chi** *sm* block; (*MIL*) blockade; (*dei fitti*) restriction; (*quadernetto*) pad; (*fig: unione*) coalition; (*il bloccare*) blocking; isolating; cutting-off; blockading; freezing; jamming; **in** ~ (*nell'insieme*) as a whole; (*COMM*) in bulk; ~ **cardiaco** cardiac arrest.

blu *ag inv, sm* dark blue.

'**blusa** *sf* (*camiciotto*) smock; (*camicetta*) blouse.

'**boa** *sm inv* (*ZOOL*) boa constrictor; (*sciarpa*) feather boa ♦ *sf* buoy.

bo'ato *sm* rumble, roar.

bo'bina *sf* reel, spool; (*di pellicola*) spool; (*di film*) reel; (*ELETTR*) coil.

'**bocca, che** *sf* mouth; **in** ~ **al lupo!** good luck!

boc'caccia, ce [bok'kattʃa] *sf* (*malalingua*) gossip; **fare le** ~**ce** to pull faces.

boc'cale *sm* jug; ~ **da birra** tankard.

boc'cetta [bot'tʃetta] *sf* small bottle.

boccheggi'are [bokked'dʒare] *vi* to gasp.

boc'chino [bok'kino] *sm* (*di sigaretta, sigaro: cannella*) cigarette-holder; cigar-holder; (*di pipa, strumenti musicali*) mouthpiece.

'**boccia, ce** [bottʃa] *sf* bottle; (*da vino*) decanter, carafe; (*palla*) bowl; **gioco delle** ~**ce** bowls *sg*.

bocci'are [bot'tʃare] *vt* (*proposta, progetto*) to reject; (*INS*) to fail;

(*BOCCE*) to hit; **boccia'tura** *sf* failure.

bocci'olo [bot'tʃolo] *sm* bud.

boc'cone *sm* mouthful, morsel.

boc'coni *av* face downwards.

'**boia** *sm inv* executioner; hangman.

boi'ata *sf* botch.

boicot'tare *vt* to boycott.

'**bolide** *sm* meteor; **come un** ~ like a flash, at top speed.

'**bolla** *sf* bubble; (*MED*) blister; ~ **papale** papal bull; ~ **di consegna** (*COMM*) delivery note.

bol'lare *vt* to stamp; (*fig*) to brand.

bol'lente *ag* boiling; boiling hot.

bol'letta *sf* bill; (*ricevuta*) receipt; **essere in** ~ to be hard up.

bollet'tino *sm* bulletin; (*COMM*) note; ~ **di spedizione** consignment note.

bol'lire *vt, vi* to boil; **bol'lito** *sm* (*CUC*) boiled meat.

bolli'tore *sm* (*CUC*) kettle; (*per riscaldamento*) boiler.

'**bollo** *sm* stamp.

'**bomba** *sf* bomb; **tornare a** ~ (*fig*) to get back to the point; ~ **atomica** atom bomb.

bombarda'mento *sm* bombardment; bombing.

bombar'dare *vt* to bombard; (*da aereo*) to bomb.

bombardi'ere *sm* bomber.

bom'betta *sf* bowler (hat).

'**bombola** *sf* cylinder.

bo'naccia, ce [bo'nattʃa] *sf* dead calm.

bo'nario, a *ag* good-natured, kind.

bo'nifica, che *sf* reclamation; reclaimed land.

bo'nifico, ci *sm* (*riduzione, abbuono*) discount; (*versamento a terzi*) credit transfer.

bontà *sf* goodness; (*cortesia*) kindness; **aver la** ~ **di fare qc** to be good o kind enough to do sth.

borbot'tare *vi* to mumble; (*stomaco*) to rumble.

'**borchia** ['borkja] *sf* stud.

borda'tura *sf* (*SARTORIA*) border, trim.

'**bordo** *sm* (*NAUT*) ship's side; (*orlo*) edge; (*striscia di guarnizione*) border, trim; **a** ~ **di** (*nave, aereo*) aboard, on board; (*macchina*) in.

bor'gata *sf* hamlet.

bor'ghese [bor'geze] *ag* (*spesso peg*) middle-class; bourgeois; **abito** ~ civilian dress; **borghe'sia** *sf* middle classes *pl*; bourgeoisie.

'borgo, ghi *sm* (*paesino*) village; (*quartiere*) district; (*sobborgo*) suburb.

'boria *sf* self-conceit, arrogance.

boro'talco *sm* talcum powder.

bor'raccia, ce [bor'rattʃa] *sf* canteen, water-bottle.

'borsa *sf* bag; (*anche:* ~ *da signora*) handbag; (*ECON*): **la B~** (*valori*) the Stock Exchange; ~ **nera** black market; ~ **della spesa** shopping bag; ~ **di studio** grant; **borsai'olo** *sm* pickpocket; **borsel'lino** *sm* purse; **bor'setta** *sf* handbag; **bor'sista, i, e** *sm/f* (*ECON*) speculator; (*INS*) grant-holder.

bos'caglia [bos'kaʎʎa] *sf* woodlands *pl*.

boscai'olo *sm* woodcutter; forester.

'bosco, schi *sm* wood; **bos'coso, a** *ag* wooded.

'bossolo *sm* cartridge-case.

bo'tanica *sf* botany.

bo'tanico, a, ci, che *ag* botanical ♦ *sm* botanist.

'botola *sf* trap door.

'botta *sf* blow; (*rumore*) bang.

'botte *sf* barrel, cask.

bot'tega, ghe *sf* shop; (*officina*) workshop; **botte'gaio, a** *sm/f* shopkeeper; **botte'ghino** *sm* ticket office; (*del lotto*) public lottery office.

bot'tiglia [bot'tiʎʎa] *sf* bottle; **bottiglie'ria** *sf* wine shop.

bot'tino *sm* (*di guerra*) booty; (*di rapina, furto*) loot.

'botto *sm* bang; crash; **di** ~ suddenly.

bot'tone *sm* button; **attaccare** ~ **a qn** (*fig*) to buttonhole sb.

bo'vino, a *ag* bovine; ~**i** *smpl* cattle.

boxe [bɔks] *sf* boxing.

'bozza ['bɔttsa] *sf* draft; sketch; (*TIP*) proof; **boz'zetto** *sm* sketch.

'bozzolo ['bɔttsolo] *sm* cocoon.

BR *sigla fpl* = **Brigate Rosse**.

brac'care *vt* to hunt.

brac'cetto [brat'tʃetto] *sm*: **a** ~ arm in

arm.

bracci'ale [brat'tʃale] *sm* bracelet; (*distintivo*) armband; **braccia'letto** *sm* bracelet, bangle.

bracci'ante [brat'tʃante] *sm* (*AGR*) day labourer.

bracci'ata [brat'tʃata] *sf* (*nel nuoto*) stroke.

'braccio ['brattʃo] (*pl(f)* **braccia**) *sm* (*ANAT*) arm; (*pl(m)* **bracci**: *di gru, fiume*) arm; (*: di edificio*) wing; ~ **di mare** sound; **bracci'olo** *sm* (*appoggio*) arm.

'bracco, chi *sm* hound.

bracconi'ere *sm* poacher.

'brace ['bratʃe] *sf* embers *pl*; **braci'ere** *sm* brazier.

braci'ola [bra'tʃɔla] *sf* (*CUC*) chop.

bra'mare *vt*: ~ **qc/di fare** to long for sth/to do.

'branca, che *sf* branch.

'branchia ['brankja] *sf* (*ZOOL*) gill.

'branco, chi *sm* (*di cani, lupi*) pack; (*di uccelli, pecore*) flock; (*peg: di persone*) gang, pack.

branco'lare *vi* to grope, feel one's way.

'branda *sf* camp bed.

bran'dello *sm* scrap, shred; **a** ~**i** in tatters, in rags.

bran'dire *vt* to brandish.

'brano *sm* piece; (*di libro*) passage.

bra'sato *sm* braised beef.

Bra'sile *sm*: **il** ~ Brazil; **brasili'ano, a** *ag*, *sm/f* Brazilian.

'bravo, a *ag* (*abile*) clever, capable, skilful; (*buono*) good, honest; (*: bambino*) good; (*coraggioso*) brave; ~! well done!; (*al teatro*) bravo!

bra'vura *sf* cleverness, skill.

'breccia, ce ['brettʃa] *sf* breach.

bre'tella *sf* (*AUT*) link; ~**e** *sfpl* (*di calzoni*) braces.

'breve *ag* brief, short; **in** ~ in short.

brevet'tare *vt* to patent.

bre'vetto *sm* patent; ~ **di pilotaggio** pilot's licence (*BRIT*) *o* license (*US*).

'brezza ['breddza] *sf* breeze.

'bricco, chi *sm* jug; ~ **del caffè** coffeepot.

bric'cone, a *sm/f* rogue, rascal.

'briciola ['britʃola] *sf* crumb.

'briciolo ['britʃolo] *sm* (*specie fig*) bit.

'briga, ghe *sf* (*fastidio*) trouble, bother; **pigliarsi la ~ di fare qc** to take the trouble to do sth.

brigadi'ere *sm* (*dei carabinieri etc*) ≈ sergeant.

bri'gante *sm* bandit.

bri'gata *sf* (MIL) brigade; (*gruppo*) group, party.

'briglia ['briʎʎa] *sf* rein; **a ~ sciolta** at full gallop; (*fig*) at full speed.

bril'lante *ag* bright; (*anche fig*) brilliant; (*che luccica*) shining ♦ *sm* diamond.

bril'lare *vi* to shine; (*mina*) to blow up ♦ *vt* (*mina*) to set off.

'brillo, a *ag* merry, tipsy.

'brina *sf* hoarfrost.

brin'dare *vi*: **~ a qn/qc** to drink to *o* toast sb/sth.

'brindisi *sm inv* toast.

'brio *sm* liveliness, go; **bri'oso, a** *ag* lively.

bri'tannico, a, ci, che *ag* British.

'brivido *sm* shiver; (*di ribrezzo*) shudder; (*fig*) thrill.

brizzo'lato, a [brittso'lato] *ag* (*persona*) going grey; (*barba, capelli*) greying.

'brocca, che *sf* jug.

broc'cato *sm* brocade.

'broccolo *sm* broccoli *sg*.

'brodo *sm* broth; (*per cucinare*) stock; **~ ristretto** consommé.

brogli'accio [broʎ'ʎattʃo] *sm* scribbling pad.

'broglio ['brɔʎʎo] *sm*: **~ elettorale** gerrymandering.

bron'chite [bron'kite] *sf* (MED) bronchitis.

'broncio ['brontʃo] *sm* sulky expression; **tenere il ~** to sulk.

'bronco, chi *sm* bronchial tube.

bronto'lare *vi* to grumble; (*tuono, stomaco*) to rumble.

'bronzo ['brondzo] *sm* bronze.

bru'care *vt* to browse on, nibble at.

brucia'pelo [brutʃa'pelo]: **a ~** *av* point-blank.

bruci'are [bru'tʃare] *vt* to burn; (*scottare*) to scald ♦ *vi* to burn; **brucia'tore** *sm* burner; **brucia'tura** *sf* (*atto*) burning *no pl*; (*segno*) burn; (*scottatura*) scald; **bruci'ore** *sm* burning *o* smarting sensation.

'bruco, chi *sm* caterpillar; grub.

brughi'era [bru'gjera] *sf* heath, moor.

bruli'care *vi* to swarm.

'brullo, a *ag* bare, bleak.

'bruma *sf* mist.

'bruno, a *ag* brown, dark; (*persona*) dark(-haired).

'brusco, a, schi, sche *ag* (*sapore*) sharp; (*modi, persona*) brusque, abrupt; (*movimento*) abrupt, sudden.

bru'sio *sm* buzz, buzzing.

bru'tale *ag* brutal.

'bruto, a *ag* (*forza*) brute *cpd* ♦ *sm* brute.

brut'tezza [brut'tettsa] *sf* ugliness.

'brutto, a *ag* ugly; (*cattivo*) bad; (*malattia, strada, affare*) nasty, bad; **~ tempo** bad weather; **brut'tura** *sf* (*cosa brutta*) ugly thing; (*sudiciume*) filth; (*azione meschina*) mean action.

Bru'xelles [bry'sɛl] *sf* Brussels.

'buca, che *sf* hole; (*avvallamento*) hollow; **~ delle lettere** letterbox.

buca'neve *sm inv* snowdrop.

bu'care *vt* (*forare*) to make a hole (*o* holes) in; (*pungere*) to pierce; (*biglietto*) to punch; **~rsi** *vr* (*con eroina*) to mainline; **~ una gomma** to have a puncture.

bu'cato *sm* (*operazione*) washing; (*panni*) wash, washing.

'buccia, ce ['buttʃa] *sf* skin, peel; (*corteccia*) bark.

bucherel'lare [bukerel'lare] *vt* to riddle with holes.

'buco, chi *sm* hole.

bu'dello *sm* (ANAT: *pl(f)* ~a) bowel, gut; (*fig: tubo*) tube; (*vicolo*) alley.

bu'dino *sm* pudding.

'bue *sm* ox; (*anche: carne di ~*) beef.

'bufalo *sm* buffalo.

bu'fera *sf* storm.

'buffo, a *ag* funny; (TEATRO) comic.

bu'gia, 'gie [bu'dʒia] *sf* lie; (*candeliere*) candleholder; **bugi'ardo, a**

ag lying, deceitful ♦ *sm/f* liar.

bugi'gattolo [budʒi'gattolo] *sm* poky little room.

'buio, a *ag* dark ♦ *sm* dark, darkness; **fa ~ pesto** it's pitch-dark.

'bulbo *sm* (*BOT*) bulb; **~ oculare** eyeball.

Bulga'ria *sf:* **la ~** Bulgaria.

bul'lone *sm* bolt.

buona'notte *escl* good night! ♦ *sf:* **dare la ~** a to say good night to.

buona'sera *escl* good evening!

buon gi'orno [bwon'dʒorno] *escl* good morning (*o* afternoon)!

buongus'taio, a *sm/f* gourmet.

buon'gusto *sm* good taste.

PAROLA CHIAVE

bu'ono, a (*ag:* dav *sm* **buon** +*C o V*, **buono** +*s impura, gn, pn, ps, x, z;* dav *sf* **buon'** +*V*) *ag* **1** (*gen*) good; **un buon pranzo/ristorante** a good lunch/restaurant; (**stai**) ~**!** behave!

2 (*benevolo*): ~ (**con**) good (to), kind (to)

3 (*giusto, valido*) right; **al momento ~** at the right moment

4 (*adatto*): ~ **a/da** fit for/to; **essere ~ a nulla** to be no good *o* use at anything

5 (*auguri*): **buon compleanno!** happy birthday!; **buon divertimento!** have a nice time!; **~a fortuna!** good luck!; **buon riposo!** sleep well!; **buon viaggio!** bon voyage!, have a good trip!

6: **a buon mercato** cheap; **di buon'ora** early; **buon senso** common sense; **alla ~a** *ag* simple ♦ *av* in a simple way, without any fuss

♦ *sm* **1** (*bontà*) goodness, good

2 (*COMM*) voucher, coupon; ~ **di cassa** cash voucher; ~ **di consegna** delivery note; ~ **del Tesoro** Treasury bill.

buontem'pone, a *sm/f* jovial person.

burat'tino *sm* puppet.

'burbero, a *ag* surly, gruff.

'burla *sf* prank, trick; **bur'lare** *vt:* **burlare qc/qn, burlarsi di qc/qn** to make fun of sth/sb.

burocra'zia [burokrat'tsia] *sf* bureaucra-cy.

bur'rasca, sche *sf* storm.

'burro *sm* butter.

bur'rone *sm* ravine.

bus'care *vt* (*anche:* ~**rsi:** *raffreddore*) to get, catch; **buscarle** (*fam*) to get a hiding.

bus'sare *vi* to knock.

'bussola *sf* compass; **perdere la ~** (*fig*) to lose one's bearings.

'busta *sf* (*da lettera*) envelope; (*astuccio*) case; **in ~ aperta/chiusa** in an unsealed/sealed envelope; **~ paga** pay packet.

busta'rella *sf* bribe, backhander.

'busto *sm* bust; (*indumento*) corset, girdle; **a mezzo ~** (*foto*) half-length.

but'tare *vt* to throw; (*anche:* ~ *via*) to throw away; ~ **giù** (*scritto*) to scribble down; (*cibo*) to gulp down; (*edificio*) to pull down, demolish; (*pasta, verdura*) to put into boiling water.

C

ca'bina *sf* (*di nave*) cabin; (*da spiaggia*) beach hut; (*di autocarro, treno*) cab; (*di aereo*) cockpit; (*di ascensore*) cage; ~ **telefonica** call *o* (tele)phone box.

ca'cao *sm* cocoa.

'caccia ['kattʃa] *sf* hunting; (*con fucile*) shooting; (*inseguimento*) chase; (*cacciagione*) game ♦ *sm inv* (*aereo*) fighter; (*nave*) destroyer; ~ **grossa** big-game hunting; ~ **all'uomo** manhunt.

cacciabombardi'ere [kattʃabombar-'djere] *sm* fighter-bomber.

cacciagi'one [kattʃa'dʒone] *sf* game.

cacci'are [kat'tʃare] *vt* to hunt; (*mandar via*) to chase away; (*ficcare*) to shove, stick ♦ *vi* to hunt; ~**rsi** *vr* (*fam: mettersi*): ~**rsi tra la folla** to plunge into the crowd; **dove s'è cacciata la mia borsa?** where has my bag got to?; ~**rsi nei guai** to get into trouble; ~ **fuori** qc to whip *o* pull sth out; ~ **un urlo** to let out a yell; **caccia'tore** *sm* hunter; **cacciatore di frodo** poacher.

caccia'vite [kattʃa'vite] *sm inv* screwdriver.

'cactus *sm inv* cactus.

ca'davere *sm* (dead) body, corpse.

ca'dente *ag* falling; (*casa*) tumbledown.

ca'denza [ka'dɛntsa] *sf* cadence; (*andamento ritmico*) rhythm; (*MUS*) cadenza.

ca'dere *vi* to fall; (*denti, capelli*) to fall out; (*tetto*) to fall in; **questa gonna cade bene** this skirt hangs well; **lasciar ~** (*anche fig*) to drop; **~ dal sonno** to be falling asleep on one's feet; **~ dalle nuvole** (*fig*) to be taken aback.

ca'detto, a *ag* younger; (*squadra*) junior *cpd* ♦ *sm* cadet.

ca'duta *sf* fall; **la ~ dei capelli** hair loss.

caffè *sm inv* coffee; (*locale*) café; **~ macchiato** coffee with a dash of milk; **~ macinato** ground coffee.

caffel'latte *sm inv* white coffee.

caffetti'era *sf* coffeepot.

cagio'nare [kadʒo'nare] *vt* to cause, be the cause of.

cagio'nevole [kadʒo'nevole] *ag* delicate, weak.

cagli'are [kaʎ'ʎare] *vi* to curdle.

'cagna [ˈkaɲɲa] *sf* (*ZOOL, peg*) bitch.

ca'gnesco, a, schi, sche [kaɲˈɲesko] *ag* (*fig*): **guardare qn in ~** to scowl at sb.

cala'brone *sm* hornet.

cala'maio *sm* inkpot; inkwell.

cala'maro *sm* squid.

cala'mita *sf* magnet.

calamità *sf inv* calamity, disaster.

ca'lare *vt* (*far discendere*) to lower; (*MAGLIA*) to decrease ♦ *vi* (*discendere*) to go (*o come*) down; (*tramontare*) to set, go down; **~ di peso** to lose weight.

'calca *sf* throng, press.

cal'cagno [kalˈkaɲɲo] *sm* heel.

cal'care *sm* limestone ♦ *vt* (*premere coi piedi*) to tread, press down; (*premere con forza*) to press down; (*mettere in rilievo*) to stress; **~ la mano** to overdo it, exaggerate.

'calce [ˈkaltʃe] *sm*: **in ~** at the foot of the page ♦ *sf* lime; **~ viva** quicklime.

calces'truzzo [kaltʃesˈtruttso] *sm* concrete.

calci'are [kalˈtʃare] *vt, vi* to kick; **calcia'tore** *sm* footballer.

cal'cina [kalˈtʃina] *sf* (lime) mortar.

'calcio [ˈkaltʃo] *sm* (*pedata*) kick; (*sport*) football, soccer; (*di pistola, fucile*) butt; (*CHIM*) calcium; **~ d'angolo** (*SPORT*) corner (kick); **~ di punizione** (*SPORT*) free kick.

'calco, chi *sm* (*ARTE*) casting, moulding; cast, mould.

calco'lare *vt* to calculate, work out, reckon; (*ponderare*) to weigh (up); **calcola'tore, 'trice** *ag* calculating ♦ *sm* calculator; (*fig*) calculating person; **calcolatore elettronico** computer; **calcola'trice** *sf* (*anche: macchina calcolatrice*) calculator.

'calcolo *sm* (*anche MAT*) calculation; (*infinitesimale etc*) calculus; (*MED*) stone; **fare i propri ~i** (*fig*) to weigh the pros and cons; **per ~** out of self-interest.

cal'daia *sf* boiler.

caldeggi'are [kaldedˈdʒare] *vt* to support.

'caldo, a *ag* warm; (*molto ~*) hot; (*fig: appassionato*) keen; hearty ♦ *sm* heat; **ho ~** I'm warm; I'm hot; **fa ~** it's warm; it's hot.

calen'dario *sm* calendar.

'calibro *sm* (*di arma*) calibre, bore; (*TECN*) callipers *pl*; (*fig*) calibre; **di grosso ~** (*fig*) prominent.

'calice [ˈkalitʃe] *sm* goblet; (*REL*) chalice.

ca'ligine [kaˈlidʒine] *sf* fog; (*mista con fumo*) smog.

'callo *sm* callus; (*ai piedi*) corn.

'calma *sf* calm.

cal'mante *sm* sedative, tranquillizer.

cal'mare *vt* to calm; (*lenire*) to soothe; **~rsi** *vr* to grow calm, calm down; (*vento*) to abate; (*dolori*) to ease.

calmi'ere *sm* controlled price.

'calmo, a *ag* calm, quiet.

'calo *sm* (*COMM: di prezzi*) fall; (*: di volume*) shrinkage; (*: di peso*) loss.

ca'lore *sm* warmth; heat; in ~ (*ZOOL*) on heat.

calo'ria *sf* calorie.

calo'roso, a *ag* warm.

calpes'tare *vt* to tread on, trample on; "è vietato ~ l'erba" "keep off the grass".

ca'lunnia *sf* slander; (*scritta*) libel.

cal'vario *sm* (*fig*) affliction, cross.

cal'vizie [kal'vittsje] *sf* baldness.

'calvo, a *ag* bald.

'calza ['kaltsa] *sf* (*da donna*) stocking; (*da uomo*) sock; fare la ~ to knit; ~e di nailon nylons, (nylon) stockings.

cal'zare [kal'tsare] *vt* (*scarpe, guanti: mettersi*) to put on; (: *portare*) to wear ♦ *vi* to fit; calza'tura *sf* footwear.

calzet'tone [kaltset'tone] *sm* heavy knee-length sock.

cal'zino [kal'tsino] *sm* sock.

calzo'laio [kaltso'lajo] *sm* shoemaker; (*che ripara scarpe*) cobbler; calzole'ria *sf* (*negozio*) shoe shop.

calzon'cini [kaltson'tʃini] *smpl* shorts.

cal'zone [kal'tsone] *sm* trouser leg; (*CUC*) *savoury turnover made with pizza dough*; ~i *smpl* (*pantaloni*) trousers (*BRIT*), pants (*US*).

cambi'ale *sf* bill (of exchange); (*pagherò cambiario*) promissory note.

cambia'mento *sm* change.

cambi'are *vt* to change; (*modificare*) to alter, change; (*barattare*): ~ (qc con qn/qc) to exchange (sth with sb/for sth) ♦ *vi* to change, alter; ~rsi *vr* (*variare abito*) to change; ~ casa to move (house); ~ idea to change one's mind; ~ treno to change trains.

'cambio *sm* change; (*modifica*) alteration, change; (*scambio, COMM*) exchange; (*corso dei cambi*) rate (of exchange); (*TECN, AUT*) gears *pl*; in ~ di in exchange for; dare il ~ a qn to take over from sb.

'camera *sf* room; (*anche:* ~ da letto) bedroom; (*POL*) chamber, house; ~ ardente mortuary chapel; ~ d'aria inner tube; (*di pallone*) bladder; C~ di Commercio Chamber of Commerce; C~ dei Deputati Chamber of Deputies, ≈

House of Commons (*BRIT*), ≈ House of Representatives (*US*); ~ a gas gas chamber; ~ a un letto/a due letti/ matrimoniale single/twin-bedded/double room; ~ oscura (*FOT*) dark room.

came'rata, i, e *sm/f* companion, mate ♦ *sf* dormitory.

cameri'era *sf* (*domestica*) maid; (*che serve a tavola*) waitress; (*che fa le camere*) chambermaid.

cameri'ere *sm* (man)servant; (*di ristorante*) waiter.

came'rino *sm* (*TEATRO*) dressing room.

'camice ['kamitʃe] *sm* (*REL*) alb; (*per medici etc*) white coat.

cami'cetta [kami'tʃetta] *sf* blouse.

ca'micia, cie [ka'mitʃa] *sf* (*da uomo*) shirt; (*da donna*) blouse; ~ di forza straitjacket; camici'otto *sm* casual shirt; (*per operai*) smock.

cami'netto *sm* hearth, fireplace.

ca'mino *sm* chimney; (*focolare*) fireplace, hearth.

'camion *sm inv* lorry (*BRIT*), truck (*US*); camion'cino *sm* van.

cam'mello *sm* (*ZOOL*) camel; (*tessuto*) camel hair.

cammi'nare *vi* to walk; (*funzionare*) to work, go.

cam'mino *sm* walk; (*sentiero*) path; (*itinerario, direzione, tragitto*) way; mettersi in ~ to set o start off.

camo'milla *sf* camomile; (*infuso*) camomile tea.

ca'morra *sf* camorra; racket.

ca'moscio [ka'moʃʃo] *sm* chamois.

cam'pagna [kam'paɲɲa] *sf* country, countryside; (*POL, COMM, MIL*) campaign; in ~ in the country; andare in ~ to go to the country; fare una ~ to campaign; campa'gnola *sf* (*AUT*) cross-country vehicle; campa'gnolo, a *ag* country cpd.

cam'pale *ag* field cpd; (*fig*): una giornata ~ a hard day.

cam'pana *sf* bell; (*anche:* ~ di vetro) bell jar; campa'nella *sf* small bell; (*di tenda*) curtain ring; campa'nello *sm* (*all'uscio, da tavola*) bell.

campa'nile *sm* bell tower, belfry;

campani'lismo *sm* parochialism.
cam'pare *vi* to live; (*tirare avanti*) to get by, manage.
cam'pato, a *ag*: ~ **in aria** unsound, unfounded.
campeggi'are [kamped'dʒare] *vi* to camp; (*risaltare*) to stand out; **campeggia'tore, 'trice** *sm/f* camper; **cam'peggio** *sm* camping; (*terreno*) camp site; **fare (del) campeggio** to go camping.
cam'pestre *ag* country *cpd*, rural.
campio'nario, a *ag*: **fiera ~a** trade fair ♦ *sm* collection of samples.
campio'nato *sm* championship.
campi'one, 'essa *sm/f* (*SPORT*) champion ♦ *sm* (*COMM*) sample.
'campo *sm* field; (*MIL*) field; (: *accampamento*) camp; (*spazio delimitato: sportivo etc*) ground; field; (*di quadro*) background; **i ~i** (*campagna*) the countryside; ~ **da aviazione** airfield; ~ **di concentramento** concentration camp; ~ **di golf** golf course; ~ **da tennis** tennis court; ~ **visivo** field of vision.
campo'santo (*pl* **campisanti**) *sm* cemetery.
camuf'fare *vt* to disguise.
'Canada *sm*: **il ~ Canada; cana'dese** *ag, sm/f* Canadian ♦ *sf* (*anche: tenda canadese*) ridge tent.
ca'naglia [ka'naʎʎa] *sf* rabble, mob; (*persona*) scoundrel, rogue.
ca'nale *sm* (*anche fig*) channel; (*artificiale*) canal.
'canapa *sf* hemp.
cana'rino *sm* canary.
cancel'lare [kantʃel'lare] *vt* (*con la gomma*) to rub out, erase; (*con la penna*) to strike out; (*annullare*) to annul, cancel; (*disdire*) to cancel.
cancelle'ria [kantʃelle'ria] *sf* chancery; (*quanto necessario per scrivere*) stationery.
cancelli'ere [kantʃel'ljɛre] *sm* chancellor; (*di tribunale*) clerk of the court.
can'cello [kan'tʃɛllo] *sm* gate.
can'crena *sf* gangrene.

'cancro *sm* (*MED*) cancer; (*dello zodiaco*): **C~** Cancer.
can'dela *sf* candle; ~ **(di accensione)** (*AUT*) spark(ing) plug.
cande'labro *sm* candelabra.
candeli'ere *sm* candlestick.
candi'dato, a *sm/f* candidate; (*aspirante a una carica*) applicant.
'candido, a *ag* white as snow; (*puro*) pure; (*sincero*) sincere, candid.
can'dito, a *ag* candied.
can'dore *sm* brilliant white; purity; sincerity, candour.
'cane *sm* dog; (*di pistola, fucile*) cock; **fa un freddo ~** it's bitterly cold; **non c'era un ~** there wasn't a soul; ~ **da caccia/guardia** hunting/guard dog; ~ **lupo** alsatian.
ca'nestro *sm* basket.
cangi'ante [kan'dʒante] *ag* iridescent.
can'guro *sm* kangaroo.
ca'nile *sm* kennel; (*di allevamento*) kennels *pl*; ~ **municipale** dog pound.
ca'nino, a *ag, sm* canine.
'canna *sf* (*pianta*) reed; (: *indica, da zucchero*) cane; (*bastone*) stick, cane; (*di fucile*) barrel; (*di organo*) pipe; ~ **fumaria** chimney flue; ~ **da pesca** (fishing) rod; ~ **da zucchero** sugar cane.
can'nella *sf* (*CUC*) cinnamon.
cannel'loni *smpl pasta tubes stuffed with sauce and baked.*
cannocchi'ale [kannok'kjale] *sm* telescope.
can'none *sm* (*MIL*) gun; (: *STORIA*) cannon; (*tubo*) pipe, tube; (*piega*) box pleat; (*fig*) ace.
can'nuccia, ce [kan'nuttʃa] *sf* (drinking) straw.
ca'noa *sf* canoe.
'canone *sm* canon, criterion; (*mensile, annuo*) rent; fee.
ca'nonico, ci *sm* (*REL*) canon.
ca'noro, a *ag* (*uccello*) singing, song *cpd*.
canot'taggio [kanot'taddʒo] *sm* rowing.
canotti'era *sf* vest.
ca'notto *sm* small boat, dinghy; canoe.
cano'vaccio [kano'vattʃo] *sm* (*tela*)

canvas; (*strofinaccio*) duster; (*trama*) plot.

can'tante *sm/f* singer.

can'tare *vt, vi* to sing; **cantau'tore, 'trice** *sm/f* singer-composer.

canti'ere *sm* (*EDIL*) (building) site; (*anche: ~ navale*) shipyard.

canti'lena *sf* (*filastrocca*) lullaby; (*fig*) sing-song voice.

can'tina *sf* (*locale*) cellar; (*bottega*) wine shop.

'canto *sm* song; (*arte*) singing; (*REL*) chant; chanting; (*poesia*) poem, lyric; (*parte di una poesia*) canto; (*parte, lato*): **da un ~** on the one hand; **d'altro ~** on the other hand.

canto'nata *sf* corner; **prendere una ~** (*fig*) to blunder.

can'tone *sm* (*in Svizzera*) canton.

can'tuccio [kan'tuttʃo] *sm* corner, nook.

canzo'nare [kantso'nare] *vt* to tease.

can'zone [kan'tsone] *sf* song; (*POESIA*) canzone; **canzoni'ere** *sm* (*MUS*) song-book; (*LETTERATURA*) collection of poems.

'caos *sm inv* chaos; **ca'otico, a, ci, che** *ag* chaotic.

C.A.P. *sigla m* = **codice di avviamento postale.**

ca'pace [ka'patʃe] *ag* able, capable; (*ampio, vasto*) large, capacious; **sei ~ di farlo?** can you *o* are you able to do it?; **capacità** *sf inv* ability; (*DIR, di recipiente*) capacity; **capaci'tarsi** *vr*: **capacitarsi di** to make out, understand.

ca'panna *sf* hut.

capan'none *sm* (*AGR*) barn; (*fabbricato industriale*) (factory) shed.

ca'parbio, a *ag* stubborn.

ca'parra *sf* deposit, down payment.

ca'pello *sm* hair; **~i** *smpl* (*capigliatura*) hair *sg*.

capez'zale [kapet'tsale] *sm* bolster; (*fig*) bedside.

ca'pezzolo [ka'pettsolo] *sm* nipple.

capi'enza [ka'pjentsa] *sf* capacity.

capiglia'tura [kapiʎʎa'tura] *sf* hair.

ca'pire *vt* to understand.

capi'tale *ag* (*mortale*) capital; (*fondamentale*) main, chief ♦ *sf* (*città*)

capital ♦ *sm* (*ECON*) capital; **capita'lismo** *sm* capitalism; **capita'lista, i, e** *ag, sm/f* capitalist.

capi'tano *sm* captain.

capi'tare *vi* (*giungere casualmente*) to happen to go, find o.s.; (*accadere*) to happen; (*presentarsi: cosa*) to turn up, present itself ♦ *vb impers* to happen; **mi è capitato un guaio** I've had a spot of trouble.

capi'tello *sm* (*ARCHIT*) capital.

ca'pitolo *sm* chapter.

capi'tombolo *sm* headlong fall, tumble.

'capo *sm* head; (*persona*) head, leader; (*: in ufficio*) head, boss; (*: in tribù*) chief; (*di oggetti*) top; end; (*GEO*) cape; **andare a ~** to start a new paragraph; **da ~** over again; **~ di bestiame** head *inv* of cattle; **~ di vestiario** item of clothing.

'capo... *prefisso*: **capocu'oco, chi** *sm* head cook; **Capo'danno** *sm* New Year; **capo'fitto: a capofitto** *av* headfirst, headlong; **capo'giro** *sm* dizziness *no pl*; **capola'voro, i** *sm* masterpiece; **capo'linea** (*pl* **capi'linea**) *sm* terminus; **capo'lino** *sm*: **fare capolino** to peep out (*o in etc*); **capolu'ogo** (*pl* **ghi** *o* **capilu'oghi**) *sm* chief town, administrative centre.

capo'rale *sm* (*MIL*) lance corporal (*BRIT*), private first class (*US*).

'capo... *prefisso*: **capostazi'one** (*pl* **capistazi'one**) *sm* station master; **capo'treno** (*pl* **capi'treno** *o* **capo'treni**) *sm* guard.

capo'volgere [kapo'vɔldʒere] *vt* to overturn; (*fig*) to reverse; **~rsi** *vr* to overturn; (*barca*) to capsize; (*fig*) to be reversed; **capo'volto, a** *pp di* capovolgere.

'cappa *sf* (*mantello*) cape, cloak; (*del camino*) hood.

cap'pella *sf* (*REL*) chapel; **cappel'lano** *sm* chaplain.

cap'pello *sm* hat.

'cappero *sm* caper.

cap'pone *sm* capon.

cap'potto *sm* (over)coat.

cappuc'cino [kapput'tʃino] *sm* (*frate*) Capuchin monk; (*bevanda*) frothy white coffee.

cap'puccio [kap'puttʃo] *sm* (*copricapo*) hood; (*della biro*) cap.

'capra *sf* (she-)goat; **ca'pretto** *sm* kid.

ca'priccio [ka'prittʃo] *sm* caprice, whim; (*bizza*) tantrum; **fare i ~i** to be very naughty; **capricci'oso, a** *ag* capricious, whimsical; naughty.

Capri'corno *sm* Capricorn.

capri'ola *sf* somersault.

capri'olo *sm* roe deer.

'capro *sm* billy-goat; **~ espiatorio** (*fig*) scapegoat.

'capsula *sf* capsule; (*di arma, per bottiglie*) cap.

cap'tare *vt* (*RADIO, TV*) to pick up; (*cattivarsi*) to gain, win.

cara'bina *sf* rifle.

carabini'ere *sm* member of Italian military police force.

ca'raffa *sf* carafe.

cara'mella *sf* sweet.

ca'rattere *sm* character; (*caratteristica*) characteristic, trait; **avere un buon ~** to be good-natured; **caratte'ristica, che** *sf* characteristic, trait, peculiarity; **caratte'ristico, a, ci, che** *ag* characteristic; **caratteriz'zare** *vt* to characterize, distinguish.

car'bone *sm* coal.

carbu'rante *sm* (*motor*) fuel.

carbura'tore *sm* carburettor.

car'cassa *sf* carcass; (*fig: peg: macchina etc*) (old) wreck.

carce'rato, a [kartʃe'rato] *sm/f* prisoner.

'carcere ['kartʃere] *sm* prison; (*pena*) imprisonment.

carci'ofo [kar'tʃɔfo] *sm* artichoke.

car'diaco, a, ci, che *ag* cardiac, heart *cpd*.

cardi'nale *ag, sm* cardinal.

'cardine *sm* hinge.

'cardo *sm* thistle.

ca'renza [ka'rɛntsa] *sf* lack, scarcity; (*vitaminica*) deficiency.

cares'tia *sf* famine; (*penuria*) scarcity, dearth.

ca'rezza [ka'rettsa] *sf* caress; **carez'zare** *vt* to caress, stroke, fondle.

'carica, che *sf* (*mansione ufficiale*) office, position; (*MIL, TECN, ELETTR*) charge; **ha una forte ~ di simpatia** he's very likeable; *vedi anche* **carico.**

cari'care *vt* to load; (*aggravare: anche fig*) to weigh down; (*orologio*) to wind up; (*batteria, MIL*) to charge.

'carico, a, chi, che *ag* (*che porta un peso*): **~ di** loaded *o* laden with; (*fucile*) loaded; (*orologio*) wound up; (*batteria*) charged; (*colore*) deep; (*caffè, tè*) strong ♦ *sm* (*il caricare*) loading; (*ciò che si carica*) load; (*fig: peso*) burden, weight; **persona a ~** dependent; **essere a ~ di qn** (*spese etc*) to be charged to sb.

'carie *sf* (*dentaria*) decay.

ca'rino,' a *ag* lovely, pretty, nice; (*simpatico*) nice.

carità *sf* charity; **per ~!** (*escl di rifiuto*) good heavens, no!

carnagi'one [karna'dʒone] *sf* complexion.

car'nale *ag* (*amore*) carnal; (*fratello*) blood *cpd*.

'carne *sf* flesh; (*bovina, ovina etc*) meat; **~ di manzo/maiale/pecora** beef/pork/mutton; **~ tritata** mince (*BRIT*), hamburger meat (*US*), minced (*BRIT*) *o* ground (*US*) meat.

car'nefice [kar'nefitʃe] *sm* executioner; hangman.

carne'vale *sm* carnival.

car'noso, a *ag* fleshy.

'caro, a *ag* (*amato*) dear; (*costoso*) dear, expensive.

ca'rogna [ka'roɲɲa] *sf* carrion; (*fig: fam*) swine.

caro'sello *sm* merry-go-round.

ca'rota *sf* carrot.

caro'vana *sf* caravan.

caro'vita *sm* high cost of living.

carpenti'ere *sm* carpenter.

car'pire *vt*: **~ qc a qn** (*segreto etc*) to get sth out of sb.

car'poni *av* on all fours.

car'rabile *ag* suitable for vehicles; **"passo ~"** "keep clear".

car'raio, a *ag*: **passo** ~ vehicle entrance.

carreggi'ata [karred'dʒata] *sf* carriageway (*BRIT*), (road)way.

car'rello *sm* trolley; (*AER*) undercarriage; (*CINEMA*) dolly; (*di macchina da scrivere*) carriage.

carri'era *sf* career; **fare** ~ to get on; **a gran** ~ at full speed.

carri'ola *sf* wheelbarrow.

'carro *sm* cart, wagon; ~ **armato** tank.

car'rozza [kar'rɔttsa] *sf* carriage, coach.

carrozze'ria [karrottse'ria] *sf* body, coachwork (*BRIT*); (*officina*) coachbuilder's workshop (*BRIT*), body shop.

carroz'zina [karrot'tsina] *sf* pram (*BRIT*), baby carriage (*US*).

'carta *sf* paper; (*al ristorante*) menu; (*GEO*) map; plan; (*documento, da gioco*) card; (*costituzione*) charter; ~**e** *sfpl* (*documenti*) papers, documents; **alla** ~ (*al ristorante*) à la carte; ~ **assegni** bank card; ~ **assorbente** blotting paper; ~ **bollata** *o* **da bollo** official stamped paper; ~ **di credito** credit card; ~ **(geografica)** map; ~ **d'identità** identity card; ~ **igienica** toilet paper; ~ **d'imbarco** (*AER, NAUT*) boarding card; ~ **da lettere** writing paper; ~ **libera** (*AMM*) unstamped paper; ~ **da parati** wallpaper; ~ **verde** (*AUT*) green card; ~ **vetrata** sandpaper; ~ **da visita** visiting card.

cartacar'bone (*pl* **cartecar'bone**) *sf* carbon paper.

car'taccia, ce [kar'tattʃa] *sf* waste paper.

cartamo'neta *sf* paper money.

carta'pecora *sf* parchment.

carta'pesta *sf* papier-mâché.

car'teggio [kar'teddʒo] *sm* correspondence.

car'tella *sf* (*scheda*) card; (*custodia: di cartone*) folder; (*: di uomo d'affari etc*) briefcase; (*: di scolaro*) schoolbag, satchel; ~ **clinica** (*MED*) case sheet.

car'tello *sm* sign; (*pubblicitario*) poster; (*stradale*) sign, signpost; (*ECON*) cartel; (*in dimostrazioni*) placard; **cartel'lone** *sm* (*pubblicitario*) advertis-

ing poster; (*della tombola*) scoring frame; (*TEATRO*) playbill; **tenere il cartellone** (*spettacolo*) to have a long run.

carti'era *sf* paper mill.

car'tina *sf* (*AUT, GEO*) map.

car'toccio [kar'tɔttʃo] *sm* paper bag.

cartole'ria *sf* stationer's (shop).

carto'lina *sf* postcard.

car'tone *sm* cardboard; (*ARTE*) cartoon; ~**i animati** *smpl* (*CINEMA*) cartoons.

car'tuccia, ce [kar'tuttʃa] *sf* cartridge.

'casa *sf* house; (*specialmente la propria casa*) home; (*COMM*) firm, house; **essere a** ~ to be at home; **vado a** ~ **mia/tua** I'm going home/to your house; ~ **di cura** nursing home; ~ **dello studente** student hostel; ~**e popolari** ≈ council houses (*o* flats) (*BRIT*), ≈ public housing units (*US*).

ca'sacca, che *sf* military coat; (*di fantino*) blouse.

casa'linga, ghe *sf* housewife.

casa'lingo, a, ghi, ghe *ag* household, domestic; (*fatto a casa*) home-made; (*semplice*) homely; (*amante della casa*) home-loving; ~**ghi** *smpl* household articles; **cucina** ~**a** plain home cooking.

cas'care *vi* to fall; **cas'cata** *sf* fall; (*d'acqua*) cascade, waterfall.

'casco, schi *sm* helmet; (*del parrucchiere*) hair-drier; (*di banane*) bunch.

casei'ficio [kazei'fitʃo] *sm* creamery.

ca'sella *sf* pigeon-hole; ~ **postale** post office box.

casel'lario *sm* filing cabinet; ~ **giudiziale** court records *pl*.

ca'sello *sm* (*di autostrada*) toll-house.

ca'serma *sf* barracks *pl*.

ca'sino *sm* (*confusione*) row, racket; (*casa di prostituzione*) brothel.

casinò *sm inv* casino.

'caso *sm* chance; (*fatto, vicenda*) event, incident; (*possibilità*) possibility; (*MED, LING*) case; **a** ~ at random; **per** ~ by chance, by accident; **in ogni** ~, **in tutti i** ~**i** in any case, at any rate; **al** ~

should the opportunity arise; **nel ~ che** in case; **~ mai** if by chance; **~ limite** borderline case.

'**cassa** *sf* case, crate, box; (*bara*) coffin; (*mobile*) chest; (*involucro: di orologio etc*) case; (*macchina*) cash register; (*luogo di pagamento*) check-out (counter); (*fondo*) fund; (*istituto bancario*) bank; **~ automatica prelievi** automatic telling machine, cash dispenser; **~ continua** night safe; **~ integrazione: mettere in ~ integrazione** ≈ to lay off; **~ mutua** *o* **malattia** health insurance scheme; **~ di risparmio** savings bank; **~ toracica** (*ANAT*) chest.

cassa'**forte** (*pl* **casseforti**) *sf* safe.
cassa'**panca** (*pl* **cassapanche** *o* **cassepanche**) *sf* settle.
casse'**rola** *sf* = **casseruola**.
casseru'**ola** *sf* saucepan.
cas'**setta** *sf* box; (*per registratore*) cassette; (*CINEMA, TEATRO*) box-office takings *pl*; **film di ~** box-office draw; **~ di sicurezza** strongbox; **~ delle lettere** letterbox.
cas'**setto** *sm* drawer; **casset'tone** *sm* chest of drawers.
cassi'**ere, a** *sm/f* cashier; (*di banca*) teller.
'**casta** *sf* caste.
cas'**tagna** [kas'taɲɲa] *sf* chestnut.
cas'**tagno** [kas'taɲɲo] *sm* chestnut (tree).
cas'**tano, a** *ag* chestnut (brown).
cas'**tello** *sm* castle; (*TECN*) scaffolding.
casti'**gare** *vt* to punish; **cas'tigo, ghi** *sm* punishment.
casti'**tà** *sf* chastity.
cas'**toro** *sm* beaver.
cas'**trare** *vt* to castrate; to geld; to doctor (*BRIT*), fix (*US*).
casu'**ale** *ag* chance *cpd*.
cata'**comba** *sf* catacomb.
ca'**talogo, ghi** *sm* catalogue.
catarifran'**gente** [catarifran'dʒɛnte] *sm* (*AUT*) reflector.
ca'**tarro** *sm* catarrh.
ca'**tasta** *sf* stack, pile.
ca'**tasto** *sm* land register; land registry office.

ca'**tastrofe** *sf* catastrophe, disaster.
catego'**ria** *sf* category.
ca'**tena** *sf* chain; **~ di montaggio** assembly line; **~e da neve** (*AUT*) snow chains; **cate'naccio** *sm* bolt.
cate'**ratta** *sf* cataract; (*chiusa*) sluice-gate.
cati'**nella** *sf*: **piovere a ~e** to pour, rain cats and dogs.
ca'**tino** *sm* basin.
ca'**trame** *sm* tar.
'**cattedra** *sf* teacher's desk; (*di università*) chair.
catte'**drale** *sf* cathedral.
catti'**veria** *sf* malice, spite; (*naughti-ness*); (*atto*) spiteful act; (*parole*) malicious *o* spiteful remark.
cattività *sf* captivity.
cat'**tivo, a** *ag* bad; (*malvagio*) bad, wicked; (*turbolento: bambino*) bad, naughty; (*: mare*) rough; (*odore, sapore*) nasty, bad.
cat'**tolico, a, ci, che** *ag, sm/f* (Roman) Catholic.
cat'**tura** *sf* capture.
cattu'**rare** *vt* to capture.
cauc'**ciù** [kaut'tʃu] *sm* rubber.
'**causa** *sf* cause; (*DIR*) lawsuit, case, action; **a ~ di, per ~ di** because of; **fare** *o* **muovere ~ a qn** to take legal action against sb.
cau'**sare** *vt* to cause.
cau'**tela** *sf* caution, prudence.
caute'**lare** *vt* to protect; **~rsi** *vr*: **~rsi (da)** to take precautions (against).
'**cauto, a** *ag* cautious, prudent.
cauzi'**one** [kaut'tsjone] *sf* security; (*DIR*) bail.
cav. *abbr* = **cavaliere**.
'**cava** *sf* quarry.
caval'**care** *vt* (*cavallo*) to ride; (*muro*) to sit astride; (*sog: ponte*) to span; **caval'cata** *sf* ride; (*gruppo di persone*) riding party.
cavalca'**via** *sm inv* flyover.
cavalci'**oni** [kaval'tʃoni]: **a ~ di** *prep* astride.
cavali'**ere** *sm* rider; (*feudale, titolo*) knight; (*soldato*) cavalryman; (*al ballo*) partner; **cavalle'resco, a, schi,**

sche *ag* chivalrous; **cavalle'ria** *sf* chivalry; *(milizia a cavallo)* cavalry.

cavalle'rizzo, a [kavalle'rittso] *sm/f* riding instructor; circus rider.

caval'letta *sf* grasshopper.

caval'letto *sm* *(FOT)* tripod; *(da pittore)* easel.

ca'vallo *sm* horse; *(SCACCHI)* knight; *(AUT: anche: ~ vapore)* horsepower; *(dei pantaloni)* crotch; **a ~** on horseback; **a ~ di** astride, straddling; **~ di battaglia** *(fig)* hobby-horse; **~ da corsa** racehorse.

ca'vare *vt (togliere)* to draw out, extract, take out; *(: giacca, scarpe)* to take off; *(: fame, sete, voglia)* to satisfy; **cavarsela** to get away with it; to manage, get on all right.

cava'tappi *sm inv* corkscrew.

ca'verna *sf* cave.

'cavia *sf* guinea pig.

cavi'ale *sm* caviar.

ca'viglia [ka'viʎʎa] *sf* ankle.

ca'villo *sm* quibble.

'cavo, a *ag* hollow ♦ *sm (ANAT)* cavity; *(grossa corda)* rope, cable; *(ELETTR, TEL)* cable.

cavolfi'ore *sm* cauliflower.

'cavolo *sm* cabbage; *(fam)*: **non m'importa un ~** I don't give a damn; **~ di Bruxelles** Brussels sprout.

cazzu'ola [kat'tswɔla] *sf* trowel.

c/c *abbr* = **conto corrente.**

ce [tʃe] *pron, av vedi* **ci.**

cece ['tʃetʃe] *sm* chickpea.

cecità [tʃetʃi'ta] *sf* blindness.

Cecoslo'vacchia [tʃekoslo'vakkja] *sf*: **la ~** Czechoslovakia; **cecoslo'vacco, a, chi, che** *ag, sm/f* Czechoslovakian.

'cedere ['tʃedere] *vt (concedere: posto)* to give up; *(DIR)* to transfer, make over ♦ *vi (cadere)* to give way, subside; **~ (a)** to surrender (to), yield (to), give in (to); **ce'devole** *ag (terreno)* soft; *(fig)* yielding.

'cedola ['tʃedola] *sf (COMM)* coupon; voucher.

'cedro ['tʃedro] *sm* cedar; *(albero da frutto, frutto)* citron.

C.E.E. ['tʃee] *sigla f* (= *Comunità*

Economica Europea) EEC.

'ceffo ['tʃeffo] *(peg)* *sm* ugly mug.

cef'fone [tʃef'fone] *sm* slap, smack.

ce'larsi [tʃe'larsi] *vr* to hide.

cele'brare [tʃele'brare] *vt* to celebrate; **celebrazi'one** *sf* celebration.

'celebre ['tʃelebre] *ag* famous, celebrated; **celebrità** *sf inv* fame; *(persona)* celebrity.

'celere ['tʃelere] *ag* fast, swift; *(corso)* crash *cpd.*

ce'leste [tʃe'leste] *ag* celestial; heavenly; *(colore)* sky-blue.

'celibe ['tʃelibe] *ag* single, unmarried ♦ *sm* bachelor.

'cella ['tʃella] *sf* cell.

'cellula ['tʃellula] *sf (BIOL, ELETTR, POL)* cell.

cemen'tare [tʃemen'tare] *vt (anche fig)* to cement.

ce'mento [tʃe'mento] *sm* cement; **~ armato** reinforced concrete.

'cena ['tʃena] *sf* dinner; *(leggera)* supper.

ce'nare [tʃe'nare] *vi* to dine, have dinner.

'cencio ['tʃentʃo] *sm* piece of cloth, rag; *(per spolverare)* duster.

'cenere ['tʃenere] *sf* ash.

'cenno ['tʃenno] *sm (segno)* sign, signal; *(gesto)* gesture; *(col capo)* nod; *(con la mano)* wave; *(allusione)* hint, mention; *(breve esposizione)* short account; **far ~ di sì/no** to nod (one's head)/shake one's head.

censi'mento [tʃensi'mento] *sm* census.

cen'sore [tʃen'sore] *sm* censor.

cen'sura [tʃen'sura] *sf* censorship; censor's office; *(fig)* censure.

cente'nario, a [tʃente'narjo] *ag (che ha cento anni)* hundred-year-old; *(che ricorre ogni cento anni)* centennial, centenary *cpd* ♦ *sm/f* centenarian ♦ *sm* centenary.

cen'tesimo, a [tʃen'tezimo] *ag, sm* hundredth.

cen'tigrado, a [tʃen'tigrado] *ag* centigrade; **20 gradi ~i** 20 degrees centigrade.

cen'timetro [tʃen'timetro] *sm* centimetre.

centi'naio [tʃenti'najo] (pl(f) **-aia**) sm: **un ~ (di)** a hundred; about a hundred.

'cento ['tʃɛnto] num a hundred, one hundred.

cen'trale [tʃen'trale] ag central ♦ sf: **~ telefonica** (telephone) exchange; **~ elettrica** electric power station; **centrali'nista** sm/f operator; **centra'lino** sm (telephone) exchange; (di albergo etc) switchboard.

cen'trare [tʃen'trare] vt to hit the centre of; (TECN) to centre.

cen'trifuga [tʃen'trifuga] sf spin-drier.

'centro ['tʃɛntro] sm centre; **~ commerciale** shopping centre; (città) commercial centre.

'ceppo ['tʃeppo] sm (di albero) stump; (pezzo di legno) log.

'cera ['tʃera] sf wax; (aspetto) appearance, look.

ce'ramica, che [tʃe'ramika] sf ceramic; (ARTE) ceramics sg.

cerbi'atto [tʃer'bjatto] sm (ZOOL) fawn.

'cerca ['tʃerka] sf: **in o alla ~ di** in search of.

cer'care [tʃer'kare] vt to look for, search for ♦ vi: **~ di fare qc** to try to do sth.

'cerchia ['tʃerkja] sf circle.

'cerchio ['tʃerkjo] sm circle; (giocattolo, di botte) hoop.

cere'ale [tʃere'ale] sm cereal.

ceri'monia [tʃeri'mɔnja] sf ceremony.

ce'rino [tʃe'rino] sm wax match.

'cernia ['tʃɛrnja] sf (ZOOL) stone bass.

cerni'era [tʃer'njera] sf hinge; **~ lampo** zip (fastener) (BRIT), zipper (US).

'cernita ['tʃernita] sf selection.

'cero ['tʃero] sm (church) candle.

ce'rotto [tʃe'rɔtto] sm sticking plaster.

certa'mente [tʃerta'mente] av certainly.

cer'tezza [tʃer'tettsa] sf certainty.

certifi'cato sm certificate; **~ medico/di nascita** medical/birth certificate.

'certo, a ['tʃerto] ag (sicuro): **~ (di/che)** certain o sure (of/that)
♦ det **1** (tale) certain; **un ~ signor Smith** a (certain) Mr Smith

2 (qualche; con valore intensivo) some; **dopo un ~ tempo** after some time; **un fatto di una ~a importanza** a matter of some importance; **di una ~a età** past one's prime, not so young
♦ pron: **~i, e** pl some
♦ av (certamente) certainly; (senz'altro) of course; **di ~** certainly; **no (di) ~!, ~ che no!** certainly not!; **sì ~** yes indeed, certainly.

cer'vello, i [tʃer'vello] (ANAT: pl(f) **-a**) sm brain.

'cervo, a ['tʃervo] sm/f stag/doe ♦ sm deer; **~ volante** stag beetle.

ce'sello [tʃe'zello] sm chisel.

ce'soie [tʃe'zoje] sfpl shears.

ces'puglio [tʃes'puʎʎo] sm bush.

ces'sare [tʃes'sare] vi, vt to stop, cease; **~ di fare qc** to stop doing sth; **cessate il fuoco** sm ceasefire.

'cesso ['tʃɛsso] (fam) sm (gabinetto) bog.

'cesta ['tʃesta] sf (large) basket.

ces'tino [tʃes'tino] sm basket; (per la carta straccia) wastepaper basket; **~ da viaggio** (FERR) packed lunch (o dinner).

'cesto ['tʃesto] sm basket.

'ceto ['tʃeto] sm (social) class.

cetrio'lino [tʃetrio'lino] sm gherkin.

cetri'olo [tʃetri'ɔlo] sm cucumber.

cfr. abbr (= confronta) cf.

CGIL sigla f (= Confederazione Generale Italiana del Lavoro) trades union organization.

che [ke] pron **1** (relativo: persona: soggetto) who; (: oggetto) whom, that; (: cosa, animale) which, that; **il ragazzo ~ è venuto** the boy who came; **l'uomo ~ io vedo** the man (whom) I see; **il libro ~ è sul tavolo** the book which o that is on the table; **il libro ~ vedi** the book (which o that) you see; **la sera ~ ti ho visto** the evening I saw you **2** (interrogativo, esclamativo) what; **~ (cosa) fai?** what are you doing?; **a ~ (cosa) pensi?** what are you thinking

about?; **non sa ~ (cosa) fare** he doesn't know what to do; **ma ~ dici!** what are you saying!
3 (*indefinito*): **quell'uomo ha un ~ di losco** there's something suspicious about that man; **un certo non so ~** an indefinable something
♦ *det* **1** (*interrogativo: tra tanti*) what; (: *tra pochi*) which; **~ tipo di film preferisci?** what sort of film do you prefer?; **~ vestito ti vuoi mettere?** what (*o* which) dress do you want to put on?
2 (*esclamativo: seguito da aggettivo*) how; (: *seguito da sostantivo*) what; **~ buono!** how delicious!; **~ bel vestito!** what a lovely dress!
♦ *cong* **1** (*con proposizioni subordinate*) that; **credo ~ verrà** I think he'll come; **voglio ~ tu studi** I want you to study; **so ~ tu c'eri** I know (that) you were there; **non ~: non ~ sia sbagliato, ma ...** not that it's wrong, but ...
2 (*finale*) so that; **vieni qua, ~ ti veda** come here, so (that) I can see you
3 (*temporale*): **arrivai ~ eri già partito** you had already left when I arrived; **sono anni ~ non lo vedo** I haven't seen him for years
4 (*in frasi imperative, concessive*): **~ venga pure!** let him come by all means!; **~ tu sia benedetto!** may God bless you!
5 (*comparativo: con più, meno*) than; *vedi anche* **più; meno; così** *etc*.

cheti'chella [keti'kɛlla]: **alla ~** *av* stealthily, unobtrusively.

PAROLA CHIAVE

chi [ki] *pron* **1** (*interrogativo: soggetto*) who; (: *oggetto*) who, whom; **~ è?** who is it?; **di ~ è questo libro?** whose book is this?, whose is this book?; **con ~ parli?** who are you talking to?; **a ~ pensi?** who are you thinking about?; **~ di voi?** which of you?; **non so a ~ rivolgermi** I don't know who to ask
2 (*relativo*) whoever, anyone who; **dillo a ~ vuoi** tell whoever you like
3 (*indefinito*): **~ ... ~ ...** some ... others

...; **~ dice una cosa, ~ dice un'altra** some say one thing, others say another.

chiacchie'rare [kjakkje'rare] *vi* to chat; (*discorrere futilmente*) to chatter; (*far pettegolezzi*) to gossip; **chiacchie'rata** *sf* chat; **chi'acchiere** *sfpl*: **fare due** *o* **quattro chiacchiere** to have a chat; **chiacchie'rone, a** *ag* talkative, chatty; gossipy ♦ *sm/f* chatterbox; gossip.
chia'mare [kja'mare] *vt* to call; (*rivolgersi a qn*) to call (in), send for; **~rsi** *vr* (*aver nome*) to be called; **mi chiamo Paolo** my name is Paolo, I'm called Paolo; **~ alle armi** to call up; **~ in giudizio** to summon; **chia'mata** *sf* (*TEL*) call; (*MIL*) call-up.
chia'rezza [kja'rettsa] *sf* clearness; clarity.
chia'rire [kja'rire] *vt* to make clear; (*fig: spiegare*) to clear up, explain; **~rsi** *vr* to become clear.
chi'aro, a ['kjaro] *ag* clear; (*luminoso*) clear, bright; (*colore*) pale, light.
chiaroveg'gente [kjaroved'dʒɛnte] *sm/f* clairvoyant.
chi'asso ['kjasso] *sm* uproar, row; **chias'soso, a** *ag* noisy, rowdy; (*vistoso*) showy, gaudy.
chi'ave ['kjave] *sf* key ♦ *ag inv* key *cpd*; **~ d'accensione** (*AUT*) ignition key; **~ inglese** monkey wrench; **~ di volta** keystone; **chiavis'tello** *sm* bolt.
chi'azza ['kjattsa] *sf* stain; splash.
'chicco, chi ['kikko] *sm* grain; (*di caffè*) bean; **~ d'uva** grape.
chi'edere ['kjɛdere] *vt* (*per sapere*) to ask; (*per avere*) to ask for ♦ *vi*: **~ di qn** to ask after sb; (*al telefono*) to ask for *o* want sb; **~ qc a qn** to ask sb sth; **to ask sb for sth**.
chi'erico, ci ['kjɛriko] *sm* cleric; altar boy.
chi'esa ['kjeza] *sf* church.
chi'esto, a *pp di* **chiedere**.
'chiglia ['kiʎʎa] *sf* keel.
'chilo ['kilo] *sm* kilo; **chilo'grammo** *sm* kilogram(me); **chi'lometro** *sm* kilometre.
'chimica ['kimika] *sf* chemistry.

'chimico, a, ci, che [ˈkimiko] *ag* chemical ♦ *sm/f* chemist.

'china [ˈkina] *sf* (*pendio*) slope, descent; (*BOT*) cinchona.

chi'nare [kiˈnare] *vt* to lower, bend; ~rsi *vr* to stoop, bend.

chi'nino [kiˈnino] *sm* quinine.

chi'occiola [ˈkjɔttʃola] *sf* snail; **scala a** ~ spiral staircase.

chi'odo [ˈkjɔdo] *sm* nail; (*fig*) obsession.

chi'oma [ˈkjɔma] *sf* (*capelli*) head of hair; (*di albero*) foliage.

chi'osco, schi [ˈkjɔsko] *sm* kiosk, stall.

chi'ostro [ˈkjɔstro] *sm* cloister.

chiro'mante [kiroˈmante] *sm/f* palmist.

chirur'gia [kirurˈdʒia] *sf* surgery; **chi'rurgo, ghi** o **gi** *sm* surgeon.

chissà [kisˈsa] *av* who knows, I wonder.

chi'tarra [kiˈtarra] *sf* guitar.

chi'udere [ˈkjudere] *vt* to close, shut; (*luce, acqua*) to put off, turn off; (*definitivamente: fabbrica*) to close down, shut down; (*strada*) to close; (*recingere*) to enclose; (*porre termine*) to end ♦ *vi* to close, shut; to close down, shut down; to end; ~rsi *vr* to shut, close; (*ritirarsi: anche fig*) to shut o.s. away; (*ferita*) to close up.

chi'unque [kiˈunkwe] *pron* (*relativo*) whoever; (*indefinito*) anyone, anybody; ~ **sia** whoever it is.

chi'uso, a [ˈkjuso] *pp di* **chiudere** ♦ *sf* (*di corso d'acqua*) sluice, lock; (*recinto*) enclosure; (*di discorso etc*) conclusion, ending; **chiu'sura** *sf* closing; shutting; closing *o* shutting down; enclosing; putting *o* turning off; ending; (*dispositivo*) catch; fastening; fastener.

PAROLA CHIAVE
---

ci [tʃi] (*dav* **lo, la, li, le, ne diventa** **ce**) *pron* **1** (*personale: complemento oggetto*) us; (: *a noi: complemento di termine*) (to) us; (: *riflessivo*) ourselves; (: *reciproco*) each other, one another; (*impersonale*): ~ **si veste** we get dressed; ~ **ha visti** he's seen us; **non** ~ **ha dato niente** he gave us nothing; ~ **vestiamo** we get dressed; ~ **amiamo** we love one another *o* each

other

2 (*dimostrativo: di ciò, su ciò, in ciò etc*) about (*o* on *o* of) it; **non so cosa far**~ I don't know what to do about it; **che c'entro io?** what have I got to do with it?

♦ *av* (*qui*) here; (*lì*) there; (*moto attraverso luogo*): ~ **passa sopra un ponte** a bridge passes over it; **non** ~ **passa più nessuno** nobody comes this way any more; **esser**~ *vedi* **essere**.

C.ia *abbr* (= *compagnia*) Co.

cia'batta [tʃaˈbatta] *sf* mule, slipper.

ci'alda [ˈtʃalda] *sf* (*CUC*) wafer.

ciam'bella [tʃamˈbella] *sf* (*CUC*) ring-shaped cake; (*salvagente*) rubber ring.

ci'ao [ˈtʃao] *escl* (*all'arrivo*) hello!; (*alla partenza*) cheerio! (*BRIT*), bye!

ciarla'tano [tʃarlaˈtano] *sm* charlatan.

cias'cuno, a [tʃasˈkuno] (*det: dav sm:* **ciascun** +*C, V,* **ciascuno** +*s impura, gn, pn, ps, x, z*; *dav sf:* **ciascuna** +*C,* **ciascun'** +*V*) *det* every, each; (*ogni*) every ♦ *pron* each (one); (*tutti*) everyone, everybody.

'cibo [ˈtʃibo] *sm* food.

ci'cala [tʃiˈkala] *sf* cicada.

cica'trice [tʃikaˈtritʃe] *sf* scar.

'cicca [ˈtʃikka] *sf* cigarette end.

'ciccia [ˈtʃittʃa] (*fam*) *sf* (*carne*) meat; (*grasso umano*) fat, flesh.

cice'rone [tʃitʃeˈrone] *sm* guide.

ci'clismo [tʃiˈklizmo] *sm* cycling; **ci'clista, i, e** *sm/f* cyclist.

'ciclo [ˈtʃiklo] *sm* cycle; (*di malattia*) course.

ciclomo'tore [tʃiklomoˈtore] *sm* moped.

ci'clone [tʃiˈklone] *sm* cyclone.

ci'cogna [tʃiˈkɔɲɲa] *sf* stork.

ci'coria [tʃiˈkɔria] *sf* chicory.

ci'eco, a, chi, che [ˈtʃɛko] *ag* blind ♦ *sm/f* blind man/woman.

ci'elo [ˈtʃɛlo] *sm* sky; (*REL*) heaven.

'cifra [ˈtʃifra] *sf* (*numero*) figure; numeral; (*somma di denaro*) sum, figure; (*monogramma*) monogram, initials *pl*; (*codice*) code, cipher.

'ciglio, i [ˈtʃiʎʎo] (*delle palpebre: pl(f)* **ciglia**) *sm* (*margine*) edge, verge;

(eye)lash; (eye)lid; (*sopracciglio*) eyebrow.

'cigno ['tʃiɲɲo] *sm* swan.

cigo'lare [tʃigo'lare] *vi* to squeak, creak.

'Cile ['tʃile] *sm*: il ~ Chile.

ci'lecca [tʃi'lekka] *sf*: far ~ to fail.

cili'egia, gie *o* **ge** [tʃi'ljedʒa] *sf* cherry; **cili'egio** *sm* cherry tree.

cilin'drata [tʃilin'drata] *sf* (*AUT*) (cubic) capacity; **una macchina di grossa ~** a big-engined car.

ci'lindro [tʃi'lindro] *sm* cylinder; (*cappello*) top hat.

'cima ['tʃima] *sf* (*sommità*) top; (*di monte*) top, summit; (*estremità*) end; **in ~ a** at the top of; **da ~ a fondo** from top to bottom; (*fig*) from beginning to end.

'cimice ['tʃimitʃe] *sf* (*ZOOL*) bug; (*puntina*) drawing pin (*BRIT*), thumbtack (*US*).

cimini'era [tʃimi'njera] *sf* chimney; (*di nave*) funnel.

cimi'tero [tʃimi'tero] *sm* cemetery.

ci'murro [tʃi'murro] *sm* (*di cani*) distemper.

'Cina ['tʃina] *sf*: la ~ China.

cin'cin [tʃin'tʃin] *escl* cheers!

cin cin [tʃin'tʃin] *escl* = cincin.

'cinema ['tʃinema] *sm inv* cinema; **cine'presa** *sf* cine-camera.

cl'nese [tʃi'nese] *ag*, *sm/f*, *sm* Chinese *inv*.

ci'netico, a, ci, che [tʃi'netiko] *ag* kinetic.

'cingere ['tʃindʒere] *vt* (*attorniare*) to surround, encircle; **~ la vita con una cintura** to put a belt round one's waist.

'cinghia ['tʃingja] *sf* strap; (*cintura, TECN*) belt.

cinghi'ale [tʃin'gjale] *sm* wild boar.

cinguet'tare [tʃingwet'tare] *vi* to twitter.

'cinico, a, ci, che ['tʃiniko] *ag* cynical ♦ *sm/f* cynic; **ci'nismo** *sm* cynicism.

cin'quanta [tʃin'kwanta] *num* fifty; **cinquan'teslmo, a** *num* fiftieth.

cinquan'tina [tʃinkwan'tina] *sf* (*serie*): **una ~ (di)** about fifty; (*età*): **essere sulla ~** to be about fifty.

'cinque ['tʃinkwe] *num* five; **avere ~**

anni to be five (years old); **il ~ dicembre 1988** the fifth of December 1988; **alle ~** (*ora*) at five (o'clock).

cinque'cento [tʃinkwe'tʃento] *num* five hundred ♦ *sm*: **il C~** the sixteenth century.

'cinto, a ['tʃinto] *pp di* cingere.

cin'tura [tʃin'tura] *sf* belt; **~ di salvataggio** lifebelt (*BRIT*), life preserver (*US*); **~ di sicurezza** (*AUT, AER*) safety *o* seat belt.

ciò [tʃɔ] *pron* this; that; **~ che** what; **~ nonostante** *o* **nondimeno** nevertheless, in spite of that.

ci'occa, che ['tʃɔkka] *sf* (*di capelli*) lock.

ciocco'lata [tʃokko'lata] *sf* chocolate; (*bevanda*) (hot) chocolate; **cioccola'tino** *sm* chocolate; **ciocco'lato** *sm* chocolate.

cioè [tʃo'ɛ] *av* that is (to say).

ciondo'lare [tʃondo'lare] *vi* to dangle; (*fig*) to loaf (about); **ci'ondolo** *sm* pendant.

ci'otola ['tʃɔtola] *sf* bowl.

ci'ottolo ['tʃɔttolo] *sm* pebble; (*di strada*) cobble(stone).

ci'polla [tʃi'polla] *sf* onion; (*di tulipano etc*) bulb.

ci'presso [tʃi'presso] *sm* cypress (tree).

'cipria ['tʃiprja] *sf* (face) powder.

'Cipro ['tʃipro] *sm* Cyprus.

'circa ['tʃirka] *av* about, roughly ♦ *prep* about, concerning; **a mezzogiorno ~** about midday.

'circo, chi ['tʃirko] *sm* circus.

circo'lare [tʃirko'lare] *vi* to circulate; (*AUT*) to drive (along), move (along) ♦ *ag* circular ♦ *sf* (*AMM*) circular; (*di autobus*) circle (line); **circolazi'one** *sf* circulation; (*AUT*): **la circolazione** (the) traffic.

'circolo ['tʃirkolo] *sm* circle.

circon'dare [tʃirkon'dare] *vt* to surround.

circonfe'renza [tʃirkonfe'rentsa] *sf* circumference.

circonvallazi'one [tʃirkonvallat'tsjone] *sf* ring road (*BRIT*), beltway (*US*); (*per evitare una città*) by-pass.

circos'critto, a [tʃirkos'kritto] *pp di* **circoscrivere**.

circos'crivere [tʃirkos'krivere] *vt* to circumscribe; *(fig)* to limit, restrict; **circoscrizi'one** *sf (AMM)* district, area; **circoscrizione elettorale** constituency.

circos'petto, a [tʃirkos'pɛtto] *ag* circumspect, cautious.

circos'tante [tʃirkos'tante] *ag* surrounding, neighbouring.

circos'tanza [tʃirkos'tantsa] *sf* circumstance; *(occasione)* occasion.

cir'cuito [tʃir'kuito] *sm* circuit.

CISL *sigla f (= Confederazione Italiana Sindacati Lavoratori) trades union organization.*

'ciste ['tʃiste] *sf* = **cisti**.

cis'terna [tʃis'tɛrna] *sf* tank, cistern.

'cisti ['tʃisti] *sf* cyst.

C.I.T. [tʃit] *sigla f* = **Compagnia Italiana Turismo**.

ci'tare [tʃi'tare] *vt (DIR)* to summon; *(autore)* to quote; *(a esempio, modello)* to cite; **citazi'one** *sf* summons *sg*; quotation; *(di persona)* mention.

ci'tofono [tʃi'tɔfono] *sm* entry phone; *(in uffici)* intercom.

città [tʃit'ta] *sf inv* town; *(importante)* city; ~ **universitaria** university campus.

cittadi'nanza [tʃittadi'nantsa] *sf* citizens *pl*, inhabitants *pl* of a town *(o* city); *(DIR)* citizenship.

citta'dino, a [tʃitta'dino] *ag* town *cpd*; city *cpd* ♦ *sm/f (di uno Stato)* citizen; *(abitante di città)* townsman, city dweller.

ci'uco, a, chi, che ['tʃuko] *sm/f* ass, donkey.

ci'uffo ['tʃuffo] *sm* tuft.

ci'vetta [tʃi'vetta] *sf (ZOOL)* owl; *(fig: donna)* coquette, flirt ♦ *ag inv*: **auto/nave** ~ decoy car/ship.

'civico, a, ci, che ['tʃivico] *ag* civic; *(museo)* municipal, town *cpd*; municipal, city *cpd*.

ci'vile [tʃi'vile] *ag* civil; *(non militare)* civilian; *(nazione)* civilized ♦ *sm* civilian.

civilizzazi'one [tʃiviliddzat'tsjone] *sf* civilization.

civiltà [tʃivil'ta] *sf* civilization; *(cortesia)* civility.

'clacson *sm inv (AUT)* horn.

cla'more *sm (frastuono)* din, uproar, clamour; *(fig)* outcry; **clamo'roso, a** *ag* noisy; *(fig)* sensational.

clandes'tino, a *ag* clandestine; *(POL)* underground, clandestine ♦ *sm/f* stowaway.

clari'netto *sm* clarinet.

'classe *sf* class; **di** ~ *(fig)* with class; of excellent quality.

'classico, a, ci, che *ag* classical; *(tradizionale: moda)* classic(al) ♦ *sm* classic; classical author.

clas'sifica *sf* classification; *(SPORT)* placings *pl*.

classifi'care *vt* to classify; *(candidato, compito)* `to grade; ~**rsi** *vr* to be placed.

'clausola *sf (DIR)* clause.

'clava *sf* club.

clavi'cembalo [klavi'tʃembalo] *sm* harpsichord.

cla'vicola *sf (ANAT)* collar bone.

cle'mente *ag* merciful; *(clima)* mild; **cle'menza** *sf* mercy, clemency; mildness.

'clero *sm* clergy.

cli'ente *sm/f* customer, client; **clien'tela** *sf* customers *pl*, clientèle.

'clima, i *sm* climate; **cli'matico, a, ci, che** *ag* climatic; **stazione climatica** health resort; **climatizzazi'one** *sf (TECN)* air conditioning.

'clinica, che *sf (scienza)* clinical medicine; *(casa di cura)* clinic, nursing home; *(settore d'ospedale)* clinic.

'clinico, a, ci, che *ag* clinical ♦ *sm (medico)* clinician.

clo'aca, che *sf* sewer.

'cloro *sm* chlorine.

cloro'formio *sm* chloroform.

club *sm inv* club.

c.m. *abbr* = **corrente mese**.

coabi'tare *vi* to live together, live under the same roof.

coagu'lare *vt* to coagulate ♦ *vi* to coagulate; *(latte)* to curdle; ~**rsi** *vr* to coagulate; to curdle.

coalizi'one [koalit'tsjone] *sf* coalition.

co'atto, a *ag* (*DIR*) compulsory, forced.

'COBAS *sigla mpl* (= *Comitati di base*) *independent trades unions.*

coca'ina *sf* cocaine.

cocci'nella [kottʃi'nɛlla] *sf* ladybird (*BRIT*), ladybug (*US*).

'coccio ['kɔttʃo] *sm* earthenware; (*vaso*) earthenware pot; ~i *smpl* (*frammenti*) fragments (of pottery).

cocci'uto, a [kot'tʃuto] *ag* stubborn, pigheaded.

'cocco, chi *sm* (*pianta*) coconut palm; (*frutto*): **noce di** ~ coconut ♦ *sm/f* (*fam*) darling.

cocco'drillo *sm* crocodile.

cocco'lare *vt* to cuddle, fondle.

co'cente [ko'tʃɛnte] *ag* (*anche fig*) burning.

co'comero *sm* watermelon.

co'cuzzolo [ko'kuttsolo] *sm* top; (*di capo, cappello*) crown.

'coda *sf* tail; (*fila di persone, auto*) queue (*BRIT*), line (*US*); (*di abiti*) train; **con la ~ dell'occhio** out of the corner of one's eye; **mettersi in** ~ to queue (up) (*BRIT*), line up (*US*); to join the queue (*BRIT*) **o line** (*US*); ~ **di cavallo** (*acconciatura*) ponytail.

co'dardo, a *ag* cowardly ♦ *sm/f* coward.

'codice ['kodiʃe] *sm* code; ~ **di avviamento postale** postcode (*BRIT*), zip code (*US*); ~ **fiscale** tax code; ~ **della strada** highway code.

coe'rente *ag* coherent; **coe'renza** *sf* coherence.

coe'taneo, a *ag, sm/f* contemporary.

'cofano *sm* (*AUT*) bonnet (*BRIT*), hood (*US*); (*forziere*) chest.

'cogli ['kɔʎʎi] *prep* + *det* = **con** + **gli**; *vedi* **con.**

'cogliere ['kɔʎʎere] *vt* (*fiore, frutto*) to pick, gather; (*sorprendere*) to catch, surprise; (*bersaglio*) to hit; (*fig: momento opportuno etc*) to grasp, seize, take; (: *capire*) to grasp; ~ **qn in flagrante o in fallo** to catch sb red-handed.

co'gnato, a [koɲ'ɲato] *sm/f* brother-/sister-in-law.

cognizi'one [koɲɲit'tsjone] *sf* knowledge.

co'gnome [koɲ'ɲome] *sm* surname.

'coi *prep* + *det* = **con** + **i**; *vedi* **con.**

coinci'denza [kointʃi'dɛntsa] *sf* coincidence; (*FERR, AER, di autobus*) connection.

coin'cidere [koin'tʃidere] *vi* to coincide; **coin'ciso, a** *pp di* **coincidere.**

coin'volgere [koin'vɔldʒere] *vt*: ~ **in** to involve in; **coin'volto, a** *pp di* **coinvolgere.**

col *prep* + *det* = **con** + **il**; *vedi* **con.**

cola'brodo *sm inv* strainer.

cola'pasta *sm inv* colander.

co'lare *vt* (*liquido*) to strain; (*pasta*) to drain; (*oro fuso*) to pour ♦ *vi* (*sudore*) to drip; (*botte*) to leak; (*cera*) to melt; ~ **a picco** *vt, vi* (*nave*) to sink.

co'lata *sf* (*di lava*) flow; (*FONDERIA*) casting.

colazi'one [kolat'tsjone] *sf* (*anche: prima* ~) breakfast; (*anche: seconda* ~) lunch; **fare** ~ to have breakfast (*o lunch*).

co'lei *pron vedi* **colui.**

co'lera *sm* (*MED*) cholera.

'colica *sf* (*MED*) colic.

'colla *sf* glue; (*di farina*) paste.

collabo'rare *vi* to collaborate; ~ **a** to collaborate on; (*giornale*) to contribute to; **collabora'tore, 'trice** *sm/f* collaborator; contributor.

col'lana *sf* necklace; (*collezione*) collection, series.

col'lant [kɔ'lã] *sm inv* tights *pl.*

col'lare *sm* collar.

col'lasso *sm* (*MED*) collapse.

collau'dare *vt* to test, try out; **col'laudo** *sm* testing *no pl*; test.

'colle *sm* hill.

col'lega, ghi, ghe *sm/f* colleague.

collega'mento *sm* connection; (*MIL*) liaison.

colle'gare *vt* to connect, join, link; ~**rsi** *vr* (*RADIO, TV*) to link up; ~**rsi con** (*TEL*) to get through to.

col'legio [kol'lɛdʒo] *sm* college; (*convitto*) boarding school; ~ **elettorale**

(*POL*) constituency.

'**collera** *sf* anger.

col'**lerico, a, ci, che** *ag* quick-tempered, irascible.

col'**letta** *sf* collection.

collettività *sf* community.

collet'**tivo, a** *ag* collective; (*interesse*) general, everybody's; (*biglietto, visita etc*) group *cpd* ♦ *sm* (*POL*) (political) group.

col'**letto** *sm* collar.

collezio'**nare** [kollettsjo'nare] *vt* to collect.

collezi'one [kollet'tsjone] *sf* collection.

colli'**mare** *vi* to correspond, coincide.

col'**lina** *sf* hill.

col'**lirio** *sm* eyewash.

collisi'one *sf* collision.

'**collo** *sm* neck; (*di abito*) neck, collar; (*pacco*) parcel; ~ **del piede** instep.

colloca'**mento** *sm* (*impiego*) employment; (*disposizione*) placing, arrangement.

collo'**care** *vt* (*libri, mobili*) to place; (*persona: trovare un lavoro per*) to find a job for, place; (*COMM: merce*) to find a market for.

col'**loquio** *sm* conversation, talk; (*ufficiale, per un lavoro*) interview; (*INS*) preliminary oral exam.

col'**mare** *vt*: ~ **di** (*anche fig*) to fill with; (*dare in abbondanza*) to load o overwhelm with; '**colmo, a** *ag*: **colmo** (**di**) full (of) ♦ *sm* summit, top; (*fig*) height; **al colmo della disperazione** in the depths of despair; **è il colmo!** it's the last straw!

co'**lombo, a** *sm/f* dove; pigeon.

co'**lonia** *sf* colony; (*per bambini*) holiday camp; (**acqua di**) ~ (eau de) cologne; **coloni'ale** *ag* colonial ♦ *sm/f* colonist, settler.

co'**lonna** *sf* column; ~ **vertebrale** spine, spinal column.

colon'**nello** *sm* colonel.

co'**lono** *sm* (*coltivatore*) tenant farmer.

colo'**rante** *sm* colouring.

colo'**rare** *vt* to colour; (*disegno*) to colour in.

co'**lore** *sm* colour; **a** ~**i** in colour,

colour *cpd*; **farne di tutti i** ~**i** to get up to all sorts of mischief.

colo'**rito, a** *ag* coloured; (*viso*) rosy, pink; (*linguaggio*) colourful ♦ *sm* (*tinta*) colour; (*carnagione*) complexion.

co'**loro** *pron pl vedi* **colui.**

co'**losso** *sm* colossus.

'**colpa** *sf* fault; (*biasimo*) blame; (*colpevolezza*) guilt; (*azione colpevole*) offence; (*peccato*) sin; **di chi è la** ~? whose fault is it?; **è** ~ **sua** it's his fault; **per** ~ **di** through, owing to; **col'pevole** *ag* guilty.

col'**pire** *vt* to hit, strike; (*fig*) to strike; **rimanere colpito da qc** to be amazed o struck by sth.

'**colpo** *sm* (*urto*) knock; (*: affettivo*) blow, shock; (*: aggressivo*) blow; (*di pistola*) shot; (*MED*) stroke; (*rapina*) raid; **di** ~ suddenly; **fare** ~ to make a strong impression; ~ **di grazia** coup de grâce; ~ **di sole** sunstroke; ~ **di Stato** coup d'état; ~ **di telefono** phone call; ~ **di testa** (sudden) impulse o whim; ~ **di vento** gust (of wind).

coltel'**lata** *sf* stab.

col'**tello** *sm* knife; ~ **a serramanico** clasp knife.

colti'**vare** *vt* to cultivate; (*verdura*) to grow, cultivate; **coltiva'tore** *sm* farmer; **coltivazi'one** *sf* cultivation; growing.

'**colto, a** *pp di* **cogliere** ♦ *ag* (*istruito*) cultured, educated.

'**coltre** *sf* blanket.

col'**tura** *sf* cultivation.

co'**lui** (*f* co'**lei**, *pl* co'**loro**) *pron* the one; ~ **che parla** the one o the man o the person who is speaking; **colei che amo** the one o the woman o the person (whom) I love.

'**coma** *sm inv* coma.

comanda'**mento** *sm* (*REL*) commandment.

coman'**dante** *sm* (*MIL*) commander, commandant; (*di reggimento*) commanding officer; (*NAUT, AER*) captain.

coman'**dare** *vi* to be in command ♦ *vt*

to command; (*imporre*) to order, command; ~ **a qn di fare** to order sb to do; **co'mando** *sm* (*ingiunzione*) order, command; (*autorità*) command; (*TECN*) control.

co'mare *sf* (*madrina*) godmother.

combaci'are [komba'tʃare] *vi* to meet; (*fig: coincidere*) to coincide.

com'battere *vt*, *vi* to fight; **combatti'mento** *sm* fight; fighting *no pl*; (*di pugilato*) match.

combi'nare *vt* to combine; (*organizzare*) to arrange; (*fam: fare*) to make, cause; **combinazi'one** *sf* combination; (*caso fortuito*) coincidence; **per combinazione** by chance.

combus'tibile *ag* combustible ♦ *sm* fuel.

com'butta (*peg*) *sf*: **in ~** in league.

PAROLA CHIAVE

'come *av* **1** (*alla maniera di*) like; **ti comporti ~ lui** you behave like him *o* like he does; **bianco ~ la neve** (as) white as snow; **~ se** as if, as though

2 (*in qualità di*) as a; **lavora ~ autista** he works as a driver

3 (*interrogativo*) how; **~ ti chiami?** what's your name?; **~ sta?** how are you?; **com'è il tuo amico?** what is your friend like?; **~?** (*prego?*) pardon?, sorry?; **~ mai?** how come?; **~ mai non ci hai avvertiti?** why on earth didn't you warn us?

4 (*esclamativo*): **~ sei bravo!** how clever you are!; **~ mi dispiace!** I'm terribly sorry!

♦ *cong* **1** (*in che modo*) how; **mi ha spiegato ~ l'ha conosciuto** he told me how he met him

2 (*correlativo*) as; (*con comparativi di maggioranza*) than; **non è bravo ~ pensavo** he isn't as clever as I thought; **è meglio di ~ pensassi** it's better than I thought

3 (*appena che, quando*) as soon as; **~ arrivò, iniziò a lavorare** as soon as he arrived, he set to work; *vedi* **così**; **tanto**.

'comico, a, ci, che *ag* (*TEATRO*) comic; (*buffo*) comical ♦ *sm* (*attore*) comedian, comic actor; (*comicità*) comic spirit, comedy.

co'mignolo [ko'miɲɲolo] *sm* chimney top.

cominci'are [komin'tʃare] *vt*, *vi* to begin, start; **~ a fare/col fare** to begin to do/by doing.

comi'tato *sm* committee.

comi'tiva *sf* party, group.

co'mizio [ko'mittsjo] *sm* (*POL*) meeting, assembly.

com'mando *sm* *inv* commando (squad).

com'media *sf* comedy; (*opera teatrale*) play; (*: che fa ridere*) comedy; (*fig*) playacting *no pl*; **commedi'ante** (*peg*) *sm/f* third-rate actor/actress; (*fig*) sham.

commemo'rare *vt* to commemorate.

commenda'tore *sm* *official title awarded for services to one's country*.

commen'tare *vt* to comment on; (*testo*) to annotate; (*RADIO*, *TV*) to give a commentary on; **commenta'tore**, **'trice** *sm/f* commentator; **com'mento** *sm* comment; (*a un testo*, *RADIO*, *TV*) commentary.

commerci'ale [kommer'tʃale] *ag* commercial, trading; (*peg*) commercial.

commerci'ante [kommer'tʃante] *sm/f* trader, dealer; (*negoziante*) shopkeeper.

commerci'are [kommer'tʃare] *vt*, *vi*: **~ in** to deal *o* trade in.

com'mercio [kom'mertʃo] *sm* trade, commerce; **essere in ~** (*prodotto*) to be on the market *o* on sale; **essere nel ~** (*persona*) to be in business; **~ all'ingrosso/al minuto** wholesale/retail trade.

com'messa *sf* (*COMM*) order.

com'messo, a *pp di* **commettere** ♦ *sm/f* shop assistant (*BRIT*), sales clerk (*US*) ♦ *sm* (*impiegato*) clerk; **~ viaggiatore** commercial traveller.

commes'tibile *ag* edible; **~i** *smpl* foodstuffs.

com'mettere vt to commit.

com'miato sm leave-taking.

commi'nare vt (DIR) to threaten; to inflict.

commissari'ato sm (AMM) commissionership; (: sede) commissioner's office; (: di polizia) police station.

commis'sario sm commissioner; (di pubblica sicurezza) ≈ (police) superintendent (BRIT), (police) captain (US); (SPORT) steward; (membro di commissione) member of a committee o board.

commissio'nario sm (COMM) agent, broker.

commissi'one sf (incarico) errand; (comitato, percentuale) commission; (COMM: ordinazione) order; ~i sfpl (acquisti) shopping sg.

commit'tente sm/f (COMM) purchaser, customer.

com'mosso, a pp di **commuovere**.

commo'vente ag moving.

commozi'one [kommot'tsjone] sf emotion, deep feeling; ~ **cerebrale** (MED) concussion.

commu'overe vt to move, affect; ~rsi vr to be moved.

commu'tare vt (pena) to commute; (ELETTR) to change o switch over.

comò sm inv chest of drawers.

como'dino sm bedside table.

comodità sf inv comfort; convenience.

'comodo, a ag comfortable; (facile) easy; (conveniente) convenient; (utile) useful, handy ♦ sm comfort; convenience; **con** ~ at one's convenience o leisure; **fare il proprio** ~ to do as one pleases; **far** ~ to be useful o handy.

compae'sano, a sm/f fellow countryman; person from the same town.

com'pagine [kom'padʒine] sf (squadra) team.

compa'gnia [kompaɲ'nia] sf company; (gruppo) gathering.

com'pagno, a [kom'paɲɲo] sm/f (di classe, gioco) companion; (POL) comrade; ~ **di lavoro** workmate.

compa'rare vt to compare.

compara'tivo, a ag, sm comparative.

compa'rire vi to appear; **com'parsa** sf appearance; (TEATRO) walk-on; (CINEMA) extra; **comparso, a** pp di **comparire**.

compartecipazi'one [kompartetʃipat-'tsjone] sf sharing; (quota) share; ~ **agli utili** profit-sharing.

comparti'mento sm compartment; (AMM) district.

compas'sato, a ag (persona) composed.

compassi'one sf compassion, pity; **avere** ~ **di qn** to feel sorry for sb, to pity sb.

com'passo sm (pair of) compasses pl; callipers pl.

compa'tibile ag (scusabile) excusable; (conciliabile, INFORM) compatible.

compa'tire vt (aver compassione di) to sympathize with, feel sorry for; (scusare) to make allowances for.

com'patto, a ag compact; (roccia) solid; (folla) dense; (fig: gruppo, partito) united, close-knit.

com'pendio sm summary; (libro) compendium.

compen'sare vt (equilibrare) to compensate for, make up for; ~ **qn di** (rimunerare) to pay o remunerate sb for; (risarcire) to pay compensation to sb for; (fig: fatiche, dolori) to reward sb for; **com'penso** sm compensation; payment, remuneration; reward; **in compenso** (d'altra parte) on the other hand.

'compera sf (acquisto) purchase; **fare le** ~**e** to do the shopping.

compe'rare vt = **comprare**.

compe'tente ag competent; (mancia) apt, suitable; **compe'tenza** sf competence; **competenze** sfpl (onorari) fees.

com'petere vi to compete, vie; (DIR: spettare): ~ **a** to lie within the competence of; **competizi'one** sf competition.

compia'cente [kompja'tʃente] ag courteous, obliging; **compia'cenza** sf courtesy.

compia'cere [kompja'tʃere] *vi*: ~ **a** to gratify, please ♦ *vt* to please; ~**rsi** *vr* (*provare soddisfazione*): ~**rsi di** *o* **per qc** to be delighted at sth; (*rallegrarsi*): ~**rsi con qn** to congratulate sb; (*degnarsi*): ~**rsi di fare** to be so good as to do; **compiaci'uto, a** *pp di* **compiacere**.

compi'angere [kom'pjandʒere] *vt* to sympathize with, feel sorry for; **compi'anto, a** *pp di* **compiangere**.

'compiere *vt* (*concludere*) to finish, complete; (*adempiere*) to carry out, fulfil; ~**rsi** *vr* (*avverarsi*) to be fulfilled, come true; ~ **gli anni** to have one's birthday.

com'pire *vt* = **compiere**.

compi'tare *vt* to spell out.

'compito *sm* (*incarico*) task, duty; (*dovere*) duty; (*INS*) exercise; (: *a casa*) piece of homework; **fare i** ~**i** to do one's homework.

com'pito, a *ag* well-mannered, polite.

comple'anno *sm* birthday.

complemen'tare *ag* complementary; (*INS: materia*) subsidiary.

comple'mento *sm* complement; (*MIL*) reserve (troops); ~ **oggetto** (*LING*) direct object.

complessità *sf* complexity.

comples'sivo, a *ag* (*globale*) comprehensive, overall; (*totale: cifra*) total.

com'plesso, a *ag* complex ♦ *sm* (*PSIC, EDIL*) complex; (*MUS: corale*) ensemble; (: *orchestrina*) band; (: *di musica pop*) group; **in** *o* **nel** ~ on the whole.

comple'tare *vt* to complete.

com'pleto, a *ag* complete; (*teatro, autobus*) full ♦ *sm* suit; **al** ~ full; (*tutti presenti*) all present.

compli'care *vt* to complicate; ~**rsi** *vr* to become complicated; **complicazi'one** *sf* complication.

'complice ['komplitʃe] *sm/f* accomplice.

complimen'tarsi *vr*: ~ **con** to congratulate.

compli'mento *sm* compliment; ~**i** *smpl* (*cortesia eccessiva*) ceremony *sg*; (*ossequi*) regards, compliments; ~**i!** congratulations!; **senza** ~**i!** don't stand on ceremony!; make yourself at home!; help yourself!

com'plotto *sm* plot, conspiracy.

compo'nente *sm/f* member ♦ *sm* component.

componi'mento *sm* (*DIR*) settlement; (*INS*) composition; (*poetico, teatrale*) work.

com'porre *vt* (*musica, testo*) to compose; (*mettere in ordine*) to arrange; (*DIR: lite*) to settle; (*TIP*) to set; (*TEL*) to dial.

comporta'mento *sm* behaviour.

compor'tare *vt* (*implicare*) to involve; (*consentire*) to permit, allow (of); ~**rsi** *vr* (*condursi*) to behave.

composi'tore, 'trice *sm/f* composer; (*TIP*) compositor, typesetter.

composizi'one [kompozit'tsjone] *sf* composition; (*DIR*) settlement.

com'posta *sf* (*CUC*) stewed fruit *no pl*; (*AGR*) compost; *vedi anche* **composto**.

compos'tezza [kompos'tettsa] *sf* composure; decorum.

com'posto, a *pp di* **comporre** ♦ *ag* (*persona*) composed, self-possessed; (: *decoroso*) dignified; (*formato da più elementi*) compound *cpd* ♦ *sm* compound.

'compra *sf* = **compera**.

com'prare *vt* to buy; **compra'tore, 'trice** *sm/f* buyer, purchaser.

com'prendere *vt* (*contenere*) to comprise, consist of; (*capire*) to understand.

comprensi'one *sf* understanding.

compren'sivo, a *ag* (*prezzo*): ~ **di** inclusive of; (*indulgente*) understanding.

com'preso, a *pp di* **comprendere** ♦ *ag* (*incluso*) included.

com'pressa *sf* (*MED*: *garza*) compress; (: *pastiglia*) tablet; *vedi anche* **compresso**.

compressi'one *sf* compression.

com'presso, a *pp di* **comprimere** ♦ *ag* (*vedi comprimere*) pressed; compressed; repressed.

com'primere *vt* (*premere*) to press;

(*FISICA*) to compress; (*fig*) to repress.

compro'messo, a *pp di* **compromettere ♦** *sm* compromise.

compro'mettere *vt* to compromise.

compro'vare *vt* to confirm.

com'punto, a *ag* contrite.

compu'tare *vt* to calculate; (*addebitare*): ~ **qc a qn** to debit sb with sth.

com'puter *sm inv* computer.

computiste'ria *sf* accounting, bookkeeping.

'computo *sm* calculation.

comu'nale *ag* municipal, town *cpd*, ≈ borough *cpd*.

co'mune *ag* common; (*consueto*) common, everyday; (*di livello medio*) average; (*ordinario*) ordinary ♦ *sm* (*AMM*) town council; (: *sede*) town hall ♦ *sf* (*di persone*) commune; **fuori del ~** out of the ordinary; **avere in ~** to have in common, share; **mettere in ~** to share.

comuni'care *vt* (*notizia*) to pass on, convey; (*malattia*) to pass on; (*ansia etc*) to communicate; (*trasmettere: calore etc*) to transmit, communicate; (*REL*) to administer communion to ♦ *vi* to communicate; ~**rsi** *vr* (*propagarsi*): ~**rsi a** to spread to; (*REL*) to receive communion.

comuni'cato *sm* communiqué; ~ **stampa** press release.

comunicazi'one [komunikat'tsjone] *sf* communication; (*annuncio*) announcement; (*TEL*): ~ (*telefonica*) (telephone) call; **dare la ~ a qn** to put sb through; **ottenere la ~** to get through.

comuni'one *sf* communion; ~ **di beni** (*DIR*) joint ownership of property.

comu'nismo *sm* communism; **comu'nista, i, e** *ag, sm/f* communist.

comunità *sf inv* community; **C~ Economica Europea** European Economic Community.

co'munque *cong* however, no matter how ♦ *av* (*in ogni modo*) in any case; (*tuttavia*) however, nevertheless.

con *prep* with; **partire col treno** to leave by train; ~ **mio grande stupore** to my great astonishment; ~ **tutto ciò** for all that.

co'nato *sm*: ~ **di vomito** retching.

'conca, che *sf* (*GEO*) valley.

con'cedere [kon'tʃedere] *vt* (*accordare*) to grant; (*ammettere*) to admit, concede; ~**rsi qc** to treat o.s. to sth, to allow o.s. sth.

concentra'mento [kontʃentra'mento] *sm* concentration.

concen'trare [kontʃen'trare] *vt* to concentrate; ~**rsi** *vr* to concentrate; **concentrazi'one** *sf* concentration.

conce'pire [kontʃe'pire] *vt* (*bambino*) to conceive; (*progetto, idea*) to conceive (of); (*metodo, piano*) to devise.

con'cernere [kon'tʃernere] *vt* to concern.

concer'tare [kontʃer'tare] *vt* (*MUS*) to harmonize; (*ordire*) to devise, plan; ~**rsi** *vr* to agree.

con'certo [kon'tʃɛrto] *sm* (*MUS*) concert; (: *componimento*) concerto.

concessio'nario [kontʃessjo'narjo] *sm* (*COMM*) agent, dealer.

con'cesso, a [kon'tʃɛsso] *pp di* **concedere**.

con'cetto [kon'tʃetto] *sm* (*pensiero, idea*) concept; (*opinione*) opinion.

concezi'one [kontʃet'tsjone] *sf* conception.

con'chiglia [kon'kiʎʎa] *sf* shell.

'concia ['kɔntʃa] *sf* (*di pelle*) tanning; (*di tabacco*) curing; (*sostanza*) tannin.

conci'are [kon'tʃare] *vt* (*pelli*) to tan; (*tabacco*) to cure; (*fig: ridurre in cattivo stato*) to beat up; ~**rsi** *vr* (*sporcarsi*) to get in a mess; (*vestirsi male*) to dress badly.

concili'are [kontʃi'ljare] *vt* to reconcile; (*contravvenzione*) to pay on the spot; (*favorire: sonno*) to be conducive to, induce; (*procurare: simpatia*) to gain; ~**rsi qc** to gain *o* win sth (for o.s.); ~**rsi qn** to win sb over; ~**rsi con** to be reconciled with; **conciliazi'one** *sf* reconciliation; (*DIR*) settlement.

con'cilio [kon'tʃiljo] *sm* (*REL*) council.

con'cime [kon'tʃime] *sm* manure; (*chimico*) fertilizer.

con'ciso, a [kon'tʃizo] *ag* concise, succinct.

conci'tato, a [kontʃi'tato] *ag* excited, emotional.

concitta'dino, a [kontʃitta'dino] *sm/f* fellow citizen.

con'cludere *vt* to conclude; *(portare a compimento)* to conclude, finish, bring to an end; *(operare positivamente)* to achieve ♦ *vi (essere convincente)* to be conclusive; ~**rsi** *vr* to come to an end, close; **conclusi'one** *sf* conclusion; *(risultato)* result; **conclu'sivo, a** *ag* conclusive; *(finale)* final; **con'cluso, a** *pp di* **concludere**.

concor'danza [konkor'dantsa] *sf (anche LING)* agreement.

concor'dare *vt (tregua, prezzo)* to agree on; *(LING)* to make agree ♦ *vi* to agree; **concor'dato** *sm* agreement; *(REL)* concordat.

con'corde *ag (d'accordo)* in agreement; *(simultaneo)* simultaneous.

concor'rente *sm/f* competitor; *(INS)* candidate; **concor'renza** *sf* competition.

con'correre *vi*: ~ **(in)** *(MAT)* to converge o meet (in); ~ **(a)** *(competere)* to compete (for); (: *INS: a una cattedra)* to apply (for); *(partecipare: a un'impresa)* to take part (in), contribute (to); **con'corso, a** *pp di* **concorrere** ♦ *sm* competition; *(INS)* competitive examination; **concorso di colpa** *(DIR)* contributory negligence.

con'creto, a *ag* concrete.

concussi'one *sf (DIR)* extortion.

con'danna *sf* sentence; conviction; condemnation.

condan'nare *vt (DIR)*: ~ **a** to sentence to; ~ **per** to convict of; *(disapprovare)* to condemn; **condan'nato, a** *sm/f* convict.

conden'sare *vt* to condense; ~**rsi** *vr* to condense; **condensazi'one** *sf* condensation.

condi'mento *sm* seasoning; dressing.

con'dire *vt* to season; *(insalata)* to dress.

condi'videre *vt* to share; **condi'viso, a** *pp di* **condividere**.

condizio'nale [kondittsjo'nale] *ag* conditional ♦ *sm (LING)* conditional ♦ *sf (DIR)* suspended sentence.

condizio'nare [kondittsjo'nare] *vt* to condition; **ad aria condizionata** air-conditioned.

condizi'one [kondit'tsjone] *sf* condition; ~**i** *sfpl (di pagamento etc)* terms, conditions; **a ~ che** on condition that, provided that.

condogli'anze [kondoʎ'ʎantse] *sfpl* condolences.

condo'minio *sm* joint ownership; *(edificio)* jointly-owned building.

condo'nare *vt (DIR)* to remit; **con'dono** *sm* remission; **condono fiscale** conditional amnesty for people evading tax.

con'dotta *sf (modo di comportarsi)* conduct, behaviour; *(di un affare etc)* handling; *(di acqua)* piping; *(incarico sanitario)* country medical practice controlled by a local authority.

con'dotto, a *pp di* **condurre** ♦ *ag*: **medico ~** local authority doctor *(in country district)* ♦ *sm (canale, tubo)* pipe, conduit; *(ANAT)* duct.

condu'cente [kondu'tʃente] *sm* driver.

con'durre *vt* to conduct; *(azienda)* to manage; *(accompagnare: bambino)* to take; *(automobile)* to drive; *(trasportare: acqua, gas)* to convey, conduct; *(fig)* to lead ♦ *vi* to lead; **condursi** *vr* to behave, conduct o.s.

condut'tore *ag*: **filo ~** *(fig)* thread ♦ *sm (di mezzi pubblici)* driver; *(FISICA)* conductor.

con'farsi *vr*: ~ **a** to suit, agree with.

confederazi'one [konfederat'tsjone] *sf* confederation.

confe'renza [konfe'rentsa] *sf (discorso)* lecture; *(riunione)* conference; ~ **stampa** press conference; **conferenzi'ere** *a sm/f* lecturer.

confe'rire *vt*: ~ **qc a qn** to give sth to sb, bestow sth on sb ♦ *vi* to confer.

con'ferma *sf* confirmation.

confer'mare *vt* to confirm.

confes'sare *vt* to confess; ~**rsi** *vr* to confess; **andare a ~rsi** *(REL)* to go to confession; **confessio'nale** *ag*, *sm* confessional; **confessi'one** *sf* confession; (*setta religiosa*) denomination; **confes'sore** *sm* confessor.

con'fetto *sm* sugared almond; (*MED*) pill.

confezio'nare [konfettsjo'nare] *vt* (*vestito*) to make (up); (*merci, pacchi*) to package.

confezi'one [konfet'tsjone] *sf* (*di abiti: da uomo*) tailoring; (: *da donna*) dressmaking; (*imballaggio*) packaging; ~ **regalo** gift pack; ~**i per signora** ladies' wear; ~**i da uomo** menswear.

confic'care *vt*: ~ **qc in** to hammer *o* drive sth into; ~**rsi** *vr* to stick.

confi'dare *vi*: ~ **in** to confide in, rely on ♦ *vt* to confide; ~**rsi con qn** to confide in sb; **confi'dente** *sm/f* (*persona amica*) confidant/confidante; (*informatore*) informer; **confi'denza** *sf* (*familiarità*) intimacy, familiarity; (*fiducia*) trust, confidence; (*rivelazione*) confidence; **confidenzi'ale** *ag* familiar, friendly; (*segreto*) confidential.

configu'rarsi *vr*: ~ **a** to assume the shape *o* form of.

confi'nare *vi*: ~ **con** to border on ♦ *vt* (*POL*) to intern; (*fig*) to confine; ~**rsi** *vr* (*isolarsi*): ~**rsi in** to shut o.s. up in.

Confin'dustria *sigla f* (= *Confederazione Generale dell'Industria Italiana*) employers' association, ≈ CBI (*BRIT*).

con'fine *sm* boundary; (*di paese*) border, frontier.

con'fino *sm* internment.

confis'care *vt* to confiscate.

con'flitto *sm* conflict.

conflu'enza [konflu'entsa] *sf* (*di fiumi*) confluence; (*di strade*) junction.

conflu'ire *vi* (*fiumi*) to flow into each other, meet; (*strade*) to meet.

con'fondere *vt* to mix up, confuse; (*imbarazzare*) to embarrass; ~**rsi** *vr* (*mescolarsi*) to mingle; (*turbarsi*) to be confused; (*sbagliare*) to get mixed up; ~ **le idee a qn** to mix sb up, confuse sb.

confor'mare *vt* (*adeguare*): ~ **a** to adapt *o* conform to; ~**rsi** *vr*: ~**rsi (a)** to conform (to).

conforme'mente *av* accordingly; ~ **a** in accordance with.

confor'tare *vt* to comfort, console; **confor'tevole** *ag* (*consolante*) comforting; (*comodo*) comfortable; **con'forto** *sm* comfort, consolation; comfort.

confron'tare *vt* to compare.

con'fronto *sm* comparison; **in** *o* **a ~ di** in comparison with, compared to; **nei miei** (*o* **tuoi** *etc*) ~**i** towards me (*o* you *etc*).

confusi'one *sf* confusion; (*chiasso*) racket, noise; (*imbarazzo*) embarrassment.

con'fuso, a *pp di* **confondere** ♦ *ag* (*vedi confondere*) confused; embarrassed.

confu'tare *vt* to refute.

conge'dare [kondʒe'dare] *vt* to dismiss; (*MIL*) to demobilize; ~**rsi** *vr* to take one's leave; **con'gedo** *sm* (*anche MIL*) leave; **prendere congedo da qn** to take one's leave of sb; **congedo assoluto** (*MIL*) discharge.

conge'gnare [kondʒeɲ'nare] *vt* to construct, put together; **con'gegno** *sm* device, mechanism.

conge'lare [kondʒe'lare] *vt* to freeze; ~**rsi** *vr* to freeze; **congela'tore** *sm* freezer.

congestio'nare [kondʒestjo'nare] *vt* to congest.

congesti'one [kondʒes'tjone] *sf* congestion.

conget'tura [kondʒet'tura] *sf* conjecture, supposition.

con'giungere [kon'dʒundʒere] *vt* to join (together); ~**rsi** *vr* to join (together).

congiunti'vite [kondʒunti'vite] *sf* conjunctivitis.

congiun'tivo [kondʒun'tivo] *sm* (*LING*) subjunctive.

congi'unto, a [kon'dʒunto] *pp di* **congiungere** ♦ *ag* (*unito*) joined ♦ *sm/f* relative.

congiun'tura [kondʒun'tura] *sf* (*giuntura*) junction, join; (*ANAT*) joint; (*circostanza*) juncture; (*ECON*) economic situation.

congiunzi'one [kondʒun'tsjone] *sf*
(*LING*) conjunction.
congi'ura [kon'dʒura] *sf* conspiracy;
congiu'rare *vi* to conspire.
conglome'rato *sm* (*GEO*) conglomer-
ate; (*fig*) conglomeration; (*EDIL*) concrete.
congratu'larsi *vr*: ~ **con qn per qc** to
congratulate sb on sth.
congratulazi'oni [kongratulat'tsjoni] *sfpl*
congratulations.
con'grega, ghe *sf* band, bunch.
con'gresso *sm* congress.
congu'aglio [kon'gwaʎʎo] *sm* balancing,
adjusting; (*somma di denaro*) balance.
coni'are *vt* to mint, coin; (*fig*) to coin.
co'niglio [ko'niʎʎo] *sm* rabbit.
coniu'gare *vt* (*LING*) to conjugate;
~**rsi** *vr* to get married; **coniu'gato, a**
ag (*sposato*) married; **coniugazi'one** *sf*
(*LING*) conjugation.
'coniuge ['kɔnjudʒe] *sm/f* spouse.
connazio'nale [konnattsjo'nale] *sm/f*
fellow-countryman/woman.
connessi'one *sf* connection.
con'nesso, a *pp di* **connettere**.
con'nettere *vt* to connect, join ♦ *vi*
(*fig*) to think straight.
conni'vente *ag* conniving.
conno'tati *smpl* distinguishing marks.
'cono *sm* cone; ~ **gelato** ice-cream
cone.
cono'scente [konoʃ'ʃente] *sm/f*
acquaintance.
cono'scenza [konoʃ'ʃentsa] *sf* (*il
sapere*) knowledge *no pl*; (*persona*)
acquaintance; (*facoltà sensoriale*) consciousness *no pl*; **perdere** ~ to lose consciousness.
co'noscere [ko'noʃʃere] *vt* to know; **ci
siamo conosciuti a Firenze** we (first)
met in Florence; **conosci'tore, 'trice**
sm/f connoisseur; **conosci'uto, a** *pp di*
conoscere ♦ *ag* well-known.
con'quista *sf* conquest.
conquis'tare *vt* to conquer; (*fig*) to
gain, win.
consa'crare *vt* (*REL*) to consecrate; (:
sacerdote) to ordain; (*dedicare*) to
dedicate; (*fig: uso etc*) to sanction;

~**rsi a** to dedicate o.s. to.
consangu'ineo, a *sm/f* blood relation.
consa'pevole *ag*: ~ **di** aware *o* conscious of; **consapevo'lezza** *sf* aware-
ness, consciousness.
'conscio, a, sci, sce ['kɔnʃo] *ag*: ~ **di**
aware *o* conscious of.
consecu'tivo, a *ag* consecutive;
(*successivo: giorno*) following, next.
con'segna [kon'seɲɲa] *sf* delivery;
(*merce consegnata*) consignment;
(*custodia*) care, custody; (*MIL: ordine*)
orders *pl*; (: *punizione*) confinement to
barracks; **pagamento alla** ~ cash on
delivery; **dare qc in** ~ **a qn** to entrust
sth to sb.
conse'gnare [konseɲ'ɲare] *vt* to
deliver; (*affidare*) to entrust, hand
over; (*MIL*) to confine to barracks.
consegu'enza [konse'gwɛntsa] *sf* consequence; **per** *o* **di** ~ consequently.
consegu'ire *vt* to achieve ♦ *vi* to
follow, result.
con'senso *sm* approval, consent.
consen'tire *vi*: ~ **a** to consent *o* agree
to ♦ *vt* to allow, permit.
con'serva *sf* (*CUC*) preserve; ~ **di
frutta** jam; ~ **di pomodoro** tomato purée.
conser'vare *vt* (*CUC*) to preserve;
(*custodire*) to keep; (: *dalla distruzione
etc*) to preserve, conserve; ~**rsi** *vr* to
keep.
conserva'tore, 'trice *sm/f* (*POL*) conservative.
conservazi'one [konservat'tsjone] *sf* pre-
servation; conservation.
conside'rare *vt* to consider; (*reputare*)
to consider, regard; ~ **molto qn** to think
highly of sb; **considerazi'one** *sf* consideration; (*stima*) regard, esteem;
prendere in considerazione to take into
consideration; **conside'revole** *ag* considerable.
consigli'are [konsiʎ'ʎare] *vt* (*persona*)
to advise; (*metodo, azione*) to recommend, advise, suggest; ~**rsi** *vr*:
~**rsi con qn** to ask sb for advice; **consigli'ere, a** *sm/f* adviser ♦ *sm*: **consigliere
d'amministrazione** board member;

consigliere comunale town councillor; **con'siglio** sm (*suggerimento*) advice *no pl*, piece of advice; (*assemblea*) council; **consiglio d'amministrazione** board; **il Consiglio dei Ministri** (*POL*) ≈ the Cabinet.

consis'tente ag thick; solid; (*fig*) sound, valid; **consis'tenza** sf consistency, thickness; solidity; validity.

con'sistere vi: ~ **in** to consist of; **consis'tito, a** pp di **consistere**.

conso'lare ag consular ♦ vt (*confortare*) to console, comfort; (*rallegrare*) to cheer up; ~rsi vr to be comforted; to cheer up.

conso'lato sm consulate.

consolazi'one [konsolat'tsjone] sf consolation, comfort.

'console[1] sm consul.

con'sole[2] [kon'sɔl] sf (*quadro di comando*) console.

conso'nante sf consonant.

'consono, a ag: ~ **a** consistent with, consonant with.

con'sorte sm/f consort.

con'sorzio [kon'sɔrtsjo] sm consortium.

con'stare vi: ~ **di** to consist of ♦ vb impers: **mi consta che** it has come to my knowledge that, it appears that.

consta'tare vt to establish, verify; **constatazi'one** sf observation; **statazione amichevole** *jointly-agreed statement for insurance purposes.*

consu'eto, a ag habitual, usual; **consue'tudine** sf habit, custom; (*usanza*) custom.

consu'lente sm/f consultant; **consu'lenza** sf consultancy.

consul'tare vt to consult; ~rsi vr: ~rsi **con qn** to seek the advice of sb; **consultazi'one** sf consultation; **consultazioni** sfpl (*POL*) talks, consultations.

consu'mare vt (*logorare: abiti, scarpe*) to wear out; (*usare*) to consume, use up; (*mangiare, bere*) to consume; (*DIR*) to consummate; ~rsi vr to wear out; to be used up; (*anche fig*) to be consumed; (*combustibile*) to burn out; **consuma'tore** sm consumer;

consumazi'one sf (*bibita*) drink; (*spuntino*) snack; (*DIR*) consummation; **con'sumo** sm consumption; wear; use.

consun'tivo sm (*ECON*) final balance.

con'tabile ag accounts cpd, accounting ♦ sm/f accountant; **contabilità** sf (*attività, tecnica*) accounting, accountancy; (*insieme dei libri etc*) books pl, accounts pl; (*ufficio*) accounts department.

conta'dino, a sm/f countryman/ woman; farm worker; (*peg*) peasant.

contagi'are [konta'dʒare] vt to infect.

con'tagio [kon'tadʒo] sm infection; (*per contatto diretto*) contagion; (*epidemia*) epidemic; **contagi'oso, a** ag infectious; contagious.

conta'gocce [konta'gottʃe] sm inv (*MED*) dropper.

contami'nare vt to contaminate.

con'tante sm cash; **pagare in** ~**i** to pay cash.

con'tare vt to count; (*considerare*) to consider ♦ vi to count, be of importance; ~ **su qn** to count o rely on sb; ~ **di fare qc** to intend to do sth; **conta'tore** sm meter.

contat'tare vt to contact.

con'tatto sm contact.

'conte sm count.

conteggi'are [konted'dʒare] vt to charge, put on the bill; **con'teggio** sm calculation.

con'tegno [kon'teɲɲo] sm (*comportamento*) behaviour; (*atteggiamento*) attitude; **darsi un** ~ to act nonchalant; to pull o.s. together.

contem'plare vt to contemplate, gaze at; (*DIR*) to make provision for.

contemporanea'mente av simultaneously; at the same time.

contempo'raneo, a ag, sm/f contemporary.

conten'dente sm/f opponent, adversary.

con'tendere vi (*competere*) to compete; (*litigare*) to quarrel ♦ vt: ~ **qc a qn** to contend with o be in competition with sb for sth.

conte'nere vt to contain; **conteni'tore**

sm container.

conten'tare *vt* to please, satisfy; **~rsi di** to be satisfied with, content o.s. with.

conten'tezza [kontenˈtettsa] *sf* contentment.

con'tento, a *ag* pleased, glad; **~ di** pleased with.

conte'nuto *sm* contents *pl*; (*argomento*) content.

con'tesa *sf* dispute, argument.

con'teso, a *pp di* **contendere.**

con'tessa *sf* countess.

contes'tare *vt* (*DIR*) to notify; (*fig*) dispute; **contestazi'one** *sf* (*DIR*) notification; dispute; (*protesta*) protest.

con'testo *sm* context.

con'tiguo, a *ag*: **~ (a)** adjacent (to).

continen'tale *ag, sm/f* continental.

conti'nente *ag* continent ♦ *sm* (*GEO*) continent; (*: terra ferma*) mainland; **conti'nenza** *sf* continence.

contin'gente [kontinˈdʒɛnte] *ag* contingent ♦ *sm* (*COMM*) quota; (*MIL*) contingent; **contin'genza** *sf* circumstance; (*ECON*): (**indennità di**) **contingenza** cost-of-living allowance.

continu'are *vt* to continue (with), go on with ♦ *vi* to continue, go on; **~ a fare qc** to go on o continue doing sth; **continuazi'one** *sf* continuation.

con'tinuo, a *ag* (*numerazione*) continuous; (*pioggia*) continual, constant; (*ELETTR*): **corrente ~a** direct current; **di ~** continually.

'**conto** *sm* (*calcolo*) calculation; (*COMM, ECON*) account; (*di ristorante, albergo*) bill; (*fig: stima*) consideration, esteem; **fare i ~i con qn** to settle one's account with sb; **fare ~ su qn/qc** to count o rely on sb; **rendere ~ a qn di qc** to be accountable to sb for sth; **tener ~ di qn/qc** to take sb/sth into account; **per ~ di** on behalf of; **per ~ mio** as far as I'm concerned; **a ~i fatti, in fin dei ~i** all things considered; **~ corrente** current account; **~ alla rovescia** countdown.

con'torcere [konˈtortʃere] *vt* to twist; (*panni*) to wring (out); **~rsi** *vr* to twist, writhe.

contor'nare *vt* to surround.

con'torno *sm* (*linea*) outline, contour; (*ornamento*) border; (*CUC*) vegetables *pl*.

con'torto, a *pp di* **contorcere.**

contrabbandi'ere, a *sm/f* smuggler.

contrab'bando *sm* smuggling, contraband; **merce di ~** contraband, smuggled goods *pl*.

contrab'basso *sm* (*MUS*) (double) bass.

contraccambi'are *vt* (*favore etc*) to return.

contraccet'tivo, a [kontrattʃetˈtivo] *ag, sm* contraceptive.

contrac'colpo *sm* rebound; (*di arma da fuoco*) recoil; (*fig*) repercussion.

con'trada *sf* street; district.

contrad'detto, a *pp di* **contraddire.**

contrad'dire *vt* to contradict; **contraddit'torio, a** *ag* contradictory; (*sentimenti*) conflicting ♦ *sm* (*DIR*) cross-examination; **contraddizi'one** *sf* contradiction.

contraf'fare *vt* (*persona*) to mimic; (*alterare: voce*) to disguise; (*firma*) to forge, counterfeit; **contraf'fatto, a** *pp di* **contraffare** ♦ *ag* counterfeit; **contraffazi'one** *sf* mimicking *no pl*; disguising *no pl*; forging *no pl*; (*cosa contraffatta*) forgery.

contrap'peso *sm* counterbalance, counterweight.

contrap'porre *vt*: **~ qc a qc** to counter sth with sth; (*paragonare*) to compare sth with sth; **contrap'posto, a** *pp di* **contrapporre.**

contraria'mente *av*: **~ a** contrary to.

contrari'are *vt* (*contrastare*) to thwart, oppose; (*irritare*) to annoy, bother; **~rsi** *vr* to get annoyed.

contrarietà *sf* adversity; (*fig*) aversion.

con'trario, a *ag* opposite; (*sfavorevole*) unfavourable ♦ *sm* opposite; **essere ~ a qc** (*persona*) to be against sth; **in caso ~** otherwise; **avere qc in ~** to have some objection; **al ~** on the contrary.

con'trarre *vt* to contract; **contrarsi** *vr*

to contract.

contrasse'gnare [kontrasseɲ'ɲare] vt to mark; **contras'segno** sm (distintivo) distinguishing mark; **spedire in contrassegno** to send C.O.D.

contras'tare vt (avversare) to oppose; (impedire) to bar; (negare: diritto) to contest, dispute ♦ vi: ~ (con) (essere in disaccordo) to contrast (with); (lottare) to struggle (with); **con'trasto** sm contrast; (conflitto) conflict; (litigio) dispute.

contrat'tacco sm counterattack.

contrat'tare vt, vi to negotiate.

contrat'tempo sm hitch.

con'tratto, a pp di **contrarre** ♦ sm contract; **contrattu'ale** ag contractual.

contravvenzi'one [contravven'tsjone] sf contravention; (ammenda) fine.

contrazi'one [kontrat'tsjone] sf contraction; (di prezzi etc) reduction.

contribu'ente sm/f taxpayer; ratepayer (BRIT), property tax payer (US).

contribu'ire vi to contribute; **contri'buto** sm contribution; (tassa) tax.

'contro prep against; ~ **di me/lui** against me/him; **pastiglie** ~ **la tosse** throat lozenges; ~ **pagamento** (COMM) on payment ♦ prefisso: **contro'battere** vt (fig: a parole) to answer back; (: confutare) to refute; **controfi'gura** sf (CINEMA) double; **controfir'mare** vt to countersign.

control'lare vt (accertare) to check; (sorvegliare) to watch, control; (tenere nel proprio potere, fig: dominare) to control; **con'trollo** sm check; watch; control; **controllo delle nascite** birth control; **control'lore** sm (FERR, AUTOBUS) (ticket) inspector.

controprodu'cente [kontroprodu'tʃente] ag counterproductive.

contro'senso sm (contraddizione) contradiction in terms; (assurdità) nonsense.

controspio'naggio [kontrospio'naddʒo] sm counterespionage.

contro'versia sf controversy; (DIR) dispute.

contro'verso, a ag controversial.

contro'voglia [kontro'vɔʎʎa] av unwillingly.

contu'macia [kontu'matʃa] sf (DIR) default.

contur'bare vt to disturb, upset.

contusi'one sf (MED) bruise.

convale'scente [konvaleʃ'ʃente] ag, sm/f convalescent; **convale'scenza** sf convalescence.

convali'dare vt (AMM) to validate; (fig: sospetto, dubbio) to confirm.

con'vegno [kon'veɲɲo] sm (incontro) meeting; (congresso) convention, congress; (luogo) meeting place.

conve'nevoli smpl civilities.

conveni'ente ag suitable; (vantaggioso) profitable; (: prezzo) cheap; **conveni'enza** sf suitability; advantage; cheapness; **le convenienze** sfpl social conventions.

conve'nire vi (riunirsi) to gather, assemble; (concordare) to agree; (tornare utile) to be worthwhile ♦ vb impers: **conviene fare questo** it is advisable to do this; **conviene andarsene** we should go; **ne convengo** I agree.

con'vento sm (di frati) monastery; (di suore) convent.

convenzio'nale [konventsjo'nale] ag conventional.

convenzi'one [konven'tsjone] sf (DIR) agreement; (nella società) convention; **le ~i** sfpl social conventions.

conver'sare vi to have a conversation, converse.

conversazi'one [konversat'tsjone] sf conversation; **fare** ~ to chat, have a chat.

conversi'one sf conversion; ~ **ad U** (AUT) U-turn.

conver'tire vt (trasformare) to change; (POL, REL) to convert; **~rsi** vr: **~rsi (a)** to be converted (to); **conver'tito, a** sm/f convert.

con'vesso, a ag convex.

con'vincere [kon'vintʃere] vt to convince; ~ **qn di qc** to convince sb of sth; ~ **qn a fare qc** to persuade sb to do sth; **con'vinto, a** pp di **convincere**; **convinzi'one** sf conviction, firm belief.

convis'suto, a *pp di* **convivere**.
con'vitto *sm* (*INS*) boarding school.
con'vivere *vi* to live together.
convo'care *vt* to call, convene; (*DIR*) to summon; **convocazi'one** *sf* meeting; summons *sg*.
convogli'are [konvoʎ'ʎare] *vt* to convey; (*dirigere*) to direct, send; **con'voglio** *sm* (*di veicoli*) convoy; (*FERR*) train.
con'vulso, a *ag* (*pianto*) violent, convulsive; (*attività*) feverish.
coope'rare *vi*: ~ **(a)** to cooperate (in); **coopera'tiva** *sf* cooperative; **cooperazi'one** *sf* cooperation.
coordi'nare *vt* to coordinate; **coordi'nate** *sfpl* (*MAT*, *GEO*) coordinates; **coordi'nati** *smpl* (*MODA*) coordinates.
co'perchio [ko'perkjo] *sm* cover; (*di pentola*) lid.
co'perta *sf* cover; (*di lana*) blanket; (*da viaggio*) rug; (*NAUT*) deck.
coper'tina *sf* (*STAMPA*) cover, jacket.
co'perto, a *pp di* **coprire** ♦ *ag* covered; (*cielo*) overcast ♦ *sm* place setting; (*posto a tavola*) place; (*al ristorante*) cover charge; ~ **di** covered in o with.
coper'tone *sm* (*telo impermeabile*) tarpaulin; (*AUT*) rubber tyre.
coper'tura *sf* (*anche ECON, MIL*) cover; (*di edificio*) roofing.
'copia *sf* copy; **brutta/bella** ~ rough/final copy.
copi'are *vt* to copy; **copia'trice** *sf* copier, copying machine.
copi'one *sm* (*CINEMA, TEATRO*) script.
'coppa *sf* (*bicchiere*) goblet; (*per frutta, gelato*) dish; (*trofeo*) cup, trophy; ~ **dell'olio** oil sump (*BRIT*) o pan (*US*).
'coppia *sf* (*di persone*) couple; (*di animali, SPORT*) pair.
coprifu'oco, chi *sm* curfew.
copri'letto *sm* bedspread.
co'prire *vt* to cover; (*occupare: carica, posto*) to hold; ~**rsi** *vr* (*cielo*) to cloud over; (*vestirsi*) to wrap up, cover up; (*ECON*) to cover o.s.; ~**rsi di** (*macchie, muffa*) to become covered in.

co'raggio [ko'raddʒo] *sm* courage, bravery; ~**!** (*forza!*) come on!; (*animo!*) cheer up!; **coraggi'oso, a** *ag* courageous, brave.
co'rallo *sm* coral.
co'rano *sm* (*REL*) Koran.
co'razza [ko'rattsa] *sf* armour; (*di animali*) carapace, shell; (*MIL*) armour(-plating); **coraz'zata** *sf* battleship.
corbelle'ria *sf* stupid remark; ~**e** *sfpl* nonsense *no pl*.
'corda *sf* cord; (*fune*) rope; (*spago, MUS*) string; **dare** ~ **a qn** to let sb have his (o her) way; **tenere sulla** ~ **qn** to keep sb on tenterhooks; **tagliare la** ~ to slip away, sneak off; ~**e vocali** vocal cords.
cordi'ale *ag* cordial, warm ♦ *sm* (*bevanda*) cordial.
cor'doglio [kor'dɔʎʎo] *sm* grief; (*lutto*) mourning.
cor'done *sm* cord, string; (*linea: di polizia*) cordon; ~ **ombelicale** umbilical cord.
Co'rea *sf*: **la** ~ Korea.
coreogra'fia *sf* choreography.
cori'andolo *sm* (*BOT*) coriander; ~**i** *smpl* confetti *sg*.
cori'care *vt* to put to bed; ~**rsi** *vr* to go to bed.
'corna *sfpl vedi* **corno**.
cor'nacchia [kor'nakkja] *sf* crow.
corna'musa *sf* bagpipes *pl*.
cor'netta *sf* (*MUS*) cornet; (*TEL*) receiver.
cor'netto *sm* (*CUC*) croissant; ~ **acustico** ear trumpet.
cor'nice [kor'nitʃe] *sf* frame; (*fig*) setting, background.
'corno (*pl(f)* -**a**) *sm* (*ZOOL*) horn; (*pl(m)* -**i**: *MUS*) horn; **fare le** ~**a a qn** to be unfaithful to sb; **cor'nuto, a** *ag* (*con corna*) horned; (*fam!: marito*) cuckolded ♦ *sm* (*fam!*) cuckold; (*: insulto*) bastard (!).
Corno'vaglia [korno'vaʎʎa] *sf*: **la** ~ Cornwall.
'coro *sm* chorus; (*REL*) choir.
co'rona *sf* crown; (*di fiori*) wreath;

coro'nare *vt* to crown.

'corpo *sm* body; (*cadavere*) (dead) body; (*militare, diplomatico*) corps *inv*; (*di opere*) corpus; prendere ~ to take shape; a ~ a ~ hand-to-hand; ~ di ballo corps de ballet; ~ di guardia guardroom; ~ insegnante teaching staff.

corpo'rale *ag* bodily; (*punizione*) corporal.

corpora'tura *sf* build, physique.

corporazi'one [korporat'tsjone] *sf* corporation.

corpu'lento, a *ag* stout.

corre'dare *vt*: ~ di to provide *o* furnish with; cor'redo *sm* equipment; (*di sposa*) trousseau.

cor'reggere [kor'reddʒere] *vt* to correct; (*compiti*) to correct, mark.

cor'rente *ag* (*fiume*) flowing; (*acqua del rubinetto*) running; (*moneta, prezzo*) current; (*comune*) everyday ♦ *sm*: essere al ~ (di) to be well-informed (about); mettere al ~ (di) to inform (of) ♦ *sf* (*movimento di liquido*) current, stream; (*spiffero*) draught; (*ELETTR, METEOR*) current; (*fig*) trend, tendency; la vostra lettera del 5 ~ mese (*COMM*) your letter of the 5th of this month; corrente'mente *av* commonly; parlare una lingua correntemente to speak a language fluently.

'correre *vi* to run; (*precipitarsi*) to rush; (*partecipare a una gara*) to race, run; (*fig: diffondersi*) to go round ♦ *vt* (*SPORT: gara*) to compete in; (*rischio*) to run; (*pericolo*) to face; ~ dietro a qn to run after sb; corre voce che ... it is rumoured that ....

cor'retto, a *pp di* correggere ♦ *ag* (*comportamento*) correct, proper; caffè ~ al cognac coffee laced with brandy.

correzi'one [korret'tsjone] *sf* correction; marking; ~ di bozze proofreading.

corri'doio *sm* corridor.

corri'dore *sm* (*SPORT*) runner; (*: su veicolo*) racer.

corri'era *sf* coach (*BRIT*), bus.

corri'ere *sm* (*diplomatico, di guerra*) courier; (*posta*) mail, post; (*COMM*) carrier.

corrispet'tivo *sm* (*somma*) amount due.

corrispon'dente *ag* corresponding ♦ *sm/f* correspondent.

corrispon'denza [korrispon'dentsa] *sf* correspondence.

corris'pondere *vi* (*equivalere*): ~ (a) to correspond (to); (*per lettera*): ~ con to correspond with ♦ *vt* (*stipendio*) to pay; (*fig: amore*) to return; corris'posto, a *pp di* corrispondere.

corrobo'rare *vt* to strengthen, fortify; (*fig*) to corroborate, bear out.

cor'rodere *vt* to corrode; ~rsi *vr* to corrode.

cor'rompere *vt* to corrupt; (*comprare*) to bribe.

corrosi'one *sf* corrosion.

cor'roso, a *pp di* corrodere.

cor'rotto, a *pp di* corrompere ♦ *ag* corrupt.

corrucci'arsi [korrut'tʃarsi] *vr* to grow angry *o* vexed.

corru'gare *vt* to wrinkle; ~ la fronte to knit one's brows.

corruzi'one [korrut'tsjone] *sf* corruption; bribery.

'corsa *sf* running *no pl*; (*gara*) race; (*di autobus, taxi*) journey, trip; fare una ~ to run, dash; (*SPORT*) to run a race.

cor'sia *sf* (*AUT, SPORT*) lane; (*di ospedale*) ward.

cor'sivo *sm* cursive (writing); (*TIP*) italics *pl*.

'corso, a *pp di* correre ♦ *sm* course; (*strada cittadina*) main street; (*di unità monetaria*) circulation; (*di titoli, valori*) rate, price; dar libero ~ a to give free expression to; in ~ in progress, under way; (*annata*) current; ~ d'acqua river, stream; (*artificiale*) waterway; ~ serale evening class.

'corte *sf* (court)yard; (*DIR, regale*) court; fare la ~ a qn to court sb; ~ marziale court-martial.

cor'teccia, ce [kor'tettʃa] *sf* bark.

corteggi'are [korted'dʒare] *vt* to court.

cor'teo *sm* procession.

cor'tese *ag* courteous; **corte'sia** *sf* courtesy; **per cortesia** ... excuse me, please ....

cortigi'ana [korti'dʒana] *sf* courtesan.

cortigi'ano, a [korti'dʒano] *sm/f* courtier.

cor'tile *sm* (court)yard.

cor'tina *sf* curtain; *(anche fig)* screen.

'corto, a *ag* short; **essere a ~ di qc** to be short of sth; **~ circuito** short-circuit.

'corvo *sm* raven.

'cosa *sf* thing; *(faccenda)* affair, matter, business *no pl*; **(che) ~?** what?; **(che) cos'è?** what is it?; **a ~ pensi?** what are you thinking about?

'coscia, sce ['kɔʃʃa] *sf* thigh; **~ di pollo** *(CUC)* chicken leg.

cosci'ente [koʃ'ʃɛnte] *ag* conscious; **~ di** conscious *o* aware of; **cosci'enza** *sf* conscience; *(consapevolezza)* consciousness; **coscienzi'oso, a** *ag* conscientious.

cosci'otto [koʃ'ʃɔtto] *sm* (CUC) leg.

cos'critto *sm* (MIL) conscript.

PAROLA CHIAVE
---

così *av* **1** *(in questo modo)* like this, (in) this way; *(in tal modo)* so; **le cose stanno ~** this is the way things stand; **non ho detto ~!** I didn't say that!; **come stai? — (e) ~** how are you? — so-so; **e ~ via** and so on; **per ~ dire** so to speak

2 *(tanto)* so; **~ lontano** so far away; **un ragazzo ~ intelligente** such an intelligent boy

♦ *ag inv (tale)*: **non ho mai visto un film ~** I've never seen such a film

♦ *cong* **1** *(perciò)* so, therefore

2: **~ ... come** as ... as; **non è ~ bravo come te** he's not as good as you; **~ ... che** so ... that.

---

cosid'detto, a *ag* so-called.

cos'metico, a, ci, che *ag, sm* cosmetic.

cos'pargere [kos'pardʒere] *vt*: **~ di** to sprinkle with, **cos'parso, a** *pp di* cospargere.

cos'petto *sm*: **al ~ di** in front of; in the presence of.

cos'picuo, a *ag* considerable, large.

cospi'rare *vi* to conspire; **cospirazi'one** *sf* conspiracy.

'costa *sf* *(tra terra e mare)* coast(line); *(litorale)* shore; *(ANAT)* rib; **la C~ Azzurra** the French Riviera.

costà *av* there.

cos'tante *ag* constant; *(persona)* steadfast ♦ *sf* constant.

cos'tare *vi, vt* to cost; **~ caro** to be expensive, cost a lot.

cos'tata *sf* (CUC) large chop.

cos'tato *sm* (ANAT) ribs *pl*.

costeggi'are [kosted'dʒare] *vt* to be close to; to run alongside.

cos'tei *pron vedi* costui.

cos'tiera *sf* stretch of coast.

costi'ero, a *ag* coastal, coast *cpd*.

costitu'ire *vt (comitato, gruppo)* to set up, form; *(collezione)* to put together, build up; *(sog: elementi, parti: comporre)* to make up, constitute; *(rappresentare)* to constitute; *(DIR)* to appoint; **~rsi alla polizia** to give o.s. up to the police.

costituzio'nale [kostitutssjo'nale] *ag* constitutional.

costituzi'one [kostitut'tsjone] *sf* setting up; building up; constitution.

'costo *sm* cost; **a ogni** *o* **qualunque ~**, **a tutti i ~i** at all costs.

'costola *sf* (ANAT) rib.

costo'letta *sf* (CUC) cutlet.

cos'toro *pron pl vedi* costui.

cos'toso, a *ag* expensive, costly.

cos'tretto, a *pp di* costringere.

cos'tringere [kos'trindʒere] *vt*: **~ qn a fare qc** to force sb to do sth; **cos-trizi'one** *sf* coercion.

costru'ire *vt* to construct, build; **cos-truzi'one** *sf* construction, building.

cos'tui *(f* cos'tei, *pl* cos'toro) *pron (soggetto)* he/she; *pl* they; *(complemento)* him/her; *pl* them; **si può sapere chi è ~?** *(peg)* just who is that fellow?

cos'tume *sm* (uʒo) custom; *(foggia di vestire, indumento)* costume; **~i** *smpl (condotta morale)* morals, morality *sg*;

il buon ~ public morality; ~ **da bagno** bathing *o* swimming costume (*BRIT*), swimsuit; (*da uomo*) bathing *o* swimming trunks *pl*.

co'tenna *sf* bacon rind.

co'togna [ko'toɲɲa] *sf* quince.

coto'letta *sf* (*di maiale, montone*) chop; (*di vitello, agnello*) cutlet.

co'tone *sm* cotton; ~ **idrofilo** cotton wool (*BRIT*), absorbent cotton (*US*).

'cotta *sf* (*fam: innamoramento*) crush.

'cottimo *sm*: **lavorare a** ~ to do piece-work.

'cotto, a *pp di* **cuocere** ♦ *ag* cooked; (*fam: innamorato*) head-over-heels in love.

cot'tura *sf* cooking; (*in forno*) baking; (*in umido*) stewing.

co'vare *vt* to hatch; (*fig: malattia*) to be sickening for; (: *odio, rancore*) to nurse ♦ *vi* (*fuoco, fig*) to smoulder.

'covo *sm* den.

co'vone *sm* sheaf.

'cozza ['kɔttsa] *sf* mussel.

coz'zare [kot'tsare] *vi*: ~ **contro** to bang into, collide with.

C.P. *abbr* (= *casella postale*) P.O. Box.

'crampo *sm* cramp.

'cranio *sm* skull.

cra'vatta *sf* tie.

cre'anza [kre'antsa] *sf* manners *pl*.

cre'are *vt* to create; **cre'ato** *sm* creation; **crea'tore, 'trice** *ag* creative ♦ *sm* creator; **crea'tura** *sf* creature; (*bimbo*) baby, infant; **creazi'one** *sf* creation; (*fondazione*) foundation, establishment.

cre'dente *sm/f* (*REL*) believer.

cre'denza [kre'dɛntsa] *sf* belief; (*armadio*) sideboard.

credenzi'ali [kreden'tsjali] *sfpl* credentials.

'credere *vt* to believe ♦ *vi*: ~ **in**, ~ **a** to believe in; ~ **qn onesto** to believe sb (*o* to be) honest; ~ **che** to believe *o* think that; ~**rsi furbo** to think one is clever.

'credito *sm* (*anche COMM*) credit; (*reputazione*) esteem, repute; **comprare a** ~ to buy on credit.

'credo *sm inv* creed.

'crema *sf* cream; (*con uova, zucchero etc*) custard; ~ **solare** sun cream.

cre'mare *vt* to cremate.

Crem'lino *sm*: **il** ~ the Kremlin.

'crepa *sf* crack.

cre'paccio [kre'pattʃo] *sm* large crack, fissure; (*di ghiacciaio*) crevasse.

crepacu'ore *sm* broken heart.

cre'pare *vi* (*fam: morire*) to snuff it, kick the bucket; ~ **dalle risa** to split one's sides laughing.

crepi'tare *vi* (*fuoco*) to crackle; (*pioggia*) to patter.

cre'puscolo *sm* twilight, dusk.

'crescere ['kreʃʃere] *vi* to grow ♦ *vt* (*figli*) to raise; **'crescita** *sf* growth; **cre-sci'uto, a** *pp di* **crescere**.

'cresima *sf* (*REL*) confirmation.

'crespo, a *ag* (*capelli*) frizzy; (*tessuto*) puckered ♦ *sm* crêpe.

'cresta *sf* crest; (*di polli, uccelli*) crest, comb.

'creta *sf* chalk; clay.

cre'tino, a *ag* stupid ♦ *sm/f* idiot, fool.

cric *sm inv* (*TECN*) jack.

'cricca, che *sf* clique.

'cricco, chi *sm*. = **cric**.

crimi'nale *ag*, *sm/f* criminal.

'crimine *sm* (*DIR*) crime.

'crine *sm* horsehair; **crini'era** *sf* mane.

crisan'temo *sm* chrysanthemum.

'crisi *sf inv* crisis; (*MED*) attack, fit; ~ **di nervi** attack *o* fit of nerves.

cristalliz'zare [kristalid'dzare] *vi* to crystallize; (*fig*) to become fossilized; ~**rsi** *vr* to crystallize; to become fossilized.

cris'tallo *sm* crystal.

cristia'nesimo *sm* Christianity.

cristi'ano, a *ag*, *sm/f* Christian.

'Cristo *sm* Christ.

cri'terio *sm* criterion; (*buon senso*) (common) sense.

'critica, che *sf* criticism; **la** ~ (*attività*) criticism; (*persone*) the critics *pl*; *vedi anche* **critico**.

criti'care *vt* to criticize.

'critico, a, ci, che *ag* critical ♦ *sm* critic.

cri'vello *sm* riddle.

'croce ['krotʃe] *sf* cross; **in** ~ (*di*

traverso) crosswise; (*fig*) on tenterhooks; la C~ Rossa the Red Cross.

croce'figgere *etc* [krotʃe'fiddʒere] = **crocifiggere** *etc*.

croce'via [krotʃe'via] *sm inv* crossroads *sg*.

croci'ata [kro'tʃata] *sf* crusade.

cro'cicchio [kro'tʃikkjo] *sm* crossroads *sg*.

croci'era [kro'tʃera] *sf* (*viaggio*) cruise; (*ARCHIT*) transept.

croci'figgere [krotʃi'fiddʒere] *vt* to crucify; **crocifissi'one** *sf* crucifixion; **croci'fisso, a** *pp di* **crocifiggere**.

crogi'olo [kro'dʒɔlo] *sm* (*fig*) melting pot.

crol'lare *vi* to collapse; **'crollo** *sm* collapse; (*di prezzi*) slump, sudden fall.

cro'mato, a *ag* chromium-plated.

'cromo *sm* chrome, chromium.

cromo'soma, i *sm* chromosome.

'cronaca, che *sf* chronicle; (*STAMPA*) news *sg*; (*: rubrica*) column; (*TV, RADIO*) commentary; **fatto** *o* **episodio di** ~ news item; ~ **nera** crime news *sg*; crime column.

'cronico, a, ci, che *ag* chronic.

cro'nista, i *sm* (*STAMPA*) reporter.

cronolo'gia [kronolo'dʒia] *sf* chronology.

cro'nometro *sm* chronometer; (*a scatto*) stopwatch.

'crosta *sf* crust.

cros'tacei [kros'tatʃei] *smpl* shellfish.

cros'tata *sf* (*CUC*) tart.

cros'tino *sm* (*CUC*) croûton; (*: da antipasto*) canapé.

'cruccio ['kruttʃo] *sm* worry, torment.

cruci'verba *sm inv* crossword (puzzle).

cru'dele *ag* cruel; **crudeltà** *sf* cruelty.

'crudo, a *ag* (*non cotto*) raw; (*aspro*) harsh, severe.

cru'miro (*peg*) *sm* blackleg (*BRIT*), scab.

'crusca *sf* bran.

crus'cotto *sm* (*AUT*) dashboard.

'Cuba *sf* Cuba.

'cubico, a, ci, che *ag* cubic.

'cubo, a *ag* cubic ♦ *sm* cube; **elevare al** ~ (*MAT*) to cube.

cuc'cagna [kuk'kaɲɲa] *sf*: **paese della** ~ land of plenty; **albero della** ~ greasy pole (*fig*).

cuc'cetta [kut'tʃetta] *sf* (*FERR*) couchette; (*NAUT*) berth.

cucchiai'ata [kukkja'jata] *sf* spoonful.

cucchia'ino [kukkja'ino] *sm* teaspoon; coffee spoon.

cucchi'aio [kuk'kjajo] *sm* spoon.

'cuccia, ce ['kuttʃa] *sf* dog's bed; **a** ~! down!

'cucciolo ['kuttʃolo] *sm* cub; (*di cane*) puppy.

cu'cina [ku'tʃina] *sf* (*locale*) kitchen; (*arte culinaria*) cooking, cookery; (*le vivande*) food, cooking; (*apparecchio*) cooker; ~ **componibile** fitted kitchen; **cuci'nare** *vt* to cook.

cu'cire [ku'tʃire] *vt* to sew, stitch; **cuci'trice** *sf* stapler; **cuci'tura** *sf* sewing, stitching; (*costura*) seam.

cucù *sm inv* = **cuculo**.

cu'culo *sm* cuckoo.

'cuffia *sf* bonnet, cap; (*da infermiera*) cap; (*da bagno*) (bathing) cap; (*per ascoltare*) headphones *pl*, headset.

cu'gino, a [ku'dʒino] *sm/f* cousin.

PAROLA CHIAVE

'cui *pron* **1** (*nei complementi indiretti: persona*) whom; (*: oggetto, animale*) which; **la persona/le persone a** ~ **accennavi** the person/people you were referring to *o* to whom you were referring; **i libri di** ~ **parlavo** the books I was talking about *o* about which I was talking; **il quartiere in** ~ **abito** the district where I live; **la ragione per** ~ the reason why

2 (*inserito tra articolo e sostantivo*) whose; **la donna i** ~ **figli sono scomparsi** the woman whose children have disappeared; **il signore, dal** ~ **figlio ho avuto il libro** the man from whose son I got the book.

culi'naria *sf* cookery.

'culla *sf* cradle.

cul'lare *vt* to rock.

culmi'nare *vi*: ~ **con** to culminate in.

'culmine *sm* top, summit.

'culo (*fam!*) *sm* arse (*Brit!*), ass (*US!*); (*fig: fortuna*): **aver ~ to** have the luck of the devil.

'culto *sm* (*religione*) religion; (*adorazione*) worship, adoration; (*venerazione: anche fig*) cult.

cul'tura *sf* culture; education, learning; **cultu'rale** *ag* cultural.

cumula'tivo, a *ag* cumulative; (*prezzo*) inclusive; (*biglietto*) group *cpd*.

'cumulo *sm* (*mucchio*) pile, heap; (*METEOR*) cumulus.

'cuneo *sm* wedge.

cu'oca *sf vedi* **cuoco.**

cu'ocere ['kwɔtʃere] *vt* (*alimenti*) to cook; (*mattoni etc*) to fire ♦ *vi* to cook; **~ al forno** (*pane*) to bake; (*arrosto*) to roast; **cu'oco, a, chi, che** *sm/f* cook; (*di ristorante*) chef.

cu'oio *sm* leather; **~ capelluto** scalp.

cu'ore *sm* heart; **~i** *smpl* (*CARTE*) hearts; **avere buon ~** to be kind-hearted; **stare a ~ a qn** to be important to sb.

cupi'digia [kupi'didʒa] *sf* greed, covetousness.

'cupo, a *ag* dark; (*suono*) dull; (*fig*) gloomy, dismal.

'cupola *sf* dome; cupola.

'cura *sf* care; (*MED: trattamento*) (course of) treatment; **aver ~ di** (*occuparsi di*) to look after; **a ~ di** (*libro*) edited by; **~ dimagrante** diet.

cu'rare *vt* (*malato, malattia*) to treat; (*: guarire*) to cure; (*aver cura di*) to take care of; (*testo*) to edit; **~rsi** *vr* to take care of o.s.; (*MED*) to follow a course of treatment; **~rsi di** to pay attention to.

cu'rato *sm* parish priest; (*protestante*) vicar, minister.

cura'tore, 'trice *sm/f* (*DIR*) trustee; (*di antologia etc*) editor.

curio'sare *vi* to look round, wander round; (*tra libri*) to browse; **~ nei negozi** to look *o* wander round the shops.

curiosità *sf inv* curiosity; (*cosa rara*) curio, curiosity.

curi'oso, a *ag* curious; **essere ~ di** to

be curious about.

cur'sore *sm* (*INFORM*) cursor.

'curva *sf* curve; (*stradale*) bend, curve.

cur'vare *vt* to bend ♦ *vi* (*veicolo*) to take a bend; (*strada*) to bend, curve; **~rsi** *vr* to bend; (*legno*) to warp.

'curvo, a *ag* curved; (*piegato*) bent.

cusci'netto [kuʃʃi'netto] *sm* pad; (*TECN*) bearing ♦ *ag inv*: **stato ~** buffer state; **~ a sfere** ball bearing.

cu'scino [kuʃ'ʃino] *sm* cushion; (*guanciale*) pillow.

'cuspide *sf* (*ARCHIT*) spire.

cus'tode *sm/f* keeper, custodian.

cus'todia *sf* care; (*DIR*) custody; (*astuccio*) case, holder.

custo'dire *vt* (*conservare*) to keep; (*assistere*) to look after, take care of; (*fare la guardia*) to guard.

'cute *sf* (*ANAT*) skin.

cu'ticola *sf* cuticle.

C.V. *abbr* (= *cavallo vapore*) h.p.

D

PAROLA CHIAVE

da (*da+il* = **dal**, *da+lo* = **dallo**, *da+l'* = **dall'**, *da+la* = **dalla**, *da+i* = **dai**, *da+gli* = **dagli**, *da+le* = **dalle**) *prep* **1** (*agente*) by; **dipinto ~ un grande artista** painted by a great artist
2 (*causa*) with; **tremare dalla paura** to tremble with fear
3 (*stato in luogo*) at; **abito ~ lui** I'm living at his house *o* with him; **sono dal giornalaio/~ Francesco** I'm at the newsagent's/Francesco's (house)
4 (*moto a luogo*) to; (*moto per luogo*) through; **vado ~ Pietro/dal giornalaio** I'm going to Pietro's (house)/to the newsagent's; **sono passati dalla finestra** they came in through the window
5 (*provenienza, allontanamento*) from; **arrivare/partire ~ Milano** to arrive/depart from Milan; **scendere dal treno/dalla macchina** to get off the train/out of the car; **si trova a 5 km ~ qui** it's 5 km from here

6 (*tempo: durata*) for; (: *a partire da: nel passato*) since; (: *nel futuro*) from; **vivo qui ~ un anno** I've been living here for a year; **è dalle 3 che ti aspetto** I've been waiting for you since 3 (o'clock); **~ oggi in poi** from today onwards; **~ bambino** as a child, when I (*o* he *etc*) was a child
7 (*modo, maniera*) like; **comportarsi ~ uomo** to behave like a man; **l'ho fatto ~ me** I did it (by) myself
8 (*descrittivo*): **una macchina ~ corsa** a racing car; **una ragazza dai capelli biondi** a girl with blonde hair; **un vestito ~ 100.000 lire** a 100,000 lire dress.

dab'bene *ag inv* honest, decent.
da 'capo *av* = daccapo.
dac'capo *av* (*di nuovo*) (once) again; (*dal principio*) all over again, from the beginning.
dacché [dak'ke] *cong* since.
'dado *sm* (*da gioco*) dice *o* die; (*CUC*) stock (*BRIT*) *o* bouillon (*US*) cube; (*TECN*) (screw)nut; **giocare a ~i** to play dice.
da 'fare *sm* = daffare.
daf'fare *sm* work, toil.
'dagli ['daʎʎi] *prep + det vedi* da.
'dai *prep + det vedi* da.
'daino *sm* (fallow) deer *inv*; (*pelle*) buckskin.
dal *prep + det vedi* da.
dall' *prep + det vedi* da.
'dalla *prep + det vedi* da.
'dalle *prep + det vedi* da.
'dallo *prep + det vedi* da.
dal'tonico, a, ci, che *ag* colour-blind.
'dama *sf* lady; (*nei balli*) partner; (*gioco*) draughts *sg* (*BRIT*), checkers *sg* (*US*).
damigi'ana [dami'dʒana] *sf* demijohn.
da'naro *sm* = denaro.
da'nese *ag* Danish ♦ *sm/f* Dane ♦ *sm* (*LING*) Danish.
Dani'marca *sf*: **la ~** Denmark.
dan'nare *vt* (*REL*) to damn; **~rsi** *vr* (*fig: tormentarsi*) to be worried to death; **far ~ qn** to drive sb mad; **dannazi'one** *sf* damnation.

danneggi'are [danned'dʒare] *vt* to damage; (*rovinare*) to spoil; (*nuocere*) to harm.
'danno *sm* damage; (*a persona*) harm, injury; **~i** *smpl* (*DIR*) damages; **dan'noso, a** *ag*: **dannoso (a, per)** harmful (to), bad (for).
Da'nubio *sm*: **il ~** the Danube.
'danza ['dantsa] *sf*: **la ~** dancing; **una ~** a dance.
dan'zare [dan'tsare] *vt, vi* to dance.
dapper'tutto *av* everywhere.
dap'poco *ag inv* inept, worthless.
dap'prima *av* at first.
'dardo *sm* dart.
'dare *sm* (*COMM*) debit ♦ *vt* to give; (*produrre: frutti, suono*) to produce ♦ *vi* (*guardare*): **~ su** to look (out) onto; **~rsi** *vr*: **~rsi a** to dedicate o.s. to; **~rsi al commercio** to go into business; **~rsi al bere** to take to drink; **~ da mangiare a qn** to give sb sth to eat; **~ per certo qc** to consider sth certain; **~ per morto qn** to give sb up for dead; **~rsi per vinto** to give in.
'darsena *sf* dock; dockyard.
'data *sf* date; **~ di nascita** date of birth.
da'tare *vt* to date ♦ *vi*: **~ da** to date from.
'dato, a *ag* (*stabilito*) given ♦ *sm* datum; **~i** *smpl* data *pl*; **~ che** given that; **un ~ di fatto** a fact.
'dattero *sm* date.
dattilogra'fare *vt* to type; **dattilogra'fia** *sf* typing; **datti'lografo, a** *sm/f* typist.
da'vanti *av* in front; (*dirimpetto*) opposite ♦ *ag inv* front ♦ *sm* front; **~ a** in front of; facing, opposite; (*in presenza di*) before, in front of.
davan'zale [davan'tsale] *sm* windowsill.
d'a'vanzo [da'vantso] *av* = davanzo.
da'vanzo [da'vantso] *av* more than enough.
dav'vero *av* really, indeed.
'dazio ['dattsjo] *sm* (*somma*) duty; (*luogo*) customs *pl*.
DC *sigla f* = Democrazia Cristiana.
d. C. *ad abbr* (= *dopo Cristo*) A.D.

'**dea** sf goddess.

'**debito, a** ag due, proper ♦ sm debt; (COMM: dare) debit; **a tempo ~** at the right time; **debi'tore, 'trice** sm/f debtor.

'**debole** ag weak, feeble; (suono) faint; (luce) dim ♦ sm weakness; **debo'lezza** sf weakness.

debut'tare vi to make one's début; **de'butto** sm début.

deca'denza [deka'dɛntsa] sf decline; (DIR) loss, forfeiture.

decaffei'nato, a ag decaffeinated.

decappot'tabile ag, sf convertible.

dece'duto, a [detʃe'duto] ag deceased.

de'cennio [de'tʃɛnnjo] sm decade.

de'cente [de'tʃɛnte] ag decent, respectable, proper; (accettabile) satisfactory, decent.

de'cesso [de'tʃɛsso] sm death; **atto di ~** death certificate.

de'cidere [de'tʃidere] vt: **~ qc** to decide on sth; (questione, lite) to settle sth; **~ di fare/che** to decide to do/that; **~ di qc** (sog: cosa) to determine sth; **~rsi (a fare)** to decide (to do), make up one's mind (to do).

deci'frare [detʃi'frare] vt to decode; (fig) to decipher, make out.

deci'male [detʃi'male] ag decimal.

'**decimo, a** ['dɛtʃimo] num tenth.

de'cina [de'tʃina] sf ten; (circa dieci): **una ~ (di)** about ten.

decisi'one [detʃi'zjone] sf decision; **prendere una ~** to make a decision.

de'ciso, a [de'tʃizo] pp di decidere.

declas'sare vt to downgrade; to lower in status.

decli'nare vi (pendio) to slope down; (fig: diminuire) to decline; (tramontare) to set, go down ♦ vt to decline; **declinazi'one** sf (LING) declension; **de'clino** sm decline.

decol'lare vi (AER) to take off; **de'collo** sm take-off.

decolo'rare vt to bleach.

decom'porre vt to decompose; **decomporsi** vr to decompose; **decom'posto, a** pp di decomporre.

deconge'lare [dekondʒe'lare] vt to defrost.

deco'rare vt to decorate; **decora'tore, 'trice** sm/f (interior) decorator; **decorazi'one** sf decoration.

de'coro sm decorum; **deco'roso, a** ag decorous, dignified.

de'correre vi to pass, elapse; (avere effetto) to run, have effect; **de'corso, a** pp di decorrere ♦ sm (evoluzione: anche MED) course.

de'crescere [de'kreʃʃere] vi (diminuire) to decrease, diminish; (acque) to subside, go down; (prezzi) to go down; **de'cresci'uto, a** pp di decrescere.

de'creto sm decree; **~ legge** decree with the force of law.

'**dedalo** sm maze, labyrinth.

'**dedica, che** sf dedication.

dedi'care vt to dedicate.

'**dedito, a** ag: **~ a** (studio etc) dedicated o devoted to; (vizio) addicted to.

de'dotto, a pp di dedurre.

de'durre vt (concludere) to deduce; (defalcare) to deduct; **deduzi'one** sf deduction.

defal'care vt to deduct.

defe'rente ag respectful, deferential.

defe'rire vt: **~ a** (DIR) to refer to.

defezi'one [defet'tsjone] sf defection, desertion.

defici'ente [defi'tʃɛnte] ag (mancante): **~ di** deficient in; (insufficiente) insufficient ♦ sm/f mental defective; (peg: cretino) idiot.

'**deficit** ['dɛfitʃit] sm inv (ECON) deficit.

defi'nire vt to define; (risolvere) to settle; **defini'tivo, a** ag definitive, final; **definizi'one** sf definition; settlement.

deflet'tore sm (AUT) quarter-light.

de'flusso sm (della marea) ebb.

defor'mare vt (alterare) to put out of shape; (corpo) to deform; (pensiero, fatto) to distort; **~rsi** vr to lose its shape.

de'forme ag deformed; disfigured; **deformità** sf inv deformity.

defrau'dare vt: **~ qn di qc** to defraud sb of sth, cheat sb out of sth.

de'funto, a ag late cpd ♦ sm/f deceased.

degene'rare [dedʒene'rare] *vi* to degenerate; **de'genere** *ag* degenerate.

de'gente [de'dʒɛnte] *sm/f* bedridden person; (*ricoverato in ospedale*) inpatient.

'degli ['deʎʎi] *prep + det vedi* **di**.

de'gnarsi [deɲ'narsi] *vr*: ~ **di fare** to deign *o* condescend to do.

'degno, a *ag* dignified; ~ **di** worthy of; ~ **di lode** praiseworthy.

degra'dare *vt* (*MIL*) to demote; (*privare della dignità*) to degrade; ~**rsi** *vr* to demean o.s.

degustazi'one [degustat'tsjone] *sf* sampling, tasting.

'dei *prep + det vedi* **di**.

del *prep + det vedi* **di**.

dela'tore, 'trice *sm/f* police informer.

'delega, ghe *sf* (*procura*) proxy.

dele'gare *vt* to delegate; **dele'gato** *sm* delegate.

del'fino *sm* (*ZOOL*) dolphin; (*STORIA*) dauphin; (*fig*) probable successor.

delibe'rare *vt* to come to a decision on ♦ *vi* (*DIR*): ~ (**su qc**) to rule (on sth).

delica'tezza [delika'tettsa] *sf* (*anche CUC*) delicacy; frailty; thoughtfulness; tactfulness.

deli'cato, a *ag* delicate; (*salute*) delicate, frail; (*fig: gentile*) thoughtful, considerate; (*: che dimostra tatto*) tactful.

deline'are *vt* to outline; ~**rsi** *vr* to be outlined; (*fig*) to emerge.

delin'quente *sm/f* criminal, delinquent; **delin'quenza** *sf* criminality, delinquency; **delinquenza minorile** juvenile delinquency.

deli'rare *vi* to be delirious, rave; (*fig*) to rave.

de'lirio *sm* delirium; (*ragionamento insensato*) raving; (*fig*): **andare/mandare in** ~ to go/send into a frenzy.

de'litto *sm* crime.

de'lizia [de'littsja] *sf* delight; **delizi'oso, a** *ag* delightful; (*cibi*) delicious.

dell' *prep + det vedi* **di**.

'della *prep + det vedi* **di**.

'delle *prep + det vedi* **di**.

'dello *prep + det vedi* **di**.

delta'plano *sm* hang-glider; **volo col** ~ hang-gliding.

de'ludere *vt* to disappoint; **delusi'one** *sf* disappointment; **de'luso, a** *pp di* **deludere**.

de'manio *sm* state property.

de'menza [de'mɛntsa] *sf* dementia; (*stupidità*) foolishness.

demo'cratico, a, ci, che *ag* democratic.

democra'zia [demokrat'tsia] *sf* democracy.

democristi'ano, a *ag, sm/f* Christian Democrat.

demo'lire *vt* to demolish.

'demone *sm* demon.

de'monio *sm* demon, devil; **il D~** the Devil.

de'naro *sm* money.

denomi'nare *vt* to name; ~**rsi** *vr* to be named *o* called; **denominazi'one** *sf* name; denomination.

densità *sf inv* density.

'denso, a *ag* thick, dense.

den'tale *ag* dental.

'dente *sm* tooth; (*di forchetta*) prong; (*GEO: cima*) jagged peak; **al** ~ (*CUC: pasta*) cooked so as to be firm when eaten; ~**i del giudizio** wisdom teeth; **denti'era** *sf* (set of) false teeth *pl.*

denti'fricio [denti'fritʃo] *sm* toothpaste.

den'tista, i, e *sm/f* dentist.

'dentro *av* inside; (*in casa*) indoors; (*fig: nell'intimo*) inwardly ♦ *prep*: ~ (**a**) in; **piegato in** ~ folded over; **qui/là** ~ in here/there; ~ **di sé** (*pensare, brontolare*) to oneself.

de'nuncia, ce *o* **cie** [de'nuntʃa] *sf* denunciation; declaration; ~ **dei redditi** (income) tax return.

denunci'are [denun'tʃare] *vt* to denounce; (*dichiarare*) to declare.

de'nunzia *etc* [de'nuntsja] = **denuncia** *etc.*

denutrizi'one [denutrit'tsjone] *sf* malnutrition.

deodo'rante *sm* deodorant.

depe'rire *vi* to waste away.

depila'torio, a *ag* hair-removing *cpd*, depilatory.

dépli'ant [depli'ã] *sm inv* leaflet; (*opuscolo*) brochure.

deplo'revole *ag* deplorable.

de'porre *vt* (*depositare*) to put down; (*rimuovere: da una carica*) to remove; (*: re*) to depose; (*DIR*) to testify.

depor'tare *vt* to deport.

deposi'tare *vt* (*gen, GEO, ECON*) to deposit; (*lasciare*) to leave; (*merci*) to store.

de'posito *sm* deposit; (*luogo*) warehouse; depot; (*: MIL*) depot; ~ **bagagli** left-luggage office.

deposizi'one [depozit'tsjone] *sf* deposition; (*da una carica*) removal.

de'posto, a *pp di* **deporre**.

depra'vato, a *ag* depraved ♦ *sm/f* degenerate.

depre'dare *vt* to rob, plunder.

depressi'one *sf* depression.

de'presso, a *pp di* **deprimere** ♦ *ag* depressed.

deprez'zare [depret'tsare] *vt* (*ECON*) to depreciate.

de'primere *vt* to depress.

depu'rare *vt* to purify.

depu'tato, a *o* **'essa** *sm/f* (*POL*) deputy, ≈ Member of Parliament (*BRIT*), ≈ Member of Congress (*US*); **deputazi'one** *sf* deputation; (*POL*) position of deputy, ≈ parliamentary seat (*BRIT*), ≈ seat in Congress (*US*).

deragli'are [deraʎ'ʎare] *vi* to be derailed; **far ~** to derail.

dere'litto, a *ag* derelict.

dere'tano (*fam*) *sm* bottom, buttocks *pl*.

de'ridere *vt* to mock, deride; **de'riso, a** *pp di* **deridere**.

de'riva *sf* (*NAUT, AER*) drift; **andare alla ~** (*anche fig*) to drift.

deri'vare *vi*: ~ **da** to derive from ♦ *vt* to derive; (*corso d'acqua*) to divert; **derivazi'one** *sf* derivation; diversion.

derma'tologo, a, gi, ghe *sm/f* dermatologist.

der'rate *sfpl* commodities; ~ **alimentari** foodstuffs.

deru'bare *vt* to rob.

des'critto, a *pp di* **descrivere**.

des'crivere *vt* to describe; **descrizi'one** *sf* description.

de'serto, a *ag* deserted ♦ *sm* (*GEO*) desert; **isola ~a** desert island.

deside'rare *vt* to want, wish for; (*sessualmente*) to desire; ~ **fare/che qn faccia** to want *o* wish to do/sb to do; **desidera fare una passeggiata?** would you like to go for a walk?

desi'derio *sm* wish; (*più intenso, carnale*) desire.

deside'roso, a *ag*: ~ **di** longing *o* eager for.

desi'nenza [dezi'nɛntsa] *sf* (*LING*) ending, inflexion.

de'sistere *vi*: ~ **da** to give up, desist from; **desis'tito, a** *pp di* **desistere**.

deso'lato, a *ag* (*paesaggio*) desolate; (*persona: spiacente*) sorry.

des'tare *vt* to wake (up); (*fig*) to awaken, arouse; ~**rsi** *vr* to wake (up).

desti'nare *vt* to destine; (*assegnare*) to appoint, assign; (*indirizzare*) to address; ~ **qc a qn** to intend to give sth to sb, intend sb to have sth; **destina'tario, a** *sm/f* (*di lettera*) addressee.

destinazi'one [destinat'tsjone] *sf* destination; (*uso*) purpose.

des'tino *sm* destiny, fate.

destitu'ire *vt* to dismiss, remove.

'desto, a *ag* (wide) awake.

'destra *sf* (*mano*) right hand; (*parte*) right (side); (*POL*): **la ~** the Right; **a ~** (*essere*) on the right; (*andare*) to the right.

destreggi'arsi [destred'dʒarsi] *vr* to manoeuvre (*BRIT*), maneuver (*US*).

des'trezza [des'trettsa] *sf* skill, dexterity.

'destro, a *ag* right, right-hand; (*abile*) skilful, adroit.

dete'nere *vt* (*incarico, primato*) to hold; (*proprietà*) to have, possess; (*in prigione*) to detain, hold; **dete'nuto, a** *sm/f* prisoner; **detenzi'one** *sf* holding; possession; detention.

deter'gente [deter'dʒɛnte] *ag* detergent; (*crema, latte*) cleansing ♦ *sm* detergent.

deterio'rare *vt* to damage; **~rsi** *vr* to deteriorate.

determi'nare *vt* to determine; **determinazi'one** *sf* determination; (*decisione*) decision.

deter'sivo *sm* detergent.

detes'tare *vt* to detest, hate.

de'trarre *vt*: **~ (da)** to deduct (from), take away (from); **de'tratto, a** *pp di* detrarre; **detrazi'one** *sf* deduction; **detrazione d'imposta** tax allowance.

de'trito *sm* (*GEO*) detritus.

dettagli'are [dettaʎ'ʎare] *vt* to detail, give full details of.

det'taglio [det'taʎʎo] *sm* detail; (*COMM*): **il ~** retail; **al ~** (*COMM*) retail; separately.

det'tare *vt* to dictate; **~ legge** (*fig*) to lay down the law; **det'tato** *sm* dictation; **detta'tura** *sf* dictation.

'detto, a *pp di* **dire** ♦ *ag* (*soprannominato*) called, known as; (*già nominato*) above-mentioned ♦ *sm* saying; **~ fatto** no sooner said than done.

detur'pare *vt* to disfigure; (*moralmente*) to sully.

devas'tare *vt* to devastate; (*fig*) to ravage.

devi'are *vi*: **~ (da)** to turn off (from) ♦ *vt* to divert; **deviazi'one** *sf* (*anche AUT*) diversion.

devo'luto, a *pp di* devolvere.

devoluzi'one [devolut'tsjone] *sf* (*DIR*) devolution, transfer.

de'volvere *vt* (*DIR*) to transfer, devolve.

de'voto, a *ag* (*REL*) devout, pious; (*affezionato*) devoted.

devozi'one [devot'tsjone] *sf* devoutness; (*anche REL*) devotion.

PAROLA CHIAVE

di (*di+il* = **del**, *di+lo* = **dello**, *di+l'* = **dell'**, *di+la* = **della**, *di+i* = **dei**, *di+gli** = **degli**, *di+le* = **delle**) *prep* **1** (*possesso, specificazione*) of; (*composto da, scritto da*) by; **la macchina ~ Paolo/mio fratello** Paolo's/my brother's car; **un amico ~ mio fratello** a friend of my brother's, one of my brother's friends; **un quadro ~ Botticelli** a painting by Botticelli

2 (*caratterizzazione, misura*) of; **una casa ~ mattoni** a brick house, a house made of bricks; **un orologio d'oro** a gold watch; **un bimbo ~ 3 anni** a child of 3, a 3-year-old child

3 (*causa, mezzo, modo*) with; **tremare ~ paura** to tremble with fear; **morire ~ cancro** to die of cancer; **spalmare ~ burro** to spread with butter

4 (*argomento*) about, of; **discutere ~ sport** to talk about sport

5 (*luogo: provenienza*) from; out of; **essere ~ Roma** to be from Rome; **uscire ~ casa** to come out of *o* leave the house

6 (*tempo*) in; **d'estate/d'inverno** in (the) summer/winter; **~ notte** by night, at night; **~ mattina/sera** in the morning/evening; **~ lunedì** on Mondays

♦ *det* (*una certa quantità di*) some; (: *negativo*) any; (: *interrogativo*) any, some; **del pane** (some) bread; **delle caramelle** (some) sweets; **degli amici miei** some friends of mine; **vuoi del vino?** do you want some *o* any wine?

---

dia'bete *sm* diabetes *sg*.

di'acono *sm* (*REL*) deacon.

dia'dema, i *sm* diadem; (*di donna*) tiara.

dia'framma, i *sm* (*divisione*) screen; (*ANAT, FOT, contraccettivo*) diaphragm.

di'agnosi [di'aɲɲozi] *sf* diagnosis *sg*.

diago'nale *ag, sf* diagonal.

dia'gramma, i *sm* diagram.

dia'letto *sm* dialect.

di'alogo, ghi *sm* dialogue.

dia'mante *sm* diamond.

di'ametro *sm* diameter.

di'amine *escl*: **che ~ ...?** what on earth ...?

diaposi'tiva *sf* transparency, slide.

di'ario *sm* diary; **~ degli esami** (*SCOL*) exam timetable.

diar'rea *sf* diarrhoea.

di'avolo *sm* devil.

di'battere *vt* to debate, discuss; **~rsi**

vr to struggle; **di'battito** *sm* debate, discussion.

dicas'tero *sm* ministry.

di'cembre [di'tʃembre] *sm* December.

dice'ria [ditʃe'ria] *sf* rumour, piece of gossip.

dichia'rare [dikja'rare] *vt* to declare; **dichiarazi'one** *sf* declaration.

dician'nove [ditʃan'nɔve] *num* nineteen.

dicias'sette [ditʃas'sette] *num* seventeen.

dici'otto [di'tʃɔtto] *num* eighteen.

dici'tura [ditʃi'tura] *sf* words *pl*, wording.

di'eci ['djetʃi] *num* ten; **die'cina** *sf* = **decina**.

'diesel ['dizəl] *sm inv* diesel engine.

di'eta *sf* diet; **essere a** ~ to be on a diet.

di'etro *av* behind; (*in fondo*) at the back ♦ *prep* behind; (*tempo: dopo*) after ♦ *sm* back, rear ♦ *ag inv* back *cpd*; **le zampe di** ~ the hind legs; ~ **richiesta** on demand; (*scritta*) on application.

di'fatti *cong* in fact, as a matter of fact.

di'fendere *vt* to defend; **difen'sivo, a** *ag* defensive ♦ *sf*: **stare sulla difensiva** (*anche fig*) to be on the defensive; **difen'sore, a** *sm/f* defender; **avvocato difensore** counsel for the defence; **di'fesa** *sf* defence; **di'feso, a** *pp di* **difendere**.

difet'tare *vi* to be defective; ~ **di** to be lacking in, lack; **difet'tivo, a** *ag* defective.

di'fetto *sm* (*mancanza*): ~ **di** lack of; shortage of; (*di fabbricazione*) fault, flaw, defect; (*morale*) fault, failing, defect; (*fisico*) defect; **far** ~ to be lacking; **in** ~ at fault; **in the wrong**; **difet'toso, a** *ag* defective, faulty.

diffa'mare *vt* to slander; to libel.

diffe'rente *ag* different.

diffe'renza [diffe'rentsa] *sf* difference; **a** ~ **di** unlike.

differenzi'are [differen'tsjare] *vt* to differentiate; ~**rsi da** to differentiate o.s. from; to differ from.

diffe'rire *vt* to postpone, defer ♦ *vi* to be different.

dif'ficile [dif'fitʃile] *ag* difficult; (*persona*) hard to please, difficult (to please); (*poco probabile*): **è** ~ **che sia libero** it is unlikely that he'll be free ♦ *sm* difficult part; difficulty; **difficoltà** *sf inv* difficulty.

dif'fida *sf* (*DIR*) warning, notice.

diffi'dare *vi*: ~ **di** to be suspicious *o* distrustful of ♦ *vt* (*DIR*) to warn; ~ **qn dal fare qc** to warn sb not to do sth, caution sb against doing sth; **diffi'dente** *ag* suspicious, distrustful; **diffi'denza** *sf* suspicion, distrust.

dif'fondere *vt* (*luce, calore*) to diffuse; (*notizie*) to spread, circulate; ~**rsi** *vr* to spread; **diffusi'one** *sf* diffusion; spread; (*anche di giornale*) circulation; (*FISICA*) scattering; **dif'fuso, a** *pp di* **diffondere** ♦ *ag* (*malattia, fenomeno*) widespread.

difi'lato *av* (*direttamente*) straight, directly; (*subito*) straight away.

difte'rite *sf* (*MED*) diphtheria.

'diga, ghe *sf* dam; (*portuale*) breakwater.

dige'rente [didʒe'rente] *ag* (*apparato*) digestive.

dige'rire [didʒe'rire] *vt* to digest; **digesti'one** *sf* digestion; **diges'tivo, a** *ag* digestive ♦ *sm* (after-dinner) liqueur.

digi'tale [didʒi'tale] *ag* digital; (*delle dita*) finger *cpd*, digital ♦ *sf* (*BOT*) foxglove.

digi'tare [didʒi'tare] *vt, vi* (*INFORM*) to key (in).

digiu'nare [didʒu'nare] *vi* to starve o.s.; (*REL*) to fast; **digi'uno, a** *ag*: **essere digiuno** not to have eaten ♦ *sm* fast; **a digiuno** on an empty stomach.

dignità [diɲɲi'ta] *sf inv* dignity; **di'gni'toso, a** *ag* dignified.

'DIGOS ['digɔs] *sigla f* (= *Divisione Investigazioni Generali e Operazioni Speciali*) police' *department dealing with political security*.

digri'gnare [digriɲ'ɲare] *vt*: ~ **i denti** to grind one's teeth.

dila'gare *vi* to flood; (*fig*) to spread.

dilani'are *vt* (*preda*) to tear to pieces.

dilapi'dare *vt* to squander, waste.

dila'tare *vt* to dilate; (*gas*) to cause to expand; (*passaggio, cavità*) to open (up); **~rsi** *vr* to dilate; (*FISICA*) to expand.

dilazio'nare [dilattsjo'nare] *vt* to delay, defer; **dilazi'one** *sf* delay; (*COMM: di pagamento etc*) extension; (*rinvio*) postponement.

dileggi'are [diled'dʒare] *vt* to mock, deride.

dilegu'are *vi* to vanish, disappear; **~rsi** *vr* to vanish, disappear.

di'lemma, i *sm* dilemma.

dilet'tante *smlf* dilettante; (*anche SPORT*) amateur.

dilet'tare *vt* to give pleasure to, delight; **~rsi** *vr*: **~rsi di** to take pleasure in, enjoy.

di'letto, a *ag* dear, beloved ♦ *sm* pleasure, delight.

dili'gente [dili'dʒɛnte] *ag* (*scrupoloso*) diligent; (*accurato*) careful, accurate; **dili'genza** *sf* diligence; care; (*carrozza*) stagecoach.

dilu'ire *vt* to dilute.

dilun'garsi *vr* (*fig*): **~ su** to talk at length on *o* about.

diluvi'are *vb impers* to pour (down).

di'luvio *sm* downpour; (*inondazione, fig*) flood.

dima'grire *vi* to get thinner, lose weight.

dime'nare *vt* to wave, shake; **~rsi** *vr* to toss and turn; (*fig*) to struggle; **~ la coda** (*sog: cane*) to wag its tail.

dimensi'one *sf* dimension; (*grandezza*) size.

dimenti'canza [dimenti'kantsa] *sf* forgetfulness; (*errore*) oversight, slip; **per ~** inadvertently.

dimenti'care *vt* to forget; **~rsi di qc** to forget sth.

di'messo, a *pp di* **dimettere** ♦ *ag* (*voce*) subdued; (*uomo, abito*) modest, humble.

dimesti'chezza [dimesti'kettsa] *sf* familiarity.

di'mettere *vt*: **~ qn da** to dismiss sb from; (*dall'ospedale*) to discharge sb from; **~rsi (da)** to resign (from).

dimez'zare [dimed'dzare] *vt* to halve.

diminu'ire *vt* to reduce, diminish; (*prezzi*) to bring down, reduce ♦ *vi* to decrease, diminish; (*rumore*) to die down, die away; (*prezzi*) to fall, go down; **diminuzi'one** *sf* decreasing, diminishing.

dimissi'oni *sfpl* resignation *sg*; **dare** *o* **presentare le ~** to resign, hand in one's resignation.

di'mora *sf* residence.

dimo'rare *vi* to reside.

dimos'trare *vt* to demonstrate, show; (*provare*) to prove, demonstrate; **~rsi** *vr*: **~rsi molto abile** to show o.s. *o* prove to be very clever; **dimostra 30 anni** he looks about 30 (years old); **dimostrazi'one** *sf* demonstration; proof.

di'namica *sf* dynamics *sg*.

di'namico, a, ci, che *ag* dynamic.

dina'mite *sf* dynamite.

'dinamo *sf inv* dynamo.

di'nanzi [di'nantsi]: **~ a** *prep* in front of.

dini'ego, ghi *sm* refusal; denial.

dinocco'lato, a *ag* lanky; **camminare ~** to walk with a slouch.

din'torno *av* round, (round) about; **~i** *smpl* outskirts; **nei ~i di** in the vicinity *o* neighbourhood of.

'dio (*pl* **'dei**) *sm* god; **D~** God; **gli dei** the gods; **D~ mio!** my goodness!, my God!

di'ocesi [di'ɔtʃezi] *sf inv* diocese.

dipa'nare *vt* (*lana*) to wind into a ball; (*fig*) to disentangle, sort out.

diparti'mento *sm* department.

dipen'dente *ag* dependent ♦ *smlf* employee; **dipen'denza** *sf* dependence; **essere alle dipendenze di qn** to be employed by sb *o* in sb's employ.

di'pendere *vi*: **~ da** to depend on; (*finanziariamente*) to be dependent on; (*derivare*) to come from, be due to; **di'peso, a** *pp di* **dipendere**.

di'pingere [di'pindʒere] *vt* to paint; **di'pinto, a** *pp di* **dipingere** ♦ *sm* painting.

di'ploma, i *sm* diploma.

diplo'mare *vt* to award a diploma to, graduate (*US*) ♦ *vi* to obtain a diploma, graduate (US).

diplo'matico, a, ci, che ag diplomatic ♦ sm diplomat.

diploma'zia [diplomat'tsia] sf diplomacy.

di'porto: imbarcazione da ~ sf pleasure craft.

dira'dare vt to thin (out); (visite) to reduce, make less frequent; **~rsi** vr to disperse; (nebbia) to clear (up).

dira'mare vt to issue ♦ vi (strade) to branch; **~rsi** vr to branch.

'dire vt to say; (segreto, fatto) to tell; **~ qc a qn** to tell sb sth; **~ a qn di fare qc** to tell sb to do sth; **~ di sì/no** to say yes/no; **si dice che ...** they say that ...; **si direbbe che ...** it looks (o sounds) as though ...; **dica, signora?** (in un negozio) yes, Madam, can I help you?

diret'tissimo sm (FERR) fast (through) train.

di'retto, a pp di **dirigere** ♦ ag direct ♦ sm (FERR) through train.

diret'tore, 'trice sm/f (di azienda) director; manager/ess; (di scuola elementare) head (teacher) (BRIT), principal (US); **~ d'orchestra** conductor.

direzi'one [diret'tsjone] sf board of directors; management; (senso di movimento) direction; **in ~ di** in the direction of, towards.

diri'gente [diri'dʒɛnte] sm/f executive; (POL) leader ♦ ag: **classe ~** ruling class.

di'rigere [di'ridʒere] vt to direct; (impresa) to run, manage; (MUS) to conduct; **~rsi** vr: **~rsi verso** o **a** to make o head for.

dirim'petto av opposite; **~ a** opposite, facing.

di'ritto, a ag straight; (onesto) straight, upright ♦ av straight, directly; **andare ~** to go straight on ♦ sm right side; (TENNIS) forehand; (MAGLIA) plain stitch; (prerogativa) right; (leggi, scienza): **il ~** law; **~i** smpl (tasse) duty sg; **stare ~** to stand up straight; **aver ~ a qc** to be entitled to sth; **~i d'autore** royalties.

dirit'tura sf (SPORT) straight; (fig) rectitude.

diroc'cato, a ag tumbledown, in ruins.

dirot'tare vt (nave, aereo) to change the course of; (aereo: sotto minaccia) to hijack; (traffico) to divert ♦ vi (nave, aereo) to change course; **dirotta'tore, 'trice** sm/f hijacker.

di'rotto, a ag (pioggia) torrential; (pianto) unrestrained; **piovere a ~** to pour, rain cats and dogs; **piangere a ~** to cry one's heart out.

di'rupo sm crag, precipice.

disabi'tato, a ag uninhabited.

disabitu'arsi vr: **~ a** to get out of the habit of.

disac'cordo sm disagreement.

disadat'tato, a ag (PSIC) maladjusted.

disa'dorno, a ag plain, unadorned.

disagi'ato, a [diza'dʒato] ag poor, needy; (vita) hard.

di'sagio [di'zadʒo] sm discomfort; (disturbo) inconvenience; (fig: imbarazzo) embarrassment; **essere a ~** to be ill at ease.

disappro'vare vt to disapprove of; **disapprovazi'one** sf disapproval.

disap'punto sm disappointment.

disar'mare vt, vi to disarm; **di'sarmo** sm (MIL) disarmament.

di'sastro sm disaster.

disat'tento, a ag inattentive; **disattenzi'one** sf carelessness, lack of attention.

disa'vanzo [diza'vantso] sm (ECON) deficit.

disavven'tura sf misadventure, mishap.

dis'brigo, ghi sm (prompt) clearing up o settlement.

dis'capito sm: **a ~ di** to the detriment of.

dis'carica, che sf (di rifiuti) rubbish tip o dump.

discen'dente [diʃʃen'dɛnte] ag descending ♦ sm/f descendant.

di'scendere [diʃ'ʃendere] vt to go (o come) down ♦ vi to go (o come) down; (strada) to go down; (smontare) to get off; **~ da** (famiglia) to be descended from; **~ dalla macchina/dal treno** to get out of the car/out of o off the train; **~**

da cavallo to dismount, get off one's horse.

di'scepolo, a [diʃ'ʃepolo] *sm/f* disciple.

di'scernere [diʃ'ʃernere] *vt* to discern.

di'scesa [diʃ'ʃesa] *sf* descent; (*pendio*) slope; **in ~** (*strada*) downhill *cpd*, sloping; **~ libera** (*SCI*) downhill (race).

di'sceso, a [diʃ'ʃeso] *pp di* discendere.

disci'ogliere [diʃ'ʃɔʎʎere] *vt* to dissolve; (*fondere*) to melt; **~rsi** *vr* to dissolve; to melt; **disci'olto, a** *pp di* disciogliere.

disci'plina [diʃʃi'plina] *sf* discipline; **disci-pli'nare** *ag* disciplinary ♦ *vt* to discipline.

'disco, schi *sm* disc; (*SPORT*) discus; (*fonografico*) record; (*INFORM*) disk; **~ orario** (*AUT*) parking disc; **~ rigido** (*IN-FORM*) hard disk; **~ volante** flying saucer.

discol'pare *vt* to clear of blame.

disco'noscere [disko'noʃʃere] *vt* (*figlio*) to disown; (*meriti*) to ignore, disregard; **disconosci'uto, a** *pp di* disconoscere.

dis'corde *ag* conflicting, clashing; **dis'cordia** *sf* discord; (*dissidio*) disagreement, clash.

dis'correre *vi:* **~ (di)** to talk (about).

dis'corso, a *pp di* discorrere ♦ *sm* speech; (*conversazione*) conversation, talk.

dis'costo, a *ag* faraway, distant ♦ *av* far away; **~ da** far from.

disco'teca, che *sf* (*raccolta*) record library; (*luogo di ballo*) disco(thèque).

discre'panza [diskre'pantsa] *sf* disagreement.

dis'creto, a *ag* discreet; (*abbastanza buono*) reasonable, fair; **discrezi'one** *sf* discretion; (*giudizio*) judgment, discernment; **a discrezione di** at the discretion of.

discriminazi'one [diskriminat'tsjone] *sf* discrimination.

discussi'one *sf* discussion; (*litigio*) argument.

dis'cusso, a *pp di* discutere.

dis'cutere *vt* to discuss, debate; (*contestare*) to question ♦ *vi* (*conversare*): **~ (di)** to discuss; (*litigare*) to argue.

disde'gnare [disdeɲ'ɲare] *vt* to scorn.

dis'detta *sf* cancellation; (*sfortuna*) bad luck.

dis'detto, a *pp di* disdire.

dis'dire *vt* (*prenotazione*) to cancel; (*DIR*): **~ un contratto d'affitto** to give notice (to quit).

dise'gnare [diseɲ'ɲare] *vt* to draw; (*progettare*) to design; (*fig*) to outline; **disegna'tore, 'trice** *sm/f* designer.

di'segno [di'seɲɲo] *sm* drawing; design; outline.

diser'bante *sm* weed-killer.

diser'tare *vt, vi* to desert; **diser'tore** *sm* (*MIL*) deserter.

dis'fare *vt* to undo; (*valigie*) to unpack; (*meccanismo*) to take to pieces; (*lavoro, paese*) to destroy; (*neve*) to melt; **~rsi** *vr* to come undone; (*neve*) to melt; **~ il letto** to strip the bed; **~rsi di qn** (*liberarsi*) to get rid of sb; **dis'fatta** *sf* (*sconfitta*) rout; **dis'fatto, a** *pp di* disfare.

dis'gelo [diz'dʒelo] *sm* thaw.

dis'grazia [diz'grattsja] *sf* (*sventura*) misfortune; (*incidente*) accident, mishap; **disgrazi'ato, a** *ag* unfortunate ♦ *sm/f* wretch.

disgre'gare *vt* to break up; **~rsi** *vr* to break up.

disgu'ido *sm:* **~ postale** error in postal delivery.

disgus'tare *vt* to disgust; **~rsi** *vr:* **~rsi di** to be disgusted by.

dis'gusto *sm* disgust; **disgus'toso, a** *ag* disgusting.

disidra'tare *vt* to dehydrate.

disil'ludere *vt* to disillusion, disenchant.

disimpa'rare *vt* to forget.

disimpe'gnare [dizimpeɲ'ɲare] *vt* (*persona: da obblighi*): **~ da** to release from; (*oggetto dato in pegno*) to redeem, get out of pawn; **~rsi** *vr:* **~rsi da** (*obblighi*) to release o.s. from, free o.s. from.

disinfet'tante *ag, sm* disinfectant.

disinfet'tare *vt* to disinfect.

disini'bito, a *ag* uninhibited.

disinte'grare *vt, vi* to disintegrate.

disinteres'sarsi *vr*: ~ **di** to take no interest in.

disinte'resse *sm* indifference; (*generosità*) unselfishness.

disintossi'care *vt* (*alcolizzato, drogato*) to treat for alcoholism (*o drug addiction*); ~ **l'organismo** to clear out one's system.

disin'volto, a *ag* casual, free and easy; **disinvol'tura** *sf* casualness, ease.

disles'sia *sf* dyslexia.

dislo'care *vt* to station, position.

dismi'sura *sf* excess; **a** ~ to excess, excessively.

disobbe'dire *etc* = **disubbidire** *etc*.

disoccu'pato, a *ag* unemployed ♦ *sm/f* unemployed person; **disoccupazi'one** *sf* unemployment.

diso'nesto, a *ag* dishonest.

diso'nore *sm* dishonour, disgrace.

di'sopra *av* (*con contatto*) on top; (*senza contatto*) above; (*al piano superiore*) upstairs ♦ *ag inv* (*superiore*) upper ♦ *sm inv* top, upper part.

disordi'nato, a *ag* untidy; (*privo di misura*) irregular, wild.

di'sordine *sm* (*confusione*) disorder, confusion; (*sregolatezza*) debauchery.

disorien'tare *vt* to disorientate; ~**rsi** *vr* (*fig*) to get confused, lose one's bearings.

di'sotto *av* below, underneath; (*in fondo*) at the bottom; (*al piano inferiore*) downstairs ♦ *ag inv* (*inferiore*) lower; bottom *cpd* ♦ *sm inv* (*parte inferiore*) lower part; bottom.

dis'paccio [dis'pattʃo] *sm* dispatch.

'dispari *ag inv* odd, uneven.

dis'parte: **in** ~ *av* (*da lato*) aside, apart; **tenersi** *o* **starsene in** ~ to keep to o.s., hold aloof.

dispendi'oso, a *ag* expensive.

dis'pensa *sf* pantry, larder; (*mobile*) sideboard; (*DIR*) exemption; (*REL*) dispensation; (*fascicolo*) number, issue.

dispen'sare *vt* (*elemosine, favori*) to distribute; (*esonerare*) to exempt.

dispe'rare *vi*: ~ (**di**) to despair (of); ~**rsi** *vr* to despair; **dispe'rato, a** *ag* (*persona*) in despair; (*caso, tentativo*) desperate; **disperazi'one** *sf* despair.

dis'perdere *vt* (*disseminare*) to disperse; (*MIL*) to scatter, rout; (*fig: consumare*) to waste, squander; ~**rsi** *vr* to disperse; to scatter; **dis'perso, a** *pp di* **disperdere** ♦ *sm/f* missing person.

dis'petto *sm* spite *no pl*, spitefulness *no pl*; **fare un** ~ **a** qn to play a (nasty) trick on sb; **a** ~ **di** in spite of; **dispet'toso, a** *ag* spiteful.

dispia'cere [dispja'tʃere] *sm* (*rammarico*) regret, sorrow; (*dolore*) grief; ~**i** *smpl* (*preoccupazioni*) troubles, worries ♦ *vi*: ~ **a** to displease ♦ *vb impers*: **mi dispiace** (**che**) I am sorry (that); **se non mi dispiace, me ne vado adesso** if you don't mind, I'll go now; **dispiaci'uto, a** *pp di* **dispiacere** ♦ *ag* sorry.

dispo'nibile *ag* available.

dis'porre *vt* (*sistemare*) to arrange; (*preparare*) to prepare; (*DIR*) to order; (*persuadere*): ~ **qn a** to incline *o* dispose sb towards ♦ *vi* (*decidere*) to decide; (*usufruire*): ~ **di** to use, have at one's disposal; (*essere dotato*): ~ **di** to have; **disporsi** *vr* (*ordinarsi*) to place o.s., arrange o.s.; **disporsi a fare** to get ready to do.

disposi'tivo *sm* (*meccanismo*) device.

disposizi'one [dispozit'tsjone] *sf* arrangement, layout; (*stato d'animo*) mood; (*tendenza*) bent, inclination; (*comando*) order; (*DIR*) provision, regulation; **a** ~ **di** qn at sb's disposal.

dis'posto, a *pp di* **disporre**.

disprez'zare [dispret'tsare] *vt* to despise.

dis'prezzo [dis'prettso] *sm* contempt.

'disputa *sf* dispute, quarrel.

dispu'tare *vt* (*contendere*) to dispute, contest; (*gara*) to take part in ♦ *vi* to quarrel; ~ **di** to discuss; ~**rsi** qc to fight for sth.

dissan'guare *vt* (*fig: persona*) to bleed white; (: *patrimonio*) to suck dry; ~**rsi** *vr* (*MED*) to lose blood; (*fig: rovinarsi*) to ruin o.s.

dissec'care *vt* to dry up; ~**rsi** *vr* to dry up.

dissemi'nare *vt* to scatter; (*fig:*

notizie) to spread.

dis'senso *sm* dissent; (*disapprovazione*) disapproval.

dissente'ria *sf* dysentery.

dissen'tire *vi*: ~ **(da)** to disagree (with).

dissertazi'one [dissertat'tsjone] *sf* dissertation.

disser'vizio [disser'vittsjo] *sm* inefficiency.

disses'tare *vt* (*ECON*) to ruin; **dis'sesto** *sm* (financial) ruin.

disse'tante *ag* refreshing.

dis'sidio *sm* disagreement.

dis'simile *ag* different, dissimilar.

dissimu'lare *vt* (*fingere*) to dissemble; (*nascondere*) to conceal.

dissi'pare *vt* to dissipate; (*scialacquare*) to squander, waste.

dis'solto, a *pp di* **dissolvere**.

disso'lubile *ag* soluble.

disso'luto, a *pp di* **dissolvere ♦** *ag* dissolute, licentious.

dis'solvere *vt* to dissolve; (*neve*) to melt; (*fumo*) to disperse; ~**rsi** *vr* to dissolve; to melt; to disperse.

dissu'adere *vt*: ~ **qn da** to dissuade sb from; **dissu'aso, a** *pp di* **dissuadere**.

distac'care *vt* to detach, separate; (*SPORT*) to leave behind; ~**rsi** *vr* to be detached; (*fig*) to stand out; ~**rsi da** (*fig: allontanarsi*) to grow away from.

dis'tacco, chi *sm* (*separazione*) separation; (*fig: indifferenza*) detachment; (*SPORT*) **vincere con un ~ di ...** to win by a distance of ....

dis'tante *av* far away ♦ *ag*: ~ **(da)** distant (from), far away (from).

dis'tanza [dis'tantsa] *sf* distance.

distanzi'are [distan'tsjare] *vt* to space out, place at intervals; (*SPORT*) to outdistance; (*fig: superare*) to outstrip, surpass.

dis'tare *vi*: **distiamo pochi chilometri da Roma** we are only a few kilometres (away) from Rome.

dis'tendere *vt* (*coperta*) to spread out; (*gambe*) to stretch (out); (*mettere a giacere*) to lay; (*rilassare: muscoli, nervi*) to relax; ~**rsi** *vr* (*rilassarsi*) to

relax; (*sdraiarsi*) to lie down; **distensi'one** *sf* stretching; relaxation; (*POL*) détente.

dis'tesa *sf* expanse, stretch.

dis'teso, a *pp di* **distendere**.

distil'lare *vt* to distil.

distille'ria *sf* distillery.

dis'tinguere *vt* to distinguish.

dis'tinta *sf* (*nota*) note; (*elenco*) list.

distin'tivo, a *ag* distinctive; distinguishing ♦ *sm* badge.

dis'tinto, a *pp di* **distinguere ♦** *ag* (*dignitoso ed elegante*) distinguished; ~**i saluti** (*in lettera*) yours faithfully.

distinzi'one [distin'tsjone] *sf* distinction.

dis'togliere [dis'tɔλλere] *vt*: ~ **da** to take away from; (*fig*) to dissuade from; **dis'tolto, a** *pp di* **distogliere**.

distorsi'one *sf* (*MED*) sprain; (*FISICA, OTTICA*) distortion.

dis'trarre *vt* to distract; (*divertire*) to entertain, amuse; **distrarsi** *vr* (*non fare attenzione*) to be distracted, let one's mind wander; (*svagarsi*) to amuse *o* enjoy o.s.; **dis'tratto, a** *pp di* **distrarre ♦** *ag* absent-minded; (*disattento*) inattentive; **distrazi'one** *sf* absent-mindedness; inattention; (*svago*) distraction, entertainment.

dis'tretto *sm* district.

distribu'ire *vt* to distribute; (*CARTE*) to deal (out); (*consegnare: posta*) to deliver; (*lavoro*) to allocate, assign; (*ripartire*) to share out; **distribu'tore** *sm* (*di benzina*) petrol (*BRIT*) *o* gas (*US*) pump; (*AUT, ELETTR*) distributor; (*automatico*) vending machine; **distribuzi'one** *sf* distribution; delivery.

distri'care *vt* to disentangle, unravel.

dis'truggere [dis'truddʒere] *vt* to destroy; **dis'trutto, a** *pp di* **distruggere**; **distruzi'one** *sf* destruction.

distur'bare *vt* to disturb, trouble; (*sonno, lezioni*) to disturb, interrupt; ~**rsi** *vr* to put o.s. out.

dis'turbo *sm* trouble, bother, inconvenience; (*indisposizione*) (slight) disorder, ailment; ~**i** *smpl* (*RADIO, TV*) static *sg*.

disubbidi'ente *ag* disobedient;

disubbidi'enza sf disobedience.
disubbi'dire vi: ~ **(a qn)** to disobey (sb).
disugu'ale ag unequal; (diverso) different; (irregolare) uneven.
disu'mano, a ag inhuman.
di'suso sm: **andare** o **cadere in** ~ to fall into disuse.
'**dita** fpl di **dito**.
di'tale sm thimble.
'**dito** (pl(f) '**dita**) sm finger; (misura) finger, finger's breadth; ~ **(del piede)** toe.
'**ditta** sf firm, business.
ditta'tore sm dictator.
ditta'tura sf dictatorship.
dit'tongo, ghi sm diphthong.
di'urno, a ag day cpd, daytime cpd ♦ sm (anche: **albergo** ~) public toilets with washing and shaving facilities etc.
'**diva** sf vedi **divo**.
diva'gare vi to digress.
divam'pare vi to flare up, blaze up.
di'vano sm sofa; divan.
divari'care vt to open wide.
di'vario sm difference.
dive'nire vi = **diventare**; **dive'nuto, a** pp di **divenire**.
diven'tare vi to become; ~ **famoso/ professore** to become famous/a teacher.
di'verbio sm altercation.
di'vergere [di'verdʒere] vi to diverge.
diversifi'care vt to diversify, vary; to differentiate.
diversi'one sf diversion.
diversità sf inv difference, diversity; (varietà) variety.
diver'sivo sm diversion, distraction.
di'verso, a ag (differente): ~ **(da)** different (from); ~**i, e** det pl several, various; (COMM) sundry ♦ pron pl several (people), many (people).
diver'tente ag amusing.
diverti'mento sm amusement, pleasure; (passatempo) pastime, recreation.
diver'tire vt to amuse, entertain; ~**rsi** vr to amuse o enjoy o.s.
divi'dendo sm dividend.
di'videre vt (anche MAT) to divide;

(distribuire, ripartire) to divide (up), split (up); ~**rsi** vr (separarsi) to separate; (strade) to fork.
divi'eto sm prohibition; "~ **di sosta**" (AUT) "no parking".
divinco'larsi vr to wriggle, writhe.
divinità sf inv divinity.
di'vino, a ag divine.
di'visa sf (MIL etc) uniform; (COMM) foreign currency.
divisi'one sf division.
di'viso, a pp di **dividere**.
'**divo, a** sm/f star.
divo'rare vt to devour.
divorzi'are [divor'tsjare] vi: ~ **(da qn)** to divorce (sb); **divorzi'ato, a** sm/f divorcee.
di'vorzio [di'vortsjo] sm divorce.
divul'gare vt to divulge, disclose; (rendere comprensibile) to popularize; ~**rsi** vr to spread.
dizio'nario [ditsjo'narjo] sm dictionary.
dizi'one [dit'tsjone] sf diction; pronunciation.
do sm (MUS) C; (: solfeggiando la scala) do(h).
DOC [dɔk] abbr (= denominazione di origine controllata) label guaranteeing the quality of wine.
'**doccia, ce** ['dottʃa] sf (bagno) shower; (condotto) pipe; **fare la** ~ to have a shower.
do'cente [do'tʃente] ag teaching ♦ sm/f teacher; (di università) lecturer; **do'cenza** sf university teaching o lecturing.
'**docile** ['dɔtʃile] ag docile.
documen'tare vt to document; ~**rsi** vr: ~**rsi (su)** to gather information o material (about).
documen'tario sm documentary.
docu'mento sm document; ~**i** smpl (d'identità etc) papers.
'**dodici** ['doditʃi] num twelve.
do'gana sf (ufficio) customs pl; (tassa) (customs) duty; **passare la** ~ to go through customs; **doga'nale** ag customs cpd; **dogani'ere** sm customs officer.
'**doglie** ['dɔʎʎe] sfpl (MED) labour sg, labour pains.

'dolce ['doltʃe] *ag* sweet; (*colore*) soft; (*carattere, persona*) gentle, mild; (*fig: mite: clima*) mild; (*non ripido: pendio*) gentle ♦ *sm* (*sapore dolce*) sweetness, sweet taste; (*CUC: portata*) sweet, dessert; (: *torta*) cake; **dol'cezza** *sf* sweetness; softness; mildness; gentleness; **dolci'umi** *smpl* sweets.

do'lente *ag* sorrowful, sad.

do'lere *vi* to be sore, hurt, ache; ~rsi *vr* to complain; (*essere spiacente*): ~rsi di to be sorry for; **mi duole la testa** my head aches, I've got a headache.

'dollaro *sm* dollar.

'dolo *sm* (*DIR*) malice.

Dolo'miti *sfpl*: le ~ the Dolomites.

do'lore *sm* (*fisico*) pain; (*morale*) sorrow, grief; **dolo'roso, a** *ag* painful; sorrowful, sad.

do'loso, a *ag* (*DIR*) malicious.

do'manda *sf* (*interrogazione*) question; (*richiesta*) demand; (: *cortese*) request; (*DIR: richiesta scritta*) application; (*ECON*): **la ~** demand; **fare una ~ a qn** to ask sb a question; **fare ~ (per un lavoro)** to apply (for a job).

doman'dare *vt* (*per avere*) to ask for; (*per sapere*) to ask; (*esigere*) to demand; ~rsi *vr* to wonder; to ask o.s.; **~ qc a qn** to ask sb for sth; to ask sb sth.

do'mani *av* tomorrow ♦ *sm*: **il ~** (*il futuro*) the future; (*il giorno successivo*) the next day; **~ l'altro** the day after tomorrow.

do'mare *vt* to tame.

domat'tina *av* tomorrow morning.

do'menica, che *sf* Sunday; **di** *o* **la ~** on Sundays; **domeni'cale** *ag* Sunday cpd.

do'mestica, che *sf vedi* **domestico**.

do'mestico, a, ci, che *ag* domestic ♦ *sm/f* servant, domestic.

domi'cilio [domi'tʃiljo] *sm* (*DIR*) domicile, place of residence.

domi'nare *vt* to dominate; (*fig: sentimenti*) to control, master ♦ *vi* to be in the dominant position; ~rsi *vr* (*controllarsi*) to control o.s.; **~ su** (*fig*) to

surpass, outclass; **dominazi'one** *sf* domination.

do'minio *sm* dominion; (*fig: campo*) field, domain.

do'nare *vt* to give, present; (*per beneficenza etc*) to donate ♦ *vi* (*fig*): **~ a** to suit, become; **~ sangue** to give blood; **dona'tore, 'trice** *sm/f* donor; **donatore di sangue/di organi** blood/organ donor.

dondo'lare *vt* (*cullare*) to rock; ~rsi *vr* to swing, sway; **'dondolo** *sm*: **sedia/cavallo a dondolo** rocking chair/horse.

'donna *sf* woman; **~ di casa** housewife; home-loving woman; **~ di servizio** maid.

donnai'olo *sm* ladykiller.

don'nesco, a, schi, sche *ag* women's, woman's.

'donnola *sf* weasel.

'dono *sm* gift.

'dopo *av* (*tempo*) afterwards; (: *più tardi*) later; (*luogo*) after, next ♦ *prep* after ♦ *cong* (*temporale*): **~ aver studiato** after having studied; **~ mangiato va a dormire** after having eaten *o* after a meal he goes for a sleep ♦ *ag inv*: **il giorno ~** the following day; **un anno ~** a year later; **~ di me/lui** after me/him.

dopo'barba *sm inv* after-shave.

dopodo'mani *av* the day after tomorrow.

dopogu'erra *sm* postwar years *pl*.

dopo'pranzo [dopo'prandzo] *av* after lunch (*o* dinner).

doposcì [dopoʃ'ʃi] *sm inv* après-ski outfit.

doposcu'ola *sm inv* school club offering extra tuition and recreational facilities.

dopo'tutto *av* (*tutto considerato*) after all.

doppi'aggio [dop'pjaddʒo] *sm* (*CINEMA*) dubbing.

doppi'are *vt* (*NAUT*) to round; (*SPORT*) to lap; (*CINEMA*) to dub.

'doppio, a *ag* double; (*fig: falso*) double-dealing, deceitful ♦ *sm* (*quantità*): **il ~** (**di**) twice as much (*o* many), double the amount (*o* number) of; (SPORT) doubles pl ♦ av double.

doppi'one sm duplicate (copy).

doppio'petto sm double-breasted jacket.

do'rare vt to gild; (CUC) to brown; **do'rato, a** ag golden; (ricoperto d'oro) gilt, gilded; **dora'tura** sf gilding.

dormicchi'are [dormik'kjare] vi to doze.

dormigli'one, a [dormiʎ'ʎone] sm/f sleepyhead.

dor'mire vt, vi to sleep; **dor'mita** sf: **farsi una dormita** to have a good sleep.

dormi'torio sm dormitory.

dormi'veglia [dormi'veʎʎa] sm drowsiness.

'dorso sm back; (di montagna) ridge, crest; (di libro) spine; **a ~ di cavallo** on horseback.

do'sare vt to measure out; (MED) to dose.

'dose sf quantity, amount; (MED) dose.

'dosso sm (rilievo) rise; (di strada) bump; (dorso): **levarsi di ~ i vestiti** to take one's clothes off.

do'tare vt: ~ **di** to provide o supply with; (fig) to endow with; **dotazi'one** sf (insieme di beni) endowment; (di macchine etc) equipment.

'dote sf (di sposa) dowry; (assegnata a un ente) endowment; (fig) gift, talent.

Dott. abbr (= dottore) Dr.

'dotto, a ag (colto) learned ♦ sm (sapiente) scholar; (ANAT) duct.

dotto'rato sm degree; ~ **di ricerca** doctorate, doctor's degree.

dot'tore, essa sm/f doctor.

dot'trina sf doctrine.

Dott.ssa abbr (= dottoressa) Dr.

'dove av (gen) where; (in cui) where, in which; (dovunque) wherever ♦ cong (mentre, laddove) whereas; ~ **sei?/vai?** where are you?/are you going?; **dimmi dov'è** tell me where it is; **di ~ sei?** where are you from?; **per ~ si passa?** which way should we go?; **la città ~ abito** the town where o in which I live; **siediti ~ vuoi** sit wherever you like

do'vere sm (obbligo) duty ♦ vt (essere debitore): ~ **qc (a qn)** to owe (sb) sth

♦ vi (seguito dall'infinito: obbligo) to have to; **rivolgersi a chi di ~** to apply to the appropriate authority o person; **lui deve farlo** he has to do it, he must do it; **è dovuto partire** he had to leave; **ha dovuto pagare** he had to pay; (: intenzione): **devo partire domani** I'm (due) to leave tomorrow; (: probabilità): **dev'essere tardi** it must be late; **come si deve** (lavorare, comportarsi) properly; **una persona come si deve** a respectable person.

dove'roso, a ag (right and) proper.

do'vunque av (in qualunque luogo) wherever; (dappertutto) everywhere; ~ **io vada** wherever I go.

do'vuto, a ag (causato): ~ **a** due to.

doz'zina [dod'dzina] sf dozen; **una ~ di uova** a dozen eggs.

dozzi'nale [doddzi'nale] ag cheap, second-rate.

dra'gare vt to dredge.

'drago, ghi sm dragon.

'dramma, i sm drama; **dram'matico a, ci, che** ag dramatic; **drammatiz'zare** vt to dramatize; **dramma'turgo, ghi** sm playwright, dramatist.

drappeggi'are [draped'dʒare] vt to drape.

drap'pello sm (MIL) squad; (gruppo) band, group.

'drastico, a, ci, che ag drastic.

dre'naggio [dre'nad_dʒo] sm drainage.

dre'nare vt to drain.

'dritto, a ag, av = **diritto.**

driz'zare [drit'tsare] vt (far tornare diritto) to straighten; (volgere: sguardo, occhi) to turn, direct; (innalzare: antenna, muro) to erect; ~**rsi** vr: ~**rsi (in piedi)** to stand up; ~ **le orecchie** to prick up one's ears.

'droga, ghe sf (sostanza aromatica) spice; (stupefacente) drug; **dro'gare** vt to season, spice; to drug, dope; **drogarsi** vr to take drugs; **dro'gato, a** sm/f drug addict.

droghe'ria [droge'ria] sf grocer's shop (BRIT), grocery (store) (US).

'dubbio, a ag (incerto) doubtful, dubious; (ambiguo) dubious ♦ sm (in-

certezza) doubt; **avere il ~ che** to be afraid that, suspect that; **mettere in ~ qc** to question sth; **dubbi'oso, a** *ag* doubtful, dubious.

dubi'tare *vi*: **~ di** to doubt; *(risultato)* to be doubtful of.

Dub'lino *sf* Dublin.

'duca, chi *sm* duke.

du'chessa [du'kessa] *sf* duchess.

'due *num* two.

due'cento [due'tʃɛnto] *num* two hundred ♦ *sm*: **il D~** the thirteenth century.

due'pezzi [due'pɛttsi] *sm (costume da bagno)* two-piece swimsuit; *(abito femminile)* two-piece suit.

du'etto *sm* duet.

'dunque *cong (perciò)* so, therefore; *(riprendendo il discorso)* well (then) ♦ *sm inv*: **venire al ~** to come to the point.

du'omo *sm* cathedral.

'duplex *sm inv (TEL)* party line.

dupli'cato *sm* duplicate.

'duplice ['duplitʃe] *ag* double, twofold; **in ~ copia** in duplicate.

du'rante *prep* during.

du'rare *vi* to last; **~ fatica a** to have difficulty in; **du'rata** *sf* length (of time); duration; **dura'turo, a** *ag* lasting; **du'revole** *ag* lasting.

du'rezza [du'rettsa] *sf* hardness; stubbornness; harshness; toughness.

'duro, a *ag (pietra, lavoro, materasso, problema)* hard; *(persona: ostinato)* stubborn, obstinate; *(: severo)* harsh, hard; *(voce)* harsh; *(carne)* tough ♦ *sm* hardness; *(difficoltà)* hard part; *(persona)* tough guy; **tener ~** to stand firm, hold out; **~ d'orecchi** hard of hearing.

du'rone *sm* hard skin.

E

e *(dav V spesso* **ed**) *cong* and; **~ lui?** what about him?; **~ compralo!** well buy it then!

E. *abbr (= est)* E.

è *vb vedi* **essere**.

'ebano *sm* ebony.

eb'bene *cong* well (then).

eb'brezza [eb'brettsa] *sf* intoxication.

'ebbro, a *ag* drunk; **~ di** *(gioia etc)* beside o.s. *o* wild with.

'ebete *ag* stupid, idiotic.

ebollizi'one [ebollit'tsjone] *sf* boiling; **punto di ~** boiling point.

e'braico, a, ci, che *ag* Hebrew, Hebraic ♦ *sm (LING)* Hebrew.

e'breo, a *ag* Jewish ♦ *sm/f* Jew/Jewess.

'Ebridi *sfpl*: **le (isole) ~** the Hebrides.

ecc *av abbr (= eccetera)* etc.

ecce'denza [ettʃe'dɛntsa] *sf* excess, surplus.

ec'cedere [et'tʃɛdere] *vt* to exceed ♦ *vi* to go too far; **~ nel bere/mangiare** to indulge in drink/food to excess.

eccel'lente [ettʃel'lɛnte] *ag* excellent; **eccel'lenza** *sf* excellence; *(titolo)* Excellency.

ec'cellere [et'tʃɛllere] *vi*: **~ (in)** to excel (at); **ec'celso, a** *pp di* **eccellere**.

ec'centrico, a, ci, che [et'tʃɛntriko] *ag* eccentric.

ecces'sivo, a [ettʃes'sivo] *ag* excessive.

ec'cesso [et'tʃɛsso] *sm* excess; **all'~** *(gentile, generoso)* to excess, excessively; **~ di velocità** *(AUT)* speeding.

ec'cetera [et'tʃetera] *av* et cetera, and so on.

ec'cetto [et'tʃetto] *prep* except, with the exception of; **~ che** except, other than; **~ che (non)** unless.

eccettu'are [ettʃettu'are] *vt* to except.

eccezio'nale [ettʃetsjo'nale] *ag* exceptional.

eccezi'one [ettʃet'tsjone] *sf* exception; *(DIR)* objection; **a ~ di** with the exception of, except for; **d'~** exceptional.

ec'cidio [et'tʃidjo] *sm* massacre.

ecci'tare [ettʃi'tare] *vt (curiosità, interesse)* to excite, arouse; *(folla)* to incite; **~rsi** *vr* to get excited; *(sessualmente)* to become aroused; **eccitazi'one** *sf* excitement.

'ecco *av (per dimostrare)*: **~ il treno!** here's *o* here comes the train!; *(dav pron)*: **~mi!** here I am!; **~ne uno!** here's one (of them)!; *(dav pp)*: **~**

fatto! there, that's it done!

echeggi'are [ekked'dʒare] vi to echo.

e'clissi sf eclipse.

'eco (pl(m) **'echi**) sm o f echo.

ecolo'gia [ekolo'dʒia] sf ecology.

econo'mia sf economy; (scienza) economics sg; (risparmio: azione) saving; **fare** ~ to economize, make economies; **eco'nomico, a, ci, che** ag economic; (poco costoso) economical; **econo'mista, i** sm economist; **economiz'zare** vt, vi to save; **e'conomo, a** ag thrifty ♦ sm/f (INS) bursar.

ed cong vedi **e**.

'edera sf ivy.

e'dicola sf newspaper kiosk o stand (US).

edifi'care vt to build; (fig: teoria, azienda) to establish; (indurre al bene) to edify.

edi'ficio [edi'fitʃo] sm building; (fig) structure.

e'dile ag building cpd; **edi'lizia** sf building, building trade; **edi'lizio, a** ag building cpd.

Edim'burgo sf Edinburgh.

edi'tore, 'trice ag publishing cpd ♦ sm/f publisher; (curatore) editor; **edito'ria** sf publishing; **editori'ale** ag publishing cpd ♦ sm editorial, leader.

edizi'one [edit'tsjone] sf edition; (tiratura) printing; (di manifestazioni, feste etc) production.

edu'care vt to educate; (gusto, mente) to train; ~ **qn a fare** to train sb to do; **edu'cato, a** ag polite, well-mannered; **educazi'one** sf education; (familiare) upbringing; (comportamento) (good) manners pl; **educazione fisica** (INS) physical training o education.

effemi'nato, a ag effeminate.

effet'tivo, a ag (reale) real, actual; (impiegato, professore) permanent; (MIL) regular ♦ sm (MIL) strength; (di patrimonio etc) sum total.

ef'fetto sm effect; (COMM: cambiale) bill; (fig: impressione) impression; **in ~i** in fact, actually; **effettu'are** vt to effect, carry out.

effi'cace [effi'katʃe] ag effective.

effici'ente [effi'tʃɛnte] ag efficient; **effici'enza** sf efficiency.

ef'fimero, a ag ephemeral.

E'geo [e'dʒɛo] sm: **l'~, il mare ~** the Aegean (Sea).

E'gitto [e'dʒitto] sm: **l'~** Egypt.

egizi'ano, a [edʒit'tsjano] ag, sm/f Egyptian.

'egli ['eʎʎi] pron he; ~ **stesso** he himself.

ego'ismo sm selfishness, egoism; **ego'ista, i, e** ag selfish, egoistic ♦ sm/f egoist.

egr. abbr = **egregio**.

e'gregio, a, gi, gie [e'grɛdʒo] ag distinguished; (nelle lettere): **E~ Signore** Dear Sir.

eguagli'anza etc [egwaʎ'ʎantsa] = **uguaglianza** etc.

E.I. abbr = **Esercito Italiano**.

elabo'rare vt (progetto) to work out, elaborate; (dati) to process; (digerire) to digest; **elabora'tore** sm (INFORM): **elaboratore elettronico** computer; **elaborazi'one** sf elaboration; digestion; **elaborazione dei dati** data processing.

e'lastico, a, ci, che ag elastic; (fig: andatura) springy; (: decisione, vedute) flexible ♦ sm (gommino) rubber band; (per il cucito) elastic no pl.

ele'fante sm elephant.

ele'gante ag elegant.

e'leggere [e'lɛddʒere] vt to elect.

elemen'tare ag elementary; **le (scuole) ~i** sfpl primary (BRIT) o grade (US) school.

ele'mento sm element; (parte componente) element, component, part; **~i** smpl (della scienza etc) elements, rudiments.

ele'mosina sf charity, alms pl; **chiedere l'~** to beg.

elen'care vt to list.

e'lenco, chi sm list; ~ **telefonico** telephone directory.

e'letto, a pp di **eleggere** ♦ sm/f (nominato) elected member; **eletto'rale** ag electoral, election cpd; **eletto'rato**

sm electorate; **elet'tore, 'trice** *sm/f* voter, elector.

elet'trauto *sm inv* workshop for car electrical repairs; (*tecnico*) car electrician.

elettri'cista, i [elettri'tʃista] *sm* electrician.

elettricità [elettritʃi'ta] *sf* electricity.

e'lettrico, a, ci, che *ag* electric(al).

elettriz'zare [elettrid'dzare] *vt* to electrify.

e'lettro... *prefisso:* **elettrocardio-'gramma, i** *sm* electrocardiogram; **elet-trodo'mestico, a, ci, che** *ag:* **apparec-chi elettrodomestici** domestic (electrical) appliances; **elet'trone** *sm* electron; **elet'tronica** *sf* electronics *sg;* **elet'tronico, a, ci, che** *ag* electronic.

ele'vare *vt* to raise; (*edificio*) to erect; (*multa*) to impose.

elezi'one [elet'tsjone] *sf* election; **~i** *sfpl* (*POL*) election(s).

'elica, che *sf* propeller.

eli'cottero *sm* helicopter.

elimi'nare *vt* to eliminate; **elimina'toria** *sf* eliminating round.

'elio *sm* helium.

'ella *pron sf* (*forma di cortesia*) you; **~ stessa** she herself; you yourself.

el'metto *sm* helmet.

e'logio [e'lɔdʒo] *sm* (*discorso, scritto*) eulogy; (*lode*) praise (*di solito no pl*).

elo'quente *ag* eloquent.

e'ludere *vt* to evade; **elu'sivo, a** *ag* evasive.

ema'nare *vt* to send out, give off; (*fig: leggi, decreti*) to issue ♦ *vi:* **~ da** to come from.

emanci'pare [emantʃi'pare] *vt* to emancipate; **~rsi** *vr* (*fig*) to become liberated *o* emancipated.

embri'one *sm* embryo.

emenda'mento *sm* amendment.

emen'dare *vt* to amend.

emer'genza [emer'dʒentsa] *sf* emergency; **in caso di ~** in an emergency.

e'mergere [e'mɛrdʒere] *vi* to emerge; (*sommergibile*) to surface; (*fig: distin-guersi*) to stand out; **e'merso, a** *pp di*

emergere.

e'messo, a *pp di* **emettere.**

e'mettere *vt* (*suono, luce*) to give out, emit; (*onde radio*) to send out; (*assegno, francobollo, ordine*) to issue; (*fig: giudizio*) to express, voice.

emi'crania *sf* migraine.

emi'grare *vi* to emigrate; **emigrazi'one** *sf* emigration.

emi'nente *ag* eminent, distinguished.

emis'fero *sm* hemisphere; **~ boreale/australe** northern/southern hemisphere.

emissi'one *sf* (*vedi emettere*) emission; sending out; issue; (*RADIO*) broadcast.

emit'tente *ag* (*banca*) issuing; (*RADIO*) broadcasting, transmitting ♦ *sf* (*RADIO*) transmitter.

emorra'gia, 'gie [emorra'dʒia] *sf* haemorrhage.

emo'tivo, a *ag* emotional.

emozio'nante [emottsjo'nante] *ag* exciting, thrilling.

emozio'nare [emottsjo'nare] *vt* (*appassionare*) to thrill, excite; (*commuovere*) to move; (*innervosire*) to upset; **~rsi** *vr* to be excited; to be moved; to be upset.

emozi'one [emot'tsjone] *sf* emotion; (*agitazione*) excitement.

'empio, a *ag* (*sacrilego*) impious; (*spietato*) cruel, pitiless; (*malvagio*) wicked, evil.

emulsi'one *sf* emulsion.

enciclope'dia [entʃiklope'dia] *sf* encyclopaedia.

endove'noso, a *ag* (*MED*) intravenous.

'ENEL ['enel] *sigla m* (= *Ente Nazionale per l'Energia Elettrica*) ≈ C.E.G.B. (= *Central Electricity Generating Board*).

ener'gia, 'gie [ener'dʒia] *sf* (*FISICA*) energy; (*fig*) energy, strength, vigour; **e'nergico, a, ci, che** *ag* energetic, vigorous.

'enfasi *sf* emphasis; (*peg*) bombast, pomposity; **en'fatico, a, ci, che** *ag* emphatic; pompous.

'ENIT ['enit] *sigla m* = **Ente Nazionale Italiano per il Turismo.**

en'nesimo, a *ag* (*MAT, fig*) nth; **per**

l'~a volta for the umpteenth time.

e'norme *ag* enormous, huge; enormità *sf inv* enormity, huge size; (*assurdità*) absurdity; non dire enormità! don't talk nonsense!

'ente *sm* (*istituzione*) body, board, corporation; (*FILOSOFIA*) being.

en'trambi, e *pron pl* both (of them) ♦ *ag pl*: ~ i ragazzi both boys, both of the boys.

en'trare *vi* to enter, go (*o come*) in; ~ in (*luogo*) to enter, go (*o come*) into; (*trovar posto, poter stare*) to fit into; (*essere ammesso a: club etc*) to join, become a member of; ~ in automobile to get into the car; far ~ qn (*visitatore etc*) to show sb in; questo non c'entra (*fig*) that's got nothing to do with it; en'trata *sf* entrance, entry; entrate *sfpl* (*COMM*) receipts, takings; (*ECON*) income *sg*.

'entro *prep* (*temporale*) within.

entusias'mare *vt* to excite, fill with enthusiasm; ~rsi (per qc/qn) to become enthusiastic (about sth/sb); entusi'asmo *sm* enthusiasm; entusi'asta, i, e *ag* enthusiastic ♦ *sm/f* enthusiast; entusi'astico, a, ci, che *ag* enthusiastic.

enunci'are [enun'tʃare] *vt* (*teoria*) to enunciate, set out.

'epico, a, ci, che *ag* epic.

epide'mia *sf* epidemic.

epi'dermide *sf* skin, epidermis.

Epifa'nia *sf* Epiphany.

epiles'sia *sf* epilepsy.

e'pilogo, ghi *sm* conclusion.

epi'sodio *sm* episode.

e'piteto *sm* epithet.

'epoca, che *sf* (*periodo storico*) age, era; (*tempo*) time; (*GEO*) age.

ep'pure *cong* and yet, nevertheless.

epu'rare *vt* (*POL*) to purge.

equa'tore *sm* equator.

equazi'one [ekwat'tsjone] *sf* (*MAT*) equation.

e'questre *ag* equestrian.

equi'latero, a *ag* equilateral.

equili'brare *vt* to balance; equi'librio *sm* balance, equilibrium; perdere l'~ to lose one's balance.

e'quino, a *ag* horse *cpd*, equine.

equipaggi'are [ekwipad'dʒare] *vt* (*di persone*) to man; (*di mezzi*) to equip; equi'paggio *sm* crew.

equipa'rare *vt* to make equal.

equità *sf* equity, fairness.

equitazi'one [ekwitat'tsjone] *sf* (horse-) riding.

equiva'lente *ag*, *sm* equivalent; equiva'lenza *sf* equivalence.

equivo'care *vi* to misunderstand; e'quivoco, a, ci, che *ag* equivocal, ambiguous; (*sospetto*) dubious ♦ *sm* misunderstanding; a scanso di equivoci to avoid any misunderstanding; giocare sull'equivoco to equivocate.

'equo, a *ag* fair, just.

'era *sf* era.

'erba *sf* grass; (*aromatica, medicinale*) herb; in ~ (*fig*) budding; er'baccia, ce *sf* weed.

e'rede *sm/f* heir; eredità *sf* (*DIR*) inheritance; (*BIOL*) heredity; lasciare qc in eredità a qn to leave *o* bequeath sth to sb; eredi'tare *vt* to inherit; eredi'tario, a *ag* hereditary.

ere'mita, i *sm* hermit.

ere'sia *sf* heresy; e'retico, a, ci, che *ag* heretical ♦ *sm/f* heretic.

e'retto, a *pp di* erigere ♦ *ag* erect, upright; erezi'one *sf* (*FISIOL*) erection.

er'gastolo *sm* (*DIR: pena*) life imprisonment.

'erica *sf* heather.

e'rigere [e'ridʒere] *vt* to erect, raise; (*fig: fondare*) to found.

ermel'lino *sm* ermine.

er'metico, a, ci, che *ag* hermetic.

'ernia *sf* (*MED*) hernia.

e'roe *sm* hero.

ero'gare *vt* (*somme*) to distribute; (: *per beneficenza*) to donate; (*gas, servizi*) to supply.

e'roico, a, ci, che *ag* heroic.

ero'ina *sf* heroine; (*droga*) heroin.

ero'ismo *sm* heroism.

erosi'one *sf* erosion.

e'rotico, a, ci, che *ag* erotic.

er'rare *vi* (*vagare*) to wander, roam;

(*sbagliare*) to be mistaken.

er'rore *sm* error, mistake; (*morale*) error; **per** ~ by mistake.

'erta *sf* steep slope; **stare all'**~ to be on the alert.

erut'tare *vt* (*sog: vulcano*) to throw out, belch.

eruzi'one [erut'tsjone] *sf* eruption.

esacer'bare [ezatfer'bare] *vt* to exacerbate.

esage'rare [ezadʒe'rare] *vt* to exaggerate ♦ *vi* to exaggerate; (*eccedere*) to go too far; **esagerazi'one** *sf* exaggeration.

e'sagono *sm* hexagon.

esal'tare *vt* to exalt; (*entusiasmare*) to excite, stir; **esal'tato, a** *sm/f* fanatic.

e'same *sm* examination; (*INS*) exam, examination; **fare** *o* **dare un** ~ to sit *o* take an exam; ~ **del sangue** blood test.

esami'nare *vt* to examine.

e'sanime *ag* lifeless.

esaspe'rare *vt* to exasperate; to exacerbate; **~rsi** *vr* to become annoyed *o* exasperated; **esasperazi'one** *sf* exasperation.

esatta'mente *av* exactly; accurately, precisely.

esat'tezza [ezat'tettsa] *sf* exactitude, accuracy, precision.

e'satto, a *pp di* **esigere** ♦ *ag* (*calcolo, ora*) correct, right, exact; (*preciso*) accurate, precise; (*puntuale*) punctual.

esat'tore *sm* (*di imposte etc*) collector.

esau'dire *vt* to grant, fulfil.

esauri'ente *ag* exhaustive.

esauri'mento *sm* exhaustion; ~ **nervoso** nervous breakdown.

esau'rire *vt* (*stancare*) to exhaust, wear out; (*provviste, miniera*) to exhaust; **~rsi** *vr* to exhaust o.s., wear o.s. out; (*provviste*) to run out; **esau'rito, a** *ag* exhausted; (*merci*) sold out; (*libri*) out of print; **registrare il tutto esaurito** (*TEATRO*) to have a full house; **e'sausto, a** *ag* exhausted.

'esca (*pl* **esche**) *sf* bait.

escande'scenza [eskandef'ʃentsa] *sf*: **dare in** ~**e** to lose one's temper, fly into a rage.

'esce *etc* ['ɛʃe] *vb vedi* **uscire**.

eschi'mese [eski'mese] *ag, sm/f* Eskimo.

escla'mare *vi* to exclaim, cry out; **esclamazi'one** *sf* exclamation.

es'cludere *vt* to exclude.

esclu'siva *sf* (*DIR, COMM*) exclusive *o* sole rights *pl*.

esclu'sivo, a *ag* exclusive.

es'cluso, a *pp di* **escludere**.

'esco *etc vb vedi* **uscire**.

escursi'one *sf* (*gita*) excursion, trip; (: *a piedi*) hike, walk; (*METEOR*) range.

ese'crare *vt* to loathe, abhor.

esecu'tivo, a *ag, sm* executive.

esecu'tore, 'trice *sm/f* (*MUS*) performer; (*DIR*) executor.

esecuzi'one [ezekut'tsjone] *sf* execution, carrying out; (*MUS*) performance; ~ **capitale** execution.

esegu'ire *vt* to carry out, execute; (*MUS*) to perform, execute.

e'sempio *sm* example; **per** ~ for example, for instance; **fare un** ~ to give an example; **esem'plare** *ag* exemplary ♦ *sm* example; (*copia*) copy; **esemplifi'care** *vt* to exemplify.

esen'tare *vt*: ~ **qn/qc da** to exempt sb/ sth from.

e'sente *ag*: ~ **da** (*dispensato da*) exempt from; (*privo di*) free from; **esenzi'one** *sf* exemption.

e'sequie *sfpl* funeral rites; funeral service *sg*.

eser'cente [ezer'tʃente] *sm/f* trader, dealer; shopkeeper.

eserci'tare [ezertʃi'tare] *vt* (*professione*) to practise (*BRIT*), practice (*US*); (*allenare: corpo, mente*) to exercise, train; (*diritto*) to exercise; (*influenza, pressione*) to exert; **~rsi** *vr* to practise; **~rsi alla lotta** to practise fighting; **esercitazi'one** *sf* (*scolastica, militare*) exercise.

e'sercito [e'zertʃito] *sm* army.

eser'cizio [ezer'tʃittsjo] *sm* practice; exercising; (*fisico, di matematica*) exercise; (*ECON*) financial year; (*azienda*) business, concern; **in** ~ (*medico etc*) practising.

esi'bire *vt* to exhibit, display; (*documenti*) to produce, present; **~rsi**

vr (*attore*) to perform; (*fig*) to show off; **esibizi'one** *sf* exhibition; (*di documento*) presentation; (*spettacolo*) show, performance.

esi'gente [ezi'dʒɛnte] *ag* demanding; **esi'genza** *sf* demand, requirement.

e'sigere [e'zidʒere] *vt* (*pretendere*) to demand; (*richiedere*) to demand, require; (*imposte*) to collect.

e'siguo, a *ag* small, slight.

'esile *ag* (*persona*) slender, slim; (*stelo*) thin; (*voce*) faint.

esili'are *vt* to exile; **e'silio** *sm* exile.

e'simere *vt*: ~ **qn/qc da** to exempt sb/ sth from; ~**rsi da** to get out of.

esis'tenza [ezis'tɛntsa] *sf* existence.

e'sistere *vi* to exist.

esis'tito, a *pp di* **esistere**.

esi'tare *vi* to hesitate; **esitazi'one** *sf* hesitation.

'esito *sm* result, outcome.

'esodo *sm* exodus.

esone'rare *vt* to exempt.

e'sordio *sm* début.

esor'tare *vt*: ~ **qn a fare** to urge sb to do.

e'sotico, a, ci, che *ag* exotic.

es'pandere *vt* to expand; (*confini*) to extend; (*influenza*) to extend, spread; ~**rsi** *vr* to expand; **espansi'one** *sf* expansion; **espan'sivo, a** *ag* expansive, communicative.

espatri'are *vi* to leave one's country.

espedi'ente *sm* expedient.

es'pellere *vt* to expel.

esperi'enza [espe'rjɛntsa] *sf* experience; (*SCIENZA: prova*) experiment.

esperi'mento *sm* experiment.

es'perto, a *ag, sm* expert.

espi'are *vt* to atone for.

espi'rare *vt, vi* to breathe out.

espli'care *vt* (*attività*) to carry out, perform.

es'plicito, a [es'plitʃito] *ag* explicit.

es'plodere *vi* (*anche fig*) to explode ♦ *vt* to fire.

esplo'rare *vt* to explore; **esplora'tore** *sm* explorer; (*anche: giovane esploratore*) (boy) scout; (*NAUT*) scout (ship).

esplosi'one *sf* explosion; **esplo'sivo, a**

ag, sm explosive; **es'ploso, a** *pp di* **esplodere**.

espo'nente *sm/f* (*rappresentante*) representative.

es'porre *vt* (*merci*) to display; (*quadro*) to exhibit, show; (*fatti, idee*) to explain, set out; (*porre in pericolo, FOT*) to expose.

espor'tare *vt* to export; **esportazi'one** *sf* exportation; export.

esposizi'one [espozit'tsjone] *sf* displaying; exhibiting; setting out; (*anche FOT*) exposure; (*mostra*) exhibition; (*narrazione*) explanation, exposition.

es'posto, a *pp di* **esporre** ♦ *ag*: ~ **a nord** facing north ♦ *sm* (*AMM*) statement, account; (*: petizione*) petition.

espressi'one *sf* expression.

espres'sivo, a *ag* expressive.

es'presso, a *pp di* **esprimere** ♦ *ag* express ♦ *sm* (*lettera*) express letter; (*anche: treno* ~) express train; (*anche: caffè* ~) espresso.

es'primere *vt* to express.

espulsi'one *sf* expulsion; **es'pulso, a** *pp di* **espellere**.

'essa (*pl* **'esse**) *pron f vedi* **esso**.

es'senza [es'sɛntsa] *sf* essence; **essenzi'ale** *ag* essential; **l'essenziale** the main *o* most important thing.

PAROLA CHIAVE

'essere *sm* being; ~ **umano** human being
♦ *vb copulativo* **1** (*con attributo, sostantivo*) to be; **sei giovane/simpatico** you are *o* you're young/nice; **è medico** he is *o* he's a doctor
2 (+*di: appartenere*) to be; **di chi è la penna?** whose pen is it?; **è di Carla** it is *o* it's Carla's, it belongs to Carla
3 (+*di: provenire*) to be; **è di Venezia** he is *o* he's from Venice
4 (*data, ora*): **è il 15 agosto/lunedì** it is *o* it's the 15th of August/Monday; **che ora è?, che ore sono?** what time is it?; **è l'una** it is *o* it's one o'clock; **sono le due** it is *o* it's two o'clock
5 (*costare*): **quant'è?** how much is it?; **sono 20.000 lire** it's 20,000 lire

♦ *vb aus* **1** (*attivo*): ~ **arrivato/venuto** to have arrived/come; **è già partita** she has already left
2 (*passivo*) to be; ~ **fatto da** to be made by; **è stata uccisa** she has been killed
3 (*riflessivo*): **si sono lavati** they washed, they got washed
4 (+*da* +*infinito*): **è da farsi subito** it must be *o* is to be done immediately
♦ *vi* **1** (*esistere, trovarsi*) to be; **sono a casa** I'm at home; ~ **in piedi/seduto** to be standing/sitting
2: **esserci**: **c'è** there is; **ci sono** there are; **che c'è?** what's the matter?, what is it?; **ci sono!** (*fig: ho capito*) I get it!; *vedi anche* **ci**
♦ *vb impers*: **è tardi/Pasqua** it's late/Easter; **è possibile che venga** he may come; **è così** that's the way it is.

'esso, a *pron* it; (*riferito a persona: soggetto*) he/she; (: *complemento*) him/her; ~**i, e** *pron pl* they; (*complemento*) them.

est *sm* east.

'estasi *sf* ecstasy.

es'tate *sf* summer.

es'tendere *vt* to extend; ~**rsi** *vr* (*diffondersi*) to spread; (*territorio, confini*) to extend; **estensi'one** *sf* extension; (*di superficie*) expanse; (*di voce*) range.

esteri'ore *ag* outward, external.

es'terno, a *ag* (*porta, muro*) outer, outside; (*scala*) outside; (*alunno, impressione*) external ♦ *sm* outside; exterior ♦ *sm/f* (*allievo*) day pupil; **per uso** ~ for external use only.

'estero, a *ag* foreign ♦ *sm*: **all'**~ abroad.

es'teso, a *pp di* **estendere** ♦ *ag* extensive, large; **scrivere per ~** to write in full.

es'tetico, a, ci, che *ag* aesthetic ♦ *sf* (*disciplina*) aesthetics *sg*; (*bellezza*) attractiveness; **este'tista, i, e** *sm/f* beautician.

'estimo *sm* valuation; (*disciplina*) surveying.

es'tinguere *vt* to extinguish, put out; (*debito*) to pay off; ~**rsi** *vr* to go out; (*specie*) to become extinct; **es'tinto, a** *pp di* **estinguere**; **estin'tore** *sm* (fire) extinguisher; **estinzi'one** *sf* putting out; (*di specie*) extinction.

estir'pare *vt* (*pianta*) to uproot, pull up; (*fig: vizio*) to eradicate.

es'tivo, a *ag* summer *cpd*.

es'torcere [es'tɔrtʃere] *vt*: ~ **qc (a qn)** to extort sth (from sb); **es'torto, a** *pp di* estorcere.

estradizi'one [estradit'tsjone] *sf* extradition.

es'traneo, a *ag* foreign; (*discorso*) extraneous, unrelated ♦ *sm/f* stranger; **rimanere** ~ **a qc** to take no part in sth.

es'trarre *vt* to extract; (*minerali*) to mine; (*sorteggiare*) to draw; **es'tratto, a** *pp di* **estrarre** ♦ *sm* extract; (*di documento*) abstract; **estratto conto** statement of account; **estratto di nascita** birth certificate; **estrazi'one** *sf* extraction; mining; drawing *no pl*; draw.

estremità *sf inv* extremity, end ♦ *sfpl* (*ANAT*) extremities.

es'tremo, a *ag* extreme; (*ultimo: ora, tentativo*) final, last ♦ *sm* extreme; (*di pazienza, forze*) limit, end; ~**i** *smpl* (*AMM: dati essenziali*) details, particulars; **l'**~ **Oriente** the Far East.

'estro *sm* (*capriccio*) whim, fancy; (*ispirazione creativa*) inspiration; **es'troso, a** *ag* whimsical, capricious; inspired.

estro'verso, a *ag, sm* extrovert.

'esule *sm/f* exile.

età *sf inv* age; **all'**~ **di 8 anni** at the age of 8, at 8 years of age; **ha la mia ~** he (*o* she) is the same age as me *o* as I am; **raggiungere la maggiore** ~ to come of age; **essere in** ~ **minore** to be under age.

'etere *sm* ether; **e'tereo, a** *ag* ethereal.

eternità *sf* eternity.

e'terno, a *ag* eternal.

etero'geneo, a [etero'dʒɛneo] *ag* heterogeneous.

'etica *sf* ethics *sg*; *vedi anche* **etico**.

eti'chetta [eti'ketta] *sf* label; (*ce-rimoniale*): l'~ etiquette.
'etico, a, ci, che *ag* ethical.
etimolo'gia, 'gie [etimolo'dʒia] *sf* etymology.
Eti'opia *sf*: l'~ Ethiopia.
'Etna *sm*: l'~ Etna.
'etnico, a, ci, che *ag* ethnic.
e'trusco, a, schi, sche *ag, sm/f* Etruscan.
'ettaro *sm* hectare (= *10,000 m²*).
'etto *sm abbr* = ettogrammo.
etto'grammo *sm* hectogram(me) (= *100 grams*).
Eucaris'tia *sf*: l'~ the Eucharist.
Eu'ropa *sf*: l'~ Europe; euro'peo, a *ag, sm/f* European.
evacu'are *vt* to evacuate.
e'vadere *vi* (*fuggire*): ~ da to escape from ♦ *vt* (*sbrigare*) to deal with, dispatch; (*tasse*) to evade.
evan'gelico, a, ci, che [evan'dʒɛliko] *ag* evangelical.
evapo'rare *vi* to evaporate; evaporazi'one *sf* evaporation.
evasi'one *sf* (*vedi evadere*) escape; dispatch; ~ fiscale tax evasion.
eva'sivo, a *ag* evasive.
e'vaso, a *pp di* evadere ♦ *sm* escapee.
eveni'enza [eve'njɛntsa] *sf*: pronto(a) per ogni ~ ready for any eventuality.
e'vento *sm* event.
eventu'ale *ag* possible.
evi'dente *ag* evident, obvious; evi'denza *sf* obviousness; mettere in evidenza to point out, highlight.
evi'tare *vt* to avoid; ~ di fare to avoid doing; ~ qc a qn to spare sb sth.
'evo *sm* age, epoch.
evo'care *vt* to evoke.
evo'luto, a *pp di* evolvere ♦ *ag* (*civiltà*) (highly) developed, advanced; (*persona*) independent.
evoluzi'one [evolut'tsjone] *sf* evolution.
e'volversi *vr* to evolve.
ev'viva *escl* hurrah!; ~ il re! long live the king!, hurrah for the king!
ex *prefisso* ex, former.
'extra *ag inv* first-rate; top-quality ♦ *sm inv* extra; extraconiu'gale *ag* extra-

marital.

F

fa *vb vedi* fare ♦ *sm inv* (*MUS*) F; (: *solfeggiando la scala*) fa ♦ *av*: 10 anni ~ 10 years ago.
fabbi'sogno [fabbi'zoɲɲo] *sm* needs *pl*, requirements *pl*.
'fabbrica *sf* factory; fabbri'cante *sm* manufacturer, maker; fabbri'care *vt* to build; (*produrre*) to manufacture, make; (*fig*) to fabricate, invent.
'fabbro *sm* (black)smith.
fac'cenda [fat'tʃɛnda] *sf* matter, affair; (*cosa da fare*) task, chore.
fac'chino [fak'kino] *sm* porter.
'faccia, ce ['fattʃa] *sf* face; (*di moneta, medaglia*) side; ~ a ~ face to face.
facci'ata [fat'tʃata] *sf* façade; (*di pagina*) side.
'faccio ['fattʃo] *vb vedi* fare.
fa'ceto, a [fa'tʃeto] *ag* witty, humorous.
'facile ['fatʃile] *ag* easy; (*affabile*) easy-going; (*disposto*): ~ a inclined to, prone to; (*probabile*): è ~ che piova it's likely to rain; facilità *sf* easiness; (*disposizione, dono*) aptitude; facili'tare *vt* to make easier.
facino'roso, a [fatʃino'roso] *ag* violent.
facoltà *sf inv* faculty; (*CHIMICA*) property; (*autorità*) power.
facolta'tivo, a *ag* optional; (*fermata d'autobus*) request *cpd*.
fac'simile *sm* facsimile.
'faggio ['faddʒo] *sm* beech.
fagi'ano [fa'dʒano] *sm* pheasant.
fagio'lino [fadʒo'lino] *sm* French (*BRIT*) o string bean.
fagi'olo [fa'dʒɔlo] *sm* bean.
fa'gotto *sm* bundle; (*MUS*) bassoon; far ~ (*fig*) to pack up and go.
'fai *vb vedi* fare.
'falce ['faltʃe] *sf* scythe; fal'cetto *sm* sickle; falci'are *vt* to cut; (*fig*) to mow down.
'falco, chi *sm* hawk.
fal'cone *sm* falcon.
'falda *sf* layer, stratum; (*di cappello*)

falegname

91

brim; (di cappotto) tails pl; (di monte) lower slope; (di tetto) pitch; **nevica a larghe ~e** the snow is falling in large flakes; **abito a ~e** tails pl.

fale'gname [faleɲ'ɲame] sm joiner.

fal'lace [fal'latʃe] ag misleading.

falli'mento sm failure; bankruptcy.

fal'lire vi (non riuscire): ~ **(in)** to fail (in); (DIR) to go bankrupt ♦ vt (colpo, bersaglio) to miss; **fal'lito, a** ag unsuccessful; bankrupt ♦ sm/f bankrupt.

'fallo sm error, mistake; (imperfezione) defect, flaw; (SPORT) foul; fault; **senza ~** without fail.

falò sm inv bonfire.

fal'sare vt to distort, misrepresent; **fal'sario** sm forger; counterfeiter; **falsifi'care** vt to forge; (monete) to forge, counterfeit.

'falso, a ag false; (errato) wrong; (falsificato) forged; fake; (: oro, gioielli) imitation cpd ♦ sm forgery; **giurare il ~** to commit perjury.

'fama sf fame; (reputazione) reputation, name.

'fame sf hunger; **aver ~** to be hungry; **fa'melico, a, ci, che** ag ravenous.

fa'miglia [fa'miʎʎa] sf family.

famili'are ag (della famiglia) family cpd; (ben noto) familiar; (rapporti, atmosfera) friendly; (LING) informal, colloquial ♦ sm/f relative, relation; **familiarità** sf familiarity; friendliness; informality.

fa'moso, a ag famous, well-known.

fa'nale sm (AUT) light, lamp (BRIT); (luce stradale, NAUT) light; (di faro) beacon.

fa'natico, a, ci, che ag fanatical; (del teatro, calcio etc): ~ **di** o **per** mad o crazy about ♦ sm/f fanatic; (tifoso) fan.

fanci'ullo, a [fan'tʃullo] sm/f child.

fan'donia sf tall story; **~e** sfpl (assurdità) nonsense sg.

fan'fara sf brass band; (musica) fanfare.

'fango, ghi sm mud; **fan'goso, a** ag muddy.

'fanno vb vedi fare.

fannul'lone, a sm/f idler, loafer.

fantasci'enza [fantaʃ'ʃɛntsa] sf science fiction.

fanta'sia sf fantasy, imagination; (capriccio) whim, caprice ♦ ag inv: **vestito ~** patterned dress.

fan'tasma, i sm ghost, phantom.

fan'tastico, a, ci, che ag fantastic; (potenza, ingegno) imaginative.

'fante sm infantryman; (CARTE) jack, knave (BRIT); **fante'ria** sf infantry.

fan'toccio [fan'tɔttʃo] sm puppet.

fara'butto sm crook.

far'dello sm bundle; (fig) burden.

PAROLA CHIAVE

'fare sm **1** (modo di fare): **con ~ distratto** absent-mindedly; **ha un ~ simpatico** he has a pleasant manner **2**: **sul far del giorno/della notte** at daybreak/nightfall

♦ vt **1** (fabbricare, creare) to make; (: casa) to build; (: assegno) to make out; ~ **un pasto/una promessa/un film** to make a meal/a promise/a film; ~ **rumore** to make a noise

2 (effettuare: lavoro, attività, studi) to do; (: sport) to play; **cosa fa?** (adesso) what are you doing?; (di professione) what do you do?; ~ **psicologia/italiano** (INS) to do psychology/Italian; ~ **un viaggio** to go on a trip o journey; ~ **una passeggiata** to go for a walk; ~ **la spesa** to do the shopping

3 (funzione) to be; (TEATRO) to play, be; ~ **il medico** to be a doctor; ~ **il malato** (fingere) to act the invalid

4 (suscitare: sentimenti): ~ **paura a qn** to frighten sb; **(non) fa niente** (non importa) it doesn't matter

5 (ammontare): **3 più 3 fa 6** 3 and 3 are o make 6; **fanno 6.000 lire** that's 6,000 lire; **Roma fa 2.000.000 di abitanti** Rome has 2,000,000 inhabitants; **che ora fai?** what time do you make it?

6 (+infinito): **far ~ qc a qn** (obbligare) to make sb do sth; (permettere) to let sb do sth; **fammi vedere** let me see; **far partire il motore** to start (up) the engine; **far riparare la macchina/costruire una casa** to get o have the car repaired/a house built

7: ~**rsi**: ~**rsi una gonna** to make o.s. a skirt; ~**rsi un nome** to make a name for o.s.; ~**rsi la permanente** to get a perm; ~**rsi tagliare i capelli** to get one's hair cut; ~**rsi operare** to have an operation

8 (*fraseologia*): **farcela** to succeed, manage; **non ce la faccio più** I can't go on; **ce la faremo** we'll make it; **me l'hanno fatta!** (*imbrogliare*) I've been done!; **lo facevo più giovane** I thought he was younger; **fare sì/no con la testa** to nod/shake one's head

♦ *vi* **1** (*agire*) to act, do; **fate come volete** do as you like; ~ **presto** to be quick; ~ **da** to act as; **non c'è niente da** ~ it's no use; **saperci** ~ **con qn/qc** to know how to deal with sb/sth; **faccia pure!** go ahead!

2 (*dire*) to say; **"davvero?" fece** "really?" he said

3: ~ **per** (*essere adatto*) to be suitable for; ~ **per** ~ **qc** to be about to do sth; **fece per andarsene** he made as if to leave

4: ~**rsi**: **si fa così** you do it like this, this is the way it's done; **non si fa così!** (*rimprovero*) that's no way to behave!; **la festa non si fa** the party is off

5: ~ **a gara con qn** to compete *o* vie with sb; ~ **a pugni** to come to blows; ~ **in tempo a** ~ to be in time to do

♦ *vb impers*: **fa bel tempo** the weather is fine; **fa caldo/freddo** it's hot/cold; **fa notte** it's getting dark

♦ *vr*: ~**rsi 1** (*diventare*) to become; ~**rsi prete** to become a priest; ~**rsi grande/vecchio** to grow tall/old

2 (*spostarsi*): ~**rsi avanti/indietro** to move forward/back

3 (*fam*: *drogarsi*) to be a junkie.

far'falla *sf* butterfly.

fa'rina *sf* flour.

farma'cia, 'cie [farma'tʃia] *sf* pharmacy; (*negozio*) chemist's (shop) (*BRIT*), pharmacy; **farma'cista, i, e** *sm/f* chemist (*BRIT*), pharmacist.

'farmaco, ci *o* **chi** *sm* drug, medicine.

'faro *sm* (*NAUT*) lighthouse; (*AER*) beacon; (*AUT*) headlight.

'farsa *sf* farce.

'fascia, sce ['faʃʃa] *sf* band, strip; (*MED*) bandage; (*di sindaco, ufficiale*) sash; (*parte di territorio*) strip, belt; (*di contribuenti etc*) group, band; **essere in ~sce** (*anche fig*) to be in one's infancy; ~ **oraria** time band.

fasci'are [faʃ'ʃare] *vt* to bind; (*MED*) to bandage; (*bambino*) to put a nappy (*BRIT*) *o* diaper (*US*) on.

fa'scicolo [faʃ'ʃikolo] *sm* (*di documenti*) file, dossier; (*di rivista*) issue, number; (*opuscolo*) booklet, pamphlet.

'fascino ['faʃʃino] *sm* charm, fascination.

'fascio ['faʃʃo] *sm* bundle, sheaf; (*di fiori*) bunch; (*di luce*) beam; (*POL*): **il F~** the Fascist Party.

fa'scismo [faʃ'ʃizmo] *sm* fascism.

'fase *sf* phase; (*TECN*) stroke; **fuori ~** (*motore*) rough.

fas'tidio *sm* bother, trouble; **dare ~ a qn** to bother *o* annoy sb; **sento ~ allo stomaco** my stomach's upset; **avere ~i con la polizia** to have trouble *o* bother with the police; **fastidi'oso, a** *ag* annoying, tiresome; (*schifiltoso*) fastidious.

'fasto *sm* pomp, splendour.

'fata *sf* fairy.

fa'tale *ag* fatal; (*inevitabile*) inevitable; (*fig*) irresistible; **fatalità** *sf inv* inevitability; (*avversità*) misfortune; (*fato*) fate, destiny.

fa'tica, che *sf* hard work, toil; (*sforzo*) effort; (*di metalli*) fatigue; **a** ~ with difficulty; **fare** ~ **a fare qc** to have a job doing sth; **fati'care** *vi* to toil; **faticare a fare qc** to have difficulty doing sth; **fati'coso, a** *ag* tiring, exhausting; (*lavoro*) laborious.

'fato *sm* fate, destiny.

'fatto, a *pp di* **fare** ♦ *ag*: **un uomo** ~ a grown man; ~ **a mano/in casa** hand-/home-made ♦ *sm* fact; (*azione*) deed; (*avvenimento*) event, occurrence; (*di romanzo, film*) action, story; **cogliere qn sul** ~ to catch sb red-handed; **il** ~ **sta** *o* **è che** the fact remains *o* is that;

in ~ **di** as for, as far as ... is concerned.
fat'tore *sm* (*AGR*) farm manager; (*MAT*, *elemento costitutivo*) factor.
fatto'ria *sf* farm; farmhouse.
fatto'rino *sm* errand-boy; (*di ufficio*) office-boy; (*d'albergo*) porter.
fat'tura *sf* (*COMM*) invoice; (*di abito*) tailoring; (*malia*) spell.
fattu'rare *vt* (*COMM*) to invoice; (*prodotto*) to produce; (*vino*) to adulterate.
'fatuo, a *ag* vain, fatuous.
'fauna *sf* fauna.
fau'tore, trice *sm/f* advocate, supporter.
fa'vella *sf* speech.
fa'villa *sf* spark.
'favola *sf* (*fiaba*) fairy tale; (*d'intento morale*) fable; (*fandonia*) yarn; **favo'loso, a** *ag* fabulous; (*incredibile*) incredible.
fa'vore *sm* favour; **per ~** please; **fare un ~ a qn** to do sb a favour; **favo'revole** *ag* favourable.
favo'rire *vt* to favour; (*il commercio, l'industria, le arti*) to promote, encourage; **vuole ~?** won't you help yourself?; **favorisca in salotto** please come into the sitting room; **favo'rito, a** *ag*, *sm/f* favourite.
fazzo'letto [fattso'letto] *sm* handkerchief; (*per la testa*) (head)scarf.
feb'braio *sm* February.
'febbre *sf* fever; **aver la ~** to have a high temperature; **~ da fieno** hay fever; **feb'brile** *ag* (*anche fig*) feverish.
'feccia, ce ['fettʃa] *sf* dregs *pl*.
'fecola *sf* potato flour.
fecondazi'one [fekondat'tsjone] *sf* fertilization; **~ artificiale** artificial insemination.
fe'condo, a *ag* fertile.
'fede *sf* (*credenza*) belief, faith; (*REL*) faith; (*fiducia*) faith, trust; (*fedeltà*) loyalty; (*anello*) wedding ring; (*attestato*) certificate; **aver ~ in qn** to have faith in sb; **in buona/cattiva ~** in good/bad faith; "**in ~**" (*DIR*) "in witness whereof"; **fe'dele** *ag*: **fedele (a)** faithful (to) ♦ *sm/f* follower; **i fedeli**

(*REL*) the faithful; **fedeltà** *sf* faithfulness; (*coniugale*) fidelity; **alta fedeltà** (*RADIO*) high fidelity.
'federa *sf* pillowslip, pillowcase.
fede'rale *ag* federal.
'fegato *sm* liver; (*fig*) guts *pl*, nerve.
'felce ['feltʃe] *sf* fern.
fe'lice [fe'litʃe] *ag* happy; (*fortunato*) lucky; **felicità** *sf* happiness.
felici'tarsi [felitʃi'tarsi] *vr* (*congratularsi*): **~ con qn per qc** to congratulate sb on sth.
fe'lino, a *ag*, *sm* feline.
'feltro *sm* felt.
'femmina *sf* (*ZOOL*, *TECN*) female; (*figlia*) girl, daughter; (*spesso peg*) woman; **femmi'nile** *ag* feminine; (*sesso*) female; (*lavoro, giornale, moda*) woman's ♦ *sm* (*LING*) feminine; **femmi'nismo** *sm* feminism.
'fendere *vt* to cut through; **fendi'nebbia** *sm inv* (*AUT*) fog lamp.
fe'nomeno *sm* phenomenon.
'feretro *sm* coffin.
feri'ale *ag* working *cpd*, work *cpd*, week *cpd*; **giorno ~** weekday.
'ferie *sfpl* holidays (*BRIT*), vacation *sg* (*US*); **andare in ~** to go on holiday *o* vacation.
fe'rire *vt* to injure; (*deliberatamente*: *MIL etc*) to wound; (*colpire*) to hurt; **fe'rita** *sf* injury, wound; **fe'rito, a** *sm/f* wounded *o* injured man/woman.
'ferma *sf* (*MIL*) (period of) service; (*CACCIA*): **cane da ~** pointer.
fer'maglio [fer'maʎʎo] *sm* clasp; (*gioiello*) brooch; (*per documenti*) clip.
fer'mare *vt* to stop, halt; (*POLIZIA*) to detain, hold; (*bottone etc*) to fasten, fix ♦ *vi* to stop; **~rsi** *vr* to stop, halt; **~rsi a fare qc** to stop to do sth.
fer'mata *sf* stop; **~ dell'autobus** bus stop.
fer'mento *sm* (*anche fig*) ferment; (*lievito*) yeast.
fer'mezza [fer'mettsa] *sf* (*fig*) firmness, steadfastness.
'fermo, a *ag* still, motionless; (*veicolo*) stationary; (*orologio*) not working; (*saldo: anche fig*) firm; (*voce, mano*)

steady ♦ *escl* stop!; keep still! ♦ *sm* (*chiusura*) catch, lock; (*DIR*): ~ **di polizia** police detention.

'**fermo** '**posta** *av, sm inv* poste restante (*BRIT*), general delivery (*US*).

fe'roce [fe'rɔtʃe] *ag* (*animale*) wild, fierce, ferocious; (*persona*) cruel, fierce; (*fame, dolore*) raging.

ferra'gosto *sm* (*festa*) feast of the Assumption; (*periodo*) August holidays *pl.*

ferra'menta *sfpl* ironmongery *sg* (*BRIT*), hardware *sg*; **negozio di** ~ ironmonger's (*BRIT*), hardware shop *o* store (*US*).

fer'rato, a *ag* (*FERR*): **strada** ~a railway (*BRIT*) *o* railroad (*US*) line; (*fig*): **essere** ~ **in** to be well up in.

'ferreo, a *ag* iron *cpd.*

'ferro *sm* iron; **una bistecca ai** ~**i a** grilled steak; ~ **battuto** wrought iron; ~ **da calza** knitting needle; ~ **di cavallo** horseshoe; ~ **da stiro** iron.

ferro'via *sf* railway (*BRIT*), railroad (*US*); ferrovi'ario, a *ag* railway *cpd* (*BRIT*), railroad *cpd* (*US*); ferrovi'ere *sm* railwayman (*BRIT*), railroad man (*US*).

'fertile *ag* fertile; fertiliz'zante *sm* fertilizer.

'fervido, a *ag* fervent.

fer'vore *sm* fervour, ardour; (*punto culminante*) height.

'fesso, a *pp di* fendere ♦ *ag* (*fam: sciocco*) crazy, cracked.

fes'sura *sf* crack, split; (*per gettone, moneta*) slot.

'festa *sf* (*religiosa*) feast; (*pubblica*) holiday; (*compleanno*) birthday; (*onomastico*) name day; (*ricevimento*) celebration, party; **far** ~ to have a holiday; to live it up; **far** ~ **a qn** to give sb a warm welcome.

festeggi'are [fested'dʒare] *vt* to celebrate; (*persona*) to have a celebration for.

fes'tino *sm* party; (*con balli*) ball.

fes'tivo, a *ag* (*atmosfera*) festive; **giorno** ~ holiday.

fes'toso, a *ag* merry, joyful.

fe'ticcio [fe'tittʃo] *sm* fetish.

'feto *sm* foetus (*BRIT*), fetus (*US*).

'fetta *sf* slice.

fettuc'cine [fettut'tʃine] *sfpl* (*CUC*) ribbon-shaped pasta.

FF.SS. *abbr* = **Ferrovie dello Stato.**

fi'aba *sf* fairy tale.

fi'acca *sf* weariness; (*svogliatezza*) listlessness.

fiac'care *vt* to weaken.

fi'acco, a, chi, che *ag* (*stanco*) tired, weary; (*svogliato*) listless; (*debole*) weak; (*mercato*) slack.

fi'accola *sf* torch.

fi'ala *sf* phial.

fi'amma *sf* flame.

fiam'mante *ag* (*colore*) flaming; **nuovo** ~ brand new.

fiammeggi'are [fjammed'dʒare] *vi* to blaze.

fiam'mifero *sm* match.

fiam'mingo, a, ghi, ghe *ag* Flemish ♦ *sm/f* Fleming ♦ *sm* (*LING*) Flemish; (*ZOOL*) flamingo; **i F~ghi** the Flemish.

fiancheggi'are [fjanked'dʒare] *vt* to border; (*fig*) to support, back (up); (*MIL*) to flank.

fi'anco, chi *sm* side; (*MIL*) flank; **di** ~ sideways, from the side; **a** ~ **a** ~ side by side.

fi'asco, schi *sm* flask; (*fig*) fiasco; **fare** ~ to be a fiasco.

fi'ato *sm* breath; (*resistenza*) stamina; **avere il** ~ **grosso** to be out of breath; **prendere** ~ to catch one's breath; ~**i** *smpl* (*MUS*) wind instruments; **strumento a** ~ wind instrument.

'fibbia *sf* buckle.

'fibra *sf* fibre; (*fig*) constitution.

fic'care *vt* to push, thrust, drive; ~**rsi** *vr* (*andare a finire*) to get to.

'fico, chi *sm* (*pianta*) fig tree; (*frutto*) fig; ~ **d'India** prickly pear; ~ **secco** dried fig.

fidanza'mento [fidantsa'mento] *sm* engagement.

fidan'zarsi [fidan'tsarsi] *vr* to get engaged; fidan'zato, a *sm/f* fiancé/fiancée.

fi'darsi *vr*: ~ **di** to trust; fi'dato, a *ag* reliable, trustworthy.

'fido, a *ag* faithful, loyal ♦ *sm* (*COMM*) credit.

fi'ducia [fi'dutʃa] *sf* confidence, trust; **incarico di ~** position of trust, responsible position; **persona di ~** reliable person.

fi'ele *sm* (*MED*) bile; (*fig*) bitterness.

fie'nile *sm* barn; hayloft.

fi'eno *sm* hay.

fi'era *sf* fair.

fie'rezza [fje'rettsa] *sf* pride.

fi'ero, a *ag* proud; (*crudele*) fierce, cruel; (*audace*) bold.

'fifa (*fam*) *sf*: **aver ~** to have the jitters.

'figlia ['fiʎʎa] *sf* daughter.

figli'astro, a [fiʎ'ʎastro] *sm/f* stepson/daughter.

'figlio ['fiʎʎo] *sm* son; (*senza distinzione di sesso*) child; **~ di papà** spoilt, wealthy young man; **~ unico** only child; **figli'occio, a, ci, ce** *sm/f* godchild, godson/daughter.

fi'gura *sf* figure; (*forma, aspetto esterno*) form, shape; (*illustrazione*) picture, illustration; **far ~** to look smart; **fare una brutta ~** to make a bad impression.

figu'rare *vi* to appear ♦ *vt*: **~rsi qc** to imagine sth; **~rsi** *vr*: **figurati!** imagine that!; **ti do noia? — ma figurati!** am I disturbing you? — not at all!

figura'tivo, a *ag* figurative.

figu'rina *sf* figurine; (*cartoncino*) picture card.

'fila *sf* row, line; (*coda*) queue; (*serie*) series, string; **di ~** in succession; **fare la ~** to queue; **in ~ indiana** in single file.

filantro'pia *sf* philanthropy.

fi'lare *vt* to spin ♦ *vi* (*baco, ragno*) to spin; (*formaggio fuso*) to go stringy; (*discorso*) to hang together; (*fam: amoreggiare*) to go steady; (*muoversi a forte velocità*) to go at full speed; (: *andarsene lestamente*) to make o.s. scarce; **~ diritto** (*fig*) to toe the line.

filas'trocca, che *sf* nursery rhyme.

filate'lia *sf* philately, stamp collecting.

fi'lato, a *ag* spun ♦ *sm* yarn; **3 giorni ~i** 3 days running *o* on end; **fila'tura** *sf* spinning; (*luogo*) spinning mill.

fi'letto *sm* (*di vite*) thread; (*di carne*) fillet.

fili'ale *ag* filial ♦ *sf* (*di impresa*) branch.

fili'grana *sf* (*in oreficeria*) filigree; (*su carta*) watermark.

film *sm inv* film; **fil'mare** *vt* to film.

'filo *sm* (*anche fig*) thread; (*filato*) yarn; (*metallico*) wire; (*di lama, rasoio*) edge; **per ~ e per segno** in detail; **~ d'erba** blade of grass; **~ di perle** string of pearls; **~ spinato** barbed wire; **con un ~ di voce** in a whisper.

'filobus *sm inv* trolley bus.

filon'cino [filon'tʃino] *sm* ≈ French stick.

fi'lone *sm* (*di minerali*) seam, vein; (*pane*) ≈ Vienna loaf; (*fig*) trend.

filoso'fia *sf* philosophy; **fi'losofo, a** *sm/f* philosopher.

fil'trare *vt, vi* to filter.

'filtro *sm* filter; **~ dell'olio** (*AUT*) oil filter.

'filza ['filtsa] *sf* (*anche fig*) string.

fin *av, prep* = **fino**.

fi'nale *ag* final ♦ *sm* (*di opera*) end, ending; (: *MUS*) finale ♦ *sf* (*SPORT*) final; **finalità** *sf* (*scopo*) aim, purpose; **final'mente** *av* finally, at last.

fi'nanza [fi'nantsa] *sf* finance; **~e** *sfpl* (*di individuo, Stato*) finances; **finanzi'ario, a** *ag* financial; **finanzi'ere** *sm* financier; - (*guardia di finanza: doganale*) customs officer; (: *tributaria*) inland revenue official.

finché [fin'ke] *cong* (*per tutto il tempo che*) as long as; (*fino al momento in cui*) until; **aspetta ~ io (non) sia ritornato** wait until I get back.

'fine *ag* -(*lamina, carta*) thin; (*capelli, polvere*) fine; (*vista, udito*) keen, sharp; (*persona: raffinata*) refined, distinguished; (*osservazione*) subtle ♦ *sf* end ♦ *sm* aim, purpose; (*esito*) result, outcome; **secondo ~** ulterior motive; **in** *o* **alla ~** in the end, finally; **~ settimana** *sm o f inv* weekend.

fi'nestra *sf* window; **fines'trino** *sm* (*di*

treno, auto) window.

'**fingere** ['findʒere] *vt* to feign; (*supporre*) to imagine, suppose; ~**rsi** *vr*: ~**rsi ubriaco/pazzo** to pretend to be drunk/mad; ~ **di fare** to pretend to do.

fini'mondo *sm* pandemonium.

fi'nire *vt* to finish ♦ *vi* to finish, end; ~ **di fare** (*compiere*) to finish doing; (*smettere*) to stop doing; ~ **in galera** to end up *o* finish up in prison; **fini'tura** *sf* finish.

finlan'dese *ag, sm* (*LING*) Finnish ♦ *sm/f* Finn.

Fin'landia *sf*: **la** ~ Finland.

'**fino, a** *ag* (*capelli, seta*) fine; (*oro*) pure; (*fig: acuto*) shrewd ♦ *av* (*spesso troncato in* **fin**: *pure, anche*) even ♦ *prep* (*spesso troncato in* **fin**: *tempo*): **fin quando?** till when?; (: *luogo*): **fin qui** as far as here; ~ **a** (*tempo*) until, till; (*luogo*) as far as, (up) to; **fin da domani** from tomorrow onwards; **fin da ieri** since yesterday; **fin dalla nascita** from *o* since birth.

fi'nocchio [fi'nɔkkjo] *sm* fennel; (*fam: peg: pederasta*) queer.

fi'nora *av* up till now.

'**finta** *sf* pretence, sham; (*SPORT*) feint; **far ~a** (**di fare**) to pretend (to do).

'**finto, a** *pp di* **fingere** ♦ *ag* false; artificial.

finzi'one [fin'tsjone] *sf* pretence, sham.

fi'occo, chi *sm* (*di nastro*) bow; (*di stoffa, lana*) flock; (*di neve*) flake; (*NAUT*) jib; **coi ~chi** (*fig*) first-rate; **~chi di granoturco** cornflakes.

fi'ocina ['fjɔtʃina] *sf* harpoon.

fi'oco, a, chi, che *ag* faint, dim.

fi'onda *sf* catapult.

fio'raio, a *sm/f* florist.

fi'ore *sm* flower; ~**i** *smpl* (*CARTE*) clubs; **a fior d'acqua** on the surface of the water; **avere i nervi a fior di pelle** to be on edge.

fioren'tino, a *ag* Florentine.

fio'retto *sm* (*SCHERMA*) foil.

fio'rire *vi* (*rosa*) to flower; (*albero*) to blossom; (*fig*) to flourish.

Fi'renze [fi'rɛntse] *sf* Florence.

'**firma** *sf* signature; (*reputazione*)

name.

fir'mare *vt* to sign.

fisar'monica, che *sf* accordion.

fis'cale *ag* fiscal, tax *cpd*; **medico ~** *doctor employed by Social Security to verify cases of sick leave*.

fischi'are [fis'kjare] *vi* to whistle ♦ *vt* to whistle; (*attore*) to boo, hiss.

'**fischio** ['fiskjo] *sm* whistle.

'**fisco** *sm* tax authorities *pl*, ≈ Inland Revenue (*BRIT*), ≈ Internal Revenue Service (*US*).

'**fisica** *sf* physics *sg*.

'**fisico, a, ci, che** *ag* physical ♦ *sm/f* physicist ♦ *sm* physique.

fisiolo'gia [fizjolo'dʒia] *sf* physiology.

fisiono'mia *sf* face, physiognomy.

fisiotera'pia *sf* physiotherapy.

fis'sare *vt* to fix, fasten; (*guardare intensamente*) to stare at; (*data, condizioni*) to fix, establish, set; (*prenotare*) to book; ~**rsi su** (*sog: sguardo, attenzione*) to focus on; (*fig: idea*) to become obsessed with; **fissazi'one** *sf* (*PSIC*) fixation.

'**fisso, a** *ag* fixed; (*stipendio, impiego*) regular ♦ *av*: **guardare ~ qc/qn** to stare at sth/sb.

'**fitta** *sf* sharp pain; *vedi anche* **fitto**.

fit'tizio, a *ag* fictitious, imaginary.

'**fitto, a** *ag* thick, dense; (*pioggia*) heavy ♦ *sm* depths *pl*, middle; (*affitto, pigione*) rent.

fi'ume *sm* river.

fiu'tare *vt* to smell, sniff; (*sog: animale*) to scent; (*fig: inganno*) to get wind of, smell; ~ **tabacco/cocaina** to take snuff/cocaine; **fi'uto** *sm* (*sense of*) smell; (*fig*) nose.

fla'gello [fla'dʒɛllo] *sm* scourge.

fla'grante *ag* flagrant; **cogliere qn in ~** to catch sb red-handed.

fla'nella *sf* flannel.

flash [flaʃ] *sm inv* (*FOT*) flash; (*giornalistico*) newsflash.

'**flauto** *sm* flute.

'**flebile** *ag* faint, feeble.

'**flemma** *sf* (*calma*) coolness, phlegm; (*MED*) phlegm.

fles'sibile *ag* pliable; (*fig: che si*

adatta) flexible.
'**flesso, a** *pp di* **flettere**.
flessu'oso, a *ag* supple, lithe; (*andatura*) flowing, graceful.
'**flettere** *vt* to bend.
F.lli *abbr* (= *fratelli*) Bros.
'**flora** *sf* flora.
'**florido, a** *ag* flourishing; (*fig*) glowing with health.
'**floscio, a, sci, sce** ['flɔʃʃo] *ag* (*cappello*) floppy, soft; (*muscoli*) flabby.
'**flotta** *sf* fleet.
'**fluido, a** *ag, sm* fluid.
flu'ire *vi* to flow.
fluo'ro *sm* fluorine.
fluo'ruro *sm* fluoride.
'**flusso** *sm* flow; (*FISICA, MED*) flux; ~ **e riflusso** ebb and flow.
fluttu'are *vi* to rise and fall; (*ECON*) to fluctuate.
fluvi'ale *ag* river *cpd*, fluvial.
'**foca, che** *sf* (*ZOOL*) seal.
fo'caccia, cc [fo'kattʃa] *sf* kind of pizza; (*dolce*) bun.
'**foce** ['fotʃe] *sf* (*GEO*) mouth.
foco'laio *sm* (*MED*) centre of infection; (*fig*) hotbed.
foco'lare *sm* hearth, fireside; (*TECN*) furnace.
'**fodera** *sf* (*di vestito*) lining; (*di libro, poltrona*) cover; **fode'rare** *vt* to line; to cover.
'**fodero** *sm* (*di spada*) scabbard; (*di pugnale*) sheath; (*di pistola*) holster.
'**foga** *sf* enthusiasm, ardour.
'**foggia, ge** ['fɔddʒa] *sf* (*maniera*) style; (*aspetto*) form, shape; (*moda*) fashion, style.
'**foglia** ['fɔʎʎa] *sf* leaf; ~ **d'argento/d'oro** silver/gold leaf; **fogli'ame** *sm* foliage, leaves *pl*.
'**foglio** ['fɔʎʎo] *sm* (*di carta*) sheet (of paper); (*di metallo*) sheet; (*documento*) document; (*banconota*) (bank)note; ~ **rosa** (*AUT*) provisional licence; ~ **di via** (*DIR*) expulsion order; ~ **volante** pamphlet.
'**fogna** ['fɔɲɲa] *sf* drain, sewer; **fogna'tura** *sf* drainage, sewerage.

folgo'rare *vt* (*sog: fulmine*) to strike down; (*: alta tensione*) to electrocute.
'**folla** *sf* crowd, throng.
'**folle** *ag* mad, insane; (*TECN*) idle; **in ~** (*AUT*) in neutral.
fol'lia *sf* folly, foolishness; foolish act; (*pazzia*) madness, lunacy.
'**folto, a** *ag* thick.
fomen'tare *vt* to stir up, foment.
fondamen'tale *ag* fundamental, basic.
fonda'mento *sm* foundation; ~**a** *sfpl* (*EDIL*) foundations.
fon'dare *vt* to found; (*fig: dar base*): ~ **qc su** to base sth on; **fondazi'one** *sf* foundation.
'**fondere** *vt* (*neve*) to melt; (*metallo*) to fuse, melt; (*fig: colori*) to merge, blend; (*: imprese, gruppi*) to merge ♦ *vi* to melt; ~**rsi** *vr* to melt; (*fig: partiti, correnti*) to unite, merge; **fonde'ria** *sf* foundry.
'**fondo, a** *ag* deep ♦ *sm* (*di recipiente, pozzo*) bottom; (*di stanza*) back; (*quantità di liquido che resta, deposito*) dregs *pl*; (*sfondo*) background; (*unità immobiliare*) property, estate; (*somma di denaro*) fund; (*SPORT*) long-distance race; ~**i** *smpl* (*denaro*) funds; **a notte** ~**a** at dead of night; **in ~ a** at the bottom of; at the back of; (*strada*) at the end of; **andare a ~** (*nave*) to sink; **conoscere a ~** to know inside out; **dar ~ a** (*fig: provviste, soldi*) to use up; **in ~** (*fig*) after all, all things considered; **andare fino in ~ a** (*fig*) to examine thoroughly; **a ~ perduto** (*COMM*) without security; ~**i di caffè** coffee grounds; ~**i di magazzino** old *o* unsold stock *sg*.
fo'netica *sf* phonetics *sg*.
fon'tana *sf* fountain.
'**fonte** *sf* spring, source; (*fig*) source ♦ *sm*: ~ **battesimale** (*REL*) font.
fo'raggio [fo'raddʒo] *sm* fodder, forage.
fo'rare *vt* to pierce, make a hole in; (*pallone*) to burst; (*biglietto*) to punch; ~ **una gomma** to burst a tyre (*BRIT*) *o* tire (*US*).
'**forbici** ['fɔrbitʃi] *sfpl* scissors.
'**forca, che** *sf* (*AGR*) fork, pitchfork;

(*patibolo*) gallows *sg*.

for'cella [for'tʃella] *sf* (*TECN*) fork; (*di monte*) pass.

for'chetta [for'ketta] *sf* fork.

for'cina [for'tʃina] *sf* hairpin.

'forcipe ['fortʃipe] *sm* forceps *pl*.

fo'resta *sf* forest.

foresti'ero, a *ag* foreign ♦ *sm/f* foreigner.

'forfora *sf* dandruff.

'forgia, ge ['fordʒa] *sf* forge; forgi'are *vt* to forge.

'forma *sf* form; (*aspetto esteriore*) form, shape; (*DIR*: *procedura*) procedure; (*per calzature*) last; (*stampo da cucina*) mould; ~e *sfpl* (*del corpo*) figure, shape; le ~e (*convenzioni*) appearances; essere in ~ to be in good shape.

formag'gino [formad'dʒino] *sm* processed cheese.

for'maggio [for'maddʒo] *sm* cheese.

for'male *ag* formal; formalità *sf inv* formality.

for'mare *vt* to form, shape, make; (*numero di telefono*) to dial; (*fig*: *carattere*) to form, mould; ~rsi *vr* to form, take shape; for'mato *sm* format, size; formazi'one *sf* formation; (*fig*: *educazione*) training.

for'mica, che *sf* ant; formi'caio *sm* anthill.

formico'lare *vi* (*gamba, braccio*) to tingle; (*brulicare*: anche *fig*): ~ di to be swarming with; mi formicola la gamba I've got pins and needles in my leg, my leg's tingling; formico'lio *sm* pins and needles *pl*; swarming.

formi'dabile *ag* powerful, formidable; (*straordinario*) remarkable.

'formula *sf* formula; ~ di cortesia courtesy form.

formu'lare *vt* to formulate; to express.

for'nace [for'natʃe] *sf* (*per laterizi etc*) kiln; (*per metalli*) furnace.

for'naio *sm* baker.

for'nello *sm* (*elettrico, a gas*) ring; (*di pipa*) bowl.

for'nire *vt*: ~ qn di qc, ~ qc a qn to provide *o* supply sb with sth, to supply

sth to sb.

'forno *sm* (*di cucina*) oven; (*panetteria*) bakery; (*TECN*: *per calce etc*) kiln; (: *per metalli*) furnace.

'foro *sm* (*buco*) hole; (*STORIA*) forum; (*tribunale*) (law) court.

'forse *av* perhaps, maybe; (*circa*) about; essere in ~ to be in doubt.

forsen'nato, a *ag* mad, insane.

'forte *ag* strong; (*suono*) loud; (*spesa*) considerable, great; (*passione, dolore*) great, deep ♦ *av* strongly; (*velocemente*) fast; (*a voce alta*) loud(ly); (*violentemente*) hard ♦ *sm* (*edificio*) fort; (*specialità*) forte, strong point; essere ~ in qc to be good at sth.

for'tezza [for'tettsa] *sf* (*morale*) strength; (*luogo fortificato*) fortress.

for'tuito, a *ag* fortuitous, chance.

for'tuna *sf* (*destino*) fortune, luck; (*buona sorte*) success, fortune; (*eredità, averi*) fortune; per ~ luckily, fortunately; di ~ makeshift, improvised; atterraggio di ~ emergency landing; fortu'nato, a *ag* lucky, fortunate; (*coronato da successo*) successful.

forvi'are *vt, vi* = fuorviare.

'forza ['fortsa] *sf* strength; (*potere*) power; (*FISICA*) force; ~e *sfpl* (*fisiche*) strength *sg*; (*MIL*) forces ♦ *escl* come on!; per ~ against one's will; (*naturalmente*) of course; a viva ~ by force; a ~ di by dint of; ~ maggiore circumstances beyond one's control; la ~ pubblica the police *pl*; le ~e armate the armed forces.

for'zare [for'tsare] *vt* to force; ~ qn a fare to force sb to do; for'zato, a *ag* forced ♦ *sm* (*DIR*) prisoner sentenced to hard labour.

fos'chia [fos'kia] *sf* mist, haze.

'fosco, a, schi, sche *ag* dark, gloomy.

'fosforo *sm* phosphorous.

'fossa *sf* pit; (*di cimitero*) grave; ~ biologica septic tank.

fos'sato *sm* ditch; (*di fortezza*) moat.

fos'setta *sf* dimple.

'fossile *ag*, *sm* fossil.

'fosso *sm* ditch; (*MIL*) trench.

'foto *sf* photo ♦ *prefisso*: foto'copia *sf*

photocopy; **fotocopi'are** *vt* to photo-copy; **fotogra'fare** *vt* to photograph; **fotogra'fia** *sf* (*procedimento*) photography; (*immagine*) photograph; **fare una fotografia** to take a photograph; **una fotografia a colori/in bianco e nero** a colour/black and white photograph; **fo'tografo, a** *sm/f* photographer; **fotoro'manzo** *sm* romantic picture story.

fra *prep* = **tra.**

fracas'sare *vt* to shatter, smash; **~rsi** *vr* to shatter, smash; (*veicolo*) to crash; **fra'casso** *sm* smash; crash; (*baccano*) din, racket.

'fradicio, a, ci, ce ['fraditʃo] *ag* (*molto bagnato*) soaking (wet); **ubriaco ~** blind drunk.

'fragile ['fradʒile] *ag* fragile; (*fig: salute*) delicate.

'fragola *sf* strawberry.

fra'gore *sm* roar; (*di tuono*) rumble.

frago'roso, a *ag* deafening.

fra'grante *ag* fragrant.

frain'tendere *vt* to misunderstand; **frain'teso, a** *pp di* **fraintendere.**

fram'mento *sm* fragment.

'frana *sf* landslide; (*fig: persona*): **essere una ~** to be useless; **fra'nare** *vi* to slip, slide down.

fran'cese [fran'tʃeze] *ag* French ♦ *sm/f* Frenchman/woman ♦ *sm* (*LING*) French; **i F~i** the French.

fran'chezza [fran'kettsa] *sf* frankness, openness.

'Francia ['frantʃa] *sf*: **la ~** France.

'franco, a, chi, che *ag* (*COMM*) free; (*sincero*) frank, open, sincere ♦ *sm* (*moneta*) franc; **farla -a** (*fig*) to get off scot-free; **~ di dogana** duty-free; **~ a domicilio** delivered free of charge; **prezzo '~ fabbrica** ex-works price; **~ tiratore** *sm* sniper.

franco'bollo *sm* (*postage*) stamp.

fran'gente [fran'dʒɛnte] *sm* (*onda*) breaker; (*scoglio emergente*) reef; (*circostanza*) situation, circumstance.

'frangia, ge ['frandʒa] *sf* fringe.

frantu'mare *vt* to break into pieces, shatter; **~rsi** *vr* to break into pieces,

shatter.

frap'pé *sm* milk shake.

'frasca, sche *sf* (leafy) branch.

'frase *sf* (*LING*) sentence; (*locuzione, espressione, MUS*) phrase; **~ fatta** set phrase.

'frassino *sm* ash (tree).

frastagli'ato, a [frastaʎ'ʎato] *ag* (*costa*) indented, jagged.

frastor'nare *vt* to daze; to befuddle.

frastu'ono *sm* hubbub, din.

'frate *sm* friar, monk.

fratel'lanza [fratel'lantsa] *sf* brotherhood; (*associazione*) fraternity.

fratel'lastro *sm* stepbrother.

fra'tello *sm* brother; **~i** *smpl* brothers; (*nel senso di fratelli e sorelle*) brothers and sisters.

fra'terno, a *ag* fraternal, brotherly.

frat'tanto *av* in the meantime, meanwhile.

frat'tempo *sm*: **nel ~** in the meantime, meanwhile.

frat'tura *sf* fracture; (*fig*) split, break.

frazi'one [frat'tsjone] *sf* fraction; (*borgata*): **~ di comune** hamlet.

'freccia, ce ['frettʃa] *sf* arrow; **~ di direzione** (*AUT*) indicator.

fred'dare *vt* to shoot dead.

fred'dezza [fred'dettsa] *sf* coldness.

'freddo, a *ag, sm* cold; **fa ~** it's cold; **aver ~** to be cold; **a ~** (*fig*) deliberately; **freddo'loso, a** *ag* sensitive to the cold.

fred'dura *sf* pun.

fre'gare *vt* to rub; (*fam: truffare*) to take in, cheat; (: *rubare*) to swipe, pinch; **fregarsene** (*fam!*): **chi se ne frega?** who gives a damn (about it)?

fre'gata *sf* rub; (*fam*) swindle; (*NAUT*) frigate.

'fregio ['fredʒo] *sm* (*ARCHIT*) frieze; (*ornamento*) decoration.

'fremere *vi*: **~ di** to tremble o quiver with; **'fremito** *sm* tremor, quiver.

fre'nare *vt* (*veicolo*) to slow down; (*cavallo*) to rein in; (*lacrime*) to restrain, hold back ♦ *vi* to brake; **~rsi** (*fig*) to restrain o.s., control o.s.; **fre'nata** *sf*: **fare una frenata** to brake.

frene'sia *sf* frenzy.

'freno *sm* brake; (*morso*) bit; ~ **a disco** disc brake; ~ **a mano** handbrake; **tenere a** ~ to restrain.

frequen'tare *vt* (*scuola, corso*) to attend; (*locale, bar*) to go to, frequent; (*persone*) to see (often).

fre'quente *ag* frequent; **di** ~ frequently; **fre'quenza** *sf* frequency; (*INS*) attendance.

fres'chezza [fres'kettsa] *sf* freshness.

'fresco, a, schi, sche *ag* fresh; (*temperatura*) cool; (*notizia*) recent, fresh ♦ *sm*: **godere il** ~ to enjoy the cool air; **stare** ~ (*fig*) to be in for it; **mettere al** ~ to put in a cool place.

'fretta *sf* hurry, haste; **in** ~ in a hurry; **in** ~ **e furia** in a mad rush; **aver** ~ to be in a hurry; **fretto'loso, a** *ag* (*persona*) in a hurry; (*lavoro etc*) hurried, rushed.

fri'abile *ag* (*terreno*) friable; (*pasta*) crumbly.

'friggere ['friddʒere] *vt* to fry ♦ *vi* (*olio etc*) to sizzle.

'frigido, a ['fridʒido] *ag* (*MED*) frigid.

'frigo *sm* fridge.

frigo'rifero, a *ag* refrigerating ♦ *sm* refrigerator.

fringu'ello *sm* chaffinch.

frit'tata *sf* omelette; **fare una** ~ (*fig*) to make a mess of things.

frit'tella *sf* (*CUC*) pancake; (*: ripiena*) fritter.

'fritto, a *pp di* **friggere** ♦ *ag* fried ♦ *sm* fried food; ~ **misto** mixed fry.

frit'tura *sf* (*CUC*): ~ **di pesce** mixed fried fish.

'frivolo, a *ag* frivolous.

frizi'one [frit'tsjone] *sf* friction; (*di pelle*) rub, rub-down; (*AUT*) clutch.

friz'zante [frid'dzante] *ag* (*anche fig*) sparkling.

'frizzo ['friddzo] *sm* witticism.

fro'dare *vt* to defraud, cheat.

'frode *sf* fraud; ~ **fiscale** tax evasion.

'froilo, a *ag* (*carne*) tender; (*: di selvaggina*) high; (*fig: persona*) soft; **pasta** ~**a** short(crust) pastry.

'fronda *sf* (leafy) branch; (*di partito* *politico*) internal opposition.

fron'tale *ag* frontal; (*scontro*) head-on.

'fronte *sf* (*ANAT*) forehead; (*di edificio*) front, façade ♦ *sm* (*MIL, POL, METEOR*) front; **a** ~, **di** ~ facing, opposite; **di** ~ **a** (*posizione*) opposite, facing, in front of; (*a paragone di*) compared with.

fronteggi'are [fronted'dʒare] *vt* (*avversari, difficoltà*) to face, stand up to; (*spese*) to cope with.

fronti'era *sf* border, frontier.

'fronzolo ['frondzolo] *sm* frill.

'frottola *sf* fib; ~**e** *sfpl* (*assurdità*) nonsense *sg*.

fru'gare *vi* to rummage ♦ *vt* to search.

frul'lare *vt* (*CUC*) to whisk ♦ *vi* (*uccelli*) to flutter; **frul'lato** *sm* milk shake; fruit drink; **frulla'tore** *sm* electric mixer; **frul'lino** *sm* whisk.

fru'mento *sm* wheat.

fru'scio [fruʃ'ʃio] *sm* rustle; rustling; (*di acque*) murmur.

'frusta *sf* whip; (*CUC*) whisk.

frus'tare *vt* to whip.

frus'tino *sm* riding crop.

frus'trare *vt* to frustrate.

'frutta *sf* fruit; (*portata*) dessert; ~ **candita/secca** candied/dried fruit.

frut'tare *vi* to bear dividends, give a return.

frut'teto *sm* orchard.

frutti'vendolo, a *sm/f* greengrocer (*BRIT*), produce dealer (*US*).

'frutto *sm* fruit; (*fig: risultato*) result(s); (*ECON: interesse*) interest; (*: reddito*) income; ~**i di mare** seafood *sg*.

FS *abbr* = **Ferrovie dello Stato.**

fu *vb vedi* **essere** ♦ *ag inv*: **il** ~ **Paolo Bianchi** the late Paolo Bianchi.

fuci'lare [futʃi'lare] *vt* to shoot; **fuci'lata** *sf* rifle shot.

fu'cile [fu'tʃile] *sm* rifle, gun; (*da caccia*) shotgun, gun.

fu'cina [fu'tʃina] *sf* forge.

'fuga *sf* escape, flight; (*di gas, liquidi*) leak; (*MUS*) fugue; ~ **di cervelli** brain drain.

fu'gace [fu'gatʃe] *ag* fleeting, transient.

fug'gevole [fud'dʒevole] *ag* fleeting.

fuggi'asco, a, schi, sche [fud'dʒasko]

_ag, sm/f_ fugitive.
fuggi'fuggi [fuddʒi'fuddʒi] _sm_ scramble, stampede.
fug'gire [fud'dʒire] _vi_ to flee, run away; _(fig: passar veloce)_ to fly ♦ _vt_ to avoid; **fuggi'tivo, a** _sm/f_ fugitive, runaway.
ful'gore _sm_ brilliance, splendour.
fu'liggine [fu'liddʒine] _sf_ soot.
fulmi'nare _vt_ _(sog: fulmine)_ to strike; (_: elettricità_) to electrocute; _(con arma da fuoco)_ to shoot dead; _(fig: con lo sguardo)_ to look daggers at.
'fulmine _sm_ thunderbolt; lightning _no pl._
fumai'olo _sm_ _(di nave)_ funnel; _(di fabbrica)_ chimney.
fu'mare _vi_ to smoke; _(emettere vapore)_ to steam ♦ _vt_ to smoke; **fu'mata** _sf_ _(segnale)_ smoke signal; **farsi una fumata** to have a smoke; **fuma'tore, 'trice** _sm/f_ smoker.
fu'metto _sm_ comic strip; **giornale** _sm_ **a ~i** comic.
'fumo _sm_ smoke; _(vapore)_ steam; _(il fumare tabacco)_ smoking; **~i** _smpl_ _(industriali etc)_ fumes; **i ~i dell'alcool** the after-effects of drink; **vendere ~** to deceive, cheat; **fu'moso, a** _ag_ smoky; _(fig)_ muddled.
fu'nambolo, a _sm/f_ tightrope walker.
'fune _sf_ rope, cord; _(più grossa)_ cable.
'funebre _ag_ _(rito)_ funeral; _(aspetto)_ gloomy, funereal.
fune'rale _sm_ funeral.
'fungere ['fundʒere] _vi_: **~ da** to act as.
'fungo, ghi _sm_ fungus; _(commestibile)_ mushroom; **~ velenoso** toadstool.
funico'lare _sf_ funicular railway.
funi'via _sf_ cable railway.
funzio'nare [funtsjo'nare] _vi_ to work, function; _(fungere)_: **~ da** to act as.
funzio'nario [funtsjo'narjo] _sm_ official.
funzi'one [fun'tsjone] _sf_ function; _(carica)_ post, position; _(REL)_ service; **in ~** _(meccanismo)_ in operation; **in ~ di** _(come)_ as; **fare la ~ di qn** _(farne le veci)_ to take sb's place.
fu'oco, chi _sm_ fire; _(fornello)_ ring; _(FOT, FISICA)_ focus; **dare ~ a qc** to set fire to sth; **far ~** _(sparare)_ to fire; **~**

d'artificio firework.
fuorché [fwor'ke] _cong, prep_ except.
fu'ori _av_ outside; _(all'aperto)_ outdoors, outside; _(fuori di casa, SPORT)_ out; _(esclamativo)_ get out! ♦ _prep:_ **~ (di)** out of, outside ♦ _sm_ outside; **lasciar ~ qc/qn** to leave sth/sb out; **far ~ qn** _(fam)_ to kill sb, do sb in; **essere ~ di sé** to be beside o.s.; **~ luogo** _(inopportuno)_ out of place, uncalled for; **~ mano** out of the way, remote; **~ pericolo** out of danger; **~ uso** old-fashioned; obsolete.
fu'ori... _prefisso:_ **fuori'bordo** _sm inv_ speedboat (with outboard motor); outboard motor; **fuori'classe** _sm/f inv_ (undisputed) champion; **fuorigi'oco** _sm_ offside; **fuori'legge** _sm/f inv_ outlaw; **fuori'serie** _ag inv_ _(auto etc)_ custombuilt ♦ _sf_ custom-built car; **fuori'strada** _sm_ _(AUT)_ cross-country vehicle; **fuor(i)u'scito, a** _sm/f_ exile; **fuorvi'are** _vt_ to mislead; _(fig)_ to lead astray ♦ _vi_ to go astray.
'furbo, a _ag_ clever, smart; _(peg)_ cunning.
fu'rente _ag:_ **~ (contro)** furious (with).
fur'fante _sm_ rascal, scoundrel.
fur'gone _sm_ van.
'furia _sf_ _(ira)_ fury, rage; _(fig: impeto)_ fury, violence; _(fretta)_ rush; **a ~ di** by dint of; **andare su tutte le ~e** to get into a towering rage; **furi'bondo, a** _ag_ furious.
furi'oso, a _ag_ furious; _(mare, vento)_ raging.
fu'rore _sm_ fury; _(esaltazione)_ frenzy; **far ~** to be all the rage.
fur'tivo, a _ag_ furtive.
'furto _sm_ theft; **~ con scasso** burglary.
'fusa _sfpl:_ **fare le ~** to purr.
fu'sibile _sm_ _(ELETTR)_ fuse.
fusi'one _sf_ _(di metalli)_ fusion, melting; _(colata)_ casting; _(COMM)_ merger; _(fig)_ merging.
'fuso, a _pp di_ **fondere** ♦ _sm_ _(FILATURA)_ spindle; **~ orario** time zone.
fus'tagno [fus'taɲɲo] _sm_ corduroy.
fus'tino _sm_ _(di detersivo)_ tub.
'fusto _sm_ stem; _(ANAT, di albero)_

trunk; (*recipiente*) drum, can.
fu'turo, a *ag*, *sm* future.

G

gab'bare *vt* to take in, dupe; ~rsi *vr*:
~rsi di qn to make fun of sb.
'gabbia *sf* cage; (*DIR*) dock; (*da imballaggio*) crate; ~ dell'ascensore lift (*BRIT*) *o* elevator (*US*) shaft; ~ toracica (*ANAT*) rib cage.
gabbi'ano *sm* (sea)gull.
gabi'netto *sm* (*MED etc*) consulting room; (*POL*) ministry; (*di decenza*) toilet, lavatory; (*INS: di fisica etc*) laboratory.
'gaffe [gaf] *sf inv* blunder.
gagli'ardo, a [gaʎˈʎardo] *ag* strong, vigorous.
'gaio, a *ag* cheerful, gay.
'gala *sf* (*sfarzo*) pomp; (*festa*) gala.
ga'lante *ag* gallant, courteous; (*avventura*) amorous; galante'ria *sf* gallantry.
galantu'omo (*pl* galantu'omini) *sm* gentleman.
ga'lassia *sf* galaxy.
gala'teo *sm* (good) manners *pl*.
gale'otto *sm* (*rematore*) galley slave; (*carcerato*) convict.
ga'lera *sf* (*NAUT*) galley; (*prigione*) prison.
'galla *sf*: a ~ afloat; venire a ~ to surface, come to the surface; (*fig: verità*) to come out.
galleggi'ante [galledˈdʒante] *ag* floating ♦ *sm* (*natante*) barge; (*di pescatore, lenza, TECN*) float.
galleggi'are [galledˈdʒare] *vi* to float.
galle'ria *sf* (*traforo*) tunnel; (*ARCHIT, d'arte*) gallery; (*TEATRO*) circle; (*strada coperta con negozi*) arcade.
'Galles *sm*: il ~ Wales; gal'lese *ag, sm* (*LING*) Welsh ♦ *sm/f* Welshman/woman.
gal'letta *sf* cracker.
gal'lina *sf* hen.
'gallo *sm* cock.
gal'lone *sm* piece of braid; (*MIL*) stripe; (*unità di misura*) gallon.

galop'pare *vi* to gallop.
ga'loppo *sm* gallop; al *o* di ~ at a gallop.
'gamba *sf* leg; (*asta: di lettera*) stem; in ~ (*in buona salute*) well; (*bravo, sveglio*) bright, smart; prendere qc sotto ~ (*fig*) to treat sth too lightly.
gambe'retto *sm* shrimp.
'gambero *sm* (*di acqua dolce*) crayfish; (*di mare*) prawn.
'gambo *sm* stem; (*di frutta*) stalk.
'gamma *sf* (*MUS*) scale; (*di colori, fig*) range.
ga'nascia, sce [gaˈnaʃʃa] *sf* jaw; ~sce del freno (*AUT*) brake shoes.
'gancio ['gantʃo] *sm* hook.
'ganghero ['gangero] *smpl*: uscire dai ~ (*fig*) to fly into a temper.
'gara *sf* competition; (*SPORT*) competition; contest; match; (: *corsa*) race; fare a ~ to compete, vie.
ga'rage [gaˈraʒ] *sm inv* garage.
garan'tire *vt* to guarantee; (*debito*) to stand surety for; (*dare per certo*) to assure.
garan'zia [garanˈtsia] *sf* guarantee; (*pegno*) security.
gar'bato, a *ag* courteous, polite.
'garbo *sm* (*buone maniere*) politeness, courtesy; (*di vestito etc*) grace, style.
gareggi'are [garedˈdʒare] *vi* to compete.
garga'rismo *sm* gargle; fare i ~i to gargle.
ga'rofano *sm* carnation; chiodo di ~ clove.
'garza ['gardza] *sf* (*per bende*) gauze.
gar'zone [garˈdzone] *sm* (*di negozio*) boy.
gas *sm inv* gas; a tutto ~ at full speed; dare ~ (*AUT*) to accelerate.
ga'solio *sm* diesel (oil).
ga's(s)ato, a *ag* (*bibita*) aerated, fizzy.
gas'sosa *sf* fizzy drink.
gas'soso, a *ag* gaseous; gassy.
gastrono'mia *sf* gastronomy.
gat'tino *sm* kitten.
'gatto, a *sm/f* cat, tomcat/she-cat; ~ selvatico wildcat; ~ delle nevi (*AUT, SCI*) snowcat.
gatto'pardo *sm*: ~ africano serval; ~

americano ocelot.

'gaudio sm joy, happiness.

ga'vetta sf (MIL) mess tin; **venire dalla ~** (MIL, fig) to rise from the ranks.

'gazza ['gaddza] sf magpie.

gaz'zella [gad'dzɛlla] sf gazelle; (dei carabinieri) (high-speed) police car.

gaz'zetta [gad'dzetta] sf news sheet; **G~ Ufficiale** official publication containing details of new laws.

gel [dʒɛl] sm inv gel.

ge'lare [dʒe'lare] vt, vi, vb impers to freeze; **ge'lata** sf frost.

gelate'ria [dʒelate'ria] sf ice-cream shop.

gela'tina [dʒela'tina] sf gelatine; **~ esplosiva** dynamite; **~ di frutta** fruit jelly.

ge'lato, a [dʒe'lato] ag frozen ♦ sm ice cream.

'gelido, a ['dʒɛlido] ag icy, ice-cold.

'gelo ['dʒɛlo] sm (temperatura) intense cold; (brina) frost; (fig) chill; **ge'lone** sm chilblain.

gelo'sia [dʒelo'sia] sf jealousy.

ge'loso, a [dʒe'loso] ag jealous.

'gelso ['dʒɛlso] sm mulberry (tree).

gelso'mino [dʒelso'mino] sm jasmine.

ge'mello, a [dʒe'mɛllo] ag, sm/f twin; **~i** smpl (di camicia) cufflinks; (dello zodiaco): **G~i** Gemini sg.

'gemere ['dʒɛmere] vi to moan, groan; (cigolare) to creak; (gocciolare) to drip, ooze; **gemito** sm moan, groan.

'gemma ['dʒɛmma] sf (BOT) bud; (pietra preziosa) gem.

gene'rale [dʒene'rale] ag, sm general; **in ~** (per sommi capi) in general terms; (di solito) usually, in general; **a ~ richiesta** by popular request; **generalità** sfpl (dati d'identità) particulars; **generaliz'zare** vt, vi to generalize; **general'mente** av generally.

gene'rare [dʒene'rare] vt (dar vita) to give birth to; (produrre) to produce; (causare) to arouse; (TECN) to produce, generate; **genera'tore** sm (TECN) generator; **generazi'one** sf generation.

'genere ['dʒɛnere] sm kind, type, sort; (BIOL) genus; (merce) article, product; (LING) gender; (ARTE, LETTERATURA) genre; **in ~** generally, as a rule; **il ~ umano** mankind; **~i alimentari** foodstuffs.

ge'nerico, a, ci, che [dʒe'nɛriko] ag generic; (vago) vague, imprecise.

'genero ['dʒɛnero] sm son-in-law.

generosità [dʒenerosi'ta] sf generosity.

gene'roso, a [dʒene'roso] ag generous.

ge'netica [dʒe'nɛtika] sf genetics sg.

ge'netico, a, ci, che [dʒe'nɛtiko] ag genetic.

gen'giva [dʒen'dʒiva] sf (ANAT) gum.

geni'ale [dʒen'jale] ag (persona) of genius; (idea) ingenious, brilliant.

'genio ['dʒɛnjo] sm genius; **andare a ~ a qn** to be to sb's liking, appeal to sb.

geni'tale [dʒeni'tale] ag genital; **~i** smpl genitals.

geni'tore [dʒeni'tore] sm parent, father o mother; **i miei ~i** my parents, my father and mother.

gen'naio [dʒen'najo] sm January.

'Genova ['dʒɛnova] sf Genoa.

gen'taglia [dʒen'taʎʎa] (peg) sf rabble.

'gente ['dʒɛnte] sf people pl.

gen'tile [dʒen'tile] ag (persona, atto) kind; (: garbato) courteous, polite; (nelle lettere): **G~ Signore** Dear Sir; (: sulla busta): **G~ Signor Fernando Villa** Mr Fernando Villa; **genti'lezza** sf kindness; courtesy, politeness; **per gentilezza** (per favore) please.

gentilu'omo [dʒenti'lwɔmo] (pl **gentilu'omini**) sm gentleman.

genu'ino, a [dʒenu'ino] ag (prodotto) natural; (persona, sentimento) genuine, sincere.

geogra'fia [dʒeogra'fia] sf geography.

geolo'gia [dʒeolo'dʒia] sf geology.

ge'ometra, i, e [dʒe'ɔmetra] sm/f (professionista) surveyor.

geome'tria [dʒeome'tria] sf geometry; **geo'metrico, a, ci, che** ag geometric(al).

ge'ranio [dʒe'ranjo] sm geranium.

gerar'chia [dʒerar'kia] sf hierarchy.

ge'rente [dʒe'rɛnte] sm/f manager/manageress.

'gergo, ghi ['dʒɛrgo] sm jargon; slang.

geria'tria [dʒerja'tria] sf geriatrics sg.

Ger'mania [dʒer'manja] sf: la ~ Germany; la ~ occidentale/orientale West/East Germany.

'germe ['dʒerme] sm germ; (fig) seed.

germogli'are [dʒermoʎ'ʎare] vi to sprout; to germinate; ger'moglio sm shoot; bud.

gero'glifico, ci [dʒero'glifiko] sm hieroglyphic.

'gesso ['dʒesso] sm chalk; (SCULTURA, MED, EDIL) plaster; (statua) plaster figure; (minerale) gypsum.

gesti'one [dʒes'tjone] sf management.

ges'tire [dʒes'tire] vt to run, manage.

'gesto ['dʒesto] sm gesture.

ges'tore [dʒes'tore] sm manager.

Gesù [dʒe'zu] sm Jesus.

gesu'ita, i [dʒezu'ita] sm Jesuit.

get'tare [dʒet'tare] vt to throw; (anche: ~ via) to throw away o out; (SCULTURA) to cast; (EDIL) to lay; (acqua) to spout; (grido) to utter; ~rsi vr: ~rsi in (sog: fiume) to flow into; ~ uno sguardo su to take a quick look at; get'tata sf (di cemento, gesso, metalli) cast; (diga) jetty.

'getto ['dʒetto] sm (di gas, liquido, AER) jet; a ~ continuo uninterruptedly; di ~ (fig) straight off, in one go.

get'tone [dʒet'tone] sm token; (per giochi) counter; (: roulette etc) chip; ~ telefonico telephone token.

ghiacci'aio [gjat'tʃajo] sm glacier.

ghiacci'are [gjat'tʃare] vt to freeze; (fig): ~ qn to make sb's blood run cold ♦ vi to freeze, ice over; ghiacci'ato, a ag frozen; (bevanda) ice-cold.

ghi'accio ['gjattʃo] sm ice.

ghiacci'olo [gjat'tʃɔlo] sm icicle; (tipo di gelato) ice lolly (BRIT), popsicle (US).

ghi'aia ['gjaja] sf gravel.

ghi'anda ['gjanda] sf (BOT) acorn.

ghi'andola ['gjandola] sf gland.

ghigliot'tina [giʎʎot'tina] sf guillotine.

ghi'gnare [gin'nare] vi to sneer.

ghi'otto, a ['gjotto] ag greedy; (cibo) delicious, appetizing; ghiot'tone, a sm/f glutton.

ghiri'bizzo [giri'biddzo] sm whim.

ghiri'goro [giri'gɔro] sm scribble, squiggle.

ghir'landa [gir'landa] sf garland, wreath.

'ghiro ['giro] sm dormouse.

'ghisa ['giza] sf cast iron.

già [dʒa] av already; (ex, in precedenza) formerly ♦ escl of course!, yes indeed!

gi'acca, che ['dʒakka] sf jacket; ~ a vento windcheater (BRIT), windbreaker (US).

giacché [dʒak'ke] cong since, as.

giac'chetta [dʒak'ketta] sf (light) jacket.

gia'cenza [dʒa'tʃentsa] sf: merce in ~ goods in stock; capitale in ~ uninvested capital; ~e di magazzino unsold stock.

gia'cere [dʒa'tʃere] vi to lie; giaci'mento sm deposit.

gia'cinto [dʒa'tʃinto] sm hyacinth.

gi'ada ['dʒada] sf jade.

giaggi'olo [dʒad'dʒɔlo] sm iris.

giagu'aro [dʒa'gwaro] sm jaguar.

gi'allo ['dʒallo] ag yellow; (carnagione) sallow ♦ sm yellow; (anche: romanzo ~) detective novel; (anche: film ~) detective film; ~ dell'uovo yolk.

giam'mai [dʒam'mai] av never.

Giap'pone [dʒap'pone] sm Japan; giappo'nese ag, sm/f, sm Japanese inv.

gi'ara ['dʒara] sf jar.

giardi'naggio [dʒardi'naddʒo] sm gardening.

giardi'netta [dʒardi'netta] sf estate car (BRIT), station wagon (US).

giardini'era [dʒardi'njera] sf (misto di sottaceti) mixed pickles pl; (automobile) = giardinetta.

giardini'ere, a [dʒardi'njere] sm/f gardener.

giar'dino [dʒar'dino] sm garden; ~ d'infanzia nursery school; ~ pubblico public gardens pl, (public) park; ~ zoologico zoo.

giarretti'era [dʒarret'tjera] sf garter.

giavel'lotto [dʒavel'lɔtto] sm javelin.

gi'gante, 'essa [dʒi'gante] sm/f giant ♦ ag giant, gigantic; (COMM) giant-size; gigan'tesco, a, schi, sche ag gigantic.

'giglio ['dʒiʎʎo] *sm* lily.

gilè [dʒi'lɛ] *sm inv* waistcoat.

gin [dʒin] *sm inv* gin.

gine'cologo, a, gi, ghe [dʒine'kɔlogo] *sm/f* gynaecologist.

gi'nepro [dʒi'nepro] *sm* juniper.

gi'nestra [dʒi'nestra] *sf* (*BOT*) broom.

Gi'nevra [dʒi'nevra] *sf* Geneva.

gingil'larsi [dʒindʒil'larsi] *vr* to fritter away one's time; (*giocare*): ~ **con** to fiddle with.

gin'gillo [dʒin'dʒillo] *sm* plaything.

gin'nasio [dʒin'nazjo] *sm the 4th and 5th year of secondary school in Italy*.

gin'nasta, i, e [dʒin'nasta] *sm/f* gymnast; **gin'nastica** *sf* gymnastics *sg*; (*esercizio fisico*) keep-fit exercises; (*INS*) physical education.

gi'nocchio [dʒi'nɔkkjo] (*pl(m)* **gi'nocchi** *o pl(f)* **gi'nocchia**) *sm* knee; **stare in** ~ to kneel, be on one's knees; **mettersi in** ~ to kneel (down); **ginocchi'oni** *av* on one's knees.

gio'care [dʒo'kare] *vt* to play; (*scommettere*) to stake, wager, bet; (*ingannare*) to take in ♦ *vi* to play; (*a roulette etc*) to gamble; (*fig*) to play a part, be important; (*TECN: meccanismo*) to be loose; ~ **a** (*gioco, sport*) to play; (*cavalli*) to bet on; **~rsi la carriera** to put one's career at risk; **gioca'tore, 'trice** *sm/f* player; gambler.

gio'cattolo [dʒo'kattolo] *sm* toy.

gio'chetto [dʒo'ketto] *sm* (*tranello*) trick; (*fig*): **è un** ~ it's child's play.

gi'oco, chi ['dʒɔko] *sm* game; (*divertimento, TECN*) play; (*al casinò*) gambling; (*CARTE*) hand; (*insieme di pezzi etc necessari per un gioco*) set; **per** ~ for fun; **fare il doppio** ~ **con qn** to double-cross sb; ~ **d'azzardo** game of chance; ~ **della palla** football; ~ **degli scacchi** chess set; **i Giochi Olimpici** the Olympic Games.

giocoli'ere [dʒoko'ljɛre] *sm* juggler.

gio'coso, a [dʒo'koso] *ag* playful, jesting.

gi'ogo, ghi ['dʒɔgo] *sm* yoke.

gi'oia ['dʒɔja] *sf* joy, delight; (*pietra preziosa*) jewel, precious stone.

gioielle'ria [dʒojelle'ria] *sf* jeweller's craft; jeweller's (shop).

gioielli'ere, a [dʒojel'ljɛre] *sm/f* jeweller.

gioi'ello [dʒo'jɛllo] *sm* jewel, piece of jewellery; **i ~i di una donna** a woman's jewels *o* jewellery.

gioi'oso, a [dʒo'joso] *ag* joyful.

Gior'dania [dʒor'danja] *sf*: **la** ~ Jordan.

giorna'laio, a [dʒorna'lajo] *sm/f* newsagent (*BRIT*), newsdealer (*US*).

gior'nale [dʒor'nale] *sm* (*news*)paper; (*diario*) journal, diary; (*COMM*) journal; ~ **di bordo** log; ~ **radio** radio news *sg*.

giornali'ero, a [dʒorna'ljɛro] *ag* daily; (*che varia: umore*) changeable ♦ *sm* day labourer.

giorna'lismo [dʒorna'lizmo] *sm* journalism.

giorna'lista, i, e [dʒorna'lista] *sm/f* journalist.

gior'nata [dʒor'nata] *sf* day; ~ **lavorativa** working day.

gi'orno ['dʒorno] *sm* day; (*opposto alla notte*) day, daytime; (*luce del* ~) daylight; **al** ~ per day; **di** ~ by day; **al** ~ **d'oggi** nowadays.

gi'ostra ['dʒɔstra] *sf* (*per bimbi*) merry-go-round; (*torneo storico*) joust.

gi'ovane ['dʒovane] *ag* young; (*aspetto*) youthful ♦ *sm/f* youth/girl, young man/woman; **i ~i** young people; **giova'nile** *ag* youthful; (*scritti*) early; (*errore*) of youth; **giova'notto** *sm* young man.

gio'vare [dʒo'vare] *vi*: ~ **a** (*essere utile*) to be useful to; (*far bene*) to be good for ♦ *vb impers* (*essere bene, utile*) to be useful; **~rsi di qc** to make use of sth.

giovedì [dʒove'di] *sm inv* Thursday; **di** *o* **il** ~ on Thursdays.

gioventù [dʒoven'tu] *sf* (*periodo*) youth; (*i giovani*) young people *pl*, youth.

giovi'ale [dʒo'vjale] *ag* jovial, jolly.

giovi'nezza [dʒovi'nettsa] *sf* youth.

gira'dischi [dʒira'diski] *sm inv* record player.

gi'raffa [dʒi'raffa] *sf* giraffe.

gi'randola [dʒi'randola] *sf* (*fuoco*

d'artificio) Catherine wheel; (*giocattolo*) toy windmill; (*banderuola*) weather vane, weathercock.

gi'rare [dʒi'rare] *vt* (*far ruotare*) to turn; (*percorrere, visitare*) to go round; (*CINEMA*) to shoot; to make; (*COMM*) to endorse ♦ *vi* to turn; (*più veloce*) to spin; (*andare in giro*) to wander, go around; **~rsi** *vr* to turn; **~ attorno a** to go round; to revolve round; **far ~ la testa a qn** to make sb dizzy; (*fig*) to turn sb's head.

girar'rosto [dʒirar'rɔsto] *sm* (*CUC*) spit.

gira'sole [dʒira'sole] *sm* sunflower.

gi'rata [dʒi'rata] *sf* (*passeggiata*) stroll; (*con veicolo*) drive; (*COMM*) endorsement.

gira'volta [dʒira'vɔlta] *sf* twirl, turn; (*curva*) sharp bend; (*fig*) about-turn.

gi'revole [dʒi'revole] *ag* revolving, turning.

gi'rino [dʒi'rino] *sm* tadpole.

'giro ['dʒiro] *sm* (*circuito, cerchio*) circle; (*di chiave, manovella*) turn; (*viaggio*) tour, excursion; (*passeggiata*) stroll, walk; (*in macchina*) drive; (*in bicicletta*) ride; (*SPORT: della pista*) lap; (*di denaro*) circulation; (*CARTE*) hand; (*TECN*) revolution; **prendere in ~ qn** (*fig*) to pull sb's leg; **fare un ~** to go for a walk (*o* a drive *o* a ride); **andare in ~** to go about, walk around; **a stretto ~ di posta** by return of post; **nel ~ di un mese** in a month's time; **essere nel ~** (*fig*) to belong to a circle (of friends); **~ d'affari** (*COMM*) turnover; **~ di parole** circumlocution; **~ di prova** (*AUT*) test drive; **~ turistico** sightseeing tour; **giro'collo** *sm*: **a girocollo** crewneck *cpd*.

gironzo'lare [dʒirondzo'lare] *vi* to stroll about.

'gita ['dʒita] *sf* excursion, trip; **fare una ~** to go for a trip, go on an outing.

gi'tano, a [dʒi'tano] *sm/f* gipsy.

giù [dʒu] *av* down; (*dabbasso*) downstairs; **in ~** downwards, down; **~ di lì** (*pressappoco*) thereabouts; **bambini dai 6 anni in ~** children aged 6 and under; **~ per: cadere ~ per le scale** to fall

down the stairs; **essere ~** (*fig: di salute*) to be run down; (: *di spirito*) to be depressed.

giub'botto [dʒub'bɔtto] *sm* jerkin; **~ antiproiettile** bulletproof vest.

gi'ubilo ['dʒubilo] *sm* rejoicing.

giudi'care [dʒudi'kare] *vt* to judge; (*accusato*) to try; (*lite*) to arbitrate in; **~ qn/qc bello** to consider sb/sth (to be) beautiful.

gi'udice ['dʒuditʃe] *sm* judge; **~ conciliatore** justice of the peace; **~ popolare** member of a jury.

giu'dizio [dʒu'dittsjo] *sm* judgment; (*opinione*) opinion;' (*DIR*) judgment, sentence; (: *processo*) trial; (: *verdetto*) verdict; **aver ~** to be wise *o* prudent; **citare in ~** to summons; **giudizi'oso, a** *ag* prudent, judicious.

gi'ugno ['dʒuɲɲo] *sm* June.

giul'lare [dʒul'lare] *sm* jester.

giu'menta [dʒu'menta] *sf* mare.

gi'unco, chi ['dʒunko] *sm* rush.

gi'ungere ['dʒundʒere] *vi* to arrive ♦ *vt* (*mani etc*) to join; **~ a** to arrive at, reach.

gi'ungla ['dʒungla] *sf* jungle.

gi'unta ['dʒunta] *sf* addition; (*organo esecutivo, amministrativo*) council, board; **per ~a** into the bargain, in addition; **~a militare** military junta.

gi'unto, a ['dʒunto] *pp di* **giungere** ♦ *sm* (*TECN*) coupling, joint; **giun'tura** *sf* joint.

giuo'care [dʒwo'kare] *vt, vi* = **giocare**; **giu'oco** *sm* = **gioco**.

giura'mento [dʒura'mento] *sm* oath; **~ falso** perjury.

giu'rare [dʒu'rare] *vt* to swear ♦ *vi* to swear, take an oath; **giu'rato, a** *ag*: **nemico giurato** sworn enemy ♦ *sm/f* juror, juryman/woman.

giu'ria [dʒu'ria] *sf* jury.

giu'ridico, a, ci, che [dʒu'ridiko] *ag* legal.

giustifi'care [dʒustifi'kare] *vt* to justify; **giustificazi'one** *sf* justification; (*INS*) (note of) excuse.

gius'tizia [dʒus'tittsja] *sf* justice; **giustizi'are** *vt* to execute, put to death;

giustizi'ere *sm* executioner.

gi'usto, a ['dʒusto] *ag* (*equo*) fair, just; (*vero*) true, correct; (*adatto*) right, suitable; (*preciso*) exact, correct ♦ *av* (*esattamente*) exactly, precisely; (*per l'appunto, appena*) just; **arrivare ~** to arrive just in time; **ho ~ bisogno di te** you're just the person I need.

glaci'ale [gla'tʃale] *ag* glacial.

'glandola *sf* = **ghiandola.**

gli [ʎi] (*dav V, s impura, gn, pn, ps, x, z*) *det mpl* the ♦ *pron* (*a lui*) to him; (*a esso*) to it; (*in coppia con lo, la, li, le, ne: a lui, a lei, a loro etc*): **gliele do** I'm giving them to him (*o* her *o* them).

gli'ela ['ʎela] *etc vedi* **gli.**

glo'bale *ag* overall.

'globo *sm* globe.

'globulo *sm* (*ANAT*): **~ rosso/bianco** red/white corpuscle.

'gloria *sf* glory; **glori'oso, a** *ag* glorious.

glos'sario *sm* glossary.

'gnocchi ['ɲɔkki] *smpl* (*CUC*) small dumplings made of semolina pasta or potato.

'gobba *sf* (*ANAT*) hump; (*protuberanza*) bump.

'gobbo, a *ag* hunchbacked; (*ricurvo*) round-shouldered ♦ *sm/f* hunchback.

'goccia, ce ['gottʃa] *sf* drop; **goccio'lare** *vi, vt* to drip.

go'dere *vi* (*compiacersi*): **~ (di)** to be delighted (at), rejoice (at); (*trarre vantaggio*): **~ di** to enjoy, benefit from ♦ *vt* to enjoy; **~rsi la vita** to enjoy life; **~sela** to have a good time, enjoy o.s.; **godi'mento** *sm* enjoyment.

'goffo, a *ag* clumsy, awkward.

'gola *sf*, (*ANAT*) throat; (*golosità*) gluttony, greed; (*di camino*) flue; (*di monte*) gorge; **fare ~** (*anche fig*) to tempt.

golf *sm inv* (*SPORT*) golf; (*maglia*) cardigan.

'golfo *sm* gulf.

go'loso, a *ag* greedy.

'gomito *sm* elbow; (*di strada etc*) sharp bend.

go'mitolo *sm* ball.

'gomma *sf* rubber; (*colla*) gum; (*per cancellare*) rubber, eraser; (*di veicolo*) tyre (*BRIT*), tire (*US*); **~ a terra** flat tyre (*BRIT*) *o* tire (*US*); **gommapi'uma** ® *sf* foam rubber.

'gondola *sf* gondola; **gondoli'ere** *sm* gondolier.

gonfa'lone *sm* banner.

gonfi'are *vt* (*pallone*) to blow up, inflate; (*dilatare, ingrossare*) to swell; (*fig: notizia*) to exaggerate; **~rsi** *vr* to swell; (*fiume*) to rise; **'gonfio, a** *ag* swollen; (*stomaco*) bloated; (*vela*) full; **gonfi'ore** *sm* swelling.

gongo'lare *vi* to look pleased with o.s.; **~ di gioia** to be overjoyed.

'gonna *sf* skirt; **~ pantalone** culottes *pl.*

'gonzo ['gondzo] *sm* simpleton, fool.

gorgheggi'are [gorged'dʒare] *vi* to warble; to trill.

'gorgo, ghi *sm* whirlpool.

gorgogli'are [gorgoʎ'ʎare] *vi* to gurgle.

go'rilla *sm inv* gorilla; (*guardia del corpo*) bodyguard.

'gotta *sf* gout.

gover'nante *sm/f* ruler ♦ *sf* (*di bambini*) governess; (*donna di servizio*) housekeeper.

gover'nare *vt* (*stato*) to govern, rule; (*pilotare, guidare*) to steer; (*bestiame*) to tend, look after; **governa'tivo, a** *ag* government *cpd*; **governa'tore** *sm* governor.

go'verno *sm* government.

gozzovigli'are [gottsoviʎ'ʎare] *vi* to make merry, carouse.

gracchi'are [grak'kjare] *vi* to caw.

graci'dare [gratʃi'dare] *vi* to croak.

'gracile ['gratʃile] *ag* frail, delicate.

gra'dasso *sm* boaster.

gradazi'one [gradat'tsjone] *sf* (*sfumatura*) gradation; **~ alcolica** alcoholic content, strength.

gra'devole *ag* pleasant, agreeable.

gradi'mento *sm* pleasure, satisfaction; **è di suo ~?** is it to your liking?

gradi'nata *sf* flight of steps; (*in teatro, stadio*) tiers *pl.*

gra'dino *sm* step; (*ALPINISMO*) foothold.

gra'dire vt (accettare con piacere) to accept; (desiderare) to wish, like; **gradisce una tazza di tè?** would you like a cup of tea?; **gra'dito, a** ag pleasing; welcome.

'grado sm (MAT, FISICA etc) degree; (stadio) degree, level; (MIL, sociale) rank; **essere in ~ di fare** to be in a position to do.

gradu'ale ag gradual.

gradu'are vt to grade; **gradu'ato, a** ag (esercizi) graded; (scala, termometro) graduated ♦ sm (MIL) non-commissioned officer.

'graffa sf (gancio) clip; (segno grafico) brace.

graffi'are vt to scratch.

'graffio sm scratch.

gra'fia sf spelling; (scrittura) handwriting.

'grafica sf graphic arts pl.

'grafico, a, ci, che ag graphic ♦ sm graph; (persona) graphic designer.

gra'migna [gra'miɲɲa] sf weed; couch grass.

gram'matica, che sf grammar; **grammati'cale** ag grammatical.

'grammo sm gram(me).

gran ag vedi **grande**.

'grana sf (granello, di minerali, corpi spezzati) grain; (fam: seccatura) trouble; (: soldi) cash ♦ sm inv Parmesan (cheese).

gra'naio sm granary, barn.

gra'nata sf (frutto) pomegranate; (pietra preziosa) garnet; (proiettile) grenade.

Gran Bre'tagna [-bre'taɲɲa] sf: **la ~** Great Britain.

'granchio ['grankjo] sm crab; (fig) blunder; **prendere un ~** (fig) to blunder.

grandango'lare sm wide-angle lens sg.

'grande (qualche volta **gran** +C, **grand'** +V) ag (grosso, largo, vasto) big, large; (alto) tall; (lungo) long; (in sensi astratti) great ♦ sm/f (persona adulta) adult, grown-up; (chi ha ingegno e potenza) great man/woman;

fare le cose in ~ to do things in style; **una gran bella donna** a very beautiful woman; **non è una gran cosa** o **un gran che** it's nothing special; **non ne so gran che** I don't know very much about it.

grandeggi'are [granded'dʒare] vi (emergere per grandezza): **~ su** to tower over; (darsi arie) to put on airs.

gran'dezza [gran'dettsa] sf (dimensione) size; magnitude; (fig) greatness; **in ~ naturale** lifesize.

grandi'nare vb impers to hail.

'grandine sf hail.

gran'duca, chi sm grand duke.

gra'nello sm (di cereali, uva) seed; (di frutta) pip; (di sabbia, sale etc) grain.

gra'nita sf kind of water ice.

gra'nito sm granite.

'grano sm (in quasi tutti i sensi) grain; (frumento) wheat; (di rosario, collana) bead; **~ di pepe** peppercorn.

gran'turco sm maize.

'granulo sm granule; (MED) pellet.

'grappa sf rough, strong brandy.

'grappolo sm bunch, cluster.

gras'setto sm (TIP) bold (type).

'grasso, a ag fat; (cibo) fatty; (pelle) greasy; (terreno) rich; (fig: guadagno, annata) plentiful; (: volgare) coarse, lewd ♦ sm (di persona, animale) fat; (sostanza che unge) grease; **gras'soccio, a, ci, ce** ag plump.

'grata sf grating.

gra'ticola sf grill.

gra'tifica, che sf bonus.

'gratis av free, for nothing.

grati'tudine sf gratitude.

'grato, a ag grateful; (gradito) pleasant, agreeable.

gratta'capo sm worry, headache.

grattaci'elo [gratta'tʃɛlo] sm skyscraper.

grat'tare vt (pelle) to scratch; (raschiare) to scrape; (pane, formaggio, carote) to grate; (fam: rubare) to pinch ♦ vi (stridere) to grate; (AUT) to grind; **~rsi** vr to scratch o.s.

grat'tugia, gie [grat'tudʒa] sf grater; **grattugi'are** vt to grate; **pane grattugiato** breadcrumbs pl.

gra'tuito, a *ag* free; *(fig)* gratuitous.
gra'vame *sm* tax; *(fig)* burden, weight.
gra'vare *vt* to burden ♦ *vi*: ~ **su** to weigh on.
'grave *ag* *(danno, pericolo, peccato etc)* grave, serious; *(responsabilità)* heavy, grave; *(contegno)* grave, solemn; *(voce, suono)* deep, low-pitched; *(LING)*: **accento** ~ grave accent; **un malato** ~ a person who is seriously ill.
gravi'danza [gravi'dantsa] *sf* pregnancy.
'gravido, a *ag* pregnant.
gravità *sf* seriousness; *(anche FISICA)* gravity.
gra'voso, a *ag* heavy, onerous.
'grazia ['grattsja] *sf* grace; *(favore)* favour; *(DIR)* pardon; **grazi'are** *vt* *(DIR)* to pardon.
'grazie ['grattsje] *escl* thank you!; ~ **mille!** *o* **tante!** *o* **infinite!** thank you very much!; ~ **a** thanks to.
grazi'oso, a [grat'tsjoso] *ag* charming, delightful; *(gentile)* gracious.
'Grecia ['grɛtʃa] *sf*: **la** ~ Greece; **'greco, a, ci, che** *ag*, *sm/f*, *sm* Greek.
'gregge ['greddʒe] *(pl(f) -i)* *sm* flock.
'greggio, a, gi, ge ['greddʒo] *ag* raw, unrefined; *(diamante)* rough, uncut; *(tessuto)* unbleached ♦ *sm* *(anche: petrolio* ~*)* crude (oil).
grembi'ule *sm* apron; *(sopravveste)* overall.
'grembo *sm* lap; *(ventre della madre)* womb.
gre'mito, a *ag*: ~ **(di)** packed *o* crowded (with).
'gretto, a *ag* mean, stingy; *(fig)* narrow-minded.
'greve *ag* heavy.
'grezzo, a ['greddzo] *ag* = **greggio**.
gri'dare *vi* *(per chiamare)* to shout, cry (out); *(strillare)* to scream, yell ♦ *vt* to shout (out), yell (out); ~ **aiuto** to cry *o* shout for help.
'grido *(pl(m) -i* *o* *pl(f) -a)* *sm* shout, cry; scream, yell; *(di animale)* cry; **di** ~ famous.
'grigio, a, gi, gie ['gridʒo] *ag*, *sm* grey.
'griglia ['griʎʎa] *sf* *(per arrostire)* grill; *(ELETTR)* grid; *(inferriata)* grating;

alla ~ *(CUC)* grilled; **grigli'ata** *sf* *(CUC)* grill.
gril'letto *sm* trigger.
'grillo *sm* *(ZOOL)* cricket; *(fig)* whim.
grimal'dello *sm* picklock.
'grinta *sf* grim expression; *(SPORT)* fighting spirit.
'grinza ['grintsa] *sf* crease, wrinkle; *(ruga)* wrinkle; **non fare una** ~ *(fig: ragionamento)* to be faultless; **grin'zoso, a** *ag* creased; wrinkled.
grip'pare *vi* *(TECN)* to seize.
gris'sino *sm* bread-stick.
'gronda *sf* eaves *pl*.
gron'daia *sf* gutter.
gron'dare *vi* to pour; *(essere bagnato)*: ~ **di** to be dripping with ♦ *vt* to drip with.
'groppa *sf* *(di animale)* back, rump; *(fam: dell'uomo)* back, shoulders *pl*.
'groppo *sm* tangle; **avere un** ~ **alla gola** *(fig)* to have a lump in one's throat.
gros'sezza [gros'settsa] *sf* size; thickness.
gros'sista, i, e *sm/f* *(COMM)* wholesaler.
'grosso, a *ag* big, large; *(di spessore)* thick; *(grossolano: anche fig)* coarse; *(grave, insopportabile)* serious, great; *(tempo, mare)* rough ♦ *sm*: **il** ~ **di** the bulk of; **un pezzo** ~ *(fig)* a VIP, a bigwig; **farla** ~**a** to do something very stupid; **dirle** ~**e** to tell tall stories; **sbagliarsi di** ~ to be completely wrong.
grosso'lano, a *ag* rough, coarse; *(fig)* coarse, crude; *(: errore)* stupid.
grosso'modo *av* roughly.
'grotta *sf* cave; grotto.
grot'tesco, a, schi, sche *ag* grotesque.
grovi'era *sm* *o* *f* gruyère (cheese).
gro'viglio [gro'viʎʎo] *sm* tangle; *(fig)* muddle.
gru *sf inv* crane.
'gruccia, ce ['gruttʃa] *sf* *(per camminare)* crutch; *(per abiti)* coathanger.
gru'gnire [gruɲ'nire] *vi* to grunt; **gru'gnito** *sm* grunt.

'grugno ['gruɲɲo] *sm* snout; (*fam: faccia*) mug.
'grullo, a *ag* silly, stupid.
'grumo *sm* (*di sangue*) clot; (*di farina etc*) lump.
'gruppo *sm* group; ~ **sanguigno** blood group.
gruvi'era *sm o f* = **groviera**.
guada'gnare [gwadaɲ'ɲare] *vt* (*ottenere*) to gain; (*soldi, stipendio*) to earn; (*vincere*) to win; (*raggiungere*) to reach.
gua'dagno [gwa'daɲɲo] *sm* earnings *pl*; (*COMM*) profit; (*vantaggio, utile*) advantage, gain; ~ **lordo/netto** gross/net earnings *pl*.
gu'ado *sm* ford; **passare a** ~ to ford.
gu'ai *escl:* ~ **a te** (*o* **lui** *etc*)! woe betide you (*o* him *etc*)!
gua'ina *sf* (*fodero*) sheath; (*indumento per donna*) girdle.
gu'aio *sm* trouble, mishap; (*inconveniente*) trouble, snag.
gua'ire *vi* to whine, yelp.
gu'ancia, ce ['gwantʃa] *sf* cheek.
guanci'ale [gwan'tʃale] *sm* pillow.
gu'anto *sm* glove.
gu'arda... *prefisso:* ~'**boschi** *sm inv* forester; ~'**caccia** *sm inv* gamekeeper; ~'**coste** *sm inv* coastguard; (*nave*) coastguard patrol vessel; ~'**linee** *sm inv* (*SPORT*) linesman.
guar'dare *vt* (*con lo sguardo: osservare*) to look at; (*film, televisione*) to watch; (*custodire*) to look after, take care of ♦ *vi* to look; (*badare*): ~ **a** to pay attention to; (*luoghi: esser orientato*): ~ **a** to face; ~**rsi** *vr* to look at o.s.; ~**rsi da** (*astenersi*) to refrain from; (*stare in guardia*) to beware of; ~**rsi da fare** to take care not to do; **guarda di non sbagliare** try not to make a mistake; ~ **a vista qn** to keep a close watch on sb.
guarda'roba *sm inv* wardrobe; (*locale*) cloakroom; **guardarobi'ere, a** *sm/f* cloakroom attendant.
gu'ardia *sf* (*individuo, corpo*) guard; (*sorveglianza*) watch; **fare la** ~ **a qc/qn** to guard sth/sb; **stare in** ~ (*fig*) to be

on one's guard; **di** ~ (*medico*) on call; ~ **carceraria** (*prison*) warder; ~ **del corpo** bodyguard; ~ **di finanza** (*corpo*) customs *pl*; (*persona*) customs officer; ~ **medica** emergency doctor service.
guardi'ano, a *sm/f* (*di carcere*) warder; (*di villa etc*) caretaker; (*di museo*) custodian; (*di zoo*) keeper; ~ **notturno** night watchman.
guar'dingo, a, ghi, ghe *ag* wary, cautious.
guardi'ola *sf* porter's lodge; (*MIL*) look-out tower.
guarigi'one [gwari'dʒone] *sf* recovery.
gua'rire *vt* (*persona, malattia*) to cure; (*ferita*) to heal ♦ *vi* to recover, be cured; to heal (up).
guarnigi'one [gwarni'dʒone] *sf* garrison.
guar'nire *vt* (*ornare: abiti*) to trim; (*CUC*) to garnish; **guarnizi'one** *sf* trimming; garnish; (*TECN*) gasket.
guasta'feste *sm/f inv* spoilsport.
guas'tare *vt* to spoil, ruin; (*meccanismo*) to break; ~**rsi** *vr* (*cibo*) to go bad; (*meccanismo*) to break down; (*tempo*) to change for the worse; (*amici*) to quarrel, fall out.
gu'asto, a *ag* (*non funzionante*) broken; (: *telefono etc*) out of order; (*andato a male*) bad, rotten; (: *dente*) decayed, bad; (*fig: corrotto*) depraved ♦ *sm* breakdown; (*avaria*) failure; ~ **al motore** engine failure.
guazza'buglio [gwattsa'buʎʎo] *sm* muddle.
gu'ercio, a, ci, ce ['gwertʃo] *ag* cross-eyed.
gu'erra *sf* war; (*tecnica: atomica, chimica etc*) warfare; **fare la** ~ **(a)** to wage war (against); ~ **mondiale** world war; **guerreggi'are** *vi* to wage war; **guerri'ero, a** *ag* warlike ♦ *sm* warrior; **guer'riglia** *sf* guerrilla warfare; **guerri'gli'ero** *sm* guerrilla.
'gufo *sm* owl.
gu'ida *sf* guide; (*comando, direzione*) guidance, direction; (: *sterzo*) steering; (*tappeto, di tenda, cassetto*) runner; ~ **a destra/sinistra** (*AUT*) right-/left-hand drive; ~

telefonica telephone directory.
gui'dare *vt* to guide; (*condurre a capo*)
to lead; (*auto*) to drive; (*aereo, nave*)
to pilot; **sai ~?** can you drive?;
guida'tore, trice *sm/f* (*conducente*)
driver.
guin'zaglio [gwin'tsaʎʎo] *sm* leash, lead.
gu'isa *sf*: **a ~ di** like, in the manner of.
guiz'zare [gwit'tsare] *vi* to dart; to flicker; to leap; **~ via** (*fuggire*) to slip
away.
'guscio ['guʃʃo] *sm* shell.
gus'tare *vt* (*cibi*) to taste; (: *assapora-
re con piacere*) to enjoy, savour; (*fig*)
to enjoy, appreciate ♦ *vi*: **~ a** to
please; **non mi gusta affatto** I don't like
it at all.
'gusto *sm* taste; (*sapore*) flavour;
(*godimento*) enjoyment; **al ~ di fragola**
strawberry-flavoured; **mangiare di ~** to
eat heartily; **prenderci ~: ci ha preso
~** he's acquired a taste for it, he's got
to like it; **gus'toso, a** *ag* tasty; (*fig*)
agreeable.

H

h *abbr* = **ora**; **altezza**.
ha *etc* [a] *vb vedi* **avere**.
hall [hɔl] *sf inv* hall, foyer.
'handicap ['handikap] *sm inv* handicap;
handicap'pato, a *ag* handicapped ♦
sm/f handicapped person, disabled
person.
'hanno ['anno] *vb vedi* **avere**.
'hascisc ['haʃiʃ] *sm* hashish.
'herpes ['ɛrpes] *sm* (*MED*) herpes *sg*; **~
zoster** shingles *sg*.
ho [ɔ] *vb vedi* **avere**.
'hobby ['hɔbi] *sm inv* hobby.
'hockey ['hɔki] *sm* hockey; **~ su
ghiaccio** ice hockey.
'hostess ['houstis] *sf inv* air hostess
(*BRIT*) *o* stewardess.
ho'tel *sm inv* hotel.

I

i *det mpl* the.
i'ato *sm* hiatus.
ibernazi'one [ibernat'tsjone] *sf* hibernation.
'ibrido, a *ag, sm* hybrid.
Id'dio *sm* God.
i'dea *sf* idea; (*opinione*) opinion, view;
(*ideale*) ideal; **dare l'~ di** to seem, look
like; **~ fissa** obsession; **neanche** *o*
neppure per ~! certainly not!
ide'ale *ag, sm* ideal.
ide'are *vt* (*immaginare*) to think up,
conceive; (*progettare*) to plan.
i'dentico, a, ci, che *ag* identical.
identifi'care *vt* to identify;
identificazi'one *sf* identification.
identità *sf inv* identity.
idi'oma, i *sm* idiom, language;
idio'matico, a, ci, che *ag* idiomatic;
frase idiomatica idiom.
idi'ota, i, e *ag* idiotic ♦ *sm/f* idiot.
idola'trare *vt* to worship; (*fig*) to
idolize.
'idolo *sm* idol.
idoneità *sf* suitability.
i'doneo, a *ag*: **~ a** suitable for, fit for;
(*MIL*) fit for; (*qualificato*) qualified for.
i'drante *sm* hydrant.
i'draulica *sf* hydraulics *sg*.
i'draulico, a, ci, che *ag* hydraulic ♦
sm plumber.
idroe'lettrico, a, ci, che *ag* hydroelectric.
i'drofilo, a *ag vedi* **cotone**.
idrofo'bia *sf* rabies *sg*.
i'drogeno [i'drɔdʒeno] *sm* hydrogen.
idros'calo *sm* seaplane base.
idrovo'lante *sm* seaplane.
i'ena *sf* hyena.
i'eri *av, sm* yesterday; **il giornale di ~**
yesterday's paper; **~ l'altro** the day
before yesterday; **~ sera** yesterday
evening.
igi'ene [i'dʒɛne] *sf* hygiene; **~ pubblica**
public health; **igi'enico, a, ci, che** *ag*
hygienic; (*salubre*) healthy.

i'**gnaro, a** [iɲ'ɲaro] *ag*: ~ **di** unaware of, ignorant of.

i'**gnobile** [iɲ'ɲɔbile] *ag* despicable, vile.

igno'**rante** [iɲɲo'rante] *ag* ignorant.

igno'**rare** [iɲɲo'rare] *vt* (*non sapere, conoscere*) to be ignorant *o* unaware of, not to know; (*fingere di non vedere, sentire*) to ignore.

i'**gnoto, a** [iɲ'ɲɔto] *ag* unknown.

PAROLA CHIAVE

il (*pl* (*m*) **i**; *diventa* **lo** (*pl* **gli**) *davanti a* s *impura, gn, pn, ps, x, z*; *f* **la** (*pl* **le**)) *det m* **1** the; ~ **libro/lo studente/l'acqua** the book/the student/the water; **gli scolari** the pupils

2 (*astrazione*): ~ **coraggio/l'amore/la giovinezza** courage/love/youth

3 (*tempo*): ~ **mattino/la sera** in the morning/evening; ~ **venerdì** *etc* (*abitualmente*) on Fridays *etc*; (*quel giorno*) on (the) Friday *etc*; **la settimana prossima** next week

4 (*distributivo*) a, an; **2.500 lire** ~ **chilo/paio** 2,500 lire a *o* per kilo/pair

5 (*partitivo*) some, any; **hai messo lo zucchero?** have you added sugar?; **hai comprato** ~ **latte?** did you buy (some *o* any) milk?

6 (*possesso*): **aprire gli occhi** to open one's eyes; **rompersi la gamba** to break one's leg; **avere i capelli neri/~ naso rosso** to have dark hair/a red nose

7 (*con nomi propri*): ~ **Petrarca** Petrarch; ~ **Presidente Reagan** President Reagan; **dov'è la Francesca?** where's Francesca?

8 (*con nomi geografici*): ~ **Tevere** the Tiber; **l'Italia** Italy; ~ **Regno Unito** the United Kingdom; **l'Everest** Everest.

'**ilare** *ag* cheerful; **ilarità** *sf* hilarity, mirth.

illangui'**dire** *vi* to grow weak *o* feeble.

illazi'**one** [illat'tsjone] *sf* inference, deduction.

ille'**gale** *ag* illegal.

illeg'**gibile** [illed'dʒibile] *ag* illegible.

ille'**gittimo, a** [ille'dʒittimo] *ag* illegitimate.

il'**leso, a** *ag* unhurt, unharmed.

illette'**rato, a** *ag* illiterate.

illi'**bato, a** *ag*: **donna** ~**a** virgin.

illimi'**tato, a** *ag* boundless; unlimited.

ill.mo *abbr* = **illustrissimo.**

il'**ludere** *vt* to deceive, delude; ~**rsi** *vr* to deceive o.s., delude o.s.

illumi'**nare** *vt* to light up, illuminate; (*fig*) to enlighten; ~**rsi** *vr* to light up; ~ **a giorno** to floodlight; **illuminazi'one** *sf* lighting; illumination; floodlighting; (*fig*) flash of inspiration.

illusi'**one** *sf* illusion; **farsi delle** ~**i** to delude o.s.

illusio'**nismo** *sm* conjuring.

il'**luso, a** *pp di* **illudere.**

illus'**trare** *vt* to illustrate; **illustra'tivo, a** *ag* illustrative; **illustrazi'one** *sf* illustration.

il'**lustre** *ag* eminent, renowned; **illus'trissimo, a** *ag* (*negli indirizzi*) very revered.

imbacuc'**care** *vt* to wrap up; ~**rsi** *vr* to wrap up.

imbal'**laggio** [imbal'laddʒo] *sm* packing *no pl*.

imbal'**lare** *vt* to pack; (*AUT*) to race; ~**rsi** *vr* (*AUT*) to race.

imbalsa'**mare** *vt* to embalm.

imbambo'**lato, a** *ag* (*sguardo*) vacant, blank.

imban'**dire** *vt*: ~ **un pranzo** to prepare a lavish meal.

imbaraz'**zare** [imbarat'tsare] *vt* (*mettere a disagio*) to embarrass; (*ostacolare: movimenti*) to hamper; (: *stomaco*) to lie heavily on.

imba'**razzo** [imba'rattso] *sm* (*disagio*) embarrassment; (*perplessità*) puzzlement, bewilderment; ~ **di stomaco** indigestion.

imbarca'**dero** *sm* landing stage.

imbar'**care** *vt* (*passeggeri*) to embark; (*merci*) to load; ~**rsi** *vr*: ~**rsi su** to board; ~**rsi per l'America** to sail for America; ~**rsi in** (*fig: affare etc*) to embark on.

imbarcazi'**one** [imbarkat'tsjone] *sf* (small) boat, (small) craft *inv*; ~ **di salvataggio** lifeboat.

im'barco, chi sm embarkation; loading; boarding; (banchina) landing stage.

imbas'tire vt (cucire) to tack; (fig: abbozzare) to sketch, outline.

im'battersi vr: ~ **in** (incontrare) to bump o run into.

imbat'tibile ag unbeatable, invincible.

imbavagli'are [imbavaʎ'ʎare] vt to gag.

imbec'cata sf (TEATRO) prompt.

imbe'cille [imbe'tʃille] ag idiotic ♦ sm/f idiot; (MED) imbecile.

imbel'lire vt to adorn, embellish ♦ vi to grow more beautiful.

im'berbe ag beardless.

im'bevere vt to soak; ~**rsi** vr: ~**rsi di** to soak up, absorb.

imbian'care vt to whiten; (muro) to whitewash ♦ vi to become o turn white.

imbian'chino [imbjan'kino] sm (house) painter, painter and decorator.

imboc'care vt (bambino) to feed; (entrare: strada) to enter, turn into ♦ vi: ~ **in** (sog: strada) to lead into; (: fiume) to flow into.

imbocca'tura sf mouth; (di strada, porto) entrance; (MUS, del morso) mouthpiece.

im'bocco, chi sm entrance.

imbos'care vt to hide; ~**rsi** vr (MIL) to evade military service.

imbos'cata sf ambush.

imbottigli'are [imbotti'ʎʎare] vt to bottle; (NAUT) to blockade; (MIL) to hem in; ~**rsi** vr to be stuck in a traffic jam.

imbot'tire vt to stuff; (giacca) to pad; **imbot'tita** sf quilt; **imbotti'tura** sf stuffing; padding.

imbrat'tare vt to dirty, smear, daub.

imbrigli'are [imbriʎ'ʎare] vt to bridle.

imbroc'care vt (fig) to guess correctly.

imbrogli'are [imbroʎ'ʎare] vt to mix up; (fig: raggirare) to deceive, cheat; (: confondere) to confuse, mix up; ~**rsi** vr to get tangled; (fig) to become confused; **im'broglio** sm (groviglio) tangle; (situazione confusa) mess; (truffa) swindle, trick; **imbrogli'one, a** sm/f cheat, swindler.

imbronci'are [imbron'tʃare] vi (anche: ~**rsi**) to sulk; **imbronci'ato, a** ag sulky.

imbru'nire vi, vb impers to grow dark; **all'~** at dusk.

imbrut'tire vt to make ugly ♦ vi to become ugly.

imbu'care vt to post.

imbur'rare vt to butter.

im'buto sm funnel.

imi'tare vt to imitate; (riprodurre) to copy; (assomigliare) to look like; **imitazi'one** sf imitation.

immaco'lato, a ag spotless; immaculate.

immagazzi'nare [immagaddzi'nare] vt to store.

immagi'nare [immadʒi'nare] vt to imagine; (supporre) to suppose; (inventare) to invent; **s'immagini!** don't mention it!, not at all!; **immagi'nario, a** ag imaginary; **immaginazi'one** sf imagination; (cosa immaginata) fancy.

im'magine [im'madʒine] sf image; (rappresentazione grafica, mentale) picture.

imman'cabile ag certain; unfailing.

immangi'abile [imman'dʒabile] ag inedible.

immatrico'lare vt to register; ~**rsi** vr (INS) to matriculate, enrol; **immatricolazi'one** sf registration; matriculation, enrolment.

imma'turo, a ag (frutto) unripe; (persona) immature; (prematuro) premature.

immedesi'marsi vr: ~ **in** to identify with.

immediata'mente av immediately, at once.

immedi'ato, a ag immediate.

im'memore ag: ~ **di** forgetful of.

im'menso, a ag immense.

im'mergere [im'merdʒere] vt to immerse, plunge; ~**rsi** vr to plunge; (sommergibile) to dive, submerge; (dedicarsi a): ~**rsi in** to immerse o.s. in.

immeri'tato, a ag undeserved.

immeri'tevole ag undeserving, unworthy.

immersi'one *sf* immersion; (*di sommergibile*) submersion, dive; (*di palombaro*) dive.

im'merso, a *pp di* **immergere**.

im'mettere *vt*: ~ (**in**) to introduce (into); ~ **dati in un computer** to enter data on a computer.

immi'grato, a *sm/f* immigrant; **immigrazi'one** *sf* immigration.

immi'nente *ag* imminent.

immischi'are [immis'kjare] *vt*: ~ **qn in** to involve sb in; **~rsi in** to interfere *o* meddle in.

immissi'one *sf* (*di aria, gas*) intake; ~ **di dati** (*INFORM*) data entry.

im'mobile *ag* motionless, still; **~i** *smpl* (*anche*: *beni ~i*) real estate *sg*; **immobili'are** *ag* (*DIR*) property *cpd*; **immobilità** *sf* stillness; immobility.

immo'desto, a *ag* immodest.

immo'lare *vt* to sacrifice, immolate.

immon'dizia [immon'dittsja] *sf* dirt, filth; (*spesso al pl: spazzatura, rifiuti*) rubbish *no pl*, refuse *no pl*.

im'mondo, a *ag* filthy, foul.

immo'rale *ag* immoral.

immor'tale *ag* immortal.

im'mune *ag* (*esente*) exempt; (*MED, DIR*) immune; **immunità** *sf* immunity; **immunità parlamentare** parliamentary privilege.

immu'tabile *ag* immutable; unchanging.

impacchet'tare [impakket'tare] *vt* to pack up.

impacci'are [impat'tʃare] *vt* to hinder, hamper; **impacci'ato, a** *ag* awkward, clumsy; (*imbarazzato*) embarrassed; **im'paccio** *sm* obstacle; (*imbarazzo*) embarrassment; (*situazione imbarazzante*) awkward situation.

im'pacco, chi *sm* (*MED*) compress.

impadro'nirsi *vr*: ~ **di** to seize, take possession of; (*fig: apprendere a fondo*) to master.

impa'gabile *ag* priceless.

impagi'nare [impadʒi'nare] *vt* (*TIP*) to paginate, page (up).

impagli'are [impaʎ'ʎare] *vt* to stuff (with straw).

impa'lato, a *ag* (*fig*) stiff as a board.

impalca'tura *sf* scaffolding.

impalli'dire *vi* to turn pale; (*fig*) to fade.

impa'nare *vt* (*CUC*) to dip in breadcrumbs.

impanta'narsi *vr* to sink (in the mud); (*fig*) to get bogged down.

impappi'narsi *vr* to stammer, falter.

impa'rare *vt* to learn.

impareggi'abile [impared'dʒabile] *ag* incomparable.

imparen'tarsi *vr*: ~ **con** to marry into.

'impari *ag inv* (*disuguale*) unequal; (*dispari*) odd.

impar'tire *vt* to bestow, give.

imparzi'ale [impar'tsjale] *ag* impartial, unbiased.

impas'sibile *ag* impassive.

impas'tare *vt* (*pasta*) to knead; (*colori*) to mix.

im'pasto *sm* (*l'impastare: di pane*) kneading; (*: di cemento*) mixing; (*pasta*) dough; (*anche fig*) mixture.

im'patto *sm* impact.

impau'rire *vt* to scare, frighten ♦ *vi* (*anche*: **~rsi**) to become scared *o* frightened.

impazi'ente [impat'tsjente] *ag* impatient; **impazi'enza** *sf* impatience.

impaz'zata [impat'tsata] *sf*: **all'~** (*precipitosamente*) at breakneck speed.

impaz'zire [impat'tsire] *vi* to go mad; ~ **per qn/qc** to be crazy about sb/sth.

impec'cabile *ag* impeccable.

impedi'mento *sm* obstacle, hindrance.

impe'dire *vt* (*vietare*): ~ **a qn di fare** to prevent sb from doing; (*ostruire*) to obstruct; (*impacciare*) to hamper, hinder.

impe'gnare [impen'ɲare] *vt* (*dare in pegno*) to pawn; (*onore etc*) to pledge; (*prenotare*) to book, reserve; (*obbligare*) to oblige; (*occupare*) to keep busy; (*MIL: nemico*) to engage; **~rsi** *vr* (*vincolarsi*): **~rsi a fare** to undertake to do; (*mettersi risolutamente*): **~rsi in qc** to devote o.s. to sth; **~rsi con qn** (*accordarsi*) to come to an agreement with sb; **impegna'tivo, a** *ag* binding;

(lavoro) demanding, exacting; **impe-'gnato, a** *ag (occupato)* busy; *(fig: romanzo, autore)* committed, engagé.

im'pegno [im'peɲɲo] *sm (obbligo)* obligation; *(promessa)* promise, pledge; *(zelo)* diligence, zeal; *(compito, d'autore)* commitment.

impel'lente *ag* pressing, urgent.

impene'trabile *ag* impenetrable.

impen'narsi *vr (cavallo)* to rear up; *(AER)* to nose up; *(fig)* to bridle.

impen'sato, a *ag* unforeseen, unexpected.

impensie'rire *vt* to worry; **~rsi** *vr* to worry.

impe'rare *vi (anche fig)* to reign, rule.

impera'tivo, a *ag, sm* imperative.

impera'tore, 'trice *sm/f* emperor/empress.

imperdo'nabile *ag* unforgivable, unpardonable.

imper'fetto, a *ag* imperfect ♦ *sm (LING)* imperfect (tense); **imperfezi'one** *sf* imperfection.

imperi'ale *ag* imperial.

imperi'oso, a *ag (persona)* imperious; *(motivo, esigenza)* urgent, pressing.

impe'rizia [impe'rittsja] *sf* lack of experience.

imperma'lirsi *vr* to take offence.

imperme'abile *ag* waterproof ♦ *sm* raincoat.

imperni'are *vt:* ~ **qc su** to hinge sth on; *(fig)* to base sth on; **~rsi** *vr (fig):* **~rsi su** to be based on.

im'pero *sm* empire; *(forza, autorità)* rule, control.

imperscru'tabile *ag* inscrutable.

imperso'nale *ag* impersonal.

imperso'nare *vt* to personify; *(TEATRO)* to play, act (the part of).

imperter'rito, a *ag* fearless, undaunted; impassive.

imperti'nente *ag* impertinent.

imperver'sare *vi* to rage.

'impeto *sm (moto, forza)* force, impetus; *(assalto)* onslaught; *(fig: impulso)* impulse; *(: slancio)* transport; **con** ~ energetically;

vehemently.

impet'tito, a *ag* stiff, erect.

impetu'oso, a *ag (vento)* strong, raging; *(persona)* impetuous.

impian'tare *vt (motore)* to install; *(azienda, discussione)* to establish, start.

impi'anto *sm (installazione)* installation; *(apparecchiature)* plant; *(sistema)* system; ~ **elettrico** wiring; ~ **sportivo** sports complex; **~i di risalita** *(SCI)* ski lifts.

impias'trare *vt* to smear, dirty.

impiastricci'are [impjastrit'tʃarc] *vt* = **impiastrare**.

impi'astro *sm* poultice.

impic'care *vt* to hang; **~rsi** *vr* to hang o.s.

impicci'are [impit'tʃare] *vt* to hinder, hamper; **~rsi** *vr* to meddle, interfere; **im'piccio** *sm (ostacolo)* hindrance; *(seccatura)* trouble, bother; *(affare imbrogliato)* mess; **essere d'impiccio** to be in the way.

impie'gare *vt (usare)* to use, employ; *(assumere)* to employ, take on; *(spendere: denaro, tempo)* to spend; *(investire)* to invest; **~rsi** *vr* to get a job, obtain employment; **impie'gato, a** *sm/f* employee.

impi'ego, ghi *sm (uso)* use; *(occupazione)* employment; *(posto di lavoro)* (regular) job, post; *(ECON)* investment.

impieto'sire *vt* to move to pity; **~rsi** *vr* to be moved to pity.

imple'trire *vt (fig)* to petrify.

impigli'are [impiʎ'ʎare] *vt* to catch, entangle; **~rsi** *vr* to get caught up o entangled.

impi'grire *vt* to make lazy ♦ *vi (anche:* **~rsi)** to grow lazy.

impli'care *vt* to imply; *(coinvolgere)* to involve; **~rsi** *vr:* **~rsi (in)** to become involved (in); **implicazi'one** *sf* implication.

im'plicito, a [im'plitʃito] *ag* implicit.

impolve'rare *vt* to cover with dust; **~rsi** *vr* to get dusty.

impo'nente *ag* imposing, impressive.

impo'nibile *ag* taxable ♦ *sm* taxable income.

impopo'lare *ag* unpopular.

im'porre *vt* to impose; (*costringere*) to force, make; (*far valere*) to impose, enforce; **imporsi** *vr* (*persona*) to assert o.s.; (*cosa: rendersi necessario*) to become necessary; (*aver successo: moda, attore*) to become popular; ~ **a qn di fare** to force sb to do, make sb do.

impor'tante *ag* important; **impor'tanza** *sf* importance; **dare importanza a qc** to attach importance to sth; **darsi importanza** to give o.s. airs.

impor'tare *vt* (*introdurre dall'estero*) to import ♦ *vi* to matter, be important ♦ *vb impers* (*essere necessario*) to be necessary; (*interessare*) to matter; **non importa!** it doesn't matter!; **non me ne importa!** I don't care!; **importazi'one** *sf* importation; (*merci importate*) imports *pl*.

im'porto *sm* (total) amount.

importu'nare *vt* to bother.

impor'tuno, a *ag* irksome, annoying.

imposizi'one [impozit'tsjone] *sf* imposition; order, command; (*onere, imposta*) tax.

imposses'sarsi *vr*: ~ **di** to seize, take possession of.

impos'sibile *ag* impossible; **fare l'~** to do one's utmost, do all one can; **impossibilità** *sf* impossibility; **essere nell'impossibilità di fare qc** to be unable to do sth.

im'posta *sf* (*di finestra*) shutter; (*tassa*) tax; ~ **sul reddito** income tax; ~ **sul valore aggiunto** value added tax (*BRIT*), sales tax (*US*).

impos'tare *vt* (*imbucare*) to post; (*preparare*) to plan, set out; (*avviare*) to begin, start off; (*voce*) to pitch.

im'posto, a *pp di* **imporre.**

impo'tente *ag* weak, powerless; (*anche MED*) impotent.

impove'rire *vt* to impoverish ♦ *vi* (*anche*: ~**rsi**) to become poor.

imprati'cabile *ag* (*strada*) impassable; (*campo da gioco*) unplayable.

imprati'chire [imprati'kire] *vt* to train; ~**rsi in qc** to practise (*BRIT*) *o* practice (*US*) sth.

impre'gnare [impreɲ'ɲare] *vt*: ~ **(di)** (*imbevere*) to soak *o* impregnate (with); (*riempire: anche fig*) to fill (with).

imprendi'tore *sm* (*industriale*) entrepreneur; (*appaltatore*) contractor; **piccolo** ~ small businessman.

im'presa *sf* (*iniziativa*) enterprise; (*azione*) exploit; (*azienda*) firm, concern.

impre'sario *sm* (*TEATRO*) manager, impresario; ~ **di pompe funebri** funeral director.

imprescin'dibile [impreʃʃin'dibile] *ag* not to be ignored.

impressio'nante *ag* impressive; upsetting.

impressio'nare *vt* to impress; (*turbare*) to upset; (*FOT*) to expose; ~**rsi** *vr* to be easily upset.

impressi'one *sf* impression; (*fig: sensazione*) sensation, feeling; (*stampa*) printing; **fare** ~ (*colpire*) to impress; (*turbare*) to frighten, upset; **fare buona/cattiva** ~ **a** to make a good/bad impression on.

im'presso, a *pp di* **imprimere.**

impres'tare *vt*: ~ **qc a qn** to lend sth to sb.

impreve'dibile *ag* unforeseeable; (*persona*) unpredictable.

imprevi'dente *ag* lacking in foresight.

impre'visto, a *ag* unexpected, unforeseen ♦ *sm* unforeseen event; **salvo** ~**i** unless anything unexpected happens.

imprigio'nare [impridʒo'nare] *vt* to imprison.

im'primere *vt* (*anche fig*) to impress, stamp; (*comunicare: movimento*) to transmit, give.

impro'babile *ag* improbable, unlikely.

im'pronta *sf* imprint, impression, sign; (*di piede, mano*) print; (*fig*) mark, stamp; ~ **digitale** fingerprint.

impro'perio *sm* insult.

im'proprio, a *ag* improper; **arma** ~**a**

offensive weapon.

improvvisa'mente *av* suddenly; unexpectedly.

improvvi'sare *vt* to improvise; **~rsi**
vr: **~rsi cuoco** to (decide to) act as
cook; **improvvi'sata** *sf* (pleasant)
surprise.

improv'viso, a *ag* (*imprevisto*) unexpected; (*subitaneo*) sudden; **all'~** unexpectedly; suddenly.

impru'dente *ag* unwise, rash.

impu'dente *ag* impudent.

impu'dico, a, chi, che *ag* immodest.

impu'gnare [impuɲ'nare] *vt* to grasp,
grip; (*DIR*) to contest.

impul'sivo, a *ag* impulsive.

im'pulso *sm* impulse.

impun'tarsi *vr* to stop dead, refuse to
budge; (*fig*) to be obstinate.

impu'tare *vt* (*ascrivere*): **~ qc a** to
attribute sth to; (*DIR: accusare*): **~ qn
di** to charge sb with, accuse sb of;
impu'tato, a *sm/f* (*DIR*) accused,
defendant; **imputazi'one** *sf* (*DIR*)
charge.

imputri'dire *vi* to rot.

PAROLA CHIAVE
---

in (*in+il* = **nel**, *in+lo* = **nello**, *in+l'* =
nell', *in+la* = **nella**, *in+i* = **nei**, *in+gli*
= **negli**, *in+le* = **nelle**) *prep* **1** (*stato in
luogo*) in; **vivere ~ Italia/città** to live in
Italy/town; **essere ~ casa/ufficio** to be
at home/the office; **se fossi ~ te** if I
were you

2 (*moto a luogo*) to; (*: dentro*) into;
andare ~ Germania/città to go to
Germany/town; **andare ~ ufficio** to go
to the office, **entrare ~ macchina/casa**
to get into the car/go into the house

3 (*tempo*) in; **nel 1989** in 1989; **~
giugno/estate** in June/summer

4 (*modo, maniera*) in; **~ silenzio** in
silence; **~ abito da sera** in evening
dress; **~ guerra** at war; **~ vacanza** on
holiday; **Maria Bianchi ~ Rossi** Maria
Rossi née Bianchi

5 (*mezzo*) by; **viaggiare ~ autobus/
treno** to travel by bus/train

6 (*materia*) made of; **~ marmo** made

of marble, marble *cpd*; **una collana ~
oro** a gold necklace

7 (*misura*) in; **siamo ~ quattro** there
are four of us; **~ tutto** in all

8 (*fine*): **dare ~ dono** to give as a gift;
spende tutto ~ alcool he spends all his
money on drink; **~ onore di** in honour
of.

i'nabile *ag*: **~ a** incapable of;
(*fisicamente, MIL*) unfit for; **inabilità** *sf*
incapacity.

inabi'tabile *ag* uninhabitable.

inacces'sibile [inattʃes'sibile] *ag* (*luogo*)
inaccessible; (*persona*) unapproach-
able; (*mistero*) unfathomable.

inaccet'tabile [inattʃet'tabile] *ag* un-
acceptable.

ina'datto, a *ag*: **~ (a)** unsuitable *o*
unfit (for).

inadegu'ato, a *ag* inadequate.

inadempi'enza [inadem'pjɛntsa] *sf*: **~
(a)** non-fulfilment (of).

inaffer'rabile *ag* elusive; (*concetto,
senso*) difficult to grasp.

ina'lare *vt* to inhale.

inalbe'rare *vt* (*NAUT*) to hoist, raise;
~rsi *vr* (*fig*) to flare up, fly off the
handle.

inalte'rabile *ag* unchangeable; (*colore*)
fast, permanent; (*affetto*) constant.

inalte'rato, a *ag* unchanged.

inami'dato, a *ag* starched.

inani'mato, a *ag* inanimate; (*senza
vita: corpo*) lifeless.

inappa'gabile *ag* insatiable.

inappel'labile *ag* (*decisione*) final,
irrevocable; (*DIR*) final, not open to
appeal.

inappe'tenza [inappe'tɛntsa] *sf* (*MED*)
lack of appetite.

inappun'tabile *ag* irreproachable.

inar'care *vt* (*schiena*) to arch;
(*sopracciglia*) to raise; **~rsi** *vr* to arch.

inari'dire *vt* to make arid, dry up ♦ *vi*
(*anche: ~rsi*) to dry up, become arid.

inaspet'tato, a *ag* unexpected.

inas'prire *vt* (*disciplina*) to tighten up,
make harsher; (*carattere*) to embitter;
~rsi *vr* to become harsher; to become

bitter; to become worse.

inattac'cabile *ag (anche fig)* unassailable; *(alibi)* cast-iron.

inatten'dibile *ag* unreliable.

inat'teso, a *ag* unexpected.

inattu'abile *ag* impracticable.

inau'dito, a *ag* unheard of.

inaugu'rare *vt* to inaugurate, open; *(monumento)* to unveil.

inavve'duto, a *ag* careless, inadvertent.

inavver'tenza [inavver'tɛntsa] *sf* carelessness, inadvertence.

incagli'are [inkaʎ'ʎare] *vi (NAUT: anche: ~rsi)* to run aground.

incal'lito, a *ag* calloused; *(fig)* hardened, inveterate; *(: insensibile)* hard.

incal'zare [inkal'tsare] *vt* to follow o pursue closely; *(fig)* to press ♦ *vi (urgere)* to be pressing; *(essere imminente)* to be imminent.

incame'rare *vt (DIR)* to expropriate.

incammi'nare *vt (fig: avviare)* to start up; ~rsi *vr* to set off.

incande'scente [inkandeʃ'ʃɛnte] *ag* incandescent, white-hot.

incan'tare *vt* to enchant, bewitch; ~rsi *vr (rimanere intontito)* to be spellbound; to be in a daze; *(meccanismo: bloccarsi)* to jam; **incanta'tore, 'trice** *ag* enchanting, bewitching ♦ *sm/f* enchanter/enchantress; **incan'tesimo** *sm* spell, charm; **incan'tevole** *ag* charming, enchanting.

in'canto *sm* spell, charm, enchantment; *(asta)* auction; **come per ~** as if by magic; **mettere all'~** to put up for auction.

incanu'tire *vi* to go white.

inca'pace [inka'patʃe] *ag* incapable; **incapacità** *sf* inability; *(DIR)* incapacity.

incapo'nirsi *vr* to be stubborn, be determined.

incap'pare *vi*: ~ **in qc/qn** *(anche fig)* to run into sth/sb.

incapsu'lare *vt (dente)* to crown.

incarce'rare [inkartʃe'rare] *vt* to imprison.

incari'care *vt*: ~ **qn di fare** to give sb the responsibility of doing; ~rsi **di** to take care o charge of; **incari'cato, a** *ag*: **incaricato (di)** in charge (of), responsible (for) ♦ *sm/f* delegate, representative; **professore incaricato** *teacher with a temporary appointment*; **incaricato d'affari** *(POL)* chargé d'affaires.

in'carico, chi *sm* task, job.

incar'nare *vt* to embody; ~rsi *vr* to be embodied; *(REL)* to become incarnate.

incarta'mento *sm* dossier, file.

incar'tare *vt* to wrap (in paper).

incas'sare *vt (merce)* to pack (in cases); *(gemma: incastonare)* to set; *(ECON: riscuotere)* to collect; *(PUGILATO: colpi)* to take, stand up to; **in'casso** *sm* cashing, encashment; *(introito)* takings *pl*.

incasto'nare *vt* to set; **incastona'tura** *sf* setting.

incas'trare *vt* to fit in, insert; *(fig: intrappolare)* to catch; ~rsi *vr (combaciare)* to fit together; *(restare bloccato)* to become stuck; **in'castro** *sm* slot, groove; *(punto di unione)* joint.

incate'nare *vt* to chain up.

incatra'mare *vt* to tar.

incatti'vire *vt* to make wicked; ~rsi *vr* to turn nasty.

in'cauto, a *ag* imprudent, rash.

inca'vare *vt* to hollow out; **inca'vato, a** *ag* hollow; *(occhi)* sunken; **in'cavo** *sm* hollow; *(solco)* groove.

incendi'are [intʃen'djare] *vt* to set fire to; ~rsi *vr* to catch fire, burst into flames.

incendi'ario, a [intʃen'djarjo] *ag* incendiary ♦ *sm/f* arsonist.

in'cendio [in'tʃendjo] *sm* fire.

incene'rire [intʃene'rire] *vt* to burn to ashes, incinerate; *(cadavere)* to cremate; ~rsi *vr* to be burnt to ashes.

in'censo [in'tʃenso] *sm* incense.

incensu'rato, a [intʃensu'rato] *ag (DIR)*: **essere ~** to have a clean record.

incen'tivo [intʃen'tivo] *sm* incentive.

incep'pare [intʃep'pare] *vt* to obstruct,

hamper; **~rsi** *vr* to jam.

ince'rata [intʃe'rata] *sf (tela)* tarpaulin; *(impermeabile)* oilskins *pl*.

incer'tezza [intʃer'tettsa] *sf* uncertainty.

in'certo, a [in'tʃerto] *ag* uncertain; *(irresoluto)* undecided, hesitating ♦ *sm* uncertainty.

in'cetta [in'tʃetta] *sf* buying up; **fare ~ di qc** to buy up sth.

inchi'esta [in'kjesta] *sf* investigation, inquiry.

inchi'nare [inki'nare] *vt* to bow; **~rsi** *vr* to bend down; *(per riverenza)* to bow; (: *donna*) to curtsy; **in'chino** *sm* bow; curtsy.

inchio'dare [inkjo'dare] *vt* to nail (down); **~ la macchina** *(AUT)* to jam on the brakes.

inchi'ostro [in'kjostro] *sm* ink; **~ simpatico** invisible ink.

inciam'pare [intʃam'pare] *vi* to trip, stumble.

inci'ampo [in'tʃampo] *sm* obstacle; **essere d'~ a qn** *(fig)* to be in sb's way.

inciden'tale [intʃiden'tale] *ag* incidental.

inci'dente [intʃi'dente] *sm* accident; **~ d'auto** car accident.

inci'denza [intʃi'dentsa] *sf* incidence; **avere una forte ~ su qc** to affect sth greatly.

in'cidere [in'tʃidere] *vi*: **~ su** to bear upon, affect ♦ *vt (tagliare incavando)* to cut into; *(ARTE)* to engrave; to etch; *(canzone)* to record.

in'cinta [in'tʃinta] *ag f* pregnant.

incipri'are [intʃi'prjare] *vt* to powder.

in'circa [in'tʃirka] *av*: **all'~** more or less, very nearly.

incisi'one [intʃi'zjone] *sf* cut; *(disegno)* engraving; etching; *(registrazione)* recording; *(MED)* incision.

in'ciso, a [in'tʃizo] *pp di* incidere ♦ *sm*: **per ~** incidentally, by the way.

inci'vile [intʃi'vile] *ag* uncivilized; *(villano)* impolite.

incivi'lire [intʃivi'lire] *vt* to civilize.

incl. *abbr* (= *incluso*) encl.

incli'nare *vt* to tilt ♦ *vi (fig)*: **~ a qc/a fare** to incline towards sth/doing; to tend towards sth/to do; **~rsi** *vr (barca)** to list; *(aereo)* to bank; **incli'nato, a** *ag* sloping; **inclinazi'one** *sf* slope; *(fig)* inclination, tendency; **in'cline** *ag*: **incline a** inclined to.

in'cludere *vt* to include; *(accludere)* to enclose; **inclu'sivo, a** *ag*: **inclusivo di** inclusive of; **in'cluso, a** *pp di* includere ♦ *ag* included; enclosed.

incoe'rente *ag* incoherent; *(contraddittorio)* inconsistent.

in'cognita [in'koɲɲita] *sf (MAT, fig)* unknown quantity.

in'cognito, a [in'koɲɲito] *ag* unknown ♦ *sm*: **in ~** incognito.

incol'lare *vt* to glue, gum; *(unire con colla)* to stick together.

incolon'nare *vt* to draw up in columns.

inco'lore *ag* colourless.

incol'pare *vt*: **~ qn di** to charge sb with.

in'colto, a *ag (terreno)* uncultivated; *(trascurato: capelli)* neglected; *(persona)* uneducated.

in'colume *ag* safe and sound, unhurt.

in'combere *vi (sovrastare minacciando)*: **~ su** to threaten, hang over.

incominci'are [inkomin'tʃare] *vi, vt* to begin, start.

in'comodo, a *ag* uncomfortable; *(inopportuno)* inconvenient ♦ *sm* inconvenience, bother.

incompe'tente *ag* incompetent.

incompi'uto, a *ag* unfinished, incomplete.

incom'pleto, a *ag* incomplete.

incompren'sibile *ag* incomprehensible.

incom'preso, a *ag* not understood; misunderstood.

inconce'pibile [inkontʃe'pibile] *ag* inconceivable.

inconcili'abile [inkontʃi'ljabile] *ag* irreconcilable.

inconclu'dente *ag* inconclusive; *(persona)* ineffectual.

incondizio'nato, a [inkondittsjo'nato] *ag* unconditional.

inconfu'tabile *ag* irrefutable.

incongru'ente *ag* inconsistent.

in'congruo, a *ag* incongruous.

inconsa'pevole *ag*: ~ **di** unaware of, ignorant of.

in'conscio, a, sci, sce [in'kɔnʃo] *ag* unconscious ♦ *sm* (PSIC): l'~ the unconscious.

inconsis'tente *ag* insubstantial; unfounded.

inconsu'eto, a *ag* unusual.

incon'sulto, a *ag* rash.

incon'trare *vt* to meet; (*difficoltà*) to meet with; ~**rsi** *vr* to meet.

incontras'tabile *ag* incontrovertible, indisputable.

in'contro *av*: ~ **a** (*verso*) towards ♦ *sm* meeting; (SPORT) match; meeting; ~ **di calcio** football match.

inconveni'ente *sm* drawback, snag.

incoraggia'mento [inkoraddʒa'mento] *sm* encouragement.

incoraggi'are [inkorad'dʒare] *vt* to encourage.

incornici'are [inkorni'tʃare] *vt* to frame.

incoro'nare *vt* to crown; **incoronazi'one** *sf* coronation.

incorpo'rare *vt* to incorporate; (*fig: annettere*) to annex.

in'correre *vi*: ~ **in** to meet with, run into.

incosci'ente [inkoʃ'ʃɛnte] *ag* (*inconscio*) unconscious; (*irresponsabile*) reckless, thoughtless; **incosci'enza** *sf* unconsciousness; recklessness, thoughtlessness.

incre'dibile *ag* incredible, unbelievable.

in'credulo, a *ag* incredulous, disbelieving.

incremen'tare *vt* to increase; (*dar sviluppo a*) to promote.

incre'mento *sm* (*sviluppo*) development; (*aumento numerico*) increase, growth.

incres'parsi *vr* (*acqua*) to ripple; (*capelli*) to go frizzy; (*pelle, tessuto*) to wrinkle.

incrimi'nare *vt* (DIR) to charge.

incri'nare *vt* to crack; (*fig: rapporti, amicizia*) to cause to deteriorate; ~**rsi** *vr* to crack; to deteriorate; **incrina'tura** *sf* crack; (*fig*) rift.

incroci'are [inkro'tʃare] *vt* to cross; (*incontrare*) to meet ♦ *vi* (NAUT, AER) to cruise; ~**rsi** *vr* (*strade*) to cross, intersect; (*persone, veicoli*) to pass each other; ~ **le braccia/le gambe** to fold one's arms/cross one's legs; **incrocia'tore** *sm* cruiser.

in'crocio [in'krotʃo] *sm* (*anche* FERR) crossing; (*di strade*) crossroads.

incros'tare *vt* to encrust.

incuba'trice [inkuba'tritʃe] *sf* incubator.

'incubo *sm* nightmare.

in'cudine *sf* anvil.

incu'rante *ag*: ~ **(di)** heedless (of), careless (of).

incurio'sire *vt* to make curious; ~**rsi** *vr* to become curious.

incursi'one *sf* raid.

incur'vare *vt* to bend, curve; ~**rsi** *vr* to bend, curve.

in'cusso, a *pp di* **incutere**.

incusto'dito, a *ag* unguarded, unattended.

in'cutere *vt* to arouse; ~ **timore/rispetto a qn** to strike fear into sb/command sb's respect.

'indaco *sm* indigo.

indaffa'rato, a *ag* busy.

inda'gare *vt* to investigate.

in'dagine [in'dadʒine] *sf* investigation, inquiry; (*ricerca*) research, study.

indebi'tarsi *vr* to run o get into debt.

in'debito, a *ag* undue; undeserved.

indebo'lire *vt, vi* (*anche:* ~**rsi**) to weaken.

inde'cente [inde'tʃɛnte] *ag* indecent; **inde'cenza** *sf* indecency.

inde'ciso, a [inde'tʃizo] *ag* indecisive; (*irresoluto*) undecided.

inde'fesso, a *ag* untiring, indefatigable.

indefi'nito, a *ag* (*anche* LING) indefinite; (*impreciso, non determinato*) undefined.

in'degno, a [in'deɲɲo] *ag* (*atto*) shameful; (*persona*) unworthy.

indelica'tezza [indelika'tettsa] *sf* tactlessness.

indemoni'ato, a *ag* possessed (by the

devil).

in'denne   *ag*   unhurt, uninjured; **indennità** *sf inv* (*rimborso: di spese*) allowance; (*: di perdita*) compensation, indemnity; **indennità di contingenza** cost-of-living allowance; **indennità di trasferta** travel expenses *pl.*

indenniz'zare [indennid'dzare] *vt* to compensate; **inden'nizzo** *sm* (*somma*) compensation, indemnity.

indero'gabile *ag* binding.

'India *sf*: **l'~** India; **indi'ano, a** *ag* Indian ♦ *smlf* (*d'India*) Indian; (*d'America*) Red Indian.

indiavo'lato, a *ag* possessed (by the devil); (*vivace, violento*) wild.

indi'care *vt* (*mostrare*) to show, indicate; (*: col dito*) to point to, point out; (*consigliare*) to suggest, recommend; **indica'tivo, a** *ag* indicative ♦ *sm* (*LING*) indicative (mood); **indica'tore** *sm* (*elenco*) guide; directory; (*TECN*) gauge; indicator; **cartello indicatore** sign; **indicatore di velocità** (*AUT*) speedometer; **indicatore della benzina** fuel gauge; **indicazi'one** *sf* indication; (*informazione*) piece of information; **indicazioni per l'uso** instructions for use.

'indice ['inditʃe] *sm* (*ANAT: dito*) index finger, forefinger; (*lancetta*) needle, pointer; (*fig: indizio*) sign; (*TECN, MAT, nei libri*) index; **~ di gradimento** (*RADIO, TV*) popularity rating.

indi'cibile [indi'tʃibile] *ag* inexpressible.

indietreggi'are [indietred'dʒare] *vi* to draw back, retreat.

indi'etro *av* back; (*guardare*) behind, back; (*andare, cadere: anche: all'~*) backwards; **rimanere ~** to be left behind; **essere ~** (*col lavoro*) to be behind; (*orologio*) to be slow; **rimandare qc ~** to send sth back.

indi'feso, a *ag* (*città etc*) undefended; (*persona*) defenceless.

indiffe'rente   *ag*   indifferent; **indiffe'renza** *sf* indifference.

in'digeno, a [in'didʒeno] *ag* indigenous, native ♦ *smlf* native.

indi'gente [indi'dʒɛnte] *ag* poverty-stricken, destitute; **indi'genza** *sf* extreme poverty.

indigesti'one [indidʒes'tjone] *sf* indigestion.

indi'gesto, a [indi'dʒɛsto] *ag* indigestible.

indi'gnare [indiɲ'ɲare] *vt* to fill with indignation; **~rsi** *vr* to be (*o* get) indignant.

indimenti'cabile *ag* unforgettable.

indipen'dente   *ag*   independent; **indipen'denza** *sf* independence.

in'dire *vt* (*concorso*) to announce; (*elezioni*) to call.

indi'retto, a *ag* indirect.

indiriz'zare [indirit'tsare] *vt* (*dirigere*) to direct; (*mandare*) to send; (*lettera*) to address.

indi'rizzo [indi'rittso] *sm* address; (*direzione*) direction; (*avvio*) trend, course.

indis'creto, a *ag* indiscreet.

indis'cusso, a *ag* unquestioned.

indispen'sabile   *ag*   indispensable, essential.

indispet'tire *vt* to irritate, annoy ♦ *vi* (*anche: ~rsi*) to get irritated *o* annoyed.

in'divia *sf* endive.

individu'ale *ag* individual; **individualità** *sf* individuality.

individu'are *vt* (*dar forma distinta a*) to characterize; (*determinare*) to locate; (*riconoscere*) to single out.

indi'viduo *sm* individual.

indizi'are [indit'tsjare] *vt*: **~ qn di qc** to cast suspicion on sb for sth; **indizi'ato, a** *ag* suspected ♦ *smlf* suspect.

in'dizio [in'dittsjo] *sm* (*segno*) sign, indication; (*POLIZIA*) clue; (*DIR*) piece of evidence.

'indole *sf* nature, character.

indolen'zito, a [indolen'tsito] *ag* stiff, aching; (*intorpidito*) numb.

indo'lore *ag* painless.

indo'mani *sm*: **l'~** the next day, the following day.

Indo'nesia *sf*: **l'~** Indonesia.

indos'sare *vt* (*mettere indosso*) to put on; (*avere indosso*) to have on; **indossa'tore, 'trice** *smlf* model.

in'dotto, a *pp di* indurre.

indottri'nare *vt* to indoctrinate.

indovi'nare *vt* (*scoprire*) to guess; (*immaginare*) to imagine, guess; (*il futuro*) to foretell; indovi'nato, a *ag* successful; (*scelta*) inspired; indovi'nello *sm* riddle; indo'vino, a *sm/f* fortuneteller.

indubbia'mente *av* undoubtedly.

in'dubbio, a *ag* certain, undoubted.

indugi'are [indu'dʒare] *vi* to take one's time, delay.

in'dugio [in'dudʒo] *sm* (*ritardo*) delay; senza ~ without delay.

indul'gente [indul'dʒɛnte] *ag* indulgent; (*giudice*) lenient; indul'genza *sf* indulgence; leniency.

in'dulgere [in'dulcʒere] *vi*: ~ a (*accondiscendere*) to comply with; (*abbandonarsi*) to indulge in; in'dulto, a *pp di* indulgere ♦ *sm* (*DIR*) pardon.

indu'mento *sm* article of clothing, garment; ~i *smpl* (*vestiti*) clothes.

indu'rire *vt* to harden ♦ *vi* (*anche*: ~rsi) to harden, become hard.

in'durre *vt*: ~ qn a fare qc to induce *o* persuade sb to do sth; ~ qn in errore to mislead sb.

in'dustria *sf* industry; industri'ale *ag* industrial ♦ *sm* industrialist.

industri'arsi *vr* to do one's best, try hard.

industri'oso, a *ag* industrious, hard-working.

induzi'one [indut'tsjone] *sf* induction.

inebe'tito, a *ag* dazed, stunned.

inebri'are *vt* (*anche fig*) to intoxicate; ~rsi *vr* to become intoxicated.

inecce'pibile [inettʃe'pibile] *ag* unexceptionable.

i'nedia *sf* starvation.

i'nedito, a *ag* unpublished.

ineffi'cace [ineffi'katʃe] *ag* ineffective.

ineffici'ente [ineffi'tʃɛnte] *ag* inefficient.

inegu'ale *ag* unequal; (*irregolare*) uneven.

ine'rente *ag*: ~ a concerning, regarding.

i'nerme *ag* unarmed; defenceless.

inerpi'carsi *vr*: ~ (su) to clamber

(up).

i'nerte *ag* inert; (*inattivo*) indolent, sluggish; i'nerzia *sf* inertia; indolence, sluggishness.

ine'satto, a *ag* (*impreciso*) inexact; (*erroneo*) incorrect; (*AMM*: *non riscosso*) uncollected.

inesis'tente *ag* non-existent.

inesperi'enza [inespe'rjɛntsa] *sf* inexperience.

ines'perto, a *ag* inexperienced.

i'netto, a *ag* (*incapace*) inept; (*che non ha attitudine*): ~ (a) unsuited (to).

ine'vaso, a *ag* (*ordine, corrispondenza*) outstanding.

inevi'tabile *ag* inevitable.

i'nezia [i'nɛttsja] *sf* trifle, thing of no importance.

infagot'tare *vt* to bundle up, wrap up; ~rsi *vr* to wrap up.

infal'libile *ag* infallible.

infa'mare *vt* to defame.

in'fame *ag* infamous; (*fig*: *cosa, compito*) awful, dreadful.

infan'tile *ag* child *cpd*; childlike; (*adulto, azione*) childish; letteratura ~ children's books *pl*.

in'fanzia [in'fantsja] *sf* childhood; (*bambini*) children *pl*; prima ~ babyhood, infancy.

infari'nare *vt* to cover with (*o* sprinkle with *o* dip in) flour; ~ di zucchero to sprinkle with sugar; infarina'tura *sf* (*fig*) smattering.

in'farto *sm* (*MED*): ~ (cardiaco) coronary.

infasti'dire *vt* to annoy, irritate; ~rsi *vr* to get annoyed *o* irritated.

infati'cabile *ag* tireless, untiring.

in'fatti *cong* as a matter of fact, in fact, actually.

infatu'arsi *vr*: ~ di *o* per to become infatuated with, fall for; infatuazi'one *sf* infatuation.

in'fausto, a *ag* unpropitious, unfavourable.

infe'condo, a *ag* infertile.

infe'dele *ag* unfaithful; infedeltà *sf* infidelity.

infe'lice [infe'litʃe] *ag* unhappy;

(*sfortunato*) unlucky, unfortunate; (*inopportuno*) inopportune, ill-timed; (*mal riuscito: lavoro*) bad, poor; **infelicità** *sf* unhappiness.

inferi'ore *ag* lower; (*per intelligenza, qualità*) inferior ♦ *sm/f* inferior; ~ **a** (*numero, quantità*) less *o* smaller than; (*meno buono*) inferior to; ~ **alla media** below average; **inferiorità** *sf* inferiority.

inferme'ria *sf* infirmary; (*di scuola, nave*) sick bay.

infermi'ere, a *sm/f* nurse.

infermità *sf inv* illness; infirmity.

in'fermo, a *ag* (*ammalato*) ill; (*debole*) infirm.

infer'nale *ag* infernal; (*proposito, complotto*) diabolical.

in'ferno *sm* hell.

inferri'ata *sf* grating.

infervo'rare *vt* to arouse enthusiasm in; ~**rsi** *vr* to get excited, get carried away.

infet'tare *vt* to infect; ~**rsi** *vr* to become infected; **infet'tivo, a** *ag* infectious; **in'fetto, a** *ag* infected; (*acque*) polluted, contaminated; **infezi'one** *sf* infection.

infiac'chire [infjak'kire] *vt* to weaken ♦ *vi* (*anche: ~rsi*) to grow weak.

infiam'mabile *ag* inflammable.

infiam'mare *vt* to set alight; (*fig, MED*) to inflame; ~**rsi** *vr* to catch fire; (*MED*) to become inflamed; (*fig*): ~**rsi di** to be fired with; **infiammazi'one** *sf* (*MED*) inflammation.

in'fido, a *ag* unreliable, treacherous.

infie'rire *vi*: ~ **su** (*fisicamente*) to attack furiously; (*verbalmente*) to rage at; (*epidemia*) to rage over.

in'figgere [in'fiddʒere] *vt*: ~ **qc in** to thrust *o* drive sth into.

infi'lare *vt* (*ago*) to thread; (*mettere: chiave*) to insert; (*: anello, vestito*) to slip *o* put on; (*strada*) to turn into, take; ~**rsi** *vr*: ~**rsi in** to slip into; (*indossare*) to slip on; ~ **l'uscio** to slip in; to slip out.

infil'trarsi *vr* to penetrate, seep through; (*MIL*) to infiltrate; **infiltrazi'one** *sf* infiltration.

infil'zare [infil'tsare] *vt* (*infilare*) to string together; (*trafiggere*) to pierce.

'infimo, a *ag* lowest.

in'fine *av* finally; (*insomma*) in short.

infinità *sf* infinity; (*in quantità*): **un'**~ **di** an infinite number of.

infi'nito, a *ag* infinite; (*LING*) infinitive ♦ *sm* infinity; (*LING*) infinitive; **all'**~ (*senza fine*) endlessly.

infinocchi'are [infinok'kjare] (*fam*) *vt* to hoodwink.

infischi'arsi [infis'kjarsi] *vr*: ~ **di** not to care about.

in'fisso, a *pp di* **infiggere** ♦ *sm* fixture; (*di porta, finestra*) frame.

infit'tire *vt, vi* (*anche: ~rsi*) to thicken.

inflazi'one [inflat'tsjone] *sf* inflation.

in'fliggere [in'fliddʒere] *vt* to inflict; **in'flitto, a** *pp di* **infliggere**.

influ'ente *ag* influential; **influ'enza** *sf* influence; (*MED*) influenza, flu.

influ'ire *vi*: ~ **su** to influence.

in'flusso *sm* influence.

infol'tire *vt, vi* to thicken.

infon'dato, a *ag* unfounded, groundless.

in'fondere *vt*: ~ **qc in qn** to instill sth in sb.

infor'care *vt* to fork (up); (*bicicletta, cavallo*) to get on; (*occhiali*) to put on.

infor'mare *vt* to inform, tell; ~**rsi** *vr*: ~**rsi (di o su)** to inquire (about).

infor'matica *sf* computer science.

informa'tivo, a *ag* informative.

informa'tore *sm* informer.

informazi'one [informat'tsjone] *sf* piece of information; **prendere ~i sul conto di qn** to get information about sb; **chiedere un'**~ to ask for (some) information.

in'forme *ag* shapeless.

informico'larsi *vr* = **informicolirsi**.

informico'lirsi *vr* to have pins and needles.

infor'tunio *sm* accident; ~ **sul lavoro** industrial accident, accident at work.

infos'sarsi *vr* (*terreno*) to sink; (*guance*) to become hollow; **infos'sato, a** *ag* hollow; (*occhi*) deep-set; (*: per malattia*) sunken.

in'frangere [in'frandʒere] *vt* to smash; (*fig: legge, patti*) to break; **~rsi** *vr* to smash, break; **infran'gibile** *ag* unbreakable; **in'franto, a** *pp di* **infrangere** ♦ *ag* broken.

infrazi'one [infrat'tsjone] *sf*: ~ **a** breaking of, violation of.

infredda'tura *sf* slight cold.

infreddo'lito, a *ag* cold, chilled.

infruttu'oso, a *ag* fruitless.

infu'ori *av* out; **all'~** outwards; **all'~ di** (*eccetto*) except, with the exception of.

infuri'are *vi* to rage; **~rsi** *vr* to fly into a rage.

infusi'one *sf* infusion.

in'fuso, a *pp di* **infondere** ♦ *sm* infusion; ~ **di camomilla** camomile tea.

Ing. *abbr* = **ingegnere**.

ingabbi'are *vt* to cage.

ingaggi'are [ingad'dʒare] *vt* (*assumere con compenso*) to take on, hire; (*SPORT*) to sign on; (*MIL*) to engage; **in'gaggio** *sm* hiring; signing on.

ingan'nare *vt* to deceive; (*coniuge*) to be unfaithful to; (*fisco*) to cheat; (*eludere*) to dodge, elude; (*fig: tempo*) to while away ♦ *vi* (*apparenza*) to be deceptive; **~rsi** *vr* to be mistaken, be wrong; **ingan'nevole** *ag* deceptive.

in'ganno *sm* deceit, deception; (*azione*) trick; (*menzogna, frode*) cheat, swindle; (*illusione*) illusion.

ingarbugli'are [ingarbuʎ'ʎare] *vt* to tangle; (*fig*) to confuse, muddle; **~rsi** *vr* to become confused o muddled.

inge'gnarsi [indʒeɲ'narsi] *vr* to do one's best, try hard; ~ **per vivere** to live by one's wits.

inge'gnere [indʒeɲ'ɲere] *sm* engineer; ~ **civile/navale** civil/naval engineer; **ingegne'ria** *sf* engineering.

in'gegno [in'dʒeɲɲo] *sm* (*intelligenza*) intelligence, brains *pl*; (*capacità creativa*) ingenuity; (*disposizione*) talent; **inge'gnoso, a** *ag* ingenious, clever.

ingelo'sire [indʒelo'zire] *vt* to make jealous ♦ *vi* (*anche:* **~rsi**) to become jealous.

in'gente [in'dʒɛnte] *ag* huge, enormous.

ingenuità [indʒenui'ta] *sf* ingenuousness.

in'genuo, a [in'dʒɛnuo] *ag* ingenuous, naïve.

inges'sare [indʒes'sare] *vt* (*MED*) to put in plaster; **ingessa'tura** *sf* plaster.

Inghil'terra [ingil'tɛrra] *sf*: **l'~** England.

inghiot'tire [ingjot'tire] *vt* to swallow.

ingial'lire [indʒal'lire] *vi* to go yellow.

ingigan'tire [indʒigan'tire] *vt* to enlarge, magnify ♦ *vi* to become gigantic o enormous.

inginocchi'arsi [indʒinok'kjarsi] *vr* to kneel (down).

ingiù [in'dʒu] *av* down, downwards.

ingi'uria [in'dʒurja] *sf* insult; (*fig: danno*) damage; **ingiuri'are** *vt* to insult, abuse; **ingiuri'oso, a** *ag* insulting, abusive.

ingius'tizia [indʒus'tittsja] *sf* injustice.

ingi'usto, a [in'dʒusto] *ag* unjust, unfair.

in'glese *ag* English ♦ *sm/f* Englishman/woman ♦ *sm* (*LING*) English; **gli I~i** the English; **andarsene** o **filare all'~** to take French leave.

ingoi'are *vt* to gulp (down); (*fig*) to swallow (up).

ingol'fare *vt* (*motore*) to flood; **~rsi** *vr* to flood.

ingom'brare *vt* (*strada*) to block; (*stanza*) to clutter up; **in'gombro, a** *ag* (*strada, passaggio*) blocked ♦ *sm* obstacle; **essere d'ingombro** to be in the way.

in'gordo, a *ag*: ~ **di** greedy for; (*fig*) greedy o avid for.

ingor'garsi *vr* to be blocked up, be choked up.

in'gorgo, ghi *sm* blockage, obstruction; (*anche:* ~ **stradale**) traffic jam.

ingoz'zare [ingot'tsare] *vt* (*animali*) to fatten; (*fig: persona*) to stuff; **~rsi** *vr*: **~rsi (di)** to stuff o.s. (with).

ingra'naggio [ingra'naddʒo] *sm* (*TECN*) gear; (*di orologio*) mechanism; **gli ~i della burocrazia** the bureaucratic machinery.

ingra'nare *vi* to mesh, engage ♦ *vt* to engage; ~ **la marcia** to get into gear.

ingrandi'mento *sm* enlargement;

extension.

ingran'dire vt (anche FOT) to enlarge; (estendere) to extend; (OTTICA, fig) to magnify ♦ vi (anche: ~rsi) to become larger o bigger; (aumentare) to grow, increase; (espandersi) to expand.

ingras'sare vt to make fat; (animali) to fatten; (AGR: terreno) to manure; (lubrificare) to oil, lubricate ♦ vi (anche: ~rsi) to get fat, put on weight.

in'grato, a ag ungrateful; (lavoro) thankless, unrewarding.

ingrazi'are [ingrat'tsjare] vt: ~rsi qn to ingratiate o.s. with sb.

ingredi'ente sm ingredient.

in'gresso sm (porta) entrance; (atrio) hall; (l'entrare) entrance, entry; (facoltà di entrare) admission; "~ libero" "admission free".

ingros'sare vt to increase; (folla, livello) to swell ♦ vi (anche: ~rsi) to increase; to swell.

in'grosso av: all'~ (COMM) wholesale; (all'incirca) roughly, about.

ingual'cibile [ingwal'tʃibile] ag crease-resistant.

ingua'ribile ag incurable.

'inguine sm (ANAT) groin.

ini'bire vt to forbid, prohibit; (PSIC) to inhibit; **inibizi'one** sf prohibition; inhibition.

iniet'tare vt to inject; ~rsi vr: ~rsi di sangue (occhi) to become bloodshot; **iniezi'one** sf injection.

inimi'carsi vr: ~ con qn to fall out with sb.

inimi'cizia [inimi'tʃittsja] sf animosity.

ininter'rotto, a ag unbroken; uninterrupted.

iniquità sf inv iniquity; (atto) wicked action.

inizi'ale [init'tsjale] ag, sf initial.

inizi'are [init'tsjare] vi, vt to begin, start; ~ qn a to initiate sb into; (pittura etc) to introduce sb to; ~ a fare qc to start doing sth.

inizia'tiva [inittsja'tiva] sf initiative; ~ privata private enterprise.

i'nizio [i'nittsjo] sm beginning; all'~ at the beginning, at the start; dare ~ a qc

to start sth, get sth going.

innaffi'are etc = **annaffiare** etc.

innal'zare [innal'tsare] vt (sollevare, alzare) to raise; (rizzare) to erect; ~rsi vr to rise.

innamo'rare vt to enchant, charm; ~rsi vr: ~rsi (di qn) to fall in love (with sb); **innamo'rato, a** ag (che nutre amore): **innamorato (di)** in love (with); (appassionato): **innamorato di** very fond of ♦ sm/f lover; sweetheart.

in'nanzi [in'nantsi] av (stato in luogo) in front, ahead; (moto a luogo) forward, on; (tempo: prima) before ♦ prep (prima) before; ~ a in front of.

in'nato, a ag innate.

innatu'rale ag unnatural.

inne'gabile ag undeniable.

innervo'sire vt: ~ qn to get on sb's nerves; ~rsi vr to get irritated o upset.

innes'care vt to prime; **in'nesco, schi** sm primer.

innes'tare vt (BOT, MED) to graft; (TECN) to engage; (inserire: presa) to insert; **in'nesto** sm graft; grafting no pl; (TECN) clutch; (ELETTR) connection.

'inno sm hymn; ~ **nazionale** national anthem.

inno'cente [inno'tʃɛnte] ag innocent; **inno'cenza** sf innocence.

in'nocuo, a ag innocuous, harmless.

inno'vare vt to change, make innovations in.

innume'revole ag innumerable.

ino'doro, a ag odourless.

inol'trare vt (AMM) to pass on, forward; ~rsi vr (addentrarsi) to advance, go forward.

i'noltre av besides, moreover.

inon'dare vt to flood; **inondazi'one** sf flooding no pl; flood.

inope'roso, a ag inactive, idle.

inoppor'tuno, a ag untimely, ill-timed; inappropriate; (momento) inopportune.

inorgo'glire [inorgoʎ'ʎire] vt to make proud ♦ vi (anche: ~rsi) to become proud; ~rsi di qc to pride o.s. on sth.

inorri'dire vt to horrify ♦ vi to be horrified.

inospi'tale *ag* inhospitable.

inosser'vato, a *ag* (*non notato*) unobserved; (*non rispettato*) not observed, not kept.

inossi'dabile *ag* stainless.

inqua'drare *vt* (*foto, immagine*) to frame; (*fig*) to situate, set.

inquie'tare *vt* (*turbare*) to disturb, worry; ~**rsi** *vr* to worry, become anxious; (*impazientirsi*) to get upset.

inqui'eto, a *ag* restless; (*preoccupato*) worried, anxious; **inquie'tudine** *sf* anxiety, worry.

inqui'lino, a *sm/f* tenant.

inquina'mento *sm* pollution.

inqui'nare *vt* to pollute.

inqui'sire *vt*, *vi* to investigate; **inquisi'tore, 'trice** *ag* (*sguardo*) inquiring; **inquisizi'one** *sf* (*STORIA*) inquisition.

insabbi'are *vt* (*fig: pratica*) to shelve; ~**rsi** *vr* (*arenarsi: barca*) to run aground; (*fig: pratica*) to be shelved.

insac'cati *smpl* (*CUC*) sausages.

insa'lata *sf* salad; ~ **mista** mixed salad; **insalati'era** *sf* salad bowl.

insa'lubre *ag* unhealthy.

insa'nabile *ag* (*piaga*) which cannot be healed; (*situazione*) irremediable; (*odio*) implacable.

insangui'nare *vt* to stain with blood.

insa'puta *sf*: **all'~ di qn** without sb knowing.

insce'nare [inʃe'nare] *vt* (*TEATRO*) to stage, put on; (*fig*) to stage.

insedi'are *vt* to install; ~**rsi** *vr* to take up office; (*popolo, colonia*) to settle.

in'segna [in'seɲɲa] *sf* sign; (*emblema*) sign, emblem; (*bandiera*) flag, banner; ~**e** *sfpl* (*decorazioni*) insignia *pl*.

insegna'mento [inseɲɲa'mento] *sm* teaching.

inse'gnante [inseɲ'ɲante] *ag* teaching ♦ *sm/f* teacher.

inse'gnare [inseɲ'ɲare] *vt*, *vi* to teach; ~ **a qn qc** to teach sb sth; ~ **a qn a fare qc** to teach sb (how) to do sth.

insegui'mento *sm* pursuit, chase.

insegu'ire *vt* to pursue, chase.

inselvati'chire [inselvati'kire] *vi* (*anche:*

~**rsi**) to grow wild.

insena'tura *sf* inlet, creek.

insen'sato, a *ag* senseless, stupid.

insen'sibile *ag* (*nervo*) insensible; (*persona*) indifferent.

inse'rire *vt* to insert; (*ELETTR*) to connect; (*allegare*) to enclose; (*annuncio*) to put in, place; ~**rsi** *vr* (*fig*): ~**rsi in** to become part of; **in'serto** *sm* (*pubblicazione*) insert.

inservi'ente *sm/f* attendant.

inserzi'one [inser'tsjone] *sf* insertion; (*avviso*) advertisement; **fare un'~ sul giornale** to put an advertisement in the paper.

insetti'cida, i [insetti'tʃida] *sm* insecticide.

in'setto *sm* insect.

in'sidia *sf* snare, trap; (*pericolo*) hidden danger; **insidi'are** *vt*: ~ **la vita di qn** to make an attempt on sb's life.

insi'eme *av* together ♦ *prep*: ~ **a** *o* **con** together with ♦ *sm* whole; (*MAT, servizio, assortimento*) set; (*MODA*) ensemble, outfit; **tutti** ~ all together; **tutto** ~ all together; (*in una volta*) at one go; **nell'~** on the whole; **d'~** (*veduta etc*) overall.

insignifi'cante [insiɲɲifi'kante] *ag* insignificant.

insi'gnire [insiɲ'ɲire] *vt*: ~ **qn di** to honour *o* decorate sb with.

insin'cero, a [insin'tʃero] *ag* insincere.

insinda'cabile *ag* unquestionable.

insinu'are *vt* (*introdurre*): ~ **qc in** to slip *o* slide sth into; (*fig*) to insinuate, imply; ~**rsi** *vr*: ~**rsi in** to seep into; (*fig*) to creep into; to worm one's way into.

insis'tente *ag* insistent; persistent.

in'sistere *vi*: ~ **su qc** to insist on sth; ~ **in qc/a fare** (*perseverare*) to persist in sth/in doing; **insis'tito, a** *pp di* **insistere.**

insoddis'fatto, a *ag* dissatisfied.

insoffe'rente *ag* intolerant.

insolazi'one [insolat'tsjone] *sf* (*MED*) sunstroke.

inso'lente *ag* insolent; **insolen'tire** *vi* to grow insolent ♦ *vt* to insult, be rude to.

in'solito, a *ag* unusual, out of the ordinary.

inso'luto, a *ag* (*non risolto*) unsolved; (*non pagato*) unpaid, outstanding.

insol'vibile *ag* insolvent.

in'somma *av* (*in breve, in conclusione*) in short; (*dunque*) well ♦ *escl* for heaven's sake!

in'sonne *ag* sleepless; **in'sonnia** *sf* insomnia, sleeplessness.

insonno'lito, a *ag* sleepy, drowsy.

insoppor'tabile *ag* unbearable.

in'sorgere [in'sordʒere] *vi* (*ribellarsi*) to rise up, rebel; (*apparire*) to come up, arise.

in'sorto, a *pp di* **insorgere** ♦ *sm/f* rebel, insurgent.

insospet'tire *vt* to make suspicious ♦ *vi* (*anche*: ~rsi) to become suspicious.

inspi'rare *vt* to breathe in, inhale.

In'stabile *ag* (*carico, indole*) unstable; (*tempo*) unsettled; (*equilibrio*) unsteady.

instal'lare *vt* to install; ~rsi *vr* (*sistemarsi*): ~rsi **in** to settle in; **installazi'one** *sf* installation.

instan'cabile *ag* untiring, indefatigable.

instau'rare *vt* to introduce, institute.

instra'dare *vt*: ~ (**verso**) to direct (towards).

insuc'cesso [insut'tʃɛsso] *sm* failure, flop.

insudici'are [insudi'tʃare] *vt* to dirty; ~rsi *vr* to get dirty.

insuffici'ente [insuffi'tʃɛnte] *ag* insufficient; (*compito, allievo*) inadequate; **insuffici'enza** *sf* insufficiency; inadequacy; (*INS*) fail.

insu'lare *ag* insular.

insu'lina *sf* insulin.

in'sulso, a *ag* (*sciocco*) inane, silly; (*persona*) dull, insipid.

insul'tare *vt* to insult, affront.

in'sulto *sm* insult, affront.

insussis'tente *ag* non-existent.

intac'care *vt* (*fare tacche*) to cut into; (*corrodere*) to corrode; (*fig: cominciare ad usare: risparmi*) to

break into; (: *ledere*) to damage.

intagli'are [intaʎ'ʎare] *vt* to carve; **in'taglio** *sm* carving.

intan'gibile [intan'dʒibile] *ag* untouchable; inviolable.

in'tanto *av* (*nel frattempo*) meanwhile, in the meantime; (*per cominciare*) just to begin with; ~ **che** while.

in'tarsio *sm* inlaying *no pl*, marquetry *no pl*; inlay.

inta'sare *vt* to choke (up), block (up); (*AUT*) to obstruct, block; ~rsi *vr* to become choked *o* blocked.

intas'care *vt* to pocket.

in'tatto, a *ag* intact; (*puro*) unsullied.

intavo'lare *vt* to start, enter into.

inte'grale *ag* complete; (*pane, farina*) wholemeal (*BRIT*), whole-wheat (*US*); (*MAT*): **calcolo** ~ integral calculus.

inte'grante *ag*: **parte** ~ integral part.

inte'grare *vt* to complete; (*MAT*) to integrate; ~rsi *vr* (*persona*) to become integrated.

integrità *sf* integrity.

'integro, a *ag* (*intatto, intero*) complete, whole; (*retto*) upright.

intelaia'tura *sf* frame; (*fig*) structure, framework.

intel'letto *sm* intellect; **intellettu'ale** *ag, sm/f* intellectual.

intelli'gente [intelli'dʒente] *ag* intelligent; **intelli'genza** *sf* intelligence.

intem'perie *sfpl* bad weather *sg*.

intempes'tivo, a *ag* untimely.

inten'dente *sm*: ~ **di Finanza** inland (*BRIT*) *o* internal (*US*) revenue officer; **inten'denza** *sf*: **intendenza di Finanza** inland (*BRIT*) *o* internal (*US*) revenue office.

in'tendere *vt* (*avere intenzione*): ~ **fare qc** to intend *o* mean to do sth; (*comprendere*) to understand; (*udire*) to hear; (*significare*) to mean; ~rsi *vr* (*conoscere*): ~rsi **di** to know a lot about, be a connoisseur of; (*accordarsi*) to get on (well); **intendersela con qn** (*avere una relazione amorosa*) to have an affair with sb; **intendi'mento** *sm* (*intelligenza*) understanding; (*proposito*) intention; **intendi'tore, 'trice** *sm/f* connoisseur, expert.

intene'rire vt (fig) to move (to pity); ~**rsi** vr (fig) to be moved.

inten'sivo, a ag intensive.

in'tenso, a ag intense.

in'tento, a ag (teso, assorto): ~ (a) intent (on), absorbed (in) ♦ sm aim, purpose.

intenzio'nale [intentsjo'nale] ag intentional.

intenzi'one [inten'tsjone] sf intention; (DIR) intent; **avere ~ di fare qc** to intend to do sth, have the intention of doing sth.

interca'lare sm pet phrase, stock phrase ♦ vt to insert.

interca'pedine sf gap, cavity.

intercet'tare [intertʃet'tare] vt to intercept.

inter'detto, a pp di **interdire** ♦ ag forbidden, prohibited; (sconcertato) dumbfounded ♦ sm (REL) interdict.

inter'dire vt to forbid, prohibit, ban; (REL) to interdict; (DIR) to deprive of civil rights; **interdizi'one** sf prohibition, ban.

interessa'mento sm interest.

interes'sante ag interesting; **essere in stato ~** to be expecting (a baby).

interes'sare vt to interest; (concernere) to concern, be of interest to; (far intervenire): ~ **qn a** to draw sb's attention to ♦ vi: ~ **a** to interest, matter to; ~**rsi** vr (mostrare interesse): ~**rsi a** to take an interest in, be interested in; (occuparsi): ~**rsi di** to take care of.

inte'resse sm (anche COMM) interest.

inter'faccia, ce [inter'fattʃa] sf (INFORM) interface.

interfe'renza [interfe'rɛntsa] sf interference.

interfe'rire vi to interfere.

interiezi'one [interjet'tsjone] sf exclamation, interjection.

interi'ora sfpl entrails.

interi'ore ag interior, inner, inside, internal; (fig) inner.

inter'ludio sm (MUS) interlude.

inter'medio, a ag intermediate.

inter'mezzo [inter'mɛddzo] sm (intervallo) interval; (breve spettacolo) intermezzo.

inter'nare vt (arrestare) to intern; (MED) to commit (to a mental institution).

internazio'nale [internattsjo'nale] ag international.

in'terno, a ag (di dentro) internal, interior, inner; (: mare) inland; (nazionale) domestic; (allievo) boarding ♦ sm inside, interior; (di paese) interior; (fodera) lining; (di appartamento) flat (number); (TEL) extension ♦ sm (INS) boarder; ~**i** smpl (CINEMA) interior shots; **all'~** inside; **Ministero degli I~i** Ministry of the Interior, ≈ Home Office (BRIT), Department of the Interior (US).

in'tero, a ag (integro, intatto) whole, entire; (completo, totale) complete; (numero) whole; (non ridotto: biglietto) full.

interpel'lare vt to consult.

inter'porre vt (ostacolo): ~ **qc a qc** to put sth in the way of sth; (influenza) to use; ~ **appello** (DIR) to appeal; **interporsi** vr to intervene; **interporsi fra** (mettersi in mezzo) to come between; **inter'posto, a** pp di **interporre**.

interpre'tare vt to interpret; **in'terprete** sm/f interpreter; (TEATRO) actor/actress, performer; (MUS) performer.

interro'gare vt to question; (INS) to test; **interroga'tivo, a** ag (occhi, sguardo) questioning, inquiring; (LING) interrogative ♦ sm question; (fig) mystery; **interroga'torio, a** ag interrogatory, questioning ♦ sm (DIR) questioning no pl; **interrogazi'one** sf questioning no pl; (INS) oral test.

inter'rompere vt to interrupt; (studi, trattative) to break off, interrupt; ~**rsi** vr to break off, stop; **inter'rotto, a** pp di **interrompere**.

interrut'tore sm switch.

interruzi'one [interrut'tsjone] sf interruption; break.

interse'care vt to intersect; ~**rsi** vr to

intersect.

inter'stizio [inter'stittsjo] *sm* interstice, crack.

interur'bana *sf* trunk call, long-distance call.

interur'bano, a *ag* inter-city; (*TEL: chiamata*) trunk *cpd*, long-distance; (: *telefono*) long-distance.

inter'vallo *sm* interval; (*spazio*) space, gap.

interve'nire *vi* (*partecipare*): ~ **a** to take part in; (*intromettersi: anche POL*) to intervene; (*MED: operare*) to operate; **inter'vento** *sm* participation; (*intromissione*) intervention; (*MED*) operation; **fare un intervento nel corso di** (*dibattito, programma*) to take part in.

inter'vista *sf* interview; **intervis'tare** *vt* to interview.

in'tesa *sf* understanding; (*accordo*) agreement, understanding.

in'teso, a *pp di* **intendere** ♦ *ag* agreed; **non darsi per ~ di qc** to take no notice of sth.

intes'tare *vt* (*lettera*) to address; (*proprietà*): ~ **a** to register in the name of; ~ **un assegno a qn** to make out a cheque to sb; **intestazi'one** *sf* heading; (*su carta da lettere*) letterhead; (*registrazione*) registration.

intes'tino, a *ag* (*lotte*) internal, civil ♦ *sm* (*ANAT*) intestine.

inti'mare *vt* to order, command; **intimazi'one** *sf* order, command.

intimi'dire *vt* to intimidate ♦ *vi* (*anche: ~rsi*) to grow shy.

intimità *sf* intimacy; privacy; (*familiarità*) familiarity.

'intimo, a *ag* intimate; (*affetti, vita*) private; (*fig: profondo*) inmost ♦ *sm* (*persona*) intimate *o* close friend; (*dell'animo*) bottom, depths *pl*; **parti ~e** (*ANAT*) private parts.

intimo'rire *vt* to frighten; **~rsi** *vr* to become frightened.

in'tingolo *sm* sauce; (*pietanza*) stew.

intiriz'zire [intirid'dzire] *vt* to numb ♦ *vi* (*anche: ~rsi*) to go numb.

intito'lare *vt* to give a title to;

(*dedicare*) to dedicate.

intolle'rabile *ag* intolerable.

intolle'rante *ag* intolerant.

in'tonaco, ci *o* **chi** *sm* plaster.

into'nare *vt* (*canto*) to start to sing; (*armonizzare*) to match; **~rsi** *vr* (*colori*) to go together; **~rsi a** (*carnagione*) to suit; (*abito*) to go with, match.

inton'tire *vt* to stun, daze ♦ *vi* to be stunned *o* dazed; **~rsi** *vr* to be stunned *o* dazed.

in'toppo *sm* stumbling block, obstacle.

in'torno *av* around; ~ **a** (*attorno a*) around; (*riguardo, circa*) about.

intorpi'dire *vt* to numb; (*fig*) to make sluggish ♦ *vi* (*anche: ~rsi*) to grow numb; (*fig*) to become sluggish.

intossi'care *vt* to poison; **intossicazi'one** *sf* poisoning.

intralci'are [intral'tʃare] *vt* to hamper, hold up.

intransi'tivo, a *ag, sm* intransitive.

intrapren'dente *ag* enterprising, go-ahead.

intra'prendere *vt* to undertake.

intrat'tabile *ag* intractable.

intratte'nere *vt* to entertain; to engage in conversation; **~rsi** *vr* to linger; **~rsi su qc** to dwell on sth.

intrave'dere *vt* to catch a glimpse of; (*fig*) to foresee.

intrecci'are [intret'tʃare] *vt* (*capelli*) to plait, braid; (*intessere: anche fig*) to weave, interweave, intertwine; **~rsi** *vr* to intertwine, become interwoven; ~ **le mani** to clasp one's hands; **in'treccio** *sm* (*fig: trama*) plot, story.

intri'gare *vi* to manoeuvre (*BRIT*), maneuver (*US*), scheme; **in'trigo, ghi** *sm* plot, intrigue.

in'trinseco, a, ci, che *ag* intrinsic.

in'triso, a *ag*: ~ (**di**) soaked (in).

intro'durre *vt* to introduce; (*chiave etc*): ~ **qc in** to insert sth into; (*persone: far entrare*) to show in; **introdursi** *vr* (*moda, tecniche*) to be introduced; **introdursi in** (*persona: penetrare*) to enter; (: *entrare furtivamente*) to steal *o* slip into; **in-**

troduzi'one *sf* introduction.
in'troito *sm* income, revenue.
intro'mettersi *vr* to interfere, meddle; (*interporsi*) to intervene.
in'truglio [in'truʎʎo] *sm* concoction.
intrusi'one *sf* intrusion; interference.
in'truso, a *sm/f* intruder.
intu'ire *vt* to perceive by intuition; (*rendersi conto*) to realize; **in'tuito** *sm* intuition; (*perspicacia*) perspicacity; **intuizi'one** *sf* intuition.
inu'mano, a *ag* inhuman.
inumi'dire *vt* to dampen, moisten; **~rsi** *vr* to become damp *o* wet.
i'nutile *ag* useless; (*superfluo*) pointless, unnecessary; **inutilità** *sf* uselessness; pointlessness.
inva'dente *ag* (*fig*) interfering, nosey.
in'vadere *vt* to invade; (*affollare*) to swarm into, overrun; (*sog: acque*) to flood; **invadi'trice** *ag vedi* **invasore.**
inva'ghirsi [inva'girsi] *vr*: ~ **di** to take a fancy to.
invalidità *sf* infirmity; disability; (*DIR*) invalidity.
in'valido, a *ag* (*infermo*) infirm, invalid; (*al lavoro*) disabled; (*DIR: nullo*) invalid ♦ *sm/f* invalid; disabled person.
in'vano *av* in vain.
invasi'one *sf* invasion.
in'vaso, a *pp di* **invadere.**
inva'sore, invadi'trice [invadi'tritʃe] *ag* invading ♦ *sm* invader.
invecchi'are [invek'kjare] *vi* (*persona*) to grow old; (*vino, popolazione*) to age; (*moda*) to become dated ♦ *vt* to age; (*far apparire più vecchio*) to make look older.
in'vece [in'vetʃe] *av* instead; (*al contrario*) on the contrary; ~ **di** instead of.
inve'ire *vi*: ~ **contro** to rail against.
inven'tare *vt* to invent; (*pericoli, pettegolezzi*) to make up, invent.
inven'tario *sm* inventory; (*COMM*) stocktaking *no pl.*
inven'tivo, a *ag* inventive ♦ *sf* inventiveness.
inven'tore *sm* inventor.
invenzi'one [inven'tsjone] *sf* invention; (*bugia*) lie, story.

inver'nale *ag* winter *cpd*; (*simile all'inverno*) wintry.
in'verno *sm* winter.
invero'simile *ag* unlikely.
inversi'one *sf* inversion; reversal; "**divieto d'~**" (*AUT*) "no U-turns".
in'verso, a *ag* opposite; (*MAT*) inverse ♦ *sm* contrary, opposite; **in senso** ~ in the opposite direction; **in ordine** ~ in reverse order.
inver'tire *vt* to invert, reverse; ~ **la marcia** (*AUT*) to do a U-turn; **inver'tito, a** *sm/f* homosexual.
investi'gare *vt, vi* to investigate; **investiga'tore, trice** *sm/f* investigator, detective; **investigazi'one** *sf* investigation, inquiry.
investi'mento *sm* (*ECON*) investment; (*scontro, urto*) crash, collision; (*incidente stradale*) road accident.
inves'tire *vt* (*denaro*) to invest; (*sog: veicolo: pedone*) to knock down; (*: altro veicolo*) to crash into; (*apostrofare*) to assail; (*incaricare*): ~ **qn di** to invest sb with.
invi'are *vt* to send; **invi'ato, a** *sm/f* envoy; (*STAMPA*) correspondent.
in'vidia *sf* envy; **invidi'are** *vt*: **invidiare qn** (**per qc**) to envy sb for sth; **invidiare qc a qn** to envy sb sth; **invidi'oso, a** *ag* envious.
in'vio, 'vii *sm* sending; (*insieme di merci*) consignment.
invipe'rito, a *ag* furious.
invischi'are [invis'kjare] *vt* (*fig*): ~ **qn in** to involve sb in; **~rsi** *vr*: **~rsi (con qn/in qc)** to get mixed up *o* involved (with sb/in sth).
invi'sibile *ag* invisible.
invi'tare *vt* to invite; ~ **qn a fare** to invite sb to do; **invi'tato, a** *sm/f* guest; **in'vito** *sm* invitation.
invo'care *vt* (*chiedere: aiuto, pace*) to cry out for; (*appellarsi: la legge, Dio*) to appeal to, invoke.
invogli'are [invoʎ'ʎare] *vt*: ~ **qn a fare** to tempt sb to do, induce sb to do.
involon'tario, a *ag* (*errore*) unintentional; (*gesto*) involuntary.
invol'tino *sm* (*CUC*) roulade.

in'volto sm (pacco) parcel; (fagotto) bundle.

in'volucro sm cover, wrapping.

involuzi'one [involut'tsjone] sf (di stile) convolutedness; (regresso): **subire un'~** to regress.

inzacche'rare [intsakke'rare] vt to spatter with mud.

inzup'pare [intsup'pare] vt to soak; **~rsi** vr to get soaked.

'io pron I ♦ sm inv: **l'~** the ego, the self; **~ stesso(a)** I myself.

i'odio sm iodine.

i'ogurt sm inv = **yoghurt**.

l'onio sm: **lo ~, il mar ~** the Ionian (Sea).

ipermer'cato sm hypermarket.

ipertensi'one sf high blood pressure, hypertension.

ip'nosi sf hypnosis; **ipno'tismo** sm hypnotism; **ipnotiz'zare** vt to hypnotize.

ipocri'sia sf hypocrisy.

i'pocrita, i, e ag hypocritical ♦ sm/f hypocrite.

ipo'teca, che sf mortgage; **ipote'care** vt to mortgage.

i'potesi sf inv hypothesis; **ipo'tetico, a, ci, che** ag hypothetical.

'ippica sf horseracing.

'ippico, a, ci, che ag horse cpd.

ippocas'tano sm horse chestnut.

ip'podromo sm racecourse.

ippo'potamo sm hippopotamus.

'ira sf anger, wrath.

l'ran sm: **l'~** Iran.

l'raq sm: **l'~** Iraq.

'iride sf (arcobaleno) rainbow; (ANAT, BOT) iris.

Ir'landa sf: **l'~** Ireland; **l'~ del Nord** Northern Ireland, Ulster; **la Repubblica d'~** Eire, the Republic of Ireland; **irlan'dese** ag Irish ♦ sm/f Irishman/woman; **gli Irlandesi** the Irish.

iro'nia sf irony; **i'ronico, a, ci, che** ag ironic(al).

irradi'are vt to radiate; (sog: raggi di luce: illuminare) to shine on ♦ vi (diffondersi: anche: **~rsi**) to radiate; **irradiazi'one** sf radiation.

irragio'nevole [irrad3o'nevole] ag irra-

tional; unreasonable.

irrazio'nale [irrattsjo'nale] ag irrational.

irre'ale ag unreal.

irrecupe'rabile ag irretrievable; (fig: person) irredeemable.

irrecu'sabile ag (offerta) not to be refused; (prova) irrefutable.

irrego'lare ag irregular; (terreno) uneven.

irremo'vibile ag (fig) unshakeable, unyielding.

irrepa'rabile ag irreparable; (fig) inevitable.

irrepe'ribile ag nowhere to be found.

irrequi'eto, a ag restless.

irresis'tibile ag irresistible.

irrespon'sabile ag irresponsible.

irridu'cibile [irridu'tʃibile] ag irreducible; (fig) indomitable.

irri'gare vt (annaffiare) to irrigate; (sog: fiume etc) to flow through; **irrigazi'one** sf irrigation.

irrigi'dire [irrid3i'dire] vt to stiffen; **~rsi** vr to stiffen.

irri'sorio, a ag derisory.

irri'tare vt (mettere di malumore) to irritate, annoy; (MED) to irritate; **~rsi** vr (stizzirsi) to become irritated o annoyed; (MED) to become irritated; **irritazi'one** sf irritation; annoyance.

ir'rompere vi: **~ in** to burst into.

irro'rare vt to sprinkle; (AGR) to spray.

irru'ente ag (fig) impetuous, violent.

irruzi'one [irrut'tsjone] sf: **fare ~ in** to burst into; (sog: polizia) to raid.

'irto, a ag bristly; **~ di** bristling with.

is'critto, a pp di **iscrivere** ♦ sm/f member; **per o in ~** in writing.

is'crivere vt to register, enter; (persona): **~ (a)** to register (in), enrol (in); **~rsi** vr: **~rsi (a)** (club, partito) to join; (università) to register o enrol (at); (esame, concorso) to register o enter (for); **iscrizi'one** sf (epigrafe etc) inscription; (a scuola, società) enrolment, registration; (registrazione) registration.

Is'lam sm: **l'~** Islam.

Is'landa sf: **l'~** Iceland.

'isola sf island; **~ pedonale** (AUT)

pedestrian precinct.

isola'mento *sm* isolation; (*TECN*) insulation.

iso'lante *ag* insulating ♦ *sm* insulator.

iso'lare *vt* to isolate; (*TECN*) to insulate; (: *acusticamente*) to soundproof; **iso'lato, a** *ag* isolated; insulated ♦ *sm* (*edificio*) block.

ispetto'rato *sm* inspectorate.

ispet'tore *sm* inspector.

ispezio'nare [ispettsjo'nare] *vt* to inspect.

ispezi'one [ispet'tsjone] *sf* inspection.

'ispido, a *ag* bristly, shaggy.

ispi'rare *vt* to inspire; **~rsi** *vr*: **~rsi a** to draw one's inspiration from.

Isra'ele *sm*: **l'~** Israel; **israeli'ano, a** *ag*, *sm/f* Israeli.

is'sare *vt* to hoist.

istan'taneo, a *ag* instantaneous ♦ *sf* (*FOT*) snapshot.

is'tante *sm* instant, moment; **all'~**, **sull'~** instantly, immediately.

is'tanza [is'tantsa] *sf* petition, request.

is'terico, a, ci, che *ag* hysterical.

iste'rismo *sm* hysteria.

isti'gare *vt* to incite; **istigazi'one** *sf* incitement; **istigazione a delinquere** (*DIR*) incitement to crime.

is'tinto *sm* instinct.

istitu'ire *vt* (*fondare*) to institute, found; (*porre: confronto*) to establish; (*intraprendere: inchiesta*) to set up.

isti'tuto *sm* institute; (*di università*) department; (*ente*, *DIR*) institution; **~ di bellezza** beauty salon.

istituzi'one [istitut'tsjone] *sf* institution.

'istmo *sm* (*GEO*) isthmus.

istra'dare *vt* = **instradare.**

'istrice ['istritʃe] *sm* porcupine.

istri'one (*peg*) *sm* ham actor.

istru'ire *vt* (*insegnare*) to teach; (*ammaestrare*) to train; (*informare*) to instruct, inform; (*DIR*) to prepare; **istrut'tore, 'trice** *sm/f* instructor ♦ *ag*: **giudice istruttore** examining (*BRIT*) *o* committing (*US*) magistrate; **istrut'toria** *sf* (*DIR*) (preliminary) investigation and hearing; **istruzi'one** *sf* education; training; (*direttiva*) instruction; (*DIR*)

= **istruttoria; istruzioni per l'uso** instructions (for use).

I'talia *sf*: **l'~** Italy.

itali'ano, a *ag* Italian ♦ *sm/f* Italian ♦ *sm* (*LING*) Italian; **gli I~i** the Italians.

itine'rario *sm* itinerary.

itte'rizia [itte'rittsja] *sf* (*MED*) jaundice.

'ittico, a, ci, che *ag* fish *cpd*; fishing *cpd.*

Iugos'lavia *sf* = **Jugoslavia.**

iugos'lavo, a *ag*, *sm/f* = **jugoslavo, a.**

i'uta *sf* jute.

I.V.A. ['iva] *sigla f* (= *imposta sul valore aggiunto*) VAT.

J

jazz [dʒaz] *sm* jazz.

jeans [dʒinz] *smpl* jeans.

Jugos'lavia [jugoz'lavja] *sf*: **la ~** Yugoslavia; **jugos'lavo, a** *ag*, *sm/f* Yugoslav(ian).

'juta ['juta] *sf* = **iuta.**

K

K *abbr* (*INFORM*) K.

k *abbr* (= *kilo*) k.

karatè *sm* karate.

Kg *abbr* (= *chilogrammo*) kg.

'killer *sm inv* gunman, hired gun.

km *abbr* (= *chilometro*) km.

'krapfen *sm inv* (*CUC*) doughnut.

L

l' *det vedi* **la; lo.**

la¹ (*dav V* **l'**) *det f* the ♦ *pron* (*oggetto: persona*) her; (: *cosa*) it; (: *forma di cortesia*) you.

la² *sm inv* (*MUS*) A; (: *solfeggiando la scala*) la.

là *av* there; **di ~** (*da quel luogo*) from there; (*in quel luogo*) in there; (*dall'altra parte*) over there; **di ~ di** beyond; **per di ~** that way; **più in ~** further on; (*tempo*) later on; **fatti in ~**

move up; ~ **dentro/sopra/sotto** in/up (*o* on)/under there; *vedi* **quello**.
'**labbro** (*pl(f)*: **labbra**: *solo nel senso ANAT*) *sm* lip.
labi'rinto *sm* labyrinth, maze.
labora'torio *sm* (*di ricerca*) laboratory; (*di arti, mestieri*) workshop; ~ **linguistico** language laboratory.
labori'oso, a *ag* (*faticoso*) laborious; (*attivo*) hard-working.
labu'rista, i, e *ag* Labour (*BRIT*) *cpd* ♦ *sm/f* Labour Party member (*BRIT*).
'**lacca, che** *sf* lacquer.
'**laccio** ['lattʃo] *sm* noose; (*legaccio, tirante*) lasso; (*di scarpa*) lace; ~ **emostatico** tourniquet.
lace'rare [latʃe'rare] *vt* to tear to shreds, lacerate; ~**rsi** *vr* to tear; '**lacero, a** *ag* (*logoro*) torn, tattered; (*MED*) lacerated.
'**lacrima** *sf* tear; **in** ~**e** in tears; **lacri'mare** *vi* to water; **lacri'mogeno, a** *ag*: **gas lacrimogeno** tear gas.
la'cuna *sf* (*fig*) gap.
'**ladro** *sm* thief; **ladro'cinio** *sm* theft, larceny.
laggiù [lad'dʒu] *av* down there; (*di là*) over there.
la'gnarsi [laɲ'ɲarsi] *vr*: ~ **(di)** to complain (about).
'**lago, ghi** *sm* lake.
'**lagrima** *etc* = **lacrima** *etc*.
la'guna *sf* lagoon.
'**laico, a, ci, che** *ag* (*apostolato*) lay; (*vita*) secular; (*scuola*) non-denominational ♦ *sm/f* layman/woman ♦ *sm* lay brother.
'**lama** *sm inv* (*ZOOL*) llama; (*REL*) lama ♦ *sf* blade.
lambic'care *vt* to distil; ~**rsi il cervello** to rack one's brains.
lam'bire *vt* to lick; to lap.
la'mella *sf* (*di metallo etc*) thin sheet, thin strip; (*di fungo*) gill.
lamen'tare *vt* to lament; ~**rsi** *vr* (*emettere lamenti*) to moan, groan; (*rammaricarsi*): ~**rsi (di)** to complain (about); **lamen'tela** *sf* complaining *no pl*; **lamen'tevole** *ag* (*voce*) complaining, plaintive; (*destino*) pitiful;

la'mento *sm* moan, groan; wail; **lamen'toso, a** *ag* plaintive.
la'metta *sf* razor blade.
lami'era *sf* sheet metal.
'**lamina** *sf* (*lastra sottile*) thin sheet (*o* layer *o* plate); ~ **d'oro** gold leaf; gold foil; **lami'nare** *vt* to laminate; **lami'nato, a** *ag* laminated; (*tessuto*) lamé ♦ *sm* laminate.
'**lampada** *sf* lamp; ~ **a gas** gas lamp; ~ **a spirito** blow lamp (*BRIT*), blow torch (*US*); ~ **da tavolo** table lamp.
lampa'dario *sm* chandelier.
lampa'dina *sf* light bulb; ~ **tascabile** pocket torch (*BRIT*) *o* flashlight (*US*).
lam'pante *ag* (*fig*: *evidente*) crystal clear, evident.
lampeggi'are [lamped'dʒare] *vi* (*luce, fari*) to flash ♦ *vb impers*: **lampeggia** there's lightning; **lampeggia'tore** *sm* (*AUT*) indicator.
lampi'one *sm* street light *o* lamp (*BRIT*).
'**lampo** *sm* (*METEOR*) flash of lightning; (*di luce, fig*) flash; ~**i** *smpl* lightning *no pl* ♦ *ag inv*: **cerniera** ~ zip (fastener) (*BRIT*), zipper (*US*); **guerra** ~ blitzkrieg.
lam'pone *sm* raspberry.
'**lana** *sf* wool; ~ **d'acciaio** steel wool; **pura** ~ **vergine** pure new wool; ~ **di vetro** glass wool.
lan'cetta [lan'tʃetta] *sf* (*indice*) pointer, needle; (*di orologio*) hand.
'**lancia** ['lantʃa] *sf* (*arma*) lance; (: *picca*) spear; (*di pompa antincendio*) nozzle; (*imbarcazione*) launch.
lanciafi'amme [lantʃa'fjamme] *sm inv* flamethrower.
lanci'are [lan'tʃare] *vt* to throw, hurl, fling; (*SPORT*) to throw; (*far partire: automobile*) to get up to full speed; (*bombe*) to drop; (*razzo, prodotto, moda*) to launch; ~**rsi** *vr*: ~**rsi contro/su** to throw *o* hurl *o* fling o.s. against/on; ~**rsi in** (*fig*) to embark on.
lanci'nante [lantʃi'nante] *ag* (*dolore*) shooting, throbbing; (*grido*) piercing.
'**lancio** ['lantʃo] *sm* throwing *no pl*; throw; dropping *no pl*; drop; launching *no pl*; launch; ~ **del peso** putting the

shot.

'landa *sf* (*GEO*) moor.

'languido, a *ag* (*fiacco*) languid, weak; (*tenero, malinconico*) languishing.

langu'ore *sm* weakness, languor.

lani'ficio [lani'fitʃo] *sm* woollen mill.

la'noso, a *ag* woolly.

lan'terna *sf* lantern; (*faro*) lighthouse.

la'nugine [la'nudʒine] *sf* down.

lapi'dare *vt* to stone.

lapi'dario, a *ag* (*fig*) terse.

'lapide *sf* (*di sepolcro*) tombstone; (*commemorativa*) plaque.

'lapis *sm inv* pencil.

Lap'ponia *sf* Lapland.

'lapsus *sm inv* slip.

'lardo *sm* bacon fat, lard.

lar'ghezza [lar'gettsa] *sf* width; breadth; looseness; generosity; ~ **di vedute** broad-mindedness.

'largo, a, ghi, ghe *ag* wide; broad; (*maniche*) wide; (*abito: troppo ampio*) loose; (*fig*) generous ♦ *sm* width; breadth; (*mare aperto*): **il** ~ the open sea ♦ *sf*: **stare** *o* **tenersi alla** ~**a** (*da qn/qc*) to keep one's distance (from sb/sth), keep away (from sb/sth); ~ **due metri** two metres wide; ~ **di spalle** broad-shouldered; **di** ~**ghe vedute** broad-minded; **su** ~**a scala** on a large scale; **di manica** ~**a** generous, open-handed; **al** ~ **di Genova** off (the coast of) Genoa; **farsi** ~ **tra la folla** to push one's way through the crowd.

'larice ['laritʃe] *sm* (*BOT*) larch.

larin'gite [larin'dʒite] *sf* laryngitis.

'larva *sf* larva; (*fig*) shadow.

la'sagne [la'zaɲɲe] *sfpl* lasagna *sg*.

lasci'are [laʃ'ʃare] *vt* to leave; (*abbandonare*) to leave, abandon, give up; (*cessare di tenere*) to let go of ♦ *vb aus*: ~ **fare qn** to let sb do ♦ *vi*: ~ **di fare** (*smettere*) to stop doing; ~**rsi** andare/truffare to let o.s. go/be cheated; ~ **andare** *o* **correre** *o* **perdere** to let things go their own way; ~ **stare qc/qn** to leave sth/sb alone.

'lascito ['laʃʃito] *sm* (*DIR*) legacy.

'laser ['lazer] *ag, sm inv*: (*raggio*) ~

laser (beam).

lassa'tivo, a *ag, sm* laxative.

'lasso *sm*: ~ **di tempo** interval, lapse of time.

lassù *av* up there.

'lastra *sf* (*di pietra*) slab; (*di metallo, FOT*) plate; (*di ghiaccio, vetro*) sheet; (*radiografica*) X-ray (plate).

lastri'care *vt* to pave; **lastri'cato** *sm*, **'lastrico, ci** *o* **chi** *sm* paving.

late'rale *ag* lateral, side *cpd*; (*uscita, ingresso etc*) side *cpd* ♦ *sm* (*CALCIO*) half-back.

late'rizio [late'rittsjo] *sm* (perforated) brick.

lati'fondo *sm* large estate.

la'tino, a *ag, sm* Latin; ~**-ameri'cano, a** *ag* Latin-American.

lati'tante *sm/f* fugitive (from justice).

lati'tudine *sf* latitude.

'lato, a *ag* (*fig*) wide, broad ♦ *sm* side; (*fig*) aspect, point of view; **in senso** ~ broadly speaking.

la'trare *vi* to bark.

latro'cinio [latro'tʃinjo] *sm* = **ladrocinio**.

'latta *sf* tin (plate); (*recipiente*) tin, can.

lat'taio, a *sm/f* milkman/woman; dairyman/woman.

lat'tante *ag* unweaned.

'latte *sm* milk; ~ **detergente** cleansing milk *o* lotion; ~ **secco** *o* **in polvere** dried *o* powdered milk; ~ **scremato** skimmed milk; **'latteo, a** *ag* milky; (*dieta, prodotto*) milk *cpd*; **latte'ria** *sf* dairy; **latti'cini** *smpl* dairy products.

lat'tina *sf* (*di birra etc*) can.

lat'tuga, ghe *sf* lettuce.

'laurea *sf* degree; **laure'ando, a** *sm/f* final-year student; **laure'are** *vt* to confer a degree on; **laurearsi** *vr* to graduate; **laure'ato, a** *ag, sm/f* graduate.

'lauro *sm* laurel.

'lauto, a *ag* (*pranzo, mancia*) lavish.

'lava *sf* lava.

la'vabo *sm* washbasin.

la'vaggio [la'vaddʒo] *sm* washing *no pl*; ~ **del cervello** brainwashing *no pl*.

la'vagna [la'vaɲɲa] *sf* (*GEO*) slate; (*di*

scuola) blackboard.

la'vanda *sf (anche MED)* wash; *(BOT)* lavender; **lavan'daia** *sf* washerwoman; **lavande'ria** *sf* laundry; **lavanderia automatica** launderette; **lavanderia a secco** dry-cleaner's; **lavan'dino** *sm* sink.

lavapi'atti *sm/f* dishwasher.

la'vare *vt* to wash; **~rsi** *vr* to wash, have a wash; **~ a secco** to dry-clean; **~rsi le mani/i denti** to wash one's hands/clean one's teeth.

lava'secco *sm o f inv* drycleaner's.

lavasto'viglie [lavastoˈviʎʎe] *sm o f inv (macchina)* dishwasher.

lava'toio *sm* (public) washhouse.

lava'trice [lavaˈtritʃe] *sf* washing machine.

lava'tura *sf* washing *no pl*; **~ di piatti** dishwater.

lavo'rante *sm/f* worker.

lavo'rare *vi* to work; *(fig: bar, studio etc)* to do good business ♦ *vt* to work; **~rsi qn** *(persuaderlo)* to work on sb; **~ a** to work on; **~ a maglia** to knit; **lavora'tivo, a** *ag* working; **lavora'tore, 'trice** *sm/f* worker ♦ *ag* working; **lavorazi'one** *sf (gen)* working; *(di legno, pietra)* carving; *(di film)* making; *(di prodotto)* manufacture; *(modo di esecuzione)* workmanship; **lavo'rio** *sm* intense activity.

la'voro *sm* work; *(occupazione)* job, work *no pl*; *(opera)* piece of work, job; *(ECON)* labour; **~i forzati** hard labour *sg*; **~i pubblici** public works.

le *det fpl* the ♦ *pron (oggetto)* them; *(: a lei, a essa)* (to) her; *(: forma di cortesia)* (to) you.

le'ale *ag* loyal; *(sincero)* sincere; *(onesto)* fair; **lealtà** *sf* loyalty; sincerity; fairness.

'lebbra *sf* leprosy.

'lecca 'lecca *sm inv* lollipop.

leccapi'edi *(peg)* *sm/f inv* toady, bootlicker.

lec'care *vt* to lick; *(sog: gatto: latte etc)* to lick *o* lap up; *(fig)* to flatter; **~rsi i baffi** to lick one's lips; **lec'cata** *sf* lick.

'leccio [ˈlettʃo] *sm* holm oak, ilex.

leccor'nia *sf* titbit, delicacy.

'lecito, a [ˈlɛtʃito] *ag* permitted, allowed.

'ledere *vt* to damage, injure.

'lega, ghe *sf* league; *(di metalli)* alloy.

le'gaccio [leˈgattʃo] *sm* string, lace.

le'gale *ag* legal ♦ *sm* lawyer; **legaliz'zare** *vt* to authenticate; *(regolarizzare)* to legalize.

le'game *sm (corda, fig: affettivo)* tie, bond; *(nesso logico)* link, connection.

le'gare *vt (prigioniero, capelli, cane)* to tie (up); *(libro)* to bind; *(CHIM)* to alloy; *(fig: collegare)* to bind, join ♦ *vi (far lega)* to unite; *(fig)* to get on well.

lega'tario, a *sm/f (DIR)* legatee.

le'gato *sm (REL)* legate; *(DIR)* legacy, bequest.

lega'tura *sf (di libro)* binding; *(MUS)* ligature.

le'genda [leˈdʒɛnda] *sf (di carta geografica etc)* = **leggenda**.

'legge [ˈleddʒe] *sf* law.

leg'genda [ledˈdʒɛnda] *sf (narrazione)* legend; *(di carta geografica etc)* key, legend.

'leggere [ˈleddʒere] *vt, vi* to read.

legge'rezza [ledˈdʒeˈrettsa] *sf* lightness; thoughtlessness; fickleness.

leg'gero, a [ledˈdʒero] *ag* light; *(agile, snello)* nimble, agile, light; *(tè, caffè)* weak; *(fig: non grave, piccolo)* slight; *(: spensierato)* thoughtless; *(: incostante)* fickle; free and easy; **alla ~a** thoughtlessly.

leggi'adro, a [ledˈdʒadro] *ag* pretty, lovely; *(movimenti)* graceful.

leg'gio, 'gii [ledˈdʒio] *sm* lectern; *(MUS)* music stand.

legisla'tura [ledʒizlaˈtura] *sf* legislature.

legislazi'one [ledʒizlatˈtsjone] *sf* legislation.

le'gittimo, a [leˈdʒittimo] *ag* legitimate; *(fig: giustificato, lecito)* justified, legitimate; **~a difesa** *(DIR)* self-defence.

'legna [ˈleɲɲa] *sf* firewood; **le'gname** *sm* wood, timber.

'legno [ˈleɲɲo] *sm* wood; *(pezzo di ~)* piece of wood; **di ~** wooden; **~**

compensato plywood; **le'gnoso, a** *ag* wooden; woody; (*carne*) tough.

le'gumi *smpl* (*BOT*) pulses.

'lei *pron* (*soggetto*) she; (*oggetto: per dare rilievo, con preposizione*) her; (*forma di cortesia: anche: L~*) you ♦ *sm*: **dare del ~ a qn** to address sb as "lei"; **~ stessa** she herself; you yourself.

'lembo *sm* (*di abito, strada*) edge; (*striscia sottile: di terra*) strip.

'lemma, i *sm* headword.

'lemme 'lemme *av* (very) very slowly.

'lena *sf* (*fig*) energy, stamina.

le'nire *vt* to soothe.

'lente *sf* (*OTTICA*) lens *sg*; **~ d'ingrandimento** magnifying glass; **~i a contatto** *o* **corneali** contact lenses.

len'tezza [len'tettsa] *sf* slowness.

len'ticchia [len'tikkja] *sf* (*BOT*) lentil.

len'tiggine [len'tiddʒine] *sf* freckle.

'lento, a *ag* slow; (*molle: fune*) slack; (*non stretto: vite, abito*) loose ♦ *sm* (*ballo*) slow dance.

'lenza ['lɛntsa] *sf* fishing-line.

lenzu'olo [len'tswɔlo] *sm* sheet; **~a** *sfpl* pair of sheets.

le'one *sm* lion; (*dello zodiaco*): **L~** Leo.

lepo'rino, a *ag*: **labbro ~** harelip.

'lepre *sf* hare.

'lercio, a, ci, cie ['lɛrtʃo] *ag* filthy.

'lesbica, che *sf* lesbian.

lesi'nare *vt* to be stingy with ♦ *vi*: **~ (su)** to skimp (on), be stingy (with).

lesi'one *sf* (*MED*) lesion; (*DIR*) injury, damage; (*EDIL*) crack.

'leso, a *pp di* **ledere** ♦ *ag* (*offeso*) injured; **parte ~a** (*DIR*) injured party.

les'sare *vt* (*CUC*) to boil.

'lessico, ci *sm* vocabulary; lexicon.

'lesso, a *ag* boiled ♦ *sm* boiled meat.

'lesto, a *ag* quick; (*agile*) nimble; **~ di mano** (*per rubare*) light-fingered; (*per picchiare*) free with one's fists.

le'tale *ag* lethal; fatal.

leta'maio *sm* dunghill.

le'tame *sm* manure, dung.

le'targo, ghi *sm* lethargy; (*ZOOL*) hibernation.

le'tizia [le'tittsja] *sf* joy, happiness.

'lettera *sf* letter; **~e** *sfpl* (*letteratura*) literature *sg*; (*studi umanistici*) arts (subjects); **alla ~** literally; **in ~e** in words, in full; **lette'rale** *ag* literal.

lette'rario, a *ag* literary.

lette'rato, a *ag* well-read, scholarly.

lettera'tura *sf* literature.

let'tiga, ghe *sf* (*portantina*) litter; (*barella*) stretcher.

let'tino *sm* cot (*BRIT*), crib (*US*).

'letto, a *pp di* **leggere** ♦ *sm* bed; **andare a ~** to go to bed; **~ a castello** bunk beds *pl*; **~ a una piazza/a due piazze** *o* **matrimoniale** single/double bed.

let'tore, 'trice *sm/f* reader; (*INS*) (foreign language) assistant (*BRIT*), (foreign) teaching assistant (*US*) ♦ *sm* (*TECN*): **~ ottico** optical character reader.

let'tura *sf* reading.

leuce'mia [leutʃe'mia] *sf* leukaemia.

'leva *sf* lever; (*MIL*) conscription; **far ~ su qn** to work on sb; **~ del cambio** (*AUT*) gear lever.

le'vante *sm* east; (*vento*) East wind; **il L~** the Levant.

le'vare *vt* (*occhi, braccio*) to raise; (*sollevare, togliere: tassa, divieto*) to lift; (*indumenti*) to take off, remove; (*rimuovere*) to take away; (: *dal di sopra*) to take off; (: *dal di dentro*) to take out; **~rsi** *vr* to get up; (*sole*) to rise; **le'vata** *sf* (*di posta*) collection.

leva'toio, a *ag*: **ponte ~** drawbridge.

leva'tura *sf* intelligence, mental capacity.

levi'gare *vt* to smooth; (*con carta vetrata*) to sand.

levri'ere *sm* greyhound.

lezi'one [let'tsjone] *sf* lesson; (*all'università, sgridata*) lecture; **fare ~** to teach; to lecture.

lezi'oso, a [let'tsjoso] *ag* affected; simpering.

'lezzo ['leddzo] *sm* stench, stink.

li *pron pl* (*oggetto*) them.

lì *av* there; **di** *o* **da ~** from there; **per di**

~ that way; **di ~ a pochi giorni** a few days later; **~ per ~** there and then; at first; **essere ~ (~) per fare** to be on the point of doing, be about to do; **~ dentro** in there; **~ sotto** under there; **~ sopra** on there; up there; *vedi* **quello**.

liba'nese *ag, sm/f* Lebanese *inv*.

Li'bano *sm*: **il ~** the Lebanon.

'libbra *sf (peso)* pound.

li'beccio [li'bettʃo] *sm* south-west wind.

li'bello *sm* libel.

li'bellula *sf* dragonfly.

libe'rale *ag, sm/f* liberal.

liberaliz'zare [liberalid'dzare] *vt* to liberalize.

libe'rare *vt (rendere libero: prigioniero)* to release; (*: popolo*) to free, liberate; (*sgombrare: passaggio*) to clear; (*: stanza*) to vacate; (*produrre: energia*) to release; **~rsi** *vr*: **~rsi di qc/qn** to get rid of sth/sb; **libera'tore, 'trice** *ag* liberating ♦ *sm/f* liberator; **liberazi'one** *sf* liberation, freeing; release; rescuing.

'libero, a *ag* free; *(strada)* clear; *(non occupato: posto etc)* vacant; not taken; empty; not engaged; **~ di fare qc** free to do sth; **~ da** free from; **~ arbitrio** free will; **~ professionista** self-employed professional person; **~ scambio** free trade; **libertà** *sf inv* freedom; *(tempo disponibile)* free time ♦ *sfpl (licenza)* liberties; **in libertà provvisoria/vigilata** released without bail/on probation; **libertà di riunione** right to hold meetings.

'Libia *sf*: **la ~** Libya; **'libico, a, ci, che** *ag, sm/f* Libyan.

li'bidine *sf* lust.

li'braio *sm* bookseller.

li'brario, a *ag* book *cpd*.

li'brarsi *vr* to hover.

libre'ria *sf (bottega)* bookshop; *(stanza)* library; *(mobile)* bookcase.

li'bretto *sm* booklet; *(taccuino)* notebook; *(MUS)* libretto; **~ degli assegni** cheque book; **~ di circolazione** *(AUT)* logbook; **~ di risparmio** *(savings)* bank-book, passbook; **~ universitario** student's report book.

'libro *sm* book; **~ bianco** *(POL)* white paper; **~ di cassa** cash book; **~ mastro** ledger; **~ paga** payroll.

li'cenza [li'tʃɛntsa] *sf (permesso)* permission, leave; *(di pesca, caccia, circolazione)* permit, licence; *(MIL)* leave; *(INS)* school leaving certificate; *(libertà)* liberty; licence; licentiousness; **andare in ~** *(MIL)* to go on leave.

licenzia'mento [litʃentsja'mento] *sm* dismissal.

licenzi'are [litʃen'tsjare] *vt (impiegato)* to dismiss; *(INS)* to award a certificate to; **~rsi** *vr (impiegato)* to resign, hand in one's notice; *(INS)* to obtain one's school-leaving certificate.

li'ceo [li'tʃɛo] *sm (INS)* secondary *(BRIT)* o high *(US)* school *(for 14- to 19-year-olds)*.

'lido *sm* beach, shore.

li'eto, a *ag* happy, glad; **"molto ~"** *(nelle presentazioni)* "pleased to meet you".

li'eve *ag* light; *(di poco conto)* slight; *(sommesso: voce)* faint, soft.

lievi'tare *vi (anche fig)* to rise ♦ *vt* to leaven.

li'evito *sm* yeast; **~ di birra** brewer's yeast.

'ligio, a, gi, gie ['lidʒo] *ag* faithful, loyal.

'lilla *sm inv* lilac.

'lillà *sm inv* = **lilla**.

'lima *sf* file.

limacci'oso, a [limat'tʃoso] *ag* slimy; muddy.

li'mare *vt* to file (down); *(fig)* to polish.

'limbo *sm (REL)* limbo.

li'metta *sf* nail file.

limi'tare *vt* to limit, restrict; *(circo-scrivere)* to bound, surround; **limita'tivo, a** *ag* limiting, restricting; **limi'tato, a** *ag* limited, restricted.

'limite *sm* limit; *(confine)* border, boundary; **~ di velocità** speed limit.

li'mitrofo, a *ag* neighbouring.

limo'nata *sf* lemonade *(BRIT)*, (lemon) soda *(US)*; lemon squash *(BRIT)*, lemonade *(US)*.

li'mone *sm (pianta)* lemon tree;

(*frutto*) lemon.
'limpido, a *ag* clear; (*acqua*) limpid, clear.
'lince ['lintʃe] *sf* lynx.
linci'are *vt* to lynch.
'lindo, a *ag* tidy, spick and span; (*biancheria*) clean.
'linea *sf* line; (*di mezzi pubblici di trasporto: itinerario*) route; (: *servizio*) service; **a grandi ~e** in outline; **mantenere la ~** to look after one's figure; **aereo di ~** airliner; **nave di ~** liner; **volo di ~** scheduled flight; **~ aerea** airline; **~ di partenza/d'arrivo** (*SPORT*) starting/finishing line; **~ di tiro** line of fire.
linea'menti *smpl* features; (*fig*) outlines.
line'are *ag* linear; (*fig*) coherent, logical.
line'etta *sf* (*trattino*) dash; (*d'unione*) hyphen.
lin'gotto *sm* ingot, bar.
'lingua *sf* (*ANAT, CUC*) tongue; (*idioma*) language; **mostrare la ~** to stick out one's tongue; **di ~ italiana** Italian-speaking; **~ madre** mother tongue; **una ~ di terra** a spit of land.
lingu'aggio [lin'gwaddʒo] *sm* language.
lingu'etta *sf* (*di strumento*) reed; (*di scarpa, TECN*) tongue; (*di busta*) flap.
lingu'istica *sf* linguistics *sg*.
'lino *sm* (*pianta*) flax; (*tessuto*) linen.
li'noleum *sm inv* linoleum, lino.
lique'fare *vt* (*render liquido*) to liquefy; (*fondere*) to melt; **~rsi** *vr* to liquefy; to melt.
liqui'dare *vt* (*società, beni; persona: uccidere*) to liquidate; (*persona: sbarazzarsene*) to get rid of; (*conto, problema*) to settle; (*COMM: merce*) to sell off, clear; **liquidazi'one** *sf* liquidation; settlement; clearance sale.
liquidità *sf* liquidity.
'liquido, a *ag, sm* liquid; **~ per freni** brake fluid.
liqui'rizia [likwi'rittsja] *sf* liquorice.
li'quore *sm* liqueur.
'lira *sf* (*unità monetaria*) lira; (*MUS*) lyre; **~ sterlina** pound sterling.

'lirica, che *sf* (*poesia*) lyric poetry; (*componimento poetico*) lyric; (*MUS*) opera.
'lirico, a, ci, che *ag* lyric(al); (*MUS*) lyric; **cantante/teatro ~** opera singer/house.
'lisca, sche *sf* (*di pesce*) fishbone.
lisci'are [liʃ'ʃare] *vt* to smooth; (*fig*) to flatter.
'liscio, a, sci, sce ['liʃʃo] *ag* smooth; (*capelli*) straight; (*mobile*) plain; (*bevanda alcolica*) neat; (*fig*) straightforward, simple ♦ *av*: **andare ~** to go smoothly; **passarla ~a** to get away with it.
'liso, a *ag* worn out, threadbare.
'lista *sf* (*striscia*) strip; (*elenco*) list; **~ elettorale** electoral roll; **~ delle vivande** menu.
lis'tino *sm* list; **~ dei cambi** (foreign) exchange rate; **~ dei prezzi** price list.
'lite *sf* quarrel, argument; (*DIR*) lawsuit.
liti'gare *vi* to quarrel; (*DIR*) to litigate.
li'tigio [li'tidʒo] *sm* quarrel; **litigi'oso, a** *ag* quarrelsome; (*DIR*) litigious.
litogra'fia *sf* (*sistema*) lithography; (*stampa*) lithograph.
lito'rale *ag* coastal, coast *cpd* ♦ *sm* coast.
'litro *sm* litre.
livel'lare *vt* to level, make level; **~rsi** *vr* to become level; (*fig*) to level out, balance out.
li'vello *sm* level; (*fig*) level, standard; **ad alto ~** (*fig*) high-level; **~ del mare** sea level.
'livido, a *ag* livid; (*per percosse*) bruised, black and blue; (*cielo*) leaden ♦ *sm* bruise.
li'vore *sm* malice, spite.
Li'vorno *sf* Livorno, Leghorn.
li'vrea *sf* livery.
'lizza ['littsa] *sf* lists *pl*; **scendere in ~** (*anche fig*) to enter the lists.
lo (*dav s impura, gn, pn, ps, x, z; dav V l'*) *det m* the ♦ *pron* (*oggetto: persona*) him; (: *cosa*) it; **~ sapevo** I knew it; **~ so** I know; **sii buono, anche se lui non ~** è be good, even if he isn't.

lo'cale *ag* local ♦ *sm* room; *(luogo pubblico)* premises *pl*; ~ **notturno** nightclub; **località** *sf inv* locality; **localiz'zare** *vt (circoscrivere)* to confine, localize; *(accertare)* to locate, place.

lo'canda *sf* inn; **locandi'ere, a** *sm/f* innkeeper.

loca'tario, a *sm/f* tenant.

loca'tore, 'trice *sm/f* landlord/lady.

locazi'one [lokat'tsjone] *sf (da parte del locatario)* renting *no pl*; *(da parte del locatore)* renting out *no pl*, letting *no pl*; **(contratto di)** ~ lease; **(canone di)** ~ rent; **dare in** ~ to rent out, let.

locomo'tiva *sf* locomotive.

locomo'tore *sm* electric locomotive.

locomozi'one [lokomot'tsjone] *sf* locomotion; **mezzi di** ~ vehicles, means of transport.

lo'custa *sf* locust.

locuzl'one [lokut'tsjone] *sf* phrase, expression.

lo'dare *vt* to praise.

'lode *sf* praise; *(INS)*: **laurearsi con 110 e** ~ ≈ to graduate with a first-class honours degree *(BRIT)*, graduate summa cum laude *(US)*.

'loden *sm inv (stoffa)* loden; *(cappotto)* loden overcoat.

lo'devole *ag* praiseworthy.

loga'ritmo *sm* logarithm.

'loggia, ge ['lɔddʒa] *sf (ARCHIT)* loggia; *(circolo massonico)* lodge; **loggi'one** *sm (di teatro)*: **il loggione** the Gods *sg*.

'logica *sf* logic.

'logico, a, ci, che ['lɔdʒiko] *ag* logical.

logo'rare *vt* to wear out; *(sciupare)* to waste; ~**rsi** *vr* to wear out; *(fig)* to wear o.s. out.

logo'rio *sm* wear and tear; *(fig)* strain.

'logoro, a *ag (stoffa)* worn out, threadbare; *(persona)* worn out.

lom'baggine [lom'baddʒine] *sf* lumbago.

Lombar'dia *sf*: **la** ~ Lombardy.

lom'bata *sf (taglio di carne)* loin.

'lombo *sm (ANAT)* loin.

lom'brico, chi *sm* earthworm.

londi'nese *ag* London *cpd* ♦ *sm/f* Londoner.

'Londra *sf* London.

lon'gevo, a [lon'dʒevo] *ag* long-lived.

longi'tudine [londʒi'tudine] *sf* longitude.

lonta'nanza [lonta'nantsa] *sf* distance; absence.

lon'tano, a *ag (distante)* distant, far-away; *(assente)* absent; *(vago: sospetto)* slight, remote; *(tempo: remoto)* far-off, distant; *(parente)* distant, remote ♦ *av* far; **è** ~**a la casa?** is it far to the house?, is the house far from here?; **è** ~ **un chilometro** it's a kilometre away *o* a kilometre from here; **più** ~ farther; **da** *o* **di** ~ from a distance; ~ **da** a long way from; **alla** ~**a** slightly, vaguely.

'lontra *sf* otter.

lo'quace [lo'kwatʃe] *ag* talkative, loquacious; *(fig: gesto etc)* eloquent.

'lordo, a *ag* dirty, filthy; *(peso, stipendio)* gross.

'loro *pron pl (oggetto, con preposizione)* them; *(complemento di termine)* to them; *(soggetto)* they; *(forma di cortesia: anche: L~)* you; to you; **il(la)** ~**, i(le)** ~ *det* their; *(forma di cortesia: anche: L~)* your ♦ *pron* theirs; *(forma di cortesia: anche: L~)* yours; ~ **stessi(e)** they themselves; ~ you yourselves.

'losco, a, schi, sche *ag (fig)* shady, suspicious.

'lotta *sf* struggle, fight; *(SPORT)* wrestling; ~ **libera** all-in wrestling; **lot'tare** *vi* to fight, struggle; to wrestle; **lotta'tore, trice** *sm/f* wrestler.

lotte'ria *sf* lottery; *(di gara ippica)* sweepstake.

'lotto *sm (gioco)* (state) lottery; *(parte)* lot; *(EDIL)* site.

lozi'one [lot'tsjone] *sf* lotion.

lubrifi'cante *sm* lubricant.

lubrifi'care *vt* to lubricate.

luc'chetto [luk'ketto] *sm* padlock.

lucci'care [luttʃi'kare] *vi* to sparkle, glitter, twinkle.

'luccio ['luttʃo] *sm (ZOOL)* pike.

'lucciola ['luttʃola] *sf (ZOOL)* firefly; glowworm.

'luce ['lutʃe] *sf* light; *(finestra)* window;

alla ~ **di** by the light of; **fare** ~ **su qc** (*fig*) to shed *o* throw light on sth; ~ **del sole/della luna** sun/moonlight; **lu'cente** *ag* shining.

lu'cerna [lu'tʃɛrna] *sf* oil-lamp.

lucer'nario [lutʃer'narjo] *sm* skylight.

lu'certola [lu'tʃertola] *sf* lizard.

luci'dare [lutʃi'dare] *vt* to polish; (*ricalcare*) to trace.

lucida'trice [lutʃida'tritʃe] *sf* floor polisher.

'lucido, a [ˈlutʃido] *ag* shining, bright; (*lucidato*) polished; (*fig*) lucid ♦ *sm* shine, lustre; (*per scarpe etc*) polish; (*disegno*) tracing.

'lucro *sm* profit, gain; **lu'croso, a** *ag* lucrative, profitable.

lu'dibrio *sm* mockery *no pl*; (*oggetto di scherno*) laughing-stock.

'luglio [ˈluʎʎo] *sm* July.

'lugubre *ag* gloomy.

'lui *pronome* (*soggetto*) he; (*oggetto: per dare rilievo, con preposizione*) him; ~ **stesso** he himself.

lu'maca, che *sf* slug; (*chiocciola*) snail.

'lume *sm* light; (*lampada*) lamp; (*fig*): **chiedere** ~**i a qn** to ask sb for advice; **a** ~ **di naso** (*fig*) by rule of thumb.

lumi'naria *sf* (*per feste*) illuminations *pl*.

lumi'noso, a *ag* (*che emette luce*) luminous; (*cielo, colore, stanza*) bright; (*sorgente*) of light, light *cpd*; (*fig: sorriso*) bright, radiant.

'luna *sf* moon; ~ **nuova/piena** new/full moon; ~ **di miele** honeymoon.

'luna park *sm inv* amusement park, funfair.

lu'nare *ag* lunar, moon *cpd*.

lu'nario *sm* almanac; **sbarcare il** ~ to make ends meet.

lu'natico, a, ci, che *ag* whimsical, temperamental.

lunedì *sm inv* Monday; **di** *o* **il** ~ on Mondays.

lun'gaggine [lun'gaddʒine] *sf* slowness; ~**i della burocrazia** red tape.

lun'ghezza [lun'gettsa] *sf* length; ~ **d'onda** (*FISICA*) wavelength.

'lungi [ˈlundʒi]: ~ **da** *prep* far from.

'lungo, a, ghi, ghe *ag* long; (*lento: persona*) slow; (*diluito: caffè, brodo*) weak, watery, thin ♦ *sm* length ♦ *prep* along; ~ **3 metri** 3 metres long; **a** ~ for a long time; **a** ~ **andare** in the long run; **di gran** ~**a** (*molto*) by far; **andare in** ~ *o* **per le lunghe** to drag on; **saperla** ~**a** to know what's what; **in** ~ **e in largo** far and wide, all over; ~ **il corso dei secoli** throughout the centuries.

lungo'mare *sm* promenade.

lu'notto *sm* (*AUT*) rear *o* back window.

lu'ogo, ghi *sm* place; (*posto: di incidente etc*) scene, site; (*punto, passo di libro*) passage; **in** ~ **di** instead of; **in primo** ~ in the first place; **aver** ~ to take place; **dar** ~ **a** to give rise to; ~ **comune** commonplace; ~ **di nascita** birthplace; (*AMM*) place of birth; ~ **di provenienza** place of origin.

luogote'nente *sm* (*MIL*) lieutenant.

lu'para *sf* sawn-off shotgun.

'lupo, a *sm/f* wolf.

'luppolo *sm* (*BOT*) hop.

'lurido, a *ag* filthy.

lu'singa, ghe *sf* (*spesso al pl*) flattery *no pl*.

lusin'gare *vt* to flatter; **lusinghi'ero, a** *ag* flattering, gratifying.

lus'sare *vt* (*MED*) to dislocate.

Lussem'burgo *sm* (*stato*): **il** ~ Luxembourg ♦ *sf* (*città*) Luxembourg.

'lusso *sm* luxury; **di** ~ luxury *cpd*; **lussu'oso, a** *ag* luxurious.

lussureggi'are [lussured'dʒare] *vi* to be luxuriant.

lus'suria *sf* lust.

lus'trare *vt* to polish, shine.

lustras'carpe *sm/f inv* shoeshine.

lus'trino *sm* sequin.

'lustro, a *ag* shiny; (*pelliccia*) glossy ♦ *sm* shine, gloss; (*fig*) prestige, glory; (*quinquennio*) five-year period.

'lutto *sm* mourning; **essere in/portare il** ~ to be in/wear mourning; **luttu'oso, a** *ag* mournful, sad.

M

ma *cong* but; ~ **insomma!** for goodness sake!; ~ **no!** of course not!

'**macabro, a** *ag* gruesome, macabre.

macché [mak'ke] *escl* not at all!, certainly not!

macche'roni [makke'roni] *smpl* macaroni *sg*.

'**macchia** ['makkja] *sf* stain, spot; (*chiazza di diverso colore*) spot; splash, patch; (*tipo di boscaglia*) scrub; **alla ~** (*fig*) in hiding; **macchi'are** *vt* (*sporcare*) to stain, mark; **macchiarsi** *vr* (*persona*) to get o.s. dirty; (*stoffa*) to stain; to get stained *o* marked.

'**macchina** ['makkina] *sf* machine; (*motore, locomotiva*) engine; (*automobile*) car; (*fig: meccanismo*) machinery; **andare in ~** (*AUT*) to go by car; (*STAMPA*) to go to press; ~ **da cucire** sewing machine; ~ **fotografica** camera; ~ **da presa** cine *o* movie camera; ~ **da scrivere** typewriter; ~ **a vapore** steam engine.

macchi'nare [makki'nare] *vt* to plot.

macchi'nario [makki'narjo] *sm* machinery.

macchi'netta [makki'netta] (*fam*) *sf* (*caffettiera*) percolator; (*accendino*) lighter.

macchi'nista, i [makki'nista] *sm* (*di treno*) engine-driver; (*di nave*) engineer; (*TEATRO, TV*) stagehand.

macchi'noso, a [makki'noso] *ag* complex, complicated.

mace'donia [matʃe'dɔnja] *sf* fruit salad.

macel'laio [matʃel'lajo] *sm* butcher.

macel'lare [matʃel'lare] *vt* to slaughter, butcher; **macelle'ria** *sf* butcher's (shop); **ma'cello** *sm* (*mattatoio*) slaughterhouse, abattoir (*BRIT*); (*fig*) slaughter, massacre; (*: disastro*) shambles *sg*.

mace'rare [matʃe'rare] *vt* to macerate; (*CUC*) to marinate; ~**rsi** *vr* (*fig*): ~**rsi in** to be consumed with.

ma'cerie [ma'tʃɛrje] *sfpl* rubble *sg*, debris *sg*.

ma'cigno [ma'tʃiɲɲo] *sm* (*masso*) rock, boulder.

maci'lento, a [matʃi'lɛnto] *ag* emaciated.

'**macina** ['matʃina] *sf* (*pietra*) millstone; (*macchina*) grinder; **macinacaffè** *sm inv* coffee grinder; **macina'pepe** *sm inv* peppermill.

maci'nare [matʃi'nare] *vt* to grind; (*carne*) to mince (*BRIT*), grind (*US*); **maci'nato** *sm* meal, flour; (*carne*) minced (*BRIT*) *o* ground (*US*) meat.

maci'nino [matʃi'nino] *sm* coffee grinder; peppermill.

'**madido, a** *ag*: ~ **(di)** wet *o* moist (with).

Ma'donna *sf* (*REL*) Our Lady.

mador'nale *ag* enormous, huge.

'**madre** *sf* mother; (*matrice di bolletta*) counterfoil ♦ *ag inv* mother *cpd*; **ragazza** ~ unmarried mother; **scena** ~ (*TEATRO*) principal scene; (*fig*) terrible scene.

madre'lingua *sf* mother tongue, native language.

madre'perla *sf* mother-of-pearl.

ma'drina *sf* godmother.

maestà *sf inv* majesty; **maes'toso, a** *ag* majestic.

ma'estra *sf vedi* **maestro**.

maes'trale *sm* north-west wind, mistral.

maes'tranze [maes'trantse] *sfpl* workforce *sg*.

maes'tria *sf* mastery, skill.

ma'estro, a *sm/f* (*INS: anche*: ~ **di scuola o elementare**) primary (*BRIT*) *o* grade school (*US*) teacher; (*esperto*) expert ♦ *sm* (*artigiano, fig: guida*) master; (*MUS*) maestro ♦ *ag* (*principale*) main; (*di grande abilità*) masterly, skilful; ~**a d'asilo** nursery teacher; ~ **di cerimonie** master of ceremonies.

'**mafia** *sf* Mafia; **mafi'oso** *sm* member of the Mafia.

'**maga** *sf* sorceress.

ma'gagna [ma'gaɲɲa] *sf* defect, flaw, blemish; (*noia, guaio*) problem.

ma'gari *escl (esprime desiderio)*: ~ **fosse vero** if only it were true!; **ti piacerebbe andare in Scozia?** — ~! would you like to go to Scotland? — and how! ♦ *av (anche)* even; *(forse)* perhaps.

magaz'zino [magad'dzino] *sm* warehouse; **grande ~** department store.

'maggio ['maddʒo] *sm* May.

maggio'rana [maddʒo'rana] *sf (BOT)* (sweet) marjoram.

maggio'ranza [maddʒo'rantsa] *sf* majority.

maggio'rare [maddʒo'rare] *vt* to increase, raise.

maggior'domo [maddʒor'dɔmo] *sm* butler.

maggi'ore [mad'dʒore] *ag (comparativo: più grande)* bigger, larger; taller; greater; (: *più vecchio: sorella, fratello)* older, elder; (: *di grado superiore)* senior; (: *più importante, MIL, MUS)* major; *(superlativo)* biggest, largest; tallest; greatest; oldest, eldest ♦ *sm/f (di grado)* superior; *(di età)* elder; *(MIL)* major; (: *AER)* squadron leader; **la maggior parte** the majority; **andare per la ~** *(cantante etc)* to be very popular; **maggio'renne** *ag* of age ♦ *sm/f* person who has come of age; **maggior'mente** *av* much more; (*con senso superlativo)* most.

ma'gia [ma'dʒia] *sf* magic; **'magico, a, ci, che** *ag* magic; *(fig)* fascinating, charming, magical.

'magio ['madʒo] *sm (REL)*: **i re Magi** the Magi, the Three Wise Men.

magis'tero [madʒis'tero] *sm* teaching; *(fig: maestria)* skill; *(INS)*: **facoltà di M~** ≈ teachers' training college; **magis'trale** *ag* primary *(BRIT)* o grade school *(US)* teachers', primary *(BRIT)* o grade school *(US)* teaching *cpd*; skilful.

magis'trato [madʒis'trato] *sm* magistrate; **magistra'tura** *sf (magistrati)*: **la magistratura** the Bench.

'maglia ['maʎʎa] *sf* stitch; *(lavoro ai ferri)* knitting *no pl*; *(tessuto, SPORT)* jersey; *(maglione)* jersey, sweater; (*di*

catena) link; *(di rete)* mesh; **~ diritta/ rovescia** plain/purl; **maglie'ria** *sf* knitwear; *(negozio)* knitwear shop; **ma- gli'etta** *sf (canottiera)* vest; *(tipo camicia)* T-shirt; **magli'ficio** *sm* knitwear factory.

'maglio ['maʎʎo] *sm* mallet; *(macchina)* power hammer.

ma'gnete [maɲ'nete] *sm* magnet; **ma'gnetico, a, ci, che** *ag* magnetic.

magne'tofono [maɲne'tɔfono] *sm* tape recorder.

ma'gnifico, a, ci, che [maɲ'ɲifiko] *ag* magnificent, splendid; *(ospite)* generous.

'magno, a ['maɲɲo] *ag*: **aula ~a** main hall.

ma'gnolia [maɲ'ɲɔlja] *sf* magnolia.

'mago, ghi *sm (stregone)* magician, wizard; *(illusionista)* magician.

ma'grezza [ma'grettsa] *sf* thinness.

'magro, a *ag (very)* thin, skinny; *(carne)* lean; *(formaggio)* low-fat; *(fig: scarso, misero)* meagre, poor; (: *meschino: scusa)* poor, lame; **mangiare di ~** not to eat meat.

'mai *av (nessuna volta)* never; *(talvolta)* ever; **non ... ~** never; **~ più** never again; **come ~?** why (o how) on earth?; **chi/dove/quando ~?** whoever/ wherever/whenever?

mai'ale *sm (ZOOL)* pig; *(carne)* pork.

maio'nese *sf* mayonnaise.

'mais *sm inv* maize.

mai'uscola *sf* capital letter.

mai'uscolo, a *ag (lettera)* capital; *(fig)* enormous, huge.

mal *av*, *sm vedi* **male**.

malac'corto, a *ag* rash, careless.

mala'fede *sf* bad faith.

mala'mente *av* badly; dangerously.

malan'dato, a *ag (persona: di salute)* in poor health; (: *di condizioni finanziarie)* badly off; *(trascurato)* shabby.

ma'lanno *sm (disgrazia)* misfortune; *(malattia)* ailment.

mala'pena *sf*: **a ~** hardly, scarcely.

ma'laria *sf (MED)* malaria.

mala'sorte *sf* bad luck.

mala'ticcio, a [mala'tittʃo] *ag* sickly.

ma'lato, a *ag* ill, sick; (*gamba*) bad; (*pianta*) diseased ♦ *sm/f* sick person; (*in ospedale*) patient; **malat'tia** *sf* (*infettiva etc*) illness, disease; (*cattiva salute*) illness, sickness; (*di pianta*) disease.

malau'gurio *sm* bad *o* ill omen.

mala'vita *sf* underworld.

mala'voglia [mala'vɔʎʎa] *sf*: **di ~** unwillingly, reluctantly.

mal'concio, a, ci, ce [mal'kontʃo] *ag* in a sorry state.

malcon'tento *sm* discontent.

malcos'tume *sm* immorality.

mal'destro, a *ag* (*inabile*) inexpert, inexperienced; (*goffo*) awkward.

maldi'cenza [maldi'tʃɛntsa] *sf* malicious gossip.

maldis'posto, a *ag*: **~ (verso)** illdisposed (towards).

'male *av* badly ♦ *sm* (*ciò che è ingiusto, disonesto*) evil; (*danno, svantaggio*) harm; (*sventura*) misfortune; (*dolore fisico, morale*) pain, ache; **di ~ in peggio** from bad to worse; **sentirsi ~** to feel ill; **far ~** (*dolere*) to hurt; **far ~ alla salute** to be bad for one's health; **far del ~ a qn** to hurt *o* harm sb; **restare** *o* **rimanere ~** to be sorry; to be disappointed; to be hurt; **andare a ~** to go bad; **come va? — non c'è** how are you? — not bad; **mal di mare** seasickness; **avere mal di gola/testa** to have a sore throat/a head ache; **aver ~ ai piedi** to have sore feet.

male'detto, a *pp di* **maledire** ♦ *ag* cursed, damned; (*fig: fam*) damned, blasted.

male'dire *vt* to curse; **maledizi'one** *sf* curse; **maledizione!** damn it!

maledu'cato, a *ag* rude, ill-mannered.

male'fatta *sf* misdeed.

male'ficio [male'fitʃo] *sm* witchcraft.

ma'lefico, a, ci, che *ag* (*aria, cibo*) harmful, bad; (*influsso, azione*) evil.

ma'lessere *sm* indisposition, slight illness; (*fig*) uneasiness.

ma'levolo, a *ag* malevolent.

malfa'mato, a *ag* notorious.

mal'fatto, a *ag* (*persona*) deformed; (*oggetto*) badly made; (*lavoro*) badly done.

malfat'tore, 'trice *sm/f* wrongdoer.

mal'fermo, a *ag* unsteady, shaky; (*salute*) poor, delicate.

malformazi'one [malformat'tsjone] *sf* malformation.

malgo'verno *sm* maladministration.

mal'grado *prep* in spite of, despite ♦ *cong* although; **mio** (*o* **tuo** *etc*) **~** against my (*o* your *etc*) will.

ma'lia *sf* spell; (*fig: fascino*) charm.

mali'gnare [maliɲ'ɲare] *vi*: **~ su** to malign, speak ill of.

ma'ligno, a [ma'liɲɲo] *ag* (*malvagio*) malicious, malignant; (*MED*) malignant.

malinco'nia *sf* melancholy, gloom; **malin'conico, a, ci, che** *ag* melancholy.

malincu'ore: a ~ *av* reluctantly, unwillingly.

malintenzio'nato, a [malintentsjo'nato] *ag* ill-intentioned.

malin'teso, a *ag* misunderstood; (*riguardo, senso del dovere*) mistaken, wrong ♦ *sm* misunderstanding.

ma'lizia [ma'littsja] *sf* (*malignità*) malice; (*furbizia*) cunning; (*espediente*) trick; **malizi'oso, a** *ag* malicious, cunning; (*vivace, birichino*) mischievous.

malme'nare *vt* to beat up; (*fig*) to illtreat.

mal'messo, a *ag* shabby.

malnu'trito, a *ag* undernourished; **malnutrizi'one** *sf* malnutrition.

ma'locchio [ma'lɔkkjo] *sm* evil eye.

ma'lora *sf*: **andare in ~** to go to the dogs.

ma'lore *sm* (sudden) illness.

mal'sano, a *ag* unhealthy.

malsi'curo, a *ag* unsafe.

'Malta *sf*: **la ~** Malta.

'malta *sf* (*EDIL*) mortar.

mal'tempo *sm* bad weather.

'malto *sm* malt.

maltrat'tare *vt* to ill-treat.

malu'more *sm* bad mood; (*irritabilità*) bad temper; (*discordia*) ill feeling; **di ~** in a bad mood.

mal'vagio, a, gi, gie [mal'vadʒo] *ag* wicked, evil.

malversazi'one [malversat'tsjone] *sf* (*DIR*) embezzlement.

mal'visto, a *ag*: ~ **(da)** disliked (by), unpopular (with).

malvi'vente *sm* criminal.

malvolenti'eri *av* unwillingly, reluctantly.

'mamma *sf* mummy, mum; ~ **mia!** my goodness!

mam'mella *sf* (*ANAT*) breast; (*di vacca, capra etc*) udder.

mam'mifero *sm* mammal.

'mammola *sf* (*BOT*) violet.

ma'nata *sf* (*colpo*) slap; (*quantità*) handful.

'manca *sf* left (hand); **a destra e a** ~ left, right and centre, on all sides.

man'canza [man'kantsa] *sf* lack; (*carenza*) shortage, scarcity; (*fallo*) fault; (*imperfezione*) failing, shortcoming; **per** ~ **di tempo** through lack of time; **in** ~ **di meglio** for lack of anything better.

man'care *vi* (*essere insufficiente*) to be lacking; (*venir meno*) to fail; (*sbagliare*) to be wrong, make a mistake; (*non esserci*) to be missing, not to be there; (*essere lontano*): ~ **(da)** to be away (from) ♦ *vt* to miss; ~ **di** to lack; ~ **a** (*promessa*) to fail to keep; **tu mi manchi** I miss you; **mancò poco che morisse** he very nearly died; **mancano ancora 10 sterline** we're still £10 short; **manca un quarto alle 6** it's a quarter to 6; **man'cato, a** *ag* (*tentativo*) unsuccessful; (*artista*) failed.

'mancia, ce ['mantʃa] *sf* tip; ~ **competente** reward.

manci'ata [man'tʃata] *sf* handful.

man'cino, a [man'tʃino] *ag* (*braccio*) left; (*persona*) left-handed; (*fig*) underhand.

'manco *av* (*nemmeno*): ~ **per sogno** o **per idea!** not on your life!

man'dare *vt* to send; (*far funzionare: macchina*) to drive; (*emettere*) to send out; (*: grido*) to give, utter, let out; ~ **a chiamare qn** to send for sb; ~ **avanti** (*fig: famiglia*) to provide for; (*: fab-*

brica) to run, look after; ~ **giù** to send down; (*anche fig*) to swallow; ~ **via** to send away; (*licenziare*) to fire.

manda'rino *sm* mandarin (orange); (*cinese*) mandarin.

man'data *sf* (*quantità*) lot, batch; (*di chiave*) turn; **chiudere a doppia** ~ to double-lock.

manda'tario *sm* (*DIR*) representative, agent.

man'dato *sm* (*incarico*) commission; (*DIR: provvedimento*) warrant; (*di deputato etc*) mandate; (*ordine di pagamento*) postal o money order; ~ **d'arresto** warrant for arrest.

man'dibola *sf* mandible, jaw.

'mandorla *sf* almond; **'mandorlo** *sm* almond tree.

'mandria *sf* herd.

maneggi'are [maned'dʒare] *vt* (*creta, cera*) to mould, work, fashion; (*arnesi, utensili*) to handle; (*: adoperare*) to use; (*fig: persone, denaro*) to handle, deal with; **ma'neggio** *sm* moulding; handling; use; (*intrigo*) plot, scheme; (*per cavalli*) riding school.

ma'nesco, a, schi, sche *ag* free with one's fists.

ma'nette *sfpl* handcuffs.

manga'nello *sm* club.

manga'nese *sm* manganese.

mange'reccio, a, ci, ce [mandʒe'rettʃo] *ag* edible.

mangia'dischi [mandʒa'diski] *sm inv* record player.

mangi'are [man'dʒare] *vt* to eat; (*intaccare*) to eat into o away; (*CARTE, SCACCHI etc*) to take ♦ *vi* to eat ♦ *sm* eating; (*cibo*) food; (*cucina*) cooking; ~**rsi le parole** to mumble; ~**rsi le unghie** to bite one's nails; **mangia'toia** *sf* feeding-trough.

man'gime [man'dʒime] *sm* fodder.

'mango, ghi *sm* mango.

ma'nia *sf* (*PSIC*) mania; (*fig*) obsession, craze; **ma'niaco, a, ci, che** *ag* suffering from a mania; **maniaco (di)** obsessed (by), crazy (about).

'manica *sf* sleeve; (*fig: gruppo*) gang, bunch; (*GEO*): **la M~, il Canale della**

M~ the (English) Channel; **essere di ~ larga/stretta** to be easy-going/strict; **~ a vento** (*AER*) wind sock.

mani'chino [mani'kino] *sm* (*di sarto, vetrina*) dummy.

'manico, ci *sm* handle; (*MUS*) neck.

mani'comio *sm* mental hospital; (*fig*) madhouse.

mani'cotto *sm* muff; (*TECN*) coupling; sleeve.

mani'cure *sm o f inv* manicure ♦ *sf inv* manicurist.

mani'era *sf* way, manner; (*stile*) style, manner; **~e** (*comportamento*) manners; **in ~ che** so that; **in ~ da** so as to; **in tutte le ~e** at all costs.

manie'rato, a *ag* affected.

manifat'tura *sf* (*lavorazione*) manufacture; (*stabilimento*) factory.

manifes'tare *vt* to show, display; (*esprimere*) to express; (*rivelare*) to reveal, disclose ♦ *vi* to demonstrate; **~rsi** *vr* to show o.s.; **~rsi amico** to prove o.s. (to be) a friend; **manifestazi'one** *sf* show, display; expression; (*sintomo*) sign, symptom; (*dimostrazione pubblica*) demonstration; (*cerimonia*) event.

mani'festo, a *ag* obvious, evident ♦ *sm* poster, bill; (*scritto ideologico*) manifesto.

ma'niglia [ma'niʎʎa] *sf* handle; (*sostegno: negli autobus etc*) strap.

manipo'lare *vt* to manipulate; (*alterare: vino*) to adulterate; **manipolazi'one** *sf* manipulation; adulteration.

manis'calco, chi *sm* blacksmith.

'manna *sf* (*REL*) manna.

man'naia *sf* (*del boia*) (executioner's) axe; (*per carni*) cleaver.

man'naro: lupo ~ *sm* werewolf.

'mano, i *sf* hand; (*strato: di vernice etc*) coat; **di prima ~** (*notizia*) first-hand; **di seconda ~** second-hand; **man ~** little by little, gradually; **man ~ che** as; **darsi o stringersi la ~** to shake hands; **mettere le ~i avanti** (*fig*) to safeguard o.s.; **restare a ~i vuote** to be left empty-handed; **venire alle ~i** to

come to blows; **a ~ by hand**; **~i in alto!** hands up!

mano'dopera *sf* labour.

mano'messo, a *pp* di **manomettere**.

ma'nometro *sm* gauge, manometer.

mano'mettere *vt* (*alterare*) to tamper with; (*aprire indebitamente*) to break open illegally.

ma'nopola *sf* (*dell'armatura*) gauntlet; (*guanto*) mitt; (*di impugnatura*) hand-grip; (*pomello*) knob.

manos'critto, a *ag* handwritten ♦ *sm* manuscript.

mano'vale *sm* labourer.

mano'vella *sf* handle; (*TECN*) crank.

ma'novra *sf* manoeuvre (*BRIT*), maneuver (*US*); (*FERR*) shunting; **mano'vrare** *vt* (*veicolo*) to manoeuvre (*BRIT*), maneuver (*US*); (*macchina, congegno*) to operate; (*fig: persona*) to manipulate ♦ *vi* to manoeuvre.

manro'vescio [manro'veʃʃo] *sm* slap (*with back of hand*).

man'sarda *sf* attic.

mansi'one *sf* task, duty, job.

mansu'eto, a *ag* gentle, docile.

man'tello *sm* cloak; (*fig: di neve etc*) blanket, mantle; (*TECN: involucro*) casing, shell; (*ZOOL*) coat.

mante'nere *vt* to maintain; (*adempiere: promesse*) to keep, abide by; (*provvedere a*) to support, maintain; **~rsi** *vr*: **~rsi calmo/giovane** to stay calm/young; **manteni'mento** *sm* maintenance.

'mantice ['mantitʃe] *sm* bellows *pl*; (*di carrozza, automobile*) hood.

'manto *sm* cloak; **~ stradale** road surface.

manu'ale *ag* manual ♦ *sm* (*testo*) manual, handbook.

ma'nubrio *sm* handle; (*di bicicletta etc*) handlebars *pl*; (*SPORT*) dumbbell.

manu'fatto *sm* manufactured article.

manutenzi'one [manuten'tsjone] *sf* maintenance, upkeep; (*d'impianti*) maintenance, servicing.

'manzo ['mandzo] *sm* (*ZOOL*) steer; (*carne*) beef.

'mappa *sf* (*GEO*) map; **mappa'mondo**

sm map of the world; (*globo girevole*) globe.

ma'rasma, i *sm* (*fig*) decay, decline.

mara'tona *sf* marathon.

'marca, che *sf* mark; (*bollo*) stamp; (*COMM*: *di prodotti*) brand; (*contrassegno, scontrino*) ticket, check; **prodotto di** ~ (*di buona qualità*) high-class product; ~ **da bollo** official stamp.

mar'care *vt* (*munire di contrassegno*) to mark; (*a fuoco*) to brand; (*SPORT*: *gol*) to score; (*: avversario*) to mark; (*accentuare*) to stress; ~ **visita** (*MIL*) to report sick.

'Marche ['marke] *sfpl*: **le** ~ the Marches (*region of central Italy*).

mar'chese, a [mar'keze] *sm/f* marquis *o* marquess/marchioness.

marchi'are [mar'kjare] *vt* to brand; **'marchio** *sm* (*di bestiame, COMM, fig*) brand; **marchio depositato** registered trademark; **marchio di fabbrica** trademark.

'marcia, ce ['martʃa] *sf* (*anche MUS, MIL*) march; (*funzionamento*) running; (*il camminare*) walking; (*AUT*) gear; **mettere in** ~ to start; **mettersi in** ~ to get moving; **far** ~ **indietro** (*AUT*) to reverse; (*fig*) to back-pedal.

marciapi'ede [martʃa'pjɛde] *sm* (*di strada*) pavement (*BRIT*), sidewalk (*US*); (*FERR*) platform.

marci'are [mar'tʃare] *vi* to march; (*andare: treno, macchina*) to go; (*funzionare*) to run, work.

'marcio, a, ci, ce ['martʃo] *ag* (*frutta, legno*) rotten, bad; (*MED*) festering; (*fig*) corrupt, rotten.

mar'cire [mar'tʃire] *vi* (*andare a male*) to go bad, rot; (*suppurare*) to fester; (*fig*) to rot, waste away.

'marco, chi *sm* (*unità monetaria*) mark.

'mare *sm* sea; **in** ~ at sea; **andare al** ~ (*in vacanza etc*) to go to the seaside; **il M~ del Nord** the North Sea.

ma'rea *sf* tide; **alta/bassa** ~ high/low tide.

mareggi'ata [mared'dʒata] *sf* heavy sea.

ma'remma *sf* (*GEO*) maremma,

swampy coastal area.

mare'moto *sm* seaquake.

maresci'allo [mareʃ'ʃallo] *sm* (*MIL*) marshal; (*: sottufficiale*) warrant officer.

marga'rina *sf* margarine.

marghe'rita [marge'rita] *sf* (ox-eye) daisy, marguerite; (*di stampante*) daisy wheel; **margheri'tina** *sf* daisy.

'margine ['mardʒine] *sm* margin; (*di bosco, via*) edge, border.

ma'rina *sf* navy; (*costa*) coast; (*quadro*) seascape; ~ **militare/mercantile** navy/merchant navy (*BRIT*) *o* marine (*US*).

mari'naio *sm* sailor.

mari'nare *vt* (*CUC*) to marinate; ~ **la scuola** to play truant; **mari'nata** *sf* marinade.

ma'rino, a *ag* sea *cpd*, marine.

mario'netta *sf* puppet.

mari'tare *vt* to marry; **~rsi** *vr*: **~rsi a** *o* **con qn** to marry sb, get married to sb.

ma'rito *sm* husband.

ma'rittimo, a *ag* maritime, sea *cpd*.

mar'maglia [mar'maʎʎa] *sf* mob, riff-raff.

marmel'lata *sf* jam; (*di agrumi*) marmalade.

mar'mitta *sf* (*recipiente*) pot; (*AUT*) silencer.

'marmo *sm* marble.

mar'mocchio [mar'mɔkkjo] (*fam*) *sm* tot, kid.

mar'motta *sf* (*ZOOL*) marmot.

Ma'rocco *sm*: **il** ~ Morocco.

ma'roso *sm* breaker.

mar'rone *ag inv* brown ♦ *sm* (*BOT*) chestnut.

mar'sala *sm inv* (*vino*) Marsala.

mar'sina *sf* tails *pl*, tail coat.

marte'dì *sm inv* Tuesday; **di** *o* **il** ~ **on** Tuesdays; ~ **grasso** Shrove Tuesday.

martel'lare *vt* to hammer ♦ *vi* (*pulsare*) to throb; (*: cuore*) to thump.

mar'tello *sm* hammer; (*di uscio*) knocker.

marti'netto *sm* (*TECN*) jack.

'martire *sm/f* martyr; **mar'tirio** *sm*

martyrdom; (*fig*) agony, torture.

'**martora** *sf* marten.

martori'are *vt* to torment, torture.

mar'xista, i, e *ag, sm/f* Marxist.

marza'pane [martsa'pane] *sm* marzipan.

'**marzo** ['martso] *sm* March.

mascal'zone [maskal'tsone] *sm* rascal, scoundrel.

ma'scella [maʃ'ʃɛlla] *sf* (*ANAT*) jaw.

'**maschera** ['maskera] *sf* mask; (*travestimento*) disguise; (: *per un ballo etc*) fancy dress; (*TEATRO, CINEMA*) usher/usherette; (*personaggio del teatro*) stock character; **masche'rare** *vt* to mask; (*travestire*) to disguise; to dress up; (*fig: celare*) to hide, conceal; (*MIL*) to camouflage; ~**rsi da** to disguise o.s. as; to dress up as; (*fig*) to masquerade as.

mas'chile [mas'kile] *ag* masculine; (*sesso, popolazione*) male; (*abiti*) men's; (*per ragazzi: scuola*) boys'.

'**maschio, a** ['maskjo] *ag* (*BIOL*) male; (*virile*) manly ♦ *sm* (*anche ZOOL, TECN*) male; (*uomo*) man; (*ragazzo*) boy; (*figlio*) son.

masco'lino, a *ag* masculine.

'**massa** *sf* mass; (*di errori etc*): **una ~ di** heaps of, masses of; (*di gente*) mass, multitude; (*ELETTR*) earth; **in ~** (*COMM*) in bulk; (*tutti insieme*) en masse; **adunata in ~** mass meeting; **di ~** (*cultura, manifestazione*) mass *cpd*; **la ~ del popolo** the masses *pl*.

mas'sacro *sm* massacre, slaughter; (*fig*) mess, disaster.

mas'saggio [mas'saddʒo] *sm* massage.

mas'saia *sf* housewife.

masse'rizie [masse'rittsje] *sfpl* (household) furnishings.

mas'siccio, a, ci, ce [mas'sittʃo] *ag* (*oro, legno*) solid; (*palazzo*) massive; (*corporatura*) stout ♦ *sm* (*GEO*) massif.

'**massima** *sf* (*sentenza, regola*) maxim; (*METEOR*) maximum temperature; **in linea di ~** generally speaking; *vedi anche* **massimo**.

massi'male *sm* maximum.

'**massimo, a** *ag, sm* maximum; **al ~** at (the) most.

'**masso** *sm* rock, boulder.

mas'sone *sm* freemason; **massone'ria** *sf* freemasonry.

masti'care *vt* to chew.

'**mastice** ['mastitʃe] *sm* mastic; (*per vetri*) putty.

mas'tino *sm* mastiff.

ma'tassa *sf* skein.

mate'matica *sf* mathematics *sg*.

mate'matico, a, ci, che *ag* mathematical ♦ *sm/f* mathematician.

mate'rasso *sm* mattress; **~ a molle** spring *o* interior-sprung mattress.

ma'teria *sf* (*FISICA*) matter; (*TECN, COMM*) material, matter *no pl*; (*disciplina*) subject; (*argomento*) subject matter, material; **~e prime** raw materials; **in ~ di** (*per quanto concerne*) on the subject of; **materi'ale** *ag* material; (*fig: grossolano*) rough, rude ♦ *sm* material, (*insieme di strumenti etc*) equipment *no pl*, materials *pl*.

maternità *sf* motherhood, maternity; (*clinica*) maternity hospital.

ma'terno, a *ag* (*amore, cura etc*) maternal, motherly; (*nonno*) maternal; (*lingua, terra*) mother *cpd*.

ma'tita *sf* pencil.

ma'trice [ma'tritʃe] *sf* matrix; (*COMM*) counterfoil; (*fig: origine*) background.

ma'tricola *sf* (*registro*) register; (*numero*) registration number; (*nell'università*) freshman, fresher.

ma'trigna [ma'triɲɲa] *sf* stepmother.

matrimoni'ale *ag* matrimonial, marriage *cpd*.

matri'monio *sm* marriage, matrimony; (*durata*) marriage, married life; (*cerimonia*) wedding.

ma'trona *sf* (*fig*) matronly woman.

mat'tina *sf* morning; **matti'nata** *sf* morning; (*spettacolo*) matinée, afternoon performance; **mattini'ero, a** *ag*: **essere mattiniero** to be an early riser; **mat'tino** *sm* morning.

'**matto, a** *ag* mad, crazy; (*fig: falso*) false, imitation; (: *opaco*) matt, dull ♦ *sm/f* madman/woman; **avere una voglia ~a di qc** to be dying for sth.

mat'tone *sm* brick; (*fig*): **questo libro/**

film è un ~ this book/film is heavy going.
matto'nella *sf* tile.
matu'rare *vi* (*anche*: *~rsi*) (*frutta, grano*) to ripen; (*ascesso*) to come to a head; (*fig*: *persona, idea,* ECON) to mature ♦ *vt* to ripen; to (make) mature.
maturità *sf* maturity; (*di frutta*) ripeness, maturity; (INS) school-leaving examination, ≈ GCE A-levels (BRIT).
ma'turo, a *ag* mature; (*frutto*) ripe, mature.
'**mazza** ['mattsa] *sf* (*bastone*) club; (*martello*) sledge-hammer; (SPORT: *da golf*) club; (: *da baseball, cricket*) bat.
maz'zata [mat'tsata] *sf* (*anche fig*) heavy blow.
'**mazzo** ['mattso] *sm* (*di fiori, chiavi etc*) bunch; (*di carte da gioco*) pack.
me *pron* me; **~ stesso(a)** myself; **sei bravo quanto ~** you are as clever as I (am) *o* as me.
me'andro *sm* meander.
M.E.C. [mɛk] *sigla m* (= *Mercato Comune Europeo*) EEC.
mec'canica, che *sf* mechanics *sg*; (*attività tecnologica*) mechanical engineering; (*meccanismo*) mechanism.
mec'canico, a, ci, che *ag* mechanical ♦ *sm* mechanic.
mecca'nismo *sm* mechanism.
me'daglia [me'daʎʎa] *sf* medal; **meda-gli'one** *sm* (ARCHIT) medallion; (*gioiello*) locket.
me'desimo, a *ag* same; (*in persona*): **io ~** I myself.
'**media** *sf* average; (MAT) mean; (INS: *voto*) end-of-term average; **in ~** on average; *vedi anche* **medio**.
medi'ano, a *ag* median; (*valore*) mean ♦ *sm* (CALCIO) half-back.
medi'ante *prep* by means of.
medi'are *vt* (*fare da mediatore*) to act as mediator in; (MAT) to average.
media'tore, 'trice *sm/f* mediator; (COMM) middle man, agent.
medica'mento *sm* medicine, drug.
medi'care *vt* to treat; (*ferita*) to

dress; **medicazi'one** *sf* treatment, medication; dressing.
medi'cina [medi'tʃina] *sf* medicine; **~ legale** forensic medicine; **medici'nale** *ag* medicinal ♦ *sm* drug, medicine.
'**medico, a, ci, che** *ag* medical ♦ *sm* doctor; **~ generico** general practitioner, GP.
medie'vale *ag* medieval.
'**medio, a** *ag* average; (*punto, ceto*) middle; (*altezza, statura*) medium ♦ *sm* (*dito*) middle finger; **licenza ~a** *leaving certificate awarded at the end of 3 years of secondary education*; **scuola ~a** *first 3 years of secondary school.*
medi'ocre *ag* mediocre, poor.
medioe'vale *ag* = **medievale.**
medio'evo *sm* Middle Ages *pl.*
medi'tare *vt* to ponder over, meditate on; (*progettare*) to plan, think out ♦ *vi* to meditate.
mediter'raneo, a *ag* Mediterranean; **il (mare) M~** the Mediterranean (Sea).
me'dusa *sf* (ZOOL) jellyfish.
me'gafono *sm* megaphone.
'**meglio** ['meʎʎo] *av, ag inv* better; (*con senso superlativo*) best ♦ *sm* (*la cosa migliore*): **il ~** the best (thing); **faresti ~ ad andartene** you had better leave; **alla ~** as best one can; **andar di bene in ~** to get better and better; **fare del proprio ~** to do one's best; **per il ~** for the best; **aver la ~ su qn** to get the better of sb.
'**mela** *sf* apple; **~ cotogna** quince.
mela'grana *sf* pomegranate.
melan'zana [melan'dzana] *sf* aubergine (BRIT), eggplant (US).
me'lassa *sf* molasses *sg*, treacle.
me'lenso, a *ag* dull, stupid.
mel'lifluo, a (*peg*) *ag* sugary, honeyed.
'**melma** *sf* mud, mire.
'**melo** *sm* apple tree.
melo'dia *sf* melody.
me'lone *sm* (musk)melon.
'**membra** *sfpl vedi* **membro.**
'**membro** *sm* member; (*pl(f)* *~a:* *arto*) limb.
memo'randum *sm inv* memorandum.

me'**moria** *sf* memory; ~**e** *sfpl* (*opera autobiografica*) memoirs; **a ~** (*imparare, sapere*) by heart; **a ~ d'uomo** within living memory; **memori'ale** *sm* (*raccolta di memorie*) memoirs *pl*; (*DIR*) memorial.

mena'**dito**: **a ~** *av* perfectly, thoroughly; **sapere qc a ~** to have sth at one's fingertips.

me'**nare** *vt* to lead; (*picchiare*) to hit, beat; (*dare: colpi*) to deal; **~ la coda** (*cane*) to wag its tail.

mendi'**cante** *sm/f* beggar.

mendi'**care** *vt* to beg for ♦ *vi* to beg.

PAROLA CHIAVE

'**meno** *av* **1** (*in minore misura*) less; **dovresti mangiare ~** you should eat less, you shouldn't eat so much

2 (*comparativo*): **~ ... di** not as ... as, less ... than; **sono ~ alto di te** I'm not as tall as you (are), I'm less tall than you (are); **~ ... che** not as ... as, less than; **~ che mai** less than ever; **è ~ intelligente che ricco** he's more rich than intelligent; **~ fumo più mangio** the less I smoke the more I eat

3 (*superlativo*) least; **il ~ dotato degli studenti** the least gifted of the students; **è quello che compro ~ spesso** it's the one I buy least often

4 (*MAT*) minus; **8 ~ 5** 8 minus 5, 8 take away 5; **sono le 8 ~ un quarto** it's a quarter to 8; **~ 5 gradi** 5 degrees below zero, minus 5 degrees; **mille lire in ~** a thousand lire less

5 (*fraseologia*): **quanto ~ poteva telefonare** he could at least have phoned; **non so se accettare o ~** I don't know whether to accept or not; **fare a ~ di qc/qn** to do without sth/sb; **non potevo fare a ~ di ridere** I couldn't help laughing; **~ male!** thank goodness!; **~ male che sei arrivato** it's a good job that you've come

♦ *ag inv* (*tempo, denaro*) less; (*errori, persone*) fewer; **ha fatto ~ errori di tutti** he made fewer mistakes than anyone, he made the fewest mistakes of all

♦ *sm inv* **1**: **il ~** (*il minimo*) the least;

parlare del più e del ~ to talk about this and that

2 (*MAT*) minus

♦ *prep* (*eccetto*) except (for), apart from; **a ~ che, a ~ di** unless; **a ~ che non piova** unless it rains; **non posso, a ~ di prendere ferie** I can't, unless I take some leave.

---

meno'**mare** *vt* (*danneggiare*) to maim, disable.

meno'**pausa** *sf* menopause.

'**mensa** *sf* (*locale*) canteen; (: *MIL*) mess; (: *nelle università*) refectory.

men'**sile** *ag* monthly ♦ *sm* (*periodico*) monthly (magazine); (*stipendio*) monthly salary.

'**mensola** *sf* bracket; (*ripiano*) shelf; (*ARCHIT*) corbel.

'**menta** *sf* mint; (*anche*: ~ *piperita*) peppermint; (*bibita*) peppermint cordial; (*caramella*) mint, peppermint.

men'**tale** *ag* mental; **mentalità** *sf inv* mentality.

'**mente** *sf* mind; **imparare/sapere qc a ~** to learn/know sth by heart; **avere in ~ qc** to have sth in mind; **passare di ~ a qn** to slip sb's mind.

men'**tire** *vi* to lie.

'**mento** *sm* chin.

men'**tolo** *sm* menthol.

'**mentre** *cong* (*temporale*) while; (*avversativo*) whereas.

menzio'**nare** [mentsjo'nare] *vt* to mention.

menzi'**one** [men'tsjone] *sf* mention; **fare ~ di** to mention.

men'**zogna** [men'tsɔɲɲa] *sf* lie.

mera'**viglia** [mera'viʎʎa] *sf* amazement, wonder; (*persona, cosa*) marvel, wonder; **a ~** perfectly, wonderfully; **meravigli'are** *vt* to amaze, astonish; **meravigliarsi (di)** to marvel (at); (*stupirsi*) to be amazed (at), be astonished (at); **meravigli'oso, a** *ag* wonderful, marvellous.

mer'**cante** *sm* merchant; **~ d'arte** art dealer; **~ di cavalli** horse dealer; **mercanteggi'are** *vt* (*onore, voto*) to sell ♦ *vi* to bargain, haggle; **mercan'tile** *ag* commercial, mercantile; *(nave, marina)* merchant *cpd* ♦ *sm (nave)* merchantman; **mercan'zia** *sf* merchandise, goods *pl*.

mer'cato *sm* market; ~ **dei cambi** exchange market; **M~ Comune (Europeo)** (European) Common Market; ~ **nero** black market.

'merce ['mɛrtʃe] *sf* goods *pl*, merchandise; ~ **deperibile** perishable goods *pl*.

mercé [mer'tʃe] *sf* mercy.

merce'nario, a [mertʃe'narjo] *ag, sm* mercenary.

merce'ria [mertʃe'ria] *sf (articoli)* haberdashery *(BRIT)*, notions *pl (US)*; *(bottega)* haberdasher's shop *(BRIT)*, notions store *(US)*.

mercoledì *sm inv* Wednesday; **di** *o* **il** ~ on Wednesdays; ~ **delle Ceneri** Ash Wednesday.

mer'curio *sm* mercury.

'merda *(fam!) sf* shit *(!)*.

me'renda *sf* afternoon snack.

meri'diana *sf (orologio)* sundial.

meridi'ano, a *ag* meridian; midday *cpd*, noonday ♦ *sm* meridian.

meridio'nale *ag* southern ♦ *sm/f* southerner.

meridi'one *sm* south.

me'ringa, ghe *sf (CUC)* meringue.

meri'tare *vt* to deserve, merit ♦ *vb impers*: **merita andare** it's worth going.

meri'tevole *ag* worthy.

'merito *sm* merit; *(valore)* worth; **in** ~ **a** as regards, with regard to; **dare** ~ **a qn di** to give sb credit for; **finire a pari** ~ to finish joint first *(o second etc)*; to tie; **meri'torio, a** *ag* praiseworthy.

mer'letto *sm* lace.

'merlo *sm (ZOOL)* blackbird; *(ARCHIT)* battlement.

mer'luzzo [mer'luttso] *sm (ZOOL)* cod.

mes'chino, a [mes'kino] *ag* wretched; *(scarso)* scanty, poor; *(persona: gretta)* mean; *(: limitata)* narrow-minded, petty.

mesco'lanza [mesko'lantsa] *sf* mixture.

mesco'lare *vt* to mix; *(vini, colori)* to blend; *(mettere in disordine)* to mix up,

muddle up; *(carte)* to shuffle; ~**rsi** *vr* to mix; to blend; to get mixed up; *(fig)*: ~**rsi in** to get mixed up in, meddle in.

'mese *sm* month.

'messa *sf (REL)* mass; *(il mettere)*: ~ **in moto** starting; ~ **in piega** set; ~ **a punto** *(TECN)* adjustment; *(AUT)* tuning; *(fig)* clarification; ~ **in scena** = **messinscena**.

messag'gero [messad'dʒero] *sm* messenger.

mes'saggio [mes'saddʒo] *sm* message.

mes'sale *sm (REL)* missal.

'messe *sf* harvest.

Mes'sia *sm inv (REL)*: **il** ~ the Messiah.

'Messico *sm*: **il** ~ Mexico.

messin'scena [messin'ʃɛna] *sf (TEATRO)* production.

'messo, a *pp di* **mettere** ♦ *sm* messenger.

mesti'ere *sm (professione)* job; *(: manuale)* trade; *(: artigianale)* craft; *(fig: abilità nel lavoro)* skill, technique; **essere del** ~ to know the tricks of the trade.

'mesto, a *ag* sad, melancholy.

'mestola *sf (CUC)* ladle; *(EDIL)* trowel.

'mestolo *sm (CUC)* ladle.

mestruazi'one [mestruat'tsjone] *sf* menstruation.

'meta *sf* destination; *(fig)* aim, goal.

metà *sf inv* half; *(punto di mezzo)* middle; **dividere qc a** *o* **per** ~ to divide sth in half, halve sth; **fare a** ~ **(di qc con qn)** to go halves (with sb in sth); **a** ~ **prezzo** at half price; **a** ~ **strada** halfway.

me'tafora *sf* metaphor.

me'tallico, a, ci, che *ag (di metallo)* metal *cpd*; *(splendore, rumore etc)* metallic.

me'tallo *sm* metal.

metalmec'canico, a, ci, che *ag* engineering *cpd* ♦ *sm* engineering worker.

me'tano *sm* methane.

meteorolo'gia [meteorolo'dʒia] *sf* meteorology; **meteoro'logico, a, ci, che**

ag meteorological, weather *cpd*.
me'ticcio, a, ci, ce [me'tittʃo] *sm/f*
half-caste, half-breed.
me'todico, a, ci, che *ag* methodical.
'metodo *sm* method; (*manuale*) tutor
(*BRIT*), manual.
'metrica *sf* metrics *sg*.
'metrico, a, ci, che *ag* metric;
(*POESIA*) metrical.
'metro *sm* metre; (*nastro*) tape
measure; (*asta*) (metre) rule.
metropoli'tana *sf* underground, subway.
metropoli'tano, a *ag* metropolitan.
'mettere *vt* to put; (*abito*) to put on;
(: *portare*) to wear; (*installare: telefono*) to put in; (*fig: provocare*): ~
fame/allegria a qn to make sb hungry/
happy; (*supporre*): **mettiamo che ...**
let's suppose *o* say that ... ; **~rsi** *vr*
(*persona*) to put o.s.; (*oggetto*) to go;
(*disporsi: faccenda*) to turn out; **~rsi a
sedere** to sit down; **~rsi a letto** to get
into bed; (*per malattia*) to take to one's
bed; **~rsi il cappello** to put on one's
hat; **~rsi a** (*cominciare*) to begin to,
start to; **~rsi al lavoro** to set to work;
~rsi con qn (*in società*) to team up
with sb; (*in coppia*) to start going out
with sb; **~rci: ~rci molta cura/molto
tempo** to take a lot of care/a lot of
time; **ci ho messo 3 ore per venire** it's
taken me 3 hours to get here; **~rcela
tutta** to do one's best; ~ **a tacere qn/qc**
to keep sb/sth quiet; ~ **su casa** to set up
house; ~ **su un negozio** to start a shop;
~ **via** to put away.
'mezza ['mɛddza] *sf*: **la** ~ half-past
twelve (*in the afternoon*); *vedi anche*
mezzo.
mez'zadro [med'dzadro] *sm* (*AGR*)
sharecropper.
mezza'luna [meddza'luna] *sf* half-moon;
(*dell'islamismo*) crescent; (*coltello*)
(semicircular) chopping knife.
mezza'nino [meddza'nino] *sm*
mezzanine (floor).
mez'zano, a [med'dzano] *ag* (*medio*)
average, medium; (*figlio*) middle *cpd* ♦
sm/f (*intermediario*) go-between;

(*ruffiano*) pimp.
mezza'notte [meddza'nɔtte] *sf* midnight.
'mezzo, a ['mɛddzo] *ag* half; **un** ~
litro/panino half a litre/roll ♦ *av* half-;
~ **morto** half-dead ♦ *sm* (*metà*) half;
(*parte centrale: di strada etc*) middle;
(*per raggiungere un fine*) means *sg*;
(*veicolo*) vehicle; (*nell'indicare l'ora*):
le nove e ~ half past nine; **mezzogiorno
e** ~ half past twelve; **~i** *smpl*
(*possibilità economiche*) means; **di ~a
età** middle-aged; **un soprabito di ~a
stagione** a spring (*o* autumn) coat; **di** ~
middle, in the middle; **andarci di** ~
(*patir danno*) to suffer; **levarsi** *o* **togliersi di** ~ to get out of the way; **in** ~
a in the middle of; **per** *o* **a** ~ **di** by
means of; **~i di comunicazione di
massa** mass media *pl*; **~i pubblici** public transport *sg*; **~i di trasporto** means
of transport.
mezzogi'orno [meddzo'dʒorno] *sm* midday, noon; (*GEO*) south; **a** ~ at 12
(o'clock) *o* midday *o* noon; **il** ~ **d'Italia**
southern Italy.
mez'z'ora [med'dzora] *sf* half-hour, half
an hour.
mez'zora [med'dzora] *sf* = **mezz'ora**.
mi (*dav lo, la, li, le, ne diventa* **me**)
pron (*oggetto*) me; (*complemento di
termine*) to me; (*riflessivo*) myself ♦
sm (*MUS*) E; (: *solfeggiando la scala*)
mi.
'mia *vedi* **mio**.
miago'lare *vi* to miaow, mew.
'mica *sf* (*CHIM*) mica ♦ *av* (*fam*): **non
... ~** not ... at all; **non sono ~ stanco**
I'm not a bit tired; **non sarà ~ partito**?
he wouldn't have left, would he?; ~
male not bad.
'miccia, ce ['mittʃa] *sf* fuse.
micidi'ale [mitʃi'djale] *ag* fatal;
(*dannosissimo*) deadly.
mi'crofono *sm* microphone.
micros'copio *sm* microscope.
mi'dollo (*pl(f)* **~a**) *sm* (*ANAT*)
marrow.
'mie *vedi* **mio**.
mi'ele *sm* honey.
mi'ei *vedi* **mio**.

mi'etere vt (AGR) to reap, harvest; (fig: vite) to take, claim.

'**miglia** ['miʎʎa] sfpl di **miglio**.

migli'aio [miʎ'ʎajo] (pl(f) ~**a**) sm thousand; **un** ~ **(di)** about a thousand; **a** ~**a** by the thousand, in thousands.

'**miglio** ['miʎʎo] sm (BOT) millet; (pl(f) ~**a**: unità di misura) mile; ~ **marino** o **nautico** nautical mile.

migliora'mento [miʎʎora'mento] sm improvement.

miglio'rare [miʎʎo'rare] vt, vi to improve.

migli'ore [miʎ'ʎore] ag (comparativo) better; (superlativo) best ♦ sm: **il** ~ the best (thing) ♦ sm/f: **il(la)** ~ the best (person); **il miglior vino di questa regione** the best wine in this area.

'**mignolo** ['miɲɲolo] sm (ANAT) little finger, pinkie; (: dito del piede) little toe.

mi'grare vi to migrate.

'**mila** pl di **mille**.

Mi'lano sf Milan.

miliar'dario, a sm/f millionaire.

mili'ardo sm thousand million, billion (US).

mili'are ag: **pietra** ~ milestone.

mili'one sm million; **un** ~ **di lire** a million lire.

mili'tante ag, sm/f militant.

mili'tare vi (MIL) to be a soldier, serve; (fig: in un partito) to be a militant ♦ ag military ♦ sm serviceman; **fare il** ~ to do one's military service.

'**milite** sm soldier.

millanta'tore, 'trice sm/f boaster.

'**mille** (pl **mila**) num a o one thousand; **dieci mila** ten thousand.

mille'foglie [mille'fɔʎʎe] sm inv (CUC) cream o vanilla slice.

mil'lennio sm millennium.

millepi'edi sm inv centipede.

mil'lesimo, a ag, sm thousandth.

milli'grammo sm milligram(me).

mil'limetro sm millimetre.

'**milza** ['miltsa] sf (ANAT) spleen.

mimetiz'zare [mimetid'dzare] vt to camouflage; ~**rsi** vr to camouflage o.s.

'**mimica** sf (arte) mime.

'**mimo** sm (attore, componimento) mime.

mi'mosa sf mimosa.

'**mina** sf (esplosiva) mine; (di matita) lead.

mi'naccia, ce [mi'nattʃa] sf threat; **minacci'are** vt to threaten; **minacciare qn di morte** to threaten to kill sb; **minacciare di fare qc** to threaten to do sth; **minacci'oso, a** ag threatening.

mi'nare vt (MIL) to mine; (fig) to undermine.

mina'tore sm miner.

mina'torio, a ag threatening.

mine'rale ag, sm mineral.

mine'rario, a ag (delle miniere) mining; (dei minerali) ore cpd.

mi'nestra sf soup; ~ **in brodo/di verdure** noodle/vegetable soup; **mines'trone** sm thick vegetable and pasta soup.

mingher'lino, a [minger'lino] ag thin, slender.

'**mini** ag inv mini ♦ sf inv miniskirt.

minia'tura sf miniature.

mini'era sf mine.

mini'gonna sf miniskirt.

'**minimo, a** ag minimum, least, slightest; (piccolissimo) very small, slight; (il più basso) lowest, minimum ♦ sm minimum; **al** ~ at least; **girare al** ~ (AUT) to idle.

minis'tero sm (POL, REL) ministry; (governo) government; **M**~ **delle Finanze** Ministry of Finance, ≈ Treasury.

mi'nistro sm (POL, REL) minister; **M**~ **delle Finanze** Minister of Finance, ≈ Chancellor of the Exchequer.

mino'ranza [mino'rantsa] sf minority.

mino'rato, a ag handicapped ♦ sm/f physically (o mentally) handicapped person.

mi'nore ag (comparativo) less; (più piccolo) smaller; (numero) lower; (inferiore) lower, inferior; (meno importante) minor; (più giovane) younger; (superlativo) least; smallest; lowest; youngest ♦ sm/f (minorenne) minor, person under age.

mino'renne *ag* under age ♦ *sm/f* minor, person under age.

mi'nuscolo, a *ag* (*scrittura, carattere*) small; (*piccolissimo*) tiny ♦ *sf* small letter.

mi'nuta *sf* rough copy, draft.

mi'nuto, a *ag* tiny, minute; (*pioggia*) fine; (*corporatura*) delicate, fine; (*lavoro*) detailed ♦ *sm* (*unità di misura*) minute; **al ~** (*COMM*) retail.

'mio (*f* **'mia,** *pl* **mi'ei, 'mie**) *det*: **il ~, la mia** *etc* my ♦ *pron*: **il ~, la mia** *etc* mine; **i miei** my family; **un ~ amico** a friend of mine.

'miope *ag* short-sighted.

'mira *sf* (*anche fig*) aim; **prendere la ~** to take aim; **prendere di ~ qn** (*fig*) to pick on sb.

mi'rabile *ag* admirable, wonderful.

mi'racolo *sm* miracle.

mi'raggio [mi'raddʒo] *sm* mirage.

mi'rare *vi*: **~ a** to aim at.

mi'rino *sm* (*TECN*) sight; (*FOT*) viewer, viewfinder.

mir'tillo *sm* bilberry (*BRIT*), blueberry (*US*), whortleberry.

mi'scela [miʃ'ʃela] *sf* mixture; (*di caffè*) blend.

miscel'lanea [miʃʃel'lanea] *sf* miscellany.

'mischia ['miskja] *sf* scuffle; (*RUGBY*) scrum, scrummage.

mischi'are [mis'kjare] *vt* to mix, blend; **~rsi** *vr* to mix, blend.

mis'cuglio [mis'kuʎʎo] *sm* mixture, hotchpotch, jumble.

mise'rabile *ag* (*infelice*) miserable, wretched; (*povero*) poverty-stricken; (*di scarso valore*) miserable.

mi'seria *sf* extreme poverty; (*infelicità*) misery; **~e** *sfpl* (*del mondo etc*) misfortunes, troubles; **porca ~!** (*fam*) blast!, damn!

miseri'cordia *sf* mercy, pity.

'misero, a *ag* miserable, wretched; (*povero*) poverty-stricken; (*insufficiente*) miserable.

mis'fatto *sm* misdeed, crime.

mi'sogino [mi'zɔdʒino] *sm* misogynist.

'missile *sm* missile.

missio'nario, a *ag, sm/f* missionary.

missi'one *sf* mission.

misteri'oso, a *ag* mysterious.

mis'tero *sm* mystery.

mistifi'care *vt* to fool, bamboozle.

'misto, a *ag* mixed; (*scuola*) mixed, coeducational ♦ *sm* mixture.

mis'tura *sf* mixture.

mi'sura *sf* measure; (*misurazione, dimensione*) measurement; (*taglia*) size; (*provvedimento*) measure, step; (*moderazione*) moderation; (*MUS*) time; (: *divisione*) bar; (*fig: limite*) bounds *pl*, limit; **nella ~ in cui** inasmuch as, insofar as; **su ~** made to measure.

misu'rare *vt* (*ambiente, stoffa*) to measure; (*terreno*) to survey; (*abito*) to try on; (*pesare*) to weigh; (*fig: parole etc*) to weigh up; (: *spese, cibo*) to limit ♦ *vi* to measure; **~rsi** *vr*; **~rsi con qn** to have a confrontation with sb; to compete with sb; **misu'rato, a** *ag* (*ponderato*) measured; (*prudente*) cautious; (*moderato*) moderate.

'mite *ag* mild; (*prezzo*) moderate, reasonable.

miti'gare *vt* to mitigate, lessen; (*lenire*) to soothe, relieve; **~rsi** *vr* (*odio*) to subside; (*tempo*) to become milder.

'mito *sm* myth; **mitolo'gia, 'gie** *sf* mythology.

'mitra *sf* (*REL*) mitre ♦ *sm inv* (*arma*) sub-machine gun.

mitraglia'trice [mitraʎʎa'tritʃe] *sf* machine gun.

mit'tente *sm/f* sender.

'mobile *ag* mobile; (*parte di macchina*) moving; (*DIR: bene*) movable, personal ♦ *sm* (*arredamento*) piece of furniture; **~i** *smpl* (*mobilia*) furniture *sg*.

mo'bilia *sf* furniture.

mobili'are *ag* (*DIR*) personal, movable.

mo'bilio *sm* = **mobilia.**

mobili'tare *vt* to mobilize.

mocas'sino *sm* moccasin.

'moccolo *sm* (*di candela*) candle-end; (*fam: bestemmia*) oath; (: *moccio*) snot; **reggere il** ~ to play gooseberry (_BRIT_), act as chaperon.

'**moda** _sf_ fashion; **alla** ~, **di** ~ fashionable, in fashion.

modalità _sf inv_ formality.

mo'della _sf_ model.

model'lare _vt_ (_creta_) to model, shape; ~**rsi** _vr_: ~**rsi su** to model o.s. on.

mo'dello _sm_ model; (_stampo_) mould ♦ _ag inv_ model _cpd_.

'**modem** _sm inv_ modem.

mode'rare _vt_ to moderate; ~**rsi** _vr_ to restrain o.s.; **mode'rato, a** _ag_ moderate.

modera'tore, 'trice _sm/f_ moderator.

mo'derno, a _ag_ modern.

mo'destia _sf_ modesty.

mo'desto, a _ag_ modest.

'**modico, a, ci, che** _ag_ reasonable, moderate.

mo'difica, che _sf_ modification.

modifi'care _vt_ to modify, alter; ~**rsi** _vr_ to alter, change.

mo'dista _sf_ milliner.

'**modo** _sm_ way, manner; (_mezzo_) means, way; (_occasione_) opportunity; (_LING_) mood; (_MUS_) mode; ~**i** _smpl_ (_comportamento_) manners; **a suo** ~, **a** ~ **suo** in his own way; **ad** _o_ **in ogni** ~ anyway; **di** _o_ **in** ~ **che** so that; **in** ~ **da** so as to; **in tutti i** ~**i** at all costs; (_comunque sia_) anyway; (_in ogni caso_) in any case; **in qualche** ~ somehow or other; ~ **di dire** turn of phrase; **per** ~ **di dire** so to speak.

modu'lare _vt_ to modulate; **modulazi'one** _sf_ modulation; **modulazione di frequenza** frequency modulation.

'**modulo** _sm_ (_modello_) form; (_ARCHIT, lunare, di comando_) module.

'**mogano** _sm_ mahogany.

'**mogio, a, gi, gie** ['mɔdʒo] _ag_ down in the dumps, dejected.

'**moglie** ['moʎʎe] _sf_ wife.

mo'ine _sfpl_ cajolery _sg_; (_leziosità_) affectation _sg_.

'**mola** _sf_ millstone; (_utensile abrasivo_) grindstone.

mo'lare _sm_ (_dente_) molar.

'**mole** _sf_ mass; (_dimensioni_) size; (_edificio grandioso_) massive structure.

moles'tare _vt_ to bother, annoy; **mo'lestia** _sf_ annoyance, bother; **recar molestia a qn** to bother sb; **mo'lesto, a** _ag_ annoying.

'**molla** _sf_ spring; ~**e** _sfpl_ (_per camino_) tongs.

mol'lare _vt_ to release, let go; (_NAUT_) to ease; (_fig: ceffone_) to give ♦ _vi_ (_cedere_) to give in.

'**molle** _ag_ soft; (_muscoli_) flabby; (_fig: debole_) weak, feeble.

mol'letta _sf_ (_per capelli_) hairgrip; (_per panni stesi_) clothes peg; ~**e** _sfpl_ (_per zucchero_) tongs.

mol'lica, che _sf_ crumb, soft part.

mol'lusco, schi _sm_ mollusc.

'**molo** _sm_ mole, breakwater; jetty.

mol'teplice [mol'teplitʃe] _ag_ (_formato di più elementi_) complex; ~**i** _pl_ (_svariati: interessi, attività_) numerous, various.

moltipli'care _vt_ to multiply; ~**rsi** _vr_ to multiply; to increase in number; **moltiplicazi'one** _sf_ multiplication.

PAROLA CHIAVE

'**molto, a** _det_ (_quantità_) a lot of, much; (_numero_) a lot of, many; ~ **pane/carbone** a lot of bread/coal; ~**a gente** a lot of people, many people; ~**i libri** a lot of books, many books; **non ho** ~ **tempo** I haven't got much time; **per** ~ (_tempo_) for a long time

♦ _av_ **1** a lot, (very) much; **viaggia** ~ he travels a lot; **non viaggia** ~ he doesn't travel much _o_ a lot

2 (_intensivo: con aggettivi, avverbi_) very; (: _con participio passato_) (very) much; ~ **buono** very good; ~ **migliore**, ~ **meglio** much _o_ a lot better

♦ _pron_ much, a lot; ~**i, e** _pron pl_ many, a lot; ~**i pensano che ...** many (people) think ....

---

momen'taneo, a _ag_ momentary, fleeting.

mo'mento _sm_ moment; **da un** ~ **all'altro** at any moment; (_all'improvviso_) suddenly; **al** ~ **di fare** just as I was (_o_ you were *o* he was *etc*) doing; **per il ~** for the time being; **dal ~ che** ever since; (*dato che*) since; **a ~i** (*da un ~ all'altro*) any time *o* moment now; (*quasi*) nearly.

'**monaca, che** *sf* nun.

'**Monaco** *sf* Monaco; **~ (di Baviera)** Munich.

'**monaco, ci** *sm* monk.

mo'**narca, chi** *sm* monarch; **monar'chia** *sf* monarchy.

monas'**tero** *sm* (*di monaci*) monastery; (*di monache*) convent; mo'**nastico, a, ci, che** *ag* monastic.

'**monco, a, chi, che** *ag* maimed; (*fig*) incomplete; **~ d'un braccio** one-armed.

mon'**dana** *sf* prostitute.

mon'**dano, a** *ag* (*anche fig*) worldly; (*dell'alta società*) society *cpd*; fashionable.

mon'**dare** *vt* (*frutta, patate*) to peel; (*piselli*) to shell; (*pulire*) to clean.

mondi'**ale** *ag* (*campionato, popolazione*) world *cpd*; (*influenza*) world-wide.

'**mondo** *sm* world; (*grande quantità*): **un ~ di** lots of, a host of; **il bel ~** high society.

mo'**nello, a** *sm/f* street urchin; (*ragazzo vivace*) scamp, imp.

mo'**neta** *sf* coin; (*ECON: valuta*) currency; (*denaro spicciolo*) (small) change; **~ estera** foreign currency; **~ legale** legal tender; **mone'tario, a** *ag* monetary.

mongo'**loide** *ag, sm/f* (*MED*) mongol.

'**monito** *sm* warning.

'**monitor** *sm inv* (*TECN, TV*) monitor.

monoco'**lore** *ag* (*POL*): **governo ~** one-party government.

mono'**polio** *sm* monopoly.

mo'**notono, a** *ag* monotonous.

monsi'**gnore** [monsiɲˈɲore] *sm* (*REL: titolo*) Your (*o* His) Grace.

mon'**sone** *sm* monsoon.

monta'**carichi** [montaˈkariki] *sm inv* hoist, goods lift.

mon'**taggio** [monˈtaddʒo] *sm* (*TECN*) assembly; (*CINEMA*) editing.

mon'**tagna** [monˈtaɲɲa] *sf* mountain;

(*zona montuosa*): **la ~** the mountains *pl*; **andare in ~** to go to the mountains; **~e russe** roller coaster *sg*, big dipper *sg* (*BRIT*); **monta'gnoso, a** *ag* mountainous.

monta'**naro, a** *ag* mountain *cpd* ♦ *sm/f* mountain dweller.

mon'**tano, a** *ag* mountain *cpd*; alpine.

mon'**tare** *vt* to go (*o* come) up; (*cavallo*) to ride; (*apparecchiatura*) to set up, assemble; (*CUC*) to whip; (*ZOOL*) to cover; (*incastonare*) to mount, set; (*CINEMA*) to edit; (*FOT*) to mount ♦ *vi* to go (*o* come) up; (*a cavallo*): **~ bene/male** to ride well/badly; (*aumentare di livello, volume*) to rise; **~rsi** *vr* to become big-headed; **~ qc** to exaggerate sth; **~ qn** *o* **la testa a qn** to turn sb's head; **~ in bicicletta/macchina/treno** to get on a bicycle/into a car/on a train; **~ a cavallo** to get on *o* mount a horse.

monta'**tura** *sf* assembling *no pl*; (*di occhiali*) frames *pl*; (*di gioiello*) mounting, setting; (*fig*): **~ pubblicitaria** publicity stunt.

'**monte** *sm* mountain; **a ~** upstream; **mandare a ~ qc** to upset sth, cause sth to fail; **il M~ Bianco** Mont Blanc; **~ di pietà** pawnshop.

mon'**tone** *sm* (*ZOOL*) ram; **carne di ~** mutton.

montu'**oso, a** *ag* mountainous.

monu'**mento** *sm* monument.

'**mora** *sf* (*del rovo*) blackberry; (*del gelso*) mulberry; (*DIR*) delay; (: *somma*) arrears *pl*.

mo'**rale** *ag* moral ♦ *sf* (*scienza*) ethics *sg*, moral philosophy; (*complesso di norme*) moral standards *pl*, morality; (*condotta*) morals *pl*; (*insegnamento morale*) moral ♦ *sm* morale; **essere giù di ~** to be feeling down; **moralità** *sf* morality; (*condotta*) morals *pl*.

'**morbido, a** *ag* soft; (*pelle*) soft, smooth.

mor'**billo** *sm* (*MED*) measles *sg*.

'**morbo** *sm* disease.

mor'**boso, a** *ag* (*fig*) morbid.

mor'**dace** [morˈdatʃe] *ag* biting, cutting.

mor'dente sm (fig: di satira, critica) bite; (: di persona) drive.

'mordere vt to bite; (addentare) to bite into; (corrodere) to eat into.

mori'bondo, a ag dying, moribund.

morige'rato, a [moridʒe'rato] ag of good morals.

mo'rire vi to die; (abitudine, civiltà) to die out; ~ **di fame** to die of hunger; (fig) to be starving; ~ **di noia/paura** to be bored/scared to death; **fa un caldo da** ~ it's terribly hot.

mormo'rare vi to murmur; (brontolare) to grumble.

'moro, a ag dark(-haired); dark(-complexioned); **i M~i** smpl (STORIA) the Moors.

mo'roso, a ag in arrears ♦ sm/f (fam: innamorato) sweetheart.

'morsa sf (TECN) vice; (fig: stretta) grip.

morsi'care vt to nibble (at), gnaw (at); (sog: insetto) to bite.

'morso, a pp di **mordere** ♦ sm bite; (di insetto) sting; (parte della briglia) bit; ~**i della fame** pangs of hunger.

mor'taio sm mortar.

mor'tale ag, sm mortal; **mortalità** sf mortality, death rate.

'morte sf death.

mortifi'care vt to mortify.

'morto, a pp di **morire** ♦ ag dead ♦ sm/f dead man/woman; **i ~i** the dead; **fare il** ~ (nell'acqua) to float on one's back; **il Mar M~** the Dead Sea.

mor'torio sm (anche fig) funeral.

mo'saico, ci sm mosaic.

'Mosca sf Moscow.

'mosca, sche sf fly; ~ **cieca** blind-man's-buff.

mos'cato sm muscatel (wine).

mosce'rino [moʃʃe'rino] sm midge, gnat.

mos'chea [mos'kɛa] sf mosque.

mos'chetto [mos'ketto] sm musket.

moscio, a, sci, sce ['mɔʃʃo] ag (fig) lifeless.

mos'cone sm (ZOOL) bluebottle; (barca) pedalo; (: a remi) kind of pedalo with oars.

'mossa sf movement; (nel gioco) move.

'mosso, a pp di **muovere** ♦ ag (mare) rough; (capelli) wavy; (FOT) blurred; (ritmo, prosa) animated.

mos'tarda sf mustard.

'mostra sf exhibition, show; (ostentazione) show; **in** ~ on show; **far** ~ **di** (fingere) to pretend; **far** ~ **di sé** to show off.

mos'trare vt to show ♦ vi: ~ **di fare** to pretend to do; ~**rsi** vr to appear.

'mostro sm monster; **mostru'oso, a** ag monstrous.

mo'tel sm inv motel.

moti'vare vt (causare) to cause; (giustificare) to justify, account for; **motivazi'one** sf justification; motive; (PSIC) motivation.

mo'tivo sm (causa) reason, cause; (movente) motive; (letterario) (central) theme; (disegno) motif, design, pattern; (MUS) motif; **per quale** ~? why?, for what reason?

'moto sm (anche FISICA) motion; (movimento, gesto) movement; (esercizio fisico) exercise; (sommossa) rising, revolt; (commozione) feeling, impulse ♦ sf inv (motocicletta) motorbike; **mettere in** ~ to set in motion; (AUT) to start up.

motoci'cletta [mototʃi'kletta] sf motorcycle; **motoci'clismo** sm motorcycling, motorcycle racing; **motoci'clista, i, e** sm/f motorcyclist.

mo'tore, 'trice ag motor; (TECN) driving ♦ sm engine, motor; **a** ~ motor cpd, power-driven; ~ **a combustione interna/a reazione** internal combustion/jet engine; **moto'rino** sm moped; **motorino di avviamento** (AUT) starter; **motoriz'zato, a** ag (truppe) motorized; (persona) having a car o transport.

motos'cafo sm motorboat.

mot'teggio [mot'teddʒo] sm banter.

'motto sm (battuta scherzosa) witty remark; (frase emblematica) motto, maxim.

mo'vente sm motive.

movimen'tare vt to liven up.

movi'mento *sm* movement; *(fig)* activity, hustle and bustle; *(MUS)* tempo, movement.

mozi'one [mot'tsjone] *sf (POL)* motion.

moz'zare [mot'tsare] *vt* to cut off; *(coda)* to dock; ~ **il fiato** *o* **il respiro a qn** *(fig)* to take sb's breath away.

mozza'rella [mottsa'rella] *sf* mozzarella *(a moist Neapolitan curd cheese)*.

mozzi'cone [mottsi'kone] *sm* stub, butt, end; *(anche:* ~ **di sigaretta)** cigarette end.

'mozzo[1] ['mɔddzo] *sm (MECCANICA)* hub.

'mozzo[2] ['mottso] *sm (NAUT)* ship's boy; ~ **di stalla** stable boy.

'mucca, che *sf* cow.

'mucchio ['mukkjo] *sm* pile, heap; *(fig):* **un** ~ **di** lots of, heaps of.

'muco, chi *sm* mucus.

'muffa *sf* mould, mildew.

mug'gire [mud'dʒire] *vi (vacca)* to low, moo; *(toro)* to bellow; *(fig)* to roar; **mug'gito** *sm* low, moo; bellow; roar.

mu'ghetto [mu'getto] *sm* lily of the valley.

mu'gnaio, a [muɲ'najo] *sm/f* miller.

mugo'lare *vi (cane)* to whimper, whine; *(fig: persona)* to moan.

muli'nare *vi* to whirl, spin (round and round).

muli'nello *sm (moto vorticoso)* eddy, whirl; *(di canna da pesca)* reel; *(NAUT)* windlass.

mu'lino *sm* mill; ~ **a vento** windmill.

'mulo *sm* mule.

'multa *sf* fine; **mul'tare** *vt* to fine.

'multiplo, a *ag, sm* multiple.

'mummia *sf* mummy.

'mungere ['mundʒere] *vt (anche fig)* to milk.

munici'pale [munitʃi'pale] *ag* municipal; town *cpd*.

muni'cipio [muni'tʃipjo] *sm* town council, corporation; *(edificio)* town hall.

mu'nire *vt:* ~ **qc/qn di** to equip sth/sb with.

munizi'oni [munit'tsjoni] *sfpl (MIL)* ammunition *sg*.

'munto, a *pp di* **mungere**.

mu'overe *vt* to move; *(ruota, macchina)* to drive; *(sollevare: questione, obiezione)* to raise, bring up; *(: accusa)* to make, bring forward; ~**rsi** *vr* to move; **muoviti!** hurry up!, get a move on!

'mura *sfpl vedi* **muro**.

mu'raglia [mu'raʎʎa] *sf* (high) wall.

mu'rale *ag* wall *cpd*; mural.

mu'rare *vt (persona, porta)* to wall up.

mura'tore *sm* mason; bricklayer.

'muro *sm* wall; ~**a** *sfpl (cinta cittadina)* walls; **a** ~ wall *cpd*; *(armadio etc)* built-in; ~ **del suono** sound barrier; **mettere al** ~ *(fucilare)* to shoot *o* execute (by firing squad).

'muschio ['muskjo] *sm (ZOOL)* musk; *(BOT)* moss.

musco'lare *ag* muscular, muscle *cpd*.

'muscolo *sm (ANAT)* muscle.

mu'seo *sm* museum.

museru'ola *sf* muzzle.

'musica *sf* music; ~ **da ballo/camera** dance/chamber music; **musi'cale** *ag* musical; **musi'cista, i, e** *sm/f* musician.

'muso *sm* muzzle; *(di auto, aereo)* nose; **tenere il** ~ to sulk; **mu'sone, a** *sm/f* sulky person.

'mussola *sf* muslin.

'muta *sf (di animali)* moulting; *(di serpenti)* sloughing; *(per immersioni subacquee)* diving suit; *(gruppo di cani)* pack.

muta'mento *sm* change.

mu'tande *sfpl (da uomo)* (under)pants; **mutan'dine** *sfpl (da donna, bambino)* pants *(BRIT)*, briefs; **mutandine di plastica** plastic pants.

mu'tare *vt, vi* to change, alter; **mutazi'one** *sf* change, alteration; *(BIOL)* mutation; **mu'tevole** *ag* changeable.

muti'lare *vt* to mutilate, maim; *(fig)* to mutilate, deface; **muti'lato, a** *sm/f* disabled person *(through loss of limbs)*.

mu'tismo *sm (MED)* mutism; *(atteggiamento)* (stubborn) silence.

'muto, a *ag (MED)* dumb; *(emozione, dolore, CINEMA)* silent; *(LING)* silent, mute; (*carta geografica*) blank; ~ **per lo stupore** *etc* speechless with amazement *etc*.

'**mutua** *sf* (*anche*: **cassa** ~) health insurance scheme.

mutu'are *vt* (*fig*) to borrow.

mutu'ato, a *sm/f* member of a health insurance scheme.

'**mutuo, a** *ag* (*reciproco*) mutual ♦ *sm* (*ECON*) (long-term) loan.

N

N. *abbr* (= *nord*) N.

'**nacchere** ['nakkere] *sfpl* castanets.

'**nafta** *sf* naphtha; (*per motori diesel*) diesel oil.

nafta'lina *sf* (*CHIM*) naphthalene; (*tarmicida*) mothballs *pl*.

'**naia** *sf* (*ZOOL*) cobra; (*MIL*) slang term *for national service*.

'**nailon** *sm* nylon.

'**nanna** *sf* (*linguaggio infantile*): **andare a ~** to go to beddy-byes.

'**nano, a** *ag*, *sm/f* dwarf.

napole'tano, a *ag*, *sm/f* Neapolitan.

'**Napoli** *sf* Naples.

'**nappa** *sf* tassel.

nar'ciso [nar't∫izo] *sm* narcissus.

nar'cosi *sf* narcosis.

nar'cotico, ci *sm* narcotic.

na'rice [na'rit∫e] *sf* nostril.

nar'rare *vt* to tell the story of, recount; **narra'tiva** *sf* (*branca letteraria*) fiction; **narra'tivo, a** *ag* narrative; **narra'tore, 'trice** *sm/f* narrator; **narrazi'one** *sf* narration; (*racconto*) story, tale.

na'sale *ag* nasal.

'**nascere** ['na∫∫ere] *vi* (*bambino*) to be born; (*pianta*) to come *o* spring up; (*fiume*) to rise, have its source; (*sole*) to rise; (*dente*) to come through; (*fig: derivare, conseguire*): ~ **da** to arise from, be born out of; **è nata nel 1952** she was born in 1952; '**nascita** *sf* birth.

nas'condere *vt* to hide, conceal; ~**rsi** *vr* to hide; **nascon'diglio** *sm* hiding place; **nascon'dino** *sm* (*gioco*) hide-and-seek; **nas'costo, a** *pp di* **na-**

scondere ♦ *ag* hidden; **di nascosto** secretly.

na'sello *sm* (*ZOOL*) hake.

'**naso** *sm* nose.

'**nastro** *sm* ribbon; (*magnetico, isolante, SPORT*) tape; ~ **adesivo** adhesive tape; ~ **trasportatore** conveyor belt.

nas'turzio [nas'turtsjo] *sm* nasturtium.

na'tale *ag* of one's birth ♦ *sm* (*REL*): **N~** Christmas; (*giorno della nascita*) birthday; **natalità** *sf* birth rate; **nata'lizio, a** *ag* (*del Natale*) Christmas *cpd*.

na'tante *sm* craft *inv*, boat.

natica, che *sf* (*ANAT*) buttock.

na'tio, a, 'tii, 'tie *ag* native.

Natività *sf* (*REL*) Nativity.

na'tivo, a *ag*, *sm/f* native.

'**nato, a** *pp di* **nascere** ♦ *ag*: **un attore** ~ a born actor; ~**a Pieri** née Pieri.

na'tura *sf* nature; **pagare in** ~ to pay in kind; ~ **morta** still life.

natu'rale *ag* natural; **natura'lezza** *sf* naturalness; **natura'lista, i, e** *sm/f* naturalist.

naturaliz'zare [naturalid'dzare] *vt* to naturalize.

natural'mente *av* naturally; (*certamente, sì*) of course.

naufra'gare *vi* (*nave*) to be wrecked; (*persona*) to be shipwrecked; (*fig*) to fall through; **nau'fragio** *sm* shipwreck; (*fig*) ruin, failure; '**naufrago, ghi** *sm* castaway, shipwreck victim.

'**nausea** *sf* nausea; **nausea'bondo, a** *ag* nauseating, sickening; **nause'are** *vt* to nauseate, make (feel) sick.

'**nautica** *sf* (art of) navigation.

'**nautico, a, ci, che** *ag* nautical.

na'vale *ag* naval.

na'vata *sf* (*anche*: ~ **centrale**) nave; (*anche*: ~ **laterale**) aisle.

'**nave** *sf* ship, vessel; ~ **cisterna** tanker; ~ **da guerra** warship; ~ **passeggeri** passenger ship; ~ **spaziale** spaceship.

na'vetta *sf* shuttle; (*servizio di collegamento*) shuttle (service).

navi'cella [navi't∫ella] *sf* (*di aerostato*) gondola.

navi'gabile *ag* navigable.

navi'gare *vi* to sail; **navigazi'one** *sf* navigation.

na'viglio [na'viλλo] *sm* fleet, ships *pl*; (*canale artificiale*) canal; **~ da pesca** fishing fleet.

nazio'nale [nattsjo'nale] *ag* national ♦ *sf* (SPORT) national team; **naziona'lismo** *sm* nationalism; **nazionalità** *sf inv* nationality.

nazi'one [nat'tsjone] *sf* nation.

PAROLA CHIAVE

ne *pron* **1** (*di lui, lei, loro*) of him/her/ them; about him/her/them; **~ riconosco la voce** I recognize his (*o* her) voice

2 (*di questa, quella cosa*) of it; about it; **~ voglio ancora** I want some more (of it *o* them); **non parliamone più!** let's not talk about it any more!

3 (*con valore partitivo*): **hai dei libri? — sì, ~ ho** have you any books? — yes, I have (some); **hai del pane? — no, non ~ ho** have you any bread? — no, I haven't any; **quanti anni hai? — ~ ho 17** how old are you? — I'm 17

♦ *av* (*moto da luogo: da lì*) from there; **~ vengo ora** I've just come from there.

---

né *cong*: **~ ... ~** neither ... nor; **~ l'uno ~ l'altro lo vuole** neither of them wants it; **non parla ~ l'italiano ~ il tedesco** he speaks neither Italian nor German, he doesn't speak either Italian or German; **non piove ~ nevica** it isn't raining or snowing.

ne'anche [ne'anke] *av, cong* not even; **non ... ~** not even; **~ se volesse potrebbe venire** he couldn't even come even if he wanted to; **non l'ho visto — ~ io** I didn't see him — neither did I *o* I didn't either; **~ per idea** *o* **sogno!** not on your life!

'nebbia *sf* fog; (*foschia*) mist; **nebbi'oso, a** *ag* foggy; misty.

nebu'loso, a *ag* (*atmosfera*) hazy; (*fig*) hazy, vague.

necessaria'mente [netʃessarja'mɛnte] *av* necessarily.

neces'sario, a [netʃes'sarjo] *ag* necessary.

necessità [netʃessi'ta] *sf inv* necessity; (*povertà*) need, poverty; **necessi'tare** *vt* to require ♦ *vi* (*aver bisogno*): **necessitare di** to need.

necro'logio [nekro'lɔdʒo] *sm* obituary notice; (*registro*) register of deaths.

ne'fando, a *ag* infamous, wicked.

ne'fasto, a *ag* inauspicious, ill-omened.

ne'gare *vt* to deny; (*rifiutare*) to deny, refuse; **~ di aver fatto/che** to deny having done/that; **nega'tivo, a** *ag*, *sf*, *sm* negative; **negazi'one** *sf* negation.

ne'gletto, a [ne'glɛtto] *ag* (*trascurato*) neglected.

'negli ['neλλi] *prep +det vedi* **in**.

negli'gente [negli'dʒɛnte] *ag* negligent, careless; **negli'genza** *sf* negligence, carelessness.

negozi'ante [negot'tsjante] *sm/f* trader, dealer; (*bottegaio*) shopkeeper (BRIT), storekeeper (US).

negozi'are [negot'tsjare] *vt* to negotiate ♦ *vi*: **~ in** to trade *o* deal in; **negozi'ato** *sm* negotiation.

ne'gozio [ne'gɔttsjo] *sm* (*locale*) shop (BRIT), store (US); (*affare*) (piece of) business *no pl*.

'negro, a *ag*, *sm/f* Negro.

'nei *prep + det vedi* **in**.

nel *prep + det vedi* **in**.

nell' *prep + det vedi* **in**.

'nella *prep + det vedi* **in**.

'nelle *prep + det vedi* **in**.

'nello *prep + det vedi* **in**.

'nembo *sm* (METEOR) nimbus.

ne'mico, a, ci, che *ag* hostile; (MIL) enemy *cpd* ♦ *sm/f* enemy; **essere ~ di** to be strongly averse *o* opposed to.

nem'meno *av, cong* = **neanche**.

'nenia *sf* dirge; (*motivo monotono*) monotonous tune.

'neo *sm* mole; (*fig*) (slight) flaw.

'neo... *prefisso* neo....

'neon *sm* (CHIM) neon.

neo'nato, a *ag* newborn ♦ *sm/f* newborn baby.

neozelan'dese [neodzelan'dese] *ag* New Zealand *cpd* ♦ *sm/f* New Zealander.

nep'pure *av, cong* = **neanche**.

'nerbo *sm* lash; (*fig*) strength, backbone; **nerbo'ruto, a** *ag* muscular; robust.

ne'retto *sm* (*TIP*) bold type.

'nero, a *ag* black; (*scuro*) dark ♦ *sm* black; **il Mar N~** the Black Sea.

nerva'tura *sf* (*ANAT*) nervous system; (*BOT*) veining; (*ARCHIT, TECN*) rib.

'nervo *sm* (*ANAT*) nerve; (*BOT*) vein; **avere i ~i** to be on edge; **dare sui ~i a qn** to get on sb's nerves; **ner'voso, a** *ag* nervous; (*irritabile*) irritable ♦ *sm* (*fam*): **far venire il nervoso a qn** to get on sb's nerves.

'nespola *sf* (*BOT*) medlar; (*fig*) blow, punch; **'nespolo** *sm* medlar tree.

'nesso *sm* connection, link.

nes'suno, a (*det: dav sm* **nessun** +*C, V,* **nessuno** +*s impura, gn, pn, ps, x, z; dav sf* **nessuna** +*C,* **nessun'** +*V*) *det* **1** (*non uno*) no, *espressione negativa* +any; **non c'è nessun libro** there isn't any book, there is no book; **nessun altro** no one else, nobody else; **nessun'altra cosa** nothing else; **in nessun luogo** nowhere

2 (*qualche*) any; **hai ~a obiezione?** do you have any objections?

♦ *pron* **1** (*non uno*) no one, nobody, *espressione negativa* +any(one); (: *cosa*) none, *espressione negativa* +any; **~ è venuto, non è venuto ~** nobody came

2 (*qualcuno*) anyone, anybody; **ha telefonato ~?** did anyone phone?

net'tare¹ *vt* to clean.

'nettare² *sm* nectar.

net'tezza [net'tettsa] *sf* cleanness, cleanliness; **~ urbana** cleansing department.

'netto, a *ag* (*pulito*) clean; (*chiaro*) clear, clear-cut; (*deciso*) definite; (*ECON*) net.

nettur'bino *sm* dustman (*BRIT*), garbage collector (*US*).

neu'rosi *sf* = **nevrosi**.

neu'trale *ag* neutral; **neutralità** *sf* neutrality; **neutraliz'zare** *vt* to neutralize.

'neutro, a *ag* neutral; (*LING*) neuter ♦ *sm* (*LING*) neuter.

ne'vaio *sm* snowfield.

'neve *sf* snow; **nevi'care** *vb impers* to snow; **nevi'cata** *sf* snowfall.

ne'vischio [ne'viskjo] *sm* sleet.

ne'voso, a *ag* snowy; snow-covered.

nevral'gia [nevral'dʒia] *sf* neuralgia.

nevras'tenico, a, ci, che *ag* (*MED*) neurasthenic; (*fig*) hot-tempered.

ne'vrosi *sf* neurosis.

'nibbio *sm* (*ZOOL*) kite.

'nicchia ['nikkja] *sf* niche; (*naturale*) cavity, hollow.

nicchi'are [nik'kjare] *vi* to shilly-shally, hesitate.

'nichel ['nikel] *sm* nickel.

nico'tina *sf* nicotine.

'nido *sm* nest; **a ~ d'ape** (*tessuto etc*) honeycomb *cpd*.

ni'ente *pron* **1** (*nessuna cosa*) nothing; **~ può fermarlo** nothing can stop him; **~ di ~** absolutely nothing; **nient'altro** nothing else; **nient'altro che** nothing but, just, only; **~ affatto** not at all, not in the least; **come se ~ fosse** as if nothing had happened; **cose da ~** trivial matters; **per ~** (*gratis, invano*) for nothing

2 (*qualcosa*): **hai bisogno di ~?** do you need anything?

3: **non ... ~** nothing, *espressione negativa* +anything; **non ho visto ~** I saw nothing, I didn't see anything; **non ho ~ da dire** I have nothing *o* haven't anything to say

♦ *sm* nothing; **un bel ~** absolutely nothing; **basta un ~ per farla piangere** the slightest thing is enough to make her cry

♦ *av* (*in nessuna misura*): **non ... ~** not ... at all; **non è (per) ~ buono** it isn't good at all.

nientedi'meno *av* actually, even ♦ *escl* really!, I say!

niente'meno av, escl = **nientedimeno**.

'**Nilo** sm: **il** ~ the Nile.

'**ninfa** sf nymph.

nin'fea sf water lily.

ninna-'nanna sf lullaby.

'**ninnolo** sm (balocco) plaything; (gingillo) knick-knack.

ni'pote sm/f (di zii) nephew/niece; (di nonni) grandson/daughter, grandchild.

'**nitido, a** ag clear; (specchio) bright.

ni'trato sm nitrate.

ni'trico, a, ci, che ag nitric.

ni'trire vi to neigh.

ni'trito sm (di cavallo) neighing no pl; neigh; (CHIM) nitrite.

nitroglice'rina [nitroglitʃe'rina] sf nitroglycerine.

'**niveo, a** ag snow-white.

no av (risposta) no; **vieni o ~?** are you coming or not?; **perché ~?** why not?; **lo conosciamo? — tu — tu io sì do we** know him? — you don't but I do; **verrai, ~?** you'll come, won't you?

'**nobile** ag noble ♦ sm/f noble, nobleman/woman; **nobili'are** ag noble; **nobiltà** sf nobility; (di azione etc) nobleness.

'**nocca, che** sf (ANAT) knuckle.

nocci'ola [not'tʃɔla] ag inv (colore) hazel, light brown ♦ sf hazelnut.

'nocciolo[1] [nɔttʃolo] sm (di frutto) stone; (fig) heart, core.

noc'ciolo[2] [not'tʃolo] sm (albero) hazel.

'**noce** ['notʃe] sm (albero) walnut tree ♦ sf (frutto) walnut; ~ **moscata** nutmeg.

no'civo, a [no'tʃivo] ag harmful, noxious.

'**nodo** sm (di cravatta, legname, NAUT) knot; (AUT, FERR) junction; (MED, ASTR, BOT) node; (fig: legame) bond, tie; (: punto centrale) heart, crux; **avere un ~ alla gola** to have a lump in one's throat; **no'doso, a** ag (tronco) gnarled.

'**noi** pron (soggetto) we; (oggetto: per dare rilievo, con preposizione) us; ~ **stessi(e)** we ourselves; (oggetto) ourselves.

'**noia** sf boredom; (disturbo, impaccio) bother no pl, trouble no pl; **avere qn/qc**

a ~ not to like sb/sth; **mi è venuto a ~** I'm tired of it; **dare ~ a** to annoy; **avere delle ~e con qn** to have trouble with sb.

noi'altri pron we.

noi'oso, a ag boring; (fastidioso) annoying, troublesome.

noleggi'are [noled'dʒare] vt (prendere a noleggio) to hire (BRIT), rent; (dare a noleggio) to hire out (BRIT), rent (out); (aereo, nave) to charter; **no'leggio** sm hire (BRIT), rental; charter.

'**nolo** sm hire (BRIT), rental; charter; (per trasporto merci) freight; **prendere/dare a ~ qc** to hire/hire out sth.

'**nomade** ag nomadic ♦ sm/f nomad.

'**nome** sm name; (LING) noun; **in/a ~ di** in the name of; **di** o **per ~** (chiamato) called, named; **conoscere qn di ~** to know sb by name; ~ **d'arte** stage name; ~ **di battesimo** Christian name; ~ **depositato** trade name; ~ **di famiglia** surname.

no'mea sf notoriety.

no'mignolo [no'miɲnolo] sm nickname.

'**nomina** sf appointment.

nomi'nale ag nominal; (LING) noun cpd.

nomi'nare vt to name; (eleggere) to appoint; (citare) to mention.

nomina'tivo, a ag (LING) nominative; (ECON) registered ♦ sm (LING: anche: caso ~) nominative (case); (AMM) name.

non av not ♦ prefisso non-; vedi **affatto**; **appena** etc.

nonché [non'ke] cong (tanto più, tanto meno) let alone; (e inoltre) as well as.

noncu'rante ag: ~ (**di**) careless (of), indifferent (to); **noncu'ranza** sf carelessness, indifference.

nondi'meno cong (tuttavia) however; (nonostante) nevertheless.

'**nonno, a** sm/f grandfather/mother; (in senso più familiare) grandma/grandpa; ~**i** smpl grandparents.

non'nulla sm inv: **un ~** nothing, a trifle.

'**nono, a** ag, sm ninth.

nonos'tante prep in spite of, notwithstanding ♦ cong although, even though.

nontiscordardimé sm inv (BOT) forget-me-not.

nord sm North ♦ ag inv north; northern; **il Mare del N~** the North Sea; **nor'dest** sm north-east; **'nordico, a, ci, che** ag nordic, northern European; **nor'dovest** sm north-west.

'norma sf (principio) norm; (regola) regulation, rule; (consuetudine) custom, rule; **a ~ di legge** according to law, as laid down by law.

nor'male ag normal; standard cpd; **normalità** sf normality; **normaliz'zare** vt to normalize, bring back to normal.

normal'mente av normally.

norve'gese [norve'dʒese] ag, sm/f, sm Norwegian.

Nor'vegia [nor'vedʒa] sf: **la ~** Norway.

nostal'gia [nostal'dʒia] sf (di casa, paese) homesickness; (del passato) nostalgia; **nos'talgico, a, ci, che** ag homesick; nostalgic.

nos'trano, a ag local; national; home-produced.

'nostro, a det: **il(la) ~(a)** etc our ♦ pron: **il(la) ~(a)** etc ours ♦ sm: **il ~** our money; our belongings; **i ~i** our family; our own people; **è dei ~i** he's one of us.

'nota sf (segno) mark; (comunicazione scritta, MUS) note; (fattura) bill; (elenco) list; **degno di ~** noteworthy, worthy of note.

no'tabile ag notable; (persona) important ♦ sm prominent citizen.

no'taio sm notary.

no'tare vt (segnare: errori) to mark; (registrare) to note (down), write down; (rilevare, osservare) to note, notice; **farsi ~** to get o.s. noticed.

notazi'one [notat'tsjone] sf (MUS) notation.

no'tevole ag (talento) notable, remarkable; (peso) considerable.

no'tifica, che sf notification.

notifi'care vt (DIR): **~ qc a qn** to notify sb of sth, give sb notice of sth.

no'tizia [no'tittsja] sf (piece of) news sg;

(informazione) piece of information; **~e** sfpl (informazioni) news sg; information sg; **notizi'ario** sm (RADIO, TV, STAMPA) news sg.

'noto, a ag (well-)known.

notorietà sf fame; notoriety.

no'torio, a ag well-known; (peg) notorious.

not'tambulo, a sm/f night-bird (fig).

not'tata sf night.

'notte sf night; **di ~** at night; (durante la notte) in the night, during the night; **peggio che andar di ~** worse than ever; **~ bianca** sleepless night; **notte'tempo** av at night; during the night.

not'turno, a ag nocturnal; (servizio, guardiano) night cpd.

no'vanta num ninety; **novan'tesimo, a** num ninetieth; **novan'tina** sf: **una novantina (di)** about ninety.

'nove num nine.

nove'cento [nove'tʃɛnto] num nine hundred ♦ sm: **il N~** the twentieth century.

no'vella sf (LETTERATURA) short story.

novel'lino, a ag (pivello) green, inexperienced.

no'vello, a ag (piante, patate) new; (insalata, verdura) early; (sposo) newly-married.

no'vembre sm November.

novi'lunio sm (ASTR) new moon.

novità sf inv novelty; (innovazione) innovation; (cosa originale, insolita) something new; (notizia) (piece of) news sg; **le ~ della moda** the latest fashions.

novizi'ato [novit'tsjato] sm (REL) novitiate; (tirocinio) apprenticeship.

no'vizio, a [no'vittsjo] sm/f (REL) novice; (tirocinante) beginner, apprentice.

nozi'one [not'tsjone] sf notion, idea; **~i** sfpl (rudimenti) basic knowledge sg, rudiments.

'nozze ['nɔttse] sfpl wedding sg, marriage sg; **~ d'argento/d'oro** silver/golden wedding sg.

ns. abbr (COMM) = **nostro**.

'nube sf cloud; **nubi'fragio** sm

cloudburst.

'nubile *ag* (*donna*) unmarried, single.

'nuca *sf* nape of the neck.

nucle'are *ag* nuclear.

'nucleo *sm* nucleus; (*gruppo*) team, unit, group; (*MIL, POLIZIA*) squad; **il ~ familiare** the family unit.

nu'dista, i, e *sm/f* nudist.

'nudo, a *ag* (*persona*) bare, naked, nude; (*membra*) bare, naked; (*montagna*) bare ♦ *sm* (*ARTE*) nude.

'nugolo *sm*: **un ~ di** a whole host of.

'nulla *pron, av* = **niente** ♦ *sm*: **il ~** nothing.

nulla'osta *sm inv* authorization.

nul'lità *sf inv* nullity; (*persona*) non-entity.

'nullo, a *ag* useless, worthless; (*DIR*) null (and void); (*SPORT*): **incontro ~** draw.

nume'rale *ag, sm* numeral.

nume'rare *vt* to number; **nume-razi'one** *sf* numbering; (*araba, decimale*) notation.

nu'merico, a, ci, che *ag* numerical.

'numero *sm* number; (*romano, arabo*) numeral; (*di spettacolo*) act, turn; **~ civico** house number; **~ 'roso, a** *ag* numerous, many; (*con sostantivo sg: adunanza etc*) large.

'nunzio ['nuntsjo] *sm* (*REL*) nuncio.

nu'ocere ['nwɔtʃere] *vi*: **~ a** to harm, damage; **nuoci'uto, a** *pp di* **nuocere**.

nu'ora *sf* daughter-in-law.

nuo'tare *vi* to swim; (*galleggiare: oggetti*) to float; **nuota'tore, 'trice** *sm/f* swimmer; **nu'oto** *sm* swimming.

nu'ova *sf* (*notizia*) (piece) of news *sg*; *vedi anche* **nuovo**.

nuova'mente *av* again.

Nu'ova Ze'landa [-dze'landa] *sf*: **la ~** New Zealand.

nu'ovo, a *ag* new; **di ~** again; **~ fiammante** *o* **di zecca** brand-new.

nutri'ente *ag* nutritious, nourishing.

nutri'mento *sm* food, nourishment.

nu'trire *vt* to feed; (*fig: sentimenti*) to harbour, nurse; **nutri'tivo, a** *ag* nutritional; (*alimento*) nutritious; **nutrizi'one** *sf* nutrition.

'nuvola *sf* cloud; **'nuvolo, a** *ag*, **nuvo'loso, a** *ag* cloudy.

nuzi'ale [nut'tsjale] *ag* nuptial; wedding *cpd*.

O

o (*dav V spesso* **od**) *cong* or; **~ ... ~** either ... or; **~ l'uno ~ l'altro** either (of them).

O. *abbr* (= *ovest*) W.

'oasi *sf inv* oasis.

obbedi'ente *etc* = **ubbidiente** *etc*.

obbli'gare *vt* (*costringere*): **~ qn a fare** to force *o* oblige sb to do; (*DIR*) to bind; **~rsi** *vr*: **~rsi a fare** to undertake to do; **obbli'gato, a** *ag* (*costretto, grato*) obliged; (*percorso, tappa*) set, fixed; **obbliga'torio, a** *ag* compulsory, obligatory; **obbligazi'one** *sf* obligation; (*COMM*) bond, debenture; **'obbligo, ghi** *sm* obligation; (*dovere*) duty; **avere l'obbligo di fare, essere nell'obbligo di fare** to be obliged to do; **essere d'obbligo** (*discorso, applauso*) to be called for.

ob'brobrio *sm* disgrace; (*fig*) mess, eyesore.

o'beso, a *ag* obese.

obiet'tare *vt*: **~ che** to object that; **~ su qc** to object to sth, raise objections concerning sth.

obiet'tivo, a *ag* objective ♦ *sm* (*OTTICA, FOT*) lens *sg*, objective; (*MIL, fig*) objective.

obiet'tore *sm* objector; **~ di coscienza** conscientious objector.

obiezi'one [objet'tsjone] *sf* objection.

obi'torio *sm* morgue, mortuary.

o'bliquo, a *ag* oblique; (*inclinato*) slanting; (*fig*) devious, underhand; **sguardo ~** sidelong glance.

oblò *sm inv* porthole.

o'blungo, a, ghi, ghe *ag* oblong.

'oboe *sm* (*MUS*) oboe.

obsole'scenza [obsoleʃ'ʃentsa] *sf* (*ECON*) obsolescence.

'oca (*pl* **'oche**) *sf* goose.

occasi'one *sf* (*caso favorevole*)

opportunity; (*causa, motivo, circostanza*) occasion; (*COMM*) bargain; **d'~** (*a buon prezzo*) bargain *cpd*; (*usato*) secondhand.

occhi'aia [ok'kjaja] *sf* eye socket; **avere le ~e** to have shadows under one's eyes.

occhi'ali [ok'kjali] *smpl* glasses, spectacles; **~ da sole** sunglasses.

occhi'ata [ok'kjata] *sf* look, glance; **dare un'~ a** to have a look at.

occhieggi'are [okkjed'dʒare] *vi* (*apparire qua e là*) to peep (out).

occhi'ello [ok'kjɛllo] *sm* buttonhole; (*asola*) eyelet.

'occhio ['ɔkkjo] *sm* eye; **~!** careful!, watch out!; **a ~ nudo** with the naked eye; **a quattr'~i** privately, tête-à-tête; **dare all'~** *o* **nell'~ a qn** to catch sb's eye; **fare l'~ a qc** to get used to sth; **tenere d'~ qn** to keep an eye on sb; **vedere di buon/mal ~ qc** to look favourably/unfavourably on sth.

occhio'lino [okkjo'lino] *sm*: **fare l'~ a qn** to wink at sb.

occiden'tale [ottʃiden'tale] *ag* western ♦ *sm/f* Westerner.

occi'dente [ottʃi'dɛnte] *sm* west; (*POL*): **l'O~** the West; **a ~** in the west.

oc'cipite [ot'tʃipite] *sm* back of the head, occiput.

oc'cludere *vt* to block; **occlusi'one** *sf* blockage, obstruction; **oc'cluso, a** *pp di* **occludere**.

occor'rente *ag* necessary ♦ *sm* all that is necessary.

occor'renza [okkor'rɛntsa] *sf* necessity, need; **all'~** in case of need.

oc'correre *vi* to be needed, be required ♦ *vb impers*: **occorre farlo** it must be done; **occorre che tu parta** you must leave, you'll have to leave; **mi occorrono i soldi** I need the money; **oc'corso, a** *pp di* **occorrere**.

occul'tare *vt* to hide, conceal.

oc'culto, a *ag* hidden, concealed; (*scienze, forze*) occult.

occu'pare *vt* to occupy; (*manodopera*) to employ; (*ingombrare*) to occupy, take up; **~rsi** *vr* to occupy o.s., keep

o.s. busy; (*impiegarsi*) to get a job; **~rsi di** (*interessarsi*) to take an interest in; (*prendersi cura di*) to look after, take care of; **occu'pato, a** *ag* (*MIL, POL*) occupied; (*persona: affaccendato*) busy; (*posto, sedia*) taken; (*toilette, TEL*) engaged; **occupazi'one** *sf* occupation; (*impiego, lavoro*) job; (*ECON*) employment.

o'ceano [o'tʃɛano] *sm* ocean.

'ocra *sf* ochre.

ocu'lare *ag* ocular, eye *cpd*; **testimone ~** eye witness.

ocu'lato, a *ag* (*attento*) cautious, prudent; (*accorto*) shrewd.

ocu'lista, i, e *sm/f* eye specialist, oculist.

'ode *sf* ode.

odi'are *vt* to hate, detest.

odi'erno, a *ag* today's, of today; (*attuale*) present.

'odio *sm* hatred; **avere in ~ qc/qn** to hate *o* detest sth/sb; **odi'oso, a** *ag* hateful, odious.

odo'rare *vt* (*annusare*) to smell; (*profumare*) to perfume, scent ♦ *vi*: **~ (di)** to smell (of); **odo'rato** *sm* sense of smell.

o'dore *sm* smell; **gli ~i** *smpl* (*CUC*) (aromatic) herbs; **odo'roso, a** *ag* sweet-smelling.

of'fendere *vt* to offend; (*violare*) to break, violate; (*insultare*) to insult; (*ferire*) to hurt; **~rsi** *vr* (*con senso reciproco*) to insult one another; (*risentirsi*): **~rsi (di)** to take offence (at), be offended (by); **offen'sivo, a** *ag*, *sf* offensive.

offe'rente *sm* (*in aste*): **al maggior ~** to the highest bidder.

of'ferta *sf* offer; (*donazione, anche REL*) offering; (*in gara d'appalto*) tender; (*in aste*) bid; (*ECON*) supply; **"~e d'impiego"** "situations vacant"; **fare un'~a** to make an offer; to tender; to bid.

of'ferto, a *pp di* **offrire**.

of'fesa *sf* insult, affront; (*MIL*) attack; (*DIR*) offence; *vedi anche* **offeso**.

of'feso, a *pp di* **offendere** ♦ *ag*

offended; (*fisicamente*) hurt, injured ♦ *sm/f* offended party; **essere ~ con qn** to be annoyed with sb; **parte ~a** (*DIR*) plaintiff.

offi'cina [offi'tʃina] *sf* workshop.

of'frire *vt* to offer; **~rsi** *vr* (*proporsi*) to offer (o.s.), volunteer; (*occasione*) to present itself; (*esporsi*): **~rsi a** to expose o.s. to; **ti offro da bere** I'll buy you a drink.

offus'care *vt* to obscure, darken; (*fig: intelletto*) to dim, cloud; (: *fama*) to obscure, overshadow; **~rsi** *vr* to grow dark; to cloud, grow dim; to be obscured.

of'talmico, a, ci, che *ag* ophthalmic.

oggettività [oddʒettivi'ta] *sf* objectivity.

ogget'tivo, a [oddʒet'tivo] *ag* objective.

og'getto [od'dʒetto] *sm* object; (*materia, argomento*) subject (matter); **~i smarriti** lost property *sg*.

'oggi ['ɔddʒi] *av, sm* today; **~ a otto a** week today; **oggigi'orno** *av* nowadays.

o'giva [o'dʒiva] *sf* ogive, pointed arch.

'ogni ['oɲɲi] *det* every, each; (*tutti*) all; (*con valore distributivo*) every; **~ uomo** è mortale all men are mortal; **viene ~ due giorni** he comes every two days; **~ cosa** everything; **ad ~ costo** at all costs, at any price; **in ~ luogo** everywhere; **~ tanto** every so often; **~ volta che** every time that.

Ognis'santi [oɲɲis'santi] *sm* All Saints' Day.

o'gnuno [oɲ'ɲuno] *pron* everyone, everybody.

'ohi *escl* oh!; (*esprimere dolore*) ow!

ohimè *escl* oh dear!

O'landa *sf*: **l'~** Holland; **olan'dese** *ag* Dutch ♦ *sm* (*LING*) Dutch ♦ *sm/f* Dutchman/woman; **gli Olandesi** the Dutch.

oleo'dotto *sm* oil pipeline.

ole'oso, a *ag* oily; (*che contiene olio*) oil-yielding.

ol'fatto *sm* sense of smell.

oli'are *vt* to oil.

oli'era *sf* oil cruet.

olim'piadi *sfpl* Olympic games; **o'limpico, a, ci, che** *ag* Olympic.

'olio *sm* oil; **sott'~** (*CUC*) in oil; **~ di fegato di merluzzo** cod liver oil; **~ d'oliva** olive oil; **~ di semi** vegetable oil.

o'liva *sf* olive; **oli'vastro, a** *ag* olive(-coloured); (*carnagione*) sallow; **oli'veto** *sm* olive grove; **o'livo** *sm* olive tree.

'olmo *sm* elm.

oltraggi'are [oltrad'dʒare] *vt* to outrage; to offend gravely.

ol'traggio [ol'traddʒo] *sm* outrage; offence, insult; **~ a pubblico ufficiale** (*DIR*) insulting a public official; **~ al pudore** (*DIR*) indecent behaviour; **oltraggi'oso, a** *ag* offensive.

ol'tralpe *av* beyond the Alps.

ol'tranza [ol'trantsa] *sf*: **a ~** to the last, to the bitter end.

'oltre *av* (*più in là*) further; (*di più: aspettare*) longer, more ♦ *prep* (*di là da*) beyond, over, on the other side of; (*più di*) more than, over; (*in aggiunta a*) besides; (*eccetto*): **~ a** except, apart from; **oltre'mare** *av* overseas; **oltrepas'sare** *vt* to go beyond, exceed.

o'maggio [o'maddʒo] *sm* (*dono*) gift; (*segno di rispetto*) homage, tribute; **~i** *smpl* (*complimenti*) respects; **rendere ~ a** to pay homage *o* tribute to; **in ~** (*copia, biglietto*) complimentary.

ombeli'cale *ag* umbilical.

ombe'lico, chi *sm* navel.

'ombra *sf* (*zona non assolata, fantasma*) shade; (*sagoma scura*) shadow; **sedere all'~** to sit in the shade; **restare nell'~** (*fig*) to remain in obscurity.

ombreggi'are [ombred'dʒare] *vt* to shade.

om'brello *sm* umbrella; **ombrel'lone** *sm* beach umbrella.

om'bretto *sm* eyeshadow.

om'broso, a *ag* shady, shaded; (*cavallo*) nervous, skittish; (*persona*) touchy, easily offended.

ome'lia *sf* (*REL*) homily, sermon.

omeopa'tia *sf* homoeopathy.

omertà *sf* conspiracy of silence.

o'messo, a *pp di* **omettere**.

o'mettere vt to omit, leave out; ~ **di fare** to omit o fail to do.

omi'cida, i, e [omi'tʃida] ag homicidal, murderous ♦ sm/f murderer/eress.

omi'cidio [omi'tʃidjo] sm murder; ~ **colposo** culpable homicide.

omissi'one sf omission; ~ **di soccorso** (DIR) failure to stop and give assistance.

omogeneiz'zato [omodʒeneid'dzato] sm baby food.

omo'geneo, a [omo'dʒɛneo] ag homogeneous.

omolo'gare vt to approve, recognize; to ratify.

o'monimo, a sm/f namesake ♦ sm (LING) homonym.

omosessu'ale ag, sm/f homosexual.

'oncia, ce ['ontʃa] sf ounce.

'onda sf wave; **mettere** o **mandare in ~** (RADIO, TV) to broadcast; **andare in ~** (RADIO, TV) to go on the air; ~**e corte/ medie/lunghe** short/medium/long wave; **on'data** sf wave, billow; (fig) wave, surge; **a ondate** in waves; **ondata di caldo** heatwave.

'onde cong (affinché: con il congiuntivo) so that, in order that; (: con l'infinito) so as to, in order to.

ondeggi'are [onded'dʒare] vi (acqua) to ripple; (muoversi sulle onde: barca) to rock, roll; (fig: muoversi come le onde, barcollare) to sway; (: essere incerto) to waver.

ondula'torio, a ag undulating; (FISICA) undulatory, wave cpd.

ondulazi'one [ondulat'tsjone] sf undulation; (acconciatura) wave.

'onere sm burden; ~**i fiscali** taxes; **one'roso, a** ag (fig) heavy, onerous.

onestà sf honesty.

o'nesto, a ag (probo, retto) honest; (giusto) fair; (casto) chaste, virtuous.

'onice ['ɔnitʃe] sf onyx.

onnipo'tente ag omnipotent.

onnisci'ente [onniʃ'ʃente] ag omniscient.

onniveg'gente [onnivedʒ'dʒɛnte] ag all-seeing.

ono'mastico, ci sm name-day.

ono'ranze [ono'rantse] sfpl honours.

ono'rare vt to honour; (far onore a) to do credit to; ~**rsi** vr: ~**rsi di** to feel honoured at, be proud of.

ono'rario, a ag honorary ♦ sm fee.

o'nore sm honour; **in ~ di** in honour of; **fare gli ~i di casa** to play host (o hostess); **fare ~ a** to honour; (pranzo) to do justice to; (famiglia) to be a credit to; **farsi ~** to distinguish o.s.; **ono'revole** ag honourable ♦ sm/f (POL) ≈ Member of Parliament (BRIT), ≈ Congressman/woman (US); **onorifi'cenza** sf honour; decoration; **ono'rifico, a, ci, che** ag honorary.

'onta sf shame, disgrace.

'O.N.U. ['ɔnu] sigla f (= Organizzazione delle Nazioni Unite) UN, UNO.

o'paco, a, chi, che ag (vetro) opaque; (metallo) dull, matt.

o'pale sm o f opal.

'opera sf work; (azione rilevante) action, deed, work; (MUS) work; opus; (: melodramma) opera; (: teatro) opera house; (ente) institution, organization; ~ **d'arte** work of art; ~ **lirica** (grand) opera; ~**e pubbliche** public works.

ope'raio, a ag working-class; workers' ♦ sm/f worker; **classe ~a** working class.

ope'rare vt to carry out, make; (MED) to operate on ♦ vi to operate, work; (rimedio) to act, work; (MED) to operate; ~**rsi** vr to occur, take place; (MED) to have an operation; ~**rsi d'appendicite** to have one's appendix out; **opera'tivo, a** ag operative, operating; **opera'tore, 'trice** sm/f operator; (TV, CINEMA) cameraman; **operatore economico** agent, broker; **operatore turistico** tour operator; **opera'torio, a** ag (MED) operating; **operazi'one** sf operation.

ope'retta sf (MUS) operetta, light opera.

ope'roso, a ag busy, active, hard-working.

opi'ficio [opi'fitʃo] sm factory, works pl.

opini'one sf opinion.

'**oppio** sm opium.

oppo'nente ag opposing ♦ sm/f opponent.

op'porre vt to oppose; **opporsi** vr: **opporsi (a qc)** to oppose (sth); to object (to sth); **~ resistenza/un rifiuto** to offer resistance/refuse.

opportu'nista, i, e sm/f opportunist.

opportunità sf inv opportunity; (convenienza) opportuneness, timeliness.

oppor'tuno, a ag timely, opportune.

opposi'tore, 'trice sm/f opposer, opponent.

opposizi'one [oppozit'tsjone] sf opposition; (DIR) objection.

op'posto, a pp di **opporre** ♦ ag opposite; (opinioni) conflicting ♦ sm opposite, contrary; **all'~** on the contrary.

oppressi'one sf oppression.

oppres'sivo, a ag oppressive.

op'presso, a pp di **opprimere**.

oppres'sore sm oppressor.

op'primere vt (premere, gravare) to weigh down; (estenuare: sog: caldo) to suffocate, oppress; (tiranneggiare: popolo) to oppress.

oppu'gnare [oppuɲ'ɲare] vt (fig) to refute.

op'pure cong or (else).

op'tare vi: **~ per** to opt for.

o'puscolo sm booklet, pamphlet.

opzi'one [op'tsjone] sf option.

'**ora**¹ sf (60 minuti) hour; (momento) time; **che ~ è?, che ~e sono?** what time is it?; **non veder l'~ di fare** to long to do, look forward to doing; **di buon'~** early; **alla buon'~**! at last!; **~ legale** o **estiva** summer time (BRIT), daylight saving time (US); **~ locale** local time; **~ di punta** (AUT) rush hour.

ora² av (adesso) now; (poco fa): **è uscito proprio ~** he's just gone out; (tra poco) presently, in a minute; (correlativo): **~ ... ~** now ... now; **d'~ in avanti** o **poi** from now on; **or ~** just now, a moment ago; **5 anni** o **sono 5 years ago; **~ come ~** right now, at present.

o'racolo sm oracle.

'**orafo** sm goldsmith.

o'rale ag, sm oral.

ora'mai av = **ormai**.

o'rario, a ag hourly; (fuso, segnale) time cpd; (velocità) per hour ♦ sm timetable, schedule; (di ufficio, visite etc) hours pl, time(s pl).

ora'tore, 'trice sm/f speaker; orator.

ora'toria sf (arte) oratory.

ora'torio, a ag oratorical ♦ sm (REL) oratory; (MUS) oratorio.

ora'zione [orat'tsjone] sf (REL) prayer; (discorso) speech, oration.

or'bene cong so, well (then).

'**orbita** sf (ASTR, FISICA) orbit; (ANAT) (eye-)socket.

or'chestra [or'kɛstra] sf orchestra; **or-ches'trale** ag orchestral ♦ sm/f orchestra player; **orches'trare** vt to orchestrate; (fig) to mount, stage-manage.

orchi'dea [orki'dɛa] sf orchid.

'**orco, chi** sm ogre.

'**orda** sf horde.

or'digno [or'diɲɲo] sm (esplosivo) explosive device.

ordi'nale ag, sm ordinal.

ordina'mento sm order, arrangement; (regolamento) regulations pl, rules pl; **~ scolastico/giuridico** education/legal system.

ordi'nanza [ordi'nantsa] sf (DIR, MIL) order; (persona: MIL) orderly, batman; **d'~** (MIL) regulation cpd.

ordi'nare vt (mettere in ordine) to arrange, organize; (COMM) to order; (prescrivere: medicina) to prescribe; (comandare): **~ a qn di fare qc** to order o command sb to do sth; (REL) to ordain.

ordi'nario, a ag (comune) ordinary; everyday; standard; (grossolano) coarse, common ♦ sm ordinary; (INS: di università) full professor.

ordi'nato, a ag tidy, orderly.

ordinazi'one [ordinat'tsjone] sf (COMM) order; (REL) ordination; **eseguire qc su ~** to make sth to order.

'**ordine** sm order; (carattere): **d'~ pratico** of a practical nature; **all'~**

(*COMM: assegno*) to order; **di prim'~** first-class; **fino a nuovo ~** until further notice; **essere in ~** (*documenti*) to be in order; (*stanza, persona*) to be tidy; **mettere in ~** to put in order, tidy (up); **~ del giorno** (*di seduta*) agenda; (*MIL*) order of the day; **~ di pagamento** (*COMM*) order for payment; **l'~ pubblico** law and order; **~i (sacri)** (*REL*) holy orders.

or'dire *vt* (*fig*) to plot, scheme; **or'dito** *sm* (*di tessuto*) warp.

orec'chino [orek'kino] *sm* earring.

o'recchio [o'rekkjo] (*pl(f)* **o'recchie**) *sm* (*ANAT*) ear.

orecchi'oni [orek'kjoni] *smpl* (*MED*) mumps *sg*.

o'refice [o'rɛfitʃe] *sm* goldsmith; jeweller; **orefice'ria** *sf* (*arte*) goldsmith's art; (*negozio*) jeweller's (shop).

'orfano, a *ag* orphan(ed) ♦ *sm/f* orphan; **~ di padre/madre** fatherless/motherless; **orfano'trofio** *sm* orphanage.

orga'netto *sm* barrel organ; (*fam: armonica a bocca*) mouth organ; (: *fisarmonica*) accordion.

or'ganico, a, ci, che *ag* organic ♦ *sm* personnel, staff.

organi'gramma, i *sm* organization chart.

orga'nismo *sm* (*BIOL*) organism; (*corpo umano*) body; (*AMM*) body, organism.

organiz'zare [organid'dzare] *vt* to organize; **~rsi** *vr* to get organized; **organizza'tore, 'trice** *ag* organizing ♦ *sm/f* organizer; **organizzazi'one** *sf* organization.

'organo *sm* organ; (*di congegno*) part; (*portavoce*) spokesman, mouthpiece.

or'gasmo *sm* (*FISIOL*) orgasm; (*fig*) agitation, anxiety.

'orgia, ge ['ordʒa] *sf* orgy.

or'goglio [or'gɔʎʎo] *sm* pride; **orgogli'oso, a** *ag* proud.

orien'tale *ag* oriental; eastern; east.

orienta'mento *sm* positioning; orientation; direction; **senso di ~** sense of direction; **perdere l'~** to lose one's bearings; **~ professionale** careers guidance.

orien'tare *vt* (*situare*) to position; (*fig*) to direct, orientate; **~rsi** *vr* to find one's bearings; (*fig: tendere*) to tend, lean; (: *indirizzarsi*): **~rsi verso** to take up, go in for.

ori'ente *sm* east; **l'O~** the East, the Orient; **a ~** in the east.

o'rigano *sm* oregano.

origi'nale [oridʒi'nale] *ag* original; (*bizzarro*) eccentric ♦ *sm* original; **originalità** *sf* originality; eccentricity.

origi'nare [oridʒi'nare] *vt* to bring about, produce ♦ *vi*: **~ da** to arise o spring from.

origi'nario, a [oridʒi'narjo] *ag* original; **essere ~ di** to be a native of; (*provenire da*) to originate from; to be native to.

o'rigine [o'ridʒine] *sf* origin; **all'~** originally; **d'~ inglese** of English origin; **dare ~ a** to give rise to.

origli'are [oriʎ'ʎare] *vi*: **~ (a)** to eavesdrop (on).

o'rina *sf* urine; **ori'nale** *sm* chamberpot.

ori'nare *vi* to urinate ♦ *vt* to pass; **orina'toio** *sm* (*public*) urinal.

ori'undo, a *ag*: **essere ~ di Milano** *etc* to be of Milanese *etc* extraction o origin ♦ *sm/f* person of foreign extraction o origin.

orizzon'tale [oriddzon'tale] *ag* horizontal.

oriz'zonte [orid'dzonte] *sm* horizon.

or'lare *vt* to hem.

'orlo *sm* edge, border; (*di recipiente*) rim, brim; (*di vestito etc*) hem.

'orma *sf* (*di persona*) footprint; (*di animale*) track; (*impronta, traccia*) mark, trace.

or'mai *av* by now, by this time; (*adesso*) now; (*quasi*) almost, nearly.

ormeggi'are [ormed'dʒare] *vt* (*NAUT*) to moor; **or'meggio** *sm* (*atto*) mooring *no pl*; (*luogo*) moorings *pl*.

or'mone *sm* hormone.

ornamen'tale *ag* ornamental, decorative.

orna'mento *sm* ornament, decoration.
or'nare *vt* to adorn, decorate; **~rsi** *vr*:
~rsi (di) to deck o.s. (out) (with);
or'nato, a *ag* ornate.
ornitolo'gia [ornitolo'dʒia] *sf* ornithology.
'oro *sm* gold; **d'~, in ~** gold *cpd*; **d'~**
(*colore, occasione*) golden; (*persona*)
marvellous.
orologe'ria [orolodʒe'ria] *sf* watchmaking *no pl*; watchmaker's (shop); clockmaker's (shop); **bomba a ~** time bomb.
orologi'aio [orolo'dʒajo] *sm* watchmaker; clockmaker.
oro'logio [oro'lɔdʒo] *sm* clock; (*da tasca, da polso*) watch; **~ da polso**
wristwatch; **~ al quarzo** quartz watch;
~ a sveglia alarm clock.
o'roscopo *sm* horoscope.
or'rendo, a *ag* (*spaventoso*) horrible,
awful; (*bruttissimo*) hideous.
or'ribile *ag* horrible.
'orrido, a *ag* fearful, horrid.
orripi'lante *ag* hair-raising, horrifying.
or'rore *sm* horror; **avere in ~** qn/qc to
loathe *o* detest sb/sth; **mi fanno ~** I
loathe *o* detest them.
orsacchi'otto [orsak'kjɔtto] *sm* teddy
bear.
'orso *sm* bear; **~ bruno/bianco** brown/
polar bear.
or'taggio [or'taddʒo] *sm* vegetable.
or'tica, che *sf* (stinging) nettle.
orti'caria *sf* nettle rash.
orticol'tura *sf* horticulture.
'orto *sm* vegetable garden, kitchen
garden; (*AGR*) market garden (*BRIT*),
truck farm (*US*).
orto'dosso, a *ag* orthodox.
ortogra'fia *sf* spelling.
orto'lano, a *sm/f* (*venditore*) greengrocer (*BRIT*), produce dealer (*US*).
ortope'dia *sf* orthopaedics *sg*;
orto'pedico, a, ci, che *ag* orthopaedic ♦
sm orthopaedic specialist.
orzai'olo [ordza'jɔlo] *sm* (*MED*) stye.
or'zata [or'dzata] *sf* barley water.
'orzo ['ordzo] *sm* barley.
o'sare *vt, vi* to dare; **~ fare** to dare
(to) do.

oscenità [oʃʃeni'ta] *sf inv* obscenity.
o'sceno, a [oʃ'ʃeno] *ag* obscene;
(*ripugnante*) ghastly.
oscil'lare [oʃʃil'lare] *vi* (*pendolo*) to
swing; (*dondolare*: al vento *etc*) to
rock; (*variare*) to fluctuate; (*TECN*) to
oscillate; (*fig*): **~ fra** to waver *o*
hesitate between; **oscillazi'one** *sf*
oscillation; (*di prezzi, temperatura*)
fluctuation.
oscura'mento *sm* darkening; obscuring; (*in tempo di guerra*) blackout.
oscu'rare *vt* to darken, obscure; (*fig*)
to obscure; **~rsi** *vr* (*cielo*) to darken,
cloud over; (*persona*): **si oscurò in**
volto his face clouded over.
os'curo, a *ag* dark; (*fig*) obscure;
humble, lowly ♦ *sm*: **all'~** in the dark;
tenere qn all'~ di qc to keep sb in the
dark about sth.
ospe'dale *sm* hospital; **ospedali'ero, a**
ag hospital *cpd*.
ospi'tale *ag* hospitable; **ospitalità** *sf*
hospitality.
ospi'tare *vt* to give hospitality to;
(*sog: albergo*) to accommodate.
'ospite *sm/f* (*persona che ospita*) host/
hostess; (*persona ospitata*) guest.
os'pizio [os'pittsjo] *sm* (*per vecchi etc*)
home.
'ossa *sfpl vedi* osso.
ossa'tura *sf* (*ANAT*) skeletal structure,
frame; (*TECN, fig*) framework.
'osseo, a *ag* bony; (*tessuto etc*) bone
cpd.
os'sequio *sm* deference, respect; **~i**
smpl (*saluto*) respects, regards;
ossequi'oso, a *ag* obsequious.
osser'vanza [osser'vantsa] *sf*
observance.
osser'vare *vt* to observe, watch;
(*esaminare*) to examine; (*notare,
rilevare*) to notice, observe; (*DIR: la
legge*) to observe, respect; (*mantenere:
silenzio*) to keep, observe; **far ~ qc a
qn** to point sth out to sb; **osserva'tore,
'trice** *ag* observant, perceptive ♦ *sm/f*
observer; **osserva'torio** *sm* (*ASTR*)
observatory; (*MIL*) observation post;
osservazi'one *sf* observation; (*di legge*

etc) observance; *(considerazione critica)* observation, remark; *(rimprovero)* reproof; **in osservazione** under observation.

ossessio'nare *vt* to obsess, haunt; *(tormentare)* to torment, harass.

ossessi'one *sf* obsession.

os'sesso, a *ag (spiritato)* possessed.

os'sia *cong* that is, to be precise.

ossi'dare *vt* to oxidize; **~rsi** *vr* to oxidize.

'ossido *sm* oxide; **~ di carbonio** carbon monoxide.

ossige'nare [ossidʒe'nare] *vt* to oxygenate; *(decolorare)* to bleach; **acqua ossigenata** hydrogen peroxide.

os'sigeno *sm* oxygen.

'osso *(pl(f)* **ossa** *nel senso ANAT) sm* bone; **d'~** *(bottone etc)* of bone, bone *cpd.*

osso'buco *(pl* **ossi'buchi)** *sm (CUC)* marrowbone; (: *piatto) stew made with knuckle of veal in tomato sauce.*

os'suto, a *ag* bony.

ostaco'lare *vt* to block, obstruct.

os'tacolo *sm* obstacle; *(EQUITAZIONE)* hurdle, jump.

os'taggio [os'taddʒo] *sm* hostage.

'oste, os'tessa *sm/f* innkeeper.

osteggi'are [osted'dʒare] *vt* to oppose, be opposed to.

os'tello *sm*: **~ della gioventù** youth hostel.

osten'tare *vt* to make a show of, flaunt; **ostentazi'one** *sf* ostentation, show.

oste'ria *sf* inn.

os'tessa *sf vedi* **oste.**

os'tetrica *sf* midwife.

os'tetrico, a, ci, che *ag* obstetric ♦ *sm* obstetrician.

'ostia *sf (REL)* host; *(per medicinali)* wafer.

'ostico, a, ci, che *ag (fig)* harsh; hard, difficult; unpleasant.

os'tile *ag* hostile; **ostilità** *sf inv* hostility ♦ *sfpl (MIL)* hostilities.

osti'narsi *vr* to insist, dig one's heels in; **~ a fare** to persist (obstinately) in doing; **osti'nato, a** *ag (caparbio)*

obstinate; *(tenace)* persistent, determined; **ostinazi'one** *sf* obstinacy; persistence.

ostra'cismo [ostra'tʃizmo] *sm* ostracism.

'ostrica, che *sf* oyster.

ostru'ire *vt* to obstruct, block; **ostruzi'one** *sf* obstruction, blockage.

'otre *sm (recipiente)* goatskin.

ottago'nale *ag* octagonal.

ot'tagono *sm* octagon.

ot'tanta *num* eighty; **ottan'tesimo, a** *num* eightieth; **ottan'tina** *sf*: **una ottantina (di)** about eighty.

ot'tava *sf* octave.

ot'tavo, a *num* eighth.

ottempe'rare *vi*: **~ a** to comply with, obey.

ottene'brare *vt* to darken; *(fig)* to cloud.

otte'nere *vt* to obtain, get; *(risultato)* to achieve, obtain.

'ottica *sf (scienza)* optics *sg; (FOT: lenti, prismi etc)* optics *pl.*

'ottico, a, ci, che *ag (della vista: nervo)* optic; *(dell'ottica)* optical ♦ *sm* optician.

ottima'mente *av* excellently, very well.

otti'mismo *sm* optimism; **otti'mista, i, e** *sm/f* optimist.

'ottimo, a *ag* excellent, very good.

'otto *num* eight.

ot'tobre *sm* October.

otto'cento [otto'tʃento] *num* eight hundred ♦ *sm*: **l'O~** the nineteenth century.

ot'tone *sm* brass; **gli ~i** *(MUS)* the brass.

ot'tundere *vt (fig)* to dull.

ottu'rare *vt* to close (up); *(dente)* to fill; **ottura'tore** *sm (FOT)* shutter; *(nelle armi)* breechblock; **otturazi'one** *sf* closing (up); *(dentaria)* filling.

ot'tuso, a *pp di* **ottundere** ♦ *ag (MAT, fig)* obtuse; *(suono)* dull.

o'vaia *sf (ANAT)* ovary.

o'vaio *sm* = **ovaia.**

o'vale *ag, sm* oval.

o'vatta *sf* cotton wool; *(per imbottire)* padding, wadding; **ovat'tare** *vt (fig:*

smorzare) to muffle.

ovazi'one [ovat'tsjone] *sf* ovation.

'ovest *sm* west.

o'vile *sm* pen, enclosure.

o'vino, a *ag* sheep *cpd*, ovine.

ovulazi'one [ovulat'tsjone] *sf* ovulation.

'ovulo *sm* (*FISIOL*) ovum.

o'vunque *av* = **dovunque**.

ov'vero *cong* (*ossia*) that is, to be precise; (*oppure*) or (else).

ovvi'are *vi*: ~ **a** to obviate.

'ovvio, a *ag* obvious.

ozi'are [ot'tsjare] *vi* to laze, idle.

'ozio ['ɔttsjo] *sm* idleness; (*tempo libero*) leisure; **ore d'**~ leisure time; **stare in** ~ to be idle; **ozi'oso, a** *ag* idle.

o'zono [o'dzɔno] *sm* ozone.

P

pa'cato, a *ag* quiet, calm.

pac'chetto [pak'ketto] *sm* packet; ~ **azionario** (*COMM*) shareholding.

'pacco, chi *sm* parcel; (*involto*) bundle.

'pace ['patʃe] *sf* peace; **darsi** ~ to resign o.s.

pacifi'care [patʃifi'kare] *vt* (*riconciliare*) to reconcile, make peace between; (*mettere in pace*) to pacify.

pa'cifico, a, ci, che [pa'tʃi:fiko] *ag* (*persona*) peaceable; (*vita*) peaceful; (*fig: indiscusso*) indisputable; (: *ovvio*) obvious, clear ♦ *sm*: **il P**~, **l'Oceano P**~ the Pacific (Ocean).

paci'fista, i, e [patʃi'fista] *sm/f* pacifist.

pa'della *sf* frying pan; (*per infermi*) bedpan.

padigli'one [padiʎ'ʎone] *sm* pavilion, (*AUT*) roof.

'Padova *sf* Padua.

'padre *sm* father; ~**i** *smpl* (*antenati*) forefathers; **pa'drino** *sm* godfather.

padro'nanza [padro'nantsa] *sf* command, mastery.

pa'drone, a *sm/f* master/mistress; (*proprietario*) owner; (*datore di lavoro*) employer; **essere** ~ **di sé** to be in control of o.s.; ~ **di casa** master/mistress

of the house; (*per gli inquilini*) landlord/lady; **padroneggi'are** *vt* (*fig: sentimenti*) to master, control; (: *materia*) to master, know thoroughly; **padroneggiarsi** *vr* to control o.s.

pae'saggio [pae'zaddʒo] *sm* landscape.

pae'sano, a *ag* country *cpd* ♦ *sm/f* villager; countryman/woman.

pa'ese *sm* (*nazione*) country, nation; (*terra*) country, land; (*villaggio*) village; ~ **di provenienza** country of origin; **i P~i Bassi** the Netherlands.

paf'futo, a *ag* chubby, plump.

'paga, ghe *sf* pay, wages *pl*.

paga'mento *sm* payment.

pa'gano, a *ag, sm/f* pagan.

pa'gare *vt* to pay; (*acquisto, fig: colpa*) to pay for; (*contraccambiare*) to repay, pay back ♦ *vi* to pay; **quanto l'hai pagato?** how much did you pay for it?; ~ **con carta di credito** to pay by credit card; ~ **in contanti** to pay cash.

pa'gella [pa'dʒɛlla] *sf* (*INS*) report card.

'paggio ['paddʒo] *sm* page(boy).

paghe'rò [page'rɔ] *sm inv* acknowledgement of a debt, IOU.

'pagina ['padʒina] *sf* page.

'paglia ['paʎʎa] *sf* straw.

pagliac'cetto [paʎʎat'tʃetto] *sm* (*per bambini*) rompers *pl*.

pagli'accio [paʎ'ʎattʃo] *sm* clown.

pagli'etta [paʎ'ʎetta] *sf* (*cappello per uomo*) (straw) boater; (*per tegami etc*) steel wool.

pa'gnotta [paɲ'ɲɔtta] *sf* round loaf.

'paio (*pl(f)* **'paia**) *sm* pair; **un** ~ **di** (*alcuni*) a couple of.

pai'olo *sm* (copper) pot.

paiu'olo *sm* = **paiolo**.

'pala *sf* shovel; (*di remo, ventilatore, elica*) blade; (*di ruota*) paddle.

pa'lato *sm* palate.

pa'lazzo [pa'lattso] *sm* (*reggia*) palace; (*edificio*) building; ~ **di giustizia** courthouse; ~ **dello sport** sports stadium.

pal'chetto [pal'ketto] *sm* shelf.

'palco, chi *sm* (*TEATRO*) box; (*tavolato*) platform, stand; (*ripiano*) layer.

palco'scenico, ci [palkoʃ'ʃeniko] *sm*

(*TEATRO*) stage.

pale'sare *vt* to reveal, disclose; ~**rsi** *vr* to reveal *o* show o.s.

pa'lese *ag* clear, evident.

Pales'tina *sf*: **la ~** Palestine.

pa'lestra *sf* gymnasium; (*esercizio atletico*) exercise, training; (*fig*) training ground, school.

pa'letta *sf* spade; (*per il focolare*) shovel; (*del capostazione*) signalling disc.

pa'letto *sm* stake, peg; (*spranga*) bolt.

palio *sm* (*gara*): **il P~** horserace run at Siena; **mettere qc in ~** to offer sth as a prize.

palla *sf* ball; (*pallottola*) bullet; **~ canestro** *sm* basketball; **~ nuoto** *sm* water polo; **~ volo** *sm* volleyball.

palleggi'are [palled'dʒare] *vi* (*CALCIO*) to practise with the ball; (*TENNIS*) to knock up.

pallia'tivo *sm* palliative; (*fig*) stopgap measure.

pallido, a *ag* pale.

pal'lina *sf* (*bilia*) marble.

pallon'cino [pallon'tʃino] *sm* balloon; (*lampioncino*) Chinese lantern.

pal'lone *sm* (*palla*) ball; (*CALCIO*) football; (*aerostato*) balloon; **gioco del ~** football.

pal'lore *sm* pallor, paleness.

pal'lottola *sf* pellet; (*proiettile*) bullet.

palma *sf* (*ANAT*) = **palmo**; (*BOT, simbolo*) palm; **~ da datteri** date palm.

palmo *sm* (*ANAT*) palm; **restare con un ~ di naso** to be badly disappointed.

palo *sm* (*legno appuntito*) stake; (*sostegno*) pole; **fare da** *o* **il ~** (*fig*) to act as look-out.

palom'baro *sm* diver.

pa'lombo *sm* (*pesce*) dogfish.

pal'pare *vt* to feel, finger.

'palpebra *sf* eyelid.

palpi'tare *vi* (*cuore, polso*) to beat; (: *più forte*) to pound, throb; (*fremere*) to quiver; **'palpito** *sm* (*del cuore*) beat; (*fig*: *d'amore etc*) throb.

paltò *sm inv* overcoat.

pa'lude *sf* marsh, swamp; **palu'doso, a** *ag* marshy, swampy.

pa'lustre *ag* marsh *cpd*, swamp *cpd*.

'pampino *sm* vine leaf.

'panca, che *sf* bench.

pan'cetta [pan'tʃetta] *sf* (*CUC*) bacon.

pan'chetto [pan'ketto] *sm* stool; footstool.

pan'china [pan'kina] *sf* garden seat; (*di giardino pubblico*) (park) bench.

'pancia, ce ['pantʃa] *sf* belly, stomach; **mettere** *o* **fare ~** to be getting a paunch; **avere mal di ~** to have stomachache *o* a sore stomach.

panci'otto [pan'tʃɔtto] *sm* waistcoat.

'pancreas *sm inv* pancreas.

'panda *sm inv* panda.

pande'monio *sm* pandemonium.

'pane *sm* bread; (*pagnotta*) loaf (of bread); (*forma*): **un ~ di burro/cera** *etc* a pat of butter/bar of wax *etc*; **guadagnarsi il ~** to earn one's living; **~ a cassetta** sliced bread; **~ integrale** wholemeal bread; **~ tostato** toast.

panette'ria *sf* (*forno*) bakery; (*negozio*) baker's (shop), bakery.

panetti'ere, a *sm/f* baker.

panet'tone *sm a kind of spiced brioche with sultanas, eaten at Christmas.*

pangrat'tato *sm* breadcrumbs *pl*.

'panico, a, ci, che *ag*, *sm* panic.

pani'ere *sm* basket.

pani'ficio [pani'fitʃo] *sm* (*forno*) bakery; (*negozio*) baker's (shop), bakery.

pa'nino *sm* roll; **~ imbottito** filled roll; sandwich; **panino'teca** *sf* sandwich bar.

'panna *sf* (*CUC*) cream; (*TECN*) = **panne**; **~ da cucina** cooking cream; **~ montata** whipped cream.

'panne *sf inv*: **essere in ~** (*AUT*) to have broken down.

pan'nello *sm* panel.

'panno *sm* cloth; **~i** *smpl* (*abiti*) clothes; **mettiti nei miei ~i** (*fig*) put yourself in my shoes.

pan'nocchia [pan'nɔkkja] *sf* (*di mais etc*) ear.

panno'lino *sm* (*per bambini*) nappy (*BRIT*), diaper (*US*).

pano'rama, i *sm* panorama; **pano'ramico, a, ci, che** *ag* panoramic; **strada panoramica** scenic route.

panta'loni *smpl* trousers (*BRIT*), pants (*US*), pair *sg* of trousers *o* pants.

pan'tano *sm* bog.

pan'tera *sf* panther.

pan'tofola *sf* slipper.

panto'mima *sf* pantomime.

pan'zana [pan'tsana] *sf* fib, tall story.

pao'nazzo, a [pao'nattso] *ag* purple.

'papa, i *sm* pope.

papà *sm inv* dad(dy).

pa'pale *ag* papal.

pa'pato *sm* papacy.

pa'pavero *sm* poppy.

'papera *sf* (*fig*) slip of the tongue, blunder; *vedi anche* **papero**.

'papero, a *sm/f* (*ZOOL*) gosling.

pa'piro *sm* papyrus.

'pappa *sf* baby cereal.

pappa'gallo *sm* parrot; (*fig*: *uomo*) Romeo, wolf.

pappa'gorgia, ge [pappa'gɔrdʒa] *sf* double chin.

pap'pare *vt* (*fam*: *anche*: ~*rsi*) to gobble up.

'para *sf*: **suole di** ~ crepe soles.

pa'rabola *sf* (*MAT*) parabola; (*REL*) parable.

para'brezza [para'breddza] *sm inv* (*AUT*) windscreen (*BRIT*), windshield (*US*).

paraca'dute *sm inv* parachute.

para'carro *sm* kerbstone (*BRIT*), curbstone (*US*).

para'diso *sm* paradise.

parados'sale *ag* paradoxical.

para'dosso *sm* paradox.

para'fango, ghi *sm* mudguard.

paraf'fina *sf* paraffin, paraffin wax.

para'fulmine *sm* lightning conductor.

pa'raggi [pa'raddʒi] *smpl*: **nei** ~ in the vicinity, in the neighbourhood.

parago'nare *vt*: ~ **con/a** to compare with/to.

para'gone *sm* comparison; (*esempio analogo*) analogy, parallel; **reggere al** ~ to stand comparison.

pa'ragrafo *sm* paragraph.

pa'ralisi *sf* paralysis; **para'litico, a, ci, che** *ag*, *sm/f* paralytic.

paraliz'zare [paralid'dzare] *vt* to paralyze.

paral'lela *sf* parallel (line); ~**e** *sfpl* (*attrezzo ginnico*) parallel bars.

paral'lelo, a *ag* parallel ♦ *sm* (*GEO*) parallel; (*comparazione*): **fare un** ~ **tra** to draw a parallel between.

pa'rame *sm* lampshade.

pa'rametro *sm* parameter.

para'noia *sf* paranoia; **para'noico, a, ci, che** *ag*, *sm/f* paranoid.

para'occhi [para'ɔkki] *smpl* blinkers.

para'piglia [para'piʎʎa] *sm* commotion, uproar.

pa'rare *vt* (*addobbare*) to adorn, deck; (*proteggere*) to shield, protect; (*scansare*: *colpo*) to parry; (*CALCIO*) to save ♦ *vi*: **dove vuole andare a** ~? what are you driving at?; ~**rsi** *vr* (*presentarsi*) to appear, present o.s.

para'sole *sm inv* parasol, sunshade.

paras'sita, i *sm* parasite.

pa'rata *sf* (*SPORT*) save; (*MIL*) review, parade.

para'tia *sf* (*di nave*) bulkhead.

para'urti *sm inv* (*AUT*) bumper.

para'vento *sm* folding screen; **fare da** ~ **a qn** (*fig*) to shield sb.

par'cella [par'tʃɛlla] *sf* account, fee (*of lawyer etc*).

parcheggi'are [parked'dʒare] *vt* to park; **par'cheggio** *sm* parking *no pl*; (*luogo*) car park; (*singolo posto*) parking space.

par'chimetro [par'kimetro] *sm* parking meter.

'parco¹, chi *sm* park; (*spazio per deposito*) depot; (*complesso di veicoli*) fleet.

'parco², a, chi, che *ag*: ~ **(in)** (*sobrio*) moderate (in); (*avaro*) sparing (with).

pa'recchio, a [pa'rekkjo] *det* quite a lot of; (*tempo*) quite a lot of, a long; ~**i, e** *det pl* quite a lot of, several ♦ *pron* quite a lot, quite a bit; (*tempo*) quite a while, a long time; ~**i, e** *pron pl* quite a lot, several ♦ *av* (*con ag*) quite, rather; (*con vb*) quite a lot, quite a bit.

pareggi'are [pared'dʒare] *vt* to make equal; (*terreno*) to level, make level; (*bilancio, conti*) to balance ♦ *vi* (*SPORT*) to draw; **pa'reggio** *sm* (ECON) balance; (SPORT) draw.

paren'tado *sm* relatives *pl*, relations *pl*.

pa'rente *sm/f* relative, relation.

paren'tela *sf* (*vincolo di sangue, fig*) relationship; (*insieme dei parenti*) relations *pl*, relatives *pl*.

pa'rentesi *sf* (*segno grafico*) bracket, parenthesis; (*frase incisa*) parenthesis; (*digressione*) parenthesis, digression.

pa'rere *sm* (*opinione*) opinion; (*consiglio*) advice, opinion; **a mio ~** in my opinion ♦ *vi* to seem, appear ♦ *vb impers*: **pare che** it seems *o* appears that, they say that; **mi pare che** it seems to me that; **mi pare di sì** I think so; **fai come ti pare** do as you like; **che ti pare del mio libro?** what do you think of my book?

pa'rete *sf* wall.

'pari *ag inv* (*uguale*) equal, same; (*in giochi*) equal; drawn, tied; (MAT) even ♦ *sm inv* (POL: di Gran Bretagna) peer ♦ *sm/f inv* peer, equal; **copiato ~ ~** copied word for word; **alla ~** on the same level; **ragazza alla ~** au pair girl; **mettersi alla ~ con** to place o.s. on the same level as; **mettersi in ~ con** to catch up with; **andare di ~ passo con** qn to keep pace with sb.

Pa'rigi [pa'ridʒi] *sf* Paris.

pa'riglia [pa'riʎʎa] *sf* pair; **rendere la ~** to give tit for tat.

parità *sf* parity, equality; (SPORT) draw, tie.

parlamen'tare *ag* parliamentary ♦ *sm/f* ≈ Member of Parliament (BRIT), ≈ Congressman/woman (US) ♦ *vi* to negotiate, parley.

parla'mento *sm* parliament.

parlan'tina (*fam*) *sf* talkativeness; **avere una buona ~** to have the gift of the gab.

par'lare *vi* to speak, talk; (*confidare cose segrete*) to talk ♦ *vt* to speak; **~ (a qn) di** to speak *o* talk (to sb) about; **parla'torio** (*di carcere etc*) visiting room; (REL) parlour.

parmigi'ano [parmi'dʒano] *sm* (*grana*)

Parmesan (cheese).

paro'dia *sf* parody.

pa'rola *sf* word; (*facoltà*) speech; **~e** *sfpl* (*chiacchiere*) talk *sg*; **chiedere la ~** to ask permission to speak; **prendere la ~** to take the floor; **~ d'onore** word of honour; **~ d'ordine** (MIL) password; **~e incrociate** crossword (puzzle) *sg*; **paro'laccia, ce** *sf* bad word, swearword.

par'rocchia [par'rɔkkja] *sf* parish; parish church.

'parroco, ci *sm* parish priest.

par'rucca, che *sf* wig.

parrucchi'ere, a [parruk'kjɛre] *sm/f* hairdresser ♦ *sm* barber.

parsi'monia *sf* frugality, thrift.

'parso, a *pp di* **parere**.

'parte *sf* part; (*lato*) side; (*quota spettante a ciascuno*) share; (*direzione*) direction; (POL) party; faction; (DIR) party; **a ~ ag** separate ♦ *av* separately; **scherzi a ~** joking aside; **a ciò** apart from that; **da ~** (*in disparte*) to one side, aside; **d'altra ~** on the other hand; **da ~ di** (*per conto di*) on behalf of; **da ~ mia** as far as I'm concerned, as for me; **da ~ a ~** right through; **da ogni ~** on all sides, everywhere; (*moto da luogo*) from all sides; **da nessuna ~** nowhere; **da questa ~** (*in questa direzione*) this way; **prendere ~ a qc** to take part in sth; **mettere da ~** to put aside; **mettere qn a ~ di qc** to inform sb of sth.

parteci'pare [partetʃi'pare] *vi*: **~ a** to take part in, participate in; (*utili etc*) to share in; (*spese etc*) to contribute to; (*dolore, successo di qn*) to share (in); **partecipazi'one** *sf* participation; sharing; (ECON) interest; **partecipazione agli utili** profit-sharing; **partecipazioni di nozze** *wedding announcement card*; **par'tecipe** *ag* participating; **essere partecipe di** to take part in, participate in; to share (in); (*consapevole*) to be aware of.

parteggi'are [parted'dʒare] *vi*: **~ per** to side with, be on the side of.

par'tenza [par'tɛntsa] *sf* departure; (SPORT) start; **essere in ~** to be about to leave, be leaving.

parti'cella [parti'tʃella] *sf* particle.

parti'cipio [parti'tʃipjo] *sm* participle.

partico'lare *ag* (*specifico*) particular; (*proprio*) personal, private; (*speciale*) special, particular; (*caratteristico*) distinctive, characteristic; (*fuori dal comune*) peculiar ♦ *sm* detail, particular; **in** ~ in particular, particularly; **particolarità** *sf inv* particularity; detail; characteristic, feature.

partigi'ano, a [parti'dʒano] *ag* partisan ♦ *sm* (*fautore*) supporter, champion; (*MIL*) partisan.

par'tire *vi* to go, leave; (*allontanarsi*) to go (*o drive etc*) away *o* off; (*petardo, colpo*) to go off; (*fig: avere inizio, SPORT*) to start; **sono partita da Roma alle 7** I left Rome at 7; **il volo parte da Ciampino** the flight leaves from Ciampino; **a** ~ **da** from.

par'tita *sf* (*COMM*) lot, consignment; (*ECON: registrazione*) entry, item; (*CARTE, SPORT: gioco*) game; (: *competizione*) match, game; ~ **di caccia** hunting party; ~ **IVA** VAT registration number.

par'tito *sm* (*POL*) party; (*decisione*) decision, resolution; (*persona da maritare*) match.

parti'tura *sf* (*MUS*) score.

'parto *sm* (*MED*) delivery, (child)birth; labour; **parto'rire** *vt* to give birth to; (*fig*) to produce.

parzi'ale [par'tsjale] *ag* (*limitato*) partial; (*non obiettivo*) biased, partial.

'pascere ['paʃʃere] *vi* to graze ♦ *vt* (*brucare*) to graze on; (*far pascolare*) to graze, pasture; **pasci'uto, a** *pp di* **pascere**.

pasco'lare *vt, vi* to graze.

'pascolo *sm* pasture.

'Pasqua *sf* Easter; **pas'quale** *ag* Easter *cpd.*

pas'sabile *ag* fairly good, passable.

pas'saggio [pas'saddʒo] *sm* passing *no pl*, passage; (*traversata*) crossing *no pl*, passage; (*luogo, prezzo della traversata, brano di libro etc*) passage;

(*su veicolo altrui*) lift (*BRIT*), ride; (*SPORT*) pass; **di** ~ (*persona*) passing through; ~ **pedonale/a livello** pedestrian/level (*BRIT*) *o* grade (*US*) crossing.

pas'sante *sm/f* passer-by ♦ *sm* loop.

passa'porto *sm* passport.

pas'sare *vi* (*andare*) to go; (*veicolo, pedone*) to pass (by), go by; (*fare una breve sosta: postino etc*) to come, call; (: *amico: per fare una visita*) to call *o* drop in; (*sole, aria, luce*) to get through; (*trascorrere: giorni, tempo*) to pass, go by; (*fig: proposta di legge*) to be passed; (: *dolore*) to pass, go away; (*CARTE*) to pass ♦ *vt* (*attraversare*) to cross; (*trasmettere: messaggio*): ~ **qc a qn** to pass sth on to sb; (*dare*): ~ **qc a qn** to pass sth to sb, give sb sth; (*trascorrere: tempo*) to spend; (*superare: esame*) to pass; (*triturare: verdura*) to strain; (*approvare*) to pass, approve; (*oltrepassare, sorpassare: anche fig*) to go beyond, pass; (*fig: subire*) to go through; ~ **da ... a** to pass from ... to; ~ **di padre in figlio** to be handed down *o* to pass from father to son; ~ **per** (*anche fig*) to go through; ~ **per stupido/un genio** to be taken for a fool/a genius; ~ **sopra** (*anche fig*) to pass over; ~ **attraverso** (*anche fig*) to go through; ~ **alla storia** to pass into history; ~ **a un esame** to go up (to the next class) after an exam; ~ **inosservato** to go unnoticed; ~ **di moda** to go out of fashion; **le passo il Signor X** (*al telefono*) here is Mr X; I'm putting you through to Mr X; **lasciar qn/qc** to let sb/sth through; **passarsela: come te la passi?** how are you getting on *o* along?

pas'sata *sf*: **dare una** ~ **di vernice a qc** to give sth a coat of paint; **dare una** ~ **al giornale** to have a look at the paper, skim through the paper.

passa'tempo *sm* pastime, hobby.

pas'sato, a *ag* past; (*sfiorito*) faded ♦ *sm* past; (*LING*) past (tense); ~ **prossimo** (*LING*) present perfect; ~ **remoto** (*LING*) past historic; ~ **di**

verdura (*CUC*) vegetable purée.

passaver'dura *sm inv* vegetable mill.

passeg'gero, a [passed'dʒero] *ag* passing ♦ *sm/f* passenger.

passeggi'are [passed'dʒare] *vi* to go for a walk; (*in veicolo*) to go for a drive; **passeggi'ata** *sf* walk; drive; (*luogo*) promenade; **fare una passeggiata** to go for a walk (*o* drive); **passeg'gino** *sm* pushchair (*BRIT*), stroller (*US*); **pas'seggio** *sm* walk, stroll; (*luogo*) promenade.

passe'rella *sf* footbridge; (*di nave, aereo*) gangway; (*pedana*) catwalk.

'passero *sm* sparrow.

pas'sibile *ag*: ~ **di** liable to.

passi'one *sf* passion.

pas'sivo, a *ag* passive ♦ *sm* (*LING*) passive; (*ECON*) debit; (: *complesso dei debiti*) liabilities *pl*.

'passo *sm* step; (*andatura*) pace; (*rumore*) (foot)step; (*orma*) footprint; (*passaggio, fig: brano*) passage; (*valico*) pass; **a ~ d'uomo** at walking pace; ~ **(a)** ~ step by step; **fare due** *o* **quattro ~i** to go for a walk *o* a stroll; **di questo** ~ at this rate; **"~ carraio"** "vehicle entrance — keep clear".

'pasta *sf* (*CUC*) dough; (: *impasto per dolce*) pastry; (: *anche:* ~ *alimentare*) pasta; (*massa molle di materia*) paste; (*fig: indole*) nature; **~e** *sfpl* (*pasticcini*) pastries; ~ **in brodo** noodle soup.

pastasci'utta [pastaʃ'ʃutta] *sf* pasta.

pas'tella *sf* batter.

pas'tello *sm* pastel.

pas'tetta *sf* (*CUC*) = **pastella**.

pas'ticca, che *sf* = **pastiglia**.

pasticce'ria [pastittʃe'ria] *sf* (*pasticcini*) pastries *pl*, cakes *pl*; (*negozio*) cake shop; (*arte*) confectionery.

pasticci'are [pastit'tʃare] *vt* to mess up, make a mess of ♦ *vi* to make a mess.

pasticci'ere, a [pastit'tʃere] *sm/f* pastrycook; confectioner.

pas'ticcio [pas'tittʃo] *sm* (*CUC*) pie; (*lavoro disordinato, imbroglio*) mess; **trovarsi nei ~i** to get into trouble.

pasti'ficio [pasti'fitʃo] *sm* pasta factory.

pas'tiglia [pas'tiʎʎa] *sf* pastille, lozenge.

pas'tina *sf* small pasta shapes used in soup.

pasti'naca, che *sf* parsnip.

'pasto *sm* meal.

pas'tore *sm* shepherd; (*REL*) pastor, minister; (*anche: cane* ~) sheepdog.

pastoriz'zare [pastorid'dzare] *vt* to pasteurize.

pas'toso, a *ag* doughy; pasty; (*fig: voce, colore*) mellow, soft.

pas'trano *sm* greatcoat.

pas'tura *sf* pasture.

pa'tata *sf* potato; **~e fritte** chips (*BRIT*), French fries; **pata'tine** *sfpl* (*potato*) crisps.

pata'trac *sm* (*crollo: anche fig*) crash.

pa'tella *sf* (*ZOOL*) limpet.

pa'tema, i *sm* anxiety, worry.

pa'tente *sf* licence; (*anche:* ~ *di guida*) driving licence (*BRIT*), driver's license (*US*).

paternità *sf* paternity, fatherhood.

pa'terno, a *ag* (*affetto, consigli*) fatherly; (*casa, autorità*) paternal.

pa'tetico, a, ci, che *ag* pathetic; (*commovente*) moving, touching.

pa'tibolo *sm* gallows *sg*, scaffold.

'patina *sf* (*su rame etc*) patina; (*sulla lingua*) fur, coating.

pa'tire *vt, vi* to suffer.

pa'tito, a *sm/f* enthusiast, fan, lover.

patolo'gia [patolo'dʒia] *sf* pathology; **pato'logico, a, ci, che** *ag* pathological.

'patria *sf* homeland.

patri'arca, chi *sm* patriarch.

pa'trigno [pa'triɲɲo] *sm* stepfather.

patri'monio *sm* estate, property; (*fig*) heritage.

patri'ota, i, e *sm/f* patriot; **patri'ottico, a, ci, che** *ag* patriotic; **patriot'tismo** *sm* patriotism.

patroci'nare [patrotʃi'nare] *vt* (*DIR: difendere*) to defend; (*sostenere*) to sponsor, support; **patro'cinio** *sm* defence; support, sponsorship.

patro'nato *sm* patronage; (*istituzione benefica*) charitable institution *o* society.

pa'trono *sm* (*REL*) patron saint; (*socio di patronato*) patron; (*DIR*) counsel.

'**patta** *sf* flap; (*dei pantaloni*) fly.
patteggi'are [patted'dʒare] *vt, vi* to negotiate.
patti'naggio [patti'naddʒo] *sm* skating.
patti'nare *vi* to skate; ~ **sul ghiaccio** to ice-skate; **pattina'tore, 'trice** *sm/f* skater; '**pattino**[1] *sm* skate; (*di slitta*) runner; (*AER*) skid; (*TECN*) sliding block; **pattini (da ghiaccio)** (ice) skates; **pattini a rotelle** roller skates; **pat'tino**[2] *sm* (*barca*) *kind of pedalo with oars.*
'**patto** *sm* (*accordo*) pact, agreement; (*condizione*) term, condition; **a** ~ **che** on condition that.
pat'tuglia [pat'tuʎʎa] *sf* (*MIL*) patrol.
pattu'ire *vt* to reach an agreement on.
pattumi'era *sf* (dust)bin (*BRIT*), ashcan (*US*).
pa'ura *sf* fear; **aver** ~ **di/di fare/che** to be frightened *o* afraid of/of doing/that; **far** ~ **a** to frighten; **per** ~ **di/che** for fear of/that; **pau'roso, a** *ag* (*che fa paura*) frightening; (*che ha paura*) fearful, timorous.
'**pausa** *sf* (*sosta*) break; (*nel parlare, MUS*) pause.
pavi'mento *sm* floor.
pa'vone *sm* peacock; **pavoneggi'arsi** *vr* to strut about, show off.
pazien'tare [pattsjen'tare] *vi* to be patient.
pazi'ente [pat'tsjɛnte] *ag, sm/f* patient; **pazi'enza** *sf* patience.
paz'zesco, a, schi, sche [pat'tsesko] *ag* mad, crazy.
paz'zia [pat'tsia] *sf* (*MED*) madness, insanity; (*azione*) folly; (*di azione, decisione*) madness, folly.
'**pazzo, a** ['pattso] *ag* (*MED*) mad, insane; (*strano*) wild, mad ♦ *sm/f* madman/woman; ~ **di** (*gioia, amore etc*) mad *o* crazy with; ~ **per qc/qn** mad *o* crazy about sth/sb.
PCI *sigla m* = **Partito Comunista Italiano.**
'**pecca, che** *sf* defect, flaw, fault.
peccami'noso, a *ag* sinful.
pec'care *vi* to sin; (*fig*) to err.
pec'cato *sm* sin; **è un** ~ **che** it's a pity

that; **che** ~! what a shame *o* pity!
pecca'tore, 'trice *sm/f* sinner.
'**pece** ['petʃe] *sf* pitch.
Pe'chino [pe'kino] *sf* Peking.
'**pecora** *sf* sheep; **peco'raio** *sm* shep herd; **peco'rino** *sm* sheep's milk cheese.
peculi'are *ag*: ~ **di** peculiar to.
pe'daggio [pe'daddʒo] *sm* toll.
pedago'gia [pedago'dʒia] *sf* pedagogy, educational methods *pl.*
peda'lare *vi* to pedal; (*andare in bicicletta*) to cycle.
pe'dale *sm* pedal.
pe'dana *sf* footboard; (*SPORT: nel salto*) springboard; (: *nella scherma*) piste.
pe'dante *ag* pedantic ♦ *sm/f* pedant.
pe'data *sf* (*impronta*) footprint; (*colpo*) kick; **prendere a** ~**e qn/qc** to kick sb/sth.
pede'rasta, i *sm* pederast; homosexual.
pedi'atra, i, e *sm/f* paediatrician; **pedia'tria** *sf* paediatrics *sg.*
pedi'cure *sm/f inv* chiropodist.
pe'dina *sf* (*della dama*) draughtsman (*BRIT*), draftsman (*US*); (*fig*) pawn.
pedi'nare *vt* to shadow, tail.
pedo'nale *ag* pedestrian.
pe'done, a *sm/f* pedestrian ♦ *sm* (*SCACCHI*) pawn.
'**peggio** ['pɛddʒo] *av, ag inv* worse ♦ *sm o f*: **il** *o* **la** ~ the worst; **alla** ~ at worst, if the worst comes to the worst; **peggiora'mento** *sm* worsening; **peggio'rare** *vt* to make worse, worsen ♦ *vi* to grow worse, worsen; **peggiora'tivo, a** *ag* pejorative; **peggi'ore** *ag* (*comparativo*) worse; (*superlativo*) worst ♦ *sm/f*: **il(la) peggiore** the worst (person).
'**pegno** ['peɲɲo] *sm* (*DIR*) security, pledge; (*nei giochi di società*) forfeit; (*fig*) pledge, token; **dare in** ~ **qc** to pawn sth.
pe'lame *sm* (*di animale*) coat, fur.
pe'lare *vt* (*spennare*) to pluck; (*spellare*) to skin; (*sbucciare*) to peel; (*fig*) to make pay through the nose; ~**rsi** *vr*

to go bald.

pel'lame _sm_ skins _pl_, hides _pl_.

'pelle _sf_ skin; (_di animale_) skin, hide; (_cuoio_) leather; **avere la ~ d'oca** to have goose pimples _o_ goose flesh.

pellegri'naggio [pellegri'naddʒo] _sm_ pilgrimage.

pelle'grino, a _sm/f_ pilgrim.

pelle'rossa (_pl_ **pelli'rosse**) _sm/f_ Red Indian.

pelli'rossa _sm/f_ = **pellerossa**.

pellette'ria _sf_ leather goods _pl_; (_negozio_) leather goods shop.

pelli'cano _sm_ pelican.

pellicce'ria [pellittʃe'ria] _sf_ (_negozio_) furrier's (shop); (_quantità di pellicce_) furs _pl_.

pel'liccia, ce [pel'littʃa] _sf_ (_mantello di animale_) coat, fur; (_indumento_) fur coat.

pel'licola _sf_ (_membrana sottile_) film, layer; (_FOT, CINEMA_) film.

'pelo _sm_ hair; (_pelame_) coat, hair; (_pelliccia_) fur; (_di tappeto_) pile; (_di liquido_) surface; **per un ~: per un ~ non ho perduto il treno** I very nearly missed the train; **c'è mancato un ~ che affogasse** he escaped drowning by the skin of his teeth; **pe'loso, a** _ag_ hairy.

'peltro _sm_ pewter.

pe'luria _sf_ down.

'pena _sf_ (_DIR_) sentence; (_punizione_) punishment; (_sofferenza_) sadness _no pl_, sorrow; (_fatica_) trouble _no pl_, effort; (_difficoltà_) difficulty; **far ~** to be pitiful; **mi fai ~** I feel sorry for you; **prendersi** _o_ **darsi la ~ di fare** to go to the trouble of doing; **~ di morte** death sentence; **~ pecuniaria** fine; **pe'nale** _ag_ penal; **penalità** _sf inv_ penalty; **penaliz'zare** _vt_ (_SPORT_) to penalize.

pe'nare _vi_ (_patire_) to suffer; (_faticare_) to struggle.

pen'dente _ag_ hanging; leaning ♦ _sm_ (_ciondolo_) pendant; (_orecchino_) drop earring; **pen'denza** _sf_ slope, slant; (_grado d'inclinazione_) gradient; (_ECON_) outstanding account.

'pendere _vi_ (_essere appeso_): **~ da** to hang from; (_essere inclinato_) to lean;

(_fig: incombere_): **~ su** to hang over.

pen'dio, 'dii _sm_ slope, slant; (_luogo in pendenza_) slope.

'pendola _sf_ pendulum clock.

pendo'lare _sm/f_ commuter.

'pendolo _sm_ (_peso_) pendulum; (_anche: orologio a ~_) pendulum clock.

'pene _sm_ penis.

pene'trante _ag_ piercing, penetrating.

pene'trare _vi_ to come _o_ get in ♦ _vt_ to penetrate; **~ in** to enter; (_sog: proiettile_) to penetrate; (: _acqua, aria_) to go _o_ come into.

penicil'lina [penitʃil'lina] _sf_ penicillin.

pe'nisola _sf_ peninsula.

peni'tenza [peni'tentsa] _sf_ penitence; (_punizione_) penance.

penitenzi'ario [peniten'tsjarjo] _sm_ prison.

'penna _sf_ (_di uccello_) feather; (_per scrivere_) pen; **~e** _sfpl_ (_CUC_) quills (_type of pasta_); **~ a feltro/stilografica/a sfera** felt-tip/fountain/ballpoint pen.

penna'rello _sm_ felt(-tip) pen.

pennel'lare _vi_ to paint.

pen'nello _sm_ brush; (_per dipingere_) (paint)brush; **a ~** (_perfettamente_) to perfection, perfectly; **~ per la barba** shaving brush.

pen'none _sm_ (_NAUT_) yard; (_stendardo_) banner, standard.

pe'nombra _sf_ half-light, dim light.

pe'noso, a _ag_ painful, distressing; (_faticoso_) tiring, laborious.

pen'sare _vi_ to think ♦ _vt_ to think; (_inventare, escogitare_) to think out; **~ a** to think of; (_amico, vacanze_) to think of _o_ about; (_problema_) to think about; **~ di fare qc** to think of doing sth; **ci penso io** I'll see to _o_ take care of it.

pensi'ero _sm_ thought; (_modo di pensare, dottrina_) thinking _no pl_; (_preoccupazione_) worry, care, trouble; **stare in ~ per qn** to be worried about sb; **pensie'roso, a** _ag_ thoughtful.

'pensile _ag_ hanging.

pensio'nante _sm/f_ (_presso una famiglia_) lodger; (_di albergo_) guest.

pensio'nato, a _sm/f_ pensioner.

pensi'one sf (al prestatore di lavoro) pension; (vitto e alloggio) board and lodging; (albergo) boarding house; **andare in ~** to retire; **mezza ~** half board; **~ completa** full board.

pen'soso, a ag thoughtful, pensive, lost in thought.

pentapar'tito sm five-party government.

Pente'coste sf Pentecost, Whit Sunday (BRIT).

penti'mento sm repentance, contrition.

pen'tirsi vr: **~ di** to repent of; (rammaricarsi) to regret, be sorry for.

'pentola sf pot; **~ a pressione** pressure cooker.

pe'nultimo, a ag last but one (BRIT), next to last, penultimate.

pe'nuria sf shortage.

penzo'lare [pendzo'lare] vi to dangle, hang loosely; **penzo'loni** av dangling, hanging down; **stare penzoloni** to dangle, hang down.

'pepe sm pepper; **~ macinato/in grani** ground/whole pepper.

pepe'rone sm pepper, capsicum; (piccante) chili.

pe'pita sf nugget.

PAROLA CHIAVE

per prep **1** (moto attraverso luogo) through; **i ladri sono passati ~ la finestra** the thieves got in (o out) through the window; **l'ho cercato ~ tutta la casa** I've searched the whole house o all over the house for it

2 (moto a luogo) for, to; **partire ~ la Germania/il mare** to leave for Germany/the sea; **il treno ~ Roma** the Rome train, the train for o to Rome

3 (stato in luogo): **seduto/sdraiato ~ terra** sitting/lying on the ground

4 (tempo) for; **~ anni/lungo tempo** for years/a long time; **~ tutta l'estate** throughout the summer, all summer long; **lo rividi ~ Natale** I saw him again at Christmas; **lo faccio ~ lunedì** I'll do it for Monday

5 (mezzo, maniera) by; **~ lettera/via**

aerea/ferrovia by letter/airmail/rail; **prendere qn ~ un braccio** to take sb by the arm

6 (causa, scopo) for; **assente ~ malattia** absent because of o through o owing to illness; **ottimo ~ il mal di gola** excellent for sore throats

7 (limitazione) for; **è troppo difficile ~ lui** it's too difficult for him; **~ quel che mi riguarda** as far as I'm concerned; **~ poco che sia** however little it may be; **~ questa volta ti perdono** I'll forgive you this time

8 (prezzo, misura) for; (distributivo) a, per; **venduto ~ 3 milioni** sold for 3 million; **1000 lire ~ persona** 1000 lire a o per person; **uno ~ volta** one at a time; **uno ~ uno** one by one; **5 ~ cento** 5 per cent; **3 ~ 4 fa 12** 3 times 4 equals 12; **dividere/moltiplicare 12 ~ 4** to divide/multiply 12 by 4

9 (in qualità di) as; (al posto di) for; **avere qn ~ professore** to have sb as a teacher; **ti ho preso ~ Mario** I mistook you for Mario, I thought you were Mario; **dare ~ morto qn** to give sb up for dead

10 (seguito da vb: finale): **~ fare qc** (so as) to do sth, in order to do sth; (: causale): **~ aver fatto qc** for having done sth; (: consecutivo): **è abbastanza grande ~ andarci da solo** he's big enough to go on his own.

'pera sf pear.

pe'raltro av moreover, what's more.

per'bene ag inv respectable, decent ♦ av (con cura) properly, well.

percentu'ale [pertʃentu'ale] sf percentage.

perce'pire [pertʃe'pire] vt (sentire) to perceive; (ricevere) to receive; **percezi'one** sf perception.

PAROLA CHIAVE

perché [per'ke] av why; **~ no?** why not?; **~ non vuoi andarci?** why don't you want to go?; **spiegami ~ l'hai fatto** tell me why you did it

♦ cong **1** (causale) because; **non posso**

uscire ~ **ho da fare** I can't go out because *o* as I've a lot to do
2 (*finale*) in order that, so that; **te lo do** ~ **tu lo legga** I'm giving it to you so (that) you can read it
3 (*consecutivo*): **è troppo forte** ~ **si possa batterlo** he's too strong to be beaten
♦ *sm inv* reason; **il** ~ **di** the reason for.

perciò [per'tʃɔ] *cong* so, for this (*o* that) reason.

per'correre *vt* (*luogo*) to go all over; (: *paese*) to travel up and down, go all over; (*distanza*) to cover.

per'corso, a *pp di* **percorrere** ♦ *sm* (*tragitto*) journey; (*tratto*) route.

per'cossa *sf* blow.

per'cosso, a *pp di* **percuotere**.

percu'otere *vt* to hit, strike.

percussi'one *sf* percussion; **strumenti a** ~ (*MUS*) percussion instruments.

'**perdere** *vt* to lose; (*lasciarsi sfuggire*) to miss; (*sprecare: tempo, denaro*) to waste; (*mandare in rovina: persona*) to ruin ♦ *vi* to lose; (*serbatoio etc*) to leak; ~**rsi** *vr* (*smarrirsi*) to get lost; (*svanire*) to disappear, vanish; **saper** ~ to be a good loser; **lascia** ~! forget it!, never mind!

perdigi'orno [perdi'dʒorno] *sm/f inv* idler, waster.

'**perdita** *sf* loss; (*spreco*) waste; (*fuoriuscita*) leak; **siamo in** ~ (*COMM*) we are running at a loss; **a** ~ **d'occhio** as far as the eye can see.

perdi'tempo *sm/f inv* waster, idler.

perdo'nare *vt* to pardon, forgive; (*scusare*) to excuse, pardon.

per'dono *sm* forgiveness; (*DIR*) pardon.

perdu'rare *vi* to go on, last; (*perseverare*) to persist.

perduta'mente *av* desperately, passionately.

per'duto, a *pp di* **perdere**.

peregri'nare *vi* to wander, roam.

pe'renne *ag* eternal, perpetual, perennial; (*BOT*) perennial.

peren'torio, a *ag* peremptory;

(*definitivo*) final.

per'fetto, a *ag* perfect ♦ *sm* (*LING*) perfect (tense).

perfezio'nare [perfettsjo'nare] *vt* to improve, perfect; ~**rsi** *vr* to improve.

perfezi'one [perfet'tsjone] *sf* perfection.

'**perfido, a** *ag* perfidious, treacherous.

per'fino *av* even.

perfo'rare *vt* to perforate; to punch a hole (*o* holes) in; (*banda, schede*) to punch; (*trivellare*) to drill; **perfora'tore, 'trice** *sm/f* punch-card operator ♦ *sm* (*utensile*) punch; (*INFORM*): **perforatore di schede** card punch; **perfora'trice** *sf* (*TECN*) boring *o* drilling machine; (*INFORM*) card punch; *vedi anche* **perforatore**; **perforazi'one** *sf* perforation; punching; drilling; (*INFORM*) punch; (*MED*) perforation.

perga'mena *sf* parchment.

perico'lante *ag* precarious.

pe'ricolo *sm* danger; **mettere in** ~ to endanger, put in danger; **perico'loso, a** *ag* dangerous.

perife'ria *sf* periphery; (*di città*) outskirts *pl*.

pe'rifrasi *sf* circumlocution.

pe'rimetro *sm* perimeter.

peri'odico, a, ci, che *ag* periodic(al); (*MAT*) recurring ♦ *sm* periodical.

pe'riodo *sm* period.

peripe'zie [peripet'tsie] *sfpl* ups and downs, vicissitudes.

pe'rire *vi* to perish, die.

pe'rito, a *ag* expert, skilled ♦ *sm/f* expert; (*agronomo, navale*) surveyor; **un** ~ **chimico** a qualified chemist.

pe'rizia [pe'rittsja] *sf* (*abilità*) ability; (*giudizio tecnico*) expert opinion; expert's report.

'**perla** *sf* pearl; **per'lina** *sf* bead.

perlus'trare *vt* to patrol.

perma'loso, a *ag* touchy.

perma'nente *ag* permanent ♦ *sf* permanent wave, perm; **perma'nenza** *sf* permanence; (*soggiorno*) stay.

perma'nere *vi* to remain.

perme'are *vt* to permeate.

per'messo, a *pp di* **permettere** ♦ *sm* (*autorizzazione*) permission, leave;

(*dato a militare, impiegato*) leave; (*licenza*) licence, permit; (*MIL: foglio*) pass; ~?, è ~? (*posso entrare?*) may I come in?; (*posso passare?*) excuse me; ~ **di lavoro/pesca** work/fishing permit.

per'mettere *vt* to allow, permit; ~ **a qn qc/di fare** to allow sb sth/to do; ~**rsi qc/di fare** to allow o.s. sth/to do; (*avere la possibilità*) to afford sth/to do.

per'nacchia [per'nakkja] (*fam*) *sf*: **fare una** ~ to blow a raspberry.

per'nice [per'nitʃe] *sf* partridge.

'perno *sm* pivot.

pernot'tare *vi* to spend the night, stay overnight.

'pero *sm* pear tree.

però *cong* (*ma*) but; (*tuttavia*) however, nevertheless.

pero'rare *vt* (*DIR, fig*): ~ **la causa di qn** to plead sb's case.

perpendico'lare *ag, sf* perpendicular.

perpe'trare *vt* to perpetrate.

perpetu'are *vt* to perpetuate.

per'petuo, a *ag* perpetual.

per'plesso, a *ag* perplexed; uncertain, undecided.

perqui'sire *vt* to search; **perquisizi'one** *sf* (police) search.

persecu'tore *sm* persecutor.

persecuzi'one [persekut'tsjone] *sf* persecution.

persegu'ire *vt* to pursue.

persegui'tare *vt* to persecute.

perseve'rante *ag* persevering.

perseve'rare *vi* to persevere.

'Persia *sf*: **la** ~ Persia.

persi'ana *sf* shutter; ~ **avvolgibile** Venetian blind.

persi'ano, a *ag, sm/f* Persian.

'persico, a, ci, che *ag*: **il golfo P**~ the Persian Gulf.

per'sino *av* = **perfino**.

persis'tente *ag* persistent.

per'sistere *vi* to persist; ~ **a fare** to persist in doing; **persis'tito, a** *pp di* **persistere**.

'perso, a *pp di* **perdere**.

per'sona *sf* person; (*qualcuno*): **una** ~ someone, somebody; (*espressione interrogativa*) +anyone *o* anybody; ~**e** *sfpl*

people; **non c'è** ~ **che ...** there's nobody who ..., there isn't anybody who ....

perso'naggio [perso'naddʒo] *sm* (*persona ragguardevole*) personality, figure; (*tipo*) character, individual; (*LETTERATURA*) character.

perso'nale *ag* personal ♦ *sm* staff; personnel; (*figura fisica*) build.

personalità *sf inv* personality.

personifi'care *vt* to personify; to embody.

perspi'cace [perspi'katʃe] *ag* shrewd, discerning.

persu'adere *vt*: ~ **qn (di qc/a fare)** to persuade sb (of sth/to do); **persuasi'one** *sf* persuasion; **persua'sivo, a** *ag* persuasive; **persu'aso, a** *pp di* **persuadere**.

per'tanto *cong* (*quindi*) so, therefore.

'pertica, che *sf* pole.

perti'nente *ag*: ~ **(a)** relevant (to), pertinent (to).

per'tosse *sf* whooping cough.

per'tugio [per'tudʒo] *sm* hole, opening.

pertur'bare *vt* to disrupt; (*persona*) to disturb, perturb; **perturbazi'one** *sf* disruption; perturbation; **perturbazione atmosferica** atmospheric disturbance.

per'vadere *vt* to pervade; **per'vaso, a** *pp di* **pervadere**.

perve'nire *vi*: ~ **a** to reach, arrive at, come to; (*venire in possesso*): **gli pervenne una fortuna** he inherited a fortune; **far** ~ **qc a** to have sth sent to; **perve'nuto, a** *pp di* **pervenire**.

per'verso, a *ag* depraved; perverse.

perver'tire *vt* to pervert.

p. es. *abbr* (= *per esempio*) e.g.

'pesa *sf* weighing *no pl*; weighbridge.

pe'sante *ag* heavy; (*fig: noioso*) dull, boring.

pe'sare *vt* to weigh ♦ *vi* (*avere un peso*) to weigh; (*essere pesante*) to be heavy; (*fig*) to carry weight; ~ **su** (*fig*) to lie heavy on; to influence; to hang over; **mi pesa sgridarlo** I find it hard to scold him.

'pesca (*pl* **pesche**: *frutto*) *sf* peach; (*il pescare*) fishing; **andare a** ~ to go fishing; ~ **di beneficenza** (*lotteria*) lucky dip; ~ **con la lenza** angling.

pes'care *vt* (*pesce*) to fish for; to catch; (*qc nell'acqua*) to fish out; (*fig*: *trovare*) to get hold of, find.

pesca'tore *sm* fisherman; angler.

'pesce ['peʃʃe] *sm* fish *gen inv*; **P~i** (*dello zodiaco*) Pisces; ~ **d'aprile!** April Fool!; ~ **spada** swordfish; **pe-sce'cane** *sm* shark.

pesche'reccio [peske'rettʃo] *sm* fishing boat.

pesche'ria [peske'ria] *sf* fishmonger's (shop) (*BRIT*), fish store (*US*).

peschi'era [pes'kjɛra] *sf* fishpond.

pesci'vendolo, a [peʃʃi'vendolo] *sm/f* fishmonger (*BRIT*), fish merchant (*US*).

'pesco, schi *sm* peach tree.

pes'coso, a *ag* abounding in fish.

'peso *sm* weight; (*SPORT*) shot; **rubare sul** ~ to give short weight; **essere di** ~ **a qn** (*fig*) to be a burden to sb; ~ **lordo/netto** gross/net weight; ~ **piuma/mosca/gallo/medio/massimo** (*PUGILATO*) feather/fly/bantam/middle/heavyweight.

pessi'mismo *sm* pessimism; **pessi'mista, i, e** *ag* pessimistic ♦ *sm/f* pessimist.

'pessimo, a *ag* very bad, awful.

pes'tare *vt* to tread on, trample on; (*sale, pepe*) to grind; (*uva, aglio*) to crush; (*fig*: *picchiare*): ~ **qn** to beat sb up.

'peste *sf* plague; (*persona*) nuisance, pest.

pes'tello *sm* pestle.

pesti'lenza [pesti'lentsa] *sf* pestilence; (*fetore*) stench.

'pesto, a *ag*: **c'è buio** ~ it's pitch-dark; **occhio** ~ black eye ♦ *sm* (*CUC*) sauce *made with basil, garlic, cheese and oil*.

'petalo *sm* (*BOT*) petal.

pe'tardo *sm* firecracker, banger (*BRIT*).

petizi'one [petit'tsjone] *sf* petition.

'peto (*fam!*) *sm* fart (!).

petrol'chimica [petrol'kimika] *sf* pet-rochemical industry.

petroli'era *sf* (*nave*) oil tanker.

petro'lifero, a *ag* oil-bearing; oil *cpd*.

pe'trolio *sm* oil, petroleum; (*per lampada, fornello*) paraffin.

pettego'lare *vi* to gossip.

pettego'lezzo [pettego'leddzo] *sm* gossip *no pl*; **fare** ~**i** to gossip.

pet'tegolo, a *ag* gossipy ♦ *sm/f* gossip.

petti'nare *vt* to comb (the hair of); ~**rsi** *vr* to comb one's hair; **pettina'tura** *sf* (*acconciatura*) hairstyle.

'pettine *sm* comb; (*ZOOL*) scallop.

petti'rosso *sm* robin.

'petto *sm* chest; (*seno*) breast, bust; (*CUC*: *di carne bovina*) brisket; (: *di pollo etc*) breast; **a doppio** ~ (*abito*) double-breasted; **petto'ruto, a** *ag* broad-chested; full-breasted.

petu'lante *ag* insolent.

'pezza ['pettsa] *sf* piece of cloth; (*toppa*) patch; (*cencio*) rag, cloth.

pez'zato, a [pet'tsato] *ag* piebald.

pez'zente [pet'tsɛnte] *sm/f* beggar.

'pezzo ['pettso] *sm* (*gen*) piece; (*brandello, frammento*) piece, bit; (*di macchina, arnese etc*) part; (*STAMPA*) article; (*di tempo*): **aspettare un** ~ to wait quite a while *o* some time; **in** *o* **a** ~**i** in pieces; **andare in** ~**i** to break into pieces; **un bel** ~ **d'uomo** a fine figure of a man; **abito a due** ~**i** two-piece suit; ~ **di cronaca** (*STAMPA*) report; ~ **grosso** (*fig*) bigwig; ~ **di ricambio** spare part.

pia'cente [pja'tʃɛnte] *ag* attractive, pleasant.

pia'cere [pja'tʃere] *vi* to please; **una ragazza che piace** a likeable girl; an attractive girl; ~ **a: mi piace** I like it; **quei ragazzi non mi piacciono** I don't like those boys; **gli piacerebbe andare al cinema** he would like to go to the cinema ♦ *sm* pleasure; (*favore*) favour; "~!" (*nelle presentazioni*) "pleased to meet you!"; **con** ~ certainly, with pleasure; **per** ~! please; **fare un** ~ **a qn** to do sb a favour; **pia'cevole** *ag* pleasant, agreeable; **piaci'uto, a** *pp di* **piacere**.

pi'aga, ghe *sf* (*lesione*) sore; (*ferita*: *anche fig*) wound; (*fig*: *flagello*) scourge, curse; (: *persona*) pest, nuisance.

piagnis'teo [pjaɲɲis'tɛo] *sm* whining, whimpering.

piagnuco'lare [pjaɲnuko'lare] *vi* to whimper.

pi'alla *sf* (*arnese*) plane; **pial'lare** *vt* to plane.

pi'ana *sf* stretch of level ground; (*più esteso*) plain.

pianeggi'ante [pjaned'dʒante] *ag* flat, level.

piane'rottolo *sm* landing.

pia'neta *sm* (ASTR) planet.

pi'angere ['pjandʒere] *vi* to cry, weep; (*occhi*) to water ♦ *vt* to cry, weep; (*lamentare*) to bewail, lament; ~ **la morte di qn** to mourn sb's death.

pianifi'care *vt* to plan; **pianificazi'one** *sf* planning.

pia'nista, i, e *sm/f* pianist.

pi'ano, a *ag* (*piatto*) flat, level; (MAT) plane; (*facile*) straightforward, simple; (*chiaro*) clear, plain ♦ *av* (*adagio*) slowly; (*a bassa voce*) softly; (*con cautela*) slowly, carefully ♦ *sm* (MAT) plane; (GEO) plain; (*livello*) level, plane; (*di edificio*) floor; (*programma*) plan; (MUS) piano; **pian** ~ very slowly; (*poco a poco*) little by little; **in primo/secondo** ~ in the foreground/background; **di primo** ~ (*fig*) prominent, high-ranking.

piano'forte *sm* piano, pianoforte.

pi'anta *sf* (BOT) plant; (ANAT: *anche*: ~ **del piede**) sole (of the foot); (*grafico*) plan; (*topografica*) map; **in** ~ **stabile** on the permanent staff; **piantagi'one** *sf* plantation; **pian'tare** *vt* to plant; (*conficcare*) to drive *o* hammer in; (*tenda*) to put up, pitch; (*fig: lasciare*) to leave, desert; **~rsi** *vr*: **~rsi davanti a qn** to plant o.s. in front of sb; **piantala!** (*fam*) cut it out!

pianter'reno *sm* ground floor.

pi'anto, a *pp di* **piangere** ♦ *sm* tears *pl*, crying.

pian'tone *sm* (*vigilante*) sentry, guard; (*soldato*) orderly; (AUT) steering column.

pia'nura *sf* plain.

pi'astra *sf* plate; (*di pietra*) slab; (*di fornello*) hotplate; ~ **di registrazione** tape deck; **panino alla** ~ ≈ toasted sandwich.

pias'trella *sf* tile.

pias'trina *sf* (MIL) identity disc.

piatta'forma *sf* (*anche fig*) platform.

piat'tino *sm* saucer.

pi'atto, a *ag* flat; (*fig: scialbo*) dull ♦ *sm* (*recipiente, vivanda*) dish; (*portata*) course; (*parte piana*) flat (part); **~i** *smpl* (MUS) cymbals; ~ **fondo** soup dish; ~ **forte** main course; ~ **del giorno** dish of the day, plat du jour; ~ **del giradischi** turntable; **~i già pronti** (CULIN) ready-cooked dishes.

pi'azza ['pjattsa] *sf* square; (COMM) market; **far** ~ **pulita** to make a clean sweep; ~ **d'armi** (MIL) parade ground; **piaz'zale** *sm* (large) square.

piaz'zare [pjat'tsare] *vt* to place; (COMM) to market, sell; **~rsi** *vr* (SPORT) to be placed.

piaz'zista, i [pjat'tsista] *sm* (COMM) commercial traveller.

piaz'zola [pjat'tsɔla] *sf* (AUT) lay-by.

'picca, che *sf* pike; **~che** *sfpl* (CARTE) spades.

pic'cante *ag* hot, pungent; (*fig*) racy; biting.

pic'carsi *vr*: ~ **di fare** to pride o.s. on one's ability to do; ~ **per qc** to take offence at sth.

pic'chetto [pik'ketto] *sm* (MIL, *di scioperanti*) picket.

picchi'are [pik'kjare] *vt* (*persona: colpire*) to hit, strike; (: *prendere a botte*) to beat (up); (*battere*) to beat; (*sbattere*) to bang ♦ *vi* (*bussare*) to knock; (: *con forza*) to bang; (*colpire*) to hit, strike; (*sole*) to beat down; **picchi'ata** *sf* (*percossa*) beating, thrashing; (AER) dive.

picchiet'tare [pikkjet'tare] *vt* (*punteggiare*) to spot, dot; (*colpire*) to tap.

'picchio ['pikkjo] *sm* woodpecker.

pic'cino, a [pit'tʃino] *ag* tiny, very small.

piccio'naia [pittʃo'naja] *sf* pigeon-loft; (TEATRO): **la** ~ the gods *sg*.

picci'one [pit'tʃone] *sm* pigeon.

'picco, chi *sm* peak; **a** ~ vertically.

'piccolo, a ag small; (oggetto, mano, di età: bambino) small, little (dav sostantivo); (di breve durata: viaggio) short; (fig) mean, petty ♦ sm/f child, little one; ~i smpl (di animale) young pl; **in ~** in miniature.
pic'cone sm pick(-axe).
pic'cozza [pik'kɔttsa] sf ice-axe.
pic'nic sm inv picnic.
pi'docchio [pi'dɔkkjo] sm louse.
pi'ede sm foot; (di mobile) leg; **in ~i** standing; **a ~i** on foot; **a ~i nudi** barefoot; **su due ~i** (fig) at once; **prendere ~** (fig) to gain ground, catch on; **sul ~ di guerra** (MIL) ready for action; **~ di porco** crowbar.
piedes'tallo sm = piedistallo.
piedis'tallo sm pedestal.
pi'ega, ghe sf (piegatura, GEO) fold; (di gonna) pleat; (di pantaloni) crease; (grinza) wrinkle, crease; **prendere una brutta ~** (avvenimento) to take a turn for the worse.
pie'gare vt to fold; (braccia, gambe, testa) to bend ♦ vi to bend; **~rsi** vr to bend; (fig): **~rsi (a)** to yield (to), submit (to); **pieghet'tare** vt to pleat; **pie'ghevole** ag pliable, flexible; (porta) folding; (fig) yielding, docile.
Pie'monte sm: **il ~** Piedmont.
pi'ena sf (di fiume) flood, spate; (gran folla) crowd, throng.
pi'eno, a ag full; (muro, mattone) solid ♦ sm (colmo) height, peak; (carico) full load; **~ di** full of; **in ~ giorno** in broad daylight; **fare il ~ (di benzina)** to fill up (with petrol).
pietà sf pity; (REL) piety; **senza ~** pitiless, merciless; **avere ~ di** (compassione) to pity, feel sorry for; (misericordia) to have pity o mercy on.
pie'tanza [pje'tantsa] sf dish; (main) course.
pie'toso, a ag (compassionevole) pitying, compassionate; (che desta pietà) pitiful.
pi'etra sf stone; **~ preziosa** precious stone, gem; **pie'traia** sf (terreno) stony ground; **pietrifi'care** vt to petrify; (fig) to transfix, paralyze.

'piffero sm (MUS) pipe.
pigi'ama, i [pi'dʒama] sm pyjamas pl.
'pigia 'pigia ['pidʒa'pidʒa] sm crowd, press.
pigi'are [pi'dʒare] vt to press.
pigi'one [pi'dʒone] sf rent.
pigli'are [piʎ'ʎare] vt to take, grab; (afferrare) to catch.
'piglio ['piʎʎo] sm look, expression.
pig'meo, a sm/f pygmy.
'pigna ['piɲɲa] sf pine cone.
pi'gnolo, a [piɲ'ɲɔlo] ag pernickety.
pigo'lare vi to cheep, chirp.
pi'grizia [pi'grittsja] sf laziness.
'pigro, a ag lazy.
'pila sf (catasta, di ponte) pile; (ELETTR) battery; (fam: torcia) torch (BRIT), flashlight.
pi'lastro sm pillar.
'pillola sf pill; **prendere la ~** to be on the pill.
pi'lone sm (di ponte) pier; (di linea elettrica) pylon.
pi'lota, i, e sm/f pilot; (AUT) driver ♦ ag inv pilot cpd; **~ automatico** automatic pilot; **pilo'tare** vt to pilot; to drive.
pi'mento sm pimento, allspice.
pinaco'teca, che sf art gallery.
pi'neta sf pinewood.
ping-'pong [piŋ'pɔŋ] sm table tennis.
'pingue ag fat, corpulent.
pingu'ino sm (ZOOL) penguin.
'pinna sf fin; (di pinguino, spatola di gomma) flipper.
'pino sm pine (tree); **pi'nolo** sm pine kernel.
'pinza ['pintsa] sf pliers pl; (MED) forceps pl; (ZOOL) pincer.
pinzette [pin'tsette] sfpl tweezers.
'pio, a, 'pii, 'pie ag pious; (opere, istituzione) charitable, charity cpd.
pi'oggia, ge ['pjɔddʒa] sf rain; **~ acida** acid rain.
pi'olo sm peg; (di scala) rung.
piom'bare vi to fall heavily; (gettarsi con impeto): **~ su** to fall upon, assail ♦ vt (dente) to fill; **piomba'tura** sf (di dente) filling.
piom'bino sm (sigillo) (lead) seal;

(*del filo a piombo*) plummet; (*PESCA*) sinker.

pi'ombo *sm* (*CHIM*) lead; (*sigillo*) (lead) seal; (*proiettile*) (lead) shot; **a ~** (*cadere*) straight down.

pioni'ere, a *sm/f* pioneer.

pi'oppo *sm* poplar.

pi'overe *vb impers* to rain ♦ *vi* (*fig: scendere dall'alto*) to rain down; (: *affluire in gran numero*): **~ in** to pour into; **pioviggi'nare** *vb impers* to drizzle; **pio'voso, a** *ag* rainy.

pi'ovra *sf* octopus.

'pipa *sf* pipe.

pipì (*fam*) *sf*: **fare ~** to have a wee (wee).

pipis'trello *sm* (*ZOOL*) bat.

pi'ramide *sf* pyramid.

pi'rata, i *sm* pirate; **~ della strada** hit-and-run driver.

Pire'nei *smpl*: **i ~** the Pyrenees.

'pirico, a, ci, che *ag*: **polvere ~a** gunpowder.

pi'rite *sf* pyrite.

pi'rofilo, a *ag* heat-resistant.

pi'roga, ghe *sf* dug-out canoe.

pi'romane *sm/f* pyromaniac; arsonist.

pi'roscafo *sm* steamer, steamship.

pisci'are [piʃ'ʃare] (*fam!*) *vi* to piss (!), pee (!).

pi'scina [piʃ'ʃina] *sf* (swimming) pool; (*stabilimento*) (swimming) baths *pl*.

pi'sello *sm* pea.

piso'lino *sm* nap.

'pista *sf* (*traccia*) track, trail; (*di stadio*) track; (*di pattinaggio*) rink; (*da sci*) run; (*AER*) runway; (*di circo*) ring; **~ da ballo** dance floor.

pis'tacchio [pis'takkjo] *sm* pistachio (tree); pistachio (nut).

pis'tola *sf* pistol, gun.

pis'tone *sm* piston.

pi'tone *sm* python.

pit'tore, 'trice *sm/f* painter; **pitto'resco, a, schi, sche** *ag* picturesque.

pit'tura *sf* painting; **pittu'rare** *vt* to paint.

più *av* **1** (*in maggiore quantità*) more; **~ del solito** more than usual; **in ~, di ~** more; **ne voglio di ~** I want some more; **ci sono 3 persone in o di ~** there are 3 more *o* extra people; **~ o meno** more or less; **per di ~** (*inoltre*) what's more, moreover

2 (*comparativo*) more, *aggettivo corto* +...er; **~ ... di/che** more ... than; **lavoro ~ di te/Paola** I work harder than you/Paola; **è ~ intelligente che ricco** he's more intelligent than rich

3 (*superlativo*) most, *aggettivo corto* +...est; **il ~ grande/intelligente** the biggest/most intelligent; **è quello che compro ~ spesso** that's the one I buy most often; **al ~ presto** as soon as possible; **al ~ tardi** at the latest

4 (*negazione*): **non ... ~** no more, no longer; **non ho ~ soldi** I've got no more money, I don't have any more money; **non lavoro ~** I'm no longer working, I don't work any more; **a ~ non posso** (*gridare*) at the top of one's voice; (*correre*) as fast as one can

5 (*MAT*) plus; **4 ~ 5 fa 9** 4 plus 5 equals 9; **~ 5 gradi** 5 degrees above freezing, plus 5

♦ *prep* plus

♦ *ag inv* **1**: **~ ... (di)** more ... (than); **~ denaro/tempo** more money/time; **~ persone di quante ci aspettassimo** more people than we expected

2 (*numerosi, diversi*) several; **l'aspettai per ~ giorni** I waited for it for several days

♦ *sm* **1** (*la maggior parte*): **il ~ è fatto** most of it is done

2 (*MAT*) plus (sign)

3: **i ~** the majority.

piucchepper'fetto [pjukkepper'fetto] *sm* (*LING*) pluperfect, past perfect.

pi'uma *sf* feather; **piu'maggio** *sm* plumage, feathers *pl*; **piu'mino** *sm* (eider)down; (*per letto*) eiderdown; (: *tipo danese*) duvet, continental quilt; (*giacca*) quilted jacket (*with goose-*

feather padding); (*per cipria*) powder puff; (*per spolverare*) feather duster.

piut'tosto *av* rather; ~ **che** (*anziché*) rather than.

pi'vello, a *sm/f* greenhorn.

'pizza ['pittsa] *sf* pizza; **pizze'ria** *sf place where pizzas are made, sold or eaten.*

pizzi'cagnolo, a [pittsi'kaɲɲolo] *sm/f* specialist grocer.

pizzi'care [pittsi'kare] *vt* (*stringere*) to nip, pinch; (*pungere*) to sting; to bite; (*MUS*) to pluck ♦ *vi* (*prudere*) to itch, be itchy; (*cibo*) to be hot *o* spicy.

pizziche'ria [pittsike'ria] *sf* delicatessen (shop).

'pizzico, chi ['pittsiko] *sm* (*pizzicotto*) pinch, nip; (*piccola quantità*) pinch, dash; (*d'insetto*) sting; bite.

pizzi'cotto [pittsi'kɔtto] *sm* pinch, nip.

'pizzo ['pittso] *sm* (*merletto*) lace; (*barbetta*) goatee beard.

pla'care *vt* to placate, soothe; ~**rsi** *vr* to calm down.

'placca, che *sf* plate; (*con iscrizione*) plaque; (*anche:* ~ *dentaria*) (dental) plaque; **plac'care** *vt* to plate; **placcato in oro/argento** gold-/silver-plated.

'placido, a ['platʃido] *ag* placid, calm.

plagi'are [pla'dʒare] *vt* (*copiare*) to plagiarize; **'plagio** *sm* plagiarism.

pla'nare *vi* (*AER*) to glide.

'plancia, ce ['plantʃa] *sf* (*NAUT*) bridge.

plane'tario, a *ag* planetary ♦ *sm* (*locale*) planetarium.

'plasma *sm* plasma.

plas'mare *vt* to mould, shape.

'plastica, che *sf* (*arte*) plastic arts *pl*; (*MED*) plastic surgery; (*sostanza*) plastic.

'plastico, a, ci, che *ag* plastic ♦ *sm* (*rappresentazione*) relief model; (*esplosivo*): **bomba al** ~ plastic bomb.

plasti'lina ® *sf* plasticine ®.

'platano *sm* plane tree.

pla'tea *sf* (*TEATRO*) stalls *pl*.

'platino *sm* platinum.

pla'tonico, a, ci, che *ag* platonic.

plau'sibile *ag* plausible.

'plauso *sm* (*fig*) approval.

ple'baglia [ple'baʎʎa] (*peg*) *sf* rabble, mob.

'plebe *sf* common people; **ple'beo, a** *ag* plebeian; (*volgare*) coarse, common.

ple'nario, a *ag* plenary.

pleni'lunio *sm* full moon.

'plettro *sm* plectrum.

pleu'rite *sf* pleurisy.

'plico, chi *sm* (*pacco*) parcel; **in** ~ **a parte** (*COMM*) under separate cover.

plo'tone *sm* (*MIL*) platoon; ~ **d'esecuzione** firing squad.

'plumbeo, a *ag* leaden.

plu'rale *ag, sm* plural; **pluralità** *sf* plurality; (*maggioranza*) majority.

plusva'lore *sm* (*ECON*) surplus.

pneu'matico, a, ci, che *ag* inflatable; pneumatic ♦ *sm* (*AUT*) tyre (*BRIT*), tire (*US*).

po' *av, sm vedi* **poco.**

PAROLA CHIAVE

'poco, a, chi, che *ag* (*quantità*) little, not much; (*numero*) few, not many; ~ **pane/denaro/spazio** little *o* not much bread/money/space; ~**che persone/idee** few *o* not many people/ideas; **ci vediamo tra** ~ (*sottinteso: tempo*) see you soon

♦ *av* **1** (*in piccola quantità*) little, not much; (*numero limitato*) few, not many; **guadagna** ~ he doesn't earn much, he earns little

2 (*con ag, av*) (a) little, not very; **sta** ~ **bene** he isn't very well; **è** ~ **più vecchia di lui** she's a little *o* slightly older than him

3 (*tempo*): ~ **dopo/prima** shortly afterwards/before; **il film dura** ~ the film doesn't last very long; **ci vediamo molto** ~ we don't see each other very often, we hardly ever see each other

4: **un po'** a little, a bit; **è un po' corto** it's a little *o* a bit short; **arriverà fra un po'** he'll arrive shortly *o* in a little while

5: **a dir** ~ to say the least; **a** ~ **a** ~ little by little; **per** ~ **non cadevo** I nearly fell; **è una cosa da** ~ it's nothing, it's of no importance; **una persona da** ~ a worthless person

♦ *pron* (a) little; ~**chi, che** *pron pl*

(*persone*) few (people); (*cose*) few
♦ *sm* **1** little; **vive del ~ che ha** he
lives on the little he has
2: **un po'** a little; **un po' di zucchero** a
little sugar; **un bel po' di denaro** quite a
lot of money; **un po' per ciascuno** a bit
each.

po'dere *sm* (*AGR*) farm.
pode'roso, a *ag* powerful.
podestà *sm inv* (*nel fascismo*) podesta,
mayor.
'podio *sm* dais, platform; (*MUS*)
podium.
po'dismo *sm* (*SPORT*) track events *pl*.
po'ema, i *sm* poem.
poe'sia *sf* (*arte*) poetry; (*componimento*) poem.
po'eta, 'essa *sm/f* poet/poetess;
po'etico, a, ci, che *ag* poetic(al).
poggi'are [pod'dʒare] *vt* to lean, rest;
(*posare*) to lay, place; poggia'testa *sm
inv* (*AUT*) headrest.
'poggio ['pɔddʒo] *sm* hillock, knoll.
'poi *av* then; (*alla fine*) finally, at last;
e ~ (*inoltre*) and besides; **questa ~** (**è
bella**)! (*ironico*) that's a good one!
poiché [poi'ke] *cong* since, as.
'poker *sm* poker.
po'lacco, a, chi, che *ag* Polish ♦ *sm/f*
Pole.
po'lare *ag* polar.
po'lemica, che *sf* controversy.
po'lemico, a, ci, che *ag* polemic(al),
controversial.
po'lenta *sf* (*CUC*) sort of thick porridge
made with maize flour.
poli'clinico, ci *sm* general hospital,
polyclinic.
poli'estere *sm* polyester.
'polio(mie'lite) *sf* polio(myelitis).
'polipo *sm* polyp.
polisti'rolo *sm* polystyrene.
poli'tecnico, ci *sm* postgraduate
technical college.
po'litica, che *sf* politics *sg*; (*linea di
condotta*) policy; *vedi anche* **politico**.
politiciz'zare [politiʃid'dzare] *vt* to
politicize.
po'litico, a, ci, che *ag* political ♦ *sm/f*

politician.
poli'zia [polit'tsia] *sf* police; **~
giudiziaria** ≈ Criminal Investigation
Department (*BRIT*), ≈ Federal Bureau
of Investigation (*US*); **~ stradale** traffic
police; polizi'esco, a, schi, sche *ag*
police *cpd*; (*film, romanzo*) detective
cpd; polizi'otto *sm* policeman; **cane
poliziotto** police dog; **donna poliziotto**
policewoman.
'polizza ['pɔlittsa] *sf* (*COMM*) bill; **~ di
assicurazione** insurance policy; **~ di
carico** bill of lading.
pol'laio *sm* henhouse.
pol'lame *sm* poultry.
pol'lastro *sm* (*ZOOL*) cockerel.
'pollice ['pɔllitʃe] *sm* thumb.
'polline *sm* pollen.
'pollo *sm* chicken.
pol'mone *sm* lung; polmo'nite *sf*
pneumonia.
'polo *sm* (*GEO, FISICA*) pole; (*gioco*)
polo; **il ~ sud/nord** the South/North
Pole.
Po'lonia *sf*: **la ~** Poland.
'polpa *sf* flesh, pulp; (*carne*) lean
meat.
pol'paccio [pol'pattʃo] *sm* (*ANAT*) calf.
pol'petta *sf* (*CUC*) meatball;
polpet'tone *sm* (*CUC*) meatloaf.
'polpo *sm* octopus.
pol'poso, a *ag* fleshy.
pol'sino *sm* cuff.
'polso *sm* (*ANAT*) wrist; (*pulsazione*)
pulse; (*fig: forza*) drive, vigour.
pol'tiglia [pol'tiʎʎa] *sf* (*composto*)
mash, mush; (*di fango e neve*) slush.
pol'trire *vi* to laze about.
pol'trona *sf* armchair; (*TEATRO: posto*)
seat in the front stalls (*BRIT*) *o*
orchestra (*US*).
pol'trone *ag* lazy, slothful.
'polvere *sf* dust; (*anche*: **~ da sparo**)
(gun)powder; (*sostanza ridotta
minutissima*) powder, dust; **latte in ~**
dried *o* powdered milk; **caffè in ~** instant coffee; **sapone in ~** soap powder;
polveri'era *sf* powder magazine;
polveriz'zare *vt* to pulverize;
(*nebulizzare*) to atomize; (*fig*) to crush,

pulverize; to smash; **polve'rone** *sm* thick cloud of dust; **polve'roso, a** *ag* dusty.

po'mata *sf* ointment, cream.

po'mello *sm* knob.

pomeridi'ano, a *ag* afternoon *cpd*; **nelle ore ~e** in the afternoon.

pome'riggio [pome'riddʒo] *sm* afternoon.

'pomice ['pɔmitʃe] *sf* pumice.

'pomo *sm* (*mela*) apple; (*ornamentale*) knob; (*di sella*) pommel; ~ **d'Adamo** (*ANAT*) Adam's apple.

pomo'doro *sm* tomato.

'pompa *sf* pump; (*sfarzo*) pomp (and ceremony); **~e funebri** funeral parlour *sg* (*BRIT*), undertaker's *sg*; **pom'pare** *vt* to pump; (*trarre*) to pump out; (*gonfiare d'aria*) to pump up.

pom'pelmo *sm* grapefruit.

pompi'ere *sm* fireman.

pom'poso, a *ag* pompous.

ponde'rare *vt* to ponder over, consider carefully.

ponde'roso, a *ag* (*anche fig*) weighty.

po'nente *sm* west.

'ponte *sm* bridge; (*di nave*) deck; (: *anche*: ~ **di comando**) bridge; (*impalcatura*) scaffold; **fare il** ~ (*fig*) to take the extra day off (*between 2 public holidays*); **governo** ~ interim government; ~ **aereo** airlift; ~ **sospeso** suspension bridge.

pon'tefice [pon'tefitʃe] *sm* (*REL*) pontiff.

pontifi'care *vi* (*anche fig*) to pontificate.

ponti'ficio, a, ci, cie [ponti'fitʃo] *ag* papal.

popo'lano, a *ag* popular, of the people.

popo'lare *ag* popular; (*quartiere, clientela*) working-class ♦ *vt* (*rendere abitato*) to populate; **~rsi** *vr* to fill with people, get crowded; **popolarità** *sf* popularity; **popolazi'one** *sf* population.

'popolo *sm* people; **popo'loso, a** *ag* densely populated.

po'pone *sm* melon.

'poppa *sf* (*di nave*) stern; (*mammella*) breast.

pop'pare *vt* to suck.

poppa'toio *sm* (feeding) bottle.

porcel'lana [portʃel'lana] *sf* porcelain, china; piece of china.

porcel'lino, a [portʃel'lino] *sm/f* piglet.

porche'ria [porke'ria] *sf* filth, muck; (*fig: oscenità*) obscenity; (: *azione disonesta*) dirty trick; (: *cosa mal fatta*) rubbish.

por'cile [por'tʃile] *sm* pigsty.

por'cino, a [por'tʃino] *ag* of pigs, pork *cpd* ♦ *sm* (*fungo*) type of edible mushroom.

'porco, ci *sm* pig; (*carne*) pork.

porcos'pino *sm* porcupine.

'porgere ['pɔrdʒere] *vt* to hand, give; (*tendere*) to hold out.

pornogra'fia *sf* pornography; **porno'grafico, a, ci, che** *ag* pornographic.

'poro *sm* pore; **po'roso, a** *ag* porous.

'porpora *sf* purple.

'porre *vt* (*mettere*) to put; (*collocare*) to place; (*posare*) to lay (down), put (down); (*fig: supporre*): **poniamo (il caso) che** ... let's suppose that ...; **porsi** *vr* (*mettersi*): **porsi a sedere/in cammino** to sit down/set off; ~ **una domanda a qn** to ask sb a question, put a question to sb.

'porro *sm* (*BOT*) leek; (*MED*) wart.

'porta *sf* door; (*SPORT*) goal; **~e** *sfpl* (*di città*) gates; **a ~e chiuse** (*DIR*) in camera.

'porta... *prefisso*: **portaba'gagli** *sm inv* (*facchino*) porter; (*AUT, FERR*) luggage rack; **portabandi'era** *sm inv* standard bearer; **porta'cenere** *sm inv* ashtray; **portachi'avi** *sm inv* keyring; **porta'cipria** *sm inv* powder compact; **porta'erei** *sf inv* (*nave*) aircraft carrier ♦ *sm inv* (*aereo*) aircraft transporter; **portafi'nestra** (*pl* **portefi'nestre**) *sf* French window; **porta'foglio** *sm* (*busta*) wallet; (*cartella*) briefcase; (*POL, BORSA*) portfolio; **portafor'tuna** *sm inv* lucky charm; mascot; **portagi'oie** *sm inv*; jewellery box; **portagioi'elli** *sm* = **portagioie**.

porta'lettere *sm/f inv* postman/woman (*BRIT*), mailman/woman (*US*).

porta'mento *sm* carriage, bearing.
portamo'nete *sm inv* purse.
por'tante *ag (muro etc)* supporting, load-bearing.
portan'tina *sf* sedan chair; *(per ammalati)* stretcher.
por'tare *vt (sostenere, sorreggere: peso, bambino, pacco)* to carry; *(indossare: abito, occhiali)* to wear; *(: capelli lunghi)* to have; *(avere: nome, titolo)* to have, bear; *(recare)*: ~ **qc a qn** to take *(o bring)* sth to sb; *(fig: sentimenti)* to bear; ~**rsi** *vr (recarsi)* to go; ~ **avanti** *(discorso, idea)* to pursue; ~ **via** to take away; *(rubare)* to take; ~ **i bambini a spasso** to take the children for a walk; ~ **fortuna** to bring good luck.
portasiga'rette *sm inv* cigarette case.
por'tata *sf (vivanda)* course; *(AUT)* carrying *(o loading)* capacity; *(di arma)* range; *(volume d'acqua)* (rate of) flow; *(fig: limite)* scope, capability; *(: importanza)* impact, import; **alla ~ di tutti** *(conoscenza)* within everybody's capabilities; *(prezzo)* within everybody's means; **a/fuori ~ (di)** within/out of reach (of); **a ~ di mano** within (arm's) reach.
por'tatile *ag* portable.
por'tato, a *ag (incline)*: ~ **a** inclined *o* apt to.
porta'tore, 'trice *sm/f (anche COMM)* bearer; *(MED)* carrier.
portau'ovo *sm inv* eggcup.
porta'voce [porta'votʃe] *sm/f inv* spokesman/woman.
por'tento *sm* wonder, marvel.
'portico, ci *sm* portico.
porti'era *sf (AUT)* door.
porti'ere *sm (portinaio)* concierge, caretaker; *(di hotel)* porter; *(nel calcio)* goalkeeper.
porti'naio, a *sm/f* concierge, caretaker.
portine'ria *sf* caretaker's lodge.
'porto, a *pp di* **porgere** ♦ *sm (NAUT)* harbour, port; *(spesa di trasporto)* carriage ♦ *sm inv* port (wine); ~ **d'armi** *(documento)* gun licence.

Porto'gallo *sm*: **il** ~ Portugal; **porto'ghese** *ag, sm/f, sm* Portuguese *inv.*
por'tone *sm* main entrance, main door.
portu'ale *ag* harbour *cpd*, port *cpd* ♦ *sm* dock worker.
porzi'one [por'tsjone] *sf* portion, share; *(di cibo)* portion, helping.
'posa *sf (FOT)* exposure; *(atteggiamento, di modello)* pose.
po'sare *vt* to put (down), lay (down) ♦ *vi (ponte, edificio, teoria)*: ~ **su** to rest on; *(FOT, atteggiarsi)* to pose; ~**rsi** *vr (aereo)* to land; *(uccello)* to alight; *(sguardo)* to settle.
po'sata *sf* piece of cutlery; ~**e** *sfpl (servizio)* cutlery *sg.*
po'sato, a *ag* serious.
pos'critto *sm* postscript.
posi'tivo, a *ag* positive.
posizi'one [pozit'tsjone] *sf* position; **prendere** ~ *(fig)* to take a stand; **luci di** ~ *(AUT)* sidelights.
posolo'gia, 'gie [pozolo'dʒia] *sf* dosage, directions *pl* for use.
pos'porre *vt* to place after; *(differire)* to postpone, defer; **pos'posto, a** *pp di* **posporre.**
posse'dere *vt* to own, possess; *(qualità, virtù)* to have, possess; *(conoscere a fondo: lingua etc)* to have a thorough knowledge of; *(sog: ira etc)* to possess; **possedi'mento** *sm* possession.
posses'sivo, a *ag* possessive.
pos'sesso *sm* ownership *no pl*; possession.
posses'sore *sm* owner.
pos'sibile *ag* possible ♦ *sm*: **fare tutto il** ~ to do everything possible; **nei limiti del** ~ as far as possible; **al più tardi** ~ as late as possible; **possibilità** *sf inv* possibility ♦ *sfpl (mezzi)* means; **aver la possibilità di fare** to be in a position to do; to have the opportunity to do.
possi'dente *sm/f* landowner.
'posta *sf (servizio)* post, postal service; *(corrispondenza)* post, mail; *(ufficio postale)* post office; *(nei giochi d'azzardo)* stake; **'~e** *sfpl*

(*amministrazione*) post office; **~ aerea** airmail; **ministro delle P~e e Telecomunicazioni** Postmaster General; **posta'giro** sm post office cheque, postal giro (*BRIT*); **pos'tale** ag postal, post office cpd.

post'bellico, a, ci, che ag postwar.

posteggi'are [posted'dʒare] vt, vi to park; **pos'teggio** sm car park (*BRIT*), parking lot (*US*); (*di taxi*) rank (*BRIT*), stand (*US*).

postelegra'fonico, a, ci, che ag postal and telecommunications cpd.

posteri'ore ag (*dietro*) back; (*dopo*) later ♦ sm (*fam: sedere*) behind.

pos'ticcio, a, ci, ce [pos'tittʃo] ag false ♦ sm hairpiece.

postici'pare [postitʃi'pare] vt to defer, postpone.

pos'tilla sf marginal note.

pos'tino sm postman (*BRIT*), mailman (*US*).

'posto, a pp di **porre** ♦ sm (*sito, posizione*) place; (*impiego*) job; (*spazio libero*) room, space; (*di parcheggio*) space; (*sedile: al teatro, in treno etc*) seat; (*MIL*) post; **a ~** (*in ordine*) in place, tidy; (: *persona*) reliable; **al ~ di** in place of; **sul ~** on the spot; **mettere a ~** to tidy (up), put in order; (*faccende*) to straighten out; **~ di blocco** roadblock; **~ di polizia** police station.

pos'tribolo sm brothel.

'postumo, a ag posthumous; (*tardivo*) belated; **~i** smpl (*conseguenze*) aftereffects, consequences.

po'tabile ag drinkable; **acqua ~** drinking water.

po'tare vt to prune.

po'tassio sm potassium.

po'tente ag (*nazione*) strong, powerful; (*veleno, farmaco*) potent, strong; **po'tenza** sf power; (*forza*) strength.

potenzi'ale [poten'tsjale] ag, sm potential.

PAROLA CHIAVE

po'tere sm power; **al ~** (*partito etc*) in power; **~ d'acquisto** purchasing power

♦ vb aus **1** (*essere in grado di*) can, be able to; **non ha potuto ripararlo** he couldn't o he wasn't able to repair it; **non è potuto venire** he couldn't o he wasn't able to come; **spiacente di non poter aiutare** sorry not to be able to help

2 (*avere il permesso*) can, may, be allowed to; **posso entrare?** can o may I come in?; **si può sapere dove sei stato?** where on earth have you been?

3 (*eventualità*) may, might, could; **potrebbe essere vero** it might o could be true; **può aver avuto un incidente** he may o might o could have had an accident; **può darsi** perhaps; **può darsi** o **essere che non venga** he may o might not come

4 (*augurio*): **potessi almeno parlargli!** if only I could speak to him!

5 (*suggerimento*): **potresti almeno scusarti!** you could at least apologize!

♦ vt can, be able to; **può molto per noi** he can do a lot for us; **non ne posso più** (*per stanchezza*) I'm exhausted; (*per rabbia*) I can't take any more.

potestà sf (*potere*) power; (*DIR*) authority.

'povero, a ag poor; (*disadorno*) plain, bare ♦ sm/f poor man/woman; **i ~i** the poor; **~ di** lacking in, having little; **povertà** sf poverty.

'pozza ['pottsa] sf pool.

poz'zanghera [pott'tsangera] sf puddle.

'pozzo ['pottso] sm well; (*cava: di carbone*) pit; (*di miniera*) shaft; **~ petrolifero** oil well.

pran'zare [pran'dzare] vi to dine, have dinner; to lunch, have lunch.

'pranzo ['prandzo] sm dinner; (*a mezzogiorno*) lunch.

'prassi sf usual procedure.

'pratica, che sf practice; (*esperienza*) experience; (*conoscenza*) knowledge, familiarity; (*tirocinio*) training, practice; (*AMM: affare*) matter, case; (: *incartamento*) file, dossier; **in ~** (*praticamente*) in practice; **mettere in ~** to put into practice.

prati'cabile ag (progetto) practicable, feasible; (luogo) passable, practicable.

prati'cante sm/f apprentice, trainee; (REL) (regular) churchgoer.

prati'care vt to practise; (SPORT: tennis etc) to play; (: nuoto, scherma etc) to go in for; (eseguire: apertura, buco) to make; ~ **uno sconto** to give a discount.

'pratico, a, ci, che ag practical; ~ **di** (esperto) experienced o skilled in; (familiare) familiar with.

'prato sm meadow; (di giardino) lawn.

preav'viso sm notice; **telefonata con** ~ personal o person to person call.

pre'cario, a ag precarious; (INS) temporary.

precauzi'one [prekaut'tsjone] sf caution, care; (misura) precaution.

prece'dente [pretʃe'dɛnte] ag previous ♦ sm precedent; **il discorso/film** ~ the previous o preceding speech/film; **senza** ~**i** unprecedented; ~**i penali** criminal record sg; **prece'denza** sf priority, precedence; (AUT) right of way.

pre'cedere [pre'tʃedere] vt to precede, go (o come) before.

pre'cetto [pre'tʃɛtto] sm precept; (MIL) call-up notice.

precet'tore [pretʃet'tore] sm (private) tutor.

precipi'tare [pretʃipi'tare] vi (cadere) to fall headlong; (fig: situazione) to get out of control ♦ vt (gettare dall'alto in basso) to hurl, fling; (fig: affrettare) to rush; ~**rsi** vr (gettarsi) to hurl o fling o.s.; (affrettarsi) to rush; **precipitazi'one** sf (METEOR) precipitation; (fig) haste; **precipi'toso, a** ag (caduta, fuga) headlong; (fig: avventato) rash, reckless; (: affrettato) hasty, rushed.

preci'pizio [pretʃi'pittsjo] sm precipice; **a** ~ (fig: correre) headlong.

preci'sare [pretʃi'zare] vt to state, specify; (spiegare) to explain (in detail).

precisi'one [pretʃi'zjone] sf precision; accuracy.

pre'ciso, a [pre'tʃizo] ag (esatto) pre-cise; (accurato) accurate, precise; (deciso: idee) precise, definite; (uguale): **2 vestiti** ~**i** 2 dresses exactly the same; **sono le 9** ~**e** it's exactly 9 o'clock.

pre'cludere vt to block, obstruct; **pre'cluso, a** pp di **precludere**.

pre'coce [pre'kɔtʃe] ag early; (bambino) precocious; (vecchiaia) premature.

precon'cetto [prekon'tʃɛtto] sm pre-conceived idea, prejudice.

precur'sore sm forerunner, precursor.

'preda sf (bottino) booty; (animale, fig) prey; **essere** ~ **di** to fall prey to; **essere in** ~ **a** to be prey to; **preda'tore** sm predator.

predeces'sore, a [predetʃes'sore] sm/f predecessor.

predesti'nare vt to predestine.

pre'detto, a pp di **predire**.

'predica, che sf sermon; (fig) lecture, talking-to.

predi'care vt, vi to preach.

predi'cato sm (LING) predicate.

predi'letto, a pp di **prediligere** ♦ ag, sm/f favourite.

predilezi'one [predilet'tsjone] sf fond-ness, partiality; **avere una** ~ **per qc/qn** to be partial to sth/fond of sb.

predi'ligere [predi'lidʒere] vt to prefer, have a preference for.

pre'dire vt to foretell, predict.

predis'porre vt to get ready, prepare; ~ **qn a qc** to predispose sb to sth; **predis'posto, a** pp di **predisporre**.

predizi'one [predit'tsjone] sf prediction.

predomi'nare vi to predominate; **predo'minio** sm predominance; su-premacy.

prefabbri'cato, a ag (EDIL) prefab-ricated.

prefazi'one [prefat'tsjone] sf preface, foreword.

prefe'renza [prefe'rɛntsa] sf preference; **preferenzi'ale** ag preferential; **corsia** ~ bus and taxi lane.

prefe'rire vt to prefer, like better; ~ **il caffè al tè** to prefer coffee to tea, like coffee better than tea.

pre'fetto sm prefect; **prefet'tura** sf prefecture.

pre'figgersi [preˈfiddʒersi] vr: ~**rsi uno scopo** to set o.s. a goal.

pre'fisso, a pp di **prefiggere** ♦ sm (LING) prefix; (TEL) dialling (BRIT) o dial (US) code.

pre'gare vi to pray ♦ vt (REL) to pray to; (implorare) to beg; (chiedere): ~ **qn di fare** to ask sb to do; **farsi** ~ to need coaxing o persuading.

pre'gevole [preˈdʒevole] ag valuable.

preghi'era [preˈgjɛra] sf (REL) prayer; (domanda) request.

pregi'ato, a [preˈdʒato] ag (di valore) valuable; **vino** ~ vintage wine.

'pregio [ˈprɛdʒo] sm (stima) esteem, regard; (qualità) (good) quality, merit; (valore) value, worth.

pregiudi'care [predʒudiˈkare] vt to prejudice, harm, be detrimental to; **pregiudi'cato, a** sm/f (DIR) previous offender.

pregiu'dizio [predʒuˈdittsjo] sm (idea errata) prejudice; (danno) harm no pl.

'pregno, a [ˈprɛɲɲo] ag (gravido) pregnant; (saturo): ~ **di** full of, saturated with.

'prego escl (a chi ringrazia) don't mention it!; (invitando qn ad accomodarsi) please sit down!; (invitando qn ad andare prima) after you!

pregus'tare vt to look forward to.

preis'torico, a, ci, che ag prehistoric.

pre'lato sm prelate.

prele'vare vt (denaro) to withdraw; (campione) to take; (sog: polizia) to take, capture.

preli'evo sm (MED): **fare un** ~ **(di)** to take a sample (of).

prelimi'nare ag preliminary; ~**i** smpl preliminary talks; preliminaries.

pre'ludio sm prelude.

pré-ma'man [premaˈmã] sm inv maternity dress.

prema'turo, a ag premature.

premeditazi'one [premeditatˈtsjone] sf (DIR) premeditation; **con** ~ ag premeditated ♦ av with intent.

'premere vt to press ♦ vi: ~ **su** to press down on; (fig) to put pressure on; ~ **a** (fig: importare) to matter to.

pre'messa sf introductory statement, introduction.

pre'messo, a pp di **premettere**.

pre'mettere vt to put before; (dire prima) to start by saying, state first.

premi'are vt to give a prize to; (fig: merito, onestà) to reward.

'premio sm prize; (ricompensa) reward; (COMM) premium; (AMM: indennità) bonus.

premu'nirsi vr: ~ **di** to provide o.s. with; ~ **contro** to protect o.s. from, guard o.s. against.

pre'mura sf (fretta) haste, hurry; (riguardo) attention, care; **premu'roso, a** ag thoughtful, considerate.

prena'tale ag antenatal.

'prendere vt to take; (andare a prendere) to get, fetch; (ottenere) to get; (guadagnare) to get, earn; (catturare: ladro, pesce) to catch; (collaboratore, dipendente) to take on; (passeggero) to pick up; (chiedere: somma, prezzo) to charge, ask; (trattare: persona) to handle ♦ vi (colla, cemento) to set; (pianta) to take; (fuoco: nel camino) to catch; (voltare): ~ **a destra** to turn (to the) right; ~**rsi** vr (azzuffarsi): ~**rsi a pugni** to come to blows; **prendi qualcosa?** (da bere, da mangiare) would you like something to eat (o drink)?; **prendo un caffè** I'll have a coffee; ~ **a fare qc** to start doing sth; ~ **qn/qc per** (scambiare) to take sb/sth for; ~ **fuoco** to catch fire; ~ **parte a** to take part in; ~**rsi cura di qn/qc** to look after sb/sth; **prendersela** (adirarsi) to get annoyed; (preoccuparsi) to get upset, worry.

prendi'sole sm inv sundress.

preno'tare vt to book, reserve; **prenotazi'one** sf booking, reservation.

preoccu'pare vt to worry; to preoccupy; ~**rsi** vr: ~**rsi di qn/qc** to worry about sb/sth; ~**rsi per qn** to be anxious for sb; **preoccupazi'one** sf worry, anxiety.

prepa'rare vt to prepare; (esame, con-

corso) to prepare for; **~rsi** *vr* (*vestirsi*) to get ready; **~rsi a qc/a fare** to get ready *o* prepare (o.s.) for sth/to do; **~ da mangiare** to prepare a meal; **prepara'tivi** *smpl* preparations; **prepa'rato** *sm* (*prodotto*) preparation; **preparazi'one** *sf* preparation.

preposizi'one [prepozit'tsjone] *sf* (*LING*) preposition.

prepo'tente *ag* (*persona*) domineering, arrogant; (*bisogno, desiderio*) overwhelming, pressing ♦ *sm/f* bully; **prepo'tenza** *sf* arrogance; arrogant behaviour.

'presa *sf* taking *no pl*; catching *no pl*; (*di città*) capture; (*indurimento: di cemento*) setting; (*appiglio, SPORT*) hold; (*di acqua, gas*) (supply) point; (*ELETTR*): **~** **(di corrente)** socket; (: *al muro*) point; (*piccola quantità: di sale etc*) pinch; (*CARTE*) trick; **far ~** (*colla*) to set; **far ~ sul pubblico** to catch the public's imagination; **~ d'aria** air inlet; **essere alle ~e con qc** (*fig*) to be struggling with sth.

pre'sagio [pre'zadʒo] *sm* omen.

presa'gire [preza'dʒiɾe] *vt* to foresee.

'presbite *ag* long-sighted.

presbi'terio *sm* presbytery.

pre'scindere [preʃ'ʃindere] *vi*: **~ da** to leave out of consideration; **a ~ da** apart from.

pres'critto, a *pp di* **prescrivere**.

pres'crivere *vt* to prescribe; **prescrizi'one** *sf* (*MED, DIR*) prescription; (*norma*) rule, regulation.

presen'tare *vt* to present; (*far conoscere*): **~ qn (a)** to introduce sb (to); (*AMM: inoltrare*) to submit; **~rsi** *vr* (*recarsi, farsi vedere*) to present o.s., appear; (*farsi conoscere*) to introduce o.s.; (*occasione*) to arise; **~rsi come candidato** (*POL*) to stand as a candidate; **~rsi bene/male** to have a good/poor appearance; **presentazi'one** *sf* presentation; introduction.

pre'sente *ag* present; (*questo*) this ♦ *sm* present; **i ~i** those present; **aver ~ qc/qn** to remember sth/sb.

presenti'mento *sm* premonition.

pre'senza [pre'zɛntsa] *sf* presence; (*aspetto esteriore*) appearance; **~ di spirito** presence of mind.

pre'sepe *sm* = **presepio**.

pre'sepio *sm* crib.

preser'vare *vt* to protect; to save; **preserva'tivo** *sm* sheath, condom.

'preside *sm/f* (*INS*) head (teacher) (*BRIT*), principal (*US*); (*di facoltà universitaria*) dean.

presi'dente *sm* (*POL*) president; (*di assemblea, COMM*) chairman; **~ del consiglio** prime minister; **presiden'tessa** *sf* president; president's wife; chairwoman; **presi'denza** *sf* presidency; office of president; chairmanship.

presidi'are *vt* to garrison; **pre'sidio** *sm* garrison.

presi'edere *vt* to preside over ♦ *vi*: **~ a** to direct, be in charge of.

'preso, a *pp di* **prendere**.

'pressa *sf* (*TECN*) press.

pressap'poco *av* about, roughly.

pres'sare *vt* to press.

pressi'one *sf* pressure; **far ~ su qn** to put pressure on sb; **~ sanguigna** blood pressure.

'presso *av* (*vicino*) nearby, close at hand ♦ *prep* (*vicino a*) near; (*accanto a*) beside, next to; (*in casa di*): **~ qn** at sb's home; (*nelle lettere*) care of, c/o; (*alle dipendenze di*): **lavora ~ di noi** he works for *o* with us ♦ *smpl*: **nei ~i di** near, in the vicinity of.

pressuriz'zare [pressurid'dzare] *vt* to pressurize.

presta'nome (*peg*) *sm/f inv* figurehead.

pres'tante *ag* good-looking.

pres'tare *vt*: **~ (qc a qn)** to lend (sb sth *o* sth to sb); **~rsi** *vr* (*offrirsi*): **~rsi a fare** to offer to do; (*essere adatto*): **~rsi a** to lend itself to, be suitable for; **~ aiuto** to lend a hand; **~ attenzione** to pay attention; **~ fede a qc/qn** to give credence to sth/sb; **~ orecchio** to listen; **prestazi'one** *sf* (*TECN, SPORT*) performance; **prestazioni** *sfpl* (*di persona: servizi*) services.

prestigia'tore, '**trice** [prestidʒa'tore] *sm/f* conjurer.

pres'tigio [pres'tidʒo] *sm* (*potere*) prestige; (*illusione*): **gioco di ~** conjuring trick.

'**prestito** *sm* lending *no pl*; loan; **dar in ~** to lend; **prendere in ~** to borrow.

'**presto** *av* (*tra poco*) soon; (*in fretta*) quickly; (*di buon'ora*) early; **a ~** see you soon; **fare ~ a fare qc** to hurry up and do sth; (*non costare fatica*) to have no trouble doing sth; **si fa ~ a criticare** it's easy to criticize.

pre'sumere *vt* to presume, assume; **pre'sunto, a** *pp di* **presumere.**

presuntu'oso, a *ag* presumptuous.

presunzi'one [prezun'tsjone] *sf* presumption.

presup'porre *vt* to suppose; to presuppose.

'**prete** *sm* priest.

preten'dente *sm/f* pretender ♦ *sm* (*corteggiatore*) suitor.

pre'tendere *vt* (*esigere*) to demand, require; (*sostenere*): **~ che** to claim that; **pretende di aver sempre ragione** he thinks he's always right.

pretenzi'oso, a [preten'tsjoso] *ag* pretentious.

pre'tesa *sf* (*esigenza*) claim, demand; (*presunzione, sfarzo*) pretentiousness; **senza ~e** unpretentious; *vedi anche* **preteso.**

pre'teso, a *pp di* **pretendere.**

pre'testo *sm* pretext, excuse.

pre'tore *sm* magistrate.

preva'lente *ag* prevailing; **preva'lenza** *sf* predominance.

preva'lere *vi* to prevail; **pre'valso, a** *pp di* **prevalere.**

preve'dere *vt* (*indovinare*) to foresee; (*presagire*) to foretell; (*considerare*) to make provision for.

preve'nire *vt* (*anticipare*) to forestall; to anticipate; (*evitare*) to avoid, prevent; (*avvertire*): **~ qn (di)** to warn sb (of); to inform sb (of).

preven'tivo, a *ag* preventive ♦ *sm* (*COMM*) estimate.

prevenzi'one [preven'tsjone] *sf* prevention; (*preconcetto*) prejudice.

previ'dente *ag* showing foresight; prudent; **previ'denza** *sf* foresight; **istituto di previdenza** provident institution; **previdenza sociale** social security (*BRIT*), welfare (*US*).

previsi'one *sf* forecast, prediction; **~i meteorologiche** *o* **del tempo** weather forecast *sg*.

pre'visto, a *pp di* **prevedere** ♦ *sm*: **più/meno del ~** more/less than expected.

prezi'oso, a [pret'tsjoso] *ag* precious; invaluable ♦ *sm* jewel; valuable.

prez'zemolo [pret'tsemolo] *sm* parsley.

'**prezzo** ['prettso] *sm* price; **~ d'acquisto/di vendita** buying/selling price.

prigi'one [pri'dʒone] *sf* prison; **prigio'nia** *sf* imprisonment; **prigioni'ero, a** *ag* captive ♦ *sm/f* prisoner.

'**prima** *sf* (*TEATRO*) first night; (*CINEMA*) première; (*AUT*) first gear; *vedi anche* **primo** ♦ *av* before; (*in anticipo*) in advance, beforehand; (*per l'addietro*) at one time, formerly; (*più presto*) sooner, earlier; (*in primo luogo*) first ♦ *cong*: **~ di fare/che parta** before doing/he leaves; **~ di** before; **~ o poi** sooner or later.

pri'mario, a *ag* primary; (*principale*) chief, leading, primary ♦ *sm* (*MED*) chief physician.

pri'mate *sm* (*REL, ZOOL*) primate.

pri'mato *sm* supremacy; (*SPORT*) record.

prima'vera *sf* spring; **primave'rile** *ag* spring *cpd*.

primeggi'are [primed'dʒare] *vi* to excel, be one of the best.

primi'tivo, a *ag* primitive; original.

pri'mizie [pri'mittsje] *sfpl* early produce *sg*.

'**primo, a** *ag* first; (*fig*) initial; basic; prime ♦ *sm/f* first (one) ♦ *sm* (*CUC*) first course; (*in date*): **il ~ luglio** the first of July; **le ~e ore del mattino** the early hours of the morning; **ai ~i di maggio** at the beginning of May;

viaggiare in ~a to travel first-class; in ~ luogo first of all, in the first place; di prim'ordine *o* ~a qualità first-class, first-rate; in un ~ tempo at first; ~a donna leading lady; (*di opera lirica*) prima donna.

primo'genito, a [primo'dʒɛnito] *ag, sm/f* firstborn.

primordi'ale *ag* primordial.

'**primula** *sf* primrose.

princi'pale [printʃi'pale] *ag* main, principal ♦ *sm* manager, boss.

princi'pato [printʃi'pato] *sm* principality.

'**principe** ['printʃipe] *sm* prince; ~ ereditario crown prince; **princi'pessa** *sf* princess.

principi'ante [printʃi'pjante] *sm/f* beginner.

prin'cipio [prin'tʃipjo] *sm* (*inizio*) beginning, start; (*origine*) origin, cause; (*concetto, norma*) principle; al *o* in ~ at first; per ~ on principle.

pri'ore *sm* (*REL*) prior.

priorità *sf* priority.

'**prisma, i** *sm* prism.

pri'vare *vt*: ~ qn di to deprive sb of; ~rsi di to go *o* do without.

priva'tiva *sf* (*ECON*) monopoly.

pri'vato, a *ag* private ♦ *sm/f* private citizen; in ~ in private.

privazi'one [privat'tsjone] *sf* privation, hardship.

privilegi'are [privile'dʒare] *vt* to grant a privilege to.

privi'legio [privi'lɛdʒo] *sm* privilege.

'**privo, a** *ag:* ~ di without, lacking.

pro *prep* for, on behalf of ♦ *sm inv* (*utilità*) advantage, benefit; a che ~? what's the use?; il ~ e il contro the pros and cons.

pro'babile *ag* probable, likely; **probabilità** *sf inv* probability.

pro'blema, i *sm* problem.

pro'boscide [pro'bɔʃʃide] *sf* (*di elefante*) trunk.

procacci'are [prokat'tʃare] *vt* to get, obtain.

pro'cedere [pro'tʃɛdere] *vi* to proceed; (*comportarsi*) to behave; (*iniziare*): ~

a to start; ~ contro (*DIR*) to start legal proceedings against; **procedi'mento** *sm* (*modo di condurre*) procedure; (*di avvenimenti*) course; (*TECN*) process; **procedimento penale** (*DIR*) criminal proceedings; **proce'dura** *sf* (*DIR*) procedure.

proces'sare [protʃes'sare] *vt* (*DIR*) to try.

processi'one [protʃes'sjone] *sf* procession.

pro'cesso [pro'tʃɛsso] *sm* (*DIR*) trial; proceedings *pl*; (*metodo*) process.

pro'cinto [pro'tʃinto] *sm*: in ~ di fare about to do, on the point of doing.

pro'clama, i *sm* proclamation.

procla'mare *vt* to proclaim.

procre'are *vt* to procreate.

pro'cura *sf* (*DIR*) proxy; power of attorney; (*ufficio*) attorney's office.

procu'rare *vt*: ~ qc a qn (*fornire*) to get *o* obtain sth for sb; (*causare: noie etc*) to bring *o* give sb sth.

procura'tore, 'trice *sm/f* (*DIR*) ≈ solicitor; (*: chi ha la procura*) attorney; proxy; ~ generale (*in corte d'appello*) public prosecutor; (*in corte di cassazione*) Attorney General; ~ della Repubblica (*in corte d'assise, tribunale*) public prosecutor.

prodi'gare *vt* to be lavish with; ~rsi per qn to do all one can for sb.

pro'digio [pro'didʒo] *sm* marvel, wonder; (*persona*) prodigy; **prodigi'oso, a** *ag* prodigious; phenomenal.

'**prodigo, a, ghi, ghe** *ag* lavish, extravagant.

pro'dotto, a *pp di* **produrre** ♦ *sm* product; ~i agricoli farm produce *sg*.

pro'durre *vt* to produce; **produttività** *sf* productivity; **produt'tivo, a** *ag* productive; **produt'tore, 'trice** *sm/f* producer; **produzi'one** *sf* production; (*rendimento*) output.

pro'emio *sm* introduction, preface.

Prof. *abbr* (= *professore*) Prof.

profa'nare *vt* to desecrate.

pro'fano, a *ag* (*mondano*) secular; profane; (*sacrilego*) profane.

profe'rire *vt* to utter.

profes'sare *vt* to profess; *(medicina etc)* to practise.

professio'nale *ag* professional.

professi'one *sf* profession; **professio'nista, i, e** *sm/f* professional.

profes'sore, 'essa *sm/f (INS)* teacher; (*: di università*) lecturer; (*: titolare di cattedra*) professor.

pro'feta, i *sm* prophet; **profe'zia** *sf* prophecy.

pro'ficuo, a *ag* useful, profitable.

profi'lare *vt* to outline; *(ornare: vestito)* to edge; **~rsi** *vr* to stand out, be silhouetted; to loom up.

pro'filo *sm* profile; *(breve descrizione)* sketch, outline; **di ~** in profile.

profit'tare *vi*: **~ di** *(trarre profitto)* to profit by; *(approfittare)* to take advantage of.

pro'fitto *sm* advantage, profit, benefit; *(fig: progresso)* progress; *(COMM)* profit.

profondità *sf inv* depth.

pro'fondo, a *ag* deep; *(rancore, meditazione)* profound ♦ *sm* depth(s *pl*), bottom; **~ 8 metri** 8 metres deep.

'profugo, a, ghi, ghe *sm/f* refugee.

profu'mare *vt* to perfume ♦ *vi* to be fragrant; **~rsi** *vr* to put on perfume *o* scent.

profume'ria *sf* perfumery; *(negozio)* perfume shop.

pro'fumo *sm (prodotto)* perfume, scent; *(fragranza)* scent, fragrance.

profusi'one *sf* profusion; **a ~** in plenty.

proget'tare [prodʒet'tare] *vt* to plan; *(TECN: edificio)* to plan, design; **pro'getto** *sm* plan; *(idea)* plan, project; **progetto di legge** bill.

pro'gramma, i *sm* programme; *(TV, RADIO)* programmes *pl*; *(INS)* syllabus, curriculum; *(INFORM)* program; **program'mare** *vt (TV, RADIO)* to put on; *(INFORM)* to program; *(ECON)* to plan; **programma'tore, 'trice** *sm/f (INFORM)* computer programmer.

progre'dire *vi* to progress, make progress.

progres'sivo, a *ag* progressive.

pro'gresso *sm* progress *no pl*; **fare ~i** to make progress.

proi'bire *vt* to forbid, prohibit; **proibi'tivo, a** *ag* prohibitive; **proibizi'one** *sf* prohibition.

proiet'tare *vt (gen, GEOM, CINEMA)* to project; (*: presentare*) to show, screen; *(luce, ombra)* to throw, cast, project; **proi'ettile** *sm* projectile, bullet *(o shell etc)*; **proiet'tore** *sm (CINEMA)* projector; *(AUT)* headlamp; *(MIL)* searchlight; **proiezi'one** *sf (CINEMA)* projection; showing.

'prole *sf* children *pl*, offspring.

prole'tario, a *ag, sm* proletarian.

prolife'rare *vi (fig)* to proliferate.

pro'lisso, a *ag* verbose.

'prologo, ghi *sm* prologue.

pro'lunga, ghe *sf (di cavo elettrico etc)* extension.

prolun'gare *vt (discorso, attesa)* to prolong; *(linea, termine)* to extend.

prome'moria *sm inv* memorandum.

pro'messa *sf* promise.

pro'messo, a *pp di* **promettere**.

pro'mettere *vt* to promise ♦ *vi* to be *o* look promising; **~ a qn di fare** to promise sb that one will do.

promi'nente *ag* prominent.

promiscuità *sf* promiscuousness.

promon'torio *sm* promontory, headland.

pro'mosso, a *pp di* **promuovere**.

promo'tore, trice *sm/f* promoter, organizer.

promozi'one [promot'tsjone] *sf* promotion.

promul'gare *vt* to promulgate.

promu'overe *vt* to promote.

proni'pote *sm/f (di nonni)* great-grandchild, great-grandson/grand-daughter; *(di zii)* great-nephew/niece; **~i** *smpl (discendenti)* descendants.

pro'nome *sm (LING)* pronoun.

pron'tezza [pron'tettsa] *sf* readiness; quickness, promptness.

'pronto, a *ag* ready; *(rapido)* fast, quick, prompt; **~!** *(TEL)* hello!; **~ all'ira** quick-tempered; **~ soccorso** first aid.

prontu'ario *sm* manual, handbook.
pro'nuncia [pro'nuntʃa] *sf* pronunciation.
pronunci'are [pronun'tʃare] *vt* (*parola*, *sentenza*) to pronounce; (*dire*) to utter; (*discorso*) to deliver; ~**rsi** *vr* to declare one's opinion; **pronunci'ato, a** *ag* (*spiccato*) pronounced, marked; (*sporgente*) prominent.
pro'nunzia *etc* [pro'nuntsja] = **pronuncia** *etc*.
propa'ganda *sf* propaganda.
propa'gare *vt* (*notizia, malattia*) to spread; (*REL, BIOL*) to propagate; ~**rsi** *vr* to spread; (*BIOL*) to propagate; (*FISICA*) to be propagated.
pro'pendere *vi*: ~ **per** to favour, lean towards; **propensi'one** *sf* inclination, propensity; **pro'penso, a** *pp di* **propendere**.
propi'nare *vt* to administer.
pro'pizio, a [pro'pittsjo] *ag* favourable.
pro'porre *vt* (*suggerire*): ~ **qc (a qn)** to suggest sth (to sb); (*candidato*) to put forward; (*legge, brindisi*) to propose; ~ **di fare** to suggest *o* propose doing; **proporsi di fare** to propose *o* intend to do; **proporsi una meta** to set o.s. a goal.
proporzio'nale [proportsjo'nale] *ag* proportional.
proporzio'nare [proportsjo'nare] *vt*: ~ **qc a** to proportion *o* adjust sth to.
proporzi'one [propor'tsjone] *sf* proportion; **in** ~ **a** in proportion to.
pro'posito *sm* (*intenzione*) intention, aim; (*argomento*) subject, matter; **a** ~ **di** regarding, with regard to; **di** ~ (*apposta*) deliberately, on purpose; **a** ~ by the way; **capitare a** ~ (*cosa, persona*) to turn up at the right time.
proposizi'one [propozit'tsjone] *sf* (*LING*) clause; (: *periodo*) sentence.
pro'posta *sf* proposal; (*suggerimento*) suggestion; ~**a di legge** bill.
pro'posto, a *pp di* **proporre**.
proprietà *sf inv* (*ciò che si possiede*) property *gen no pl*, estate; (*caratteristica*) property; (*correttezza*) correctness; **proprie'tario, a** *sm/f* owner; (*di*

albergo etc) proprietor, owner; (*per l'inquilino*) landlord/lady.
'proprio, a *ag* (*possessivo*) own; (: *impersonale*) one's; (*esatto*) exact, correct, proper; (*senso, significato*) literal; (*LING: nome*) proper; (*particolare*): ~ **di** characteristic of, peculiar to ♦ *av* (*precisamente*) just, exactly; (*davvero*) really; (*affatto*): **non ... ~** not ... at all; **l'ha visto con i (suoi) ~i occhi** he saw it with his own eyes.
'prora *sf* (*NAUT*) bow(s *pl*), prow.
'proroga, ghe *sf* extension; postponement; **proro'gare** *vt* to extend; (*differire*) to postpone, defer.
pro'rompere *vi* to burst out; **pro'rotto, a** *pp di* **prorompere**.
'prosa *sf* prose; **pro'saico, a, ci, che** *ag* (*fig*) prosaic, mundane.
pro'sciogliere [proʃ'ʃɔʎʎere] *vt* to release; (*DIR*) to acquit; **prosci'olto, a** *pp di* **prosciogliere**.
prosciu'gare [proʃʃu'gare] *vt* (*terreni*) to drain, reclaim; ~**rsi** *vr* to dry up.
prosci'utto [proʃ'ʃutto] *sm* ham.
prosegui'mento *sm* continuation; **buon** ~! all the best!; (*a chi viaggia*) enjoy the rest of your journey!
prosegu'ire *vt* to carry on with, continue ♦ *vi* to carry on, go on.
prospe'rare *vi* to thrive; **prosperità** *sf* prosperity; **'prospero, a** *ag* (*fiorente*) flourishing, thriving, prosperous; **pro-spe'roso, a** *ag* (*robusto*) hale and hearty; (: *ragazza*) buxom.
prospet'tare *vt* (*esporre*) to point out, show; ~**rsi** *vr* to carry on, appear.
prospet'tiva *sf* (*ARTE*) perspective; (*veduta*) view; (*fig: previsione, possibilità*) prospect.
pros'petto *sm* (*DISEGNO*) elevation; (*veduta*) view, prospect; (*facciata*) façade, front; (*tabella*) table; (*sommario*) summary.
prospici'ente [prospi'tʃɛnte] *ag*: ~ **qc** facing *o* overlooking sth.
prossimità *sf* nearness, proximity; **in** ~ **di** near (to), close to.
'prossimo, a *ag* (*vicino*): ~ **a** near

(to), close to; (*che viene subito dopo*) next; (*parente*) close ♦ *sm* neighbour, fellow man.

prosti'tuta *sf* prostitute; **prostituzi'one** *sf* prostitution.

pros'trare *vt* (*fig*) to exhaust, wear out; **~rsi** *vr* (*fig*) to humble o.s.

protago'nista, i, e *sm/f* protagonist.

pro'teggere [pro'tɛddʒere] *vt* to protect.

prote'ina *sf* protein.

pro'tendere *vt* to stretch out; **pro'teso, a** *pp di* **protendere**.

pro'testa *sf* protest.

protes'tante *ag, sm/f* Protestant.

protes'tare *vt, vi* to protest; **~rsi** *vr*: **~rsi innocente** *etc* to protest one's innocence *o* that one is innocent *etc*.

protet'tivo, a *ag* protective.

pro'tetto, a *pp di* **proteggere**.

protet'tore, 'trice *sm/f* protector; (*sostenitore*) patron.

protezi'one [protet'tsjone] *sf* protection; (*patrocinio*) patronage.

protocol'lare *vt* to register ♦ *ag* formal; of protocol.

proto'collo *sm* protocol; (*registro*) register of documents.

pro'totipo *sm* prototype.

pro'trarre *vt* (*prolungare*) to prolong; **pro'tratto, a** *pp di* **protrarre**.

protube'ranza [protube'rantsa] *sf* protuberance, bulge.

'prova *sf* (*esperimento, cimento*) test, trial; (*tentativo*) attempt, try; (*MAT, testimonianza, documento etc*) proof; (*DIR*) evidence *no pl*, proof; (*INS*) exam, test; (*TEATRO*) rehearsal; (*di abito*) fitting; **a ~ di** (*in testimonianza di*) as proof of; **a ~ di fuoco** fireproof; **fino a ~ contraria** until it is proved otherwise; **mettere alla ~** to put to the test; **giro di ~ test** *o* trial run; **~ generale** (*TEATRO*) dress rehearsal.

pro'vare *vt* (*sperimentare*) to test; (*tentare*) to try, attempt; (*assaggiare*) to try, taste; (*sperimentare in sé*) to experience; (*sentire*) to feel; (*cimentare*) to put to the test; (*dimostrare*) to prove; (*abito*) to try on; **~rsi** *vr*: **~rsi (a fare)** to try *o*

attempt (to do); **~ a fare** to try *o* attempt to do.

proveni'enza [prove'njɛntsa] *sf* origin, source.

prove'nire *vi*: **~ da** to come from.

pro'venti *smpl* revenue *sg*.

prove'nuto, a *pp di* **provenire**.

pro'verbio *sm* proverb.

pro'vetta *sf* test tube; **bambino in ~** test-tube baby.

pro'vetto, a *ag* skilled, experienced.

pro'vincia, ce *o* **cie** [pro'vintʃa] *sf* province; **provinci'ale** *ag* provincial; (*strada*) **provinciale** main road (*BRIT*), highway (*US*).

pro'vino *sm* (*CINEMA*) screen test; (*campione*) specimen.

provo'cante *ag* (*attraente*) provocative.

provo'care *vt* (*causare*) to cause, bring about; (*eccitare: riso, pietà*) to arouse; (*irritare, sfidare*) to provoke; **provoca'torio, a** *ag* provocative; **provocazi'one** *sf* provocation.

provve'dere *vi* (*disporre*): **~ (a)** to provide (for); (*prendere un provvedimento*) to take steps, act ♦ *vt*: **~ qc a qn** to supply sth to sb; **~rsi** *vr*: **~rsi di** to provide o.s. with; **provvedi'mento** *sm* measure; (*di previdenza*) precaution.

provvi'denza [provvi'dɛntsa] *sf*: **la ~** providence; **provvidenzi'ale** *ag* providential.

provvigi'one [provvi'dʒone] *sf* (*COMM*) commission.

provvi'sorio, a *ag* temporary.

prov'vista *sf* provision, supply.

'prua *sf* (*NAUT*) = **prora**.

pru'dente *ag* cautious, prudent; (*assennato*) sensible, wise; **pru'denza** *sf* prudence, caution; wisdom.

'prudere *vi* to itch, be itchy.

'prugna ['pruɲɲa] *sf* plum; **~ secca** prune.

prurigi'noso, a [pruridʒi'noso] *ag* itchy.

pru'rito *sm* itchiness *no pl*; itch.

P.S. *abbr* (= *postscriptum*) P.S.; (*POLIZIA*) = **Pubblica Sicurezza**.

pseu'donimo *sm* pseudonym.

PSI *sigla m* = **Partito Socialista Italiano**.

psicana'lista, i, e *sm/f* psychoanalyst.

'psiche ['psike] *sf* (*PSIC*) psyche.

psichi'atra, i, e [psi'kjatra] *sm/f* psychiatrist; **psichi'atrico, a, ci, che** *ag* psychiatric.

'psichico, a, ci, che ['psikiko] *ag* psychological.

psicolo'gia [psikolo'dʒia] *sf* psychology; **psico'logico, a, ci, che** *ag* psychological; **psi'cologo, a, gi, ghe** *sm/f* psychologist.

psico'patico, a, ci, che *ag* psychopathic ♦ *sm/f* psychopath.

P.T. *abbr* = Posta e Telegrafi.

pubbli'care *vt* to publish.

pubblicazi'one [pubblikat'tsjone] *sf* publication; **~i (matrimoniali)** *sfpl* (marriage) banns.

pubbli'cista, i, e [pubbli'tʃista] *sm/f* (*STAMPA*) occasional contributor.

pubblicità [pubblitʃi'ta] *sf* (*diffusione*) publicity; (*attività*) advertising; (*annunci nei giornali*) advertisements *pl*; **pubblici'tario, a** *ag* advertising *cpd*; (*trovata, film*) publicity *cpd*.

'pubblico, a, ci, che *ag* public; (*statale: scuola etc*) state *cpd* ♦ *sm* public; (*spettatori*) audience; **in ~** in public; **~ funzionario** civil servant; **P~ Ministero** Public Prosecutor's Office; **la P~a Sicurezza** the police.

'pube *sm* (*ANAT*) pubis.

pubertà *sf* puberty.

'pudico, a, ci, che *ag* modest.

pu'dore *sm* modesty.

puericul'tura *sf* paediatric nursing; infant care.

pue'rile *ag* childish.

pugi'lato [pudʒi'lato] *sm* boxing.

'pugile ['pudʒile] *sm* boxer.

pugna'lare [puɲɲa'lare] *vt* to stab.

pu'gnale [puɲ'ɲale] *sm* dagger.

'pugno ['puɲɲo] *sm* fist; (*colpo*) punch; (*quantità*) fistful.

'pulce ['pultʃe] *sf* flea.

pul'cino [pul'tʃino] *sm* chick.

pu'ledro, a *sm/f* colt/filly.

pu'leggia, ge [pu'leddʒa] *sf* pulley.

pu'lire *vt* to clean; (*lucidare*) to polish; **pu'lita** *sf* quick clean; **pu'lito, a** *ag* (*anche fig*) clean; (*ordinato*) neat, tidy; **puli'tura** *sf* cleaning; **pulitura a secco** dry cleaning; **pu'lizia** *sf* cleaning; cleanness; **fare le pulizie** to do the cleaning, do the housework.

'pullman *sm inv* coach.

pul'lover *sm inv* pullover, jumper.

pullu'lare *vi* to swarm, teem.

pul'mino *sm* minibus.

'pulpito *sm* pulpit.

pul'sante *sm* (push-)button.

pul'sare *vi* to pulsate, beat; **pulsazi'one** *sf* beat.

pul'viscolo *sm* fine dust.

'puma *sm inv* puma.

pun'gente [pun'dʒɛnte] *ag* prickly; stinging; (*anche fig*) biting.

'pungere ['pundʒere] *vt* to prick; (*sog: insetto, ortica*) to sting; (: *freddo*) to bite.

pungigli'one [pundʒiʎ'ʎone] *sm* sting.

pu'nire *vt* to punish; **punizi'one** *sf* punishment; (*SPORT*) penalty.

'punta *sf* point; (*parte terminale*) tip, end; (*di monte*) peak; (*di costa*) promontory; (*minima parte*) touch, trace; **in ~ di piedi** on tip-toe; **ore di ~** peak hours; **uomo di ~** front-rank *o* leading man.

pun'tare *vt* (*piedi a terra, gomiti sul tavolo*) to plant; (*dirigere: pistola*) to point; (*scommettere*) to bet ♦ *vi* (*mirare*): **~ a** to aim at; (*avviarsi*): **~ su** to head *o* make for; (*fig: contare*): **~ su** to count *o* rely on.

pun'tata *sf* (*gita*) short trip; (*scommessa*) bet; (*parte di opera*) instalment; **romanzo a ~e** serial.

punteggia'tura [punteddʒa'tura] *sf* (*LING*) punctuation.

pun'teggio [pun'teddʒo] *sm* score.

puntel'lare *vt* to support.

pun'tello *sm* prop, support.

puntigli'oso, a [puntiʎ'ʎoso] *ag* punctilious.

pun'tina *sf*: **~ da disegno** drawing pin.

pun'tino *sm* dot; **fare qc a ~** to do sth properly.

'punto, a *pp di* pungere ♦ *sm* (*segno*, *macchiolina*) dot; (*LING*) full stop; (*MAT, momento, di punteggio, fig*: *argomento*) point; (*posto*) spot; (*a scuola*) mark; (*nel cucire, nella maglia, MED*) stitch ♦ *av*: **non ... ~** not at all; **due ~i** *sm* (*LING*) colon; **sul ~ di fare** (just) about to do; **fare il ~** (*NAUT*) to take a bearing; (*fig*): **fare il ~ della situazione** to take stock of the situation; to sum up the situation; **alle 6 in ~** at 6 o'clock sharp *o* on the dot; **essere a buon ~** to have reached a satisfactory stage; **mettere a ~** to adjust; (*motore*) to tune; (*cannocchiale*) to focus; (*fig*) to settle; **di ~ in bianco** point-blank; **~ cardinale** point of the compass, cardinal point; **~ debole** weak point; **~ esclamativo/interrogativo** exclamation/question mark; **~ di riferimento** landmark; (*fig*) point of reference; **~ di vendita** retail outlet; **~ e virgola** semicolon; **~ di vista** (*fig*) point of view; **~i di sospensione** suspension points.

puntu'ale *ag* punctual; **puntualità** *sf* punctuality.

pun'tura *sf* (*di ago*) prick; (*di insetto*) sting, bite; (*MED*) puncture; (: *iniezione*) injection; (*dolore*) sharp pain.

punzecchi'are [puntsek'kjare] *vt* to prick; (*fig*) to tease.

pun'zone [pun'tsone] *sm* (*per metalli*) stamp, die.

'pupa *sf* doll.

pu'pazzo [pu'pattso] *sm* puppet.

pu'pilla *sf* (*ANAT*) pupil; *vedi anche* pupillo.

pu'pillo, a *sm/f* (*DIR*) ward; (*prediletto*) favourite, pet.

purché [pur'ke] *cong* provided that, on condition that.

'pure *cong* (*tuttavia*) and yet, nevertheless; (*anche se*) even if ♦ *av* (*anche*) too, also; **pur di** (*al fine di*) just to; **faccia ~!** go ahead!, please do!

purè *sm* (*CUC*) purée; (: *di patate*) mashed potatoes.

pu'rea *sf* = purè.

pu'rezza [pu'rettsa] *sf* purity.

'purga, ghe *sf* (*MED*) purging *no pl*; purge; (*POL*) purge.

pur'gante *sm* (*MED*) purgative, purge.

pur'gare *vt* (*MED, POL*) to purge; (*pulire*) to clean.

purga'torio *sm* purgatory.

purifi'care *vt* to purify; (*metallo*) to refine.

puri'tano, a *ag, sm/f* puritan.

'puro, a *ag* pure; (*acqua*) clear, limpid; (*vino*) undiluted; **puro'sangue** *sm/f inv* thoroughbred.

pur'troppo *av* unfortunately.

'pustola *sf* pimple.

puti'ferio *sm* rumpus, row.

putre'fare *vi* to putrefy, rot; **putre'fatto, a** *pp di* putrefare.

'putrido, a *ag* putrid, rotten.

put'tana (*fam!*) *sf* whore (!).

'puzza ['puttsa] *sf* = puzzo.

puz'zare [put'tsare] *vi* to stink.

'puzzo ['puttso] *sm* stink, foul smell.

'puzzola ['puttsola] *sf* polecat.

puzzo'lente [puttso'lɛnte] *ag* stinking.

Q

qua *av* here; **in ~** (*verso questa parte*) this way; **da un anno in ~** for a year now; **da quando in ~?** since when?; **per di ~** (*passare*) this way; **al di ~ di** (*fiume, strada*) on this side of; **~ dentro/fuori** *etc* in/out here *etc*; *vedi* questo.

qua'derno *sm* notebook; (*per scuola*) exercise book.

qua'drante *sm* quadrant; (*di orologio*) face.

qua'drare *vi* (*bilancio*) to balance, tally; (*descrizione*) to correspond; (*fig*): **~ a** to please, be to one's liking ♦ *vt* (*MAT*) to square; **non mi quadra** I don't like it; **qua'drato, a** *ag* square; (*fig*: *equilibrato*) level-headed, sensible; (: *peg*) square ♦ *sm* (*MAT*) square; (*PUGILATO*) ring; **5 al quadrato** 5 squared.

qua'dretto *sm*: **a ~i** (*tessuto*) checked; (*foglio*) squared.

quadri'foglio [kwadri'fɔʎʎo] *sm* four-leaf clover.

'quadro *sm* (*pittura*) painting, picture; (*quadrato*) square; (*tabella*) table, chart; (*TECN*) board, panel; (*TEATRO*) scene; (*fig: scena, spettacolo*) sight; (: *descrizione*) outline, description; **~i** *smpl* (*POL*) party organizers; (*MIL*) cadres; (*COMM*) managerial staff; (*CARTE*) diamonds.

'quadruplo, a *ag, sm* quadruple.

quaggiù [kwad'dʒu] *av* down here.

'quaglia ['kwaʎʎa] *sf* quail.

PAROLA CHIAVE

'qualche ['kwalke] *det* **1** some, a few; (*in interrogative*) any; **ho comprato ~ libro** I've bought some *o* a few books; **~ volta** sometimes; **hai ~ sigaretta?** have you any cigarettes?
2 (*uno*): **c'è ~ medico?** is there a doctor?; **in ~ modo** somehow
3 (*un certo, parecchio*) some; **un personaggio di ~ rilievo** a figure of some importance
4: **~ cosa** = **qualcosa**.

---

qualche'duno [kwalke'duno] *pron* = **qualcuno**.

qual'cosa *pron* something; (*in espressioni interrogative*) anything; **qualcos'altro** something else; anything else; **~ di nuovo** something new; anything new; **~ da mangiare** something to eat; **anything to eat**; **~ che non va?** is there something *o* anything wrong?

qual'cuno *pron* (*persona*) someone, somebody; (: *in espressioni interrogative*) anyone, anybody; (*alcuni*) some; **~ è favorevole a noi** some are on our side; **qualcun altro** someone *o* somebody else; anyone *o* anybody else.

PAROLA CHIAVE

'quale (*spesso troncato in* **qual**) *det* **1** (*interrogativo*) what; (: *scegliendo tra due o più cose o persone*) which; **~ uomo/denaro?** what man/money?; which man/money?; **~i sono i tuoi programmi?** what are your plans?; **~**

stanza preferisci? which room do you prefer?
2 (*relativo: come*): **il risultato fu ~ ci si aspettava** the result was as expected
3 (*esclamativo*) what; **~ disgrazia!** what bad luck!
♦ *pron* **1** (*interrogativo*) which; **~ dei due scegli?** which of the two do you want?
2 (*relativo*): **il(la) ~** (*persona: soggetto*) who; (: *oggetto, con preposizione*) whom; (*cosa*) which; (*possessivo*) whose; **suo padre, il ~ è avvocato, ...** his father, who is a lawyer, ...; **il signore con il ~ parlavo** the gentleman to whom I was speaking; **l'albergo al ~ ci siamo fermati** the hotel where we stayed *o* which we stayed at; **la signora della ~ ammiriamo la bellezza** the lady whose beauty we admire
3 (*relativo: in elenchi*) such as, like; **piante ~i l'edera** plants like *o* such as ivy; **~ sindaco di questa città** as mayor of this town.

---

qua'lifica, che *sf* qualification; (*titolo*) title.

qualifi'care *vt* to qualify; (*definire*): **~ qn/qc come** to describe sb/sth as; **~rsi** *vr* (*anche SPORT*) to qualify; **qualifica'tivo, a** *ag* qualifying; **qualificazi'one** *sf* qualification; **gara di qualificazione** (*SPORT*) qualifying event.

qualità *sf inv* quality; **in ~ di** in one's capacity as.

qua'lora *cong* in case, if.

qual'siasi *det inv* = **qualunque**.

qua'lunque *det inv* any; (*quale che sia*) whatever; (*discriminativo*) whichever; (*posposto: mediocre*) poor, indifferent; ordinary; **mettiti un vestito ~** put on any old dress; **~ cosa** anything; **~ cosa accada** whatever happens; **a ~ costo** at any cost, whatever the cost; **l'uomo ~** the man in the street; **~ persona** anyone, anybody.

'quando *cong, av* when; **~ sarò ricco** when I'm rich; **da ~** (*dacché*) since; (*interrogativo*): **da ~ sei qui?** how long have you been here?; **quand'anche** even if.

quantità *sf inv* quantity; (*gran numero*): **una ~ di** a great deal of; a lot of; **in grande ~** in large quantities; **quantita'tivo** *sm* (*COMM*) amount, quantity.

PAROLA CHIAVE

'quanto, a *det* **1** (*interrogativo: quantità*) how much; (: *numero*) how many; **~ pane/denaro?** how much bread/money?; **~i libri/ragazzi?** how many books/boys?; **~ tempo?** how long?; **~i anni hai?** how old are you? **2** (*esclamativo*): **~e storie!** what a lot of nonsense!; **~ tempo sprecato!** what a waste of time! **3** (*relativo: quantità*) as much ... as; (: *numero*) as many ... as; **ho ~ denaro mi occorre** I have as much money as I need; **prendi ~i libri vuoi** take as many books as you like

♦ *pron* **1** (*interrogativo: quantità*) how much; (: *numero*) how many; (: *tempo*) how long; **~ mi dai?** how much will you give me?; **~i me ne hai portati?** how many did you bring me?; **da ~ sei qui?** how long have you been here?; **~i ne abbiamo oggi?** what's the date today? **2** (*relativo: quantità*) as much as; (: *numero*) as many as; **farò ~ posso** I'll do as much as I can; **possono venire ~i sono stati invitati** all those who have been invited can come

♦ *av* **1** (*interrogativo: con ag, av*) how; (: *con vb*) how much; **~ stanco ti sembrava?** how tired did he seem to be?; **~ corre la tua moto?** how fast can your motorbike go?; **~ costa?** how much does it cost?; **quant'è?** how much is it? **2** (*esclamativo: con ag, av*) how; (: *con vb*) how much; **~ sono felice!** how happy I am!; **sapessi ~ abbiamo camminato!** if you knew how far we've walked!; **studierò ~ posso** I'll study as much as *o* all I can; **~ prima** as soon as possible **3**: **in ~** (*in qualità di*) as; (*perché, per*

il fatto che) as, since; (**in**) **~ a** (*per ciò che riguarda*) as for, as regards **4**: **per ~** (*nonostante, anche se*) however; **per ~ si sforzi, non ce la farà** try as he may, he won't manage it; **per ~ sia brava, fa degli errori** however good she may be, she makes mistakes; **per ~ io sappia** as far as I know.

quan'tunque *cong* although, though.
qua'ranta *num* forty.
quaran'tena *sf* quarantine.
quaran'tesimo, a *num* fortieth.
quaran'tina *sf*: **una ~ (di)** about forty.
qua'resima *sf*: **la ~** Lent.
'quarta *sf* (*AUT*) fourth (gear); *vedi anche* **quarto.**
quar'tetto *sm* quartet(te).
quarti'ere *sm* district, area; (*MIL*) quarters *pl*; **~ generale** headquarters *pl*, HQ.
'quarto, a *ag* fourth ♦ *sm* fourth; (*quarta parte*) quarter; **le 6 e un ~** a quarter past six; **~ d'ora** quarter of an hour; **~i di finale** quarter final.
'quarzo ['kwartso] *sm* quartz.
'quasi *av* almost, nearly ♦ *cong* (*anche: ~ che*) as if; (**non**) **... ~ mai** hardly ever; **~ me ne andrei** I've half a mind to leave.
quas'sù *av* up here.
'quatto, a *ag* crouched, squatting; (*silenzioso*) silent; **~ ~** very quietly, stealthily.
quat'tordici [kwat'torditʃi] *num* fourteen.
quat'trini *smpl* money *sg*, cash *sg*.
'quattro *num* four; **in ~ e quattr'otto** in less than no time; **quattro'cento** *num* four hundred ♦ *sm*: **il Quattrocento** the fifteenth century; **quattro'mila** *num* four thousand.

PAROLA CHIAVE

'quello, a (*dav sm* **quel** +*C*, **quell'** +*V*, **quello** +*s impura, gn, pn, ps, x, z; pl* **quei** +*C*, **quegli** +*V o s impura, gn, pn, ps, x, z; dav sf* **quella** +*C*, **quell'** +*V; pl* **quelle**) *det* that; those *pl*; **~a casa** that house; **quegli uomini** those men; **voglio**

~a camicia (lì o là) I want that shirt
♦ pron 1 (dimostrativo) that (one);
those (ones) pl; (ciò) that; conosci ~a?
do you know that woman?; prendo ~
bianco I'll take the white one; chi è ~?
who's that?; prendiamo ~ (lì o là) let's
take that one (there)
2 (relativo): ~(a) che the
one (who); (cosa) the one (which), the
one (that); ~i(e) che (persone) those
who; (cose) those which; è lui ~ che
non voleva venire he's the one who
didn't want to come; ho fatto ~ che
potevo I did what I could.

'**quercia, ce** ['kwɛrtʃa] sf oak (tree);
(legno) oak.
que'rela sf (DIR) (legal) action;
quere'lare vt to bring an action against.
que'sito sm question, query; problem.
questio'nare vi: ~ di/su qc to argue
about/over sth.
questio'nario sm questionnaire.
questi'one sf problem, question; (controversia) issue; (litigio) quarrel; in ~
in question; fuor di ~ out of the question; è ~ di tempo it's a matter o question of time.

PAROLA CHIAVE

'**questo, a** det 1 (dimostrativo) this;
these pl; ~ libro (qui o qua) this book;
io prendo ~ cappotto, tu quello I'll take
this coat, you take that one; quest'oggi
today; ~a sera this evening
2 (enfatico): non fatemi più prendere
di ~e paure don't frighten me like that
again
♦ pron (dimostrativo) this (one); these
(ones) pl; (ciò) this; prendo ~ (qui o
qua) I'll take this one; preferisci ~i o
quelli? do you prefer these (ones) or
those (ones)?; ~ intendevo io this is
what I meant; vengono Paolo e Luca:
~ da Roma, quello da Palermo Paolo
and Luca are coming: the former from
Palermo, the latter from Rome.

ques'tore sm ≈ chief constable (BRIT),
≈ police commissioner (US).

'**questua** sf collection (of alms).
ques'tura sf police headquarters pl.
qui av here; da o di ~ from here; di ~
in avanti from now on; di ~ a poco/una
settimana in a little while/a week's
time; ~ dentro/sopra/vicino in/up/near
here; vedi questo.
quie'tanza [kwje'tantsa] sf receipt.
quie'tare vt to calm, soothe.
qui'ete sf quiet, quietness; calmness;
stillness; peace.
qui'eto, a ag quiet; (notte) calm, still;
(mare) calm.
'**quindi** av then ♦ cong therefore, so.
'**quindici** ['kwinditʃi] num fifteen;
giorni a fortnight (BRIT), two weeks.
quindi'cina [kwindi'tʃina] sf (serie): una
~ (di) about fifteen; fra una ~ di giorni
in a fortnight.
quin'quennio sm period of five years.
quin'tale sm quintal (100 kg).
'**quinte** sfpl (TEATRO) wings.
'**quinto, a** num fifth.
'**quota** sf (parte) quota, share; (AER)
height, altitude; (IPPICA) odds pl;
prendere/perdere ~ (AER) to gain/lose
height o altitude; ~ d'iscrizione enrolment fee; (ad un club) membership
fee.
quo'tare vt (BORSA) to quote;
quotazi'one sf quotation.
quotidi'ano, a ag daily; (banale)
everyday ♦ sm (giornale) daily
(paper).
quozi'ente [kwot'tsjɛnte] sm (MAT)
quotient; ~ d'intelligenza intelligence
quotient, IQ.

R

ra'barbaro sm rhubarb.
'**rabbia** sf (ira) anger, rage;
(accanimento, furia) fury; (MED:
idrofobia) rabies sg.
rab'bino sm rabbi.
rabbi'oso, a ag angry, furious; (facile
all'ira) quick-tempered; (forze, acqua
etc) furious, raging; (MED) rabid, mad.
rabbo'nire vt to calm down; ~rsi vr to

calm down.

rabbrivi'dire *vi* to shudder, shiver.

rabbui'arsi *vr* to grow dark.

raccapez'zarsi [rakkapet'tsarsi] *vr*: **non ~** to be at a loss.

raccapricci'ante [rakkaprit'tʃante] *ag* horrifying.

raccatta'palle *sm inv* (SPORT) ballboy.

raccat'tare *vt* to pick up.

rac'chetta [rak'ketta] *sf* (*per tennis*) racket; (*per ping-pong*) bat; **~ da neve** snowshoe; **~ da sci** ski stick.

racchi'udere [rak'kjudere] *vt* to contain; **racchi'uso, a** *pp di* **racchiudere**.

rac'cogliere [rak'kɔʎʎere] *vt* to collect; (*raccattare*) to pick up; (*frutti, fiori*) to pick, pluck; (AGR) to harvest; (*approvazione, voti*) to win; (*profughi*) to take in; **~rsi** *vr* to gather; (*fig*) to gather one's thoughts; to meditate; **raccogli'mento** *sm* meditation; **raccogli'tore** *sm* (*cartella*) folder, binder; **raccoglitore a fogli mobili** loose-leaf binder.

rac'colta *sf* collecting *no pl*; collection; (AGR) harvesting *no pl*, gathering *no pl*; harvest, crop; (*adunata*) gathering.

rac'colto, a *pp di* **raccogliere** ♦ *ag* (*persona: pensoso*) thoughtful; (*luogo: appartato*) secluded, quiet ♦ *sm* (AGR) crop, harvest.

raccoman'dare *vt* to recommend; (*affidare*) to entrust; (*esortare*): **~ a qn di non fare** to tell *o* warn sb not to do; **~rsi** *vr*: **~rsi a qn** to commend o.s. to sb; **mi raccomando!** don't forget!; **raccoman'data** *sf* (*anche: lettera raccomandata*) recorded-delivery letter; **raccomandazi'one** *sf* recommendation.

raccon'tare *vt*: **~ (a qn)** (*dire*) to tell (sb); (*narrare*) to relate (to sb), tell (sb) about; **rac'conto** *sm* telling *no pl*, relating *no pl*; (*fatto raccontato*) story, tale.

raccorci'are [rakkor'tʃare] *vt* to shorten.

rac'cordo *sm* (TECN: *giunzione*) connection, joint; (AUT: *di autostrada*) slip road* (BRIT), entrance (*o* exit) ramp (US); **~ anulare** (AUT) ring road (BRIT), beltway (US).

ra'chitico, a, ci, che [ra'kitiko] *ag* suffering from rickets; (*fig*) scraggy, scrawny.

racimo'lare [ratʃimo'lare] *vt* (*fig*) to scrape together, glean.

'rada *sf* (natural) harbour.

'radar *sm* radar.

raddol'cire [raddol'tʃire] *vt* (*persona, carattere*) to soften; **~rsi** *vr* (*tempo*) to grow milder; (*persona*) to soften, mellow.

raddoppi'are *vt, vi* to double.

raddriz'zare [raddrit'tsare] *vt* to straighten; (*fig: correggere*) to put straight, correct.

'radere *vt* (*barba*) to shave off; (*mento*) to shave; (*fig: rasentare*) to graze; to skim; **~rsi** *vr* to shave (o.s.); **~ al suolo** to raze to the ground.

radi'ale *ag* radial.

radi'are *vt* to strike off.

radia'tore *sm* radiator.

radiazi'one [radjat'tsjone] *sf* (FISICA) radiation; (*cancellazione*) striking off.

radi'cale *ag* radical ♦ *sm* (LING) root.

ra'dicchio [ra'dikkjo] *sm* chicory.

ra'dice [ra'ditʃe] *sf* root.

'radio *sf inv* radio ♦ *sm* (CHIM) radium; **radioat'tivo, a** *ag* radioactive; **radiodiffusi'one** *sf* (radio) broadcasting; **radiogra'fare** *vt* to X-ray; **radiogra'fia** *sf* radiography; (*foto*) X-ray photograph.

radi'oso, a *ag* radiant.

radiostazi'one [radjostat'tsjone] *sf* radio station.

radiotera'pia *sf* radiotherapy.

'rado, a *ag* (*capelli*) sparse, thin; (*visite*) infrequent; **di ~** rarely.

radu'nare *vt*, to gather, assemble; **~rsi** *vr* to gather, assemble.

ra'dura *sf* clearing.

'rafano *sm* horseradish.

raffazzo'nare [raffattso'nare] *vt* to patch up.

raf'fermo, a *ag* stale.

'raffica, che *sf* (METEOR) gust (of wind); (*di colpi: scarica*) burst of gunfire.

raffigu'rare *vt* to represent.

raffi'nare *vt* to refine; **raffina'tezza** *sf* refinement; **raffi'nato, a** *ag* refined; **raffine'ria** *sf* refinery.

raffor'zare [raffor'tsare] *vt* to reinforce.

raffredda'mento *sm* cooling.

raffred'dare *vt* to cool; (*fig*) to dampen, have a cooling effect on; **~rsi** *vr* to grow cool *o* cold; (*prendere un raffreddore*) to catch a cold; (*fig*) to cool (off).

raffred'dato, a *ag* (*MED*): **essere ~** to have a cold.

raffred'dore *sm* (*MED*) cold.

raf'fronto *sm* comparison.

'rafia *sf* (*fibra*) raffia.

ra'gazzo, a [ra'gattso] *sm/f* boy/girl; (*fam: fidanzato*) boyfriend/girlfriend.

raggi'ante [rad'dʒante] *ag* radiant, shining.

'raggio ['raddʒo] *sm* (*di sole etc*) ray; (*MAT, distanza*) radius; (*di ruota etc*) spoke; **~ d'azione** range; **~i X** X-rays.

raggi'rare [raddʒi'rare] *vt* to take in, trick; **rag'giro** *sm* trick.

raggi'ungere [rad'dʒundʒere] *vt* to reach; (*persona: riprendere*) to catch up (with); (*bersaglio*) to hit; (*fig: meta*) to achieve; **raggi'unto, a** *pp di* **raggiungere**.

raggomito'larsi *vr* to curl up.

raggranel'lare *vt* to scrape together.

raggrin'zare [raggrin'tsare] *vt, vi* (*anche: ~rsi*) to wrinkle.

raggrup'pare *vt* to group (together).

raggu'aglio [rag'gwaʎʎo] *sm* comparison; (*informazione, relazione*) piece of information.

ragguar'devole *ag* (*degno di riguardo*) distinguished, notable; (*notevole: somma*) considerable.

ragiona'mento [radʒona'mento] *sm* reasoning *no pl*; arguing *no pl*; argument.

ragio'nare [radʒo'nare] *vi* (*usare la ragione*) to reason; (*discorrere*): **~ (di)** to argue (about).

ragi'one [ra'dʒone] *sf* reason; (*dimostrazione, prova*) argument, reason; (*diritto*) right; **aver ~** to be right; **aver ~ di qn** to get the better of

sb; **dare ~ a qn** to agree with sb; to prove sb right; **perdere la ~** to become insane; (*fig*) to take leave of one's senses; **in ~ di** at the rate of; to the amount of; according to; **a o con ~** rightly, justly; **~ sociale** (*COMM*) corporate name; **a ragion veduta** after due consideration.

ragione'ria [radʒone'ria] *sf* accountancy; accounts department.

ragio'nevole [radʒo'nevole] *ag* reasonable.

ragioni'ere, a [radʒo'njɛre] *sm/f* accountant.

ragli'are [raʎ'ʎare] *vi* to bray.

ragna'tela [raɲɲa'tela] *sf* cobweb, spider's web.

'ragno ['raɲɲo] *sm* spider.

ragù *sm inv* (*CUC*) meat sauce; stew.

RAI-TV [raiti'vu] *sigla f* = **Radio televisione italiana**.

rallegra'menti *smpl* congratulations.

ralle'grare *vt* to cheer up; **~rsi** *vr* to cheer up; (*provare allegrezza*) to rejoice; **~rsi con qn** to congratulate sb.

rallen'tare *vt* to slow down; (*fig*) to lessen, slacken ♦ *vi* to slow down.

raman'zina [raman'dzina] *sf* lecture, telling-off.

'rame *sm* (*CHIM*) copper.

rammari'carsi *vr*: **~ (di)** (*rincrescersi*) to be sorry (about), regret; (*lamentarsi*) to complain (about); **ram'marico, chi** *sm* regret.

rammen'dare *vt* to mend; (*calza*) to darn; **ram'mendo** *sm* mending *no pl*; darning *no pl*; mend; darn.

rammen'tare *vt* to remember, recall; (*richiamare alla memoria*): **~ qc a qn** to remind sb of sth; **~rsi** *vr*: **~rsi (di qc)** to remember (sth).

rammol'lire *vt* to soften ♦ *vi* (*anche: ~rsi*) to go soft.

'ramo *sm* branch.

ramo'scello [ramoʃ'ʃello] *sm* twig.

'rampa *sf* flight (of stairs); **~ di lancio** launching pad.

rampi'cante *ag* (*BOT*) climbing.

ram'pone *sm* harpoon; (*ALPINISMO*) crampon.

'**rana** *sf* frog.
'**rancido, a** ['rantʃido] *ag* rancid.
ran'core *sm* rancour, resentment.
ran'dagio, a, gi, gie *o* **ge** [ran'dadʒo] *ag* (*gatto, cane*) stray.
ran'dello *sm* club, cudgel.
'**rango, ghi** *sm* (*condizione sociale*, *MIL: riga*) rank.
rannicchi'arsi [rannik'kjarsi] *vr* to crouch, huddle.
rannuvo'larsi *vr* to cloud over, become overcast.
ra'nocchio [ra'nɔkkjo] *sm* (edible) frog.
'**rantolo** *sm* wheeze; (*di agonizzanti*) death rattle.
'**rapa** *sf* (*BOT*) turnip.
ra'pace [ra'patʃe] *ag* (*animale*) predatory; (*fig*) rapacious, grasping ♦ *sm* bird of prey.
ra'pare *vt* (*capelli*) to crop, cut very short.
'**rapida** *sf* (*di fiume*) rapid; *vedi anche* **rapido**.
rapida'mente *av* quickly, rapidly.
rapidità *sf* speed.
'**rapido, a** *ag* fast; (*esame, occhiata*) quick, rapid ♦ *sm* (*FERR*) express (train).
rapi'mento *sm* kidnapping; (*fig*) rapture.
ra'pina *sf* robbery; ~ **a mano armata** armed robbery; **rapi'nare** *vt* to rob; **rapina'tore, 'trice** *sm/f* robber.
ra'pire *vt* (*cose*) to steal; (*persone*) to kidnap; (*fig*) to enrapture, delight; **rapi'tore, 'trice** *sm/f* kidnapper.
rappor'tare *vt* (*confrontare*) to compare; (*riprodurre*) to reproduce.
rap'porto *sm* (*resoconto*) report; (*legame*) relationship; (*MAT, TECN*) ratio; ~**i smpl** (*fra persone, paesi*) relations; ~**i sessuali** sexual intercourse *sg*.
rap'prendersi *vr* to coagulate, clot; (*latte*) to curdle.
rappre'saglia [rappre'saʎʎa] *sf* reprisal, retaliation.
rappresen'tante *sm/f* representative; **rappresen'tanza** *sf* delegation, deputation; (*COMM: ufficio, sede*) agency.
rappresen'tare *vt* to represent; (*TEA-*

TRO) to perform; **rappresenta'tivo, a** *ag* representative; **rappresentazi'one** *sf* representation; performing *no pl*; (*spettacolo*) performance.
rap'preso, a *pp di* **rapprendere**.
rapso'dia *sf* rhapsody.
rara'mente *av* seldom, rarely.
rare'fatto, a *ag* rarefied.
'**raro, a** *ag* rare.
ra'sare *vt* (*barba etc*) to shave off; (*siepi, erba*) to trim, cut; ~**rsi** *vr* to shave (o.s.).
raschi'are [ras'kjare] *vt* to scrape; (*macchia, fango*) to scrape off ♦ *vi* to clear one's throat.
rasen'tare *vt* (*andar rasente*) to keep close to; (*sfiorare*) to skim along (*o* over); (*fig*) to border on.
ra'sente *prep:* ~ (**a**) close to, very near.
'**raso, a** *pp di* **radere** ♦ *ag* (*barba*) shaved; (*capelli*) cropped; (*con misure di capacità*) level; (*pieno: bicchiere*) full to the brim ♦ *sm* (*tessuto*) satin; ~ **terra** close to the ground; **un cucchiaio** ~ **a** level spoonful.
ra'soio *sm* razor; ~ **elettrico** electric shaver *o* razor.
ras'segna [ras'seɲɲa] *sf* (*MIL*) inspection, review; (*esame*) inspection; (*resoconto*) review, survey; (*pubblicazione letteraria etc*) review; (*mostra*) exhibition, show; **passare in** ~ (*MIL, fig*) to review.
rasse'gnare [rasseɲ'ɲare] *vt:* ~ **le dimissioni** to resign, hand in one's resignation; ~**rsi** *vr* (*accettare*): ~**rsi (a qc/a fare)** to resign o.s. (to sth/to doing); **rassegnazi'one** *sf* resignation.
rassere'narsi *vr* (*tempo*) to clear up.
rasset'tare *vt* to tidy, put in order; (*aggiustare*) to repair, mend.
rassicu'rare *vt* to reassure.
rasso'dare *vt* to harden, stiffen.
rassomigli'anza [rassomiʎ'ʎantsa] *sf* resemblance.
rassomigli'are [rassomiʎ'ʎare] *vi:* ~ **a** to resemble, look like.
rastrel'lare *vt* to rake; (*fig: perlustrare*) to comb.

rastrelli'era sf rack; (per piatti) dish rack.

ras'trello sm rake.

'rata sf (quota) instalment; **pagare a ~e** to pay by instalments o on hire purchase (BRIT).

ratifi'care vt (DIR) to ratify.

'ratto sm (DIR) abduction; (ZOOL) rat.

rattop'pare vt to patch; **rat'toppo** sm patching no pl; patch.

rattrap'pire vt to make stiff; **~rsi** vr to be stiff.

rattris'tare vt to sadden; **~rsi** vr to become sad.

'rauco, a, chi, che ag hoarse.

rava'nello sm radish.

ravi'oli smpl ravioli sg.

ravve'dersi vr to mend one's ways.

ravvici'nare [ravvitʃi'nare] vt (avvicinare): **~ qc a** to bring sth nearer to; (: due tubi) to bring closer together; (riconciliare) to reconcile, bring together.

ravvi'sare vt to recognize.

ravvi'vare vt to revive; (fig) to brighten up, enliven; **~rsi** vr to revive; to brighten up.

razio'cinio [ratsjo'tʃinjo] sm reasoning no pl; reason; (buon senso) common sense.

razio'nale [rattsjo'nale] ag rational.

razio'nare [rattsjo'nare] vt to ration.

razi'one [rat'tsjone] sf ration; (porzione) portion, share.

'razza ['rattsa] sf race; (ZOOL) breed; (discendenza, stirpe) stock, race; (sorta) sort, kind.

raz'zia [rat'tsia] sf raid, foray.

razzi'ale [rat'tsjale] ag racial.

raz'zismo [rat'tsizmo] sm racism, racialism.

raz'zista, i, e [rat'tsista] ag, sm/f racist, racialist.

'razzo ['raddzo] sm rocket.

razzo'lare [rattso'lare] vi (galline) to scratch about.

re sm inv king; (MUS) D; (: solfeggiando la scala) re.

rea'gire [rea'dʒire] vi to react.

re'ale ag real; (di, da re) royal ♦ sm:

il ~ reality; **rea'lismo** sm realism; **rea'lista, i, e** sm/f realist; (POL) royalist.

realiz'zare [realid'dzare] vt (progetto etc) to realize, carry out; (sogno, desiderio) to realize, fulfil; (scopo) to achieve; (COMM: titoli etc) to realize; (CALCIO etc) to score; **~rsi** vr to be realized; **realizzazi'one** sf realization; fulfilment; achievement.

real'mente av really, actually.

realtà sf inv reality.

re'ato sm offence.

reat'tore sm (FISICA) reactor; (AER: aereo) jet; (: motore) jet engine.

reazio'nario, a [reattsjo'narjo] ag (POL) reactionary.

reazi'one [reat'tsjone] sf reaction.

'rebbio sm prong.

recapi'tare vt to deliver.

re'capito sm (indirizzo) address; (consegna) delivery.

re'care vt (portare) to bring; (avere su di sé) to carry, bear; (cagionare) to cause, bring; **~rsi** vr to go.

re'cedere [re'tʃɛdere] vi to withdraw.

recensi'one [retʃen'sjone] sf review; **recen'sire** vt to review.

re'cente [re'tʃɛnte] ag recent; **di ~** recently; **recente'mente** av recently.

recessi'one [retʃes'sjone] sf (ECON) recession.

re'cidere [re'tʃidere] vt to cut off, chop off.

reci'divo, a [retʃi'divo] sm/f (DIR) second (o habitual) offender, recidivist.

re'cinto [re'tʃinto] sm enclosure; (ciò che recinge) fence; surrounding wall.

recipi'ente [retʃi'pjɛnte] sm container.

re'ciproco, a, ci, che [re'tʃiproko] ag reciprocal.

re'ciso, a [re'tʃizo] pp di recidere.

'recita ['rɛtʃita] sf performance.

reci'tare [retʃi'tare] vt (poesia, lezione) to recite; (dramma) to perform; (ruolo) to play o act (the part of); **recitazi'one** sf recitation; (di attore) acting.

recla'mare vi to complain ♦ vt (richiedere) to demand.

ré'clame [re'klam] *sf inv* advertising *no pl*; advertisement, advert (*BRIT*), ad (*fam*).

re'clamo *sm* complaint.

reclusi'one *sf* (*DIR*) imprisonment.

'recluta *sf* recruit; **reclu'tare** *vt* to recruit.

re'condito, a *ag* secluded; (*fig*) secret, hidden.

recriminazi'one [rekriminat'tsjone] *sf* recrimination.

recrude'scenza [rekrudeʃ'ʃɛntsa] *sf* fresh outbreak.

recupe'rare *vt* = **ricuperare**.

redargu'ire *vt* to rebuke.

re'datto, a *pp di* **redigere**; **redat'tore, 'trice** *sm/f* (*STAMPA*) editor; (: *di articolo*) writer; (*di dizionario etc*) compiler; **redattore capo** chief editor; **redazi'one** *sf* editing; writing; (*sede*) editorial office(s); (*personale*) editorial staff; (*versione*) version.

reddi'tizio, a [reddi'tittsjo] *ag* profitable.

'reddito *sm* income; (*dello Stato*) revenue; (*di un capitale*) yield.

re'dento, a *pp di* **redimere**.

redenzi'one [reden'tsjone] *sf* redemption.

re'digere [re'didʒere] *vt* to write; (*contratto*) to draw up.

re'dimere *vt* to deliver; (*REL*) to redeem.

'redini *sfpl* reins.

'reduce ['rɛdutʃe] *ag*: ~ **da** returning from, back from ♦ *sm/f* survivor.

refe'rendum *sm inv* referendum.

refe'renza [refe'rɛntsa] *sf* reference.

re'ferto *sm* medical report.

refet'torio *sm* refectory.

refrat'tario, a *ag* refractory.

refrige'rare [refridʒe'rare] *vt* to refrigerate; (*rinfrescare*) to cool, refresh.

rega'lare *vt* to give (as a present), make a present of.

re'gale *ag* regal.

re'galo *sm* gift, present.

re'gata *sf* regatta.

reg'gente [red'dʒɛnte] *sm/f* regent.

'reggere ['rɛddʒere] *vt* (*tenere*) to hold; (*sostenere*) to support, bear, hold up; (*portare*) to carry, bear; (*resistere*) to withstand; (*dirigere*: *impresa*) to manage, run; (*governare*) to rule, govern; (*LING*) to take, be followed by ♦ *vi* (*resistere*): ~ **a** to stand up to, hold out against; (*sopportare*): ~ **a** to stand; (*durare*) to last; (*fig: teoria etc*) to hold water; ~**rsi** *vr* (*stare ritto*) to stand; (*fig: dominarsi*) to control o.s.; ~**rsi sulle gambe** *o* **in piedi** to stand up.

'reggia, ge ['rɛddʒa] *sf* royal palace.

reggi'calze [reddʒi'kaltse] *sm inv* suspender belt.

reggi'mento [reddʒi'mento] *sm* (*MIL*) regiment.

reggi'petto [reddʒi'pɛtto] *sm* = **reggiseno**.

reggi'seno [reddʒi'seno] *sm* bra.

re'gia, 'gie [re'dʒia] *sf* (*TV, CINEMA etc*) direction.

re'gime [re'dʒime] *sm* (*POL*) regime; (*DIR*: *aureo, patrimoniale etc*) system; (*MED*) diet; (*TECN*) (engine) speed.

re'gina [re'dʒina] *sf* queen.

'regio, a, gi, gie ['rɛdʒo] *ag* royal.

regio'nale [redʒo'nale] *ag* regional.

regi'one [re'dʒone] *sf* region; (*territorio*) region, district, area.

re'gista, i, e [re'dʒista] *sm/f* (*TV, CINEMA etc*) director.

regis'trare [redʒis'trare] *vt* (*AMM*) to register; (*COMM*) to enter; (*notare*) to note, take note of; (*canzone, conversazione, sog: strumento di misura*) to record; (*mettere a punto*) to adjust, regulate; (*bagagli*) to check in; **registra'tore** *sm* (*strumento*) recorder, register; (*magnetofono*) tape recorder; **registratore di cassa** cash register; **registrazi'one** *sf* recording; (*AMM*) registration; (*COMM*) entry; (*di bagagli*) check-in.

re'gistro [re'dʒistro] *sm* (*libro*) register; ledger; logbook; (*DIR*) registry; (*MUS, TECN*) register.

re'gnare [reɲ'ɲare] *vi* to reign, rule; (*fig*) to reign.

'regno ['reɲɲo] *sm* kingdom; (*periodo*) reign; (*fig*) realm; **il ~ animale/vegetale** the animal/vegetable kingdom;

il R~ Unito the United Kingdom.

'**regola** *sf* rule; **a ~ d'arte** duly; perfectly; **in ~** in order.

regola'mento *sm* (*complesso di norme*) regulations *pl*; (*di debito*) settlement; **~ di conti** (*fig*) settling of scores.

rego'lare *ag* regular; (*in regola: domanda*) in order, lawful ♦ *vt* to regulate, control; (*apparecchio*) to adjust, regulate; (*questione, conto, debito*) to settle; **~rsi** *vr* (*moderarsi*): **~rsi nel bere/nello spendere** to control one's drinking/spending; (*comportarsi*) to behave, act; **regolarità** *sf inv* regularity.

'**regolo** *sm* ruler; **~ calcolatore** slide rule.

reinte'grare *vt* (*energie*) to recover; (*in una carica*) to reinstate.

rela'tivo, a *ag* relative.

relazi'one [relat'tsjone] *sf* (*fra cose, persone*) relation(ship); (*resoconto*) report, account; **~i** *sfpl* (*conoscenze*) connections.

rele'gare *vt* to banish; (*fig*) to relegate.

religi'one [reli'dʒone] *sf* religion; **religi'oso, a** *ag* religious ♦ *sm/f* monk/nun.

re'liquia *sf* relic.

re'litto *sm* wreck; (*fig*) down-and-out.

re'mare *vi* to row.

remini'scenze [reminiʃ'ʃɛntse] *sfpl* reminiscences.

remissi'one *sf* remission.

remis'sivo, a *ag* submissive, compliant.

'**remo** *sm* oar.

re'moto, a *ag* remote.

'**rendere** *vt* (*ridare*) to return, give back; (: *saluto etc*) to return; (*produrre*) to yield, bring in; (*esprimere, tradurre*) to render; (*far diventare*): **~ qc possibile** to make sth possible; **~ grazie a qn** to thank sb; **~rsi utile** to make o.s. useful; **~rsi conto di qc** to realize sth.

rendi'conto *sm* (*rapporto*) report, account; (*AMM, COMM*) statement of account.

rendi'mento *sm* (*reddito*) yield; (*di manodopera, TECN*) efficiency; (*capacità di produrre*) output; (*di studenti*) performance.

'**rendita** *sf* (*di individuo*) private *o* unearned income; (*COMM*) revenue; **~ annua** annuity.

'**rene** *sm* kidney.

'**reni** *sfpl* back *sg*.

reni'tente *ag* reluctant, unwilling; **~ ai consigli di qn** unwilling to follow sb's advice; **essere ~ alla leva** (*MIL*) to fail to report for military service.

'**renna** *sf* reindeer *inv*.

'**Reno** *sm*: **il ~** the Rhine.

'**reo, a** *sm/f* (*DIR*) offender.

re'parto *sm* department, section; (*MIL*) detachment.

repel'lente *ag* repulsive.

repen'taglio [repen'taʎʎo] *sm*: **mettere a ~** to jeopardize, risk.

repen'tino, a *ag* sudden, unexpected.

repe'rire *vt* to find, trace.

re'perto *sm* (*ARCHEOLOGIA*) find; (*MED*) report; (*DIR: anche: ~ giudiziario*) exhibit.

reper'torio *sm* (*TEATRO*) repertory; (*elenco*) index, (alphabetical) list.

'**replica, che** *sf* repetition; reply, answer; (*obiezione*) objection; (*TEATRO, CINEMA*) repeat performance; (*copia*) replica.

repli'care *vt* (*ripetere*) to repeat; (*rispondere*) to answer, reply.

repressi'one *sf* repression.

re'presso, a *pp di* **reprimere**.

re'primere *vt* to suppress, repress.

re'pubblica, che *sf* republic; **repubbli'cano, a** *ag, sm/f* republican.

repu'tare *vt* to consider, judge.

reputazi'one [reputat'tsjone] *sf* reputation.

'**requie** *sf*: **senza ~** unceasingly.

requi'sire *vt* to requisition.

requi'sito *sm* requirement.

requisizi'one [rekwizit'tsjone] *sf* requisition.

'**resa** *sf* (*l'arrendersi*) surrender; (*restituzione, rendimento*) return; **~ dei conti** rendering of accounts; (*fig*) day of reckoning.

resi'dente *ag* resident; **resi'denza** *sf* residence; **residenzi'ale** *ag* residential.

re'siduo, a *ag* residual, remaining ♦ *sm* remainder; (*CHIM*) residue.

'resina *sf* resin.

resis'tente *ag* (*che resiste*): ~ a resistant to; (*forte*) strong; (*duraturo*) long-lasting, durable; ~ **al caldo** heat-resistant; **resis'tenza** *sf* resistance; (*di persona: fisica*) stamina, endurance; (: *mentale*) endurance, resistance.

re'sistere *vi* to resist; ~ a (*assalto, tentazioni*) to resist; (*dolore, sog: pianta*) to withstand; (*non patir danno*) to be resistant to; **resis'tito, a** *pp di* **resistere.**

'reso, a *pp di* **rendere.**

reso'conto *sm* report, account.

res'pingere [res'pindʒere] *vt* to drive back, repel; (*rifiutare*) to reject; (*INS: bocciare*) to fail; **res'pinto, a** *pp di* **respingere.**

respi'rare *vi* to breathe; (*fig*) to get one's breath; to breathe again ♦ *vt* to breathe (in), inhale; **respira'tore** *sm* respirator; **respirazi'one** *sf* breathing; **respirazione artificiale** artificial respiration; **res'piro** *sm* breathing *no pl*; (*singolo atto*) breath; (*fig*) respite, rest; **mandare un respiro di sollievo** to give a sigh of relief.

respon'sabile *ag* responsible ♦ *sm/f* person responsible; (*capo*) person in charge; ~ **di** responsible for; (*DIR*) liable for; **responsabilità** *sf inv* responsibility; (*legale*) liability.

res'ponso *sm* answer.

'ressa *sf* crowd, throng.

res'tare *vi* (*rimanere*) to remain, stay; (*diventare*): ~ **orfano/cieco** to become o be left an orphan/become blind; (*trovarsi*): ~ **sorpreso** to be surprised; (*avanzare*) to be left, remain; ~ **d'accordo** to agree; **non resta più niente** there's nothing left; **restano pochi giorni** there are only a few days left.

restau'rare *vt* to restore; **restaurazi'one** *sf* (*POL*) restoration; **res'tauro** *sm* (*di edifici etc*) restoration.

res'tio, a, 'tii, 'tie *ag* restive; (*persona*): ~ **a** reluctant to.

restitu'ire *vt* to return, give back; (*energie, forze*) to restore.

'resto *sm* remainder, rest; (*denaro*) change; (*MAT*) remainder; ~**i** *smpl* (*di cibo*) leftovers; (*di città*) remains; **del** ~ moreover, besides; ~**i mortali** (*mortal*) remains.

res'tringere [res'trindʒere] *vt* to reduce; (*vestito*) to take in; (*stoffa*) to shrink; (*fig*) to restrict, limit; ~**rsi** *vr* (*strada*) to narrow; (*stoffa*) to shrink; **restrizi'one** *sf* restriction.

'rete *sf* net; (*fig*) trap, snare; (*di recinzione*) wire netting; (*AUT, FERR, di spionaggio etc*) network; **segnare una** ~ (*CALCIO*) to score a goal; ~ **del letto** (*sprung*) bed base.

reti'cente [reti'tʃente] *ag* reticent.

retico'lato *sm* grid; (*rete metallica*) wire netting; (*di filo spinato*) barbed wire (fence).

'retina *sf* (*ANAT*) retina.

re'torica *sf* rhetoric.

re'torico, a, ci, che *ag* rhetorical.

retribu'ire *vt* to pay; (*premiare*) to reward; **retribuzi'one** *sf* payment; reward.

'retro *sm inv* back ♦ *av* (*dietro*): **vedi** ~ see over(leaf).

retro'cedere [retro'tʃedere] *vi* to withdraw ♦ *vt* (*CALCIO*) to relegate; (*MIL*) to degrade.

re'trogrado, a *ag* (*fig*) reactionary, backward-looking.

retro'marcia [retro'martʃa] *sf* (*AUT*) reverse; (: *dispositivo*) reverse gear.

retrospet'tivo, a *ag* retrospective.

retrovi'sore *sm* (*AUT*) (rear-view) mirror.

'retta *sf* (*MAT*) straight line; (*di convitto*) charge for bed and board; (*fig: ascolto*): **dar** ~ **a** to listen to, pay attention to.

rettango'lare *ag* rectangular.

ret'tangolo, a *ag* right-angled ♦ *sm* rectangle.

ret'tifica, che *sf* rectification, correction.

rettifi'care vt (curva) to straighten; (fig) to rectify, correct.

'rettile sm reptile.

retti'lineo, a ag rectilinear.

retti'tudine sf rectitude, uprightness.

'retto, a pp di **reggere** ♦ ag straight; (MAT): **angolo** ~ right angle; (onesto) honest, upright; (giusto, esatto) correct, proper, right.

ret'tore sm (REL) rector; (di università) ≈ chancellor.

reuma'tismo sm rheumatism.

reve'rendo, a ag: **il** ~ **padre Belli** the Reverend Father Belli.

rever'sibile ag reversible.

revisio'nare vt (conti) to audit; (TECN) to overhaul, service; (DIR: processo) to review; (componimento) to revise.

revisi'one sf auditing no pl; audit; servicing no pl; overhaul; review; revision.

revi'sore sm: ~ **di conti/bozze** auditor/proofreader.

'revoca sf revocation.

revo'care vt to revoke.

re'volver sm inv revolver.

riabili'tare vt to rehabilitate; (fig) to restore to favour.

rial'zare [rial'tsare] vt to raise, lift; (alzare di più) to heighten, raise; (aumentare: prezzi) to increase, raise ♦ vi (prezzi) to rise, increase; **ri'alzo** sm (di prezzi) increase, rise; (sporgenza) rise.

rianimazi'one [rianimat'tsjone] sf (MED) resuscitation; **centro di** ~ intensive care unit.

riap'pendere vt to rehang; (TEL) to hang up.

ria'prire vt to reopen, open again; ~**rsi** vr to reopen, open again.

ri'armo sm (MIL) rearmament.

rias'setto sm (di stanza etc) rearrangement; (ordinamento) reorganization.

rias'sumere vt (riprendere) to resume; (impiegare di nuovo) to reemploy; (sintetizzare) to summarize; **rias'sunto, a** pp di **riassumere** ♦ sm summary.

ria'vere vt to have again; (avere indietro) to get back; (riacquistare) to recover; ~**rsi** vr to recover.

riba'dire vt (fig) to confirm.

ri'balta sf flap; (TEATRO: proscenio) front of the stage; (: apparecchio d'illuminazione) footlights pl; (fig) limelight.

ribal'tabile ag (sedile) tip-up.

ribal'tare vt, vi (anche: ~**rsi**) to turn over, tip over.

ribas'sare vt to lower, bring down ♦ vi to come down, fall; **ri'basso** sm reduction, fall.

ri'battere vt to return, hit back; (confutare) to refute; ~ **che** to retort that.

ribel'larsi vr: ~ **(a)** to rebel (against); **ri'belle** ag (soldati) rebel; (ragazzo) rebellious ♦ sm/f rebel; **ribelli'one** sf rebellion.

'ribes sm inv currant; ~ **nero** blackcurrant; ~ **rosso** redcurrant.

ribol'lire vi (fermentare) to ferment; (fare bolle) to bubble, boil; (fig) to seethe.

ri'brezzo [ri'breddzo] sm disgust, loathing; **far** ~ **a** to disgust.

ribut'tante ag disgusting, revolting.

rica'dere vi to fall again; (scendere a terra, fig: nel peccato etc) to fall back; (vestiti, capelli etc) to hang (down); (riversarsi: fatiche, colpe): ~ **su** to fall on; **rica'duta** sf (MED) relapse.

rical'care vt (disegni) to trace; (fig) to follow faithfully.

rica'mare vt to embroider.

ricambi'are vt to change again; (contraccambiare) to repay, return; **ri'cambio** sm exchange, return; (FISIOL) metabolism; **ricambi** smpl (TECN) spare parts.

ri'camo sm embroidery.

ricapito'lare vt to recapitulate, sum up.

ricari'care vt (arma, macchina fotografica) to reload; (pipa) to refill; (orologio) to rewind; (batteria) to recharge.

ricat'tare vt to blackmail; **ricatta'tore, 'trice** sm/f blackmailer; **ri'catto** sm blackmail.

rica'vare vt (*estrarre*) to draw out, extract; (*ottenere*) to obtain, gain; **ri'cavo** sm proceeds pl.

ric'chezza [rik'kettsa] sf wealth; (*fig*) richness; ~**e** sfpl (*beni*) wealth sg, riches.

'riccio, a ['rittʃo] ag curly ♦ sm (ZOOL) hedgehog; (: *anche:* ~ *di mare*) sea urchin; **'ricciolo** sm curl; **ricci'uto, a** ag curly.

'ricco, a, chi, che ag rich; (*persona, paese*) rich, wealthy ♦ sm/f rich man/ woman; **i** ~**chi** the rich; ~ **di** full of; rich in.

ri'cerca, che [ri'tʃerka] sf search; (*indagine*) investigation, inquiry; (*studio*): **la** ~ research; **una** ~ piece of research.

ricer'care [ritʃer'kare] vt (*motivi, cause*) to look for, try to determine; (*successo, piacere*) to pursue; (*onore, gloria*) to seek; **ricer'cato, a** ag (*apprezzato*) much sought-after; (*affettato*) studied, affected ♦ sm/f (POLIZIA) wanted man/ woman.

ri'cetta [ri'tʃetta] sf (MED) prescription; (CUC) recipe.

ricettazi'one [ritʃettat'tsjone] sf (DIR) receiving (stolen goods).

ri'cevere [ri'tʃevere] vt to receive; (*stipendio, lettera*) to get, receive; (*accogliere: ospite*) to welcome; (*vedere: cliente, rappresentante etc*) to see; **ricevi'mento** sm receiving no pl; (*trattenimento*) reception; **ricevi'tore** sm (TECN) receiver; **ricevitore delle imposte** tax collector; **rice'vuta** sf receipt; **ricevuta fiscale** receipt for tax purposes; **ricezi'one** sf (RADIO, TV) reception.

richia'mare [rikja'mare] vt (*chiamare indietro, ritelefonare*) to call back; (*ambasciatore, truppe*) to recall; (*rimproverare*) to reprimand; (*attirare*) to attract, draw; ~**rsi a** (*riferirsi a*) to refer to; **richi'amo** sm call; recall; reprimand; attraction.

richi'edere [ri'kjɛdere] vt to ask again for; (*chiedere indietro*): ~ **qc** to ask for sth back; (*chiedere: per sapere*) to

ask; (: *per avere*) to ask for; (AMM: *documenti*) to apply for; (*esigere*) to need, require; **richi'esta** sf (*domanda*) request; (AMM) application, request; (*esigenza*) demand, request; **a richiesta** on request; **richi'esto, a** pp di **richiedere**.

'ricino ['ritʃino] sm: **olio di** ~ castor oil.

ricognizi'one [rikoɲɲit'tsjone] sf (MIL) reconnaissance; (DIR) recognition, acknowledgement.

ricominci'are [rikomin'tʃare] vt, vi to start again, begin again.

ricom'pensa sf reward.

ricompen'sare vt to reward.

riconcili'are [rikontʃi'ljare] vt to reconcile; ~**rsi** vr to be reconciled; **riconciliazi'one** sf reconciliation.

ricono'scente [rikonoʃ'ʃɛnte] ag grateful; **ricono'scenza** sf gratitude.

rico'noscere [riko'noʃʃere] vt to recognize; (DIR: *figlio, debito*) to acknowledge; (*ammettere: errore*) to admit, acknowledge; **riconosci'mento** sm recognition; acknowledgement; (*identificazione*) identification; **riconosci'uto, a** pp di **riconoscere**.

rico'prire vt (*coprire*) to cover; (*occupare: carica*) to hold.

ricor'dare vt to remember, recall; (*richiamare alla memoria*): ~ **qc a qn** to remind sb of sth; ~**rsi** vr: ~**rsi (di)** to remember; ~**rsi di qc/di aver fatto** to remember sth/having done.

ri'cordo sm memory; (*regalo*) keepsake, souvenir; (*di viaggio*) souvenir; ~**i** smpl (*memorie*) memoirs.

ricor'rente ag recurrent, recurring; **ricor'renza** sf recurrence; (*festività*) anniversary.

ri'correre vi (*ripetersi*) to recur; ~ **a** (*rivolgersi*) to turn to; (: DIR) to appeal to; (*servirsi di*) to have recourse to; **ri'corso, a** pp di **ricorrere** ♦ sm recurrence; (DIR) appeal; **far ricorso a** = **ricorrere a**.

ricostru'ire vt (*casa*) to rebuild; (*fatti*) to reconstruct; **ricostruzi'one** sf rebuilding no pl; reconstruction.

ri'cotta sf soft white unsalted cheese

made from sheep's milk.

ricove'rare *vt* to give shelter to; ~ qn in ospedale to admit sb to hospital.

ri'covero *sm* shelter, refuge; (*MIL*) shelter; (*MED*) admission (to hospital).

ricre'are *vt* to recreate; (*rinvigorire*) to restore; (*fig: distrarre*) to amuse.

ricreazi'one [rikreat'tsjone] *sf* recreation, entertainment; (*INS*) break.

ri'credersi *vr* to change one's mind.

ricupe'rare *vt* (*rientrare in possesso di*) to recover, get back; (*tempo perduto*) to make up for; (*NAUT*) to salvage; (: *naufraghi*) to rescue; (*delinquente*) to rehabilitate; ~ lo svantaggio (*SPORT*) to close the gap.

ridacchi'are [ridak'kjare] *vi* to snigger.

ri'dare *vt* to return, give back.

'ridere *vi* to laugh; (*deridere, beffare*): ~ di to laugh at, make fun of.

ri'detto, a *pp di* ridire.

ri'dicolo, a *ag* ridiculous, absurd.

ridimensio'nare *vt* to reorganize; (*fig*) to see in the right perspective.

ri'dire *vt* to repeat; (*criticare*) to find fault with; to object to; **trova sempre qualcosa da** ~ he always manages to find fault.

ridon'dante *ag* redundant.

ri'dotto, a *pp di* ridurre.

ri'durre *vt* (*anche CHIM, MAT*) to reduce; (*prezzo, spese*) to cut, reduce; (*accorciare: opera letteraria*) to abridge; (: *RADIO, TV*) to adapt; **ridursi** *vr* (*diminuirsi*) to be reduced, shrink; **ridursi a** to be reduced to; **ridursi pelle e ossa** to be reduced to skin and bone; **riduzi'one** *sf* reduction; abridgement; adaptation.

riem'pire *vt* to fill (up); (*modulo*) to fill in *o* out; ~**rsi** *vr* to fill (up); (*mangiare troppo*) to stuff o.s.; ~ **qc di** to fill sth (up) with.

rien'tranza [rien'trantsa] *sf* recess; indentation.

rien'trare *vi* (*entrare di nuovo*) to go (*o* come) back in; (*tornare*) to return; (*fare una rientranza*) to go in, curve inwards; to be indented; (*riguardare*): ~ in to be included among, form part of;

ri'entro *sm* (*ritorno*) return; (*di astronave*) re-entry.

riepilo'gare *vt* to summarize ♦ *vi* to recapitulate.

ri'fare *vt* to do again; (*ricostruire*) to make again; (*nodo*) to tie again, do up again; (*imitare*) to imitate, copy; ~**rsi** *vr* (*risarcirsi*): ~**rsi di** to make up for; (*vendicarsi*): ~**rsi di qc su qn** to get one's own back on sb for sth; (*riferirsi*): ~**rsi a** to go back to; to follow; ~ **il letto** to make the bed; ~**rsi una vita** to make a new life for o.s.; **ri'fatto, a** *pp di* rifare.

riferi'mento *sm* reference; **in** *o* **con** ~ **a** with reference to.

rife'rire *vt* (*riportare*) to report; (*ascrivere*): ~ **qc a** to attribute sth to ♦ *vi* to do a report; ~**rsi** *vr*: ~**rsi a** to refer to.

rifi'nire *vt* to finish off, put the finishing touches to; **rifini'tura** *sf* finishing touch; **rifiniture** *sfpl* (*di mobile, auto*) finish *sg*.

rifiu'tare *vt* to refuse; ~ **di fare** to refuse to do; **rifi'uto** *sm* refusal; **rifiuti** *smpl* (*spazzatura*) rubbish *sg*, refuse *sg*.

riflessi'one *sf* (*FISICA, meditazione*) reflection; (*il pensare*) thought, reflection; (*osservazione*) remark.

rifles'sivo, a *ag* (*persona*) thoughtful, reflective; (*LING*) reflexive.

ri'flesso, a *pp di* riflettere ♦ *sm* (*di luce, rispecchiamento*) reflection; (*FISIOL*) reflex; **di** *o* **per** ~ indirectly.

ri'flettere *vt* to reflect ♦ *vi* to think; ~**rsi** *vr* to be reflected; ~**rsi su** to think over.

riflet'tore *sm* reflector; (*proiettore*) floodlight; searchlight.

ri'flusso *sm* flowing back; (*della marea*) ebb; **un'epoca di** ~ an era of nostalgia.

ri'fondere *vt* (*rimborsare*) to refund, repay.

ri'forma *sf* reform; **la R**~ (*REL*) the Reformation.

rifor'mare *vt* to re-form; (*cambiare, innovare*) to reform; (*MIL: recluta*) to declare unfit for service; (: *soldato*) to invalid out, discharge; **riforma'torio** *sm* (*DIR*) community home (*BRIT*), reformatory (*US*).

riforni'mento *sm* supplying, providing; restocking; **~i** *smpl* (*provviste*) supplies, provisions.

rifor'nire *vt* (*provvedere*): **~ di** to supply *o* provide with; (*fornire di nuovo: casa etc*) to restock.

ri'frangere [ri'frandʒere] *vt* to refract; **ri'fratto, a** *pp di* **rifrangere**; **rifrazi'one** *sf* refraction.

rifug'gire [rifud'dʒire] *vi* to escape again; (*fig*): **~ da** to shun.

rifugi'arsi [rifu'dʒarsi] *vr* to take refuge; **rifugi'ato, a** *sm/f* refugee.

ri'fugio [ri'fudʒo] *sm* refuge, shelter; (*in montagna*) shelter; **~ antiaereo** air-raid shelter.

'riga, ghe *sf* line; (*striscia*) stripe; (*di persone, cose*) line, row; (*regolo*) ruler; (*scriminatura*) parting; **mettersi in ~** to line up; **a ~ghe** (*foglio*) lined; (*vestito*) striped.

ri'gagnolo [ri'gaɲɲolo] *sm* rivulet.

ri'gare *vt* (*foglio*) to rule ♦ *vi*: **~ diritto** (*fig*) to toe the line.

rigatti'ere *sm* junk dealer.

riget'tare [ridʒet'tare] *vt* (*gettare indietro*) to throw back; (*fig: respingere*) to reject; (*vomitare*) to bring *o* throw up; **ri'getto** *sm* (*anche MED*) rejection.

rigidità [ridʒidi'ta] *sf* rigidity; stiffness; severity, rigours *pl*; strictness.

'rigido, a ['ridʒido] *ag* rigid, stiff; (*membra etc: indurite*) stiff; (*METEOR*) harsh, severe; (*fig*) strict.

rigi'rare [ridʒi'rare] *vt* to turn; **~rsi** *vr* to turn round; (*nel letto*) to turn over; **~ qc tra le mani** to turn sth over in one's hands; **~ il discorso** to change the subject.

'rigo, ghi *sm* line; (*MUS*) staff, stave.

rigogli'oso, a [rigoʎ'ʎoso] *ag* (*pianta*) luxuriant; (*fig: commercio, sviluppo*) thriving.

ri'gonfio, a *ag* swollen.

ri'gore *sm* (*METEOR*) harshness, rigours *pl*; (*fig*) severity, strictness; (*anche:*

calcio di ~) penalty; **di ~ compulsory; a rigor di termini** strictly speaking; **rigo'roso, a** *ag* (*severo: persona, ordine*) strict; (*preciso*) rigorous.

rigover'nare *vt* to wash (up).

riguar'dare *vt* to look at again; (*considerare*) to regard, consider; (*concernere*) to regard, concern; **~rsi** *vr* (*aver cura di sé*) to look after o.s.

rigu'ardo *sm* (*attenzione*) care; (*considerazione*) regard, respect; **~ a** concerning, with regard to; **non aver ~i nell'agire/nel parlare** to act/speak freely.

rilasci'are [rilaʃ'ʃare] *vt* (*rimettere in libertà*) to release; (*AMM: documenti*) to issue; **ri'lascio** *sm* release; issue.

rilas'sare *vt* to relax; **~rsi** *vr* to relax; (*fig: disciplina*) to become slack.

rile'gare *vt* (*libro*) to bind; **rilega'tura** *sf* binding.

ri'leggere [ri'leddʒere] *vt* to reread, read again; (*rivedere*) to read over.

ri'lento: a ~ *av* slowly.

rileva'mento *sm* (*topografico, statistico*) survey; (*NAUT*) bearing.

rile'vante *ag* considerable; important.

rile'vare *vt* (*ricavare*) to find; (*notare*) to notice; (*mettere in evidenza*) to point out; (*venire a conoscere: notizia*) to learn; (*raccogliere: dati*) to gather, collect; (*TOPOGRAFIA*) to survey; (*MIL*) to relieve; (*COMM*) to take over.

rili'evo *sm* (*ARTE, GEO*) relief; (*fig: rilevanza*) importance; (*osservazione*) point, remark; (*TOPOGRAFIA*) survey; **dar ~ a** *o* **mettere in ~ qc** (*fig*) to bring sth out, highlight sth.

rilut'tante *ag* reluctant; **rilut'tanza** *sf* reluctance.

'rima *sf* rhyme; (*verso*) verse.

riman'dare *vt* to send again; (*restituire, rinviare*) to send back, return; (*differire*): **~ qc (a)** to postpone sth *o* put sth off (till); (*fare riferimento*): **~ qn a** to refer sb to; **essere rimandato** (*INS*) to have to repeat one's exams; **ri'mando** *sm* (*rinvio*) return; (*dilazione*) postponement; (*riferimento*) cross-reference.

rima'nente *ag* remaining ♦ *sm* rest, remainder; **i** ~**i** (*persone*) the rest of them, the others; **rima'nenza** *sf* rest, remainder; **rimanenze** *sfpl* (*COMM*) unsold stock *sg*.

rima'nere *vi* (*restare*) to remain, stay; (*avanzare*) to be left, remain; (*restare stupito*) to be amazed; (*restare, mancare*): **rimangono poche settimane a Pasqua** there are only a few weeks left till Easter; **rimane da vedere se it** remains to be seen whether; (*diventare*): ~ **vedovo** to be left a widower; (*trovarsi*): ~ **confuso/sorpreso** to be confused/surprised.

ri'mare *vt*, *vi* to rhyme.

rimargi'nare [rimardʒi'nare] *vt*, *vi* (*anche*: ~**rsi**) to heal.

ri'masto, a *pp di* **rimanere**.

rima'sugli [rima'suʎʎi] *smpl* leftovers.

rimbal'zare [rimbal'tsare] *vi* to bounce back, rebound; (*proiettile*) to ricochet; **rim'balzo** *sm* rebound; ricochet.

rimbam'bito, a *ag* senile, in one's dotage.

rimboc'care *vt* (*orlo*) to turn up; (*coperta*) to tuck in; (*maniche, pantaloni*) to turn *o* roll up.

rimbom'bare *vi* to resound.

rimbor'sare *vt* to pay back, repay; **rim'borso** *sm* repayment.

rimedi'are *vi*: ~ **a** to remedy ♦ *vt* (*fam*: *procurarsi*) to get *o* scrape together.

ri'medio *sm* (*medicina*) medicine; (*cura, fig*) remedy, cure.

rimesco'lare *vt* to mix well, stir well; (*carte*) to shuffle; **sentirsi** ~ **il sangue** (*per paura*) to feel one's blood run cold; (*per rabbia*) to feel one's blood boil.

ri'messa *sf* (*locale*: *per veicoli*) garage; (: *per aerei*) hangar; (*COMM*: *di merce*) consignment; (: *di denaro*) remittance; (*TENNIS*) return; (*CALCIO*: *anche*: ~ **in gioco**) throw-in.

ri'messo, a *pp di* **rimettere**.

ri'mettere *vt* (*mettere di nuovo*) to put back; (*indossare di nuovo*): ~ **qc** to put sth back on, put sth on again; (*resti-*

tuire) to return, give back; (*affidare*) to entrust; (: *decisione*) to refer; (*condonare*) to remit; (*COMM*: *merci*) to deliver; (: *denaro*) to remit; (*vomitare*) to bring up; (*perdere*: *anche*: **rimetterci**) to lose; ~**rsi al bello** (*tempo*) to clear up; ~**rsi in salute** to get better, recover one's health.

'rimmel ® *sm inv* mascara.

rimoder'nare *vt* to modernize.

rimon'tare *vt* (*meccanismo*) to reassemble; (: *tenda*) to put up again ♦ *vi* (*salire di nuovo*): ~ **in** (*macchina, treno*) to get back into; (*SPORT*) to close the gap.

rimorchi'are [rimor'kjare] *vt* to tow; (*fig*: *ragazza*) to pick up; **rimorchia'tore** *sm* (*NAUT*) tug(boat).

ri'morchio [ri'mɔrkjo] *sm* tow; (*veicolo*) trailer.

ri'morso *sm* remorse.

rimozi'one [rimot'tsjone] *sf* removal; (*da un impiego*) dismissal; (*PSIC*) repression.

rim'pasto *sm* (*POL*) reshuffle.

rimpatri'are *vi* to return home ♦ *vt* to repatriate; **rim'patrio** *sm* repatriation.

rimpi'angere [rim'pjandʒere] *vt* to regret; (*persona*) to miss; **rimpi'anto, a** *pp di* **rimpiangere** ♦ *sm* regret.

rimpiat'tino *sm* hide-and-seek.

rimpiaz'zare [rimpjat'tsare] *vt* to replace.

rimpiccio'lire [rimpittʃo'lire] *vt* to make smaller ♦ *vi* (*anche*: ~**rsi**) to become smaller.

rimpin'zare [rimpin'tsare] *vt*: ~ **di** to cram *o* stuff with.

rimprove'rare *vt* to rebuke, reprimand; **rim'provero** *sm* rebuke, reprimand.

rimugi'nare [rimudʒi'nare] *vt* (*fig*) to turn over in one's mind.

rimunerazi'one [rimunerat'tsjone] *sf* remuneration; (*premio*) reward.

rimu'overe *vt* to remove; (*destituire*) to dismiss.

Rinasci'mento [rinaʃʃi'mento] *sm*: **il** ~ the Renaissance.

ri'nascita [ri'naʃʃita] *sf* rebirth, revival.

rincal'zare [rinkal'tsare] vt (palo, albero) to support, prop up; (lenzuola) to tuck in.

rinca'rare vt to increase the price of ♦ vi to go up, become more expensive.

rinca'sare vi to go home.

rinchi'udere [rin'kjudere] vt to shut (o lock) up; ~rsi vr: ~rsi in to shut o.s. up in; ~rsi in se stesso to withdraw into o.s.; rinchi'uso, a pp di rinchiudere.

rin'correre vt to chase, run after; rin'corsa sf short run; rin'corso, a pp di rincorrere.

rin'crescere [rin'kreʃʃere] vb impers: mi rincresce che/di non poter fare I'm sorry that/I can't do, I regret that/being unable to do; rincresci'mento sm regret; rincresci'uto, a pp di rincrescere.

rincu'lare vi to draw back; (arma) to recoil.

rinfacci'are [rinfatt'ʃare] vt (fig): ~ qc a qn to throw sth in sb's face.

rinfor'zare [rinfor'tsare] vt to reinforce, strengthen ♦ vi (anche: ~rsi) to grow stronger; rin'forzo sm: mettere un rinforzo a to strengthen; di rinforzo (asse, sbarra) strengthening; (esercito) supporting; (personale) extra, additional; rinforzi smpl (MIL) reinforcements.

rinfran'care vt to encourage, reassure.

rinfres'care vt (atmosfera, temperatura) to cool (down); (abito, pareti) to freshen up ♦ vi (tempo) to grow cooler; ~rsi vr (ristorarsi) to refresh o.s.; (lavarsi) to freshen up; rin'fresco, schi sm (festa) party; rinfreschi smpl refreshments.

rin'fusa sf: alla ~ in confusion, higgledy-piggledy.

ringhi'are [rin'gjare] vi to growl, snarl.

ringhi'era [rin'gjera] sf railing; (delle scale) banister(s pl).

ringiova'nire [rindʒova'nire] vt (sog: vestito, acconciatura etc): ~ qn to make sb look younger; (: vacanze etc) to rejuvenate ♦ vi (anche: ~rsi) to become (o look) younger.

ringrazia'mento [ringrattsja'mento] sm thanks pl.

ringrazi'are [ringrat'tsjare] vt to thank; ~ qn di qc to thank sb for sth.

rinne'gare vt (fede) to renounce; (figlio) to disown, repudiate; rinne'gato, a sm/f renegade.

rinnova'mento sm renewal; (economico) revival.

rinno'vare vt to renew; (ripetere) to repeat, renew; ~rsi vr (fenomeno) to be repeated, recur; rin'novo sm (di contratto) renewal; "chiuso per rinnovo dei locali" "closed for alterations".

rinoce'ronte [rinotʃe'ronte] sm rhinoceros.

rino'mato, a ag renowned, celebrated.

rinsal'dare vt to strengthen.

rintoc'care vi (campana) to toll; (orologio) to strike.

rintracci'are [rintrat'tʃare] vt to track down.

rintro'nare vi to boom, roar ♦ vt (assordare) to deafen; (stordire) to stun.

ri'nuncia [ri'nuntʃa] etc = rinunzia etc.

ri'nunzia [ri'nuntsja] sf renunciation.

rinunzi'are [rinun'tsjare] vi: ~ a to give up, renounce.

rinve'nire vt to find, recover; (scoprire) to discover, find out ♦ vi (riprendere i sensi) to come round; (riprendere l'aspetto naturale) to revive.

rinvi'are vt (rimandare indietro) to send back, return; (differire): ~ qc (a) to postpone sth o put sth off (till); to adjourn sth (till); (fare un rimando): ~ qn a to refer sb to.

rinvigo'rire vt to strengthen.

rin'vio, 'vii sm (rimando) return; (differimento) postponement; (: di seduta) adjournment; (in un testo) cross-reference.

ri'one sm district, quarter.

riordi'nare vt (rimettere in ordine) to tidy; (riorganizzare) to reorganize.

riorganiz'zare [riorganid'dzare] vt to reorganize.

ripa'gare vt to repay.

ripa'rare vt (proteggere) to protect, defend; (correggere: male, torto) to make up for; (: *errore*) to put right; (*aggiustare*) to repair ♦ *vi* (*mettere rimedio*): ~ **a** to make up for; ~**rsi** *vr* (*rifugiarsi*) to take refuge *o* shelter; **riparazi'one** *sf* (*di un torto*) reparation; (*di guasto, scarpe*) repairing *no pl*; repair; (*risarcimento*) compensation.

ri'paro *sm* (*protezione*) shelter, protection; (*rimedio*) remedy.

ripar'tire *vt* (*dividere*) to divide up; (*distribuire*) to share out ♦ *vi* to set off again; to leave again.

ripas'sare *vi* to come (*o* go) back ♦ *vt* (*scritto, lezione*) to go over (again).

ripen'sare *vi* to think; (*cambiare pensiero*) to change one's mind; (*tornare col pensiero*): ~ **a** to recall.

ripercu'otersi *vr*: ~ **su** (*fig*) to have repercussions on.

ripercussi'one *sf* (*fig*): avere una ~ *o* delle ~i **su** to have repercussions on.

ripes'care *vt* (*pesce*) to catch again; (*persona, cosa*) to fish out; (*fig: ritrovare*) to dig out.

ri'petere *vt* to repeat; (*ripassare*) to go over; **ripetizi'one** *sf* repetition; (*di lezione*) revision; **ripetizioni** *sfpl* (*INS*) private tutoring *o* coaching *sg*.

ripi'ano *sm* (*GEO*) terrace; (*di mobile*) shelf.

ri'picca *sf*: **per** ~ out of spite.

'ripido, a *ag* steep.

ripie'gare *vt* to refold; (*piegare più volte*) to fold (up) ♦ *vi* (*MIL*) to retreat, fall back; (*fig: accontentarsi*): ~ **su** to make do with; ~**rsi** *vr* to bend; **ripi'ego, ghi** *sm* expedient.

ripi'eno, a *ag* full; (*CUC*) stuffed; (: *panino*) filled ♦ *sm* (*CUC*) stuffing.

ri'porre *vt* (*porre al suo posto*) to put back, replace; (*mettere via*) to put away; (*fiducia, speranza*): ~ **qc in qn** to place *o* put sth in sb.

ripor'tare *vt* (*portare indietro*) to bring (*o* take) back; (*riferire*) to report; (*citare*) to quote; (*ricevere*) to receive, get; (*vittoria*) to gain; (*successo*) to have; (*MAT*) to carry; ~**rsi a** (*anche fig*) to go back to; (*riferirsi a*) to refer to; ~ **danni** to suffer damage.

ripo'sare *vt* (*bicchiere, valigia*) to put down; (*dare sollievo*) to rest ♦ *vi* to rest; ~**rsi** *vr* to rest; **ri'poso** *sm* rest; (*MIL*): **riposo!** at ease!; **a riposo** (*in pensione*) retired; **giorno di riposo** day off.

ripos'tiglio [ripos'tiʎʎo] *sm* lumberroom.

ri'posto, a *pp di* **riporre**.

ri'prendere *vt* (*prigioniero, fortezza*) to recapture; (*prendere indietro*) to take back; (*ricominciare: lavoro*) to resume; (*andare a prendere*) to fetch, come back for; (*assumere di nuovo: impiegati*) to take on again, re-employ; (*rimproverare*) to tell off; (*restringere: abito*) to take in; (*CINEMA*) to shoot; ~**rsi** *vr* to recover; (*correggersi*) to correct o.s.; **ri'presa** *sf* recapture; resumption; (*economica, da malattia, emozione*) recovery; (*AUT*) acceleration *no pl*; (*TEATRO, CINEMA*) rerun; (*CINEMA: presa*) shooting *no pl*; shot; (*SPORT*) second half; (: *PUGILATO*) round; **a più riprese** on several occasions, several times; **ripreso, a** *pp di* **riprendere**.

ripristi'nare *vt* to restore.

ripro'durre *vt* to reproduce; **riprodursi** *vr* (*BIOL*) to reproduce; (*riformarsi*) to form again; **riprodut'tivo, a** *ag* reproductive; **riproduzi'one** *sf* reproduction; **riproduzione vietata** all rights reserved.

ripudi'are *vt* to repudiate, disown.

ripu'gnante [ripuɲ'ɲante] *ag* disgusting, repulsive.

ripu'gnare [ripuɲ'ɲare] *vi*: ~ **a qn** to repel *o* disgust sb.

ripu'lire *vt* to clean up; (*sog: ladri*) to clean out; (*perfezionare*) to polish, refine.

ri'quadro *sm* square; (*ARCHIT*) panel.

ri'saia *sf* paddy field.

risa'lire *vi* (*ritornare in su*) to go back up; ~ **a** (*ritornare con la mente*) to go back to; (*datare da*) to date back to, go back to.

risal'tare *vi* (*fig: distinguersi*) to stand out; (*ARCHIT*) to project, jut out;

ri'salto sm prominence; (sporgenza) projection; **mettere** o **porre in risalto qc** to make sth stand out.

risa'nare vt (guarire) to heal, cure; (palude) to reclaim; (economia) to improve; (bilancio) to reorganize.

risa'puto, a ag: **è ~ che ...** everyone knows that ..., it is common knowledge that ....

risarci'mento [risartʃi'mento] sm: **~ (di)** compensation (for).

risar'cire [risar'tʃire] vt (cose) to pay compensation for; (persona): **~ qn di qc** to compensate sb for sth.

ri'sata sf laugh.

riscalda'mento sm heating; **~ cen-trale** central heating.

riscal'dare vt (scaldare) to heat; (: mani, persona) to warm; (minestra) to reheat; **~rsi** vr to warm up.

riscat'tare vt (prigioniero) to ransom, pay a ransom for; (DIR) to redeem; **~rsi** vr (da disonore) to redeem o.s.; **ris'catto** sm ransom; redemption.

rischia'rare [riskja'rare] vt (illuminare) to light up; (colore) to make lighter; **~rsi** vr (tempo) to clear up; (cielo) to clear; (fig: volto) to brighten up; **~rsi la voce** to clear one's throat.

rischi'are [ris'kjare] vt to risk ♦ vi: **~ di fare qc** to risk o run the risk of doing sth.

'rischio ['riskjo] sm risk; **rischi'oso, a** ag risky, dangerous.

riscia'cquare [riʃʃa'kware] vt to rinse.

riscon'trare vt (confrontare: due cose) to compare; (esaminare) to check, verify; (rilevare) to find; **ris'contro** sm comparison; check, verification; (AMM: lettera di risposta) reply.

ris'cossa sf (riconquista) recovery, re-conquest; vedi anche **riscosso**.

riscossi'one sf collection.

ris'cosso, a pp di **riscuotere**.

ris'cuotere vt (ritirare una somma dovuta) to collect; (: stipendio) to draw, collect; (assegno) to cash; (fig: successo etc) to win, earn; **~rsi** vr: **~rsi (da)** to shake o.s. (out of), rouse o.s. (from).

risenti'mento sm resentment.

risen'tire vt to hear again; (provare) to feel ♦ vi: **~ di** to feel (o show) the effects of; **~rsi** vr: **~rsi di** o **per** to take offence at, resent; **risen'tito, a** ag re-sentful.

ri'serbo sm reserve.

ri'serva sf reserve; (di caccia, pesca) preserve; (restrizione, di indigeni) re-servation; **di ~** (provviste etc) in re-serve.

riser'vare vt (tenere in serbo) to keep, put aside; (prenotare) to book, reserve; **~rsi** vr: **~rsi di fare qc** to intend to do sth; **riser'vato, a** ag (prenotato, fig: persona) reserved; (confidenziale) con-fidential; **riserva'tezza** sf reserve.

risi'edere vi: **~ a** o **in** to reside in.

'risma sf (di carta) ream; (fig) kind, sort.

'riso (pl(f) ~a: il ridere) sm: **un ~ a** laugh; **il ~** laughter; (pianta) rice ♦ pp di **ridere**.

riso'lino sm snigger.

ri'solto, a pp di **risolvere**.

risolu'tezza [risolu'tettsa] sf determina-tion.

riso'luto, a ag determined, resolute.

risoluzi'one [risolut'tsjone] sf solving no pl; (MAT) solution; (decisione, di immagine) resolution.

ri'solvere vt (difficoltà, controversia) to resolve; (problema) to solve; (decidere): **~ di fare** to resolve to do; **~rsi** vr (decidersi): **~rsi a fare** to make up one's mind to do; (andare a finire): **~rsi in** to end up, turn out; **~rsi in nulla** to come to nothing.

riso'nanza [riso'nantsa] sf resonance; **aver vasta ~** (fig: fatto etc) to be known far and wide.

riso'nare vt, vi = **risuonare**.

ri'sorgere [ri'sordʒere] vi to rise again; **risorgi'mento** sm revival; **il Risorgimento** (STORIA) the Risorgi-mento.

ri'sorsa sf expedient, resort; **~e** sfpl (naturali, finanziarie etc) resources; **persona piena di ~e** resourceful person.

ri'sorto, a pp di **risorgere**.

ri'sotto *sm* (*CUC*) risotto.
risparmi'are *vt* to save; (*non uccidere*) to spare ♦ *vi* to save; ~ **qc a qn** to spare sb sth.
ris'parmio *sm* saving *no pl*; (*denaro*) savings *pl*.
rispec'chiare [rispek'kjare] *vt* to reflect.
rispet'tabile *ag* respectable.
rispet'tare *vt* to respect; **farsi** ~ to command respect.
rispet'tivo, a *ag* respective.
ris'petto *sm* respect; ~**i** *smpl* (*saluti*) respects, regards; ~ **a** (*in paragone a*) compared to; (*in relazione a*) as regards, as for; **rispet'toso, a** *ag* respectful.
ris'plendere *vi* to shine.
ris'pondere *vi* to answer, reply; (*freni*) to respond; ~ **a** (*domanda*) to answer, reply to; (*persona*) to answer; (*invito*) to reply to; (*provocazione, sog: veicolo, apparecchio*) to respond to; (*corrispondere a*) to correspond to; (. *speranze, bisogno*) to answer; ~ **di** to answer for; **ris'posta** *sf* answer, reply; **in risposta a** in reply to; **risposto, a** *pp di* rispondere.
'rissa *sf* brawl.
ristabi'lire *vt* to re-establish, restore; (*persona: sog: riposo etc*) to restore to health; ~**rsi** *vr* to recover.
rista'gnare [rista̱ɲ'nare] *vi* (*acqua*) to become stagnant; (*sangue*) to cease flowing; (*fig: industria*) to stagnate; **ris'tagno** *sm* stagnation.
ris'tampa *sf* reprinting *no pl*; reprint.
risto'rante *sm* restaurant.
risto'rarsi *vr* to have something to eat and drink; (*riposarsi*) to rest, have a rest; **ris'toro** *sm* (*bevanda, cibo*) refreshment; **servizio di ristoro** (*FERR*) refreshments *pl*.
ristret'tezza [ristret'tettsa] *sf* (*strettezza*) narrowness; (*fig: scarsezza*) scarcity, lack; (: *meschinità*) meanness; ~**e** *sfpl* (*povertà*) financial straits.
ris'tretto, a *pp di* **restringere** ♦ *ag* (*racchiuso*) enclosed, hemmed in; (*angusto*) narrow; (*limitato*): ~ **(a)** restricted *o* limited (to); (*CUC: brodo*)

thick; (: *caffè*) extra strong.
risucchi'are [risuk'kjare] *vt* to suck in.
risul'tare *vi* (*dimostrarsi*) to prove (to be), turn out (to be); (*riuscire*): ~ **vincitore** to emerge as the winner; ~ **da** (*provenire*) to result from, be the result of; **mi risulta che** ... I understand that ...; **non mi risulta** not as far as I know; **risul'tato** *sm* result.
risuo'nare *vi* (*rimbombare*) to resound.
risurrezi'one [risurret'tsjone] *sf* (*REL*) resurrection.
risusci'tare [risuʃʃi'tare] *vt* to resuscitate, restore to life; (*fig*) to revive, bring back ♦ *vi* to rise (from the dead).
ris'veglio [riz'veʎʎo] *sm* waking up; (*fig*) revival.
ris'volto *sm* (*di giacca*) lapel; (*di pantaloni*) turn-up; (*di manica*) cuff; (*di tasca*) flap; (*di libro*) inside flap; (*fig*) implication.
ritagli'are [ritaʎ'ʎare] *vt* (*tagliar via*) to cut out; **ri'taglio** *sm* (*di giornale*) cutting, clipping; (*di stoffa etc*) scrap; **nei ritagli di tempo** in one's spare time.
ritar'dare *vi* (*persona, treno*) to be late; (*orologio*) to be slow ♦ *vt* (*rallentare*) to slow down; (*impedire*) to delay, hold up; (*differire*) to postpone, delay; **ritarda'tario, a** *sm/f* latecomer.
ri'tardo *sm* delay; (*di persona aspettata*) lateness *no pl*; (*fig: mentale*) backwardness; **in** ~ late.
ri'tegno [ri'teɲɲo] *sm* restraint.
rite'nere *vt* (*trattenere*) to hold back; (: *somma*) to deduct; (*giudicare*) to consider, believe; **rite'nuta** *sf* (*sul salario*) deduction.
riti'rare *vt* to withdraw; (*POL: richiamare*) to recall; (*andare a prendere: pacco etc*) to collect, pick up; ~**rsi** *vr* to withdraw; (*da un'attività*) to retire; (*stoffa*) to shrink; (*marea*) to recede; **riti'rata** *sf* (*MIL*) retreat; (*latrina*) lavatory; **ri'tiro** *sm* withdrawal; recall; collection; (*luogo appartato*) retreat.
'ritmo *sm* rhythm; (*fig*) rate; (: *della*

vita) pace, tempo.

'**rito** *sm* rite; **di** ~ usual, customary.

ritoc'care *vt* (*disegno, fotografia*) to touch up; (*testo*) to alter; **ri'tocco, chi** *sm* touching up *no pl*; alteration.

ritor'nare *vi* to return, go (*o come*) back; (*ripresentarsi*) to recur; (*ridiventare*): ~ **ricco** to become rich again ♦ *vt* (*restituire*) to return, give back.

ritor'nello *sm* refrain.

ri'torno *sm* return; **essere di** ~ to be back; **avere un** ~ **di fiamma** (*AUT*) to backfire; (*fig: persona*) to be back in love again.

ri'trarre *vt* (*trarre indietro, via*) to withdraw; (*distogliere: sguardo*) to turn away; (*rappresentare*) to portray, depict; (*ricavare*) to get, obtain.

ritrat'tare *vt* (*disdire*) to retract, take back; (*trattare nuovamente*) to deal with again.

ri'tratto, a *pp di* **ritrarre** ♦ *sm* portrait.

ri'troso, a *ag* (*restio*): ~ **(a)** reluctant (to); (*schivo*) shy; **andare a** ~ to go backwards.

ritro'vare *vt* to find; (*salute*) to regain; (*persona*) to find; to meet again; **~rsi** *vr* (*essere, capitare*) to find o.s.; (*raccapezzarsi*) to find one's way; (*con senso reciproco*) to meet (again); **ri'trovo** *sm* meeting place; **ritrovo notturno** night club.

'**ritto, a** *ag* (*in piedi*) standing, on one's feet; (*levato in alto*) erect, raised; (: *capelli*) standing on end; (*posto verticalmente*) upright.

ritu'ale *ag, sm* ritual.

riuni'one *sf* (*adunanza*) meeting; (*riconciliazione*) reunion.

riu'nire *vt* (*ricongiungere*) to join (together); (*riconciliare*) to reunite, bring together (again); **~rsi** *vr* (*adunarsi*) to meet; (*tornare a stare insieme*) to be reunited.

riu'scire [riuʃʃire] *vi* (*uscire di nuovo*) to go out again, go back out; (*aver esito: fatti, azioni*) to go, turn out; (*aver successo*) to succeed, be successful; (*essere, apparire*) to be, prove;

(*raggiungere il fine*) to manage, succeed; ~ **a fare qc** to manage to do *o* succeed in doing *o* be able to do sth; **questo mi riesce nuovo** this is new to me; **riu'scita** *sf* (*esito*) result, outcome; (*buon esito*) success.

'**riva** *sf* (*di fiume*) bank; (*di lago, mare*) shore.

ri'vale *sm/f* rival; **rivalità** *sf* rivalry.

ri'valsa *sf* (*rivincita*) revenge; (*risarcimento*) compensation.

rivalu'tare *vt* (*ECON*) to revalue.

rivan'gare *vt* (*ricordi etc*) to dig up (again).

rive'dere *vt* to see again; (*ripassare*) to revise; (*verificare*) to check.

rive'lare *vt* to reveal; (*divulgare*) to reveal, disclose; (*dare indizio*) to reveal, show; **~rsi** *vr* (*manifestarsi*) to be revealed; **~rsi onesto** *etc* to prove to be honest *etc*; **rivela'tore** *sm* (*TECN*) detector; (*FOT*) developer; **rivelazi'one** *sf* revelation.

rivendi'care *vt* to claim, demand.

ri'vendita *sf* (*bottega*) retailer's (shop).

rivendi'tore, 'trice *sm/f* retailer; ~ **autorizzato** (*COMM*) authorized dealer.

ri'verbero *sm* (*di luce, calore*) reflection; (*di suono*) reverberation.

rive'renza [rive'rɛntsa] *sf* reverence; (*inchino*) bow; curtsey.

rive'rire *vt* (*rispettare*) to revere; (*salutare*) to pay one's respects to.

river'sare *vt* (*anche fig*) to pour; **~rsi** *vr* (*fig: persone*) to pour out.

rivesti'mento *sm* covering; coating.

rives'tire *vt* to dress again; (*ricoprire*) to cover; to coat; (*fig: carica*) to hold; **~rsi** *vr* to get dressed again; to change (one's clothes).

rivi'era *sf* coast; **la** ~ **italiana** the Italian Riviera.

ri'vincita [ri'vintʃita] *sf* (*SPORT*) return match; (*fig*) revenge.

rivis'suto, a *pp di* **rivivere**.

ri'vista *sf* review; (*periodico*) magazine, review; (*TEATRO*) revue; variety show.

ri'vivere *vi* (*riacquistare forza*) to

come alive again; (*tornare in uso*) to be revived ♦ *vt* to relive.

ri'volgere [ri'vɔldʒere] *vt* (*attenzione, sguardo*) to turn, direct; (*parole*) to address; **~rsi** *vr* to turn round; (*fig: dirigersi per informazioni*): **~rsi a** to go and see, go and speak to; (: *ufficio*) to enquire at.

ri'volta *sf* revolt, rebellion.

rivol'tare *vt* to turn over; (*con l'interno all'esterno*) to turn inside out; (*disgustare: stomaco*) to upset, turn; **~rsi** *vr* (*ribellarsi*): **~rsi (a)** to rebel (against).

rivol'tella *sf* revolver.

ri'volto, a *pp di* **rivolgere**.

rivoluzio'nare [rivolutsjo'nare] *vt* to revolutionize.

rivoluzio'nario, a [rivoluttsjo'narjo] *ag, sm/f* revolutionary.

rivoluzi'one [rivolut'tsjone] *sf* revolution.

riz'zare [rit'tsare] *vt* to raise, erect; **~rsi** *vr* to stand up; (*capelli*) to stand on end.

'roba *sf* stuff, things *pl*; (*possessi, beni*) belongings *pl*, things *pl*, possessions *pl*; **~ da mangiare** things *pl* to eat, food; **~ da matti** sheer madness *o* lunacy.

'robot *sm inv* robot.

ro'busto, a *ag* robust, sturdy; (*solido: catena*) strong.

'rocca, che *sf* fortress.

rocca'forte *sf* stronghold.

roc'chetto [rok'ketto] *sm* reel, spool.

'roccia, ce ['rɔttʃa] *sf* rock; **fare ~** (*SPORT*) to go rock climbing; **roc'cioso, a** *ag* rocky.

ro'daggio [ro'daddʒo] *sm* running (*BRIT*) *o* breaking (*US*) in; **in ~** running (*BRIT*) *o* breaking (*US*) in.

'Rodano *sm*: **il ~** the Rhone.

'rodere *vt* to gnaw (at); (*distruggere poco a poco*) to eat into.

rodi'tore *sm* (*ZOOL*) rodent.

rodo'dendro *sm* rhododendron.

'rogna ['rɔɲɲa] *sf* (*MED*) scabies *sg*; (*fig*) bother, nuisance.

ro'gnone [roɲ'ɲone] *sm* (*CUC*) kidney.

'rogo, ghi *sm* (*per cadaveri*) (funeral) pyre; (*supplizio*): **il ~** the stake.

rol'lio *sm* roll(ing).

'Roma *sf* Rome.

Roma'nia *sf*: **la ~** Romania.

ro'manico, a, ci, che *ag* Romanesque.

ro'mano, a *ag, sm/f* Roman.

romanti'cismo [romanti'tʃizmo] *sm* romanticism.

ro'mantico, a, ci, che *ag* romantic.

ro'manza [ro'mandza] *sf* (*MUS, LETTERATURA*) romance.

roman'zesco, a, schi, sche [roman'dzesko] *ag* (*stile, personaggi*) fictional; (*fig*) storybook *cpd*.

romanzi'ere [roman'dzjere] *sm* novelist.

ro'manzo, a [ro'mandzo] *ag* (*LING*) romance *cpd* ♦ *sm* (*medievale*) romance; (*moderno*) novel; **~ d'appendice** serial (story).

rom'bare *vi* to rumble, thunder, roar.

'rombo *sm* rumble, thunder, roar; (*MAT*) rhombus; (*ZOOL*) turbot; brill.

ro'meno, a *ag, sm/f, sm* = **rumeno, a**.

'rompere *vt* to break; (*conversazione, fidanzamento*) to break off ♦ *vi* to break; **~rsi** *vr* to break; **mi rompe le scatole** (*fam*) he (*o* she) is a pain in the neck; **~rsi un braccio** to break an arm; **rompi'capo** *sm* worry, headache; (*indovinello*) puzzle; (*in enigmistica*) brainteaser; **rompighi'accio** *sm* (*NAUT*) icebreaker; **rompis'catole** (*fam*) *sm/f inv* pest, pain in the neck.

'ronda *sf* (*MIL*) rounds *pl*, patrol.

ron'della *sf* (*TECN*) washer.

'rondine *sf* (*ZOOL*) swallow.

ron'done *sm* (*ZOOL*) swift.

ron'zare [ron'dzare] *vi* to buzz, hum.

ron'zino [ron'dzino] *sm* (*peg: cavallo*) nag.

'rosa *sf* rose ♦ *ag inv, sm* pink; **ro'saio** *sm* (*pianta*) rosebush, rose tree; (*giardino*) rose garden; **ro'sario** *sm* (*REL*) rosary; **ro'sato, a** *ag* pink, rosy ♦ *sm* (*vino*) rosé (wine); **ro'seo, a** *ag* (*anche fig*) rosy.

rosicchi'are [rosik'kjare] *vt* to gnaw (at); (*mangiucchiare*) to nibble (at).

rosma'rino *sm* rosemary.

'roso, a *pp di* **rodere**.

roso'lare vt (CUC) to brown.

roso'lia sf (MED) German measles sg, rubella.

ro'sone sm rosette; (vetrata) rose window.

'rospo sm (ZOOL) toad.

ros'setto sm (per labbra) lipstick; (per guance) rouge.

'rosso, a ag, sm, sm/f red; **il mar R~** the Red Sea; **~ d'uovo** egg yolk; **ros'sore** sm flush, blush.

rosticce'ria [rostittʃe'ria] sf shop selling roast meat and other cooked food.

'rostro sm rostrum; (becco) beak.

ro'tabile ag (percorribile): **strada ~** roadway; (FERR): **materiale ~** rolling stock.

ro'taia sf rut, track; (FERR) rail.

ro'tare vt, vi to rotate; **rotazi'one** sf rotation.

rote'are vt, vi to whirl; **~ gli occhi** to roll one's eyes.

ro'tella sf small wheel; (di mobile) castor.

roto'lare vt, vi to roll; **~rsi** vr to roll (about).

'rotolo sm roll; **andare a ~i** (fig) to go to rack and ruin.

ro'tonda sf rotunda.

ro'tondo, a ag round.

ro'tore sm rotor.

'rotta sf (AER, NAUT) course, route; (MIL) rout; **a ~ di collo** at breakneck speed; **essere in ~ con qn** to be on bad terms with sb.

rot'tame sm fragment, scrap, broken bit; **~i** smpl (di nave, aereo etc) wreckage sg; **~i di ferro** scrap iron sg.

'rotto, a pp di **rompere** ♦ ag broken; (calzoni) torn, split; (persona: pratico, resistente): **~ a** accustomed o inured to; **per il ~ della cuffia** by the skin of one's teeth.

rot'tura sf breaking no pl; break; breaking off; (MED) fracture, break.

rou'lotte [ru'lɔt] sf caravan.

ro'vente ag red-hot.

'rovere sm oak.

rovesci'are [roveʃ'ʃare] vt (versare in giù) to pour; (: accidentalmente) to spill; (capovolgere) to turn upside down; (gettare a terra) to knock down; (: fig: governo) to overthrow; (piegare all'indietro: testa) to throw back; **~rsi** vr (sedia, macchina) to overturn; (barca) to capsize; (liquido) to spill; (fig: situazione) to be reversed.

ro'vescio, sci [ro'veʃʃo] sm other side, wrong side; (della mano) back; (di moneta) reverse; (pioggia) sudden downpour; (fig) setback; (MAGLIA: anche: punto ~) purl (stitch); (TENNIS) backhand (stroke); **a ~** upside-down; inside-out; **capire qc a ~** to misunderstand sth.

ro'vina sf ruin; **andare in ~** (andare a pezzi) to collapse; (fig) to go to rack and ruin.

rovi'nare vi to collapse, fall down ♦ vt (far cadere giù: casa) to demolish; (danneggiare, fig) to ruin; **rovi'noso, a** ag disastrous; damaging; violent.

rovis'tare vt (casa) to ransack; (tasche) to rummage in (o through).

'rovo sm (BOT) blackberry bush, bramble bush.

'rozzo, a ['roddzo] ag rough, coarse.

'ruba sf: **andare a ~** to sell like hot cakes.

ru'bare vt to steal; **~ qc a qn** to steal sth from sb.

rubi'netto sm tap, faucet (US).

ru'bino sm ruby.

ru'brica, che sf (STAMPA) column; (quadernetto) index book; address book.

'rude ag tough, rough.

'rudere sm (rovina) ruins pl.

rudimen'tale ag rudimentary, basic.

rudi'menti smpl rudiments; basic principles; basic knowledge sg.

ruffi'ano sm pimp.

'ruga, ghe sf wrinkle.

'ruggine ['ruddʒine] sf rust.

rug'gire [rud'dʒire] vi to roar.

rugi'ada [ru'dʒada] sf dew.

ru'goso, a ag wrinkled.

rul'lare vi (tamburo, nave) to roll; (aereo) to taxi.

'rullo sm (di tamburi) roll; (arnese

cilindrico, *TIP*) roller; ~ **compressore** steam roller; ~ **di pellicola** roll of film.
rum *sm* rum.
ru'meno, a *ag*, *sm/f*, *sm* Romanian.
rumi'nare *vt* (*ZOOL*) to ruminate.
ru'more *sm*: **un** ~ a noise, a sound; (*fig*) a rumour; **il** ~ noise; **rumo'roso, a** *ag* noisy.
ru'olo *sm* (*TEATRO*, *fig*) role, part; (*elenco*) roll, register, list; **di** ~ permanent, on the permanent staff.
ru'ota *sf* wheel; **a** ~ (*forma*) circular; ~ **anteriore/posteriore** front/back wheel; ~ **di scorta** spare wheel.
ruo'tare *vt*, *vi* = **rotare**.
'rupe *sf* cliff.
ru'rale *ag* rural, country *cpd*.
ru'scello [ruʃˈʃɛllo] *sm* stream.
'ruspa *sf* excavator.
rus'sare *vi* to snore.
'Russia *sf*: **la** ~ Russia; **'russo, a** *ag*, *sm/f*, *sm* Russian.
'rustico, a, ci, che *ag* rustic; (*fig*) rough, unrefined.
rut'tare *vi* to belch; **'rutto** *sm* belch.
'ruvido, a *ag* rough, coarse.
ruzzo'lare [ruttsoˈlare] *vi* to tumble down; **ruzzo'loni** *av*: **cadere ruzzoloni** to tumble down; **fare le scale ruzzoloni** to tumble down the stairs.

S

S. *abbr* (= *sud*) S.
sa *vb vedi* **sapere**.
'sabato *sm* Saturday; **di** *o* **il** ~ on Saturdays.
'sabbia *sf* sand; ~**e mobili** quicksand(s); **sabbi'oso, a** *ag* sandy.
sabo'taggio [saboˈtaddʒo] *sm* sabotage.
sabo'tare *vt* to sabotage.
'sacca, che *sf* bag; (*bisaccia*) haversack; (*insenatura*) inlet; ~ **da viaggio** travelling bag.
sacca'rina *sf* saccharin(e).
sac'cente [satˈtʃɛnte] *sm/f* know-all (*BRIT*), know-it-all (*US*).
saccheggi'are [sakkedˈdʒare] *vt* to sack, plunder; **sac'cheggio** *sm* sack(ing).

sac'chetto [sakˈketto] *sm* (small) bag; (small) sack.
'sacco, chi *sm* bag; (*per carbone etc*) sack; (*ANAT*, *BIOL*) sac; (*tela*) sacking; (*saccheggio*) sack(ing); (*fig: grande quantità*): **un** ~ **di** lots of, heaps of; ~ **a pelo** sleeping bag; ~ **per i rifiuti** bin bag.
sacer'dote [satʃerˈdɔte] *sm* priest; **sacer'dozio** *sm* priesthood.
sacra'mento *sm* sacrament.
sacrifi'care *vt* to sacrifice; ~**rsi** *vr* to sacrifice o.s.; (*privarsi di qc*) to make sacrifices.
sacri'ficio [sakriˈfitʃo] *sm* sacrifice.
sacri'legio [sakriˈlɛdʒo] *sm* sacrilege.
'sacro, a *ag* sacred.
'sadico, a, ci, che *ag* sadistic ♦ *sm/f* sadist.
sa'etta *sf* arrow; (*fulmine: anche fig*) thunderbolt; flash of lightning.
sa'fari *sm inv* safari.
sa'gace [saˈgatʃe] *ag* shrewd, sagacious.
sag'gezza [sadˈdʒettsa] *sf* wisdom.
saggi'are [sadˈdʒare] *vt* (*metalli*) to assay; (*fig*) to test.
'saggio, a, gi, ge [ˈsaddʒo] *ag* wise ♦ *sm* (*persona*) sage; (*operazione sperimentale*) test; (: *dell'oro*) assay; (*fig: prova*) proof; (*campione indicativo*) sample; (*ricerca, esame critico*) essay.
Sagit'tario [sadʒitˈtarjo] *sm* Sagittarius.
'sagoma *sf* (*profilo*) outline, profile; (*forma*) form, shape; (*TECN*) template; (*bersaglio*) target; (*fig: persona*) character.
'sagra *sf* festival.
sagres'tano *sm* sacristan; sexton.
sagres'tia *sf* sacristy; (*culto protestante*) vestry.
Sa'hara [saˈara] *sm*: **il (deserto del)** ~ the Sahara (Desert).
'sai *vb vedi* **sapere**.
'sala *sf* hall; (*stanza*) room; ~ **d'aspetto** waiting room; ~ **da ballo** ballroom; ~ **per concerti** concert hall; ~ **da gioco** gaming room; ~ **operatoria** operating theatre; ~ **da pranzo** dining room.
sa'lame *sm* salami *no pl*, salami sau-

sage.

sala'moia sf (CUC) brine.

sa'lare vt to salt.

salari'ato, a sm/f wage-earner.

sa'lario sm pay, wages pl.

sa'lato, a ag (sapore) salty; (CUC) salted, salt cpd; (fig: discorso etc) biting, sharp; (: prezzi) steep, stiff.

sal'dare vt (congiungere) to join, bind; (parti metalliche) to solder; (: con saldatura autogena) to weld; (conto) to settle, pay; **salda'tura** sf soldering; welding; (punto saldato) soldered joint; weld.

sal'dezza [sal'dettsa] sf firmness; strength.

'saldo, a ag (resistente, forte) strong, firm; (fermo) firm, steady, stable; (fig) firm, steadfast ♦ sm (svendita) sale; (di conto) settlement; (ECON) balance.

'sale sm salt; (fig): **ha poco ~ in zucca** he doesn't have much sense; **~ fino/grosso** table/cooking salt.

'salice [salitfe] sm willow; **~ piangente** weeping willow.

sali'ente ag (fig) salient, main.

sali'era sf salt cellar.

sa'lina sf saltworks sg.

sa'lino, a ag saline.

sa'lire vi to go (o come) up; (aereo etc) to climb, go up; (passeggero) to get on; (sentiero, prezzi, livello) to go up, rise ♦ vt (scale, gradini) to go (o come) up; **~ su** to climb (up); **~ sul treno/sull'autobus** to board the train/the bus; **~ in macchina** to get into the car; **sa'lita** sf climb, ascent; (erta) hill, slope; **in salita** ag, av uphill.

sa'liva sf saliva.

'salma sf corpse.

'salmo sm psalm.

sal'mone sm salmon.

sa'lone sm (stanza) sitting room, lounge; (in albergo) lounge; (su nave) lounge, saloon; (mostra) show, exhibition; **~ di bellezza** beauty salon.

sa'lotto sm lounge, sitting room; (mobilio) lounge suite.

sal'pare vi (NAUT) to set sail; (anche: **~ l'ancora**) to weigh anchor.

'salsa sf (CUC) sauce; **~ di pomodoro** tomato sauce.

sal'siccia, ce [sal'sittfa] sf pork sausage.

sal'tare vi to jump, leap; (esplodere) to blow up, explode; (: valvola) to blow; (venir via) to pop off; (non aver luogo: corso etc) to be cancelled ♦ vt to jump (over), leap (over); (fig: pranzo, capitolo) to skip, miss (out); (CUC) to sauté; **far ~** to blow up; to burst open; **~ fuori** (fig: apparire all'improvviso) to turn up.

saltel'lare vi to skip; to hop.

saltim'banco sm acrobat.

'salto sm jump; (SPORT) jumping; **fare un ~** to jump, leap; **fare un ~ da qn** to pop over to sb's (place); **~ in alto/lungo** high/long jump; **~ con l'asta** pole vaulting; **~ mortale** somersault.

saltu'ario, a ag occasional, irregular.

sa'lubre ag healthy, salubrious.

salume'ria sf delicatessen.

sa'lumi smpl salted pork meats.

salu'tare ag healthy; (fig) salutary, beneficial ♦ vt (per dire buon giorno, fig) to greet; (per dire addio) to say goodbye to; (MIL) to salute.

sa'lute sf health; **~!** (a chi starnutisce) bless you!; (nei brindisi) cheers!; **bere alla ~ di qn** to drink (to) sb's health.

sa'luto sm (gesto) wave; (parola) greeting; (MIL) salute; **~i** smpl (formula di cortesia) greetings; **cari ~i** best regards; **vogliate gradire i nostri più distinti ~i** Yours faithfully.

salvacon'dotto sm (MIL) safe-conduct.

salva'gente [salva'dʒente] sm (NAUT) lifebuoy; (stradale) traffic island; **~ a ciambella** life belt; **~ a giubbotto** life-jacket.

salvaguar'dare vt to safeguard.

sal'vare vt to save; (trarre da un pericolo) to rescue; (proteggere) to protect; **~rsi** vr to save o.s.; to escape; **salva'taggio** sm rescue; **salva'tore, 'trice** sm/f saviour.

'salve (fam) escl hi!

sal'vezza [sal'vettsa] sf salvation; (sicurezza) safety.

'salvia sf (BOT) sage.

'**salvo, a** *ag* safe, unhurt, unharmed; (*fuori pericolo*) safe, out of danger ♦ *sm*: **in** ~ safe ♦ *prep* (*eccetto*) except; **mettere qc in** ~ to put sth in a safe place; ~ **che** (*a meno che*) unless; (*eccetto che*) except (that); ~ **imprevisti** barring accidents.

sam'buco *sm* elder (tree).

san *ag vedi* **santo**.

sa'nare *vt* to heal, cure; (*economia*) to put right.

san'cire [san'tʃire] *vt* to sanction.

'**sandalo** *sm* (*BOT*) sandalwood; (*calzatura*) sandal.

'**sangue** *sm* blood; **farsi cattivo** ~ to fret, get in a state; ~ **freddo** (*fig*) sang-froid, calm; **a** ~ **freddo** in cold blood; **sangu'igno, a** *ag* blood *cpd*; (*colore*) blood-red; **sangui'nare** *vi* to bleed; **sangui'noso, a** *ag* bloody; **sangui'suga** *sf* leech.

sanità *sf* health; (*salubrità*) healthiness; **Ministero della S~** Department of Health; ~ **mentale** sanity.

sani'tario, a *ag* health *cpd*; (*condizioni*) sanitary ♦ *sm* (*AMM*) doctor; (**impianti**) ~**i** *smpl* bathroom *o* sanitary fittings.

'**sanno** *vb vedi* **sapere**.

'**sano, a** *ag* healthy; (*denti, costituzione*) healthy, sound; (*integro*) whole, unbroken; (*fig: politica, consigli*) sound; ~ **di mente** sane; **di** ~**a pianta** completely, entirely; ~ **e salvo** safe and sound.

sant' *ag vedi* **santo**.

santifi'care *vt* to sanctify; (*feste*) to observe.

santità *sf* sanctity; holiness; **Sua/Vostra** ~ (*titolo di Papa*) His/Your Holiness.

'**santo, a** *ag* holy; (*fig*) saintly; (*seguito da nome proprio*) saint ♦ *sm/f* saint; **la S~a Sede** the Holy See.

santu'ario *sm* sanctuary.

sanzio'nare [santsjo'nare] *vt* to sanction.

sanzi'one [san'tsjone] *sf* sanction; (*penale, civile*) sanction, penalty.

sa'pere *vt* to know; (*essere capace di*): **so nuotare** I know how to swim, I can

swim ♦ *vi*: ~ **di** (*aver sapore*) to taste of; (*aver odore*) to smell of ♦ *sm* knowledge; **far** ~ **qc a qn** to inform sb about sth, let sb know sth; **mi sa che non sia vero** I don't think that's true.

sapi'enza [sa'pjentsa] *sf* wisdom.

sa'pone *sm* soap; ~ **da bucato** washing soap; **sapo'netta** *sf* cake *o* bar *o* tablet of soap.

sa'pore *sm* taste, flavour; **sapo'rito, a** *ag* tasty.

sappi'amo *vb vedi* **sapere**.

saraci'nesca [saratʃi'neska] *sf* (*serranda*) rolling shutter.

sar'casmo *sm* sarcasm *no pl*; sarcastic remark.

Sar'degna [sar'deɲɲa] *sf*: **la** ~ Sardinia.

sar'dina *sf* sardine.

'**sardo, a** *ag, sm/f* Sardinian.

'**sarto, a** *sm/f* tailor/dressmaker; **sarto'ria** *sf* tailor's (shop); dressmaker's (shop); (*casa di moda*) fashion house; (*arte*) couture.

'**sasso** *sm* stone; (*ciottolo*) pebble; (*masso*) rock.

sas'sofono *sm* saxophone.

sas'soso, a *ag* stony; pebbly.

'**Satana** *sm* Satan; **sa'tanico, a, ci, che** *ag* satanic, fiendish.

sa'tellite *sm, ag* satellite.

'**satira** *sf* satire.

'**saturo, a** *ag* saturated; (*fig*): ~ **di** full of.

S.A.U.B. ['saub] *sigla f* (= *Struttura Amministrativa Unificata di Base*) *state welfare system*.

'**sauna** *sf* sauna.

Sa'voia *sf*: **la** ~ Savoy.

savoi'ardo, a *ag* of Savoy, Savoyard ♦ *sm* (*biscotto*) sponge finger.

sazi'are [sat'tsjare] *vt* to satisfy, satiate; ~**rsi** *vr* (*riempirsi di cibo*): ~**rsi** (**di**) to eat one's fill (of); (*fig*): ~**rsi di** to grow tired *o* weary of.

'**sazio, a** ['sattsjo] *ag*: ~ (**di**) sated (with), full (of); (*fig: stufo*) fed up (with), sick (of).

sba'dato, a *ag* careless, inattentive.

sbadigli'are [zbadiʎ'ʎare] *vi* to yawn; **sba'diglio** *sm* yawn.

sbagli'are [zbaʎ'ʎare] vt to make a mistake in, get wrong ♦ vi to make a mistake, be mistaken, be wrong; (*operare in modo non giusto*) to err; **~rsi** vr to make a mistake, be mistaken, be wrong; **~ la mira/strada** to miss one's aim/take the wrong road; **'sbaglio** sm mistake, error; (*morale*) error; **fare uno sbaglio** to make a mistake.

sbal'lare vt (*merce*) to unpack ♦ vi (*nel fare un conto*) to overestimate; (*fam: gergo della droga*) to get high.

sballot'tare vt to toss (about).

sbalor'dire vt to stun, amaze ♦ vi to be stunned, be amazed; **sbalordi'tivo, a** ag amazing; (*prezzo*) incredible, absurd.

sbal'zare [zbal'tsare] vt to throw, hurl ♦ vi (*balzare*) to bounce; (*saltare*) to leap, bound; **'sbalzo** sm (*spostamento improvviso*) jolt, jerk; **a sbalzi** jerkily; (*fig*) in fits and starts; **uno sbalzo di temperatura** a sudden change in temperature.

sban'dare vi (NAUT) to list; (AER) to bank; (AUT) to skid; **~rsi** vr (*folla*) to disperse; (*fig: famiglia*) to break up.

sbandie'rare vt (*bandiera*) to wave; (*fig*) to parade, show off.

sbaragli'are [zbaraʎ'ʎare] vt (MIL) to rout; (*in gare sportive etc*) to beat, defeat.

sba'raglio [zba'raʎʎo] sm rout; defeat; **gettarsi allo ~** to risk everything.

sbaraz'zarsi [zbarat'tsarsi] vr: **~ di** to get rid of, rid o.s. of.

sbar'care vt (*passeggeri*) to disembark; (*merci*) to unload ♦ vi to disembark; **'sbarco** sm disembarkation; unloading; (MIL) landing.

'sbarra sf bar; (*di passaggio a livello*) barrier; (DIR): **presentarsi alla ~** to appear before the court.

sbarra'mento sm (*stradale*) barrier; (*diga*) dam, barrage; (MIL) barrage.

sbar'rare vt (*strada etc*) to block, bar; (*assegno*) to cross; **~ il passo** to bar the way; **~ gli occhi** to open one's eyes wide.

'sbattere vt (*porta*) to slam, bang; (*tappeti, ali,* CUC) to beat; (*urtare*) to

knock, hit ♦ vi (*porta, finestra*) to bang; (*agitarsi: ali, vele etc*) to flap; **me ne sbatto!** (*fam*) I don't give a damn!; **sbat'tuto, a** ag (*viso, aria*) dejected, worn out; (*uovo*) beaten.

sba'vare vi to dribble; (*colore*) to smear, smudge.

sbia'dire vi, vt to fade; **~rsi** vr to fade, **sbia'dito, a** ag faded; (*fig*) colourless, dull.

sbian'care vt to whiten; (*tessuto*) to bleach ♦ vi (*impallidire*) to grow pale o white.

sbi'eco, a, chi, che ag (*storto*) squint, askew; **di ~: guardare qn di ~** (*fig*) to look askance at sb; **tagliare una stoffa di ~** to cut a material on the bias.

sbigot'tire vt to dismay, stun ♦ vi (*anche: ~rsi*) to be dismayed.

sbilanci'are [zbilan'tʃare] vt to throw off balance; **~rsi** vr (*perdere l'equilibrio*) to overbalance, lose one's balance; (*fig: compromettersi*) to compromise o.s.

sbirci'are [zbir'tʃare] vt to cast sidelong glances at, eye.

'sbirro (*peg*) sm cop.

sbizzar'rirsi [zbiddzar'rirsi] vr to indulge one's whims.

sbloc'care vt to unblock, free; (*freno*) to release; (*prezzi, affitti*) to decontrol.

sboc'care vi: **~ in** (*fiume*) to flow into; (*strada*) to lead into; (*persona*) to come (out) into; (*fig: concludersi*) to end (up) in.

sboc'cato, a ag (*persona*) foul-mouthed; (*linguaggio*) foul.

sbocci'are [zbot'tʃare] vi (*fiore*) to bloom, open (out).

'sbocco, chi sm (*di fiume*) mouth; (*di strada*) end; (*di tubazione,* COMM) outlet; (*uscita: anche fig*) way out; **siamo in una situazione senza ~chi** there's no way out of this for us.

sbol'lire vi (*fig*) to cool down, calm down.

'sbornia (*fam*) sf: **prendersi una ~** to get plastered.

sbor'sare vt (*denaro*) to pay out.

sbot'tare vi: **~ in una risata/per la collera** to burst out laughing/explode with anger.

sbotto'nare *vt* to unbutton, undo.

sbracci'ato, a [zbrat'tʃato] *ag* (*camicia*) sleeveless; (*persona*) bare-armed.

sbrai'tare *vi* to yell, bawl.

sbra'nare *vt* to tear to pieces.

sbricio'lare [zbritʃo'lare] *vt* to crumble; ~rsi *vr* to crumble.

sbri'gare *vt* to deal with, get through; (*cliente*) to attend to, deal with; ~rsi *vr* to hurry (up); **sbriga'tivo, a** *ag* (*persona, modo*) quick, expeditious; (*giudizio*) hasty.

sbrindel'lato, a *ag* tattered, in tatters.

sbrodo'lare *vt* to stain, dirty.

'sbronza ['zbrontsa] (*fam*) *sf* (*ubriaco*): **prendersi una** ~ to get tight *o* plastered.

'sbronzo, a ['zbrontso] (*fam*) *ag* (*ubriaco*) tight.

sbu'care *vi* to come out, emerge; (*apparire improvvisamente*) to pop out (*o* up).

sbucci'are [zbut'tʃare] *vt* (*arancia, patata*) to peel; (*piselli*) to shell; ~rsi **un ginocchio** to graze one's knee.

sbudel'larsi *vr*: ~ **dalle risa** to split one's sides laughing.

sbuf'fare *vi* (*persona, cavallo*) to snort; (: *ansimare*) to puff, pant; (*treno*) to puff; **'sbuffo** *sm* (*di aria, fumo, vapore*) puff; **maniche a sbuffo** puff(ed) sleeves.

'scabbia *sf* (*MED*) scabies *sg*.

sca'broso, a *ag* (*fig: difficile*) difficult, thorny; (: *imbarazzante*) embarrassing; (: *sconcio*) indecent.

scacchi'era [skak'kjɛra] *sf* chessboard.

scacci'are [skat'tʃare] *vt* to chase away *o* out, drive away *o* out.

'scacco, chi *sm* (*pezzo del gioco*) chessman; (*quadretto di scacchiera*) square; (*fig*) setback, reverse; ~**chi** *smpl* (*gioco*) chess *sg*; **a** ~**chi** (*tessuto*) check(ed); **scacco'matto** *sm* checkmate.

sca'dente *ag* shoddy, of poor quality.

sca'denza [ska'dɛntsa] *sf* (*di cambiale, contratto*) maturity; (*di passaporto*) expiry date; **a breve/lunga** ~ short-/

long-term; **data di** ~ expiry date.

sca'dere *vi* (*contratto etc*) to expire; (*debito*) to fall due; (*valore, forze, peso*) to decline, go down.

sca'fandro *sm* (*di palombaro*) diving suit; (*di astronauta*) space-suit.

scaf'fale *sm* shelf; (*mobile*) set of shelves.

'scafo *sm* (*NAUT, AER*) hull.

scagio'nare [skadʒo'nare] *vt* to exonerate, free from blame.

'scaglia ['skaʎʎa] *sf* (*ZOOL*) scale; (*scheggia*) chip, flake.

scagli'are [skaʎ'ʎare] *vt* (*lanciare: anche fig*) to hurl, fling; ~rsi *vr*: ~rsi **su** *o* **contro** to hurl *o* fling o.s. at; (*fig*) to rail at.

scaglio'nare [skaʎʎo'nare] *vt* (*pagamenti*) to space out, spread out; (*MIL*) to echelon; **scagli'one** *sm* echelon; (*GEO*) terrace; **a scaglioni** in groups.

'scala *sf* (*a gradini etc*) staircase, stairs *pl*; (*a pioli, di corda*) ladder; (*MUS, GEO, di colori, valori, fig*) scale; ~**e** *sfpl* (*scalinata*) stairs; **su vasta** ~/~ **ridotta** on a large/small scale; ~ **a libretto** stepladder; ~ **mobile** escalator; (*ECON*) sliding scale; ~ **mobile** (**dei salari**) index-linked pay scale.

sca'lare *vt* (*ALPINISMO, muro*) to climb, scale; (*debito*) to scale down, reduce; **sca'lata** *sf* scaling *no pl*, climbing *no pl*; (*arrampicata, fig*) climb; **scala'tore, 'trice** *sm/f* climber.

scalda'bagno [skalda'baɲɲo] *sm* waterheater.

scal'dare *vt* to heat; ~rsi *vr* to warm up, heat up; (*al fuoco, al sole*) to warm o.s.; (*fig*) to get excited.

scal'fire *vt* to scratch.

scali'nata *sf* staircase.

sca'lino *sm* (*anche fig*) step; (*di scala a pioli*) rung.

'scalo *sm* (*NAUT*) slipway; (: *porto d'approdo*) port of call; (*AER*) stopover; **fare** ~ (**a**) (*NAUT*) to call (at), put in (at); (*AER*) to land (at), make a stop (at); ~ **merci** (*FERR*) goods (*BRIT*) *o* freight yard.

scalop'pina *sf* (*CUC*) escalope.

scal'pello *sm* chisel.

scal'pore *sm* noise, row; **far ~** (*notizia*) to cause a sensation *o* a stir.

'scaltro, a *ag* cunning, shrewd.

scal'zare [skal'tsare] *vt* (*albero*) to bare the roots of; (*muro, fig: autorità*) to undermine.

'scalzo, a ['skaltso] *ag* barefoot.

scambi'are *vt* to exchange; (*confondere*): **~ qn/qc per** to take *o* mistake sb/sth for; **mi hanno scambiato il cappello** they've given me the wrong hat.

scambi'evole *ag* mutual, reciprocal.

'scambio *sm* exchange; (*FERR*) points *pl*; **fare (uno) ~** to make a swap.

scampa'gnata [skampaɲ'ɲata] *sf* trip to the country.

scampa'nare *vi* to peal.

scam'pare *vt* (*salvare*) to rescue, save; (*evitare: morte, prigione*) to escape ♦ *vi*: ~ **(a qc)** to survive (sth), escape (sth); **scamparla bella** to have a narrow escape.

'scampo *sm* (*salvezza*) escape; (*ZOOL*) prawn; **cercare ~ nella fuga** to seek safety in flight.

'scampolo *sm* remnant.

scanala'tura *sf* (*incavo*) channel, groove.

scandagli'are [skandaʎ'ʎare] *vt* (*NAUT*) to sound; (*fig*) to sound out; to probe.

scandaliz'zare [skandalid'dzare] *vt* to shock, scandalize; **~rsi** *vr* to be shocked.

'scandalo *sm* scandal.

Scandi'navia *sf*: **la ~** Scandinavia; **scandi'navo, a** *ag, sm/f* Scandinavian.

scan'dire *vt* (*versi*) to scan; (*parole*) to articulate, pronounce distinctly; **~ il tempo** (*MUS*) to beat time.

scan'nare *vt* (*animale*) to butcher, slaughter; (*persona*) to cut *o* slit the throat of.

'scanno *sm* seat, bench.

scansafa'tiche [skansafa'tike] *sm/f inv* idler, loafer.

scan'sare *vt* (*rimuovere*) to move (aside), shift; (*schivare: schiaffo*) to dodge; (*sfuggire*) to avoid; **~rsi** *vr* to move aside.

scan'sia *sf* shelves *pl*; (*per libri*) bookcase.

'scanso *sm*: **a ~ di** in order to avoid, as a precaution against.

scanti'nato *sm* basement.

scanto'nare *vi* to turn the corner; (*svignarsela*) to sneak off.

scapes'trato, a *ag* dissolute.

'scapito *sm* (*perdita*) loss; (*danno*) damage, detriment; **a ~ di** to the detriment of.

'scapola *sf* shoulder blade.

'scapolo *sm* bachelor.

scappa'mento *sm* (*AUT*) exhaust.

scap'pare *vi* (*fuggire*) to escape; (*andare via in fretta*) to rush off; **lasciarsi ~ un'occasione** to let an opportunity go by; **~ di prigione** to escape from prison; **~ di mano** (*oggetto*) to slip out of one's hands; **~ di mente a qn** to slip sb's mind; **mi scappò detto** I let it slip; **scap'pata** *sf* quick visit *o* call; **scappa'tella** *sf* escapade; **scappa'toia** *sf* way out.

scara'beo *sm* beetle.

scarabocchi'are [skarabok'kjare] *vt* to scribble, scrawl; **scara'bocchio** *sm* scribble, scrawl.

scara'faggio [skara'faddʒo] *sm* cockroach.

scaraven'tare *vt* to fling, hurl.

scarce'rare [skartʃe'rare] *vt* to release (from prison).

'scarica, che *sf* (*di più armi*) volley of shots; (*di sassi, pugni*) hail, shower; (*ELETTR*) discharge; **~ di mitra** burst of machine-gun fire.

scari'care *vt* (*merci, camion etc*) to unload; (*passeggeri*) to set down, put off; (*arma*) to unload; (*: sparare, ELETTR*) to discharge; (*sog: corso d'acqua*) to empty, pour; (*fig: liberare da un peso*) to unburden, relieve; **~rsi** *vr* (*orologio*) to run *o* wind down; (*batteria, accumulatore*) to go flat *o* dead; (*fig: rilassarsi*) to unwind; (*: sfogarsi*) to let off steam; **il fulmine si scaricò su un albero** the lightning struck a tree;

scarica'tore *sm* loader; (*di porto*) dock-er.

'scarico, a, chi, che *ag* unloaded; (*orologio*) run down; (*accumulatore*) dead, flat ♦ *sm* (*di merci, materiali*) unloading; (*di immondizie*) dumping, tipping (*BRIT*); (: *luogo*) rubbish dump; (*TECN: deflusso*) draining; (: *dispositivo*) drain; (*AUT*) exhaust.

scar'latto, a *ag* scarlet.

'scarno, a *ag* thin, bony.

'scarpa *sf* shoe; ~e da ginnastica/tennis gym/tennis shoes.

scar'pata *sf* escarpment.

scarseggi'are [skarsed'dʒare] *vi* to be scarce; ~ di to be short of, lack.

scar'sezza [skar'settsa] *sf* scarcity, lack.

'scarso, a *ag* (*insufficiente*) insufficient, meagre; (*povero: annata*) poor, lean; (*INS: voto*) poor; ~ di lacking in; 3 chili ~i just under 3 kilos, barely 3 kilos.

scarta'mento *sm* (*FERR*) gauge; ~ normale/ridotto standard/narrow gauge.

scar'tare *vt* (*pacco*) to unwrap; (*idea*) to reject; (*MIL*) to declare unfit for military service; (*carte da gioco*) to discard; (*CALCIO*) to dodge (past) ♦ *vi* to swerve.

'scarto *sm* (*cosa scartata, anche COMM*) reject; (*di veicolo*) swerve; (*differenza*) gap, difference.

scassi'nare *vt* to break, force.

'scasso *sm vedi* furto.

scate'nare *vt* (*fig*) to incite, stir up; ~rsi *vr* (*temporale*) to break; (*rivolta*) to break out; (*persona: infuriarsi*) to rage.

'scatola *sf* box; (*di latta*) tin (*BRIT*), can; cibi in ~ tinned (*BRIT*) o canned foods; ~ cranica cranium.

scat'tare *vt* (*fotografia*) to take ♦ *vi* (*congegno, molla etc*) to be released; (*balzare*) to spring up; (*SPORT*) to put on a spurt; (*fig: per l'ira*) to fly into a rage; ~ in piedi to spring to one's feet.

'scatto *sm* (*dispositivo*) release; (: *di arma da fuoco*) trigger mechanism; (*rumore*) click; (*balzo*) jump, start; (*SPORT*) spurt; (*fig: di ira etc*) fit; (: *di*

stipendio) increment; di ~ suddenly.

scatu'rire *vi* to gush, spring.

scaval'care *vt* (*ostacolo*) to pass (o climb) over; (*fig*) to get ahead of, overtake.

sca'vare *vt* (*terreno*) to dig; (*legno*) to hollow out; (*pozzo, galleria*) to bore; (*città sepolta etc*) to excavate.

'scavo *sm* excavating *no pl*; excavation.

'scegliere ['ʃeʎʎere] *vt* to choose, select.

sce'icco, chi [ʃe'ikko] *sm* sheik.

scelle'rato, a [ʃelle'rato] *ag* wicked, evil.

scel'lino [ʃel'lino] *sm* shilling.

'scelta ['ʃelta] *sf* choice; selection; di prima ~ top grade o quality; frutta o formaggi a ~ choice of fruit or cheese.

'scelto, a ['ʃelto] *pp di* scegliere ♦ *ag* (*gruppo*) carefully selected; (*frutta, verdura*) choice, top quality; (*MIL: specializzato*) crack *cpd*, highly skilled.

sce'mare [ʃe'mare] *vt, vi* to diminish.

'scemo, a ['ʃemo] *ag* stupid, silly.

'scempio ['ʃempjo] *sm* slaughter, massacre; (*fig*) ruin; far ~ di (*fig*) to play havoc with, ruin.

'scena ['ʃɛna] *sf* (*gen*) scene; (*palcoscenico*) stage; le ~e (*fig: teatro*) the stage; fare una ~ to make a scene; andare in ~ to be staged o put on o performed; mettere in ~ to stage.

sce'nario [ʃe'narjo] *sm* scenery; (*di film*) scenario.

sce'nata [ʃe'nata] *sf* row, scene.

'scendere ['ʃendere] *vi* to go (o come) down; (*strada, sole*) to go down; (*notte*) to fall; (*passeggero: fermarsi*) to get out, alight; (*fig: temperatura, prezzi*) to go o come down, fall, drop ♦ *vt* (*scale, pendio*) to go (o come) down; ~ dalle scale to go (o come) down the stairs; ~ dal treno to get off o out of the train; ~ dalla macchina to get out of the car; ~ da cavallo to dismount, get off one's horse.

'scenico, a, ci, che ['ʃɛniko] *ag* stage *cpd*, scenic.

scervel'lato, a [ʃervel'lato] *ag* feather-brained, scatterbrained.

'**sceso, a** ['ʃeso] *pp di* scendere.

'**scettico, a, ci, che** ['ʃettiko] *ag* sceptical.

'**scettro** ['ʃettro] *sm* sceptre.

'**scheda** ['skɛda] *sf* (index) card; ~ **elettorale** ballot paper; ~ **perforata** punch card; **sche'dare** *vt* (*dati*) to file; (*libri*) to catalogue; (*registrare: anche POLIZIA*) to put on one's files; **sche'dario** *sm* file; (*mobile*) filing cabinet.

'**scheggia, ge** ['skeddʒa] *sf* splinter, sliver.

'**scheletro** ['skeletro] *sm* skeleton.

'**schema, i** ['skɛma] *sm* (*diagramma*) diagram, sketch; (*progetto, abbozzo*) outline, plan.

'**scherma** ['skerma] *sf* fencing.

scher'maglia [sker'maʎʎa] *sf* (*fig*) skirmish.

'**schermo** ['skermo] *sm* shield, screen; (*CINEMA, TV*) screen.

scher'nire [sker'nire] *vt* to mock, sneer at; **'scherno** *sm* mockery, derision.

scher'zare [sker'tsare] *vi* to joke.

'**scherzo** ['skertso] *sm* joke; (*tiro*) trick; (*MUS*) scherzo; **è uno** ~! (*una cosa facile*) it's child's play!, it's easy!; **per** ~ in jest; for a joke *o* a laugh; **fare un brutto** ~ **a qn** to play a nasty trick on sb; **scher'zoso, a** *ag* (*tono, gesto*) playful; (*osservazione*) facetious; **è un tipo scherzoso** he likes a joke.

schiaccia'noci [skjattʃa'notʃi] *sm inv* nutcracker.

schiacci'are [skjat'tʃare] *vt* (*dito*) to crush; (*noci*) to crack; ~ **un pisolino** to have a nap.

schiaffeggi'are [skjaffed'dʒare] *vt* to slap.

schi'affo ['skjaffo] *sm* slap.

schiamaz'zare [skjamat'tsare] *vi* to squawk, cackle.

schian'tare [skjan'tare] *vt* to break, tear apart; ~**rsi** *vr* to break (up), shatter; **schi'anto** *sm* (*rumore*) crash; tearing sound; **è uno schianto!** (*fam*) it's (*o* he's *o* she's) terrific!; **di schianto** all of a sudden.

schia'rire [skja'rire] *vt* to lighten, make

lighter ♦ *vi* (*anche*: ~**rsi**) to grow lighter; (*tornar sereno*) to clear, brighten up; ~**rsi la voce** to clear one's throat.

schiavitù [skjavi'tu] *sf* slavery.

schi'avo, a ['skjavo] *sm/f* slave.

schi'ena ['skjena] *sf* (*ANAT*) back; **schie'nale** *sm* (*di sedia*) back.

schi'era ['skjera] *sf* (*MIL*) rank; (*gruppo*) group, band.

schiera'mento [skjera'mento] *sm* (*MIL, SPORT*) formation; (*fig*) alliance.

schie'rare [skje'rare] *vt* (*esercito*) to line up, draw up, marshal; ~**rsi** *vr* to line up; (*fig*) ~**rsi con** *o* **dalla parte di/contro qn** to side with/oppose sb.

schi'etto, a ['skjetto] *ag* (*puro*) pure; (*fig*) frank, straightforward; sincere.

'**schifo** ['skifo] *sm* disgust; **fare** ~ (*essere fatto male, dare pessimi risultati*) to be awful; **mi fa** ~ it makes me sick, it's disgusting; **quel libro è uno** ~ that book's rotten; **schi'foso, a** *ag* disgusting, revolting; (*molto scadente*) rotten, lousy.

schioc'care [skjɔk'kare] *vt* (*frusta*) to crack; (*dita*) to snap; (*lingua*) to click; ~ **le labbra** to smack one's lips.

schi'udere ['skjudere] *vt* to open; ~**rsi** *vr* to open.

schi'uma ['skjuma] *sf* foam; (*di sapone*) lather; (*di latte*) froth; (*fig: feccia*) scum; **schiu'mare** *vt* to skim ♦ *vi* to foam.

schi'uso, a ['skjuso] *pp di* schiudere.

schi'vare [ski'vare] *vt* to dodge, avoid.

'**schivo, a** ['skivo] *ag* (*ritroso*) standoffish, reserved; (*timido*) shy.

schiz'zare [skit'tsare] *vt* (*spruzzare*) to spurt, squirt; (*sporcare*) to splash, spatter; (*fig: abbozzare*) to sketch ♦ *vi* to spurt, squirt; (*saltar fuori*) to dart up (*o* off *etc*).

schizzi'noso, a [skittsi'noso] *ag* fussy, finicky.

'**schizzo** ['skittso] *sm* (*di liquido*) spurt; splash, spatter; (*abbozzo*) sketch.

sci [ʃi] *sm* (*attrezzo*) ski; (*attività*) skiing; ~ **nautico** water-skiing.

'**scia** ['ʃia] (*pl* '**scie**) *sf* (*di imbarcazione*) wake; (*di profumo*) trail.

scià [ʃa] *sm inv* shah.

sci'abola ['ʃabola] *sf* sabre.

scia'callo [ʃa'kallo] *sm* jackal.

sciac'quare [ʃak'kware] *vt* to rinse.

scia'gura [ʃa'gura] *sf* disaster, calamity; misfortune; **sciagu'rato, a** *ag* unfortunate; (*malvagio*) wicked.

scialac'quare [ʃalak'kware] *vt* to squander.

scia'lare [ʃa'lare] *vi* to lead a life of luxury.

sci'albo, a ['ʃalbo] *ag* pale, dull; (*fig*) dull, colourless.

sci'alle ·['ʃalle] *sm* shawl.

scia'luppa [ʃa'luppa] *sf* (*NAUT*) sloop; (*anche*: ~ *di salvataggio*) lifeboat.

sci'ame ['ʃame] *sm* swarm.

scian'cato, a [ʃan'kato] *ag* lame; (*mobile*) rickety.

sci'are [ʃi'are] *vi* to ski.

sci'arpa ['ʃarpa] *sf* scarf; (*fascia*) sash.

scia'tore, 'trice [ʃia'tore] *sm/f* skier.

sci'atto, a ['ʃatto] *ag* (*persona: nell'aspetto*) slovenly, unkempt; (: *nel lavoro*) sloppy, careless.

scien'tifico, a, ci, che [ʃen'tifiko] *ag* scientific.

sci'enza ['ʃɛntsa] *sf* science; (*sapere*) knowledge; ~**e** *sfpl* (*INS*) science *sg*; ~**e naturali** natural sciences; **scienzi'ato, a** *sm/f* scientist.

'scimmia ['ʃimmja] *sf* monkey; **scimmiot'tare** *vt* to ape, mimic.

scimpanzé [ʃimpan'tse] *sm inv* chimpanzee.

scimu'nito, a [ʃimu'nito] *ag* silly, idiotic.

'scindere ['ʃindere] *vt* to split (up); ~**rsi** *vr* to split (up).

scin'tilla [ʃin'tilla] *sf* spark; **scintil'lare** *vi* to spark; (*acqua, occhi*) to sparkle.

scioc'chezza [ʃok'kettsa] *sf* stupidity *no pl*; stupid *o* foolish thing; **dire ~e** to talk nonsense.

sci'occo, a, chi, che ['ʃɔkko] *ag* stupid, foolish.

sci'ogliere ['ʃɔʎʎere] *vt* (*nodo*) to untie; (*capelli*) to loosen; (*persona, animale*) to untie, release; (*fig: persona*): ~ **da** to release from; (*neve*) to melt; (*nell'acqua: zucchero etc*) to dissolve; (*fig: mistero*) to solve; (*porre fine a: contratto*) to cancel; (: *società, matrimonio*) to dissolve; (: *riunione*) to bring to an end; ~**rsi** *vr* to loosen, come untied; to melt; to dissolve; (*assemblea etc*) to break up; ~ **i muscoli** to limber up.

sciol'tezza [ʃol'tettsa] *sf* agility; suppleness; ease.

sci'olto, a ['ʃɔlto] *pp di* **sciogliere** ♦ *ag* loose; (*agile*) agile, nimble; supple; (*disinvolto*) free and easy; **versi ~i** (*POESIA*) blank verse.

sciope'rante [ʃope'rante] *sm/f* striker.

sciope'rare [ʃope'rare] *vi* to strike, go on strike.

sci'opero ['ʃɔpero] *sm* strike; **fare ~** to strike; ~ **bianco** work-to-rule (*BRIT*), slowdown (*US*); ~ **selvaggio** wildcat strike; ~ **a singhiozzo** on-off strike.

sci'rocco [ʃi'rɔkko] *sm* sirocco.

sci'roppo [ʃi'rɔppo] *sm* syrup.

'scisma, i ['ʃizma] *sm* (*REL*) schism.

scissi'one [ʃis'sjone] *sf* (*anche fig*) split, division; (*FISICA*) fission.

'scisso, a ['ʃisso] *pp di* **scindere**.

sciu'pare [ʃu'pare] *vt* (*abito, libro, appetito*) to spoil, ruin; (*tempo, denaro*) to waste; ~**rsi** *vr* to get spoilt *o* ruined; (*rovinarsi la salute*) to ruin one's health.

scivo'lare [ʃivo'lare] *vi* to slide *o* glide along; (*involontariamente*) to slip, slide; **'scivolo** *sm* slide; (*TECN*) chute.

scle'rosi *sf* sclerosis.

scoc'care *vt* (*freccia*) to shoot ♦ *vi* (*guizzare*) to shoot up; (*battere: ora*) to strike.

scocci'are [skot'tʃare] (*fam*) *vt* to bother, annoy; ~**rsi** *vr* to be bothered *o* annoyed.

sco'della *sf* bowl.

scodinzo'lare [skodintso'lare] *vi* to wag its tail.

scogli'era [skoʎ'ʎɛra] *sf* reef; cliff.

'scoglio ['skoʎʎo] *sm* (*al mare*) rock.

scoi'attolo *sm* squirrel.

sco'lare *ag*: **età ~** school age ♦ *vt* to

drain ♦ *vi* to drip.

scola'resca *sf* schoolchildren *pl*, pupils *pl*.

sco'laro, a *sm/f* pupil, schoolboy/girl.

sco'lastico, a, ci, che *ag* school *cpd*; scholastic.

scol'lare *vt* (*staccare*) to unstick; ~**rsi** *vr* to come unstuck.

scolla'tura *sf* neckline.

'scolo *sm* drainage.

scolo'rire *vt* to fade; to discolour ♦ *vi* (*anche:* ~**rsi**) to fade; to become discoloured; (*impallidire*) to turn pale.

scol'pire *vt* to carve, sculpt.

scombi'nare *vt* to mess up, upset.

scombusso'lare *vt* to upset.

scom'messa *sf* bet, wager.

scom'messo, a *pp di* **scommettere**.

scom'mettere *vt, vi* to bet.

scomo'dare *vt* to trouble, bother; to disturb; ~**rsi** *vr* to put o.s. out; ~**rsi a fare** to go to the bother o trouble of doing.

'scomodo, a *ag* uncomfortable; (*sistemazione, posto*) awkward, inconvenient.

scompa'rire *vi* (*sparire*) to disappear, vanish; (*fig*) to be insignificant; **scom'parsa** *sf* disappearance; **scom'parso, a** *pp di* **scomparire**.

scomparti'mento *sm* (FERR) compartment.

scom'parto *sm* compartment, division.

scompigli'are [skompiʎ'ʎare] *vt* (*cassetto, capelli*) to mess up, disarrange; (*fig: piani*) to upset; **scom'piglio** *sm* mess, confusion.

scom'porre *vt* (*parola, numero*) to break up; (CHIM) to decompose; **scomporsi** *vr* (*fig*) to get upset, lose one's composure; **scom'posto, a** *pp di* **scomporre** ♦ *ag* (*gesto*) unseemly; (*capelli*) ruffled, dishevelled.

sco'munica *sf* excommunication.

scomuni'care *vt* to excommunicate.

sconcer'tare [skontʃer'tare] *vt* to disconcert, bewilder.

'sconcio, a, ci, ce ['skontʃo] *ag* (*osceno*) indecent, obscene ♦ *sm* (*cosa riprovevole, mal fatta*) disgrace.

sconfes'sare *vt* to renounce, disavow; to repudiate.

scon'figgere [skon'fiddʒere] *vt* to defeat, overcome.

sconfi'nare *vi* to cross the border; (*in proprietà privata*) to trespass; (*fig*): ~ **da** to stray o digress from; **sconfi'nato, a** *ag* boundless, unlimited.

scon'fitta *sf* defeat.

scon'fitto, a *pp di* **sconfiggere**.

scon'forto *sm* despondency.

scongiu'rare [skondʒu'rare] *vt* (*implorare*) to entreat, beseech, implore; (*eludere: pericolo*) to ward off, avert; **scongi'uro** *sm* entreaty; (*esorcismo*) exorcism; **fare gli scongiuri** to touch wood (BRIT), knock on wood (US).

scon'nesso, a *ag* (*fig: discorso*) incoherent, rambling.

sconosci'uto, a [skonoʃ'ʃuto] *ag* unknown; new, strange ♦ *sm/f* stranger; unknown person.

sconquas'sare *vt* to shatter, smash.

sconside'rato, a *ag* thoughtless, rash.

sconsigli'are [skonsiʎ'ʎare] *vt*: ~ **qc a qn** to advise sb against sth; ~ **qn dal fare qc** to advise sb not to do o against doing sth.

sconso'lato, a *ag* inconsolable; desolate.

scon'tare *vt* (COMM: *detrarre*) to deduct; (: *debito*) to pay off; (: *cambiale*) to discount; (*pena*) to serve; (*colpa, errori*) to pay for, suffer for.

scon'tato, a *ag* (*previsto*) foreseen, taken for granted; **dare per** ~ **che** to take it for granted that.

scon'tento, a *ag*: ~ (**di**) discontented o dissatisfied (with) ♦ *sm* discontent, dissatisfaction.

'sconto *sm* discount; **fare uno** ~ to give a discount.

scon'trarsi *vr* (*treni etc*) to crash, collide; (*venire ad uno scontro, fig*) to clash; ~ **con** to crash into, collide with.

scon'trino *sm* ticket.

'scontro *sm* clash, encounter; crash, collision.

scon'troso, a *ag* sullen, surly; (*permaloso*) touchy.

sconveni'ente *ag* unseemly, improper.

scon'volgere [skon'vɔldʒere] *vt* to throw into confusion, upset; (*turbare*) to shake, disturb, upset; **scon'volto, a** *pp di* **sconvolgere**.

'scopa *sf* broom; (*CARTE*) *Italian card game*; **sco'pare** *vt* to sweep.

sco'perta *sf* discovery.

sco'perto, a *pp di* **scoprire ♦** *ag* uncovered; (*capo*) uncovered, bare; (*macchina*) open; (*MIL*) exposed, without cover; (*conto*) overdrawn.

'scopo *sm* aim, purpose; **a che ~?** what for?

scoppi'are *vi* (*spaccarsi*) to burst; (*esplodere*) to explode; (*fig*) to break out; **~ in pianto** *o* **a piangere** to burst out crying; **~ dalle risa** *o* **dal ridere** to split one's sides laughing.

scoppiet'tare *vi* to crackle.

'scoppio *sm* explosion; (*di tuono, arma etc*) crash, bang; (*fig: di risa, ira*) fit, outburst; (: *di guerra*) outbreak; **a ~ ritardato** delayed-action.

sco'prire *vt* to discover; (*liberare da ciò che copre*) to uncover; (: *monumento*) to unveil; **~rsi** *vr* to put on lighter clothes; (*fig*) to give o.s. away.

scoraggi'are [skorad'dʒare] *vt* to discourage; **~rsi** *vr* to become discouraged, lose heart.

scorcia'toia [skortʃa'toja] *sf* short cut.

'scorcio ['skortʃo] *sm* (*ARTE*) foreshortening; (*di secolo, periodo*) end, close.

scor'dare *vt* to forget; **~rsi** *vr*: **~rsi di qc/di fare** to forget sth/to do.

'scorgere ['skɔrdʒere] *vt* to make out, distinguish, see.

sco'ria *sf* (*di metalli*) slag; (*vulcanica*) scoria; **~e radioattive** (*FISICA*) radioactive waste *sg*.

'scorno *sm* ignominy, disgrace.

scorpacci'ata [skorpat'tʃata] *sf*: **fare una ~ (di)** to stuff o.s. (with), eat one's fill (of).

scorpi'one *sm* scorpion; (*dello zodiaco*): **S~** Scorpio.

scorraz'zare [skorrat'tsare] *vi* to run about.

'scorrere *vt* (*giornale, lettera*) to run *o* skim through ♦ *vi* (*liquido, fiume*) to run, flow; (*fune*) to run; (*cassetto, porta*) to slide easily; (*tempo*) to pass (by).

scor'retto, a *ag* incorrect; (*sgarbato*) impolite; (*sconveniente*) improper.

scor'revole *ag* (*porta*) sliding; (*fig: stile*) fluent, flowing.

scorri'banda *sf* (*MIL*) raid; (*escursione*) trip, excursion.

'scorsa *sf* quick look, glance.

'scorso, a *pp di* **scorrere ♦** *ag* last.

scor'soio, a *ag*: **nodo ~** noose.

'scorta *sf* (*di personalità, convoglio*) escort; (*provvista*) supply, stock; **scor'tare** *vt* to escort.

scor'tese *ag* discourteous, rude; **scorte'sia** *sf* discourtesy, rudeness; (*azione*) discourtesy.

scorti'care *vt* to skin.

'scorto, a *pp di* **scorgere**.

'scorza ['skɔrdza] *sf* (*di albero*) bark; (*di agrumi*) peel, skin.

sco'sceso, a [skoʃ'feso] *ag* steep.

'scossa *sf* jerk, jolt, shake; (*ELETTR, fig*) shock.

'scosso, a *pp di* **scuotere ♦** *ag* (*turbato*) shaken, upset.

scos'tante *ag* (*fig*) off-putting (*BRIT*), unpleasant.

scos'tare *vt* to move (away), shift; **~rsi** *vr* to move away.

scostu'mato, a *ag* immoral, dissolute.

scot'tare *vt* (*ustionare*) to burn; (: *con liquido bollente*) to scald ♦ *vi* to burn; (*caffè*) to be too hot; **scotta'tura** *sf* burn; scald.

'scotto, a *ag* overcooked ♦ *sm* (*fig*): **pagare lo ~ (di)** to pay the penalty (for).

sco'vare *vt* to drive out, flush out; (*fig*) to discover.

'Scozia ['skɔttsia] *sf*: **la ~** Scotland; **scoz'zese** *ag* Scottish ♦ *sm/f* Scot.

scredi'tare *vt* to discredit.

screpo'lare *vt* to crack; **~rsi** *vr* to crack; **screpola'tura** *sf* cracking *no pl*; crack.

screzi'ato, a [skret'tsjato] *ag* streaked.

'**screzio** ['skrettsjo] *sm* disagreement.

scricchio'lare [skrikkjo'lare] *vi* to creak, squeak.

'**scricciolo** ['skrittʃolo] *sm* wren.

'**scrigno** ['skriɲɲo] *sm* casket.

scrimina'tura *sf* parting.

'**scritta** *sf* inscription.

'**scritto, a** *pp di* **scrivere ♦** *ag* written ♦ *sm* writing; (*lettera*) letter, note; ~**i** *smpl* (*letterari etc*) writing *sg*; **per** *o* **in** ~ in writing.

scrit'toio *sm* writing desk.

scrit'tore, 'trice *sm/f* writer.

scrit'tura *sf* writing; (*COMM*) entry; (*contratto*) contract; (*REL*): **la Sacra S~** the Scriptures *pl*; ~**e** *sfpl* (*COMM*) accounts, books.

scrittu'rare *vt* (*TEATRO, CINEMA*) to sign up, engage; (*COMM*) to enter.

scriva'nia *sf* desk.

scri'vente *sm/f* writer.

'**scrivere** *vt* to write; **come si scrive?** how is it spelt?, how do you write it?

scroc'cone, a *sm/f* scrounger.

'**scrofa** *sf* (*ZOOL*) sow.

scrol'lare *vt* to shake; ~**rsi** *vr* (*anche fig*) to give o.s. a shake; ~ **le spalle/il capo** to shrug one's shoulders/shake one's head.

scrosci'are [skroʃ'ʃare] *vi* (*pioggia*) to pour down, pelt down; (*torrente, fig: applausi*) to thunder, roar; '**scroscio** *sm* pelting; thunder, roar; (*di applausi*) burst.

scros'tare *vt* (*intonaco*) to scrape off, strip; ~**rsi** *vr* to peel off, flake off.

'**scrupolo** *sm* scruple; (*meticolosità*) care, conscientiousness.

scru'tare *vt* to scrutinize; (*intenzioni, causa*) to examine, scrutinize.

scruti'nare *vt* (*voti*) to count; **scru'tinio** *sm* (*votazione*) ballot; (*insieme delle operazioni*) poll; (*INS*) (*meeting for*) assignment of marks at end of a term or year.

scu'cire [sku'tʃire] *vt* (*orlo etc*) to unpick, undo.

scude'ria *sf* stable.

scu'detto *sm* (*SPORT*) (championship) shield; (*distintivo*) badge.

'**scudo** *sm* shield.

scul'tore, 'trice *sm/f* sculptor.

scul'tura *sf* sculpture.

scu'ola *sf* school; ~ **elementare/ materna/media** primary (*BRIT*) *o* grade (*US*)/nursery/secondary (*BRIT*) *o* high (*US*) school; ~ **guida** driving school; ~ **dell'obbligo** compulsory education; ~**e serali** evening classes, night school *sg*; ~ **tecnica** technical college.

scu'otere *vt* to shake; ~**rsi** *vr* to jump, be startled; (*fig: muoversi*) to rouse o.s., stir o.s.; (: *turbarsi*) to be shaken.

'**scure** *sf* axe.

'**scuro, a** *ag* dark; (*fig: espressione*) grim ♦ *sm* darkness; dark colour; (*imposta*) (window) shutter; **verde/ rosso** *etc* ~ dark green/red *etc*.

scur'rile *ag* scurrilous.

'**scusa** *sf* apology; (*pretesto*) excuse; **chiedere** ~ **a qn** (**per**) to apologize to sb (for); **chiedo** ~ I'm sorry; (*disturbando etc*) excuse me.

scu'sare *vt* to excuse; ~**rsi** *vr*: ~**rsi** (**di**) to apologize (for); (**mi**) **scusi** I'm sorry; (*per richiamare l'attenzione*) excuse me.

sde'gnato, a [zdeɲ'ɲato] *ag* indignant, angry.

'**sdegno** ['zdeɲɲo] *sm* scorn, disdain; **sde'gnoso, a** *ag* scornful, disdainful.

sdoga'nare *vt* (*merci*) to clear through customs.

sdolci'nato, a [zdoltʃi'nato] *ag* mawkish, oversentimental.

sdoppi'are *vt* (*dividere*) to divide *o* split in two.

sdrai'arsi *vr* to stretch out, lie down.

'**sdraio** *sm*: **sedia a** ~ deck chair.

sdruccio'levole [zdruttʃo'levole] *ag* slippery.

PAROLA CHIAVE

se *pron vedi* **si**

♦ *cong* **1** (*condizionale, ipotetica*) if; ~ **nevica non vengo** I won't come if it snows; **sarei rimasto** ~ **me l'avessero chiesto** I would have stayed if they'd asked me; **non puoi fare altro** ~ **non telefonare** all you can do is phone; ~

mai if, if ever; **siamo noi ~ mai che le siamo grati** it is we who should be grateful to you; **~ no** *(altrimenti)* or (else), otherwise

2 *(in frasi dubitative, interrogative indirette)* if, whether; **non so ~ scrivere o telefonare** I don't know whether *o* if I should write or phone.

sé *pron (gen)* oneself; *(esso, essa, lui, lei, loro)* itself; himself; herself; themselves; **~ stesso(a)** *pron* oneself; itself; himself; herself; **~ stessi(e)** *pron pl* themselves.

seb'bene *cong* although, though.

sec. *abbr* (= *secolo*) c.

'secca *sf (del mare)* shallows *pl*; *vedi anche* **secco**.

sec'care *vt* to dry; *(prosciugare)* to dry up; *(fig: importunare)* to annoy, bother ♦ *vi* to dry; to dry up; **~rsi** *vr* to dry; to dry up; *(fig)* to grow annoyed; **secca'tura** *sf (fig)* bother *no pl*, trouble *no pl*.

'secchia ['sekkja] *sf* bucket, pail.

'secco, a, chi, che *ag* dry; *(fichi, pesce)* dried; *(foglie, ramo)* withered; *(magro: persona)* thin, skinny; *(fig: risposta, modo di fare)* curt, abrupt; (: *colpo)* clean, sharp ♦ *sm (siccità)* drought; *(fig: morire sul colpo)* to drop dead; **mettere in ~** *(barca)* to beach; **rimanere in** *o* **a ~** *(NAUT)* to run aground; *(fig)* to be left in the lurch.

seco'lare *ag* age-old, centuries-old; *(laico, mondano)* secular.

'secolo *sm* century; *(epoca)* age.

se'conda *sf (AUT)* second *(gear)*; **viaggiare in ~** to travel second-class; *vedi anche* **secondo**.

secon'dario, a *ag* secondary.

se'condo, a *ag* second ♦ *sm* second; *(di pranzo)* main course ♦ *prep* according to; *(nel modo prescritto)* in accordance with; **~ me** in my opinion, to my mind; **di ~a classe** second-class; **di ~a mano** second-hand; **a ~a di** according to; in accordance with.

'sedano *sm* celery.

seda'tivo, a *ag, sm* sedative.

'sede *sf* seat; *(di ditta)* head office; *(di organizzazione)* headquarters *pl*; **in ~ di** *(in occasione di)* during; **~ sociale** registered office.

seden'tario, a *ag* sedentary.

se'dere *vi* to sit, be seated; **~rsi** *vr* to sit down ♦ *sm (deretano)* behind, bottom.

'sedia *sf* chair.

sedi'cente [sedi't ʃɛnte] *ag* self-styled.

'sedici ['seditʃi] *num* sixteen.

se'dile *sm* seat; *(panchina)* bench.

sedizi'one [sedit'tsjone] *sf* revolt, rebellion.

se'dotto, a *pp di* **sedurre**.

sedu'cente [sedu'tʃɛnte] *ag* seductive; *(proposta)* very attractive.

se'durre *vt* to seduce.

se'duta *sf* session, sitting; *(riunione)* meeting; **~ spiritica** séance; **~ stante** *(fig)* immediately.

seduzi'one [sedut'tsjone] *sf* seduction; *(fascino)* charm, appeal.

'sega, ghe *sf* saw.

'segale *sf* rye.

se'gare *vt* to saw; *(recidere)* to saw off; **sega'tura** *sf (residuo)* sawdust.

'seggio ['sɛddʒo] *sm* seat; **~ elettorale** polling station.

seggi'ola ['sɛddʒola] *sf* chair; **seggio'lino** *sm* seat; *(per bambini)* child's chair; **seggio'lone** *sm (per bambini)* highchair.

seggio'via [sɛddʒo'via] *sf* chairlift.

seghe'ria [sege'ria] *sf* sawmill.

se'gnalare [seɲɲa'lare] *vt (manovra etc)* to signal; to indicate; *(annunciare)* to announce; to report; *(fig: far conoscere)* to point out; (: *persona)* to single out; **~rsi** *vr (distinguersi)* to distinguish o.s.

se'gnale [seɲ'ɲale] *sm* signal; *(cartello)* **~ stradale** road sign; **~ d'allarme** alarm; *(FERR)* communication cord; **~ orario** *(RADIO)* time signal; **segna'letica** *sf* signalling, signposting; **segnaletica stradale** road signs *pl*.

se'gnare [seɲ'ɲare] *vt* to mark; *(pren-*

dere nota) to note; (*indicare*) to indicate, mark; (*SPORT: goal*) to score; **~rsi** *vr* (*REL*) to make the sign of the cross, cross o.s.

'segno ['seɲɲo] *sm* sign; (*impronta, contrassegno*) mark; (*limite*) limit, bounds *pl*; (*bersaglio*) target; **fare ~ di sì/no** to nod (one's head)/shake one's head; **fare ~ a qn di fermarsi** to motion (to) sb to stop; **cogliere** *o* **colpire nel ~** (*fig*) to hit the mark.

segre'gare *vt* to segregate, isolate; **segregazi'one** *sf* segregation.

segre'tario, a *sm/f* secretary; **~ comunale** town clerk; **S~ di Stato** Secretary of State.

segrete'ria *sf* (*di ditta, scuola*) (secretary's) office; (*d'organizzazione internazionale*) secretariat; (*POL etc: carica*) office of Secretary; **~ telefonica** answering service.

segre'tezza [segre'tettsa] *sf* secrecy.

se'greto, a *ag* secret ♦ *sm* secret; **secrecy** *no pl*; **in ~**, in secret, secretly.

segu'ace [se'gwatʃe] *sm/f* follower, disciple.

segu'ente *ag* following, next.

segu'ire *vt* to follow; (*frequentare: corso*) to attend ♦ *vi* to follow; (*continuare: testo*) to continue.

segui'tare *vt* to continue, carry on with ♦ *vi* to continue, carry on.

'seguito *sm* (*scorta*) suite, retinue; (*discepoli*) followers *pl*; (*favore*) following; (*serie*) sequence, series *sg*; (*continuazione*) continuation; (*conseguenza*) result; **di ~** at a stretch, on end; **in ~** later on; **in ~ a, a ~ di** following; (*a causa di*) as a result of, owing to.

'sei *vb vedi* **essere** ♦ *num* six.

sei'cento [sei'tʃento] *num* six hundred ♦ *sm*: **il S~** the seventeenth century.

selci'ato [sel'tʃato] *sm* cobbled surface.

selezio'nare [selettsjo'nare] *vt* to select.

selezi'one [selet'tsjone] *sf* selection.

'sella *sf* saddle; **sel'lare** *vt* to saddle.

selvag'gina [selvad'dʒina] *sf* (*animali*) game.

sel'vaggio, a, gi, ge [sel'vaddʒo] *ag* wild; (*tribù*) savage, uncivilized; (*fig*)

savage, brutal ♦ *sm/f* savage.

sel'vatico, a, ci, che *ag* wild.

se'maforo *sm* (*AUT*) traffic lights *pl*.

sem'brare *vi* to seem ♦ *vb impers*: **sembra che** it seems that; **mi sembra che** it seems to me that; I think (that); **~ di essere** to seem to be.

'seme *sm* seed; (*sperma*) semen; (*CARTE*) suit.

se'mestre *sm* half-year, six-month period.

'semi... *prefisso* semi...; **semi'cerchio** *sm* semicircle; **semifi'nale** *sf* semifinal; **semi'freddo, a** *ag* (*CUC*) chilled ♦ *sm* ice-cream cake.

'semina *sf* (*AGR*) sowing.

semi'nare *vt* to sow.

semi'nario *sm* seminar; (*REL*) seminary.

seminter'rato *sm* basement; (*appartamento*) basement flat.

se'mitico, a, ci, che *ag* semitic.

sem'mai = **se mai**; *vedi* **se**.

'semola *sf* bran; **~ di grano duro** durum wheat.

semo'lino *sm* semolina.

'semplice ['semplitʃe] *ag* simple; (*di un solo elemento*) single; **semplice'mente** *av* simply; **semplicità** *sf* simplicity.

'sempre *av* always; (*ancora*) still; **posso ~ tentare** I can always *o* still try; **da ~** always; **per ~** forever; **una volta per ~** once and for all; **~ che** provided (that); **~ più** more and more; **~ meno** less and less.

sempre'verde *ag*, *sm o f* (*BOT*) evergreen.

'senape *sf* (*CUC*) mustard.

se'nato *sm* senate; **sena'tore, 'trice** *sm/f* senator.

sennò *av* = **se no**; *vedi* **se**.

'senno *sm* judgment, (common) sense; **col ~ di poi** with hindsight.

'seno *sm* (*ANAT: petto, mammella*) breast; (: *grembo, fig*) womb; (: *cavità*) sinus; (*GEO*) inlet, creek; (*MAT*) sine.

sen'sato, a *ag* sensible.

sensazio'nale [sensattsjo'nale] *ag* sensational.

sensazi'one [sensat'tsjone] *sf* feeling, sensation; **avere la ~ che** to have a feeling that; **fare ~** to cause a sensation, create a stir.

sen'sibile *ag* sensitive; *(ai sensi)* perceptible; *(rilevante, notevole)* appreciable, noticeable; **~ a** sensitive to; **sensibilità** *sf* sensitivity.

'senso *sm* (FISIOL, *istinto)* sense; *(impressione, sensazione)* feeling, sensation; *(significato)* meaning, sense; *(direzione)* direction; **~i** *smpl (coscienza)* consciousness *sg*; *(sensualità)* senses; **ciò non ha ~** that doesn't make sense; **fare ~ a** *(ripugnare)* to disgust, repel; **~ comune** common sense; **in ~ orario/antiorario** clockwise/anticlockwise; **a ~ unico** *(strada)* one-way; **"~ vietato"** *(AUT)* "no entry".

sensu'ale *ag* sensual; sensuous; **sensualità** *sf* sensuality; sensuousness.

sen'tenza [sen'tentsa] *sf* (DIR) sentence; *(massima)* maxim; **sentenzi'are** *vi* (DIR) to pass judgment.

senti'ero *sm* path.

sentimen'tale *ag* sentimental; *(vita, avventura)* love *cpd*.

senti'mento *sm* feeling.

senti'nella *sf* sentry.

sen'tire *vt (percepire al tatto, fig)* to feel; *(udire)* to hear; *(ascoltare)* to listen to; *(odore)* to smell; *(avvertire con il gusto, assaggiare)* to taste ♦ *vi*: **~ di** *(avere sapore)* to taste of; *(avere odore)* to smell of; **~rsi** *vr (uso reciproco)* to be in touch; **~rsi bene/male** to feel well/unwell *o* ill; **~rsi di fare qc** *(essere disposto)* to feel like doing sth.

sen'tito, a *ag (sincero)* sincere, warm; **per ~ dire** by hearsay.

'senza ['sɛntsa] *prep, cong* without; **~ dir nulla** without saying a word; **fare ~ qc** to do without sth; **~ di me** without me; **~ che io lo sapessi** without me *o* my knowing; **senz'altro** of course, certainly; **~ dubbio** no doubt; **~ scrupoli** unscrupulous; **~ amici** friendless.

sepa'rare *vt* to separate; *(dividere)* to

divide; *(tenere distinto)* to distinguish; **~rsi** *vr (coniugi)* to separate, part; *(amici)* to part, leave each other; **~rsi da** *(coniuge)* to separate *o* part from; *(amico, socio)* to part company with; *(oggetto)* to part with; **sepa'rato, a** *ag (letti, conto etc)* separate; *(coniugi)* separated; **separazi'one** *sf* separation.

se'polcro *sm* sepulchre.

se'polto, a *pp di* **seppellire**.

seppel'lire *vt* to bury.

'seppia *sf* cuttlefish ♦ *ag inv* sepia.

se'quenza [se'kwɛntsa] *sf* sequence.

seques'trare *vt* (DIR) to impound; *(rapire)* to kidnap; *(costringere in un luogo)* to keep, confine; **se'questro** *sm* (DIR) impoundment; **sequestro di persona** kidnapping.

'sera *sf* evening; **di ~** in the evening; **domani ~** tomorrow evening, tomorrow night; **se'rale** *ag* evening *cpd*; **se'rata** *sf* evening; *(ricevimento)* party.

ser'bare *vt* to keep; *(mettere da parte)* to put aside; **~ rancore/odio verso qn** to bear sb a grudge/hate sb.

serba'toio *sm* tank; *(cisterna)* cistern.

'serbo *sm*: **mettere/tenere** *o* **avere in ~ qc** to put/keep sth aside.

se'reno, a *ag (tempo, cielo)* clear; *(fig)* serene, calm.

ser'gente [ser'dʒɛnte] *sm* (MIL) sergeant.

'serie *sf inv (successione)* series *inv*; *(gruppo, collezione: di chiavi etc)* set; *(SPORT)* division; league; *(COMM)*: **modello da ~/fuori ~** standard/custom-built model; **in ~** in quick succession; *(COMM)* mass *cpd*.

serietà *sf* seriousness; reliability.

'serio, a *ag* serious; *(impiegato)* responsible, reliable; *(ditta, cliente)* reliable, dependable; **sul ~** *(davvero)* really, truly; *(seriamente)* seriously, in earnest.

ser'mone *sm* sermon.

serpeggi'are [serped'dʒare] *vi* to wind; *(fig)* to spread.

ser'pente *sm* snake; **~ a sonagli** rattlesnake.

'serra *sf* greenhouse; hothouse.

ser'randa *sf* roller shutter.

ser'rare *vt* to close, shut; (*a chiave*) to lock; (*stringere*) to tighten; (*premere: nemico*) to close in on; ~ **i pugni/i denti** to clench one's fists/teeth; ~ **le file** to close ranks.

serra'tura *sf* lock.

'serva *sf vedi* **servo**.

ser'vire *vt* to serve; (*clienti: al ristorante*) to wait on; (*: al negozio*) to serve, attend to; (*fig: giovare*) to aid, help; (*CARTE*) to deal ♦ *vi* (*TENNIS*) to serve; (*essere utile*): ~ **a qn** to be of use to sb; ~ **a qc/a fare** (*utensile etc*) to be used for sth/for doing; ~ (**a qn**) **da** to serve as (for sb); **~rsi** *vr* (*usare*): **~rsi di** to use; (*prendere: cibo*): **~rsi (di)** to help o.s. (to); (*essere cliente abituale*): **~rsi da** to be a regular customer at, go to.

servitù *sf* servitude; slavery; (*personale di servizio*) servants *pl*, domestic staff.

servizi'evole [servit'tsjevole] *ag* obliging, willing to help.

ser'vizio [ser'vittsjo] *sm* service; (*al ristorante: sul conto*) service (charge); (*STAMPA, TV, RADIO*) report; (*da tè, caffè etc*) set, service; **~i** *smpl* (*di casa*) kitchen and bathroom; (*ECON*) services; **essere di** ~ to be on duty; **fuori** ~ (*telefono etc*) out of order; ~ **compreso** service included; ~ **militare** military service; **~i segreti** secret service *sg*.

'servo, a *sm/f* servant.

ses'santa *num* sixty; **sessan'tesimo, a** *num* sixtieth.

sessan'tina *sf*: **una** ~ (**di**) about sixty.

sessi'one *sf* session.

'sesso *sm* sex; **sessu'ale** *ag* sexual, sex *cpd*.

ses'tante *sm* sextant.

'sesto, a *ag, sm* sixth.

'seta *sf* silk.

'sete *sf* thirst; **avere** ~ to be thirsty.

'setola *sf* bristle.

'setta *sf* sect.

set'tanta *num* seventy; **settan'tesimo, a** *num* seventieth.

settan'tina *sf*: **una** ~ (**di**) about seventy.

'sette *num* seven.

sette'cento [sette'tʃento] *num* seven hundred ♦ *sm*: **il S~** the eighteenth century.

set'tembre *sm* September.

settentrio'nale *ag* northern.

settentri'one *sm* north.

'settico, a, ci, che *ag* (*MED*) septic.

setti'mana *sf* week; **settima'nale** *ag, sm* weekly.

'settimo, a *ag, sm* seventh.

set'tore *sm* sector.

severità *sf* severity.

se'vero, a *ag* severe.

sevizi'are [sevit'tsjare] *vt* to torture.

se'vizie [se'vittsje] *sfpl* torture *sg*.

sezio'nare [settsjo'nare] *vt* to divide into sections; (*MED*) to dissect.

sezi'one [set'tsjone] *sf* section; (*MED*) dissection.

sfaccen'dato, a [sfattʃen'dato] *ag* idle.

sfacci'ato, a [sfat'tʃato] *ag* (*maleducato*) cheeky, impudent; (*vistoso*) gaudy.

sfa'celo [sfa'tʃɛlo] *sm* (*fig*) ruin, collapse.

sfal'darsi *vr* to flake (off).

'sfarzo ['sfartso] *sm* pomp, splendour.

sfasci'are [sfaʃ'ʃare] *vt* (*ferita*) to unbandage; (*distruggere: porta*) to smash, shatter; **~rsi** *vr* (*rompersi*) to smash, shatter.

sfa'tare *vt* (*leggenda*) to explode.

sfavil'lare *vi* to spark, send out sparks; (*risplendere*) to sparkle.

sfavo'revole *ag* unfavourable.

'sfera *sf* sphere; **'sferico, a, ci, che** *ag* spherical.

sfer'rare *vt* (*fig: colpo*) to land, deal; (*: attacco*) to launch.

sfer'zare [sfer'tsare] *vt* to whip; (*fig*) to lash out at.

sfi'brare *vt* (*indebolire*) to exhaust, enervate.

'sfida *sf* challenge; **sfi'dare** *vt* to challenge; (*fig*) to defy, brave.

sfi'ducia [sfi'dutʃa] *sf* distrust, mistrust.

sfigu'rare *vt* (*persona*) to disfigure;

(*quadro, statua*) to deface ♦ *vi* (*far cattiva figura*) to make a bad impression.

sfi'lare *vt* (*ago*) to unthread; (*abito, scarpe*) to slip off ♦ *vi* (*truppe*) to march past; (*atleti*) to parade; ~**rsi** *vr* (*perle etc*) to come unstrung; (*orlo, tessuto*) to fray; (*calza*) to run, ladder; **sfi'lata** *sf* march past; parade; **sfilata di moda** fashion show.

'sfinge ['sfindʒe] *sf* sphinx.

sfi'nito, a *ag* exhausted.

sfio'rare *vt* to brush (against); (*argomento*) to touch upon.

sfio'rire *vi* to wither, fade.

sfo'cato, a *ag* (*FOT*) out of focus.

sfoci'are [sfo'tʃare] *vi*: ~ **in** to flow into; (*fig: malcontento*) to develop into.

sfo'gare *vt* to vent, pour out; ~**rsi** *vr* (*sfogare la propria rabbia*) to give vent to one's anger; (*confidarsi*): ~**rsi** (**con**) to pour out one's feelings (to); **non sfogarti su di me!** don't take your bad temper out on me!

sfoggi'are [sfod'dʒare] *vt, vi* to show off.

'sfoglia ['sfoʎʎa] *sf* sheet of pasta dough; **pasta** ~ (*CUC*) puff pastry.

sfogli'are [sfoʎ'ʎare] *vt* (*libro*) to leaf through.

'sfogo, ghi *sm* outlet; (*eruzione cutanea*) rash; (*fig*) outburst; **dare** ~ **a** (*fig*) to give vent to.

sfolgo'rante *ag* (*luce*) blazing; (*fig: vittoria*) brilliant.

sfol'lare *vt* to empty, clear ♦ *vi* to disperse; ~ **da** (*città*) to evacuate.

sfon'dare *vt* (*porta*) to break down; (*scarpe*) to wear a hole in; (*cesto, scatola*) to burst, knock the bottom out of; (*MIL*) to break through ♦ *vi* (*riuscire*) to make a name for o.s.

'sfondo *sm* background.

sfor'mato *sm* (*CUC*) type of soufflé.

sfor'nito, a *ag*: ~ **di** lacking in, without; (*negozio*) out of.

sfor'tuna *sf* misfortune, ill luck *no pl*; **avere** ~ to be unlucky; **sfortu'nato, a** *ag* unlucky; (*impresa, film*) unsuccessful.

sfor'zare [sfor'tsare] *vt* to force; (*voce,*

occhi) to strain; ~**rsi** *vr*: ~**rsi di** *o* **a** *o* **per fare** to try hard to do.

'sforzo ['sfɔrtso] *sm* effort; (*tensione eccessiva, TECN*) strain; **fare uno** ~ to make an effort.

sfrat'tare *vt* to evict; **'sfratto** *sm* eviction.

sfrecci'are [sfret'tʃare] *vi* to shoot *o* flash past.

sfregi'are [sfre'dʒare] *vt* to slash, gash; (*persona*) to disfigure; (*quadro*) to deface; **'sfregio** *sm* gash; scar; (*fig*) insult.

sfre'nato, a *ag* (*fig*) unrestrained, unbridled.

sfron'tato, a *ag* shameless.

sfrutta'mento *sm* exploitation.

sfrut'tare *vt* (*terreno*) to overwork, exhaust; (*miniera*) to exploit, work; (*fig: operai, occasione, potere*) to exploit.

sfug'gire [sfud'dʒire] *vi* to escape; ~ **a** (*custode*) to escape (from); (*morte*) to escape; ~ **a qn** (*dettaglio, nome*) to escape sb; ~ **di mano a qn** to slip out of sb's hand (*o* hands); **sfug'gita: di sfuggita** *ad* (*rapidamente, in fretta*) in passing.

sfu'mare *vt* (*colori, contorni*) to soften, shade off ♦ *vi* to shade (off), fade; (*fig: svanire*) to vanish, disappear; (: *speranze*) to come to nothing; **sfuma'tura** *sf* shading off *no pl*; (*tonalità*) shade, tone; (*fig*) touch, hint.

sfuri'ata *sf* (*scatto di collera*) fit of anger; (*rimprovero*) sharp rebuke.

sga'bello *sm* stool.

sgabuz'zino [sgabud'dzino] *sm* lumber room.

sgambet'tare *vi* to kick one's legs about.

sgam'betto *sm*: **far lo** ~ **a qn** to trip sb up; (*fig*) to oust sb.

sganasci'arsi [zganaʃ'ʃarsi] *vr*: ~ **dalle risa** to roar with laughter.

sganci'are [zgan'tʃare] *vt* to unhook; (*FERR*) to uncouple; (*bombe: da aereo*) to release, drop; (*fig: fam: soldi*) to fork out; ~**rsi** *vr* (*fig*): ~**rsi** (**da**) to get away (from).

sganghe'rato, a [zgange'rato] *ag* (*porta*) off its hinges; (*auto*) ramshackle; (*risata*) wild, boisterous.

sgar'bato, a *ag* rude, impolite.

'sgarbo *sm*: **fare uno ~ a qn** to be rude to sb.

sgattaio'lare *vi* to sneak away *o* off.

sge'lare [zdʒe'lare] *vi, vt* to thaw.

'sghembo, a ['zgembo] *ag* (*obliquo*) slanting; (*storto*) crooked.

sghignaz'zare [zgiɲɲat'tsare] *vi* to laugh scornfully.

sgob'bare (*fam*) *vi* (*scolaro*) to swot; (*operaio*) to slog.

sgoccio'lare [zgottʃo'lare] *vt* (*vuotare*) to drain (to the last drop) ♦ *vi* (*acqua*) to drip; (*recipiente*) to drain.

sgo'larsi *vr* to talk (*o* shout *o* sing) o.s. hoarse.

sgomb(e)'rare *vt* to clear; (*andarsene da: stanza*) to vacate; (*evacuare*) to evacuate.

'sgombro, a *ag*: **~ (di)** clear (of), free (from) ♦ *sm* (ZOOL) mackerel; (*anche: sgombero*) clearing; vacating; evacuation; (*: trasloco*) removal.

sgomen'tare *vt* to dismay; **~rsi** *vr* to be dismayed; **sgo'mento, a** *ag* dismayed ♦ *sm* dismay, consternation.

sgonfi'are *vt* to let down, deflate; **~rsi** *vr* to go down.

'sgorbio *sm* blot; scribble.

sgor'gare *vi* to gush (out).

sgoz'zare [zgot'tsare] *vt* to cut the throat of.

sgra'devole *ag* unpleasant, disagreeable.

sgra'dito, a *ag* unpleasant, unwelcome.

sgra'nare *vt* (*piselli*) to shell; **~ gli occhi** to open one's eyes wide.

sgran'chirsi [zgran'kirsi] *vr* to stretch; **~ le gambe** to stretch one's legs.

sgranocchi'are [zgranok'kjare] *vt* to munch.

'sgravio *sm*: **~ fiscale** tax relief.

sgrazi'ato, a [zgrat'tsjato] *ag* clumsy, ungainly.

sgreto'lare *vt* to cause to crumble; **~rsi** *vr* to crumble.

sgri'dare *vt* to scold; **sgri'data** *sf* scolding.

sguai'ato, a *ag* coarse, vulgar.

sgual'cire [zgwal'tʃire] *vt* to crumple (up), crease.

sgual'drina (*peg*) *sf* slut.

sgu'ardo *sm* (*occhiata*) look, glance; (*espressione*) look (in one's eye).

sguaz'zare [zgwat'tsare] *vi* (*nell'acqua*) to splash about; (*nella melma*) to wallow; **~ nell'oro** to be rolling in money.

sguinzagli'are [zgwintsaʎ'ʎare] *vt* to let off the leash; (*fig: persona*): **~ qn dietro a qn** to set sb on sb.

sgusci'are [zguʃ'ʃare] *vt* to shell ♦ *vi* (*sfuggire di mano*) to slip; **~ via** to slip *o* slink away.

'shampoo ['ʃampo] *sm inv* shampoo.

shock [ʃɔk] *sm inv* shock.

PAROLA CHIAVE

si¹ (*dav lo, la, li, le, ne diventa* **se**) *pron*
1 (*riflessivo: maschile*) himself; (: *femminile*) herself; (: *neutro*) itself; (: *impersonale*) oneself; (: *pl*) themselves; **lavarsi** to wash (oneself); **~ è tagliato** he has cut himself; **~ credono importanti** they think a lot of themselves

2 (*riflessivo: con complemento oggetto*): **lavarsi le mani** to wash one's hands; **~ sta lavando i capelli** he (*o* she) is washing his (*o* her) hair

3 (*reciproco*) one another, each other; **si amano** they love one another *o* each other

4 (*passivo*): **~ ripara facilmente** it is easily repaired

5 (*impersonale*): **~ dice che ...** they *o* people say that ...; **~ vede che è vecchio** one *o* you can see that it's old

6 (*noi*) we; **tra poco ~ parte** we're leaving soon.

si² *sm* (MUS) B; (*solfeggiando la scala*) ti.

sì *av* yes; **un giorno ~ e uno no** every other day.

'sia *cong*: **~ ... ~** (*o ... o*): **~ che lavori,**

~ che **non lavori** whether he works or not; (*tanto ... quanto*): **verranno ~ Luigi ~ suo fratello** both Luigi and his brother will be coming.

si'**amo** *vb vedi* **essere**.

sibi'**lare** *vi* to hiss; (*fischiare*) to whistle; '**sibilo** *sm* hiss; whistle.

si'**cario** *sm* hired killer.

sicché [sik'ke] *cong* (*perciò*) so (that), therefore; (*e quindi*) (and) so.

siccità [sittʃi'ta] *sf* drought.

sic'**come** *cong* since, as.

Si'**cilia** [si'tʃilja] *sf*: **la ~** Sicily; **sicili'ano, a** *ag*, *sm/f* Sicilian.

sicu'**rezza** [siku'rettsa] *sf* safety; security; (*fiducia*) confidence; (*certezza*) certainty; **di ~** safety *cpd*; **la ~ stradale** road safety.

si'**curo, a** *ag* safe; (*ben difeso*) secure; (*fiducioso*) confident; (*certo*) sure, certain; (*notizia, amico*) reliable; (*esperto*) skilled ♦ *av* (*anche*: **di ~**) certainly; **essere/mettere al ~** to be safe/put in a safe place; **~ di sé** self-confident, sure of o.s.; **sentirsi ~** to feel safe *o* secure.

siderur'**gia** [siderur'dʒia] *sf* iron and steel industry.

'**sidro** *sm* cider.

si'**epe** *sf* hedge.

si'**ero** *sm* (*MED*) serum.

si'**esta** *sf* siesta, (afternoon) nap.

si'**ete** *vb vedi* **essere**.

si'**filide** *sf* syphilis.

si'**fone** *sm* siphon.

Sig. *abbr* (= *signore*) Mr.

siga'**retta** *sf* cigarette.

'**sigaro** *sm* cigar.

Sigg. *abbr* (= *signori*) Messrs.

sigil'**lare** [sidʒil'lare] *vt* to seal.

si'**gillo** [si'dʒillo] *sm* seal.

'**sigla** *sf* initials *pl*; acronym, abbreviation; **~ automobilistica** *abbreviation of province on vehicle number plate*; **~ musicale** signature tune.

si'**glare** *vt* to initial.

Sig.na *abbr* (= *signorina*) Miss.

signifi'**care** [siɲɲifi'kare] *vt* to mean; **significa'tivo, a** *ag* significant; **signi-ficato** *sm* meaning.

si'**gnora** [siɲ'ɲora] *sf* lady; **la ~ X** Mrs X; **buon giorno S~/Signore/Signorina** good morning; (*deferente*) good morning Madam/Sir/Madam; (*quando si conosce il nome*) good morning Mrs/Mr/Miss X; **Gentile S~/Signore/Signorina** (*in una lettera*) Dear Madam/Sir/Madam; **il signor Rossi e ~** Mr Rossi and his wife; **~e e signori** ladies and gentlemen.

si'**gnore** [siɲ'ɲore] *sm* gentleman; (*padrone*) lord, master; (*REL*): **il S~** the Lord; **il signor X Mr X; i ~i Bianchi** (*coniugi*) Mr and Mrs Bianchi; *vedi anche* **signora**.

signo'**rile** [siɲɲo'rile] *ag* refined.

signo'**rina** [siɲɲo'rina] *sf* young lady; **la ~ X** Miss X; *vedi anche* **signora**.

Sig.ra *abbr* (= *signora*) Mrs.

silenzia'**tore** [silentsja'tore] *sm* silencer.

si'**lenzio** [si'lentsjo] *sm* silence; **fare ~** to be quiet, stop talking; **silenzi'oso, a** *ag* silent, quiet.

si'**licio** [si'litʃo] *sm* silicon; **piastrina di ~** silicon chip.

'**sillaba** *sf* syllable.

silu'**rare** *vt* to torpedo; (*fig: privare del comando*) to oust.

si'**luro** *sm* torpedo.

simboleggi'**are** [simboled'dʒare] *vt* to symbolize.

'**simbolo** *sm* symbol.

'**simile** *ag* (*analogo*) similar; (*di questo tipo*): **un uomo ~** such a man, a man like this; **libri ~i** such books; **~ a** a similar to; **i suoi ~i** one's fellow men; one's peers.

simme'**tria** *sf* symmetry.

simpa'**tia** *sf* (*qualità*) pleasantness; (*inclinazione*) liking; **avere ~ per qn** to like sb, have a liking for sb; **sim'patico, a, ci, che** *ag* (*persona*) nice, pleasant, likeable; (*casa, albergo etc*) nice, pleasant.

simpatiz'**zare** [simpatid'dzare] *vi*: **~ con** to take a liking to.

sim'**posio** *sm* symposium.

simu'**lare** *vt* to sham, simulate; (*TECN*) to simulate; **simulazi'one** *sf* shamming; simulation.

simul'taneo, a *ag* simultaneous.

sina'goga, ghe *sf* synagogue.

sincerità [sintʃeri'ta] *sf* sincerity.

sin'cero, a [sin'tʃero] *ag* sincere; genuine; heartfelt.

'sincope *sf* syncopation; (*MED*) black-out.

sinda'cale *ag* (trade-)union *cpd*; **sindaca'lista, i, e** *sm/f* trade unionist.

sinda'cato *sm* (*di lavoratori*) (trade) union; (*AMM*, *ECON*, *DIR*) syndicate, trust, pool; **~ dei datori di lavoro** employers' association, employers' federation.

'sindaco, ci *sm* mayor.

sinfo'nia *sf* (*MUS*) symphony.

singhioz'zare [singjot'tsare] *vi* to sob; to hiccup.

singhi'ozzo [sin'gjottso] *sm* sob; (*MED*) hiccup; **avere il ~** to have the hiccups; **a ~** (*fig*) by fits and starts.

singo'lare *ag* (*insolito*) remarkable, singular; (*LING*) singular ♦ *sm* (*LING*) singular; (*TENNIS*): **~ maschile/femminile** men's/women's singles.

'singolo, a *ag* single, individual ♦ *sm* (*persona*) individual; (*TENNIS*) = singolare.

si'nistra *sf* (*POL*) left (wing); **a ~ on** the left; (*direzione*) to the left.

si'nistro, a *ag* left, left-hand; (*fig*) sinister ♦ *sm* (*incidente*) accident.

'sino *prep* = **fino**.

si'nonimo, a *ag* synonymous ♦ *sm* synonym; **~ di** synonymous with.

sin'tassi *sf* syntax.

'sintesi *sf* synthesis; (*riassunto*) summary, résumé.

sin'tetico, a, ci, che *ag* synthetic.

sintetiz'zare [sintetid'dzare] *vt* to synthesize; (*riassumere*) to summarize.

sinto'matico, a, ci, che *ag* sympto-matic.

'sintomo *sm* symptom.

sinu'oso, a *ag* (*strada*) winding.

S.I.P. *sigla f* (= *Società italiana per l'esercizio telefonico*) *Italian telephone company*.

si'pario *sm* (*TEATRO*) curtain.

si'rena *sf* (*apparecchio*) siren; (*nella*

mitologia, *fig*) siren, mermaid.

'Siria *sf*: **la ~** Syria.

si'ringa, ghe *sf* syringe.

'sismico, a, ci, che *ag* seismic.

sis'mografo *sm* seismograph.

sis'tema, i *sm* system; method, way; **~ di vita** way of life.

siste'mare *vt* (*mettere a posto*) to tidy, put in order; (*risolvere*: *questione*) to sort out, settle; (*procurare un lavoro a*) to find a job for; (*dare un alloggio a*) to settle, find accommodation for; **~rsi** *vr* (*problema*) to be settled; (*persona*: *trovare alloggio*) to find accommodation (*BRIT*) *o* accommodations (*US*); (: *trovarsi un lavoro*) to get fixed up with a job; **ti sistemo io!** I'll soon sort you out!

siste'matico, a, ci, che *ag* systematic.

sistemazi'one [sistemat'tsjone] *sf* arrangement, order; settlement; employment; accommodation (*BRIT*), accommodations (*US*).

'sito *sm* (*letterario*) place.

situ'are *vt* to site, situate; **situ'ato, a** *ag*: **situato a/su** situated at/on.

situazi'one [situat'tsjone] *sf* situation.

slacci'are [zlat'tʃare] *vt* to undo, un-fasten.

slanci'arsi [zlan'tʃarsi] *vr* to dash, fling o.s.; **slanci'ato, a** *ag* slender; **'slancio** *sm* dash, leap; (*fig*) surge; **di slancio** impetuously.

sla'vato, a *ag* faded, washed out; (*fig*: *viso*, *occhi*) pale, colourless.

'slavo, a *ag* Slav(onic), Slavic.

sle'ale *ag* disloyal; (*concorrenza etc*) unfair.

sle'gare *vt* to untie.

'slitta *sf* sledge; (*trainata*) sleigh.

slit'tare *vi* to slip, slide; (*AUT*) to skid.

slo'gare *vt* (*MED*) to dislocate.

sloggi'are [zlod'dʒare] *vt* (*inquilino*) to turn out; (*nemico*) to drive out, dis-lodge ♦ *vi* to move out.

smacchi'are [zmak'kjare] *vt* to remove stains from.

'smacco, chi *sm* humiliating defeat.

smagli'ante [zmaʎ'ʎante] *ag* brilliant,

dazzling.

smaglia'tura [zmaʎʎa'tura] *sf* (*su maglia, calza*) ladder; (*della pelle*) stretch mark.

smalizi'ato, a [smalit'tsjato] *ag* shrewd, cunning.

smal'tare *vt* to enamel; (*ceramica*) to glaze; (*unghie*) to varnish.

smal'tire *vt* (*merce*) to sell off; (*rifiuti*) to dispose of; (*cibo*) to digest; (*peso*) to lose; (*rabbia*) to get over; ~ **la sbornia** to sober up.

'smalto *sm* (*anche: di denti*) enamel; (*per ceramica*) glaze; ~ **per unghie** nail varnish.

'smania *sf* agitation, restlessness; (*fig*): ~ **di** thirst for, craving for; **avere la ~ addosso** to have the fidgets; **avere la ~ di fare** to be desperate to do.

smantel'lare *vt* to dismantle.

smarri'mento *sm* loss; (*fig*) bewilderment; dismay.

smar'rire *vt* to lose; (*non riuscire a trovare*) to mislay; ~**rsi** *vr* (*perdersi*) to lose one's way, get lost; (*: oggetto*) to go astray; **smar'rito, a** *ag* (*sbigottito*) bewildered.

smasche'rare [zmaske'rare] *vt* to unmask.

smemo'rato, a *ag* forgetful.

smen'tire *vt* (*negare*) to deny; (*testimonianza*) to refute; (*reputazione*) to give the lie to; ~**rsi** *vr* to be inconsistent; **smen'tita** *sf* denial; retraction.

sme'raldo *sm* emerald.

smerci'are [zmer'tʃare] *vt* (*COMM*) to sell; (*: svendere*) to sell off.

sme'riglio [zme'riʎʎo] *sm* emery.

'smesso, a *pp di* smettere.

'smettere *vt* to stop; (*vestiti*) to stop wearing ♦ *vi* to stop, cease; ~ **di fare** to stop doing.

'smilzo, a ['zmiltso] *ag* thin, lean.

sminu'ire *vt* to diminish, lessen; (*fig*) to belittle.

sminuz'zare [zminut'tsare] *vt* to break into small pieces; to crumble.

smis'tare *vt* (*pacchi etc*) to sort; (*FERR*) to shunt.

smisu'rato, a *ag* boundless, immeasurable; (*grandissimo*) immense, enormous.

smobili'tare *vt* to demobilize.

smo'dato, a *ag* immoderate.

smoking ['smǝukiŋ] *sm inv* dinner jacket.

smon'tare *vt* (*mobile, macchina etc*) to take to pieces, dismantle; (*fig: scoraggiare*) to dishearten ♦ *vi* (*scendere: da cavallo*) to dismount; (*: da treno*) to get off; (*terminare il lavoro*) to stop (work); ~**rsi** *vr* to lose heart; to lose one's enthusiasm.

'smorfia *sf* grimace; (*atteggiamento lezioso*) simpering; **fare** ~ to make faces; to simper; **smorfi'oso, a** *ag* simpering.

'smorto, a *ag* (*viso*) pale, wan; (*colore*) dull.

smor'zare [zmor'tsare] *vt* (*suoni*) to deaden; (*colori*) to tone down; (*luce*) to dim; (*sete*) to quench; (*entusiasmo*) to dampen; ~**rsi** *vr* (*suono, luce*) to fade; (*entusiasmo*) to dampen.

'smosso, a *pp di* smuovere.

smotta'mento *sm* landslide.

'smunto, a *ag* haggard, pinched.

smu'overe *vt* to move, shift; (*fig: commuovere*) to move; (*: dall'inerzia*) to rouse, stir; ~**rsi** *vr* to move, shift.

smus'sare *vt* (*angolo*) to round off, smooth; (*lama etc*) to blunt; ~**rsi** *vr* to become blunt.

snatu'rato, a *ag* inhuman, heartless.

'snello, a *ag* (*agile*) agile; (*svelto*) slender, slim.

sner'vare *vt* to enervate, wear out; ~**rsi** *vr* to become enervated.

sni'dare *vt* to drive out, flush out.

snob'bare *vt* to snub.

sno'bismo *sm* snobbery.

snoccio'lare [znottʃo'lare] *vt* (*frutta*) to stone; (*fig: orazioni*) to rattle off; (*: verità*) to blab.

sno'dare *vt* (*rendere agile, mobile*) to loosen; ~**rsi** *vr* to come loose; (*articolarsi*) to bend; (*strada, fiume*) to wind.

so *vb vedi* sapere.

so'ave *ag* sweet, gentle, soft.

sobbal'zare [sobbal'tsare] *vi* to jolt, jerk; (*trasalire*) to jump, start; **sob'balzo** *sm* jerk, jolt; jump, start.

sobbar'carsi *vr*: ~ **a** to take on, undertake.

sob'borgo, ghi *sm* suburb.

sobil'lare *vt* to stir up, incite.

'sobrio, a *ag* sober.

socchi'udere [sok'kjudere] *vt* (*porta*) to leave ajar; (*occhi*) to half-close; **socchi'uso, a** *pp di* **socchiudere**.

soc'correre *vt* to help, assist; **soc'corso, a** *pp di* **soccorrere** ♦ *sm* help, aid, assistance; **soccorsi** *smpl* relief *sg*, aid *sg*; **soccorso stradale** breakdown service.

socialdemo'cratico, a, ci, che [sotʃaldemo'kratiko] *sm/f* Social Democrat.

soci'ale [so'tʃale] *ag* social; (*di associazione*) club *cpd*, association *cpd*.

socia'lismo [sotʃa'lizmo] *sm* socialism; **socia'lista, i, e** *ag, sm/f* socialist.

società [sotʃe'ta] *sf inv* society; (*sportiva*) club; (*COMM*) company; ~ **per azioni** limited (*BRIT*) *o* incorporated (*US*) company; ~ **a responsabilità limitata** *type of limited liability company.*

soci'evole [so'tʃevole] *ag* sociable.

'socio ['sɔtʃo] *sm* (*DIR, COMM*) partner; (*membro di associazione*) member.

'soda *sf* (*CHIM*) soda; (*acqua gassata*) soda (water).

soda'lizio [soda'littsjo] *sm* association, society.

soddisfa'cente [soddisfa'tʃente] *ag* satisfactory.

soddis'fare *vt, vi*: ~ **a** to satisfy; (*impegno*) to fulfil; (*debito*) to pay off; (*richiesta*) to meet, comply with; (*offesa*) to make amends for; **soddis'fatto, a** *pp di* **soddisfare** ♦ *ag* satisfied; **soddisfatto di** happy *o* satisfied with; pleased with; **soddisfazi'one** *sf* satisfaction.

'sodo, a *ag* firm, hard ♦ *av* (*picchiare, lavorare*) hard; **dormire** ~ to sleep soundly.

sofà *sm inv* sofa.

soffe'renza [soffe'rɛntsa] *sf* suffering.

sof'ferto, a *pp di* **soffrire**.

soffi'are *vt* to blow; (*notizia, segreto*) to whisper ♦ *vi* to blow; (*sbuffare*) to puff (and blow); ~**rsi il naso** to blow one's nose; ~ **qc/qn a qn** (*fig*) to pinch *o* steal sth/sb from sb; ~ **via qc** to blow sth away.

'soffice ['sɔffitʃe] *ag* soft.

'soffio *sm* (*di vento*) breath; (*di fumo*) puff; (*MED*) murmur.

sof'fitta *sf* attic.

sof'fitto *sm* ceiling.

soffo'care *vi* (*anche*: ~**rsi**) to suffocate, choke ♦ *vt* to suffocate, choke; (*fig*) to stifle, suppress.

sof'friggere [sof'friddʒere] *vt* to fry lightly.

sof'frire *vt* to suffer, endure; (*sopportare*) to bear, stand ♦ *vi* to suffer; to be in pain; ~ (**di**) **qc** (*MED*) to suffer from sth.

sof'fritto, a *pp di* **soffriggere** ♦ *sm* (*CUC*) *fried mixture of herbs, bacon and onions.*

sofisti'cato, a *ag* sophisticated; (*vino*) adulterated.

sogget'tivo, a [soddʒet'tivo] *ag* subjective.

sog'getto, a [sod'dʒetto] *ag*: ~ **a** (*sottomesso*) subject to; (*esposto: a variazioni, danni etc*) subject *o* liable to ♦ *sm* subject.

soggezi'one [soddʒet'tsjone] *sf* subjection; (*timidezza*) awe; **avere** ~ **di qn** to stand in awe of sb; to be ill at ease in sb's presence.

sogghi'gnare [soggiɲ'ɲare] *vi* to sneer.

soggior'nare [soddʒor'nare] *vi* to stay; **soggi'orno** *sm* (*invernale, marino*) stay; (*stanza*) living room.

sog'giungere [sod'dʒundʒere] *vt* to add.

'soglia ['sɔʎʎa] *sf* doorstep; (*anche fig*) threshold.

'sogliola ['sɔʎʎola] *sf* (*ZOOL*) sole.

so'gnare [soɲ'ɲare] *vt, vi* to dream; ~ **a occhi aperti** to daydream; **sogna'tore, 'trice** *sm/f* dreamer.

'sogno ['soɲɲo] *sm* dream.

'soia sf (BOT) soya.

sol sm (MUS) G; (: solfeggiando la scala) so(h).

so'laio sm (soffitta) attic.

sola'mente av only, just.

so'lare ag solar, sun cpd.

'solco, chi sm (scavo, fig: ruga) furrow; (incavo) rut, track; (di disco) groove; (scia) wake.

sol'dato sm soldier; ~ **semplice** private.

'soldo sm (fig): **non avere un** ~ to be penniless; **non vale un** ~ it's not worth a penny; ~**i** smpl (denaro) money sg.

'sole sm sun; (luce) sun(light); (tempo assolato) sun(shine); **prendere il** ~ to sunbathe.

soleggi'ato, a [soled'dʒato] ag sunny.

so'lenne ag solemn; **solennità** sf solemnity; (festività) holiday, feast day.

sol'fato sm (CHIM) sulphate.

soli'dale ag: **essere** ~ **(con)** to be in agreement (with).

solidarietà sf solidarity.

'solido, a ag solid; (forte, robusto) sturdy, solid; (fig: ditta) sound, solid ♦ sm (MAT) solid.

soli'loquio sm soliloquy.

so'lista, i, e ag solo ♦ sm/f soloist.

solita'mente av usually, as a rule.

soli'tario, a ag (senza compagnia) solitary, lonely; (solo, isolato) solitary, lone; (deserto) lonely ♦ sm (gioiello, gioco) solitaire.

'solito, a ag usual; **essere** ~ **fare** to be in the habit of doing; **di** ~ usually; **più tardi del** ~ later than usual; **come al** ~ as usual.

soli'tudine sf solitude.

solleci'tare [solletʃi'tare] vt (lavoro) to speed up; (persona) to urge on; (chiedere con insistenza) to press for, request urgently; (stimolare): ~ **qn a fare** to urge sb to do; (TECN) to stress; **sollecitazi'one** sf entreaty, request; (fig) incentive; (TECN) stress.

sol'lecito, a [sol'letʃito] ag prompt, quick ♦ sm (lettera) reminder; **solleci'tudine** sf promptness, speed.

solleti'care vt to tickle.

sol'letico sm tickling; **soffrire il** ~ to be ticklish.

solleva'mento sm raising; lifting; revolt; ~ **pesi** (SPORT) weight-lifting.

solle'vare vt to lift, raise; (fig: persona: allegerire): ~ **(da)** to relieve (of); (: dar conforto) to comfort, relieve; (: questione) to raise; (: far insorgere) to stir (to revolt); ~**rsi** vr to rise; (fig: riprendersi) to recover; (: ribellarsi) to rise up.

solli'evo sm relief; (conforto) comfort.

'solo, a ag alone; (in senso spirituale: isolato) lonely; (unico): **un** ~ **libro** only one book, a single book; (con ag numerale): **veniamo noi tre** ~**i** just o only the three of us are coming ♦ av (soltanto) only, just; **non** ~ ... **ma anche** not only ... but also; **fare qc da** ~ to do sth (all) by oneself; **da me** ~ single-handed, on my own.

sol'tanto av only.

so'lubile ag (sostanza) soluble.

soluzi'one [solut'tsjone] sf solution.

sol'vente ag, sm solvent.

'soma sf: **bestia da** ~ beast of burden.

so'maro sm ass, donkey.

somigli'anza [somiʎ'ʎantsa] sf resemblance.

somigli'are [somiʎ'ʎare] vi: ~ **a** to be like, resemble; (nell'aspetto fisico) to look like; ~**rsi** vr to be (o look) alike.

'somma sf (MAT) sum; (di denaro) sum (of money); (complesso di varie cose) whole amount, sum total.

som'mare vt to add up; (aggiungere) to add; **tutto sommato** all things considered.

som'mario, a ag (racconto, indagine) brief; (giustizia) summary ♦ sm summary.

som'mergere [som'mɛrdʒere] vt to submerge.

sommer'gibile [sommer'dʒibile] sm submarine.

som'merso, a pp di **sommergere**.

som'messo, a ag (voce) soft, subdued.

somminis'trare vt to give, administer.

sommità *sf inv* summit, top; *(fig)* height.

'sommo, a *ag* highest; *(rispetto etc)* highest, greatest; *(poeta, artista)* great, outstanding ♦ *sm (fig)* height; **per ~i capi** briefly, covering the main points.

som'mossa *sf* uprising.

so'nare *etc* = **suonare** *etc*.

son'daggio [son'daddʒo] *sm* sounding; probe; boring, drilling; *(indagine)* survey; **~ d'opinioni** opinion poll.

son'dare *vt (NAUT)* to sound; *(atmosfera, piaga)* to probe; *(MINE-RALOGIA)* to bore, drill; *(fig: opinione etc)* to survey, poll.

so'netto *sm* sonnet.

son'nambulo, a *sm/f* sleepwalker.

sonnecchi'are [sonnek'kjare] *vi* to doze, nod.

son'nifero *sm* sleeping drug (*o* pill).

'sonno *sm* sleep; **prendere ~** to fall asleep; **aver ~** to be sleepy.

'sono *vb vedi* **essere**.

so'noro, a *ag (ambiente)* resonant; *(voce)* sonorous, ringing; *(onde, film)* sound *cpd*.

sontu'oso, a *ag* sumptuous; lavish.

sopo'rifero, a *ag* soporific.

soppe'sare *vt* to weigh in one's hand(s), feel the weight of; *(fig)* to weigh up.

soppi'atto: di ~ *av* secretly; furtively.

soppor'tare *vt (reggere)* to support; *(subire: perdita, spese)* to bear, sustain; *(soffrire: dolore)* to bear, endure; *(sog: cosa: freddo)* to withstand; *(sog: persona: freddo, vino)* to take; *(tollerare)* to put up with, tolerate.

sop'presso, a *pp di* **sopprimere**.

sop'primere *vt (carica, privilegi, testimone)* to do away with; *(pubblicazione)* to suppress; *(parola, frase)* to delete.

'sopra *prep (gen)* on; *(al di sopra di, più in alto di)* above; over; *(riguardo a)* on, about ♦ *av* on top; *(attaccato, scritto)* on it; *(al di sopra)* above; *(al piano superiore)* upstairs; **donne ~ i 30 anni** women over 30 (years of age); **abito di ~** I live upstairs; **dormirci ~**

(fig) to sleep on it.

so'prabito *sm* overcoat.

soprac'ciglio [soprat'tʃiʎʎo] *(pl(f)* **soprac'ciglia)** *sm* eyebrow.

sopracco'perta *sf (di letto)* bedspread; *(di libro)* jacket.

soprad'detto, a *ag* aforesaid.

sopraf'fare *vt* to overcome, overwhelm; **sopraf'fatto, a** *pp di* **sopraffare**.

sopraf'fino, a *ag (pranzo, vino)* excellent.

sopraggi'ungere [soprad'dʒundʒere] *vi (giungere all'improvviso)* to arrive (unexpectedly); *(accadere)* to occur (unexpectedly).

sopral'luogo, ghi *sm (di esperti)* inspection; *(di polizia)* on-the-spot investigation.

sopram'mobile *sm* ornament.

soprannatu'rale *ag* supernatural.

sopran'nome *sm* nickname.

so'prano, a *sm/f (persona)* soprano ♦ *sm (voce)* soprano.

soprappensi'ero *av* lost in thought.

sopras'salto *sm*: **di ~** with a start; suddenly.

soprasse'dere *vi*: **~ a** to delay, put off.

soprat'tutto *av (anzitutto)* above all; *(specialmente)* especially.

soprav'vento *sm*: **avere/prendere il ~ su** to have/get the upper hand over.

sopravvis'suto, a *pp di* **sopravvivere**.

soprav'vivere *vi* to survive; *(continuare a vivere)*: **~ (in)** to live on (in); **~ a** *(incidente etc)* to survive; *(persona)* to outlive.

soprinten'dente *sm/f* supervisor; *(statale: di belle arti etc)* keeper; **soprinten'denza** *sf* supervision; *(ente)*: **soprintendenza alle Belle Arti** government department responsible for monuments and artistic treasures.

so'pruso *sm* abuse of power; **subire un ~** to be abused.

soq'quadro *sm*: **mettere a ~** to turn upside-down.

sor'betto *sm* sorbet, water ice.

sor'bire *vt* to sip; *(fig)* to put up with.

'sorcio, ci ['sortʃo] *sm* mouse.

'**sordido, a** *ag* sordid; (*fig*: *gretto*) stingy.

sor'**dina** *sf*: in ~ softly; (*fig*) on the sly.

sordità *sf* deafness.

'**sordo, a** *ag* deaf; (*rumore*) muffled; (*dolore*) dull; (*odio, rancore*) veiled ♦ *sm/f* deaf person; **sordo'muto, a** *ag* deaf-and-dumb ♦ *sm/f* deaf-mute.

so'**rella** *sf* sister; **sorel'lastra** *sf* stepsister.

sor'**gente** [sor'dʒɛnte] *sf* (*acqua che sgorga*) spring; (*di fiume, FISICA, fig*) source.

'**sorgere** ['sordʒere] *vi* to rise; (*scaturire*) to spring, rise; (*fig: difficoltà*) to arise.

sormon'**tare** *vt* (*fig*) to overcome, surmount.

sorni'**one, a** *ag* sly.

sorpas'**sare** *vt* (*AUT*) to overtake; (*fig*) to surpass; (: *eccedere*) to exceed, go beyond; ~ in altezza to be higher than; (*persona*) to be taller than.

sorpren'**dente** *ag* surprising.

sor'**prendere** *vt* (*cogliere: in flagrante etc*) to catch; (*stupire*) to surprise; ~rsi *vr*: ~rsi (di) to be surprised (at); sor'presa *sf* surprise; fare una sorpresa a qn to give sb a surprise; sor'preso, a *pp di* sorprendere.

sor'**reggere** [sor'reddʒere] *vt* to support, hold up; (*fig*) to sustain; sor'retto, a *pp di* sorreggere.

sor'**ridere** *vi* to smile; sor'riso, a *pp di* sorridere ♦ *sm* smile.

'**sorso** *sm* sip.

'**sorta** *sf* sort, kind; di ~ whatever, of any kind, at all.

'**sorte** *sf* (*fato*) fate, destiny; (*evento fortuito*) chance; tirare a ~ to draw lots.

sor'**teggio** [sor'teddʒo] *sm* draw.

sorti'**legio** [sorti'lɛdʒo] *sm* witchcraft *no pl*; (*incantesimo*) spell; fare un ~ a qn to cast a spell on sb.

sor'**tita** *sf* (*MIL*) sortie.

'**sorto, a** *pp di* sorgere.

sorvegli'**anza** [sorveʎ'ʎantsa] *sf* watch; supervision; (*POLIZIA, MIL*)

surveillance.

sorvegli'**are** [sorveʎ'ʎare] *vt* (*bambino, bagagli, prigioniero*) to watch, keep an eye on; (*malato*) to watch over; (*territorio, casa*) to watch o keep watch over; (*lavori*) to supervise.

sorvo'**lare** *vt* (*territorio*) to fly over ♦ *vi*: ~ su (*fig*) to skim over.

'**sosia** *sm inv* double.

sos'**pendere** *vt* (*appendere*) to hang (up); (*interrompere, privare di una carica*) to suspend; (*rimandare*) to defer; ~ un quadro al muro/un lampadario al soffitto to hang a picture on the wall/a chandelier from the ceiling; sospensi'one *sf* (*anche CHIM, AUT*) suspension; deferment; sos'peso, a *pp di* sospendere ♦ *ag* (*appeso*): sospeso a hanging on (o from); (*treno, autobus*) cancelled; in sospeso in abeyance; (*conto*) outstanding; tenere in sospeso (*fig*) to keep in suspense.

sospet'**tare** *vt* to suspect ♦ *vi*: ~ di to suspect; (*diffidare*) to be suspicious of.

sos'**petto, a** *ag* suspicious ♦ *sm* suspicion; sospet'toso, a *ag* suspicious.

sos'**pingere** [sos'pindʒere] *vt* to drive, push; sos'pinto, a *pp di* sospingere.

sospi'**rare** *vi* to sigh ♦ *vt* to long for, yearn for; sos'piro *sm* sigh.

'**sosta** *sf* (*fermata*) stop, halt; (*pausa*) pause, break; senza ~ non-stop, without a break.

sostan'**tivo** *sm* noun, substantive.

sos'**tanza** [sos'tantsa] *sf* substance; ~e *sfpl* (*ricchezze*) wealth *sg*, possessions; in ~ in short, to sum up; sostanzi'oso, a *ag* (*cibo*) nourishing, substantial.

sos'**tare** *vi* (*fermarsi*) to stop (for a while), stay; (*fare una pausa*) to take a break.

sos'**tegno** [sos'teɲɲo] *sm* support.

soste'**nere** *vt* to support; (*prendere su di sé*) to take on, bear; (*resistere*) to withstand, stand up to; (*affermare*): ~ che to maintain that; ~rsi *vr* to hold o.s. up, support o.s.; (*fig*) to keep up one's strength; ~ gli esami to sit exams; sosteni'tore, 'trice *sm/f* supporter.

sostenta'mento *sm* maintenance, support.

soste'nuto, a *ag* (*stile*) elevated; (*velocità, ritmo*) sustained; (*prezzo*) high ♦ *sm/f*: **fare il(la)** ~(**a**) to be standoffish, keep one's distance.

sostitu'ire *vt* (*mettere al posto di*): ~ **qn/qc a** to substitute sb/sth for; (*prendere il posto di: persona*) to substitute for; (: *cosa*) to take the place of.

sosti'tuto, a *sm/f* substitute.

sostituzi'one *sf* substitution; **in** ~ **di** as a substitute for, in place of.

sotta'ceti [sotta'tʃeti] *smpl* pickles.

sot'tana *sf* (*sottoveste*) underskirt; (*gonna*) skirt; (*REL*) soutane, cassock.

sotter'fugio [sotter'fudʒo] *sm* subterfuge.

sotter'raneo, a *ag* underground ♦ *sm* cellar.

sotter'rare *vt* to bury.

sottigli'ezza [sottiʎ'ʎettsa] *sf* thinness; slimness; (*fig: acutezza*) subtlety; shrewdness; ~**e** *sfpl* (*pedanteria*) quibbles.

sot'tile *ag* thin; (*figura, caviglia*) thin, slim, slender; (*fine: polvere, capelli*) fine; (*fig: leggero*) light; (: *vista*) sharp, keen; (: *olfatto*) fine, discriminating; (: *mente*) subtle; shrewd ♦ *sm*: **non andare per il** ~ not to mince matters.

sottin'tendere *vt* (*intendere qc non espresso*) to understand; (*implicare*) to imply; **sottin'teso, a** *pp di* **sottintendere** ♦ *sm* allusion; **parlare senza sottintesi** to speak plainly.

'sotto *prep* (*gen*) under; (*più in basso di*) below ♦ *av* underneath, beneath; below; (*al piano inferiore*): (**al piano**) **di** ~ downstairs; ~ **forma di** in the form of; ~ **il monte** at the foot of the mountain; **siamo** ~ **Natale** it's nearly Christmas; ~ **la pioggia/il sole** in the rain/sun(shine); ~ **terra** underground; ~ **voce** in a low voice; **chiuso** ~ **vuoto** vacuum-packed.

sottoline'are *vt* to underline; (*fig*) to emphasize, stress.

sottoma'rino, a *ag* (*flora*) submarine; (*cavo, navigazione*) underwater ♦ *sm* (*NAUT*) submarine.

sotto'messo, a *pp di* **sottomettere**.

sotto'mettere *vt* to subdue, subjugate; ~**rsi** *vr* to submit.

sottopas'saggio [sottopas'saddʒo] *sm* (*AUT*) underpass; (*pedonale*) subway, underpass.

sotto'porre *vt* (*costringere*) to subject; (*fig: presentare*) to submit; **sottoporsi** *vr* to submit; **sottoporsi a** (*subire*) to undergo; **sotto'posto, a** *pp di* **sottoporre**.

sottos'critto, a *pp di* **sottoscrivere**.

sottos'crivere *vt* to sign ♦ *vi*: ~ **a** to subscribe to; **sottoscrizi'one** *sf* signing; subscription.

sottosegre'tario *sm*: ~ **di Stato** Under-Secretary of State (*BRIT*), Assistant Secretary of State (*US*).

sotto'sopra *av* upside-down.

sotto'terra *av* underground.

sotto'titolo *sm* subtitle.

sotto'veste *sf* underskirt.

sotto'voce [sotto'votʃe] *av* in a low voice.

sot'trarre *vt* (*MAT*) to subtract, take away; ~ **qn/qc a** (*togliere*) to remove sb/sth from; (*salvare*) to save *o* rescue sb/sth from; ~ **qc a qn** (*rubare*) to steal sth from sb; **sottrarsi** *vr*: **sottrarsi a** (*sfuggire*) to escape; (*evitare*) to avoid; **sot'tratto, a** *pp di* **sottrarre**; **sottrazi'one** *sf* subtraction; removal.

sovi'etico, a, ci, che *ag* Soviet ♦ *sm/f* Soviet citizen.

sovraccari'care *vt* to overload.

sovrannatu'rale *ag* = **soprannaturale**.

so'vrano, a *ag* sovereign; (*fig: sommo*) supreme ♦ *sm/f* sovereign, monarch.

sovrap'porre *vt* to place on top of, put on top of.

sovras'tare *vi*: ~ **a** (*vallata, fiume*) to overhang; (*fig*) to hang over, threaten ♦ *vt* to overhang; to hang over, threaten.

sovrinten'dente *sm/f* = **soprintendente**; **sovrinten'denza** *sf* = **soprintendenza**.

sovru'mano, a *ag* superhuman.

sovvenzi'one [sovven'tsjone] *sf* subsidy, grant.

sovver'sivo, a *ag* subversive.

'sozzo, a ['sottso] *ag* filthy, dirty.

S.p.A. *abbr* = **società per azioni.**

spac'care *vt* to split, break; (*legna*) to chop; **~rsi** *vr* to split, break; **spacca'tura** *sf* split.

spacci'are [spat'tʃare] *vt* (*vendere*) to sell (off); (*mettere in circolazione*) to circulate; (*droga*) to peddle, push; **~rsi** *vr*: **~rsi per** (*farsi credere*) to pass o.s. off as, pretend to be; **spaccia'tore, 'trice** *sm/f* (*di droga*) pusher; (*di denaro falso*) dealer; **'spaccio** *sm* (*di merce rubata, droga*): **spaccio (di)** trafficking (in); (*in denaro falso*): **spaccio (di)** passing (of); (*vendita*) sale; (*bottega*) shop.

'spacco, chi *sm* (*fenditura*) split, crack; (*strappo*) tear; (*di gonna*) slit.

spac'cone *sm/f* boaster, braggart.

'spada *sf* sword.

spae'sato, a *ag* disorientated, lost.

spa'ghetti [spa'getti] *smpl* (*CUC*) spaghetti *sg*.

'Spagna ['spaɲɲa] *sf*: **la ~** Spain; **~e** *sfpl* (*dorso*) back; **spa'gnolo, a** *ag* Spanish ♦ *sm/f* Spaniard ♦ *sm* (*LING*) Spanish; **gli Spagnoli** the Spanish.

'spago, ghi *sm* string, twine.

spai'ato, a *ag* (*calza, guanto*) odd.

spalan'care *vt* to open wide; **~rsi** *vr* to open wide.

spa'lare *vt* to shovel.

'spalla *sf* shoulder; (*fig: TEATRO*) stooge; **~e** *sfpl* (*dorso*) back; **spalleggi'are** *vt* to back up, support.

spal'letta *sf* (*parapetto*) parapet.

spalli'era *sf* (*di sedia etc*) back; (*di letto: da capo*) head(board); (: *da piedi*) foot(board); (*GINNASTICA*) wall bars *pl*.

spal'mare *vt* to spread.

'spalti *smpl* (*di stadio*) terracing.

'spandere *vt* to spread; (*versare*) to pour (out); **~rsi** *vr* to spread; **'spanto, a** *pp di* **spandere.**

spa'rare *vt* to fire ♦ *vi* (*far fuoco*) to

fire; (*tirare*) to shoot; **spara'tore** *sm* gunman; **spara'toria** *sf* exchange of shots.

sparecchi'are [sparek'kjare] *vt*: **~ (la tavola)** to clear the table.

spa'reggio [spa'reddʒo] *sm* (*SPORT*) play-off.

'spargere ['spardʒere] *vt* (*sparpagliare*) to scatter; (*versare: vino*) to spill; (: *lacrime, sangue*) to shed; (*diffondere*) to spread; (*emanare*) to give off (*o* out); **~rsi** *vr* to spread; **spargi'mento** *sm* scattering, strewing; spilling; shedding; **spargimento di sangue** bloodshed.

spa'rire *vi* to disappear, vanish.

spar'lare *vi*: **~ di** to run down, speak ill of.

'sparo *sm* shot.

sparpagli'are [sparpaʎ'ʎare] *vt* to scatter; **~rsi** *vr* to scatter.

'sparso, a *pp di* **spargere** ♦ *ag* scattered; (*sciolto*) loose.

spar'tire *vt* (*eredità, bottino*) to share out; (*avversari*) to separate.

sparti'traffico *sm inv* (*AUT*) central reservation (*BRIT*), median (strip) (*US*).

spa'ruto, a *ag* (*viso etc*) haggard.

sparvi'ero *sm* (*ZOOL*) sparrowhawk.

spasi'mare *vi* to be in agony; **~ di fare** (*fig*) to yearn to do; **~ per qn** to be madly in love with sb.

'spasimo *sm* pang; **'spasmo** *sm* (*MED*) spasm; **spas'modico, a, ci, che** *ag* (*angoscioso*) agonizing; (*MED*) spasmodic.

spassio'nato, a *ag* dispassionate, impartial.

'spasso *sm* (*divertimento*) amusement, enjoyment; **andare a ~** to go out for a walk; **essere a ~** (*fig*) to be out of work; **mandare qn a ~** (*fig*) to give sb the sack.

spau'racchio [spau'rakkjo] *sm* scarecrow.

spau'rire *vt* to frighten, terrify.

spa'valdo, a *ag* arrogant, bold.

spaventa'passeri *sm inv* scarecrow.

spaven'tare *vt* to frighten, scare; **~rsi** *vr* to be frightened, be scared; to get a fright; **spa'vento** *sm* fear, fright; **far**

spavento a qn to give sb a fright; **spaven'toso, a** *ag* frightening, terrible; *(fig: fam)* tremendous, fantastic.

spazien'tire [spattsjen'tire] *vi (anche:* ~*rsi)* to lose one's patience.

'spazio ['spattsjo] *sm* space; ~ **aereo** airspace; **spazi'oso, a** *ag* spacious.

spazzaca'mino [spattsaka'mino] *sm* chimney sweep.

spaz'zare [spat'tsare] *vt* to sweep; *(foglie etc)* to sweep up; *(cacciare)* to sweep away; **spazza'tura** *sf* sweepings *pl; (immondizia)* rubbish; **spaz'zino** *sm* street sweeper.

'spazzola ['spattsola] *sf* brush; ~ **per abiti** clothesbrush; ~ **da capelli** hairbrush; **spazzo'lare** *vt* to brush; **spazzo'lino** *sm* (small) brush; **spazzolino da denti** toothbrush.

specchi'arsi [spek'kjarsi] *vr* to look at o.s. in a mirror; *(riflettersi)* to be mirrored, be reflected.

'specchio ['spekkjo] *sm* mirror.

speci'ale [spe'tʃale] *ag* special; **specia'lista, i, e** *sm/f* specialist; **specialità** *sf inv* speciality; *(branca di studio)* special field, speciality; **specializ'zarsi** *vr:* **specializzarsi (in)** to specialize (in); **special'mente** *av* especially, particularly.

'specie ['spetʃe] *sf inv* (BIOL, BOT, ZOOL) species *inv; (tipo)* kind, sort ♦ *av* especially, particularly; **una ~ di** a kind of; **fare ~ a qn** to surprise sb; **la ~ umana** mankind.

specifi'care [spetʃifi'kare] *vt* to specify, state.

spe'cifico, a, ci, che [spe'tʃifiko] *ag* specific.

specu'lare *vi:* ~ **su** (COMM) to speculate in; *(sfruttare)* to exploit; *(meditare)* to speculate on; **speculazi'one** *sf* speculation.

spe'dire *vt* to send; **spedizi'one** *sf* sending; *(collo)* consignment; *(scientifica etc)* expedition.

'spegnere ['speɲɲere] *vt (fuoco, sigaretta)* to put out, extinguish; *(apparecchio elettrico)* to turn o switch off; *(gas)* to turn off; *(fig: suoni, passioni)* to stifle; *(debito)* to extinguish; ~**rsi** *vr* to go out; to go off; *(morire)* to pass away.

spel'lare *vt (scuoiare)* to skin; *(scorticare)* to graze; ~**rsi** *vr* to peel.

'spendere *vt* to spend.

spen'nare *vt* to pluck.

spensie'rato, a *ag* carefree.

'spento, a *pp di* **spegnere** ♦ *ag (suono)* muffled; *(colore)* dull; *(sigaretta)* out; *(civiltà, vulcano)* extinct.

spe'ranza [spe'rantsa] *sf* hope.

spe'rare *vt* to hope for ♦ *vi:* ~ **in** to trust in; ~ **che/di fare** to hope that/to do; **lo spero, spero di sì** I hope so.

sper'duto, a *ag (isolato)* out-of-the-way; *(persona: smarrita, a disagio)* lost.

spergi'uro, a [sper'dʒuro] *sm/f* perjurer ♦ *sm* perjury.

sperimen'tale *ag* experimental.

sperimen'tare *vt* to experiment with, test; *(fig)* to test, put to the test.

'sperma, i *sm* (BIOL) sperm.

spe'rone *sm* spur.

sperpe'rare *vt* to squander.

'spesa *sf (somma di denaro)* expense; *(costo)* cost; *(acquisto)* purchase; *(fam: acquisto del cibo quotidiano)* shopping; ~**e** *sfpl (soldi spesi)* expenses; (COMM) costs; charges; **fare la ~** to do the shopping; **a ~e di** *(a carico di)* at the expense of; ~**e generali** overheads; ~**e postali** postage *sg;* ~**e di viaggio** travelling expenses.

'speso, a *pp di* **spendere**.

'spesso, a *ag (fitto)* thick; *(frequente)* frequent ♦ *av* often; ~**e volte** frequently, often.

spes'sore *sm* thickness.

spet'tabile *(abbr:* **Spett.**: *in lettere) ag:* ~ **ditta X** Messrs X and Co.

spet'tacolo *sm (rappresentazione)* performance, show; *(vista, scena)* sight; **dare ~ di sé** to make an exhibition o a spectacle of o.s.; **spettaco'loso, a** *ag* spectacular.

spet'tare *vi:* ~ **a** *(decisione)* to be up to; *(stipendio)* to be due to; **spetta a te decidere** it's up to you decide.

spetta'tore, 'trice *sm/f* (CINEMA, TEATRO) member of the audience; (*di avvenimento*) onlooker, witness.

spetti'nare *vt*: ~ **qn** to ruffle sb's hair; ~**rsi** *vr* to get one's hair in a mess.

'spettro *sm* (*fantasma*) spectre; (FISICA) spectrum.

'spezie ['spɛttsje] *sfpl* (CUC) spices.

spez'zare [spet'tsare] *vt* (*rompere*) to break; (*fig: interrompere*) to break up; ~**rsi** *vr* to break.

spezza'tino [spettsa'tino] *sm* (CUC) stew.

spezzet'tare [spettset'tare] *vt* to break up (*o chop*) into small pieces.

'spia *sf* spy; (*confidente della polizia*) informer; (ELETTR) indicating light; warning light; (*fessura*) peep-hole; (*fig: sintomo*) sign, indication.

spia'cente [spja'tʃɛnte] *ag* sorry; essere ~ **di qc/di fare qc** to be sorry about sth/for doing sth.

spia'cevole [spja'tʃevole] *ag* unpleasant, disagreeable.

spi'aggia, ge ['spjaddʒa] *sf* beach.

spia'nare *vt* (*terreno*) to level, make level; (*edificio*) to raze to the ground; (*pasta*) to roll out; (*rendere liscio*) to smooth (out).

spi'ano *sm*: **a tutto ~** (*lavorare*) nonstop, without a break; (*spendere*) lavishly.

spian'tato, a *ag* penniless, ruined.

spi'are *vt* to spy on; (*occasione etc*) to watch *o* wait for.

spi'azzo ['spjattso] *sm* open space; (*radura*) clearing.

spic'care *vt* (*assegno, mandato di cattura*) to issue ♦ *vi* (*risaltare*) to stand out; ~ **il volo** to fly off; (*fig*) to spread one's wings; ~ **un balzo** to leap; **spic'cato, a** *ag* (*marcato*) marked, strong; (*notevole*) remarkable.

'spicchio ['spikkjo] *sm* (*di agrumi*) segment; (*di aglio*) clove; (*parte*) piece, slice.

spicci'arsi [spit'tʃarsi] *vr* to hurry up.

'spicciolo, a ['spittʃolo] *ag*: **moneta ~a**, ~**i** *smpl* (small) change.

'spicco, chi *sm*: **di ~** outstanding;

(*tema*) main, principal; **fare ~** to stand out.

spi'edo *sm* (CUC) spit.

spie'gare *vt* (*far capire*) to explain; (*tovaglia*) to unfold; (*vele*) to unfurl; ~**rsi** *vr* to explain o.s., make o.s. clear; ~ **qc a qn** to explain sth to sb; **il problema si spiega** one can understand the problem; **spiegazi'one** *sf* explanation.

spiegaz'zare [spjegat'tsare] *vt* to crease, crumple.

spie'tato, a *ag* ruthless, pitiless.

spiffe'rare (*fam*) *vt* to blurt out, blab.

'spiga, ghe *sf* (BOT) ear.

spigli'ato, a [spiʎ'ʎato] *ag* self-possessed, self-confident.

'spigolo *sm* corner; (MAT) edge.

'spilla *sf* brooch; (*da cravatta, cappello*) pin.

spil'lare *vt* (*vino, fig*) to tap; ~ **denaro/notizie a qn** to tap sb for money/information.

'spillo *sm* pin; (*spilla*) brooch; ~ **di sicurezza** *o* **da balia** safety pin; ~ **di sicurezza** (MIL) (safety) pin.

spi'lorcio, a, ci, ce [spi'lortʃo] *ag* mean, stingy.

'spina *sf* (BOT) thorn; (ZOOL) spine, prickle; (*di pesce*) bone; (ELETTR) plug; (*di botte*) bunghole; **birra alla ~** draught beer; ~ **dorsale** (ANAT) backbone.

spi'nacio [spi'natʃo] *sm* spinach; (CUC): ~**i** spinach *sg*.

spi'nale *ag* (ANAT) spinal.

'spingere ['spindʒere] *vt* to push; (*condurre: anche fig*) to drive; (*stimolare*): ~ **qn a fare** to urge *o* press sb to do; ~**rsi** *vr* (*inoltrarsi*) to push on, carry on; ~**rsi troppo lontano** (*anche fig*) to go too far.

spi'noso, a *ag* thorny, prickly.

'spinta *sf* (*urto*) push; (FISICA) thrust; (*fig: stimolo*) incentive, spur; (: *appoggio*) string-pulling *no pl*; **dare una ~a a qn** (*fig*) to pull strings for sb.

'spinto, a *pp di* **spingere**.

spio'naggio [spio'naddʒo] *sm* espionage, spying.

spi'overe *vi* (*scorrere*) to flow down;

(*ricadere*) to hang down, fall.

'**spira** *sf* coil.

spi'raglio [spi'raʎʎo] *sm* (*fessura*) chink, narrow opening; (*raggio di luce, fig*) glimmer, gleam.

spi'rale *sf* spiral; (*contraccettivo*) coil; **a ~** spiral(-shaped).

spi'rare *vi* (*vento*) to blow; (*morire*) to expire, pass away.

spiri'tato, a *ag* possessed; (*fig: persona, espressione*) wild.

spiri'tismo *sm* spiritualism.

'**spirito** *sm* (REL, CHIM, *disposizione d'animo, di legge etc, fantasma*) spirit; (*pensieri, intelletto*) mind; (*arguzia*) wit; (*umorismo*) humour, wit; **lo S~** Santo the Holy Spirit *o* Ghost.

spirito'saggine [spirito'saddʒine] *sf* witticism; (*peg*) wisecrack.

spiri'toso, a *ag* witty.

spiritu'ale *ag* spiritual.

'**splendere** *vi* to shine.

'**splendido, a** *ag* splendid; (*splendente*) shining; (*sfarzoso*) magnificent, splendid.

splen'dore *sm* splendour; (*luce intensa*) brilliance, brightness.

spodes'tare *vt* to deprive of power; (*sovrano*) to depose.

'**spoglia** ['spɔʎʎa] *sf* (ZOOL) skin, hide; (: *di rettile*) slough; **~e** *sfpl* (*salma*) remains; (*preda*) spoils, booty *sg*; *vedi anche* **spoglio**.

spogli'are [spoʎ'ʎare] *vt* (*svestire*) to undress; (*privare, fig: depredare*): **~ qn di qc** to deprive sb of sth; (*togliere ornamenti: anche fig*): **~ qn/qc di** to strip sb/sth of; **~rsi** *vr* to undress, strip; **~rsi di** (*ricchezze etc*) to deprive o.s. of, give up; (*pregiudizi*) to rid o.s. of; **spoglia'toio** *sm* dressing room; (*di scuola etc*) cloakroom; (SPORT) changing room; '**spoglio, a** *ag* (*pianta, terreno*) bare; (*privo*): **spoglio di** stripped of; lacking in, without ♦ *sm* (*di voti*) counting.

'**spola** *sf* shuttle; (*bobina di filo*) cop; **fare la ~ (fra)** to go to and fro *o* shuttle (between).

spol'pare *vt* to strip the flesh off.

spolve'rare *vt* (*anche* CUC) to dust; (*con spazzola*) to brush; (*con battipanni*) to beat; (*fig*) to polish off ♦ *vi* to dust.

'**sponda** *sf* (*di fiume*) bank; (*di mare, lago*) shore; (*bordo*) edge.

spon'taneo, a *ag* spontaneous; (*persona*) unaffected, natural.

spopo'lare *vt* to depopulate ♦ *vi* (*attirare folla*) to draw the crowds; **~rsi** *vr* to become depopulated.

spor'care *vt* to dirty, make dirty; (*fig*) to sully, soil; **~rsi** *vr* to get dirty.

spor'cizia [spor'tʃittsja] *sf* (*stato*) dirtiness; (*sudiciume*) dirt, filth; (*cosa sporca*) dirt *no pl*, something dirty; (*fig: cosa oscena*) obscenity.

'**sporco, a, chi, che** *ag* dirty, filthy.

spor'genza [spor'dʒɛntsa] *sf* projection.

'**sporgere** ['spɔrdʒere] *vt* to put out, stretch out ♦ *vi* (*venire in fuori*) to stick out; **~rsi** *vr* to lean out; **~ querela contro qn** (DIR) to take legal action against sb.

sport *sm inv* sport.

'**sporta** *sf* shopping bag.

spor'tello *sm* (*di treno, auto etc*) door; (*di banca, ufficio*) window, counter; **~ automatico** (BANCA) cash dispenser, automated telling machine.

spor'tivo, a *ag* (*gara, giornale*) sports *cpd*; (*persona*) sporty; (*abito*) casual; (*spirito, atteggiamento*) sporting.

'**sporto, a** *pp di* **sporgere**.

'**sposa** *sf* bride; (*moglie*) wife.

sposa'lizio [spoza'littsjo] *sm* wedding.

spo'sare *vt* to marry; (*fig: idea, fede*) to espouse; **~rsi** *vr* to get married, marry; **~rsi con qn** to marry sb, get married to sb; **spo'sato, a** *ag* married.

'**sposo** *sm* (*bride*)groom; (*marito*) husband; **gli ~i** *smpl* the newlyweds.

spos'sato, a *ag* exhausted, weary.

spos'tare *vt* to move, shift; (*cambiare: orario*) to change; **~rsi** *vr* to move.

'**spranga, ghe** *sf* (*sbarra*) bar.

'**sprazzo** ['sprattso] *sm* (*di sole etc*) flash; (*fig: di gioia etc*) burst.

spre'care *vt* to waste; **~rsi** *vr*

(*persona*) to waste one's energy; **'spreco** *sm* waste.

spre'gevole [spre'dʒevole] *ag* contempt-ible, despicable.

spregiudi'cato, a [spredʒudi'kato] *ag* unprejudiced, unbiased; (*peg*) un-scrupulous.

'spremere *vt* to squeeze.

spre'muta *sf* fresh juice; ~ **d'arancia** fresh orange juice.

sprez'zante [spret'tsante] *ag* scornful, contemptuous.

sprigio'nare [spridʒo'nare] *vt* to give off, emit; ~**rsi** *vr* to emanate; (*uscire con impeto*) to burst out.

spriz'zare [sprit'tsare] *vt, vi* to spurt; ~ **gioia/salute** to be bursting with joy/health.

sprofon'dare *vi* to sink; (*casa*) to collapse; (*suolo*) to give way, subside; ~**rsi** *vr*: ~**rsi in** (*poltrona*) to sink into, (*fig*) to become immersed *o* absorbed in.

spro'nare *vt* to spur (on).

'sprone *sm* (*sperone, fig*) spur.

sproporzio'nato, a [sproportsjo'nato] *ag* disproportionate, out of all proportion.

sproporzi'one [sropor'tsjone] *sf* dis-proportion.

sproposi'tato, a *ag* (*lettera, discorso*) full of mistakes; (*fig: costo*) excessive, enormous.

spro'posito *sm* blunder; **a** ~ at the wrong time; (*rispondere, parlare*) irrelevantly.

sprovve'duto, a *ag* inexperienced, naïve.

sprov'visto, a *ag* (*mancante*): ~ **di** lacking in, without; **alla** ~**a** unawares.

spruz'zare [sprut'tsare] *vt* (*a nebulizzazione*) to spray; (*aspergere*) to sprinkle; (*inzaccherare*) to splash; **'spruzzo** *sm* spray; splash.

'spugna ['spuɲɲa] *sf* (*ZOOL*) sponge; (*tessuto*) towelling; **spu'gnoso, a** *ag* spongy.

'spuma *sf* (*schiuma*) foam; (*bibita*) mineral water.

spu'mante *sm* sparkling wine.

spumeggi'ante [spumed'dʒante] *ag* (*birra*) foaming; (*vino, fig*) sparkling.

spu'mone *sm* (*CUC*) mousse.

spun'tare *vt* (*coltello*) to break the point of; (*capelli*) to trim ♦ *vi* (*uscire: germogli*) to sprout; (: *capelli*) to begin to grow; (: *denti*) to come through; (*apparire*) to appear (suddenly); ~**rsi** *vr* to become blunt, lose its point; **spuntarla** (*fig*) to make it, win through.

spun'tino *sm* snack.

'spunto *sm* (*TEATRO, MUS*) cue; (*fig*) starting point; **dare lo** ~ **a** (*fig*) to give rise to.

spur'gare *vt* (*fogna*) to clean, clear; ~**rsi** *vr* (*MED*) to expectorate.

spu'tare *vt* to spit out; (*fig*) to belch (out) ♦ *vi* to spit; **'sputo** *sm* spittle *no pl*, spit *no pl*.

'squadra *sf* (*strumento*) (set) square; (*gruppo*) team, squad; (*di operai*) gang, squad; (*MIL*) squad; (: *AER, NAUT*) squadron; (*SPORT*) team; **lavoro a** ~**e** teamwork.

squa'drare *vt* to square, make square; (*osservare*) to look at closely.

squa'driglia [skwa'driʎʎa] *sf* (*AER*) flight; (*NAUT*) squadron.

squa'drone *sm* squadron.

squagli'arsi [skwaʎ'ʎarsi] *vr* to melt; (*fig*) to sneak off.

squa'lifica *sf* disqualification.

squalifi'care *vt* to disqualify.

'squallido, a *ag* wretched, bleak.

squal'lore *sm* wretchedness, bleakness.

'squalo *sm* shark.

'squama *sf* scale; **squa'mare** *vt* to scale; **squamarsi** *vr* to flake *o* peel (off).

squarcia'gola [skwartʃa'gola]: **a** ~ *av* at the top of one's voice.

squar'tare *vt* to quarter, cut up.

squattri'nato, a *ag* penniless.

squili'brare *vt* to unbalance; **squili'brato, a** *ag* (*PSIC*) unbalanced; **squi'librio** *sm* (*differenza, sbilancio*) imbalance; (*PSIC*) unbalance.

squil'lante *ag* shrill, sharp.

squil'lare *vi* (*campanello, telefono*) to ring (out); (*tromba*) to blare; **'squillo** *sm* ring, ringing *no pl*; blare; **ragazza** *f*

squillo *inv* call girl.

squi'sito, a *ag* exquisite; (*cibo*) delicious; (*persona*) delightful.

squit'tire *vi* (*uccello*) to squawk; (*topo*) to squeak.

sradi'care *vt* to uproot; (*fig*) to eradicate.

sragio'nare [zradʒo'nare] *vi* to talk nonsense, rave.

srego'lato, a *ag* (*senza ordine: vita*) disorderly; (*smodato*) immoderate; (*dissoluto*) dissolute.

S.r.l. *abbr* = **società a responsabilità limitata.**

'stabile *ag* stable, steady; (*tempo: non variabile*) settled; (*TEATRO: compagnia*) resident ♦ *sm* (*edificio*) building.

stabili'mento *sm* (*edificio*) establishment; (*fabbrica*) plant, factory.

stabi'lire *vt* to establish; (*fissare: prezzi, data*) to fix; (*decidere*) to decide; ~**rsi** *vr* (*prendere dimora*) to settle.

stac'care *vt* (*levare*) to detach, remove; (*separare: anche fig*) to separate, divide; (*strappare*) to tear off (*o* out); (*scandire: parole*) to pronounce clearly; (*SPORT*) to leave behind; ~**rsi** *vr* (*bottone etc*) to come off; (*scostarsi*): ~**rsi (da)** to move away (from); (*fig: separarsi*): ~**rsi da** to leave; **non ~ gli occhi da qn** not to take one's eyes off sb.

'stadio *sm* (*SPORT*) stadium; (*periodo, fase*) phase, stage.

'staffa *sf* (*di sella, TECN*) stirrup; **perdere le ~e** (*fig*) to fly off the handle.

staf'fetta *sf* (*messo*) dispatch rider; (*SPORT*) relay race.

stagio'nale [stadʒo'nale] *ag* seasonal.

stagio'nare [stadʒo'nare] *vt* (*legno*) to season; (*formaggi, vino*) to mature.

stagi'one [sta'dʒone] *sf* season; **alta/bassa ~** high/low season.

stagli'arsi [staʎ'ʎarsi] *vr* to stand out, be silhouetted.

sta'gnare [staɲ'ɲare] *vt* (*vaso, tegame*) to tin-plate; (*barca, botte*) to make watertight; (*sangue*) to stop ♦ *vi* to stagnate.

'stagno, a ['staɲɲo] *ag* watertight; (*a tenuta d'aria*) airtight ♦ *sm* (*acquitrino*) pond; (*CHIM*) tin.

sta'gnola [staɲ'ɲɔla] *sf* tinfoil.

'stalla *sf* (*per bovini*) cowshed; (*per cavalli*) stable.

stal'lone *sm* stallion.

sta'mani *av* = **stamattina.**

stamat'tina *av* this morning.

'stampa *sf* (*TIP, FOT: tecnica*) printing; (*impressione, copia fotografica*) print; (*insieme di quotidiani, giornalisti etc*) press; "~**e**" *sfpl* "printed matter".

stam'pante *sf* (*INFORM*) printer.

stam'pare *vt* to print; (*pubblicare*) to publish; (*coniare*) to strike, coin; (*imprimere: anche fig*) to impress.

stampa'tello *sm* block letters *pl*.

stam'pella *sf* crutch.

'stampo *sm* mould; (*fig: indole*) type, kind, sort.

sta'nare *vt* to drive out.

stan'care *vt* to tire, make tired; (*annoiare*) to bore; (*infastidire*) to annoy; ~**rsi** *vr* to get tired, tire o.s. out; ~**rsi (di)** to grow weary (of), grow tired (of).

stan'chezza [stan'kettsa] *sf* tiredness, fatigue.

'stanco, a, chi, che *ag* tired; **~ di** tired of, fed up with.

'stanga, ghe *sf* bar; (*di carro*) shaft.

stan'gata *sf* (*colpo: anche fig*) blow; (*cattivo risultato*) poor result; (*CALCIO*) shot.

sta'notte *av* tonight; (*notte passata*) last night.

'stante *prep*: **a sé ~** (*appartamento, casa*) independent, separate.

stan'tio, a, 'tii, 'tie *ag* stale; (*burro*) rancid; (*fig*) old.

stan'tuffo *sm* piston.

'stanza ['stantsa] *sf* room; (*POESIA*) stanza; **~ da letto** bedroom.

stanzi'are [stan'tsjare] *vt* to allocate.

stap'pare *vt* to uncork; to uncap.

'stare *vi* (*restare in un luogo*) to stay, remain; (*abitare*) to stay, live; (*essere situato*) to be, be situated; (*anche*: **~ in piedi**) to be, stand; (*essere, trovarsi*) to be; *(dipendere)*: **se stesse in me** if it were up to me, if it depended on me; *(seguito da gerundio)*: **sta studiando** he's studying; **starci** *(esserci spazio)*: **nel baule non ci sta più niente** there's no more room in the boot; *(accettare)* to accept; **ci stai?** is that okay with you?; ~ **a** *(attenersi a)* to follow, stick to; *(seguito dall'infinito)*: **stiamo a discutere** we're talking; *(toccare a)*: **sta a te giocare** it's your turn to play; ~ **per fare qc** to be about to do sth; **come sta?** how are you?; **io sto bene/male** I'm very well/not very well; ~ **a qn** *(abiti etc)* to fit sb; **queste scarpe mi stanno strette** these shoes are tight for me; **il rosso ti sta bene** red suits you.

starnu'tire *vi* to sneeze; **star'nuto** *sm* sneeze.

sta'sera *av* this evening, tonight.

sta'tale *ag* state *cpd*; government *cpd* ♦ *sm/f* state employee, local authority employee; *(nell'amministrazione)* ≈ civil servant.

sta'tista, i *sm* statesman.

sta'tistica *sf* statistics *sg*.

'stato, a *pp di* essere; **stare** ♦ *sm* *(condizione)* state, condition; *(POL)* state; *(DIR)* status; **essere in** ~ **d'accusa** *(DIR)* to be committed for trial; ~ **d'assedio/d'emergenza** state of siege/emergency; ~ **civile** *(AMM)* marital status; ~ **maggiore** *(MIL)* staff; **gli S~i Uniti (d'America)** the United States (of America).

'statua *sf* statue.

statuni'tense *ag* United States *cpd*, of the United States.

sta'tura *sf* *(ANAT)* height, stature; *(fig)* stature.

sta'tuto *sm* *(DIR)* statute; constitution.

sta'volta *av* this time.

stazio'nario, a [stattsjo'narjo] *ag* stationary; *(fig)* unchanged.

stazi'one [stat'tsjone] *sf* station; *(balneare, termale)* resort; ~ **degli autobus** bus station; ~ **balneare** seaside resort; ~ **ferroviaria** railway *(BRIT)* o railroad *(US)* station; ~ **invernale** winter sports resort; ~ **di polizia** police

station *(in small town)*; ~ **di servizio** service o petrol *(BRIT)* o filling station.

'stecca, che *sf* stick; *(di ombrello)* rib; *(di sigarette)* carton; *(MED)* splint; *(stonatura)*: **fare una** ~ to sing (o play) a wrong note.

stec'cato *sm* fence.

stec'chito, a [stek'kito] *ag* dried up; *(persona)* skinny; **lasciar** ~ **qn** *(fig)* to leave sb flabbergasted; **morto** ~ stone dead.

'stella *sf* star; ~ **alpina** *(BOT)* edelweiss; ~ **di mare** *(ZOOL)* starfish.

'stelo *sm* stem; *(asta)* rod; **lampada a** ~ standard lamp.

'stemma, i *sm* coat of arms.

stempe'rare *vt* to dilute; to dissolve; *(colori)* to mix.

sten'dardo *sm* standard.

'stendere *vt* *(braccia, gambe)* to stretch (out); *(tovaglia)* to spread (out); *(bucato)* to hang out; *(mettere a giacere)* to lay (down); *(spalmare: colore)* to spread; *(mettere per iscritto)* to draw up; ~**rsi** *vr* *(coricarsi)* to stretch out, lie down; *(estendersi)* to extend, stretch.

stenodatti'lografo, a *sm/f* shorthand typist *(BRIT)*, stenographer *(US)*.

stenogra'fare *vt* to take down in shorthand; **stenogra'fia** *sf* shorthand.

sten'tare *vi*: ~ **a fare** to find it hard to do, have difficulty doing.

'stento *sm* *(fatica)* difficulty; ~**i** *smpl* *(privazioni)* hardship *sg*, privation *sg*; **a** ~ with difficulty, barely.

'sterco *sm* dung.

'stereo('fonico, a, ci, che) *ag* stereo(phonic).

'sterile *ag* sterile; *(terra)* barren; *(fig)* futile, fruitless; **sterilità** *sf* sterility.

sterili'zzare [sterilid'dzare] *vt* to sterilize; **sterilizzazi'one** *sf* sterilization.

ster'lina *sf* pound (sterling).

stermi'nare *vt* to exterminate, wipe out.

stermi'nato, a *ag* immense; endless.

ster'minio *sm* extermination, destruction.

'sterno *sm* *(ANAT)* breastbone.

ster'zare [ster'tsare] *vt, vi* (*AUT*) to steer; **'sterzo** *sm* steering; (*volante*) steering wheel.

'steso, a *pp di* **stendere**.

'stesso, a *ag* same; (*rafforzativo: in persona, proprio*): **il re** ~ the king himself *o* in person ♦ *pron*: **lo(la)** ~(**a**) the same (one); **i suoi** ~**i avversari lo ammirano** even his enemies admire him; **fa lo** ~ it doesn't matter; **per me è lo** ~ it's all the same to me, it doesn't matter to me; *vedi* **io**; **tu** *etc*.

ste'sura *sf* drafting *no pl*, drawing up *no pl*; draft.

'stigma, i *sm* stigma.

'stigmate *sfpl* (*REL*) stigmata.

sti'lare *vt* to draw up, draft.

'stile *sm* style; **sti'lista, i** *sm* designer.

stil'lare *vi* (*trasudare*) to ooze; (*gocciolare*) to drip; **stilli'cidio** *sm* (*fig*) continual pestering (*o* moaning *etc*).

stilo'grafica, che *sf* (*anche: penna* ~) fountain pen.

'stima *sf* esteem; valuation; assessment, estimate.

sti'mare *vt* (*persona*) to esteem, hold in high regard; (*terreno, 'casa etc*) to value; (*stabilire in misura approssimativa*) to estimate, assess; (*ritenere*): ~ **che** to consider that; ~**rsi fortunato** to consider o.s. (to be) lucky.

stimo'lare *vt* to stimulate; (*incitare*): ~ **qn** (**a fare**) to spur sb on (to do).

'stimolo *sm* (*anche fig*) stimulus.

'stinco, chi *sm* shin; shinbone.

'stingere ['stindʒere] *vt, vi* (*anche:* ~**rsi**) to fade; **'stinto, a** *pp di* **stingere**.

sti'pare *vt* to cram, pack; ~**rsi** *vr* (*accalcarsi*) to crowd, throng.

sti'pendio *sm* salary.

'stipite *sm* (*di porta, finestra*) jamb.

stipu'lare *vt* (*redigere*) to draw up.

sti'rare *vt* (*abito*) to iron; (*distendere*) to stretch; (*strappare: muscolo*) to strain; ~**rsi** *vr* to stretch (o.s.); **stira'tura** *sf* ironing.

'stirpe *sf* birth, stock; descendants *pl*.

stiti'chezza [stiti'kettsa] *sf* constipation.

'stitico, a, ci, che *ag* constipated.

'stiva *sf* (*di nave*) hold.

sti'vale *sm* boot.

'stizza ['stittsa] *sf* anger, vexation; **stiz'zirsi** *vr* to lose one's temper; **stiz'zoso, a** *ag* (*persona*) quick-tempered, irascible; (*risposta*) angry.

stocca'fisso *sm* stockfish, dried cod.

stoc'cata *sf* (*colpo*) stab, thrust; (*fig*) gibe, cutting remark.

'stoffa *sf* material, fabric; (*fig*): **aver la** ~ **di** to have the makings of.

'stola *sf* stole.

'stolto, a *ag* stupid, foolish.

'stomaco, chi *sm* stomach; **dare di** ~ to vomit, be sick.

sto'nare *vt* to sing (*o* play) out of tune ♦ *vi* to be out of tune, sing (*o* play) out of tune; (*fig*) to be out of place, jar; (*: colori*) to clash; **stona'tura** *sf* (*suono*) false note.

stop *sm inv* (*TEL*) stop; (*AUT: cartello*) stop sign; (*: fanalino d'arresto*) brake-light.

'stoppa *sf* tow.

'stoppia *sf* (*AGR*) stubble.

stop'pino *sm* wick; (*miccia*) fuse.

'storcere ['stortʃere] *vt* to twist; ~**rsi** *vr* to writhe, twist; ~ **il naso** (*fig*) to turn up one's nose; ~**rsi la caviglia** to twist one's ankle.

stor'dire *vt* (*intontire*) to stun, daze; ~**rsi** *vr*: ~**rsi col bere** to dull one's senses with drink; **stor'dito, a** *ag* stunned; (*sventato*) scatterbrained, heedless.

'storia *sf* (*scienza, avvenimenti*) history; (*racconto, bugia*) story; (*faccenda, questione*) business *no pl*; (*pretesto*) excuse, pretext; ~**e** *sfpl* (*smancerie*) fuss *sg*; **'storico, a, ci, che** *ag* historic(al) ♦ *sm* historian.

stori'one *sm* (*ZOOL*) sturgeon.

stor'mire *vi* to rustle.

'stormo *sm* (*di uccelli*) flock.

stor'nare *vt* (*COMM*) to transfer.

'storno *sm* starling.

storpi'are *vt* to cripple, maim; (*fig: parole*) to mangle; (*: significato*) to twist.

'storpio, a *ag* crippled, maimed.

'storta *sf* (*distorsione*) sprain, twist;

(*recipiente*) retort.

'**storto, a** *pp di* **storcere** ♦ *ag* (*chiodo*) twisted, bent; (*gamba, quadro*) crooked; (*fig: ragionamento*) false, wrong.

sto'viglie [sto'viʎʎe] *sfpl* dishes *pl*, crockery.

'strabico, a, ci, che *ag* squint-eyed; (*occhi*) squint.

stra'bismo *sm* squinting.

stra'carico, a, chi, che *ag* overloaded.

stracci'are [strat'tʃare] *vt* to tear.

'**straccio, a, ci, ce** ['strattʃo] *ag*: **carta ∼** waste paper ♦ *sm* rag; (*per pulire*) cloth, duster; **stracci'vendolo** *sm* ragman.

stra'cotto, a *ag* overcooked ♦ *sm* (*CUC*) beef stew.

'**strada** *sf* road; (*di città*) street; (*cammino, via, fig*) way; **farsi ∼** (*fig*) to do well for o.s.; **essere fuori ∼** (*fig*) to be on the wrong track; **∼ facendo** on the way; **∼ senza uscita** dead end; **stra'dale** *ag* road *cpd*.

strafalcio'ne [strafal'tʃone] *sm* blunder, howler.

stra'fare *vi* to overdo it; **stra'fatto, a** *pp di* **strafare**.

strafot'tente *ag*: **è ∼** he doesn't give a damn, he couldn't care less.

'**strage** ['stradʒe] *sf* massacre, slaughter.

stralu'nato, a *ag* (*occhi*) rolling; (*persona*) beside o.s., very upset.

stramaz'zare [stramat'tsare] *vi* to fall heavily.

'**strambo, a** *ag* strange, queer.

strampa'lato, a *ag* odd, eccentric.

stra'nezza [stra'nettsa] *sf* strangeness.

strango'lare *vt* to strangle; **∼rsi** *vr* to choke.

strani'ero, a *ag* foreign ♦ *sm/f* foreigner.

'**strano, a** *ag* strange, odd.

straordi'nario, a *ag* extraordinary; (*treno etc*) special ♦ *sm* (*lavoro*) overtime.

strapaz'zare [strapat'tsare] *vt* to illtreat; **∼rsi** *vr* to tire o.s. out, overdo things; **stra'pazzo** *sm* strain, fatigue;

da **strapazzo** (*fig*) third-rate.

strapi'ombo *sm* overhanging rock; **a ∼** overhanging.

strapo'tere *sm* excessive power.

strap'pare *vt* (*gen*) to tear, rip; (*pagina etc*) to tear off, tear out; (*sradicare*) to pull up; (*togliere*): **∼ qc a qn** to snatch sth from sb; (*fig*) to wrest sth from sb; **∼rsi** *vr* (*lacerarsi*) to rip, tear; (*rompersi*) to break; **∼rsi un muscolo** to tear a muscle; **strappo** *sm* pull, tug; tear, rip; **fare uno strappo alla regola** to make an exception to the rule; **strappo muscolare** torn muscle.

strapun'tino *sm* jump *o* foldaway seat.

strari'pare *vi* to overflow.

strasci'care [straʃʃi'kare] *vt* to trail; (*piedi*) to drag; **∼ le parole** to drawl.

'**strascico, chi** ['straʃʃiko] *sm* (*di abito*) train; (*conseguenza*) after-effect.

strata'gemma, i [strata'dʒemma] *sm* stratagem.

strate'gia, 'gie [strate'dʒia] *sf* strategy; **stra'tegico, a, ci, che** *ag* strategic.

'**strato** *sm* layer; (*rivestimento*) coat, coating; (*GEO, fig*) stratum; (*METEOR*) stratus.

stratos'fera *sf* stratosphere.

strava'gante *ag* odd, eccentric; **strava'ganza** *sf* eccentricity.

stra'vecchio, a [stra'vekkjo] *ag* very old.

stra'vizio [stra'vittsjo] *sm* excess.

stra'volgere [stra'vɔldʒere] *vt* (*volto*) to contort; (*fig: animo*) to trouble deeply; (: *verità*) to twist, distort; **stra'volto, a** *pp di* **stravolgere**.

strazi'are [strat'tsjare] *vt* to torture, torment; **'strazio** *sm* torture; (*fig: cosa fatta male*): **essere uno ∼** to be appalling.

'**strega, ghe** *sf* witch.

stre'gare *vt* to bewitch.

stre'gone *sm* (*mago*) wizard; (*di tribù*) witch doctor.

'**stregua** *sf*: **alla ∼ di** by the same standard as.

stre'mare *vt* to exhaust.

'**stremo** *sm* very end; **essere allo ∼** to be at the end of one's tether.

'**strenna** *sf* Christmas present.

'**strenuo, a** *ag* brave, courageous.

strepi'toso, a *ag* clamorous, deafening; (*fig: successo*) resounding.

stres'sante *ag* stressful.

'**stretta** *sf* (*di mano*) grasp; (*finanziaria*) squeeze; (*fig: dolore, turbamento*) pang; **una ~a di mano** a handshake; **essere alle ~e** to have one's back to the wall; *vedi anche* **stretto**.

stretta'mente *av* tightly; (*rigorosamente*) strictly.

stret'tezza [stret'tettsa] *sf* narrowness; ~e *sfpl* (*povertà*) poverty *sg*, straitened circumstances.

'**stretto, a** *pp di* **stringere** ♦ *ag* (*corridoio, limiti*) narrow; (*gonna, scarpe, nodo, curva*) tight; (*intimo: parente, amico*) close; (*rigoroso: osservanza*) strict; (*preciso: significato*) precise, exact ♦ *sm* (*braccio di mare*) strait; **a denti ~i** with clenched teeth; **lo ~ necessario** the bare minimum; **stret'toia** *sf* bottleneck; (*fig*) tricky situation.

stri'ato, a *ag* streaked.

'**stridere** *vi* (*porta*) to squeak; (*animale*) to screech, shriek; (*colori*) to clash; '**strido** (*pl*(*f*) **strida**) *sm* screech, shriek; **stri'dore** *sm* screeching, shrieking; '**stridulo, a** *ag* shrill.

stril'lare *vt, vi* to scream, shriek; '**strillo** *sm* scream, shriek.

stril'lone *sm* newspaper seller.

strimin'zito, a [strimin'tsito] *ag* (*misero*) shabby; (*molto magro*) skinny.

strimpel'lare *vt* (*MUS*) to strum.

'**stringa, ghe** *sf* lace.

strin'gato, a *ag* (*fig*) concise.

'**stringere** ['strind ʒere] *vt* (*avvicinare due cose*) to press (together), squeeze (together); (*tenere stretto*) to hold tight, clasp, clutch; (*pugno, mascella, denti*) to clench; (*labbra*) to compress; (*avvitare*) to tighten; (*abito*) to take in; (*sog: scarpe*) to pinch, be tight for; (*fig: concludere: patto*) to make; (: *accelerare: passo, tempo*) to quicken ♦ *vi* (*essere stretto*) to be tight; (*tempo: incalzare*) to be pressing; ~**rsi** *vr*

(*accostarsi*): ~**rsi a** to press o.s. up against; ~ **la mano a qn** to shake sb's hand; ~ **gli occhi** to screw up one's eyes.

'**striscia, sce** ['striʃʃa] *sf* (*di carta, tessuto etc*) strip; (*riga*) stripe; ~**sce** (**pedonali**) zebra crossing *sg*.

strisci'are [striʃ'ʃare] *vt* (*piedi*) to drag; (*muro, macchina*) to graze ♦ *vi* to crawl, creep.

'**striscio** ['striʃʃo] *sm* graze; (*MED*) smear; **colpire di** ~ to graze.

strito'lare *vt* to grind.

striz'zare [strit'tsare] *vt* (*arancia*) to squeeze; (*panni*) to wring (out); ~ **l'occhio a** to wink.

'**strofa** *sf* = **strofe**.

'**strofe** *sf inv* strophe.

strofi'naccio [strofi'nattʃo] *sm* duster, cloth; (*per piatti*) dishcloth; (*per pavimenti*) floorcloth.

strofi'nare *vt* to rub.

stron'care *vt* to break off; (*fig: ribellione*) to suppress, put down; (: *film, libro*) to tear to pieces.

stropicci'are [stropit'tʃare] *vt* to rub.

stroz'zare [strot'tsare] *vt* (*soffocare*) to choke, strangle; ~**rsi** *vr* to choke; **strozza'tura** *sf* (*restringimento*) narrowing; (*di strada etc*) bottleneck.

'**struggere** ['struddʒere] *vt* (*fig*) to consume; ~**rsi** *vr* (*fig*): ~**rsi di** to be consumed with.

strumen'tale *ag* (*MUS*) instrumental.

strumentaliz'zare [strumentalid'dzare] *vt* to exploit, use to one's own ends.

stru'mento *sm* (*arnese, fig*) instrument, tool; (*MUS*) instrument; ~ **a corda** *o* **ad arco/a fiato** stringed/wind instrument.

'**strutto** *sm* lard.

strut'tura *sf* structure; **struttu'rare** *vt* to structure.

'**struzzo** ['struttso] *sm* ostrich.

stuc'care *vt* (*muro*) to plaster; (*vetro*) to putty; (*decorare con stucchi*) to stucco.

stuc'chevole [stuk'kevole] *ag* nauseating; (*fig*) tedious, boring.

'**stucco, chi** *sm* plaster; (*da vetri*)

putty; (*ornamentale*) stucco; **rimanere di ~** (*fig*) to be dumbfounded.

stu'dente, **'essa** *sm/f* student; (*scolaro*) pupil, schoolboy/girl; **studen'tesco, a, schi, sche** *ag* student *cpd*; school *cpd*.

studi'are *vt* to study.

'studio *sm* studying; (*ricerca, saggio, stanza*) study; (*di professionista*) office; (*di artista, CINEMA, TV, RADIO*) studio; **~i** *smpl* (*INS*) studies; **~ medico** doctor's surgery (*BRIT*) o office (*US*).

studi'oso, a *ag* studious, hard-working ♦ *sm/f* scholar.

'stufa *sf* stove; **~ elettrica** electric fire o heater.

stu'fare *vt* (*CUC*) to stew; (*fig: fam*) to bore; **stu'fato** *sm* (*CUC*) stew; **'stufo, a** (*fam*) *ag*: **essere stufo di** to be fed up with, be sick and tired of.

stu'oia *sf* mat.

stupefa'cente [stupefa'tʃɛnte] *ag* stunning, astounding ♦ *sm* drug, narcotic.

stu'pendo, a *ag* marvellous, wonderful.

stupi'daggine [stupi'daddʒine] *sf* stupid thing (to do o say).

stupidità *sf* stupidity.

'stupido, a *ag* stupid.

stu'pire *vt* to amaze, stun ♦ *vi* (*anche: ~rsi*): **~ (di)** to be amazed (at), be stunned (by).

stu'pore *sm* amazement, astonishment.

'stupro *sm* rape.

stu'rare *vt* (*lavandino*) to clear.

stuzzica'denti [stuttsika'dɛnti] *sm* toothpick.

stuzzi'care [stuttsi'kare] *vt* (*ferita etc*) to poke (at), prod (at); (*fig*) to tease; (: *appetito*) to whet; (: *curiosità*) to stimulate; **~ i denti** to pick one's teeth.

su (*su +il* = **sul**, *su +lo* = **sullo**, *su +l'* = **sull'**, *su +la* = **sulla**, *su +i* = **sui**, *su +gli* = **sugli**, *su +le* = **sulle**) *prep* **1** (*gen*) on; (*moto*) on(to); (*in cima a*) on (top of); **mettilo sul tavolo** put it on the table; **un paesino sul mare** a village by the sea

2 (*argomento*) about, on; **un libro ~ Cesare** a book on o about Caesar

3 (*circa*) about; **costerà sui 3 milioni** it will cost about 3 million; **una ragazza sui 17 anni** a girl of about 17 (years of age)

4: **~ misura** made to measure; **~ richiesta** on request; **3 casi ~ dieci** 3 cases out of 10

♦ *av* **1** (*in alto, verso l'alto*) up; **vieni ~** come on up; **guarda ~** look up; **~ le mani!** hands up!; **in ~** (*verso l'alto*) up(wards); (*in poi*) onwards; **dai 20 anni in ~** from the age of 20 onwards

2 (*addosso*) on; **cos'hai ~?** what have you got on?

♦ *escl* come on!; **~ coraggio!** come on, cheer up!

'sua *vedi* **suo.**

su'bacqueo, a *ag* underwater ♦ *sm* skindiver.

sub'buglio [sub'buʎʎo] *sm* confusion, turmoil.

subcosci'ente [subkoʃ'ʃɛnte] *ag, sm* subconscious.

'subdolo, a *ag* underhand, sneaky.

suben'trare *vi*: **~ a qn in qc** to take over sth from sb.

su'bire *vt* to suffer, endure.

subis'sare *vt* (*fig*): **~ di** to overwhelm with, load with.

subi'taneo, a *ag* sudden.

'subito *av* immediately, at once, straight away.

subodo'rare *vt* (*insidia etc*) to smell, suspect.

subordi'nato, a *ag* subordinate; (*dipendente*): **~ a** dependent on, subject to.

subur'bano, a *ag* suburban.

succe'daneo [suttʃe'daneo] *sm* substitute.

suc'cedere [sut'tʃɛdere] *vi* (*prendere il posto di qn*): **~ a** to succeed; (*venire dopo*): **~ a** to follow; (*accadere*) to happen; **~rsi** *vr* to follow each other; **~ al trono** to succeed to the throne; **successi'one** *sf* succession; **succes'sivo, a** *ag* successive; **suc'cesso, a** *pp di*

succedere ♦ *sm* (*esito*) outcome; (*buona riuscita*) success; **di successo** (*libro, personaggio*) successful.

succhi'are [suk'kjare] *vt* to suck (up).

suc'cinto, a [sut'tʃinto] *ag* (*discorso*) succinct; (*abito*) brief.

'succo, chi *sm* juice; (*fig*) essence, gist; **~ di frutta** fruit juice; **suc'coso, a** *ag* juicy; (*fig*) pithy.

succur'sale *sf* branch (office).

sud *sm* south ♦ *ag inv* south; (*lato*) south, southern.

Su'dafrica *sm*: **il ~** South Africa; **sudafri'cano, a** *ag, sm/f* South African.

Suda'merica *sm*: **il ~** South America; **sudameri'cano, a** *ag, sm/f* South American.

su'dare *vi* to perspire, sweat; **~ freddo** to come out in a cold sweat; **su'data** *sf* sweat; **ho fatto una bella sudata per finirlo in tempo** it was a real sweat to get it finished in time.

sud'detto, a *ag* above-mentioned.

sud'dito, a *sm/f* subject.

suddi'videre *vt* to subdivide.

su'dest *sm* south-east.

'sudicio, a, ci, ce ['suditʃo] *ag* dirty, filthy; **sudici'ume** *sm* dirt, filth.

su'dore *sm* perspiration, sweat.

su'dovest *sm* south-west.

'sue *vedi* suo.

suffici'ente [suffi'tʃɛnte] *ag* enough, sufficient; (*borioso*) self-important; (*INS*) satisfactory; **suffici'enza** *sf* self-importance; pass mark; **a sufficienza** enough; **ne ho avuto a sufficienza!** I've had enough of this!

suf'fisso *sm* (*LING*) suffix.

suf'fragio [suf'fradʒo] *sm* (*voto*) vote; **~ universale** universal suffrage.

suggel'lare [suddʒel'lare] *vt* (*fig*) to seal.

suggeri'mento [suddʒeri'mento] *sm* suggestion; (*consiglio*) piece of advice, advice *no pl*.

sugge'rire [suddʒe'rire] *vt* (*risposta*) to tell; (*consigliare*) to advise; (*proporre*) to suggest; (*TEATRO*) to prompt; **suggeri'tore, 'trice** *sm/f* (*TEATRO*) prompter.

suggestio'nare [suddʒestjo'nare] *vt* to influence.

suggesti'one [suddʒes'tjone] *sf* (*PSIC*) suggestion; (*istigazione*) instigation.

sugges'tivo, a [suddʒes'tivo] *ag* (*paesaggio*) evocative; (*teoria*) interesting, attractive.

'sughero ['sugero] *sm* cork.

'sugli ['suʎʎi] *prep + det vedi* su.

'sugo, ghi *sm* (*succo*) juice; (*di carne*) gravy; (*condimento*) sauce; (*fig*) gist, essence.

'sui *prep + det vedi* su.

sui'cida, i, e [sui'tʃida] *ag* suicidal ♦ *sm/f* suicide.

suici'darsi [suitʃi'darsi] *vr* to commit suicide.

sui'cidio [sui'tʃidjo] *sm* suicide.

su'ino, a *ag*: **carne ~a** pork ♦ *sm* pig; **~i** *smpl* swine *pl*.

sul *prep + det vedi* su.

sull' *prep + det vedi* su.

'sulla *prep + det vedi* su.

'sulle *prep + det vedi* su.

'sullo *prep + det vedi* su.

sulta'nina *ag f*: (*uva*) **~** sultana.

sul'tano, a *sm/f* sultan/sultana.

'sunto *sm* summary.

'suo (*f* **'sua**, *pl* **'sue, su'oi**) *det*: **il ~, la sua** *etc* (*di lui*) his; (*di lei*) her; (*di esso*) its; (*con valore indefinito*) one's, his/her; (*forma di cortesia: anche: S~*) your ♦ *pron*: **il ~, la sua** *etc* his; hers; yours; **i suoi** (*parenti*) his (*o her o* one's *o* your) family.

su'ocero, a ['swɔtʃero] *sm/f* father/mother-in-law; **i ~i** *smpl* father-and mother-in-law.

su'oi *vedi* suo.

su'ola *sf* (*di scarpa*) sole.

su'olo *sm* (*terreno*) ground; (*terra*) soil.

suo'nare *vt* (*MUS*) to play; (*campana*) to ring; (*ore*) to strike; (*clacson, allarme*) to sound ♦ *vi* to play; (*telefono, campana*) to ring; (*ore*) to strike; (*clacson, fig: parole*) to sound.

su'ono *sm* sound.

su'ora *sf* (*REL*) sister.

'super *sf* (*anche: benzina ~*) ≈ four-star (petrol) (*BRIT*), premium (*US*).

supe'rare *vt* (*oltrepassare: limite*) to exceed, surpass; (*percorrere*) to cover; (*attraversare: fiume*) to cross; (*sorpassare: veicolo*) to overtake; (*fig: essere più bravo di*) to surpass, outdo; (*: difficoltà*) to overcome; (*: esame*) to get through; ~ **qn in altezza/peso** to be taller/heavier than sb; **ha superato la cinquantina** he's over fifty (years of age).

su'perbia *sf* pride.

su'perbo, a *ag* proud; (*fig*) magnificent, superb.

superfici'ale [superfi'tʃale] *ag* superficial.

super'ficie, ci [super'fitʃe] *sf* surface.

su'perfluo, a *ag* superfluous.

superi'ore *ag* (*piano, arto, classi*) upper; (*più elevato: temperatura, livello*): ~ **(a)** higher (than); (*migliore*): ~ **(a)** superior (to); ~, **a** *sm/f* (*anche REL*) superior ♦ *sf* superiority.

superla'tivo, a *ag, sm* superlative.

supermer'cato *sm* supermarket.

su'perstite *ag* surviving ♦ *sm/f* survivor.

superstizi'one [superstit'tsjone] *sf* superstition; **superstizi'oso, a** *ag* superstitious.

su'pino, a *ag* supine.

suppel'lettile *sf* furnishings *pl*.

suppergiù [supper'dʒu] *av* more or less, roughly.

supplemen'tare *ag* extra; (*treno*) relief *cpd*; (*entrate*) additional.

supple'mento *sm* supplement.

sup'plente *ag* temporary; (*insegnante*) supply *cpd* (*BRIT*), substitute *cpd* (*US*) ♦ *sm/f* temporary member of staff; supply (*o* substitute) teacher.

'supplica, che *sf* (*preghiera*) plea; (*domanda scritta*) petition, request.

suppli'care *vt* to implore, beseech.

sup'plire *vi*: ~ **a** to make up for, compensate for.

sup'plizio [sup'plittsjo] *sm* torture.

sup'porre *vt* to suppose.

sup'porto *sm* (*sostegno*) support.

sup'posta *sf* (*MED*) suppository.

sup'posto, a *pp di* **supporre**.

su'premo, a *ag* supreme.

surge'lare [surdʒe'lare] *vt* to (deep-)freeze; **surge'lati** *smpl* frozen food *sg*.

sur'plus *sm inv* (*ECON*) surplus.

surriscal'dare *vt* to overheat.

surro'gato *sm* substitute.

suscet'tibile [suʃʃet'tibile] *ag* (*sensibile*) touchy, sensitive; (*soggetto*): ~ **di miglioramento** that can be improved, open to improvement.

susci'tare [suʃʃi'tare] *vt* to provoke, arouse.

su'sina *sf* plum; **su'sino** *sm* plum (tree).

sussegu'ire *vt* to follow; ~**rsi** *vr* to follow one another.

sussidi'ario, a *ag* subsidiary; auxiliary.

sus'sidio *sm* subsidy.

sussis'tenza [sussis'tɛntsa] *sf* subsistence.

sus'sistere *vi* to exist; (*essere fondato*) to be valid *o* sound.

sussul'tare *vi* to shudder.

sussur'rare *vt, vi* to whisper, murmur; **sus'surro** *sm* whisper, murmur.

sutu'rare *vt* (*MED*) to stitch up, suture.

sva'gare *vt* (*distrarre*) to distract; (*divertire*) to amuse; ~**rsi** *vr* to amuse o.s.; to enjoy o.s.

'svago, ghi *sm* (*riposo*) relaxation; (*ricreazione*) amusement; (*passatempo*) pastime.

svaligi'are [zvali'dʒare] *vt* to rob, burgle (*BRIT*), burglarize (*US*).

svalu'tare *vt* (*ECON*) to devalue; (*fig*) to belittle; ~**rsi** *vr* (*ECON*) to be devalued; **svalutazi'one** *sf* devaluation.

sva'nire *vi* to disappear, vanish.

svan'taggio [zvan'taddʒo] *sm* disadvantage; (*inconveniente*) drawback, disadvantage.

svapo'rare *vi* to evaporate.

svari'ato, a *ag* varied; various.

'svastica *sf* swastika.

sve'dese *ag* Swedish ♦ *sm/f* Swede ♦ *sm* (*LING*) Swedish.

'sveglia ['zveʎʎa] *sf* waking up; (*oro-*

logio) alarm (clock); **suonare la ~** (*MIL*) to sound the reveille.

svegli'are [zveʎ'ʎare] *vt* to wake up; (*fig*) to awaken, arouse; **~rsi** *vr* to wake up; (*fig*) to be revived, reawaken.

'sveglio, a ['zveʎʎo] *ag* awake; (*fig*) quick-witted.

sve'lare *vt* to reveal.

'svelto, a *ag* (*passo*) quick; (*mente*) quick, alert; (*linea*) slim, slender; **alla ~a** quickly.

'svendita *sf* (*COMM*) (clearance) sale.

sveni'mento *sm* fainting fit, faint.

sve'nire *vi* to faint.

sven'tare *vt* to foil, thwart.

sven'tato, a *ag* (*distratto*) scatterbrained; (*imprudente*) rash.

svento'lare *vt, vi* to wave, flutter.

sven'trare *vt* to disembowel.

sven'tura *sf* misfortune; **sventu'rato, a** *ag* unlucky, unfortunate.

sve'nuto, a *pp di* svenire.

svergo'gnato, a [zvergoɲ'ɲato] *ag* shameless.

sver'nare *vi* to spend the winter.

sves'tire *vt* to undress; **~rsi** *vr* to get undressed.

'Svezia ['zvɛttsja] *sf*: **la ~** Sweden.

svez'zare [zvet'tsare] *vt* to wean.

svi'are *vt* to divert; (*fig*) to lead astray; **~rsi** *vr* to go astray.

svi'gnarsela [zviɲ'narsela] *vr* to slip away, sneak off.

svilup'pare *vt* to develop; **~rsi** *vr* to develop.

svi'luppo *sm* development.

'svincolo *sm* (*COMM*) clearance; (*stradale*) motorway (*BRIT*) *o* expressway (*US*) intersection.

svisce'rare [zviʃʃe'rare] *vt* (*fig: argomento*) to examine in depth; **svisce'rato, a** *ag* (*amore*) passionate; (*lodi*) obsequious.

'svista *sf* oversight.

svi'tare *vt* to unscrew.

'Svizzera ['zvittsera] *sf*: **la ~** Switzerland.

'svizzero, a ['zvittsero] *ag, sm/f* Swiss.

svogli'ato, a [zvoʎ'ʎato] *ag* listless; (*pigro*) lazy.

svolaz'zare [zvolat'tsare] *vi* to flutter.

'svolgere ['zvɔldʒere] *vt* to unwind; (*srotolare*) to unroll; (*fig: argomento*) to develop; (*: piano, programma*) to carry out; **~rsi** *vr* to unwind; to unroll; (*fig: aver luogo*) to take place; (*: procedere*) to go on; **svolgi'mento** *sm* development; carrying out; (*andamento*) course.

'svolta *sf* (*atto*) turning *no pl*; (*curva*) turn, bend; (*fig*) turning-point.

svol'tare *vi* to turn.

'svolto, a *pp di* svolgere.

svuo'tare *vt* to empty (out).

T

tabac'caio, a *sm/f* tobacconist.

tabacche'ria [tabakke'ria] *sf* tobacconist's (shop).

ta'bacco, chi *sm* tobacco.

ta'bella *sf* (*tavola*) table; (*elenco*) list.

taber'nacolo *sm* tabernacle.

tabu'lato *sm* (*INFORM*) printout.

'tacca, che *sf* notch, nick; **di mezza ~** (*fig*) mediocre.

tac'cagno, a [tak'kaɲɲo] *ag* mean, stingy.

tac'cheggio [tak'keddʒo] *sm* shoplifting.

tac'chino [tak'kino] *sm* turkey.

tacci'are [tat'tʃare] *vt*: **~ qn di** to accuse sb of.

'tacco, chi *sm* heel.

taccu'ino *sm* notebook.

ta'cere [ta'tʃere] *vi* to be silent *o* quiet; (*smettere di parlare*) to fall silent ♦ *vt* to keep to oneself, say nothing about; **far ~ qn** to make sb be quiet; (*fig*) to silence sb.

ta'chimetro [ta'kimetro] *sm* speedometer.

'tacito, a ['tatʃito] *ag* silent; (*sottinteso*) tacit, unspoken.

ta'fano *sm* horsefly.

taffe'ruglio [taffe'ruʎʎo] *sm* brawl, scuffle.

taffettà *sm* taffeta.

'taglia ['taʎʎa] *sf* (*statura*) height; (*misura*) size; (*riscatto*) ransom;

(*ricompensa*) reward.
taglia'carte [taʎʎa'karte] *sm inv* paper-knife.
tagli'ando [taʎ'ʎando] *sm* coupon.
tagli'are [taʎ'ʎare] *vt* to cut; (*recidere, interrompere*) to cut off; (*intersecare*) to cut across, intersect; (*carne*) to carve; (*vini*) to blend ♦ *vi* to cut; (*prendere una scorciatoia*) to take a short-cut; ~ **corto** (*fig*) to cut short.
taglia'telle [taʎʎa'tɛlle] *sfpl* tagliatelle *pl*.
tagli'ente [taʎ'ʎɛnte] *ag* sharp.
'taglio ['taʎʎo] *sm* cutting *no pl*; cut; (*parte tagliente*) cutting edge; (*di abito*) cut, style; (*di stoffa: lunghezza*) length; (*di vini*) blending; **di** ~ on edge, edgeways; **banconote di piccolo/grosso** ~ notes of small/large denomination.
tagli'ola [taʎ'ʎola] *sf* trap, snare.
tagliuz'zare [taʎʎut'tsare] *vt* to cut into small pieces.
'talco *sm* talcum powder.

'tale *det* **1** (*simile, così grande*) such; **un(a)** ~ ... such (a) ...; **non accetto** ~**i discorsi** I won't allow such talk; **è di una** ~ **arroganza** he is so arrogant; **fa una** ~ **confusione!** he makes such a mess!
2 (*persona o cosa indeterminata*) such-and-such; **il giorno** ~ **all'ora** ~ on such-and-such a day at such-and-such a time; **la tal persona** that person; **ha telefonato una** ~ **Giovanna** somebody called Giovanna phoned
3 (*nelle similitudini*): ~ ... ~ like ... like; ~ **padre** ~ **figlio** like father, like son; **hai il vestito** ~ **quale il mio** your dress is just *o* exactly like mine
♦ *pron* (*indefinito: persona*): **un(a)** ~ someone; **quel** (*o* **quella**) ~ that person, that man (*o* woman); **il tal dei** ~**i** what's-his-name.

ta'lento *sm* talent.
talis'mano *sm* talisman.
tallon'cino [tallon'tʃino] *sm* counterfoil.

tal'lone *sm* heel.
tal'mente *av* so.
ta'lora *av* = talvolta.
'talpa *sf* (*ZOOL*) mole.
tal'volta *av* sometimes, at times.
tambu'rello *sm* tambourine.
tam'buro *sm* drum.
Ta'migi [ta'midʒi] *sm*: **il** ~ the Thames.
tampo'nare *vt* (*otturare*) to plug; (*urtare: macchina*) to crash *o* ram into.
tam'pone *sm* (*MED*) wad, pad; (*per timbri*) ink-pad; (*respingente*) buffer; ~ **assorbente** tampon.
'tana *sf* lair, den.
'tanfo *sm* stench; musty smell.
tan'gente [tan'dʒɛnte] *ag* (*MAT*): ~ **a** tangential to ♦ *sf* tangent; (*quota*) share.
tan'tino: **un** ~ *av* a little, a bit.

'tanto, a *det* **1** (*molto: quantità*) a lot of, much; (: *numero*) a lot of, many; (*così* ~: *quantità*) so much, such a lot of; (: *numero*) so many, such a lot of; ~**e volte** so many times, so often; ~**i auguri!** all the best!; ~**e grazie** many thanks; ~ **tempo** so long, such a long time; **ogni** ~**i chilometri** every so many kilometres
2: ~ ... **quanto** (*quantità*) as much ... as; (*numero*) as many ... as; **ho** ~**a pazienza quanta ne hai tu** I have as much patience as you have *o* as you; **ha** ~**i amici quanti nemici** he has as many friends as he has enemies
3 (*rafforzativo*) such; **ho aspettato per** ~ **tempo** I waited so long *o* for such a long time
♦ *pron* **1** (*molto*) much, a lot; (*così* ~) so much, such a lot; ~**i, e** many, a lot; so many, such a lot; **credevo ce ne fosse** ~ I thought there was (such) a lot, I thought there was plenty
2: ~ **quanto** (*denaro*) as much as; (*cioccolatini*) as many as; **ne ho** ~ **quanto basta** I have as much as I need; **due volte** ~ twice as much
3 (*indeterminato*) so much; ~ **per l'affitto**, ~ **per il gas** so much for the

rent, so much for the gas; **costa un ~ al metro** it costs so much per metre; **di ~ in ~, ogni ~** every so often; **~ vale che ... I** (o we etc) may as well ...; **~ meglio!** so much the better!; **~ peggio per lui!** so much the worse for him!

♦ *av* **1** (molto) very; **vengo ~ volentieri** I'd be very glad to come; **non ci vuole ~ a capirlo** it doesn't take much to understand it

2 (così ~: con ag, av) so; (: con vb) so much, such a lot; **è ~ bella!** she's so beautiful!; **non urlare ~** don't shout so much; **sto ~ meglio adesso** I'm so much better now; **~ ... che** so ... (that); **~ ... da** so ... as

3: **~ ... quanto** as ... as; **conosco ~ Carlo quanto suo padre** I know both Carlo and his father; **non è poi ~ complicato quanto sembri** it's not as difficult as it seems; **~ più insisti, ~ più non mollerà** the more you insist, the more stubborn he'll be; **quanto più ... ~ meno** the more ... the less

4 (solamente) just; **~ per cambiare/ scherzare** just for a change/a joke; **una volta ~** for once

5 (a lungo) (for) long

♦ *cong* after all.

'**tappa** sf (luogo di sosta, fermata) stop, halt; (parte di un percorso) stage, leg; (SPORT) lap; **a ~e** in stages.

tap'pare vt to plug, stop up; (bottiglia) to cork.

tap'peto sm carpet; (anche: tappetino) rug; (di tavolo) cloth; (SPORT): **andare al ~** to go down for the count; **mettere sul ~** (fig) to bring up for discussion.

tappez'zare [tappet'tsare] vt (con carta) to paper; (rivestire): **~ qc (di)** to cover sth (with); **tappezze'ria** sf (tessuto) tapestry; (carta da parato) wallpaper; (arte) upholstery; **far da tappezzeria** (fig) to be a wallflower; **tappezzi'ere** sm upholsterer.

'**tappo** sm stopper; (in sughero) cork.

tarchi'ato, a [tar'kjato] ag stocky, thickset.

tar'dare vi to be late ♦ vt to delay; **~ a**

fare to delay doing.

'**tardi** av late; **più ~** later (on); **al più ~** at the latest; **sul ~** (verso sera) late in the day; **far ~** to be late; (restare alzato) to stay up late.

tar'divo, a ag (primavera) late; (rimedio) belated, tardy; (fig: bambino) retarded.

'**tardo, a** ag (lento, fig: ottuso) slow; (tempo: avanzato) late.

'**targa, ghe** sf plate; (AUT) number (BRIT) o license (US) plate.

ta'riffa sf (gen) rate, tariff; (di trasporti) fare; (elenco) price list; tariff.

'**tarlo** sm woodworm.

'**tarma** sf moth.

ta'rocco, chi sm tarot card; **~chi** smpl (gioco) tarot sg.

tartagli'are [tartaʎ'ʎare] vi to stutter, stammer.

'**tartaro, a** ag, sm (in tutti i sensi) tartar.

tarta'ruga, ghe sf tortoise; (di mare) turtle; (materiale) tortoiseshell.

tar'tina sf canapé.

tar'tufo sm (BOT) truffle.

'**tasca, sche** sf pocket; **tas'cabile** ag (libro) pocket cpd; **tasca'pane** sm haversack; **tas'chino** sm breast pocket.

'**tassa** sf (imposta) tax; (doganale) duty; (per iscrizione: a scuola etc) fee; **~ di circolazione/di soggiorno** road/ tourist tax.

tas'sametro sm taximeter.

tas'sare vt to tax; to levy a duty on.

tassa'tivo, a ag peremptory.

tassazi'one [tassat'tsjone] sf taxation.

tas'sello sm plug; wedge.

tassì sm inv = **taxi**; **tas'sista, i, e** sm/f taxi driver.

'**tasso** sm (di natalità, d'interesse etc) rate; (BOT) yew; (ZOOL) badger; **~ di cambio/d'interesse** rate of exchange/ interest.

tas'tare vt to feel; **~ il terreno** (fig) to see how the land lies.

tasti'era sf keyboard.

'**tasto** sm key; (tatto) touch, feel.

tas'toni av: **procedere (a) ~** to grope

one's way forward.

'tattica *sf* tactics *pl.*

'tattico, a, ci, che *ag* tactical.

'tatto *sm* (*senso*) touch; (*fig*) tact; **duro al** ~ hard to the touch; **aver** ~ to be tactful, have tact.

tatu'aggio [tatu'addʒo] *sm* tattooing; (*disegno*) tattoo.

tatu'are *vt* to tattoo.

'tavola *sf* table; (*asse*) plank, board; (*lastra*) tablet; (*quadro*) panel (painting); (*illustrazione*) plate; ~ **calda** snack bar; ~ **pieghevole** folding table.

tavo'lato *sm* boarding; (*pavimento*) wooden floor.

tavo'letta *sf* tablet, bar; **a** ~ (*AUT*) flat out.

tavo'lino *sm* small table; (*scrivania*) desk.

'tavolo *sm* table.

tavo'lozza [tavo'lɔttsa] *sf* (*ARTE*) palette.

'taxi *sm inv* taxi.

'tazza ['tattsa] *sf* cup; ~ **da caffè/tè** coffee/tea cup; **una** ~ **di caffè/tè** a cup of coffee/tea.

te *pron* (*soggetto: in forme comparative, oggetto*) you.

tè *sm inv* tea; (*trattenimento*) tea party.

tea'trale *ag* theatrical.

te'atro *sm* theatre.

'tecnica, che *sf* technique; (*tecnologia*) technology.

'tecnico, a, ci, che *ag* technical ♦ *sm/f* technician.

tecnolo'gia [teknolo'dʒia] *sf* technology.

te'desco, a, schi, sche *ag, sm/f, sm* German.

'tedio *sm* tedium, boredom.

te'game *sm* (*CUC*) pan.

'tegola *sf* tile.

tei'era *sf* teapot.

'tela *sf* (*tessuto*) cloth; (*per vele, quadri*) canvas; (*dipinto*) canvas, painting; **di** ~ (*calzoni*) (heavy) cotton *cpd*; (*scarpe, borsa*) canvas *cpd*; ~ **cerata** oilcloth; (*copertone*) tarpaulin.

te'laio *sm* (*apparecchio*) loom; (*struttura*) frame.

tele'camera *sf* television camera.

tele'cronaca *sf* television report.

tele'ferica, che *sf* cableway.

telefo'nare *vi* to telephone, ring; to make a phone call ♦ *vt* to telephone; ~ **a** to phone up, ring up, call up.

telefo'nata *sf* (*telephone*) call; ~ **a carico del destinatario** reverse charge (*BRIT*) o collect (*US*) call.

tele'fonico, a, ci, che *ag* (tele)phone *cpd*.

telefo'nista, i, e *sm/f* telephonist; (*d'impresa*) switchboard operator.

te'lefono *sm* telephone; ~ **a gettoni** ≈ pay phone.

telegior'nale [teledʒor'nale] *sm* television news (programme).

te'legrafo *sm* telegraph; (*ufficio*) telegraph office.

tele'gramma, i *sm* telegram.

tele'matica *sf* data transmission; telematics *sg*.

telepa'tia *sf* telepathy.

teles'copio *sm* telescope.

teleselezi'one [teleselet'tsjone] *sf* direct dialling.

telespetta'tore, 'trice *sm/f* (television) viewer.

televisi'one *sf* television.

televi'sore *sm* television set.

'telex *sm inv* telex.

'tema, i *sm* theme; (*INS*) essay, composition.

teme'rario, a *ag* rash, reckless.

te'mere *vt* to fear, be afraid of; (*essere sensibile a: freddo, calore*) to be sensitive to ♦ *vi* to be afraid; (*essere preoccupato*): ~ **per** to worry about, fear for; ~ **di/che** to be afraid of/that.

temperama'tite *sm inv* pencil sharpener.

tempera'mento *sm* temperament.

tempe'rare *vt* (*aguzzare*) to sharpen; (*fig*) to moderate, control, temper.

tempe'rato, a *ag* moderate, temperate; (*clima*) temperate.

tempera'tura *sf* temperature.

tempe'rino *sm* penknife.

tem'pesta *sf* storm; ~ **di sabbia/neve** sand/snowstorm.

tempes'tare *vt*: ~ **qn di domande** to

bombard sb with questions; ~ **qn di colpi** to rain blows on sb.

tempes'tivo, a *ag* timely.

tempes'toso, a *ag* stormy.

'tempia *sf* (*ANAT*) temple.

'tempio *sm* (*edificio*) temple.

'tempo *sm* (*METEOR*) weather; (*cronologico*) time; (*epoca*) time, times *pl*; (*di film, gioco: parte*) part; (*MUS*) time; (: *battuta*) beat; (*LING*) tense; **un ~ once**; **~ fa** some time ago; **al ~ stesso** *o* **a un ~** at the same time; **per ~** early; **aver fatto il suo ~** to have had its (*o* his *etc*) day; **primo/secondo ~** (*TEATRO*) first/second ⁻ part; (*SPORT*) first/second half; **in ~ utile** in due time *o* course.

tempo'rale *ag* temporal ♦ *sm* (*METEOR*) (thunder)storm.

tempo'raneo, a *ag* temporary.

temporeggi'are [tempored'dʒare] *vi* to play for time, temporize.

tem'prare *vt* to temper.

te'nace [te'natʃe] *ag* strong, tough; (*fig*) tenacious; **te'nacia** *sf* tenacity.

te'naglie [te'naʎʎe] *sfpl* pincers *pl*.

'tenda *sf* (*riparo*) awning; (*di finestra*) curtain; (*per campeggio etc*) tent.

ten'denza [ten'dentsa] *sf* tendency; (*orientamento*) trend; **avere ~ a** *o* **per qc** to have a bent for sth.

'tendere *vt* (*allungare al massimo*) to stretch, draw tight; (*porgere: mano*) to hold out; (*fig: trappola*) to lay, set ♦ *vi*: **~ a qc/a fare** to tend towards sth/to do; **~ l'orecchio** to prick up one's ears; **il tempo tende al caldo** the weather is getting hot; **un blu che tende al verde** a greenish blue.

ten'dina *sf* curtain.

'tendine *sm* tendon, sinew.

ten'done *sm* (*da circo*) tent.

'tenebre *sfpl* darkness *sg*; **tene'broso, a** *ag* dark, gloomy.

te'nente *sm* lieutenant.

te'nere *vt* to hold; (*conservare, mantenere*) to keep; (*ritenere, considerare*) to consider; (*spazio: occupare*) to take up, occupy; (*seguire: strada*) to keep to ♦ *vi* to hold; (*colori*)

to be fast; (*dare importanza*): **~ a** to care about; **~ a fare** to want to do, be keen to do; **~rsi** *vr* (*stare in una determinata posizione*) to stand; (*stimarsi*) to consider o.s.; (*aggrapparsi*): **~rsi a** to hold on to; (*attenersi*): **~rsi a** to stick to; **~ una conferenza** to give a lecture; **~ conto di qc** to take sth into consideration; **~ presente qc** to bear sth in mind.

'tenero, a *ag* tender; (*pietra, cera, colore*) soft; (*fig*) tender, loving.

'tenia *sf* tapeworm.

'tennis *sm* tennis.

te'nore *sm* (*tono*) tone; (*MUS*) tenor; **~ di vita** way of life; (*livello*) standard of living.

tensi'one *sf* tension.

ten'tare *vt* (*indurre*) to tempt; (*provare*): **~ qc/di fare** to attempt *o* try sth/to do; **tenta'tivo** *sm* attempt; **tentazi'one** *sf* temptation.

tenten'nare *vi* to shake, be unsteady; (*fig*) to hesitate, waver ♦ *vt*: **~ il capo** to shake one's head.

ten'toni *av*: **andare a ~** (*anche fig*) to grope one's way.

'tenue *ag* (*sottile*) fine; (*colore*) soft; (*fig*) slender, slight.

te'nuta *sf* (*capacità*) capacity; (*divisa*) uniform; (*abito*) dress; (*AGR*) estate; **a ~ d'aria** airtight; **~ di strada** roadholding power.

teolo'gia [teolo'dʒia] *sf* theology; **te'ologo, gi** *sm* theologian.

teo'rema, i *sm* theorem.

teo'ria *sf* theory; **te'orico, a, ci, che** *ag* theoretic(al).

'tepido, a *ag* = tiepido.

te'pore *sm* warmth.

'teppa *sf* mob, hooligans *pl*; **tep'pismo** *sm* hooliganism; **tep'pista, i** *sm* hooligan.

tera'pia *sf* therapy.

tergicris'tallo [terdʒikris'tallo] *sm* windscreen (*BRIT*) *o* windshield (*US*) wiper.

tergiver'sare [terdʒiver'sare] *vi* to shilly-shally.

'tergo *sm*: **a ~** behind; **vedi a ~** please turn over.

ter'male *ag* thermal; **stazione** *sf* ~ spa.
'terme *sfpl* thermal baths.
'termico, a, ci, che *ag* thermic; (*unità*) thermal.
termi'nale *ag*, *sm* terminal.
termi'nare *vt* to end; (*lavoro*) to finish ♦ *vi* to end.
'termine *sm* term; (*fine*, *estremità*) end; (*di territorio*) boundary, limit; **contratto a** ~ (*COMM*) forward contract; **a breve/lungo** ~ short-/long-term; **parlare senza mezzi** ~**i** to talk frankly, not to mince one's words.
ter'mometro *sm* thermometer.
termonucle'are *ag* thermonuclear.
'termos *sm inv* = **thermos**.
termosi'fone *sm* radiator; (**riscaldamento a**) ~ central heating.
ter'mostato *sm* thermostat.
'terra *sf* (*gen*, *ELETTR*) earth; (*sostanza*) soil, earth; (*opposto al mare*) land *no pl*; (*regione*, *paese*) land; (*argilla*) clay; ~**e** *sfpl* (*possedimento*) lands, land *sg*; **a o per** ~ (*stato*) on the ground (*o floor*); (*moto*) to the ground, down; **mettere a** ~ (*ELETTR*) to earth.
terra'cotta *sf* terracotta; **vasellame** *sm* **di** ~ earthenware.
terra'ferma *sf* dry land, terra firma; (*continente*) mainland.
terrapi'eno *sm* embankment, bank.
ter'razza [teʼrattsa] *sf* terrace.
ter'razzo [terʼrattso] *sm* = **terrazza**.
terre'moto *sm* earthquake.
ter'reno, a *ag* (*vita*, *beni*) earthly ♦ *sm* (*suolo*, *fig*) ground; (*COMM*) land *no pl*, plot (of land); site; (*SPORT*, *MIL*) field.
ter'restre *ag* (*superficie*) of the earth, earth's; (*di terra: battaglia*, *animale*) land *cpd*; (*REL*) earthly, worldly.
ter'ribile *ag* terrible, dreadful.
terrifi'cante *ag* terrifying.
territori'ale *ag* territorial.
terri'torio *sm* territory.
ter'rore *sm* terror; **terro'rismo** *sm* terrorism; **terro'rista, i, e** *sm/f* terrorist.
'terso, a *ag* clear.

'terzo, a [ˈtɛrtso] *ag* third ♦ *sm* (*frazione*) third; (*DIR*) third party; ~**i** *smpl* (*altri*) others, other people; **la** ~**a pagina** (*STAMPA*) the Arts page.
'tesa *sf* brim.
'teschio [ˈteskjo] *sm* skull.
'tesi *sf* thesis.
'teso, a *pp di* **tendere** ♦ *ag* (*tirato*) taut, tight; (*fig*) tense.
tesore'ria *sf* treasury.
tesori'ere *sm* treasurer.
te'soro *sm* treasure; **il Ministero del T**~ the Treasury.
'tessera *sf* (*documento*) card.
'tessere *vt* to weave; **'tessile** *ag*, *sm* textile; **tessi'tore, 'trice** *sm/f* weaver; **tessi'tura** *sf* weaving.
tes'suto *sm* fabric, material; (*BIOL*) tissue; (*fig*) web.
'testa *sf* head; (*di cose: estremità*, *parte anteriore*) head, front; **di** ~ (*vettura etc*) front; **tenere** ~ **a qn** (*nemico etc*) to stand up to sb; **fare di** ~ **propria** to go one's own way; **in** ~ (*SPORT*) in the lead; ~ **o croce?** heads or tails?; **avere la** ~ **dura** to be stubborn; ~ **di serie** (*TENNIS*) seed, seeded player.
testa'mento *sm* (*atto*) will; **l'Antico/il Nuovo T**~ (*REL*) the Old/New Testament.
tes'tardo, a *ag* stubborn, pig-headed.
tes'tata *sf* (*parte anteriore*) head; (*intestazione*) heading.
'teste *sm/f* witness.
tes'ticolo *sm* testicle.
testi'mone *sm/f* (*DIR*) witness.
testimoni'anza [testimoˈnjantsa] *sf* testimony.
testimoni'are *vt* to testify; (*fig*) to bear witness to, testify to ♦ *vi* to give evidence, testify.
'testo *sm* text; **fare** ~ (*opera*, *autore*) to be authoritative; **questo libro non fa** ~ this book is not essential reading; **te-stu'ale** *ag* textual; literal, word for word.
tes'tuggine [tesˈtuddʒine] *sf* tortoise; (*di mare*) turtle.
'tetano *sm* (*MED*) tetanus.

'**tetro, a** *ag* gloomy.

'**tetto** *sm* roof; **tet'toia** *sf* roofing; canopy.

'**Tevere** *sm*: **il** ~ the Tiber.

Tg. *abbr* = **telegiornale**.

'**thermos** ['tɛrmos] ® *sm inv* vacuum *o* Thermos ® flask.

ti *pron* (*dav lo, la, li, le, ne diventa* **te**) *pron* (*oggetto*) you; (*complemento di termine*) (to) you; (*riflessivo*) yourself.

ti'ara *sf* (*REL*) tiara.

'**tibia** *sf* tibia, shinbone.

tic *sm inv* tic, (*nervous*) twitch; (*fig*) mannerism.

ticchet'tio [tikket'tio] *sm* (*di macchina da scrivere*) clatter; (*di orologio*) ticking; (*della pioggia*) patter.

'**ticchio** ['tikkjo] *sm* (*ghiribizzo*) whim; (*tic*) tic, (*nervous*) twitch.

ti'epido, a *ag* lukewarm, tepid.

ti'fare *vi*: ~ **per** to be a fan of; (*parteggiare*) to side with.

'**tifo** *sm* (*MED*) typhus; (*fig*): **fare il** ~ **per** to be a fan of.

tifoi'dea *sf* typhoid.

ti'fone *sm* typhoon.

ti'foso, a *sm/f* (*SPORT etc*) fan.

'**tiglio** ['tiʎʎo] *sm* lime (tree), linden (tree).

'**tigre** *sf* tiger.

tim'ballo *sm* (*strumento*) kettledrum; (*CUC*) timbale.

'**timbro** *sm* stamp; (*MUS*) timbre, tone.

'**timido, a** *ag* shy; timid.

'**timo** *sm* thyme.

ti'mone *sm* (*NAUT*) rudder; **timoni'ere** *sm* helmsman.

ti'more *sm* (*paura*) fear; (*rispetto*) awe; **timo'roso, a** *ag* timid, timorous.

'**timpano** *sm* (*ANAT*) eardrum; (*MUS*): ~**i** *smpl* kettledrums, timpani.

'**tingere** ['tindʒere] *vt* to dye.

'**tino** *sm* vat.

ti'nozza [ti'nɔttsa] *sf* tub.

'**tinta** *sf* (*materia colorante*) dye; (*colore*) colour, shade; **tinta'rella** (*fam*) *sf* (sun)tan.

tintin'nare *vi* to tinkle.

'**tinto, a** *pp di* **tingere**.

tinto'ria *sf* (*officina*) dyeworks *sg*;

(*lavasecco*) dry cleaner's (shop).

tin'tura *sf* (*operazione*) dyeing; (*colorante*) dye; ~ **di iodio** tincture of iodine.

'**tipico, a, ci, che** *ag* typical.

'**tipo** *sm* type; (*genere*) kind, type; (*fam*) chap, fellow.

tipogra'fia *sf* typography; (*procedimento*) letterpress (printing); (*officina*) printing house; **tipo'grafico, a, ci, che** *ag* typographic(al); letterpress *cpd*; **ti-'pografo** *sm* typographer.

ti'ranno, a *ag* tyrannical ♦ *sm* tyrant.

ti'rante *sm* (*per tenda*) guy.

ti'rare *vt* (*gen*) to pull; (*estrarre*): ~ **qc da** to take *o* pull sth out of; to get sth out of; to extract sth from; (*chiudere: tenda etc*) to draw, pull; (*tracciare, disegnare*) to draw, trace; (*lanciare: sasso, palla*) to throw; (*stampare*) to print; (*pistola, freccia*) to fire ♦ *vi* (*pipa, camino*) to draw; (*vento*) to blow; (*abito*) to be tight; (*fare fuoco*) to fire; (*fare del tiro, CALCIO*) to shoot; ~ **avanti** *vi* to struggle on ♦ *vt* to keep going; ~ **fuori** (*estrarre*) to take out, pull out; ~ **giù** (*abbassare*) to bring down; ~ **su** to pull up; (*capelli*) to put up; (*fig: bambino*) to bring up; ~**rsi indietro** to move back.

tira'tore *sm* gunman; **un buon** ~ a good shot; ~ **scelto** marksman.

tira'tura *sf* (*azione*) printing; (*di libro*) (print) run; (*di giornale*) circulation.

'**tirchio, a** ['tirkjo] *ag* mean, stingy.

'**tiro** *sm* shooting *no pl*, firing *no pl*; (*colpo, sparo*) shot; (*di palla: lancio*) throwing *no pl*; throw; (*fig*) trick; **cavallo da** ~ draught (*BRIT*) *o* draft (*US*) horse; ~ **a segno** target shooting; (*luogo*) shooting range.

tiro'cinio [tiro'tʃinjo] *sm* apprenticeship; (*professionale*) training.

ti'roide *sf* thyroid (gland).

Tir'reno *sm*: **il (mar)** ~ the Tyrrhenian Sea.

ti'sana *sf* herb tea.

tito'lare *ag* appointed; (*sovrano*) titular ♦ *sm/f* incumbent; (*proprietario*) owner; (*CALCIO*) regular player.

'**titolo** *sm* title; (*di giornale*) headline;

(*diploma*) qualification; (*COMM*) security; (: *azione*) share; **a che ~?** for what reason?; **a ~ di amicizia** out of friendship; **a ~ di premio** as a prize; **~ di credito** share; **~ di proprietà** title deed.

titu'bante *ag* hesitant, irresolute.

'tizio, a ['tittsjo] *sm/f* fellow, chap.

tiz'zone [tit'tsone] *sm* brand.

toc'cante *ag* touching.

toc'care *vt* to touch; (*tastare*) to feel; (*fig: riguardare*) to concern; (: *commuovere*) to touch, move; (: *pungere*) to hurt, wound; (: *far cenno a: argomento*) to touch on, mention ♦ *vi*: **~ a** (*accadere*) to happen to; (*spettare*) to be up to; **~ (il fondo)** (*in acqua*) to touch the bottom; **tocca a te difenderci** it's up to you to defend us; **a chi tocca?** whose turn is it?; **mi toccò pagare** I had to pay.

'tocco, chi *sm* touch; (*ARTE*) stroke, touch.

'toga, ghe *sf* toga; (*di magistrato, professore*) gown.

'togliere ['tɔʎʎere] *vt* (*rimuovere*) to take away (o off), remove; (*riprendere, non concedere più*) to take away, remove; (*MAT*) to take away, subtract; (*liberare*) to free; **~ qc a qn** to take sth (away) from sb; **ciò non toglie che** nevertheless, be that as it may; **~rsi il cappello** to take off one's hat.

toi'lette [twa'lɛt] *sf inv* toilet; (*mobile*) dressing table.

to'letta *sf* = **toilette**.

tolle'ranza [tolle'rantsa] *sf* tolerance.

tolle'rare *vt* to tolerate.

'tolto, a *pp di* **togliere**.

to'maia *sf* (*di scarpa*) upper.

'tomba *sf* tomb.

tom'bino *sm* manhole cover.

'tombola *sf* (*gioco*) tombola; (*ruzzolone*) tumble.

'tomo *sm* volume.

'tonaca, che *sf* (*REL*) habit.

to'nare *vi* = **tuonare**.

'tondo, a *ag* round.

'tonfo *sm* splash; (*rumore sordo*) thud; (*caduta*): **fare un ~** to take a tumble.

'tonico, a, ci, che *ag, sm* tonic.

tonifi'care *vt* (*muscoli, pelle*) to tone up; (*irrobustire*) to invigorate, brace.

tonnel'laggio [tonnel'laddʒo] *sm* (*NAUT*) tonnage.

tonnel'lata *sf* ton.

'tonno *sm* tuna (fish).

'tono *sm* (*gen*) tone; (*MUS: di pezzo*) key; (*di colore*) shade, tone.

ton'silla *sf* tonsil; **tonsil'lite** *sf* tonsillitis.

'tonto, a *ag* dull, stupid.

to'pazio [to'pattsjo] *sm* topaz.

'topo *sm* mouse.

topogra'fia *sf* topography.

'toppa *sf* (*serratura*) keyhole; (*pezza*) patch.

to'race [to'ratʃe] *sm* chest.

'torba *sf* peat.

'torbido, a *ag* (*liquido*) cloudy; (: *fiume*) muddy; (*fig*) dark; troubled ♦ *sm*: **pescare nel ~** (*fig*) to fish in troubled water.

'torcere ['tɔrtʃere] *vt* to twist; (*biancheria*) to wring (out); **~rsi** *vr* to twist, writhe.

torchi'are [tor'kjare] *vt* to press; **torchio** *sm* press; **torchio tipografico** printing press.

'torcia, ce ['tɔrtʃa] *sf* torch; **~ elettrica** torch (*BRIT*), flashlight (*US*).

torci'collo [tortʃi'kɔllo] *sm* stiff neck.

'tordo *sm* thrush.

To'rino *sf* Turin.

tor'menta *sf* snowstorm.

tormen'tare *vt* to torment; **~rsi** *vr* to fret, worry o.s.; **tor'mento** *sm* torment.

torna'conto *sm* advantage, benefit.

tor'nado *sm* tornado.

tor'nante *sm* hairpin bend.

tor'nare *vi* to return, go (o come) back; (*ridiventare: anche fig*) to become (again); (*riuscire giusto, esatto: conto*) to work out; (*risultare*) to turn out (to be), prove (to be); **~ utile** to prove o turn out (to be) useful; **~ a casa** to go (o come) home.

torna'sole *sm inv* litmus.

tor'neo *sm* tournament.

'tornio *sm* lathe.

'**toro** _sm_ bull; (_dello zodiaco_): **T~** Taurus.

tor'**pedine** _sf_ torpedo; **torpedini'era** _sf_ torpedo boat.

'**torre** _sf_ tower; (_SCACCHI_) rook, castle; **~ di controllo** (_AER_) control tower.

torrefazi'one [torrefat'tsjone] _sf_ roasting.

tor'**rente** _sm_ torrent.

tor'**retta** _sf_ turret.

torri'**one** _sm_ keep.

tor'**rone** _sm_ nougat.

torsi'**one** _sf_ twisting; torsion.

'**torso** _sm_ torso, trunk; (_ARTE_) torso.

'**torsolo** _sm_ (_di cavolo etc_) stump; (_di frutta_) core.

'**torta** _sf_ cake.

'**torto, a** _pp di_ **torcere** ♦ _ag_ (_ritorto_) twisted; (_storto_) twisted, crooked ♦ _sm_ (_ingiustizia_) wrong; (_colpa_) fault; **a ~** wrongly; **aver ~** to be wrong.

'**tortora** _sf_ turtle dove.

tortu'**oso, a** _ag_ (_strada_) twisting; (_fig_) tortuous.

tor'**tura** _sf_ torture; **tortu'rare** _vt_ to torture.

'**torvo, a** _ag_ menacing, grim.

tosa'**erba** _sm o f inv_ (lawn)mower.

to'**sare** _vt_ (_pecora_) to shear; (_siepe_) to clip, trim.

Tos'**cana** _sf_: **la ~** Tuscany; **tos'cano, a** _ag_, _sm/f_ Tuscan ♦ _sm_ (_sigaro_) strong Italian cigar.

'**tosse** _sf_ cough.

'**tossico, a, ci, che** _ag_ toxic.

tossicodipen'**dente** _sm/f_ drug addict.

tossi'**comane** _sm/f_ drug addict.

tos'**sire** _vi_ to cough.

tosta'**pane** _sm inv_ toaster.

tos'**tare** _vt_ to toast; (_caffè_) to roast.

'**tosto, a** _ag_: **faccia ~a** cheek.

to'**tale** _ag_, _sm_ total; **totalità** _sf_: **la totalità di** all of, the total amount (_o_ number) of; the whole +_sg_; **totaliz'zare** _vt_ to total; (_SPORT_) to score.

toto'**calcio** [toto'kaltʃo] _sm_ gambling _pool betting on football results_, ≈ (football) pools _pl_ (_BRIT_).

to'**vaglia** [to'vaʎʎa] _sf_ tablecloth; **tova-gli'olo** _sm_ napkin.

'**tozzo, a** ['tɔttso] _ag_ squat ♦ _sm_: **~ di pane** crust of bread.

tra _prep_ (_di due persone, cose_) between; (_di più persone, cose_) among(st); (_tempo: entro_) within, in; **~ 5 giorni** in 5 days' time; **sia detto ~ noi ...** between you and me ...; **litigano ~ (di) loro** they're fighting amongst themselves; **~ breve** soon; **~ sé e sé** (_parlare etc_) to oneself.

trabal'**lare** _vi_ to stagger, totter.

traboc'**care** _vi_ to overflow.

traboc'**chetto** [trabok'ketto] _sm_ (_fig_) trap.

tracan'**nare** _vt_ to gulp down.

'**traccia, ce** ['trattʃa] _sf_ (_segno, striscia_) trail, track; (_orma_) tracks _pl_; (_residuo, testimonianza_) trace, sign; (_abbozzo_) outline.

tracci'**are** [trat'tʃare] _vt_ to trace, mark (out); (_disegnare_) to draw; (_fig: abbozzare_) to outline; **tracci'ato** _sm_ (_grafico_) layout, plan.

tra'**chea** [tra'kɛa] _sf_ windpipe, trachea.

tra'**colla** _sf_ shoulder strap; **borsa a ~** shoulder bag.

tra'**collo** _sm_ (_fig_) collapse, crash.

traco'**tante** _ag_ overbearing, arrogant.

tradi'**mento** _sm_ betrayal; (_DIR, MIL_) treason.

tra'**dire** _vt_ to betray; (_coniuge_) to be unfaithful to; (_doveri: mancare_) to fail in; (_rivelare_) to give away, reveal; **tradi'tore, 'trice** _sm/f_ traitor.

tradizio'**nale** [traditsjo'nale] _ag_ traditional.

tradizi'**one** [tradit'tsjone] _sf_ tradition.

tra'**dotto, a** _pp di_ **tradurre**.

tra'**durre** _vt_ to translate; (_spiegare_) to render, convey; **tradut'tore, 'trice** _sm/f_ translator; **traduzi'one** _sf_ translation.

tra'**ente** _sm/f_ (_ECON_) drawer.

trafe'**lato, a** _ag_ out of breath.

traffi'**cante** _sm/f_ dealer; (_peg_) trafficker.

traffi'**care** _vi_ (_commerciare_): **~ (in)** to trade (in), deal (in); (_affaccendarsi_) to busy o.s. ♦ _vt_ (_peg_) to traffic in.

'**traffico, ci** _sm_ traffic; (_commercio_) trade, traffic.

tra'figgere [traˈfiddʒere] *vt* to run through, stab; (*fig*) to pierce; **tra'fitto, a** *pp di* **trafiggere**.

trafo'rare *vt* to bore, drill; **tra'foro** *sm* (*azione*) boring, drilling; (*galleria*) tunnel.

tra'gedia [traˈdʒɛdja] *sf* tragedy.

tra'ghetto [traˈgetto] *sm* crossing; (*barca*) ferry(boat).

'tragico, a, ci, che [ˈtradʒiko] *ag* tragic.

tra'gitto [traˈdʒitto] *sm* (*passaggio*) crossing; (*viaggio*) journey.

tragu'ardo *sm* (*SPORT*) finishing line; (*fig*) goal, aim.

traiet'toria *sf* trajectory.

trai'nare *vt* to drag, haul; (*rimorchiare*) to tow; **traino** *sm* (*carro*) wagon; (*slitta*) sledge; (*carico*) load.

tralasci'are [tralaʃˈʃare] *vt* (*studi*) to neglect; (*dettagli*) to leave out, omit.

'tralcio [ˈtraltʃo] *sm* (*BOT*) shoot.

tra'liccio [traˈlittʃo] *sm* (*tela*) ticking; (*struttura*) trellis; (*ELETTR*) pylon.

tram *sm inv* tram.

'trama *sf* (*filo*) weft, woof; (*fig: argomento, maneggio*) plot.

traman'dare *vt* to pass on, hand down.

tra'mare *vt* (*fig*) to scheme, plot.

tram'busto *sm* turmoil.

trames'tio *sm* bustle.

tramez'zino [tramedˈdzino] *sm* sandwich.

tra'mezzo [traˈmɛddzo] *sm* (*EDIL*) partition.

'tramite *prep* through.

tramon'tare *vi* to set, go down; **tra'monto** *sm* setting; (*del sole*) sunset.

tramor'tire *vi* to faint ♦ *vt* to stun.

trampo'lino *sm* (*per tuffi*) springboard, diving board; (*per lo sci*) ski-jump.

'trampolo *sm* stilt.

tramu'tare *vt*: ~ **in** to change into, turn into.

tra'nello *sm* trap.

trangugi'are [tranguˈdʒare] *vt* to gulp down.

'tranne *prep* except (for), but (for); ~ che unless.

tranquil'lante *sm* (*MED*) tranquillizer.

tranquillità *sf* calm, stillness; quietness; peace of mind.

tranquilliz'zare [trankwillidˈdzare] *vt* to reassure.

tran'quillo, a *ag* calm, quiet; (*bambino, scolaro*) quiet; (*sereno*) with one's mind at rest; **sta'** ~ don't worry.

transat'lantico, a, ci, che *ag* transatlantic ♦ *sm* transatlantic liner.

tran'satto, a *pp di* **transigere**.

transazi'one [transatˈtsjone] *sf* compromise; (*DIR*) settlement; (*COMM*) transaction, deal.

tran'senna *sf* barrier.

tran'sigere [tranˈsidʒere] *vi* (*DIR*) to reach a settlement; (*venire a patti*) to compromise, come to an agreement.

tran'sistor *sm inv* transistor.

transis'tore *sm* = **transistor**.

transi'tabile *ag* passable.

transi'tare *vi* to pass.

transi'tivo, a *ag* transitive.

'transito *sm* transit; **di** ~ (*merci*) in transit; (*stazione*) transit *cpd*; **"divieto di ~"** "no entry".

transi'torio, a *ag* transitory, transient; (*provvisorio*) provisional.

tran'via *sf* tramway (*BRIT*), streetcar line (*US*).

'trapano *sm* (*utensile*) drill; (*: MED*) trepan.

trapas'sare *vt* to pierce.

tra'passo *sm* passage.

trape'lare *vi* to leak, drip; (*fig*) to leak out.

tra'pezio [traˈpɛttsjo] *sm* (*MAT*) trapezium; (*attrezzo ginnico*) trapeze.

trapian'tare *vt* to transplant; **trapi'anto** *sm* transplanting; (*MED*) transplant.

'trappola *sf* trap.

tra'punta *sf* quilt.

'trarre *vt* to draw, pull; (*portare*) to take; (*prendere, tirare fuori*) to take (out), draw; (*derivare*) to obtain; ~ **origine da qc** to have its origins o originate in sth.

trasa'lire *vi* to start, jump.

trasan'dato, a *ag* shabby.

trasbor'dare *vt* to transfer; (*NAUT*) to tran(s)ship ♦ *vi* (*NAUT*) to change ship; (*AER*) to change plane; (*FERR*) to change (trains).

trasci'nare [traʃʃi'nare] *vt* to drag; ~**rsi** *vr* to drag o.s. along; (*fig*) to drag on.

tras'correre *vt* (*tempo*) to spend, pass ♦ *vi* to pass; **tras'corso, a** *pp di* **trascorrere**.

tras'critto, a *pp di* **trascrivere**.

tras'crivere *vt* to transcribe.

trascu'rare *vt* to neglect; (*non considerare*) to disregard; **trascura'tezza** *sf* carelessness, negligence; **trascu'rato, a** *ag* (*casa*) neglected; (*persona*) careless, negligent.

traseco'lato, a *ag* astounded, amazed.

trasferi'mento *sm* transfer; (*trasloco*) removal, move.

trasfe'rire *vt* to transfer; ~**rsi** *vr* to move; **tras'ferta** *sf* transfer; (*indennità*) travelling expenses *pl*; (*SPORT*) away game.

trasfigu'rare *vt* to transfigure.

trasfor'mare *vt* to transform, change.

trasfusi'one *sf* (*MED*) transfusion.

trasgre'dire *vt* to disobey, contravene.

tras'lato, a *ag* metaphorical, figurative.

traslo'care *vt* to move, transfer; ~**rsi** *vr* to move; **tras'loco, chi** *sm* removal.

tras'messo, a *pp di* **trasmettere**.

tras'mettere *vt* (*passare*): ~ **qc a qn** to pass sth on to sb; (*mandare*) to send; (*TECN, TEL, MED*) to transmit; (*TV, RADIO*) to broadcast; **trasmetti'tore** *sm* transmitter; **trasmissi'one** *sf* (*gen, FISICA, TECN*) transmission; (*passaggio*) transmission, passing on; (*TV, RADIO*) broadcast; **trasmit'tente** *sf* transmitting *o* broadcasting station.

traso'gnato, a [trasoɲ'ɲato] *ag* dreamy.

traspa'rente *ag* transparent.

traspa'rire *vi* to show (through).

traspi'rare *vi* to perspire; (*fig*) to come to light, leak out; **traspirazi'one** *sf* perspiration.

traspor'tare *vt* to carry, move; (*merce*) to transport, convey; **lasciarsi** ~ **(da qc)** (*fig*) to let o.s. be carried away (by sth); **tras'porto** *sm* transport.

trastul'lare *vt* to amuse; ~**rsi** *vr* to amuse o.s.

trasu'dare *vi* (*filtrare*) to ooze; (*sudare*) to sweat ♦ *vt* to ooze with.

trasver'sale *ag* transverse, cross(-); running at right angles.

trasvo'lare *vt* to fly over.

'tratta *sf* (*ECON*) draft; (*di persone*): **la** ~ **delle bianche** the white slave trade.

tratta'mento *sm* treatment; (*servizio*) service.

trat'tare *vt* (*gen*) to treat; (*commerciare*) to deal in; (*svolgere: argomento*) to discuss, deal with; (*negoziare*) to negotiate ♦ *vi*: ~ **di** to deal with; ~ **con** (*persona*) to deal with; **si tratta di ...** it's about ...; **tratta'tive** *sfpl* negotiations; **trat'tato** *sm* (*testo*) treatise; (*accordo*) treaty; **trattazi'one** *sf* treatment.

tratteggi'are [tratted'dʒare] *vt* (*disegnare: a tratti*) to sketch, outline; (: *col tratteggio*) to hatch.

tratte'nere *vt* (*far rimanere: persona*) to detain; (*intrattenere: ospiti*) to entertain; (*tenere, frenare, reprimere*) to hold back, keep back; (*astenersi dal consegnare*) to hold, keep; (*detrarre: somma*) to deduct; ~**rsi** *vr* (*astenersi*) to restrain o.s., stop o.s.; (*soffermarsi*) to stay, remain.

tratteni'mento *sm* entertainment; (*festa*) party.

tratte'nuta *sf* deduction.

trat'tino *sm* dash; (*in parole composte*) hyphen.

'tratto, a *pp di* **trarre** ♦ *sm* (*di penna, matita*) stroke; (*parte*) part, piece; (*di strada*) stretch; (*di mare, cielo*) expanse; (*di tempo*) period (of time); ~**i** *smpl* (*caratteristiche*) features; (*modo di fare*) ways, manners; **a un** ~, **d'un** ~ suddenly.

trat'tore *sm* tractor.

tratto'ria *sf* restaurant.

'trauma, i *sm* trauma; **trau'matico, a, ci, che** *ag* traumatic.

tra'vaglio [tra'vaʎʎo] *sm* (*angoscia*) pain, suffering; (*MED*) pains *pl*; ~ **di parto** labour pains.

trava'sare *vt* to decant.

'trave *sf* beam.

tra'versa *sf* (*trave*) crosspiece; (*via*) sidestreet; (*FERR*) sleeper (*BRIT*), (railroad) tie (*US*); (*CALCIO*) crossbar.

traver'sare *vt* to cross; **traver'sata** *sf* crossing; (*AER*) flight, trip.

traver'sie *sfpl* mishaps, misfortunes.

traver'sina *sf* (*FERR*) sleeper (*BRIT*), (railroad) tie (*US*).

tra'verso, a *ag* oblique; **di** ~ *ag* askew ♦ *av* sideways; **andare di** ~ (*cibo*) to go down the wrong way; **guardare di** ~ to look askance at.

travesti'mento *sm* disguise.

traves'tire *vt* to disguise; ~**rsi** *vr* to disguise o.s.

travi'are *vt* (*fig*) to lead astray.

travi'sare *vt* (*fig*) to distort, misrepresent.

tra'volgere [tra'vɔldʒere] *vt* to sweep away, carry away; (*fig*) to overwhelm; **tra'volto, a** *pp di* **travolgere.**

tre *num* three.

trebbi'are *vt* to thresh.

'treccia, ce ['trettʃa] *sf* plait, braid.

tre'cento [tre'tʃento] *num* three hundred ♦ *sm:* **il T~** the fourteenth century.

'tredici ['treditʃi] *num* thirteen.

'tregua *sf* truce; (*fig*) respite.

tre'mare *vi:* ~ **di** (*freddo etc*) to shiver *o* tremble with; (*paura, rabbia*) to shake *o* tremble with.

tre'mendo, a *ag* terrible, awful.

tre'mila *num* three thousand.

'tremito *sm* trembling *no pl*; shaking *no pl*; shivering *no pl*.

tremo'lare *vi* to tremble; (*luce*) to flicker; (*foglie*) to quiver.

tre'more *sm* tremor.

'treno *sm* train; ~ **di gomme** set of tyres (*BRIT*) *o* tires (*US*); ~ **merci** goods (*BRIT*) *o* freight train; ~ **viaggiatori** passenger train.

'trenta *num* thirty; **tren'tesimo, a** *num* thirtieth; **tren'tina** *sf:* **una trentina (di)** thirty or so, about thirty.

'trepido, a *ag* anxious.

treppi'ede *sm* tripod; (*CUC*) trivet.

'tresca, sche *sf* (*fig*) intrigue; (*: relazione amorosa*) affair.

'trespolo *sm* trestle.

tri'angolo *sm* triangle.

tribù *sf inv* tribe.

tri'buna *sf* (*podio*) platform; (*in aule etc*) gallery; (*di stadio*) stand.

tribu'nale *sm* court.

tribu'tare *vt* to bestow.

tri'buto *sm* tax; (*fig*) tribute.

tri'checo, chi [tri'kɛko] *sm* (*ZOOL*) walrus.

tri'ciclo [tri'tʃiklo] *sm* tricycle.

trico'lore *ag* three-coloured ♦ *sm* tricolour; (*bandiera italiana*) Italian flag.

tri'dente *sm* trident.

tri'foglio [tri'fɔʎʎo] *sm* clover.

'triglia ['triʎʎa] *sf* red mullet.

tril'lare *vi* (*MUS*) to trill.

tri'mestre *sm* period of three months; (*INS*) term, quarter (*US*); (*COMM*) quarter.

'trina *sf* lace.

trin'cea [trin'tʃea] *sf* trench; **trince'rare** *vt* to entrench.

trinci'are [trin'tʃare] *vt* to cut up.

trion'fare *vi* to triumph, win; ~ **su** to triumph over, overcome; **tri'onfo** *sm* triumph.

tripli'care *vt* to triple.

'triplice ['triplitʃe] *ag* triple; **in** ~ **copia** in triplicate.

'triplo, a *ag* triple; treble ♦ *sm:* **il** ~ **(di)** three times as much (as); **la spesa è** ~**a** it costs three times as much.

'tripode *sm* tripod.

'trippa *sf* (*CUC*) tripe.

'triste *ag* sad; (*luogo*) dreary, gloomy; **tris'tezza** *sf* sadness; gloominess.

trita'carne *sm inv* mincer, grinder (*US*).

tri'tare *vt* to mince, grind (*US*).

'trito, a *ag* (*tritato*) minced, ground (*US*); ~ **e ritrito** (*fig*) trite, hackneyed.

'trittico, ci *sm* (*ARTE*) triptych.

trivel'lare *vt* to drill.

trivi'ale *ag* vulgar, low.

tro'feo sm trophy.

'trogolo sm (per maiali) trough.

'tromba sf (MUS) trumpet; (AUT) horn; ~ d'aria whirlwind; ~ delle scale stairwell.

trom'bone sm trombone.

trom'bosi sf thrombosis.

tron'care vt to cut off; (spezzare) to break off.

'tronco, a, chi, che ag cut off; broken off; (LING) truncated; (fig) cut short ♦ sm (BOT, ANAT) trunk; (fig: tratto) section; (: pezzo: di lancia) stump; licenziare qn in ~ to fire sb on the spot.

troneggi'are [troned'dʒare] vi: ~ (su) to tower (over).

'tronfio, a ag conceited.

'trono sm throne.

tropi'cale ag tropical.

'tropico, ci sm tropic; ~ci smpl (GEO) tropics.

PAROLA CHIAVE

'troppo, a det (in eccesso: quantità) too much; (: numero) too many; c'era ~a gente there were too many people; fa ~ caldo it's too hot

♦ pron (in eccesso: quantità) too much; (: numero) too many; ne hai messo ~ you've put in too much; meglio ~i che pochi better too many than too few

♦ av (eccessivamente: con ag, av) too; (: con vb) too much; ~ amaro/tardi too bitter/late; lavora ~ he works too much; di ~ too much; too many; qualche tazza di ~ a few cups too many; 3000 lire di ~ 3000 lire too much; essere di ~ to be in the way.

'trota sf trout.

trot'tare vi to trot; trotterel'lare vi to trot along; (bambino) to toddle; 'trotto sm trot.

'trottola sf spinning top.

tro'vare vt to find; (giudicare): trovo che I find o think that; ~rsi vr (reciproco: incontrarsi) to meet; (essere, stare) to be; (arrivare, capitare) to find o.s.; andare a ~ qn to go and see sb; ~

qn colpevole to find sb guilty; ~rsi bene (in un luogo, con qn) to get on well; tro'vata sf good idea.

truc'care vt (falsare) to fake; (attore etc) to make up; (travestire) to disguise; (SPORT) to fix; (AUT) to soup up; ~rsi vr to make up (one's face); trucca'tore, 'trice sm/f (CINEMA, TEATRO) make-up artist.

'trucco, chi sm trick; (cosmesi) make-up.

'truce ['trutʃe] ag fierce.

truci'dare [trutʃi'dare] vt to slaughter.

'truciolo ['trutʃolo] sm shaving.

'truffa sf fraud, swindle; truf'fare vt to swindle, cheat.

'truppa sf troop.

tu pron you; ~ stesso(a) you yourself; dare del ~ a qn to address sb as "tu".

'tuba sf (MUS) tuba; (cappello) top hat.

tu'bare vi to coo.

tuba'tura sf piping q, pipes pl.

tubazi'one [tubat'tsjone] sf = tubatura.

tu'betto sm tube.

'tubo sm tube; pipe; ~ digerente (ANAT) alimentary canal, digestive tract; ~ di scappamento (AUT) exhaust pipe.

'tue vedi tuo.

tuf'fare vt to plunge, dip; ~rsi vr to plunge, dive; 'tuffo sm dive; (breve bagno) dip.

tu'gurio sm hovel.

tuli'pano sm tulip.

tume'farsi vr (MED) to swell.

'tumido, a ag swollen.

tu'more sm (MED) tumour.

tu'multo sm uproar, commotion; (sommossa) riot; (fig) turmoil; tumultu'oso, a ag rowdy, unruly; (fig) turbulent, stormy.

'tunica, che sf tunic.

Tuni'sia sf: la ~ Tunisia.

'tuo (f 'tua, pl tu'oi, 'tue) det: il ~, la tua etc your ♦ pron: il ~, la tua etc yours.

tuo'nare vi to thunder; tuona it is thundering, there's some thunder.

tu'ono sm thunder.

tu'orlo *sm* yolk.

tu'racciolo [tu'rattʃolo] *sm* cap, top; (*di sughero*) cork.

tu'rare *vt* to stop, plug; (*con sughero*) to cork; **~rsi il naso** to hold one's nose.

turba'mento *sm* disturbance; (*di animo*) anxiety, agitation.

tur'bante *sm* turban.

tur'bare *vt* to disturb, trouble.

turbi'nare *vi* to whirl.

'turbine *sm* whirlwind; **~ di neve** swirl of snow; **~ di polvere/sabbia** dust/sandstorm.

turbo'lento, a *ag* turbulent; (*ragazzo*) boisterous, unruly.

turbo'lenza [turbo'lɛntsa] *sf* turbulence.

tur'chese [tur'kese] *sf* turquoise.

Tur'chia [tur'kia] *sf*: **la ~** Turkey.

tur'chino, a [tur'kino] *ag* deep blue.

'turco, a, chi, che *ag* Turkish ♦ *sm/f* Turk/Turkish woman ♦ *sm* (*LING*) Turkish; **parlare ~** (*fig*) to talk double-dutch.

tu'rismo *sm* tourism; tourist industry; **tu'rista, i, e** *sm/f* tourist; **tu'ristico, a, ci, che** *ag* tourist *cpd*.

'turno *sm* turn; (*di lavoro*) shift; **di ~** (*soldato, medico, custode*) on duty; **a ~** (*rispondere*) in turn; (*lavorare*) in shifts; **fare a ~ a fare qc** to take turns to do sth; **è il suo ~** it's your (*o his etc*) turn.

'turpe *ag* filthy, vile; **turpi'loquio** *sm* obscene language.

'tuta *sf* overalls *pl*; (*SPORT*) tracksuit.

tu'tela *sf* (*DIR: di minore*) guardianship; (: *protezione*) protection; (*difesa*) defence; **tute'lare** *vt* to protect, defend.

tu'tore, 'trice *sm/f* (*DIR*) guardian.

tutta'via *cong* nevertheless, yet.

PAROLA CHIAVE

'tutto, a *det* **1** (*intero*) all; **~ il latte** all the milk; **~a la notte** all night, the whole night; **~ il libro** the whole book; **~a una bottiglia** a whole bottle

2 (*pl, collettivo*) all; every; **~i i libri** all the books; **~e le notti** every night; **~i i venerdì** every Friday; **~i gli uomini** all the men; (*collettivo*) all

men; **~i e due** both *o* each of us (*o* them *o* you); **~i e cinque** all five of us (*o* them *o* you)

3 (*completamente*): **era ~a sporca** she was all dirty; **tremava ~** he was trembling all over; **è ~a sua madre** she's just *o* exactly like her mother

4: **a tutt'oggi** so far, up till now; **a ~a velocità** at full *o* top speed

♦ *pron* **1** (*ogni cosa*) everything, all; (*qualsiasi cosa*) anything; **ha mangiato ~** he's eaten everything; **~ considerato** all things considered; **in ~ 10.000 lire** in all: **10,000 lire** in **~** 10.000 lire in all; **in ~ eravamo 50** there were 50 of us in all

2: **~i, e** (*ognuno*) all, everybody; **vengono ~i** they are all coming, everybody's coming; **~i quanti** all and sundry

♦ *av* (*completamente*) entirely, quite; **è ~ il contrario** it's quite *o* exactly the opposite; **tutt'al più**: **saranno stati tutt'al più una cinquantina** there were about fifty of them at (the very) most; **tutt'al più possiamo prendere un treno** if the worst comes to the worst we can take a train; **tutt'altro** on the contrary; **è tutt'altro che felice** he's anything but happy; **tutt'a un tratto** suddenly

♦ *sm*: **il ~** the whole lot, all of it.

tutto'fare *ag inv*: **domestica ~** general maid; **ragazzo ~** office boy ♦ *sm/f inv* handyman/woman.

tut'tora *av* still.

U

ubbidi'ente *ag* obedient; **ubbidi'enza** *sf* obedience.

ubbi'dire *vi* to obey; **~ a** to obey; (*sog: veicolo, macchina*) to respond to.

ubiquità *sf*: **non ho il dono dell'~** I can't be everywhere at once.

ubria'care *vt*: **~ qn** to get sb drunk; (*sog: alcool*) to make sb drunk; (*fig*) to make sb's head spin *o* reel; **~rsi** *vr* to get drunk; **~rsi di** (*fig*) to become intoxicated with.

ubri'aco, a, chi, che *ag, sm/f* drunk.
uccelli'era [uttʃel'ljɛra] *sf* aviary.
uccel'lino [uttʃel'lino] *sm* baby bird, chick.
uc'cello [ut'tʃello] *sm* bird.
uc'cidere [ut'tʃidere] *vt* to kill; **~rsi** *vr* (*suicidarsi*) to kill o.s.; (*perdere la vita*) to be killed; **uccisi'one** *sf* killing; **uc'ciso, a** *pp di* **uccidere; ucci'sore, uccidi'trice** *sm/f* killer.
udi'enza [u'djɛntsa] *sf* audience; (*DIR*) hearing; **dare ~ (a)** to grant an audience (to).
u'dire *vt* to hear; **udi'tivo, a** *ag* auditory; **u'dito** *sm* (sense of) hearing; **udi'tore, 'trice** *sm/f* listener; (*INS*) unregistered student (*attending lectures*); **udi'torio** *sm* (*persone*) audience.
uffa *escl* tut!
uffici'ale [uffi'tʃale] *ag* official ♦ *sm* (*AMM*) official, officer; (*MIL*) officer; **~ di stato civile** registrar.
uf'ficio [uf'fitʃo] *sm* (*gen*) office; (*dovere*) duty; (*mansione*) task, function, job; (*agenzia*) agency, bureau; (*REL*) service; **d'~** *ag* office *cpd*; official ♦ *av* officially; **~ di collocamento** employment office; **~ informazioni** information bureau; **~ oggetti smarriti** lost property office (*BRIT*), lost and found (*US*); **~ postale** post office.
uffici'oso, a [uffi'tʃoso] *ag* unofficial.
'ufo: a ~ *av* free, for nothing.
uggi'oso, a [ud'dʒoso] *ag* tiresome; (*tempo*) dull.
uguagli'anza [ugwaʎ'ʎantsa] *sf* equality.
uguagli'are [ugwaʎ'ʎare] *vt* to make equal; (*essere uguale*) to equal, be equal to; (*livellare*) to level; **~rsi a o con qn** (*paragonarsi*) to compare o.s. to sb.
ugu'ale *ag* equal; (*identico*) identical, the same; (*uniforme*) level, even ♦ *av*: **costano ~** they cost the same; **sono bravi ~** they're equally good; **ugual'mente** *av* equally; (*lo stesso*) all the same.
'ulcera ['ultʃera] *sf* ulcer.
u'liva *etc* = **oliva** *etc.*
ulteri'ore *ag* further.

ulti'mare *vt* to finish, complete.
'ultimo, a *ag* (*finale*) last; (*estremo*) farthest, utmost; (*recente: notizia, moda*) latest; (*fig: sommo, fondamentale*) ultimate ♦ *sm/f* last (one); **fino all'~** to the last, until the end; **da ~, in ~** in the end; **abitare all'~ piano** to live on the top floor; **per ~** (*entrare, arrivare*) last.
ulu'lare *vi* to howl; **ulu'lato** *sm* howling *no pl*; howl.
umanità *sf* humanity; **umani'tario, a** *ag* humanitarian.
u'mano, a *ag* human; (*comprensivo*) humane.
umbi'lico *sm* = **ombelico.**
umet'tare *vt* to dampen, moisten.
umidità *sf* dampness; humidity.
'umido, a *ag* damp; (*mano, occhi*) moist; (*clima*) humid ♦ *sm* dampness, damp; **carne in ~** stew.
'umile *ag* humble.
umili'are *vt* to humiliate; **~rsi** *vr* to humble o.s.; **umiliazi'one** *sf* humiliation.
umiltà *sf* humility, humbleness.
u'more *sm* (*disposizione d'animo*) mood; (*carattere*) temper; **di buon/ cattivo ~** in a good/bad mood.
umo'rismo *sm* humour; **avere il senso dell'~** to have a sense of humour; **umo'rista, i, e** *sm/f* humorist; **umo'ristico, a, ci, che** *ag* humorous, funny.
un *vedi* **uno.**
un' *vedi* **uno.**
'una *vedi* **uno.**
u'nanime *ag* unanimous; **unanimità** *sf* unanimity; **all'unanimità** unanimously.
unci'netto [untʃi'netto] *sm* crochet hook.
un'cino [un'tʃino] *sm* hook.
'undici ['unditʃi] *num* eleven.
'ungere ['undʒere] *vt* to grease, oil; (*REL*) to anoint; (*fig*) to flatter, butter up; **~rsi** *vr* (*sporcarsi*) to get covered in grease; **~rsi con la crema** to put on cream.
unghe'rese [unge'rese] *ag, sm/f, sm* Hungarian.
Unghe'ria [unge'ria] *sf*: **l'~** Hungary.

'**unghia** ['ungja] *sf* (*ANAT*) nail; (*di animale*) claw; (*di rapace*) talon; (*di cavallo*) hoof; **unghi'ata** *sf* (*graffio*) scratch.

ungu'ento *sm* ointment.

'**unico, a, ci, che** *ag* (*solo*) only; (*ineguagliabile*) unique; (*singolo: binario*) single; **figlio(a)** ~(a) only son/daughter, only child.

unifi'care *vt* to unite, unify; (*sistemi*) to standardize; **unificazi'one** *sf* uniting; unification; standardization.

uni'forme *ag* uniform; (*superficie*) even ♦ *sf* (*divisa*) uniform.

unilate'rale *ag* one-sided; (*DIR*) unilateral.

uni'one *sf* union; (*fig: concordia*) unity, harmony; **l'U~ Sovietica** the Soviet Union.

u'nire *vt* to unite; (*congiungere*) to join, connect; (*: ingredienti, colori*) to combine; (*in matrimonio*) to unite, join together; ~**rsi** *vr* to unite; (*in matrimonio*) to be joined together; ~ **qc a** to unite sth with; to join o connect sth with; to combine sth with; ~**rsi a** (*gruppo, società*) to join.

unità *sf inv* (*unione, concordia*) unity; (*MAT, MIL, COMM, di misura*) unit; **uni'tario, a** *ag* unitary; **prezzo unitario** price per unit.

u'nito, a *ag* (*paese*) united; (*amici, famiglia*) close; **in tinta** ~**a** plain, self-coloured.

univer'sale *ag* universal; general.

università *sf inv* university; **universi'tario, a** *ag* university *cpd* ♦ *sm/f* (*studente*) university student; (*insegnante*) academic, university lecturer.

uni'verso *sm* universe.

PAROLA CHIAVE

'**uno, a** (*dav sm* **un** +*C, V,* **uno** +*s impura, gn, pn, ps, x, z; dav sf* **un'** +*V,* **una** +*C*) *art indef* **1** a; (*dav vocale*) an; **un bambino** a child; ~**a strada** a street; ~ **zingaro** a gypsy
2 (*intensivo*): **ho avuto** ~**a paura!** I got such a fright!

♦ *pron* **1** one; **prendine** ~ take one (of them); **l'~ o l'altro** either (of them); **l'~ e l'altro** both (of them); **aiutarsi l'un l'altro** to help one another o each other; **sono entrati l'~ dopo l'altro** they came in one after the other
2 (*un tale*) someone, somebody
3 (*con valore impersonale*) one, you; **se** ~ **vuole** if one wants, if you want
♦ *num* one; ~**a mela e due pere** one apple and two pears; ~ **più** ~ **fa due** one plus one equals two, one and one are two
♦ *sf*: **è l'~a** it's one (o'clock).

'**unto, a** *pp di* **ungere** ♦ *ag* greasy, oily ♦ *sm* grease; **untu'oso, a** *ag* greasy, oily.

u'omo (*pl* **u'omini**) *sm* man; **da** ~ (*abito, scarpe*) men's, for men; ~ **d'affari** businessman; ~ **di paglia** stooge; ~ **rana** frogman.

u'opo *sm*: **all'**~ if necessary.

u'ovo (*pl(f)* **u'ova**) *sm* egg; ~ **affogato** poached egg; ~ **bazzotto/sodo** soft-/hard-boiled egg; ~ **alla coque** boiled egg; ~ **di Pasqua** Easter egg; **uova strapazzate** scrambled eggs.

ura'gano *sm* hurricane.

urba'nistica *sf* town planning.

ur'bano, a *ag* urban, city *cpd*, town *cpd*; (*TEL: chiamata*) local; (*fig*) urbane.

ur'gente [ur'dʒɛnte] *ag* urgent; **ur'genza** *sf* urgency; **in caso d'urgenza** in (case of) an emergency; **d'urgenza** *ag* emergency ♦ *av* urgently, as a matter of urgency.

'**urgere** ['urdʒere] *vi* to be urgent; to be needed urgently.

u'rina *sf* = **orina**.

ur'lare *vi* (*persona*) to scream, yell; (*animale, vento*) to howl ♦ *vt* to scream, yell.

'**urlo** (*pl(m)* '**urli**, *pl(f)* '**urla**) *sm* scream, yell; howl.

'**urna** *sf* urn; (*elettorale*) ballot-box; **andare alle** ~**e** to go to the polls.

urrà *escl* hurrah!

U.R.S.S. *abbr f*: **l'**~ the USSR.

ur'tare *vt* to bump into, knock against; *(fig: irritare)* to annoy ♦ *vi*: ~ **contro** o **in** to bump into, knock against, crash into; *(fig: imbattersi)* to come up against; ~**rsi** *vr (reciproco: scontrarsi)* to collide; *(: fig)* to clash; *(irritarsi)* to get annoyed; **'urto** *sm (colpo)* knock, bump; *(scontro)* crash, collision; *(fig)* clash.

U.S.A. ['uza] *smpl*: **gli** ~ the USA.

u'sanza [u'zantsa] *sf* custom; *(moda)* fashion.

u'sare *vt* to use, employ ♦ *vi (servirsi)*: ~ **di** to use; *(: diritto)* to exercise; *(essere di moda)* to be fashionable; *(essere solito)*: ~ **fare** to be in the habit of doing, be accustomed to doing ♦ *vb impers*: **qui usa così** it's the custom round here; **u'sato, a** *ag* used; *(consumato)* worn; *(di seconda mano)* used, second-hand ♦ *sm* second-hand goods *pl*.

usci'ere [uʃ'ʃɛre] *sm* usher.

'uscio ['uʃʃo] *sm* door.

u'scire [uʃ'ʃire] *vi (gen)* to come out; *(partire, andare a passeggio, a uno spettacolo etc)* to go out; *(essere sorteggiato: numero)* to come up; ~ **da** *(gen)* to leave; *(posto)* to go (o come) out of, leave; *(solco, vasca etc)* to come out of; *(muro)* to stick out of; *(competenza etc)* to be outside; *(infanzia, adolescenza)* to leave behind; *(famiglia nobile etc)* to come from; ~ **da** o **di casa** to go out; *(fig)* to leave home; ~ **in automobile** to go out in the car, go for a drive; ~ **di strada** *(AUT)* to go off o leave the road.

u'scita [uʃ'ʃita] *sf (passaggio, varco)* exit, way out; *(per divertimento)* outing; *(ECON: somma)* expenditure; *(TEATRO)* entrance; *(fig: battuta)* witty remark; ~ **di sicurezza** emergency exit.

usi'gnolo [uziɲ'ɲɔlo] *sm* nightingale.

U.S.L. [uzl] *sigla f (= unità sanitaria locale)* local health centre.

'uso *sm (utilizzazione)* use; *(esercizio)* practice; *(abitudine)* custom; **a** ~ **di** for (the use of); **d'**~ *(corrente)* in use; **fuori** ~ out of use.

usti'one *sf* burn.

usu'ale *ag* common, everyday.

u'sura *sf* usury; *(logoramento)* wear (and tear).

uten'sile *sm* tool, implement; ~**i da cucina** kitchen utensils.

u'tente *sm/f* user.

'utero *sm* uterus.

'utile *ag* useful ♦ *sm (vantaggio)* advantage, benefit; *(ECON: profitto)* profit; **utilità** *sf* usefulness *no pl*; use; *(vantaggio)* benefit; **utili'taria** *sf (AUT)* economy car; **utili'tario, a** *ag* utilitarian.

utiliz'zare [utilid'dzare] *vt* to use, make use of, utilize.

'uva *sf* grapes *pl*; ~ **passa** raisins *pl*; ~ **spina** gooseberry.

V

v. *abbr (= vedi)* v.

va *vb vedi* **andare**.

va'cante *ag* vacant.

va'canza [va'kantsa] *sf (l'essere vacante)* vacancy; *(riposo, ferie)* holiday(s *pl*) *(BRIT)*, vacation *(US)*; *(giorno di permesso)* day off, holiday; ~**e** *sfpl (periodo di ferie)* holidays *(BRIT)*, vacation *sg (US)*; **essere/andare in** ~ to be/go on holiday o vacation; ~**e estive** summer holiday(s) o vacation.

'vacca, che *sf* cow.

vacci'nare [vattʃi'nare] *vt* to vaccinate.

vacil'lare [vatʃil'lare] *vi* to sway, wobble; *(luce)* to flicker; *(fig: memoria, coraggio)* to be failing, falter.

'vacuo, a *ag (fig)* empty, vacuous ♦ *sm* vacuum.

'vado *vb vedi* **andare**.

vaga'bondo, a *sm/f* tramp, vagrant; *(fannullone)* idler, loafer.

va'gare *vi* to wander.

vagheggi'are [vaged'dʒare] *vt* to long for, dream of.

va'gina [va'dʒina] *sf* vagina.

va'gire [va'dʒire] *vi* to whimper.

'vaglia ['vaʎʎa] *sm inv* money order; ~ **postale** postal order.

vagli'are [vaʎ'ʎare] *vt* to sift; *(fig)* to

weigh up; **'vaglio** sm sieve.

'vago, a, ghi, ghe ag vague.

va'gone sm (FERR: per passeggeri) coach; (: per merci) truck, wagon; ~ **letto** sleeper, sleeping car; ~ **ristorante** dining o restaurant car.

'vai vb vedi **andare**.

vai'olo sm smallpox.

va'langa, ghe sf avalanche.

va'lente ag able, talented.

va'lere vi (avere forza, potenza) to have influence; (essere valido) to be valid; (avere vigore, autorità) to hold, apply; (essere capace: poeta, studente) to be good, be able ♦ vt (prezzo, sforzo) to be worth; (corrispondere) to correspond to; (procurare): ~ **qc a qn** to earn sb sth; **~rsi di** to make use of, take advantage of; **far** ~ (autorità etc) to assert; **vale a dire** that is to say; ~ **la pena** to be worth the effort o worth it.

va'levole ag valid.

vali'care vt to cross.

'valico, chi sm (passo) pass.

'valido, a ag valid; (rimedio) effective; (aiuto) real; (persona) worthwhile.

valige'ria [validʒe'ria] sf leather goods pl; leather goods factory; leather goods shop.

va'ligia, gie o **ge** [va'lidʒa] sf (suit)case; **fare le ~gie** to pack (up); ~ **diplomatica** diplomatic bag.

val'lata sf valley.

'valle sf valley; **a** ~ (di fiume) downstream; **scendere a** ~ to go downhill.

val'letto sm valet.

va'lore sm (gen) value; (merito) merit, worth; (coraggio) valour, courage; (COMM: titolo) security; ~**i** smpl (oggetti preziosi) valuables.

valoriz'zare [valorid'dzare] vt (terreno) to develop; (fig) to make the most of.

'valso, a pp di **valere**.

va'luta sf currency, money; (BANCA): ~ **15 gennaio** interest to run from January 15th.

valu'tare vt (casa, gioiello, fig) to value; (stabilire: peso, entrate, fig) to

estimate; **valutazi'one** sf valuation; estimate.

'valvola sf (TECN, ANAT) valve; (ELETTR) fuse.

'valzer ['valtser] sm inv waltz.

vam'pata sf (di fiamma) blaze; (di calore) blast; (: al viso) flush.

vam'piro sm vampire.

vanda'lismo sm vandalism.

'vandalo sm vandal.

vaneggi'are [vaned'dʒare] vi to rave.

'vanga, ghe sf spade; **van'gare** vt to dig.

van'gelo [van'dʒelo] sm gospel.

va'niglia [va'niʎʎa] sf vanilla.

vanità sf vanity; (di promessa) emptiness; (di sforzo) futility; **vani'toso, a** ag vain, conceited.

'vanno vb vedi **andare**.

'vano, a ag vain ♦ sm (spazio) space; (apertura) opening; (stanza) room.

van'taggio [van'taddʒo] sm advantage; **essere/portarsi in** ~ (SPORT) to be in/take the lead; **vantaggi'oso, a** ag advantageous; favourable.

van'tare vt to praise, speak highly of; **~rsi** vr: **~rsi (di/di aver fatto)** to boast o brag (about/about having done); **vante'ria** sf boasting; **'vanto** sm boasting; (merito) virtue, merit; (gloria) pride.

'vanvera sf: **a** ~ haphazardly; **parlare a** ~ to talk nonsense.

va'pore sm vapour; (anche: ~ acqueo) steam, (nave) steamer; **a** ~ (turbina etc) steam cpd; **al** ~ (CUC) steamed; **vapo'retto** sm steamer; **vapori'era** sf (FERR) steam engine; **vaporiz'zare** vt to vaporize; **vapo'roso, a** ag (tessuto) filmy; (capelli) soft and full.

va'rare vt (NAUT, fig) to launch; (DIR) to pass.

var'care vt to cross.

'varco, chi sm passage; **aprirsi un** ~ **tra la folla** to push one's way through the crowd.

vari'abile ag variable; (tempo, umore) changeable, variable ♦ sf (MAT) variable.

vari'are vt, vi to vary; ~ **di opinione** to

change one's mind; **variazi'one** sf variation; change.

va'rice [va'ritʃe] sf varicose vein.

vari'cella [vari'tʃɛlla] sf chickenpox.

vari'coso, a ag varicose.

varie'gato, a ag variegated.

varietà sf inv variety ♦ sm inv variety show.

'vario, a ag varied; (parecchi: col sostantivo al pl) various; (mutevole: umore) changeable; **vario'pinto, a** ag multicoloured.

'varo sm (NAUT, fig) launch; (di leggi) passing.

va'saio sm potter.

'vasca, sche sf basin; (anche: ~ da bagno) bathtub, bath.

va'scello [vaʃ'ʃello] sm (NAUT) vessel, ship.

vase'lina sf vaseline.

vasel'lame sm (stoviglie) crockery; (: di porcellana) china; ~ **d'oro/d'argento** gold/silver plate.

'vaso sm (recipiente) pot; (: barattolo) jar; (: decorativo) vase; (ANAT) vessel; ~ **da fiori** vase; (per piante) flowerpot.

vas'soio sm tray.

'vasto, a ag vast, immense.

Vati'cano sm: **il** ~ the Vatican.

ve pron, av vedi **vi**.

vecchi'aia [vek'kjaja] sf old age.

'vecchio, a ['vɛkkjo] ag old ♦ sm/f old man/woman; **i** ~**i** the old.

'vece ['vetʃe] sf: **in** ~ **di** in the place of, for; **fare le** ~**i di qn** to take sb's place.

ve'dere vt, vi to see; ~**rsi** vr to meet, see one another; **avere a che** ~ **con** to have something to do with; **far** ~ **qc a qn** to show sb sth; **farsi** ~ to show o.s.; (farsi vivo) to show one's face; **vedi di non farlo** make sure o see you don't do it; **non (ci) si vede** (è buio etc) you can't see a thing; **non lo posso** ~ (fig) I can't stand him.

ve'detta sf (sentinella, posto) look-out; (NAUT) patrol boat.

'vedovo, a sm/f widower/widow.

ve'duta sf view.

vee'mente ag vehement; violent.

vege'tale [vedʒe'tale] ag, sm vegetable.

vegetari'ano, a [vedʒeta'rjano] ag, sm/f vegetarian.

'vegeto, a ['vɛdʒeto] ag (pianta) thriving; (persona) strong, vigorous.

'veglia ['veʎʎa] sf wakefulness; (sorveglianza) watch; (trattenimento) evening gathering; **fare la** ~ **a un malato** to watch over a sick person.

vegli'are [veʎ'ʎare] vi to be awake; to stay o sit up; (stare vigile) to watch; to keep watch ♦ vt (malato, morto) to watch over, sit up with.

ve'icolo sm vehicle; ~ **spaziale** spacecraft inv.

'vela sf (NAUT: tela) sail; (sport) sailing.

ve'lare vt to veil; ~**rsi** vr (occhi, luna) to mist over; (voce) to become husky; ~**rsi il viso** to cover one's face (with a veil); **ve'lato, a** ag veiled.

veleggi'are [veled'dʒare] vi to sail; (AER) to glide.

ve'leno sm poison; **vele'noso, a** ag poisonous.

veli'ero sm sailing ship.

ve'lina sf (anche: carta ~: per imballare) tissue paper; (: per copie) flimsy paper; (copia) carbon copy.

ve'livolo sm aircraft.

velleità sf inv vain ambition, vain desire.

'vello sm fleece.

vel'luto sm velvet; ~ **a coste** cord.

'velo sm veil; (tessuto) voile.

ve'loce [ve'lotʃe] ag fast, quick ♦ av fast, quickly; **velo'cista, i, e** sm/f (SPORT) sprinter; **velocità** sf speed; **a forte velocità** at high speed; **velocità di crociera** cruising speed.

ve'lodromo sm velodrome.

'vena sf (gen) vein; (filone) vein, seam; (fig: ispirazione) inspiration; (: umore) mood; **essere in** ~ **di qc** to be in the mood for.

ve'nale ag (prezzo, valore) market cpd; (fig) venal; mercenary.

ven'demmia sf (raccolta) grape harvest; (quantità d'uva) grape crop, grapes pl; (vino ottenuto) vintage;

vendemmi'are *vt* to harvest ♦ *vi* to harvest the grapes.

'**vendere** *vt* to sell; "**vendesi**" "for sale".

ven'detta *sf* revenge.

vendi'care *vt* to avenge; ~**rsi** *vr*: ~**rsi (di)** to avenge o.s. (for); (*per rancore*) to take one's revenge (for); ~**rsi su qn** to revenge o.s. on sb; **vendica'tivo, a** *ag* vindictive.

'**vendita** *sf* sale; **la** ~ (*attività*) selling; (*smercio*) sales *pl*; **in** ~ on sale; ~ **all'asta** sale by auction; **vendi'tore** *sm* seller, vendor; (*gestore di negozio*) trader, dealer.

ve'nefico, a, ci, che *ag* poisonous.

vene'rabile *ag* venerable.

venerando, a *ag* = **venerabile**.

vene'rare *vt* to venerate.

venerdì *sm inv* Friday; **di** *o* **il** ~ on 'Fridays; **V~ Santo** Good Friday.

ve'nereo, a *ag* venereal.

'**veneto, a** *ag, sm/f* Venetian.

Ve'nezia [ve'nɛttsja] *sf* Venice; **venezi'ano, a** *ag, sm/f* Venetian.

veni'ale *ag* venial.

ve'nire *vi* to come; (*riuscire: dolce, fotografia*) to turn out; (*come ausiliare: essere*): **viene ammirato da tutti** he is admired by everyone; ~ **da** to come from; **quanto viene?** how much does it cost?; **far** ~ (*mandare a chiamare*) to send for; ~ **giù** to come down; ~ **meno** (*svenire*) to faint; ~ **meno a qc** not to fulfil sth; ~ **su** to come up; ~ **a trovare qn** to come and see sb; ~ **via** to come away.

ven'taglio [ven'taʎʎo] *sm* fan.

ven'tata *sf* gust (of wind).

ven'tenne *ag*: **una ragazza** ~ a twenty-year-old girl, a girl of twenty.

ven'tesimo, a *num* twentieth.

'**venti** *num* twenty.

venti'lare *vt* (*stanza*) to air, ventilate; (*fig: idea, proposta*) to air; **ventila'tore** *sm* ventilator, fan.

ven'tina *sf*: **una** ~ (**di**) around twenty, twenty or so.

venti'sette *num* twenty-seven; **il** ~ (*giorno di paga*) (monthly) pay day.

'**vento** *sm* wind.

'**ventola** *sf* (*AUT, TECN*) fan.

ven'tosa *sf* (*ZOOL*) sucker; (*di gomma*) suction pad.

ven'toso, a *ag* windy.

'**ventre** *sm* stomach.

ven'tura *sf*: **andare alla** ~ to trust to luck; **soldato di** ~ mercenary.

ven'turo, a *ag* next, coming.

ve'nuta *sf* coming, arrival.

ve'nuto, a *pp di* **venire**.

vera'mente *av* really.

ver'bale *ag* verbal ♦ *sm* (*di riunione*) minutes *pl*.

'**verbo** *sm* (*LING*) verb; (*parola*) word; (*REL*): **il V~** the Word.

'**verde** *ag, sm* green; **essere al** ~ to be broke; ~ **bottiglia/oliva** bottle/olive green.

verde'rame *sm* verdigris.

ver'detto *sm* verdict.

ver'dura *sf* vegetables *pl*.

vere'condo, a *ag* modest.

'**verga, ghe** *sf* rod.

ver'gato, a *ag* (*foglio*) ruled.

'**vergine** ['verdʒine] *sf* virgin; (*dello zodiaco*): **V~** Virgo ♦ *ag* virgin; (*ragazza*): **essere** ~ to be a virgin.

ver'gogna [ver'goɲɲa] *sf* shame; (*timidezza*) shyness, embarrassment; **vergo'gnarsi** *vr*: **vergognarsi (di)** to be *o* feel ashamed (of); to be shy (about), be embarrassed (about); **vergo'gnoso, a** *ag* ashamed; (*timido*) shy, embarrassed; (*causa di vergogna: azione*) shameful.

ve'rifica, che *sf* checking *no pl*, check.

verifi'care *vt* (*controllare*) to check; (*confermare*) to confirm, bear out.

verità *sf inv* truth.

veriti'ero, a *ag* (*che dice la verità*) truthful; (*conforme a verità*) true.

'**verme** *sm* worm.

vermi'celli [vermi'tʃɛlli] *smpl* vermicelli *sg*.

ver'miglio [ver'miʎʎo] *sm* vermilion, scarlet.

'**vermut** *sm inv* vermouth.

ver'nice [ver'nitʃe] *sf* (*colorazione*) paint; (*trasparente*) varnish; (*pelle*) patent leather; "~ **fresca**" "wet paint"; **vernici'are** vt to paint; to varnish.

'**vero, a** ag (veridico: fatti, testimonianza) true; (autentico) real ♦ sm (verità) truth; (realtà) (real) life; **un ~ e proprio delinquente** a real criminal, an out-and-out criminal.

vero'simile ag likely, probable.

ver'ruca, che sf wart.

versa'mento sm (pagamento) payment; (deposito di denaro) deposit.

ver'sante sm slopes pl, side.

ver'sare vt (fare uscire: vino, farina) to pour (out); (spargere: lacrime, sangue) to shed; (rovesciare) to spill; (ECON) to pay; (: depositare) to deposit, pay in; ~**rsi** vr (rovesciarsi) to spill; (fiume, folla): ~**rsi (in)** to pour (into).

versa'tile ag versatile.

ver'setto sm (REL) verse.

versi'one sf version; (traduzione) translation.

'**verso** sm (di poesia) verse, line; (di animale, uccello, venditore ambulante) cry; (direzione) direction; (modo) way; (di foglio di carta) verso; (di moneta) reverse; ~**i** smpl (poesia) verse sg; **non c'è ~ di persuaderlo** there's no way of persuading him, he can't be persuaded ♦ prep (in direzione di) toward(s); (nei pressi di) near, around (about); (in senso temporale) about, around; (nei confronti di) for; ~ **di me** towards me; ~ **sera** towards evening.

verti'cale ag, sf vertical.

'**vertice** ['vertitʃe] sm summit, top; (MAT) vertex; **conferenza al ~** (POL) summit conference.

ver'tigine [ver'tidʒine] sf dizziness no pl; dizzy spell; (MED) vertigo; **avere le ~i** to feel dizzy; **vertigi'noso, a** ag (altezza) dizzy; (fig) breathtakingly high (o deep etc).

ve'scica, che [veʃ'ʃika] sf (ANAT) bladder; (MED) blister.

'**vescovo** sm bishop.

'**vespa** sf wasp.

'**vespro** sm (REL) vespers pl.

ves'sillo sm standard; (bandiera) flag.

ves'taglia [ves'taʎʎa] sf dressing gown.

'**veste** sf garment; (rivestimento) covering; (qualità, facoltà) capacity; **in ~ ufficiale** (fig) in an official capacity; **in ~ di** in the guise of, as; **vesti'ario** sm wardrobe, clothes pl.

ves'tibolo sm (entrance) hall.

ves'tire vt (bambino, malato) to dress; (avere indosso) to have on, wear; ~**rsi** vr to dress, get dressed; **ves'tito, a** ag dressed ♦ sm garment; (da donna) dress; (da uomo) suit; **vestiti** smpl (indumenti) clothes; **vestito di bianco** dressed in white.

Ve'suvio sm: **il ~** Vesuvius.

vete'rano, a ag, sm/f veteran.

veteri'naria sf veterinary medicine.

veteri'nario, a ag veterinary ♦ sm veterinary surgeon (BRIT), veterinarian (US), vet.

'**veto** sm inv veto.

ve'traio sm glassmaker; glazier.

ve'trata sf glass door (o window); (di chiesa) stained glass window.

ve'trato, a ag (porta, finestra) glazed; (che contiene vetro) glass cpd.

vetre'ria sf (stabilimento) glassworks sg; (oggetti di vetro) glassware.

ve'trina sf (di negozio) (shop) window; (armadio) display cabinet; **vetri'nista, i, e** sm/f window dresser.

vetri'olo sm vitriol.

'**vetro** sm glass; (per finestra, porta) pane (of glass).

'**vetta** sf peak, summit, top.

vet'tore sm (MAT, FISICA) vector; (chi trasporta) carrier.

vetto'vaglie [vetto'vaʎʎe] sfpl supplies.

vet'tura sf (carrozza) carriage; (FERR) carriage (BRIT), car (US); (auto) car (BRIT), automobile (US).

vezzeggi'are [vettsed'dʒare] vt to fondle, caress; **vezzeggia'tivo** sm (LING) term of endearment.

'**vezzo** ['vettso] sm habit; ~**i** smpl (smancerie) affected ways; (leggiadria) charms; **vez'zoso, a** ag (grazioso) charming, pretty; (lezioso) affected.

vi (*dav lo, la, li, le, ne diventa* **ve**) *pron* (*oggetto*) you; (*complemento di termine*) (to) you; (*riflessivo*) yourselves; (*reciproco*) each other ♦ *av* (*lì*) there; (*qui*) here; (*per questo/quel luogo*) through here/there; ~ **è/sono** there is/are.

'**via** *sf* (*gen*) way; (*strada*) street; (*sentiero, pista*) path, track; (AMM: *procedimento*) channels *pl* ♦ *prep* (*passando per*) via, by way of ♦ *av* away ♦ *escl* go away!; (*suvvia*) come on!; (SPORT) go! ♦ *sm* (SPORT) starting signal; **in** ~ **di guarigione** on the road to recovery; **per** ~ **di** (*a causa di*) because of, on account of; **in o per** ~ on the way; **per** ~ **aerea** by air; (*lettere*) by airmail; **andare/essere** ~ to go/be away; ~ ~ **che** (*a mano a mano*) as; **dare il** ~ (SPORT) to give the starting signal; **dare il** ~ **a** (*fig*) to start; **V~ lattea** (ASTR) Milky Way; ~ **di mezzo** middle course; **in** ~ **provvisoria** provisionally.

viabilità *sf* (*di strada*) practicability; (*rete stradale*) roads *pl*, road network.

via'dotto *sm* viaduct.

viaggi'are [viad'dʒare] *vi* to travel; **viaggia'tore, 'trice** *ag* travelling ♦ *sm* traveller; (*passeggero*) passenger.

vi'aggio ['vjaddʒo] *sm* travel(ling); (*tragitto*) journey, trip; **buon** ~! have a good trip!; ~ **di nozze** honeymoon.

vi'ale *sm* avenue.

via'vai *sm* coming and going, bustle.

vi'brare *vi* to vibrate; (*agitarsi*): ~ (**di**) to quiver (with).

vi'cario *sm* (*apostolico etc*) vicar.

'**vice** ['vitʃe] *sm/f* deputy ♦ *prefisso*: ~'**console** *sm* vice-consul; ~**diret'tore** *sm* assistant manager.

vi'cenda [vi'tʃenda] *sf* event; **a** ~ in turn; **vicen'devole** *ag* mutual, reciprocal.

vice'versa [vitʃe'vɛrsa] *av* vice versa; **da Roma a Pisa e** ~ from Rome to Pisa and back.

vici'nanza [vitʃi'nantsa] *sf* nearness, closeness; ~**e** *sfpl* (*paraggi*) neighbourhood, vicinity.

vici'nato [vitʃi'nato] *sm* neighbourhood; (*vicini*) neighbours *pl*.

vi'cino, a [vi'tʃino] *ag* (*gen*) near; (*nello spazio*) near, nearby; (*accanto*) next; (*nel tempo*) near, close at hand ♦ *sm/f* neighbour ♦ *av* near, close; **da** ~ (*guardare*) close up; (*esaminare, seguire*) closely; (*conoscere*) well, intimately; ~ **a** near (to), close to; (*accanto a*) beside; ~ **di casa** neighbour.

'**vicolo** *sm* alley; ~ **cieco** blind alley.

'**video** *sm inv* (TV: *schermo*) screen; ~**cas'setta** *sf* videocassette; ~**regi-stra'tore** *sm* video (recorder).

vie'tare *vt* to forbid; (AMM) to prohibit; ~ **a qn di fare** to forbid sb to do; to prohibit sb from doing; "**vietato fumare/l'ingresso**" "no smoking/admittance".

Viet'nam *sm*: **il** ~ Vietnam; **vietna'mita, i, e** *ag, sm/f, sm* Vietnamese *inv*.

vi'gente [vi'dʒɛnte] *ag* in force.

vigi'lante [vidʒi'lante] *ag* vigilant, watchful.

vigi'lare [vidʒi'lare] *vt* to watch over, keep an eye on; ~ **che** to make sure that, see to it that.

'**vigile** ['vidʒile] *ag* watchful ♦ *sm* (*anche:* ~ **urbano**) policeman (*in towns*); ~ **del fuoco** fireman.

vi'gilia [vi'dʒilja] *sf* (*giorno antecedente*) eve; **la** ~ **di Natale** Christmas Eve.

vigli'acco, a, chi, che [viʎ'ʎakko] *ag* cowardly ♦ *sm/f* coward.

'**vigna** ['viɲɲa] *sf* = **vi'gneto**.

vi'gneto [viɲ'ɲeto] *sm* vineyard.

vi'gnetta [viɲ'ɲetta] *sf* cartoon.

vi'gore *sm* vigour; (DIR): **essere/entrare in** ~ to be in/come into force; **vigo'roso, a** *ag* vigorous.

'**vile** *ag* (*spregevole*) low, mean, base; (*codardo*) cowardly.

vili'pendio *sm* contempt, scorn; public insult.

'**villa** *sf* villa.

vil'laggio [vil'laddʒo] *sm* village.

villa'nia *sf* rudeness, lack of manners; **fare** (*o* **dire**) **una** ~ **a qn** to be rude to sb.

vil'lano, a *ag* rude, ill-mannered ♦ *sm* boor.

villeggia'tura [villeddʒa'tura] *sf* holiday(s *pl*) (*BRIT*), vacation (*US*).

vil'lino *sm* small house (with a garden), cottage.

vil'loso, a *ag* hairy.

viltà *sf* cowardice *no pl*; cowardly act.

'vimine *sm* wicker; **mobili di ~i** wicker furniture *sg*.

'vincere ['vintʃere] *vt* (*in guerra, al gioco, a una gara*) to defeat, beat; (*premio, guerra, partita*) to win; (*fig*) to overcome, conquer ♦ *vi* to win; **~ qn in bellezza** to be better-looking than sb; **'vincita** *sf* win; (*denaro vinto*) winnings *pl*; **vinci'tore** *sm* winner; (*MIL*) victor.

vinco'lare *vt* to bind; (*COMM: denaro*) to tie up; **'vincolo** *sm* (*fig*) bond, tie; (*DIR: servitù*) obligation.

vi'nicolo, a *ag* wine *cpd*.

'vino *sm* wine; **~ bianco/rosso** white/red wine.

'vinto, a *pp di* **vincere**.

vi'ola *sf* (*BOT*) violet; (*MUS*) viola ♦ *ag*, *sm inv* (*colore*) purple.

vio'lare *vt* (*chiesa*) to desecrate, violate; (*giuramento, legge*) to violate.

violen'tare *vt* to use violence on; (*donna*) to rape.

vio'lento, a *ag* violent; **vio'lenza** *sf* violence; **violenza carnale** rape.

vio'letta *sf* (*BOT*) violet.

vio'letto, a *ag, sm* (*colore*) violet.

violi'nista, i, e *sm/f* violinist.

vio'lino *sm* violin.

violon'cello [violon'tʃello] *sm* cello.

vi'ottolo *sm* path, track.

'vipera *sf* viper, adder.

vi'raggio [vi'raddʒo] *sm* (*NAUT, AER*) turn; (*FOT*) toning.

vi'rare *vt* (*NAUT*) to haul (in), heave (in) ♦ *vi* (*NAUT, AER*) to turn; (*FOT*) to tone; **~ di bordo** (*NAUT*) to tack.

'virgola *sf* (*LING*) comma; (*MAT*) point; **virgo'lette** *sfpl* inverted commas, quotation marks.

vi'rile *ag* (*proprio dell'uomo*) masculine; (*non puerile, da uomo*) manly, vir-

ile.

virtù *sf inv* virtue; **in o per ~ di** by virtue of, by.

virtu'ale *ag* virtual.

virtu'oso, a *ag* virtuous ♦ *sm/f* (*MUS etc*) virtuoso.

'virus *sm inv* virus.

'viscere ['viʃʃere] *sm* (*ANAT*) internal organ ♦ *sfpl* (*di animale*) entrails *pl*; (*fig*) bowels *pl*.

'vischio ['viskjo] *sm* (*BOT*) mistletoe; (*pania*) birdlime; **vischi'oso, a** *ag* sticky.

'viscido, a ['viʃʃido] *ag* slimy.

vi'sibile *ag* visible.

visi'bilio *sm*: **andare in ~** to go into raptures.

visibilità *sf* visibility.

visi'era *sf* (*di elmo*) visor; (*di berretto*) peak.

visi'one *sf* vision; **prendere ~ di qc** to examine sth, look sth over; **prima/seconda ~** (*CINEMA*) first/second showing.

'visita *sf* visit; (*MED*) visit, call; (: *esame*) examination; **visi'tare** *vt* to visit; (*MED*) to visit, call on; (: *esaminare*) to examine; **visita'tore, 'trice** *sm/f* visitor.

vi'sivo, a *ag* visual.

'viso *sm* face.

vi'sone *sm* mink.

'vispo, a *ag* quick, lively.

vis'suto, a *pp di* **vivere** ♦ *ag* (*aria, modo di fare*) experienced.

'vista *sf* (*facoltà*) (eye)sight; (*fatto di vedere*): **la ~ di** the sight of; (*veduta*) view; **sparare a ~** to shoot on sight; **in ~** in sight; **perdere qn di ~** to lose sight of sb; (*fig*) to lose touch with sb; **a ~ d'occhio** as far as the eye can see; (*fig*) before one's very eyes; **far ~ di fare** to pretend to do.

'visto, a *pp di* **vedere** ♦ *sm* visa; **~ che** seeing (that).

vis'toso, a *ag* gaudy, garish; (*ingente*) considerable.

visu'ale *ag* visual; **visualizza'tore** *sm* (*INFORM*) visual display unit, VDU.

'vita *sf* life; (*ANAT*) waist; **a ~** for life.

vi'tale ag vital; vita'lizio, a ag life cpd
♦ sm life annuity.
vita'mina sf vitamin.
'vite sf (BOT) vine; (TECN) screw.
vi'tello sm (ZOOL) calf; (carne) veal;
(pelle) calfskin.
vi'ticcio [vi'tittʃo] sm (BOT) tendril.
viticol'tore sm wine grower;
viticol'tura sf wine growing.
'vitreo, a ag vitreous; (occhio,
sguardo) glassy.
'vittima sf victim.
'vitto sm food; (in un albergo etc)
board; ~ e alloggio board and lodging.
vit'toria sf victory.
'viva escl: ~ il re! long live the king!
vi'vace [vi'vatʃe] ag (vivo, animato)
lively; (: mente) lively, sharp; (colore)
bright; vivacità sf vivacity; liveliness;
brightness.
vi'vaio sm (di pesci) hatchery; (AGR)
nursery.
vi'vanda sf food; (piatto) dish.
vi'vente ag living, alive; i ~i the living.
'vivere vi to live ♦ vt to live; (passare:
brutto momento) to live through, go
through; (sentire: gioie, pene di qn) to
share ♦ sm life; (anche: modo di ~)
way of life; ~i smpl (cibo) food sg,
provisions; ~ di to live on.
'vivido, a ag (colore) vivid, bright.
'vivo, a ag (vivente) alive, living; (:
animale) live; (fig) lively; (: colore)
bright, brilliant; i ~i the living; nel ~ e
vegeto hale and hearty; farsi ~ to show
one's face; to be heard from; ritrarre
dal ~ to paint from life; pungere qn nel
~ (fig) to cut sb to the quick.
vizi'are [vit'tsjare] vt (bambino) to spoil;
(corrompere moralmente) to corrupt;
vizi'ato, a ag spoilt; (aria, acqua)
polluted.
'vizio ['vittsjo] sm (morale) vice;
(cattiva abitudine) bad habit;
(imperfezione) flaw, defect; (errore)
fault, mistake; vizi'oso, a ag depraved;
defective; (inesatto) incorrect, wrong.
vocabo'lario sm (dizionario) dictionary; (lessico) vocabulary.

vo'cabolo sm word.
vo'cale ag vocal ♦ sf vowel.
vocazi'one [vokat'tsjone] sf vocation;
(fig) natural bent.
'voce ['votʃe] sf voice; (diceria)
rumour; (di un elenco, in bilancio)
item; aver ~ in capitolo (fig) to have a
say in the matter.
voci'are [vo'tʃare] vi to shout, yell.
'voga sf (NAUT) rowing; (usanza):
essere in ~ to be in fashion o in vogue.
vo'gare vi to row.
'voglia ['vɔʎʎa] sf desire, wish;
(macchia) birthmark; aver ~ di qc/di
fare to feel like sth/like doing; (più
forte) to want sth/to do.
'voi pron you; voi'altri pron you.
vo'lano sm (SPORT) shuttlecock; (TECN)
flywheel.
vo'lante ag flying ♦ sm (steering)
wheel.
volan'tino sm leaflet.
vo'lare vi (uccello, aereo, fig) to fly;
(cappello) to blow away o off, fly away
o off; ~ via to fly away o off.
vo'latile ag (CHIM) volatile ♦ sm
(ZOOL) bird.
volente'roso, a ag willing.
volenti'eri av willingly; "~" "with
pleasure", "I'd be glad to".

PAROLA CHIAVE

vo'lere sm will, wish(es); contro il ~ di
against the wishes of; per ~ di qn in
obedience to sb's will o wishes
♦ vt 1 (esigere, desiderare) to want;
voler fare/che qn faccia to want to do/sb
to do; volete del caffè? would you like o
do you want some coffee?; vorrei
questo/fare I would o I'd like this/to do;
come vuoi as you like; senza ~ (inavvertitamente) without meaning to,
unintentionally
2 (consentire): vogliate attendere, per
piacere please wait; vogliamo andare?
shall we go?; vuole essere così gentile
da ...? would you be so kind as to ...?;
non ha voluto ricevermi he wouldn't see
me
3: volerci (essere necessario: mate-

riale, attenzione) to need; (: *tempo*) to take; **quanta farina ci vuole per questa torta?** how much flour do you need for this cake?; **ci vuole un'ora per arrivare a Venezia** it takes an hour to get to Venice
4: voler bene a qn (*amore*) to love sb; (*affetto*) to be fond of sb, like sb very much; **voler male a qn** to dislike sb; **volerne a qn** to bear sb a grudge; **voler dire** to mean.

vol'gare *ag* vulgar; **volgariz'zare** *vt* to popularize.
'volgere ['vɔldʒere] *vt* to turn ♦ *vi* to turn; (*tendere*): ~ **a: il tempo volge al brutto** the weather is breaking; **un rosso che volge al viola** a red verging on purple; ~**rsi** *vr* to turn; ~ **al peggio** to take a turn for the worse; ~ **al termine** to draw to an end.
'volgo *sm* common people.
voli'era *sf* aviary.
voli'tivo, a *ag* strong-willed.
'volo *sm* flight; **al ~: colpire qc al ~** to hit sth as it flies past; **capire al ~** to understand straight away.
volontà *sf* will; **a ~** (*mangiare, bere*) as much as one likes; **buona/cattiva ~** goodwill/lack of goodwill.
volon'tario, a *ag* voluntary ♦ *sm* (*MIL*) volunteer.
'volpe *sf* fox.
'volta *sf* (*momento, circostanza*) time; (*turno, giro*) turn; (*curva*) turn, bend; (*ARCHIT*) vault; (*direzione*): **partire alla ~ di** to set off for; **a mia** (*o* **tua** *etc*) ~ in turn; **una ~ once**; **una ~ sola** only once; **due ~e** twice; **una cosa per ~** one thing at a time; **una ~ per tutte** once and for all; **a ~e** at times, sometimes; **una ~ che** (*temporale*) once; (*causale*) since; **3 ~e 4 3** times 4.
volta'faccia [volta'fattʃa] *sm inv* (*fig*) volte-face.
vol'taggio [vol'taddʒo] *sm* (*ELETTR*) voltage.
vol'tare *vt* to turn; (*girare: moneta*) to turn over; (*rigirare*) to turn round ♦ *vi* to turn; ~**rsi** *vr* to turn; to turn over;

to turn round.
volteggi'are [volted'dʒare] *vi* (*volare*) to circle; (*in equitazione*) to do trick riding; (*in ginnastica*) to vault; to perform acrobatics.
'volto, a *pp di* **volgere** ♦ *sm* face.
vo'lubile *ag* changeable, fickle.
vo'lume *sm* volume; **volumi'noso, a** *ag* voluminous, bulky.
voluttà *sf* sensual pleasure *o* delight; **voluttu'oso, a** *ag* voluptuous.
vomi'tare *vt, vi* to vomit; 'vomito *sm* vomiting *no pl*; vomit.
'vongola *sf* clam.
vo'race [vo'ratʃe] *ag* voracious, greedy.
vo'ragine [vo'radʒine] *sf* abyss, chasm.
'vortice ['vɔrtitʃe] *sm* whirlwind; whirlpool; (*fig*) whirl.
'vostro, a *det*: **il(la)** ~**(a)** *etc* your ♦ *pron*: **il(la)** ~**(a)** *etc* yours.
vo'tante *sm/f* voter.
vo'tare *vi* to vote ♦ *vt* (*sottoporre a votazione*) to take a vote on; (*approvare*) to vote for; (*REL*): ~ **qc a** to dedicate sth to; **votazi'one** *sf* vote, voting; **votazioni** *sfpl* (*POL*) votes; (*INS*) marks.
'voto *sm* (*POL*) vote; (*INS*) mark; (*REL*) vow; (: *offerta*) votive offering; **aver** ~**i belli/brutti** (*INS*) to get good/bad marks.
vs. *abbr* (*COMM*) = **vostro**.
vul'cano *sm* volcano.
vulne'rabile *ag* vulnerable.
vuo'tare *vt* to empty; ~**rsi** *vr* to empty.
vu'oto, a *ag* empty; (*fig: privo*): ~ **di** (*senso etc*) devoid of ♦ *sm* empty space, gap; (*spazio in bianco*) blank; (*FISICA*) vacuum; (*fig: mancanza*) gap, void; **a mani** ~**e** empty-handed; ~ **d'aria** air pocket; ~ **a rendere** return-able bottle.

W X Y

watt [vat] *sm inv* watt.
'weekend ['wi:kend] *sm inv* weekend.
'whisky ['wiski] *sm inv* whisky.

'**xeres** ['ksɛres] *sm inv* sherry.
xero'copia [ksero'kɔpja] *sf* xerox ®, photocopy.
xi'lofono [ksi'lɔfono] *sm* xylophone.
yacht [jɔt] *sm inv* yacht.
'**yoghurt** ['jɔgurt] *sm inv* yoghourt.

Z

zabai'one [dzaba'jone] *sm dessert made of egg yolks, sugar and marsala.*
zaf'fata [tsaf'fata] *sf (tanfo)* stench.
zaffe'rano [dzaffe'rano] *sm* saffron.
zaf'firo [dzaf'firo] *sm* sapphire.
'**zaino** ['dzaino] *sm* rucksack.
'**zampa** ['tsampa] *sf (di animale: gamba)* leg; (: *piede*) paw; **a quattro** ~**e** on all fours.
zampil'lare [tsampil'lare] *vi* to gush, spurt; **zam'pillo** *sm* gush, spurt.
zam'pogna [tsam'poɲɲa] *sf instrument similar to bagpipes.*
'**zanna** ['tsanna] *sf (di elefante)* tusk; (*di carnivoro*) fang.
zan'zara [dzan'dzara] *sf* mosquito; **zanzari'era** *sf* mosquito net.
'**zappa** ['tsappa] *sf* hoe; **zap'pare** *vt* to hoe.
zar, za'rina [tsar, tsa'rina] *sm/f* tsar/tsarina.
'**zattera** ['dzattɛra] *sf* raft.
za'vorra [dza'vɔrra] *sf* ballast.
'**zazzera** ['tsattsera] *sf* shock of hair.
'**zebra** ['dzɛbra] *sf* zebra; ~**e** *sfpl (AUT)* zebra crossing *sg (BRIT)*, crosswalk *sg (US)*.
'**zecca, che** ['tsekka] *sf (ZOOL)* tick; (*officina di monete*) mint.
'**zelo** ['dzɛlo] *sm* zeal.
'**zenit** ['dzɛnit] *sm* zenith.
'**zenzero** ['dzendzero] *sm* ginger.
'**zeppa** ['tseppa] *sf* wedge.
'**zeppo, a** ['tseppo] *ag*: ~ **di** crammed *o* packed with.
zer'bino [dzer'bino] *sm* doormat.
'**zero** ['dzɛro] *sm* zero, nought; **vincere per tre a** ~ (*SPORT*) to win three-nil.
'**zeta** ['dzɛta] *sm o f* zed, (the letter) z.
'**zia** ['tsia] *sf* aunt.

zibel'lino [dzibel'lino] *sm* sable.
'**zigomo** ['dzigomo] *sm* cheekbone.
zig'zag [dzig'dzag] *sm inv* zigzag; **andare a** ~ to zigzag.
zim'bello [dzim'bello] *sm (oggetto di burle)* laughing-stock.
'**zinco** ['dzinko] *sm* zinc.
'**zingaro, a** ['dzingaro] *sm/f* gipsy.
'**zio** ['tsio] (*pl* '**zii**) *sm* uncle; **zii** *smpl (zio e zia)* uncle and aunt.
zi'tella [dzi'tɛlla] *sf* spinster; (*peg*) old maid.
'**zitto, a** ['tsitto] *ag* quiet, silent; **sta'** ~**!** be quiet!
ziz'zania [dzid'dzanja] *sf (fig)*: **gettare** *o* **seminare** ~ to sow discord.
'**zoccolo** ['tsɔkkolo] *sm (calzatura)* clog; (*di cavallo etc*) hoof; (*basamento*) base; plinth.
zo'diaco [dzo'diako] *sm* zodiac.
'**zolfo** ['tsolfo] *sm* sulphur.
'**zolla** ['dzɔlla] *sf* clod (of earth).
zol'letta [dzol'letta] *sf* sugar lump.
'**zona** ['dzɔna] *sf* zone, area; ~ **di depressione** (*METEOR*) trough of low pressure; ~ **pedonale** pedestrian precinct; ~ **verde** (*di abitato*) green area.
'**zonzo** ['dzondzo]: **a** ~ *av*: **andare a** ~ to wander about, stroll about.
zoo ['dzɔo] *sm inv* zoo.
zoolo'gia [dzoolo'dʒia] *sf* zoology.
zoppi'care [tsoppi'kare] *vi* to limp; to be shaky, rickety.
'**zoppo, a** ['tsɔppo] *ag* lame; (*fig: mobile*) shaky, rickety.
zoti'cone [dzoti'kone] *sm* lout.
'**zucca, che** ['tsukka] *sf (BOT)* marrow; pumpkin.
zucche'rare [tsukke'rare] *vt* to put sugar in; **zucche'rato, a** *ag* sweet, sweetened.
zuccheri'era [tsukke'rjera] *sf* sugar bowl.
zuccheri'ficio [tsukkeri'fitʃo] *sm* sugar refinery.
zucche'rino, a [tsukke'rino] *ag* sugary, sweet.
'**zucchero** ['tsukkero] *sm* sugar.
zuc'china [tsuk'kina] *sf* courgette (*BRIT*), zucchini (*US*).
zuc'chino [tsuk'kino] *sm* = **zucchina**.

'**zuffa** ['tsuffa] *sf* brawl.
'**zuppa** ['tsuppa] *sf* soup; (*fig*) mixture, muddle; ~ **inglese** (*CUC*) *dessert made with sponge cake, custard and* chocolate, ≈ trifle (*BRIT*); **zuppi'era** *sf* soup tureen.
'**zuppo, a** ['tsuppo] *ag:* ~ (**di**) drenched (with), soaked (with).

ENGLISH - ITALIAN
INGLESE - ITALIANO

A

A [eɪ] n (MUS) la m.

a [ə] (before vowel or silent h: an) indef art **1** un (uno +s impure, gn, pn, ps, x, z), f una (un' +vowel); ~ **book** un libro; ~ **mirror** uno specchio; **an apple** una mela; **she's** ~ **doctor** è medico
2 (instead of the number "one") un(o), f una; ~ **year ago** un anno fa; ~ **hundred/thousand** etc **pounds** cento/mille etc sterline
3 (in expressing ratios, prices etc) a, per; **3** ~ **day/week** 3 al giorno/alla settimana; **10 km an hour** 10 km all'ora; £5 ~ **person** 5 sterline a persona or per persona.

A.A. n abbr (= Alcoholics Anonymous) AA; (BRIT: = Automobile Association) ≈ A.C.I. m.
A.A.A. (US) n abbr (= American Automobile Association) ≈ A.C.I. m.
aback [ə'bæk] adv: **to be taken** ~ essere sbalordito(a).
abandon [ə'bændən] vt abbandonare ♦ n: **with** ~ sfrenatamente, spensieratamente.
abashed [ə'bæʃt] adj imbarazzato(a).
abate [ə'beɪt] vi calmarsi.
abattoir ['æbətwɑ:*] (BRIT) n mattatoio.
abbey ['æbɪ] n abbazia, badia.
abbot ['æbət] n abate m.
abbreviation [əbri:vɪ'eɪʃən] n abbreviazione f.
abdicate ['æbdɪkeɪt] vt abdicare a ♦ vi abdicare.
abdomen ['æbdəmɛn] n addome m.
abduct [æb'dʌkt] vt rapire.
aberration [æbə'reɪʃən] n aberrazione f.
abet [ə'bɛt] vt see **aid**.
abeyance [ə'beɪəns] n: **in** ~ (law) in

disuso; (matter) in sospeso.
abide [ə'baɪd] vt: **I can't** ~ **it/him** non lo posso soffrire or sopportare; ~ **by** vt fus conformarsi a.
ability [ə'bɪlɪtɪ] n abilità f inv.
abject ['æbdʒɛkt] adj (poverty) abietto(a); (apology) umiliante.
ablaze [ə'bleɪz] adj in fiamme.
able ['eɪbl] adj capace; **to be** ~ **to do sth** essere capace di fare qc, poter fare qc; ~-**bodied** adj robusto(a); **ably** adv abilmente.
abnormal [æb'nɔ:məl] adj anormale.
aboard [ə'bɔ:d] adv a bordo ♦ prep a bordo di.
abode [ə'bəud] n: **of no fixed** ~ senza fissa dimora.
abolish [ə'bɔlɪʃ] vt abolire.
abominable [ə'bɔmɪnəbl] adj abominevole.
aborigine [æbə'rɪdʒɪnɪ] n aborigeno/a.
abort [ə'bɔ:t] vt abortire; ~**ion** [ə'bɔ:ʃən] n aborto; **to have an** ~**ion** abortire; ~**ive** adj abortivo(a).
abound [ə'baund] vi abbondare; **to** ~ **in** or **with** abbondare di.

about [ə'baut] adv **1** (approximately) circa, quasi; ~ **a hundred/thousand** etc un centinaio/migliaio etc, circa cento/mille etc; **it takes** ~ **10 hours** ci vogliono circa 10 ore; **at** ~ **2 o'clock** verso le 2; **I've just** ~ **finished** ho quasi finito
2 (referring to place) qua e là, in giro; **to leave things lying** ~ lasciare delle cose in giro; **to run** ~ correre qua e là; **to walk** ~ camminare
3: to be ~ **to do sth** stare per fare qc
♦ prep **1** (relating to) su, di; **a book** ~ **London** un libro su Londra; **what is it** ~? di che si tratta?; (book, film etc) di

cosa tratta?; **we talked ~ it** ne abbiamo parlato; **what** or **how ~ doing this?** che ne dici di fare questo?

2 (*referring to place*): **to walk ~ the town** camminare per la città; **her clothes were scattered ~ the room** i suoi vestiti erano sparsi or in giro per tutta la stanza.

about-face *n* dietro front *m inv*.

about-turn *n* dietro front *m inv*.

above [əˈbʌv] *adv*, *prep* sopra; **mentioned ~** suddetto; **~ all** soprattutto; **~board** aperto(a); onesto(a).

abrasive [əˈbreɪzɪv] *adj* abrasivo(a); (*fig*) caustico(a).

abreast [əˈbrɛst] *adv* di fianco; **to keep ~ of** tenersi aggiornato su.

abridge [əˈbrɪdʒ] *vt* ridurre.

abroad [əˈbrɔːd] *adv* all'estero.

abrupt [əˈbrʌpt] *adj* (*sudden*) improvviso(a); (*gruff, blunt*) brusco(a).

abscess [ˈæbsɪs] *n* ascesso.

abscond [əbˈskɔnd] *vi* scappare.

absence [ˈæbsəns] *n* assenza.

absent [ˈæbsənt] *adj* assente; **~ee** [-ˈtiː] *n* assente *m/f*; **~-minded** *adj* distratto(a).

absolute [ˈæbsəluːt] *adj* assoluto(a); **~ly** [-ˈluːtlɪ] *adv* assolutamente.

absolve [əbˈzɔlv] *vt*: **to ~ sb (from)** (*sin*) assolvere qn (da); (*oath*) sciogliere qn (da).

absorb [əbˈzɔːb] *vt* assorbire; **to be ~ed in a book** essere immerso in un libro; **~ent cotton** (*US*) *n* cotone *m* idrofilo; **~ing** *adj* avvincente.

absorption [əbˈsɔːpʃən] *n* assorbimento.

abstain [əbˈsteɪn] *vi*: **to ~ (from)** astenersi (da).

abstemious [əbˈstiːmɪəs] *adj* astemio(a).

abstract [ˈæbstrækt] *adj* astratto(a).

absurd [əbˈsɔːd] *adj* assurdo(a).

abuse [*n* əˈbjuːs, *vb* əˈbjuːz] *n* abuso; (*insults*) ingiurie *fpl* ♦ *vt* abusare di; **abusive** *adj* ingiurioso(a).

abysmal [əˈbɪzməl] *adj* spaventoso(a).

abyss [əˈbɪs] *n* abisso.

AC *abbr* (= *alternating current*) c.a.

academic [ækəˈdɛmɪk] *adj* accademico(a); (*pej: issue*) puramente formale ♦ *n* universitario/a.

academy [əˈkædəmɪ] *n* (*learned body*) accademia; (*school*) scuola privata; **~ of music** conservatorio.

accelerate [ækˈsɛləreɪt] *vt*, *vi* accelerare; **accelerator** *n* acceleratore *m*.

accent [ˈæksɛnt] *n* accento.

accept [əkˈsɛpt] *vt* accettare; **~able** *adj* accettabile; **~ance** *n* accettazione *f*.

access [ˈæksɛs] *n* accesso; **~ible** [ækˈsɛsəbl] *adj* accessibile.

accessory [ækˈsɛsərɪ] *n* accessorio; (*LAW*): **~ to** complice *m/f* di.

accident [ˈæksɪdənt] *n* incidente *m*; (*chance*) caso; **by ~** per caso; **~al** [-ˈdɛntl] *adj* accidentale; **~ally** [-ˈdɛntəlɪ] *adv* per caso; **~-prone** *adj*: **he's very ~-prone** è un vero passaguai.

acclaim [əˈkleɪm] *n* acclamazione *f*.

accolade [ˈækəleɪd] *n* encomio.

accommodate [əˈkɔmədeɪt] *vt* alloggiare; (*oblige, help*) favorire.

accommodating [əˈkɔmədeɪtɪŋ] *adj* compiacente.

accommodation [əkɔməˈdeɪʃən] *n* alloggio; **~s** (*US*) *npl* alloggio.

accompany [əˈkʌmpənɪ] *vt* accompagnare.

accomplice [əˈkʌmplɪs] *n* complice *m/f*.

accomplish [əˈkʌmplɪʃ] *vt* compiere; (*goal*) raggiungere; **~ed** *adj* esperto(a); **~ment** *n* compimento; realizzazione *f*; **~ments** *npl* (*skills*) doti *fpl*.

accord [əˈkɔːd] *n* accordo ♦ *vt* accordare; **of his own ~** di propria iniziativa; **~ance** *n*: **in ~ance with** in conformità con; **~ing**: **~ing to** *prep* secondo; **~ingly** *adv* in conformità.

accordion [əˈkɔːdɪən] *n* fisarmonica.

accost [əˈkɔst] *vt* avvicinare.

account [əˈkaunt] *n* (*COMM*) conto; (*report*) descrizione *f*; **~s** *npl* (*COMM*) conti *mpl*; **of no ~** di nessuna importanza; **on ~** in acconto; **on no ~** per nessun motivo; **on ~ of** a causa di; **to take into ~, take ~ of** tener conto di;

~ **for** vt fus spiegare; giustificare; **~able** adj: **~able (to)** responsabile (verso).

accountancy [ə'kauntənsɪ] n ragioneria.

accountant [ə'kauntənt] n ragioniere/a.

account number n numero di conto.

accrued interest [ə'kru:d-] n interesse m maturato.

accumulate [ə'kju:mjuleɪt] vt accumulare ♦ vi accumularsi.

accuracy ['ækjurəsɪ] n precisione f.

accurate ['ækjurɪt] adj preciso(a); **~ly** adv precisamente.

accusation [ækju'zeɪʃən] n accusa.

accuse [ə'kju:z] vt accusare; **~d** n accusato/a.

accustom [ə'kʌstəm] vt abituare; **~ed** adj: **~ed to** abituato(a) a.

ace [eɪs] n asso.

ache [eɪk] n male m, dolore m ♦ vi (be sore) far male, dolere; **my head ~s** mi fa male la testa.

achieve [ə'tʃi:v] vt (aim) raggiungere; (victory, success) ottenere; **~ment** n compimento; successo.

acid ['æsɪd] adj acido(a) ♦ n acido; ~ **rain** n pioggia acida.

acknowledge [ək'nɔlɪdʒ] vt (letter: also: ~ **receipt of**) confermare la ricevuta di; (fact) riconoscere; **~ment** n conferma; riconoscimento.

acne ['æknɪ] n acne f.

acorn ['eɪkɔ:n] n ghianda.

acoustic [ə'ku:stɪk] adj acustico(a); **~s** n, npl acustica.

acquaint [ə'kweɪnt] vt: **to ~ sb with sth** far sapere qc a qn; **to be ~ed with** (person) conoscere; **~ance** n conoscenza; (person) conoscente m/f.

acquiesce [ækwɪ'es] vi: **to ~ (to)** acconsentire (a).

acquire [ə'kwaɪə*] vt acquistare.

acquisition [ækwɪ'zɪʃən] n acquisto.

acquit [ə'kwɪt] vt assolvere; **to ~ o.s. well** comportarsi bene; **~tal** n assoluzione f.

acre ['eɪkə*] n acro (= 4047 m²).

acrid ['ækrɪd] adj acre; pungente.

acrimonious [ækrɪ'məunɪəs] adj astioso(a).

acrobat ['ækrəbæt] n acrobata m/f.

across [ə'krɔs] prep (on the other side) dall'altra parte di; (crosswise) attraverso ♦ adv dall'altra parte; in larghezza; **to run/swim ~** attraversare di corsa/a nuoto; **~ from** di fronte a.

acrylic [ə'krɪlɪk] adj acrilico(a).

act [ækt] n atto; (in music-hall etc) numero; (LAW) decreto ♦ vi agire; (THEATRE) recitare; (pretend) fingere ♦ vt (part) recitare; **to ~ as** agire da; **~ing** adj che fa le funzioni di ♦ n (of actor) recitazione f; (activity): **to do some ~ing** fare del teatro (or del cinema).

action ['ækʃən] n azione f; (MIL) combattimento; (LAW) processo; **out of ~** fuori combattimento; fuori servizio; **to take ~** agire; **~ replay** n (TV) replay m inv.

activate ['æktɪveɪt] vt (mechanism) attivare.

active ['æktɪv] adj attivo(a); **~ly** adv (participate) attivamente; (discourage, dislike) vivamente.

activity [æk'tɪvɪtɪ] n attività f inv.

actor ['æktə*] n attore m.

actress ['æktrɪs] n attrice f.

actual ['æktjuəl] adj reale, vero(a); **~ly** adv veramente; (even) addirittura.

acumen ['ækjumən] n acume m.

acute [ə'kju:t] adj acuto(a); (mind, person) perspicace.

ad [æd] n abbr = **advertisement**.

A.D. adv abbr (= Anno Domini) d.C.

adamant ['ædəmənt] adj irremovibile.

adapt [ə'dæpt] vt adattare ♦ vi: **to ~ (to)** adattarsi (a); **~able** adj (device) adattabile; (person) che sa adattarsi; **~er** or **~or** n (ELEC) adattatore m.

add [æd] vt aggiungere; (figures: also: ~ **up**) addizionare ♦ vi: **to ~ to** (increase) aumentare; **it doesn't ~ up** (fig) non quadra, non ha senso.

adder ['ædə*] n vipera.

addict ['ædɪkt] n tossicomane m/f; (fig) fanatico/a; **~ed** [ə'dɪktɪd] adj: **to be ~ed to** (drink etc) essere dedito(a) a; (fig: football etc) essere tifoso(a) di; **~ion** [ə'dɪkʃən] n (MED) tossicodipendenza;

~**ive** [ə'dɪktɪv] *adj* che dà assuefazione.

addition [ə'dɪʃən] *n* addizione *f*; (*thing added*) aggiunta; **in** ~ inoltre; **in** ~ **to** oltre; ~**al** *adj* supplementare.

additive ['ædɪtɪv] *n* additivo.

address [ə'dres] *n* indirizzo; (*talk*) discorso ♦ *vt* indirizzare; (*speak to*) fare un discorso a; (*issue*) affrontare.

adept ['ædept] *adj*: ~ **at** esperto(a) in.

adequate ['ædɪkwɪt] *adj* adeguato(a); sufficiente.

adhere [əd'hɪə*] *vi*: **to** ~ **to** aderire a; (*fig*: *rule, decision*) seguire.

adhesive [əd'hi:zɪv] *n* adesivo; ~ **tape** *n* (*BRIT: for parcels etc*) nastro adesivo; (*US: MED*) cerotto adesivo.

adjective ['ædʒektɪv] *n* aggettivo.

adjoining [ə'dʒɔɪnɪŋ] *adj* accanto *inv*, adiacente.

adjourn [ə'dʒɜ:n] *vt* rimandare ♦ *vi* essere aggiornato(a).

adjudicate [ə'dʒu:dɪkeɪt] *vt* (*contest*) giudicare; (*claim*) decidere su.

adjust [ə'dʒʌst] *vt* aggiustare; (*change*) rettificare ♦ *vi*: **to** ~ (**to**) adattarsi (a); ~**able** *adj* regolabile; ~**ment** *n* (*PSYCH*) adattamento; (*of machine*) regolazione *f*; (*of prices, wages*) modifica.

ad-lib [æd'lɪb] *vi* improvvisare ♦ *adv*: **ad lib** a piacere, a volontà.

administer [əd'mɪnɪstə*] *vt* amministrare; (*justice, drug*) somministrare.

administration [ədmɪnɪs'treɪʃən] *n* amministrazione *f*.

administrative [əd'mɪnɪstrətɪv] *adj* amministrativo(a).

admiral ['ædmərəl] *n* ammiraglio; **A~ty** (*BRIT*) *n* Ministero della Marina.

admiration [ædmə'reɪʃən] *n* ammirazione *f*.

admire [əd'maɪə*] *vt* ammirare.

admission [əd'mɪʃən] *n* ammissione *f*; (*to exhibition, night club etc*) ingresso; (*confession*) confessione *f*.

admit [əd'mɪt] *vt* ammettere; far entrare; (*agree*) riconoscere; **to** ~ **to** riconoscere; ~**tance** *n* ingresso; ~**tedly** *adv* bisogna pur riconoscere (che).

admonish [əd'mɒnɪʃ] *vt* ammonire.

ad nauseam [æd'nɔ:sɪæm] *adv* fino alla

nausea, a non finire.

ado [ə'du:] *n*: **without (any) more** ~ senza più indugi.

adolescence [ædəu'lesns] *n* adolescenza.

adolescent [ædəu'lesnt] *adj, n* adolescente *m/f*.

adopt [ə'dɒpt] *vt* adottare; ~**ed** *adj* adottivo(a); ~**ion** [ə'dɒpʃən] *n* adozione *f*.

adore [ə'dɔ:*] *vt* adorare.

Adriatic [eɪdrɪ'ætɪk] *n*: **the** ~ (**Sea**) il mare Adriatico, l'Adriatico.

adrift [ə'drɪft] *adv* alla deriva.

adult ['ædʌlt] *adj* adulto(a); (*work, education*) per adulti ♦ *n* adulto/a.

adultery [ə'dʌltərɪ] *n* adulterio.

advance [əd'vɑ:ns] *n* avanzamento; (*money*) anticipo ♦ *adj* (*booking etc*) in anticipo ♦ *vt* (*money*) anticipare ♦ *vi* avanzare; **in** ~ in anticipo; ~**d** *adj* avanzato(a); (*SCOL*: *studies*) superiore.

advantage [əd'vɑ:ntɪdʒ] *n* (*also*: *TENNIS*) vantaggio; **to take** ~ **of** approfittarsi di.

advent ['ædvənt] *n* avvento; (*REL*): **A~** Avvento.

adventure [əd'ventʃə*] *n* avventura.

adverb ['ædvə:b] *n* avverbio.

adverse ['ædvə:s] *adj* avverso(a).

advert ['ædvə:t] (*BRIT*) *n abbr* = **advertisement**.

advertise ['ædvətaɪz] *vi* (*vt*) fare pubblicità *or* réclame (a); fare un'inserzione (per vendere); **to** ~ **for** (*staff*) mettere un annuncio sul giornale per trovare.

advertisement [əd'və:tɪsmənt] *n* (*COMM*) réclame *f inv*, pubblicità *f inv*; (*in classified ads*) inserzione *f*.

advertiser ['ædvətaɪzə*] *n* (*in newspaper etc*) inserzionista *m/f*.

advertising ['ædvətaɪzɪŋ] *n* pubblicità.

advice [əd'vaɪs] *n* consigli *mpl*; (*notification*) avviso; **piece of** ~ consiglio; **to take legal** ~ consultare un avvocato.

advisable [əd'vaɪzəbl] *adj* consigliabile.

advise [əd'vaɪz] *vt* consigliare; **to** ~ **sb of sth** informare qn di qc; **to** ~ **sb against sth/doing sth** sconsigliare qc a qn/a qn di fare qc; ~**dly** [-ədlɪ] *adv* (*deliberately*) di proposito; ~**r** *or* **advisor** *n* consigliere/a; **advisory** [-ərɪ] *adj* consultivo(a).

advocate [*n* 'ædvəkɪt, *vb* 'ædvəkeɪt] *n* (*upholder*) sostenitore/trice; (*LAW*) avvocato (difensore) ♦ *vt* propugnare.

Aegean [ɪ'dʒi:ən] *n*: **the ~** (*Sea*) il mar Egeo, l'Egeo.

aerial ['ɛərɪəl] *n* antenna ♦ *adj* aereo(a).

aerobics [ɛə'rəubɪks] *n* aerobica.

aeroplane ['ɛərəpleɪn] (*BRIT*) *n* aeroplano.

aerosol ['ɛərəsɔl] (*BRIT*) *n* aerosol *m inv*.

aesthetic [ɪs'θetɪk] *adj* estetico(a).

afar [ə'fɑ:*] *adv*: **from ~** da lontano.

affair [ə'fɛə*] *n* affare *m*; (*also: love ~*) relazione *f* amorosa.

affect [ə'fɛkt] *vt* toccare; (*influence*) influire su, incidere su; (*feign*) fingere; **~ed** *adj* affettato(a).

affection [ə'fɛkʃən] *n* affezione *f*; **~ate** *adj* affettuoso(a).

affix [ə'fɪks] *vt* apporre; attaccare.

afflict [ə'flɪkt] *vt* affliggere.

affluence ['æfluəns] *n* abbondanza; opulenza.

affluent ['æfluənt] *adj* ricco(a); **the ~ society** la società del benessere.

afford [ə'fɔ:d] *vt* permettersi; (*provide*) fornire.

afield [ə'fi:ld] *adv*: **far ~** lontano.

afloat [ə'fləut] *adv* a galla.

afoot [ə'fut] *adv*: **there is something ~** si sta preparando qualcosa.

afraid [ə'freɪd] *adj* impaurito(a); **to be ~ of** *or* **to/that** aver paura di/che; **I am ~ so/not** ho paura di sì/no.

afresh [ə'frɛʃ] *adv* di nuovo.

Africa ['æfrɪkə] *n* Africa; **~n** *adj*, *n* africano(a).

aft [ɑ:ft] *adv* a poppa, verso poppa.

after ['ɑ:ftə*] *prep*, *adv* dopo ♦ *conj* dopo che; **what/who are you ~?** che/chi cerca?; **~ he left/having done** dopo che se ne fu andato/dopo aver fatto; **to name sb ~ sb** dare a qn il nome di qn; **it's twenty ~ eight** (*US*) sono le otto e venti; **to ask ~ sb** chiedere di qn; **~ all** dopo tutto; **~ you!** dopo di lei!; **~-**

effects *npl* conseguenze *fpl*; (*of illness*) postumi *mpl*; **~math** *n* conseguenze *fpl*; **in the ~math of** nel periodo dopo; **~noon** *n* pomeriggio; **~s** *n* (*inf*: *dessert*) dessert *m inv*; **~-sales service** (*BRIT*) *n* servizio assistenza clienti; **~-shave (lotion)** *n* dopobarba *m inv*; **~thought** *n*: **as an ~thought** come aggiunta; **~wards** (*US* **~ward**) *adv* dopo.

again [ə'gɛn] *adv* di nuovo; **to begin/see ~** ricominciare/rivedere; **not ... ~** non ... più; **~ and ~** ripetutamente.

against [ə'gɛnst] *prep* contro.

age [eɪdʒ] *n* età *f inv* ♦ *vt*, *vi* invecchiare; **it's been ~s since** sono secoli che; **he is 20 years of ~** ha 20 anni; **to come of ~** diventare maggiorenne; **~d 10** di 10 anni; **the ~d** ['eɪdʒɪd] gli anziani; **~ group** *n* generazione *f*; **~ limit** *n* limite *m* d'età.

agency ['eɪdʒənsɪ] *n* agenzia.

agenda [ə'dʒɛndə] *n* ordine *m* del giorno.

agent ['eɪdʒənt] *n* agente *m*.

aggravate ['ægrəveɪt] *vt* aggravare; (*person*) irritare.

aggregate ['ægrɪgeɪt] *n* aggregato.

aggressive [ə'grɛsɪv] *adj* aggressivo(a).

aggrieved [ə'gri:vd] *adj* addolorato(a).

aghast [ə'gɑ:st] *adj* sbigottito(a).

agitate ['ædʒɪteɪt] *vt* turbare; agitare ♦ *vi*: **to ~ for** agitarsi per.

AGM *n abbr* = **annual general meeting.**

ago [ə'gəu] *adv*: **2 days ~** 2 giorni fa; **not long ~** poco tempo fa; **how long ~?** quanto tempo fa?

agog [ə'gɔg] *adj* ansioso(a), emozionato(a).

agonizing ['ægənaɪzɪŋ] *adj* straziante.

agony ['ægənɪ] *n* dolore *m* atroce; **to be in ~** avere dolori atroci.

agree [ə'gri:] *vt* (*price*) pattuire ♦ *vi*: **to ~ (with)** essere d'accordo (con); (*LING*) concordare (con); **to ~ to sth/to do sth** accettare qc/di fare qc; **to ~ that** (*admit*) ammettere che; **to ~ on sth** accordarsi su qc; **garlic doesn't ~ with me** l'aglio non mi va; **~able** *adj* gradevole; (*willing*) disposto(a); **~d**

adj (time, place) stabilito(a); ~**ment** *n* accordo; **in** ~**ment** d'accordo.
agricultural [ægrɪ'kʌltʃərəl] *adj* agricolo(a).
agriculture ['ægrɪkʌltʃə*] *n* agricoltura.
aground [ə'graʊnd] *adv*: **to run** ~ arenarsi.
ahead [ə'hɛd] *adv* avanti; davanti; ~ **of** davanti a; *(fig: schedule etc)* in anticipo su; ~ **of time** in anticipo; **go right** *or* **straight** ~ tiri diritto.
aid [eɪd] *n* aiuto ♦ *vt* aiutare; **in** ~ **of** a favore di; **to** ~ **and abet** *(LAW)* essere complice di.
aide [eɪd] *n (person)* aiutante *m*.
AIDS [eɪdz] *n abbr* (= *acquired immune deficiency syndrome*) AIDS *f*.
ailing ['eɪlɪŋ] *adj* sofferente.
ailment ['eɪlmənt] *n* indisposizione *f*.
aim [eɪm] *vt*: **to** ~ **sth at** *(such as gun)* mirare qc a, puntare qc a; *(camera)* rivolgere qc a; *(missile)* lanciare qc contro ♦ *vi* *(also: to take* ~*)* prendere la mira ♦ *n* mira; **to** ~ **at** mirare; **to** ~ **to do** aver l'intenzione di fare; ~**less** *adj* senza scopo.
ain't [eɪnt] *(inf)* = **am not; aren't; isn't**.
air [ɛə*] *n* aria ♦ *vt (room)* arieggiare; *(clothes)* far prendere aria a; *(grievances, ideas)* esprimere pubblicamente ♦ *cpd (currents)* d'aria; *(attack)* aereo(a); **to throw sth into the** ~ lanciare qc in aria; **by** ~ *(travel)* in aereo; **on the** ~ *(RADIO, TV)* in onda; ~**bed** *(BRIT)* *n* materassino; ~**borne** *adj* in volo; aerotrasportato(a); ~ **conditioning** *n* condizionamento d'aria; ~**craft** *n inv* apparecchio; ~**craft carrier** *n* portaerei *f inv*; ~**field** *n* campo d'aviazione; **A**~ **Force** *n* aviazione *f* militare; ~ **freshener** *n* deodorante *m* per ambienti; ~**gun** *n* fucile *m* ad aria compressa; ~ **hostess** *(BRIT)* *n* hostess *f inv*; ~ **letter** *(BRIT)* *n* aerogramma *m*; ~**lift** *n* ponte *m* aereo; ~**line** *n* linea aerea; ~**liner** *n* aereo di linea; ~**mail** *n*: **by** ~**mail** per via aerea; ~**plane** *(US)* *n* aeroplano; ~**port** *n* aeroporto; ~ **raid** *n* incursione *f* aerea; ~**sick** *adj*: **to be** ~**sick** soffrire di mal d'aria; ~

terminal *n* air-terminal *m inv*; ~**tight** *adj* ermetico(a); ~ **traffic controller** *n* controllore *m* del traffico aereo; ~**y** *adj* arioso(a); *(manners)* noncurante.
aisle [aɪl] *n (of church)* navata laterale; navata centrale; *(of plane)* corridoio.
ajar [ə'dʒɑː*] *adj* socchiuso(a).
akin [ə'kɪn] *adj*: ~ **to** simile a.
alacrity [ə'lækrɪtɪ] *n*: **with** ~ con prontezza.
alarm [ə'lɑːm] *n* allarme *m* ♦ *vt* allarmare; ~ **call** *n (in hotel etc)* sveglia; ~ **clock** *n* sveglia.
alas [ə'læs] *excl* ohimè!, ahimè!
albeit [ɔːl'biːɪt] *conj* sebbene +*sub*, benché +*sub*.
album ['ælbəm] *n* album *m inv*.
alcohol ['ælkəhɔl] *n* alcool *m*; ~**ic** [-'hɔlɪk] *adj* alcolico(a) ♦ *n* alcolizzato/a.
ale [eɪl] *n* birra.
alert [ə'ləːt] *adj* vigile ♦ *n* allarme *m* ♦ *vt* avvertire; mettere in guardia; **on the** ~ all'erta.
algebra ['ældʒɪbrə] *n* algebra.
alias ['eɪlɪəs] *adv* alias ♦ *n* pseudonimo, falso nome *m*.
alibi ['ælɪbaɪ] *n* alibi *m inv*.
alien ['eɪlɪən] *n* straniero/a; *(extraterrestrial)* alieno/a ♦ *adj*: ~ **(to)** estraneo(a) (a); ~**ate** *vt* alienare.
alight [ə'laɪt] *adj* acceso(a) ♦ *vi* scendere; *(bird)* posarsi.
align [ə'laɪn] *vt* allineare.
alike [ə'laɪk] *adj* simile ♦ *adv* sia ... sia; **to look** ~ assomigliarsi.
alimony ['ælɪmənɪ] *n (payment)* alimenti *mpl*.
alive [ə'laɪv] *adj* vivo(a); *(lively)* vivace.

KEYWORD

all [ɔːl] *adj* tutto(a); ~ **day** tutto il giorno; ~ **night** tutta la notte; ~ **men** tutti gli uomini; ~ **five came** sono venuti tutti e cinque; ~ **the books** tutti i libri; ~ **the food** tutto il cibo; ~ **the time** sempre; tutto il tempo; ~ **his life** tutta la vita
♦ *pron* **1** tutto(a); **I ate it** ~, **I ate** ~ **of** it l'ho mangiato tutto; ~ **of us went**

tutti noi siamo andati; ~ **of the boys went** tutti i ragazzi sono andati **2** (*in phrases*): **above** ~ soprattutto; **after** ~ dopotutto; **at** ~: **not at** ~ (*in answer to question*) niente affatto; (*in answer to thanks*) prego!, di niente!, s'immagini!; **I'm not at** ~ **tired** non sono affatto stanco(a); **anything at** ~ **will do** andrà bene qualsiasi cosa; ~ **in** ~ tutto sommato
♦ *adv*: ~ **alone** tutto(a) solo(a); **it's not as hard as** ~ **that** non è poi così difficile; ~ **the more/the better** tanto più/meglio; ~ **but** quasi; **the score is two** ~ il punteggio è di due a due.

allay [ə'leɪ] *vt* (*fears*) dissipare.
all clear *n* (*also fig*) segnale *m* di cessato allarme.
allegation [ælɪ'geɪʃən] *n* asserzione *f*.
allege [ə'lɛdʒ] *vt* asserire; ~**dly** [ə'lɛdʒɪdlɪ] *adv* secondo quanto si asserisce.
allegiance [ə'liːdʒəns] *n* fedeltà.
allergic [ə'lə:dʒɪk] *adj*: ~ **to** allergico(a) a.
allergy [ælədʒɪ] *n* allergia.
alleviate [ə'liːvɪeɪt] *vt* sollevare.
alley [ælɪ] *n* vicolo.
alliance [ə'laɪəns] *n* alleanza.
allied [ælaɪd] *adj* alleato(a).
all-in *adj* (*BRIT: also adv: charge*) tutto compreso; ~ **wrestling** *n* lotta americana.
all-night *adj* aperto(a) (*or* che dura) tutta la notte.
allocate [æləkeɪt] *vt* assegnare.
allot [ə'lɔt] *vt* assegnare; ~**ment** *n* assegnazione *f*; (*garden*) lotto di terra.
all-out *adj* (*effort etc*) totale ♦ *adv*: **to go all out for** mettercela tutta per.
allow [ə'lau] *vt* (*practice, behaviour*) permettere; (*sum, to spend etc*) accordare; (*sum, time estimated*) dare; (*concede*): **to** ~ **that** ammettere che; **to** ~ **sb to do** permettere a qn di fare; **he is** ~**ed to** lo può fare; ~ **for** *vt fus* tener conto di; ~**ance** *n* (*money received*) assegno; indennità *f inv*; (*TAX*) detrazione *f* di imposta; **to make**

~**ances for** tener conto di.
alloy [ælɔɪ] *n* lega.
all right *adv* (*feel, work*) bene; (*as answer*) va bene.
all-round *adj* completo(a).
all-time *adj* (*record*) assoluto(a).
allude [ə'luːd] *vi*: **to** ~ **to** alludere a.
alluring [ə'ljuərɪŋ] *adj* seducente.
ally [ælaɪ] *n* alleato.
almighty [ɔːl'maɪtɪ] *adj* onnipotente; (*row etc*) colossale.
almond [ˈɑːmənd] *n* mandorla.
almost [ˈɔːlməust] *adv* quasi.
alms [ɑːmz] *npl* elemosina *sg*.
aloft [ə'lɔft] *adv* in alto.
alone [ə'ləun] *adj*, *adv* solo(a); **to leave sb** ~ lasciare qn in pace; **to leave sth** ~ lasciare stare qc, **let** ~ ... figuriamoci poi ..., tanto meno ....
along [ə'lɔŋ] *prep* lungo ♦ *adv*: **is he coming** ~? viene con noi?; **he was limping** ~ veniva zoppicando; ~ **with** insieme con; **all** ~ (*all the time*) sempre, fin dall'inizio; ~**side** *prep* accanto a; lungo ♦ *adv* accanto.
aloof [ə'luːf] *adj* distaccato(a) ♦ *adv*: **to stand** ~ tenersi a distanza *or* in disparte.
aloud [ə'laud] *adv* ad alta voce.
alphabet [ælfəbɛt] *n* alfabeto.
alpine [ælpaɪn] *adj* alpino(a).
Alps [ælps] *npl*: **the** ~ le Alpi.
already [ɔːl'rɛdɪ] *adv* già.
alright [ˈɔːlraɪt] (*BRIT*) *adv* = **all right**.
Alsatian [æl'seɪʃən] (*BRIT*) *n* (*dog*) pastore *m* tedesco, (cane *m*) lupo.
also [ˈɔːlsəu] *adv* anche.
altar [ˈɔltə*] *n* altare *m*.
alter [ˈɔltə*] *vt*, *vi* alterare.
alternate [*adj* ɔl'tə:nɪt, *vb* ˈɔltə:neɪt] *adj* alterno(a); (*US: plan etc*) alternativo(a) ♦ *vi*: **to** ~ (**with**) alternarsi (con); **on** ~ **days** ogni due giorni; **alternating** *adj* (*current*) alternato(a).
alternative [ɔl'tə:nətɪv] *adj* alternativo(a) ♦ *n* (*choice*) alternativa; ~**ly** *adv*: ~**ly one could** ... come alternativa si potrebbe ....
alternator [ˈɔltə:neɪtə*] *n* (*AUT*)

alternatore *m*.

although [ɔːl'ðəu] *conj* benché +*sub*, sebbene +*sub*.

altitude ['æltɪtjuːd] *n* altitudine *f*.

alto ['æltəu] *n* contralto; (*male*) contraltino.

altogether [ɔːltə'gɛðə*] *adv* del tutto, completamente; (*on the whole*) tutto considerato; (*in all*) in tutto.

aluminium [ælju'mɪnɪəm] *n* alluminio.

aluminum [ə'luːmɪnəm] (*US*) *n* = **aluminium**.

always ['ɔːlweɪz] *adv* sempre.

am [æm] *vb see* **be**.

a.m. *adv abbr* (= *ante meridiem*) della mattina.

amalgamate [ə'mælgəmeɪt] *vt* amalgamare ♦ *vi* amalgamarsi.

amateur ['æmətə*] *n* dilettante *m/f* ♦ *adj* (*SPORT*) dilettante; ~**ish** (*pej*) *adj* da dilettante.

amaze [ə'meɪz] *vt* stupire; **to be ~d** (**at**) essere sbalordito (da); ~**ment** *n* stupore *m*; **amazing** *adj* sorprendente, sbalorditivo(a).

ambassador [æm'bæsədə*] *n* ambasciatore/trice.

amber ['æmbə*] *n* ambra; **at ~** (*BRIT: AUT*) giallo.

ambiguous [æm'bɪgjuəs] *adj* ambiguo(a).

ambition [æm'bɪʃən] *n* ambizione *f*.

ambitious [æm'bɪʃəs] *adj* ambizioso(a).

amble ['æmbl] *vi* (*gen*: **to ~ along**) camminare tranquillamente.

ambulance ['æmbjuləns] *n* ambulanza.

ambush ['æmbuʃ] *n* imboscata ♦ *vt* fare un'imboscata a.

amenable [ə'miːnəbl] *adj*: ~ **to** (*advice etc*) ben disposto(a) a.

amend [ə'mɛnd] *vt* (*law*) emendare; (*text*) correggere; **to make ~s** fare ammenda.

amenities [ə'miːnɪtɪz] *npl* attrezzature *fpl* ricreative e culturali.

America [ə'mɛrɪkə] *n* America; ~**n** *adj*, *n* americano(a).

amiable ['eɪmɪəbl] *adj* amabile, gentile.

amicable ['æmɪkəbl] *adj* amichevole.

amid(st) [ə'mɪd(st)] *prep* fra, tra, in

mezzo a.

amiss [ə'mɪs] *adj*, *adv*: **there's something ~** c'è qualcosa che non va bene; **don't take it ~** non prendertela (a male).

ammonia [ə'məunɪə] *n* ammoniaca.

ammunition [æmju'nɪʃən] *n* munizioni *fpl*.

amok [ə'mɔk] *adv*: **to run ~** diventare pazzo(a) furioso(a).

among(st) [ə'mʌŋ(st)] *prep* fra, tra, in mezzo a.

amorous ['æmərəs] *adj* amoroso(a).

amount [ə'maunt] *n* somma; ammontare *m*; quantità *f inv* ♦ *vi*: **to ~ to** (*total*) ammontare a; (*be same as*) essere come.

amp(ère) ['æmp(ɛə*)] *n* ampère *m inv*.

ample ['æmpl] *adj* ampio(a); spazioso(a); (*enough*): **this is ~** questo è più che sufficiente.

amplifier ['æmplɪfaɪə*] *n* amplificatore *m*.

amuck [ə'mʌk] *adv* = **amok**.

amuse [ə'mjuːz] *vt* divertire; ~**ment** *n* divertimento; ~**ment arcade** *n* sala giochi.

an [æn] *indef art see* **a**.

anaemic [ə'niːmɪk] *adj* anemico(a).

anaesthetic [ænɪs'θɛtɪk] *adj* anestetico(a) ♦ *n* anestetico.

analog(ue) ['ænəlɔg] *adj* (*watch*, *computer*) analogico(a).

analyse ['ænəlaɪz] (*BRIT*) *vt* analizzare.

analyses [ə'næləsiːz] *npl of* **analysis**.

analysis [ə'næləsɪs] (*pl* **analyses**) *n* analisi *f inv*.

analyst ['ænəlɪst] *n* (*POL etc*) analista *m/f*; (*US*) (psic)analista *m/f*.

analyze ['ænəlaɪz] (*US*) *vt* = **analyse**.

anarchist ['ænəkɪst] *n* anarchico/a.

anarchy ['ænəkɪ] *n* anarchia.

anathema [ə'næθɪmə] *n*: **that is ~ to him** non vuole nemmeno sentirne parlare.

anatomy [ə'nætəmɪ] *n* anatomia.

ancestor ['ænsɪstə*] *n* antenato/a.

anchor ['æŋkə*] *n* ancora ♦ *vi* (*also*: **to drop ~**) gettare l'ancora ♦ *vt* ancorare; **to weigh ~** salpare *or* levare l'ancora.

anchovy ['æntʃəvɪ] *n* acciuga.
ancient ['eɪnʃənt] *adj* antico(a); (*person, car*) vecchissimo(a).
ancillary [æn'sɪlərɪ] *adj* ausiliario(a).
and [ænd] *conj* e (*often* ed *before vowel*); ~ **so on** e così via; **try** ~ **come** cerca di venire; **he talked** ~ **talked** non la finiva di parlare; **better** ~ **better** sempre meglio.
anemic [ə'niːmɪk] (*US*) *adj* = anaemic.
anesthetic [ænɪs'θɛtɪk] (*US*) *adj, n* = anaesthetic.
anew [ə'njuː] *adv* di nuovo.
angel ['eɪndʒəl] *n* angelo.
anger ['æŋgə*] *n* rabbia.
angina [æn'dʒaɪnə] *n* angina pectoris.
angle ['æŋgl] *n* angolo; **from their** ~ dal loro punto di vista.
Anglican ['æŋglɪkən] *adj, n* anglicano(a).
angling ['æŋglɪŋ] *n* pesca con la lenza.
Anglo- ['æŋgləʊ] *prefix* anglo....
angrily ['æŋgrɪlɪ] *adv* con rabbia.
angry ['æŋgrɪ] *adj* arrabbiato(a), furioso(a); (*wound*) infiammato(a); **to be** ~ **with sb/at sth** essere in collera con qn/per qc; **to get** ~ arrabbiarsi; **to make sb** ~ fare arrabbiare qn.
anguish ['æŋgwɪʃ] *n* angoscia.
animal ['ænɪməl] *adj* animale ♦ *n* animale *m*.
animate ['ænɪmɪt] *adj* animato(a).
animated ['ænɪmeɪtɪd] *adj* animato(a).
aniseed ['ænɪsiːd] *n* semi *mpl* di anice.
ankle ['æŋkl] *n* caviglia; ~ **sock** *n* calzino.
annex [*n* 'ænɛks, *vb* ə'nɛks] *n* (*also*: *BRIT*: **annexe**) (edificio) annesso ♦ *vt* annettere.
annihilate [ə'naɪəleɪt] *vt* annientare.
anniversary [ænɪ'vɜːsərɪ] *n* anniversario.
announce [ə'naʊns] *vt* annunciare; ~**ment** *n* annuncio; (*letter, card*) partecipazione *f*; ~**r** *n* (*RADIO, TV*: *between programmes*) annunciatore/trice; (: *in a programme*) presentatore/trice.
annoy [ə'nɔɪ] *vt* dare fastidio a; **don't get** ~**ed!** non irritarti!; ~**ance** *n* fa-

stidio; (*cause of* ~*ance*) noia; ~**ing** *adj* noioso(a).
annual ['ænjʊəl] *adj* annuale ♦ *n* (*BOT*) pianta annua; (*book*) annuario.
annul [ə'nʌl] *vt* annullare.
annum ['ænəm] *n see* **per.**
anonymous [ə'nɒnɪməs] *adj* anonimo(a).
anorak ['ænəræk] *n* giacca a vento.
another [ə'nʌðə*] *adj*: ~ **book** (*one more*) un altro libro, ancora un libro; (*a different one*) un altro libro ♦ *pron* un altro(un'altra), ancora uno(a); *see also* **one.**
answer ['ɑːnsə*] *n* risposta; soluzione *f* ♦ *vi* rispondere ♦ *vt* (*reply to*) rispondere a; (*problem*) risolvere; (*prayer*) esaudire; **in** ~ **to your letter** in risposta alla sua lettera; **to** ~ **the phone** rispondere (al telefono); **to** ~ **the bell** rispondere al campanello; **to** ~ **the door** aprire la porta; ~ **back** *vi* ribattere; ~ **for** *vt fus* essere responsabile di; ~ **to** *vt fus* (*description*) corrispondere a; ~**able** *adj*: ~**able (to sb/for sth)** responsabile (verso qn/di qc); ~**ing machine** *n* segreteria (telefonica) automatica.
ant [ænt] *n* formica.
antagonism [æn'tægənɪzəm] *n* antagonismo.
antagonize [æn'tægənaɪz] *vt* provocare l'ostilità di.
Antarctic [ænt'ɑːktɪk] *n*: **the** ~ l'Antartide *f*.
antenatal ['æntɪ'neɪtl] *adj* prenatale; ~ **clinic** *n* assistenza medica preparto.
anthem ['ænθəm] *n*: **national** ~ inno nazionale.
anthology [æn'θɒlədʒɪ] *n* antologia.
antibiotic ['æntɪbaɪ'ɔtɪk] *n* antibiotico.
antibody ['æntɪbɒdɪ] *n* anticorpo.
anticipate [æn'tɪsɪpeɪt] *vt* prevedere; pregustare; (*wishes, request*) prevenire.
anticipation [æntɪsɪ'peɪʃən] *n* anticipazione *f*; (*expectation*) aspettativa *fpl*.
anticlimax ['æntɪ'klaɪmæks] *n*: **it was an** ~ fu una completa delusione.

anticlockwise ['ænti'klɔkwaiz] adj, adv in senso antiorario.

antics ['æntiks] npl buffonerie fpl.

antifreeze ['ænti'fri:z] n anticongelante m.

antihistamine [ænti'histəmin] n antistaminico.

antiquated ['æntikweitid] adj antiquato(a).

antique [æn'ti:k] n antichità f inv ♦ adj antico(a); ~ **dealer** n antiquario/a; ~ **shop** n negozio d'antichità.

antiquity [æn'tikwiti] n antichità f inv.

anti-Semitism ['ænti'semitizəm] n antisemitismo.

antiseptic [ænti'septik] n antisettico.

antisocial ['ænti'səuʃəl] adj asociale.

antlers ['æntləz] npl palchi mpl.

anvil ['ænvil] n incudine f.

anxiety [æŋ'zaiəti] n ansia; (keenness): ~ **to do** smania di fare.

anxious ['æŋkʃəs] adj ansioso(a), inquieto(a); (worrying) angosciante; (keen): ~ **to do/that** impaziente di fare/che +sub.

KEYWORD
---

any ['ɛni] adj 1 (in questions etc): **have you ~ butter?** hai del burro?, hai un po' di burro?; **have you ~ children?** hai bambini?; **if there are ~ tickets left** se ci sono ancora (dei) biglietti, se c'è ancora qualche biglietto
2 (with negative): **I haven't ~ money/books** non ho soldi/libri
3 (no matter which) qualsiasi, qualunque; **choose ~ book you like** scegli un libro qualsiasi
4 (in phrases): **in ~ case** in ogni caso; **~ day now** da un giorno all'altro; **at ~ moment** in qualsiasi momento, da un momento all'altro; **at ~ rate** ad ogni modo
♦ pron 1 (in questions, with negative): **have you got ~?** ne hai?; **can ~ of you sing?** qualcuno di voi sa cantare?; **I haven't ~ (of them)** non ne ho
2 (no matter which one(s)): **take ~ of those books (you like)** prendi uno qualsiasi di quei libri

♦ adv 1 (in questions etc): **do you want ~ more soup/sandwiches?** vuoi ancora un po' di minestra/degli altri panini?; **are you feeling ~ better?** ti senti meglio?
2 (with negative): **I can't hear him ~ more** non lo sento più; **don't wait ~ longer** non aspettare più.

anybody ['ɛnibɔdi] pron (in questions etc) qualcuno, nessuno; (with negative) nessuno; (no matter who) chiunque; **can you see ~?** vedi qualcuno or nessuno?; **if ~ should phone ...** se telefona qualcuno ...; **I can't see ~** non vedo nessuno; **~ could do it** chiunque potrebbe farlo.

anyhow ['ɛnihau] adv (at any rate) ad ogni modo, comunque; (haphazard): **do it ~** you like fallo come ti pare; **I shall go ~** ci andrò lo stesso or comunque; **she leaves things just ~** lascia tutto come capita.

anyone ['ɛniwʌn] pron = anybody.

anything ['ɛniθiŋ] pron (in question etc) qualcosa, niente; (with negative) niente; (no matter what): **you can say ~ you like** puoi dire quello che ti pare; **can you see ~?** vedi niente or qualcosa?; **if ~ happens to me ...** se mi dovesse succedere qualcosa ...; **I can't see ~** non vedo niente; **~ will do** va bene qualsiasi cosa or tutto.

anyway ['ɛniwei] adv (at any rate) ad ogni modo, comunque; (besides) ad ogni modo.

anywhere ['ɛniwɛə*] adv (in questions etc) da qualche parte; (with negative) da nessuna parte; (no matter where) da qualsiasi or qualunque parte, dovunque; **can you see him ~?** lo vedi da qualche parte?; **I can't see him ~** non lo vedo da nessuna parte; **~ in the world** dovunque nel mondo.

apart [ə'pɑːt] adv (to one side) a parte; (separately) separatamente; **with one's legs ~** con le gambe divaricate; **10 miles ~** a 10 miglia di distanza (l'uno dall'altro); **to take ~** smontare; **~ from** a parte, eccetto.

apartheid [ə'pɑːteɪt] n apartheid f.
apartment [ə'pɑːtmənt] n (US) appartamento; (room) locale m; ~ **building** (US) n stabile m, caseggiato.
apathetic [æpə'θetɪk] adj apatico(a).
ape [eɪp] n scimmia ♦ vt scimmiottare.
apéritif [ə'perɪtɪv] n aperitivo.
aperture ['æpətʃjuə*] n apertura.
apex ['eɪpɛks] n apice m.
apiece [ə'piːs] adv ciascuno(a).
aplomb [ə'plɔm] n disinvoltura.
apologetic [əpɔlə'dʒetɪk] adj (tone, letter) di scusa.
apologize [ə'pɔlədʒaɪz] vi: to ~ (for sth to sb) scusarsi (di qc a qn), chiedere scusa (a qn per qc).
apology [ə'pɔlədʒɪ] n scuse fpl.
apostle [ə'pɔsl] n apostolo.
apostrophe [ə'pɔstrəfɪ] n (sign) apostrofo.
appal [ə'pɔːl] vt scioccare; ~ing adj spaventoso(a).
apparatus [æpə'reɪtəs] n apparato; (in gymnasium) attrezzatura.
apparel [ə'pærl] n (US) n abbigliamento, confezioni fpl.
apparent [ə'pærənt] adj evidente; ~ly adv evidentemente.
apparition [æpə'rɪʃən] n apparizione f.
appeal [ə'piːl] vi (LAW) appellarsi alla legge ♦ n (LAW) appello; (request) richiesta; (charm) attrattiva; to ~ for chiedere (con insistenza); to ~ to (subj: person) appellarsi a; (subj: thing) piacere a; it doesn't ~ to me mi dice poco; ~ing adj (nice) attraente.
appear [ə'pɪə*] vi apparire; (LAW) comparire; (publication) essere pubblicato(a); (seem) sembrare; it would ~ that sembra che; ~ance n apparizione f; apparenza; (look, aspect) aspetto.
appease [ə'piːz] vt calmare, appagare.
appendices [ə'pendɪsiːz] npl of **appendix**.
appendicitis [əpendɪ'saɪtɪs] n appendicite f.
appendix [ə'pendɪks] (pl **appendices**) n appendice f.
appetite ['æpɪtaɪt] n appetito.

appetizer ['æpɪtaɪzə*] n stuzzichino.
applaud [ə'plɔːd] vt, vi applaudire.
applause [ə'plɔːz] n applauso.
apple ['æpl] n mela; ~ **tree** n melo.
appliance [ə'plaɪəns] n apparecchio.
applicant ['æplɪkənt] n candidato/a.
application [æplɪ'keɪʃən] n applicazione f; (for a job, a grant etc) domanda; ~ **form** n modulo per la domanda.
applied [ə'plaɪd] adj applicato(a).
apply [ə'plaɪ] vt: to ~ (to) (paint, ointment) dare (a); (theory, technique) applicare (a) ♦ vi: to ~ to (ask) rivolgersi a; (be suitable for, relevant to) riguardare, riferirsi a; to ~ (for) (permit, grant, job) fare domanda (per); to ~ o.s. to dedicarsi a.
appoint [ə'pɔɪnt] vt nominare; ~ed adj: at the ~ed time all'ora stabilita; ~ment n nomina; (arrangement to meet) appuntamento; to make an ~ment (with) prendere un appuntamento (con).
appraisal [ə'preɪzl] n valutazione f.
appreciate [ə'priːʃeɪt] vt (like) apprezzare; (be grateful for) essere riconoscente di; (be aware of) rendersi conto di ♦ vi (FINANCE) aumentare.
appreciation [əpriːʃɪ'eɪʃən] n apprezzamento; (FINANCE) aumento del valore.
appreciative [ə'priːʃɪətɪv] adj (person) sensibile; (comment) elogiativo(a).
apprehend [æprɪ'hend] vt (arrest) arrestare.
apprehension [æprɪ'henʃən] n (fear) inquietudine f.
apprehensive [æprɪ'hensɪv] adj apprensivo(a).
apprentice [ə'prentɪs] n apprendista m/f; ~ship n apprendistato.
approach [ə'prəutʃ] vi avvicinarsi ♦ vt (come near) avvicinarsi a; (ask, apply to) rivolgersi a; (subject, passer-by) avvicinare ♦ n approccio; accesso; (to problem) modo di affrontare; ~able adj accessibile.
appropriate [adj ə'prəuprɪɪt, vb ə'prəuprɪeɪt] adj appropriato(a); adatto(a) ♦ vt (take) appropriarsi.

approval [ə'pru:vəl] *n* approvazione *f*; **on ~** (*COMM*) in prova, in esame.
approve [ə'pru:v] *vt, vi* approvare; **~ of** *vt fus* approvare.
approximate [ə'prɔksɪmɪt] *adj* approssimativo(a); **~ly** *adv* circa.
apricot ['eɪprɪkɔt] *n* albicocca.
April ['eɪprəl] *n* aprile *m*; **~ fool!** pesce d'aprile!
apron ['eɪprən] *n* grembiule *m*.
apt [æpt] *adj* (*suitable*) adatto(a); (*able*) capace; (*likely*): **to be ~ to do** avere tendenza a fare.
aptitude ['æptɪtju:d] *n* abilità *f inv*.
aqualung ['ækwəlʌŋ] *n* autorespiratore *m*.
aquarium [ə'kwɛərɪəm] *n* acquario.
Aquarius [ə'kwɛərɪəs] *n* Acquario.
Arab ['ærəb] *adj, n* arabo(a).
Arabian [ə'reɪbɪən] *adj* arabo(a).
Arabic ['ærəbɪk] *adj* arabico(a), arabo(a) ♦ *n* arabo; **~ numerals** numeri *mpl* arabi, numerazione *f* araba.
arbitrary ['ɑ:bɪtrərɪ] *adj* arbitrario(a).
arbitration [ɑ:bɪ'treɪʃən] *n* (*LAW*) arbitrato; (*INDUSTRY*) arbitraggio.
arcade [ɑ:'keɪd] *n* portico; (*passage with shops*) galleria.
arch [ɑ:tʃ] *n* arco; (*of foot*) arco plantare ♦ *vt* inarcare.
archaeologist [ɑ:kɪ'ɔlədʒɪst] *n* archeologo/a.
archaeology [ɑ:kɪ'ɔlədʒɪ] *n* archeologia.
archbishop [ɑ:tʃ'bɪʃəp] *n* arcivescovo.
arch-enemy *n* arcinemico/a.
archeology [ɑ:kɪ'ɔlədʒɪ] *etc* (*US*) = **archaeology** *etc*.
archery ['ɑ:tʃərɪ] *n* tiro all'arco.
architect ['ɑ:kɪtɛkt] *n* architetto; **~ure** ['ɑ:kɪtɛktʃə*] *n* architettura.
archives ['ɑ:kaɪvz] *npl* archivi *mpl*.
Arctic ['ɑ:ktɪk] *adj* artico(a) ♦ *n*: **the ~** l'Artico.
ardent ['ɑ:dənt] *adj* ardente.
are [ɑ:*] *vb see* **be**.
area ['ɛərɪə] *n* (*GEOM*) area; (*zone*) zona; (: *smaller*) settore *m*.
aren't [ɑ:nt] = **are not**.
Argentina [ɑ:dʒən'ti:nə] *n* Argentina;

Argentinian [-'tɪnɪən] *adj, n* argentino(a).
arguably [ɑ:gjuəblɪ] *adv*: **it is ~ ...** si può sostenere che sia ....
argue ['ɑ:gju:] *vi* (*quarrel*) litigare; (*reason*) ragionare; **to ~ that** sostenere che.
argument ['ɑ:gjumənt] *n* (*reasons*) argomento; (*quarrel*) lite *f*; **~ative** [ɑ:gju'mɛntətɪv] *adj* litigioso(a).
Aries ['ɛərɪz] *n* Ariete *m*.
arise [ə'raɪz] (*pt* **arose**, *pp* **arisen**) *vi* (*opportunity, problem*) presentarsi;
arisen [ə'rɪzn] *pp of* **arise**.
aristocrat ['ærɪstəkræt] *n* aristocratico/a.
arithmetic [ə'rɪθmətɪk] *n* aritmetica.
ark [ɑ:k] *n*: **Noah's A~** l'arca di Noè.
arm [ɑ:m] *n* braccio ♦ *vt* armare; **~s** *npl* (*weapons*) armi *fpl*; **~ in ~** a braccetto.
armaments ['ɑ:məmənts] *npl* armamenti *mpl*.
arm: **~chair** *n* poltrona; **~ed** *adj* armato(a); **~ed robbery** *n* rapina a mano armata.
armour ['ɑ:mə*] (*US* **armor**) *n* armatura; (*MIL*: *tanks*) mezzi *mpl* blindati; **~ed car** *n* autoblinda *f inv*.
armpit ['ɑ:mpɪt] *n* ascella.
armrest ['ɑ:mrɛst] *n* bracciolo.
army ['ɑ:mɪ] *n* esercito.
aroma [ə'rəumə] *n* aroma.
arose [ə'rəuz] *pt of* **arise**.
around [ə'raund] *adv* attorno, intorno ♦ *prep* intorno a; (*fig*: *about*): **~ £5/3 o'clock** circa 5 sterline/le 3; **is he ~?** è in giro?
arouse [ə'rauz] *vt* (*sleeper*) svegliare; (*curiosity, passions*) suscitare.
arrange [ə'reɪndʒ] *vt* sistemare; (*programme*) preparare; **to ~ to do sth** mettersi d'accordo per fare qc; **~ment** *n* sistemazione *f*; (*agreement*) accordo; **~ments** *npl* (*plans*) progetti *mpl*, piani *mpl*.
array [ə'reɪ] *n*: **~ of** fila di.
arrears [ə'rɪəz] *npl* arretrati *mpl*; **to be in ~ with one's rent** essere in arretrato con l'affitto.
arrest [ə'rɛst] *vt* arrestare; (*sb's*

attention) attirare ♦ *n* arresto; **under ~** in arresto.

arrival [əˈraɪvəl] *n* arrivo; (*person*) arrivato/a; **a new ~** un nuovo venuto; (*baby*) un neonato.

arrive [əˈraɪv] *vi* arrivare.

arrogant [ˈærəgənt] *adj* arrogante.

arrow [ˈærəu] *n* freccia.

arse [ɑːs] (*inf!*) *n* culo (*!*).

arson [ˈɑːsn] *n* incendio doloso.

art [ɑːt] *n* arte *f*; (*craft*) mestiere *m*; **A~s** *npl* (*SCOL*) Lettere *fpl*.

artefact [ˈɑːtɪfækt] *n* manufatto.

artery [ˈɑːtərɪ] *n* arteria.

artful [ˈɑːtful] *adj* abile.

art gallery *n* galleria d'arte.

arthritis [ɑːˈθraɪtɪs] *n* artrite *f*.

artichoke [ˈɑːtɪtʃəuk] *n* carciofo; **Jerusalem ~** topinambur *m inv*.

article [ˈɑːtɪkl] *n* articolo; **~s** *npl* (*BRIT: LAW. training*) contratto di tirocinio; **~ of clothing** capo di vestiario.

articulate [*adj* ɑːˈtɪkjulɪt, *vb* ɑːˈtɪkjuleɪt] *adj* (*person*) che si esprime forbitamente; (*speech*) articolato(a) ♦ *vi* articolare; **~d lorry** (*BRIT*) *n* autotreno.

artificial [ɑːtɪˈfɪʃəl] *adj* artificiale; **~ respiration** *n* respirazione *f* artificiale.

artillery [ɑːˈtɪlərɪ] *n* artiglieria.

artisan [ˈɑːtɪzæn] *n* artigiano/a.

artist [ˈɑːtɪst] *n* artista *m/f*; **~ic** [ɑːˈtɪstɪk] *adj* artistico(a); **~ry** *n* arte *f*.

artless [ˈɑːtlɪs] *adj* semplice, ingenuo(a).

art school *n* scuola d'arte.

KEYWORD

as [æz] *conj* **1** (*referring to time*) mentre; **~ the years went by** col passare degli anni; **he came in ~ I was leaving** arrivò mentre stavo uscendo; **~ from tomorrow** da domani

2 (*in comparisons*): **~ big ~** grande come; **twice ~ big ~** due volte più grande di; **~ much/many ~** tanto quanto/tanti quanti; **~ soon ~ possible** prima possibile

3 (*since, because*) dal momento che, siccome

4 (*referring to manner, way*) come; **do** **~ you wish** fa' come vuoi; **~ she said** come ha detto lei

5 (*concerning*): **~ for** *or* **to that** per quanto riguarda *or* quanto a quello

6: **~ if** *or* **though** come se; **he looked ~ if he was ill** sembrava stare male; *see also* **long; such; well**

♦ *prep*: **he works ~ a driver** fa l'autista; **~ chairman of the company, he ...** come presidente della compagnia, lui ...; **he gave me it ~ a present** me lo ha regalato.

---

a.s.a.p. *abbr* **= as soon as possible.**

ascend [əˈsɛnd] *vt* salire; **~ancy** *n* ascendente *m*.

ascent [əˈsɛnt] *n* salita; (*of mountain*) ascensione *f*.

ascertain [æsəˈteɪn] *vt* accertare.

ascribe [əˈskraɪb] *vt*: **to ~ sth to** attribuire qc a.

ash [æʃ] *n* (*dust*) cenere *f*; (*wood, tree*) frassino.

ashamed [əˈʃeɪmd] *adj* vergognoso(a); **to be ~ of** vergognarsi di.

ashen [ˈæʃn] *adj* (*pale*) livido(a).

ashore [əˈʃɔː*] *adv* a terra.

ashtray [ˈæʃtreɪ] *n* portacenere *m*.

Ash Wednesday *n* mercoledì *m inv* delle Ceneri.

Asia [ˈeɪʃə] *n* Asia; **~n** *adj*, *n* asiatico(a).

aside [əˈsaɪd] *adv* da parte ♦ *n* a parte *m*.

ask [ɑːsk] *vt* (*question*) domandare; (*invite*) invitare; **to ~ sb sth/sb to do sth** chiedere qc a qn/a qn di fare qc; **to ~ sb about sth** chiedere a qn di qc; **to ~ (sb) a question** fare una domanda (a qn); **to ~ sb out to dinner** invitare qn a mangiare fuori; **~ after** *vt fus* chiedere di; **~ for** *vt fus* chiedere; (*trouble etc*) cercare.

askance [əˈskɑːns] *adv*: **to look ~ at sb** guardare qn di traverso.

askew [əˈskjuː] *adv* di traverso, storto.

asleep [əˈsliːp] *adj* addormentato(a); **to be ~** dormire; **to fall ~** addormentarsi.

asparagus [əsˈpærəgəs] *n* asparagi *mpl*.

aspect [ˈæspɛkt] *n* aspetto.

aspersions [əs'pəːʃənz] *npl*: **to cast ~ on** diffamare.

asphyxiation [æsfɪksɪ'eɪʃən] *n* asfissia.

aspire [əs'paɪə*] *vi*: **to ~ to** aspirare a.

aspirin ['æsprɪn] *n* aspirina.

ass [æs] *n* asino; (*inf*) scemo/a; (*US: inf!*) culo (!).

assailant [ə'seɪlənt] *n* assalitore *m*.

assassinate [ə'sæsɪneɪt] *vt* assassinare; **assassination** [əsæsɪ'neɪʃən] *n* assassinio.

assault [ə'sɔːlt] *n* (*MIL*) assalto; (*gen: attack*) aggressione *f* ♦ *vt* assaltare; aggredire; (*sexually*) violentare.

assemble [ə'sɛmbl] *vt* riunire; (*TECH*) montare ♦ *vi* riunirsi.

assembly [ə'sɛmblɪ] *n* (*meeting*) assemblea; (*construction*) montaggio; **~ line** *n* catena di montaggio.

assent [ə'sɛnt] *n* assenso, consenso.

assert [ə'səːt] *vt* asserire; (*insist on*) far valere.

assess [ə'sɛs] *vt* valutare; **~ment** *n* valutazione *f*.

asset ['æsɛt] *n* vantaggio; **~s** *npl* (*FINANCE: of individual*) beni *mpl*; (: *of company*) attivo.

assign [ə'saɪn] *vt*: **to ~ (to)** (*task*) assegnare (a); (*resources*) riservare (a); (*cause, meaning*) attribuire (a); **to ~ a date to sth** fissare la data di qc; **~ment** *n* compito.

assist [ə'sɪst] *vt* assistere, aiutare; **~ance** *n* assistenza, aiuto; **~ant** *n* assistente *m/f*; (*BRIT: also: shop ~ant*) commesso/a.

associate [*adj, n* ə'səʊʃɪɪt, *vb* ə'səʊʃɪeɪt] *adj* associato(a); (*member*) aggiunto(a) ♦ *n* collega *m/f* ♦ *vt* associare ♦ *vi*: **to ~ with sb** frequentare qn.

association [əsəʊsɪ'eɪʃən] *n* associazione *f*.

assorted [ə'sɔːtɪd] *adj* assortito(a).

assortment [ə'sɔːtmənt] *n* assortimento.

assume [ə'sjuːm] *vt* supporre; (*responsibilities etc*) assumere; (*attitude, name*) prendere; **~d name** *n* nome *m* falso.

assumption [ə'sʌmpʃən] *n* supposizione *f*, ipotesi *f inv*; (*of power*) assunzione *f*.

assurance [ə'ʃuərəns] *n* assicurazione *f*;

(*self-confidence*) fiducia in se stesso.

assure [ə'ʃuə*] *vt* assicurare.

asthma ['æsmə] *n* asma.

astonish [ə'stɔnɪʃ] *vt* stupire; **~ment** *n* stupore *m*.

astound [ə'staund] *vt* sbalordire.

astray [ə'streɪ] *adv*: **to go ~** smarrirsi; **to lead ~** portare sulla cattiva strada.

astride [ə'straɪd] *prep* a cavalcioni di.

astrology [əs'trɔlədʒɪ] *n* astrologia.

astronaut ['æstrənɔːt] *n* astronauta *m/f*.

astronomy [əs'trɔnəmɪ] *n* astronomia.

astute [əs'tjuːt] *adj* astuto(a).

asylum [ə'saɪləm] *n* asilo; (*building*) manicomio.

KEYWORD
---

at [æt] *prep* **1** (*referring to position, direction*) a; **~ the top** in cima; **~ the desk** al banco, alla scrivania; **~ home/ school** a casa/scuola; **~ the baker's** dal panettiere; **to look ~ sth** guardare qc; **to throw sth ~ sb** lanciare qc a qn

2 (*referring to time*) a; **~ 4 o'clock** alle 4; **~ night** di notte; **~ Christmas** a Natale; **~ times** a volte

3 (*referring to rates, speed etc*) a; **~ £1 a kilo** a 1 sterlina al chilo; **two ~ a time** due per volta, due per volta; **~ 50 km/h** a 50 km/h

4 (*referring to manner*): **~ a stroke** d'un solo colpo; **~ peace** in pace

5 (*referring to activity*): **to be ~ work** essere al lavoro; **to play ~ cowboys** giocare ai cowboy; **to be good ~ sth/ doing sth** essere bravo in qc/a fare qc

6 (*referring to cause*): **shocked/ surprised/annoyed ~ sth** colpito da/ sorpreso da/arrabbiato per qc; **I went ~ his suggestion** ci sono andato dietro suo consiglio.

---

ate [eɪt] *pt of* **eat**.

atheist ['eɪθɪɪst] *n* ateo/a.

Athens ['æθɪnz] *n* Atene *f*.

athlete ['æθliːt] *n* atleta *m/f*.

athletic [æθ'lɛtɪk] *adj* atletico(a); **~s** *n* atletica.

Atlantic [ət'læntɪk] *adj* atlantico(a) ♦ *n*: **the ~ (Ocean)** l'Atlantico, l'Oceano

Atlantico.

atlas ['ætləs] *n* atlante *m*.

atmosphere ['ætməsfɪə*] *n* atmosfera.

atom ['ætəm] *n* atomo; ~**ic** [ə'tɔmɪk] *adj* atomico(a); ~(**ic**) **bomb** *n* bomba atomica; ~**izer** ['ætəmaɪzə*] *n* atomizzatore *m*.

atone [ə'təun] *vi*: to ~ for espiare.

atrocious [ə'trəuʃəs] *adj* pessimo(a), atroce.

attach [ə'tætʃ] *vt* attaccare; (*document, letter*) allegare; (*importance etc*) attribuire; **to be** ~**ed to sb/sth** (*to like*) essere affezionato(a) a qn/qc.

attaché case [ə'tæʃeɪ-] *n* valigetta per documenti.

attachment [ə'tætʃmənt] *n* (*tool*) accessorio; (*love*): ~ (**to**) affetto (per).

attack [ə'tæk] *vt* attaccare; (*person*) aggredire; (*task etc*) iniziare; (*problem*) affrontare ♦ *n* attacco; **heart** ~ infarto; ~**er** *n* aggressore *m*.

attain [ə'teɪn] *vt* (*also*: to ~ to) arrivare a, raggiungere; ~**ments** *npl* cognizioni *fpl*.

attempt [ə'tɛmpt] *n* tentativo ♦ *vt* tentare; **to make an** ~ **on sb's life** attentare alla vita di qn.

attend [ə'tɛnd] *vt* frequentare; (*meeting, talk*) andare a; (*patient*) assistere; ~ **to** *vt fus* (*needs, affairs etc*) prendersi cura di; (*customer*) occuparsi di; ~**ance** *n* (*being present*) presenza; (*people present*) gente *f* presente; ~**ant** *n* custode *m/f*; persona di servizio ♦ *adj* concomitante.

attention [ə'tɛnʃən] *n* attenzione *f* ♦ *excl* (*MIL*) attenti!; **for the** ~ **of** (*ADMIN*) per l'attenzione di.

attentive [ə'tɛntɪv] *adj* attento(a); (*kind*) premuroso(a).

attic ['ætɪk] *n* soffitta.

attitude ['ætɪtjuːd] *n* atteggiamento; posa.

attorney [ə'tɔːnɪ] *n* (*lawyer*) avvocato; (*having proxy*) mandatario; A~ **General** *n* (*BRIT*) Procuratore *m* Generale; (*US*) Ministro della Giustizia.

attract [ə'trækt] *vt* attirare; ~**ion** [ə'trækʃən] *n* (*gen pl: pleasant things*)

attrattiva; (*PHYSICS, fig*: *towards sth*) attrazione *f*; ~**ive** *adj* attraente.

attribute [*n* 'ætrɪbjuːt, *vb* ə'trɪbjuːt] *n* attributo ♦ *vt*: **to** ~ **sth to** attribuire qc a.

attrition [ə'trɪʃən] *n*: **war of** ~ guerra di logoramento.

aubergine ['əubəʒiːn] *n* melanzana.

auburn ['ɔːbən] *adj* tizianesco(a).

auction ['ɔːkʃən] *n* (*also*: *sale by* ~) asta ♦ *vt* (*also*: *to sell by* ~) vendere all'asta; (*also*: *to put up for* ~) mettere all'asta; ~**eer** [-'nɪə*] *n* banditore *m*.

audible ['ɔːdɪbl] *adj* udibile.

audience ['ɔːdɪəns] *n* (*people*) pubblico; spettatori *mpl*; ascoltatori *mpl*; (*interview*) udienza.

audio-typist ['ɔːdɪəu'taɪpɪst] *n* dattilografo/a che trascrive da nastro.

audio-visual ['ɔːdɪəu'vɪzjuəl] *adj* audiovisivo(a); ~ **aid** *n* sussidio audiovisivo.

audit ['ɔːdɪt] *vt* rivedere, verificare.

audition [ɔː'dɪʃən] *n* audizione *f*.

auditor ['ɔːdɪtə*] *n* revisore *m*.

augment [ɔːg'mɛnt] *vt*, *vi* aumentare.

augur ['ɔːgə*] *vi*: **it** ~**s well** promette bene.

August ['ɔːgəst] *n* agosto.

aunt [ɑːnt] *n* zia; ~**ie** *n* zietta; ~**y** *n* zietta.

au pair ['əu'pɛə*] *n* (*also*: ~ *girl*) (ragazza *f*) alla pari *inv*.

aura ['ɔːrə] *n* aura.

auspicious [ɔːs'pɪʃəs] *adj* propizio(a).

austerity [ɔs'tɛrɪtɪ] *n* austerità.

Australia [ɔs'treɪlɪə] *n* Australia; ~**n** *adj*, *n* australiano(a).

Austria ['ɔstrɪə] *n* Austria; ~**n** *adj*, *n* austriaco(a).

authentic [ɔː'θɛntɪk] *adj* autentico(a).

author ['ɔːθə*] *n* autore/trice.

authoritarian [ɔːθɔrɪ'tɛərɪən] *adj* autoritario(a).

authoritative [ɔː'θɔrɪtətɪv] *adj* (*account etc*) autorevole; (*manner*) autoritario(a).

authority [ɔː'θɔrɪtɪ] *n* autorità *f inv*; (*permission*) autorizzazione *f*; **the authorities** *npl* (*government etc*) le autorità.

authorize ['ɔ:θəraɪz] vt autorizzare.
auto ['ɔ:təʊ] (US) n auto f inv.
autobiography [ɔ:təbaɪ'ɔgrəfɪ] n autobiografia.
autograph ['ɔ:təgrɑ:f] n autografo ♦ vt firmare.
automata [ɔ:'tɔmətə] npl of automaton.
automatic [ɔ:tə'mætɪk] adj automatico(a) ♦ n (gun) arma automatica; (washing machine) lavatrice f automatica; (car) automobile f con cambio automatico; ~ally adv automaticamente.
automation [ɔ:tə'meɪʃən] n automazione f.
automaton [ɔ:'tɔmətən] (pl automata) n automa m.
automobile ['ɔ:təməbi:l] (US) n automobile f.
autonomy [ɔ:'tɔnəmɪ] n autonomia.
autumn ['ɔ:təm] n autunno.
auxiliary [ɔ:g'zɪlɪərɪ] adj ausiliario(a) ♦ n ausiliare m/f.
Av. abbr = avenue.
avail [ə'veɪl] vt: to ~ o.s. of servirsi di; approfittarsi di ♦ n: to no ~ inutilmente.
available [ə'veɪləbl] adj disponibile.
avalanche ['ævəlɑ:nʃ] n valanga.
avant-garde ['ævɑ̃'gɑ:d] adj d'avanguardia.
Ave. abbr = avenue.
avenge [ə'vendʒ] vt vendicare.
avenue ['ævənju:] n viale m; (fig) strada, via.
average ['ævərɪdʒ] n media ♦ adj medio(a) ♦ vt (a certain figure) fare di or in media; **on** ~ in media; ~ **out** vi: to ~ out at aggirarsi in media su, essere in media di.
averse [ə'vɜ:s] adj: to be ~ to sth/doing essere contrario a qc/a fare.
avert [ə'vɜ:t] vt evitare, prevenire; (one's eyes) distogliere.
aviary ['eɪvɪərɪ] n voliera, uccelliera.
avid ['ævɪd] adj (supporter etc) accanito(a).
avocado [ævə'kɑ:dəʊ] n (also: BRIT: ~ pear) avocado m inv.
avoid [ə'vɔɪd] vt evitare.

avuncular [ə'vʌŋkjʊlə*] adj paterno(a).
await [ə'weɪt] vt aspettare.
awake [ə'weɪk] (pt awoke, pp awoke, awaked) adj sveglio(a) ♦ vt svegliare ♦ vi svegliarsi; ~ning [ə'weɪknɪŋ] n risveglio.
award [ə'wɔ:d] n premio; (LAW) risarcimento ♦ vt assegnare; (LAW: damages) accordare.
aware [ə'weə*] adj: ~ of (conscious) conscio(a) di; (informed) informato(a) di; **to become** ~ of accorgersi di; ~ness n consapevolezza.
awash [ə'wɔʃ] adj: ~ (with) inondato(a) (da).
away [ə'weɪ] adj, adv via; lontano(a); **two kilometres** ~ a due chilometri di distanza; **two hours** ~ **by car** a due ore di distanza in macchina; **the holiday was two weeks** ~ mancavano due settimane alle vacanze; **he's** ~ **for a week** è andato via per una settimana; **to take** ~ togliere; **he was working/pedalling** etc ~ la particella indica la continuità e l'energia dell'azione: lavorava/pedalava etc più che poteva; **to fade/wither** etc ~ la particella rinforza l'idea della diminuzione; ~ **game** n (SPORT) partita fuori casa.
awe [ɔ:] n timore m; ~-**inspiring** imponente; ~**some** adj imponente.
awful ['ɔ:fəl] adj terribile; **an** ~ **lot of** un mucchio di; ~**ly** adv (very) terribilmente.
awhile [ə'waɪl] adv (per) un po'.
awkward ['ɔ:kwəd] adj (clumsy) goffo(a); (inconvenient) scomodo(a); (embarrassing) imbarazzante.
awning ['ɔ:nɪŋ] n (of shop, hotel etc) tenda.
awoke [ə'wəʊk] pt of awake.
awoken [ə'wəʊkn] pp of awake.
awry [ə'raɪ] adv di traverso; **to go** ~ andare a monte.
axe [æks] (US ax) n scure f ♦ vt (project etc) abolire; (jobs) sopprimere.
axes ['æksi:z] npl of axis.
axis ['æksɪs] (pl axes) n asse m.
axle ['æksl] n (also: ~-tree) asse m.
ay(e) [aɪ] excl (yes) sì.

B

B [bi:] *n* (*MUS*) si *m*.

B.A. *n abbr* = **Bachelor of Arts**.

babble ['bæbl] *vi* (*person, voices*) farfugliare; (*brook*) gorgogliare.

baby ['beɪbɪ] *n* bambino/a; ~ **carriage** (*US*) *n* carrozzina; ~-**sit** *vi* fare il (*or* la) babysitter; ~-**sitter** *n* baby-sitter *m/f inv*.

bachelor ['bætʃələ*] *n* scapolo; **B~ of Arts/Science** ≈ laureato/a in lettere/scienze.

back [bæk] *n* (*of person, horse*) dorso, schiena; (*as opposed to front*) dietro; (*of hand*) dorso; (*of train*) coda; (*of chair*) schienale *m*; (*of page*) rovescio; (*of book*) retro; (*FOOTBALL*) difensore *m* ♦ *vt* (*candidate: also:* ~ **up**) appoggiare; (*horse: at races*) puntare su; (*car*) guidare a marcia indietro ♦ *vi* indietreggiare; (*car etc*) fare marcia indietro ♦ *cpd* posteriore, di dietro; (*AUT: seat, wheels*) posteriore ♦ *adv* (*not forward*) indietro; (*returned*): **he's** ~ è tornato; **he ran** ~ tornò indietro di corsa; (*restitution*): **throw the ball** ~ ritira la palla; **can I have it** ~? posso riaverlo?; (*again*): **he called** ~ ha richiamato; ~ **down** *vi* fare marcia indietro; ~ **out** *vi* (*of promise*) tirarsi indietro; ~ **up** *vt* (*support*) appoggiare, sostenere; (*COMPUT*) fare una copia di riserva di; ~**bencher** (*BRIT*) *n membro del Parlamento senza potere amministrativo*; ~**bone** *n* spina dorsale; ~**cloth** *n* scena di sfondo; ~**date** *vt* (*letter*) retrodatare; ~**dated pay rise** aumento retroattivo; ~**drop** *n* = ~**cloth**; ~**fire** *vi* (*AUT*) dar ritorni di fiamma; (*plans*) fallire; ~**ground** *n* sfondo; (*of events*) background *m inv*; (*basic knowledge*) base *f*; (*experience*) esperienza; **family** ~**ground** ambiente *m* familiare; ~**hand** *n* (*TENNIS: also:* ~**hand stroke**) rovescio; ~**handed** *adj* (*fig*) ambiguo(a); ~**hander** (*BRIT*) *n* (*bribe*) bustarella; ~**ing** *n* (*fig*)

appoggio; ~**lash** *n* contraccolpo, ripercussione *f*; ~**log** *n*: ~**log of work** lavoro arretrato; ~ **number** *n* (*of magazine etc*) numero arretrato; ~**pack** *n* zaino; ~ **pay** *n* arretrato di paga; ~ **payments** *npl* arretrati *mpl*; ~**side** (*inf*) *n* sedere *m*; ~**stage** *adv* nel retroscena; ~**stroke** *n* nuoto sul dorso; ~**up** *adj* (*train, plane*) supplementare; (*COMPUT*) di riserva ♦ *n* (*support*) appoggio, sostegno; (*also:* ~**up file**) file *m inv* di riserva; ~**ward** *adj* (*movement*) indietro *inv*; (*person*) tardivo(a); (*country*) arretrato(a); ~**wards** *adv* indietro; (*fall, walk*) all'indietro; ~**water** *n* (*fig*) posto morto; ~**yard** *n* cortile *m* dietro la casa.

bacon ['beɪkən] *n* pancetta.

bad [bæd] *adj* cattivo(a); (*accident, injury*) brutto(a); (*meat, food*) andato(a) a male; **his** ~ **leg** la sua gamba malata; **to go** ~ andare a male.

bade [bæd] *pt of* **bid**.

badge [bædʒ] *n* insegna; (*of policeman*) stemma *m*.

badger ['bædʒə*] *n* tasso.

badly ['bædlɪ] *adv* (*work, dress etc*) male; ~ **wounded** gravemente ferito; **he needs it** ~ ne ha un gran bisogno; ~ **off** *adj* povero(a).

badminton ['bædmɪntən] *n* badminton *m*.

bad-tempered ['bæd'tempəd] *adj* irritabile; di malumore.

baffle ['bæfl] *vt* (*puzzle*) confondere.

bag [bæg] *n* sacco; (*handbag etc*) borsa; ~**s of** (*inf: lots of*) un sacco di; ~**gage** *n* bagagli *mpl*; ~**gy** *adj* largo(a), sformato(a); ~**pipes** *npl* cornamusa.

bail [beɪl] *n* cauzione *f* ♦ *vt* (*prisoner: also: grant* ~ *to*) concedere la libertà provvisoria su cauzione a; (*boat: also:* ~ **out**) aggottare; **on** ~ in libertà provvisoria su cauzione; ~ **out** *vt* (*prisoner*) ottenere la libertà provvisoria su cauzione di; *see also* **bale**.

bailiff ['beɪlɪf] *n* (*LAW: BRIT*) ufficiale *m* giudiziario; (: *US*) usciere *m*.

bait [beɪt] n esca ♦ vt (hook) innescare; (trap) munire di esca; (fig) tormentare.

bake [beɪk] vt cuocere al forno ♦ vi cuocersi al forno; ~d beans npl fagioli mpl in salsa di pomodoro; ~r n fornaio/a, panettiere/a; ~ry n panetteria; baking n cottura (al forno); baking powder n lievito in polvere.

balance ['bæləns] n equilibrio; (COMM: sum) bilancio; (remainder) resto; (scales) bilancia ♦ vt tenere in equilibrio; (budget) far quadrare; (account) pareggiare; (compensate) contrappesare; ~ of trade/payments bilancia commerciale/dei pagamenti; ~d adj (personality, diet) equilibrato(a); ~ sheet n bilancio.

balcony ['bælkənɪ] n balcone m; (in theatre) balconata.

bald [bɔːld] adj calvo(a); (tyre) liscio(a).

bale [beɪl] n balla; ~ out vi (of a plane) gettarsi col paracadute.

baleful ['beɪlful] adj funesto(a).

ball [bɔːl] n palla; (football) pallone m; (for golf) pallina; (of wool, string) gomitolo; (dance) ballo; to play ~ (fig) stare al gioco.

ballast ['bæləst] n zavorra.

ball bearings npl cuscinetti a sfere.

ballerina [bælə'riːnə] n ballerina.

ballet ['bæleɪ] n balletto; ~ dancer n ballerino(a) classico(a).

balloon [bə'luːn] n pallone m.

ballot paper ['bælət-] n scheda.

ball-point pen n penna a sfera.

ballroom ['bɔːlrum] n sala da ballo.

balm [bɑːm] n balsamo.

ban [bæn] n interdizione f ♦ vt interdire.

banana [bə'nɑːnə] n banana.

band [bænd] n banda; (at a dance) orchestra; (MIL) fanfara; ~ together vi collegarsi.

bandage ['bændɪdʒ] n benda, fascia.

bandaid ['bændeɪd] ® (US) n cerotto.

bandwagon ['bændwægən] n: to jump on the ~ (fig) seguire la corrente.

bandy ['bændɪ] vt (jokes, insults) scambiare.

bandy-legged [-'lɛgɪd] adj dalle gambe storte.

bang [bæŋ] n (of door) lo sbattere; (of gun, blow) colpo ♦ vt battere (violentemente); (door) sbattere ♦ vi scoppiare; sbattere.

bangle ['bæŋgl] n braccialetto.

bangs [bæŋz] (US) npl (fringe) frangia, frangetta.

banish ['bænɪʃ] vt bandire.

banister(s) ['bænɪstə(z)] n(pl) ringhiera.

bank [bæŋk] n banca, banco; (of river, lake) riva, sponda; (of earth) banco ♦ vi (AVIAT) inclinarsi in virata; ~ on vt fus contare su; ~ account n conto in banca; ~ card n carta assegni; ~er n banchiere m; ~er's card (BRIT) n = ~ card; B~ holiday (BRIT) n giorno di festa (in cui le banche sono chiuse); ~ing n attività bancaria; professione f di banchiere; ~note n banconota; ~ rate n tasso bancario.

bankrupt ['bæŋkrʌpt] adj fallito(a); to go ~ fallire; ~cy n fallimento.

bank statement n estratto conto.

banner ['bænə*] n striscione m.

banns [bænz] npl pubblicazioni fpl di matrimonio.

baptism ['bæptɪzəm] n battesimo.

bar [bɑː*] n (place) bar m inv; (counter) banco; (rod) barra; (of window etc) sbarra; (of chocolate) tavoletta; (fig) ostacolo; restrizione f; (MUS) battuta ♦ vt (road, window) sbarrare; (person) escludere; (activity) interdire; ~ of soap saponetta; the B~ (LAW) l'Ordine m degli avvocati; behind ~s (prisoner) dietro le sbarre; ~ none senza eccezione.

barbaric [bɑː'bærɪk] adj barbarico(a).

barbecue ['bɑːbɪkjuː] n barbecue m inv.

barbed wire ['bɑːbd-] n filo spinato.

barber ['bɑːbə*] n barbiere m.

bar code n (on goods) codice m a barre.

bare [bɛə*] adj nudo(a) ♦ vt scoprire, denudare; (teeth) mostrare; the ~ necessities lo stretto necessario; ~back adv senza sella; ~faced adj sfacciato(a); ~foot adj, adv scalzo(a);

~**ly** *adv* appena.
bargain ['bɑ:gɪn] *n* (*transaction*) contratto; (*good buy*) affare *m* ♦ *vi* trattare; **into the** ~ per giunta; ~ **for** *vt fus*: **he got more than he** ~**ed for** gli è andata peggio di quel che si aspettasse.
barge [bɑ:dʒ] *n* chiatta; ~ **in** *vi* (*walk in*) piombare dentro; (*interrupt talk*) intromettersi a sproposito.
bark [bɑ:k] *n* (*of tree*) corteccia; (*of dog*) abbaio ♦ *vi* abbaiare.
barley ['bɑ:lɪ] *n* orzo.
barmaid ['bɑ:meɪd] *n* cameriera al banco.
barman ['bɑ:mən] *n* barista *m*.
barn [bɑ:n] *n* granaio.
barometer [bə'rɔmɪtə*] *n* barometro.
baron ['bærən] *n* barone *m*; ~**ess** *n* baronessa.
barracks ['bærəks] *npl* caserma.
barrage ['bærɑ:ʒ] *n* (*MIL*, *dam*) sbarramento; (*fig*) fiume *m*.
barrel ['bærəl] *n* barile *m*; (*of gun*) canna.
barren ['bærən] *adj* sterile; (*soil*) arido(a).
barricade [bærɪ'keɪd] *n* barricata.
barrier ['bærɪə*] *n* barriera.
barring ['bɑ:rɪŋ] *prep* salvo.
barrister ['bærɪstə*] (*BRIT*) *n* avvocato/essa (*con diritto di parlare davanti a tutte le corti*).
barrow ['bærəu] *n* (*cart*) carriola.
bartender ['bɑ:tɛndə*] (*US*) *n* barista *m*.
barter ['bɑ:tə*] *vt*: **to** ~ **sth for** barattare qc con.
base [beɪs] *n* base *f* ♦ *vt*: **to** ~ **sth on** basare qc su ♦ *adj* vile.
baseball ['beɪsbɔ:l] *n* baseball *m*.
basement ['beɪsmənt] *n* seminterrato; (*of shop*) interrato.
bases¹ ['beɪsi:z] *npl of* **basis.**
bases² ['beɪsɪz] *npl of* **base.**
bash [bæʃ] (*inf*) *vt* picchiare.
bashful ['bæʃful] *adj* timido(a).
basic ['beɪsɪk] *adj* rudimentale; essenziale; ~**ally** [-lɪ] *adv* fondamentalmente; sostanzialmente; ~**s** *npl*: **the** ~**s** l'essenziale *m*.

basil ['bæzl] *n* basilico.
basin ['beɪsn] *n* (*vessel, also GEO*) bacino; (*also: wash*~) lavabo.
basis ['beɪsɪs] (*pl* **bases**) *n* base *f*; **on a part-time** ~ part-time; **on a trial** ~ in prova.
bask [bɑ:sk] *vi*: **to** ~ **in the sun** crogiolarsi al sole.
basket ['bɑ:skɪt] *n* cesta; (*smaller*) cestino; (*with handle*) paniere *m*; ~**ball** *n* pallacanestro *f*.
bass [beɪs] *n* (*MUS*) basso.
bassoon [bə'su:n] *n* fagotto.
bastard ['bɑ:stəd] *n* bastardo/a; (*inf!*) stronzo (*!*).
bat [bæt] *n* pipistrello; (*for baseball etc*) mazza; (*BRIT: for table tennis*) racchetta ♦ *vt*: **he didn't** ~ **an eyelid** non battè ciglio.
batch [bætʃ] *n* (*of bread*) infornata; (*of papers*) cumulo.
bated ['beɪtɪd] *adj*: **with** ~ **breath** col fiato sospeso.
bath [bɑ:θ] *n* bagno; (*bathtub*) vasca da bagno ♦ *vt* far fare il bagno a; **to have a** ~ fare un bagno; *see also* **baths.**
bathe [beɪð] *vi* fare il bagno ♦ *vt* (*wound*) lavare; ~**r** *n* bagnante *m/f*.
bathing ['beɪðɪŋ] *n* bagni *mpl*; ~ **cap** *n* cuffia da bagno; ~ **costume** (*US* ~ **suit**) *n* costume *m* da bagno.
bathrobe ['bɑ:θrəub] *n* accappatoio.
bathroom ['bɑ:θrum] *n* stanza da bagno.
baths [bɑ:ðz] *npl* bagni *mpl* pubblici.
bath towel *n* asciugamano da bagno.
baton ['bætən] *n* (*MUS*) bacchetta; (*ATHLETICS*) testimone *m*; (*club*) manganello.
batter ['bætə*] *vt* battere ♦ *n* pastetta; ~**ed** *adj* (*hat*) sformato(a); (*pan*) ammaccato(a).
battery ['bætərɪ] *n* batteria; (*of torch*) pila.
battle ['bætl] *n* battaglia ♦ *vi* battagliare, lottare; ~**field** *n* campo di battaglia; ~**ship** *n* nave *f* da guerra.
bawdy ['bɔ:dɪ] *adj* piccante.
bawl [bɔ:l] *vi* urlare.
bay [beɪ] *n* (*of sea*) baia; **to hold sb at** ~ tenere qn a bada; ~ **leaf** *n* foglia

d'alloro; ~ **window** n bovindo.
bazaar [bə'zɑ:*] n bazar m inv; vendita
di beneficenza.
B. & B. abbr = **bed and breakfast.**
BBC n abbr (= British Broadcasting
Corporation) rete nazionale di
radiotelevisione in Gran Bretagna.
B.C. adv abbr (= before Christ) a.C.

KEYWORD

be [bi:] (pt **was, were,** pp **been**) aux vb
1 (with present participle: forming
continuous tenses): **what are you
doing?** che fa?, che sta facendo?;
they're coming tomorrow vengono
domani; **I've been waiting for her for
hours** sono ore che l'aspetto
2 (with pp: forming passives) essere;
to ~ killed essere or venire ucciso(a);
the box had been opened la scatola era
stata aperta; **the thief was nowhere to
~ seen** il ladro non si trovava da
nessuna parte
3 (in tag questions): **it was fun, wasn't
it?** è stato divertente, no?; **he's good-
looking, isn't he?** è un bell'uomo,
vero?; **she's back, is she?** così è
tornata, eh?
4 (+ to + infinitive): **the house is to ~
sold** abbiamo (or hanno etc) intenzione
di vendere casa; **you're to ~ con-
gratulated for all your work** dovremo
farvi i complimenti per tutto il vostro
lavoro; **he's not to open it** non deve
aprirlo
♦ vb + complement 1 (gen) essere; **I'm
English** sono inglese; **I'm tired** sono
stanco(a); **I'm hot/cold** ho caldo/freddo;
he's a doctor è medico; **2 and 2 are 4** 2
più 2 fa 4; **~ careful!** sta attento(a)!; **~
good** sii buono(a)
2 (of health) stare; **how are you?** come
sta?; **he's very ill** sta molto male
3 (of age): **how old are you?** quanti
anni hai?; **I'm sixteen (years old)** ho
sedici anni
4 (cost) costare; **how much was the
meal?** quant'era or quanto costava il
pranzo?; **that'll ~ £5, please** (fa) 5
sterline, per favore

♦ vi 1 (exist, occur etc) essere, esistere; **the best singer that ever was** il
migliore cantante mai esistito or di tutti
tempi; **~ that as it may** comunque sia,
sia come sia; **so ~ it** sia pure, e sia
2 (referring to place) essere, trovarsi;
I won't ~ here tomorrow non ci sarò
domani; **Edinburgh is in Scotland**
Edimburgo si trova in Scozia
3 (referring to movement): **where have
you been?** dov'è stato?; **I've been to
China** sono stato in Cina
♦ impers vb 1 (referring to time, distance) essere; **it's 5 o'clock** sono le 5;
it's the 28th of April è il 28 aprile; **it's
10 km to the village** di qui al paese sono
10 km
2 (referring to the weather) fare; **it's
too hot/cold** fa troppo caldo/freddo; **it's
windy** c'è vento
3 (emphatic): **it's me** sono io; **it was
Maria who paid the bill** è stata Maria
che ha pagato il conto.

beach [bi:tʃ] n spiaggia ♦ vt tirare in
secco.
beacon ['bi:kən] n (lighthouse) faro;
(marker) segnale m.
bead [bi:d] n perlina.
beak [bi:k] n becco.
beaker ['bi:kə*] n coppa.
beam [bi:m] n trave f; (of light) raggio
♦ vi brillare.
bean [bi:n] n fagiolo; (of coffee) chicco;
runner ~ fagiolino; **broad ~** fava;
~sprouts npl germogli mpl di soia.
bear [beə*] (pt **bore,** pp **borne**) n orso ♦
vt portare; (endure) sopportare;
(produce) generare ♦ vi: **to ~ right/left**
piegare a destra/sinistra; **~ out** vt
(suspicions) confermare, convalidare;
(person) dare il proprio appoggio a; **~
up** vi (person) fare buon viso a cattiva
sorte.
beard [bɪəd] n barba.
bearer ['beərə*] n portatore m.
bearing ['beərɪŋ] n portamento;
(connection) rapporto; **~s** npl (also:
ball ~s) cuscinetti mpl a sfere; **to take
a ~** fare un rilevamento; **to find one's**

beast 21 belated

~s orientarsi.

beast [bi:st] *n* bestia; **~ly** *adj* meschino(a); (*weather*) da cani.

beat [bi:t] (*pt* beat, *pp* beaten) *n* colpo; (*of heart*) battito; (*MUS*) tempo; battuta; (*of policeman*) giro ♦ *vt* battere; (*eggs, cream*) sbattere ♦ *vi* battere; **off the ~en track** fuori mano; **~ it!** (*inf*) fila!, fuori dai piedi!; **~ off** *vt* respingere; **~ up** *vt* (*person*) picchiare; (*eggs*) sbattere; **beaten** *pp of* beat; **~ing** *n* bastonata.

beautiful ['bju:tɪful] *adj* bello(a); **~ly** *adv* splendidamente.

beauty ['bju:tɪ] *n* bellezza; **~ salon** *n* istituto di bellezza; **~ spot** (*BRIT*) *n* (*TOURISM*) luogo pittoresco.

beaver ['bi:və*] *n* castoro.

became [bɪ'keɪm] *pt of* become.

because [bɪ'kɔz] *conj* perché; **~ of** a causa di.

beck [bɛk] *n*: **to be at sb's ~ and call** essere a completa disposizione di qn.

beckon ['bɛkən] *vt* (*also*: **~ to**) chiamare con un cenno.

become [bɪ'kʌm] (*irreg: like* come) *vt* diventare; **to ~ fat/thin** ingrassarsi/dimagrire.

becoming [bɪ'kʌmɪŋ] *adj* (*behaviour*) che si conviene; (*clothes*) grazioso(a).

bed [bɛd] *n* letto; (*of flowers*) aiuola; (*of coal, clay*) strato; **single/double ~** letto a una piazza/a due piazze *or* matrimoniale; **~ and breakfast** *n* (*place*) ≈ pensione *f* familiare; (*terms*) camera con colazione; **~clothes** *npl* biancheria e coperte *fpl* da letto; **~ding** *n* coperte e lenzuola *fpl*.

bedlam ['bɛdləm] *n* baraonda.

bedraggled [bɪ'dræɡld] *adj* fradicio(a).

bed: ~ridden *adj* costretto(a) a letto; **~room** *n* camera da letto; **~side** *n*: **at sb's ~side** al capezzale di qn; **~sit(ter)** (*BRIT*) *n* monolocale *m*; **~spread** *n* copriletto; **~time** *n*: **it's ~time** è ora di andare a letto.

bee [bi:] *n* ape *f*.

beech [bi:tʃ] *n* faggio.

beef [bi:f] *n* manzo; **roast ~** arrosto di manzo; **~burger** *n* hamburger *m inv*;

B~eater *n* guardia della Torre di Londra.

beehive ['bi:haɪv] *n* alveare *m*.

beeline ['bi:laɪn] *n*: **to make a ~ for** buttarsi a capo fitto verso.

been [bi:n] *pp of* be.

beer [bɪə*] *n* birra.

beetle ['bi:tl] *n* scarafaggio; coleottero.

beetroot ['bi:tru:t] (*BRIT*) *n* barbabietola.

before [bɪ'fɔ:*] *prep* (*in time*) prima di; (*in space*) davanti a ♦ *conj* prima che +*sub*; prima di ♦ *adv* prima; **~ going** prima di andare; **~ she goes** prima che vada; **the week ~** la settimana prima; **I've seen it ~** l'ho già visto; **I've never seen it ~** è la prima volta che lo vedo; **~hand** *adv* in anticipo.

beg [bɛɡ] *vi* chiedere l'elemosina ♦ *vt* (*also*: **~ for**) chiedere in elemosina; (: *favour*) chiedere; **to ~ sb to do sth** pregare qn di fare.

began [bɪ'ɡæn] *pt of* begin.

beggar ['bɛɡə*] *n* mendicante *m/f*.

begin [bɪ'ɡɪn] (*pt* began, *pp* begun) *vt*, *vi* cominciare; **to ~ doing *or* to do sth** incominciare *or* iniziare a fare qc; **~ner** *n* principiante *m/f*; **~ning** *n* inizio, principio.

begun [bɪ'ɡʌn] *pp of* begin.

behalf [bɪ'hɑ:f] *n*: **on ~ of** per conto di; a nome di.

behave [bɪ'heɪv] *vi* comportarsi; (*well*: *also*: **~ o.s.**) comportarsi bene.

behaviour [bɪ'heɪvjə*] (*US* **behavior**) *n* comportamento, condotta.

behead [bɪ'hed] *vt* decapitare.

beheld [bɪ'held] *pt, pp of* behold.

behind [bɪ'haɪnd] *prep* dietro; (*followed by pronoun*) dietro di; (*time*) in ritardo con ♦ *adv* dietro; (*leave, stay*) indietro ♦ *n* didietro; **to be ~ (schedule)** essere in ritardo rispetto al programma; **~ the scenes** (*fig*) dietro le quinte.

behold [bɪ'həʊld] (*irreg: like* hold) *vt* vedere, scorgere.

beige [beɪʒ] *adj* beige *inv*.

Beijing ['beɪ'dʒɪŋ] *n* Pechino *f*.

being ['bi:ɪŋ] *n* essere *m*.

belated [bɪ'leɪtɪd] *adj* tardo(a).

belch [beltʃ] *vi* ruttare ♦ *vt* (*gen*: ~ *out*: *smoke etc*) eruttare.

belfry ['bɛlfrɪ] *n* campanile *m*.

Belgian ['bɛldʒən] *adj, n* belga *m/f*.

Belgium ['bɛldʒəm] *n* Belgio.

belie [bɪ'laɪ] *vt* smentire.

belief [bɪ'liːf] *n* (*opinion*) opinione *f*, convinzione *f*; (*trust, faith*) fede *f*.

believe [bɪ'liːv] *vt, vi* credere; **to ~ in** (*God*) credere in; (*ghosts*) credere a; (*method*) avere fiducia in; **~r** *n* (*REL*) credente *m/f*; (*in idea, activity*): **to be a ~r in** credere in.

belittle [bɪ'lɪtl] *vt* sminuire.

bell [bɛl] *n* campana; (*small, on door, electric*) campanello.

belligerent [bɪ'lɪdʒərənt] *adj* bellicoso(a).

bellow ['bɛləu] *vi* muggire.

bellows ['bɛləuz] *npl* soffietto.

belly ['bɛlɪ] *n* pancia.

belong [bɪ'lɔŋ] *vi*: **to ~ to** appartenere a; (*club etc*) essere socio di; **this book ~s here** questo libro va qui; **~ings** *npl* cose *fpl*, roba.

beloved [bɪ'lʌvɪd] *adj* adorato(a).

below [bɪ'ləu] *prep* sotto, al di sotto di ♦ *adv* sotto, di sotto; giù; **see ~** vedi sotto *or* oltre.

belt [bɛlt] *n* cintura; (*TECH*) cinghia ♦ *vt* (*thrash*) picchiare ♦ *vi* (*inf*) filarsela; **~way** (*US*) *n* (*AUT*: *ring road*) circonvallazione *f*; (: *motorway*) autostrada.

bemused [bɪ'mjuːzd] *adj* perplesso(a), stupito(a).

bench [bɛntʃ] *n* panca; (*in workshop, POL*) banco; **the B~** (*LAW*) la Corte.

bend [bɛnd] (*pt, pp* **bent**) *vt* curvare; (*leg, arm*) piegare ♦ *vi* curvarsi; piegarsi ♦ *n* (*BRIT: in road*) curva; (*in pipe, river*) gomito; **~ down** *vi* chinarsi; **~ over** *vi* piegarsi.

beneath [bɪ'niːθ] *prep* sotto, al di sotto di; (*unworthy of*) indegno(a) di ♦ *adv* sotto, di sotto.

benefactor ['bɛnɪfæktə*] *n* benefattore *m*.

beneficial [bɛnɪ'fɪʃəl] *adj* che fa bene; vantaggioso(a).

benefit ['bɛnɪfɪt] *n* beneficio, vantaggio; (*allowance of money*) indennità *f inv* ♦ *vt* far bene a ♦ *vi*: **he'll ~ from it** ne trarrà beneficio *or* profitto.

benevolent [bɪ'nɛvələnt] *adj* benevolo(a).

benign [bɪ'naɪn] *adj* (*person, smile*) benevolo(a); (*MED*) benigno(a).

bent [bɛnt] *pt, pp of* **bend** ♦ *n* inclinazione *f* ♦ *adj* (*inf: dishonest*) losco(a); **to be ~ on** essere deciso(a) a.

bequest [bɪ'kwɛst] *n* lascito.

bereaved [bɪ'riːvd] *n*: **the ~** i familiari in lutto.

beret ['bɛreɪ] *n* berretto.

berm [bəːm] (*US*) *n* (*AUT*) corsia d'emergenza.

berry ['bɛrɪ] *n* bacca.

berserk [bə'səːk] *adj*: **to go ~** montare su tutte le furie.

berth [bəːθ] *n* (*bed*) cuccetta; (*for ship*) ormeggio ♦ *vi* (*in harbour*) entrare in porto; (*at anchor*) gettare l'ancora.

beseech [bɪ'siːtʃ] (*pt, pp* **besought**) *vt* implorare.

beset [bɪ'sɛt] (*pt, pp* **beset**) *vt* assalire.

beside [bɪ'saɪd] *prep* accanto a; **to be ~ o.s. (with anger)** essere fuori di sé (dalla rabbia); **that's ~ the point** non c'entra.

besides [bɪ'saɪdz] *adv* inoltre, per di più ♦ *prep* oltre a; a parte.

besiege [bɪ'siːdʒ] *vt* (*town*) assediare; (*fig*) tempestare.

besought [bɪ'sɔːt] *pt, pp of* **beseech**.

best [bɛst] *adj* migliore ♦ *adv* meglio; **the ~ part of** (*quantity*) la maggior parte di; **at ~** tutt'al più; **to make the ~ of sth** cavare il meglio possibile da qc; **to do one's ~** fare del proprio meglio; **to the ~ of my knowledge** per quel che ne so; **to the ~ of my ability** al massimo delle mie capacità; **~ man** *n* testimone *m* dello sposo.

bestow [bɪ'stəu] *vt* accordare; (*title*) conferire.

bet [bɛt] (*pt, pp* **bet** *or* **betted**) *n* scommessa ♦ *vt, vi* scommettere; **to ~ sb sth** scommettere qc con qn.

betray [bɪ'treɪ] *vt* tradire; **~al** *n*

tradimento.

better ['bɛtə*] *adj* migliore ♦ *adv* meglio ♦ *vt* migliorare ♦ *n*: to get the ~ of avere la meglio su; you had ~ do it è meglio che lo faccia; he thought ~ of it cambiò idea; to get ~ migliorare; ~ off *adj* più ricco(a); (*fig*): you'd be ~ off this way starebbe meglio così.

betting ['bɛtɪŋ] *n* scommesse *fpl*; ~ shop (*BRIT*) *n* ufficio dell'allibratore.

between [bɪ'twi:n] *prep* tra ♦ *adv* in mezzo, nel mezzo.

beverage ['bɛvərɪdʒ] *n* bevanda.

beware [bɪ'wɛə*] *vt, vi*: to ~ (of) stare attento(a) (a); "~ of the dog" "attenti al cane".

bewildered [bɪ'wɪldəd] *adj* sconcertato(a), confuso(a).

bewitching [bɪ'wɪtʃɪŋ] *adj* affascinante.

beyond [bɪ'jɔnd] *prep* (*in space*) oltre; (*exceeding*) al di sopra di ♦ *adv* di là; ~ doubt senza dubbio; ~ repair irreparabile.

bias ['baɪəs] *n* (*prejudice*) pregiudizio; (*preference*) preferenza; ~(s)ed *adj* parziale.

bib [bɪb] *n* bavaglino.

Bible ['baɪbl] *n* Bibbia.

bicarbonate of soda [baɪ'kɑːbənɪt-] *n* bicarbonato (di sodio).

bicker ['bɪkə*] *vi* bisticciare.

bicycle ['baɪsɪkl] *n* bicicletta.

bid [bɪd] (*pt* bade *or* bid, *pp* bidden *or* bid) *n* offerta; (*attempt*) tentativo ♦ *vi* fare un'offerta ♦ *vt* fare un'offerta di; to ~ sb good day dire buon giorno a qn; bidden *pp of* bid; ~der *n*: the highest ~der il maggior offerente; ~ding *n* offerte *fpl*.

bide [baɪd] *vt*: to ~ one's time aspettare il momento giusto.

bifocals [baɪ'fəuklz] *npl* occhiali *mpl* bifocali.

big [bɪg] *adj* grande; grosso(a).

big dipper [-'dɪpə*] *n* montagne *fpl* russe, otto *m inv* volante.

bigheaded ['bɪg'hɛdɪd] *adj* presuntuoso(a).

bigot ['bɪgət] *n* persona gretta; ~ed *adj* gretto(a); ~ry *n* grettezza.

big top *n* tendone *m* del circo.

bike [baɪk] *n* bici *f inv*.

bikini [bɪ'kiːnɪ] *n* bikini *m inv*.

bilingual [baɪ'lɪŋgwəl] *adj* bilingue.

bill [bɪl] *n* conto; (*POL*) atto; (*US: banknote*) banconota; (*of bird*) becco; (*of show*) locandina; "post no ~s" "divieto di affissione"; to fit *or* fill the ~ (*fig*) fare al caso; ~board *n* tabellone *m*.

billet ['bɪlɪt] *n* alloggio.

billfold ['bɪlfəuld] (*US*) *n* portafoglio.

billiards ['bɪljədz] *n* biliardo.

billion ['bɪljən] *n* (*BRIT*) bilione *m*; (*US*) miliardo.

bin [bɪn] *n* (*for coal, rubbish*) bidone *m*; (*for bread*) cassetta; (*dust~*) pattumiera; (*litter ~*) cestino.

bind [baɪnd] (*pt, pp* bound) *vt* legare; (*oblige*) obbligare ♦ *n* (*inf*) scocciatura; ~ing *adj* (*contract*) vincolante.

binge [bɪndʒ] (*inf*) *n*: to go on a ~ fare baldoria.

bingo ['bɪŋgəu] *n* gioco simile alla tombola.

binoculars [bɪ'nɔkjuləz] *npl* binocolo.

bio... [baɪə'...] *prefix*: ~chemistry *n* biochimica; ~graphy [baɪ'ɔgrəfɪ] *n* biografia; ~logical *adj* biologico(a); ~logy [baɪ'ɔlədʒɪ] *n* biologia.

birch [bəːtʃ] *n* betulla.

bird [bəːd] *n* uccello; (*BRIT*: *inf*: *girl*) bambola; ~'s eye view *n* vista panoramica; ~ watcher *n* ornitologo/a dilettante.

Biro ['baɪrəu] ® *n* biro *f inv* ®.

birth [bəːθ] *n* nascita; to give ~ to partorire; ~ certificate *n* certificato di nascita; ~ control *n* controllo delle nascite; contraccezione *f*; ~day *n* compleanno ♦ *cpd* di compleanno; ~ rate *n* indice *m* di natalità.

biscuit ['bɪskɪt] (*BRIT*) *n* biscotto.

bisect [baɪ'sɛkt] *vt* tagliare in due (parti).

bishop ['bɪʃəp] *n* vescovo.

bit [bɪt] *pt of* bite ♦ *n* pezzo; (*COMPUT*) bit *m inv*; (*of horse*) morso; a ~ of un po' di; a ~ mad un po' matto; ~ by ~ a poco a poco.

bitch [bɪtʃ] n (dog) cagna; (inf!) vacca.
bite [baɪt] (pt **bit**, pp **bitten**) vt, vi mordere; (subj: insect) pungere ♦ n morso; (insect ~) puntura; (mouthful) boccone m; **let's have a ~ (to eat)** mangiamo un boccone; **to ~ one's nails** mangiarsi le unghie; **bitten** ['bɪtn] pp of **bite**.
bitter ['bɪtə*] adj amaro(a); (wind, criticism) pungente ♦ n (BRIT: beer) birra amara; **~ness** n amarezza; gusto amaro.
blab [blæb] vi parlare troppo.
black [blæk] adj nero(a) ♦ n nero; (person): B~ negro/a ♦ vt (BRIT: INDUSTRY) boicottare; **to give sb a ~ eye** fare un occhio nero a qn; **in the ~** (bank account) in attivo; **~ and blue** adj tutto(a) pesto(a); **~berry** n mora; **~bird** n merlo; **~board** n lavagna; **~currant** n ribes m inv; **~en** vt annerire; **~ ice** n strato trasparente di ghiaccio; **~leg** (BRIT) n crumiro; **~list** n lista nera; **~mail** n ricatto ♦ vt ricattare; **~ market** n mercato nero; **~out** n oscuramento; (TV, RADIO) interruzione f delle trasmissioni; (fainting) svenimento; B~ Sea n: **the** B~ Sea il Mar Nero; **~ sheep** n pecora nera; **~smith** n fabbro ferraio; **~ spot** n (AUT) luogo famigerato per gli incidenti; (for unemployment etc) zona critica.
bladder ['blædə*] n vescica.
blade [bleɪd] n lama; (of oar) pala; **~ of grass** filo d'erba.
blame [bleɪm] n colpa ♦ vt: **to ~ sb/sth for sth** dare la colpa di qc a qn/qc; **who's to ~?** chi è colpevole?
bland [blænd] adj mite; (taste) blando(a).
blank [blæŋk] adj bianco(a); (look) distratto(a) ♦ n spazio vuoto; (cartridge) cartuccia a salve; **~ cheque** n assegno in bianco.
blanket ['blæŋkɪt] n coperta.
blare [blɛə*] vi strombettare.
blasphemy ['blæsfɪmɪ] n bestemmia.
blast [blɑːst] n (of wind) raffica; (of bomb etc) esplosione f ♦ vt far saltare;

~-off n (SPACE) lancio.
blatant ['bleɪtənt] adj flagrante.
blaze [bleɪz] n (fire) incendio; (fig) vampata; splendore m ♦ vi (fire) ardere, fiammeggiare; (guns) sparare senza sosta; (fig: eyes) ardere ♦ vt: **to ~ a trail** (fig) tracciare una via nuova; **in a ~ of publicity** circondato da grande pubblicità.
blazer ['bleɪzə*] n blazer m inv.
bleach [bliːtʃ] n (also: household ~) varechina ♦ vt (material) candeggiare; **~ed** adj (hair) decolorato(a); **~ers** (US) npl (SPORT) posti mpl di gradinata.
bleak [bliːk] adj tetro(a).
bleary-eyed ['blɪərɪ'aɪd] adj dagli occhi offuscati.
bleat [bliːt] vi belare.
bled [bled] pt, pp of **bleed**.
bleed [bliːd] (pt, pp **bled**) vi sanguinare; **my nose is ~ing** mi viene fuori sangue dal naso.
bleeper ['bliːpə*] n (device) cicalino.
blemish ['blemɪʃ] n macchia.
blend [blend] n miscela ♦ vt mescolare ♦ vi (colours etc: also: ~ **in**) armonizzare.
bless [bles] (pt, pp **blessed** or **blest**) vt benedire; **~ you!** (after sneeze) salute!; **~ing** n benedizione f; fortuna; **blest** [blest] pt, pp of **bless**.
blew [bluː] pt of **blow**.
blight [blaɪt] vt (hopes etc) deludere; (life) rovinare.
blimey ['blaɪmɪ] (BRIT: inf) excl accidenti!
blind [blaɪnd] adj cieco(a) ♦ n (for window) avvolgibile m; (Venetian ~) veneziana ♦ vt accecare; **the ~** npl i ciechi; **~ alley** n vicolo cieco; **~ corner** (BRIT) n svolta cieca; **~fold** n benda ♦ adj, adv bendato(a) ♦ vt bendare gli occhi a; **~ly** adv ciecamente; **~ness** n cecità; **~ spot** n (AUT etc) punto cieco; (fig) punto debole.
blink [blɪŋk] vi battere gli occhi; (light) lampeggiare; **~ers** npl paraocchi mpl.
bliss [blɪs] n estasi f.
blister ['blɪstə*] n (on skin) vescica; (on paintwork) bolla ♦ vi (paint) coprirsi di

bolle.

blithely ['blaɪðlɪ] *adv* allegramente.

blizzard ['blɪzəd] *n* bufera di neve.

bloated ['bləʊtɪd] *adj* gonfio(a).

blob [blɔb] *n* (*drop*) goccia; (*stain*, *spot*) macchia.

bloc [blɔk] *n* (*POL*) blocco.

block [blɔk] *n* blocco; (*in pipes*) ingombro; (*toy*) cubo; (*of buildings*) isolato ♦ *vt* bloccare; ~ **of flats** (*BRIT*) *n* caseggiato; ~**ade** [-'keɪd] *n* blocco; ~**age** *n* ostacolo; ~**buster** *n* (*film*, *book*) grande successo; ~ **letters** *npl* stampatello.

bloke [bləʊk] (*BRIT*: *inf*) *n* tizio.

blonde [blɔnd] *adj*, *n* biondo(a).

blood [blʌd] *n* sangue *m*; ~ **donor** *n* donatore/trice di sangue; ~ **group** *n* gruppo sanguigno; ~**hound** *n* segugio; ~ **poisoning** *n* setticemia, ~ **pressure** *n* pressione *f* sanguigna; ~**shed** *n* spargimento di sangue; ~**shot** *adj*: ~**shot eyes** occhi iniettati di sangue; ~**stream** *n* flusso del sangue; ~ **test** *n* analisi *f inv* del sangue; ~**thirsty** *adj* assetato(a) di sangue; ~**y** *adj* (*fight*) sanguinoso(a); (*nose*) sanguinante; (*BRIT*: *inf!*): **this** ~**y** ... questo maledetto ...; ~**y awful/good** (*inf!*) veramente terribile/forte; ~**y-minded** (*BRIT*: *inf*) *adj* indisponente.

bloom [blu:m] *n* fiore *m* ♦ *vi* (*tree*) essere in fiore; (*flower*) aprirsi.

blossom ['blɔsəm] *n* fiore *m*; (*with pl sense*) fiori *mpl* ♦ *vi* essere in fiore.

blot [blɔt] *n* macchia ♦ *vt* macchiare; ~ **out** *vt* (*memories*) cancellare; (*view*) nascondere.

blotchy ['blɔtʃɪ] *adj* (*complexion*) coperto(a) di macchie.

blotting paper ['blɔtɪŋ-] *n* carta assorbente.

blouse [blauz] *n* (*feminine garment*) camicetta.

blow [bləʊ] (*pt* blew, *pp* blown) *n* colpo ♦ *vi* soffiare ♦ *vt* (*fuse*) far saltare; (*subj*: *wind*) spingere; (*instrument*) suonare; **to** ~ **one's nose** soffiarsi il naso; **to** ~ **a whistle** fischiare; ~ **away** *vt* portare via; ~ **down** *vt* abbattere;

~ **off** *vt* far volare via; ~ **out** *vi* scoppiare; ~ **over** *vi* calmarsi; ~ **up** *vi* saltare in aria ♦ *vt* far saltare in aria; (*tyre*) gonfiare; (*PHOT*) ingrandire; ~-**dry** *n* messa in piega a föhn; ~**lamp** (*BRIT*) *n* lampada a benzina per saldare; **blown** *pp of* blow; ~-**out** *n* (*of tyre*) scoppio; ~**torch** *n* = ~**lamp**.

blue [blu:] *adj* azzurro(a); (*depressed*) giù *inv*; ~ **film/joke** film/barzelletta pornografico(a); **out of the** ~ (*fig*) all'improvviso; ~**bell** *n* giacinto dei boschi; ~**bottle** *n* moscone *m*; ~**print** *n* (*fig*): ~**print (for)** formula (di).

bluff [blʌf] *vi* bluffare ♦ *n* bluff *m inv* ♦ *adj* (*person*) brusco(a); **to call sb's** ~ mettere alla prova il bluff di qn.

blunder ['blʌndə*] *n* abbaglio ♦ *vi* prendere un abbaglio.

blunt [blʌnt] *adj* smussato(a); spuntato(a); (*person*) brusco(a).

blur [blə:*] *n* forma indistinta ♦ *vt* offuscare.

blurb [blə:b] *n* trafiletto pubblicitario.

blurt out [blə:t-] *vt* lasciarsi sfuggire.

blush [blʌʃ] *vi* arrossire ♦ *n* rossore *m*.

blustering ['blʌstərɪŋ] *adj* infuriato(a).

blustery ['blʌstərɪ] *adj* (*weather*) burrascoso(a).

boar [bɔ:*] *n* cinghiale *m*.

board [bɔ:d] *n* tavola; (*on wall*) tabellone *m*; (*committee*) consiglio, comitato; (*in firm*) consiglio d'amministrazione; (*NAUT*, *AVIAT*): **on** ~ a bordo ♦ *vt* (*ship*) salire a bordo di; (*train*) salire su; **full** ~ (*BRIT*) pensione completa; **half** ~ (*BRIT*) mezza pensione; ~ **and lodging** vitto e alloggio; **which goes by the** ~ (*fig*) che viene abbandonato; ~ **up** *vt* (*door*) chiudere con assi; ~**er** *n* (*SCOL*) convittore/trice; ~**ing card** *n* = ~**ing pass**; ~**ing house** *n* pensione *f*; ~**ing pass** *n* (*AVIAT*, *NAUT*) carta d'imbarco; ~**ing school** *n* collegio; ~ **room** *n* sala del consiglio.

boast [bəʊst] *vi*: **to** ~ (**about** *or* **of**) vantarsi (di).

boat [bəʊt] *n* nave *f*; (*small*) barca; ~**er** *n* (*hat*) paglietta; ~**swain** ['bəʊsn] *n* nostromo.

bob [bɔb] *vi* (*boat, cork on water: also:* ~ *up and down*) andare su e giù; ~ **up** *vi* saltare fuori.

bobby ['bɔbɪ] (*BRIT: inf*) *n* poliziotto.

bobsleigh ['bɔbsleɪ] *n* bob *m inv*.

bode [bəud] *vi:* **to** ~ **well/ill (for)** essere di buon/cattivo auspicio (per).

bodily ['bɔdɪlɪ] *adj* fisico(a), corporale ♦ *adv* corporalmente; interamente; in persona.

body ['bɔdɪ] *n* corpo; (*of car*) carrozzeria; (*of plane*) fusoliera; (*fig: group*) gruppo; (: *organization*) organizzazione *f*; (: *quantity*) quantità *f inv*; ~-**building** *n* culturismo; ~**guard** *n* guardia del corpo; ~**work** *n* carrozzeria.

bog [bɔg] *n* palude *f* ♦ *vt:* **to get** ~**ged down** (*fig*) impantanarsi.

boggle ['bɔgl] *vi:* **the mind** ~**s è in-credibile.**

bogus ['bəugəs] *adj* falso(a); finto(a).

boil [bɔɪl] *vt, vi* bollire ♦ *n* (*MED*) foruncolo; **to come to the** (*BRIT*) **or a** (*US*) ~ raggiungere l'ebollizione; ~ **down to** *vt fus* (*fig*) ridursi a; ~ **over** *vi* traboccare (bollendo); ~**ed egg** *n* uovo alla coque; ~**ed potatoes** *npl* patate *fpl* bollite *or* lesse; ~**er** *n* caldaia; ~**er suit** (*BRIT*) *n* tuta; ~**ing point** *n* punto di ebollizione.

boisterous ['bɔɪstərəs] *adj* chiassoso(a).

bold [bəuld] *adj* audace; (*child*) impudente; (*colour*) deciso(a).

bollard ['bɔləd] (*BRIT*) *n* (*AUT*) colonnina luminosa.

bolster ['bəulstə*] *n* capezzale *m*; ~ **up** *vt* sostenere.

bolt [bəult] *n* chiavistello; (*with nut*) bullone *m* ♦ *adv:* ~ **upright** diritto(a) come un fuso ♦ *vt* serrare; (*also:* ~ *together*) imbullonare; (*food*) mangiare in fretta ♦ *vi* scappare via.

bomb [bɔm] *n* bomba ♦ *vt* bombardare.

bombastic [bɔm'bæstɪk] *adj* ma-gniloquente.

bomb: ~ **disposal unit** *n* corpo degli artificieri; ~**er** *n* (*AVIAT*) bombardiere *m*; ~**shell** *n* (*fig*) notizia bomba.

bona fide ['bəunə'faɪdɪ] *adj* sincero(a); (*offer*) onesto(a).

bond [bɔnd] *n* legame *m*; (*binding promise, FINANCE*) obbligazione *f*; (*COMM*): **in** ~ in attesa di sdoganamento.

bondage ['bɔndɪdʒ] *n* schiavitù *f*.

bone [bəun] *n* osso; (*of fish*) spina, lisca ♦ *vt* disossare; togliere le spine a; ~ **idle** *adj* pigrissimo(a).

bonfire ['bɔnfaɪə*] *n* falò *m inv*.

bonnet ['bɔnɪt] *n* cuffia; (*BRIT: of car*) cofano.

bonus ['bəunəs] *n* premio; (*fig*) so-vrappiù *m inv*.

bony ['bəunɪ] *adj* (*MED: tissue*) osseo(a); (*arm, face*) ossuto(a); (*meat*) pieno(a) di ossi; (*fish*) pieno(a) di spine.

boo [bu:] *excl* ba! ♦ *vt* fischiare.

booby trap ['bu:bɪ-] *n* trappola.

book [buk] *n* libro; (*of stamps etc*) blocchetto ♦ *vt* (*ticket, seat, room*) prenotare; (*driver*) multare; (*football player*) ammonire; ~**s** *npl* (*COMM*) conti *mpl*; ~**case** *n* scaffale *m*; ~**ing office** (*BRIT*) *n* (*RAIL*) biglietteria; (*THEATRE*) botteghino; ~-**keeping** *n* contabilità; ~**let** *n* libricino; ~**maker** *n* allibratore *m*; ~**seller** *n* libraio; ~**shop** *n* libreria; ~**store** *n* libreria.

boom [bu:m] *n* (*noise*) rimbombo; (*in prices etc*) boom *m inv* ♦ *vi* rimbombare; andare a gonfie vele.

boon [bu:n] *n* vantaggio.

boost [bu:st] *n* spinta ♦ *vt* spingere; ~**er** *n* (*MED*) richiamo.

boot [bu:t] *n* stivale *m*; (*for hiking*) scarpone *m* da montagna; (*for football etc*) scarpa; (*BRIT: of car*) portabagagli *m inv* ♦ *vt* (*COMPUT*) inizializzare; **to** ~ (*in addition*) per giunta, in più.

booth [bu:ð] *n* cabina; (*at fair*) baraccone *m*.

booty ['bu:tɪ] *n* bottino.

booze [bu:z] (*inf*) *n* alcool *m*.

border ['bɔ:də*] *n* orlo; margine *m*; (*of a country*) frontiera; (*for flowers*) aiuola (laterale) ♦ *vt* (*road*) co-steggiare; (*another country: also:* ~ **on**) confinare con; **the B~s** *la zona di*

bore 27 **B.R.**

confine tra l'Inghilterra e la Scozia; ~ **on** vt fus (fig: insanity etc) sfiorare; ~**line** n (fig): **on the ~line** incerto(a); ~**line case** n caso incerto.

bore [bɔ:*] pt of **bear** ♦ vt (hole etc) scavare; (person) annoiare ♦ n (person) seccatore/trice; (of gun) calibro; **to be ~d** annoiarsi; ~**dom** n noia; **boring** adj noioso(a).

born [bɔ:n] adj: **to be ~** nascere; **I was ~ in 1960** sono nato nel 1960.

borne [bɔ:n] pp of **bear**.

borough ['bʌrə] n comune m.

borrow ['bɔrəu] vt: **to ~ sth (from sb)** prendere in prestito qc (da qn).

bosom ['buzəm] n petto; **~ friend** n amico/a del cuore.

boss [bɔs] n capo ♦ vt comandare; **~y** adj prepotente.

bosun ['bəusn] n nostromo.

botany ['bɔtəni] n botanica.

botch [bɔtʃ] vt (also: ~ up) fare un pasticcio di.

both [bəuθ] adj entrambi(e), tutt'e due ♦ pron: ~ (of them) entrambi(e); ~ of us went, we ~ went ci siamo andati tutt'e due ♦ adv: **they sell ~ meat and poultry** vendono insieme la carne ed il pollame.

bother ['bɔðə*] vt (worry) preoccupare; (annoy) infastidire ♦ vi (also: ~ o.s.) preoccuparsi ♦ n: **it is a ~ to have to do** è una seccatura dover fare; **it was no ~** non c'era problema; **to ~ doing sth** darsi la pena di fare qc.

bottle ['bɔtl] n bottiglia; (baby's) biberon m inv ♦ vt imbottigliare; ~ **up** vt contenere; **~neck** n imbottigliamento; **~-opener** n apribottiglie m inv.

bottom ['bɔtəm] n fondo; (buttocks) sedere m ♦ adj più basso(a); ultimo(a); **at the ~ of** in fondo a.

bough [bau] n ramo.

bought [bɔ:t] pt, pp of **buy**.

boulder ['bəuldə*] n masso (tondeggiante).

bounce [bauns] vi (ball) rimbalzare; (cheque) essere restituito(a) ♦ vt far rimbalzare ♦ n (rebound) rimbalzo; ~**r**

(inf) n buttafuori m inv.

bound [baund] pt, pp of **bind** ♦ n (gen pl) limite m; (leap) salto ♦ vi saltare ♦ vt (limit) delimitare ♦ adj: ~ **by law** obbligato(a) per legge; **to be ~ to do sth** (obliged) essere costretto(a) a fare qc; **he's ~ to fail** (likely) fallirà di certo; ~ **for** diretto(a) a; **out of ~s** il cui accesso è vietato.

boundary ['baundri] n confine m.

boundless ['baundlis] adj senza limiti.

bourgeois ['buəʒwa:] adj borghese.

bout [baut] n periodo; (of malaria etc) attacco; (BOXING etc) incontro.

bow1 [bəu] n nodo; (weapon) arco; (MUS) archetto.

bow2 [bau] n (with body) inchino; (NAUT: also: ~s) prua ♦ vi inchinarsi; (yield): **to ~ to** or **before** sottomettersi a.

bowels ['bauəlz] npl intestini mpl; (fig) viscere fpl.

bowl [bəul] n (for eating) scodella; (for washing) bacino; (ball) boccia ♦ vi (CRICKET) servire (la palla).

bow-legged ['bəu'legid] adj dalle gambe storte.

bowler ['bəulə*] n (CRICKET, BASEBALL) lanciatore m; (BRIT: also: ~ hat) bombetta.

bowling ['bəuliŋ] n (game) gioco delle bocce; ~ **alley** n pista da bowling; ~ **green** n campo di bocce.

bowls [bəulz] n gioco delle bocce.

bow tie n cravatta a farfalla.

box [bɔks] n scatola; (also: cardboard ~) cartone m; (THEATRE) palco ♦ vt inscatolare ♦ vi fare del pugilato; ~**er** n (person) pugile m; ~**ing** n (SPORT) pugilato; **B~ing Day** (BRIT) n Santo Stefano; ~**ing gloves** npl guantoni mpl da pugile; ~**ing ring** n ring m inv; ~ **office** n biglietteria; ~ **room** n ripostiglio.

boy [bɔi] n ragazzo.

boycott ['bɔikɔt] n boicottaggio ♦ vt boicottare.

boyfriend ['bɔifrend] n ragazzo.

boyish ['bɔiiʃ] adj da ragazzo.

B.R. abbr = **British Rail**.

bra [brɑː] n reggipetto, reggiseno.

brace [breɪs] n (on teeth) apparecchio correttore; (tool) trapano ♦ vt rinforzare, sostenere; ~s (BRIT) npl (DRESS) bretelle fpl; to ~ o.s. (also fig) tenersi forte.

bracelet ['breɪslɪt] n braccialetto.

bracing ['breɪsɪŋ] adj invigorante.

bracken ['brækən] n felce f.

bracket ['brækɪt] n (TECH) mensola; (group) gruppo; (TYP) parentesi f inv ♦ vt mettere fra parentesi.

brag [bræg] vi vantarsi.

braid [breɪd] n (trimming) passamano; (of hair) treccia.

brain [breɪn] n cervello; ~s npl (intelligence) cervella fpl; he's got ~s è intelligente; ~child n creatura, creazione f; ~wash vt fare un lavaggio di cervello a; ~wave n lampo di genio; ~y adj intelligente.

braise [breɪz] vt brasare.

brake [breɪk] n (on vehicle) freno ♦ vi frenare; ~ fluid n liquido dei freni; ~ light n (fanalino dello) stop m inv.

bramble ['bræmbl] n rovo.

bran [bræn] n crusca.

branch [brɑːntʃ] n ramo; (COMM) succursale f; ~ out vi (fig) intraprendere una nuova attività.

brand [brænd] n (also: ~ name) marca; (fig) tipo ♦ vt (cattle) marcare (a ferro rovente).

brand-new adj nuovo(a) di zecca.

brandy ['brændɪ] n brandy m inv.

brash [bræʃ] adj sfacciato(a).

brass [brɑːs] n ottone m; the ~ (MUS) gli ottoni; ~ band n fanfara.

brassière ['bræsɪə*] n reggipetto, reggiseno.

brat [bræt] (pej) n marmocchio, monello/a.

bravado [brə'vɑːdəu] n spavalderia.

brave [breɪv] adj coraggioso(a) ♦ vt affrontare; ~ry n coraggio.

brawl [brɔːl] n rissa.

brawny ['brɔːnɪ] adj muscoloso(a).

bray [breɪ] vi ragliare.

brazen ['breɪzn] adj sfacciato(a) ♦ vt: to ~ it out fare lo sfacciato.

brazier ['breɪzɪə*] n braciere m.

Brazil [brə'zɪl] n Brasile m.

breach [briːtʃ] vt aprire una breccia in ♦ n (gap) breccia, varco; (breaking): ~ of contract rottura di contratto; ~ of the peace violazione f dell'ordine pubblico.

bread [brɛd] n pane m; ~ and butter n pane e burro; (fig) mezzi mpl di sussistenza; ~bin n (US ~box) n cassetta f portapane inv; ~crumbs npl briciole fpl; (CULIN) pangrattato; ~line n: to be on the ~line avere appena il denaro per vivere.

breadth [brɛtθ] n larghezza; (fig: of knowledge etc) ampiezza.

breadwinner ['brɛdwɪnə*] n chi guadagna il pane per tutta la famiglia.

break [breɪk] (pt broke, pp broken) vt rompere; (law) violare; (record) battere ♦ vi rompersi; (storm) scoppiare; (weather) cambiare; (dawn) spuntare; (news) saltare fuori ♦ n (gap) breccia; (fracture) rottura; (rest, also SCOL) intervallo; (: short) pausa; (chance) possibilità f inv; to ~ one's leg etc rompersi la gamba etc; to ~ the news to sb comunicare per primo la notizia a qn; to ~ even coprire le spese; to ~ free or loose spezzare i legami; to ~ open (door etc) sfondare; ~ down vt (figures, data) analizzare ♦ vi (person) avere un esaurimento (nervoso); (AUT) guastarsi; ~ in vt (horse etc) domare ♦ vi (burglar) fare irruzione; (interrupt) interrompere; ~ into vt fus (house) fare irruzione in; ~ off vi (speaker) interrompersi; (branch) troncarsi; ~ out vi evadere; (war, fight) scoppiare; to ~ out in spots coprirsi di macchie; ~ up vi (ship) sfondarsi; (meeting) sciogliersi; (crowd) disperdersi; (marriage) andare a pezzi; (SCOL) chiudere ♦ vt fare a pezzi, spaccare; (fight etc) interrompere, far cessare; ~age n rottura; (object broken) cosa rotta; ~down n (AUT) guasto; (in communications) interruzione f; (of marriage) rottura; (MED: also: nervous

~*down*) esaurimento nervoso; (*of statistics*) resoconto; ~**down van** (*BRIT*) *n* carro *m* attrezzi *inv*; ~**er** *n* frangente *m*.

breakfast ['brɛkfəst] *n* colazione *f*.

break: ~**-in** *n* irruzione *f*; ~**ing and entering** *n* (*LAW*) violazione *f* di domicilio con scasso; ~**through** *n* (*fig*) passo avanti; ~**water** *n* frangiflutti *m inv*.

breast [brɛst] *n* (*of woman*) seno; (*chest*, *CULIN*) petto; ~**-feed** (*irreg*: *like* **feed**) *vt*, *vi* allattare (al seno); ~**stroke** *n* nuoto a rana.

breath [brɛθ] *n* respiro; **out of** ~ senza fiato.

Breathalyser ['brɛθəlaɪzə*] ® (*BRIT*) *n* alcoltest *m inv*.

breathe [bri:ð] *vt*, *vi* respirare; ~ **in** *vt* respirare ♦ *vi* inspirare; ~ **out** *vt*, *vi* espirare; ~**r** *n* attimo di respiro; **breathing** *n* respiro, respirazione *f*.

breathless ['brɛθlɪs] *adj* senza fiato.

breathtaking ['brɛθteɪkɪŋ] *adj* mozzafiato *inv*.

bred [brɛd] *pt*, *pp of* **breed**.

breed [bri:d] (*pt*, *pp* **bred**) *vt* allevare ♦ *vi* riprodursi ♦ *n* razza; (*type*, *class*) varietà *f inv*; ~**ing** *n* riproduzione *f*; allevamento; (*upbringing*) educazione *f*.

breeze [bri:z] *n* brezza.

breezy ['bri:zɪ] *adj* allegro(a); ventilato(a).

brew [bru:] *vt* (*tea*) fare un infuso di; (*beer*) fare ♦ *vi* (*storm*, *fig*: *trouble etc*) prepararsi; ~**er** *n* birraio; ~**ery** *n* fabbrica di birra.

bribe [braɪb] *n* bustarella ♦ *vt* comprare; ~**ry** *n* corruzione *f*.

brick [brɪk] *n* mattone *m*; ~**layer** *n* muratore *m*.

bridal ['braɪdl] *adj* nuziale.

bride [braɪd] *n* sposa; ~**groom** *n* sposo; ~**smaid** *n* damigella d'onore.

bridge [brɪdʒ] *n* ponte *m*; (*NAUT*) ponte di comando; (*of nose*) dorso; (*CARDS*) bridge *m inv* ♦ *vt* (*fig*: *gap*) colmare.

bridle ['braɪdl] *n* briglia; ~ **path** *n* sentiero (per cavalli).

brief [bri:f] *adj* breve ♦ *n* (*LAW*)

comparsa; (*gen*) istruzioni *fpl* ♦ *vt* mettere al corrente; ~**s** *npl* (*underwear*) mutande *fpl*; ~**case** *n* cartella; ~**ing** *n* briefing *m inv*; ~**ly** *adv* (*glance*) di sfuggita; (*explain*, *say*) brevemente.

bright [braɪt] *adj* luminoso(a); (*clever*) sveglio(a); (*lively*) vivace; ~**en** (*also*: ~**en up**) *vt* (*room*) rendere luminoso(a) ♦ *vi* schiarirsi; (*person*) rallegrarsi.

brilliance ['brɪljəns] *n* splendore *m*.

brilliant ['brɪljənt] *adj* brillante; (*light*, *smile*) radioso(a); (*inf*) splendido(a).

brim [brɪm] *n* orlo.

brine [braɪn] *n* (*CULIN*) salamoia.

bring [brɪŋ] (*pt*, *pp* **brought**) *vt* portare; ~ **about** *vt* causare; ~ **back** *vt* riportare; ~ **down** *vt* portare giù; abbattere; ~ **forward** *vt* (*proposal*) avanzare; (*meeting*) anticipare; ~ **off** *vt* (*task*, *plan*) portare a compimento; ~ **out** *vt* tirar fuori; (*meaning*) mettere in evidenza; (*book*, *album*) far uscire; ~ **round** *vt* (*unconscious person*) far rinvenire; ~ **up** *vt* (*carry up*) portare su; (*child*) allevare; (*question*) introdurre; (*food*: *vomit*) rimettere, rigurgitare.

brink [brɪŋk] *n* orlo.

brisk [brɪsk] *adj* (*manner*) spiccio(a); (*trade*) vivace; (*pace*) svelto(a).

bristle ['brɪsl] *n* setola ♦ *vi* rizzarsi; **bristling with** irto(a) di.

Britain ['brɪtən] *n* (*also*: *Great* ~) Gran Bretagna.

British ['brɪtɪʃ] *adj* britannico(a); **the** ~ *npl* i Britannici; **the** ~ **Isles** *npl* le Isole Britanniche; ~ **Rail** *n* compagnia ferroviaria britannica, ≈ Ferrovie *fpl* dello Stato.

Briton ['brɪtən] *n* britannico/a.

brittle ['brɪtl] *adj* fragile.

broach [brəutʃ] *vt* (*subject*) affrontare.

broad [brɔ:d] *adj* largo(a); (*distinction*) generale; (*accent*) spiccato(a); **in** ~ **daylight** in pieno giorno; ~**cast** (*pt*, *pp* ~**cast**) *n* trasmissione *f* ♦ *vt* trasmettere per radio (*or* per televisione) ♦ *vi* fare una trasmissione; ~**en** *vt* allargare ♦ *vi* allargarsi; ~**ly** *adv* (*fig*) in generale; **~-minded** adj di mente aperta.

broccoli ['brɔkəlɪ] n broccoli mpl.

brochure ['brəʊfjʊə*] n dépliant m inv.

broil [brɔɪl] vt cuocere a fuoco vivo.

broke [brəʊk] pt of **break** ♦ adj (inf) squattrinato(a).

broken ['brəʊkn] pp of **break** ♦ adj rotto(a); **a ~ leg** una gamba rotta; **in ~ English** in un inglese stentato; **~-hearted** adj: **to be ~-hearted** avere il cuore spezzato.

broker ['brəʊkə*] n agente m.

brolly ['brɔlɪ] (BRIT: inf) n ombrello.

bronchitis [brɔŋ'kaɪtɪs] n bronchite f.

bronze [brɔnz] n bronzo.

brooch [brəʊtʃ] n spilla.

brood [bruːd] n covata ♦ vi (person) rimuginare.

brook [brʊk] n ruscello.

broom [brʊm] n scopa; (BOT) ginestra; **~stick** n manico di scopa.

Bros. abbr (= Brothers) F.lli.

broth [brɔθ] n brodo.

brothel ['brɔθl] n bordello.

brother ['brʌðə*] n fratello; **~-in-law** n cognato.

brought [brɔːt] pt, pp of **bring**.

brow [braʊ] n fronte f; (rare, gen: eye~) sopracciglio; (of hill) cima.

brown [braʊn] adj bruno(a), marrone; (tanned) abbronzato(a) ♦ n (colour) color m bruno or marrone ♦ vt (CULIN) rosolare; **~ bread** n pane m integrale, pane nero.

brownie ['braʊnɪ] n giovane esploratrice f; (US: cake) dolce al cioccolato e nocciole.

brown paper n carta da pacchi or da imballaggio.

brown sugar n zucchero greggio.

browse [braʊz] vi (among books) curiosare fra i libri; **to ~ through a book** sfogliare un libro.

bruise [bruːz] n (on person) livido ♦ vt farsi un livido a.

brunette [bruː'nɛt] n bruna.

brunt [brʌnt] n: **the ~ of** (attack, criticism etc) il peso maggiore di.

brush [brʌʃ] n spazzola; (for painting, shaving) pennello; (quarrel) schermaglia ♦ vt spazzolare; (also: ~ against) sfiorare; **~ aside** vt scostare; **~ up** vt (knowledge) rinfrescare; **~wood** n macchia.

Brussels ['brʌslz] n Bruxelles f; **~ sprout** n cavolo di Bruxelles.

brutal ['bruːtl] adj brutale.

brute [bruːt] n bestia ♦ adj: **by ~ force** con la forza, a viva forza.

B.Sc. n abbr = **Bachelor of Science**.

bubble ['bʌbl] n bolla ♦ vi ribollire; (sparkle, fig) essere effervescente; **~ bath** n bagnoschiuma m inv; **~ gum** n gomma americana.

buck [bʌk] n maschio (di camoscio, caprone, coniglio etc); (US: inf) dollaro ♦ vi sgroppare; **to pass the ~ (to sb)** scaricare (su di qn) la propria responsabilità; **~ up** vi (cheer up) rianimarsi.

bucket ['bʌkɪt] n secchio.

buckle ['bʌkl] n fibbia ♦ vt allacciare ♦ vi (wheel etc) piegarsi.

bud [bʌd] n gemma; (of flower) bocciolo ♦ vi germogliare; (flower) sbocciare.

Buddhism ['bʊdɪzəm] n buddismo.

budding ['bʌdɪŋ] adj (poet etc) in erba.

buddy ['bʌdɪ] (US) n compagno.

budge [bʌdʒ] vt scostare; (fig) smuovere ♦ vi spostarsi; smuoversi.

budgerigar ['bʌdʒərɪgɑː*] n pappagallino.

budget ['bʌdʒɪt] n bilancio preventivo ♦ vi: **to ~ for sth** fare il bilancio per qc.

budgie ['bʌdʒɪ] n = **budgerigar**.

buff [bʌf] adj color camoscio ♦ n (inf: enthusiast) appassionato/a.

buffalo ['bʌfələʊ] (pl ~ or ~es) n bufalo; (US) bisonte m.

buffer ['bʌfə*] n respingente m; (COMPUT) memoria tampone, buffer m inv.

buffet¹ ['bʊfeɪ] n (food, BRIT: bar) buffet m inv; **~ car** (BRIT) n (RAIL) ≈ servizio ristoro.

buffet² ['bʌfɪt] vt sferzare.

bug [bʌg] n (esp US: insect) insetto; (COMPUT, fig: germ) virus m inv; (spy device) microfono spia ♦ vt mettere

buggy 31 **burn**

sotto controllo; (*inf*: *annoy*) scocciare.
buggy ['bʌgɪ] n (*baby* ~) passeggino.
bugle ['bjuːgl] n tromba.
build [bɪld] (*pt, pp* **built**) n (*of person*) corporatura ♦ *vt* costruire; ~ **up** *vt* accumulare; aumentare; ~**er** n costruttore m; ~**ing** n costruzione f; edificio; (*industry*) edilizia; ~**ing society** (*BRIT*) n società f inv immobiliare.
built [bɪlt] *pt, pp of* **build** ♦ *adj*: ~**-in** (*cupboard*) a muro; (*device*) incorporato(a); ~**-up area** n abitato.
bulb [bʌlb] n (*BOT*) bulbo; (*ELEC*) lampadina.
bulge [bʌldʒ] n rigonfiamento ♦ *vi* essere protuberante *or* rigonfio(a); **to be bulging with** essere pieno(a) *or* zeppo(a) di.
bulk [bʌlk] n massa, volume m; **in ~ a** pacchi (*or* cassette *etc*); (*COMM*) all'ingrosso; **the ~ of** il grosso di; ~**y** *adj* grosso(a); voluminoso(a).
bull [bul] n toro; (*male elephant, whale*) maschio; ~**dog** n bulldog m inv.
bulldozer ['buldəuzə*] n bulldozer m inv.
bullet ['bulɪt] n pallottola.
bulletin ['bulɪtɪn] n bollettino.
bulletproof ['bulɪtpruːf] *adj* (*car*) blindato(a); (*vest etc*) antiproiettile inv.
bullfight ['bulfaɪt] n corrida; ~**er** n torero; ~**ing** n tauromachia.
bullion ['buljən] n oro *or* argento in lingotti.
bullock ['bulək] n manzo.
bullring ['bulrɪŋ] n arena (per corride).
bull's-eye ['bulzaɪ] n centro del bersaglio.
bully ['bulɪ] n prepotente m ♦ *vt* angariare; (*frighten*) intimidire.
bum [bʌm] (*inf*) n (*backside*) culo; (*tramp*) vagabondo/a.
bumblebee ['bʌmblbiː] n bombo.
bump [bʌmp] n (*in car*) piccolo tamponamento; (*jolt*) scossa; (*on road etc*) protuberanza; (*on head*) bernoccolo ♦ *vt* battere; ~ **into** *vt fus* scontrarsi con; (*person*) imbattersi in;

~**er** n paraurti m inv ♦ *adj*: ~**er harvest** raccolto eccezionale; ~**er cars** npl autoscontri mpl.
bumptious ['bʌmpʃəs] *adj* presuntuoso(a).
bumpy ['bʌmpɪ] *adj* (*road*) dissestato(a).
bun [bʌn] n focaccia; (*of hair*) crocchia.
bunch [bʌntʃ] n (*of flowers, keys*) mazzo; (*of bananas*) casco; (*of people*) gruppo; ~ **of grapes** grappolo d'uva; ~**es** npl (*in hair*) codine fpl.
bundle ['bʌndl] n fascio ♦ *vt* (*also:* ~ **up**) legare in un fascio; (*put*): **to ~ sth/sb into** spingere qc/qn in.
bungalow ['bʌŋgələu] n bungalow m inv.
bungle ['bʌŋgl] *vt* fare un pasticcio di.
bunion ['bʌnjən] n callo (al piede).
bunk [bʌŋk] n cuccetta; ~ **beds** npl letti mpl a castello.
bunker ['bʌŋkə*] n (*coal store*) ripostiglio per il carbone; (*MIL, GOLF*) bunker m inv.
bunny ['bʌnɪ] n (*also:* ~ **rabbit**) coniglietto.
bunting ['bʌntɪŋ] n pavesi mpl, bandierine fpl.
buoy [bɔɪ] n boa; ~ **up** *vt* (*fig*) sostenere; ~**ant** *adj* galleggiante; (*fig*) vivace.
burden ['bəːdn] n carico, fardello ♦ *vt*: **to ~ sb with** caricare di.
bureau [bjuə'rəu] (*pl* **bureaux**) n (*BRIT*: *writing desk*) scrivania; (*US*: *chest of drawers*) cassettone m; (*office*) ufficio, agenzia.
bureaucracy [bjuə'rɔkrəsɪ] n burocrazia.
bureaux [bjuə'rəuz] npl of **bureau**.
burglar ['bəːglə*] n scassinatore m; ~ **alarm** n campanello antifurto; ~**y** n furto con scasso.
burial ['berɪəl] n sepoltura.
burly ['bəːlɪ] *adj* robusto(a).
Burma ['bəːmə] n Birmania.
burn [bəːn] (*pt, pp* **burned** *or* **burnt**) *vt, vi* bruciare ♦ *n* bruciatura, scottatura; ~ **down** *vt* distruggere col fuoco; ~**er** n (*on cooker*) fornello; (*TECH*) bruciatore m, becco (a gas); ~**ing** *adj*

burrow 32 by

in fiamme; (sand) che scotta; (ambition) bruciante; **burnt** pt, pp of burn.
burrow ['bʌrəu] n tána ♦ vt scavare.
bursary ['bɜːsərɪ] (BRIT) n (SCOL) borsa di studio.
burst [bɜːst] (pt, pp **burst**) vt far scoppiare ♦ vi esplodere; (tyre) scoppiare ♦ n scoppio; (also: ~ pipe) rottura nel tubo, perdita; **a ~ of speed** uno scatto di velocità; **to ~ into flames/tears** scoppiare in fiamme/lacrime; **to ~ out laughing** scoppiare a ridere; **to be ~ing with** scoppiare di; **~ into** vt fus (room etc) irrompere in.
bury ['berɪ] vt seppellire.
bus [bʌs] (pl ~es) n autobus m inv.
buses ['bʌsɪz] npl of **bus**.
bush [buʃ] n cespuglio; (scrub land) macchia; **to beat about the ~** menare il cane per l'aia.
bushy ['buʃɪ] adj cespuglioso(a).
busily ['bɪzɪlɪ] adv con impegno, alacremente.
business ['bɪznɪs] n (matter) affare m; (trading) affari mpl; (firm) azienda; (job, duty) lavoro; **to be away on ~** essere andato via per affari; **it's none of my ~** questo non mi riguarda; **he means ~** non scherza; **~like** adj serio(a); efficiente; **~man/woman** n uomo/donna d'affari; **~ trip** n viaggio d'affari.
busker ['bʌskə*] (BRIT) n suonatore/trice ambulante.
bus-stop n fermata d'autobus.
bust [bʌst] n busto; (ANAT) seno ♦ adj (inf: broken) rotto(a); **to go ~** fallire.
bustle ['bʌsl] n movimento, attività ♦ vi darsi da fare; **bustling** adj movimentato(a).
busy ['bɪzɪ] adj occupato(a); (shop, street) molto frequentato(a) ♦ vt: **to ~ o.s.** darsi da fare; **~body** n ficcanaso m/f inv; **~ signal** (US) n (TEL) segnale m di occupato.

KEYWORD

but [bʌt] conj ma; **I'd love to come, ~ I'm busy** vorrei tanto venire, ma ho da fare
♦ prep (apart from, except) eccetto, tranne, meno; **he was nothing ~ trouble** non dava altro che guai; **no-one ~ him can do it** nessuno può farlo tranne lui; **~ for you/your help** se non fosse per te/per il tuo aiuto; **anything ~ that** tutto ma non questo
♦ adv (just, only) solo, soltanto; **she's ~ a child** è solo una bambina; **had I ~ known** se solo avessi saputo; **I can ~ try** tentar non nuoce; **all ~ finished** quasi finito.

butcher ['butʃə*] n macellaio ♦ vt macellare; **~'s (shop)** n macelleria.
butler ['bʌtlə*] n maggiordomo.
butt [bʌt] n (cask) grossa botte f; (of gun) calcio; (of cigarette) mozzicone m; (BRIT: fig: target) oggetto ♦ vt cozzare; **~ in** vi (interrupt) interrompere.
butter ['bʌtə*] n burro ♦ vt imburrare; **~cup** n ranuncolo.
butterfly ['bʌtəflaɪ] n farfalla; (SWIMMING: also: ~ stroke) (nuoto a) farfalla.
buttocks ['bʌtəks] npl natiche fpl.
button ['bʌtn] n bottone m; (US: badge) distintivo ♦ vt (also: ~ up) abbottonare ♦ vi abbottonarsi.
buttress ['bʌtrɪs] n contrafforte f.
buxom ['bʌksəm] adj formoso(a).
buy [baɪ] (pt, pp **bought**) vt comprare ♦ n acquisto; **to ~ sb sth/sth from sb** comprare qc per qn/qc da qn; **to ~ sb a drink** offrire da bere a qn; **~er** n compratore/trice.
buzz [bʌz] n ronzio; (inf: phone call) colpo di telefono ♦ vi ronzare.
buzzer ['bʌzə*] n cicalino.
buzz word (inf) n termine m di gran moda.

KEYWORD

by [baɪ] prep **1** (referring to cause, agent) da; **killed ~ lightning** ucciso da un fulmine; **surrounded ~ a fence** circondato da uno steccato; **a painting ~ Picasso** un quadro di Picasso

2 (*referring to method, manner, means*): ~ **bus/car/train** in autobus/macchina/treno, con l'autobus/la macchina/il treno; **to pay** ~ **cheque** pagare con (un) assegno; ~ **moonlight** al chiaro di luna; ~ **saving hard, he** ... risparmiando molto, lui ...

3 (*via, through*) per; **we came** ~ **Dover** siamo venuti via Dover

4 (*close to, past*) accanto a; **the house** ~ **the river** la casa sul fiume; **a holiday** ~ **the sea** una vacanza al mare; **she sat** ~ **his bed** si sedette accanto al suo letto; **she rushed** ~ **me** mi è passata accanto correndo; **I go** ~ **the post office every day** passo davanti all'ufficio postale ogni giorno

5 (*not later than*) per, entro; ~ **4 o'clock** per *or* entro le 4; ~ **this time tomorrow** domani a quest'ora; ▪ **the time I got here it was too late** quando sono arrivato era ormai troppo tardi

6 (*during*): ~ **day/night** di giorno/notte

7 (*amount*) a; ~ **the kilo/metre** a chili/metri; **paid** ~ **the hour** pagato all'ora; **one** ~ **one** uno per uno; **little** ~ **little** a poco a poco

8 (*MATH, measure*): **to divide/multiply** ~ **3** dividere/moltiplicare per 3; **it's broader** ~ **a metre** è un metro più largo, è più largo di un metro

9 (*according to*) per; **to play** -- **the rules** attenersi alle regole; **it's all right** ~ **me** per me va bene

10: **(all)** ~ **oneself** *etc* (tutto(a)) solo(a); **he did it (all)** ~ **himself** lo ha fatto (tutto) da solo

11: ~ **the way** a proposito; **this wasn't my idea** ~ **the way** tra l'altro l'idea non è stata mia

♦ *adv* **1** *see* **go; pass** *etc*

2: ~ **and** ~ (*in past*) poco dopo; (*in future*) fra breve; ~ **and large** nel complesso.

bye(-bye) ['baɪ('baɪ)] *excl* ciao!, arrivederci!

by(e)-law *n* legge *f* locale.

by-election (*BRIT*) *n* elezione *f* straordinaria.

bygone ['baɪgɒn] *adj* passato(a) ♦ *n*: **let** ~**s be** ~**s** mettiamoci una pietra sopra.

bypass ['baɪpɑ:s] *n* circonvallazione *f*; (*MED*) by-pass *m inv* ♦ *vt* fare una deviazione intorno a.

by-product *n* sottoprodotto; (*fig*) conseguenza secondaria.

bystander ['baɪstændə*] *n* spettatore/trice.

byte [baɪt] *n* (*COMPUT*) byte *m inv*, bicarattere *m*.

byword ['baɪwə:d] *n*: **to be a** ~ **for** essere sinonimo di.

by-your-leave *n*: **without so much as a** ~ senza nemmeno chiedere il permesso.

C

C [si:] *n* (*MUS*) do.

C.A. *n abbr* = **chartered accountant**.

cab [kæb] *n* taxi *m inv*; (*of train, truck*) cabina.

cabaret ['kæbəreɪ] *n* cabaret *m inv*.

cabbage ['kæbɪdʒ] *n* cavolo.

cabin ['kæbɪn] *n* capanna; (*on ship*) cabina; ~ **cruiser** *n* cabinato.

cabinet ['kæbɪnɪt] *n* (*POL*) consiglio dei ministri; (*furniture*) armadietto; (*also*: *display* ~) vetrinetta.

cable ['keɪbl] *n* cavo; fune *f*; (*TEL*) cablogramma *m* ♦ *vt* telegrafare; ~**-car** *n* funivia; ~ **television** *n* televisione *f* via cavo.

cache [kæʃ] *n* deposito segreto.

cackle ['kækl] *vi* schiamazzare.

cacti ['kæktaɪ] *npl of* **cactus**.

cactus ['kæktəs] (*pl* **cacti**) *n* cactus *m inv*.

cadet [kə'dɛt] *n* (*MIL*) cadetto.

cadge [kædʒ] (*inf*) *vt* scroccare.

café ['kæfeɪ] *n* caffè *m inv*.

cafeteria [kæfɪ'tɪərɪə] *n* self-service *m inv*.

cage [keɪdʒ] *n* gabbia.

cagey ['keɪdʒɪ] (*inf*) *adj* chiuso(a); guardingo(a).

cagoule [kə'gu:l] *n* K-way *m inv* ®.

cajole [kə'dʒəul] *vt* allettare.

cake [keɪk] *n* (*large*) torta; (*small*) pasticcino; ~ **of soap** saponetta; ~**d** *adj*: ~**d with** incrostato(a) di.

calculate ['kælkjuleɪt] *vt* calcolare; **calculation** [-'leɪʃən] *n* calcolo; **calculator** *n* calcolatrice *f*.

calendar ['kæləndə*] *n* calendario; ~ **year** *n* anno civile.

calf [kɑːf] (*pl* **calves**) *n* (*of cow*) vitello; (*of other animals*) piccolo; (*also*: ~**skin**) (pelle *f* di) vitello; (*ANAT*) polpaccio.

calibre ['kælɪbə*] (*US* **caliber**) *n* calibro.

call [kɔːl] *vt* (*gen, also TEL*) chiamare; (*meeting*) indire ♦ *vi* chiamare; (*visit: also*: ~ **in**, ~ **round**) passare ♦ *n* (*shout*) grido, urlo; (*TEL*) telefonata; **to be** ~**ed** (*person, object*) chiamarsi; **to be on** ~ essere a disposizione; ~ **back** *vi* (*return*) ritornare; (*TEL*) ritelefonare, richiamare; ~ **for** *vt fus* richiedere; (*fetch*) passare a prendere; ~ **off** *vt* disdire; ~ **on** *vt fus* (*visit*) passare da; (*appeal to*) chiedere a; ~ **out** *vi* (*in pain*) urlare; (*to person*) chiamare; ~ **up** *vt* (*MIL*) richiamare; (*TEL*) telefonare a; ~**box** (*BRIT*) *n* cabina telefonica; ~**er** *n* persona che chiama; visitatore/trice; ~ **girl** *n* ragazza *f* squillo *inv*; ~**-in** (*US*) *n* (*phone-in*) trasmissione *f* a filo diretto con gli ascoltatori; ~**ing** *n* vocazione *f*; ~**ing card** (*US*) *n* biglietto da visita.

callous ['kæləs] *adj* indurito(a), insensibile.

calm [kɑːm] *adj* calmo(a) ♦ *n* calma ♦ *vt* calmare; ~ **down** *vi* calmarsi ♦ *vt* calmare.

Calor gas ['kælə*-] ® *n* butano.

calorie ['kælərɪ] *n* caloria.

calves [kɑːvz] *npl* of **calf**.

camber ['kæmbə*] *n* (*of road*) bombatura.

Cambodia [kæm'bəudjə] *n* Cambogia.

came [keɪm] *pt* of **come**.

camel ['kæməl] *n* cammello.

camera ['kæmərə] *n* macchina fotografica; (*CINEMA, TV*) cinepresa; **in** ~ a porte chiuse; ~**man** *n* cameraman *m inv*.

camouflage ['kæməflɑːʒ] *n* (*MIL, ZOOL*)

mimetizzazione *f* ♦ *vt* mimetizzare.

camp [kæmp] *n* campeggio; (*MIL*) campo ♦ *vi* accamparsi ♦ *adj* effeminato(a).

campaign [kæm'peɪn] *n* (*MIL, POL etc*) campagna ♦ *vi* (*also fig*) fare una campagna.

camp bed (*BRIT*) *n* brandina.

camper ['kæmpə*] *n* campeggiatore/trice; (*vehicle*) camper *m inv*.

camping ['kæmpɪŋ] *n* campeggio; **to go** ~ andare in campeggio.

campsite ['kæmpsaɪt] *n* campeggio.

campus ['kæmpəs] *n* campus *m inv*.

can¹ [kæn] *n* (*of milk*) scatola; (*of oil*) bidone *m*; (*of water*) tanica; (*tin*) scatola ♦ *vt* mettere in scatola.

KEYWORD

can² [kæn] (*negative* **cannot, can't**; *conditional and pt* **could**) *aux vb* **1** (*be able to*) potere; **I** ~**'t go any further** non posso andare oltre; **you** ~ **do it if you try** sei in grado di farlo — basta provarci; **I'll help you all I** ~ ti aiuterò come potrò; **I** ~**'t see you** non ti vedo
2 (*know how to*) sapere, essere capace di; **I** ~ **swim** so nuotare; ~ **you speak French?** parla francese?
3 (*may*) potere; **could I have a word with you?** posso parlarle un momento?
4 (*expressing disbelief, puzzlement etc*): **it** ~**'t be true!** non può essere vero!; **what** CAN **he want?** cosa può mai volere?
5 (*expressing possibility, suggestion etc*): **he could be in the library** può darsi che sia in biblioteca; **she could have been delayed** può aver avuto un contrattempo.

Canada ['kænədə] *n* Canada *m*.

Canadian [kə'neɪdɪən] *adj, n* canadese *m/f*.

canal [kə'næl] *n* canale *m*.

canary [kə'nɛərɪ] *n* canarino.

cancel ['kænsəl] *vt* annullare; (*train*) sopprimere; (*cross out*) cancellare; ~**lation** [-'leɪʃən] *n* annullamento; soppressione *f*; cancellazione *f*; (*TOURISM*) prenotazione *f* annullata.

cancer ['kænsə*] *n* cancro; **C~** (*sign*) Cancro.

candid ['kændɪd] *adj* onesto(a).

candidate ['kændɪdeɪt] *n* candidato/a.

candle ['kændl] *n* candela; (*in church*) cero; **~light** *n*: **by ~light** a lume di candela; **~stick** *n* bugia; (*bigger, ornate*) candeliere *m*.

candour ['kændə*] (*US* **candor**) *n* sincerità.

candy ['kændɪ] *n* zucchero candito; (*US*) caramella; **caramelle** *fpl*; **~-floss** (*BRIT*) *n* zucchero filato.

cane [keɪn] *n* canna; (*for furniture*) bambù *m*; (*stick*) verga ♦ *vt* (*BRIT: SCOL*) punire a colpi di verga.

canister ['kænɪstə*] *n* scatola metallica.

cannabis ['kænəbɪs] *n* canapa indiana.

canned ['kænd] *adj* (*food*) in scatola.

cannon ['kænən] (*pl* ~ *or* ~s) *n* (*gun*) cannone *m*.

cannot ['kænɒt] = **can not**.

canny ['kænɪ] *adj* furbo(a).

canoe [kə'nu:] *n* canoa.

canon ['kænən] *n* (*clergyman*) canonico; (*standard*) canone *m*.

can opener [-'əupnə*] *n* apriscatole *m inv*.

canopy ['kænəpɪ] *n* baldacchino.

can't [kænt] = **can not**.

cantankerous [kæn'tæŋkərəs] *adj* stizzoso(a).

canteen [kæn'ti:n] *n* mensa; (*BRIT: of cutlery*) portaposate *m inv*.

canter ['kæntə*] *vi* andare al piccolo galoppo.

canvas ['kænvəs] *n* tela.

canvass ['kænvəs] *vi* (*POL*): **to ~ for** raccogliere voti per ♦ *vt* fare un sondaggio di.

canyon ['kænjən] *n* canyon *m inv*.

cap [kæp] *n* (*hat*) berretto; (*of pen*) coperchio; (*of bottle, toy gun*) tappo; (*contraceptive*) diaframma *m* ♦ *vt* (*outdo*) superare.

capability [keɪpə'bɪlɪtɪ] *n* capacità *f inv*, abilità *f inv*.

capable ['keɪpəbl] *adj* capace.

capacity [kə'pæsɪtɪ] *n* capacità *f inv*; (*of*

lift etc) capienza.

cape [keɪp] *n* (*garment*) cappa; (*GEO*) capo.

caper ['keɪpə*] *n* (*CULIN*) cappero; (*prank*) scherzetto.

capital ['kæpɪtl] *n* (*also*: ~ *city*) capitale *f*; (*money*) capitale *m*; (*also*: ~ *letter*) (*lettera*) maiuscola; ~ **gains tax** *n* imposta sulla plusvalenza; **~ism** *n* capitalismo; **~ist** *adj*, *n* capitalista (*m/f*); **~ize**: **to ~ize on** *vt fus* trarre vantaggio da; ~ **punishment** *n* pena capitale.

Capricorn ['kæprɪkɔ:n] *n* Capricorno.

capsize [kæp'saɪz] *vt* capovolgere ♦ *vi* capovolgersi.

capsule ['kæpsju:l] *n* capsula.

captain ['kæptɪn] *n* capitano.

caption ['kæpʃən] *n* leggenda.

captivate ['kæptɪveɪt] *vt* avvincere.

captive ['kæptɪv] *adj*, *n* prigioniero(a).

captivity [kæp'tɪvɪtɪ] *n* cattività.

capture ['kæptʃə*] *vt* catturare; (*COMPUT*) registrare ♦ *n* cattura; (*data* ~) registrazione *f or* rilevazione *f* di dati.

car [ka:*] *n* (*AUT*) macchina, automobile *f*; (*RAIL*) vagone *m*.

carafe [kə'ræf] *n* caraffa.

caramel ['kærəməl] *n* caramello.

caravan ['kærəvæn] *n* (*BRIT*) roulotte *f inv*; (*of camels*) carovana; ~ **site** (*BRIT*) *n* campeggio per roulotte.

carbohydrates [ka:bəu'haɪdreɪts] *npl* (*foods*) carboidrati *mpl*.

carbon ['ka:bən] *n* carbonio; ~ **paper** *n* carta carbone.

carburettor [ka:bju'rɛtə*] (*US* **carburetor**) *n* carburatore *m*.

card [ka:d] *n* carta; (*visiting* ~ *etc*) biglietto; (*Christmas* ~ *etc*) cartolina; **~board** *n* cartone *m*; ~ **game** *n* gioco di carte.

cardiac ['ka:dɪæk] *adj* cardiaco(a).

cardigan ['ka:dɪgən] *n* cardigan *m inv*.

cardinal ['ka:dɪnl] *adj* cardinale ♦ *n* cardinale *m*.

card index *n* schedario.

care [kɛə*] *n* cura, attenzione *f*; (*worry*) preoccupazione *f* ♦ *vi*: **to ~ about**

curarsi di; (*thing, idea*) interessarsi di; ~ **of** presso; **in sb's** ~ alle cure di qn; **to take** ~ **(to do)** fare attenzione (a fare); **to take** ~ **of** curarsi di; (*bill, problem*) occuparsi di; **I don't** ~ non me ne importa; **I couldn't** ~ **less** non m'interessa affatto; ~ **for** *vt fus* aver cura di; (*like*) volere bene a.

career [kə'rıə*] *n* carriera ♦ *vi* (*also:* ~ *along*) andare di (gran) carriera.

carefree ['kɛəfri:] *adj* sgombro(a) di preoccupazioni.

careful ['kɛəful] *adj* attento(a); (*cautious*) cauto(a); **(be)** ~! attenzione!; ~**ly** *adv* con cura; cautamente.

careless ['kɛəlıs] *adj* negligente; (*heedless*) spensierato(a).

caress [kə'rɛs] *n* carezza ♦ *vt* accarezzare.

caretaker ['kɛəteıkə*] *n* custode *m*.

car-ferry *n* traghetto.

cargo ['ka:gəu] (*pl* ~**es**) *n* carico.

car hire *n* autonoleggio.

Caribbean [kærı'bi:ən] *adj*: **the** ~ **(Sea)** il Mar dei Caraibi.

caring ['kɛərıŋ] *adj* (*person*) premuroso(a); (*society, organization*) umanitario(a).

carnage ['ka:nıdʒ] *n* carneficina.

carnation [ka:'neıʃən] *n* garofano.

carnival ['ka:nıvəl] *n* (*public celebration*) carnevale *m*; (*US: funfair*) luna park *m inv*.

carol ['kærəl] *n*: **(Christmas)** ~ canto di Natale.

carp [ka:p] *n* (*fish*) carpa; ~ **at** *vt fus* trovare a ridire su.

car park (*BRIT*) *n* parcheggio.

carpenter ['ka:pıntə*] *n* carpentiere *m*.

carpentry ['ka:pıntrı] *n* carpenteria.

carpet ['ka:pıt] *n* tappeto ♦ *vt* coprire con tappeto; ~ **slippers** *npl* pantofole *fpl*; ~ **sweeper** *n* scopatappeti *m inv*.

carriage ['kærıdʒ] *n* vettura; (*of goods*) trasporto; ~ **return** *n* (*on typewriter etc*) leva (*or* tasto) del ritorno a capo; ~**way** (*BRIT*) *n* (*part of road*) carreggiata.

carrier ['kærıə*] *n* (*of disease*) portatore/trice; (*COMM*) impresa di trasporti; ~ **bag** (*BRIT*) *n* sacchetto.

carrot ['kærət] *n* carota.

carry ['kærı] *vt* (*subj: person*) portare; (: *vehicle*) trasportare; (*involve: responsibilities etc*) comportare; (*MED*) essere portatore/trice di ♦ *vi* (*sound*) farsi sentire; **to be** *or* **get carried away** (*fig*) entusiasmarsi; ~ **on** *vi*: **to** ~ **on with sth/doing** continuare qc/a fare ♦ *vt* mandare avanti; ~ **out** *vt* (*orders*) eseguire; (*investigation*) svolgere; ~**cot** (*BRIT*) *n* culla portabile; ~**-on** (*inf*) *n* (*fuss*) casino, confusione *f*.

cart [ka:t] *n* carro ♦ *vt* (*inf*) trascinare.

carton ['ka:tən] *n* (*box*) scatola di cartone; (*of yogurt*) cartone *m*; (*of cigarettes*) stecca.

cartoon [ka:'tu:n] *n* (*PRESS*) disegno umoristico; (*comic strip*) fumetto; (*CINEMA*) disegno animato.

cartridge ['ka:trıdʒ] *n* (*for gun, pen*) cartuccia; (*music tape*) cassetta.

carve [ka:v] *vt* (*meat*) trinciare; (*wood, stone*) intagliare; ~ **up** *vt* (*fig: country*) suddividere; **carving** *n* (*in wood etc*) scultura; **carving knife** *n* trinciante *m*.

car wash *n* lavaggio auto.

cascade [kæs'keıd] *n* cascata.

case [keıs] *n* caso; (*LAW*) causa, processo; (*box*) scatola; (*BRIT: also: suit~*) valigia; **in** ~ **of** in caso di; **in** ~ **he** in caso mai lui; **in any** ~ in ogni caso; **just in** ~ in caso di bisogno.

cash [kæʃ] *n* denaro; (*coins, notes*) denaro liquido ♦ *vt* incassare; **to pay (in)** ~ pagare in contanti; ~ **on delivery** pagamento alla consegna; ~**book** *n* giornale *m* di cassa; ~ **card** (*BRIT*) *n* tesserino di prelievo; ~ **desk** (*BRIT*) *n* cassa; ~ **dispenser** (*BRIT*) *n* sportello automatico.

cashew [kæ'ʃu:] *n* (*also:* ~ **nut**) anacardio.

cashier [kæ'ʃıə*] *n* cassiere/a.

cashmere ['kæʃmıə*] *n* cachemire *m*.

cash register *n* registratore *m* di cassa.

casing ['keısıŋ] *n* rivestimento.

casino [kə'si:nəu] n casinò m inv.

cask [kɑ:sk] n botte f.

casket ['kɑ:skɪt] n cofanetto; (US: coffin) bara.

casserole ['kæsərəul] n casseruola; (food): **chicken** ~ pollo in casseruola.

cassette [kæ'sɛt] n cassetta; ~ **player** n riproduttore m a cassette; ~ **recorder** n registratore m a cassette.

cast [kɑ:st] (pt, pp **cast**) vt (throw) gettare; (metal) gettare, fondere; (THEATRE): **to** ~ **sb as Hamlet** scegliere qn per la parte di Amleto ♦ n (THEATRE) cast m inv; (also: plaster ~) ingessatura; **to** ~ **one's vote** votare, dare il voto; ~ **off** vi (NAUT) salpare; (KNITTING) calare; ~ **on** vi (KNITTING) avviare le maglie.

castaway ['kɑ:stəwəɪ] n naufrago/a.

caster sugar ['kɑ:stə*-] (BRIT) n zucchero semolato.

casting vote ['kɑ:stɪŋ-] (BRIT) n voto decisivo.

cast iron n ghisa.

castle ['kɑ:sl] n castello.

castor ['kɑ:stə*] n (wheel) rotella; ~ **oil** n olio di ricino.

castrate [kæs'treɪt] vt castrare.

casual ['kæʒjul] adj (by chance) casuale, fortuito(a); (irregular: work etc) avventizio(a); (unconcerned) non-curante, indifferente; ~ **wear** casual m; ~**ly** adv (in a relaxed way) con noncuranza; (dress) casual.

casualty ['kæʒjultı] n ferito/a; (dead) morto/a, vittima; (MED: department) pronto soccorso.

cat [kæt] n gatto.

catalogue ['kætəlɒg] (US **catalog**) n catalogo ♦ vt catalogare.

catalyst ['kætəlɪst] n catalizzatore m.

catapult ['kætəpʌlt] n catapulta; fionda.

cataract ['kætərækt] n (also MED) cateratta.

catarrh [kə'tɑ:*] n catarro.

catastrophe [kə'tæstrəfı] n catastrofe f.

catch [kætʃ] (pt, pp **caught**) vt prendere; (ball) afferrare; (surprise: person) sorprendere; (attention) attirare; (comment, whisper) cogliere; (person: also: ~ up) raggiungere ♦ vi (fire) prendere ♦ n (fish etc caught) retata; (of ball) presa; (trick) inganno; (TECH) gancio; (game) catch m inv; **to** ~ **fire** prendere fuoco; **to** ~ **sight of** scorgere; ~ **on** vi capire; (become popular) affermarsi, far presa; ~ **up** vi mettersi in pari ♦ vt (also: ~ up with) raggiungere.

catching ['kætʃɪŋ] adj (MED) contagioso(a).

catchment area ['kætʃmənt-] (BRIT) n (SCOL) circoscrizione f scolare.

catch phrase n slogan m inv; frase f fatta.

catchy ['kætʃı] adj orecchiabile.

category ['kætɪgərı] n categoria.

cater ['keɪtə*] vi: ~ **for** (BRIT: needs) provvedere a; (: readers, consumers) incontrare i gusti di; (COMM: provide food) provvedere alla ristorazione di; ~**er** n fornitore m; ~**ing** n approvvigionamento.

caterpillar ['kætəpɪlə*] n bruco; ~ **track** n catena a cingoli.

cathedral [kə'θi:drəl] n cattedrale f, duomo.

catholic ['kæθəlık] adj universale; aperto(a); eclettico(a); **C**~ adj, n (REL) cattolico(a).

cat's-eye [kæts'aɪ] (BRIT) n (AUT) catarifrangente m.

cattle ['kætl] npl bestiame m, bestie fpl.

catty ['kætı] adj maligno(a), dispettoso(a).

caucus ['kɔ:kəs] n (POL: group) comitato di dirigenti; (: US) (riunione f del) comitato elettorale.

caught [kɔ:t] pt, pp of **catch**.

cauliflower ['kɒlıflauə*] n cavolfiore m.

cause [kɔ:z] n causa ♦ vt causare.

caution ['kɔ:ʃən] n prudenza; (warning) avvertimento ♦ vt avvertire; ammonire.

cautious ['kɔ:ʃəs] adj cauto(a), prudente.

cavalier [kævə'lıə*] adj brusco(a).

cavalry ['kævəlrı] n cavalleria.

cave [keɪv] n caverna, grotta; ~ **in** vi (roof etc) crollare; ~**man** n uomo delle

caverne.
caviar(e) ['kævɪɑ:*] n caviale m.
cavort [kə'vɔ:t] vi far capriole.
CB n abbr (= Citizens' Band (Radio)):
~ **radio (set)** baracchino.
CBI n abbr (= Confederation of British Industries) ≈ Confindustria.
cc abbr = **cubic centimetres**; **carbon copy**.
cease [si:s] vt, vi cessare; ~**fire** n cessate il fuoco m inv; ~**less** adj incessante, continuo(a).
cedar ['si:də*] n cedro.
ceiling ['si:lɪŋ] n soffitto; (on wages etc) tetto.
celebrate ['sɛlɪbreɪt] vt, vi celebrare; ~**d** adj celebre; **celebration** [-'breɪʃən] n celebrazione f.
celery ['sɛlərɪ] n sedano.
cell [sɛl] n cella; (of revolutionaries, BIOL) cellula; (ELEC) elemento (di batteria).
cellar ['sɛlə*] n sottosuolo; cantina.
'**cello** ['tʃɛləʊ] n violoncello.
Celt [kɛlt, sɛlt] n celta m/f.
Celtic ['kɛltɪk, 'sɛltɪk] adj celtico(a).
cement [sə'mɛnt] n cemento; ~ **mixer** n betoniera.
cemetery ['sɛmɪtrɪ] n cimitero.
censor ['sɛnsə*] n censore m ♦ vt censurare; ~**ship** n censura.
censure ['sɛnʃə*] vt riprovare, censurare.
census ['sɛnsəs] n censimento.
cent [sɛnt] n (US: coin) centesimo (= 1:100 di un dollaro); see also **per**.
centenary [sɛn'ti:nərɪ] n centenario.
center ['sɛntə*] (US) n, vt = **centre**.
centigrade ['sɛntɪgreɪd] adj centigrado(a).
centimetre ['sɛntɪmi:tə*] (US **centimeter**) n centimetro.
centipede ['sɛntɪpi:d] n centopiedi m inv.
central ['sɛntrəl] adj centrale; **C~ America** n America centrale; ~ **heating** n riscaldamento centrale; ~**ize** vt accentrare.
centre ['sɛntə*] (US **center**) n centro ♦ vt centrare; ~-**forward** n (SPORT) cen-

troavanti m inv; ~-**half** n (SPORT) centromediano.
century ['sɛntjʊrɪ] n secolo; **20th** ~ ventesimo secolo.
ceramic [sɪ'ræmɪk] adj ceramico(a); ~**s** npl ceramica.
cereal ['si:rɪəl] n cereale m.
ceremony ['sɛrɪmənɪ] n cerimonia; **to stand on** ~ fare complimenti.
certain ['sɜ:tən] adj certo(a); **to make** ~ **of** assicurarsi di; **for** ~ per certo, di sicuro; ~**ly** adv certamente, certo; ~**ty** n certezza.
certificate [sə'tɪfɪkɪt] n certificato; diploma m.
certified ['sɜ:tɪfaɪd]: ~ **mail** (US) n posta raccomandata con ricevuta di ritorno; ~ **public accountant** (US) n ≈ commercialista m/f.
certify ['sɜ:tɪfaɪ] vt certificare; (award diploma to) conferire un diploma a; (declare insane) dichiarare pazzo(a).
cervical ['sɜ:vɪkl] adj: ~ **cancer** cancro della cervice; ~ **smear** Pap-test m inv.
cervix ['sɜ:vɪks] n cervice f.
cesspit ['sɛspɪt] n pozzo nero.
cf. abbr (= compare) cfr.
ch. abbr (= chapter) cap.
chafe [tʃeɪf] vt fregare, irritare.
chagrin ['ʃægrɪn] n disappunto.
chain [tʃeɪn] n catena ♦ vt (also: ~ up) incatenare; ~ **reaction** n reazione f a catena; ~-**smoke** vi fumare una sigaretta dopo l'altra; ~ **store** n negozio a catena.
chair [tʃɛə*] n sedia; (armchair) poltrona; (of university) cattedra; (of meeting) presidenza ♦ vt (meeting) presiedere; ~**lift** n seggiovia; ~**man** n presidente m.
chalice ['tʃælɪs] n calice m.
chalk [tʃɔ:k] n gesso.
challenge ['tʃælɪndʒ] n sfida ♦ vt sfidare; (statement, right) mettere in dubbio; **to** ~ **sb to do** sfidare qn a fare; **challenging** adj (task) impegnativo(a); (look) di sfida.
chamber ['tʃeɪmbə*] n camera; ~ **of commerce** n camera di commercio; ~**maid** n cameriera; ~ **music** n musica

da camera.

chamois ['ʃæmwɑ:] n camoscio; (also: ~ leather) panno in pelle di camoscio.

champagne [ʃæm'peɪn] n champagne m inv.

champion ['tʃæmpɪən] n campione/essa; ~ship n campionato.

chance [tʃɑ:ns] n caso; (opportunity) occasione f; (likelihood) possibilità f inv ♦ vt: to ~ it rischiare, provarci ♦ adj fortuito(a); to take a ~ rischiare; by ~ per caso.

chancellor ['tʃɑ:nsələ*] n cancelliere m; C~ of the Exchequer (BRIT) n Cancelliere dello Scacchiere.

chandelier [ʃændə'lɪə*] n lampadario.

change ['tʃeɪndʒ] vt cambiare; (transform): to ~ sb into trasformare qn in ♦ vi cambiare; (~ one's clothes) cambiarsi; (be transformed): to ~ into trasformarsi in ♦ n cambiamento; (of clothes) cambio; (money) resto; to ~ one's mind cambiare idea; for a ~ tanto per cambiare; ~able adj (weather) variabile; ~ machine n distributore automatico di monete; ~over n cambiamento, passaggio.

changing ['tʃeɪndʒɪŋ] adj che cambia; (colours) cangiante; ~ room n (BRIT: in shop) camerino; (: SPORT) spogliatoio.

channel ['tʃænl] n canale m; (of river, sea) alveo ♦ vt canalizzare; the (English) C~ la Manica; the C~ Islands npl le Isole Normanne.

chant [tʃɑ:nt] n canto; salmodia ♦ vt cantare, salmodiare.

chaos ['keɪɔs] n caos m.

chap [tʃæp] (BRIT: inf) n (man) tipo.

chapel ['tʃæpəl] n cappella.

chaperone ['ʃæpərəʊn] n accompagnatrice f ♦ vt accompagnare.

chaplain ['tʃæplɪn] n cappellano.

chapped [tʃæpt] adj (skin, lips) screpolato(a).

chapter ['tʃæptə*] n capitolo.

char [tʃɑ:*] vt (burn) carbonizzare ♦ n (BRIT) = **charlady**.

character ['kærɪktə*] n carattere m; (in novel, film) personaggio; ~istic [-'rɪstɪk]

adj caratteristico(a) ♦ n caratteristica.

charade [ʃə'rɑ:d] n sciarada.

charcoal ['tʃɑ:kəʊl] n carbone m di legna.

charge [tʃɑ:dʒ] n accusa; (cost) prezzo; (responsibility) responsabilità ♦ vt (gun, battery, MIL: enemy) caricare; (customer) fare pagare a; (sum) fare pagare; (LAW): to ~ sb (with) accusare qn (di) ♦ vi (gen with: up, along etc) lanciarsi; ~s npl (bank - s etc) tariffe fpl; to reverse the ~s (TEL) fare una telefonata a carico del destinatario; to take ~ incaricarsi di; to be in ~ of essere responsabile per; how much do you ~? quanto chiedete?; to ~ an expense (up) to sb addebitare una spesa a qn; ~ card n carta f clienti inv.

charitable ['tʃærɪtəbl] adj caritatevole.

charity ['tʃærɪtɪ] n carità; (organization) opera pia.

charlady ['tʃɑ:leɪdɪ] (BRIT) n domestica a ore.

charlatan ['ʃɑ:lətən] n ciarlatano.

charm [tʃɑ:m] n fascino; (on bracelet) ciondolo ♦ vt affascinare, incantare; ~ing adj affascinante.

chart [tʃɑ:t] n tabella; grafico; (map) carta nautica ♦ vt fare una carta nautica di; ~s npl (MUS) hit parade f.

charter ['tʃɑ:tə*] vt (plane) noleggiare ♦ n (document) carta; ~ed accountant (BRIT) n ragioniere/a professionista; ~ flight n volo m charter inv.

charwoman ['tʃɑ:wʊmən] n = **charlady**.

chase [tʃeɪs] vt inseguire; (also: ~ away) cacciare ♦ n caccia.

chasm ['kæzəm] n abisso.

chassis ['ʃæsɪ] n telaio.

chastity ['tʃæstɪtɪ] n castità.

chat [tʃæt] vi (also: have a ~) chiacchierare ♦ n chiacchierata; ~ show (BRIT) n talk show m inv.

chatter ['tʃætə*] vi (person) ciarlare; (bird) cinguettare; (teeth) battere ♦ n ciarle fpl; cinguettio; ~box (inf) n chiacchierone/a.

chatty ['tʃætɪ] adj (style) familiare; (person) chiacchierino(a).

chauffeur ['ʃəʊfə*] n autista m.

e

chauvinist ['ʃəʊvɪnɪst] n (male ~) maschilista m; (nationalist) sciovinista m/f.

cheap [tʃiːp] adj a buon mercato; (joke) grossolano(a); (poor quality) di cattiva qualità ♦ adv a buon mercato; ~er adj meno caro(a); ~ly adv a buon prezzo, a buon mercato.

cheat [tʃiːt] vi imbrogliare; (at school) copiare ♦ vt ingannare ♦ n imbroglione m; to ~ sb out of sth defraudare qn di qc.

check [tʃɛk] vt verificare; (passport, ticket) controllare; (halt) fermare; (restrain) contenere ♦ n verifica; controllo; (curb) freno; (US: bill) conto; (pattern: gen pl) quadretti mpl; (US) = **cheque** ♦ adj (pattern, cloth) a quadretti; ~ in vi (in hotel) registrare; (at airport) presentarsi all'accettazione ♦ vt (luggage) depositare; ~ out vi (in hotel) saldare il conto; ~ up vi: to ~ up (on sth) investigare (qc); to ~ up on sb informarsi sul conto di qn; ~ered (US) adj = **chequered**; ~ers (US) n dama; ~-in (desk) n check-in m inv, accettazione f (bagagli inv); ~ing account (US) n conto corrente; ~mate n scaccomatto; ~out n (in supermarket) cassa; ~point n posto di blocco; ~room (US) n deposito m bagagli inv; ~up n (MED) controllo medico.

cheek [tʃiːk] n guancia; (impudence) faccia tosta; ~bone n zigomo; ~y adj sfacciato(a).

cheep [tʃiːp] vi pigolare.

cheer [tʃɪə*] vt applaudire; (gladden) rallegrare ♦ vi applaudire ♦ n grido (di incoraggiamento); ~s npl (of approval, encouragement) applausi mpl; evviva mpl; ~s! salute!; ~ up vi rallegrarsi, farsi animo ♦ vt rallegrare; ~ful adj allegro(a).

cheerio ['tʃɪərɪ'əʊ] (BRIT) excl ciao!

cheese [tʃiːz] n formaggio; ~board n piatto del (or per il) formaggio.

cheetah ['tʃiːtə] n ghepardo.

chef [ʃɛf] n capocuoco.

chemical ['kɛmɪkəl] adj chimico(a) ♦ n prodotto chimico.

chemist ['kɛmɪst] n (BRIT: pharmacist)

farmacista m/f; (scientist) chimico/a; ~ry n chimica; ~'s (shop) (BRIT) n farmacia.

cheque [tʃɛk] (BRIT) n assegno; ~book n libretto degli assegni; ~ card n carta f assegni inv.

chequered ['tʃɛkəd] (US **checkered**) adj (fig) movimentato(a).

cherish ['tʃɛrɪʃ] vt aver caro.

cherry ['tʃɛrɪ] n ciliegia; (also: ~ tree) ciliegio.

chess [tʃɛs] n scacchi mpl; ~board n scacchiera.

chest [tʃɛst] n petto; (box) cassa; ~ of drawers n cassettone m.

chestnut ['tʃɛsnʌt] n castagna; (also: ~ tree) castagno.

chew [tʃuː] vt masticare; ~ing gum n chewing gum m.

chic [ʃiːk] adj elegante.

chick [tʃɪk] n pulcino; (inf) pollastrella.

chicken ['tʃɪkɪn] n pollo; (inf: coward) coniglio; ~ out vi (inf) avere fifa; ~pox n varicella.

chicory ['tʃɪkərɪ] n cicoria.

chief [tʃiːf] n capo ♦ adj principale; ~ executive n direttore m generale; ~ly adv per lo più, soprattutto.

chilblain ['tʃɪlbleɪn] n gelone m.

child [tʃaɪld] (pl ~ren) n bambino/a; ~birth n parto; ~hood n infanzia; ~ish adj puerile; ~like adj fanciullesco(a); ~ minder (BRIT) n bambinaia.

children ['tʃɪldrən] npl of child.

Chile ['tʃɪlɪ] n Cile m.

chill [tʃɪl] n freddo; (MED) infreddatura ♦ vt raffreddare.

chil(l)i ['tʃɪlɪ] n peperoncino.

chilly ['tʃɪlɪ] adj freddo(a), fresco(a); to feel ~ sentirsi infreddolito(a).

chime [tʃaɪm] n carillon m inv ♦ vi suonare, scampanare.

chimney ['tʃɪmnɪ] n camino; ~ sweep n spazzacamino.

chimpanzee [tʃɪmpæn'ziː] n scimpanzé m inv.

chin [tʃɪn] n mento.

China ['tʃaɪnə] n Cina.

china ['tʃaɪnə] n porcellana.

Chinese [tʃaɪ'niːz] adj cinese ♦ n inv

cinese *m/f*; (*LING*) cinese *m*.
chink [tʃɪŋk] *n* (*opening*) fessura; (*noise*) tintinnio.
chip [tʃɪp] *n* (*gen pl*: *CULIN*) patatina fritta; (: *US*: *also*: *potato* ~) patatina; (*of wood, glass, stone*) scheggia; (*also*: *micro~*) chip *m inv* ♦ *vt* (*cup, plate*) scheggiare; ~ **in** (*inf*) *vi* (*contribute*) contribuire; (*interrupt*) intromettersi.
chiropodist [kɪ'rɔpədɪst] (*BRIT*) *n* pedicure *m/f inv*.
chirp [tʃə:p] *vi* cinguettare; fare cri cri.
chisel [ˈtʃɪzl] *n* cesello.
chit [tʃɪt] *n* biglietto.
chitchat [ˈtʃɪttʃæt] *n* chiacchiere *fpl*.
chivalry [ˈʃɪvəlrɪ] *n* cavalleria; cortesia.
chives [tʃaɪvz] *npl* erba cipollina.
chock-a-block [ˈtʃɔk-] *adj* pieno(a) zeppo(a).
chock-full [ˈtʃɔk-] *adj* = **chock-a-block**.
chocolate [ˈtʃɔklɪt] *n* (*substance*) cioccolato, cioccolata; (*drink*) cioccolata; (*a sweet*) cioccolatino.
choice [tʃɔɪs] *n* scelta ♦ *adj* scelto(a).
choir [ˈkwaɪə*] *n* coro; ~**boy** *n* corista *m* fanciullo.
choke [tʃəuk] *vi* soffocare ♦ *vt* soffocare; (*block*): **to be ~d with** essere intasato(a) di ♦ *n* (*AUT*) valvola dell'aria.
cholera [ˈkɔlərə] *n* colera *m*.
cholesterol [kəˈlɛstərɔl] *n* colesterolo.
choose [tʃu:z] (*pt* **chose**, *pp* **chosen**) *vt* scegliere; **to** ~ **to do** decidere di fare; preferire fare.
choosy [ˈtʃu:zɪ] *adj* schizzinoso(a).
chop [tʃɔp] *vt* (*wood*) spaccare; (*CULIN*: *also*: ~ *up*) tritare ♦ *n* (*CULIN*) costoletta; ~**s** *npl* (*jaws*) mascelle *fpl*.
chopper [ˈtʃɔpə*] *n* (*helicopter*) elicottero.
choppy [ˈtʃɔpɪ] *adj* (*sea*) mosso(a).
chopsticks [ˈtʃɔpstɪks] *npl* bastoncini *mpl* cinesi.
choral [ˈkɔːrəl] *adj* corale.
chord [kɔ:d] *n* (*MUS*) accordo.
chore [tʃɔ:*] *n* faccenda; **household ~s** faccende *fpl* domestiche.
choreographer [kɔrɪˈɔgrəfə*] *n* coreografo/a.

chortle [ˈtʃɔ:tl] *vi* ridacchiare.
chorus [ˈkɔ:rəs] *n* coro; (*repeated part of song, also fig*) ritornello.
chose [tʃəuz] *pt of* **choose**.
chosen [ˈtʃəuzn] *pp of* **choose**.
Christ [kraɪst] *n* Cristo.
christen [ˈkrɪsn] *vt* battezzare.
Christian [ˈkrɪstɪən] *adj, n* cristiano(a); ~**ity** [-ˈænɪtɪ] *n* cristianesimo; ~ **name** *n* nome *m* (di battesimo).
Christmas [ˈkrɪsməs] *n* Natale *m*; **Merry ~!** Buon Natale!; ~ **card** *n* cartolina di Natale; ~ **Day** *n* il giorno di Natale; ~ **Eve** *n* la vigilia di Natale; ~ **tree** *n* albero di Natale.
chrome [krəum] *n* cromo.
chromium [ˈkrəumɪəm] *n* cromo.
chronic [ˈkrɔnɪk] *adj* cronico(a).
chronicle [ˈkrɔnɪkl] *n* cronaca.
chronological [krɔnəˈlɔdʒɪkəl] *adj* cronologico(a).
chrysanthemum [krɪˈsænθəməm] *n* crisantemo.
chubby [ˈtʃʌbɪ] *adj* paffuto(a).
chuck [tʃʌk] (*inf*) *vt* buttare, gettare; (*BRIT*: *also*: ~ *up*) piantare; ~ **out** *vt* buttar fuori.
chuckle [ˈtʃʌkl] *vi* ridere sommessamente.
chug [tʃʌg] *vi* fare ciuf ciuf.
chum [tʃʌm] *n* compagno/a.
chunk [tʃʌŋk] *n* pezzo.
church [tʃə:tʃ] *n* chiesa; ~**yard** *n* sagrato.
churlish [ˈtʃə:lɪʃ] *adj* rozzo(a), sgarbato(a).
churn [tʃə:n] *n* (*for butter*) zangola; (*for milk*) bidone *m*; ~ **out** *vt* sfornare.
chute [ʃu:t] *n* (*also*: *rubbish* ~) canale *m* di scarico; (*BRIT*: *children's slide*) scivolo.
chutney [ˈtʃʌtnɪ] *n* salsa piccante (*di frutta, zucchero e spezie*).
CIA (*US*) *n abbr* (= *Central Intelligence Agency*) CIA *f*.
CID (*BRIT*) *n abbr* (= *Criminal Investigation Department*) ≈ polizia giudiziaria.
cider [ˈsaɪdə*] *n* sidro.
cigar [sɪˈgɑ:*] *n* sigaro.

cigarette [sɪgə'rɛt] n sigaretta; ~ **case** n portasigarette m inv; ~ **end** n mozzicone m.

Cinderella [sɪndə'rɛlə] n Cenerentola.

cinders ['sɪndəz] npl ceneri fpl.

cine camera ['sɪnɪ-] (BRIT) n cinepresa.

cine-film ['sɪnɪ-] (BRIT) n pellicola.

cinema ['sɪnəmə] n cinema m inv.

cinnamon ['sɪnəmən] n cannella.

cipher ['saɪfə*] n cifra.

circle ['sə:kl] n cerchio; (of friends etc) circolo; (in cinema) galleria ♦ vi girare in circolo ♦ vt (surround) circondare; (move round) girare intorno a.

circuit ['sə:kɪt] n circuito; ~ous [sə:'kjuɪtəs] adj indiretto(a).

circular ['sə:kjulə*] adj circolare ♦ n circolare f.

circulate ['sə:kjuleɪt] vi circolare ♦ vt far circolare; **circulation** [-'leɪʃən] n circolazione f; (of newspaper) tiratura.

circumstances ['sə:kəmstənsɪz] npl circostanze fpl; (financial condition) condizioni fpl finanziarie.

circumvent [sə:kəm'vɛnt] vt aggirare.

circus ['sə:kəs] n circo.

cistern ['sɪstən] n cisterna; (in toilet) serbatoio d'acqua.

citizen ['sɪtɪzn] n (of country) cittadino/a; (of town) abitante m/f; ~ship n cittadinanza.

citrus fruit ['sɪtrəs-] n agrume m.

city ['sɪtɪ] n città f inv; **the C~** la Città di Londra (centro commerciale).

civic ['sɪvɪk] adj civico(a); ~ **centre** (BRIT) n centro civico.

civil ['sɪvɪl] adj civile; ~ **engineer** n ingegnere m civile; ~ian [sɪ'vɪlɪən] adj, n borghese m/f.

civilization [sɪvɪlaɪ'zeɪʃən] n civiltà f inv.

civilized ['sɪvɪlaɪzd] adj civilizzato(a); (fig) cortese.

civil: ~ **law** n codice m civile; (study) diritto civile; ~ **servant** n impiegato/a statale; **C~ Service** n amministrazione f statale; ~ **war** n guerra civile.

clad [klæd] adj: ~ (**in**) vestito(a) (di).

claim [kleɪm] vt (assert): **to** ~ (**that**)/**to be** sostenere (che)/di essere; (credit, rights etc) rivendicare; (damages) ri-

chiedere ♦ vi (for insurance) fare una domanda d'indennizzo ♦ n pretesa; rivendicazione f; richiesta; ~ant n (ADMIN, LAW) richiedente m/f.

clairvoyant [kleə'vɔɪənt] n chiaroveggente m/f.

clam [klæm] n vongola.

clamber ['klæmbə*] vi arrampicarsi.

clammy ['klæmɪ] adj (weather) caldo(a) umido(a); (hands) viscido(a).

clamour ['klæmə*] (US **clamor**) vi: **to** ~ **for** chiedere a gran voce.

clamp [klæmp] n pinza; morsa ♦ vt stringere con una morsa; ~ **down on** vt fus dare un giro di vite a.

clan [klæn] n clan m inv.

clang [klæŋ] vi emettere un suono metallico.

clap [klæp] vi applaudire; ~**ping** n applausi mpl.

claret ['klærət] n vino di Bordeaux.

clarify ['klærɪfaɪ] vt chiarificare, chiarire.

clarinet [klærɪ'nɛt] n clarinetto.

clarity ['klærɪtɪ] n clarità.

clash [klæʃ] n frastuono; (fig) scontro ♦ vi scontrarsi; cozzare.

clasp [klɑ:sp] n (hold) stretta; (of necklace, bag) fermaglio, fibbia ♦ vt stringere.

class [klɑ:s] n classe f ♦ vt classificare.

classic ['klæsɪk] adj classico(a) ♦ n classico; ~**al** adj classico(a).

classified ['klæsɪfaɪd] adj (information) segreto(a), riservato(a); ~ **advertisement** n annuncio economico.

classmate ['klɑ:smeɪt] n compagno/a di classe.

classroom ['klɑ:srum] n aula.

clatter ['klætə*] n tintinnio; scalpitio ♦ vi tintinnare; scalpitare.

clause [klɔ:z] n clausola; (LING) proposizione f.

claw [klɔ:] n (of bird of prey) artiglio; (of lobster) pinza; ~ **at** vt fus graffiare; afferrare.

clay [kleɪ] n argilla.

clean [kli:n] adj pulito(a); (clear, smooth) liscio(a) ♦ vt pulire; ~ **out** vt ripulire; ~ **up** vt (also fig) ripulire; ~-

cut adj (man) curato(a); ~**er** n (person) donna delle pulizie; ~**er's** n (also: dry ~**er's**) tintoria; ~**ing** n pulizia; ~**liness** ['klɛnlɪnɪs] n pulizia.
cleanse [klɛnz] vt pulire; purificare; ~**r** n detergente m.
clean-shaven [-'ʃeɪvn] adj sbarbato(a).
cleansing department ['klɛnzɪŋ-] (BRIT) n nettezza urbana.
clear [klɪə*] adj chiaro(a); (glass etc) trasparente; (road, way) libero(a); (conscience) pulito(a) ♦ vt sgombrare; liberare; (table) sparecchiare; (cheque) fare la compensazione di; (LAW: suspect) discolpare; (obstacle) superare ♦ vi (weather) rasserenarsi; (fog) andarsene ♦ adv: ~ **of** distante da; ~ **up** vt mettere in ordine; (mystery) risolvere; ~**ance** n (removal) sgombro; (permission) autorizzazione f, permesso; ~**-cut** adj ben delineato(a), distinto(a); ~**ing** n radura; ~**ing bank** (BRIT) n banca (che fa uso della camera di compensazione); ~**ly** adv chiaramente; ~**way** (BRIT) n strada con divieto di sosta.
cleaver ['kliːvə*] n mannaia.
clef [klɛf] n (MUS) chiave f.
cleft [klɛft] n (in rock) crepa, fenditura.
clench [klɛntʃ] vt stringere.
clergy ['klɜːdʒɪ] n clero; ~**man** n ecclesiastico.
clerical ['klɛrɪkəl] adj d'impiegato; (REL) clericale.
clerk [klɑːk, (US) klɜːrk] n (BRIT) impiegato/a; (US) commesso/a.
clever ['klɛvə*] adj (mentally) intelligente; (deft, skilful) abile; (device, arrangement) ingegnoso(a).
click [klɪk] vi scattare ♦ vt (heels etc) battere; (tongue) far schioccare.
client ['klaɪənt] n cliente m/f.
cliff [klɪf] n scogliera scoscesa, rupe f.
climate ['klaɪmɪt] n clima m.
climax ['klaɪmæks] n culmine m; (sexual) orgasmo.
climb [klaɪm] vi salire; (clamber) arrampicarsi ♦ vt salire; (CLIMBING) scalare ♦ n salita; arrampicata, scalata; ~**-down** n marcia indietro;

~**er** n rocciatore/trice; alpinista m/f; ~**ing** n alpinismo.
clinch [klɪntʃ] vt (deal) concludere.
cling [klɪŋ] (pt, pp clung) vi: **to** ~ (**to**) aggrapparsi (a); (of clothes) aderire strettamente (a).
clinic ['klɪnɪk] n clinica; ~**al** adj clinico(a); (fig) distaccato(a); (: room) freddo(a).
clink [klɪŋk] vi tintinnare.
clip [klɪp] n (for hair) forcina; (also: paper ~) graffetta; (TV, CINEMA) sequenza ♦ vt attaccare insieme; (hair, nails) tagliare; (hedge) tosare; ~**pers** npl (for gardening) cesoie fpl; (also: nail ~**pers**) forbicine fpl per le unghie; ~**ping** n (from newspaper) ritaglio.
clique [kliːk] n cricca.
cloak [kləuk] n mantello ♦ vt avvolgere; ~**room** n (for coats etc) guardaroba m inv; (BRIT: W.C.) gabinetti mpl.
clock [klɔk] n orologio; ~ **in** or **on** vi timbrare il cartellino (all'entrata); ~ **off** or **out** vi timbrare il cartellino (all'uscita); ~**wise** adv in senso orario; ~**work** n movimento or meccanismo a orologeria ♦ adj a molla.
clog [klɔg] n zoccolo ♦ vt intasare ♦ vi (also: ~ **up**) intasarsi, bloccarsi.
cloister ['klɔɪstə*] n chiostro.
clone [kləun] n clone m.
close¹ [kləus] adj: ~ (**to**) vicino(a) (a); (watch, link, relative) stretto(a); (examination) attento(a); (contest) combattuto(a); (weather) afoso(a) ♦ adv vicino, dappresso; ~ **to** vicino a; ~ **by**, ~ **at hand** a portata di mano; **a** ~ **friend** un amico intimo; **to have a** ~ **shave** (fig) scamparla bella.
close² [kləuz] vt chiudere ♦ vi (shop etc) chiudere; (lid, door etc) chiudersi; (end) finire ♦ n (end) fine f; ~ **down** vi cessare (definitivamente); ~**d** adj chiuso(a); ~**d shop** n azienda o fabbrica che impiega solo aderenti ai sindacati.
close-knit [kləus'nɪt] adj (family, community) molto unito(a).
closely ['kləuslɪ] adv (examine, watch) da vicino; (related) strettamente.

closet ['klɔzɪt] n (cupboard) armadio.

close-up ['kləusʌp] n primo piano.

closure ['kləuʒə*] n chiusura.

clot [klɔt] n (also: blood ~) coagulo; (inf: idiot) scemo/a ♦ vi coagularsi.

cloth [klɔθ] n (material) tessuto, stoffa; (rag) strofinaccio.

clothe [kləuð] vt vestire; ~s npl abiti mpl, vestiti mpl; ~s brush n spazzola per abiti; ~s line n corda (per stendere il bucato); ~s peg (US ~s pin) n molletta.

clothing ['kləuðɪŋ] n = **clothes**.

cloud [klaud] n nuvola; ~burst n acquazzone m; ~y adj nuvoloso(a); (liquid) torbido(a).

clout [klaut] vt dare un colpo a.

clove [kləuv] n chiodo di garofano; ~ of garlic spicchio d'aglio.

clover ['kləuvə*] n trifoglio.

clown [klaun] n pagliaccio ♦ vi (also: ~ about, ~ around) fare il pagliaccio.

cloying ['klɔɪɪŋ] adj (taste, smell) nauseabondo(a).

club [klʌb] n (society) club m inv, circolo; (weapon, GOLF) mazza ♦ vt bastonare ♦ vi: to ~ together associarsi; ~s npl (CARDS) fiori mpl; ~ car (US) n (RAIL) vagone m ristorante; ~house n sede f del circolo.

cluck [klʌk] vi chiocciare.

clue [klu:] n indizio; (in crosswords) definizione f; I haven't a ~ non ho la minima idea.

clump [klʌmp] n (of flowers, trees) gruppo; (of grass) ciuffo.

clumsy ['klʌmzɪ] adj goffo(a).

clung [klʌŋ] pt, pp of **cling**.

cluster ['klʌstə*] n gruppo ♦ vi raggrupparsi.

clutch [klʌtʃ] n (grip, grasp) presa, stretta; (AUT) frizione f ♦ vt afferrare, stringere forte.

clutter ['klʌtə*] vt ingombrare.

CND n abbr = **Campaign for Nuclear Disarmament**.

Co. abbr = **county; company**.

c/o abbr (= care of) presso.

coach [kəutʃ] n (bus) pullman m inv; (horse-drawn, of train) carrozza; (SPORT) allenatore/trice; (tutor) chi dà ripetizioni ♦ vt allenare; dare ripetizioni a; ~ trip n viaggio in pullman.

coal [kəul] n carbone m; ~ face n fronte f; ~field n bacino carbonifero.

coalition [kəuə'lɪʃən] n coalizione f.

coal: ~**man** n negoziante m di carbone; ~ **merchant** n = ~**man**; ~**mine** n miniera di carbone.

coarse [kɔ:s] adj (salt, sand etc) grosso(a); (cloth, person) rozzo(a).

coast [kəust] n costa ♦ vi (with cycle etc) scendere a ruota libera; ~al adj costiero(a); ~guard n guardia costiera; ~line n linea costiera.

coat [kəut] n cappotto; (of animal) pelo; (of paint) mano f ♦ vt coprire; ~ of arms n stemma m; ~ hanger n attaccapanni m inv; ~ing n rivestimento.

coax [kəuks] vt indurre (con moine).

cob [kɔb] n see **corn**.

cobbler ['kɔblə*] n calzolaio.

cobbles ['kɔblz] npl ciottoli mpl.

cobblestones ['kɔblstəunz] npl ciottoli mpl.

cobweb ['kɔbwεb] n ragnatela.

cocaine [kə'keɪn] n cocaina.

cock [kɔk] n (rooster) gallo; (male bird) maschio ♦ vt (gun) armare; ~erel n galletto; ~-eyed adj (fig) storto(a); strampalato(a).

cockle ['kɔkl] n cardio.

cockney ['kɔknɪ] n cockney m/f inv (abitante dei quartieri popolari dell'East End di Londra).

cockpit ['kɔkpɪt] n abitacolo.

cockroach ['kɔkrəutʃ] n blatta.

cocktail ['kɔkteɪl] n cocktail m inv; ~ cabinet n mobile m bar inv; ~ party n cocktail m inv.

cocoa ['kəukəu] n cacao.

coconut ['kəukənʌt] n noce f di cocco.

cocoon [kə'ku:n] n bozzolo.

cod [kɔd] n merluzzo.

C.O.D. abbr = **cash on delivery**.

code [kəud] n codice m.

cod-liver oil n olio di fegato di merluzzo.

coercion [kəu'ə:ʃən] *n* coercizione *f*.
coffee ['kɒfɪ] *n* caffè *m inv*; ~ **bar**
(*BRIT*) *n* caffè *m inv*; ~ **break** *n* pausa
per il caffè; ~**pot** *n* caffettiera; ~
table *n* tavolino.
coffin ['kɒfɪn] *n* bara.
cog [kɒg] *n* dente *m*.
cogent ['kəudʒənt] *adj* convincente.
coherent [kəu'hɪərənt] *adj* coerente.
coil [kɔɪl] *n* rotolo; (*ELEC*) bobina; (*contraceptive*) spirale *f* ♦ *vt* avvolgere.
coin [kɔɪn] *n* moneta ♦ *vt* (*word*)
coniare; ~**age** *n* sistema *m* monetario;
~**-box** (*BRIT*) *n* telefono a gettoni.
coincide [kəuɪn'saɪd] *vi* coincidere;
~**nce** [kəu'ɪnsɪdəns] *n* combinazione *f*.
Coke [kəuk] ® *n* coca.
coke [kəuk] *n* coke *m*.
colander ['kɒləndə*] *n* colino.
cold [kəuld] *adj* freddo(a) ♦ *n* freddo;
(*MED*) raffreddore *m*; **it's** ~ fa freddo;
to be ~ (*person*) aver freddo; (*object*)
essere freddo(a); **to catch** ~ prendere
freddo; **to catch a** ~ prendere un raffreddore; **in** ~ **blood** a sangue freddo;
~**-shoulder** *vt* trattare con freddezza;
~ **sore** *n* erpete *m*.
coleslaw ['kəulslɔ:] *n* insalata di cavolo
bianco.
colic ['kɒlɪk] *n* colica.
collapse [kə'læps] *vi* crollare ♦ *n* crollo;
(*MED*) collasso.
collapsible [kə'læpsəbl] *adj* pieghevole.
collar ['kɒlə*] *n* (*of coat, shirt*) colletto;
(*of dog, cat*) collare *m*; ~**bone** *n*
clavicola.
collateral [kə'lætərl] *n* garanzia.
colleague ['kɒli:g] *n* collega *m/f*.
collect [kə'lekt] *vt* (*gen*) raccogliere;
(*as a hobby*) fare collezione di; (*BRIT*:
call and pick up) prendere; (*money
owed, pension*) riscuotere; (*donations,
subscriptions*) fare una colletta di ♦ *vi*
adunarsi, riunirsi; ammucchiarsi; **to
call** ~ (*US*: *TEL*) fare una chiamata a
carico del destinatario; ~**ion** [kə'lekʃən]
n raccolta; collezione *f*; (*for money*)
colletta.
collector [kə'lektə*] *n* collezionista *m/f*;
(*of taxes*) esattore *m*.

college ['kɒlɪdʒ] *n* college *m inv*; (*of
technology etc*) istituto superiore.
collide [kə'laɪd] *vi*: **to** ~ (**with**) scontrarsi (con).
collie ['kɒlɪ] *n* (*dog*) collie *m inv*.
colliery ['kɒlɪərɪ] (*BRIT*) *n* miniera di
carbone.
collision [kə'lɪʒən] *n* collisione *f*, scontro.
colloquial [kə'ləukwɪəl] *adj* familiare.
colon ['kəulən] *n* (*sign*) due punti *mpl*;
(*MED*) colon *m inv*.
colonel ['kə:nl] *n* colonnello.
colonial [kə'ləunɪəl] *adj* coloniale.
colony ['kɒlənɪ] *n* colonia.
colour ['kʌlə*] (*US* **color**) *n* colore *m* ♦
vt colorare; (*tint, dye*) tingere; (*fig:
affect*) influenzare ♦ *vi* (*blush*)
arrossire; ~**s** *npl* (*of party, club*) colori
mpl; **in** ~ a colori; ~ **in** *vt* colorare; ~
bar *n* discriminazione *f* razziale (*in
locali etc*); ~**-blind** *adj* daltonico(a);
~**ed** *adj* (*photo*) a colori; (*person*) di
colore; ~ **film** *n* (*for camera*) pellicola
a colori; ~**ful** *adj* pieno(a) di colore, a
vivaci colori; (*personality*) colorato(a);
~**ing** *n* (*substance*) colorante *m*; (*complexion*) colorito; ~ **scheme** *n*
combinazione *f* di colori; ~ **television** *n*
televisione *f* a colori.
colt [kəult] *n* puledro.
column ['kɒləm] *n* colonna; ~**ist**
['kɒləmnɪst] *n* articolista *m/f*.
coma ['kəumə] *n* coma *m inv*.
comb [kəum] *n* pettine *m* ♦ *vt* (*hair*)
pettinare; (*area*) battere a tappeto.
combat ['kɒmbæt] *n* combattimento ♦ *vt*
combattere, lottare contro.
combination [kɒmbɪ'neɪʃən] *n*
combinazione *f*.
combine [*vb* kəm'baɪn, *n* 'kɒmbaɪn] *vt*: **to**
~ (**with**) combinare (con); (*one quality
with another*) unire (a) ♦ *vi* unirsi;
(*CHEM*) combinarsi ♦ *n* (*ECON*)
associazione *f*; ~ (**harvester**) *n* mieti-
trebbia.
come [kʌm] (*pt* **came**, *pp* **come**) *vi*
venire; arrivare; **to** ~ **to** (*decision etc*)
raggiungere; **I've** ~ **to like him** ha
cominciato a piacermi; **to** ~ **undone**

slacciarsi; **to ~ loose** allentarsi; ~
about *vi* succedere; ~ **across** *vt fus*
trovare per caso; ~ **away** *vi* venire
via; staccarsi; ~ **back** *vi* ritornare; ~
by *vt fus* (*acquire*) ottenere;
procurarsi; ~ **down** *vi* scendere;
(*prices*) calare; (*buildings*) essere
demolito(a); ~ **forward** *vi* farsi avanti;
presentarsi; ~ **from** *vt fus* venire da;
provenire da; ~ **in** *vi* entrare; ~ **in for**
vt fus (*criticism etc*) ricevere; ~ **into**
vt fus (*money*) ereditare; ~ **off** *vi*
(*button*) staccarsi; (*stain*) andar via;
(*attempt*) riuscire; ~ **on** *vi* (*pupil*,
work, *project*) fare progressi; (*lights*)
accendersi; (*electricity*) entrare in
funzione; ~ **on!** avanti!, andiamo!,
forza!; ~ **out** *vi* uscire; (*stain*) andare
via; ~ **round** *vi* (*after faint*, *operation*)
riprendere conoscenza, rinvenire; ~ **to**
vi rinvenire; ~ **up** *vi* (*sun*) salire;
(*problem*) sorgere; (*event*) essere in
arrivo; (*in conversation*) saltar fuori;
~ **up against** *vt fus* (*resistance*,
difficulties) urtare contro; ~ **up with**
vt fus: **he came up with an idea** venne
fuori con un'idea; ~ **upon** *vt fus*
trovare per caso; ~**back** *n* (*THEATRE
etc*) ritorno.
comedian [kə'mi:dɪən] *n* comico.
comedienne [kəmi:dɪ'ɛn] *n* attrice *f*
comica.
comedy ['kɔmɪdɪ] *n* commedia.
comeuppance [kʌm'ʌpəns] *n*: **to get
one's ~** ricevere ciò che si merita.
comfort ['kʌmfət] *n* comodità *f inv*,
benessere *m*; (*relief*) consolazione *f*,
conforto ♦ *vt* consolare, confortare; ~**s**
npl comodità *fpl*; ~**able** *adj*
comodo(a); (*financially*) agiato(a);
~**ably** *adv* (*sit etc*) comodamente;
(*live*) bene; ~ **station** (*US*) *n* gabinetti
mpl.
comic ['kɔmɪk] *adj* (*also*: ~**al**)
comico(a) ♦ *n* comico; (*BRIT*:
magazine) giornaletto; ~ **strip** *n*
fumetto.
coming ['kʌmɪŋ] *n* arrivo ♦ *adj* (*next*)
prossimo(a); (*future*) futuro(a); ~**(s)
and going(s)** *n(pl)* andirivieni *m inv*.

comma ['kɔmə] *n* virgola.
command [kə'mɑ:nd] *n* ordine *m*,
comando; (*MIL*: *authority*) comando;
(*mastery*) padronanza ♦ *vt* comandare;
to ~ sb to do ordinare a qn di fare;
~**eer** [kɔmən'dɪə*] *vt* requisire; ~**er** *n*
capo; (*MIL*) comandante *m*.
commando [kə'mɑ:ndəu] *n* commando
m inv; membro di un commando.
commence [kə'mɛns] *vt*, *vi* cominciare.
commend [kə'mɛnd] *vt* lodare;
raccomandare.
commensurate [kə'mɛnsərɪt] *adj*: ~
with proporzionato(a) a.
comment ['kɔmɛnt] *n* commento ♦ *vi*:
to ~ (on) fare commenti (su); ~**ary**
['kɔməntərɪ] *n* commentario; (*SPORT*)
radiocronaca; telecronaca; ~**ator**
['kɔməntɛɪtə*] *n* commentatore/trice;
radiocronista *m/f*; telecronista *m/f*.
commerce ['kɔmə:s] *n* commercio.
commercial [kə'mə:ʃəl] *adj*
commerciale ♦ *n* (*TV*, *RADIO*:
advertisement) pubblicità *f inv*; ~
radio/television *n* radio *f inv*/televisione
f privata.
commiserate [kə'mɪzəreɪt] *vi*: **to ~ with**
partecipare al dolore di.
commission [kə'mɪʃən] *n* commissione
f ♦ *vt* (*work of art*) commissionare; **out
of ~** (*NAUT*) in disarmo; ~**aire**
[kəmɪʃə'nɛə*] (*BRIT*) *n* (*at shop*, *cinema
etc*) portiere *m* in livrea; ~**er** *n*
(*POLICE*) questore *m*.
commit [kə'mɪt] *vt* (*act*) commettere;
(*to sb's care*) affidare; **to ~ o.s. (to do)**
impegnarsi (a fare); **to ~ suicide**
suicidarsi; ~**ment** *n* impegno;
promessa.
committee [kə'mɪtɪ] *n* comitato.
commodity [kə'mɔdɪtɪ] *n* prodotto,
articolo.
common ['kɔmən] *adj* comune; (*pej*)
volgare; (*usual*) normale ♦ *n* terreno
comune; **the C~s** (*BRIT*) *npl* la Camera
dei Comuni; **in ~** in comune; ~**er** *n*
cittadino/a (non nobile); ~ **law** *n* diritto
consuetudinario; ~**ly** *adv* comunemen-
te, usualmente; **C~ Market** *n* Mercato
Comune; ~**place** *adj* banale,

ordinario(a); **~room** n sala di riunione; (SCOL) sala dei professori; **~ sense** n buon senso; **the C~wealth** n il Commonwealth.

commotion [kə'məuʃən] n confusione f, tumulto.

communal ['kɔmjuːnl] adj (for common use) pubblico(a).

commune [n 'kɔmjuːn, vb kə'mjuːn] n (group) comune f ♦ vi: **to ~ with** mettersi in comunione con.

communicate [kə'mjuːnɪkeɪt] vt comunicare, trasmettere ♦ vi: **to ~ (with)** comunicare (con).

communication [kəmjuːnɪ'keɪʃən] n comunicazione f; **~ cord** (BRIT) n segnale m d'allarme.

communion [kə'mjuːnɪən] n (also: Holy C~) comunione f.

communiqué [kə'mjuːnɪkeɪ] n comunicato.

communism ['kɔmjunɪzəm] n comunismo; **communist** adj, n comunista m/f.

community [kə'mjuːnɪtɪ] n comunità f inv; **~ centre** n circolo ricreativo; **~ chest** (US) n fondo di beneficenza; **~ home** (BRIT) n riformatorio.

commutation ticket [kɔmjuˈteɪʃən-] (US) n biglietto di abbonamento.

commute [kə'mjuːt] vi fare il pendolare ♦ vt (LAW) commutare; **~r** n pendolare m/f.

compact [adj kəm'pækt, n 'kɔmpækt] adj compatto(a) ♦ n (also: powder ~) portacipria m inv; **~ disk** n compact disc m inv.

companion [kəm'pænɪən] n compagno/a; **~ship** n compagnia.

company ['kʌmpənɪ] n (also COMM, MIL, THEATRE) compagnia; **to keep sb ~** tenere compagnia a qn; **~ secretary** (BRIT) n segretario/a generale.

comparable ['kɔmpərəbl] adj simile.

comparative [kəm'pærətɪv] adj relativo(a); (adjective etc) comparativo(a); **~ly** adv relativamente.

compare [kəm'pɛə*] vt: **to ~ sth/sb with/to** confrontare qc/qn con/a ♦ vi: **to ~ (with)** reggere il confronto (con); **comparison** [-'pærɪsn] n confronto; **in**

comparison (with) in confronto (a).

compartment [kəm'pɑːtmənt] n compartimento; (RAIL) scompartimento.

compass ['kʌmpəs] n bussola; **~es** npl (MATH) compasso.

compassion [kəm'pæʃən] n compassione f.

compatible [kəm'pætɪbl] adj compatibile.

compel [kəm'pɛl] vt costringere, obbligare; **~ling** adj (fig: argument) irresistibile.

compensate ['kɔmpənseɪt] vt risarcire ♦ vi: **to ~ for** compensare; **compensation** [-'seɪʃən] n compensazione f; (money) risarcimento.

compère ['kɔmpɛə*] n presentatore/trice.

compete [kəm'piːt] vi (take part) concorrere; (vie): **to ~ (with)** fare concorrenza (a).

competent ['kɔmpɪtənt] adj competente.

competition [kɔmpɪ'tɪʃən] n gara; concorso; (ECON) concorrenza.

competitive [kəm'pɛtɪtɪv] adj (ECON) concorrenziale; (sport) agonistico(a); (person) che ha spirito di competizione; che ha spirito agonistico.

competitor [kəm'pɛtɪtə*] n concorrente m/f.

complacency [kəm'pleɪsnsɪ] n compiacenza di sé.

complain [kəm'pleɪn] vi lagnarsi, lamentarsi; **~t** n lamento; (in shop etc) reclamo; (MED) malattia.

complement [n 'kɔmplɪmənt, vb 'kɔmplɪment] n complemento; (especially of ship's crew etc) effettivo ♦ vt (enhance) accompagnarsi bene a; **~ary** [kɔmplɪ'mentərɪ] adj complementare.

complete [kəm'pliːt] adj completo(a) ♦ vt completare; (a form) riempire; **~ly** adv completamente; **completion** n completamento.

complex ['kɔmplɛks] adj complesso(a) ♦ n (PSYCH, buildings etc) complesso.

complexion [kəm'plɛkʃən] n (of face) carnagione f.

compliance [kəm'plaɪəns] n acquiescenza; **in** ~ **with** (*orders, wishes etc*) in conformità con.

complicate ['kɒmplɪkeɪt] *vt* complicare; ~**d** *adj* complicato(a); **complication** [-'keɪʃən] *n* complicazione *f*.

compliment [*n* 'kɒmplɪmənt, *vb* 'kɒmplɪment] *n* complimento ♦ *vt* fare un complimento a; ~**s** *npl* (*greetings*) complimenti *mpl*; rispetti *mpl*; **to pay sb a** ~ fare un complimento a qn; ~**ary** [-'mentərɪ] *adj* complimentoso(a), elogiativo(a); (*free*) in omaggio; ~**ary ticket** *n* biglietto omaggio.

comply [kəm'plaɪ] *vi*: **to** ~ **with** assentire a; conformarsi a.

component [kəm'pəʊnənt] *a* componente ♦ *n* componente *m*.

compose [kəm'pəʊz] *vt* (*form*): **to be** ~**d of** essere composto di; (*music, poem etc*) comporre; **to** ~ **o.s.** ricomporsi; ~**d** *adj* calmo(a); ~**r** *n* (*MUS*) compositore/trice.

composition [kɒmpə'zɪʃən] *n* composizione *f*.

composure [kəm'pəʊʒə*] *n* calma.

compound ['kɒmpaʊnd] *n* (*CHEM, LING*) composto; (*enclosure*) recinto ♦ *adj* composto(a); ~ **fracture** *n* frattura esposta.

comprehend [kɒmprɪ'hend] *vt* comprendere, capire; **comprehension** [-'henʃən] *n* comprensione *f*.

comprehensive [kɒmprɪ'hensɪv] *adj* comprensivo(a); ~ **policy** *n* (*INSURANCE*) polizza che copre tutti i rischi; ~ (**school**) (*BRIT*) *n* scuola *secondaria aperta a tutti*.

compress [*vb* kəm'pres, *n* 'kɒmpres] *vt* comprimere ♦ *n* (*MED*) compressa.

comprise [kəm'praɪz] *vt* (*also:* **be** ~**d of**) comprendere.

compromise ['kɒmprəmaɪz] *n* compromesso ♦ *vt* compromettere ♦ *vi* venire a un compromesso.

compulsion [kəm'pʌlʃən] *n* costrizione *f*.

compulsive [kəm'pʌlsɪv] *adj* (*liar, gambler*) che non riesce a controllarsi; (*viewing, reading*) cui non si può fare a meno.

compulsory [kəm'pʌlsərɪ] *adj* obbligatorio(a).

computer [kəm'pju:tə*] *n* computer *m inv*, elaboratore *m* elettronico; ~**ize** *vt* computerizzare; ~ **programmer** *n* programmatore/trice; ~ **programming** *n* programmazione *f* di computer; ~ **science** *n* informatica; **computing** *n* informatica.

comrade ['kɒmrɪd] *n* compagno/a; ~**ship** *n* cameratismo.

con [kɒn] (*inf*) *vt* truffare ♦ *n* truffa.

conceal [kən'si:l] *vt* nascondere.

concede [kən'si:d] *vt* ammettere.

conceit [kən'si:t] *n* presunzione *f*, vanità; ~**ed** *adj* presuntuoso(a), vanitoso(a).

conceive [kən'si:v] *vt* concepire ♦ *vi* concepire un bambino.

concentrate ['kɒnsəntreɪt] *vi* concentrarsi ♦ *vt* concentrare.

concentration [kɒnsən'treɪʃən] *n* concentrazione *f*; ~ **camp** *n* campo di concentramento.

concept ['kɒnsept] *n* concetto.

concern [kən'sə:n] *n* affare *m*; (*COMM*) azienda, ditta; (*anxiety*) preoccupazione *f* ♦ *vt* riguardare; **to be** ~**ed** (**about**) preoccuparsi (di); ~**ing** *prep* riguardo a, circa.

concert ['kɒnsət] *n* concerto; ~**ed** [kən'sə:tɪd] *adj* concertato(a); ~ **hall** *n* sala da concerti.

concertina [kɒnsə'ti:nə] *n* piccola fisarmonica.

concerto [kən'tʃə:təʊ] *n* concerto.

conclude [kən'klu:d] *vt* concludere; **conclusion** [-'klu:ʒən] *n* conclusione *f*; **conclusive** [-'klu:sɪv] *adj* conclusivo(a).

concoct [kən'kɒkt] *vt* inventare; ~**ion** [-'kɒkʃən] *n* miscuglio.

concourse ['kɒŋkɔ:s] *n* (*hall*) atrio.

concrete ['kɒŋkri:t] *n* calcestruzzo ♦ *adj* concreto(a); di calcestruzzo.

concur [kən'kə:*] *vi* concordare.

concurrently [kən'kʌrntlɪ] *adv* simultaneamente.

concussion [kən'kʌʃən] *n* commozione *f* cerebrale.

condemn [kən'dem] *vt* condannare;

(*building*) dichiarare pericoloso(a).
condensation [kɔndɛn'seɪʃən] *n* condensazione *f*.
condense [kən'dɛns] *vi* condensarsi ♦ *vt* condensare; **~d milk** *n* latte *m* condensato.
condescending [kɔndɪ'sɛndɪŋ] *adj* (*person*) che ha un'aria di superiorità.
condition [kən'dɪʃən] *n* condizione *f*; (*MED*) malattia ♦ *vt* condizionare; **on ~ that** a condizione che + *sub*, a condizione di; **~al** *adj* condizionale; **~er** *n* (*for hair*) balsamo; (*for fabrics*) ammorbidente *m*.
condolences [kən'dəʊlənsɪz] *npl* condoglianze *fpl*.
condom ['kɔndəm] *n* preservativo.
condominium [kɔndə'mɪnɪəm] (*US*) *n* condominio.
conducive [kən'djuːsɪv] *adj*: **~ to** favorevole a.
conduct [*n* 'kɔndʌkt, *vb* kən'dʌkt] *n* condotta ♦ *vt* condurre; (*manage*) dirigere; amministrare; (*MUS*) dirigere; **to ~ o.s.** comportarsi; **~ed tour** *n* gita accompagnata; **~or** *n* (*of orchestra*) direttore *m* d'orchestra; (*on bus*) bigliettaio; (*US: on train*) controllore *m*; (*ELEC*) conduttore *m*; **~ress** *n* (*on bus*) bigliettaia.
cone [kəʊn] *n* cono; (*BOT*) pigna; (*traffic*) ♥ birillo.
confectioner [kən'fɛkʃənə*] *n* pasticciere *m*; **~'s (shop)** *n* ≈ pasticceria; **~y** *n* dolciumi *mpl*.
confer [kən'fɔː*] *vt*: **to ~ sth on** conferire qc a ♦ *vi* conferire.
conference ['kɔnfərns] *n* congresso.
confess [kən'fɛs] *vt* confessare, ammettere ♦ *vi* confessare; **~ion** [-'fɛʃən] *n* confessione *f*.
confetti [kən'fɛtɪ] *n* coriandoli *mpl*.
confide [kən'faɪd] *vi*: **to ~ in** confidarsi con.
confidence ['kɔnfɪdns] *n* confidenza; (*trust*) fiducia; (*self-assurance*) sicurezza di sé; **in ~** (*speak, write*) in confidenza, confidenzialmente; **~ trick** *n* truffa; **confident** *adj* sicuro(a); sicuro(a) di sé; **confidential**

[kɔnfɪ'dɛnʃəl] *adj* riservato(a), confidenziale.
confine [kən'faɪn] *vt* limitare; (*shut up*) rinchiudere; **~d** *adj* (*space*) ristretto(a); **~ment** *n* prigionia; **~s** ['kɔnfaɪnz] *npl* confini *mpl*.
confirm [kən'fɜːm] *vt* confermare; **~ation** [kɔnfə'meɪʃən] *n* conferma; (*REL*) cresima; **~ed** *adj* inveterato(a).
confiscate ['kɔnfɪskeɪt] *vt* confiscare.
conflict [*n* 'kɔnflɪkt, *vb* kən'flɪkt] *n* conflitto ♦ *vi* essere in conflitto; **~ing** *adj* contrastante.
conform [kən'fɔːm] *vi*: **to ~ (to)** conformarsi (a).
confound [kən'faʊnd] *vt* confondere.
confront [kən'frʌnt] *vt* (*enemy, danger*) affrontare; **~ation** [kɔnfrən'teɪʃən] *n* scontro.
confuse [kən'fjuːz] *vt* (*one thing with another*) confondere; **~d** *adj* confuso(a); **confusing** *adj* che fa confondere; **confusion** [-'fjuːʒən] *n* confusione *f*.
congeal [kən'dʒiːl] *vi* (*blood*) congelarsi.
congenial [kən'dʒiːnɪəl] *adj* (*person*) simpatico(a); (*thing*) congeniale.
congested [kən'dʒɛstɪd] *adj* congestionato(a).
congestion [kən'dʒɛstʃən] *n* congestione *f*.
congratulate [kən'grætjuleɪt] *vt*: **to ~ sb (on)** congratularsi con qn (per *or* di); **congratulations** [-'leɪʃənz] *npl* auguri *mpl*; (*on success*) complimenti *mpl*, congratulazioni *fpl*.
congregate ['kɔŋgrɪgeɪt] *vi* congregarsi, riunirsi.
congress ['kɔŋgrɛs] *n* congresso; **~man** (*US*) *n* membro del Congresso.
conjecture [kən'dʒɛktʃə*] *n* congettura.
conjunction [kən'dʒʌŋkʃən] *n* congiunzione *f*.
conjunctivitis [kəndʒʌŋktɪ'vaɪtɪs] *n* congiuntivite *f*.
conjure ['kʌndʒə*] *vi* fare giochi di prestigio; **~ up** *vt* (*ghost, spirit*) evocare; (*memories*) rievocare; **~r** *n* prestidigitatore/trice, prestigiatore/trice.
conk out [kɔŋk-] (*inf*) *vi* andare in

panne.
con man n truffatore m.
connect [kə'nɛkt] vt connettere, collegare; (ELEC, TEL) collegare; (fig) associare ♦ vi (train): **to ~ with** essere in coincidenza con; **to be ~ed with** (associated) aver rapporti con; **~ion** [-ʃən] n relazione f, rapporto; (ELEC) connessione f; (train, plane) coincidenza; (TEL) collegamento.
connive [kə'naɪv] vi: **to ~ at** essere connivente in.
connoisseur [kɒnɪ'sə*] n conoscitore/trice.
conquer ['kɒŋkə*] vt conquistare; (feelings) vincere.
conquest ['kɒŋkwɛst] n conquista.
cons [kɒnz] npl see **convenience**; **pro**.
conscience ['kɒnʃəns] n coscienza.
conscientious [kɒnʃɪ'ɛnʃəs] adj coscienzioso(a).
conscious ['kɒnʃəs] adj consapevole; (MED) cosciente; **~ness** n consapevolezza; coscienza.
conscript ['kɒnskrɪpt] n coscritto; **~ion** [-'skrɪpʃən] n arruolamento (obbligatorio).
consent [kən'sɛnt] n consenso ♦ vi: **to ~ (to)** acconsentire (a).
consequence ['kɒnsɪkwəns] n conseguenza, risultato; importanza.
consequently ['kɒnsɪkwəntlɪ] adv di conseguenza, dunque.
conservation [kɒnsə'veɪʃən] n conservazione f.
conservative [kən'sə:vətɪv] adj conservatore(trice); (cautious) cauto(a); **C~** (BRIT) adj, n (POL) conservatore(trice).
conservatory [kən'sə:vətrɪ] n (greenhouse) serra; (MUS) conservatorio.
conserve [kən'sə:v] vt conservare ♦ n conserva.
consider [kən'sɪdə*] vt considerare; (take into account) tener conto di; **to ~ doing sth** considerare la possibilità di fare qc.
considerable [kən'sɪdərəbl] adj considerevole, notevole; **considerably**

adv notevolmente, decisamente.
considerate [kən'sɪdərɪt] adj premuroso(a).
consideration [kənsɪdə'reɪʃən] n considerazione f.
considering [kən'sɪdərɪŋ] prep in considerazione di.
consign [kən'saɪn] vt: **to ~ to** (sth unwanted) relegare in; (person: to sb's care) consegnare a; (: to poverty) condannare a; **~ment** n (of goods) consegna; spedizione f.
consist [kən'sɪst] vi: **to ~ of** constare di, essere composto(a) di.
consistency [kən'sɪstənsɪ] n consistenza; (fig) coerenza.
consistent [kən'sɪstənt] adj coerente.
consolation [kɒnsə'leɪʃən] n consolazione f.
console[1] [kən'səul] vt consolare.
console[2] ['kɒnsəul] n quadro di comando.
consonant ['kɒnsənənt] n consonante f.
consortium [kən'sɔ:tɪəm] n consorzio.
conspicuous [kən'spɪkjuəs] adj cospicuo(a).
conspiracy [kən'spɪrəsɪ] n congiura, cospirazione f.
constable ['kʌnstəbl] (BRIT) n ≈ poliziotto, agente m di polizia; **chief ~** ≈ questore m.
constabulary [kən'stæbjulərɪ] n forze fpl dell'ordine.
constant ['kɒnstənt] adj costante; continuo(a); **~ly** adv costantemente; continuamente.
constipated ['kɒnstɪpeɪtɪd] adj stitico(a).
constipation [kɒnstɪ'peɪʃən] n stitichezza.
constituency [kən'stɪtjuənsɪ] n collegio elettorale.
constituent [kən'stɪtjuənt] n elettore/trice; (part) elemento componente.
constitution [kɒnstɪ'tju:ʃən] n costituzione f; **~al** adj costituzionale.
constraint [kən'streɪnt] n costrizione f.
construct [kən'strʌkt] vt costruire; **~ion** [-ʃən] n costruzione f; **~ive** adj costruttivo(a).

construe [kən'stru:] vt interpretare.

consul ['kɔnsl] n console m; ~**ate** ['kɔnsjulıt] n consolato.

consult [kən'sʌlt] vt consultare; ~**ant** n (MED) consulente m medico; (other specialist) consulente; ~**ation** [-'teıʃən] n (MED) consulto; (discussion) consultazione f; ~**ing room** (BRIT) n ambulatorio.

consume [kən'sju:m] vt consumare; ~**r** n consumatore/trice; ~**r goods** npl beni mpl di consumo; ~**r society** n società dei consumi.

consumption [kən'sʌmpʃən] n consumo.

cont. abbr = **continued**.

contact ['kɔntækt] n contatto; (person) conoscenza ♦ vt mettersi in contatto con; ~ **lenses** npl lenti fpl a contatto.

contagious [kən'teıdʒəs] adj (also fig) contagioso(a).

contain [kən'teın] vt contenere; **to** ~ **o.s.** contenersi; ~**er** n recipiente m; (for shipping etc) container m inv.

contaminate [kən'tæmıneıt] vt contaminare.

cont'd abbr = **continued**.

contemplate ['kɔntəmpleıt] vt contemplare; (consider) pensare a (or di).

contemporary [kən'tempərərı] adj, n contemporaneo(a).

contempt [kən'tempt] n disprezzo; ~ **of court** (LAW) oltraggio alla Corte; ~**ible** adj deprecabile; ~**uous** adj sdegnoso(a).

contend [kən'tend] vt: **to** ~ **that** sostenere che ♦ vi: **to** ~ **with** lottare contro; ~**er** n contendente m/f; concorrente m/f.

content¹ ['kɔntent] n contenuto; ~**s** npl (of box, case etc) contenuto; **(table of)** ~**s** indice m.

content² [kən'tent] adj contento(a), soddisfatto(a) ♦ vt contentare, soddisfare; ~**ed** adj contento(a), soddisfatto(a).

contention [kən'tenʃən] n contesa; (assertion) tesi f inv.

contentment [kən'tentmənt] n contentezza.

contest [n 'kɔntest, vb kən'test] n lotta;

(competition) gara, concorso ♦ vt contestare; impugnare; (compete for) essere in lizza per; ~**ant** [kən'testənt] n concorrente m/f; (in fight) avversario/a.

context ['kɔntekst] n contesto.

continent ['kɔntınənt] n continente m; **the C~** (BRIT) l'Europa continentale; ~**al** [-'nentl] adj continentale; ~**al quilt** (BRIT) n piumino.

contingency [kən'tındʒənsı] n eventualità f inv.

continual [kən'tınjuəl] adj continuo(a).

continuation [kəntınju'eıʃən] n continuazione f; (after interruption) ripresa; (of story) seguito.

continue [kən'tınju:] vi continuare ♦ vt continuare; (start again) riprendere.

continuity [kɔntı'nju:ıtı] n continuità; (TV, CINEMA) (ordine m della) sceneggiatura.

continuous [kən'tınjuəs] adj continuo(a); ininterrotto(a); ~ **stationery** n carta a moduli continui.

contort [kən'tɔ:t] vt contorcere.

contour ['kɔntuə*] n contorno, profilo; (also: ~ line) curva di livello.

contraband ['kɔntrəbænd] n contrabbando.

contraceptive [kɔntrə'septıv] adj contraccettivo(a) ♦ n contraccettivo.

contract [n 'kɔntrækt, vb kən'trækt] n contratto ♦ vi (become smaller) contrarsi; (COMM): **to** ~ **to do sth** fare un contratto per fare qc ♦ vt (illness) contrarre; ~**ion** [-ʃən] n contrazione f; ~**or** n imprenditore m.

contradict [kɔntrə'dıkt] vt contraddire.

contraption [kən'træpʃən] (pej) n aggeggio.

contrary¹ ['kɔntrərı] adj contrario(a); (unfavourable) avverso(a), contrario(a) ♦ n contrario; **on the** ~ al contrario; **unless you hear to the** ~ salvo contrordine.

contrary² [kən'treərı] adj (perverse) bisbetico(a).

contrast [n 'kɔntra:st, vb kən'tra:st] n contrasto ♦ vt mettere in contrasto; **in** ~ **to** contrariamente a.

contribute [kən'trıbju:t] vi contribuire ♦

vt: **to ~ £10/an article to** dare 10 sterline/un articolo a; **to ~ to** contribuire a; (*newspaper*) scrivere per; **contribution** [kɔntrɪ'bjuːʃən] *n* contributo; **contributor** *n* (*to newspaper*) collaboratore/trice.

contrivance [kən'traɪvəns] *n* congegno; espediente *m*.

contrive [kən'traɪv] *vi*: **to ~ to do** fare in modo di fare.

control [kən'trəul] *vt* controllare; (*firm, operation etc*) dirigere ♦ *n* controllo; **~s** *npl* (*of vehicle etc*) comandi *mpl*; (*governmental*) controlli *mpl*; **under ~** sotto controllo; **to be in ~ of** avere il controllo di; **to go out of ~** (*car*) non rispondere ai comandi; (*situation*) sfuggire di mano; **~ panel** *n* quadro dei comandi; **~ room** *n* (*NAUT, MIL*) sala di comando; (*RADIO, TV*) sala di regia; **~ tower** *n* (*AVIAT*) torre *f* di controllo.

controversial [kɔntrə'vəːʃl] *adj* controverso(a), polemico(a).

controversy ['kɔntrəvəːsɪ] *n* controversia, polemica.

convalesce [kɔnvə'lɛs] *vi* rimettersi in salute.

convene [kən'viːn] *vt* convocare ♦ *vi* convenire, adunarsi.

convenience [kən'viːnɪəns] *n* comodità *f inv*; **at your ~** a suo comodo; **all modern ~s**, (*BRIT*) **all mod cons** tutte le comodità moderne.

convenient [kən'viːnɪənt] *adj* conveniente, comodo(a).

convent ['kɔnvənt] *n* convento.

convention [kən'vɛnʃən] *n* convenzione *f*; (*meeting*) convegno; **~al** *adj* convenzionale.

conversant [kən'vəːsnt] *adj*: **to be ~ with** essere al corrente di; essere pratico(a) di.

conversation [kɔnvə'seɪʃən] *n* conversazione *f*; **~al** *adj* non formale.

converse¹ [kən'vəːs] *vi* conversare.

converse² ['kɔnvəːs] *n* contrario, opposto; **~ly** [-'vəːslɪ] *adv* al contrario, per contro.

convert [*vb* kən'vəːt, *n* 'kɔnvəːt] *vt* (*COMM, REL*) convertire; (*alter*) tra-

sformare ♦ *n* convertito/a; **~ible** *n* macchina decappottabile.

convex ['kɔnvɛks] *adj* convesso(a).

convey [kən'veɪ] *vt* trasportare; (*thanks*) comunicare; (*idea*) dare; **~or belt** *n* nastro trasportatore.

convict [*vb* kən'vɪkt, *n* 'kɔnvɪkt] *vt* dichiarare colpevole ♦ *n* carcerato/a; **~ion** [-ʃən] *n* condanna; (*belief*) convinzione *f*.

convince [kən'vɪns] *vt* convincere, persuadere; **convincing** *adj* convincente.

convoluted [kɔnvə'luːtɪd] *adj* (*argument etc*) involuto(a).

convoy ['kɔnvɔɪ] *n* convoglio.

convulse [kən'vʌls] *vt*: **to be ~d with laughter** contorcersi dalle risa.

coo [kuː] *vi* tubare.

cook [kuk] *vt* cucinare, cuocere ♦ *vi* cuocere; (*person*) cucinare ♦ *n* cuoco/a; **~book** *n* libro di cucina; **~er** *n* fornello, cucina; **~ery** *n* cucina; **~ery book** (*BRIT*) *n* = **~book**; **~ie** (*US*) *n* biscotto; **~ing** *n* cucina.

cool [kuːl] *adj* fresco(a); (*not afraid, calm*) calmo(a); (*unfriendly*) freddo(a) ♦ *vt* raffreddare; (*room*) rinfrescare ♦ *vi* (*water*) raffreddarsi; (*air*) rinfrescarsi.

coop [kuːp] *n* stia ♦ *vt*: **to ~ up** (*fig*) rinchiudere.

cooperate [kəu'ɔpəreɪt] *vi* cooperare, collaborare; **cooperation** [-'reɪʃən] *n* cooperazione *f*, collaborazione *f*.

cooperative [kəu'ɔpərətɪv] *adj* cooperativo(a) ♦ *n* cooperativa.

coordinate [*vb* kəu'ɔːdɪneɪt, *n* kəu'ɔːdɪnət] *vt* coordinare ♦ *n* (*MATH*) coordinata; **~s** *npl* (*clothes*) coordinati *mpl*.

co-ownership [kəu'əunəʃɪp] *n* comproprietà.

cop [kɔp] (*inf*) *n* sbirro.

cope [kəup] *vi*: **to ~ with** (*problems*) far fronte a.

copper ['kɔpə*] *n* rame *m*; (*inf: policeman*) sbirro; **~s** *npl* (*coins*) spiccioli *mpl*.

coppice ['kɔpɪs] *n* bosco ceduo.

copse [kɔps] n bosco ceduo.
copulate ['kɔpjuleɪt] vi accoppiarsi.
copy ['kɔpɪ] n copia ♦ vt copiare; **~right** n diritto d'autore.
coral ['kɔrəl] n corallo; **~ reef** n barriera corallina.
cord [kɔːd] n corda; (ELEC) filo; (fabric) velluto a coste.
cordial ['kɔːdɪəl] adj cordiale ♦ n (BRIT) cordiale m.
cordon ['kɔːdn] n cordone m; **~ off** vt fare cordone a.
corduroy ['kɔːdərɔɪ] n fustagno.
core [kɔː*] n (of fruit) torsolo; (of organization etc) cuore m ♦ vt estrarre il torsolo da.
cork [kɔːk] n sughero; (of bottle) tappo; **~screw** n cavatappi m inv.
corn [kɔːn] n (BRIT: wheat) grano; (US: maize) granturco; (on foot) callo; **~ on the cob** (CULIN) pannocchia cotta.
corned beef ['kɔːnd-] n carne f di manzo in scatola.
corner ['kɔːnə*] n angolo; (AUT) curva ♦ vt intrappolare; mettere con le spalle al muro; (COMM: market) accaparrare ♦ vi prendere una curva; **~stone** n pietra angolare.
cornet ['kɔːnɪt] n (MUS) cornetta; (BRIT: of ice-cream) cono.
cornflakes ['kɔːnfleɪks] npl fiocchi mpl di granturco.
cornflour ['kɔːnflauə*] (BRIT) n farina finissima di granturco.
cornstarch ['kɔːnstɑːtʃ] (US) n = cornflour.
Cornwall ['kɔːnwəl] n Cornovaglia.
corny ['kɔːnɪ] (inf) adj trito(a).
coronary ['kɔrənərɪ] n: **~ (thrombosis)** trombosi f coronaria.
coronation [kɔrə'neɪʃən] n incoronazione f.
coroner ['kɔrənə*] n magistrato incaricato di indagare la causa di morte in circostanze sospette.
coronet ['kɔrənɪt] n diadema m.
corporal ['kɔːpərl] n caporalmaggiore m ♦ adj: **~ punishment** pena corporale.
corporate ['kɔːpərɪt] adj costituito(a) (in corporazione); comune.

corporation [kɔːpə'reɪʃən] n (of town) consiglio comunale; (COMM) ente m.
corps [kɔː*, pl kɔːz] n inv corpo.
corpse [kɔːps] n cadavere m.
corral [kə'rɑːl] n recinto.
correct [kə'rɛkt] adj (accurate) corretto(a), esatto(a); (proper) corretto(a) ♦ vt correggere; **~ion** [-ʃən] n correzione f.
correspond [kɔrɪs'pɔnd] vi corrispondere; **~ence** n corrispondenza; **~ence course** n corso per corrispondenza; **~ent** n corrispondente m/f.
corridor ['kɔrɪdɔː*] n corridoio.
corrode [kə'rəud] vt corrodere ♦ vi corrodersi.
corrugated ['kɔrəgeɪtɪd] adj increspato(a); ondulato(a); **~ iron** n lamiera di ferro ondulata.
corrupt [kə'rʌpt] adj corrotto(a); (COMPUT) alterato(a) ♦ vt corrompere; **~ion** [-ʃən] n corruzione f.
corset ['kɔːsɪt] n busto.
Corsica ['kɔːsɪkə] n Corsica.
cosh [kɔʃ] (BRIT) n randello (corto).
cosmetic [kɔz'metɪk] n cosmetico ♦ adj (fig: measure etc) superficiale.
cosset ['kɔsɪt] vt vezzeggiare.
cost [kɔst] (pt, pp cost) n costo ♦ vi stare; (find out the ~ of) stabilire il prezzo di; **~s** npl (COMM, LAW) spese fpl; **how much does it ~?** quanto costa?; **at all ~s** a ogni costo.
co-star ['kəu-] n attore/trice della stessa importanza del protagonista.
cost-effective adj conveniente.
costly ['kɔstlɪ] adj costoso(a), caro(a).
cost-of-living adj: **~ allowance** indennità f inv di contingenza.
cost price (BRIT) n prezzo all'ingrosso.
costume ['kɔstjuːm] n costume m; (lady's suit) tailleur m inv; (BRIT: also: **swimming ~**) costume da bagno; **~ jewellery** n bigiotteria.
cosy ['kəuzɪ] (US **cozy**) adj intimo(a); **I'm very ~ here** sto proprio bene qui.
cot [kɔt] n (BRIT: child's) lettino; (US: campbed) brandina.
cottage ['kɔtɪdʒ] n cottage m inv; **~ cheese** n fiocchi mpl di latte magro.

cotton ['kɔtn] n cotone m; ~ **on to**
(inf) vt fus afferrare; ~ **candy** (US) n
zucchero filato; ~ **wool** (BRIT) n cotone
idrofilo.
couch [kautʃ] n sofà m inv.
couchette [ku:'ʃet] n (on train, boat)
cuccetta.
cough [kɔf] vi tossire ♦ n tosse f; ~
drop n pasticca per la tosse.
could [kud] pt of **can**; ~**n't** = **could not**.
council ['kaunsl] n consiglio; **city** or
town ~ consiglio comunale; ~ **estate**
(BRIT) n quartiere m di case popolari;
~ **house** (BRIT) n casa popolare; ~**lor**
n consigliere/a.
counsel ['kaunsl] n avvocato;
consultazione f ♦ vt consigliare; ~**lor** n
consigliere/a; (US) avvocato.
count [kaunt] vt, vi contare ♦ n (of
votes etc) conteggio; (of pollen etc)
livello; (nobleman) conte m; ~ **on** vt
fus contare su; ~**down** n conto alla
rovescia.
countenance ['kauntɪnəns] n volto,
aspetto ♦ vt approvare.
counter ['kauntə*] n banco ♦ vt opporsi
a ♦ adv: ~ **to** contro; in opposizione a;
~**act** vt agire in opposizione a; (poison
etc) annullare gli effetti di; ~**espionage** n controspionaggio.
counterfeit ['kauntəfɪt] n contraffazione
f, falso ♦ vt contraffare, falsificare ♦
adj falso(a).
counterfoil ['kauntəfɔɪl] n matrice f.
countermand [kauntə'mɑ:nd] vt
annullare.
counterpart ['kauntəpɑ:t] n (of
document etc) copia; (of person) corrispondente m/f.
counter-productive [-prə'dʌktɪv] adj
controproducente.
countersign ['kauntəsaɪn] vt con-
trofirmare.
countess ['kauntɪs] n contessa.
countless ['kauntlɪs] adj innumerevole.
country ['kʌntrɪ] n paese m; (native
land) patria; (as opposed to town)
campagna; (region) regione f; ~ **dancing** (BRIT) n danza popolare; ~ **house**
n villa in campagna; ~**man** n

(national) compatriota m; (rural)
contadino; ~**side** n campagna.
county ['kauntɪ] n contea.
coup [ku:] (pl **coups**) n colpo; (also: ~
d'état) colpo di Stato.
couple ['kʌpl] n coppia; **a** ~ **of** un paio
di.
coupon ['ku:pɔn] n buono; (detachable
form) coupon m inv.
courage ['kʌrɪdʒ] n coraggio.
courgette [kuə'ʒet] (BRIT) n zucchina.
courier ['kurɪə*] n corriere m; (for
tourists) guida.
course [kɔ:s] n corso; (of ship) rotta;
(for golf) campo; (part of meal) piatto;
of ~ senz'altro, naturalmente; ~ **of**
action modo d'agire; **a** ~ **of treatment**
(MED) una cura.
court [kɔ:t] n corte f; (TENNIS) campo ♦
vt (woman) fare la corte a; **to take to**
~ citare in tribunale.
courteous ['kɔ:tɪəs] adj cortese.
courtesan [kɔ:tɪ'zæn] n cortigiana.
courtesy ['kɔ:təsɪ] n cortesia; (by) ~ **of**
per gentile concessione di.
court-house (US) n palazzo di giustizia.
courtier ['kɔ:tɪə*] n cortigiano/a.
court-martial [-'mɑ:ʃəl] (pl **courts-
martial**) n corte f marziale.
courtroom ['kɔ:trum] n tribunale m.
courtyard ['kɔ:tjɑ:d] n cortile m.
cousin ['kʌzn] n cugino/a; **first** ~ cugino
di primo grado.
cove [kəuv] n piccola baia.
covenant ['kʌvənənt] n accordo.
cover ['kʌvə*] vt coprire; (book, table)
rivestire; (include) comprendere;
(PRESS) fare un servizio su ♦ n (of pan)
coperchio; (over furniture) fodera; (of
bed) copriletto; (of book) copertina;
(shelter) riparo; (COMM, INSURANCE, of
spy) copertura; **to take** ~ (shelter)
ripararsi; **under** ~ al riparo; **under** ~
of darkness protetto dall'oscurità;
under separate ~ (COMM) a parte, in
plico separato; ~ **up** vi: **to** ~ **up for sb**
coprire qn; ~**age** n (PRESS, RADIO, TV);
to give full ~**age to sth** fare un ampio
servizio su qc; ~ **charge** n coperto;

~**ing** n copertura; ~**ing letter** (US ~ **letter**) n lettera d'accompagnamento; ~ **note** n (INSURANCE) polizza (di assicurazione) provvisoria.

covert ['kʌvət] adj (hidden) nascosto(a); (glance) furtivo(a).

cover-up n occultamento (di informazioni).

covet ['kʌvɪt] vt bramare.

cow [kau] n vacca ♦ vt (person) intimidire.

coward ['kauəd] n vigliacco/a; ~**ice** [-ɪs] n vigliaccheria; ~**ly** adj vigliacco(a).

cowboy ['kaubɔɪ] n cow-boy m inv.

cower ['kauə*] vi acquattarsi.

coxswain ['kɔksn] (abbr: **cox**) n timoniere m.

coy [kɔɪ] adj falsamente timido(a).

cozy ['kəuzɪ] (US) adj = **cosy**.

CPA (US) n abbr = **certified public accountant**.

crab [kræb] n granchio; ~ **apple** n mela selvatica.

crack [kræk] n fessura, crepa; incrinatura; (noise) schiocco; (: of gun) scoppio ♦ vt spaccare; incrinare; (whip) schioccare; (nut) schiacciare; (problem) risolvere; (code) decifrare ♦ adj (troops) fuori classe; **to ~ a joke** fare una battuta; ~ **down on** vt fus porre freno a; ~ **up** vi crollare; ~**er** n cracker m inv; petardo.

crackle ['krækl] vi crepitare.

cradle ['kreɪdl] n culla.

craft [krɑ:ft] n mestiere m; (cunning) astuzia; (boat) naviglio; ~**sman** n artigiano; ~**smanship** n abilità; ~**y** adj furbo(a), astuto(a).

crag [kræg] n roccia.

cram [kræm] vt (fill): **to ~ sth with** riempire qc di; (put): **to ~ sth into** stipare qc in ♦ vi (for exams) prepararsi (in gran fretta).

cramp [kræmp] n crampo; ~**ed** adj ristretto(a).

crampon ['kræmpən] n (CLIMBING) rampone m.

cranberry ['krænbərɪ] n mirtillo.

crane [kreɪn] n gru f inv.

crank [kræŋk] n manovella; (person)

persona stramba; ~**shaft** n albero a gomiti.

cranny ['krænɪ] n see **nook**.

crash [kræʃ] n fragore m; (of car) incidente m; (of plane) caduta; (of business etc) crollo ♦ vt fracassare ♦ vi (plane) fracassarsi; (car) avere un incidente; (two cars) scontrarsi; (business etc) fallire, andare in rovina; ~ **course** n corso intensivo; ~ **helmet** n casco; ~ **landing** n atterraggio di fortuna.

crate [kreɪt] n cassa.

cravat(e) [krə'væt] n fazzoletto da collo.

crave [kreɪv] vt, vi: **to ~ (for)** desiderare ardentemente.

crawl [krɔ:l] vi strisciare carponi; (vehicle) avanzare lentamente ♦ n (SWIMMING) crawl m.

crayfish ['kreɪfɪʃ] n inv (freshwater) gambero (d'acqua dolce); (saltwater) gambero.

crayon ['kreɪən] n matita colorata.

craze [kreɪz] n mania.

crazy ['kreɪzɪ] adj matto(a); (inf: keen): ~ **about sb** pazzo(a) di qn; ~ **about sth** matto(a) per qc; ~ **paving** (BRIT) n lastricato a mosaico irregolare.

creak [kri:k] vi cigolare, scricchiolare.

cream [kri:m] n crema; (fresh) panna ♦ adj (colour) color crema inv; ~ **cake** n torta alla panna; ~ **cheese** n formaggio fresco; ~**y** adj cremoso(a).

crease [kri:s] n grinza; (deliberate) piega ♦ vt sgualcire ♦ vi sgualcirsi.

create [kri:'eɪt] vt creare; **creation** [-ʃən] n creazione f; **creative** adj creativo(a).

creature ['kri:tʃə*] n creatura.

crèche [kreʃ] n asilo infantile.

credence ['kri:dns] n: **to lend** or **give ~ to** prestar fede a.

credentials [krɪ'dɛnʃlz] npl credenziali fpl.

credit ['krɛdɪt] n credito; onore m ♦ vt (COMM) accreditare; (believe: also): **give ~ to**) credere, prestar fede a; ~**s** npl (CINEMA) titoli mpl; **to ~ sb with** (fig) attribuire a qn; **to be in ~** (person) essere creditore (trice); (bank account) essere coperto(a); ~ **card** n

creed 56 crow

creed [kri:d] n credo; dottrina.
creek [kri:k] n insenatura; (US) piccolo fiume m.
creep [kri:p] (pt, pp **crept**) vi avanzare furtivamente (or pian piano); ~**er** n pianta rampicante; ~**y** adj (frightening) che fa accapponare la pelle.
crematoria [krɛməˈtɔ:rɪə] npl of **crematorium**.
crematorium [krɛməˈtɔ:rɪəm] (pl **crematoria**) n forno crematorio.
crêpe [kreɪp] n crespo; ~ **bandage** (BRIT) n fascia elastica.
crept [krɛpt] pt, pp of **creep**.
crescent [ˈkrɛsnt] n (shape) mezzaluna; (street) strada semicircolare.
cress [krɛs] n crescione m.
crest [krɛst] n cresta; (of coat of arms) cimiero; ~**fallen** adj mortificato(a).
Crete [kri:t] n Creta.
crevasse [krɪˈvæs] n crepaccio.
crevice [ˈkrɛvɪs] n fessura, crepa.
crew [kru:] n equipaggio; **to have a** ~-**cut** avere i capelli a spazzola; ~-**neck** n girocollo.
crib [krɪb] n culla ♦ vt (inf) copiare.
crick [krɪk] n crampo.
cricket [ˈkrɪkɪt] n (insect) grillo; (game) cricket m.
crime [kraɪm] n crimine m; **criminal** [ˈkrɪmɪnl] adj, n criminale m/f.
crimson [ˈkrɪmzn] adj color cremisi inv.
cringe [krɪndʒ] vi acquattarsi; (in embarrassment) sentirsi sprofondare.
crinkle [ˈkrɪŋkl] vt arricciare, increspare.
cripple [ˈkrɪpl] n zoppo/a ♦ vt azzoppare.
crises [ˈkraɪsi:z] npl of **crisis**.
crisis [ˈkraɪsɪs] (pl **crises**) n crisi f inv.
crisp [krɪsp] adj croccante; (fig) frizzante; vivace; deciso(a); ~**s** (BRIT) npl patatine fpl.
criss-cross [ˈkrɪs-] adj incrociato(a).
criteria [kraɪˈtɪərɪə] npl of **criterion**.
criterion [kraɪˈtɪərɪən] (pl **criteria**) n criterio.
critic [ˈkrɪtɪk] n critico; ~**al** adj critico(a); ~**ally** adv (speak etc)

criticamente; ~**ally ill** gravemente malato; ~**ism** [ˈkrɪtɪsɪzm] n critica; ~**ize** [ˈkrɪtɪsaɪz] vt criticare.
croak [krəuk] vi gracchiare; (frog) gracidare.
crochet [ˈkrəuʃeɪ] n lavoro all'uncinetto.
crockery [ˈkrɔkərɪ] n vasellame m.
crocodile [ˈkrɔkədaɪl] n coccodrillo.
crocus [ˈkrəukəs] n croco.
croft [krɔft] (BRIT) n piccolo podere m.
crony [ˈkrəunɪ] (inf: pej) n compare m.
crook [kruk] n truffatore m; (of shepherd) bastone m; ~**ed** [ˈkrukɪd] adj curvo(a), storto(a); (action) disonesto(a).
crop [krɔp] n (produce) coltivazione f; (amount produced) raccolto; (riding ~) frustino ♦ vt (hair) rapare; ~ **up** vi presentarsi.
croquette [krəˈkɛt] n crocchetta.
cross [krɔs] n croce f; (BIOL) incrocio ♦ vt (street etc) attraversare; (arms, legs, BIOL) incrociare; (cheque) sbarrare ♦ adj di cattivo umore; ~ **out** vt cancellare; ~ **over** vi attraversare; ~**bar** n traversa; ~**country** (race) n cross-country m inv; ~-**examine** vt (LAW) interrogare in contraddittorio; ~-**eyed** adj strabico(a); ~**fire** n fuoco incrociato; ~**ing** n incrocio; (sea passage) traversata; (also: pedestrian ~ing) passaggio pedonale; ~**ing guard** (US) n dipendente comunale che aiuta i bambini ad attraversare la strada; ~ **purposes** npl: **to be at** ~ **purposes** non parlare della stessa cosa; ~-**reference** n rinvio, rimando; ~**roads** n incrocio; ~-**section** n sezione f trasversale; (in population) settore m rappresentativo; ~**walk** (US) n strisce fpl pedonali, passaggio pedonale; ~**wind** n vento di traverso; ~**word** n cruciverba m inv.
crotch [krɔtʃ] n (ANAT) inforcatura; (of garment) pattina.
crotchet [ˈkrɔtʃɪt] n (MUS) semiminima.
crotchety [ˈkrɔtʃɪtɪ] adj (person) burbero(a).
crouch [krautʃ] vi acquattarsi; rannicchiarsi.
crow [krəu] n (bird) cornacchia; (of

cock) canto del gallo ♦ *vi* (*cock*) cantare.

crowbar ['krəuba:*] *n* piede *m* di porco.

crowd [kraud] *n* folla ♦ *vt* affollare, stipare ♦ *vi*: **to ~ round/in** affollarsi intorno a/in; **~ed** *adj* affollato(a); **~ed with** stipato(a) di.

crown [kraun] *n* corona; (*of head*) calotta cranica; (*of hat*) cocuzzolo; (*of hill*) cima ♦ *vt* incoronare; (*fig: career*) coronare; **~ jewels** *npl* gioielli *mpl* della Corona; **~ prince** *n* principe *m* ereditario.

crow's feet *npl* zampe *fpl* di gallina.

crucial ['kru:ʃl] *adj* cruciale, decisivo(a).

crucifix ['kru:sɪfɪks] *n* crocifisso; **~ion** [-'fɪkʃən] *n* crocifissione *f*.

crude [kru:d] *adj* (*materials*) greggio(a); non raffinato(a); (*fig: basic*) crudo(a), primitivo(a); (: *vulgar*) rozzo(a), grossolano(a); **~ (oil)** *n* (petrolio) greggio.

cruel ['kruəl] *adj* crudele; **~ty** *n* crudeltà *f inv*.

cruise [kru:z] *n* crociera ♦ *vi* andare a velocità di crociera; (*taxi*) circolare; **~r** *n* incrociatore *m*.

crumb [krʌm] *n* briciola.

crumble ['krʌmbl] *vt* sbriciolare ♦ *vi* sbriciolarsi; (*plaster etc*) sgretolarsi; (*land, earth*) franare; (*building, fig*) crollare; **crumbly** *adj* friabile.

crumpet ['krʌmpɪt] *n* specie di frittella.

crumple ['krʌmpl] *vt* raggrinzare, spiegazzare.

crunch [krʌntʃ] *vt* sgranocchiare; (*underfoot*) scricchiolare ♦ *n* (*fig*) punto *or* momento cruciale; **~y** *adj* croccante.

crusade [kru:'seɪd] *n* crociata.

crush [krʌʃ] *n* folla; (*love*): **to have a ~ on sb** avere una cotta per qn; (*drink*): **lemon ~** spremuta di limone ♦ *vt* schiacciare; (*crumple*) sgualcire.

crust [krʌst] *n* crosta.

crutch [krʌtʃ] *n* gruccia.

crux [krʌks] *n* nodo.

cry [kraɪ] *vi* piangere; (*shout: also: ~ out*) urlare ♦ *n* urlo, grido; **~ off** *vi* ritirarsi.

cryptic ['krɪptɪk] *adj* ermetico(a).

crystal ['krɪstl] *n* cristallo; **~-clear** *adj* cristallino(a).

cub [kʌb] *n* cucciolo; (*also: ~ scout*) lupetto.

Cuba ['kju:bə] *n* Cuba.

cubbyhole ['kʌbɪhəul] *n* angolino.

cube [kju:b] *n* cubo ♦ *vt* (*MATH*) elevare al cubo; **cubic** *adj* cubico(a); (*metre, foot*) cubo(a); **cubic capacity** *n* cilindrata.

cubicle ['kju:bɪkl] *n* scompartimento separato; cabina.

cuckoo ['kuku:] *n* cucù *m inv*; **~ clock** *n* orologio a cucù.

cucumber ['kju:kʌmbə*] *n* cetriolo.

cuddle ['kʌdl] *vt* abbracciare, coccolare ♦ *vi* abbracciarsi.

cue [kju:] *n* (*snooker ~*) stecca; (*THEATRE etc*) segnale *m*.

cuff [kʌf] *n* (*BRIT: of shirt, coat etc*) polsino; (*US: of trousers*) risvolto; **off the ~** improvvisando; **~link** *n* gemello.

cuisine [kwɪ'zi:n] *n* cucina.

cul-de-sac ['kʌldəsæk] *n* vicolo cieco.

cull [kʌl] *vt* (*ideas etc*) scegliere ♦ *n* (*of animals*) abbattimento selettivo.

culminate ['kʌlmɪneɪt] *vi*: **to ~ in** culminare con; **culmination** [-'neɪʃən] *n* culmine *m*.

culottes [kju:'lɔts] *npl* gonna *f* pantalone *inv*.

culpable ['kʌlpəbl] *adj* colpevole.

culprit ['kʌlprɪt] *n* colpevole *m/f*.

cult [kʌlt] *n* culto.

cultivate ['kʌltɪveɪt] *vt* (*also fig*) coltivare; **cultivation** [-'veɪʃən] *n* coltivazione *f*.

cultural ['kʌltʃərəl] *adj* culturale.

culture ['kʌltʃə*] *n* (*also fig*) cultura; **~d** *adj* colto(a).

cumbersome ['kʌmbəsəm] *adj* ingombrante.

cunning ['kʌnɪŋ] *n* astuzia, furberia ♦ *adj* astuto(a), furbo(a).

cup [kʌp] *n* tazza; (*prize, of bra*) coppa.

cupboard ['kʌbəd] *n* armadio.

cup-tie (*BRIT*) *n* partita di coppa.

curate ['kjuərɪt] *n* cappellano.

curator [kjuə'reɪtə*] n direttore m (di museo etc).

curb [kə:b] vt tenere a freno ♦ n freno; (US) bordo del marciapiede.

curdle ['kə:dl] vi cagliare.

cure [kjuə*] vt guarire; (CULIN) trattare; affumicare; essiccare ♦ n rimedio.

curfew ['kə:fju:] n coprifuoco.

curio ['kjuərɪəu] n curiosità f inv.

curiosity [kjuərɪ'ɔsɪtɪ] n curiosità.

curious ['kjuərɪəs] adj curioso(a).

curl [kə:l] n riccio ♦ vt ondulare; (tightly) arricciare ♦ vi arricciarsi; ~ up vi rannicchiarsi; ~er n bigodino.

curly ['kə:lɪ] adj ricciuto(a).

currant ['kʌrnt] n (dried) sultanina; (bush, fruit) ribes m inv.

currency ['kʌrnsɪ] n moneta; **to gain** ~ (fig) acquistare larga diffusione.

current ['kʌrnt] adj corrente ♦ n corrente f; ~ **account** (BRIT) n conto corrente; ~ **affairs** npl attualità fpl; ~**ly** adv attualmente.

curricula [kə'rɪkjulə] npl of **curriculum**.

curriculum [kə'rɪkjuləm] (pl ~s or **curricula**) n curriculum m inv; ~ **vitae** n curriculum vitae m inv.

curry ['kʌrɪ] n curry m inv ♦ vt: **to** ~ **favour with** cercare di attirarsi i favori di; ~ **powder** n curry m.

curse [kə:s] vt maledire ♦ vi bestemmiare ♦ n maledizione f; bestemmia.

cursor ['kə:sə*] n (COMPUT) cursore m.

cursory ['kə:sərɪ] adj superficiale.

curt [kə:t] adj secco(a).

curtail [kə:'teɪl] vt (freedom etc) limitare; (visit etc) accorciare; (expenses etc) ridurre, decurtare.

curtain ['kə:tn] n tenda; (THEATRE) sipario.

curts(e)y ['kə:tsɪ] vi fare un inchino or una riverenza.

curve [kə:v] n curva ♦ vi curvarsi.

cushion ['kuʃən] n cuscino ♦ vt (shock) fare da cuscinetto a.

custard ['kʌstəd] n (for pouring) crema.

custodian [kʌs'təudɪən] n custode m/f.

custody ['kʌstədɪ] n (of child) tutela; **to**

take **into** ~ (suspect) mettere in detenzione preventiva.

custom ['kʌstəm] n costume m, consuetudine f; (COMM) clientela; ~**ary** adj consueto(a).

customer ['kʌstəmə*] n cliente m/f.

customized ['kʌstəmaɪzd] adj (car etc) fuoriserie inv.

custom-made adj (clothes) fatto(a) su misura; (other goods) fatto(a) su ordinazione.

customs ['kʌstəmz] npl dogana; ~ **duty** n tassa doganale; ~ **officer** n doganiere m.

cut [kʌt] (pt, pp **cut**) vt tagliare; (shape, make) intagliare; (reduce) ridurre ♦ vi tagliare ♦ n taglio; (in salary etc) riduzione f; **to** ~ **a tooth** mettere un dente; (reduce) ~ **down** vt (tree etc) abbattere ♦ vt fus (also: ~ down on) ridurre; ~ **off** vt tagliare; (fig) isolare; ~ **out** vt tagliare fuori; eliminare; ritagliare; ~ **up** vt (paper, meat) tagliare a pezzi; ~**back** n riduzione f.

cute [kju:t] adj (sweet) carino(a).

cuticle ['kju:tɪkl] n (on nail) pellicina, cuticola.

cutlery ['kʌtlərɪ] n posate fpl.

cutlet ['kʌtlɪt] n costoletta; (nut etc ~) cotoletta vegetariana.

cut: ~**out** n interruttore m; (cardboard ~out) ritaglio; ~-**price** (US ~-**rate**) adj a prezzo ridotto; ~**throat** n assassino ♦ adj (competition) spietato(a).

cutting ['kʌtɪŋ] adj tagliente ♦ n (from newspaper) ritaglio (di giornale); (from plant) talea.

CV n abbr = **curriculum vitae**.

cwt abbr = **hundredweight**(s).

cyanide ['saɪənaɪd] n cianuro.

cycle ['saɪkl] n ciclo; (bicycle) bicicletta ♦ vi andare in bicicletta.

cycling ['saɪklɪŋ] n ciclismo.

cyclist ['saɪklɪst] n ciclista m/f.

cygnet ['sɪgnɪt] n cigno giovane.

cylinder ['sɪlɪndə*] n cilindro; ~-**head gasket** n guarnizione f della testata del cilindro.

cymbals ['sɪmblz] *npl* cembali *mpl*.
cynic ['sɪnɪk] *n* cinico/a; ~**al** *adj*
cinico(a); ~**ism** ['sɪnɪsɪzəm] *n* cinismo.
Cyprus ['saɪprəs] *n* Cipro.
cyst [sɪst] *n* cisti *f inv*.
cystitis [sɪs'taɪtɪs] *n* cistite *f*.
czar [zɑ:*] *n* zar *m inv*.
Czech [tʃɛk] *adj* ceco(a) ♦ *n* ceco/a;
(*LING*) ceco.
Czechoslovakia [tʃɛkəslə'vækɪə] *n* Ceco-
slovacchia; ~**n** *adj, n* cecoslovacco(a).

D

D [di:] *n* (*MUS*) re *m*.
dab [dæb] *vt* (*eyes, wound*) tamponare;
(*paint, cream*) applicare (con leggeri
colpetti).
dabble ['dæbl] *vi*: **to** ~ **in** occuparsi (da
dilettante) di.
dad(dy) [dæd(ɪ)] (*inf*) *n* babbo, papà *m
inv*.
daffodil ['dæfədɪl] *n* trombone *m*, giun-
chiglia.
daft [dɑ:ft] *adj* sciocco(a).
dagger ['dægə*] *n* pugnale *m*.
daily ['deɪlɪ] *adj* quotidiano(a),
giornaliero(a) ♦ *n* quotidiano ♦ *adv* tutti
i giorni.
dainty ['deɪntɪ] *adj* delicato(a),
grazioso(a).
dairy ['dɛərɪ] *n* (*BRIT: shop*) latteria;
(*on farm*) caseificio ♦ *adj* caseario(a);
~ **farm** *n* caseificio; ~ **products** *npl*
latticini *mpl*; ~ **store** (*US*) *n* latteria.
dais ['deɪɪs] *n* pedana, palco.
daisy ['deɪzɪ] *n* margherita; ~ **wheel** *n*
(*on printer*) margherita.
dale [deɪl] (*BRIT*) *n* valle *f*.
dam [dæm] *n* diga ♦ *vt* sbarrare; costruire dighe su.
damage ['dæmɪdʒ] *n* danno, danni *mpl*;
(*fig*) danno ♦ *vt* danneggiare; ~**s** *npl*
(*LAW*) danni.
damn [dæm] *vt* condannare; (*curse*)
maledire ♦ *n* (*inf*): **I don't give a** ~ non
me ne frega niente ♦ *adj* (*inf: also*:
~**ed**): **this** ~ ... questo maledetto ...; ~
(**it**)! accidenti!; ~**ing** *adj* (*evidence*)

schiacciante.
damp [dæmp] *adj* umido(a) ♦ *n* umidità,
umido ♦ *vt* (*also*: ~**en**: *cloth, rag*)
inumidire, bagnare; (: *enthusiasm etc*)
spegnere.
damson ['dæmzən] *n* susina dama-
schina.
dance [dɑ:ns] *n* danza, ballo; (*ball*)
ballo ♦ *vi* ballare; ~ **hall** *n* dancing *m
inv*, sala da ballo; ~**r** *n* danzatore/trice;
(*professional*) ballerino/a.
dancing ['dɑ:nsɪŋ] *n* danza, ballo.
dandelion ['dændɪlaɪən] *n* dente *m* di
leone.
dandruff ['dændrəf] *n* forfora.
Dane [deɪn] *n* danese *m/f*.
danger ['deɪndʒə*] *n* pericolo; **there is a**
~ **of fire** c'è pericolo di incendio; **in** ~
in pericolo; **he was in** ~ **of falling** ri-
schiava di cadere; ~**ous** *adj*
pericoloso(a).
dangle ['dæŋgl] *vt* dondolare; (*fig*) far
balenare ♦ *vi* pendolare.
Danish ['deɪnɪʃ] *adj* danese ♦ *n* (*LING*)
danese *m*.
dapper ['dæpə*] *adj* lindo(a).
dare [dɛə*] *vt*: **to** ~ **sb to do** sfidare qn
a fare ♦ *vi*: **to** ~ (**to**) **do sth** osare fare
qc; **I** ~ **say** (*I suppose*) immagino
(che); ~**devil** *n* scavezzacollo *m/f*; **daring** *adj* audace, ardito(a) ♦ *n* audacia.
dark [dɑ:k] *adj* (*night, room*) buio(a),
scuro(a); (*colour, complexion*)
scuro(a); (*fig*) cupo(a), tetro(a),
nero(a) ♦ *n*: **in the** ~ al buio; **in the** ~
about (*fig*) all'oscuro di; **after** ~ a notte
fatta; ~**en** *vt* (*colour*) scurire ♦ *vi*
(*sky, room*) oscurarsi; ~ **glasses** *npl*
occhiali *mpl* scuri; ~**ness** *n* oscurità,
buio; ~ **room** *n* camera oscura.
darling ['dɑ:lɪŋ] *adj* caro(a) ♦ *n* tesoro.
darn [dɑ:n] *vt* rammendare.
dart [dɑ:t] *n* freccetta; (*SEWING*) pince *f
inv* ♦ *vi*: **to** ~ **towards** precipitarsi
verso; **to** ~ **away/along** sfrecciare via/
lungo; ~**board** *n* bersaglio (per
freccette); ~**s** *n* tiro al bersaglio (con
freccette).
dash [dæʃ] *n* (*sign*) lineetta; (*small
quantity*) punta ♦ *vt* (*missile*) gettare;

(*hopes*) infrangere ♦ *vi*: **to ~ towards** precipitarsi verso; **~ away** *or* **off** *vi* scappare via.

dashboard ['dæʃbɔːd] *n* (*AUT*) cruscotto.

dashing ['dæʃɪŋ] *adj* ardito(a).

data ['deɪtə] *npl* dati *mpl*; **~base** *n* base *f* di dati, data base *m inv*; **~ processing** *n* elaborazione *f* (elettronica) dei dati.

date [deɪt] *n* data; appuntamento; (*fruit*) dattero ♦ *vt* datare; (*person*) uscire con; **~ of birth** data di nascita; **to ~** (*until now*) fino a oggi; **~d** *adj* passato(a) di moda.

daub [dɔːb] *vt* imbrattare.

daughter ['dɔːtə*] *n* figlia; **~-in-law** *n* nuora.

daunting ['dɔːntɪŋ] *adj* non invidiabile.

dawdle ['dɔːdl] *vi* bighellonare.

dawn [dɔːn] *n* alba ♦ *vi* (*day*) spuntare; (*fig*): **it ~ed on him that ...** gli è venuto in mente che ....

day [deɪ] *n* giorno; (*as duration*) giornata; (*period of time, age*) tempo, epoca; **the ~ before** il giorno avanti *or* prima; **the ~ after, the following ~** il giorno dopo *or* seguente; **the ~ after tomorrow** dopodomani; **the ~ before yesterday** l'altroieri; **by ~** di giorno; **~break** *n* spuntar *m* del giorno; **~dream** *vi* sognare a occhi aperti; **~light** *n* luce *f* del giorno; **~ return** (*BRIT*) *n* biglietto giornaliero di andata e ritorno; **~time** *n* giorno; **~-to-~** *adj* (*life, organization*) quotidiano(a).

daze [deɪz] *vt* (*subject: drug*) inebetire; (: *blow*) stordire ♦ *n*: **in a ~** inebetito(a); stordito(a).

dazzle ['dæzl] *vt* abbagliare.

DC *abbr* (= *direct current*) c.c.

D-day *n* giorno dello sbarco alleato in Normandia.

dead [dɛd] *adj* morto(a); (*numb*) intirizzito(a); (*telephone*) muto(a); (*battery*) scarico(a) ♦ *adv* assolutamente, perfettamente ♦ *npl*: **the ~** i morti; **he was shot ~** fu colpito a morte; **~ tired** stanco(a) morto(a); **to stop ~** fermarsi di colpo; **~en** *vt* (*blow, sound*) ammortire; **~ end** *n* vicolo

cieco; **~ heat** *n* (*SPORT*): **to finish in a ~ heat** finire alla pari; **~line** *n* scadenza; **~lock** *n* punto morto; **~ loss** *n*: **to be a ~ loss** (*inf: person, thing*) non valere niente; **~ly** *adj* mortale; (*weapon, poison*) micidiale; **~pan** *adj* a faccia impassibile.

deaf [dɛf] *adj* sordo(a); **~en** *vt* assordare; **~ness** *n* sordità.

deal [diːl] (*pt, pp* **dealt**) *n* accordo; (*business* ~) affare *m* ♦ *vt* (*blow, cards*) dare; **a great ~ (of)** molto(a); **~ in** *vt fus* occuparsi di; **~ with** *vt fus* (*COMM*) fare affari con, trattare con; (*handle*) occuparsi di; (*be about: book etc*) trattare di; **~er** *n* commerciante *m/f*; **~ings** *npl* (*COMM*) relazioni *fpl*; (*relations*) rapporti *mpl*; **dealt** [dɛlt] *pt, pp* of **deal**.

dean [diːn] *n* (*REL*) decano; (*SCOL*) preside *m* di facoltà (*or* di collegio).

dear [dɪə*] *adj* caro(a) ♦ *n*: **my ~** caro mio/cara mia ♦ *excl*: **~ me!** Dio mio!; **D~ Sir/Madam** (*in letter*) Egregio Signore/Egregia Signora; **D~ Mr/Mrs X** Gentile Signor/Signora X; **~ly** *adv* (*love*) moltissimo; (*pay*) a caro prezzo.

death [dɛθ] *n* morte *f*; (*ADMIN*) decesso; **~ certificate** *n* atto di decesso; **~ly** *adj* di morte; **~ penalty** *n* pena di morte; **~ rate** *n* indice *m* di mortalità; **~ toll** *n* vittime *fpl*.

debacle [dɪ'bækl] *n* fiasco.

debar [dɪ'bɑː*] *vt*: **to ~ sb from doing** impedire a qn di fare.

debase [dɪ'beɪs] *vt* (*currency*) adulterare; (*person*) degradare.

debatable [dɪ'beɪtəbl] *adj* discutibile.

debate [dɪ'beɪt] *n* dibattito ♦ *vt* dibattere; discutere.

debauchery [dɪ'bɔːtʃərɪ] *n* dissolutezza.

debit ['dɛbɪt] *n* debito ♦ *vt*: **to ~ a sum to sb** *or* **to sb's account** addebitare una somma a qn.

debris ['dɛbriː] *n* detriti *mpl*.

debt [dɛt] *n* debito; **to be in ~** essere indebitato(a); **~or** *n* debitore/trice.

debunk [diː'bʌŋk] *vt* (*theory, claim*) smentire.

début ['deɪbjuː] *n* debutto.

decade ['dɛkeɪd] *n* decennio.

decadence ['dɛkədəns] *n* decadenza.

decaffeinated [dɪ'kæfɪneɪtɪd] *adj* decaffeinato(a).

decanter [dɪ'kæntə*] *n* caraffa.

decay [dɪ'keɪ] *n* decadimento; (*also*: *tooth* ~) carie *f* ♦ *vi* (*rot*) imputridire.

deceased [dɪ'si:st] *n* defunto/a.

deceit [dɪ'si:t] *n* inganno; ~**ful** *adj* ingannevole, perfido(a).

deceive [dɪ'si:v] *vt* ingannare.

December [dɪ'sɛmbə*] *n* dicembre *m*.

decent ['di:sənt] *adj* decente; (*respectable*) per bene; (*kind*) gentile.

deception [dɪ'sɛpʃən] *n* inganno.

deceptive [dɪ'sɛptɪv] *adj* ingannevole.

decide [dɪ'saɪd] *vt* (*person*) far prendere una decisione a; (*question, argument*) risolvere, decidere ♦ *vi* decidere, decidersi; **to ~ to do/that** decidere di fare/che; **to ~ on** decidere per; ~**d** *adj* (*resolute*) deciso(a); (*clear, definite*) netto(a), chiaro(a); ~**dly** [-dɪdlɪ] *adv* indubbiamente; decisamente.

decimal ['dɛsɪməl] *adj* decimale ♦ *n* decimale *m*; ~ **point** *n* ≈ virgola.

decipher [dɪ'saɪfə*] *vt* decifrare.

decision [dɪ'sɪʒən] *n* decisione *f*.

decisive [dɪ'saɪsɪv] *adj* decisivo(a); (*person*) deciso(a).

deck [dɛk] *n* (*NAUT*) ponte *m*; (*of bus*): **top** ~ imperiale *m*; (*record* ~) piatto; (*of cards*) mazzo; ~**chair** *n* sedia a sdraio.

declaration [dɛklə'reɪʃən] *n* dichiarazione *f*.

declare [dɪ'klɛə*] *vt* dichiarare.

decline [dɪ'klaɪn] *n* (*decay*) declino; (*lessening*) ribasso ♦ *vt* declinare; rifiutare ♦ *vi* declinare; diminuire.

decode [di:'kəud] *vt* decifrare.

decompose [di:kəm'pəuz] *vi* decomporre.

décor ['deɪkɔ:*] *n* decorazione *f*.

decorate ['dɛkəreɪt] *vt* (*adorn, give a medal to*) decorare; (*paint and paper*) tinteggiare e tappezzare; **decoration** [-'reɪʃən] *n* (*medal etc, adornment*) decorazione *f*; **decorator** *n* decoratore *m*.

decorum [dɪ'kɔ:rəm] *n* decoro.

decoy ['di:kɔɪ] *n* zimbello.

decrease [*n* 'di:kri:s, *vb* di:'kri:s] *n* diminuzione *f* ♦ *vt, vi* diminuire.

decree [dɪ'kri:] *n* decreto; ~ **nisi** [-'naɪsaɪ] *n* sentenza provvisoria di divorzio.

dedicate ['dɛdɪkeɪt] *vt* consacrare; (*book etc*) dedicare.

dedication [dɛdɪ'keɪʃən] *n* (*devotion*) dedizione *f*; (*in book etc*) dedica.

deduce [dɪ'dju:s] *vt* dedurre.

deduct [dɪ'dʌkt] *vt*: **to ~ sth (from)** dedurre qc (da); ~**ion** [dɪ'dʌkʃən] *n* deduzione *f*.

deed [di:d] *n* azione *f*, atto; (*LAW*) atto.

deem [di:m] *vt* giudicare, ritenere.

deep [di:p] *adj* profondo(a); **4 metres ~** profondo(a) 4 metri ♦ *adv*: **spectators stood 20** ~ c'erano 20 file di spettatori; ~**en** *vt* (*hole*) approfondire ♦ *vi* approfondirsi; (*darkness*) farsi più buio; ~**-freeze** *n* congelatore *m*; ~**-fry** *vt* friggere in olio abbondante; ~**ly** *adv* profondamente; ~**-sea diving** *n* immersione *f* in alto mare; ~**-seated** *adj* radicato(a).

deer [dɪə*] *n inv*: **the** ~ i cervidi; (**red**) ~ cervo; (**fallow**) ~ daino; (**roe**) ~ capriolo; ~**skin** *n* pelle *f* di daino.

deface [dɪ'feɪs] *vt* imbrattare.

default [dɪ'fɔ:lt] *n* (*COMPUT*: *also*: ~ *value*) default *m inv*; **by** ~ (*SPORT*) per abbandono.

defeat [dɪ'fi:t] *n* sconfitta ♦ *vt* (*team, opponents*) sconfiggere; ~**ist** *adj, n* disfattista *m/f*.

defect [*n* 'di:fɛkt, *vb* dɪ'fɛkt] *n* difetto ♦ *vi*: **to** ~ **to the enemy** passare al nemico; ~**ive** [dɪ'fɛktɪv] *adj* difettoso(a).

defence [dɪ'fɛns] (*US* **defense**) *n* difesa; ~**less** *adj* senza difesa.

defend [dɪ'fɛnd] *vt* difendere; ~**ant** *n* imputato/a; ~**er** *n* difensore/a.

defense [dɪ'fɛns] (*US*) *n* = **defence**.

defensive [dɪ'fɛnsɪv] *adj* difensivo(a) ♦ *n*: **on the** ~ sulla difensiva.

defer [dɪ'fə:*] *vt* (*postpone*) differire, rinviare.

defiance [dɪ'faɪəns] *n* sfida; **in** ~ **of** a dispetto di.

defiant [dɪ'faɪənt] *adj* (*attitude*) di sfida; (*person*) ribelle.

deficiency [dɪ'fɪʃənsɪ] *n* deficienza; carenza.

deficit ['dɛfɪsɪt] *n* deficit *m inv*.

defile [dɪ'faɪl] *vt* deturpare.

define [dɪ'faɪn] *vt* definire.

definite ['dɛfɪnɪt] *adj* (*fixed*) definito(a), preciso(a); (*clear, obvious*) ben definito(a), esatto(a); (*LING*) determinativo(a); **he was ~ about it** ne era sicuro; ~**ly** *adv* indubbiamente.

definition [dɛfɪ'nɪʃən] *n* definizione *f*.

deflate [di:'fleɪt] *vt* sgonfiare.

deflect [dɪ'flɛkt] *vt* deflettere, deviare.

deformed [dɪ'fɔːmd] *adj* deforme.

defraud [dɪ'frɔːd] *vt* defraudare.

defrost [di:'frɒst] *vt* (*fridge*) disgelare; ~**er** (*US*) *n* (*demister*) sbrinatore *m*.

deft [dɛft] *adj* svelto(a), destro(a).

defunct [dɪ'fʌŋkt] *adj* che non esiste più.

defuse [di:'fju:z] *vt* disinnescare; (*fig*) distendere.

defy [dɪ'faɪ] *vt* sfidare; (*efforts etc*) resistere a; **it defies description** supera ogni descrizione.

degenerate [*vb* dɪ'dʒɛnəreɪt, *adj* dɪ'dʒɛnərɪt] *vi* degenerare ♦ *adj* degenere.

degree [dɪ'griː] *n* grado; (*SCOL*) laurea (universitaria); **a (first) ~ in maths** una laurea in matematica; **by ~s** (*gradually*) gradualmente, a poco a poco; **to some ~** fino a un certo punto, in certa misura.

dehydrated [di:haɪ'dreɪtɪd] *adj* disidratato(a); (*milk, eggs*) in polvere.

de-ice [di:'aɪs] *vt* (*windscreen*) disgelare.

deign [deɪn] *vi*: **to ~ to do** degnarsi di fare.

deity ['di:ɪtɪ] *n* divinità *f inv*.

dejected [dɪ'dʒɛktɪd] *adj* abbattuto(a), avvilito(a).

delay [dɪ'leɪ] *vt* ritardare ♦ *vi*: **to ~ (in doing sth)** ritardare (a fare qc) ♦ *n* ritardo; **to be ~ed** subire un ritardo; (*person*) essere trattenuto(a).

delectable [dɪ'lɛktəbl] *adj* (*person, food*)

delizioso(a).

delegate [*n* 'dɛlɪgɪt, *vb* 'dɛlɪgeɪt] *n* delegato/a ♦ *vt* delegare; **delegation** [-'geɪʃən] *n* (*group*) delegazione *f*; (*by manager*) delega.

delete [dɪ'liːt] *vt* cancellare.

deliberate [*adj* dɪ'lɪbərɪt, *vb* dɪ'lɪbəreɪt] *adj* (*intentional*) intenzionale; (*slow*) misurato(a) ♦ *vi* deliberare, riflettere; ~**ly** *adv* (*on purpose*) deliberatamente.

delicacy ['dɛlɪkəsɪ] *n* delicatezza.

delicate ['dɛlɪkɪt] *adj* delicato(a).

delicatessen [dɛlɪkə'tɛsn] *n* ≈ salumeria.

delicious [dɪ'lɪʃəs] *adj* delizioso(a), squisito(a).

delight [dɪ'laɪt] *n* delizia, gran piacere *m* ♦ *vt* dilettare; **to take (a) ~ in** dilettarsi in; ~**ed** *adj*: ~**ed (at** *or* **with)** contentissimo(a) (di), felice (di); ~**ed to do** felice di fare; ~**ful** *adj* delizioso(a); incantevole.

delinquent [dɪ'lɪŋkwənt] *adj*, *n* delinquente *m/f*.

delirious [dɪ'lɪrɪəs] *adj*: **to be ~** delirare.

deliver [dɪ'lɪvə*] *vt* (*mail*) distribuire; (*goods*) consegnare; (*speech*) pronunciare; (*MED*) far partorire; ~**y** *n* distribuzione *f*; consegna; (*of speaker*) dizione *f*; (*MED*) parto.

delude [dɪ'luːd] *vt* illudere.

deluge ['dɛljuːdʒ] *n* diluvio.

delusion [dɪ'luːʒən] *n* illusione *f*.

delve [dɛlv] *vi*: **to ~ into** frugare in; (*subject*) far ricerche in.

demand [dɪ'mɑːnd] *vt* richiedere; (*rights*) rivendicare ♦ *n* domanda; (*claim*) rivendicazione *f*; **in ~** ricercato(a), richiesto(a); **on ~** a richiesta; ~**ing** *adj* (*boss*) esigente; (*work*) impegnativo(a).

demean [dɪ'miːn] *vt*: **to ~ o.s.** umiliarsi.

demeanour [dɪ'miːnə*] (*US* **demeanor**) *n* comportamento; contegno.

demented [dɪ'mɛntɪd] *adj* demente, impazzito(a).

demise [dɪ'maɪz] *n* decesso.

demister [di:'mɪstə*] (*BRIT*) *n* (*AUT*) sbrinatore *m*.

demo ['dɛməu] (*inf*) *n abbr* (= *demonstration*) manifestazione *f*.

democracy [dɪ'mɔkrəsɪ] *n* democrazia.

democrat ['dɛməkræt] *n* democratico/a; **~ic** [dɛmə'krætɪk] *adj* democratico(a).

demolish [dɪ'mɔlɪʃ] *vt* demolire.

demonstrate ['dɛmənstreɪt] *vt* dimostrare, provare ♦ *vi* dimostrare, manifestare; **demonstration** [-'streɪʃən] *n* dimostrazione *f*; (*POL*) dimostrazione, manifestazione *f*; **demonstrator** *n* (*POL*) dimostrante *m/f*; (*COMM*) dimostratore/trice.

demote [dɪ'məut] *vt* far retrocedere.

demure [dɪ'mjuə*] *adj* contegnoso(a).

den [dɛn] *n* tana, covo; (*room*) buco.

denatured alcohol [di:'neɪtʃəd-] (*US*) *n* alcool *m inv* denaturato.

denial [dɪ'naɪəl] *n* diniego; rifiuto.

denim ['dɛnɪm] *n* tessuto di cotone ritorto; **~s** *npl* (*jeans*) blue jeans *mpl*.

Denmark ['dɛnmɑ:k] *n* Danimarca.

denomination [dɪnɔmɪ'neɪʃən] *n* (*money*) valore *m*; (*REL*) confessione *f*.

denounce [dɪ'nauns] *vt* denunciare.

dense [dɛns] *adj* fitto(a); (*smoke*) denso(a); (*inf*: *person*) ottuso(a), duro(a).

density ['dɛnsɪtɪ] *n* densità *f inv*.

dent [dɛnt] *n* ammaccatura ♦ *vt* (*also*: *make a ~ in*) ammaccare.

dental ['dɛntl] *adj* dentale; **~ surgeon** *n* medico *m* dentista.

dentist ['dɛntɪst] *n* dentista *m/f*; **~ry** *n* odontoiatria.

dentures ['dɛntʃəz] *npl* dentiera *f*.

deny [dɪ'naɪ] *vt* negare; (*refuse*) rifiutare.

deodorant [di:'əudərənt] *n* deodorante *m*.

depart [dɪ'pɑ:t] *vi* partire; **to ~ from** (*fig*) deviare da.

department [dɪ'pɑ:tmənt] *n* (*COMM*) reparto; (*SCOL*) sezione *f*, dipartimento; (*POL*) ministero; **~ store** *n* grande magazzino.

departure [dɪ'pɑ:tʃə*] *n* partenza; (*fig*): **~ from** deviazione *f* da; **a new ~** una svolta (decisiva); **~ lounge** *n* (*at airport*) sala d'attesa.

depend [dɪ'pɛnd] *vi*: **to ~ on** dipendere da; (*rely on*) contare su; **it ~s** dipende; **~ing on the result ...** a seconda del risultato ...; **~able** *adj* fidato(a); (*car etc*) affidabile; **~ant** *n* persona a carico; **~ent** *adj*: **to be ~ent on** dipendere da; (*child*, *relative*) essere a carico di ♦ *n* = **~ant**.

depict [dɪ'pɪkt] *vt* (*in picture*) dipingere; (*in words*) descrivere.

depleted [dɪ'pli:tɪd] *adj* diminuito(a).

deploy [dɪ'plɔɪ] *vt* dispiegare.

depopulation ['di:pɔpju'leɪʃən] *n* spopolamento.

deport [dɪ'pɔ:t] *vt* deportare; espellere; **~ment** [dɪ'pɔ:tmənt] *n* portamento.

depose [dɪ'pəuz] *vt* deporre.

deposit [dɪ'pɔzɪt] *n* (*COMM*, *GEO*) deposito; (*of ore, oil*) giacimento; (*CHEM*) sedimento; (*part payment*) acconto; (*for hired goods etc*) cauzione *f* ♦ *vt* depositare; dare in acconto; mettere *or* lasciare in deposito; **~ account** *n* conto vincolato.

depot ['dɛpəu] *n* deposito; (*US*) stazione *f* ferroviaria.

depreciate [dɪ'pri:ʃɪeɪt] *vi* svalutarsi.

depress [dɪ'prɛs] *vt* deprimere; (*price*, *wages*) abbassare; (*press down*) premere; **~ed** *adj* (*person*) depresso(a), abbattuto(a); (*price*) in ribasso; (*industry*) in crisi; **~ing** *adj* deprimente; **~ion** [dɪ'prɛʃən] *n* depressione *f*.

deprivation [dɛprɪ'veɪʃən] *n* privazione *f*.

deprive [dɪ'praɪv] *vt*: **to ~ sb of** privare qn di; **~d** *adj* disgraziato(a).

depth [dɛpθ] *n* profondità *f inv*; **in the ~s of** nel profondo di; nel cuore di; **out of one's ~** (*in water*) dove non si tocca; (*fig*) a disagio.

deputize ['dɛpjutaɪz] *vi*: **to ~ for** svolgere le funzioni di.

deputy ['dɛpjutɪ] *adj*: **~ head** (*BRIT*: *SCOL*) vicepreside *m/f* ♦ *n* (*assistant*) vice *m/f inv*; (*US*: *also*: **~ sheriff**) vicesceriffo.

derail [dɪ'reɪl] *vt*: **to be ~ed** deragliare.

deranged [dɪ'reɪndʒd] *adj*: **to be**

(mentally) ~ essere pazzo(a).
derby ['dɑːbɪ] (US) n (bowler hat)
bombetta.
derelict ['dɛrɪlɪkt] adj abbandonato(a).
derisory [dɪ'raɪsərɪ] adj (sum)
irrisorio(a); (laughter, person)
beffardo(a).
derive [dɪ'raɪv] vt: to ~ sth from
derivare qc da; trarre qc da ♦ vi: to ~
from derivare da.
derogatory [dɪ'rɔgətərɪ] adj deni-
gratorio(a).
derv [dəːv] (BRIT) n gasolio.
descend [dɪ'sɛnd] vt, vi discendere,
scendere; to ~ from discendere da; to
~ to (lying, begging) abbassarsi a;
~ant n discendente m/f.
descent [dɪ'sɛnt] n discesa; (origin) discendenza, famiglia.
describe [dɪs'kraɪb] vt descrivere; **description** [-'krɪpʃən] n descrizione f;
(sort) genere m, specie f.
desecrate ['dɛsɪkreɪt] vt profanare.
desert [n 'dɛzət, vb dɪ'zəːt] n deserto ♦ vt
lasciare, abbandonare ♦ vi (MIL)
disertare; ~er n disertore m; ~ion
[dɪ'zəːʃən] n (MIL) diserzione f; (LAW)
abbandono del tetto coniugale; ~ island
n isola deserta; ~s [dɪ'zəːts] npl: to get
one's just ~s avere ciò che si merita.
deserve [dɪ'zəːv] vt meritare; **deserving**
adj (person) meritevole, degno(a); (cause)
meritorio(a).
design [dɪ'zaɪn] n (art, sketch) disegno;
(layout, shape) linea; (pattern)
fantasia; (intention) intenzione f ♦ vt
disegnare; progettare.
designer [dɪ'zaɪnə*] n (ART, TECH)
disegnatore/trice; (of fashion) modelli-
sta m/f.
desire [dɪ'zaɪə*] n desiderio, voglia ♦ vt
desiderare, volere.
desk [dɛsk] n (in office) scrivania; (for
pupil) banco; (BRIT: in shop, restaurant) cassa; (in hotel) ricevimento;
(at airport) accettazione f.
desolate ['dɛsəlɪt] adj desolato(a).
despair [dɪs'pɛə*] n disperazione f ♦ vi:
to ~ of disperare di.
despatch [dɪs'pætʃ] n, vt = dispatch.

desperate ['dɛspərɪt] adj disperato(a);
(fugitive) capace di tutto; to be ~ for
sth/to do volere disperatamente qc/fare;
~ly adv disperatamente; (very)
terribilmente, estremamente.
desperation [dɛspə'reɪʃən] n disperazione f.
despicable [dɪs'pɪkəbl] adj di-
sprezzabile.
despise [dɪs'paɪz] vt disprezzare, sdegnare.
despite [dɪs'paɪt] prep malgrado, a dispetto di, nonostante.
despondent [dɪs'pɔndənt] adj
abbattuto(a), scoraggiato(a).
dessert [dɪ'zəːt] n dolce m; frutta;
~spoon n cucchiaio da dolci.
destination [dɛstɪ'neɪʃən] n destinazione
f.
destined ['dɛstɪnd] adj: to be ~ to do/
for essere destinato(a) a fare/per.
destiny ['dɛstɪnɪ] n destino.
destitute ['dɛstɪtjuːt] adj indigente, biso-
gnoso(a).
destroy [dɪs'trɔɪ] vt distruggere; ~er n
(NAUT) cacciatorpediniere m.
destruction [dɪs'trʌkʃən] n distruzione f.
detach [dɪ'tætʃ] vt staccare, distaccare;
~ed adj (attitude) distante; ~ed house
n villa; ~ment n (MIL) distaccamento;
(fig) distacco.
detail ['diːteɪl] n particolare m, dettaglio
♦ vt dettagliare, particolareggiare; in ~
nei particolari; ~ed adj particola-
reggiato(a).
detain [dɪ'teɪn] vt trattenere; (in
captivity) detenere.
detect [dɪ'tɛkt] vt scoprire, scorgere;
(MED, POLICE, RADAR etc) individuare;
~ion [dɪ'tɛkʃən] n scoperta;
individuazione f; ~ive n investigatore/
trice; ~ive story n giallo.
détente [deɪ'tɑːnt] n (POL) distensione f.
detention [dɪ'tɛnʃən] n detenzione f;
(SCOL) permanenza forzata per
punizione.
deter [dɪ'təː*] vt dissuadere.
detergent [dɪ'təːdʒənt] n detersivo.
deteriorate [dɪ'tɪərɪəreɪt] vi deteriorarsi.
determine [dɪ'təːmɪn] vt determinare;

~**d** *adj* (*person*) risoluto(a), deciso(a);
~**d to do** deciso(a) a fare.
detour ['di:tuə*] *n* deviazione *f*.
detract [dɪ'trækt] *vi*: **to ~ from** detrarre
da.
detriment ['dɛtrɪmənt] *n*: **to the ~ of** a
detrimento di; **~al** [dɛtrɪ'mɛntl] *adj*: ~**al**
to dannoso(a) a, nocivo(a) a.
devaluation [dɪvælju'eɪʃən] *n*
svalutazione *f*.
devastate ['dɛvəsteɪt] *vt* devastare;
(*fig*): ~**d by** sconvolto(a) da; **devas-**
tating *adj* devastatore(trice); sconvolgente.
develop [dɪ'vɛləp] *vt* sviluppare; (*habit*)
prendere (gradualmente) ♦ *vi*
svilupparsi; (*facts, symptoms: appear*)
manifestarsi, rivelarsi; ~**er** *n* (*also*:
property ~**er**) costruttore *m* edile;
~**ing country** *n* paese *m* in via di
sviluppo; ~**ment** *n* sviluppo.
device [dɪ'vaɪs] *n* (*apparatus*) congegno.
devil ['dɛvl] *n* diavolo; demonio.
devious ['di:vɪəs] *adj* (*person*)
subdolo(a).
devise [dɪ'vaɪz] *vt* escogitare, concepire.
devoid [dɪ'vɔɪd] *adj*: ~ **of** privo(a) di.
devolution [di:və'lu:ʃən] *n* (*POL*) decen-
tramento.
devote [dɪ'vəut] *vt*: **to ~ sth to** dedicare
qc a; ~**d** *adj* devoto(a); **to be ~d to sb**
essere molto affezionato(a) a qn; ~**e**
[dɛvəu'ti:] *n* (*MUS, SPORT*) appassionato/a.
devotion [dɪ'vəuʃən] *n* devozione *f*,
attaccamento; (*REL*) atto di devozione,
preghiera.
devour [dɪ'vauə*] *vt* divorare.
devout [dɪ'vaut] *adj* pio(a), devoto(a).
dew [dju:] *n* rugiada.
dexterity [dɛks'tɛrɪtɪ] *n* destrezza.
diabetes [daɪə'bi:ti:z] *n* diabete *m*; **dia-**
betic [-'bɛtɪk] *adj*, *n* diabetico(a).
diabolical [daɪə'bɔlɪkl] (*inf*) *adj*
(*weather, behaviour*) orribile.
diagnoses [daɪəg'nəusi:z] *npl of* **diag-**
nosis.
diagnosis [daɪəg'nəusɪs] (*pl* **diagnoses**) *n*
diagnosi *f inv*.
diagonal [daɪ'ægənl] *adj* diagonale ♦ *n*
diagonale *f*.

diagram ['daɪəgræm] *n* diagramma *m*.
dial ['daɪəl] *n* quadrante *m*; (*on radio*)
lancetta; (*on telephone*) disco
combinatore ♦ *vt* (*number*) fare.
dialect ['daɪəlɛkt] *n* dialetto.
dialling code ['daɪəlɪŋ-] (*US* **dial code**) *n*
prefisso.
dialling tone ['daɪəlɪŋ-] (*US* **dial tone**) *n*
segnale *m* di linea libera.
dialogue ['daɪəlɔg] (*US* **dialog**) *n* dialogo.
diameter [daɪ'æmɪtə*] *n* diametro.
diamond ['daɪəmənd] *n* diamante *m*;
(*shape*) rombo; ~**s** *npl* (*CARDS*) quadri
mpl.
diaper ['daɪəpə*] (*US*) *n* pannolino.
diaphragm ['daɪəfræm] *n* diaframma *m*.
diarrhoea [daɪə'ri:ə] (*US* **diarrhea**) *n*
diarrea.
diary ['daɪərɪ] *n* (*daily account*) diario;
(*book*) agenda.
dice [daɪs] *n inv* dado ♦ *vt* (*CULIN*) tagliare a dadini.
Dictaphone ['dɪktəfəun] ® *n* dittafono
®.
dictate [dɪk'teɪt] *vt* dettare.
dictation [dɪk'teɪʃən] *n* dettatura;
(*SCOL*) dettato.
dictator [dɪk'teɪtə*] *n* dittatore *m*;
~**ship** *n* dittatura.
dictionary ['dɪkʃənrɪ] *n* dizionario.
did [dɪd] *pt of* **do**.
didn't = **did not**.
die [daɪ] *vi* morire; **to be dying for sth/**
to do sth morire dalla voglia di qc/di
fare qc; ~ **away** *vi* spegnersi a poco a
poco; ~ **down** *vi* abbassarsi; ~ **out** *vi*
estinguersi.
diehard ['daɪhɑ:d] *n* reazionario/a.
diesel ['di:zəl] *n* (*vehicle*) diesel *m inv*;
~ **engine** *n* motore *m* diesel *inv*; ~
(**oil**) *n* gasolio (per motori diesel),
diesel *m inv*.
diet ['daɪət] *n* alimentazione *f*; (*re-*
stricted food) dieta ♦ *vi* (*also*: *be on a*
~) stare a dieta.
differ ['dɪfə*] *vi*: **to ~ from sth** differire
da qc; essere diverso(a) da qc; **to ~**
from sb over sth essere in disaccordo
con qn su qc; ~**ence** *n* differenza;
(*disagreement*) screzio; ~**ent** *adj*

diverso(a); ~**entiate** [-'rɛnʃɪeɪt] vi: to ~**entiate between** discriminare or fare differenza fra.
difficult ['dɪfɪkəlt] adj difficile; ~**y** n difficoltà f inv.
diffident ['dɪfɪdənt] adj sfiduciato(a).
diffuse [adj dɪ'fju:s, vb dɪ'fju:z] adj diffuso(a) ♦ vt diffondere.
dig [dɪg] (pt, pp **dug**) vt (hole) scavare; (garden) vangare ♦ n (prod) gomitata; (archaeological) scavo; (fig) frecciata; ~ **into** vt fus (savings) scavare in; **to** ~ **one's nails into** conficcare le unghie in; ~ **up** vt (tree etc) sradicare; (information) scavare fuori.
digest [vb daɪ'dʒɛst, n 'daɪdʒɛst] vt digerire ♦ n compendio; ~**ion** [dɪ'dʒɛstʃən] n digestione f; ~**ive** adj (juices, system) digerente.
digit ['dɪdʒɪt] n cifra; (finger) dito; ~**al** adj digitale.
dignified ['dɪgnɪfaɪd] adj dignitoso(a).
dignity ['dɪgnɪtɪ] n dignità.
digress [daɪ'grɛs] vi: **to** ~ **from** divagare da.
digs [dɪgz] (BRIT: inf) npl camera ammobiliata.
dike [daɪk] n = **dyke**.
dilapidated [dɪ'læpɪdeɪtɪd] adj cadente.
dilemma [daɪ'lɛmə] n dilemma m.
diligent ['dɪlɪdʒənt] adj diligente.
dilute [daɪ'lu:t] vt diluire; (with water) annacquare.
dim [dɪm] adj (light) debole; (outline, figure) vago(a); (room) in penombra; (inf: person) tonto(a) ♦ vt (light) abbassare.
dime [daɪm] (US) n = 10 cents.
dimension [daɪ'mɛnʃən] n dimensione f.
diminish [dɪ'mɪnɪʃ] vt, vi diminuire.
diminutive [dɪ'mɪnjutɪv] adj minuscolo(a) ♦ n (LING) diminutivo.
dimmers ['dɪməz] (US) npl (AUT) anabbaglianti mpl; luci fpl di posizione.
dimple ['dɪmpl] n fossetta.
din [dɪn] n chiasso, fracasso.
dine [daɪn] vi pranzare; ~**r** n (person) cliente m/f; (US: place) tavola calda.
dinghy ['dɪngɪ] n battello pneumatico; (also: rubber ~) gommone m.

dingy ['dɪndʒɪ] adj grigio(a).
dining car ['daɪnɪn-] (BRIT) n vagone m ristorante.
dining room ['daɪnɪn-] n sala da pranzo.
dinner ['dɪnə*] n (lunch) pranzo; (evening meal) cena; (public) banchetto; ~ **jacket** n smoking m inv; ~ **party** n cena; ~ **time** n ora di pranzo (or cena).
dint [dɪnt] n: **by** ~ **of** a forza di.
dip [dɪp] n discesa; (in sea) bagno; (CULIN) salsetta ♦ vt immergere; bagnare; (BRIT: AUT: lights) abbassare ♦ vi abbassarsi.
diphthong ['dɪfθɔŋ] n dittongo.
diploma [dɪ'pləumə] n diploma m.
diplomacy [dɪ'pləuməsɪ] n diplomazia.
diplomat ['dɪpləmæt] n diplomatico; ~**ic** [dɪplə'mætɪk] adj diplomatico(a).
diprod ['dɪprɔd] (US) n = **dipstick**.
dipstick ['dɪpstɪk] n (AUT) indicatore m di livello dell'olio.
dipswitch ['dɪpswɪtʃ] (BRIT) n (AUT) levetta dei fari.
dire [daɪə*] adj terribile; estremo(a).
direct [daɪ'rɛkt] adj diretto(a) ♦ vt dirigere; (order): **to** ~ **sb to do sth** dare direttive a qn di fare qc ♦ adv direttamente; **can you** ~ **me to ...?** mi può indicare la strada per ...?
direction [dɪ'rɛkʃən] n direzione f; ~**s** npl (advice) chiarimenti mpl; **sense of** ~ senso dell'orientamento; ~**s for use** istruzioni fpl.
directly [dɪ'rɛktlɪ] adv (in straight line) direttamente; (at once) subito.
director [dɪ'rɛktə*] n direttore/trice; amministratore/trice; (THEATRE, CINEMA) regista m/f.
directory [dɪ'rɛktərɪ] n elenco.
dirt [də:t] n sporcizia; immondizia; (earth) terra; ~-**cheap** adj da due soldi; ~**y** adj sporco(a) ♦ vt sporcare; ~**y trick** n brutto scherzo.
disability [dɪsə'bɪlɪtɪ] n invalidità f inv; (LAW) incapacità f inv.
disabled [dɪs'eɪbld] adj invalido(a); (mentally) ritardato(a) ♦ npl: **the** ~ gli invalidi.

disadvantage [dɪsəd'vɑ:ntɪdʒ] n svantaggio.

disaffection [dɪsə'fɛkʃən] n: ~ **(with)** allontanamento (da).

disagree [dɪsə'gri:] vi (differ) discordare; (be against, think otherwise): **to ~ (with)** essere in disaccordo (con), dissentire (da); **~able** adj sgradevole; (person) antipatico(a); **~ment** n disaccordo; (argument) dissapore m.

disallow [dɪsə'lau] vt (appeal) respingere.

disappear [dɪsə'pɪə*] vi scomparire; **~ance** n scomparsa.

disappoint [dɪsə'pɔɪnt] vt deludere; **~ed** adj deluso(a); **~ing** adj deludente; **~ment** n delusione f.

disapproval [dɪsə'pru:vəl] n disapprovazione f.

disapprove [dɪsə'pru:v] vi: **to ~ of** disapprovare.

disarm [dɪs'ɑ:m] vt disarmare; **~ament** n disarmo.

disarray [dɪsə'reɪ] n: **in ~** (army) in rotta; (organization) in uno stato di confusione; (clothes, hair) in disordine.

disaster [dɪ'zɑ:stə*] n disastro.

disband [dɪs'bænd] vt sbandare; (MIL) congedare ♦ vi sciogliersi.

disbelief ['dɪsbə'li:f] n incredulità.

disc [dɪsk] n disco; (COMPUT) = **disk**.

discard [dɪs'kɑ:d] vt (old things) scartare; (fig) abbandonare.

discern [dɪ'sɑ:n] vt discernere, distinguere; **~ing** adj perspicace.

discharge [vb dɪs'tʃɑ:dʒ, n 'dɪstʃɑ:dʒ] vt (duties) compiere; (ELEC, waste etc) scaricare; (MED) emettere; (patient) dimettere; (employee) licenziare; (soldier) congedare; (defendant) liberare ♦ n (ELEC) scarica; (MED) emissione f; (dismissal) licenziamento; congedo; liberazione f.

disciple [dɪ'saɪpl] n discepolo.

discipline ['dɪsɪplɪn] n disciplina ♦ vt disciplinare; (punish) punire.

disc jockey n disc jockey m inv.

disclaim [dɪs'kleɪm] vt negare, smentire.

disclose [dɪs'kləuz] vt rivelare, svelare; **disclosure** [-'kləuʒə*] n rivelazione f.

disco ['dɪskəu] n abbr = **discothèque**.

discoloured [dɪs'kʌləd] (US **discolored**) adj scolorito(a); ingiallito(a).

discomfort [dɪs'kʌmfət] n disagio; (lack of comfort) scomodità f inv.

disconcert [dɪskən'sɔ:t] vt sconcertare.

disconnect [dɪskə'nɛkt] vt sconnettere, staccare; (ELEC, RADIO) staccare; (gas, water) chiudere.

discontent [dɪskən'tɛnt] n scontentezza; **~ed** adj scontento(a).

discontinue [dɪskən'tɪnju:] vt smettere, cessare; **"~d"** (COMM) "fuori produzione".

discord ['dɪskɔ:d] n disaccordo; (MUS) dissonanza.

discothèque ['dɪskəutɛk] n discoteca.

discount [n 'dɪskaunt, vb dɪs'kaunt] n sconto ♦ vt scontare; (idea) non badare a.

discourage [dɪs'kʌrɪdʒ] vt scoraggiare.

discourteous [dɪs'kɜ:tɪəs] adj scortese.

discover [dɪs'kʌvə*] vt scoprire; **~y** n scoperta.

discredit [dɪs'krɛdɪt] vt screditare; mettere in dubbio.

discreet [dɪ'skri:t] adj discreto(a).

discrepancy [dɪ'skrɛpənsɪ] n discrepanza.

discriminate [dɪ'skrɪmɪneɪt] vi: **to ~ between** distinguere tra; **to ~ against** discriminare contro; **discriminating** adj fine, giudizioso(a); **discrimination** [-'neɪʃən] n discriminazione f; (judgment) discernimento.

discuss [dɪs'kʌs] vt discutere; (debate) dibattere; **~ion** [dɪ'skʌʃən] n discussione f.

disdain [dɪs'deɪn] n disdegno.

disease [dɪ'zi:z] n malattia.

disembark [dɪsɪm'bɑ:k] vt, vi sbarcare.

disengage [dɪsɪn'geɪdʒ] vt (AUT: clutch) disinnestare.

disentangle [dɪsɪn'tæŋgl] vt liberare; (wool etc) sbrogliare.

disfigure [dɪs'fɪgə*] vt sfigurare.

disgrace [dɪs'greɪs] n vergogna; (disfavour) disgrazia ♦ vt disonorare, far cadere in disgrazia; **~ful** adj scandaloso(a), vergognoso(a).

disgruntled [dɪs'grʌntld] *adj* scontento(a), di cattivo umore.

disguise [dɪs'gaɪz] *n* travestimento ♦ *vt*: to ~ (as) travestire (da); in ~ travestito(a).

disgust [dɪs'gʌst] *n* disgusto, nausea ♦ *vt* disgustare, far schifo a; ~ing *adj* disgustoso(a); ripugnante.

dish [dɪʃ] *n* piatto; to do *or* wash the ~es fare i piatti; ~ out *vt* distribuire; ~ up *vt* servire; ~cloth *n* strofinaccio.

dishearten [dɪs'hɑ:tn] *vt* scoraggiare.

dishevelled [dɪ'ʃevəld] *adj* arruffato(a); scapigliato(a).

dishonest [dɪs'ɔnɪst] *adj* disonesto(a).

dishonour [dɪs'ɔnə*] (*US* **dishonor**) *n* disonore *m*; ~able *adj* disonorevole.

dishtowel ['dɪʃtauəl] (*US*) *n* strofinaccio dei piatti.

dishwasher ['dɪʃwɔʃə*] *n* lavastoviglie *f inv*.

disillusion [dɪsɪ'lu:ʒən] *vt* disilludere, disingannare.

disincentive [dɪsɪn'sɛntɪv] *n*: to be a ~ non essere un incentivo.

disinfect [dɪsɪn'fɛkt] *vt* disinfettare; ~ant *n* disinfettante *m*.

disintegrate [dɪs'ɪntɪgreɪt] *vi* disintegrarsi.

disinterested [dɪs'ɪntrəstɪd] *adj* disinteressato(a).

disjointed [dɪs'dʒɔɪntɪd] *adj* sconnesso(a).

disk [dɪsk] *n* (*COMPUT*) disco; single-/double-sided ~ disco a facciata singola/doppia; ~ drive *n* lettore *m*; ~ette (*US*) *n* = **disk**.

dislike [dɪs'laɪk] *n* antipatia, avversione *f*; (*gen pl*) cosa che non piace ♦ *vt*: he ~s it non gli piace.

dislocate ['dɪsləkeɪt] *vt* slogare.

dislodge [dɪs'lɔdʒ] *vt* rimuovere.

disloyal [dɪs'lɔɪəl] *adj* sleale.

dismal ['dɪzml] *adj* triste, cupo(a).

dismantle [dɪs'mæntl] *vt* (*machine*) smontare.

dismay [dɪs'meɪ] *n* costernazione *f* ♦ *vt* sgomentare.

dismiss [dɪs'mɪs] *vt* congedare; (*employee*) licenziare; (*idea*) scacciare;

(*LAW*) respingere; ~al *n* congedo; licenziamento.

dismount [dɪs'maunt] *vi* scendere.

disobedience [dɪsə'bi:dɪəns] *n* disubbidienza.

disobedient [dɪsə'bi:dɪənt] *adj* disubbidiente.

disobey [dɪsə'beɪ] *vt* disubbidire a.

disorder [dɪs'ɔ:də*] *n* disordine *m*; (*rioting*) tumulto; (*MED*) disturbo; ~ly *adj* disordinato(a); tumultuoso(a).

disorientated [dɪs'ɔ:rɪenteɪtɪd] *adj* disorientato(a).

disown [dɪs'əun] *vt* rinnegare.

disparaging [dɪs'pærɪdʒɪŋ] *adj* spregiativo(a), sprezzante.

dispassionate [dɪs'pæʃənət] *adj* calmo(a), freddo(a); imparziale.

dispatch [dɪs'pætʃ] *vt* spedire, inviare ♦ *n* spedizione *f*, invio; (*MIL, PRESS*) dispaccio.

dispel [dɪs'pɛl] *vt* dissipare, scacciare.

dispense [dɪs'pɛns] *vt* distribuire, amministrare; ~ with *vt fus* fare a meno di; ~r *n* (*container*) distributore *m*; **dispensing chemist** (*BRIT*) *n* farmacista *m/f*.

disperse [dɪs'pə:s] *vt* disperdere; (*knowledge*) disseminare ♦ *vi* disperdersi.

dispirited [dɪs'pɪrɪtɪd] *adj* scoraggiato(a), abbattuto(a).

displace [dɪs'pleɪs] *vt* spostare; ~d person *n* (*POL*) profugo/a.

display [dɪs'pleɪ] *n* esposizione *f*; (*of feeling etc*) manifestazione *f*; (*screen*) schermo ♦ *vt* mostrare; (*goods*) esporre; (*pej*) ostentare.

displease [dɪs'pli:z] *vt* dispiacere a, scontentare; ~d with scontento di; **displeasure** [-'plɛʒə*] *n* dispiacere *m*.

disposable [dɪs'pəuzəbl] *adj* (*pack etc*) a perdere; (*income*) disponibile; ~ **nappy** *n* pannolino di carta.

disposal [dɪs'pəuzl] *n* eliminazione *f*; (*of property*) cessione *f*; at one's ~ alla sua disposizione.

dispose [dɪs'pəuz] *vi*: ~ of sbarazzarsi di; ~d *adj*: ~d to do disposto(a) a fare; **disposition** [-'zɪʃən] *n* disposizione *f*; (*temperament*) carattere *m*.

disproportionate [dɪsprə'pɔ:ʃənət] *adj* sproporzionato(a).

disprove [dɪs'pru:v] *vt* confutare.

dispute [dɪs'pju:t] *n* disputa; (*also: industrial* ~) controversia (sindacale) ♦ *vt* contestare; (*matter*) discutere; (*victory*) disputare.

disqualify [dɪs'kwɔlɪfaɪ] *vt* (*SPORT*) squalificare; **to** ~ **sb from sth/from doing** rendere qn incapace a qc/a fare; squalificare qn da qc/da fare; **to** ~ **sb from driving** ritirare la patente a qn.

disquiet [dɪs'kwaɪət] *n* inquietudine *f*.

disregard [dɪsrɪ'gɑ:d] *vt* non far caso a, non badare a.

disrepair [dɪsrɪ'pɛə*] *n*: **to fall into** ~ (*building*) andare in rovina; (*machine*) deteriorarsi.

disreputable [dɪs'rɛpjutəbl] *adj* poco raccomandabile; indecente.

disrupt [dɪs'rʌpt] *vt* disturbare; creare scompiglio in.

dissatisfaction [dɪssætɪs'fækʃən] *n* scontentezza, insoddisfazione *f*.

dissect [dɪ'sɛkt] *vt* sezionare.

dissent [dɪ'sɛnt] *n* dissenso.

dissertation [dɪsə'teɪʃən] *n* tesi *f inv*, dissertazione *f*.

disservice [dɪs'sə:vɪs] *n*: **to do sb a** ~ fare un cattivo servizio a qn.

dissimilar [dɪ'sɪmɪlə*] *adj*: ~ (**to**) dissimile *or* diverso(a) (da).

dissipate ['dɪsɪpeɪt] *vt* dissipare.

dissolute ['dɪsəlu:t] *adj* dissoluto(a), licenzioso(a).

dissolution [dɪsə'lu:ʃən] *n* (*of organization, marriage, POL*) scioglimento.

dissolve [dɪ'zɔlv] *vt* dissolvere, sciogliere; (*POL, marriage etc*) sciogliere ♦ *vi* dissolversi, sciogliersi.

distance ['dɪstns] *n* distanza; **in the** ~ in lontananza.

distant ['dɪstnt] *adj* lontano(a), distante; (*manner*) riservato(a), freddo(a).

distaste [dɪs'teɪst] *n* ripugnanza; ~**ful** *adj* ripugnante, sgradevole.

distended [dɪs'tɛndɪd] *adj* (*stomach*) dilatato(a).

distil [dɪs'tɪl] (*US* **distill**) *vt* distillare; ~**lery** *n* distilleria.

distinct [dɪs'tɪŋkt] *adj* distinto(a); **as** ~ **from** a differenza di; ~**ion** [dɪs'tɪŋkʃən] *n* distinzione *f*; (*in exam*) lode *f*; ~**ive** *adj* distintivo(a).

distinguish [dɪs'tɪŋgwɪʃ] *vt* distinguere; discernere; ~**ed** *adj* (*eminent*) eminente; ~**ing** *adj* (*feature*) distinto(a), caratteristico(a).

distort [dɪs'tɔ:t] *vt* distorcere; (*TECH*) deformare.

distract [dɪs'trækt] *vt* distrarre; ~**ed** *adj* distratto(a); ~**ion** [dɪs'trækʃən] *n* distrazione *f*.

distraught [dɪs'trɔ:t] *adj* stravolto(a).

distress [dɪs'trɛs] *n* angoscia ♦ *vt* affliggere; ~**ing** *adj* doloroso(a); ~ **signal** *n* segnale *m* di soccorso.

distribute [dɪs'trɪbju:t] *vt* distribuire; **distribution** [-'bju:ʃən] *n* distribuzione *f*; **distributor** *n* distributore *m*.

district ['dɪstrɪkt] *n* (*of country*) regione *f*; (*of town*) quartiere *m*; (*ADMIN*) distretto; ~ **attorney** (*US*) *n* ≈ sostituto procuratore *m* della Repubblica; ~ **nurse** (*BRIT*) *n* infermiera di quartiere.

distrust [dɪs'trʌst] *n* diffidenza, sfiducia ♦ *vt* non aver fiducia in.

disturb [dɪs'tə:b] *vt* disturbare; ~**ance** *n* disturbo; (*political etc*) disordini *mpl*; ~**ed** *adj* (*worried, upset*) turbato(a); **emotionally** ~**ed** con turbe emotive; ~**ing** *adj* sconvolgente.

disuse [dɪs'ju:s] *n*: **to fall into** ~ cadere in disuso.

disused [dɪs'ju:zd] *adj* abbandonato(a).

ditch [dɪtʃ] *n* fossa ♦ *vt* (*inf*) piantare in asso.

dither ['dɪðə*] (*pej*) *vi* vacillare.

ditto ['dɪtəu] *adv* idem.

dive [daɪv] *n* tuffo; (*of submarine*) immersione *f* ♦ *vi* tuffarsi; immergersi; ~**r** *n* tuffatore/trice; palombaro.

diverse [daɪ'və:s] *adj* vario(a).

diversion [daɪ'və:ʃən] *n* (*BRIT: AUT*) deviazione *f*; (*distraction*) divertimento.

divert [daɪ'və:t] *vt* deviare.

divide [dɪ'vaɪd] *vt* dividere; (*separate*) separare ♦ *vi* dividersi; ~**d highway**

(US) n strada a doppia carreggiata.

dividend ['dɪvɪdend] n dividendo; (fig):
to pay ~s dare dei frutti.

divine [dɪ'vaɪn] adj divino(a).

diving ['daɪvɪŋ] n tuffo; ~ **board** n
trampolino.

divinity [dɪ'vɪnɪtɪ] n divinità f inv;
teologia.

division [dɪ'vɪʒən] n divisione f;
separazione f; (esp FOOTBALL) serie f.

divorce [dɪ'vɔ:s] n divorzio ♦ vt
divorziare da; (dissociate) separare;
~d adj divorziato(a); ~e ['si:] n
divorziato/a.

D.I.Y. (BRIT) n abbr = do-it-yourself.

dizzy ['dɪzɪ] adj: to feel ~ avere il
capogiro.

DJ n abbr = disc jockey.

KEYWORD

---

do [du:] (pt did, pp done) n (inf: party
etc) festa; it was rather a grand ~ è
stato un ricevimento piuttosto
importante

♦ vb 1 (in negative constructions) non
tradotto; I don't understand non capisco
2 (to form questions) non tradotto;
didn't you know? non lo sapevi?; why
didn't you come? perché non sei
venuto?
3 (for emphasis, in polite expressions):
she does seem rather late sembra
essere piuttosto in ritardo; ~ sit down
si accomodi la prego, prego si sieda; ~
take care! mi raccomando, sta
attento!
4 (used to avoid repeating vb): she
swims better than I ~ lei nuota meglio
di me; ~ you agree? — yes, I ~/no, I
don't sei d'accordo? — sì/no; she lives
in Glasgow — so ~ I lei vive a Glasgow
— anch'io; he asked me to help him
and I did mi ha chiesto di aiutarlo ed io
l'ho fatto
5 (in question tags): you like him,
don't you? ti piace, vero?; I don't know
him, ~ I? non lo conosco, vero?

♦ vt (gen, carry out, perform etc) fare;
what are you ~ing tonight? che fa
stasera?; to ~ the cooking cucinare; to

~ the washing-up fare i piatti; to ~
one's teeth lavarsi i denti; to ~ one's
hair/nails farsi i capelli/le unghie; the
car was ~ing 100 la macchina faceva i
100 all'ora

♦ vi 1 (act, behave) fare; ~ as I ~
faccia come me, faccia come faccio io
2 (get on, fare) andare; he's ~ing
well/badly at school va bene/male a
scuola; how ~ you ~? piacere!
3 (suit) andare bene; this room will ~
questa stanza va bene
4 (be sufficient) bastare; will £10 ~?
basteranno 10 sterline?; that'll ~ basta
così; that'll ~! (in annoyance) ora basta!; to make ~ (with) arrangiarsi
(con)

do away with vt fus (kill) far fuori;
(abolish) abolire

do up vt (laces) allacciare; (dress,
buttons) abbottonare; (renovate: room,
house) rimettere a nuovo, rifare

do with vt fus (need) aver bisogno di;
(be connected): what has it got to ~
with you? e tu che c'entri?; I won't
have anything to ~ with it non voglio
avere niente a che farci; it has to ~
with money si tratta di soldi

do without vi fare senza ♦ vt fus fare
a meno di.

---

dock [dɔk] n (NAUT) bacino; (LAW)
banco degli imputati ♦ vi entrare in
bacino; (SPACE) agganciarsi; ~s npl
(NAUT) dock m inv; ~er n scaricatore
m; ~yard n cantiere m (navale).

doctor ['dɔktə*] n medico/a; (Ph.D. etc)
dottore/essa ♦ vt (drink etc) adulterare;
D~ of Philosophy n dottorato di
ricerca; (person) titolare m/f di un
dottorato di ricerca.

doctrine ['dɔktrɪn] n dottrina.

document ['dɔkjumənt] n documento;
~ary ['mentərɪ] adj (evidence) docu-
mentato(a) ♦ n documentario.

dodge [dɔdʒ] n trucco; schivata ♦ vt
schivare, eludere.

dodgems ['dɔdʒəmz] (BRIT) npl autoscontri mpl.

doe [dəu] n (deer) femmina di daino;

(*rabbit*) coniglia.

does [dʌz] *vb see* **do; doesn't** = **does not.**

dog [dɔg] *n* cane *m* ♦ *vt* (*follow closely*) pedinare; (*fig: memory etc*) perseguitare; ~ **collar** *n* collare *m* di cane; (*fig*) collarino; ~-**eared** *adj* (*book*) con orecchie.

dogged ['dɔgɪd] *adj* ostinato(a), tenace.

dogsbody ['dɔgzbɔdɪ] (*BRIT: inf*) *n* factotum *m inv.*

doings ['duɪŋz] *npl* attività *fpl.*

do-it-yourself *n* il far da sé.

doldrums ['dɔldrəmz] *npl* (*fig*): **to be in the** ~ avere un brutto periodo.

dole [dəul] (*BRIT*) *n* sussidio di disoccupazione; **to be on the** ~ vivere del sussidio; ~ **out** *vt* distribuire.

doleful ['dəulful] *adj* triste.

doll [dɔl] *n* bambola; ~**ed up** (*inf*) *adj* in ghingheri.

dollar ['dɔlə*] *n* dollaro.

dolphin ['dɔlfɪn] *n* delfino.

domain [də'meɪn] *n* dominio.

dome [dəum] *n* cupola.

domestic [də'mɛstɪk] *adj* (*duty, happiness, animal*) domestico(a); (*policy, affairs, flights*) nazionale; ~**ated** *adj* addomesticato(a).

dominate ['dɔmɪneɪt] *vt* dominare.

domineering [dɔmɪ'nɪərɪŋ] *adj* dispotico(a), autoritario(a).

dominion [də'mɪnɪən] *n* dominio; sovranità; dominion *m inv.*

domino ['dɔmɪnəu] (*pl* ~**es**) *n* domino; ~**es** *n* (*game*) gioco del domino.

don [dɔn] (*BRIT*) *n* docente *m/f* universitario(a).

donate [də'neɪt] *vt* donare.

done [dʌn] *pp of* **do.**

donkey ['dɔŋkɪ] *n* asino.

donor ['dəunə*] *n* donatore/trice.

don't [dəunt] = **do not.**

doodle ['du:dl] *vi* scarabocchiare.

doom [du:m] *n* destino; rovina ♦ *vt*: **to be** ~**ed** (**to failure**) essere predestinato(a) (a fallire); ~**sday** *n* il giorno del Giudizio.

door [dɔ:*] *n* porta; ~**bell** *n* campanello; ~ **handle** *n* maniglia;

~**man** *n* (*in hotel*) portiere *m* in livrea; ~**mat** *n* stuoia della porta; ~**step** *n* gradino della porta; ~**way** *n* porta.

dope [dəup] *n* (*inf: drugs*) roba ♦ *vt* (*horse etc*) drogare.

dopey ['dəupɪ] (*inf*) *adj* inebetito(a).

dormant ['dɔ:mənt] *adj* inattivo(a).

dormice ['dɔ:maɪs] *npl of* **dormouse.**

dormitory ['dɔ:mɪtrɪ] *n* dormitorio; (*US*) casa dello studente.

dormouse ['dɔ:maus] (*pl* **dormice**) *n* ghiro.

dosage ['dəusɪdʒ] *n* posologia.

dose [dəus] *n* dose *f*; (*bout*) attacco.

doss house ['dɔs-] (*BRIT*) *n* asilo notturno.

dot [dɔt] *n* punto; macchiolina ♦ *vt*: ~**ted with** punteggiato(a) di; **on the** ~ in punto.

dote [dəut]: ~ **on** *vt fus* essere infatuato(a) di.

dot-matrix printer [dɔt'meɪtrɪks-] *n* stampante *f* a matrice a punti.

dotted line ['dɔtɪd-] *n* linea punteggiata.

double ['dʌbl] *adj* doppio(a) ♦ *adv* (*twice*): **to cost** ~ (**sth**) costare il doppio (di qc) ♦ *n* sosia *m inv* ♦ *vt* raddoppiare; (*fold*) piegare doppio *or* in due ♦ *vi* raddoppiarsi; **at the** ~ (*BRIT*), **on the** ~ a passo di corsa; ~ **bass** *n* contrabbasso; ~ **bed** *n* letto matrimoniale; ~-**breasted** *adj* a doppio petto; ~**cross** *vt* fare il doppio gioco con; ~**decker** *n* autobus *m inv* a due piani; ~ **glazing** (*BRIT*) *n* doppi vetri *mpl*; ~ **room** *n* camera per due; ~**s** *n* (*TENNIS*) doppio; **doubly** *adv* doppiamente.

doubt [daut] *n* dubbio ♦ *vt* dubitare di; **to** ~ **that** dubitare che + *sub*; ~**ful** *adj* dubbioso(a), incerto(a); (*person*) equivoco(a); ~**less** *adv* indubbiamente.

dough [dəu] *n* pasta, impasto; ~**nut** *n* bombolone *m.*

douse [dauz] *vt* (*drench*) inzuppare; (*extinguish*) spegnere.

dove [dʌv] *n* colombo/a.

dovetail ['dʌvteɪl] *vi* (*fig*) combaciare.

dowdy ['daudɪ] *adj* trasandato(a);

malvestito(a).

down [daun] n piume fpl ♦ adv giù, di sotto ♦ prep giù per ♦ vt (inf: drink) scolarsi; ~ **with X!** abbasso X!; ~-**and-out** n barbone m; ~-**at-heel** adj scalcagnato(a); ~**cast** adj abbattuto(a); ~**fall** n caduta; rovina; ~**hearted** adj scoraggiato(a); ~**hill** adv: **to go** ~**hill** andare in discesa; (fig) lasciarsi andare; andare a rotoli; ~ **payment** n acconto; ~**pour** n scroscio di pioggia; ~**right** adj franco(a); (refusal) assoluto(a); ~**stairs** adv di sotto; al piano inferiore; ~**stream** adv a valle; ~-**to-earth** adj pratico(a); ~**town** adv in città; ~ **under** adv (Australia etc) agli antipodi; ~**ward** ['daunwəd] adj, adv in giù, in discesa; ~**wards** ['daunwədz] adv = ~**ward**.

dowry ['dauri] n dote f.

doz. abbr = **dozen**.

doze [dəuz] vi sonnecchiare; ~ **off** vi appisolarsi.

dozen ['dʌzn] n dozzina; **a** ~ **books** una dozzina di libri; ~**s of** decine fpl di.

Dr. abbr (= doctor) dott.; (in street names) = **drive** n.

drab [dræb] adj tetro(a), grigio(a).

draft [drɑ:ft] n abbozzo; (POL) bozza; (COMM) tratta; (US: call-up) leva ♦ vt abbozzare; see also **draught**.

draftsman ['drɑ:ftsmən] (US) n = **draughtsman**.

drag [dræg] vt trascinare; (river) dragare ♦ vi trascinarsi ♦ n (inf) noioso/a; noia, fatica; (women's clothing): **in** ~ travestito (da donna); ~ **on** vi tirar avanti lentamente.

dragon ['drægən] n drago.

dragonfly ['drægənflaɪ] n libellula.

drain [dreɪn] n (for sewage) fogna; (on resources) salasso ♦ vt (land, marshes) prosciugare; (vegetables) scolare ♦ vi (water) defluire (via); ~**age** n prosciugamento; fognatura; ~**ing board** (US ~**board**) n piano del lavello; ~**pipe** n tubo di scarico.

drama ['drɑ:mə] n (art) dramma m, teatro; (play) commedia; (event) dramma; ~**tic** [drə'mætɪk] adj

drammatico(a); ~**tist** ['dræmətɪst] n drammaturgo/a; ~**tize** vt (events) drammatizzare; (adapt: for TV/cinema) ridurre or adattare per la televisione/lo schermo.

drank [dræŋk] pt of **drink**.

drape [dreɪp] vt drappeggiare; ~**r** (BRIT) n negoziante m/f di stoffe; ~**s** (US) npl (curtains) tende fpl.

drastic ['dræstɪk] adj drastico(a).

draught [drɑ:ft] (US **draft**) n corrente f d'aria; (NAUT) pescaggio; **on** ~ (beer) alla spina; ~**board** (BRIT) n scacchiera; ~**s** (BRIT) n (gioco della) dama.

draughtsman ['drɑ:ftsmən] (US **draftsman**) n disegnatore m.

draw [drɔ:] (pt **drew**, pp **drawn**) vt tirare; (take out) estrarre; (attract) attirare; (picture) disegnare; (line, circle) tracciare; (money) ritirare ♦ vi (SPORT) pareggiare ♦ n pareggio; (in lottery) estrazione f; **to** ~ **near** avvicinarsi; ~ **out** vi (lengthen) allungarsi ♦ vt (money) ritirare; ~ **up** vi (stop) arrestarsi, fermarsi ♦ vt (chair) avvicinare; (document) compilare; ~**back** n svantaggio, inconveniente m; ~**bridge** n ponte m levatoio.

drawer [drɔ:*] n cassetto.

drawing ['drɔ:ɪŋ] n disegno; ~ **board** n tavola da disegno; ~ **pin** (BRIT) n puntina da disegno; ~ **room** n salotto.

drawl [drɔ:l] n pronuncia strascicata.

drawn [drɔ:n] pp of **draw**.

dread [dred] n terrore m ♦ vt tremare all'idea di; ~**ful** adj terribile.

dream [dri:m] (pt, pp **dreamed** or **dreamt**) n sogno ♦ vt, vi sognare; **dreamt** [dremt] pt, pp of **dream**; ~**y** adj sognante.

dreary ['drɪəri] adj tetro(a); monotono(a).

dredge [dredʒ] vt dragare.

dregs [dregz] npl feccia.

drench [drentʃ] vt inzuppare.

dress [dres] n vestito; (no pl: clothing) abbigliamento ♦ vt vestire; (wound) fasciare ♦ vi vestirsi; **to get** ~**ed** vestirsi; ~ **up** vi vestirsi a festa; (in fancy *dress*) vestirsi in costume; ~ **circle** (*BRIT*) *n* prima galleria; ~**er** *n* (*BRIT*: *cupboard*) credenza; (*US*) cassettone *m*; ~**ing** *n* (*MED*) benda; (*CULIN*) condimento; ~**ing gown** (*BRIT*) *n* vestaglia; ~**ing room** *n* (*THEATRE*) camerino; (*SPORT*) spogliatoio; ~**ing table** *n* toilette *f inv*; ~**maker** *n* sarta; ~ **rehearsal** *n* prova generale; ~**y** (*inf*) *adj* elegante.

drew [druː] *pt of* **draw.**

dribble ['drɪbl] *vi* (*baby*) sbavare ♦ *vt* (*ball*) dribblare.

dried [draɪd] *adj* (*fruit, beans*) secco(a), (*eggs, milk*) in polvere.

drier ['draɪə*] *n* = **dryer.**

drift [drɪft] *n* (*of current etc*) direzione *f*; forza; (*of snow*) cumulo; turbine *m*; (*general meaning*) senso ♦ *vi* (*boat*) essere trasportato(a) dalla corrente; (*sand, snow*) ammucchiarsi; ~**wood** *n* resti *mpl* della mareggiata.

drill [drɪl] *n* trapano; (*MIL*) esercitazione *f* ♦ *vt* trapanare; (*troops*) addestrare ♦ *vi* (*for oil*) fare trivellazioni.

drink [drɪŋk] (*pt* **drank**, *pp* **drunk**) *n* bevanda, bibita; (*alcoholic* ~) bicchierino; (*sip*) sorso ♦ *vt, vi* bere; **to have a** ~ bere qualcosa; **a** ~ **of water** un po' d'acqua; ~**er** *n* bevitore/trice; ~**ing water** *n* acqua potabile.

drip [drɪp] *n* goccia; gocciolamento; (*MED*) fleboclisi *f inv* ♦ *vi* gocciolare; (*tap*) sgocciolare; ~**-dry** *adj* (*shirt*) che non si stira; ~**ping** *n* grasso d'arrosto.

drive [draɪv] (*pt* **drove**, *pp* **driven**) *n* passeggiata *or* giro in macchina; (*also:* ~*way*) viale *m* d'accesso; (*energy*) energia; (*campaign*) campagna; (*also: disk* ~) lettore *m* ♦ *vt* guidare; (*nail*) piantare; (*push*) cacciare, spingere; (*TECH: motor*) azionare; far funzionare ♦ *vi* (*AUT: at controls*) guidare; (: *travel*) andare in macchina; **left-/right-hand** ~ guida a sinistra/destra; **to** ~ **sb mad** far impazzire qn.

drivel ['drɪvl] (*inf*) *n* idiozie *fpl*.

driven ['drɪvn] *pp of* **drive.**

driver ['draɪvə*] *n* conducente *m/f*; (*of taxi*) tassista *m*; (*chauffeur, of bus*)

autista *m/f*; ~'**s license** (*US*) *n* patente *f* di guida.

driveway ['draɪvweɪ] *n* viale *m* d'accesso.

driving ['draɪvɪŋ] *n* guida; ~ **instructor** *n* istruttore/trice di scuola guida; ~ **lesson** *n* lezione *f* di guida; ~ **licence** (*BRIT*) *n* patente *f* di guida; ~ **mirror** *n* specchietto retrovisore; ~ **school** *n* scuola *f* guida *inv*; ~ **test** *n* esame *m* di guida.

drizzle ['drɪzl] *n* pioggerella.

drone [drəʊn] *n* ronzio; (*male bee*) fuco.

drool [druːl] *vi* sbavare.

droop [druːp] *vi* (*flower*) appassire; (*head, shoulders*) chinarsi.

drop [drɒp] *n* (*of water*) goccia; (*lessening*) diminuzione *f*; (*fall*) caduta ♦ *vt* lasciare cadere; (*voice, eyes, price*) abbassare; (*set down from car*) far scendere; (*name from list*) lasciare fuori ♦ *vi* cascare; (*wind*) abbassarsi; ~**s** *npl* (*MED*) gocce *fpl*; ~ **off** *vi* (*sleep*) addormentarsi ♦ *vt* (*passenger*) far scendere; ~ **out** *vi* (*withdraw*) ritirarsi; (*student etc*) smettere di studiare; ~**-out** *n* (*from society/from university*) chi ha abbandonato (la società/gli studi); ~**per** *n* contagocce *m inv*; ~**pings** *npl* sterco.

drought [draʊt] *n* siccità *f inv*.

drove [drəʊv] *pt of* **drive.**

drown [draʊn] *vt* affogare; (*fig: noise*) soffocare ♦ *vi* affogare.

drowsy ['draʊzɪ] *adj* sonnolento(a), assonnato(a).

drudgery ['drʌdʒərɪ] *n* lavoro faticoso.

drug [drʌg] *n* farmaco; (*narcotic*) droga ♦ *vt* drogare; **to be on** ~**s** drogarsi; (*MED*) prendere medicinali; **hard/soft** ~**s** droghe pesanti/leggere; ~ **addict** *n* tossicomane *m/f*; ~**gist** (*US*) *n* persona che gestisce un *drugstore*; ~**store** (*US*) *n* drugstore *m inv*.

drum [drʌm] *n* tamburo; (*for oil, petrol*) fusto ♦ *vi* tamburellare; ~**s** *npl* (*set of* ~*s*) batteria; ~**mer** *n* batterista *m/f*.

drunk [drʌŋk] *pp of* **drink** ♦ *adj* ubriaco(a), ebbro(a) ♦ *n* (*also:* ~*ard*) ubriacone/a; ~**en** *adj* ubriaco(a); da ubriaco.

dry [draɪ] *adj* secco(a); *(day, clothes)* asciutto(a) ♦ *vt* seccare; *(clothes, hair, hands)* asciugare ♦ *vi* asciugarsi; ~ **up** *vi* seccarsi; ~**-cleaner's** *n* lavasecco *m inv*; ~**-cleaning** *n* pulitura a secco; ~**er** *n (for hair)* föhn *m inv*, asciugacapelli *m inv*; *(for clothes)* asciugabiancheria; *(US: spin-dryer)* centrifuga; ~ **goods store** *(US) n* negozio di stoffe; ~ **rot** *n* fungo del legno.

DSS *n abbr (= Department of Social Security) ministero della Previdenza sociale.*

dual ['djuəl] *adj* doppio(a); ~ **carriageway** *(BRIT) n* strada a doppia carreggiata; ~**-purpose** *adj* a doppio uso.

dubbed [dʌbd] *adj (CINEMA)* doppiato(a).

dubious ['djuːbɪəs] *adj* dubbio(a).

Dublin ['dʌblɪn] *n* Dublino *f*.

duchess ['dʌtʃɪs] *n* duchessa.

duck [dʌk] *n* anatra ♦ *vi* abbassare la testa; ~**ling** *n* anatroccolo.

duct [dʌkt] *n* condotto; *(ANAT)* canale *m*.

dud [dʌd] *n (object, tool)*: **it's a** ~ è inutile, non funziona ♦ *adj*: ~ **cheque** *(BRIT)* assegno a vuoto.

due [djuː] *adj* dovuto(a); *(expected)* atteso(a); *(fitting)* giusto(a) ♦ *n* dovuto ♦ *adv*: ~ **north** diritto verso nord; ~**s** *npl (for club, union)* quota; *(in harbour)* diritti *mpl* di porto; **in** ~ **course** a tempo debito; finalmente; ~ **to** dovuto a; a causa di; **to be** ~ **to do** dover fare.

duet [djuːˈɛt] *n* duetto.

duffel bag ['dʌfl-] *n* sacca da viaggio di tela.

duffel coat ['dʌfl-] *n* montgomery *m inv*.

dug [dʌg] *pt, pp of* **dig**.

duke [djuːk] *n* duca *m*.

dull [dʌl] *adj (light)* debole; *(boring)* noioso(a); *(slow-witted)* ottuso(a); *(sound, pain)* sordo(a); *(weather, day)* fosco(a), scuro(a) ♦ *vt (pain, grief)* attutire; *(mind, senses)* intorpidire.

duly ['djuːlɪ] *adv (on time)* a tempo debito; *(as expected)* debitamente.

dumb [dʌm] *adj* muto(a); *(pej)* stupido(a); ~**founded** [dʌmˈfaundɪd] *adj* stupito(a), stordito(a).

dummy ['dʌmɪ] *n (tailor's model)* manichino; *(TECH, COMM)* riproduzione *f*; *(BRIT: for baby)* tettarella ♦ *adj* falso(a), finto(a).

dump [dʌmp] *n (also: rubbish ~)* discarica di rifiuti; *(inf: place)* buco ♦ *vt (put down)* scaricare; mettere giù; *(get rid of)* buttar via.

dumpling ['dʌmplɪŋ] *n* specie di gnocco.

dumpy ['dʌmpɪ] *adj* tracagnotto(a).

dunce [dʌns] *n (SCOL)* somaro/a.

dung [dʌŋ] *n* concime *m*.

dungarees [dʌŋgəˈriːz] *npl* tuta.

dungeon ['dʌndʒən] *n* prigione *f* sotterranea.

dupe [djuːp] *n* zimbello ♦ *vt* gabbare, ingannare.

duplex ['djuːplɛks] *(US) n (house) casa con muro divisorio in comune con un'altra; (apartment)* appartamento su due piani.

duplicate [*n* 'djuːplɪkət, *vb* 'djuːplɪkeɪt] *n* doppio ♦ *vt* duplicare; **in** ~ in doppia copia.

durable ['djuərəbl] *adj* durevole; *(clothes, metal)* resistente.

duration [djuəˈreɪʃən] *n* durata.

duress [djuəˈrɛs] *n*: **under** ~ sotto costrizione.

during ['djuərɪŋ] *prep* durante, nel corso di.

dusk [dʌsk] *n* crepuscolo.

dust [dʌst] *n* polvere *f* ♦ *vt (furniture)* spolverare; *(cake etc)*: **to** ~ **with** cospargere con; ~**bin** *(BRIT) n* pattumiera; ~**er** *n* straccio per la polvere; ~**man** *(BRIT) n* netturbino; ~**y** *adj* polveroso(a).

Dutch [dʌtʃ] *adj* olandese ♦ *n (LING)* olandese *m*; **the** ~ *npl* gli Olandesi; **to go** ~ *(inf)* fare alla romana; ~**man/woman** *n* olandese *m/f*.

dutiful ['djuːtɪful] *adj (child)* rispettoso(a).

duty ['djuːtɪ] *n* dovere *m*; *(tax)* dazio, tassa; **on** ~ di servizio; **off** ~ libero(a), fuori servizio; ~-**free** adj esente da dazio.

duvet ['du:veɪ] (BRIT) n piumino, piumone m.

dwarf [dwɔːf] n nano/a ♦ vt far apparire piccolo.

dwell [dwɛl] (pt, pp **dwelt**) vi dimorare; ~ **on** vt fus indugiare su; ~**ing** n dimora; **dwelt** pt, pp of **dwell**.

dwindle ['dwɪndl] vi diminuire, decrescere.

dye [daɪ] n tinta ♦ vt tingere.

dying ['daɪɪŋ] adj morente, moribondo(a).

dyke [daɪk] (BRIT) n diga.

dynamic [daɪ'næmɪk] adj dinamico(a).

dynamite ['daɪnəmaɪt] n dinamite f.

dynamo ['daɪnəməʊ] n dinamo f inv.

dyslexia [dɪs'lɛksɪə] n dislessia.

E

E [iː] n (MUS) mi m.

each [iːtʃ] adj ogni, ciascuno(a) ♦ pron ciascuno(a), ognuno(a); ~ **one** ognuno(a); ~ **other** si (or ci etc); **they hate** ~ **other** si odiano (l'un l'altro); **you are jealous of** ~ **other** siete gelosi l'uno dell'altro; **they have 2 books** ~ hanno 2 libri ciascuno.

eager ['iːgə*] adj impaziente; desideroso(a); ardente; **to be** ~ **for** essere desideroso di, aver gran voglia di.

eagle ['iːgl] n aquila.

ear [ɪə*] n orecchio; (of corn) pannocchia; ~**ache** n mal m d'orecchi; ~**drum** n timpano m.

earl [əːl] (BRIT) n conte m.

earlier ['əːlɪə*] adj precedente ♦ adv prima.

early ['əːlɪ] adv presto, di buon'ora; (ahead of time) in anticipo ♦ adj (near the beginning) primo(a); (sooner than expected) prematuro(a); (quick: reply) veloce; **at an** ~ **hour** di buon'ora; **to have an** ~ **night** andare a letto presto; **in the** ~ or ~ **in the spring/19th century** all'inizio della primavera/

dell'Ottocento; ~ **retirement** n ritiro anticipato.

earmark ['ɪəmɑːk] vt: **to** ~ **sth for** destinare qc a.

earn [əːn] vt guadagnare; (rest, reward) meritare.

earnest ['əːnɪst] adj serio(a); **in** ~ sul serio.

earnings ['əːnɪŋz] npl guadagni mpl; (salary) stipendio.

earphones ['ɪəfəʊnz] npl cuffia.

earring ['ɪərɪŋ] n orecchino.

earshot ['ɪəʃɔt] n: **within** ~ a portata d'orecchio.

earth [əːθ] n terra ♦ vt (BRIT: ELEC) mettere a terra; ~**enware** n terracotta; stoviglie fpl di terracotta; ~**quake** n terremoto; ~**y** adj (fig) grossolano(a).

ease [iːz] n agio, comodo ♦ vt (soothe) calmare; (loosen) allentare; **to** ~ **sth out/in** tirare fuori/infilare qc con delicatezza; facilitare l'uscita/l'entrata di qc; **at** ~ a proprio agio; (MIL) a riposo; ~ **off** or **up** vi diminuire; (slow down) rallentare.

easel ['iːzl] n cavalletto.

easily ['iːzɪlɪ] adv facilmente.

east [iːst] n est m ♦ adj dell'est ♦ adv a oriente; **the E**~ l'Oriente m; (POL) l'Est.

Easter ['iːstə*] n Pasqua; ~ **egg** n uovo di Pasqua.

easterly ['iːstəlɪ] adj dall'est, d'oriente.

eastern ['iːstən] adj orientale, d'oriente; dell'est.

East Germany n Germania dell'Est.

eastward(s) ['iːstwəd(z)] adv verso est, verso levante.

easy ['iːzɪ] adj facile; (manner) disinvolto(a) ♦ adv: **to take it** or **things** ~ prendersela con calma; ~ **chair** n poltrona; ~-**going** adj accomodante.

eat [iːt] (pt **ate**, pp **eaten**) vt, vi mangiare; ~ **away** at vt fus rodere; ~ **into** vt fus rodere; ~**en** ['iːtn] pp of **eat**.

eaves [iːvz] npl gronda.

eavesdrop ['iːvzdrɔp] vi: **to** ~ (**on a conversation**) origliare (una conversazione).

ebb [ɛb] *n* riflusso ♦ *vi* rifluire; *(fig: also:* ~ *away)* declinare.

ebony ['ɛbənɪ] *n* ebano.

EC *n abbr* (= *European Community)* CEE *f*.

eccentric [ɪk'sɛntrɪk] *adj, n* eccentrico(a).

echo ['ɛkəu] *(pl* ~**es)** *n* eco *m or f* ♦ *vt* ripetere; fare eco a ♦ *vi* echeggiare; dare un eco.

éclair [eɪ'klɛə*] *n* ≈ bignè *m inv*.

eclipse [ɪ'klɪps] *n* eclissi *f inv*.

ecology [ɪ'kɔlədʒɪ] *n* ecologia.

economic [i:kə'nɔmɪk] *adj* economico(a); ~**al** *adj* economico(a); *(person)* economo(a); ~**s** *n* economia ♦ *npl* lato finanziario.

economize [ɪ'kɔnəmaɪz] *vi* risparmiare, fare economia.

economy [ɪ'kɔnəmɪ] *n* economia; ~ **class** *n* (*AVIAT)* classe *f* turistica; ~ **size** *n* (*COMM)* confezione *f* economica.

ecstasy ['ɛkstəsɪ] *n* estasi *f inv*.

eczema ['ɛksɪmə] *n* eczema *m*.

edge [ɛdʒ] *n* margine *m*; *(of table, plate, cup)* orlo; *(of knife etc)* taglio ♦ *vt* bordare; **on** ~ *(fig)* = **edgy; to** ~ **away from** sgattaiolare da; ~**ways** *adv*: **he couldn't get a word in** ~**ways** non riuscì a dire una parola; **edgy** *adj* nervoso(a).

edible ['ɛdɪbl] *adj* commestibile; *(meal)* mangiabile.

edict ['i:dɪkt] *n* editto.

Edinburgh ['ɛdɪnbərə] *n* Edimburgo *f*.

edit ['ɛdɪt] *vt* curare; ~**ion** [ɪ'dɪʃən] *n* edizione *f*; ~**or** *n* (*in newspaper)* redattore/trice; redattore/trice capo; *(of sb's work)* curatore/trice; ~**orial** [-'tɔ:rɪəl] *adj* redazionale, editoriale ♦ *n* editoriale *m*.

educate ['ɛdjukeɪt] *vt* istruire; educare.

education [ɛdju'keɪʃən] *n* educazione *f*; *(schooling)* istruzione *f*; ~**al** *adj* pedagogico(a); scolastico(a); istruttivo(a).

EEC *n abbr* = **EC.**

eel [i:l] *n* anguilla.

eerie ['ɪərɪ] *adj* che fa accapponare la pelle.

effect [ɪ'fɛkt] *n* effetto ♦ *vt* effettuare; **to take** ~ *(law)* entrare in vigore; *(drug)* fare effetto; **in** ~ effettivamente; ~**ive** *adj* efficace; *(actual)* effettivo(a); ~**ively** *adv* efficacemente; effettivamente; ~**iveness** *n* efficacia.

effeminate [ɪ'fɛmɪnɪt] *adj* effeminato(a).

efficiency [ɪ'fɪʃənsɪ] *n* efficienza; rendimento effettivo.

efficient [ɪ'fɪʃənt] *adj* efficiente.

effort ['ɛfət] *n* sforzo.

effrontery [ɪ'frʌntərɪ] *n* sfrontatezza.

effusive [ɪ'fju:sɪv] *adj* *(handshake, welcome)* caloroso(a).

e.g. *adv abbr* (= *exempli gratia)* per esempio, p.es.

egg [ɛg] *n* uovo; **hard-boiled/soft-boiled** ~ uovo sodo/alla coque; ~ **on** *vt* incitare; ~**cup** *n* portauovo *m inv*; ~**plant** *n* *(especially US)* melanzana; ~**shell** *n* guscio d'uovo.

ego ['i:gəu] *n* ego *m inv*.

egotism ['ɛgəutɪzəm] *n* egotismo.

Egypt ['i:dʒɪpt] *n* Egitto; ~**ian** [ɪ'dʒɪpʃən] *adj, n* egiziano(a).

eiderdown ['aɪdədaun] *n* piumino.

eight [eɪt] *num* otto; ~**een** *num* diciotto; **eighth** [eɪtθ] *num* ottavo(a); ~**y** *num* ottanta.

Eire ['ɛərə] *n* Repubblica d'Irlanda.

either ['aɪðə*] *adj* l'uno(a) o l'altro(a); *(both, each)* ciascuno(a) ♦ *pron*: ~ *(of them)* (o) l'uno(a) o l'altro(a) ♦ *adv* neanche ♦ *conj*: ~ **good or bad** o buono o cattivo; **on** ~ **side** su ciascun lato; **I don't like** ~ non mi piace né l'uno né l'altro; **no, I don't** ~ no, neanch'io.

eject [ɪ'dʒɛkt] *vt* espellere; lanciare.

eke [i:k]: **to** ~ **out** *vt* far durare; aumentare.

elaborate [*adj* ɪ'læbərɪt, *vb* ɪ'læbəreɪt] *adj* elaborato(a), minuzioso(a) ♦ *vt* elaborare ♦ *vi* fornire i particolari.

elapse [ɪ'læps] *vi* trascorrere, passare.

elastic [ɪ'læstɪk] *adj* elastico(a) ♦ *n* elastico; ~ **band** *(BRIT)* *n* elastico.

elated [ɪ'leɪtɪd] *adj* pieno(a) di gioia.

elbow ['ɛlbəu] *n* gomito.

elder ['ɛldə*] *adj* maggiore, più vec-

chio(a) ♦ n (tree) sambuco; **one's ~s** i più anziani; **~ly** adj anziano(a) ♦ npl: **the ~ly** gli anziani.
eldest ['ɛldɪst] adj, n: **the ~ (child)** il(la) maggiore (dei bambini).
elect [ɪ'lɛkt] vt eleggere ♦ adj: **the president ~** il presidente designato; **to ~ to do** decidere di fare; **~ion** [ɪ'lɛkʃən] n elezione f; **~ioneering** [ɪlɛkʃə'nɪərɪŋ] n propaganda elettorale; **~or** n elettore/trice; **~orate** n elettorato.
electric [ɪ'lɛktrɪk] adj elettrico(a); **~al** adj elettrico(a); **~ blanket** n coperta elettrica; **~ fire** n stufa elettrica.
electrician [ɪlɛk'trɪʃən] n elettricista m.
electricity [ɪlɛk'trɪsɪtɪ] n elettricità.
electrify [ɪ'lɛktrɪfaɪ] vt (RAIL) elettrificare; (audience) elettrizzare.
electrocute [ɪ'lɛktrəukjuːt] vt fulminare.
electronic [ɪlɛk'trɔnɪk] adj elettronico(a); **~ mail** n posta elettronica; **~s** n elettronica.
elegant ['ɛlɪɡənt] adj elegante.
element ['ɛlɪmənt] n elemento; (of heater, kettle etc) resistenza; **~ary** [-'mɛntərɪ] adj elementare.
elephant ['ɛlɪfənt] n elefante/essa.
elevation [ɛlɪ'veɪʃən] n elevazione f.
elevator ['ɛlɪveɪtə*] n elevatore m; (US: lift) ascensore m.
eleven [ɪ'lɛvn] num undici; **~ses** (BRIT) n caffè m a metà mattina; **~th** adj undicesimo(a).
elicit [ɪ'lɪsɪt] vt: **to ~ (from)** trarre (da), cavare fuori (da).
eligible ['ɛlɪdʒəbl] adj eleggibile; (for membership) che ha i requisiti.
elm [ɛlm] n olmo.
elocution [ɛlə'kjuːʃən] n dizione f.
elongated ['iːlɔŋɡeɪtɪd] adj allungato(a).
elope [ɪ'ləup] vi (lovers) scappare; **~ment** n fuga.
eloquent ['ɛləkwənt] adj eloquente.
else [ɛls] adv altro; **something ~** qualcos'altro; **somewhere ~** altrove; **everywhere ~** in qualsiasi altro luogo; **nobody ~** nessun altro; **where ~?** in quale altro luogo?; **little ~** poco altro; **~where** adv altrove.
elucidate [ɪ'luːsɪdeɪt] vt delucidare.

elude [ɪ'luːd] vt eludere.
elusive [ɪ'luːsɪv] adj elusivo(a).
emaciated [ɪ'meɪsɪeɪtɪd] adj emaciato(a).
emanate ['ɛməneɪt] vi: **to ~ from** provenire da.
emancipate [ɪ'mænsɪpeɪt] vt emancipare.
embankment [ɪm'bæŋkmənt] n (of road, railway) terrapieno.
embark [ɪm'bɑːk] vi: **to ~ (on)** imbarcarsi (su) ♦ vt imbarcare; **to ~ on** (fig) imbarcarsi in; **~ation** [ɛmbɑː'keɪʃən] n imbarco.
embarrass [ɪm'bærəs] vt imbarazzare; **~ed** adj imbarazzato(a); **~ing** adj imbarazzante; **~ment** n imbarazzo.
embassy ['ɛmbəsɪ] n ambasciata.
embedded [ɪm'bɛdɪd] adj incastrato(a).
embellish [ɪm'bɛlɪʃ] vt abbellire.
embers ['ɛmbəz] npl braci fpl.
embezzle [ɪm'bɛzl] vt appropriarsi indebitamente di.
embitter [ɪm'bɪtə*] vt amareggiare; inasprire.
embody [ɪm'bɔdɪ] vt (features) racchiudere, comprendere; (ideas) dar forma concreta a, esprimere.
embossed [ɪm'bɔst] adj in rilievo; goffrato(a).
embrace [ɪm'breɪs] vt abbracciare ♦ vi abbracciarsi ♦ n abbraccio.
embroider [ɪm'brɔɪdə*] vt ricamare; **~y** n ricamo.
embryo ['ɛmbrɪəu] n embrione m.
emerald ['ɛmərəld] n smeraldo.
emerge [ɪ'məːdʒ] vi emergere.
emergency [ɪ'məːdʒənsɪ] n emergenza; **in an ~** in caso di emergenza; **~ cord** (US) n segnale m d'allarme; **~ exit** n uscita di sicurezza; **~ landing** n atterraggio forzato; **~ services** npl (fire, police, ambulance) servizi mpl di pronto intervento.
emery board ['ɛmərɪ-] n limetta di carta smerigliata.
emigrate ['ɛmɪɡreɪt] vi emigrare.
eminent ['ɛmɪnənt] adj eminente.
emit [ɪ'mɪt] vt emettere.
emotion [ɪ'məuʃən] n emozione f; **~al**

adj (*person*) emotivo(a); (*scene*) commovente; (*tone, speech*) carico(a) d'emozione.

emperor ['ɛmpərə*] *n* imperatore *m*.

emphases ['ɛmfəsi:z] *npl of* **emphasis**.

emphasis ['ɛmfəsɪs] (*pl* -**ases**) *n* enfasi *f inv*; importanza.

emphasize ['ɛmfəsaɪz] *vt* (*word, point*) sottolineare; (*feature*) mettere in evidenza.

emphatic [ɛm'fætɪk] *adj* (*strong*) vigoroso(a); (*unambiguous, clear*) netto(a); ~**ally** *adv* vigorosamente; nettamente.

empire ['ɛmpaɪə*] *n* impero.

employ [ɪm'plɔɪ] *vt* impiegare; ~**ee** [-'i:] *n* impiegato/a; ~**er** *n* principale *m/f*, datore *m* di lavoro; ~**ment** *n* impiego; ~**ment agency** *n* agenzia di collocamento.

empower [ɪm'pauə*] *vt*: **to ~ sb to do** concedere autorità a qn di fare.

empress ['ɛmprɪs] *n* imperatrice *f*.

emptiness ['ɛmptɪnɪs] *n* vuoto.

empty ['ɛmptɪ] *adj* vuoto(a); (*threat, promise*) vano(a) ♦ *vt* vuotare ♦ *vi* vuotarsi; (*liquid*) scaricarsi; ~-**handed** *adj* a mani vuote.

emulate ['ɛmjuleɪt] *vt* emulare.

emulsion [ɪ'mʌlʃən] *n* emulsione *f*; ~ (**paint**) *n* colore *m* a tempera.

enable [ɪ'neɪbl] *vt*: **to ~ sb to do** permettere a qn di fare.

enact [ɪn'ækt] *vt* (*law*) emanare; (*play, scene*) rappresentare.

enamel [ɪ'næməl] *n* smalto; (*also: ~ paint*) vernice *f* a smalto.

encased [ɪn'keɪst] *adj*: ~ **in** racchiuso(a) in; rivestito(a) di.

enchant [ɪn'tʃɑːnt] *vt* incantare; (*subj: magic spell*) catturare; ~**ing** *adj* incantevole, affascinante.

encircle [ɪn'sə:kl] *vt* accerchiare.

encl. *abbr* (= *enclosed*) all.

enclave ['ɛnkleɪv] *n* enclave *f*.

enclose [ɪn'kləuz] *vt* (*land*) circondare, recingere; (*letter etc*): **to ~ (with)** allegare (con); **please find ~d** trovi qui accluso.

enclosure [ɪn'kləuʒə*] *n* recinto.

encompass [ɪn'kʌmpəs] *vt* comprendere.

encore [ɔŋ'kɔː*] *excl* bis ♦ *n* bis *m inv*.

encounter [ɪn'kauntə*] *n* incontro ♦ *vt* incontrare.

encourage [ɪn'kʌrɪdʒ] *vt* incoraggiare; ~**ment** *n* incoraggiamento.

encroach [ɪn'krəutʃ] *vi*: **to ~ (up)on** (*rights*) usurpare; (*time*) abusare di; (*land*) oltrepassare i limiti di.

encumber [ɪn'kʌmbə*] *vt*: **to be ~ed with** essere carico(a) di.

encyclop(a)edia [ɛnsaɪkləu'piːdɪə] *n* enciclopedia.

end [ɛnd] *n* fine *f*; (*aim*) fine *m*; (*of table*) bordo estremo; (*of pointed object*) punta ♦ *vt* finire; (*also: bring to an ~, put an ~ to*) mettere fine a ♦ *vi* finire; **in the ~** alla fine; **on ~** (*object*) ritto(a); **to stand on ~** (*hair*) rizzarsi; **for hours on ~** per ore ed ore; ~ **up** *vi*: **to ~ up in** finire in.

endanger [ɪn'deɪndʒə*] *vt* mettere in pericolo.

endearing [ɪn'dɪərɪŋ] *adj* accattivante.

endeavour [ɪn'devə*] (*US* **endeavor**) *n* sforzo, tentativo ♦ *vi*: **to ~ to do** cercare *or* sforzarsi di fare.

ending ['ɛndɪŋ] *n* fine *f*, conclusione *f*; (*LING*) desinenza.

endive ['ɛndaɪv] *n* (*curly*) indivia (riccia); (*smooth, flat*) indivia belga.

endless ['ɛndlɪs] *adj* senza fine.

endorse [ɪn'dɔːs] *vt* (*cheque*) girare; (*approve*) approvare, appoggiare; ~**ment** *n* approvazione *f*; (*on driving licence*) *contravvenzione registrata sulla patente*.

endow [ɪn'dau] *vt* (*provide with money*) devolvere denaro a; (*equip*): **to ~ with** fornire di, dotare di.

endurance [ɪn'djuərəns] *n* resistenza; pazienza.

endure [ɪn'djuə*] *vt* sopportare, resistere a ♦ *vi* durare.

enemy ['ɛnəmɪ] *adj, n* nemico(a).

energetic [ɛnə'dʒɛtɪk] *adj* energico(a); attivo(a).

energy ['ɛnədʒɪ] *n* energia.

enforce [ɪn'fɔːs] *vt* (*LAW*) applicare, far

osservare.

engage [ɪn'geɪdʒ] *vt* (*hire*) assumere; (*lawyer*) incaricare; (*attention, interest*) assorbire; (*TECH*): **to ~ gear/ the clutch** innestare la marcia/la frizione ♦ *vi* (*TECH*) ingranare; **to ~ in** impegnarsi in; **~d** *adj* (*BRIT: busy, in use*) occupato(a); (*betrothed*) fidanzato(a); **to get ~d** fidanzarsi; **~d tone** (*BRIT*) *n* (*TEL*) segnale *m* di occupato; **~ment** *n* impegno, obbligo; appuntamento; (*to marry*) fidanzamento; **~ment ring** *n* anello di fidanzamento.

engaging [ɪn'geɪdʒɪŋ] *adj* attraente.

engender [ɪn'dʒendə*] *vt* produrre, causare.

engine ['endʒɪn] *n* (*AUT*) motore *m*; (*RAIL*) locomotiva; **~ driver** *n* (*of train*) macchinista *m*.

engineer [endʒɪ'nɪə*] *n* ingegnere *m*; (*BRIT: for repairs*) tecnico; (*on ship, US: RAIL*) macchinista *m*; **~ing** *n* ingegneria.

England ['ɪŋglənd] *n* Inghilterra.

English ['ɪŋglɪʃ] *adj* inglese ♦ *n* (*LING*) inglese *m*; **the ~** *npl* gli Inglesi; **the ~ Channel** *n* la Manica; **~man/woman** *n* inglese *m/f*.

engraving [ɪn'greɪvɪŋ] *n* incisione *f*.

engrossed [ɪn'grəust] *adj*: **~ in** assorbito(a) da, preso(a) da.

engulf [ɪn'gʌlf] *vt* inghiottire.

enhance [ɪn'hɑ:ns] *vt* accrescere.

enjoy [ɪn'dʒɔɪ] *vt* godere, (*have: success, fortune*) avere; **to ~ o.s.** godersela, divertirsi; **~able** *adj* piacevole; **~ment** *n* piacere *m*, godimento.

enlarge [ɪn'lɑ:dʒ] *vt* ingrandire ♦ *vi*: **to ~ on** (*subject*) dilungarsi su.

enlighten [ɪn'laɪtn] *vt* illuminare; dare schiarimenti a; **~ed** *adj* illuminato(a); **~ment** *n*: **the E~ment** (*HISTORY*) l'Illuminismo.

enlist [ɪn'lɪst] *vt* arruolare; (*support*) procurare ♦ *vi* arruolarsi.

enmity ['enmɪtɪ] *n* inimicizia.

enormous [ɪ'nɔ:məs] *adj* enorme.

enough [ɪ'nʌf] *adj, n*: **~ time/books**

assai tempo/libri; **have you got ~?** ne ha abbastanza *or* a sufficienza? ♦ *adv*: **big ~** abbastanza grande; **he has not worked ~** non ha lavorato abbastanza; **~!** basta!; **that's ~,** thanks basta così, grazie; **I've had ~ of him** ne ho abbastanza di lui; **... which, funnily** *or* **oddly ~ ...** che, strano a dirsi.

enquire [ɪn'kwaɪə*] *vt, vi* = **inquire.**

enrage [ɪn'reɪdʒ] *vt* fare arrabbiare.

enrich [ɪn'rɪtʃ] *vt* arricchire.

enrol [ɪn'rəul] *vt* iscrivere ♦ *vi* iscriversi; **~ment** *n* iscrizione *f*.

ensue [ɪn'sju:] *vi* seguire, risultare.

ensure [ɪn'ʃuə*] *vt* assicurare; garantire.

entail [ɪn'teɪl] *vt* comportare.

entangled [ɪn'tæŋgld] *adj*: **to become ~ (in)** impigliarsi (in).

enter ['entə*] *vt* entrare in; (*army*) arruolarsi in; (*competition*) partecipare a; (*sb for a competition*) iscrivere; (*write down*) registrare; (*COMPUT*) inserire ♦ *vi* entrare; **~ for** *vt fus* iscriversi a; **~ into** *vt fus* (*explanation*) cominciare a dare; (*debate*) partecipare a; (*agreement*) concludere.

enterprise ['entəpraɪz] *n* (*undertaking, company*) impresa; (*spirit*) iniziativa; **free ~** liberalismo economico; **private ~** iniziativa privata.

enterprising ['entəpraɪzɪŋ] *adj* intraprendente.

entertain [entə'teɪn] *vt* divertire; (*invite*) ricevere; (*idea, plan*) nutrire; **~er** *n* comico/a; **~ing** *adj* divertente; **~ment** *n* (*amusement*) divertimento; (*show*) spettacolo.

enthralled [ɪn'θrɔ:ld] *adj* affascinato(a).

enthusiasm [ɪn'θu:zɪæzəm] *n* entusiasmo.

enthusiast [ɪn'θu:zɪæst] *n* entusiasta *m/f*; **~ic** [-'æstɪk] *adj* entusiasta, entusiastico(a); **to be ~ic about sth/sb** essere appassionato(a) di qc/entusiasta di qn.

entice [ɪn'taɪs] *vt* allettare, sedurre.

entire [ɪn'taɪə*] *adj* intero(a); **~ly** *adv* completamente, interamente; **~ty** [ɪn'taɪərətɪ] *n*: **in its ~ty** nel suo complesso.

entitle [ɪn'taɪtl] vt (give right): to ~ sb to sth/to do dare diritto a qn a qc/a fare; ~d adj (book) che si intitola; to be ~d to do avere il diritto di fare.

entrails ['entreɪlz] npl interiora fpl.

entrance [n 'entrns, vb ɪn'trɑ:ns] n entrata, ingresso; (of person) entrata ♦ vt incantare, rapire; **to gain** ~ **to** (university etc) essere ammesso a; ~ **examination** n esame m di ammissione; ~ **fee** n tassa d'iscrizione; (to museum etc) prezzo d'ingresso; ~ **ramp** (US) n (AUT) rampa di accesso.

entrant ['entrnt] n partecipante m/f; concorrente m/f.

entreat [ɛn'tri:t] vt supplicare.

entrenched [ɛn'trɛntʃt] adj radicato(a).

entrepreneur [ɒntrəprə'nə:*] n imprenditore m.

entrust [ɪn'trʌst] vt: to ~ sth to affidare qc a.

entry ['entrɪ] n entrata; (way in) entrata, ingresso; (item: on list) iscrizione f; (in dictionary) voce f; **no** ~ vietato l'ingresso; (AUT) divieto di accesso; ~ **form** n modulo d'iscrizione; ~ **phone** n citofono.

envelop [ɪn'vɛləp] vt avvolgere, avviluppare.

envelope ['ɛnvələup] n busta.

envious ['ɛnvɪəs] adj invidioso(a).

environment [ɪn'vaɪərnmənt] n ambiente m; ~**al** [-'mentl] adj ecologico(a); ambientale.

envisage [ɪn'vɪzɪdʒ] vt immaginare; prevedere.

envoy ['ɛnvɔɪ] n inviato/a.

envy ['ɛnvɪ] n invidia ♦ vt invidiare; to ~ sb sth invidiare qn per qc.

epic ['ɛpɪk] n poema m epico ♦ adj epico(a).

epidemic [ɛpɪ'dɛmɪk] n epidemia.

epilepsy ['ɛpɪlɛpsɪ] n epilessia.

episode ['ɛpɪsəud] n episodio.

epistle [ɪ'pɪsl] n epistola.

epitome [ɪ'pɪtəmɪ] n epitome f; quintessenza; **epitomize** vt (fig) incarnare.

equable ['ɛkwəbl] adj uniforme; equilibrato(a).

equal ['i:kwl] adj uguale ♦ n pari m/f inv ♦ vt uguagliare; ~ **to** (task) all'altezza di; ~**ity** [i:'kwɔlɪtɪ] n uguaglianza; ~**ize** vi pareggiare; ~**ly** adv ugualmente.

equanimity [ɛkwə'nɪmɪtɪ] n serenità.

equate [ɪ'kweɪt] vt: to ~ sth with considerare qc uguale a; (compare) paragonare qc con; **equation** [ɪ'kweɪʃən] n (MATH) equazione f.

equator [ɪ'kweɪtə*] n equatore m.

equilibrium [i:kwɪ'lɪbrɪəm] n equilibrio.

equip [ɪ'kwɪp] vt equipaggiare, attrezzare; to ~ sb/sth with fornire qn/qc di; to be well ~ped (office etc) essere ben attrezzato(a); he is well ~ped for the job ha i requisiti necessari per quel lavoro; ~**ment** n attrezzatura; (electrical etc) apparecchiatura.

equitable ['ɛkwɪtəbl] adj equo(a), giusto(a).

equities ['ɛkwɪtɪz] (BRIT) npl (COMM) azioni fpl ordinarie.

equivalent [ɪ'kwɪvəlnt] adj equivalente ♦ n equivalente m; to be ~ to equivalere a.

equivocal [ɪ'kwɪvəkl] adj equivoco(a); (open to suspicion) dubbio(a).

era ['ɪərə] n era, età f inv.

eradicate [ɪ'rædɪkeɪt] vt sradicare.

erase [ɪ'reɪz] vt cancellare; ~**r** n gomma.

erect [ɪ'rɛkt] adj eretto(a) ♦ vt costruire; (assemble) montare; ~**ion** [ɪ'rɛkʃən] n costruzione f; montaggio; (PHYSIOL) erezione f.

ermine ['ə:mɪn] n ermellino.

erode [ɪ'rəud] vt erodere; (metal) corrodere.

erotic [ɪ'rɔtɪk] adj erotico(a).

err [ə:*] vi errare.

errand ['ɛrnd] n commissione f.

erratic [ɪ'rætɪk] adj imprevedibile; (person, mood) incostante.

error ['ɛrə*] n errore m.

erupt [ɪ'rʌpt] vi (volcano) mettersi (or essere) in eruzione; (war, crisis) scoppiare; ~**ion** [ɪ'rʌpʃən] n eruzione f; scoppio.

escalate ['ɛskəleɪt] vi intensificarsi.

escalator ['eskəleɪtə*] n scala mobile.
escapade [eskə'peɪd] n scappatella; avventura.
escape [ɪ'skeɪp] n evasione f; fuga; (of gas etc) fuga, fuoriuscita ♦ vi fuggire; (from jail) evadere, scappare; (leak) uscire ♦ vt sfuggire a; to ~ from (place) fuggire da; (person) sfuggire a; **escapism** n evasione f (dalla realtà).
escort [n 'eskɔːt, vb ɪ'skɔːt] n scorta; (male companion) cavaliere m ♦ vt scortare; accompagnare.
Eskimo ['eskɪməu] n eschimese m/f.
especially [ɪ'speʃlɪ] adv specialmente; soprattutto; espressamente.
espionage ['espɪənɑːʒ] n spionaggio.
esplanade [esplə'neɪd] n lungomare m inv.
Esq. abbr = **Esquire**.
Esquire [ɪ'skwaɪə*] n: **J. Brown, ~ Signor J. Brown.**
essay ['eseɪ] n (SCOL) composizione f; (LITERATURE) saggio.
essence ['esns] n essenza.
essential [ɪ'senʃl] adj essenziale ♦ n elemento essenziale; **~ly** adv essenzialmente.
establish [ɪ'stæblɪʃ] vt stabilire; (business) mettere su; (one's power etc) affermare; **~ed** adj (business etc) affermato(a); **~ment** n stabilimento; **the E~ment** la classe dirigente, l'establishment m.
estate [ɪ'steɪt] n proprietà f inv; beni mpl, patrimonio; (BRIT: also: housing ~)· complesso edilizio; **~ agent** (BRIT) n agente m immobiliare; **~ car** (BRIT) n giardiniera.
esteem [ɪ'stiːm] n stima ♦ vt (think highly of) stimare; (consider) considerare.
esthetic [ɪs'θetɪk] (US) adj = **aesthetic**.
estimate [n 'estɪmət, vb 'estɪmeɪt] n stima; (COMM) preventivo ♦ vt stimare, valutare; **estimation** [-'meɪʃən] n stima; opinione f.
estranged [ɪ'streɪndʒd] adj separato(a).
etc abbr (= et cetera) etc, ecc.
etching ['etʃɪŋ] n acquaforte f.
eternal [ɪ'təːnl] adj eterno(a)

eternity [ɪ'təːnɪtɪ] n eternità.
ether ['iːθə*] n etere m.
ethical ['eθɪkl] adj etico(a), morale.
ethics ['eθɪks] n etica ♦ npl morale f.
Ethiopia [iːθɪ'əupɪə] n Etiopia.
ethnic ['eθnɪk] adj etnico(a).
ethos ['iːθɔs] n norma di vita.
etiquette ['etɪket] n etichetta.
Eurocheque ['juərəutʃek] n eurochèque m inv.
Europe ['juərəp] n Europa; **~an** [-'pɪːən] adj, n europeo(a).
evacuate [ɪ'vækjueɪt] vt evacuare.
evade [ɪ'veɪd] vt (tax) evadere; (duties etc) sottrarsi a; (person) schivare.
evaluate [ɪ'væljueɪt] vt valutare.
evaporate [ɪ'væpəreɪt] vi evaporare; **~d milk** n latte m concentrato.
evasion [ɪ'veɪʒən] n evasione f.
evasive [ɪ'veɪsɪv] adj evasivo(a).
eve [iːv] n: **on the ~ of** alla vigilia di.
even ['iːvn] adj regolare; (number) pari inv ♦ adv anche, perfino; **~ if, ~ though** anche se; **~ more** ancora di più; **~ so** ciò nonostante; **not ~** nemmeno; **to get ~ with sb** dare la pari a qn; **~ out** vi pareggiare.
evening ['iːvnɪŋ] n sera; (as duration, event) serata; **in the ~** la sera; **~ class** n corso serale; **~ dress** n (woman's) abito da sera; **in ~ dress** (man) in abito scuro; (woman) in abito lungo.
event [ɪ'vent] n avvenimento; (SPORT) gara; **in the ~ of** in caso di; **~ful** adj denso(a) di eventi.
eventual [ɪ'ventʃuəl] adj finale; **~ity** [-'ælɪtɪ] n possibilità f inv, eventualità f inv; **~ly** adv alla fine.
ever ['evə*] adv mai; (at all times) sempre; **the best ~** il migliore che ci sia mai stato; **have you ~ seen it?** l'ha mai visto?; **~ since** adv da allora ♦ conj sin da quando; **~ so pretty** così bello(a); **~green** n sempreverde m; **~lasting** adj eterno(a).
every ['evrɪ] adj ogni; **~ day** tutti i giorni, ogni giorno; **~ other/third day** ogni due/tre giorni; **~ other car** una macchina su due; **~ now and then** ogni tanto, di quando in quando; **~body**

pron = ~**one**; ~**day** *adj* quotidiano(a); di ogni giorno; ~**one** *pron* ognuno, tutti pl; ~**thing** *pron* tutto, ogni cosa; ~**where** *adv* (*gen*) dappertutto; (*wherever*) ovunque.

evict [ɪ'vɪkt] *vt* sfrattare.

evidence ['ɛvɪdns] *n* (*proof*) prova; (*of witness*) testimonianza; (*sign*): **to show ~ of** dare segni di; **to give ~** deporre.

evident ['ɛvɪdnt] *adj* evidente; ~**ly** *adv* evidentemente.

evil ['i:vl] *adj* cattivo(a), maligno(a) ♦ *n* male *m*.

evoke [ɪ'vəuk] *vt* evocare.

evolution [i:və'lu:ʃən] *n* evoluzione *f*.

evolve [ɪ'vɔlv] *vt* elaborare ♦ *vi* svilupparsi, evolversi.

ewe [ju:] *n* pecora.

ex- [ɛks] *prefix* ex.

exacerbate [ɛks'æsəbeɪt] *vt* aggravare.

exact [ɪg'zækt] *adj* esatto(a) ♦ *vt*: **to ~ sth** (**from**) estorcere qc (da); esigere qc (da); ~**ing** *adj* esigente; (*work*) faticoso(a); ~**ly** *adv* esattamente.

exaggerate [ɪg'zædʒəreɪt] *vt*, *vi* esagerare; **exaggeration** [-'reɪʃən] *n* esagerazione *f*.

exalted [ɪg'zɔ:ltɪd] *adj* esaltato(a); elevato(a).

exam [ɪg'zæm] *n abbr* (*SCOL*) = **examination**.

examination [ɪgzæmɪ'neɪʃən] *n* (*SCOL*) esame *m*; (*MED*) controllo.

examine [ɪg'zæmɪn] *vt* esaminare; ~**r** *n* esaminatore/trice.

example [ɪg'zɑ:mpl] *n* esempio; **for ~** ad *or* per esempio.

exasperate [ɪg'zɑ:spəreɪt] *vt* esasperare; **exasperating** *adj* esasperante; **exasperation** [-'reɪʃən] *n* esasperazione *f*.

excavate ['ɛkskəveɪt] *vt* scavare.

exceed [ɪk'si:d] *vt* superare; (*one's powers, time limit*) oltrepassare; ~**ing-ly** *adv* eccessivamente.

excellent ['ɛksələnt] *adj* eccellente.

except [ɪk'sɛpt] *prep* (*also:* ~ **for**, ~**ing**) salvo, all'infuori di, eccetto ♦ *vt* escludere; ~ **if/when** salvo se/quando; ~ **that** salvo che; ~**ion** [ɪk'sɛpʃən] *n*

eccezione *f*; **to take ~ion to** trovare a ridire su; ~**ional** [ɪk'sɛpʃənl] *adj* eccezionale.

excerpt ['ɛksə:pt] *n* estratto.

excess [ɪk'sɛs] *n* eccesso; ~ **baggage** *n* bagaglio in eccedenza; ~ **fare** *n* supplemento; ~**ive** *adj* eccessivo(a).

exchange [ɪks'tʃeɪndʒ] *n* scambio; (*also: telephone ~*) centralino ♦ *vt*: **to ~** (**for**) scambiare (con); ~ **rate** *n* tasso di cambio.

Exchequer [ɪks'tʃekə*] *n*: **the ~** (*BRIT*) lo Scacchiere, ≈ il ministero delle Finanze.

excise ['ɛksaɪz] *n* imposta, dazio.

excite [ɪk'saɪt] *vt* eccitare; **to get ~d** eccitarsi; ~**ment** *n* eccitazione *f*; agitazione *f*; **exciting** *adj* avventuroso(a); (*film, book*) appassionante.

exclaim [ɪk'skleɪm] *vi* esclamare; **exclamation** [ɛksklə'meɪʃən] *n* esclamazione *f*; **exclamation mark** *n* punto esclamativo.

exclude [ɪk'sklu:d] *vt* escludere.

exclusive [ɪk'sklu:sɪv] *adj* esclusivo(a); ~ **of VAT** I.V.A. esclusa.

excommunicate [ɛkskə'mju:nɪkeɪt] *vt* scomunicare.

excruciating [ɪk'skru:ʃɪeɪtɪŋ] *adj* straziante, atroce.

excursion [ɪk'skə:ʃən] *n* escursione *f*, gita.

excuse [*n* ɪk'skju:s, *vb* ɪk'skju:z] *n* scusa ♦ *vt* scusare; **to ~ sb from** (*activity*) dispensare qn da; ~ **me!** mi scusi!; **now, if you will ~ me ...** ora, mi scusi ma ....

ex-directory (*BRIT*) *adj* (*TEL*): **to be ~** non essere sull'elenco.

execute ['ɛksɪkju:t] *vt* (*prisoner*) giustiziare; (*plan etc*) eseguire.

execution [ɛksɪ'kju:ʃən] *n* esecuzione *f*; ~**er** *n* boia *m inv*.

executive [ɪg'zekjutɪv] *n* (*COMM*) dirigente *m*; (*POL*) esecutivo ♦ *adj* esecutivo(a).

exemplify [ɪg'zemplɪfaɪ] *vt* esemplificare.

exempt [ɪg'zempt] *adj* esentato(a) ♦ *vt*:

to ~ sb from esentare qn da; ~ion [ɪg'zɛmpʃən] n esenzione f.

exercise ['ɛksəsaɪz] n (keep fit) moto; (SCOL, MIL etc) esercizio ♦ vt esercitare; (patience) usare; (dog) portar fuori ♦ vi (also: take ~) fare del moto; ~ book n quaderno.

exert [ɪg'zə:t] vt esercitare; to ~ o.s. sforzarsi; ~ion [-ʃən] n sforzo.

exhale [ɛks'heɪl] vt, vi espirare.

exhaust [ɪg'zɔ:st] n (also: ~ fumes) scappamento; (also: ~ pipe) tubo di scappamento ♦ vt esaurire; ~ed adj esaurito(a); ~ion [ɪg'zɔ:stʃən] n esaurimento; **nervous** ~ion sovraffaticamento mentale; ~ive adj esauriente.

exhibit [ɪg'zɪbɪt] n (ART) oggetto esposto; (LAW) documento or oggetto esibito ♦ vt esporre; (courage, skill) dimostrare; ~ion [ɛksɪ'bɪʃən] n mostra, esposizione f.

exhilarating [ɪg'zɪləreɪtɪŋ] adj esilarante; stimolante.

exhort [ɪg'zɔ:t] vt esortare.

exile ['ɛksaɪl] n esilio; (person) esiliato/a ♦ vt esiliare.

exist [ɪg'zɪst] vi esistere; ~ence n esistenza; ~ing adj esistente.

exit ['ɛksɪt] n uscita ♦ vi (THEATRE, COMPUT) uscire; ~ ramp (US) n (AUT) rampa di uscita.

exodus ['ɛksədəs] n esodo.

exonerate [ɪg'zɔnəreɪt] vt: to ~ from discolpare da.

exotic [ɪg'zɔtɪk] adj esotico(a).

expand [ɪk'spænd] vt espandere; estendere; allargare ♦ vi (business, gas) espandersi; (metal) dilatarsi.

expanse [ɪk'spæns] n distesa, estensione f.

expansion [ɪk'spænʃən] n (gen) espansione f; (of town, economy) sviluppo; (of metal) dilatazione f.

expect [ɪk'spɛkt] vt (anticipate) prevedere, aspettarsi, prevedere or aspettarsi che +sub; (require) richiedere, esigere; (suppose) supporre; (await, also baby) aspettare ♦ vi: to be ~ing essere in stato interessante; to ~

sb to do aspettarsi che qn faccia; ~ancy n (anticipation) attesa; **life** ~ancy probabilità fpl di vita; ~ant **mother** n gestante f; ~ation [ɛkspɛk'teɪʃən] n aspettativa; speranza.

expedience [ɪk'spi:dɪəns] n convenienza.

expediency [ɪk'spi:dɪənsɪ] n convenienza.

expedient [ɪk'spi:dɪənt] adj conveniente; vantaggioso(a) ♦ n espediente m.

expedition [ɛkspə'dɪʃən] n spedizione f.

expel [ɪk'spɛl] vt espellere.

expend [ɪk'spɛnd] vt spendere; (use up) consumare; ~able adj sacrificabile; ~iture [ɪk'spɛndɪtʃə*] n spesa.

expense [ɪk'spɛns] n spesa; (high cost) costo; ~s npl (COMM) spese fpl, indennità fpl; **at the ~ of** a spese di; ~ **account** n conto m spese inv.

expensive [ɪk'spɛnsɪv] adj caro(a), costoso(a).

experience [ɪk'spɪərɪəns] n esperienza ♦ vt (pleasure) provare; (hardship) soffrire; ~d adj esperto(a).

experiment [n ɪk'spɛrɪmənt, vb ɪk'spɛrɪment] n esperimento, esperienza ♦ vi: to ~ (with/on) fare esperimenti (con/su).

expert ['ɛkspə:t] adj, n esperto(a); ~ise [-'ti:z] n competenza.

expire [ɪk'spaɪə*] vi (period of time, licence) scadere; **expiry** n scadenza.

explain [ɪk'spleɪn] vt spiegare; **explanation** [ɛksplə'neɪʃən] n spiegazione f; **explanatory** [ɪk'splænətrɪ] adj esplicativo(a).

explicit [ɪk'splɪsɪt] adj esplicito(a).

explode [ɪk'spləud] vi esplodere.

exploit [n 'ɛksplɔɪt, vb ɪk'splɔɪt] n impresa ♦ vt sfruttare; ~ation [-'teɪʃən] n sfruttamento.

exploratory [ɪk'splɔrətrɪ] adj esplorativo(a).

explore [ɪk'splɔ:*] vt esplorare; (possibilities) esaminare; ~r n esploratore/trice.

explosion [ɪk'spləuʒən] n esplosione f.

explosive [ɪk'spləusɪv] adj esplosivo(a) ♦ n esplosivo.

exponent [ɪk'spəunənt] n esponente m/f.

export [vb ɛk'spɔ:t, n 'ɛkspɔ:t] vt esportare ♦ n esportazione f; articolo di esportazione ♦ cpd d'esportazione; ~**er** n esportatore m.

expose [ɪk'spəuz] vt esporre; (unmask) smascherare; ~**d** adj (position) esposto(a).

exposure [ɪk'spəuʒə*] n esposizione f; (PHOT) posa; (MED) assideramento; ~ **meter** n esposimetro.

expound [ɪk'spaund] vt esporre.

express [ɪk'sprɛs] adj (definite) chiaro(a), espresso(a); (BRIT: letter etc) espresso inv ♦ n (train) espresso ♦ vt esprimere; ~**ion** [ɪk'sprɛʃən] n espressione f; ~**ive** adj espressivo(a); ~**ly** adv espressamente; ~**way** n (US) n (urban motorway) autostrada che attraversa la città.

exquisite [ɛk'skwɪzɪt] adj squisito(a).

extend [ɪk'stɛnd] vt (visit) protrarre; (road, deadline) prolungare; (building) ampliare; (offer) offrire, porgere ♦ vi (land, period) estendersi.

extension [ɪk'stɛnʃən] n (of road, term) prolungamento; (of contract, deadline) proroga; (building) annesso; (to wire, table) prolunga; (telephone) interno; (: in private house) apparecchio supplementare.

extensive [ɪk'stɛnsɪv] adj esteso(a), ampio(a); (damage) su larga scala; (coverage, discussion) esauriente; (use) grande; ~**ly** adv: **he's travelled** ~**ly** ha viaggiato molto.

extent [ɪk'stɛnt] n estensione f; **to some** ~ fino a un certo punto; **to such an** ~ **that** ... a un tal punto che ...; **to what** ~? fino a che punto?; **to the** ~ **of** ... fino al punto di ....

extenuating [ɪks'tɛnjueɪtɪŋ] adj: ~ **circumstances** attenuanti fpl.

exterior [ɛk'stɪərɪə*] adj esteriore, esterno(a) ♦ n esteriore m, esterno; aspetto (esteriore).

exterminate [ɪk'stə:mɪneɪt] vt sterminare.

external [ɛk'stə:nl] adj esterno(a), esteriore.

extinct [ɪk'stɪŋkt] adj estinto(a).

extinguish [ɪk'stɪŋgwɪʃ] vt estinguere; ~**er** n estintore m.

extort [ɪk'stɔ:t] vt: **to** ~ **sth** (**from**) estorcere qc (da); ~**ionate** [ɪk'stɔ:ʃnət] adj esorbitante.

extra ['ɛkstrə] adj extra inv, supplementare ♦ adv (in addition) di più ♦ n extra m inv; (surcharge) supplemento; (CINEMA, THEATRE) comparsa.

extra... ['ɛkstrə] prefix extra....

extract [vb ɪk'strækt, n 'ɛkstrækt] vt estrarre; (money, promise) strappare ♦ n estratto; (passage) brano.

extracurricular ['ɛkstrəkə'rɪkjulə*] adj extrascolastico(a).

extradite ['ɛkstrədaɪt] vt estradare.

extramarital [ɛkstrə'mærɪtl] adj extraconiugale.

extramural [ɛkstrə'mjuərl] adj fuori dell'università.

extraordinary [ɪk'strɔ:dnrɪ] adj straordinario(a).

extravagance [ɪk'strævəgəns] n sperpero; stravaganza.

extravagant [ɪk'strævəgənt] adj (lavish) prodigo(a); (wasteful) dispendioso(a).

extreme [ɪk'stri:m] adj estremo(a) ♦ n estremo; ~**ly** adv estremamente.

extricate ['ɛkstrɪkeɪt] vt: **to** ~ **sth** (**from**) districare qc (da).

extrovert ['ɛkstrəvə:t] n estroverso/a.

exude [ɪg'zju:d] vt trasudare; (fig) emanare.

eye [aɪ] n occhio; (of needle) cruna ♦ vt osservare; **to keep an** ~ **on** tenere d'occhio; ~**ball** n globo dell'occhio; ~**bath** n occhino; ~**brow** n sopracciglio; ~**brow pencil** n matita per le sopracciglia; ~**drops** npl gocce fpl oculari, collirio; ~**lash** n ciglio; ~**lid** n palpebra; ~ **liner** n eye-liner m inv; ~**opener** n rivelazione f; ~**shadow** n ombretto; ~**sight** n vista; ~**sore** n pugno nell'occhio; ~ **witness** n testimone m/f oculare.

F

F [εf] *n* (*MUS*) fa *m*.

fable ['feɪbl] *n* favola.

fabric ['fæbrɪk] *n* stoffa, tessuto.

fabrication [fæbrɪ'keɪʃən] *n* fabbricazione *f*; falsificazione *f*.

fabulous ['fæbjuləs] *adj* favoloso(a); (*super*) favoloso(a), fantastico(a).

façade [fə'sɑːd] *n* (*also fig*) facciata.

face [feɪs] *n* faccia, viso, volto; (*expression*) faccia; (*of clock*) quadrante *m*; (*of building*) facciata ♦ *vt* essere di fronte a; (*facts, situation*) affrontare; ~ **down** a faccia in giù; **to make** *or* **pull a** ~ fare una smorfia; **in the** ~ **of** (*difficulties etc*) di fronte a; **on the** ~ **of it** a prima vista; ~ **to** ~ faccia a faccia; ~ **up to** *vt fus* affrontare, far fronte a; ~ **cloth** (*BRIT*) *n* guanto di spugna; ~ **cream** *n* crema per il viso; ~ **lift** *n* lifting *m inv*; (*of façade etc*) ripulita; ~ **powder** *n* cipria; ~**-saving** *adj* per salvare la faccia.

facet ['fæsɪt] *n* sfaccettatura.

facetious [fə'siːʃəs] *adj* faceto(a).

face value *n* (*of coin*) valore *m* facciale *or* nominale; **to take sth at** ~ (*fig*) giudicare qc dalle apparenze.

facial ['feɪʃəl] *adj* del viso.

facile ['fæsaɪl] *adj* superficiale.

facilities [fə'sɪlɪtɪz] *npl* attrezzature *fpl*; **credit** ~ facilitazioni *fpl* di credito.

facing ['feɪsɪŋ] *prep* di fronte a.

facsimile [fæk'sɪmɪlɪ] *n* facsimile *m inv*; ~ **machine** *n* telecopiatrice *f*.

fact [fækt] *n* fatto; **in** ~ infatti.

factor ['fæktə*] *n* fattore *m*.

factory ['fæktərɪ] *n* fabbrica, stabilimento.

factual ['fæktjuəl] *adj* che si attiene ai fatti.

faculty ['fækəltɪ] *n* facoltà *f inv*; (*US*) corpo insegnante.

fad [fæd] *n* mania; capriccio.

fade [feɪd] *vi* sbiadire, sbiadirsi; (*light, sound, hope*) attenuarsi, affievolirsi; (*flower*) appassire.

fag [fæg] (*BRIT*: *inf*) *n* (*cigarette*) cicca.

fail [feɪl] *vt* (*exam*) non superare; (*candidate*) bocciare; (*subj: courage, memory*) mancare a ♦ *vi* fallire; (*student*) essere respinto(a); (*eyesight, health, light*) venire a mancare; **to** ~ **to do sth** (*neglect*) mancare di fare qc; (*be unable*) non riuscire a fare qc; **without** ~ senza fallo; certamente; ~**ing** *n* difetto ♦ *prep* in mancanza di; ~**ure** ['feɪljə*] *n* fallimento; (*person*) fallito/a; (*mechanical etc*) guasto.

faint [feɪnt] *adj* debole; (*recollection*) vago(a); (*mark*) indistinto(a) ♦ *n* (*MED*) svenimento ♦ *vi* svenire; **to feel** ~ sentirsi svenire.

fair [fεə*] *adj* (*person, decision*) giusto(a), equo(a); (*quite large, quite good*) discreto(a); (*hair etc*) biondo(a); (*skin, complexion*) chiaro(a); (*weather*) bello(a), clemente ♦ *adv* (*play*) lealmente ♦ *n* fiera; (*BRIT: funfair*) luna park *m inv*; ~**ly** *adv* equamente; (*quite*) abbastanza; ~**ness** *n* equità, giustizia; ~ **play** *n* correttezza.

fairy ['fεərɪ] *n* fata; ~ **tale** *n* fiaba.

faith [feɪθ] *n* fede *f*; (*trust*) fiducia; (*sect*) religione *f*, fede *f*; ~**ful** *adj* fedele; ~**fully** *adv* fedelmente; **yours** ~**fully** (*BRIT: in letters*) distinti saluti.

fake [feɪk] *n* imitazione *f*; (*picture*) falso; (*person*) impostore/a ♦ *adj* falso(a) ♦ *vt* (*accounts*) falsificare; (*illness*) fingere; (*painting*) contraffare.

falcon ['fɔːlkən] *n* falco, falcone *m*.

fall [fɔːl] (*pt* **fell**, *pp* **fallen**) *n* caduta; (*in temperature*) abbassamento; (*in price*) ribasso; (*US: autumn*) autunno ♦ *vi* cadere; (*temperature, price, night*) scendere; ~**s** *npl* (*waterfall*) cascate *fpl*; **to** ~ **flat** (*on one's face*) cadere bocconi; (*joke*) fare cilecca; (*plan*) fallire; ~ **back** *vi* (*retreat*) indietreggiare; (*MIL*) ritirarsi; ~ **back on** *vt fus* (*remedy etc*) ripiegare su; ~ **behind** *vi* rimanere indietro; ~ **down** *vi* (*person*) cadere; (*building*) crollare; ~ **for** *vt fus* (*trick*) prendere una cotta per; **to** ~ **for a trick** (*or a story etc*) cascarci; ~ **in** *vi* crollare; (*MIL*)

etc) cascarci; ~ **in** *vi* crollare; (*MIL*) mettersi in riga; ~ **off** *vi* cadere; (*diminish*) diminuire, abbassarsi; ~ **out** *vi* (*hair, teeth*) cadere; (*friends etc*) litigare; ~ **through** *vi* (*plan, project*) fallire.

fallacy ['fæləsɪ] *n* errore *m*.

fallen ['fɔ:lən] *pp of* **fall**.

fallout ['fɔ:laut] *n* fall-out *m*; ~ **shelter** *n* rifugio antiatomico.

fallow ['fæləu] *adj* incolto(a), a maggese.

false [fɔ:ls] *adj* falso(a); **under** ~ **pretences** con l'inganno; ~ **teeth** (*BRIT*) *npl* denti *mpl* finti.

falter ['fɔ:ltə*] *vi* esitare, vacillare.

fame [feɪm] *n* fama, celebrità.

familiar [fə'mɪlɪə*] *adj* familiare; (*close*) intimo(a); **to be** ~ **with** (*subject*) conoscere; ~**ize** [fə'mɪlɪəraɪz] *vt*: **to** ~**ize o.s. with** familiarizzare con.

family ['fæmɪlɪ] *n* famiglia; ~ **business** *n* ditta a conduzione familiare.

famine ['fæmɪn] *n* carestia.

famished ['fæmɪʃt] *adj* affamato(a).

famous ['feɪməs] *adj* famoso(a); ~**ly** *adv* (*get on*) a meraviglia.

fan [fæn] *n* (*folding*) ventaglio; (*ELEC*) ventilatore *m*; (*person*) ammiratore/trice; tifoso/a ♦ *vt* far vento a; (*fire, quarrel*) alimentare; ~ **out** *vi* spargersi (a ventaglio).

fanatic [fə'nætɪk] *n* fanatico/a.

fan belt *n* cinghia del ventilatore.

fanciful ['fænsɪful] *adj* fantasioso(a).

fancy ['fænsɪ] *n* immaginazione *f*, fantasia; (*whim*) capriccio ♦ *adj* (*hat*) stravagante; (*hotel, food*) speciale ♦ *vt* (*feel like, want*) aver voglia di; (*imagine, think*) immaginare; **to take a** ~ **to** incapricciarsi di; **he fancies her** (*inf*) gli piace; ~ **dress** *n* costume *m* (per maschera); ~**-dress ball** *n* ballo in maschera.

fang [fæŋ] *n* zanna; (*of snake*) dente *m*.

fantastic [fæn'tæstɪk] *adj* fantastico(a).

fantasy ['fæntəsɪ] *n* fantasia, immaginazione *f*; fantasticheria; chimera.

far [fɑ:*] *adj* lontano(a) ♦ *adv* lontano; (*much, greatly*) molto; ~ **away**, ~ **off** lontano, distante; ~ **better** assai migliore; ~ **from** lontano da; **by** ~ di gran lunga; **go as** ~ **as the farm** vada fino alla fattoria; **as** ~ **as I know** per quel che so; **how** ~? quanto lontano?; (*referring to activity etc*) fino a dove?; ~**away** *adj* lontano(a).

farce [fɑ:s] *n* farsa.

farcical ['fɑ:sɪkəl] *adj* farsesco(a).

fare [fɛə*] *n* (*on trains, buses*) tariffa; (*in taxi*) prezzo della corsa; (*food*) vitto, cibo; **half** ~ metà tariffa; **full** ~ tariffa intera.

Far East *n*: **the** ~ l'Estremo Oriente *m*.

farewell [fɛə'wɛl] *excl, n* addio.

farm [fɑ:m] *n* fattoria, podere *m* ♦ *vt* coltivare; ~**er** *n* coltivatore/trice; agricoltore/trice; ~**hand** *n* bracciante *m* agricolo; ~**house** *n* fattoria; ~**ing** *n* (*gen*) agricoltura; (*of crops*) coltivazione *f*; (*of animals*) allevamento; ~**land** *n* terreno coltivabile; ~ **worker** *n* = ~**hand**; ~**yard** *n* aia.

far-reaching [-'ri:tʃɪŋ] *adj* di vasta portata.

fart [fɑ:t] (*inf!*) *vi* scoreggiare (*!*).

farther ['fɑ:ðə*] *adv* più lontano ♦ *adj* più lontano(a).

farthest ['fɑ:ðɪst] *superl of* **far**.

fascinate ['fæsɪneɪt] *vt* affascinare; **fascinating** *adj* affascinante; **fascination** [-'neɪʃən] *n* fascino.

fascism ['fæʃɪzəm] *n* fascismo.

fashion ['fæʃən] *n* moda; (*manner*) maniera, modo ♦ *vt* foggiare, formare; **in** ~ alla moda; **out of** ~ passato(a) di moda; ~**able** *adj* alla moda, di moda; ~ **show** *n* sfilata di moda.

fast [fɑ:st] *adj* rapido(a), svelto(a), veloce; (*clock*): **to be** ~ andare avanti; (*dye, colour*) solido(a) ♦ *adv* rapidamente; (*stuck, held*) saldamente ♦ *n* digiuno ♦ *vi* digiunare; ~ **asleep** profondamente addormentato.

fasten ['fɑ:sn] *vt* chiudere, fissare; (*coat*) abbottonare, allacciare ♦ *vi* chiudersi, fissarsi; abbottonarsi, allacciarsi; ~**er** *n* fermaglio, chiusura; ~**ing** *n* = ~**er**.

fast food *n* fast food *m*.

fastidious [fæs'tɪdɪəs] *adj* esigente, difficile.

fat [fæt] *adj* grasso(a); (*book, profit etc*) grosso(a) ♦ *n* grasso.

fatal ['feɪtl] *adj* fatale; mortale; disastroso(a); ~**ity** [fə'tælɪtɪ] *n* (*road death etc*) morto/a, vittima; ~**ly** *adv* a morte.

fate [feɪt] *n* destino; (*of person*) sorte *f*; ~**ful** *adj* fatidico(a).

father ['fɑːðə*] *n* padre *m*; ~**-in-law** *n* suocero; ~**ly** *adj* paterno(a).

fathom ['fæðəm] *n* braccio (= *1828 mm*) ♦ *vt* (*mystery*) penetrare, sondare.

fatigue [fə'tiːg] *n* stanchezza.

fatten ['fætn] *vt, vi* ingrassare.

fatty ['fætɪ] *adj* (*food*) grasso(a) ♦ *n* (*inf*) ciccione/a.

fatuous ['fætjuəs] *adj* fatuo(a).

faucet ['fɔːsɪt] (*US*) *n* rubinetto.

fault [fɔːlt] *n* colpa; (*TENNIS*) fallo; (*defect*) difetto; (*GEO*) faglia ♦ *vt* criticare; **it's my** ~ è colpa mia; **to find** ~ **with** trovare da ridire su; **at** ~ in fallo; ~**y** *adj* difettoso(a).

fauna ['fɔːnə] *n* fauna.

faux pas ['fəu'pɑː] *n* gaffe *f inv*.

favour ['feɪvə*] (*US* **favor**) *n* favore *m* ♦ *vt* (*proposition*) favorire, essere favorevole a; (*pupil etc*) favorire; (*team, horse*) dare per vincente; **to do sb a** ~ fare un favore *or* una cortesia a qn; **to find** ~ **with** (*subj: person*) entrare nelle buone grazie di; (: *suggestion*) avere l'approvazione di; **in** ~ **of** in favore di; ~**able** *adj* favorevole; ~**ite** [-rɪt] *adj, n* favorito(a).

fawn [fɔːn] *n* daino ♦ *adj* (*also:* ~-*coloured*) marrone chiaro *inv* ♦ *vi*: **to** ~ (**up**)**on** adulare servilmente.

fax [fæks] *n* (*document*) facsimile *m inv*, telecopia; (*machine*) telecopiatrice *f* ♦ *vt* telecopiare, trasmettere in facsimile.

FBI (*US*) *n abbr* (= *Federal Bureau of Investigation*) F.B.I. *f*.

fear [fɪə*] *n* paura, timore *m* ♦ *vt* aver paura di, temere; **for** ~ **of** per paura di; ~**ful** *adj* pauroso(a); (*sight, noise*) terribile, spaventoso(a).

feasible ['fiːzəbl] *adj* possibile, realizzabile.

feast [fiːst] *n* festa, banchetto; (*REL: also:* ~ *day*) festa ♦ *vi* banchettare.

feat [fiːt] *n* impresa, fatto insigne.

feather ['feðə*] *n* penna.

feature ['fiːtʃə*] *n* caratteristica; (*PRESS, TV*) articolo ♦ *vt* (*subj: film*) avere come protagonista ♦ *vi* figurare; ~**s** *npl* (*of face*) fisionomia; ~ **film** *n* film *m inv* principale.

February ['fɛbruərɪ] *n* febbraio.

fed [fɛd] *pt, pp of* **feed**.

federal ['fɛdərəl] *adj* federale.

fed-up *adj*: **to be** ~ essere stufo(a).

fee [fiː] *n* pagamento; (*of doctor, lawyer*) onorario; (*for examination*) tassa d'esame; **school** ~**s** tasse *fpl* scolastiche.

feeble ['fiːbl] *adj* debole.

feed [fiːd] (*pt, pp* **fed**) *n* (*of baby*) pappa; (*of animal*) mangime *m*; (*on printer*) meccanismo di alimentazione ♦ *vt* nutrire; (*baby*) allattare; (*horse etc*) dare da mangiare a; (*fire, machine*) alimentare; (*data, information*): **to** ~ **into** inserire in; ~ **on** *vt fus* nutrirsi di; ~**back** *n* feed-back *m*; ~**ing bottle** (*BRIT*) *n* biberon *m inv*.

feel [fiːl] (*pt, pp* **felt**) *n* consistenza; (*sense of touch*) tatto ♦ *vt* toccare; palpare; tastare; (*cold, pain, anger*) sentire; (*think, believe*): **to** ~ (**that**) pensare che; **to** ~ **hungry/cold** aver fame/freddo; **to** ~ **lonely/better** sentirsi solo/meglio; **I don't** ~ **well** non mi sento bene; **it** ~**s soft** è morbido al tatto; **to** ~ **like** (*want*) aver voglia di; **to** ~ **about** *or* **around for** cercare a tastoni; ~**er** *n* (*of insect*) antenna; **to put out a** ~**er** *or* ~**ers** (*fig*) fare un sondaggio; ~**ing** *n* sensazione *f*; (*emotion*) sentimento.

feet [fiːt] *npl of* **foot**.

feign [feɪn] *vt* fingere, simulare.

fell [fɛl] *pt of* **fall** ♦ *vt* (*tree*) abbattere.

fellow ['fɛləu] *n* individuo, tipo; compagno; (*of learned society*) membro ♦ *cpd*: ~ **citizen** *n* concittadino/a; ~ **countryman** *n* compatriota *m*; ~ **men** *npl* simili *mpl*; ~**ship** *n* associazione *f*; compagnia; *specie di borsa di studio* *universitaria.*

felony ['fɛlənɪ] *n* reato, crimine *m*.

felt [fɛlt] *pt, pp of* **feel** ♦ *n* feltro; **~-tip pen** *n* pennarello.

female ['fiːmeɪl] *n* (ZOOL) femmina; (*pej: woman*) donna, femmina ♦ *adj* (BIOL, ELEC) femmina *inv*; (*sex, character*) femminile; (*vote etc*) di donne.

feminine ['fɛmɪnɪn] *adj* femminile.

feminist ['fɛmɪnɪst] *n* femminista *m/f*.

fence [fɛns] *n* recinto ♦ *vt* (*also: ~ in*) recingere ♦ *vi* (SPORT) tirare di scherma; **fencing** *n* (SPORT) scherma.

fend [fɛnd] *vi:* **to ~ for o.s.** arrangiarsi; **~ off** *vt* (*attack, questions*) respingere, difendersi da.

fender ['fɛndə*] *n* parafuoco; (*on boat*) parabordo; (US) parafango; paraurti *m inv*.

ferment [vb fə'mɛnt, n 'fəːmɛnt] *vi* fermentare ♦ *n* (*fig*) agitazione *f*, eccitazione *f*.

fern [fəːn] *n* felce *f*.

ferocious [fə'rəʊʃəs] *adj* feroce.

ferret ['fɛrɪt] *n* furetto; **~ out** *vt* (*information*) scovare.

ferry ['fɛrɪ] *n* (*small*) traghetto; (*large: also:* **~boat**) nave *f* traghetto *inv* ♦ *vt* traghettare.

fertile ['fəːtaɪl] *adj* fertile; (BIOL) fecondo(a); **fertilizer** ['fəːtɪlaɪzə*] *n* fertilizzante *m*.

fester ['fɛstə*] *vi* suppurare.

festival ['fɛstɪvəl] *n* (REL) festa; (ART, MUS) festival *m inv*.

festive ['fɛstɪv] *adj* di festa; **the ~ season** (BRIT: *Christmas*) il periodo delle feste.

festivities [fɛs'tɪvɪtɪz] *npl* festeggiamenti *mpl*.

festoon [fɛs'tuːn] *vt:* **to ~ with** ornare di.

fetch [fɛtʃ] *vt* andare a prendere; (*sell for*) essere venduto(a) per.

fetching ['fɛtʃɪŋ] *adj* attraente.

fête [feɪt] *n* festa.

fetish ['fɛtɪʃ] *n* feticcio.

fetus ['fiːtəs] (US) *n* = **foetus**.

feud [fjuːd] *n* contesa, lotta.

feudal ['fjuːdl] *adj* feudale.

fever ['fiːvə*] *n* febbre *f*; **~ish** *adj* febbrile.

few [fjuː] *adj* pochi(e); **a ~** *adj* qualche *inv* ♦ *pron* alcuni(e); **~er** *adj* meno *inv*; meno numerosi(e); **~est** *adj* il minor numero di.

fiancé [fɪ'ɑ̃ːŋseɪ] *n* fidanzato; **~e** *n* fidanzata.

fib [fɪb] *n* piccola bugia.

fibre ['faɪbə*] (US **fiber**) *n* fibra; **~-glass** *n* fibra di vetro.

fickle ['fɪkl] *adj* incostante, capriccioso(a).

fiction ['fɪkʃən] *n* narrativa, romanzi *mpl*; (*sth made up*) finzione *f*; **~al** *adj* immaginario(a).

fictitious [fɪk'tɪʃəs] *adj* fittizio(a).

fiddle ['fɪdl] *n* (MUS) violino; (*cheating*) imbroglio; truffa ♦ *vt* (BRIT: *accounts*) falsificare, falsare; **~ with** *vt fus* gingillarsi con.

fidelity [fɪ'dɛlɪtɪ] *n* fedeltà; (*accuracy*) esattezza.

fidget ['fɪdʒɪt] *vi* agitarsi.

field [fiːld] *n* campo; **~ marshal** *n* feldmaresciallo; **~work** *n* ricerche *fpl* esterne.

fiend [fiːnd] *n* demonio; **~ish** ['fiːndɪʃ] *adj* (*person, problem*) diabolico(a).

fierce [fɪəs] *adj* (*animal, person, fighting*) feroce; (*loyalty*) assoluto(a); (*wind*) furioso(a); (*heat*) intenso(a).

fiery ['faɪərɪ] *adj* ardente; infocato(a).

fifteen [fɪf'tiːn] *num* quindici.

fifth [fɪfθ] *num* quinto(a).

fifty ['fɪftɪ] *num* cinquanta; **~-~** *adj:* **a ~-~ chance** una possibilità su due ♦ *adv* fifty-fifty, metà per ciascuno.

fig [fɪg] *n* fico.

fight [faɪt] (*pt, pp* **fought**) *n* zuffa, rissa; (MIL) battaglia, combattimento; (*against cancer etc*) lotta ♦ *vt* (*person*) azzuffarsi con; (*enemy: also: MIL*) combattere; (*cancer, alcoholism, emotion*) lottare contro, combattere; (*election*) partecipare a ♦ *vi* combattere; **~er** *n* combattente *m*; (*plane*) aeroplano da caccia; **~ing** *n* combattimento.

figment ['fɪgmənt] *n*: a ~ of the imagination un parto della fantasia.

figurative ['fɪgjurətɪv] *adj* figurato(a).

figure ['fɪgə*] *n* figura; (*number, cipher*) cifra ♦ *vt* (*think: esp US*) pensare ♦ *vi* (*appear*) figurare; ~ **out** *vt* riuscire a capire; calcolare; ~**head** *n* (*NAUT*) polena; (*pej*) prestanome *m/f inv*; ~ **of speech** *n* figura retorica.

filch [fɪltʃ] (*inf*) *vt* sgraffignare.

file [faɪl] *n* (*tool*) lima; (*dossier*) incartamento; (*folder*) cartellina; (*COMPUT*) archivio; (*row*) fila ♦ *vt* (*nails, wood*) limare; (*papers*) archiviare; (*LAW: claim*) presentare; passare agli atti; ~ **in/out** *vi* entrare/uscire in fila.

filing cabinet ['faɪlɪŋ-] *n* casellario.

fill [fɪl] *vt* riempire; (*job*) coprire ♦ *n*: to eat one's ~ mangiare a sazietà; ~ **in** *vt* (*hole*) riempire; (*form*) compilare; ~ **up** *vt* riempire ♦ *vi* (*AUT*) fare il pieno.

fillet ['fɪlɪt] *n* filetto; ~ **steak** *n* bistecca di filetto.

filling ['fɪlɪŋ] *n* (*CULIN*) impasto, ripieno; (*for tooth*) otturazione *f*; ~ **station** *n* stazione *f* di rifornimento.

film [fɪlm] *n* (*CINEMA*) film *m inv*; (*PHOT*) pellicola; (*of powder, liquid*) sottile strato ♦ *vt*, *vi* girare; ~ **star** *n* divo/a dello schermo; ~ **strip** *n* filmina.

filter ['fɪltə*] *n* filtro ♦ *vt* filtrare; ~ **lane** (*BRIT*) *n* (*AUT*) corsia di svincolo; ~-**tipped** *adj* con filtro.

filth [fɪlθ] *n* sporcizia; ~**y** *adj* lordo(a), sozzo(a); (*language*) osceno(a).

fin [fɪn] *n* (*of fish*) pinna.

final ['faɪnl] *adj* finale, ultimo(a); definitivo(a) ♦ *n* (*SPORT*) finale *f*; ~**s** *npl* (*SCOL*) esami *mpl* finali.

finale [fɪ'nɑːlɪ] *n* finale *m*.

finalize ['faɪnəlaɪz] *vt* mettere a punto.

finally ['faɪnəlɪ] *adv* (*lastly*) alla fine; (*eventually*) alla fine.

finance [faɪ'næns] *n* finanza; (*capital*) capitale *m* ♦ *vt* finanziare; ~**s** *npl* (*funds*) finanze *fpl*.

financial [faɪ'nænʃəl] *adj* finanziario(a).

financier [faɪ'nænsɪə*] *n* finanziatore *m*.

find [faɪnd] (*pt, pp* **found**) *vt* trovare;

(*lost object*) ritrovare ♦ *n* trovata, scoperta; to ~ sb guilty (*LAW*) giudicare qn colpevole; ~ **out** *vt* (*truth, secret*) scoprire; (*person*) cogliere in fallo; to ~ **out about** informarsi su; (*by chance*) scoprire; ~**ings** *npl* (*LAW*) sentenza, conclusioni *fpl*; (*of report*) conclusioni.

fine [faɪn] *adj* bello(a); ottimo(a); (*thin, subtle*) fine ♦ *adv* (*well*) molto bene ♦ *n* (*LAW*) multa ♦ *vt* (*LAW*) multare; to be ~ (*person*) stare bene; (*weather*) far bello; ~ **arts** *npl* belle arti *fpl*.

finery ['faɪnərɪ] *n* abiti *mpl* eleganti.

finger ['fɪŋgə*] *n* dito ♦ *vt* toccare, tastare; **little/index** ~ mignolo/(dito) indice *m*; ~**nail** *n* unghia; ~**print** *n* impronta digitale; ~**tip** *n* punta del dito.

finicky ['fɪnɪkɪ] *adj* esigente, pignolo(a); minuzioso(a).

finish ['fɪnɪʃ] *n* fine *f*; (*polish etc*) finitura ♦ *vt*, *vi* finire; to ~ **doing sth** finire di fare qc; to ~ **third** arrivare terzo(a); ~ **off** *vt* compiere; (*kill*) uccidere; ~ **up** *vi*, *vt* finire; ~**ing line** *n* linea d'arrivo; ~**ing school** *n* scuola privata di perfezionamento (*per signorine*).

finite ['faɪnaɪt] *adj* limitato(a); (*verb*) finito(a).

Finland ['fɪnlənd] *n* Finlandia.

Finn [fɪn] *n* finlandese *m/f*; ~**ish** *adj* finlandese ♦ *n* (*LING*) finlandese *m*.

fir [fəː*] *n* abete *m*.

fire [faɪə*] *n* fuoco; (*destructive*) incendio; (*gas* ~, *electric* ~) stufa ♦ *vt* (*gun*) far fuoco con; (*arrow*) sparare; (*fig*) infiammare; (*inf: dismiss*) licenziare ♦ *vi* sparare, far fuoco; **on** ~ in fiamme; ~ **alarm** *n* allarme *m* d'incendio; ~**arm** *n* arma da fuoco; ~ **brigade** (*US* ~ **department**) *n* (corpo dei) pompieri *mpl*; ~ **engine** *n* autopompa; ~ **escape** *n* scala di sicurezza; ~ **extinguisher** *n* estintore *m*; ~**guard** *n* parafuoco; ~**man** *n* pompiere *m*; ~**place** *n* focolare *m*; ~**side** *n* angolo del focolare; ~ **station** *n* caserma dei pompieri; ~**wood** *n* legna; ~**works** *npl* fuochi *mpl* d'artificio.

firing squad ['faɪərɪŋ-] *n* plotone *m* d'esecuzione.

firm [fɔ:m] *adj* fermo(a) ♦ *n* ditta, azienda; **~ly** *adv* fermamente.

first [fɔ:st] *adj* primo(a) ♦ *adv* (*before others*) il primo, la prima; (*before other things*) per primo; (*when listing reasons etc*) per prima cosa ♦ *n* (*person: in race*) primo/a; (*BRIT: SCOL*) laurea con lode; (*AUT*) prima; **at ~** dapprima, all'inizio; **~ of all** prima di tutto; **~ aid** *n* pronto soccorso; **~-aid kit** *n* cassetta pronto soccorso; **~-class** *adj* di prima classe; **~-hand** *adj* di prima mano; **~ lady** (*US*) *n* moglie *f* del presidente; **~ly** *adv* in primo luogo; **~ name** *n* prenome *m*; **~-rate** *adj* di prima qualità, ottimo(a).

fish [fɪʃ] *n inv* pesce *m* ♦ *vt* (*river, area*) pescare in ♦ *vi* pescare; **to go ~ing** andare a pesca; **~erman** *n* pescatore *m*; **~ farm** *n* vivaio; **~ fingers** (*BRIT*) *npl* bastoncini *mpl* di pesce (surgelati); **~ing boat** *n* barca da pesca; **~ing line** *n* lenza; **~ing rod** *n* canna da pesca; **~monger** *n* pescivendolo; **~monger's (shop)** *n* pescheria; **~ sticks** (*US*) *npl* = **~ fingers**; **~y** (*inf*) *adj* (*tale, story*) sospetto(a).

fist [fɪst] *n* pugno.

fit [fɪt] *adj* (*MED, SPORT*) in forma; (*proper*) adatto(a), appropriato(a); conveniente ♦ *vt* (*subj: clothes*) stare bene a; (*put in, attach*) mettere; installare; (*equip*) fornire, equipaggiare ♦ *vi* (*clothes*) stare bene; (*parts*) andare bene, adattarsi; (*in space, gap*) entrare ♦ *n* (*MED*) accesso, attacco; **~ to** in grado di; **~ for** adatto a; degno(a) di; **a ~ of anger** un accesso d'ira; **this dress is a good ~** questo vestito sta bene; **by ~s and starts** a sbalzi; **~ in** *vi* accordarsi; adattarsi; **~ful** *adj* saltuario(a); **~ment** *n* componibile *m*; **~ness** *n* (*MED*) forma fisica; **~ted carpet** *n* moquette *f*; **~ted kitchen** *n* cucina componibile; **~ter** *n* aggiustatore *m* or montatore *m* meccanico; **~ting** *adj* appropriato(a) ♦ *n* (*of dress*) prova; (*of piece of equipment*) montaggio, aggiustaggio; **~tings** *npl* (*in building*) impianti *mpl*; **~ting room** *n* camerino.

five [faɪv] *num* cinque; **~r** (*inf*) *n* (*BRIT*) biglietto da cinque sterline; (*US*) biglietto da cinque dollari.

fix [fɪks] *vt* fissare; (*mend*) riparare; (*meal, drink*) preparare ♦ *n*: **to be in a ~** essere nei guai; **~ up** *vt* (*meeting*) fissare; **to ~ sb up with sth** procurare qc a qn; **~ation** *n* fissazione *f*; **~ed** [fɪkst] *adj* (*prices etc*) fisso(a); **~ture** ['fɪkstʃə*] *n* impianto (fisso); (*SPORT*) incontro (del calendario sportivo).

fizzle out ['fɪzl-] *vi* finire in nulla.

fizzy ['fɪzɪ] *adj* frizzante; gassato(a).

flabbergasted ['flæbəgɑːstɪd] *adj* sbalordito(a).

flabby ['flæbɪ] *adj* flaccido(a).

flag [flæg] *n* bandiera; (*also*: **~stone**) pietra da lastricare ♦ *vi* stancarsi; affievolirsi; **~ down** *vt* fare segno (di fermarsi) a.

flagpole ['flægpəʊl] *n* albero.

flagship ['flægʃɪp] *n* nave *f* ammiraglia.

flair [flɛə*] *n* (*for business etc*) fiuto; (*for languages etc*) facilità; (*style*) stile *m*.

flak [flæk] *n* (*MIL*) fuoco d'artiglieria; (*inf: criticism*) critiche *fpl*.

flake [fleɪk] *n* (*of rust, paint*) scaglia; (*of snow, soap powder*) fiocco ♦ *vi* (*also*: **~ off**) sfaldarsi.

flamboyant [flæm'bɔɪənt] *adj* sgargiante.

flame [fleɪm] *n* fiamma.

flamingo [flə'mɪŋgəʊ] *n* fenicottero, fiammingo.

flammable ['flæməbl] *adj* infiammabile.

flan [flæn] (*BRIT*) *n* flan *m inv*.

flank [flæŋk] *n* fianco ♦ *vt* fiancheggiare.

flannel ['flænl] *n* (*BRIT: also*: **face ~**) guanto di spugna; (*fabric*) flanella; **~s** *npl* (*trousers*) pantaloni *mpl* di flanella.

flap [flæp] *n* (*of pocket*) patta; (*of envelope*) lembo ♦ *vt* (*wings*) battere ♦ *vi* (*sail, flag*) sbattere; (*inf: also: be in a ~*) essere in agitazione.

flare [flɛə*] *n* razzo; (*in skirt etc*) svasatura; **~ up** *vi* andare in fiamme;

(*fig: person*) infiammarsi di rabbia; (: *revolt*) scoppiare.

flash [flæʃ] *n* vampata; (*also: news ~*) notizia *f* lampo *inv*; (*PHOT*) flash *m inv* ♦ *vt* accendere e spegnere; (*send: message*) trasmettere; (: *look, smile*) lanciare ♦ *vi* brillare; (*light on ambulance, eyes etc*) lampeggiare; **in a ~** in un lampo; **to ~ one's headlights** lampeggiare; **he ~ed by** *or* **past** ci passò davanti come un lampo; **~bulb** *n* cubo *m* flash *inv*; **~cube** *n* flash *m inv*; **~light** *n* lampadina tascabile.

flashy ['flæʃɪ] (*pej*) *adj* vistoso(a).

flask [flɑːsk] *n* fiasco; (*also: vacuum ~*) thermos *m inv* ®.

flat [flæt] *adj* piatto(a); (*tyre*) sgonfio(a), a terra; (*battery*) scarico(a); (*beer*) svampito(a); (*denial*) netto(a); (*MUS*) bemolle *inv*; (: *voice*) stonato(a); (*rate, fee*) unico(a) ♦ *n* (*BRIT: rooms*) appartamento; (*AUT*) pneumatico sgonfio; (*MUS*) bemolle *m*; **to work ~ out** lavorare a più non posso; **~ly** *adv* categoricamente; **~ten** *vt* (*also: ~ten out*) appiattire; (*building, city*) spianare.

flatter ['flætə*] *vt* lusingare; **~ing** *adj* lusinghiero(a); (*dress*) che dona; **~y** *n* adulazione *f*.

flaunt [flɔːnt] *vt* fare mostra di.

flavour ['fleɪvə*] (*US* **flavor**) *n* gusto ♦ *vt* insaporire, aggiungere sapore a; **strawberry-~ed** al gusto di fragola; **~ing** *n* essenza (artificiale).

flaw [flɔː] *n* difetto.

flax [flæks] *n* lino; **~en** *adj* biondo(a).

flea [fliː] *n* pulce *f*.

fleck [flɛk] *n* (*mark*) macchiolina; (*pattern*) screziatura.

fled [flɛd] *pt, pp of* **flee**.

flee [fliː] (*pt, pp* **fled**) *vt* fuggire da ♦ *vi* fuggire, scappare.

fleece [fliːs] *n* vello ♦ *vt* (*inf*) pelare.

fleet [fliːt] *n* flotta; (*of lorries etc*) convoglio; parco.

fleeting ['fliːtɪŋ] *adj* fugace, fuggitivo(a); (*visit*) volante.

Flemish ['flemɪʃ] *adj* fiammingo(a).

flesh [flɛʃ] *n* carne *f*; (*of fruit*) polpa; ~

wound *n* ferita superficiale.

flew [fluː] *pt of* **fly**.

flex [flɛks] *n* filo (flessibile) ♦ *vt* flettere; (*muscles*) contrarre; **~ible** *adj* flessibile.

flick [flɪk] *n* colpetto; scarto ♦ *vt* dare un colpetto a; **~ through** *vt fus* sfogliare.

flicker ['flɪkə*] *vi* tremolare.

flier ['flaɪə*] *n* aviatore *m*.

flight [flaɪt] *n* volo; (*escape*) fuga; (*also: ~ of steps*) scalinata; **~ attendant** (*US*) *n* steward *m inv*, hostess *f inv*; **~ deck** *n* (*AVIAT*) cabina di controllo; (*NAUT*) ponte *m* di comando.

flimsy ['flɪmzɪ] *adj* (*shoes, clothes*) leggero(a); (*building*) poco solido(a); (*excuse*) che non regge.

flinch [flɪntʃ] *vi* ritirarsi; **to ~ from** tirarsi indietro di fronte a.

fling [flɪŋ] (*pt, pp* **flung**) *vt* lanciare, gettare.

flint [flɪnt] *n* selce *f*; (*in lighter*) pietrina.

flip [flɪp] *vt* (*switch*) far scattare; (*coin*) lanciare in aria.

flippant ['flɪpənt] *adj* senza rispetto, irriverente.

flipper ['flɪpə*] *n* pinna.

flirt [flɜːt] *vi* flirtare ♦ *n* civetta.

flit [flɪt] *vi* svolazzare.

float [fləʊt] *n* galleggiante *m*; (*in procession*) carro; (*money*) somma ♦ *vi* galleggiare.

flock [flɔk] *n* (*of sheep, REL*) gregge *m*; (*of birds*) stormo ♦ *vi*: **to ~ to** accorrere in massa a.

flog [flɔg] *vt* flagellare.

flood [flʌd] *n* alluvione *m*; (*of letters etc*) marea ♦ *vt* allagare; (*subj: people*) invadere ♦ *vi* (*place*) allagarsi; (*people*): **to ~ into** riversarsi in; **~ing** *n* inondazione *f*; **~light** *n* riflettore *m* ♦ *vt* illuminare a giorno.

floor [flɔː*] *n* pavimento; (*storey*) piano; (*of sea, valley*) fondo ♦ *vt* (*subj: blow*) atterrare; (: *question*) ridurre al silenzio; **ground ~**, (*US*) **first ~** pianterreno; **first ~**, (*US*) **second ~** primo piano; **~board** *n* tavellone *m* di

legno; ~ **show** n spettacolo di varietà.
flop [flɔp] n fiasco ♦ vi far fiasco; (fall) lasciarsi cadere.
floppy ['flɔpɪ] adj floscio(a), molle; ~ **(disk)** n (COMPUT) floppy disk m inv.
flora ['flɔːrə] n flora.
Florence ['flɔrəns] n Firenze f; **Florentine** ['flɔrəntaɪn] adj fiorentino(a).
florid ['flɔrɪd] adj (complexion) florido(a); (style) fiorito(a).
florist ['flɔrɪst] n fioraio/a.
flounce [flauns] n balzo; ~ **out** vi uscire stizzito(a).
flounder ['flaundə*] vi annaspare ♦ n (ZOOL) passera di mare.
flour ['flauə*] n farina.
flourish ['flʌrɪʃ] vi fiorire ♦ n (bold gesture): **with a** ~ con ostentazione; ~**ing** adj florido(a).
flout [flaut] vt (order) contravvenire a.
flow [fləu] n flusso; circolazione f ♦ vi fluire; (traffic, blood in veins) circolare; (hair) scendere; ~ **chart** n schema m di flusso.
flower ['flauə*] n fiore m ♦ vi fiorire; ~ **bed** n aiuola; ~**pot** n vaso da fiori; ~**y** adj (perfume) di fiori; (pattern) a fiori; (speech) fiorito(a).
flown [fləun] pp di **fly**.
flu [fluː] n influenza.
fluctuate ['flʌktjueɪt] vi fluttuare, oscillare.
fluent ['fluːənt] adj (speech) facile, sciolto(a); corrente; **he speaks ~ Italian, he's ~ in Italian** parla l'italiano correntemente.
fluff [flʌf] n lanugine f; ~**y** adj lanuginoso(a); (toy) di peluche.
fluid ['fluːɪd] adj fluido(a) ♦ n fluido.
fluke [fluːk] (inf) n colpo di fortuna.
flung [flʌŋ] pt, pp di **fling**.
fluoride ['fluəraɪd] n fluoruro.
flurry ['flʌrɪ] n (of snow) tempesta; **a ~ of activity** uno scoppio di attività.
flush [flʌʃ] n rossore m; (fig: of youth, beauty etc) rigoglio, pieno vigore ♦ vt ripulire con un getto d'acqua ♦ vi arrossire ♦ adj: ~ **with** a livello di, pari a; **to ~ the toilet** tirare l'acqua; ~ **out** vt (birds) far alzare in volo; (animals,

fig) stanare; ~**ed** adj tutto(a) rosso(a).
flustered ['flʌstəd] adj sconvolto(a).
flute [fluːt] n flauto.
flutter ['flʌtə*] n agitazione f; (of wings) battito ♦ vi (bird) battere le ali.
flux [flʌks] n: **in a state of** ~ in continuo mutamento.
fly [flaɪ] (pt **flew**, pp **flown**) n (insect) mosca; (on trousers: also: **flies**) chiusura ♦ vt pilotare; (passengers, cargo) trasportare (in aereo); (distances) percorrere ♦ vi volare; (passengers) andare in aereo; (escape) fuggire; (flag) sventolare; ~ **away** or **off** vi volare via; ~**ing** n (activity) aviazione f; (action) volo ♦ adj: ~**ing visit** visita volante; **with ~ing colours** con risultati brillanti; ~**ing saucer** n disco volante; ~**ing start** n: **to get off to a ~ing start** partire come un razzo; ~**over** (BRIT) n (bridge) cavalcavia m inv; ~**sheet** n (for tent) sopratetto.
foal [fəul] n puledro.
foam [fəum] n schiuma; (also: ~ **rubber**) gommapiuma ® ♦ vi schiumare; (soapy water) fare la schiuma.
fob [fɔb] vt: **to ~ sb off with** rifilare a qn.
focus ['fəukəs] (pl ~**es**) n fuoco; (of interest) centro ♦ vt (field glasses etc) mettere a fuoco ♦ vi: **to ~ on** (with camera) mettere a fuoco; (person) fissare lo sguardo su; **in ~** a fuoco; **out of ~** sfocato(a).
fodder ['fɔdə*] n foraggio.
foe [fəu] n nemico.
foetus ['fiːtəs] (US **fetus**) n feto.
fog [fɔg] n nebbia; ~**gy** adj: **it's ~gy** c'è nebbia; ~ **lamp** (US ~ **light**) n (AUT) faro m antinebbia inv.
foil [fɔɪl] vt confondere, frustrare ♦ n lamina di metallo; (kitchen ~) foglio di alluminio; (FENCING) fioretto; **to act as a ~ to** (fig) far risaltare.
fold [fəuld] n (bend, crease) piega; (AGR) ovile m; (fig) gregge m ♦ vt piegare; (arms) incrociare; ~ **up** vi (map, bed, table) piegarsi; (business) crollare ♦ vt (map etc) piegare,

ripiegare; ~**er** n (for papers) cartella; cartellina; ~**ing** adj (chair, bed) pieghevole.

foliage ['fəʊlɪdʒ] n fogliame m.

folk [fəʊk] npl gente f ♦ adj popolare; ~**s** npl (family) famiglia; ~**lore** ['fəʊklɔ:*] n folclore m; ~ **song** n canto popolare.

follow ['fɒləʊ] vt seguire ♦ vi seguire; (result) conseguire, risultare; **to** ~ **suit** fare lo stesso; ~ **up** vt (letter, offer) fare seguito a; (case) seguire; ~**er** n seguace m/f, discepolo/a; ~**ing** adj seguente ♦ n seguito, discepoli mpl.

folly ['fɒlɪ] n pazzia, follia.

fond [fɒnd] adj (memory, look) tenero(a), affettuoso(a); **to be** ~ **of sb** volere bene a qn; **he's** ~ **of walking** gli piace fare camminate.

fondle ['fɒndl] vt accarezzare.

font [fɒnt] n (in church) fonte m battesimale; (TYP) caratteri mpl.

food [fu:d] n cibo; ~ **mixer** n frullatore m; ~ **poisoning** n intossicazione f; ~ **processor** n tritatutto m inv elettrico; ~**stuffs** npl generi fpl alimentari.

fool [fu:l] n sciocco/a; (CULIN) frullato ♦ vt ingannare ♦ vi (gen: ~ around) fare lo sciocco; ~**hardy** adj avventato(a); ~**ish** adj scemo(a), stupido(a); imprudente; ~**proof** adj (plan etc) sicurissimo(a).

foot [fʊt] (pl **feet**) n piede m; (measure) piede (= 304 mm; 12 inches); (of animal) zampa ♦ vt (bill) pagare; **on** ~ a piedi; ~**age** n (CINEMA: length) ≈ metraggio; (: material) sequenza; ~**ball** n pallone m; (sport: BRIT) calcio; (: US) football m americano; ~**ball player** n (BRIT: also: ~**baller**) calciatore m; (US) giocatore m di football americano; ~**brake** n freno a pedale; ~**bridge** n passerella; ~**hills** npl contrafforti fpl; ~**hold** n punto d'appoggio; ~**ing** n (fig) posizione f; **to lose one's** ~**ing** mettere un piede in fallo; ~**lights** npl luci fpl della ribalta; ~**man** n lacchè m inv; ~**note** n nota (a piè di pagina); ~**path** n sentiero, (in street) marciapiede m; ~**print** n orma,

impronta; ~**step** n passo; (~print) orma, impronta; ~**wear** n calzatura.

for [fɔ:*] prep **1** (indicating destination, intention, purpose) per; **the train** ~ **London** il treno per Londra; **he went** ~ **the paper** è andato a prendere il giornale; **it's time** ~ **lunch** è ora di pranzo; **what's it** ~? a che serve?; **what** ~? (why) perché?

2 (on behalf of, representing) per; **to work** ~ **sb/sth** lavorare per qn/qc; **I'll ask him** ~ **you** glielo chiederò a nome tuo; **G** ~ **George** G come George

3 (because of) per, a causa di; ~ **this reason** per questo motivo

4 (with regard to) per, It's cold ~ **July** è freddo per luglio; ~ **everyone who voted yes, 50 voted no** per ogni voto a favore ce n'erano 50 contro

5 (in exchange for) per; **I sold it** ~ £5 l'ho venduto per 5 sterline

6 (in favour of) per, a favore di; **are you** ~ **or against us?** è con noi o contro di noi?; **I'm all** ~ **it** sono completamente a favore

7 (referring to distance, time) per; **there are roadworks** ~ **5 km** ci sono lavori in corso per 5 km; **he was away** ~ **2 years** è stato via per 2 anni; **she will be away** ~ **a month** starà via un mese; **it hasn't rained** ~ **3 weeks** non piove da 3 settimane; **can you do it** ~ **tomorrow?** può farlo per domani?

8 (with infinitive clauses): **it is not** ~ **me to decide** non sta a me decidere; **it would be best** ~ **you to leave** sarebbe meglio che lei se ne andasse; **there is still time** ~ **you to do it** ha ancora tempo per farlo; ~ **this to be possible** ... perché ciò sia possibile ...

9 (in spite of) nonostante; ~ **all his complaints, he's very fond of her** nonostante tutte le sue lamentele, le vuole molto bene

♦ conj (since, as: rather formal) dal momento che, poiché.

forage ['fɒrɪdʒ] vi: **to** ~ **(for)** andare in

cerca (di).

foray ['fɔreɪ] n incursione f.

forbad(e) [fə'bæd] pt of forbid.

forbid [fə'bɪd] (pt forbad(e), pp forbidden) vt vietare, interdire; to ~ sb to do sth proibire a qn di fare qc; ~den pp of forbid; ~ding adj minaccioso(a).

force [fɔ:s] n forza ♦ vt forzare; the F~s (BRIT) npl le forze armate; to ~ o.s. to do costringersi a fare; in ~ (in large numbers) in gran numero; (law) in vigore; ~d adj forzato(a); ~-feed vt (animal, prisoner) sottoporre ad alimentazione forzata; ~ful adj forte, vigoroso(a).

forceps ['fɔ:sɛps] npl forcipe m.

forcibly ['fɔ:səblɪ] adv con la forza; (vigorously) vigorosamente.

ford [fɔ:d] n guado.

fore [fɔ:*] n: to come to the ~ mettersi in evidenza.

forearm ['fɔ:rɑ:m] n avambraccio.

foreboding [fɔ:'bəudɪŋ] n cattivo presagio.

forecast ['fɔ:kɑ:st] (irreg: like cast) n previsione f ♦ vt prevedere.

forecourt ['fɔ:kɔ:t] n (of garage) corte f esterna.

forefathers ['fɔ:fɑ:ðəz] npl antenati mpl, avi mpl.

forefinger ['fɔ:fɪŋgə*] n (dito) indice m.

forefront ['fɔ:frʌnt] n: in the ~ of all'avanguardia in.

forego [fɔ:'gəu] (irreg: like go) vt rinunciare a.

foregone [fɔ:'gɒn] pp of forego ♦ adj: it's a ~ conclusion è una conclusione scontata.

foreground ['fɔ:graund] n primo piano.

forehead ['fɒrɪd] n fronte f.

foreign ['fɒrɪn] adj straniero(a); (trade) estero(a); (object, matter) estraneo(a); ~er n straniero/a; ~ exchange n cambio con l'estero; (currency) valuta estera; F~ Office (BRIT) n Ministero degli Esteri; F~ Secretary (BRIT) n ministro degli Affari esteri.

foreleg ['fɔ:lɛg] n zampa anteriore.

foreman ['fɔ:mən] n caposquadra m.

foremost ['fɔ:məust] adj principale; più

in vista ♦ adv: first and ~ innanzitutto.

forensic [fə'rɛnsɪk] adj: ~ medicine medicina legale.

forerunner ['fɔ:rʌnə*] n precursore m.

foresaw [fɔ:'sɔ:] pt of foresee.

foresee [fɔ:'si:] (irreg: like see) vt prevedere; ~able adj prevedibile: foreseen pp of foresee.

foreshadow [fɔ:'ʃædəu] vt presagire, far prevedere.

foresight ['fɔ:saɪt] n previdenza.

forest ['fɒrɪst] n foresta.

forestall [fɔ:'stɔ:l] vt prevenire.

forestry ['fɒrɪstrɪ] n silvicoltura.

foretaste ['fɔ:teɪst] n pregustazione f.

foretell [fɔ:'tɛl] (irreg: like tell) vt predire; foretold [fɔ:'təuld] pt, pp of foretell.

forever [fə'rɛvə*] adv per sempre; (endlessly) sempre, di continuo.

forewent [fɔ:'wɛnt] pt of forego.

foreword ['fɔ:wə:d] n prefazione f.

forfeit ['fɔ:fɪt] vt perdere; (one's happiness, health) giocarsi.

forgave [fə'geɪv] pt of forgive.

forge [fɔ:dʒ] n fucina ♦ vt (signature, money) contraffare, falsificare; (wrought iron) fucinare, foggiare; ~ ahead vi tirare avanti; ~r n contraffattore m; ~ry n falso; (activity) contraffazione f.

forget [fə'gɛt] (pt forgot, pp forgotten) vt, vi dimenticare; ~ful adj di corta memoria; ~ful of dimentico(a) di; ~-me-not n nontiscordardimé m inv.

forgive [fə'gɪv] (pt forgave, pp forgiven) vt perdonare; to ~ sb for sth perdonare qc a qn; forgiven pp of forgive; ~ness n perdono.

forgo [fɔ:'gəu] = forego.

forgot [fə'gɒt] pt of forget.

forgotten [fə'gɒtn] pp of forget.

fork [fɔ:k] n (for eating) forchetta; (for gardening) forca; (of roads, rivers, railways) biforcazione f ♦ vi (road etc) biforcarsi; ~ out (inf) vt (pay) sborsare; ~-lift truck n carrello elevatore.

forlorn [fə'lɔ:n] adj (person) sconsolato(a); (place) abbandonato(a);

(*attempt*) disperato(a); (*hope*) vano(a).

form [fɔːm] *n* forma; (*SCOL*) classe *f*; (*questionnaire*) scheda ♦ *vt* formare; **in top ~** in gran forma.

formal ['fɔːməl] *adj* formale; (*gardens*) simmetrico(a), regolare; **~ly** *adv* formalmente.

format ['fɔːmæt] *n* formato ♦ *vt* (*COMPUT*) formattare.

formation [fɔː'meɪʃən] *n* formazione *f*.

formative ['fɔːmətɪv] *adj*: **~ years** anni *mpl* formativi.

former ['fɔːmə*] *adj* vecchio(a) (*before n*), ex *inv* (*before n*); **the ~ ... the latter** quello ... questo; **~ly** *adv* in passato.

formula ['fɔːmjulə] *n* formula.

forsake [fə'seɪk] (*pt* **forsook**, *pp* **forsaken**) *vt* abbandonare; **forsaken** *pp of* **forsake**; **forsook** [fə'suk] *pt of* **forsake**.

fort [fɔːt] *n* forte *m*.

forth [fɔːθ] *adv* in avanti; **back and ~** avanti e indietro; **and so ~** e così via; **~coming** *adj* (*event*) prossimo(a); (*help*) disponibile; (*character*) aperto(a), comunicativo(a); **~right** *adj* franco(a), schietto(a); **~with** *adv* immediatamente, subito.

fortify ['fɔːtɪfaɪ] *vt* (*city*) fortificare; (*person*) armare.

fortitude ['fɔːtɪtjuːd] *n* forza d'animo.

fortnight ['fɔːtnaɪt] (*BRIT*) *n* quindici giorni *mpl*, due settimane *fpl*; **~ly** *adj* himensile ♦ *adv* ogni quindici giorni.

fortress ['fɔːtrɪs] *n* fortezza, rocca.

fortunate ['fɔːtʃənɪt] *adj* fortunato(a); **it is ~ that** è una fortuna che; **~ly** *adv* fortunatamente.

fortune ['fɔːtʃən] *n* fortuna; **~teller** *n* indovino/a.

forty ['fɔːtɪ] *num* quaranta.

forum ['fɔːrəm] *n* foro.

forward ['fɔːwəd] *adj* (*ahead of schedule*) in anticipo; (*movement, position*) in avanti; (*not shy*) aperto(a); diretto(a) ♦ *n* (*SPORT*) avanti *m inv* ♦ *vt* (*letter*) inoltrare; (*parcel, goods*) spedire; (*career, plans*)

promuovere, appoggiare; **to move ~** avanzare; **~(s)** *adv* avanti.

fossil ['fɔsl] *adj* fossile ♦ *n* fossile *m*.

foster ['fɔstə*] *vt* incoraggiare, nutrire; (*child*) avere in affidamento; **~ child** *n* bambino(a) preso(a) in affidamento.

fought [fɔːt] *pt, pp of* **fight**.

foul [faul] *adj* (*smell, food, temper etc*) cattivo(a); (*weather*) brutto(a); (*language*) osceno(a) ♦ *n* (*SPORT*) fallo ♦ *vt* sporcare; **~ play** *n* (*LAW*): **the police suspect ~ play** la polizia sospetta un atto criminale.

found [faund] *pt, pp of* **find** ♦ *vt* (*establish*) fondare; **~ation** [-'deɪʃən] *n* (*act*) fondazione *f*; (*base*) base *f*; (*also:* **~ation cream**) fondo tinta; **~ations** *npl* (*of building*) fondamenta *fpl*.

founder ['faundə*] *n* fondatore/trice ♦ *vi* affondare.

foundry ['faundrɪ] *n* fonderia.

fountain ['fauntɪn] *n* fontana; **~ pen** *n* penna stilografica.

four [fɔː*] *num* quattro; **on all ~s** a carponi; **~-poster** *n* (*also:* **~-poster bed**) letto a quattro colonne; **~some** ['fɔːsəm] *n* partita a quattro; uscita in quattro; **~teen** *num* quattordici; **~th** *num* quarto(a).

fowl [faul] *n* pollame *m*; volatile *m*.

fox [fɔks] *n* volpe *f* ♦ *vt* confondere.

foyer ['fɔɪeɪ] *n* atrio; (*THEATRE*) ridotto.

fraction ['frækʃən] *n* frazione *f*.

fracture ['fræktʃə*] *n* frattura.

fragile ['frædʒaɪl] *adj* fragile.

fragment ['frægmənt] *n* frammento.

fragrant ['freɪgrənt] *adj* fragrante, profumato(a).

frail [freɪl] *adj* debole, delicato(a).

frame [freɪm] *n* (*of building*) armatura; (*of human, animal*) ossatura, corpo; (*of picture*) cornice *f*; (*of door, window*) telaio; (*of spectacles: also:* **~s**) montatura ♦ *vt* (*picture*) incorniciare; **~ of mind** *n* stato d'animo; **~work** *n* struttura.

France [frɑːns] *n* Francia.

franchise ['fræntʃaɪz] *n* (*POL*) diritto di voto; (*COMM*) concessione *f*.

frank [fræŋk] *adj* franco(a), aperto(a) ♦

vt (*letter*) affrancare; **~ly** *adv* francamente, sinceramente.

frantic ['fræntɪk] *adj* frenetico(a).

fraternity [frə'təːnɪtɪ] *n* (*club*) associazione *f*; (*spirit*) fratellanza.

fraud [frɔːd] *n* truffa; (*LAW*) frode *f*; (*person*) impostore/a.

fraught [frɔːt] *adj*: ~ **with** pieno(a) di, intriso(a) da.

fray [freɪ] *n* baruffa ♦ *vt* logorare ♦ *vi* logorarsi; **her nerves were ~ed** aveva i nervi a pezzi.

freak [friːk] *n* fenomeno, mostro.

freckle ['frɛkl] *n* lentiggine *f*.

free [friː] *adj* libero(a); (*gratis*) gratuito(a) ♦ *vt* (*prisoner, jammed person*) liberare; (*jammed object*) districare; ~ (**of charge**), **for** ~ gratuitamente; **~dom** ['friːdəm] *n* libertà; **~-for-all** *n* parapiglia *m* generale; ~ **gift** *n* regalo, omaggio; **~hold** *n* proprietà assoluta; ~ **kick** *n* calcio libero; **~lance** *adj* indipendente; **~ly** *adv* liberamente; (*liberally*) liberalmente; **F~mason** *n* massone *m*; **F~post** ® *n* affrancatura a carico del destinatario; **~-range** *adj* (*hen*) ruspante; (*eggs*) di gallina ruspante; ~ **trade** *n* libero scambio; **~way** (*US*) *n* superstrada; ~ **will** *n* libero arbitrio; **of one's own ~ will** di spontanea volontà.

freeze [friːz] (*pt* **froze**, *pp* **frozen**) *vi* gelare ♦ *vt* gelare; (*food*) congelare; (*prices, salaries*) bloccare ♦ *n* gelo; blocco; **~-dried** *adj* liofilizzato(a); **~r** *n* congelatore *m*.

freezing ['friːzɪŋ] *adj* (*wind, weather*) gelido(a); ~ **point** *n* punto di congelamento; **3 degrees below ~ point** 3 gradi sotto zero.

freight [freɪt] *n* (*goods*) merce *f*, merci *fpl*; (*money charged*) spese *fpl* di trasporto; ~ **train** (*US*) *n* treno *m* merci *inv*.

French [frɛntʃ] *adj* francese ♦ *n* (*LING*) francese *m*; **the ~** *npl* i Francesi; ~ **bean** *n* fagiolino; ~ **fried potatoes** (*US* ~ **fries**) *npl* patate *fpl* fritte; **~man** *n* francese *m*; ~ **window** *n* portafinestra; **~woman** *n* francese *f*.

frenzy ['frɛnzɪ] *n* frenesia.

frequent [*adj* 'friːkwənt, *vb*frɪ'kwɛnt] *adj* frequente ♦ *vt* frequentare; **~ly** *adv* frequentemente, spesso.

fresco ['frɛskəu] *n* affresco.

fresh [frɛʃ] *adj* fresco(a); (*new*) nuovo(a); (*cheeky*) sfacciato(a); **~en** *vi* (*wind, air*) rinfrescare; **~en up** *vi* rinfrescarsi; **~er** (*BRIT*: *inf*) *n* (*SCOL*) matricola; **~ly** *adv* di recente, di fresco; **~man** (*US*) *n* = **~er**; **~ness** *n* freschezza; **~water** *adj* (*fish*) d'acqua dolce.

fret [frɛt] *vi* agitarsi, affliggersi.

friar ['fraɪə*] *n* frate *m*.

friction ['frɪkʃən] *n* frizione *f*, attrito.

Friday ['fraɪdɪ] *n* venerdì *m inv*.

fridge [frɪdʒ] (*BRIT*) *n* frigo, frigorifero.

fried [fraɪd] *pt*, *pp* of **fry** ♦ *adj* fritto(a).

friend [frɛnd] *n* amico/a; **~ly** *adj* amichevole; **~ship** *n* amicizia.

frieze [friːz] *n* fregio.

fright [fraɪt] *n* paura, spavento; **to take ~** spaventarsi; **~en** *vt* spaventare, far paura a; **~ened** *adj* spaventato(a); **~ening** *adj* spaventoso(a), pauroso(a); **~ful** *adj* orribile.

frigid ['frɪdʒɪd] *adj* (*woman*) frigido(a).

frill [frɪl] *n* balza.

fringe [frɪndʒ] *n* (*decoration, BRIT: of hair*) frangia; (*edge: of forest etc*) margine *m*; ~ **benefits** *npl* vantaggi *mpl*.

frisk [frɪsk] *vt* perquisire.

frisky ['frɪskɪ] *adj* vivace, vispo(a).

fritter ['frɪtə*] *n* frittella; ~ **away** *vt* sprecare.

frivolous ['frɪvələs] *adj* frivolo(a).

frizzy ['frɪzɪ] *adj* crespo(a).

fro [frəu] *see* **to**.

frock [frɔk] *n* vestito.

frog [frɔg] *n* rana; **~man** *n* uomo *m* rana *inv*.

frolic ['frɔlɪk] *vi* sgambettare.

KEYWORD
---

from [frɔm] *prep* **1** (*indicating starting place, origin etc*) da; **where do you come ~?, where are you ~?** da dove viene?, di dov'è?; ~ **London to Glasgow**

da Londra a Glasgow; **a letter ~ my sister** una lettera da mia sorella; **tell him ~ me that ...** gli dica da parte mia che ...
2 (*indicating time*) da; **~ one o'clock to** *or* **until** *or* **till two** dall'una alle due; **~ January (on)** da gennaio, a partire da gennaio
3 (*indicating distance*) da; **the hotel is 1 km ~ the beach** l'albergo è a 1 km dalla spiaggia
4 (*indicating price, number etc*) da; **prices range ~ £10 to £50** i prezzi vanno dalle 10 alle 50 sterline
5 (*indicating difference*) da; **he can't tell red ~ green** non sa distinguere il rosso dal verde
6 (*because of, on the basis of*): **~ what he says** da quanto dice lui; **weak ~ hunger** debole per la fame.

front [frʌnt] *n* (*of house, dress*) davanti *m inv*; (*of train*) testa; (*of book*) copertina; (*promenade*: *also*: **sea ~**) lungomare *m*; (*fig: appearances*) fronte *f* ♦ *adj* primo(a); anteriore, davanti *inv*; **in ~ of** davanti a; **~age** *n* facciata; **~ door** *n* porta d'entrata; (*of car*) sportello anteriore; **~ier** ['frʌntɪə*] *n* frontiera; **~ page** *n* prima pagina; **~ room** (*BRIT*) *n* salotto; **~-wheel drive** *n* trasmissione *f* anteriore.
frost [frɔst] *n* gelo; (*also: hoar~*) brina; **~bite** *n* congelamento; **~ed** *adj* (*glass*) smerigliato(a); **~y** *adj* (*weather, look*) gelido(a).
froth ['frɔθ] *n* spuma; schiuma.
frown [fraun] *vi* acciglarsi.
froze [frɔuz] *pt of* **freeze**; **frozen** *pp of* **freeze**.
fruit [fru:t] *n inv* (*also fig*) frutto; (*collectively*) frutta; **~erer** *n* fruttivendolo; **~erer's (shop)** *n*: **at the ~erer's (shop)** dal fruttivendolo; **~ful** *adj* fruttuoso(a); **~ion** [fru:'ɪʃən] *n*: **to come to ~ion** realizzarsi; **~ juice** *n* succo di frutta; **~ machine** (*BRIT*) *n* macchina *f* mangiasoldi *inv*; **~ salad** *n* macedonia.

frustrate [frʌs'treɪt] *vt* frustrare.
fry [fraɪ] (*pt, pp* **fried**) *vt* friggere; *see also* **small**; **~ing pan** *n* padella.
ft. *abbr* = **foot**; **feet**.
fuddy-duddy ['fʌdɪdʌdɪ] *n* matusa.
fudge [fʌdʒ] *n* (*CULIN*) *specie di caramella a base di latte, burro e zucchero.*
fuel [fjuəl] *n* (*for heating*) combustibile *m*; (*for propelling*) carburante *m*; **~ tank** *n* deposito *m* nafta *inv*; (*on vehicle*) serbatoio (della benzina).
fugitive ['fju:dʒɪtɪv] *n* fuggitivo/a, profugo/a.
fulfil [ful'fɪl] *vt* (*function*) compiere; (*order*) eseguire; (*wish, desire*) soddisfare, appagare; **~ment** *n* (*of wishes*) soddisfazione *f*, appagamento; **sense of ~ment** soddisfazione.
full [ful] *adj* pieno(a); (*details, skirt*) ampio(a) ♦ *adv*: **to know ~ well that** sapere benissimo che; **I'm ~ (up)** sono pieno; **a ~ two hours** due ore intere; **at ~ speed** a tutta velocità; **in ~** per intero; **~ employment** *n* piena occupazione; **~-length** *adj* (*film*) lungometraggio; (*coat, novel*) lungo(a); (*portrait*) in piedi; **~ moon** *n* luna piena; **~-scale** *adj* (*attack, war*) su larga scala; (*model*) in grandezza naturale; **~ stop** *n* punto; **~-time** *adj, adv* (*work*) a tempo pieno; **~y** *adv* interamente, pienamente, completamente; (*at least*) almeno; **~y-fledged** *adj* (*teacher, member etc*) a tutti gli effetti.
fulsome ['fulsəm] (*pej*) *adj* (*praise, compliments*) esagerato(a).
fumble ['fʌmbl] *vi*: **to ~ with sth** armeggiare con qc.
fume [fju:m] *vi* essere furioso(a); **~s** *npl* esalazioni *fpl*, vapori *mpl*.
fun [fʌn] *n* divertimento, spasso; **to have ~** divertirsi; **for ~** per scherzo; **to make ~ of** prendersi gioco di.
function ['fʌŋkʃən] *n* funzione *f*; cerimonia, ricevimento ♦ *vi* funzionare; **~al** *adj* funzionale.
fund [fʌnd] *n* fondo, cassa; (*source*) fondo; (*store*) riserva; **~s** *npl* (*money*)

fondi *mpl*.
fundamental [fʌndə'mɛntl] *adj* fondamentale.
funeral ['fjuːnərəl] *n* funerale *m*; ~ **parlour** *n* impresa di pompe funebri; ~ **service** *n* ufficio funebre.
fun fair (*BRIT*) *n* luna park *m inv*.
fungi ['fʌngaɪ] *npl of* **fungus**.
fungus ['fʌngəs] (*pl* **fungi**) *n* fungo; (*mould*) muffa.
funnel ['fʌnl] *n* imbuto; (*of ship*) ciminiera.
funny ['fʌnɪ] *adj* divertente, buffo(a); (*strange*) strano(a), bizzarro(a).
fur [fəː*] *n* pelo; pelliccia; (*BRIT: in kettle etc*) deposito calcare; ~ **coat** *n* pelliccia.
furious ['fjuərɪəs] *adj* furioso(a); (*effort*) accanito(a).
furlong ['fəːlɔŋ] *n* = *201.17 m* (*termine ippico*).
furlough ['fəːləu] *n* congedo, permesso.
furnace ['fəːnɪs] *n* fornace *f*.
furnish ['fəːnɪʃ] *vt* ammobiliare; (*supply*) fornire; ~**ings** *npl* mobili *mpl*, mobilia.
furniture ['fəːnɪtʃə*] *n* mobili *mpl*; **piece of** ~ mobile *m*.
furrow ['fʌrəu] *n* solco.
furry ['fəːrɪ] *adj* (*animal*) peloso(a).
further ['fəːðə*] *adj* supplementare, altro(a); nuovo(a); più lontano(a) ♦ *adv* più lontano; (*more*) di più; (*moreover*) inoltre ♦ *vt* favorire, promuovere; **college of** ~ **education** *n* istituto statale con corsi specializzati (*di formazione professionale, aggiornamento professionale etc*); ~**more** [fəːðə'mɔː*] *adv* inoltre, per di più.
furthest ['fəːðɪst] *superl of* **far**.
fury ['fjuərɪ] *n* furore *m*.
fuse [fjuːz] *n* fusibile *m*; (*for bomb etc*) miccia, spoletta ♦ *vt* fondere ♦ *vi* fondersi; **to** ~ **the lights** (*BRIT: ELEC*) far saltare i fusibili; ~ **box** *n* cassetta dei fusibili.
fuselage ['fjuːzəlɑːʒ] *n* fusoliera.
fuss [fʌs] *n* agitazione *f*; (*complaining*) storie *fpl*; **to make a** ~ fare delle storie; ~**y** *adj* (*person*) puntiglioso(a),

esigente; che fa le storie; (*dress*) carico(a) di fronzoli; (*style*) elaborato(a).
future ['fjuːtʃə*] *adj* futuro(a) ♦ *n* futuro, avvenire *m*; (*LING*) futuro; **in** ~ in futuro.
fuze [fjuːz] (*US*) = **fuse**.
fuzzy ['fʌzɪ] *adj* (*PHOT*) indistinto(a), sfocato(a); (*hair*) crespo(a).

G

G [dʒiː] *n* (*MUS*) sol *m*.
gabble ['gæbl] *vi* borbottare; farfugliare.
gable ['geɪbl] *n* frontone *m*.
gadget ['gædʒɪt] *n* aggeggio.
Gaelic ['geɪlɪk] *adj* gaelico(a) ♦ *n* (*LING*) gaelico.
gag [gæg] *n* bavaglio; (*joke*) facezia, scherzo ♦ *vt* imbavagliare.
gaiety ['geɪɪtɪ] *n* gaiezza.
gaily ['geɪlɪ] *adv* allegramente.
gain [geɪn] *n* guadagno, profitto ♦ *vt* guadagnare ♦ *vi* (*clock, watch*) andare avanti; (*benefit*): **to** ~ (**from**) trarre beneficio (da); **to** ~ **3lbs** (**in weight**) aumentare di 3 libbre; **to** ~ **on sb** (*in race etc*) guadagnare su qn.
gait [geɪt] *n* andatura.
gal. *abbr* = **gallon**.
galaxy ['gæləksɪ] *n* galassia.
gale [geɪl] *n* vento forte; burrasca.
gallant ['gælənt] *adj* valoroso(a); (*towards ladies*) galante, cortese.
gall bladder ['gɔːl-] *n* cistifellea.
gallery ['gælərɪ] *n* galleria.
galley ['gælɪ] *n* (*ship's kitchen*) cambusa.
gallon ['gælən] *n* gallone *m* (= *8 pints*; *BRIT* = *4.543l*; *US* = *3.785l*).
gallop ['gæləp] *n* galoppo ♦ *vi* galoppare.
gallows ['gæləuz] *n* forca.
gallstone ['gɔːlstəun] *n* calcolo biliare.
galore [gə'lɔː*] *adv* a iosa, a profusione.
galvanize ['gælvənaɪz] *vt* galvanizzare.
gambit ['gæmbɪt] *n* (*fig*): (**opening**) ~ prima mossa.
gamble ['gæmbl] *n* azzardo, rischio

calcolato ♦ *vt, vi* giocare; **to ~ on** (*fig*) giocare su; **~r** *n* giocatore/trice d'azzardo; **gambling** *n* gioco d'azzardo.

game [geɪm] *n* gioco; (*event*) partita; (*TENNIS*) game *m inv*; (*CULIN, HUNTING*) selvaggina ♦ *adj* (*ready*): **to be ~ (for sth/to do)** essere pronto(a) (a qc/a fare); **big ~** selvaggina grossa; **~keeper** *n* guardacaccia *m inv*.

gammon ['gæmən] *n* (*bacon*) quarto di maiale; (*ham*) prosciutto affumicato.

gamut ['gæmət] *n* gamma.

gang [gæŋ] *n* banda, squadra ♦ *vi*: **to ~ up on sb** far combutta contro qn.

gangrene ['gæŋgriːn] *n* cancrena.

gangster ['gæŋstə*] *n* gangster *m inv*.

gangway ['gæŋweɪ] *n* passerella; (*BRIT: of bus*) corridoio.

gaol [dʒeɪl] (*BRIT*) *n, vt* = **jail**.

gap [gæp] *n* (*space*) buco; (*in time*) intervallo; (*difference*): ~ **(between)** divario (tra).

gape [geɪp] *vi* (*person*) restare a bocca aperta; (*shirt, hole*) essere spalancato(a); **gaping** *adj* spalancato(a).

garage ['gærɑːʒ] *n* garage *m inv*.

garbage ['gɑːbɪdʒ] *n* (*US*) immondizie *fpl*, rifiuti *mpl*; (*inf*) sciocchezze *fpl*; ~ **can** (*US*) *n* bidone *m* della spazzatura.

garbled ['gɑːbld] *adj* deformato(a); ingarbugliato(a).

garden ['gɑːdn] *n* giardino; **~s** *npl* (*public park*) giardini pubblici; **~er** *n* giardiniere/a; **~ing** *n* giardinaggio.

gargle ['gɑːgl] *vi* fare gargarismi.

garish ['gɛərɪʃ] *adj* vistoso(a).

garland ['gɑːlənd] *n* ghirlanda; corona.

garlic ['gɑːlɪk] *n* aglio.

garment ['gɑːmənt] *n* indumento.

garnish ['gɑːnɪʃ] *vt* (*food*) guarnire.

garrison ['gærɪsn] *n* guarnigione *f*.

garrulous ['gærjuləs] *adj* ciarliero(a), loquace.

garter ['gɑːtə*] *n* giarrettiera.

gas [gæs] *n* gas *m inv*; (*US: gasoline*) benzina ♦ *vt* asfissiare con il gas; ~ **cooker** (*BRIT*) *n* cucina a gas; ~ **cylinder** *n* bombola del gas; ~ **fire** (*BRIT*) *n* radiatore *m* a gas.

gash [gæʃ] *n* sfregio ♦ *vt* sfregiare.

gasket ['gæskɪt] *n* (*AUT*) guarnizione *f*.

gas mask *n* maschera *f* antigas *inv*.

gas meter *n* contatore *m* del gas.

gasoline ['gæsəliːn] (*US*) *n* benzina.

gasp [gɑːsp] *n* respiro affannoso, ansito ♦ *vi* ansare, ansimare; (*in surprise*) restare senza fiato; ~ **out** *vt* dire affannosamente.

gas station (*US*) *n* distributore *m* di benzina.

gassy ['gæsɪ] *adj* gassoso(a).

gate [geɪt] *n* cancello; (*at airport*) uscita; **~crash** (*BRIT*) *vt* partecipare senza invito a; **~way** *n* porta.

gather ['gæðə*] *vt* (*flowers, fruit*) cogliere; (*pick up*) raccogliere; (*assemble*) radunare; raccogliere; (*understand*) capire; (*SEWING*) increspare ♦ *vi* (*assemble*) radunarsi; **to ~ speed** acquistare velocità; **~ing** *n* adunanza.

gauche [gəʊʃ] *adj* goffo(a), maldestro(a).

gaudy ['gɔːdɪ] *adj* vistoso(a).

gauge [geɪdʒ] *n* (*instrument*) indicatore *m* ♦ *vt* misurare; (*fig*) valutare.

gaunt [gɔːnt] *adj* scarno(a); (*grim, desolate*) desolato(a).

gauntlet ['gɔːntlɪt] *n* guanto; (*fig*): **to run the ~ through an angry crowd** passare sotto il fuoco di una folla ostile; **to throw down the ~** gettare il guanto.

gauze [gɔːz] *n* garza.

gave [geɪv] *pt of* **give**.

gay [geɪ] *adj* (*homosexual*) omosessuale; (*cheerful*) gaio(a), allegro(a); (*colour*) vivace, vivo(a).

gaze [geɪz] *n* sguardo fisso ♦ *vi*: **to ~ at** guardare fisso.

gazetteer [gæzɪ'tɪə*] *n* indice *m* dei nomi geografici.

GB *abbr* = **Great Britain**.

GCE (*BRIT*) *n abbr* (= *General Certificate of Education*) ≈ maturità.

GCSE (*BRIT*) *n abbr* = *General Certificate of Secondary Education*.

gear [gɪə*] *n* attrezzi *mpl*, equipaggiamento; (*TECH*) ingranaggio; (*AUT*) marcia ♦ *vt* (*fig: adapt*): **to ~ sth to** adattare qc a; **in top** *or* (*US*) **high/low ~** in quarta (*or* quinta)/

seconda; **in ~** in marcia; **~ box** *n* scatola del cambio; **~ lever** (*US* **~ shift**) *n* leva del cambio.

geese [gi:s] *npl of* **goose.**

gel [dʒɛl] *n* gel *m inv.*

gelignite ['dʒɛlɪgnaɪt] *n* nitroglicerina.

gem [dʒɛm] *n* gemma.

Gemini ['dʒɛmɪnaɪ] *n* Gemelli *mpl.*

gender ['dʒɛndə*] *n* genere *m.*

general ['dʒɛnərl] *n* generale *m* ♦ *adj* generale; **in ~** in genere; **~ delivery** (*US*) *n* fermo posta *m*; **~ election** *n* elezioni *fpl* generali; **~ly** *adv* generalmente; **~ practitioner** *n* medico generico.

generate ['dʒɛnəreɪt] *vt* generare.

generation [dʒɛnə'reɪʃən] *n* generazione *f.*

generator ['dʒɛnəreɪtə*] *n* generatore *m.*

generosity [dʒɛnə'rɒsɪtɪ] *n* generosità.

generous ['dʒɛnərəs] *adj* generoso(a); (*copious*) abbondante.

Geneva [dʒɪ'ni:və] *n* Ginevra.

genial ['dʒi:nɪəl] *adj* geniale, cordiale.

genitals ['dʒɛnɪtlz] *npl* genitali *mpl.*

genius ['dʒi:nɪəs] *n* genio.

Genoa ['dʒɛnəuə] *n* Genova.

gent [dʒɛnt] *n abbr* = **gentleman.**

genteel [dʒɛn'ti:l] *adj* raffinato(a), distinto(a).

gentle ['dʒɛntl] *adj* delicato(a); (*persona*) dolce.

gentleman ['dʒɛntlmən] *n* signore *m*; (*well-bred man*) gentiluomo.

gently ['dʒɛntlɪ] *adv* delicatamente.

gentry ['dʒɛntrɪ] *n* nobiltà minore.

gents [dʒɛnts] *n* W.C. *m* (per signori).

genuine ['dʒɛnjuɪn] *adj* autentico(a); sincero(a).

geography [dʒɪ'ɒɡrəfɪ] *n* geografia.

geology [dʒɪ'ɒlədʒɪ] *n* geologia.

geometric(al) [dʒɪə'mɛtrɪk(l)] *adj* geometrico(a).

geometry [dʒɪ'ɒmətrɪ] *n* geometria.

geranium [dʒɪ'reɪnjəm] *n* geranio.

geriatric [dʒɛrɪ'ætrɪk] *adj* geriatrico(a).

germ [dʒə:m] *n* (*MED*) microbo; (*BIOL, fig*) germe *m.*

German ['dʒə:mən] *adj* tedesco(a) ♦ *n* tedesco/a; (*LING*) tedesco; **~ measles**

(*BRIT*) *n* rosolia.

Germany ['dʒə:mənɪ] *n* Germania.

gesture ['dʒɛstjə*] *n* gesto.

KEYWORD

get [ɡɛt] (*pt, pp* **got**, (*US*) *pp* **gotten**) *vi*
1 (*become, be*) diventare, farsi; **to ~ old** invecchiare; **to ~ tired** stancarsi; **to ~ drunk** ubriacarsi; **to ~ killed** venire *or* rimanere ucciso(a); **when do I ~ paid?** quando mi pagate?; **it's ~ting late** si sta facendo tardi

2 (*go*) **to ~ to/from** andare a/da; **to ~ home** arrivare *or* tornare a casa; **how did you ~ here?** come sei venuto?

3 (*begin*) mettersi a, cominciare a; **to ~ to know sb** incominciare a conoscere qn; **let's ~ going** *or* **started** muoviamoci

4 (*modal aux vb*): **you've got to do it** devi farlo

♦ *vt* **1**: **to ~ sth done** (*do*) fare qc; (*have done*) far fare qc; **to ~ one's hair cut** farsi tagliare i capelli; **to ~ sb to do sth** far fare qc a qn

2 (*obtain: money, permission, results*) ottenere; (*find: job, flat*) trovare; (*fetch: person, doctor*) chiamare; (: *object*) prendere; **to ~ sth for sb** prendere *or* procurare qc a qn; **~ me Mr Jones, please** (*TEL*) mi passi il signor Jones, per favore; **can I ~ you a drink?** le posso offrire da bere?

3 (*receive: present, letter, prize*) ricevere; (*acquire: reputation*) farsi; **how much did you ~ for the painting?** quanto le hanno dato per il quadro?

4 (*catch*) prendere; (*hit: target etc*) colpire; **to ~ sb by the arm/throat** afferrare qn per un braccio/alla gola; **~ him!** prendetelo!

5 (*take, move*) portare; **to ~ sth to sb** far avere qc a qn; **do you think we'll ~ it through the door?** pensi che riusciremo a farlo passare per la porta?

6 (*catch, take: plane, bus etc*) prendere

7 (*understand*) afferrare; (*hear*) sentire; **I've got it!** ci sono arrivato!, ci sono!; **I'm sorry, I didn't ~ your name** scusi, non ho capito (*or* sentito) il suo nome

8 (*have, possess*): **to have got** avere; **how many have you got?** quanti ne ha?

get about *vi* muoversi; (*news*) diffondersi

get along *vi* (*agree*) andare d'accordo; (*depart*) andarsene; (*manage*) = **get by**

get at *vt fus* (*attack*) prendersela con; (*reach*) raggiungere, arrivare a

get away *vi* partire, andarsene; (*escape*) scappare

get away with *vt fus* cavarsela; farla franca

get back *vi* (*return*) ritornare, tornare ♦ *vt* riottenere, riavere

get by *vi* (*pass*) passare; (*manage*) farcela

get down *vi, vt fus* scendere ♦ *vt* far scendere; (*depress*) buttare giù

get down to *vt fus* (*work*) mettersi a (fare)

get in *vi* entrare; (*train*) arrivare; (*arrive home*) ritornare, tornare

get into *vt fus* entrare in; **to ~ into a rage** incavolarsi

get off *vi* (*from train etc*) scendere; (*depart: person, car*) andare via; (*escape*) cavarsela ♦ *vt* (*remove: clothes, stain*) levare ♦ *vt fus* (*train, bus*) scendere da

get on *vi* (*at exam etc*) andare; (*agree*): **to ~ on (with)** andare d'accordo (con) ♦ *vt fus* montare in; (*horse*) montare su

get out *vi* uscire; (*of vehicle*) scendere ♦ *vt* tirar fuori, far uscire

get out of *vt fus* uscire da; (*duty etc*) evitare

get over *vt fus* (*illness*) riaversi da

get round *vt fus* aggirare; (*fig: person*) rigirare

get through *vi* (*TEL*) avere la linea

get through to *vt fus* (*TEL*) parlare a

get together *vi* riunirsi ♦ *vt* raccogliere; (*people*) adunare

get up *vi* (*rise*) alzarsi ♦ *vt fus* salire su per

get up to *vt fus* (*reach*) raggiungere; (*prank etc*) fare.

getaway ['gɛtəweɪ] *n* fuga.

geyser ['giːzə*] *n* (*BRIT*) scaldabagno; (*GEO*) geyser *m inv*.

Ghana ['gɑːnə] *n* Ghana *m*.

ghastly ['gɑːstlɪ] *adj* orribile, orrendo(a); (*pale*) spettrale.

gherkin ['gəːkɪn] *n* cetriolino.

ghost [gəust] *n* fantasma *m*, spettro.

giant ['dʒaɪənt] *n* gigante *m* ♦ *adj* gigantesco(a), enorme.

gibberish ['dʒɪbərɪʃ] *n* parole *fpl* senza senso.

gibe [dʒaɪb] *n* = **jibe**.

giblets ['dʒɪblɪts] *npl* frattaglie *fpl*.

Gibraltar [dʒɪ'brɔːltə*] *n* Gibilterra.

giddy ['gɪdɪ] *adj* (*dizzy*): **to be ~** aver le vertigini.

gift [gɪft] *n* regalo; (*donation, ability*) dono; **~ed** *adj* dotato(a); **~ token** *n* buono *m* omaggio *inv*; **~ voucher** *n* = **~ token**.

gigantic [dʒaɪ'gæntɪk] *adj* gigantesco(a).

giggle ['gɪgl] *vi* ridere scioccamente.

gill [dʒɪl] *n* (*measure*) = *0.25 pints* (*BRIT* = *0.148l*, *US* = *0.118l*).

gills [gɪlz] *npl* (*of fish*) branchie *fpl*.

gilt [gɪlt] *n* doratura ♦ *adj* dorato(a); **~-edged** *adj* (*COMM*) della massima sicurezza.

gimmick ['gɪmɪk] *n* trucco.

gin [dʒɪn] *n* (*liquor*) gin *m inv*.

ginger ['dʒɪndʒə*] *n* zenzero; **~ ale** *n* bibita gassosa allo zenzero; **~ beer** *n* = **~ ale**; **~bread** *n* pan *m* di zenzero.

gingerly ['dʒɪndʒəlɪ] *adv* cautamente.

gipsy ['dʒɪpsɪ] *n* zingaro/a.

giraffe [dʒɪ'rɑːf] *n* giraffa.

girder ['gəːdə*] *n* trave *f*.

girdle ['gəːdl] *n* (*corset*) guaina.

girl [gəːl] *n* ragazza; (*young unmarried woman*) signorina; (*daughter*) figlia, figliola; **~friend** *n* (*of girl*) amica; (*of boy*) ragazza; **~ish** *adj* da ragazza.

giro ['dʒaɪrəu] *n* (*bank ~*) versamento bancario; (*post office ~*) postagiro; (*BRIT: welfare cheque*) assegno del sussidio di assistenza sociale.

girth [gəːθ] *n* circonferenza; (*of horse*) cinghia.

gist [dʒɪst] *n* succo.

give [gɪv] (*pt* **gave**, *pp* **given**) *vt* dare ♦ *vi* cedere; **to ~ sb sth**, **~ sth to sb** dare qc a qn; **I'll ~ you £5 for it** te lo pago 5 sterline; **to ~ a cry/sigh** emettere un grido/sospiro; **to ~ a speech** fare un discorso; **~ away** *vt* dare via; (*disclose*) rivelare; (*bride*) condurre all'altare; **~ back** *vt* rendere; **~ in** *vi* cedere ♦ *vt* consegnare; **~ off** *vt* emettere; **~ out** *vt* distribuire; annunciare; **~ up** *vi* rinunciare ♦ *vt* rinunciare a; **to ~ up smoking** smettere di fumare; **to ~ o.s. up** arrendersi; **~ way** *vi* cedere; (*BRIT: AUT*) dare la precedenza; **given** *pp of* **give**.

glacier ['glæsɪə*] *n* ghiacciaio.
glad [glæd] *adj* lieto(a), contento(a).
gladly ['glædlɪ] *adv* volentieri.
glamorous ['glæmərəs] *adj* affascinante, seducente.
glamour ['glæmə*] *n* fascino.
glance [glɑ:ns] *n* occhiata, sguardo ♦ *vi*: **to ~** dare un'occhiata a; **to ~ off** (*bullet*) rimbalzare su; **glancing** *adj* (*blow*) che colpisce di striscio.
gland [glænd] *n* ghiandola.
glare [glɛə*] *n* (*of anger*) sguardo furioso; (*of light*) riverbero, luce *f* abbagliante; (*of publicity*) chiasso ♦ *vi* abbagliare; **to ~ at** guardare male; **glaring** *adj* (*mistake*) madornale.
glass [glɑ:s] *n* (*substance*) vetro; (*tumbler*) bicchiere *m*; **~es** *npl* (*spectacles*) occhiali *mpl*; **~house** *n* serra; **~ware** *n* vetrame *m*; **~y** *adj* (*eyes*) vitreo(a).
glaze [gleɪz] *vt* (*door*) fornire di vetri; (*pottery*) smaltare ♦ *n* smalto; **~d** *adj* (*eyes*) vitreo(a); (*pottery*) smaltato(a).
glazier ['gleɪzɪə*] *n* vetraio.
gleam [gli:m] *vi* luccicare.
glean [gli:n] *vt* (*information*) racimolare.
glee [gli:] *n* allegrezza, gioia.
glen [glɛn] *n* valletta.
glib [glɪb] *adj* dalla parola facile; facile.
glide [glaɪd] *vi* scivolare; (*AVIAT, birds*) planare; **~r** *n* (*AVIAT*) aliante *m*; **gliding** *n* (*AVIAT*) volo a vela.
glimmer ['glɪmə*] *n* barlume *m*.
glimpse [glɪmps] *n* impressione *f* fugace

♦ *vt* vedere al volo.
glint [glɪnt] *vi* luccicare.
glisten ['glɪsn] *vi* luccicare.
glitter ['glɪtə*] *vi* scintillare.
gloat [gləut] *vi*: **to ~ (over)** gongolare di piacere (per).
global ['gləubl] *adj* globale.
globe [gləub] *n* globo, sfera.
gloom [glu:m] *n* oscurità, buio; (*sadness*) tristezza, malinconia; **~y** *adj* scuro(a); fosco(a), triste.
glorious ['glɔ:rɪəs] *adj* glorioso(a); magnifico(a).
glory ['glɔ:rɪ] *n* gloria; splendore *m*.
gloss [glɔs] *n* (*shine*) lucentezza; (*also*: **~ paint**) vernice *f* a olio; **~ over** *vt fus* scivolare su.
glossary ['glɔsərɪ] *n* glossario.
glossy ['glɔsɪ] *adj* lucente.
glove [glʌv] *n* guanto; **~ compartment** *n* (*AUT*) vano portaoggetti.
glow [gləu] *vi* ardere; (*face*) essere luminoso(a).
glower ['glauə*] *vi*: **to ~ (at sb)** guardare (qn) in cagnesco.
glue [glu:] *n* colla ♦ *vt* incollare.
glum [glʌm] *adj* abbattuto(a).
glut [glʌt] *n* eccesso.
glutton ['glʌtn] *n* ghiottone/a; **a ~ for work** un(a) patito(a) del lavoro.
gnarled [nɑ:ld] *adj* nodoso(a).
gnat [næt] *n* moscerino.
gnaw [nɔ:] *vt* rodere.
go [gəu] (*pt* **went**, *pp* **gone**; *pl* **~es**) *vi* andare; (*depart*) partire, andarsene; (*work*) funzionare; (*time*) passare; (*break etc*) rompersi; (*be sold*): **to ~ for £10** essere venduto per 10 sterline; (*fit, suit*): **to ~ with** andare bene con; (*become*): **to ~ pale** diventare pallido(a); **to ~ mouldy** ammuffire ♦ *n*: **to have a ~ (at)** provare; **to be on the ~** essere in moto; **whose ~ is it?** a chi tocca?; **he's going to do** sta per fare; **to ~ for a walk** andare a fare una passeggiata; **to ~ dancing/shopping** andare a ballare/fare la spesa; **just then the bell went** proprio allora suonò il campanello; **how did it ~?** com'è andato?; **to ~ round the back/by the**

shop passare da dietro/davanti al negozio; ~ **about** vi (also: ~ **round**: rumour) correre, circolare ♦ vt fus: **how do I ~ about this?** qual'è la prassi per questo?; ~ **ahead** vi andare avanti; ~ **along** vi andare, avanzare ♦ vt fus percorrere; **to ~ along with** (plan, idea) appoggiare; ~ **away** vi partire, andarsene; ~ **back** vi tornare, ritornare; ~ **back on** vt fus (promise) non mantenere; ~ **by** vi (years, time) scorrere ♦ vt fus attenersi a, seguire (alla lettera): prestar fede a; ~ **down** vi scendere; (ship) affondare; (sun) tramontare ♦ vt fus scendere; ~ **for** vt fus (fetch) andare a prendere; (like) andar matto(a) per; (attack) attaccare; saltare addosso a; ~ **in** vi entrare; ~ **in for** vt fus (competition) iscriversi a; (be interested in) interessarsi di; ~ **into** vt fus entrare in; (investigate) indagare, esaminare; (embark on) lanciarsi in; ~ **off** vi partire, andar via; (food) guastarsi; (explode) esplodere, scoppiare; (event) passare ♦ vt fus: **I've gone off chocolate** la cioccolata non mi piace più; **the gun went off** il fucile si scaricò; ~ **on** vi continuare; (happen) succedere; **to ~ on doing** continuare a fare; ~ **out** vi uscire; (couple) **they went out for 3 years** sono stati insieme per 3 anni; (fire, light) spegnersi; ~ **over** vi (ship) ribaltarsi ♦ vt fus (check) esaminare; ~ **through** vt fus (town etc) attraversare; (files, papers) passare in rassegna; (examine: list etc) leggere da cima a fondo; ~ **up** vi salire; ~ **without** vt fus fare a meno di.

goad [gəud] vt spronare.

go-ahead adj intraprendente ♦ n via m.

goal [gəul] n (SPORT) gol m, rete f; (: place) porta; (fig: aim) fine m, scopo; ~**keeper** n portiere m; ~-**post** n palo (della porta).

goat [gəut] n capra.

gobble ['gɔbl] vt (also: ~ **down**, ~ **up**) ingoiare.

go-between n intermediario/a.

god [gɔd] n dio; **G~** n Dio; ~**child** n figlioccio/a; ~**daughter** n figlioccia; ~**dess** n dea; ~**father** n padrino; ~-**forsaken** adj desolato(a), sperduto(a); ~**mother** n madrina; ~**send** n dono del cielo; ~**son** n figlioccio.

goggles ['gɔglz] npl occhiali mpl (di protezione).

going ['gəuiŋ] n (conditions) andare m, stato del terreno ♦ adj: **the ~ rate** la tariffa in vigore.

gold [gəuld] n oro ♦ adj d'oro; ~**en** adj (made of ~) d'oro; (~ in colour) dorato(a); (~ fish n pesce m dorato or rosso; ~**mine** n (also fig) miniera d'oro; ~-**plated** adj placcato(a) oro inv; ~**smith** n orefice m, orafo.

golf [gɔlf] n golf m; ~-**ball** n (for game) pallina da golf; (on typewriter) pallina; ~ **club** n circolo di golf; (stick) bastone m or mazza da golf; ~ **course** n campo di golf; ~**er** n giocatore/trice di golf.

gondola ['gɔndələ] n gondola.

gone [gɔn] pp of **go** ♦ adj partito(a).

gong [gɔŋ] n gong m inv.

good [gud] adj buono(a); (kind) buono(a), gentile; (child) bravo(a) ♦ n bene m; ~**s** npl (COMM etc) beni mpl; merci fpl; ~! bene!, ottimo!; **to be ~ at** essere bravo(a) in; **to be ~ for** andare bene per; **it's ~ for you** fa bene; **would you be ~ enough to ...?** avrebbe la gentilezza di ...?; **a ~ deal (of)** molto(a), una buona quantità (di); **a ~ many** molti(e); **to make ~** (loss, damage) compensare; **it's no ~ complaining** brontolare non serve a niente; **for ~** per sempre, definitivamente; ~ **morning!** buon giorno!; ~ **afternoon/evening!** buona sera!; ~ **night!** buona notte!; ~**bye** excl arrivederci!; **G~ Friday** n Venerdì Santo; ~-**looking** adj bello(a); ~-**natured** adj affabile; ~**ness** n (of person) bontà; **for ~ness sake!** per amor di Dio!; ~**ness gracious!** santo cielo!, mamma mia!; ~**s train** (BRIT) n treno m merci inv; ~**will** n amicizia, benevolenza.

goose [gu:s] (pl **geese**) n oca.
gooseberry ['guzbərɪ] n uva spina; **to play** ~ (BRIT) tenere la candela.
gooseflesh ['gu:sflɛʃ] n pelle f d'oca.
goose pimples npl pelle f d'oca.
gore [gɔ:*] vt incornare ♦ n sangue m (coagulato).
gorge [gɔ:dʒ] n gola ♦ vt: **to** ~ **o.s. (on)** ingozzarsi (di).
gorgeous ['gɔ:dʒəs] adj magnifico(a).
gorilla [gə'rɪlə] n gorilla m inv.
gorse [gɔ:s] n ginestrone m.
gory ['gɔ:rɪ] adj sanguinoso(a).
go-slow (BRIT) n rallentamento dei lavori (per agitazione sindacale).
gospel ['gɔspl] n vangelo.
gossip ['gɔsɪp] n chiacchiere fpl; pettegolezzi mpl; (person) pettegolo/a ♦ vi chiacchierare.
got [gɔt] pt, pp of **get**; ~**ten** (US) pp of **get**.
gout [gaut] n gotta.
govern ['gʌvən] vt governare.
governess ['gʌvənɪs] n governante f.
government ['gʌvnmənt] n governo.
governor ['gʌvənə*] n (of state, bank) governatore m; (of school, hospital) amministratore m; (BRIT: of prison) direttore/trice.
gown [gaun] n vestito lungo; (of teacher, BRIT: of judge) toga.
G.P. n abbr = **general practitioner**.
grab [græb] vt afferrare, arraffare; (property, power) impadronirsi di ♦ vi: **to** ~ **at** cercare di afferrare.
grace [greɪs] n grazia ♦ vt onorare; 5 **days'** ~ dilazione f di 5 giorni; ~**ful** adj elegante, aggraziato(a); **gracious** ['greɪʃəs] adj grazioso(a); misericordioso(a).
grade [greɪd] n (COMM) qualità f inv; classe f; categoria; (in hierarchy) grado; (SCOL: mark) voto; (US: school class) classe ♦ vt classificare; ordinare; graduare; ~ **crossing** (US) n passaggio a livello; ~ **school** (US) n scuola elementare.
gradient ['greɪdɪənt] n pendenza, inclinazione f.
gradual ['grædjuəl] adj graduale; ~**ly**

adv man mano, a poco a poco.
graduate [n 'grædjuɪt, vb 'grædjueɪt] n (of university) laureato/a; (US: of high school) diplomato/a ♦ vi laurearsi; diplomarsi; **graduation** [-'eɪʃən] n (ceremony) consegna delle lauree (or dei diplomi).
graffiti [grə'fi:tɪ] npl graffiti mpl.
graft [grɑ:ft] n (AGR, MED) innesto; (bribery) corruzione f; (BRIT: hard work): **it's hard** ~ è un lavoraccio ♦ vt innestare.
grain [greɪn] n grano; (of sand) granello; (of wood) venatura.
gram [græm] n grammo.
grammar ['græmə*] n grammatica; ~ **school** (BRIT) n ≈ liceo.
grammatical [grə'mætɪkl] adj grammaticale.
gramme [græm] n = **gram**.
grand [grænd] adj grande, magnifico(a); grandioso(a); ~**children** npl nipoti mpl; ~**dad** (inf) n nonno; ~**daughter** n nipote f; ~**eur** ['grændjə*] n grandiosità; ~**father** n nonno; ~**ma** (inf) n nonna; ~**mother** n nonna; ~**pa** (inf) n = ~**dad**; ~**parents** npl nonni mpl; ~ **piano** n pianoforte m a coda; ~**son** n nipote m; ~**stand** n (SPORT) tribuna.
granite ['grænɪt] n granito.
granny ['grænɪ] (inf) n nonna.
grant [grɑ:nt] vt accordare; (a request) accogliere; (admit) ammettere, concedere ♦ n (SCOL) borsa; (ADMIN) sussidio, sovvenzione f; **to take sth for** ~**ed** dare qc per scontato; **to take sb for** ~**ed** dare per scontata la presenza di qn.
granulated ['grænjuleɪtɪd] adj: ~ **sugar** zucchero cristallizzato.
granule ['grænju:l] n granello.
grape [greɪp] n chicco d'uva, acino.
grapefruit ['greɪpfru:t] n pompelmo.
graph [grɑ:f] n grafico; ~**ic** adj grafico(a); (vivid) vivido(a); ~**ics** n grafica ♦ npl illustrazioni fpl.
grapple ['græpl] vi: **to** ~ **with** essere alle prese con.
grasp [grɑ:sp] vt afferrare ♦ n (grip) presa; (fig) potere m; comprensione f;

~**ing** adj avido(a).

grass [grɑːs] n erba; ~**hopper** n cavalletta; ~-**roots** adj di base.

grate [greɪt] n graticola (del focolare) ♦ vi cigolare, stridere ♦ vt (CULIN) grattugiare.

grateful ['greɪtful] adj grato(a), riconoscente.

grater ['greɪtə*] n grattugia.

grating ['greɪtɪŋ] n (iron bars) grata ♦ adj (noise) stridente, stridulo(a).

gratitude ['grætɪtjuːd] n gratitudine f.

gratuity [grə'tjuːɪtɪ] n mancia.

grave [greɪv] n tomba ♦ adj grave, serio(a).

gravel ['grævl] n ghiaia.

gravestone ['greɪvstəun] n pietra tombale.

graveyard ['greɪvjɑːd] n cimitero.

gravity ['grævɪtɪ] n (PHYSICS) gravità; pesantezza; (seriousness) gravità, serietà.

gravy ['greɪvɪ] n intingolo della carne; salsa.

gray [greɪ] adj = **grey**.

graze [greɪz] vi pascolare, pascere ♦ vt (touch lightly) sfiorare; (scrape) escoriare ♦ n (MED) escoriazione f.

grease [griːs] n (fat) grasso; (lubricant) lubrificante m ♦ vt ingrassare; lubrificare; ~**proof paper** (BRIT) n carta oleata; **greasy** adj grasso(a), untuoso(a).

great [greɪt] adj grande; (inf) magnifico(a), meraviglioso(a); **G~ Britain** n Gran Bretagna; ~-**grandfather** n bisnonno; ~-**grandmother** n bisnonna; ~**ly** adv molto; ~**ness** n grandezza.

Greece [griːs] n Grecia.

greed [griːd] n (also: ~**iness**) avarizia; (for food) golosità, ghiottoneria; ~**y** adj avido(a); goloso(a), ghiotto(a).

Greek [griːk] adj greco(a) ♦ n greco/a; (LING) greco.

green [griːn] adj verde; (inexperienced) inesperto(a), ingenuo(a) ♦ n verde m; (stretch of grass) prato; (on golf course) green m inv; ~**s** npl (vegetables) verdura; ~ **belt** n (round town) cintura di verde; ~ **card** n (BRIT: AUT) carta verde; (US: ADMIN) permesso di soggiorno e di lavoro; ~**ery** n verde m; ~**grocer** (BRIT) n fruttivendolo/a, erbivendolo/a; ~**house** n serra; ~**ish** adj verdastro(a).

Greenland ['griːnlənd] n Groenlandia.

greet [griːt] vt salutare; ~**ing** n saluto; ~**ing(s) card** n cartolina d'auguri.

gregarious [grə'gɛərɪəs] adj (person) socievole.

grenade [grə'neɪd] n (also: hand ~) granata.

grew [gruː] pt of **grow**.

grey [greɪ] adj grigio(a); ~-**haired** adj dai capelli grigi; ~**hound** n levriere m.

grid [grɪd] n grata; (ELEC) rete f.

grief [griːf] n dolore m.

grievance ['griːvəns] n lagnanza.

grieve [griːv] vi addolorarsi; rattristarsi ♦ vt addolorare; **to ~ for sb** (dead person) piangere qn.

grievous ['griːvəs] adj: ~ **bodily harm** (LAW) aggressione f.

grill [grɪl] n (on cooker) griglia; (also: mixed ~) grigliata mista ♦ vt (BRIT) cuocere ai ferri; (inf: question) interrogare senza sosta.

grille [grɪl] n grata; (AUT) griglia.

grim [grɪm] adj sinistro(a), brutto(a).

grimace [grɪ'meɪs] n smorfia ♦ vi fare smorfie; fare boccacce.

grime [graɪm] n sudiciume m.

grin [grɪn] n sorriso smagliante ♦ vi fare un gran sorriso.

grind [graɪnd] (pt, pp **ground**) vt macinare; (make sharp) arrotare ♦ n (work) sgobbata.

grip [grɪp] n impugnatura; presa; (holdall) borsa da viaggio ♦ vt (object) afferrare; (attention) catturare; **to come to ~s with** affrontare; cercare di risolvere.

gripping ['grɪpɪŋ] adj avvincente.

grisly ['grɪzlɪ] adj macabro(a), orrido(a).

gristle ['grɪsl] n cartilagine f.

grit [grɪt] n ghiaia; (courage) fegato ♦ vt (road) coprire di sabbia; **to ~ one's teeth** stringere i denti.

groan [grəun] n gemito ♦ vi gemere.

grocer ['grǝusǝ*] n negoziante m di generi alimentari; ~ies npl provviste fpl; ~'s **(shop)** n negozio di (generi) alimentari.

groggy ['grɔgɪ] adj barcollante.

groin [grɔɪn] n inguine m.

groom [gru:m] n palafreniere m; (also: bride~) sposo ♦ vt (horse) strigliare; (fig): **to ~ sb for** avviare qn a; **well-~ed** (person) curato(a).

groove [gru:v] n scanalatura, solco.

grope [grǝup] vi: **to ~ for** cercare a tastoni.

gross [grǝus] adj grossolano(a); (COMM) lordo(a); ~**ly** adv (greatly) molto.

grotesque [grǝu'tɛsk] adj grottesco(a).

grotto ['grɔtǝu] n grotta.

grotty ['grɔtɪ] (inf) adj terribile.

ground [graund] pt, pp of **grind** ♦ n suolo, terra; (land) terreno; (SPORT) campo; (reason: gen pl) ragione f; (US: also: ~ wire) terra ♦ vt (plane) tenere a terra; (US: ELEC) mettere la presa a terra a; ~**s** npl (of coffee etc) fondi mpl; (gardens etc) terreno, giardini mpl; **on/to the ~** per/a terra; **to gain/lose ~** guadagnare/perdere terreno; ~ **cloth** (US) n = ~**sheet**; ~**ing** n (in education) basi fpl; ~**less** adj infondato(a); ~**sheet** (BRIT) n telone m impermeabile; ~ **staff** n personale m di terra; ~ **swell** n (fig) movimento; ~**work** n preparazione f.

group [gru:p] n gruppo ♦ vt (also: ~ together) raggruppare ♦ vi (also: ~ together) raggrupparsi.

grouse [graus] n inv (bird) tetraone m ♦ vi (complain) brontolare.

grove [grǝuv] n boschetto.

grovel ['grɔvl] vi (fig): **to ~ (before)** strisciare (di fronte a).

grow [grǝu] (pt **grew**, pp **grown**) vi crescere; (increase) aumentare; (develop) svilupparsi; (become): **to ~ rich/weak** arricchirsi/indebolirsi ♦ vt coltivare, far crescere; ~ **up** vi farsi grande, crescere; ~**er** n coltivatore/trice; ~**ing** adj (fear, amount) crescente.

growl [graul] vi ringhiare.

grown [grǝun] pp of **grow**; ~**-up** n

adulto/a, grande m/f.

growth [grǝuθ] n crescita, sviluppo; (what has grown) crescita; (MED) escrescenza, tumore m.

grub [grʌb] n larva; (inf: food) roba (da mangiare).

grubby ['grʌbɪ] adj sporco(a).

grudge [grʌdʒ] n rancore m ♦ vt: **to ~ sb sth** dare qc a qn di malavoglia; invidiare qc a qn; **to bear sb a ~ (for)** serbar rancore a qn (per).

gruelling ['gruǝlɪŋ] adj estenuante.

gruesome ['gru:sǝm] adj orribile.

gruff [grʌf] adj rozzo(a).

grumble ['grʌmbl] vi brontolare, lagnarsi.

grumpy ['grʌmpɪ] adj scorbutico(a).

grunt [grʌnt] vi grugnire.

G-string n tanga m inv.

guarantee [gærǝn'ti:] n garanzia ♦ vt garantire.

guard [gɑ:d] n guardia; (one man) guardia, sentinella; (BRIT: RAIL) capotreno; (on machine) schermo protettivo; (also: fire~) parafuoco ♦ vt fare la guardia a; (protect): **to ~ (against)** proteggere (da); **to be on one's ~** stare in guardia; ~ **against** vt fus guardarsi da; ~**ed** adj (fig) cauto(a), guardingo(a); ~**ian** n custode m; (of minor) tutore/trice; ~**'s van** (BRIT) n (RAIL) vagone m di servizio.

guerrilla [gǝ'rɪlǝ] n guerrigliero.

guess [gɛs] vi indovinare ♦ vt indovinare; (US) credere, pensare ♦ n: **to take** or **have a ~** provare a indovinare; ~**work** n: **I got the answer by ~work** ho azzeccato la risposta.

guest [gɛst] n ospite m/f; (in hotel) cliente m/f; ~**-house** n pensione f; ~ **room** n camera degli ospiti.

guffaw [gʌ'fɔ:] vi scoppiare in una risata sonora.

guidance ['gaɪdǝns] n guida, direzione f.

guide [gaɪd] n (person, book etc) guida; (BRIT: also: **girl ~**) giovane esploratrice f ♦ vt guidare; ~**book** n guida; ~ **dog** n cane m guida inv; ~**lines** npl (fig) indicazioni fpl, linee fpl direttive.

guild [gɪld] n arte f, corporazione f;

associazione f.
guile [gaɪl] n astuzia.
guillotine ['gɪlətiːn] n ghigliottina; (for paper) taglierina.
guilt [gɪlt] n colpevolezza; ~y adj colpevole.
guinea pig ['gɪnɪ-] n cavia.
guise [gaɪz] n maschera.
guitar [gɪ'tɑ:ˑ] n chitarra.
gulf [gʌlf] n golfo; (abyss) abisso.
gull [gʌl] n gabbiano.
gullet ['gʌlɪt] n gola.
gullible ['gʌlɪbl] adj credulo(a).
gully ['gʌlɪ] n burrone m; gola; canale m.
gulp [gʌlp] vi deglutire; (from emotion) avere il nodo in gola ♦ vt (also: ~ down) tracannare, inghiottire.
gum [gʌm] n (ANAT) gengiva; (glue) colla; (also: ~drop) caramella gommosa; (also: chewing ~) chewing-gum m ♦ vt: to ~ (together) incollare; ~boots (BRIT) npl stivali mpl di gomma.
gumption ['gʌmpʃən] n spirito d'iniziativa, buonsenso.
gun [gʌn] n fucile m; (small) pistola, rivoltella; (rifle) carabina; (shotgun) fucile da caccia; (cannon) cannone m; ~boat n cannoniera; ~fire n spari mpl; ~man n bandito armato; ~point n: at ~point sotto minaccia di fucile; ~powder n polvere f da sparo; ~shot n sparo.
gurgle ['gə:gl] vi gorgogliare.
guru ['guru:] n guru m inv.
gush [gʌʃ] vi sgorgare; (fig) abbandonarsi ad effusioni.
gusset ['gʌsɪt] n gherone m.
gust [gʌst] n (of wind) raffica; (of smoke) buffata.
gusto ['gʌstəu] n entusiasmo.
gut [gʌt] n intestino, budello; ~s npl (ANAT) interiora fpl; (courage) fegato.
gutter ['gʌtəˑ] n (of roof) grondaia; (in street) cunetta.
guy [gaɪ] n (inf: man) tipo, elemento; (also: ~rope) cavo or corda di fissaggio; (figure) effigie di Guy Fawkes.

guzzle ['gʌzl] vt tranguiare.
gym [dʒɪm] n (also: gymnasium) palestra; (also: gymnastics) ginnastica.
gymnast ['dʒɪmnæst] n ginnasta m/f; ~ics [-'næstɪks] n, npl ginnastica.
gym shoes npl scarpe fpl da ginnastica.
gym slip (BRIT) n grembiule m da scuola (per ragazze).
gynaecologist [gaɪnɪ'kɔlədʒɪst] (US gynecologist) n ginecologo/a.
gypsy ['dʒɪpsɪ] n = gipsy.
gyrate [dʒaɪ'reɪt] vi girare.

H

haberdashery ['hæbə'dæʃərɪ] (BRIT) n merceria.
habit ['hæbɪt] n abitudine f; (costume) abito; (REL) tonaca.
habitual [hə'bɪtjuəl] adj abituale; (drinker, liar) inveterato(a).
hack [hæk] vt tagliare, fare a pezzi ♦ n (pej: writer) scribacchino/a.
hacker ['hækəˑ] n (COMPUT) pirata m informatico.
hackneyed ['hæknɪd] adj comune, trito(a).
had [hæd] pt, pp of have.
haddock ['hædək] (pl ~ or ~s) n eglefino.
hadn't ['hædnt] = had not.
haemorrhage ['hemərɪdʒ] (US hemorrhage) n emorragia.
haemorrhoids ['hemərɔɪdz] (US hemorrhoids) npl emorroidi fpl.
haggard ['hægəd] adj smunto(a).
haggle ['hægl] vi mercanteggiare.
Hague [heɪg] n: The ~ L'Aia.
hail [heɪl] n grandine f; (of criticism etc) pioggia ♦ vt (call) chiamare; (flag down: taxi) fermare; (greet) salutare ♦ vi grandinare; ~stone n chicco di grandine.
hair [hɛəˑ] n capelli mpl; (single hair: on head) capello; (: on body) pelo; to do one's ~ pettinarsi; ~brush n spazzola per capelli; ~cut n taglio di capelli; ~do ['hɛədu:] n acconciatura,

pettinatura; ~**dresser** n parrucchiere/a; ~-**dryer** n asciugacapelli m inv; ~**grip** n forcina; ~**net** n retina per capelli; ~**pin** n forcina; ~**pin bend** (US ~**pin curve**) n tornante m; ~**raising** adj orripilante; ~ **remover** n crema depilatoria; ~ **spray** n lacca per capelli; ~**style** n pettinatura, acconciatura; ~**y** adj irsuto(a); peloso(a); (inf: frightening) spaventoso(a).

hake [heɪk] (pl ~ or ~s) n nasello.

half [hɑ:f] (pl **halves**) n mezzo, metà f inv ♦ adj mezzo(a) ♦ adv a mezzo, a metà; ~ **an hour** mezz'ora; ~ **a dozen** mezza dozzina; ~ **a pound** mezza libbra; **two and a** ~ due e mezzo; **a week and a** ~ una settimana e mezza; ~ (**of it**) la metà; ~ (**of**) la metà di; **to cut sth in** ~ tagliare qc in due; ~**asleep** mezzo(a) addormentato(a); ~-**baked** adj (scheme) che non sta in piedi; ~-**caste** n meticcio/a; ~-**hearted** adj tiepido(a); ~-**hour** n mezz'ora; ~-**mast**: **at** ~-**mast** adv (flag) a mezz'asta; ~-**penny** ['heɪpnɪ] (BRIT) n mezzo penny m inv; ~-**price** adj, adv a metà prezzo; ~ **term** (BRIT) n (SCOL) vacanza a or di metà trimestre; ~-**time** n (SPORT) intervallo; ~**way** adv a metà strada.

halibut ['hælɪbət] n inv ippoglosso.

hall [hɔ:l] n sala, salone m; (entrance way) entrata; ~ **of residence** (BRIT) n casa dello studente.

hallmark ['hɔ:lmɑ:k] n marchio di garanzia; (fig) caratteristica.

hallo [hə'ləu] excl = **hello**.

Hallowe'en [hæləu'i:n] n vigilia d'Ognissanti.

hallucination [həlu:sɪ'neɪʃən] n allucinazione f.

hallway ['hɔ:lweɪ] n corridoio; (entrance) ingresso.

halo ['heɪləu] n (of saint etc) aureola.

halt [hɔ:lt] n fermata ♦ vt fermare ♦ vi fermarsi.

halve [hɑ:v] vt (apple etc) dividere a metà; (expense) ridurre di metà.

halves [hɑ:vz] npl of **half**.

ham [hæm] n prosciutto.

hamburger ['hæmbə:gə*] n hamburger m inv.

hamlet ['hæmlɪt] n paesetto.

hammer ['hæmə*] n martello ♦ vt martellare ♦ vi: **to** ~ **on** or **at the door** picchiare alla porta.

hammock ['hæmək] n amaca.

hamper ['hæmpə*] vt impedire ♦ n cesta.

hamster ['hæmstə*] n criceto.

hand [hænd] n mano f; (of clock) lancetta; (handwriting) scrittura; (at cards) mano; (: game) partita; (worker) operaio/a ♦ vt dare, passare; **to give sb a** ~ dare una mano a qn; **at** ~ a portata di mano; **in** ~ a disposizione; (work) in corso; **on** ~ (person) disponibile; (services) pronto(a) a intervenire; **to** ~ (information etc) a portata di mano; **on the one** ~ ..., **on the other** ~ da un lato ..., dall'altro; ~ **in** vt consegnare; ~ **out** vt distribuire; ~ **over** vt passare; cedere; ~**bag** n borsetta; ~**book** n manuale m; ~**brake** n freno a mano; ~**cuffs** npl manette fpl; ~**ful** n manciata, pugno.

handicap ['hændɪkæp] n handicap m inv ♦ vt handicappare; **to be physically** ~**ped** essere handicappato(a); **to be mentally** ~**ped** essere un(a) handicappato(a) mentale.

handicraft ['hændɪkrɑ:ft] n lavoro d'artigiano.

handiwork ['hændɪwə:k] n opera.

handkerchief ['hæŋkətʃɪf] n fazzoletto.

handle ['hændl] n (of door etc) maniglia; (of cup etc) ansa; (of knife etc) impugnatura; (of saucepan) manico; (for winding) manovella ♦ vt toccare, maneggiare; (deal with) occuparsi di; (treat: people) trattare; "~ **with care**" "fragile"; **to fly off the** ~ (fig) perdere le staffe, uscire dai gangheri; ~**bar(s)** n(pl) manubrio.

hand: ~ **luggage** n bagagli mpl a mano; ~**made** adj fatto(a) a mano; ~**out** n (money, food) elemosina; (leaflet) volantino; (at lecture) prospetto; ~**rail** n corrimano; ~**shake** n stretta di mano.

handsome ['hænsəm] *adj* bello(a); (*profit, fortune*) considerevole.

handwriting ['hændraɪtɪŋ] *n* scrittura.

handy ['hændɪ] *adj* (*person*) bravo(a); (*close at hand*) a portata di mano; (*convenient*) comodo(a); ~**man** *n* tuttofare *m inv*.

hang [hæŋ] (*pt, pp* hung) *vt* appendere; (*criminal*: *pt, pp* hanged) impiccare ♦ *vi* (*painting*) essere appeso(a); (*hair*) scendere; (*drapery*) cadere; **to get the ~ of sth** (*inf*) capire come qc funziona; ~ **about** *or* **around** *vi* bighellonare, ciondolare; ~ **on** *vi* (*wait*) aspettare; ~ **up** *vi* (*TEL*) riattaccare ♦ *vt* appendere.

hangar ['hæŋə*] *n* hangar *m inv*.

hanger ['hæŋə*] *n* gruccia.

hanger-on *n* parassita *m*.

hang-gliding ['-glaɪdɪŋ] *n* volo col deltaplano.

hangover ['hæŋəʊvə*] *n* (*after drinking*) postumi *mpl* di sbornia.

hang-up *n* complesso.

hanker ['hæŋkə*] *vi*: **to ~ after** bramare.

hankie ['hæŋkɪ] *n abbr* = **handkerchief**.

hanky ['hæŋkɪ] *n abbr* = **handkerchief**.

haphazard [hæp'hæzəd] *adj* a casaccio, alla carlona.

happen ['hæpən] *vi* accadere, succedere; (*chance*): **to ~ to do sth** fare qc per caso; **as it ~s** guarda caso; ~**ing** *n* avvenimento.

happily ['hæpɪlɪ] *adv* felicemente; fortunatamente.

happiness ['hæpɪnɪs] *n* felicità, contentezza.

happy ['hæpɪ] *adj* felice, contento(a); ~ **with** (*arrangements etc*) soddisfatto(a) di; **to be ~ to do** (*willing*) fare volentieri; ~ **birthday!** buon compleanno!; ~**-go-lucky** *adj* spensierato(a).

harangue [hə'ræŋ] *vt* arringare.

harass ['hærəs] *vt* molestare; ~**ment** *n* molestia.

harbour ['hɑ:bə*] (*US* harbor) *n* porto ♦ *vt* (*hope, fear*) nutrire; (*criminal*) dare

rifugio a.

hard [hɑ:d] *adj* duro(a) ♦ *adv* (*work*) sodo; (*think, try*) bene; **to look ~ at** guardare fissamente; esaminare attentamente; **no ~ feelings!** senza rancore!; **to be ~ of hearing** essere duro(a) d'orecchio; **to be ~ done by** essere trattato(a) ingiustamente; ~**back** *n* libro rilegato; ~ **cash** *n* denaro in contanti; ~ **disk** *n* (*COMPUT*) disco rigido; ~**en** *vt, vi* indurire; ~**headed** *adj* pratico(a); ~ **labour** *n* lavori forzati *mpl*.

hardly ['hɑ:dlɪ] *adv* (*scarcely*) appena; **it's ~ the case** non è proprio il caso; ~ **anyone/anywhere** quasi nessuno/da nessuna parte; ~ **ever** quasi mai.

hardship ['hɑ:dʃɪp] *n* avversità *f inv*; privazioni *fpl*.

hard-up (*inf*) *adj* al verde.

hardware ['hɑ:dwɛə*] *n* ferramenta *fpl*; (*COMPUT*) hardware *m*; (*MIL*) armamenti *mpl*; ~ **shop** *n* (negozio di) ferramenta *fpl*.

hard-wearing [-'wɛərɪŋ] *adj* resistente; (*shoes*) robusto(a).

hard-working [-'wə:kɪŋ] *adj* lavoratore(trice).

hardy ['hɑ:dɪ] *adj* robusto(a); (*plant*) resistente al gelo.

hare [hɛə*] *n* lepre *f*; ~**-brained** *adj* folle; scervellato(a).

harm [hɑ:m] *n* male *m*; (*wrong*) danno ♦ *vt* (*person*) fare male a; (*thing*) danneggiare; **out of ~'s way** al sicuro; ~**ful** *adj* dannoso(a); ~**less** *adj* innocuo(a); inoffensivo(a).

harmonica [hɑ:'mɔnɪkə] *n* armonica.

harmonious [hɑ:'məʊnɪəs] *adj* armonioso(a).

harmony ['hɑ:mənɪ] *n* armonia.

harness ['hɑ:nɪs] *n* (*for horse*) bardatura, finimenti *mpl*; (*for child*) briglie *fpl*; (*safety ~*) imbracatura ♦ *vt* (*horse*) bardare; (*resources*) sfruttare.

harp [hɑ:p] *n* arpa ♦ *vi*: **to ~ on about** insistere tediosamente su.

harpoon [hɑ:'pu:n] *n* arpione *m*.

harrowing ['hærəʊɪŋ] *adj* straziante.

harsh [hɑ:ʃ] *adj* (*life, winter*) duro(a);

(*judge, criticism*) severo(a); (*sound*) rauco(a); (*light*) violento(a).

harvest ['hɑːvɪst] *n* raccolto; (*of grapes*) vendemmia ♦ *vt* fare il raccolto di, raccogliere; vendemmiare.

has [hæz] *vb see* **have**.

hash [hæʃ] *n* (CULIN) *specie di spezzatino fatto con carne già cotta*; (*fig: mess*) pasticcio.

hashish ['hæʃɪʃ] *n* hascisc *m*.

hasn't ['hæznt] = **has not**.

hassle ['hæsl] (*inf*) *n* sacco di problemi.

haste [heɪst] *n* fretta; precipitazione *f*; ~**n** ['heɪsn] *vt* affrettare ♦ *vi*: **to** ~**n (to)** affrettarsi (a); **hastily** *adv* in fretta; precipitosamente; **hasty** *adj* affrettato(a); precipitoso(a).

hat [hæt] *n* cappello.

hatch [hætʃ] *n* (NAUT: *also:* ~*way*) boccaporto; (*also: service* ~) portello di servizio ♦ *vi* (*bird*) uscire dal guscio; (*egg*) schiudersi.

hatchback ['hætʃbæk] *n* (AUT) tre (*or* cinque) porte *f inv*.

hatchet ['hætʃɪt] *n* accetta.

hate [heɪt] *vt* odiare, detestare ♦ *n* odio; ~**ful** *adj* odioso(a), detestabile.

hatred ['heɪtrɪd] *n* odio.

haughty ['hɔːtɪ] *adj* altero(a), arrogante.

haul [hɔːl] *vt* trascinare, tirare ♦ *n* (*of fish*) pescata; (*of stolen goods etc*) bottino; ~**age** *n* trasporto; autotrasporto; ~**ier** (US ~**er**) *n* trasportatore *m*.

haunch [hɔːntʃ] *n* anca; (*of meat*) coscia.

haunt [hɔːnt] *vt* (*subj: fear*) pervadere; (: *person*) frequentare ♦ *n* rifugio; **this house is** ~**ed** questa casa è abitata da un fantasma.

KEYWORD

have [hæv] (*pt, pp* **had**) *aux vb* **1** (*gen*) avere; essere; **to** ~ **arrived/gone** essere arrivato(a)/andato(a); **to** ~ **eaten/slept** avere mangiato/dormito; **he has been kind/promoted** è stato gentile/promosso; **having finished** *or* **when he had finished, he left** dopo aver finito, se n'è andato

2 (*in tag questions*): **you've done it, ~n't you?** l'ha fatto, (non è) vero?; **he hasn't done it, has he?** non l'ha fatto, vero?

3 (*in short answers and questions*): **you've made a mistake — no I ~n't/so I ~** ha fatto un errore — ma no, niente affatto/sì, è vero; **we ~n't paid — yes we ~!** non abbiamo pagato — ma sì che abbiamo pagato!; **I've been there before, ~ you?** ci sono già stato, e lei?

♦ *modal aux vb* (*be obliged*): **to ~ (got) to do sth** dover fare qc; **I ~n't got** *or* **I don't ~ to wear glasses** non ho bisogno di portare gli occhiali

♦ *vt* **1** (*possess, obtain*) avere; **he has (got) blue eyes/dark hair** ha gli occhi azzurri/i capelli scuri; **do you ~** *or* ~ **you got a car/phone?** ha la macchina/il telefono?; **may I ~ your address?** potrebbe darmi il suo indirizzo?; **you can ~ it for £5** te lo lascio per 5 sterline

2 (+*noun: take, hold etc*): **to ~ breakfast/a swim/a bath** fare colazione/una nuotata/un bagno; **to ~ lunch** pranzare; **to ~ dinner** cenare; **to ~ a drink** bere qualcosa; **to ~ a cigarette** fumare una sigaretta

3: **to ~ done** far fare qc; **to ~ one's hair cut** farsi tagliare i capelli; **to ~ sb do sth** far fare qc a qn

4 (*experience, suffer*) avere; **to ~ a cold/flu** avere il raffreddore/l'influenza; **she had her bag stolen** le hanno rubato la borsa

5 (*inf: dupe*): **you've been had!** ci sei cascato!

have out *vt*: **to ~ it out with sb** (*settle a problem etc*) mettere le cose in chiaro con qn.

haven ['heɪvn] *n* porto; (*fig*) rifugio.

haven't ['hævnt] = **have not**.

haversack ['hævəsæk] *n* zaino.

havoc ['hævək] *n* caos *m*.

hawk [hɔːk] *n* falco.

hay [heɪ] *n* fieno; ~ **fever** *n* febbre *f* da fieno; ~**stack** *n* pagliaio.

haywire ['heɪwaɪə*] (*inf*) *adj*: **to go ~** impazzire.

hazard 111 **heavy**

hazard ['hæzəd] n azzardo, ventura; pericolo, rischio ♦ vt (guess etc) azzardare; ~**ous** adj pericoloso(a); ~ **(warning) lights** npl (AUT) luci fpl di emergenza.
haze [heɪz] n foschia.
hazelnut ['heɪzlnʌt] n nocciola.
hazy ['heɪzɪ] adj fosco(a); (idea) vago(a).
he [hiː] pronoun lui, egli; **it is ~ who ...** è lui che ....
head [hɛd] n testa; (leader) capo; (of school) preside m/f ♦ vt (list) essere in testa a; (group) essere a capo di; ~**s (or tails)** testa (o croce), pari (o dispari); ~ **first** a capofitto, di testa; ~ **over heels in love** pazzamente innamorato(a); **to ~ the ball** colpire una palla di testa; ~ **for** vt fus dirigersi verso; ~**ache** n mal m di testa; ~**dress** (BRIT) n (of bride) acconciatura; ~**ing** n titolo; intestazione f; ~**lamp** (BRIT) n = ~**light**; ~**land** n promontorio; ~**light** n fanale m; ~**line** n titolo; ~**long** adv (fall) a capofitto; (rush) precipitosamente; ~**master/mistress** n preside m/f; ~ **office** n sede f (centrale); ~**-on** adj (collision) frontale; ~**phones** npl cuffia; ~**quarters** npl ufficio centrale; (MIL) quartiere m generale; ~**-rest** n poggiacapo; ~**room** n (in car) altezza dell'abitacolo; (under bridge) altezza limite; ~**scarf** n foulard m inv; ~**strong** adj testardo(a); ~ **waiter** n capocameriere m; ~**way** n: **to make ~way** fare progressi; ~**wind** n controvento; ~**y** adj (experience, period) inebriante.
heal [hiːl] vt, vi guarire.
health [hɛlθ] n salute f; ~ **food(s)** n(pl) alimenti mpl integrali; **the H~ Service** (BRIT) n ≈ il Servizio Sanitario Statale; ~**y** adj (person) sano(a), in buona salute; (climate) salubre; (appetite, economy etc) sano(a).
heap [hiːp] n mucchio ♦ vt (stones, sand): **to ~ (up)** ammucchiare; (plate, sink): **to ~ sth with** riempire qc di; ~**s of** (inf) un mucchio di.

hear [hɪə*] (pt, pp **heard**) vt sentire; (news) ascoltare ♦ vi sentire; **to ~ about** avere notizie di; sentire parlare di; **to ~ from sb** ricevere notizie da qn; ~**ing** n (sense) udito; (of witnesses) audizione f; (of a case) udienza; ~**ing aid** n apparecchio acustico; ~**say** n dicerie fpl, chiacchiere fpl.
hearse [həːs] n carro funebre.
heart [hɑːt] n cuore m; ~**s** npl (CARDS) cuori mpl; **to lose ~** scoraggiarsi; **to take ~** farsi coraggio; **at ~** in fondo; **by ~** (learn, know) a memoria; ~ **attack** n attacco di cuore; ~**beat** n battito del cuore; ~**breaking** adj straziante; ~**broken** adj: **to be ~broken** avere il cuore spezzato; ~**burn** n bruciore m di stomaco; ~ **failure** n arresto cardiaco; ~**felt** adj sincero(a).
hearth [hɑːθ] n focolare m.
heartland ['hɑːtlænd] n regione f centrale.
heartless ['hɑːtlɪs] adj senza cuore.
hearty ['hɑːtɪ] adj caloroso(a); robusto(a), sano(a); vigoroso(a).
heat [hiːt] n calore m; (fig) ardore m; fuoco; (SPORT: also: qualifying ~) prova eliminatoria ♦ vt scaldare; ~ **up** vi (liquids) scaldarsi; (room) riscaldarsi ♦ vt riscaldare; ~**ed** adj riscaldato(a); (argument) acceso(a); ~**er** n radiatore m; (stove) stufa.
heath [hiːθ] (BRIT) n landa.
heathen ['hiːðn] n pagano/a.
heather ['hɛðə*] n erica.
heating ['hiːtɪŋ] n riscaldamento.
heatstroke ['hiːtstrəuk] n colpo di sole.
heatwave ['hiːtweɪv] n ondata di caldo.
heave [hiːv] vt (pull) tirare (con forza); (push) spingere (con forza); (lift) sollevare (con forza) ♦ vi sollevarsi; (retch) aver conati di vomito ♦ n (push) grande spinta; **to ~ a sigh** emettere un sospiro.
heaven ['hɛvn] n paradiso, cielo; ~**ly** adj divino(a), celeste.
heavily ['hɛvɪlɪ] adv pesantemente; (drink, smoke) molto.
heavy ['hɛvɪ] adj pesante; (sea)

grosso(a); (*rain*, *blow*) forte; (*weather*) afoso(a); (*drinker*, *smoker*) gran (*before noun*); ~ **goods vehicle** *n* veicolo per trasporti pesanti; ~**weight** *n* (SPORT) peso massimo.

Hebrew ['hi:bru:] *adj* ebreo(a) ♦ *n* (LING) ebraico.

Hebrides ['hɛbrɪdi:z] *npl*: **the** ~ le Ebridi.

heckle ['hɛkl] *vt* interpellare e dare noia a (*un oratore*).

hectic ['hɛktɪk] *adj* movimentato(a).

he'd [hi:d] = **he would**; **he had**.

hedge [hɛdʒ] *n* siepe *f* ♦ *vi* essere elusivo(a); **to** ~ **one's bets** (*fig*) coprirsi dai rischi.

hedgehog ['hɛdʒhɔg] *n* riccio.

heed [hi:d] *vt* (*also*: take ~ of) badare a, far conto di; ~**less** *adj*: ~ (**of**) sordo(a) (a).

heel [hi:l] *n* (ANAT) calcagno; (*of shoe*) tacco ♦ *vt* (*shoe*) rifare i tacchi a.

hefty ['hɛftɪ] *adj* (*person*) robusto(a); (*parcel*) pesante; (*profit*) grosso(a).

heifer ['hɛfə*] *n* giovenca.

height [haɪt] *n* altezza; (*high ground*) altura; (*fig*: of glory) apice *m*; (: of stupidity) colmo; ~**en** *vt* (*fig*) accrescere.

heir [ɛə*] *n* erede *m*; ~**ess** *n* erede *f*; ~**loom** *n* mobile *m* (or gioiello or quadro) di famiglia.

held [hɛld] *pt, pp of* **hold**.

helicopter ['hɛlɪkɔptə*] *n* elicottero.

heliport ['hɛlɪpɔ:t] *n* eliporto.

helium ['hi:lɪəm] *n* elio.

hell [hɛl] *n* inferno; ~! (*inf*) porca miseria!, accidenti!

he'll [hi:l] = **he will**; **he shall**.

hellish ['hɛlɪʃ] (*inf*) *adj* infernale.

hello [hə'ləu] *excl* buon giorno!; ciao! (*to sb one addresses as "tu"*); (*surprise*) ma guarda!

helm [hɛlm] *n* (NAUT) timone *m*.

helmet ['hɛlmɪt] *n* casco.

help [hɛlp] *n* aiuto; (*charwoman*) donna di servizio ♦ *vt* aiutare; ~! aiuto!; ~ **yourself** (**to bread**) si serva (del pane); **he can't** ~ **it** non ci può far niente; ~**er** *n* aiutante *m/f*, assistente *m/f*; ~**ful** *adj*

di grande aiuto; (*useful*) utile; ~**ing** *n* porzione *f*; ~**less** *adj* impotente; debole.

hem [hɛm] *n* orlo ♦ *vt* fare l'orlo a; ~ **in** *vt* cingere.

hemisphere ['hɛmɪsfɪə*] *n* emisfero.

hemorrhage ['hɛmərɪdʒ] (US) *n* = **haemorrhage**.

hemorrhoids ['hɛmərɔɪdz] (US) *npl* = **haemorroids**.

hen [hɛn] *n* gallina; (*female bird*) femmina.

hence [hɛns] *adv* (*therefore*) dunque; **2 years** ~ di qui a 2 anni; ~**forth** *adv* d'ora in poi.

henchman ['hɛntʃmən] (*pej*) *n* caudatario.

henpecked ['hɛnpɛkt] *adj* dominato dalla moglie.

hepatitis [hɛpə'taɪtɪs] *n* epatite *f*.

her [hə:*] *pron* (*direct*) la, l' +vowel; (*indirect*) le; (*stressed, after prep*) lei ♦ *adj* il(la) suo(a), i(le) sùoi(sue); *see also* **me**; **my**.

herald ['hɛrəld] *n* araldo ♦ *vt* annunciare.

heraldry ['hɛrəldrɪ] *n* araldica.

herb [hə:b] *n* erba.

herd [hə:d] *n* mandria.

here [hɪə*] *adv* qui, qua ♦ *excl* ehi!; ~! (*at roll call*) presente!; ~ **is/are** ecco; ~ **he/she is** eccolo/eccola; ~**after** *adv* in futuro; dopo questo; ~**by** *adv* (*in letter*) con la presente.

hereditary [hɪ'rɛdɪtrɪ] *adj* ereditario(a).

heresy ['hɛrəsɪ] *n* eresia.

heretic ['hɛrətɪk] *n* eretico/a.

heritage ['hɛrɪtɪdʒ] *n* eredità; (*fig*) retaggio.

hermetically [hə:'mɛtɪklɪ] *adv*: ~ **sealed** ermeticamente chiuso(a).

hermit ['hə:mɪt] *n* eremita *m*.

hernia ['hə:nɪə] *n* ernia.

hero ['hɪərəu] (*pl* ~es) *n* eroe *m*.

heroin ['hɛrəuɪn] *n* eroina.

heroine ['hɛrəuɪn] *n* eroina.

heron ['hɛrən] *n* airone *m*.

herring ['hɛrɪŋ] *n* aringa.

hers [hə:z] *pron* il(la) suo(a), i(le) suoi(sue); *see also* **mine**.

herself [hɔ:'self] *pron* (*reflexive*) si; (*emphatic*) lei stessa; (*after prep*) se stessa, sé; *see also* oneself.

he's [hi:z] = **he is**; **he has**.

hesitant ['hezɪtənt] *adj* esitante, indeciso(a).

hesitate ['hezɪteɪt] *vi*: **to ~** (*about/to do*) esitare (su/a fare); **hesitation** [-'teɪʃən] *n* esitazione *f*.

heterosexual ['hetərəu'seksjuəl] *adj*, *n* eterosessuale *m/f*.

hew [hju:] *vt* (*stone*) scavare; (*wood*) tagliare.

hexagonal [hek'sægənəl] *adj* esagonale.

heyday ['heɪdeɪ] *n*: **the ~ of** i bei giorni di, l'età d'oro di.

HGV *n abbr* = **heavy goods vehicle**.

hi [haɪ] *excl* ciao!

hiatus [haɪ'eɪtəs] *n* vuoto; (*LING*) iato.

hibernate ['haɪbəneɪt] *vi* ibernare.

hiccough ['hɪkʌp] *vi* singhiozzare; **~s** *npl*: **to have ~s** avere il singhiozzo.

hiccup ['hɪkʌp] = **hiccough**.

hid [hɪd] *pt of* **hide**; **~den** ['hɪdn] *pp of* **hide**.

hide [haɪd] (*pt* **hid**, *pp* **hidden**) *n* (*skin*) pelle *f* ♦ *vt*: **to ~ sth** (**from sb**) nascondere qc (a qn) ♦ *vi*: **to ~** (**from sb**) nascondersi (da qn); **~-and-seek** *n* rimpiattino; **~away** *n* nascondiglio.

hideous ['hɪdɪəs] *adj* laido(a); orribile.

hiding ['haɪdɪŋ] *n* (*beating*) bastonata; **to be in ~** (*concealed*) tenersi nascosto(a).

hierarchy ['haɪərɑːkɪ] *n* gerarchia.

hi-fi ['haɪfaɪ] *n* stereo ♦ *adj* ad alta fedeltà, hi-fi *inv*.

high [haɪ] *adj* alto(a); (*speed, respect, number*) grande; (*wind*) forte; (*voice*) acuto(a) ♦ *adv* alto, in alto; **20m ~** alto(a) 20m; **~brow** *adj*, *n* intellettuale *m/f*; **~chair** *n* seggiolone *m*; **~er education** *n* studi *mpl* superiori; **~-handed** *adj* prepotente; **~-heeled** *adj* con i tacchi alti; **~ jump** *n* (*SPORT*) salto in alto; **the H~lands** *npl* le Highlands scozzesi; **~light** *n* (*fig: of event*) momento culminante; (*in hair*) colpo di sole ♦ *vt* mettere in evidenza; **~ly** *adv* molto; **to speak ~ly of** parlare

molto bene di; **~ly strung** *adj* teso(a) di nervi, eccitabile; **~ness** *n*: **Her H~ness** Sua Altezza; **~-pitched** *adj* acuto(a); **~-rise block** *n* palazzone *m*; **~ school** *n* scuola secondaria; (*US*) istituto superiore d'istruzione; **~ season** (*BRIT*) *n* alta stagione; **~ street** (*BRIT*) *n* strada principale.

highway ['haɪweɪ] *n* strada maestra; **H~ Code** (*BRIT*) *n* codice *m* della strada.

hijack ['haɪdʒæk] *vt* dirottare; **~er** *n* dirottatore/trice.

hike [haɪk] *vi* fare un'escursione a piedi ♦ *n* escursione *f* a piedi; **~r** *n* escursionista *m/f*.

hilarious [hɪ'lɛərɪəs] *adj* (*behaviour, event*) spassosissimo(a).

hill [hɪl] *n* collina, colle *m*; (*fairly high*) montagna; (*on road*) salita; **~side** *n* fianco della collina; **~y** *adj* collinoso(a); montagnoso(a).

hilt [hɪlt] *n* (*of sword*) elsa; **to the ~** (*fig: support*) fino in fondo.

him [hɪm] *pron* (*direct*) lo, l' +*vowel*; (*indirect*) gli; (*stressed, after prep*) lui; *see also* me; **~self** *pron* (*reflexive*) si; (*emphatic*) lui stesso; (*after prep*) se stesso, sé; *see also* oneself.

hind [haɪnd] *adj* posteriore.

hinder ['hɪndə*] *vt* ostacolare; **hindrance** ['hɪndrəns] *n* ostacolo, impedimento.

hindsight ['haɪndsaɪt] *n*: **with ~** con il senno di poi.

Hindu ['hɪndu:] *n* indù *m/f inv*.

hinge [hɪndʒ] *n* cardine *m* ♦ *vi* (*fig*): **to ~ on** dipendere da.

hint [hɪnt] *n* (*suggestion*) allusione *f*; (*advice*) consiglio; (*sign*) accenno ♦ *vt*: **to ~ that** lasciar capire che ♦ *vi*: **to ~ at** alludere a.

hip [hɪp] *n* anca, fianco.

hippopotami [hɪpə'pɒtəmaɪ] *npl of* **hippopotamus**.

hippopotamus [hɪpə'pɒtəməs] (*pl* **~es** *or* **hippopotami**) *n* ippopotamo.

hire ['haɪə*] *vt* (*BRIT: car, equipment*) noleggiare; (*worker*) assumere, dare lavoro a ♦ *n* nolo, noleggio; **for ~** da

nolo; (taxi) libero(a); ~ **purchase**
(BRIT) n acquisto (or vendita) rateale.
his [hɪz] adj, pron il(la) suo(sua), i(le)
suoi(sue); see also **my**; **mine**.
hiss [hɪs] vi fischiare; (cat, snake)
sibilare.
historic(al) [hɪ'stɔrɪk(l)] adj storico(a).
history ['hɪstərɪ] n storia.
hit [hɪt] (pt, pp hit) vt colpire, picchiare; (knock against) battere;
(reach: target) raggiungere; (collide
with: car) urtare contro; (fig: affect)
colpire; (find: problem etc) incontrare
♦ n colpo; (success, song) successo; to
~ it off with sb andare molto d'accordo
con qn; ~-**and-run driver** n pirata m
della strada.
hitch [hɪtʃ] vt (fasten) attaccare; (also:
~ up) tirare su ♦ n (difficulty) intoppo,
difficoltà f inv; to ~ **a lift** fare l'autostop.
hitch-hike vi fare l'autostop; ~**r** n
autostoppista m/f.
hi-tech ['haɪtɛk] adj di alta tecnologia ♦
n alta tecnologia.
hitherto [hɪðə'tu:] adv in precedenza.
hive [haɪv] n alveare m; ~ **off** vt
separare.
H.M.S. abbr = His(Her) Majesty's
Ship.
hoard [hɔ:d] n (of food) provviste fpl;
(of money) gruzzolo ♦ vt ammassare.
hoarding ['hɔ:dɪŋ] (BRIT) n (for posters)
tabellone m per affissioni.
hoarfrost ['hɔ:frɔst] n brina.
hoarse [hɔ:s] adj rauco(a).
hoax [həʊks] n scherzo; falso allarme.
hob [hɔb] n piastra (con fornelli).
hobble ['hɔbl] vi zoppicare.
hobby ['hɔbɪ] n hobby m inv,
passatempo; ~-**horse** n (fig) chiodo
fisso.
hobo ['həʊbəʊ] (US) n vagabondo.
hockey ['hɔkɪ] n hockey m.
hoe [həʊ] n zappa.
hog [hɔg] n maiale m ♦ vt (fig)
arraffare; **to go the whole ~** farlo fino
in fondo.
hoist [hɔɪst] n paranco ♦ vt issare.
hold [həʊld] (pt, pp held) vt tenere;

(contain) contenere; (keep back)
trattenere; (believe) mantenere;
considerare; (possess) avere,
possedere; detenere ♦ vi (withstand
pressure) tenere; (be valid) essere
valido(a) ♦ n presa; (control): **to have
a ~ over** avere controllo su; (NAUT)
stiva; ~ **the line!** (TEL) resti in linea!;
to ~ one's own (fig) difendersi bene; **to
catch** or **get (a) ~ of** afferrare; ~ **back**
vt trattenere; (secret) tenere celato(a);
~ **down** vt (person) tenere a terra;
(job) tenere; ~ **off** vt tener lontano; ~
on vi tener fermo; (wait) aspettare; ~
on! (TEL) resti in linea!; ~ **on to** vt
fus tenersi stretto(a) a; (keep)
conservare; ~ **out** vt offrire ♦ vi
(resist) resistere; ~ **up** vt (raise)
alzare; (support) sostenere; (delay)
ritardare; (rob) assaltare; ~**all** (BRIT)
n borsone m; ~**er** n (container)
contenitore m; (of ticket, title)
possessore/posseditrice; (of office etc)
incaricato/a; (of record) detentore/
trice; ~**ing** n (share) azioni fpl, titoli
mpl; (farm) podere m, tenuta; ~**up** n
(robbery) rapina a mano armata;
(delay) ritardo; (BRIT: in traffic)
blocco.
hole [həʊl] n buco, buca ♦ vt bucare.
holiday ['hɔlədɪ] n vacanza; (day off)
giorno di vacanza; (public) giorno festivo; **on ~** in vacanza; ~ **camp** (BRIT)
n (also: ~ centre) ≈ villaggio (di
vacanze); ~-**maker** (BRIT) n
villeggiante m/f; ~ **resort** n luogo di
villeggiatura.
holiness ['həʊlɪnɪs] n santità.
Holland ['hɔlənd] n Olanda.
hollow ['hɔləʊ] adj cavo(a); (container,
claim) vuoto(a); (laugh, sound)
cupo(a) ♦ n cavità f inv; (in land)
valletta, depressione f ♦ vt: **to ~ out**
scavare.
holly ['hɔlɪ] n agrifoglio.
holocaust ['hɔləkɔːst] n olocausto.
holster ['həʊlstə*] n fondina (di pistola).
holy ['həʊlɪ] adj santo(a); (bread)
benedetto(a), consacrato(a); (ground)
consacrato(a).

homage ['hɔmɪdʒ] *n* omaggio; **to pay ~ to** rendere omaggio a.

home [həum] *n* casa; (*country*) patria; (*institution*) casa, ricovero ♦ *cpd* familiare; (*cooking etc*) casalingo(a); (*ECON, POL*) nazionale, interno(a); (*SPORT*) di casa ♦ *adv* a casa; in patria; (*right in: nail etc*) fino in fondo; **at ~** a casa; (*in situation*) a proprio agio; **to go** (*or* **come**) **~** tornare a casa (*or* in patria); **make yourself at ~** si metta a suo agio; **~ address** *n* indirizzo di casa; **~ computer** *n* home computer *m inv*; **~land** *n* patria; **~less** *adj* senza tetto; spatriato(a); **~ly** *adj* semplice, alla buona; accogliente; **~-made** *adj* casalingo(a); **H~ Office** (*BRIT*) *n* ministero degli Interni; **~ rule** *n* autogoverno; **H~ Secretary** (*BRIT*) *n* ministro degli Interni; **~sick** *adj*: **to be ~sick** avere la nostalgia; **~ town** *n* città *f inv* natale; **~ward** ['həumwəd] *adj* (*journey*) di ritorno; **~work** *n* compiti *mpl* (per casa).

homicide ['hɔmɪsaɪd] (*US*) *n* omicidio.

homogeneous [hɔməu'dʒiːnɪəs] *adj* omogeneo(a).

homosexual [hɔməu'sɛksjuəl] *adj, n* omosessuale *m/f*.

honest ['ɔnɪst] *adj* onesto(a); sincero(a); **~ly** *adv* onestamente; sinceramente; **~y** *n* onestà.

honey ['hʌnɪ] *n* miele *m*; **~comb** *n* favo; **~moon** *n* luna di miele, viaggio di nozze; **~suckle** *n* (*BOT*) caprifoglio.

honk [hɔŋk] *vi* suonare il clacson.

honorary ['ɔnərərɪ] *adj* onorario(a); (*duty, title*) onorifico(a).

honour ['ɔnə*] (*US* **honor**) *vt* onorare ♦ *n* onore *m*; **~able** *adj* onorevole; **~s degree** *n* (*SCOL*) *laurea specializzata*.

hood [hud] *n* cappuccio; (*on cooker*) cappa; (*BRIT: AUT*) capote *f*; (*US: AUT*) cofano.

hoodlum ['huːdləm] *n* teppista *m/f*.

hoodwink ['hudwɪŋk] *vt* infinocchiare.

hoof [huːf] *n* (*pl* **hooves**) *n* zoccolo.

hook [huk] *n* gancio; (*for fishing*) amo ♦ *vt* uncinare; (*dress*) agganciare.

hooligan ['huːlɪgən] *n* giovinastro, teppista *m*.

hoop [huːp] *n* cerchio.

hooray [huː'reɪ] *excl* = **hurray**.

hoot [huːt] *vi* (*AUT*) suonare il clacson; (*siren*) ululare; (*owl*) gufare; **~er** *n* (*BRIT: AUT*) clacson *m inv*; (*NAUT*) sirena.

hoover ['huːvə*] ® (*BRIT*) *n* aspirapolvere *m inv* ♦ *vt* pulire con l'aspirapolvere.

hooves [huːvz] *npl of* **hoof**.

hop [hɔp] *vi* saltellare, saltare; (*on one foot*) saltare su una gamba.

hope [həup] *vt*: **to ~ that/to do** sperare che/di fare ♦ *vi* sperare ♦ *n* speranza; **I ~ so/not** spero di sì/no; **~ful** *adj* (*person*) pieno(a) di speranza; (*situation*) promettente; **~fully** *adv* con speranza; **~fully he will recover** speriamo che si riprenda; **~less** *adj* senza speranza, disperato(a); (*useless*) inutile.

hops [hɔps] *npl* luppoli *mpl*.

horde [hɔːd] *n* orda.

horizon [hə'raɪzn] *n* orizzonte *m*; **~tal** [hɔrɪ'zɔntl] *adj* orizzontale.

hormone ['hɔːməun] *n* ormone *m*.

horn [hɔːn] *n* (*ZOOL, MUS*) corno; (*AUT*) clacson *m inv*.

hornet ['hɔːnɪt] *n* calabrone *m*.

horny ['hɔːnɪ] (*inf*) *adj* arrapato(a).

horoscope ['hɔrəskəup] *n* oroscopo.

horrendous [hə'rɛndəs] *adj* orrendo(a).

horrible ['hɔrɪbl] *adj* orribile, tremendo(a).

horrid ['hɔrɪd] *adj* orrido(a); (*person*) odioso(a).

horrify ['hɔrɪfaɪ] *vt* scandalizzare.

horror ['hɔrə*] *n* orrore *m*; **~ film** *n* film *m inv* dell'orrore.

hors d'œuvre [ɔː'dəːvrə] *n* antipasto.

horse [hɔːs] *n* cavallo; **~back: on ~back** *adj, adv* a cavallo; **~ chestnut** *n* ippocastano; **~man** *n* cavaliere *m*; **~power** *n* cavallo (vapore); **~-racing** *n* ippica; **~radish** *n* rafano; **~shoe** *n* ferro di cavallo; **~woman** *n* amazzone *f*.

horticulture ['hɔːtɪkʌltʃə*] *n* orticoltura.

hose [həuz] *n* (*also:* **~pipe**) tubo; (*also:*

garden ~) tubo per annaffiare.
hosiery ['həʊʒərɪ] *n* maglieria.
hospice ['hɒspɪs] *n* ricovero, ospizio.
hospitable [hɒs'pɪtəbl] *adj* ospitale.
hospital ['hɒspɪtl] *n* ospedale *m*.
hospitality [hɒspɪ'tælɪtɪ] *n* ospitalità.
host [həʊst] *n* ospite *m*; (*REL*) ostia;
(*large number*): **a** ~ **of** una schiera di.
hostage ['hɒstɪdʒ] *n* ostaggio/a.
hostel ['hɒstl] *n* ostello; (*also: youth* ~)
ostello della gioventù.
hostess ['həʊstɪs] *n* ospite *f*; (*BRIT*: *air*
~) hostess *f inv*.
hostile ['hɒstaɪl] *adj* ostile.
hostility [hɒ'stɪlɪtɪ] *n* ostilità *f inv*.
hot [hɒt] *adj* caldo(a); (*as opposed to*
only warm) molto caldo(a); (*spicy*)
piccante; (*fig*) accanito(a); ardente;
violento(a), focoso(a); **to be** ~ (*person*)
aver caldo; (*object*) essere caldo(a);
(*weather*) far caldo; ~**bed** *n* (*fig*)
focolaio; ~ **dog** *n* hot dog *m inv*.
hotel [həʊ'tɛl] *n* albergo; ~**ier** *n*
albergatore/trice.
hot: ~**headed** *adj* focoso(a), eccitabile;
~**house** *n* serra; ~ **line** *n* (*POL*)
telefono rosso; ~**ly** *adv* violentemente;
~**plate** *n* (*on cooker*) piastra ri-
scaldante; ~**-water bottle** *n* borsa
dell'acqua calda.
hound [haʊnd] *vt* perseguitare ♦ *n*
segugio.
hour ['aʊə*] *n* ora; ~**ly** *adj* all'ora.
house [*n* haus, *pl* 'haʊzɪz, *vb* haʊz] *n*
(*also: firm*) casa; (*POL*) camera;
(*THEATRE*) sala; pubblico; spettacolo;
(*dynasty*) casata ♦ *vt* (*person*) ospitare,
alloggiare; **on the** ~ (*fig*) offerto(a)
dalla casa; ~ **arrest** *n* arresti *mpl*
domiciliari; ~**boat** *n* house boat *f inv*;
~**bound** *adj* confinato(a) in casa;
~**breaking** *n* furto con scasso; ~**coat** *n*
vestaglia; ~**hold** *n* famiglia; casa;
~**keeper** *n* governante *f*; ~**keeping** *n*
(*work*) governo della casa; (*money*)
soldi *mpl* per le spese di casa; ~**-**
warming party *n* festa per inaugurare
la casa nuova; ~**wife** *n* massaia,
casalinga; ~**work** *n* faccende *fpl* domestiche.

housing ['haʊzɪŋ] *n* alloggio; ~
development (*BRIT* ~ **estate**) *n* zona
residenziale con case popolari e/o
private.
hovel ['hɒvl] *n* casupola.
hover ['hɒvə*] *vi* (*bird*) librarsi; ~**craft**
n hovercraft *m inv*.
how [haʊ] *adv* come; ~ **are you?** come
sta?; ~ **do you do?** piacere!; ~ **far is it**
to the river? quanto è lontano il
fiume?; ~ **long have you been here?** da
quando è qui?; ~ **lovely!/awful!** che
bello!/orrore!; ~ **many?** quanti(e)?; ~
much? quanto(a)?; ~ **much milk?**
quanto latte?; ~ **many people?** quante
persone?; ~ **old are you?** quanti anni
ha?; ~**ever** *adv* in qualsiasi modo *or*
maniera che; (+*adjective*) per quanto
+*sub*; (*in questions*) come ♦ *conj*
comunque, però.
howl [haʊl] *vi* ululare; (*baby, person*)
urlare.
H.P. *abbr* = **hire purchase; horsepower.**
h.p. *n abbr* = **H.P.**
HQ *n abbr* = **headquarters.**
hub [hʌb] *n* (*of wheel*) mozzo; (*fig*) ful-
cro.
hubbub ['hʌbʌb] *n* baccano.
hubcap ['hʌbkæp] *n* coprimozzo.
huddle ['hʌdl] *vi*: **to** ~ **together** rannicchiarsi l'uno contro l'altro.
hue [hju:] *n* tinta; ~ **and cry** *n* clamore
m.
huff [hʌf] *n*: **in a** ~ stizzito(a).
hug [hʌg] *vt* abbracciare; (*shore, kerb*)
stringere.
huge [hju:dʒ] *adj* enorme, immenso(a).
hulk [hʌlk] *n* (*ship*) nave *f* in disarmo;
(*building, car*) carcassa; (*person*) ma-
stodonte *m.*
hull [hʌl] *n* (*of ship*) scafo.
hullo [hə'ləʊ] *excl* = **hello.**
hum [hʌm] *vt* (*tune*) canticchiare ♦ *vi*
canticchiare; (*insect, plane, tool*)
ronzare.
human ['hju:mən] *adj* umano(a) ♦ *n*
essere *m* umano.
humane [hju:'meɪn] *adj* umanitario(a).
humanitarian [hju:mænɪ'tɛərɪən] *adj*
umanitario(a).

humanity [hju:'mænɪtɪ] n umanità.
humble ['hʌmbl] adj umile, modesto(a) ♦ vt umiliare.
humbug ['hʌmbʌg] n sciocchezze fpl; (BRIT: sweet) caramella alla menta.
humdrum ['hʌmdrʌm] adj monotono(a), tedioso(a).
humid ['hju:mɪd] adj umido(a).
humiliate [hju:'mɪlɪeɪt] vt umiliare; **humiliation** [-'eɪʃən] n umiliazione f.
humility [hju:'mɪlɪtɪ] n umiltà.
humorous ['hju:mərəs] adj umoristico(a); (person) buffo(a).
humour ['hju:mə*] (US **humor**) n umore m ♦ vt accontentare.
hump [hʌmp] n gobba; ~**backed** adj: ~**backed bridge** ponte m a schiena d'asino.
hunoh [hʌntʃ] n (premonition) intuizione f; ~**back** n gobbo/a; ~**ed** adj incurvato(a).
hundred ['hʌndrəd] num cento; ~**s of** centinaia fpl di; ~**weight** n (BRIT) = 50.8 kg; 112 lb; (US) = 45.3 kg; 100 lb.
hung [hʌŋ] pt, pp of **hang**.
Hungary ['hʌŋgərɪ] n Ungheria.
hunger ['hʌŋgə*] n fame f ♦ vi: **to** ~ **for** desiderare ardentemente; ~ **strike** n sciopero della fame.
hungry ['hʌŋgrɪ] adj affamato(a); (avid): ~ **for** avido(a) di; **to be** ~ aver fame.
hunk [hʌŋk] n (of bread etc) bel pezzo.
hunt [hʌnt] vt (seek) cercare; (SPORT) cacciare ♦ vi: **to** ~ **(for)** andare a caccia (di) ♦ n caccia; ~**er** n cacciatore m; ~**ing** n caccia.
hurdle ['hə:dl] n (SPORT, fig) ostacolo.
hurl [hə:l] vt lanciare con violenza.
hurrah [hu'rɑ:] excl = **hurray**.
hurray [hu'reɪ] excl urra!, evviva!
hurricane ['hʌrɪkən] n uragano.
hurried ['hʌrɪd] adj affrettato(a); (work) fatto(a) in fretta; ~**ly** adv in fretta.
hurry ['hʌrɪ] n fretta ♦ vi (also: ~ **up**) affrettarsi ♦ vt (also: ~ **up**: person) affrettare; (: work) far in fretta; **to be in a** ~ aver fretta.
hurt [hə:t] (pt, pp **hurt**) vt (cause pain

to) far male a; (injure, fig) ferire ♦ vi far male; ~**ful** adj (remark) che ferisce.
hurtle ['hə:tl] vi: **to** ~ **past/down** passare/scendere a razzo.
husband ['hʌzbənd] n marito.
hush [hʌʃ] n silenzio, calma ♦ vt zittire; ~**!** zitto(a)!; ~ **up** vt (scandal) mettere a tacere.
husk [hʌsk] n (of wheat) cartoccio; (of rice, maize) buccia.
husky ['hʌskɪ] adj roco(a) ♦ n cane m eschimese.
hustle ['hʌsl] vt spingere, incalzare ♦ n: ~ **and bustle** trambusto.
hut [hʌt] n rifugio; (shed) ripostiglio.
hutch [hʌtʃ] n gabbia.
hyacinth ['haɪəsɪnθ] n giacinto.
hybrid ['haɪbrɪd] n ibrido.
hydrant ['haɪdrənt] n (also: fire ~) idrante m.
hydraulic [haɪ'drɔ:lɪk] adj idraulico(a).
hydroelectric [haɪdrəu'lektrɪk] adj idroelettrico(a).
hydrofoil ['haɪdrəufɔɪl] n aliscafo.
hydrogen ['haɪdrədʒən] n idrogeno.
hyena [haɪ'i:nə] n iena.
hygiene ['haɪdʒi:n] n igiene f.
hymn [hɪm] n inno; cantica.
hype [haɪp] (inf) n campagna pubblicitaria.
hypermarket ['haɪpəmɑ:kɪt] (BRIT) n ipermercato.
hyphen ['haɪfn] n trattino.
hypnotism ['hɪpnətɪzm] n ipnotismo.
hypnotize ['hɪpnətaɪz] vt ipnotizzare.
hypocrisy [hɪ'pɔkrɪsɪ] n ipocrisia.
hypocrite ['hɪpəkrɪt] n ipocrita m/f; **hypocritical** [-'krɪtɪkl] adj ipocrita.
hypothermia [haɪpəu'θə:mɪə] n ipotermia.
hypotheses [haɪ'pɔθɪsi:z] npl of **hypothesis**.
hypothesis [haɪ'pɔθɪsɪs] (pl **hypotheses**) n ipotesi f inv.
hypothetical [haɪpəu'θetɪkl] adj ipotetico(a).
hysterical [hɪ'sterɪkl] adj isterico(a).
hysterics [hɪ'sterɪks] npl accesso di isteria; (laughter) attacco di riso.

I

I [aɪ] *pron* io.
ice [aɪs] *n* ghiaccio; (*on road*) gelo; (~ *cream*) gelato ♦ *vt* (*cake*) glassare ♦ *vi* (*also:* ~ *over*) ghiacciare; (*also:* ~ *up*) gelare; ~**berg** *n* iceberg *m inv*; ~**box** *n* (*US*) frigorifero; (*BRIT*) reparto ghiaccio; (*insulated box*) frigo portatile; ~ **cream** *n* gelato; ~ **hockey** *n* hockey *m* su ghiaccio.
Iceland ['aɪslənd] *n* Islanda.
ice: ~ **lolly** (*BRIT*) *n* ghiacciolo; ~ **rink** *n* pista di pattinaggio; ~ **skating** *n* pattinaggio sul ghiaccio.
icicle ['aɪsɪkl] *n* ghiacciolo.
icing ['aɪsɪŋ] *n* (*CULIN*) glassa; ~ **sugar** (*BRIT*) *n* zucchero a velo.
icy ['aɪsɪ] *adj* ghiacciato(a); (*weather, temperature*) gelido(a).
I'd [aɪd] = I would; I had.
idea [aɪ'dɪə] *n* idea.
ideal [aɪ'dɪəl] *adj* ideale ♦ *n* ideale *m*.
identical [aɪ'dɛntɪkl] *adj* identico(a).
identification [aɪdɛntɪfɪ'keɪʃən] *n* identificazione *f*; (**means of**) ~ carta d'identità.
identify [aɪ'dɛntɪfaɪ] *vt* identificare.
identikit picture [aɪ'dɛntɪkɪt-] *n* identikit *m inv*.
identity [aɪ'dɛntɪtɪ] *n* identità *f inv*; ~ **card** *n* carta d'identità.
idiom ['ɪdɪəm] *n* idioma *m*; (*phrase*) espressione *f* idiomatica.
idiot ['ɪdɪət] *n* idiota *m/f*; ~**ic** [-'ɔtɪk] *adj* idiota.
idle ['aɪdl] *adj* inattivo(a); (*lazy*) pigro(a), ozioso(a); (*unemployed*) disoccupato(a); (*question, pleasures*) ozioso(a) ♦ *vi* (*engine*) girare al minimo; ~ **away** *vt*: **to** ~ **away the time** buttar via il tempo.
idol ['aɪdl] *n* idolo; ~**ize** *vt* idoleggiare.
i.e. *adv abbr* (= *that is*) cioè.
if [ɪf] *conj* se; **I were you ...** se fossi in te ..., io al tuo posto ...; ~ **so** se è così; ~ **not** se no; ~ **only** se solo *or* soltanto.
ignite [ɪg'naɪt] *vt* accendere ♦ *vi* accendersi.
ignition [ɪg'nɪʃən] *n* (*AUT*) accensione *f*; **to switch on/off the** ~ accendere/spegnere il motore; ~ **key** *n* (*AUT*) chiave *f* dell'accensione.
ignorant ['ɪgnərənt] *adj* ignorante; **to be** ~ **of** (*subject*) essere ignorante in; (*events*) essere ignaro(a) di.
ignore [ɪg'nɔ:*] *vt* non tener conto di; (*person, fact*) ignorare.
I'll [aɪl] = I will; I shall.
ill [ɪl] *adj* (*sick*) malato(a); (*bad*) cattivo(a) ♦ *n* male *m* ♦ *adv*: **to speak** *etc* ~ **of sb** parlare *etc* male di qn; **to take** *or* **be taken** ~ ammalarsi; ~-**advised** *adj* (*decision*) poco giudizioso(a); (*person*) mal consigliato(a); ~-**at-ease** *adj* a disagio.
illegal [ɪ'li:gl] *adj* illegale.
illegible [ɪ'lɛdʒɪbl] *adj* illeggibile.
illegitimate [ɪlɪ'dʒɪtɪmət] *adj* illegittimo(a).
ill-fated [ɪl'feɪtɪd] *adj* nefasto(a).
ill feeling *n* rancore *m*.
illiterate [ɪ'lɪtərət] *adj* analfabeta, illetterato(a); (*letter*) scorretto(a).
ill-mannered [ɪl'mænəd] *adj* maleducato(a).
illness ['ɪlnɪs] *n* malattia.
ill-treat *vt* maltrattare.
illuminate [ɪ'lu:mɪneɪt] *vt* illuminare; **illumination** [-'neɪʃən] *n* illuminazione *f*; **illuminations** *npl* (*decorative*) luminarie *fpl*.
illusion [ɪ'lu:ʒən] *n* illusione *f*.
illustrate ['ɪləstreɪt] *vt* illustrare; **illustration** [-'streɪʃən] *n* illustrazione *f*.
ill will *n* cattiva volontà.
I'm [aɪm] = I am.
image ['ɪmɪdʒ] *n* immagine *f*; (*public face*) immagine (pubblica); ~**ry** *n* immagini *fpl*.
imaginary [ɪ'mædʒɪnərɪ] *adj* immaginario(a).
imagination [ɪmædʒɪ'neɪʃən] *n* immaginazione *f*, fantasia.
imaginative [ɪ'mædʒɪnətɪv] *adj* immaginoso(a).
imagine [ɪ'mædʒɪn] *vt* immaginare.
imbalance [ɪm'bæləns] *n* squilibrio.

imbue [ɪm'bju:] *vt*: to ~ sb/sth with permeare qn/qc di.

imitate ['ɪmɪteɪt] *vt* imitare; **imitation** [-'teɪʃən] *n* imitazione *f*.

immaculate [ɪ'mækjulət] *adj* immacolato(a); (*dress, appearance*) impeccabile.

immaterial [ɪmə'tɪərɪəl] *adj* immateriale, indifferente.

immature [ɪmə'tjuə*] *adj* immaturo(a).

immediate [ɪ'mi:dɪət] *adj* immediato(a); ~**ly** *adv* (*at once*) subito, immediatamente; ~**ly next to** proprio accanto a.

immense [ɪ'mɛns] *adj* immenso(a); enorme.

immerse [ɪ'mə:s] *vt* immergere.

immersion heater [ɪ'mə:ʃən-] (*BRIT*) *n* scaldaacqua *m inv* a immersione.

immigrant ['ɪmɪgrənt] *n* immigrante *m/f*; immigrato/a.

immigration [ɪmɪ'greɪʃən] *n* immigrazione *f*.

imminent ['ɪmɪnənt] *adj* imminente.

immoral [ɪ'mɔrl] *adj* immorale.

immortal [ɪ'mɔ:tl] *adj, n* immortale *m/f*.

immune [ɪ'mju:n] *adj*: ~ (**to**) immune (da); **immunity** *n* immunità *f*.

imp [ɪmp] *n* folletto, diavoletto; (*child*) diavoletto.

impact ['ɪmpækt] *n* impatto.

impair [ɪm'pɛə*] *vt* danneggiare.

impale [ɪm'peɪl] *vt* infilzare.

impart [ɪm'pɑ:t] *vt* (*make known*) comunicare; (*bestow*) impartire.

impartial [ɪm'pɑ:ʃl] *adj* imparziale.

impassable [ɪm'pɑ:səbl] *adj* insuperabile; (*road*) impraticabile.

impassive [ɪm'pæsɪv] *adj* impassibile.

impatience [ɪm'peɪʃəns] *n* impazienza.

impatient [ɪm'peɪʃənt] *adj* impaziente; **to get** *or* **grow** ~ perdere la pazienza.

impeccable [ɪm'pɛkəbl] *adj* impeccabile.

impede [ɪm'pi:d] *vt* impedire.

impediment [ɪm'pɛdɪmənt] *n* impedimento; (*also: speech* ~) difetto di pronuncia.

impending [ɪm'pɛndɪŋ] *adj* imminente.

imperative [ɪm'pɛrətɪv] *adj* imperativo(a); necessario(a), urgente; (*voice*) imperioso(a) ♦ *n* (*LING*) imperativo.

imperfect [ɪm'pə:fɪkt] *adj* imperfetto(a); (*goods etc*) difettoso(a) ♦ *n* (*LING: also:* ~ *tense*) imperfetto.

imperial [ɪm'pɪərɪəl] *adj* imperiale; (*measure*) legale.

impersonal [ɪm'pə:sənl] *adj* impersonale.

impersonate [ɪm'pə:səneɪt] *vt* impersonare; (*THEATRE*) fare la mimica di.

impertinent [ɪm'pə:tɪnənt] *adj* insolente, impertinente.

impervious [ɪm'pə:vɪəs] *adj* (*fig*): ~ **to** insensibile a; impassibile di fronte a.

impetuous [ɪm'pɛtjuəs] *adj* impetuoso(a), precipitoso(a).

impetus ['ɪmpətəs] *n* impeto.

impinge on [ɪm'pɪndʒ-] *vt fus* (*person*) colpire; (*rights*) ledere.

implement [*n* 'ɪmplɪmənt, *vb* 'ɪmplɪmɛnt] *n* attrezzo; (*for cooking*) utensile *m* ♦ *vt* effettuare.

implicit [ɪm'plɪsɪt] *adj* implicito(a); (*complete*) completo(a).

imply [ɪm'plaɪ] *vt* insinuare; suggerire.

impolite [ɪmpə'laɪt] *adj* scortese.

import [*vb* ɪm'pɔ:t, *n* 'ɪmpɔ:t] *vt* importare ♦ *n* (*COMM*) importazione *f*.

importance [ɪm'pɔ:tns] *n* importanza.

important [ɪm'pɔ:tnt] *adj* importante; **it's not** ~ non ha importanza.

importer [ɪm'pɔ:tə*] *n* importatore/trice.

impose [ɪm'pəuz] *vt* imporre ♦ *vi*: to ~ **on sb** sfruttare la bontà di qn.

imposing [ɪm'pəuzɪŋ] *adj* imponente.

imposition [ɪmpə'zɪʃən] *n* (*of tax etc*) imposizione *f*; **to be an** ~ **on** (*person*) abusare della gentilezza di.

impossibility [ɪmpɔsə'bɪlɪtɪ] *n* impossibilità.

impossible [ɪm'pɔsɪbl] *adj* impossibile.

impotent ['ɪmpɔtnt] *adj* impotente.

impound [ɪm'paund] *vt* confiscare.

impoverished [ɪm'pɔvərɪʃt] *adj* impoverito(a).

impracticable [ɪm'præktɪkəbl] *adj* inattuabile.

impractical [ɪm'præktɪkl] *adj* non pratico(a).

impregnable [ɪm'prɛgnəbl] *adj* (*fortress*) inespugnabile.

impress [ɪm'prɛs] *vt* impressionare; (*mark*) imprimere, stampare; **to ~ sth on sb** far capire qc a qn.

impression [ɪm'prɛʃən] *n* impressione *f*; **to be under the ~ that** avere l'impressione che.

impressive [ɪm'prɛsɪv] *adj* notevole.

imprint ['ɪmprɪnt] *n* (*of hand etc*) impronta; (*PUBLISHING*) sigla editoriale.

imprison [ɪm'prɪzn] *vt* imprigionare; **~ment** *n* imprigionamento.

improbable [ɪm'prɔbəbl] *adj* improbabile; (*excuse*) inverosimile.

impromptu [ɪm'prɔmptju:] *adj* improvvisato(a).

improper [ɪm'prɔpə*] *adj* scorretto(a); (*unsuitable*) inadatto(a), improprio(a); sconveniente, indecente.

improve [ɪm'pru:v] *vt* migliorare ♦ *vi* migliorare; (*pupil etc*) fare progressi; **~ment** *n* miglioramento; progresso.

improvise ['ɪmprəvaɪz] *vt*, *vi* improvvisare.

impudent ['ɪmpjudnt] *adj* impudente, sfacciato(a).

impulse ['ɪmpʌls] *n* impulso; **on ~** d'impulso, impulsivamente.

impulsive [ɪm'pʌlsɪv] *adj* impulsivo(a).

KEYWORD

in [ɪn] *prep* **1** (*indicating place, position*) in; **~ the house/garden** in casa/giardino; **~ the box** nella scatola; **~ the fridge** nel frigorifero; **I have it ~ my hand** ce l'ho in mano; **~ town/the country** in città/campagna; **~ school** a scuola; **~ here/there** qui/lì dentro

2 (*with place names: of town, region, country*): **~ London** a Londra; **~ England** in Inghilterra; **~ the United States** negli Stati Uniti; **~ Yorkshire** nello Yorkshire

3 (*indicating time: during, in the space of*) in; **~ spring/summer** in primavera/estate; **~ 1988** nel 1988; **~ May** in *or* a maggio; **I'll see you ~ July** ci vediamo

a luglio; **~ the afternoon** nel pomeriggio; **at 4 o'clock ~ the afternoon** alle 4 del pomeriggio; **I did it ~ 3 hours/days** l'ho fatto in 3 ore/giorni; **I'll see you ~ 2 weeks** *or* **~ 2 weeks' time** ci vediamo tra 2 settimane

4 (*indicating manner etc*) a; **~ a loud/soft voice** a voce alta/bassa; **~ pencil** a matita; **~ English/French** in inglese/francese; **the boy ~ the blue shirt** il ragazzo con la camicia blu

5 (*indicating circumstances*): **~ the sun** al sole; **~ the shade** all'ombra; **~ the rain** sotto la pioggia; **a rise ~ prices** un aumento dei prezzi

6 (*indicating mood, state*): **~ tears** in lacrime; **~ anger** per la rabbia; **~ despair** disperato(a); **~ good condition** in buono stato, in buone condizioni; **to live ~ luxury** vivere nel lusso

7 (*with ratios, numbers*): **1 ~ 10** 1 su 10; **20 pence ~ the pound** 20 pence per sterlina; **they lined up ~ twos** si misero in fila a due a due

8 (*referring to people, works*) in; **the disease is common ~ children** la malattia è comune nei bambini; **~ (the works of) Dickens** in Dickens

9 (*indicating profession etc*) in; **to be ~ teaching** fare l'insegnante, insegnare; **to be ~ publishing** essere nell'editoria

10 (*after superlative*) di; **the best ~ the class** il migliore della classe

11 (*with present participle*): **~ saying this** dicendo questo, nel dire questo

♦ *adv*: **to be ~** (*person: at home, work*) esserci; (*train, ship, plane*) essere arrivato(a); (*in fashion*) essere di moda; **to ask sb ~** invitare qn ad entrare; **to run/limp etc ~** entrare di corsa/zoppicando *etc*

♦ *n*: **the ~s and outs of the problem** tutti i particolari del problema.

in. *abbr* = **inch**.

inability [ɪnə'bɪlɪtɪ] *n*: **~ (to do)** incapacità (di fare).

inaccurate [ɪn'ækjurət] *adj* inesatto(a), impreciso(a).

inadequate [ɪn'ædɪkwət] *adj*

insufficiente.

inadvertently [ɪnəd'vəːtntlɪ] *adv* senza volerlo.

inadvisable [ɪnəd'vaɪzəbl] *adj* consigliabile.

inane [ɪ'neɪn] *adj* vacuo(a), stupido(a).

inanimate [ɪn'ænɪmət] *adj* inanimato(a).

inappropriate [ɪnə'prəuprɪət] *adj* non adatto(a); (*word, expression*) improprio(a).

inarticulate [ɪnaː'tɪkjulət] *adj* (*person*) che si esprime male; (*speech*) inarticolato(a).

inasmuch as [ɪnəz'mʌtʃæz] *adv* in quanto che; (*insofar as*) poiché.

inaudible [ɪn'ɔːdɪbl] *adj* che non si riesce a sentire.

inauguration [ɪnɔːgju'reɪʃən] *n* inaugurazione *f*; insediamento in carica.

in-between *adj* fra i (*or* le) due.

inborn [ɪn'bɔːn] *adj* innato(a).

inbred [ɪn'bred] *adj* innato(a); (*family*) connaturato(a).

Inc. (*US*) *abbr* (= *incorporated*) S.A.

incapable [ɪn'keɪpəbl] *adj* incapace.

incapacitate [ɪnkə'pæsɪteɪt] *vt*: to ~ sb from doing rendere qn incapace di fare.

incense [*n* 'ɪnsens, *vb* ɪn'sens] *n* incenso ♦ *vt* (*anger*) infuriare.

incentive [ɪn'sentɪv] *n* incentivo.

incessant [ɪn'sesnt] *adj* incessante; ~ly *adv* di continuo, senza sosta.

inch [ɪntʃ] *n* pollice *m* (= 25 *mm*; 12 *in a foot*); **within an ~ of** a un pelo da; **he didn't give an ~** non ha ceduto di un millimetro; ~ **forward** *vi* avanzare pian piano.

incidence ['ɪnsɪdns] *n* (*of crime, disease*) incidenza.

incident ['ɪnsɪdnt] *n* incidente *m*; (*in book*) episodio.

incidental [ɪnsɪ'dentl] *adj* accessorio(a), d'accompagnamento; (*unplanned*) incidentale; ~ **to** marginale a; ~**ly** [-'dentəlɪ] *adv* (*by the way*) a proposito.

inclination [ɪnklɪ'neɪʃən] *n* inclinazione *f*.

incline [*n* 'ɪnklaɪn, *vb* ɪn'klaɪn] *n* pendenza, pendio ♦ *vt* inclinare ♦ *vi*

(*surface*) essere inclinato(a); **to be ~d to do** tendere a fare; essere propenso(a) a fare.

include [ɪn'kluːd] *vt* includere, comprendere; **including** *prep* compreso(a), incluso(a).

inclusive [ɪn'kluːsɪv] *adj* incluso(a), compreso(a); ~ **of tax** *etc* tasse *etc* comprese.

incoherent [ɪnkəu'hɪərənt] *adj* incoerente.

income ['ɪnkʌm] *n* reddito; ~ **tax** *n* imposta sul reddito.

incoming ['ɪnkʌmɪŋ] *adj* (*flight, mail*) in arrivo; (*government*) subentrante; (*tide*) montante.

incompetent [ɪn'kɔmpɪtnt] *adj* incompetente, incapace.

incomplete [ɪnkəm'pliːt] *adj* incompleto(a).

incongruous [ɪn'kɔŋgruəs] *adj* poco appropriato(a); (*remark, act*) incongruo(a).

inconsiderate [ɪnkən'sɪdərət] *adj* sconsiderato(a).

inconsistency [ɪnkən'sɪstənsɪ] *n* incoerenza.

inconsistent [ɪnkən'sɪstənt] *adj* incoerente; ~ **with** non coerente con.

inconspicuous [ɪnkən'spɪkjuəs] *adj* incospicuo(a); (*colour*) poco appariscente; (*dress*) dimesso(a).

inconvenience [ɪnkən'viːnjəns] *n* inconveniente *m*; (*trouble*) disturbo ♦ *vt* disturbare.

inconvenient [ɪnkən'viːnjənt] *adj* scomodo(a).

incorporate [ɪn'kɔːpəreɪt] *vt* incorporare; (*contain*) contenere; ~**d** *adj*: ~**d company** (*US*) società *f inv* anonima.

incorrect [ɪnkə'rekt] *adj* scorretto(a); (*statement*) inesatto(a).

increase [*n* 'ɪnkriːs, *vb* ɪn'kriːs] *n* aumento ♦ *vi, vt* aumentare.

increasing [ɪn'kriːsɪŋ] *adj* (*number*) crescente; ~**ly** *adv* sempre più.

incredible [ɪn'kredɪbl] *adj* incredibile.

incredulous [ɪn'kredjuləs] *adj* incredulo(a).

increment ['ɪnkrɪmənt] n aumento, incremento.

incriminate [ɪn'krɪmɪneɪt] vt compromettere.

incubator ['ɪnkjubeɪtə*] n incubatrice f.

incumbent [ɪn'kʌmbənt] n titolare m/f ♦ adj: **to be ~ on sb** spettare a qn.

incur [ɪn'kə:*] vt (expenses) incorrere; (anger, risk) esporsi a; (debt) contrarre; (loss) subire.

indebted [ɪn'detɪd] adj: **to be ~ to sb (for)** essere obbligato(a) verso qn (per).

indecent [ɪn'di:snt] adj indecente; **~ assault** (BRIT) n aggressione f a scopo di violenza sessuale; **~ exposure** n atti mpl osceni in luogo pubblico.

indecisive [ɪndɪ'saɪsɪv] adj indeciso(a).

indeed [ɪn'di:d] adv infatti; veramente; **yes ~!** certamente!

indefinite [ɪn'defɪnɪt] adj indefinito(a); (answer) vago(a); (period, number) indeterminato(a); **~ly** adv (wait) indefinitamente.

indemnity [ɪn'demnɪtɪ] n (insurance) assicurazione f; (compensation) indennità, indennizzo.

independence [ɪndɪ'pendns] n indipendenza.

independent [ɪndɪ'pendnt] adj indipendente.

index ['ɪndeks] (pl ~es) n (in book) indice m; (: in library etc) catalogo; (pl indices: ratio, sign) indice m; **~ card** n scheda; **~ finger** n (dito) indice m; **~-linked** (US **~ed**) adj legato(a) al costo della vita.

India ['ɪndɪə] n India; **~n** adj, n indiano(a); **Red ~n** pellerossa m/f.

indicate ['ɪndɪkeɪt] vt indicare; **indication** [-'keɪʃən] n indicazione f, segno.

indicative [ɪn'dɪkətɪv] adj: **~ of** indicativo(a) di ♦ n (LING) indicativo.

indicator ['ɪndɪkeɪtə*] n indicatore m; (AUT) freccia.

indices ['ɪndɪsi:z] npl of **index**.

indictment [ɪn'daɪtmənt] n accusa.

indifference [ɪn'dɪfrəns] n indifferenza.

indifferent [ɪn'dɪfrənt] adj indifferente; (poor) mediocre.

indigenous [ɪn'dɪdʒɪnəs] adj indigeno(a).

indigestion [ɪndɪ'dʒestʃən] n indigestione f.

indignant [ɪn'dɪgnənt] adj: **~ (at sth/ with sb)** indignato(a) (per qc/contro qn).

indignity [ɪn'dɪgnɪtɪ] n umiliazione f.

indigo ['ɪndɪgəu] n indaco.

indirect [ɪndɪ'rekt] adj indiretto(a).

indiscreet [ɪndɪ'skri:t] adj indiscreto(a); (rash) imprudente.

indiscriminate [ɪndɪ'skrɪmɪnət] adj indiscriminato(a).

indisputable [ɪndɪ'spju:təbl] adj incontestabile, indiscutibile.

individual [ɪndɪ'vɪdjuəl] n individuo ♦ adj individuale; (characteristic) particolare, originale; **~ist** n individualista m/f.

indoctrination [ɪndɒktrɪ'neɪʃən] n indottrinamento.

Indonesia [ɪndə'ni:zɪə] n Indonesia.

indoor ['ɪndɔ:*] adj da interno; (plant) d'appartamento; (swimming pool) coperto(a); (sport, games) fatto(a) al coperto; **~s** [ɪn'dɔ:z] adv all'interno.

induce [ɪn'dju:s] vt persuadere; (bring about, MED) provocare; **~ment** n incentivo.

indulge [ɪn'dʌldʒ] vt (whim) compiacere, soddisfare; (child) viziare ♦ vi: **to ~ in sth** concedersi qc; abbandonarsi a qc; **~nce** n lusso (che uno si permette); (leniency) indulgenza; **~nt** adj indulgente.

industrial [ɪn'dʌstrɪəl] adj industriale; (injury) sul lavoro; **~ action** n azione f rivendicativa; **~ estate** (BRIT) n zona industriale; **~ park** (US) n = **~ estate**.

industrious [ɪn'dʌstrɪəs] adj industrioso(a), assiduo(a).

industry ['ɪndəstrɪ] n industria; (diligence) operosità.

inebriated [ɪ'ni:brɪeɪtɪd] adj ubriaco(a).

inedible [ɪn'edɪbl] adj immangiabile; (poisonous) non commestibile.

ineffective [ɪnɪ'fektɪv] adj inefficace; incompetente.

ineffectual [ɪnɪ'fektʃuəl] adj inefficace;

incompetente.
inefficiency [ɪnɪˈfɪʃənsɪ] n inefficienza.
inefficient [ɪnɪˈfɪʃənt] adj inefficiente.
inept [ɪˈnɛpt] adj inetto(a).
inequality [ɪnɪˈkwɔlɪtɪ] n ineguaglianza.
inescapable [ɪnɪˈskeɪpəbl] adj
inevitabile.
inevitable [ɪnˈɛvɪtəbl] adj inevitabile;
inevitably adv inevitabilmente.
inexact [ɪnɪɡˈzækt] adj inesatto(a).
inexcusable [ɪnɪksˈkjuːzəbl] adj ingiu-
stificabile.
inexpensive [ɪnɪkˈspɛnsɪv] adj poco co-
stoso(a).
inexperienced [ɪnɪksˈpɪərɪənst] adj ine-
sperto(a), senza esperienza.
infallible [ɪnˈfælɪbl] adj infallibile.
infamous [ˈɪnfəməs] adj infame.
infancy [ˈɪnfənsɪ] n infanzia.
infant [ˈɪnfənt] n bambino/a; ~ **school**
(BRIT) n scuola elementare (per
bambini dall'età di 5 a 7 anni).
infantry [ˈɪnfəntrɪ] n fanteria.
infatuated [ɪnˈfætjueɪtɪd] adj: ~ **with**
infatuato(a) di.
infatuation [ɪnfætjuˈeɪʃən] n infatuazione
f.
infect [ɪnˈfɛkt] vt infettare; ~**ion**
[ɪnˈfɛkʃən] n infezione f; ~**ious**
[ɪnˈfɛkʃəs] adj (disease) infettivo(a),
contagioso(a); (person, fig: enthusiasm) contagioso(a).
infer [ɪnˈfɜː*] vt inferire, dedurre.
inferior [ɪnˈfɪərɪə*] adj inferiore; (goods)
di qualità scadente ♦ n inferiore m/f;
(in rank) subalterno/a; ~**ity**
[ɪnfɪərɪˈɔrɪtɪ] n inferiorità; ~**ity complex**
n complesso di inferiorità.
inferno [ɪnˈfɜːnəʊ] n rogo.
infertile [ɪnˈfɜːtaɪl] adj sterile.
in-fighting [ˈɪnfaɪtɪŋ] n lotte fpl intestine.
infiltrate [ˈɪnfɪltreɪt] vt infiltrarsi in.
infinite [ˈɪnfɪnɪt] adj infinito(a).
infinitive [ɪnˈfɪnɪtɪv] n infinito.
infinity [ɪnˈfɪnɪtɪ] n infinità; (also MATH)
infinito.
infirmary [ɪnˈfɜːmərɪ] n ospedale m; (in
school, factory) infermeria.
infirmity [ɪnˈfɜːmɪtɪ] n infermità f inv.

inflamed [ɪnˈfleɪmd] adj infiammato(a).
inflammable [ɪnˈflæməbl] adj
infiammabile.
inflammation [ɪnfləˈmeɪʃən] n
infiammazione f.
inflatable [ɪnˈfleɪtəbl] adj gonfiabile.
inflate [ɪnˈfleɪt] vt (tyre, balloon)
gonfiare; (fig) esagerare; gonfiare; in-
flation [ɪnˈfleɪʃən] n (ECON) inflazione f;
inflationary [ɪnˈfleɪʃnərɪ] adj inflazioni-
stico(a).
inflict [ɪnˈflɪkt] vt: to ~ **on** infliggere a.
influence [ˈɪnfluəns] n influenza ♦ vt
influenzare; **under the** ~ **of alcohol** sotto
l'effetto dell'alcool.
influential [ɪnfluˈɛnʃl] adj influente.
influenza [ɪnfluˈɛnzə] n (MED) influenza.
influx [ˈɪnflʌks] n afflusso.
inform [ɪnˈfɔːm] vt: to ~ **sb** (of)
informare qn (di) ♦ vi: to ~ **on sb**
denunciare qn.
informal [ɪnˈfɔːml] adj informale; (announcement, invitation) non ufficiale;
~**ity** [-ˈmælɪtɪ] n informalità; carattere
m non ufficiale.
informant [ɪnˈfɔːmənt] n informatore/
trice.
information [ɪnfəˈmeɪʃən] n
informazioni fpl; particolari mpl; **a
piece of** ~ un'informazione; ~ **office** n
ufficio m informazioni inv.
informative [ɪnˈfɔːmətɪv] adj
istruttivo(a).
informer [ɪnˈfɔːmə*] n (also: police ~)
informatore/trice.
infringe [ɪnˈfrɪndʒ] vt infrangere ♦ vi: to
~ **on** calpestare; ~**ment** n infrazione f.
infuriating [ɪnˈfjuərɪeɪtɪŋ] adj molto
irritante.
ingenious [ɪnˈdʒiːnjəs] adj ingegnoso(a).
ingenuity [ɪndʒɪˈnjuːɪtɪ] n ingegnosità.
ingenuous [ɪnˈdʒɛnjuəs] adj ingenuo(a).
ingot [ˈɪŋɡət] n lingotto.
ingrained [ɪnˈɡreɪnd] adj radicato(a).
ingratiate [ɪnˈɡreɪʃɪeɪt] vt: to ~ **o.s. with**
sb ingraziarsi qn.
ingredient [ɪnˈɡriːdɪənt] n ingrediente
m; elemento.
inhabit [ɪnˈhæbɪt] vt abitare.
inhabitant [ɪnˈhæbɪtnt] n abitante m/f.

inhale [ɪn'heɪl] vt inalare ♦ vi (*in smoking*) aspirare.

inherent [ɪn'hɪərənt] adj: ~ (**in** or **to**) inerente (a).

inherit [ɪn'hɛrɪt] vt ereditare; ~**ance** n eredità.

inhibit [ɪn'hɪbɪt] vt (*PSYCH*) inibire; ~**ion** [-'bɪʃən] n inibizione f.

inhospitable [ɪnhɔs'pɪtəbl] adj inospitale.

inhuman [ɪn'hju:mən] adj inumano(a).

initial [ɪ'nɪʃl] adj iniziale ♦ n iniziale f ♦ vt siglare; ~**s** npl (*of name*) iniziali fpl; (*as signature*) sigla; ~**ly** adv inizialmente, all'inizio.

initiate [ɪ'nɪʃɪeɪt] vt (*start*) avviare; intraprendere; iniziare; (*person*) iniziare; **to ~ sb into a secret** mettere qn a parte di un segreto; **to ~ proceedings against sb** (*LAW*) intentare causa contro qn.

initiative [ɪ'nɪʃətɪv] n iniziativa.

inject [ɪn'dʒɛkt] vt (*liquid*) iniettare; (*patient*): **to ~ sb with sth** fare a qn un'iniezione di qc; (*funds*) immettere; ~**ion** [ɪn'dʒɛkʃən] n iniezione f, puntura.

injure ['ɪndʒə*] vt ferire; (*damage: reputation etc*) nuocere a; ~**d** adj ferito(a).

injury ['ɪndʒərɪ] n ferita; ~ **time** n (*SPORT*) tempo di ricupero.

injustice [ɪn'dʒʌstɪs] n ingiustizia.

ink [ɪŋk] n inchiostro.

inkling ['ɪŋklɪŋ] n sentore m, vaga idea.

inlaid ['ɪnleɪd] adj incrostato(a); (*table etc*) intarsiato(a).

inland [adj 'ɪnlənd, adv ɪn'lænd] adj interno(a) ♦ adv all'interno; **I~ Revenue** (*BRIT*) n Fisco.

in-laws ['ɪnlɔ:z] npl suoceri mpl; famiglia del marito (or della moglie).

inlet ['ɪnlɛt] n (*GEO*) insenatura, baia.

inmate ['ɪnmeɪt] n (*in prison*) carcerato/a; (*in asylum*) ricoverato/a.

inn [ɪn] n locanda.

innate [ɪ'neɪt] adj innato(a).

inner ['ɪnə*] adj interno(a), interiore; ~ **city** n centro di una zona urbana; ~ **tube** n camera d'aria.

innings ['ɪnɪŋz] n (*CRICKET*) turno di battuta.

innocence ['ɪnəsns] n innocenza.

innocent ['ɪnəsnt] adj innocente.

innocuous [ɪ'nɔkjuəs] adj innocuo(a).

innuendo [ɪnju'ɛndəu] (pl ~**es**) n insinuazione f.

innumerable [ɪ'nju:mrəbl] adj innumerevole.

inordinately [ɪ'nɔ:dɪnətlɪ] adv smoderatamente.

in-patient n ricoverato/a.

input ['ɪnput] n input m.

inquest ['ɪnkwɛst] n inchiesta.

inquire [ɪn'kwaɪə*] vi informarsi ♦ vt domandare, informarsi su; ~ **about** vt fus informarsi di or su; ~ **into** vt fus fare indagini su; **inquiry** n domanda; (*LAW*) indagine f, investigazione f; **inquiry office** (*BRIT*) n ufficio m informazioni inv.

inquisitive [ɪn'kwɪzɪtɪv] adj curioso(a).

inroads ['ɪnrəudz] npl: **to make ~ into** (*savings etc*) intaccare (pesantemente).

ins. abbr = **inches**.

insane [ɪn'seɪn] adj matto(a), pazzo(a); (*MED*) alienato(a).

insanity [ɪn'sænɪtɪ] n follia; (*MED*) alienazione f mentale.

inscription [ɪn'skrɪpʃən] n iscrizione f; dedica.

inscrutable [ɪn'skru:təbl] adj imperscrutabile.

insect ['ɪnsɛkt] n insetto; ~**icide** [ɪn'sɛktɪsaɪd] n insetticida m.

insecure [ɪnsɪ'kjuə*] adj malsicuro(a); (*person*) insicuro(a).

insemination [ɪnsɛmɪ'neɪʃən] n: **artificial ~** fecondazione f artificiale.

insensible [ɪn'sɛnsɪbl] adj (*unconscious*) privo(a) di sensi.

insensitive [ɪn'sɛnsɪtɪv] adj insensibile.

insert [ɪn'sə:t] vt inserire, introdurre; ~**ion** [ɪn'sə:ʃən] n inserzione f.

in-service adj (*training, course*) durante l'orario di lavoro.

inshore [ɪn'fɔ:*] adj costiero(a) ♦ adv presso la riva; verso la riva.

inside ['ɪn'saɪd] n interno, parte f interiore ♦ adj interno(a), interiore ♦ adv dentro, all'interno ♦ prep dentro, all'interno di; *(of time)*: ~ **10 minutes** entro 10 minuti; ~s *npl (inf: stomach)* ventre *m*; ~ **forward** *n (SPORT)* mezzala, interno; ~ **lane** *n (AUT)* corsia di marcia; ~ **out** *adv (turn)* a rovescio; *(know)* in fondo.

insight ['ɪnsaɪt] *n* acume *m*, perspicacia; *(glimpse, idea)* percezione *f*.

insignia [ɪn'sɪgnɪə] *npl* insegne *fpl*.

insignificant [ɪnsɪg'nɪfɪkənt] *adj* insignificante.

insincere [ɪnsɪn'sɪə*] *adj* insincero(a).

insinuate [ɪn'sɪnjueɪt] *vt* insinuare.

insist [ɪn'sɪst] *vi* insistere; **to ~ on doing** insistere per fare; **to ~ that** insistere perché ~ sub; *(claim)* sostenere che; ~**ent** *adj* insistente.

insole ['ɪnsəʊl] *n* soletta.

insolent ['ɪnsələnt] *adj* insolente.

insomnia [ɪn'sɒmnɪə] *n* insonnia.

inspect [ɪn'spɛkt] *vt* ispezionare; *(BRIT: ticket)* controllare; ~**ion** [ɪn'spɛkʃən] *n* ispezione *f*; controllo; ~**or** *n* ispettore/trice; *(BRIT: on buses, trains)* controllore *m*.

inspire [ɪn'spaɪə*] *vt* ispirare.

install [ɪn'stɔːl] *vt* installare; ~**ation** [ɪnstə'leɪʃən] *n* installazione *f*.

instalment, *(US* **installment)** [ɪn'stɔːlmənt] *n* rata; *(of TV serial etc)* puntata; **in ~s** *(pay)* a rate; *(receive)* una parte per volta; *(: publication)* a fascicoli.

instance ['ɪnstəns] *n* esempio, caso; **for ~** per *or* ad esempio; **in the first ~** in primo luogo.

instant ['ɪnstənt] *n* istante *m*, attimo ♦ *adj* immediato(a); urgente; *(coffee, food)* in polvere; ~**ly** *adv* immediatamente, subito.

instead [ɪn'stɛd] *adv* invece; ~ **of** invece di.

instep ['ɪnstɛp] *n* collo del piede; *(of shoe)* collo della scarpa.

instil [ɪn'stɪl] *vt*: **to ~ (into)** inculcare (in).

instinct ['ɪnstɪŋkt] *n* istinto.

institute ['ɪnstɪtjuːt] *n* istituto ♦ *vt* istituire, stabilire; *(inquiry)* avviare; *(proceedings)* iniziare.

institution [ɪnstɪ'tjuːʃən] *n* istituzione *f*; *(educational ~, mental ~)* istituto.

instruct [ɪn'strʌkt] *vt*: **to ~ sb in sth** insegnare qc a qn; **to ~ sb to do** dare ordini a qn di fare; ~**ion** [ɪn'strʌkʃən] *n* istruzione *f*; ~**ions (for use)** istruzioni per l'uso; ~**or** *n* istruttore/trice; *(for skiing)* maestro/a.

instrument ['ɪnstrəmənt] *n* strumento; ~**al** [-'mɛntl] *adj (MUS)* strumentale; **to be ~al in** essere d'aiuto in; ~ **panel** *n* quadro *m* portastrumenti *inv*.

insufferable [ɪn'sʌfərəbl] *adj* insopportabile.

insufficient [ɪnsə'fɪʃənt] *adj* insufficiente.

insular ['ɪnsjulə*] *adj* insulare; *(person)* di mente ristretta.

insulate ['ɪnsjuleɪt] *vt* isolare; **insulating tape** *n* nastro isolante; **insulation** [-'leɪʃən] *n* isolamento.

insulin ['ɪnsjulɪn] *n* insulina.

insult [*n* 'ɪnsʌlt, *vb* ɪn'sʌlt] *n* insulto, affronto ♦ *vt* insultare; ~**ing** *adj* offensivo(a), ingiurioso(a).

insuperable [ɪn'sjuːprəbl] *adj* insormontabile, insuperabile.

insurance [ɪn'ʃuərəns] *n* assicurazione *f*; **fire/life** ~ assicurazione contro gli incendi/sulla vita; ~ **policy** *n* polizza d'assicurazione.

insure [ɪn'ʃuə*] *vt* assicurare.

intact [ɪn'tækt] *adj* intatto(a).

intake ['ɪnteɪk] *n (TECH)* immissione *f*; *(of food)* consumo; *(BRIT: of pupils etc)* afflusso.

integral ['ɪntɪgrəl] *adj* integrale; *(part)* integrante.

integrate ['ɪntɪgreɪt] *vt* integrare ♦ *vi* integrarsi.

integrity [ɪn'tɛgrɪtɪ] *n* integrità.

intellect ['ɪntəlɛkt] *n* intelletto; ~**ual** [-'lɛktjuəl] *adj, n* intellettuale *m/f*.

intelligence [ɪn'tɛlɪdʒəns] *n* intelligenza; *(MIL etc)* informazioni *fpl*; ~ **service** *n* servizio segreto.

intelligent [ɪn'tɛlɪdʒənt] *adj* intelligente.

intend [ɪn'tɛnd] *vt (gift etc)*: **to ~ sth for** destinare qc a; **to ~ to do** aver l'intenzione di fare; ~**ed** *adj (effect)* voluto(a).

intense [ɪnˈtɛns] *adj* intenso(a); (*person*) di forti sentimenti; ~**ly** *adv* intensamente; profondamente.

intensive [ɪnˈtɛnsɪv] *adj* intensivo(a); ~ **care unit** *n* reparto terapia intensiva.

intent [ɪnˈtɛnt] *n* intenzione *f* ♦ *adj*: ~ (**on**) intento(a) (a), immerso(a) (in); **to all ~s and purposes** a tutti gli effetti; **to be ~ on doing sth** essere deciso a fare qc.

intention [ɪnˈtɛnʃən] *n* intenzione *f*; ~**al** *adj* intenzionale, deliberato(a); ~**ally** *adv* apposta.

intently [ɪnˈtɛntlɪ] *adv* attentamente.

inter [ɪnˈtɜ:*] *vt* sotterrare.

interact [ɪntərˈækt] *vi* interagire.

interchange [ˈɪntətʃeɪndʒ] *n* (*exchange*) scambio; (*on motorway*) incrocio pluridirezionale; ~**able** [-ˈtʃeɪndʒəbl] *adj* intercambiabile.

intercom [ˈɪntəkɔm] *n* interfono.

intercourse [ˈɪntəkɔ:s] *n* rapporti *mpl*.

interest [ˈɪntrɪst] *n* interesse *m*; (*COMM: stake, share*) interessi *mpl* ♦ *vt* interessare; ~**ed** *adj* interessato(a); **to be ~ed in** interessarsi di; ~**ing** *adj* interessante; ~ **rate** *n* tasso di interesse.

interface [ˈɪntəfeɪs] *n* (*COMPUT*) interfaccia.

interfere [ɪntəˈfɪə*] *vi*: **to ~ in** (*quarrel, other people's business*) immischiarsi in; **to ~ with** (*object*) toccare; (*plans, duty*) interferire con.

interference [ɪntəˈfɪərəns] *n* interferenza.

interim [ˈɪntərɪm] *adj* provvisorio(a) ♦ *n*: **in the ~** nel frattempo.

interior [ɪnˈtɪərɪə*] *n* interno; (*of country*) entroterra ♦ *adj* interno(a); (*minister*) degli Interni; ~ **designer** *n* arredatore/trice.

interlock [ɪntəˈlɔk] *vi* ingranarsi.

interloper [ˈɪntələupə*] *n* intruso/a.

interlude [ˈɪntəlu:d] *n* intervallo; (*THEATRE*) intermezzo.

intermarry [ɪntəˈmærɪ] *vi* fare un matrimonio misto.

intermediate [ɪntəˈmi:dɪət] *adj* intermedio(a).

intermission [ɪntəˈmɪʃən] *n* pausa; (*THEATRE, CINEMA*) intermissione *f*, intervallo.

intern [*vb* ɪnˈtɜ:n, *n* ˈɪntə:n] *vt* internare ♦ *n* (*US*) medico interno.

internal [ɪnˈtɜ:nl] *adj* interno(a); ~**ly** *adv*: "**not to be taken ~ly**" "per uso esterno"; **I~ Revenue Service** (*US*) *n* Fisco.

international [ɪntəˈnæʃənl] *adj* internazionale ♦ *n* (*BRIT: SPORT*) incontro internazionale.

interplay [ˈɪntəpleɪ] *n* azione e reazione *f*.

interpret [ɪnˈtə:prɪt] *vt* interpretare ♦ *vi* fare da interprete; ~**er** *n* interprete *m/f*.

interrelated [ɪntərɪˈleɪtɪd] *adj* correlato(a).

interrogate [ɪnˈtɛrəugeɪt] *vt* interrogare; **interrogation** [-ˈgeɪʃən] *n* interrogazione *f*; (*of suspect etc*) interrogatorio; **interrogative** [ɪntəˈrɔgətɪv] *adj* interrogativo(a).

interrupt [ɪntəˈrʌpt] *vt, vi* interrompere; ~**ion** [-ˈrʌpʃən] *n* interruzione *f*.

intersect [ɪntəˈsɛkt] *vi* (*roads*) incrociarsi; ~**ion** [-ˈsɛkʃən] *n* intersezione *f*; (*of roads*) incrocio.

intersperse [ɪntəˈspə:s] *vt*: **to ~ with** costellare di.

intertwine [ɪntəˈtwaɪn] *vi* intrecciarsi.

interval [ˈɪntəvl] *n* intervallo; **at ~s** a intervalli.

intervene [ɪntəˈvi:n] *vi* (*time*) intercorrere; (*event, person*) intervenire; **intervention** [-ˈvɛnʃən] *n* intervento.

interview [ˈɪntəvju:] *n* (*RADIO, TV etc*) intervista; (*for job*) colloquio ♦ *vt* intervistare; avere un colloquio con; ~**er** *n* intervistatore/trice.

intestine [ɪnˈtɛstɪn] *n* intestino.

intimacy [ˈɪntɪməsɪ] *n* intimità.

intimate [*adj* ˈɪntɪmət, *vb* ˈɪntɪmeɪt] *adj* intimo(a); (*knowledge*) profondo(a) ♦ *vt* lasciar capire.

into [ˈɪntu:] *prep* dentro, in; **come ~ the house** entra in casa; **he worked late ~**

the **night** lavorò fino a tarda notte; ~
Italian in italiano.
intolerable [ɪn'tɔlərəbl] *adj* intollerabile.
intolerance [ɪn'tɔlərns] *n* intolleranza.
intolerant [ɪn'tɔlərnt] *adj*: ~ **of**
intollerante di.
intoxicated [ɪn'tɔksɪkeɪtɪd] *adj* ine-
briato(a).
intoxication [ɪntɔksɪ'keɪʃən] *n* ebbrezza.
intractable [ɪn'træktəbl] *adj* intrattabile.
intransitive [ɪn'trænsɪtɪv] *adj* in-
transitivo(a).
intravenous [ɪntrə'viːnəs] *adj*
endovenoso(a).
in-tray *n* contenitore *m* per la corrispondenza in arrivo.
intricate ['ɪntrɪkət] *adj* intricato(a),
complicato(a).
intrigue [ɪn'triːg] *n* intrigo ♦ *vt* affascinare; **intriguing** *adj* affascinante.
intrinsic [ɪn'trɪnsɪk] *adj* intrinseco(a).
introduce [ɪntrə'djuːs] *vt* introdurre; **to**
~ **sb** (**to sb**) presentare qn (a qn); **to** ~
sb to (*pastime, technique*) iniziare qn
a; **introduction** [-'dʌkʃən] *n* introduzione
f; (*of person*) presentazione *f*; (*to new
experience*) iniziazione *f*; **introductory**
adj introduttivo(a).
intrude [ɪn'truːd] *vi* (*person*): **to** ~ (**on**)
intromettersi (in); ~**r** *n* intruso/a.
intuition [ɪntjuː'ɪʃən] *n* intuizione *f*.
inundate ['ɪnʌndeɪt] *vt*: **to** ~ **with**
inondare di.
invade [ɪn'veɪd] *vt* invadere.
invalid [*n* 'ɪnvəlɪd, *adj* ɪn'vælɪd] *n*
malato/a; (*with disability*) invalido/a ♦
adj (*not valid*) invalido(a), non
valido(a).
invaluable [ɪn'væljuəbl] *adj* prezioso(a);
inestimabile.
invariably [ɪn'vɛərɪəblɪ] *adv*
invariabilmente; sempre.
invasion [ɪn'veɪʒən] *n* invasione *f*.
invent [ɪn'vɛnt] *vt* inventare; ~**ion**
[ɪn'vɛnʃən] *n* invenzione *f*; ~**ive** *adj*
inventivo(a); ~**or** *n* inventore *m*.
inventory ['ɪnvəntrɪ] *n* inventario.
invert [ɪn'vɜːt] *vt* invertire; (*cup,
object*) rovesciare; ~**ed commas**
(*BRIT*) *npl* virgolette *fpl*.

invest [ɪn'vɛst] *vt* investire ♦ *vi*: **to** ~
(**in**) investire (in).
investigate [ɪn'vɛstɪgeɪt] *vt* investigare,
indagare; (*crime*) fare indagini su; **investigation** [-'geɪʃən] *n* investigazione *f*;
(*of crime*) indagine *f*.
investment [ɪn'vɛstmənt] *n* inve-
stimento.
investor [ɪn'vɛstə*] *n* investitore/trice;
azionista *m/f*.
invidious [ɪn'vɪdɪəs] *adj* odioso(a);
(*task*) spiacevole.
invigilator [ɪn'vɪdʒɪleɪtə*] *n* (*in exam*)
sorvegliante *m/f*.
invigorating [ɪn'vɪgəreɪtɪŋ] *adj*
stimolante; vivificante.
invisible [ɪn'vɪzɪbl] *adj* invisibile.
invitation [ɪnvɪ'teɪʃən] *n* invito.
invite [ɪn'vaɪt] *vt* invitare; (*opinions etc*)
sollecitare; **inviting** *adj* invitante, attraente.
invoice ['ɪnvɔɪs] *n* fattura ♦ *vt* fatturare.
involuntary [ɪn'vɔləntrɪ] *adj*
involontario(a).
involve [ɪn'vɔlv] *vt* (*entail*) richiedere,
comportare; (*associate*): **to** ~ **sb** (**in**)
implicare qn (in); coinvolgere qn (in);
~**d** *adj* involuto(a), complesso(a); **to be**
~**d in** essere coinvolto(a) in; ~**ment** *n*
implicazione *f*; coinvolgimento.
inward ['ɪnwəd] *adj* (*movement*) verso
l'interno; (*thought, feeling*) interiore,
intimo(a); ~(**s**) *adv* verso l'interno.
I/O *abbr* (*COMPUT*: = *input/output*) I/O.
iodine ['aɪədiːn] *n* iodio.
iota [aɪ'əutə] *n* (*fig*) briciolo.
IOU *n* *abbr* (= *I owe you*) pagherò *m
inv*.
IQ *n* *abbr* (= *intelligence quotient*)
quoziente *m* d'intelligenza.
IRA *n* *abbr* (= *Irish Republican Army*)
IRA *f*.
Iran [ɪ'rɑːn] *n* Iran *m*; ~**ian** *adj*, *n*
iraniano(a).
Iraq [ɪ'rɑːk] *n* Iraq *m*; ~**i** *adj*, *n* ira-
cheno(a).
irate [aɪ'reɪt] *adj* adirato(a).
Ireland ['aɪələnd] *n* Irlanda.
iris ['aɪrɪs] (*pl* ~**es**) *n* iride *f*; (*BOT*)
giaggiolo, iride.

Irish [ˈaɪrɪʃ] adj irlandese ♦ npl: **the ~** gli Irlandesi; **~man** n irlandese m; **~ Sea** n Mar m d'Irlanda; **~woman** n irlandese f.

irksome [ˈəːksəm] adj seccante.

iron [ˈaɪən] n ferro; (for clothes) ferro da stiro ♦ adj di or in ferro ♦ vt (clothes) stirare; **~ out** vt (crease) appianare; (fig) spianare; far sparire; **the I~ Curtain** n la cortina di ferro.

ironic(al) [aɪˈrɔnɪk(l)] adj ironico(a).

ironing [ˈaɪənɪŋ] n (act) stirare m; (clothes) roba da stirare; **~ board** n asse f da stiro.

ironmonger [ˈaɪənmʌŋgə*] (BRIT) n negoziante m in ferramenta; **~'s (shop)** n negozio di ferramenta.

irony [ˈaɪrənɪ] n ironia.

irrational [ɪˈræʃənl] adj irrazionale.

irregular [ɪˈrɛgjulə*] adj irregolare.

irrelevant [ɪˈrɛləvənt] adj non pertinente.

irreplaceable [ɪrɪˈpleɪsəbl] adj insostituibile.

irrepressible [ɪrɪˈprɛsəbl] adj irrefrenabile.

irresistible [ɪrɪˈzɪstɪbl] adj irresistibile.

irrespective [ɪrɪˈspɛktɪv]: **~ of** prep senza riguardo a.

irresponsible [ɪrɪˈspɔnsɪbl] adj irresponsabile.

irrigate [ˈɪrɪgeɪt] vt irrigare; **irrigation** [-ˈgeɪʃən] n irrigazione f.

irritable [ˈɪrɪtəbl] adj irritabile.

irritate [ˈɪrɪteɪt] vt irritare; **irritating** adj (person, sound etc) irritante; **irritation** [-ˈteɪʃən] n irritazione f.

IRS (US) n abbr = **Internal Revenue Service**.

is [ɪz] vb see **be**.

Islam [ˈɪzlɑːm] n Islam m.

island [ˈaɪlənd] n isola; **~er** n isolano/a.

isle [aɪl] n isola.

isn't [ˈɪznt] = **is not**.

isolate [ˈaɪsəleɪt] vt isolare; **~d** adj isolato(a); **isolation** [-ˈleɪʃən] n isolamento.

Israel [ˈɪzreɪl] n Israele m; **~i** [ɪzˈreɪlɪ] adj, n israeliano(a).

issue [ˈɪʃjuː] n questione f, problema m;

(of banknotes etc) emissione f; (of newspaper etc) numero ♦ vt (statement) rilasciare; (rations, equipment) distribuire; (book) pubblicare; (banknotes, cheques, stamps) emettere; **at ~** in gioco, in discussione; **to take ~ with sb (over sth)** prendere posizione contro qn (riguardo a qc); **to make an ~ of sth** fare un problema di qc.

isthmus [ˈɪsməs] n istmo.

KEYWORD

it [ɪt] pron **1** (specific: subject) esso(a); (: direct object) lo(la), l'; (: indirect object) gli(le); **where's my book? — ~'s on the table** dov'è il mio libro? — è sulla tavola; **I can't find ~** non lo (or la) trovo; **give ~ to me** dammelo (or dammela); **about/from/of ~** ne; **I spoke to him about ~** gliene ho parlato; **what did you learn from ~?** quale insegnamento ne hai tratto?; **I'm proud of ~** ne sono fiero; **did you go to ~?** ci sei andato?; **put the book in ~** mettici il libro

2 (impers): **~'s raining** piove; **~'s Friday tomorrow** domani è venerdì; **~'s 6 o'clock** sono le 6; **who is ~? — ~'s me** chi è? — sono io.

Italian [ɪˈtæljən] adj italiano(a) ♦ n italiano/a; (LING) italiano; **the ~s** gli Italiani.

italics [ɪˈtælɪks] npl corsivo m.

Italy [ˈɪtəlɪ] n Italia.

itch [ɪtʃ] n prurito ♦ vi (person) avere il prurito; (part of body) prudere; **to ~ to do sth** aver una gran voglia di fare qc; **~y** adj che prude; **to be ~y** = **to ~**.

it'd [ˈɪtd] = **it would**; **it had**.

item [ˈaɪtəm] n articolo; (on agenda) punto; (also: news ~) notizia; **~ize** vt specificare, dettagliare.

itinerant [ɪˈtɪnərənt] adj ambulante.

itinerary [aɪˈtɪnərərɪ] n itinerario.

it'll [ˈɪtl] = **it will**; **it shall**.

its [ɪts] adj il(la) suo(a), i(le) suoi(sue).

it's [ɪts] = **it is**; **it has**.

itself [ɪtˈsɛlf] pron (emphatic) esso(a)

stesso(a); *(reflexive)* si.
ITV *(BRIT)* *n abbr* (= *Independent Television*) rete televisiva in concorrenza con la BBC.
I.U.D. *n abbr* (= *intra-uterine device*) spirale *f*.
I've [aɪv] = **I have**.
ivory ['aɪvərɪ] *n* avorio.
ivy ['aɪvɪ] *n* edera.

J

jab [dʒæb] *vt* dare colpetti a ♦ *n* *(MED: inf)* puntura; **to ~ sth into** affondare *or* piantare qc dentro.
jack [dʒæk] *n* *(AUT)* cricco; *(CARDS)* fante *m*; **~ up** *vt* sollevare col cricco.
jackal ['dʒækl] *n* sciacallo.
jackdaw ['dʒækdɔ:] *n* taccola.
jacket ['dʒækɪt] *n* giacca; *(of book)* copertura.
jack-knife *vi*: **the lorry ~d** l'autotreno si è piegato su se stesso.
jack plug *n* *(ELEC)* jack *m inv*.
jackpot ['dʒækpɔt] *n* primo premio (in denaro).
jade [dʒeɪd] *n* *(stone)* giada.
jaded ['dʒeɪdɪd] *adj* sfinito(a), spossato(a).
jagged ['dʒægɪd] *adj* seghettato(a); *(cliffs etc)* frastagliato(a).
jail [dʒeɪl] *n* prigione *f* ♦ *vt* mandare in prigione.
jam [dʒæm] *n* marmellata; *(also: traffic ~)* ingorgo; *(inf)* pasticcio ♦ *vt* *(passage etc)* ingombrare, ostacolare; *(mechanism, drawer etc)* bloccare; *(RADIO)* disturbare con interferenze ♦ *vi* incepparsi; **to ~ sth into** forzare qc dentro; infilare qc a forza dentro.
Jamaica [dʒə'meɪkə] *n* Giamaica.
jangle ['dʒæŋgl] *vi* risuonare; *(bracelet)* tintinnare.
janitor ['dʒænɪtə*] *n* *(caretaker)* portiere *m*; *(: SCOL)* bidello.
January ['dʒænjuərɪ] *n* gennaio.
Japan [dʒə'pæn] *n* Giappone *m*; **~ese** [dʒæpə'ni:z] *adj* giapponese ♦ *n inv* giapponese *m/f*; *(LING)* giapponese *m*.

jar [dʒɑ:*] *n* *(glass)* barattolo, vasetto ♦ *vi* *(sound)* stridere; *(colours etc)* stonare.
jargon ['dʒɑ:gən] *n* gergo.
jasmin(e) ['dʒæzmɪn] *n* gelsomino.
jaundice ['dʒɔ:ndɪs] *n* itterizia; **~d** *adj* *(fig)* cupo(a).
jaunt [dʒɔ:nt] *n* gita; **~y** *adj* vivace; disinvolto(a).
javelin ['dʒævlɪn] *n* giavellotto.
jaw [dʒɔ:] *n* mascella.
jay [dʒeɪ] *n* ghiandaia.
jaywalker ['dʒeɪwɔ:kə*] *n* pedone(a) indisciplinato(a).
jazz [dʒæz] *n* jazz *m*; **~ up** *vt* rendere vivace.
jealous ['dʒeləs] *adj* geloso(a); **~y** *n* gelosia.
jeans [dʒi:nz] *npl* (blue-)jeans *mpl*.
jeer [dʒɪə*] *vi*: **to ~ (at)** fischiare; beffeggiare.
jelly ['dʒelɪ] *n* gelatina; **~fish** *n* medusa.
jeopardy ['dʒepədɪ] *n*: **in ~** in pericolo.
jerk [dʒə:k] *n* sobbalzo, scossa; sussulto; *(inf: idiot)* tonto/a ♦ *vt* dare una scossa a ♦ *vi* *(vehicles)* sobbalzare.
jerkin ['dʒə:kɪn] *n* giubbotto.
jersey ['dʒə:zɪ] *n* maglia; *(fabric)* jersey *m*.
jest [dʒest] *n* scherzo.
Jesus ['dʒi:zəs] *n* Gesù *m*.
jet [dʒet] *n* *(of gas, liquid)* getto; *(AVIAT)* aviogetto; **~-black** *adj* nero(a) come l'ebano, corvino(a); **~ engine** *n* motore *m* a reazione; **~ lag** *n* (problemi *mpl* dovuti allo) sbalzo dei fusi orari.
jettison ['dʒetɪsn] *vt* gettare in mare.
jetty ['dʒetɪ] *n* molo.
Jew [dʒu:] *n* ebreo.
jewel ['dʒu:əl] *n* gioiello; **~ler** *(US* **~er)** *n* orefice *m*, gioielliere/a; **~(l)er's (shop)** *n* oreficeria, gioielleria; **~lery** *(US* **~ery)** *n* gioielli *mpl*.
Jewess ['dʒu:ɪs] *n* ebrea.
Jewish ['dʒu:ɪʃ] *adj* ebreo(a), ebraico(a).
jibe [dʒaɪb] *n* beffa.
jiffy ['dʒɪfɪ] *(inf)* *n*: **in a ~** in un batter d'occhio.

jig [dʒɪg] n giga.

jigsaw ['dʒɪgsɔ:] n (also: ~ puzzle) puzzle m inv.

jilt [dʒɪlt] vt piantare in asso.

jingle ['dʒɪŋgl] n (for advert) sigla pubblicitaria ♦ vi tintinnare, scampanellare.

jinx [dʒɪŋks] n iettatura; (person) iettatore/trice.

jitters ['dʒɪtəz] (inf) npl: **to get the ~** aver fifa.

job [dʒɔb] n lavoro; (employment) impiego, posto; **it's not my ~** (duty) non è compito mio; **it's a good ~ that** ... meno male che ...; **just the ~!** proprio quello che ci vuole; **~ centre** (BRIT) n ufficio di collocamento; **~less** adj senza lavoro, disoccupato(a).

jockey ['dʒɔkɪ] n fantino, jockey m inv ♦ vi: **to ~ for position** manovrare per una posizione di vantaggio.

jocular ['dʒɔkjulə*] adj gioviale; scherzoso(a).

jog [dʒɔg] vt urtare ♦ vi (SPORT) fare footing, fare jogging; **to ~ sb's memory** rinfrescare la memoria a qn; **to ~ along** trottare; (fig) andare avanti piano piano; **~ging** n footing m, jogging m.

join [dʒɔɪn] vt unire, congiungere; (become member of) iscriversi a; (meet) raggiungere; riunirsi a ♦ vi (roads, rivers) confluire ♦ n giuntura; **~ in** vi partecipare ♦ vt fus unirsi a; **~ up** vi incontrarsi; (MIL) arruolarsi.

joiner ['dʒɔɪnə*] (BRIT) n falegname m.

joint [dʒɔɪnt] n (TECH) giuntura; giunto; (ANAT) articolazione f, giuntura; (BRIT: CULIN) arrosto; (inf: place) locale m; (: of cannabis) spinello ♦ adj comune; **~ account** n (at bank etc) conto in partecipazione, conto comune.

joist [dʒɔɪst] n trave f.

joke [dʒəuk] n scherzo; (funny story) barzelletta; (also: practical ~) beffa ♦ vi scherzare; **to play a ~ on sb** fare uno scherzo a qn; **~r** n (CARDS) matta, jolly m inv.

jolly ['dʒɔlɪ] adj allegro(a), gioioso(a) ♦ adv (BRIT: inf) veramente, proprio.

jolt [dʒəult] n scossa, sobbalzo ♦ vt urtare.

Jordan ['dʒɔ:dən] n (country) Giordania; (river) Giordano.

jostle ['dʒɔsl] vt spingere coi gomiti.

jot [dʒɔt] n: **not one ~** nemmeno un po'; **~ down** vt annotare in fretta, buttare giù; **~ter** (BRIT) n blocco.

journal ['dʒə:nl] n giornale m; rivista; diario; **~ism** n giornalismo; **~ist** n giornalista m/f.

journey ['dʒə:nɪ] n viaggio; (distance covered) tragitto.

joy [dʒɔɪ] n gioia; **~ful** adj gioioso(a), allegro(a); **~ ride** n gita in automobile (specialmente rubata); **~stick** n (AVIAT) barra di comando; (COMPUT) joystick m inv.

JP n abbr = **Justice of the Peace**.

Jr abbr = **junior**.

jubilant ['dʒu:bɪlnt] adj giubilante; trionfante.

jubilee ['dʒu:bɪli:] n giubileo; **silver ~** venticinquesimo anniversario.

judge [dʒʌdʒ] n giudice m/f ♦ vt giudicare; **judg(e)ment** n giudizio.

judicial [dʒu:'dɪʃl] adj giudiziale, giudiziario(a).

judiciary [dʒu:'dɪʃɪərɪ] n magistratura.

judo ['dʒu:dəu] n judo.

jug [dʒʌg] n brocca, bricco.

juggernaut ['dʒʌgənɔ:t] (BRIT) n (huge truck) bestione m.

juggle ['dʒʌgl] vi fare giochi di destrezza; **~r** n giocoliere/a.

Jugoslav etc ['ju:gəuslɑ:v] = **Yugoslav** etc.

juice [dʒu:s] n succo.

juicy ['dʒu:sɪ] adj succoso(a).

jukebox ['dʒu:kbɔks] n juke-box m inv.

July [dʒu:'laɪ] n luglio.

jumble ['dʒʌmbl] n miscuglio ♦ vt (also: ~ up) mischiare; **~ sale** (BRIT) n vendita di oggetti per beneficenza.

jumbo (jet) ['dʒʌmbəu-] n jumbo-jet m inv.

jump [dʒʌmp] vi saltare, balzare; (start) sobbalzare; (increase) rincarare ♦ vt saltare ♦ n salto, balzo; sobbalzo.

jumper ['dʒʌmpə*] n (BRIT: pullover)

maglione *m*, pullover *m inv*; (*US: dress*) scamiciato; ~ **cables** (*US*) *npl* = **jump leads**.

jump leads (*BRIT*) *npl* cavi *mpl* per batteria.

jumpy ['dʒʌmpɪ] *adj* nervoso(a), agitato(a).

Jun. *abbr* = **junior**.

junction ['dʒʌŋkʃən] *n* (*BRIT: of roads*) incrocio; (*of rails*) nodo ferroviario.

juncture ['dʒʌŋktʃə*] *n*: **at this ~** in questa congiuntura.

June [dʒuːn] *n* giugno.

jungle ['dʒʌŋgl] *n* giungla.

junior ['dʒuːnɪə*] *adj*, *n*: **he's ~ to me (by 2 years), he's my ~ (by 2 years)** è più giovane di me (di 2 anni); **he's ~ to me** (*seniority*) è al di sotto di me, ho più anzianità di lui; (*of rails*) **~ school** (*BRIT*) *n* scuola elementare (*da 8 a 11 anni*).

junk [dʒʌŋk] *n* cianfrusaglie *fpl*; (*cheap goods*) robaccia; **~ food** *n* porcherie *fpl*.

junkie ['dʒʌŋkɪ] (*inf*) *n* drogato/a.

junk shop *n* chincaglieria.

Junr *abbr* = **junior**.

juror ['dʒuərə*] *n* giurato/a.

jury ['dʒuərɪ] *n* giuria.

just [dʒʌst] *adj* giusto(a) ♦ *adv*: **he's ~ done it/left** lo ha appena fatto/è appena partito; **~ right** proprio giusto; **~ 2 o'clock** le 2 precise; **she's ~ as clever as you** è in gamba proprio quanto te; **it's ~ as well that ...** meno male che ...; **~ as I arrived** proprio mentre arrivavo; **it was ~ before/enough/here** era poco prima/appena assai/proprio qui; **it's ~ me** sono solo io; **~ missed/caught** appena perso/preso; **~ listen to this!** senta un po' questo!

justice ['dʒʌstɪs] *n* giustizia; **J~ of the Peace** *n* giudice *m* conciliatore.

justify ['dʒʌstɪfaɪ] *vt* giustificare.

jut [dʒʌt] *vi* (*also:* **~ out**) sporgersi.

juvenile ['dʒuːvənaɪl] *adj* giovane, giovanile; (*court*) dei minorenni; (*books*) per ragazzi ♦ *n* giovane *m/f*, minorenne *m/f*.

juxtapose ['dʒʌkstəpəuz] *vt* giustapporre.

K

K *abbr* (= *one thousand*) mille; (= *kilobyte*) K.

Kampuchea [kæmpu'tʃɪə] *n* Cambogia.

kangaroo [kæŋgə'ruː] *n* canguro.

karate [kə'rɑːtɪ] *n* karatè *m*.

kebab [kə'bæb] *n* spiedino.

keel [kiːl] *n* chiglia; **on an even ~** (*fig*) in uno stato normale.

keen [kiːn] *adj* (*interest, desire*) vivo(a); (*eye, intelligence*) acuto(a); (*competition*) serrato(a); (*edge*) affilato(a); (*eager*) entusiasta; **to be ~ to do** *or* **on doing sth** avere una gran voglia di fare qc; **to be ~ on sth** essere appassionato(a) di qc; **to be ~ on sb** avere un debole per qn.

keep [kiːp] (*pt, pp* **kept**) *vt* tenere; (*hold back*) trattenere; (*feed: one's family etc*) mantenere, sostentare; (*a promise*) mantenere; (*chickens, bees, pigs etc*) allevare ♦ *vi* (*food*) mantenersi; (*remain: in a certain state or place*) restare ♦ *n* (*of castle*) maschio; (*food etc*): **enough for his ~** abbastanza per vitto e alloggio; (*inf*): **for ~s** per sempre; **to ~ doing sth** continuare a fare qc; fare qc di continuo; **to ~ sb from doing** impedire a qn di fare; **to ~ sb busy/a place tidy** tenere qn occupato(a)/un luogo in ordine; **to ~ sth to o.s.** tenere qc per sé; **to ~ sth (back) from sb** celare qc a qn; **to ~ time** (*clock*) andar bene; **~ on** *vi*: **to ~ on doing** continuare a fare; **to ~ on (about sth)** continuare a insistere (su qc); **~ out** *vt* tener fuori; **"~ out"** "vietato l'accesso"; **~ up** *vt* continuare, mantenere ♦ *vi*: **to ~ up with** tener dietro a, andare di pari passo con; (*work etc*) farcela a seguire; **~er** *n* custode *m/f*, guardiano/a; **~fit** *n* ginnastica; **~ing** *n* (*care*) custodia; **in ~ing with** in armonia con; in accordo con; **~sake** *n* ricordo.

kennel ['kɛnl] *n* canile *m*; **to put a dog in ~s** mettere un cane al canile.

kept [kɛpt] *pt, pp of* **keep**.
kerb [kə:b] (*BRIT*) *n* orlo del marciapiede.
kernel ['kə:nl] *n* nocciolo.
kettle ['kɛtl] *n* bollitore *m*.
kettle drum *n* timpano.
key [ki:] *n* (*gen, MUS*) chiave *f*; (*of piano, typewriter*) tasto ♦ *adj* chiave *inv* ♦ *vt* (*also: ~ in*) digitare; **~board** *n* tastiera; **~ed up** *adj* (*person*) agitato(a); **~hole** *n* buco della serratura; **~note** *n* (*MUS*) tonica; (*fig*) nota dominante; **~ ring** *n* portachiavi *m inv*.
khaki ['kɑ:kɪ] *adj* cachi ♦ *n* cachi *m*.
kick [kɪk] *vt* calciare, dare calci a; (*inf: habit etc*) liberarsi di ♦ *vi* (*horse*) tirar calci ♦ *n* calcio; (*thrill*): **he does it for ~s** lo fa giusto per il piacere di farlo; **~ off** *vi* (*SPORT*) dare il primo calcio.
kid [kɪd] *n* (*inf: child*) ragazzino/a; (*animal, leather*) capretto ♦ *vi* (*inf*) scherzare.
kidnap ['kɪdnæp] *vt* rapire, sequestrare; **~per** *n* rapitore/trice; **~ping** *n* sequestro (di persona).
kidney ['kɪdnɪ] *n* (*ANAT*) rene *m*; (*CULIN*) rognone *m*.
kill [kɪl] *vt* uccidere, ammazzare ♦ *n* uccisione *f*; **~er** *n* uccisore *m*, killer *m inv*; assassino/a; **~ing** *n* assassinio; **to make a ~ing** (*inf*) fare un bel colpo; **~joy** *n* guastafeste *m/f inv*.
kiln [kɪln] *n* forno.
kilo ['ki:ləʊ] *n* chilo; **~byte** *n* (*COMPUT*) kilobyte *m inv*; **~gram(me)** ['kɪləʊɡræm] *n* chilogrammo; **~metre** ['kɪləmi:tə*] (*US* **~meter**) *n* chilometro; **~watt** ['kɪləʊwɔt] *n* chilowatt *m inv*.
kilt [kɪlt] *n* gonnellino scozzese.
kin [kɪn] *n see* **next**; **kith**.
kind [kaɪnd] *adj* gentile, buono(a) ♦ *n* sorta, specie *f*; (*species*) genere *m*; **to be two of a ~** essere molto simili; **in ~** (*COMM*) in natura.
kindergarten ['kɪndəɡɑ:tn] *n* giardino d'infanzia.
kind-hearted [-'hɑ:tɪd] *adj* di buon cuore.
kindle ['kɪndl] *vt* accendere,

infiammare.
kindly ['kaɪndlɪ] *adj* pieno(a) di bontà, benevolo(a) ♦ *adv* con bontà, gentilmente; **will you ~** ... vuole ... per favore.
kindness ['kaɪndnɪs] *n* bontà, gentilezza.
kindred ['kɪndrɪd] *adj*: **~ spirit** spirito affine.
king [kɪŋ] *n* re *m inv*; **~dom** *n* regno, reame *m*; **~fisher** *n* martin *m inv* pescatore; **~-size** *adj* super *inv*; gigante.
kinky ['kɪŋkɪ] (*pej*) *adj* eccentrico(a); dai gusti particolari.
kiosk ['ki:ɔsk] *n* edicola, chiosco; (*BRIT: TEL*) cabina (telefonica).
kipper ['kɪpə*] *n* aringa affumicata.
kiss [kɪs] *n* bacio ♦ *vt* baciare; **to ~ (each other)** baciarsi; **~ of life** *n* respirazione *f* bocca a bocca.
kit [kɪt] *n* equipaggiamento, corredo; (*set of tools etc*) attrezzi *mpl*; (*for assembly*) scatola di montaggio.
kitchen ['kɪtʃɪn] *n* cucina; **~ sink** *n* acquaio.
kite [kaɪt] *n* (*toy*) aquilone *m*.
kith [kɪθ] *n*: **~ and kin** amici e parenti *mpl*.
kitten ['kɪtn] *n* gattino/a, micino/a.
kitty ['kɪtɪ] *n* (*money*) fondo comune.
knack [næk] *n*: **to have the ~ of** avere l'abilità di.
knapsack ['næpsæk] *n* zaino, sacco da montagna.
knead [ni:d] *vt* impastare.
knee [ni:] *n* ginocchio; **~cap** *n* rotula.
kneel [ni:l] (*pt, pp* **knelt**) *vi* (*also: ~ down*) inginocchiarsi; **knelt** [nɛlt] *pt, pp of* **kneel**.
knew [nju:] *pt of* **know**.
knickers ['nɪkəz] (*BRIT*) *npl* mutandine *fpl*.
knife [naɪf] (*pl* **knives**) *n* coltello ♦ *vt* accoltellare, dare una coltellata a.
knight [naɪt] *n* cavaliere *m*; (*CHESS*) cavallo; **~hood** (*BRIT*) *n* (*title*): **to get a ~hood** essere fatto cavaliere.
knit [nɪt] *vt* fare a maglia ♦ *vi* lavorare a maglia; (*broken bones*) saldarsi; **to ~ one's brows** aggrottare le sopracciglia; **~ting** *n* lavoro a maglia; **~ting**

machine *n* macchina per maglieria; **~ting needle** *n* ferro (da calza); **~wear** *n* maglieria.

knives [naɪvz] *npl of* **knife**.

knob [nɔb] *n* bottone *m*; manopola.

knock [nɔk] *vt* colpire; urtare; (*fig: inf*) criticare ♦ *vi* (*at door etc*): **to ~ at/on** bussare a ♦ *n* bussata; colpo, botta; **~ down** *vt* abbattere; **~ off** *vi* (*inf: finish*) smettere (di lavorare) ♦ *vt* (*from price*) far abbassare; (*inf: steal*) sgraffignare; **~ out** *vt* stendere; (*BOXING*) mettere K.O.; (*defeat*) battere; **~ over** *vt* (*person*) investire; (*object*) far cadere; **~er** *n* (*on door*) battente *m*; **~out** *n* (*BOXING*) knock out *m inv* ♦ *cpd* a eliminazione.

knot [nɔt] *n* nodo ♦ *vt* annodare; **~ty** *adj* (*fig*) spinoso(a).

know [nəʊ] (*pt* **knew**, *pp* **known**) *vt* sapere; (*person, author, place*) conoscere; **to ~ how to do** sapere fare; **to ~ about** *or* **of sth/sb** conoscere qc/qn; **~-all** *n* sapientone/a; **~-how** *n* tecnica; pratica; **~ing** *adj* (*look etc*) d'intesa; **~ingly** *adv* (*purposely*) consapevolmente; (*smile, look*) con aria d'intesa.

knowledge ['nɔlɪdʒ] *n* consapevolezza; (*learning*) conoscenza, sapere *m*; **~able** *adj* ben informato(a).

known [nəʊn] *pp of* **know**.

knuckle ['nʌkl] *n* nocca.

Koran [kɔ'rɑːn] *n* Corano.

Korea [kə'rɪə] *n* Corea.

kosher ['kəʊʃə*] *adj* kasher *inv*.

L

L (*BRIT*) *abbr* = **learner driver**.

lab [læb] *n abbr* (= *laboratory*) laboratorio.

label ['leɪbl] *n* etichetta, cartellino; (*brand: of record*) casa ♦ *vt* etichettare.

labor *etc* ['leɪbə*] (*US*) = **labour** *etc*.

laboratory [lə'bɔrətərɪ] *n* laboratorio.

labour ['leɪbə*] (*US* **labor**) *n* (*task*) lavoro; (*workmen*) manodopera;

(*MED*): **to be in ~** avere le doglie ♦ *vi*: **to ~ (at)** lavorare duro (a); **L~, the L~ party** (*BRIT*) il partito laburista, i laburisti; **hard ~** lavori *mpl* forzati; **~ed** *adj* (*breathing*) affannoso(a); **~er** *n* manovale *m*; **farm ~er** lavoratore *m* agricolo.

lace [leɪs] *n* merletto, pizzo; (*of shoe etc*) laccio ♦ *vt* (*shoe: also: ~ up*) allacciare.

lack [læk] *n* mancanza ♦ *vt* mancare di; **through** *or* **for ~ of** per mancanza di; **to be ~ing** mancare; **to be ~ing in** mancare di.

lackadaisical [lækə'deɪzɪkl] *adj* disinteressato(a), noncurante.

lacquer ['lækə*] *n* lacca.

lad [læd] *n* ragazzo, giovanotto.

ladder ['lædə*] *n* scala; (*BRIT: in tights*) smagliatura.

laden ['leɪdn] *adj*: **~ (with)** carico(a) *or* caricato(a) (di).

ladle ['leɪdl] *n* mestolo.

lady ['leɪdɪ] *n* signora; dama; **L~ Smith** lady Smith; **the ladies' (room)** i gabinetti per signore; **~bird** (*US* **~bug**) *n* coccinella; **~like** *adj* da signora, distinto(a); **~ship** *n*: **your ~ship** signora contessa (*or* baronessa *etc*).

lag [læg] *n* (*of time*) lasso, intervallo ♦ *vi* (*also: ~ behind*) trascinarsi ♦ *vt* (*pipes*) rivestire di materiale isolante.

lager ['lɑːgə*] *n* lager *m inv*.

lagoon [lə'guːn] *n* laguna.

laid [leɪd] *pt, pp of* **lay**; **~ back** (*inf*) *adj* rilassato(a), tranquillo(a); **~ up** *adj*: **~ up (with)** costretto(a) a letto (da).

lain [leɪn] *pp of* **lie**.

lair [lɛə*] *n* covo, tana.

lake [leɪk] *n* lago.

lamb [læm] *n* agnello.

lame [leɪm] *adj* zoppo(a); (*excuse etc*) zoppicante.

lament [lə'mɛnt] *n* lamento ♦ *vt* lamentare, piangere.

laminated ['læmɪneɪtɪd] *adj* laminato(a).

lamp [læmp] *n* lampada.

lamppost ['læmppəʊst] (*BRIT*) *n* lampione *m*.

lampshade ['læmpʃeɪd] *n* paralume *m*.

lance [lɑ:ns] n lancia ♦ vt (MED) incidere.

land [lænd] n (as opposed to sea) terra (ferma); (country) paese m; (soil) terreno; suolo; (estate) terreni mpl, terre fpl ♦ vi (from ship) sbarcare; (AVIAT) atterrare; (fig: fall) cadere ♦ vt (passengers) sbarcare; (goods) scaricare; **to ~ sb with sth** affibbiare qc a qn; **~ up** vi andare a finire; **~ing** n atterraggio; (of staircase) pianerottolo; **~ing gear** n carrello di atterraggio; **~ing strip** n pista di atterraggio; **~lady** n padrona or proprietaria di casa; **~locked** adj senza sbocco sul mare; **~lord** n padrone m or proprietario di casa; (of pub etc) padrone m; **~mark** n punto di riferimento; (fig) pietra miliare; **~owner** n proprietario(a) terriero(a).

landscape ['lænskeɪp] n paesaggio.

landslide ['lændslaɪd] n (GEO) frana; (fig: POL) valanga.

lane [leɪn] n stradina; (AUT, in race) corsia.

language ['læŋgwɪdʒ] n lingua; (way one speaks) linguaggio; **bad ~** linguaggio volgare; **~ laboratory** n laboratorio linguistico.

languid ['læŋgwɪd] adj languido(a).

lank [læŋk] adj (hair) liscio(a) e opaco(a).

lanky ['læŋkɪ] adj allampanato(a).

lantern ['læntn] n lanterna.

lap [læp] n (of track) giro; (of body): **in** or **on one's ~** in grembo ♦ vt (also: ~ up) papparsi, leccare ♦ vi (waves) sciabordare; **~ up** vt (fig) bearsi di.

lapel [lə'pɛl] n risvolto.

Lapland ['læplænd] n Lapponia.

lapse [læps] n lapsus m inv; (longer) caduta ♦ vi (law) cadere; (membership, contract) scadere; **to ~ into bad habits** pigliare cattive abitudini; **~ of time** spazio di tempo.

larceny ['lɑ:sənɪ] n furto.

larch [lɑ:tʃ] n larice m.

lard [lɑ:d] n lardo.

larder ['lɑ:də*] n dispensa.

large [lɑ:dʒ] adj grande; (person,

animal) grosso(a); **at ~** (free) in libertà; (generally) in generale; nell'insieme; **~ly** adv in gran parte.

largesse [lɑ:'ʒɛs] n generosità.

lark [lɑ:k] n (bird) allodola; (joke) scherzo, gioco; **~ about** vi fare lo stupido.

laryngitis [lærɪn'dʒaɪtɪs] n laringite f.

laser ['leɪzə*] n laser m; **~ printer** n stampante f laser inv.

lash [læʃ] n frustata; (also: eye~) ciglio ♦ vt frustare; (tie): **to ~ to/together** legare a insieme; **~ out** vi: **to ~ out** (at or against sb) attaccare violentemente (qn).

lass [læs] n ragazza.

lasso [læ'su:] n laccio.

last [lɑ:st] adj ultimo(a); (week, month, year) scorso(a), passato(a) ♦ adv per ultimo ♦ vi durare; **~ week** la settimana scorsa; **~ night** ieri sera, la notte scorsa; **at ~** finalmente, alla fine; **~ but one** penultimo(a); **~-ditch** adj (attempt) estremo(a); **~ing** adj durevole; **~ly** adv infine, per finire; **~-minute** adj fatto(a) (or preso(a) etc) all'ultimo momento.

latch [lætʃ] n chiavistello.

late [leɪt] adj (not on time) in ritardo; (far on in day etc) tardi inv; tardo(a); (former) ex; (dead) defunto(a) ♦ adv tardi; (behind time, schedule) in ritardo; **of ~** di recente; **in the ~ afternoon** nel tardo pomeriggio; **in ~ May** verso la fine di maggio; **~comer** n ritardatario/a; **~ly** adv recentemente.

later ['leɪtə*] adj (date etc) posteriore; (version etc) successivo(a) ♦ adv più tardi; **~ on** più avanti.

lateral ['lætərl] adj laterale.

latest ['leɪtɪst] adj ultimo(a), più recente; **at the ~** al più tardi.

lathe [leɪð] n tornio.

lather ['lɑ:ðə*] n schiuma di sapone ♦ vt insaponare.

Latin ['lætɪn] n latino ♦ adj latino(a); **~ America** n America Latina; **~-American** adj, n sudamericano(a).

latitude ['lætɪtju:d] n latitudine f; (fig) libertà d'azione.

latter ['lætə*] adj secondo(a); più recente ♦ n: **the ~** quest'ultimo, il secondo; **~ly** adv recentemente, negli ultimi tempi.

lattice ['lætɪs] n traliccio; graticolato.

laudable ['lɔːdəbl] adj lodevole.

laugh [lɑːf] n risata ♦ vi ridere; **~ at** vt fus (misfortune etc) ridere di; **~ off** vt prendere alla leggera; **~able** adj ridicolo(a); **~ing stock** n: **the ~ing stock of** lo zimbello di; **~ter** n riso; risate fpl.

launch [lɔːntʃ] n (of rocket, COMM) lancio; (of new ship) varo; (also: **motor ~**) lancia ♦ vt (rocket, COMM) lanciare; (ship, plan) varare; **~ into** vt fus lanciarsi in; **~(ing) pad** n rampa di lancio.

launder ['lɔːndə*] vt lavare e stirare.

launderette [lɔːn'drɛt] (BRIT) n lavanderia (automatica).

laundromat ['lɔːndrəmæt] (US) n lavanderia automatica.

laundry ['lɔːndrɪ] n lavanderia; (clothes) biancheria; (: dirty) panni mpl da lavare.

laureate ['lɔːrɪət] adj see **poet**.

laurel ['lɔrl] n lauro.

lava ['lɑːvə] n lava.

lavatory ['lævətərɪ] n gabinetto.

lavender ['lævəndə*] n lavanda.

lavish ['lævɪʃ] adj copioso(a); abbondante; (giving freely): **~ with** di, largo(a) in ♦ vt: **to ~ sth on sb** colmare qn di qc.

law [lɔː] n legge f; **civil/criminal ~** diritto civile/penale; **~-abiding** adj ubbidiente alla legge; **~ and order** n l'ordine m pubblico; **~ court** n tribunale m, corte f di giustizia; **~ful** adj legale; lecito(a); **~less** adj che non conosce nessuna legge.

lawn [lɔːn] n tappeto erboso; **~mower** n tosaerba m or f inv; **~ tennis** n tennis m su prato.

law school n facoltà f inv di legge.

lawsuit ['lɔːsuːt] n processo, causa.

lawyer ['lɔːjə*] n (for sales, wills etc) ≈ notaio; (partner, in court) ≈ avvocato/essa.

lax [læks] adj rilassato(a); negligente.

laxative ['læksətɪv] n lassativo.

lay [leɪ] (pt, pp laid) pt of **lie** ♦ adj laico(a); (not expert) profano(a) ♦ vt posare, mettere; (eggs) fare; (trap) tendere; (plans) fare, elaborare; **to ~ the table** apparecchiare la tavola; **~ aside** or **by** vt mettere da parte; **~ down** vt mettere giù; (rules etc) formulare, fissare; **to ~ down the law** dettar legge; **to ~ down one's life** dare la propria vita; **~ off** vt (workers) licenziare; **~ on** vt (provide) fornire; **~ out** vt (display) presentare, disporre; **~about** n sfaccendato/a, fannullone/a; **~-by** (BRIT) n piazzola (di sosta).

layer ['leɪə*] n strato.

layman ['leɪmən] n laico; profano.

layout ['leɪaut] n lay-out m inv, disposizione f; (PRESS) impaginazione f.

laze [leɪz] vi oziare.

lazy ['leɪzɪ] adj pigro(a).

lb. abbr = **pound** (weight).

lead¹ [liːd] (pt, pp led) n (front position) posizione f di testa; (distance, time ahead) vantaggio; (clue) indizio; (ELEC) filo (elettrico); (for dog) guinzaglio; (THEATRE) parte f principale ♦ vt guidare, condurre; (induce) indurre; (be leader of) essere a capo di ♦ vi condurre; (SPORT) essere in testa; **in the ~** in testa; **to ~ the way** fare strada; **~ away** vt condurre via; **~ back** vt: **to ~ back to** ricondurre a; **~ on** vt (tease) tenere sulla corda; **~ to** vt fus condurre a; portare a; **~ up to** vt fus portare a.

lead² [lɛd] n (metal) piombo; (in pencil) mina.

leaden ['lɛdn] adj (sky, sea) plumbeo(a).

leader ['liːdə*] n capo; leader m inv; (in newspaper) articolo di fondo; (SPORT) chi è in testa; **~ship** n direzione f; capacità di comando.

leading ['liːdɪŋ] adj primo(a); principale; **~ man/lady** n (THEATRE) primo attore/prima attrice; **~ light** n (person) personaggio di primo piano.

lead singer n cantante alla testa di un gruppo.

leaf [li:f] (pl **leaves**) n foglia ♦ vi: to ~ **through sth** sfogliare qc; **to turn over a new** ~ cambiar vita.

leaflet ['li:flɪt] n dépliant m inv; (POL, REL) volantino.

league [li:g] n lega; (FOOTBALL) campionato; **to be in** ~ **with** essere in lega con.

leak [li:k] n (out) fuga; (in) infiltrazione f; (security ~) fuga d'informazioni ♦ vi (roof, bucket) perdere; (liquid) uscire; (shoes) lasciar passare l'acqua ♦ vt (information) divulgare; ~ **out** vi uscire; (information) trapelare.

lean [li:n] (pt, pp **leaned** or **leant**) adj magro(a) ♦ vt: to ~ **sth on sth** appoggiare qc su qc ♦ vi (slope) pendere; (rest): to ~ **against** appoggiarsi contro; essere appoggiato(a) a; to ~ **on** appoggiarsi a; ~ **forward/back** vi sporgersi in avanti/indietro; ~ **out** vi sporgersi; ~ **over** vi inclinarsi; ~**ing** n: ~**ing** (**towards**) propensione f (per); **leant** [lɛnt] pt, pp of **lean**.

leap [li:p] (pt, pp **leaped** or **leapt**) n salto, balzo ♦ vi saltare, balzare; ~**frog** n gioco della cavallina; **leapt** [lɛpt] pt, pp of **leap**; ~ **year** n anno bisestile.

learn [lə:n] (pt, pp **learned** or **learnt**) vt, vi imparare; to ~ **about sth** (hear, read) apprendere qc; to ~ **to do sth** imparare a fare qc; ~**ed** ['lə:nɪd] adj erudito(a), dotto(a); ~**er** n principiante m/f; apprendista m/f; (BRIT: also: ~**er driver**) guidatore/trice principiante; ~**ing** n erudizione f, sapienza; **learnt** pt, pp of **learn**.

lease [li:s] n contratto d'affitto ♦ vt affittare.

leash [li:ʃ] n guinzaglio.

least [li:st] adj: **the** ~ (+ noun) il(la) più piccolo(a), il(la) minimo(a); (smallest amount of) il(la) meno ♦ adv (+ verb) meno; **the** ~ (+ adjective): **the** ~ **beautiful girl** la ragazza meno bella; **the** ~ **possible effort** il minimo sforzo possibile; **I have the** ~ **money** ho meno denaro di tutti; **at** ~ almeno; **not in the** ~ affatto, per nulla.

leather ['lɛðə*] n cuoio.

leave [li:v] (pt, pp **left**) vt lasciare; (go away from) ♦ vi partire, andarsene; (bus, train) partire ♦ n (time off) congedo; (MIL, also: consent) licenza; **to be left** rimanere; **there's some milk left** over c'è rimasto del latte; **on** ~ in congedo; ~ **behind** vt (person, object) lasciare; (: forget) dimenticare; ~ **out** vt omettere, tralasciare; ~ **of absence** n congedo.

leaves [li:vz] npl of **leaf**.

Lebanon ['lɛbənən] n Libano.

lecherous ['lɛtʃərəs] adj lascivo(a), lubrico(a).

lecture ['lɛktʃə*] n conferenza; (SCOL) lezione f ♦ vi fare conferenze; fare lezioni ♦ vt (scold): to ~ **sb on** or **about sth** rimproverare qn or fare una ramanzina a qn per qc; **to give a** ~ **on** tenere una conferenza su.

lecturer ['lɛktʃərə*] (BRIT) n (at university) professore/essa, docente m/f.

led [lɛd] pt, pp of **lead**.

ledge [lɛdʒ] n (of window) davanzale m; (on wall etc) sporgenza; (of mountain) cornice f, cengia.

ledger ['lɛdʒə*] n libro maestro, registro.

lee [li:] n lato sottovento.

leech [li:tʃ] n sanguisuga.

leek [li:k] n porro.

leer [lɪə*] vi: to ~ **at sb** gettare uno sguardo voglioso (or maligno) su qn.

leeway ['li:weɪ] n (fig): **to have some** ~ avere una certa libertà di azione.

left [lɛft] pt, pp of **leave** ♦ adj sinistro(a) ♦ adv a sinistra ♦ n sinistra; **on the** ~, **to the** ~ a sinistra; **the L**~ (POL) la sinistra; ~-**handed** adj mancino(a); ~-**hand side** n lato or fianco sinistro; ~ **luggage** (**office**) (BRIT) n deposito m bagagli inv; ~**overs** npl avanzi mpl, resti mpl; ~-**wing** adj (POL) di sinistra.

leg [lɛg] n gamba; (of animal) zampa; (of furniture) piede m; (CULIN: of chicken) coscia; (of journey) tappa; **1st/2nd** ~ (SPORT) partita di andata/

ritorno.

legacy ['lɛgəsɪ] n eredità f inv.

legal ['li:gl] adj legale; ~ **holiday** (US) n giorno festivo, festa nazionale; ~ **tender** n moneta legale.

legend ['lɛdʒənd] n leggenda.

legislation [lɛdʒɪs'leɪʃən] n legislazione f; **legislature** ['lɛdʒɪslətʃə*] n corpo legislativo.

legitimate [lɪ'dʒɪtɪmət] adj legittimo(a).

leg-room n spazio per le gambe.

leisure ['lɛʒə*] n agio, tempo libero; ricreazioni fpl; **at** ~ con comodo; ~ **centre** n centro di ricreazione; ~**ly** adj tranquillo(a); fatto(a) con comodo or senza fretta.

lemon ['lɛmən] n limone m; ~**ade** [-'neɪd] n limonata; ~ **tea** n tè m inv al limone.

lend [lɛnd] (pt, pp lent) vt: **to** ~ **sth** (**to sb**) prestare qc (a qn); ~**ing library** n biblioteca che consente prestiti di libri.

length [lɛŋθ] n lunghezza; (distance) distanza; (section: of road, pipe etc) pezzo, tratto; (of time) periodo; **at** ~ (at last) finalmente, alla fine; (lengthily) a lungo; ~**en** vt allungare, prolungare ♦ vi allungarsi; ~**ways** adv per il lungo; ~**y** adj molto lungo(a).

lenient ['li:nɪənt] adj indulgente, clemente.

lens [lɛnz] n lente f; (of camera) obiettivo.

Lent [lɛnt] n Quaresima.

lent [lɛnt] pt, pp of **lend**.

lentil ['lɛntl] n lenticchia.

Leo ['li:əu] n Leone m.

leotard ['li:əta:d] n calzamaglia.

leprosy ['lɛprəsɪ] n lebbra.

lesbian ['lɛzbɪən] n lesbica.

less [lɛs] adj, pron, adv meno ♦ prep: ~ **tax/10% discount** meno tasse/il 10% di sconto; ~ **than ever** meno che mai; ~ **than half** meno della metà; ~ **and** ~ sempre meno; **the** ~ **he works** ... ~ meno lavora ....

lessen ['lɛsn] vi diminuire, attenuarsi ♦ vt diminuire, ridurre.

lesser ['lɛsə*] adj minore, più piccolo(a); **to a** ~ **extent** in grado or misura minore.

lesson ['lɛsn] n lezione f; **to teach sb a** ~ dare una lezione a qn.

lest [lɛst] conj per paura di + infinitive, per paura che + sub.

let [lɛt] (pt, pp let) vt lasciare; (BRIT: lease) dare in affitto; **to** ~ **sb do sth** lasciar fare qc a qn, lasciare che qn faccia qc; **to** ~ **sb know sth** far sapere qc a qn; ~'**s go** andiamo; ~ **him come** lo lasci venire; "**to** ~" "affittasi"; ~ **down** vt (lower) abbassare; (dress) allungare; (hair) sciogliere; (tyre) sgonfiare; (disappoint) deludere; ~ **go** vt, vi mollare; ~ **in** vt lasciare entrare; (visitor etc) far entrare; ~ **off** vt (allow to go) lasciare andare; (firework etc) far partire; ~ **on** (inf) vi dire; ~ **out** vt lasciare uscire; (scream) emettere; ~ **up** vi diminuire.

lethal ['li:θl] adj letale, mortale.

lethargic [lɛ'θa:dʒɪk] adj letargico(a).

letter ['lɛtə*] n lettera; ~ **bomb** n lettera esplosiva; ~**box** (BRIT) n buca delle lettere; ~**ing** n iscrizione f; caratteri mpl.

lettuce ['lɛtɪs] n lattuga, insalata.

let-up n pausa.

leukaemia [lu:'ki:mɪə] (US **leukemia**) n leucemia.

level ['lɛvl] adj piatto(a), piano(a); orizzontale ♦ adv: **to draw** ~ **with** mettersi alla pari di ♦ n livello ♦ vt livellare, spianare; **to be** ~ **with** essere alla pari di; **A** ~**s** (BRIT) npl ≈ esami mpl di maturità; **O** ~**s** (BRIT) npl esami fatti in Inghilterra all'età di 16 anni; **on the** ~ piatto(a); (fig) onesto(a); ~ **off** or **out** vi (prices etc) stabilizzarsi; ~ **crossing** (BRIT) n passaggio a livello; ~-**headed** adj equilibrato(a).

lever ['li:və*] n leva; ~**age** n: ~**age** (**on** or **with**) forza (su); (fig) ascendente m (su).

levity ['lɛvɪtɪ] n leggerezza, frivolezza.

levy ['lɛvɪ] n tassa, imposta ♦ vt imporre.

lewd [lu:d] adj osceno(a), lascivo(a).

liability [laɪə'bɪlətɪ] n responsabilità f inv; (handicap) peso; **liabilities** npl debiti *mpl*; (*on balance sheet*) passivo.

liable ['laɪəbl] *adj* (*subject*): ~ **to** soggetto(a) a; passibile di; (*responsible*): ~ (**for**) responsabile (di); (*likely*): ~ **to do** propenso(a) a fare.

liaise [li:'eɪz] *vi*: **to** ~ (**with**) mantenere i contatti (con).

liaison [li:'eɪzɒn] *n* relazione *f*; (*MIL*) collegamento.

liar ['laɪə*] *n* bugiardo/a.

libel ['laɪbl] *n* libello, diffamazione *f* ♦ *vt* diffamare.

liberal ['lɪbərl] *adj* liberale; (*generous*): **to be** ~ **with** distribuire liberalmente.

liberty ['lɪbətɪ] *n* libertà *f inv*; **at** ~ (*criminal*) in libertà; **at** ~ **to do** libero(a) di fare.

Libra ['li:brə] *n* Bilancia.

librarian [laɪ'brɛərɪən] *n* bibliotecario/a.

library ['laɪbrərɪ] *n* biblioteca.

Libya ['lɪbɪə] *n* Libia; ~**n** *adj, n* libico(a).

lice [laɪs] *npl of* louse.

licence ['laɪsns] (*US* **license**) *n* autorizzazione *f*, permesso; (*COMM*) licenza; (*RADIO, TV*) canone *m*, abbonamento; (*also*: *driving* ~, (*US*) *driver's* ~) patente *f* di guida; (*excessive freedom*) licenza; ~ **number** *n* numero di targa; ~ **plate** *n* targa.

license ['laɪsns] *n* (*US*) = **licence** ♦ *vt* dare una licenza a; ~**d** *adj* (*for alcohol*) che ha la licenza di vendere bibite alcoliche.

lick [lɪk] *vt* leccare; (*inf*: *defeat*) stracciare; **to** ~ **one's lips** (*fig*) leccarsi i baffi.

licorice ['lɪkərɪs] (*US*) *n* = **liquorice**.

lid [lɪd] *n* coperchio; (*eye*~) palpebra.

lie [laɪ] (*pt* **lay**, *pp* **lain**) *vi* (*rest*) giacere; star disteso(a); (*of object*: *be situated*) trovarsi, essere; (*tell lies*: *pt, pp* **lied**) mentire, dire bugie ♦ *n* bugia, menzogna; **to** ~ **low** (*fig*) latitare; ~ **about** *or* **around** *vi* (*things*) essere in giro; (*person*) bighellonare; ~-**down** (*BRIT*) *n*: **to have a** ~-**down** sdraiarsi, riposarsi; ~-**in** (*BRIT*) *n*: **to have a** ~-**in** rimanere a letto.

lieu [lu:]: **in** ~ **of** *prep* invece di, al po-

sto di.

lieutenant [lɛf'tɛnənt, (*US*) lu:'tɛnənt] *n* tenente *m*.

life [laɪf] (*pl* **lives**) *n* vita *f* ♦ *cpd* di vita; della vita; a vita; **to come to** ~ rianimarsi; ~ **assurance** (*BRIT*) *n* = ~ **insurance**; ~**belt** (*BRIT*) *n* salvagente *m*; ~**boat** *n* scialuppa di salvataggio; ~**guard** *n* bagnino; ~ **imprisonment** *n* carcere *m* a vita; ~ **insurance** *n* assicurazione *f* sulla vita; ~ **jacket** *n* giubbotto di salvataggio; ~**less** *adj* senza vita; ~**like** *adj* verosimile; rassomigliante; ~**line** *n*: **it was his** ~**line** era vitale per lui; ~**long** *adj* per tutta la vita; ~ **preserver** (*US*) *n* salvagente *m*; giubbotto di salvataggio; ~ **sentence** *n* ergastolo; ~-**size(d)** *adj* a grandezza naturale; ~ **span** *n* (durata della) vita; ~**style** *n* stile *m* di vita; ~ **support system** *n* respiratore *m* automatico; ~**time** *n*: **in his** ~**time** durante la sua vita; **once in a** ~**time** una volta nella vita.

lift [lɪft] *vt* sollevare; (*ban, rule*) levare ♦ *vi* (*fog*) alzarsi ♦ *n* (*BRIT*: *elevator*) ascensore *m*; **to give sb a** ~ (*BRIT*) dare un passaggio a qn; ~-**off** *n* decollo.

light [laɪt] (*pt, pp* **lighted** *or* **lit**) *n* luce *f*, lume *m*; (*daylight*) luce *f*, giorno; (*lamp*) lampada; (*AUT*: *rear* ~) luce *f* di posizione; (: *headlamp*) fanale *m*; (*for cigarette etc*): **have you got a** ~? ha da accendere?; ~**s** *npl* (*AUT*: *traffic* ~**s**) semaforo ♦ *vt* (*candle, cigarette, fire*) accendere; (*room*): **to be lit by** essere illuminato(a) da ♦ *adj* (*room, colour*) chiaro(a); (*not heavy, also fig*) leggero(a); **to come to** ~ venire alla luce, emergere; ~ **up** *vi* illuminarsi ♦ *vt* illuminare; ~ **bulb** *n* lampadina; ~**en** *vt* (*make less heavy*) alleggerire; ~**er** *n* (*also*: *cigarette* ~**er**) accendino; ~-**headed** *adj* stordito(a); ~-**hearted** *adj* gioioso(a), gaio(a); ~**house** *n* faro; ~**ing** *n* illuminazione *f*; ~**ly** *adv* leggermente; **to get off** ~**ly** cavarsela a buon mercato; ~**ness** *n* chiarezza; (*in weight*) leggerezza.

lightning ['laɪtnɪŋ] n lampo, fulmine m; ~ **conductor** (US ~ **rod**) n parafulmine m.

light pen n penna ottica.

lightweight ['laɪtweɪt] adj (suit) leggero(a) ♦ n (BOXING) peso leggero.

light year n anno m luce inv.

like [laɪk] vt (person) volere bene a; (activity, object, food): **I** ~ **swimming/ that book/chocolate** mi piace nuotare/ quel libro/il cioccolato ♦ prep come ♦ adj simile, uguale ♦ n: **the** ~ uno(a) uguale; **his** ~**s and dislikes** i suoi gusti; **I would** ~, **I'd** ~ mi piacerebbe, vorrei; **would you** ~ **a coffee?** gradirebbe un caffè?; **to be/look** ~ **sb/sth** somigliare a qn/qc; **what does it look/taste** ~? che aspetto/gusto ha?; **what does it sound** ~? come fa?; **that's just** ~ **him** è proprio da lui; **do it** ~ **this** fallo così; **it is nothing** ~ ... non è affatto come ...; ~**able** adj simpatico(a).

likelihood ['laɪklɪhud] n probabilità.

likely ['laɪklɪ] adj probabile; plausibile; **he's** ~ **to leave** probabilmente partirà, è probabile che parta; **not** ~! neanche per sogno!

likeness ['laɪknɪs] n somiglianza.

likewise ['laɪkwaɪz] adv similmente, nello stesso modo.

liking ['laɪkɪŋ] n: ~ (**for**) debole m (per); **to be to sb's** ~ piacere a qn.

lilac ['laɪlək] n lilla m inv.

lily ['lɪlɪ] n giglio; ~ **of the valley** n mughetto.

limb [lɪm] n arto.

limber up ['lɪmbə*-] vi riscaldarsi i muscoli.

limbo ['lɪmbəu] n: **to be in** ~ (fig) essere lasciato(a) nel dimenticatoio.

lime [laɪm] n (tree) tiglio; (fruit) limetta; (GEO) calce f.

limelight ['laɪmlaɪt] n: **in the** ~ (fig) alla ribalta, in vista.

limerick ['lɪmərɪk] n poesiola umoristica di 5 versi.

limestone ['laɪmstəun] n pietra calcarea; (GEO) calcare m.

limit ['lɪmɪt] n limite m ♦ vt limitare; ~**ed** adj limitato(a), ristretto(a); **to be** ~**ed to** limitarsi a; ~**ed** (**liability**) **company** (BRIT) n ≈ società f inv a responsabilità limitata.

limp [lɪmp] n: **to have a** ~ zoppicare ♦ vi zoppicare ♦ adj floscio(a), flaccido(a).

limpet ['lɪmpɪt] n patella.

line [laɪn] n linea; (rope) corda; (for fishing) lenza; (wire) filo; (of poem) verso; (row, series) fila, riga; coda; (on face) ruga ♦ vt (clothes): **to** ~ (**with**) foderare (di); (box): **to** ~ (**with**) rivestire or foderare (di); (subj: trees, crowd) fiancheggiare; ~ **of business** settore m or ramo d'attività; **in** ~ **with** in linea con; ~ **up** vi allinearsi, mettersi in fila ♦ vt mettere in fila; (event, celebration) preparare.

lined [laɪnd] adj (face) rugoso(a); (paper) a righe, rigato(a).

linen ['lɪnɪn] n biancheria, panni mpl; (cloth) tela di lino.

liner ['laɪnə*] n nave f di linea; (for bin) sacchetto.

linesman ['laɪnzmən] n guardalinee m inv.

line-up n allineamento, fila; (SPORT) formazione f di gioco.

linger ['lɪŋgə*] vi attardarsi; indugiare; (smell, tradition) persistere.

lingerie ['lænʒəri:] n biancheria intima femminile.

lingo ['lɪŋgəu] (pl ~**es**) (pej) n gergo.

linguistics [lɪŋ'gwɪstɪks] n linguistica.

lining ['laɪnɪŋ] n fodera.

link [lɪŋk] n (of a chain) anello; (relationship) legame m; (connection) collegamento ♦ vt collegare, unire, congiungere; (associate): **to** ~ **with** or **to** collegare a; ~**s** npl (GOLF) pista or terreno da golf; ~ **up** vt collegare, unire ♦ vi riunirsi; associarsi.

lino ['laɪnəu] n = **linoleum**.

linoleum [lɪ'nəuliəm] n linoleum m inv.

lion ['laɪən] n leone m; ~**ess** n leonessa.

lip [lɪp] n labbro; (of cup etc) orlo; ~**read** vi leggere sulle labbra; ~ **salve** n burro di cacao; ~ **service** n: **to pay** ~ **service to sth** essere favorevole a qc solo a parole; ~**stick** n rossetto.

liqueur [lɪ'kjuə*] n liquore m.
liquid ['lɪkwɪd] n liquido ♦ adj liquido(a).
liquidize ['lɪkwɪdaɪz] vt (CULIN) passare al frullatore; ~r n frullatore m (a brocca).
liquor ['lɪkə*] n alcool m.
liquorice ['lɪkərɪs] (BRIT) n liquirizia.
liquor store (US) n negozio di liquori.
lisp [lɪsp] n pronuncia blesa della "s".
list [lɪst] n lista, elenco ♦ vt (write down) mettere in lista; fare una lista di; (enumerate) elencare; ~ed build-ing (BRIT) n edificio sotto la protezione delle Belle Arti.
listen ['lɪsn] vi ascoltare; **to** ~ **to** ascoltare; ~er n ascoltatore/trice.
listless ['lɪstlɪs] adj apatico(a).
lit [lɪt] pt, pp of **light**.
liter ['li:tə*] (US) n = **litre**.
literacy ['lɪtərəsɪ] n il sapere leggere e scrivere.
literal ['lɪtərl] adj letterale.
literary ['lɪtərərɪ] adj letterario(a).
literate ['lɪtərət] adj che sa leggere e scrivere.
literature ['lɪtərɪtʃə*] n letteratura; (brochures etc) materiale m.
lithe [laɪð] adj agile, snello(a).
litigation [lɪtɪ'geɪʃən] n causa.
litre ['li:tə*] (US **liter**) n litro.
litter ['lɪtə*] n (rubbish) rifiuti mpl; (young animals) figliata; ~ **bin** (BRIT) n cestino per rifiuti; ~ed adj: ~ed with coperto(a) di.
little ['lɪtl] adj (small) piccolo(a); (not much) poco(a) ♦ adv poco; **a** ~ un po' (di); **a** ~ **bit** un pochino; ~ **by** ~ a poco a poco; ~ **finger** n mignolo.
live¹ [lɪv] vi vivere; (reside) vivere, abitare; ~ **down** vt far dimenticare (alla gente); ~ **on** vt fus (food) vivere di; ~ **together** vi vivere insieme, convivere; ~ **up to** vt fus tener fede a, non venir meno a.
live² [laɪv] adj (animal) vivo(a); (wire) sotto tensione; (bullet, missile) ine-sploso(a); (broadcast) diretto(a); (performance) dal vivo.
livelihood ['laɪvlɪhud] n mezzi mpl di so-

stentamento.
lively ['laɪvlɪ] adj vivace, vivo(a).
liven up ['laɪvn'ʌp] vt (discussion, evening) animare ♦ vi ravvivarsi.
liver ['lɪvə*] n fegato.
livery ['lɪvərɪ] n livrea.
lives [laɪvz] npl of **life**.
livestock ['laɪvstɔk] n bestiame m.
livid ['lɪvɪd] adj livido(a); (furious) livido(a) di rabbia, furibondo(a).
living ['lɪvɪŋ] adj vivo(a), vivente ♦ n: **to earn** or **make a** ~ guadagnarsi la vita; ~ **conditions** npl condizioni fpl di vita; ~ **room** n soggiorno; ~ **standards** npl tenore m di vita; ~ **wage** n salario sufficiente per vivere.
lizard ['lɪzəd] n lucertola.
load [ləud] n (weight) peso; (thing carried) carico ♦ vt (also: ~ **up**): **to** ~ (**with**) (lorry, ship) caricare (di); (gun, camera, COMPUT) caricare (con); **a** ~ **of**, ~**s of** (fig) un sacco di; ~**ed** adj (vehicle): ~**ed** (**with**) carico(a) (di); (question) capzioso(a); (inf: rich) carico(a) di soldi.
loaf [ləuf] (pl **loaves**) n pane m, pa-gnotta.
loan [ləun] n prestito ♦ vt dare in pre-stito; **on** ~ in prestito.
loath [ləuθ] adj: **to be** ~ **to do** essere re-stio(a) a fare.
loathe [ləuð] vt detestare, aborrire.
loaves [ləuvz] npl of **loaf**.
lobby ['lɔbɪ] n atrio, vestibolo; (POL: pressure group) gruppo di pressione ♦ vt fare pressione su.
lobster ['lɔbstə*] n aragosta.
local ['ləukl] adj locale ♦ n (BRIT: pub) ≈ bar m inv all'angolo; **the** ~**s** npl (local inhabitants) la gente della zona; ~ **authority** n ente m locale; ~ **call** n (TEL) telefonata urbana; ~ **govern-ment** n amministrazione f locale.
locality [ləu'kælɪtɪ] n località f inv; (position) posto, luogo.
locally ['ləukəlɪ] adv da queste parti; nel vicinato.
locate [ləu'keɪt] vt (find) trovare; (situate) collocare; situare.
location [ləu'keɪʃən] n posizione f; **on** ~

(*CINEMA*) all'esterno.

loch [lɔx] *n* lago.

lock [lɔk] *n* (*of door, box*) serratura; (*of canal*) chiusa; (*of hair*) ciocca, riccio ♦ *vt* (*with key*) chiudere a chiave ♦ *vi* (*door etc*) chiudersi; (*wheels*) bloccarsi, incepparsi; ~ **in** *vt* chiudere dentro (a chiave); ~ **out** *vt* chiudere fuori; ~ **up** *vt* (*criminal, mental patient*) rinchiudere; (*house*) chiudere (a chiave) ♦ *vi* chiudere tutto (a chiave).

locker [ˈlɔkə*] *n* armadietto.

locket [ˈlɔkɪt] *n* medaglione *m*.

locksmith [ˈlɔksmɪθ] *n* magnano.

lock-up (*US*) *n* prigione *f*; guardina.

locomotive [ləukəˈməutɪv] *n* locomotiva.

locum [ˈləukəm] *n* (*MED*) medico sostituto.

locust [ˈləukəst] *n* locusta.

lodge [lɔdʒ] *n* casetta, portineria; (*hunting* ~) casino di caccia ♦ *vi* (*person*): **to** ~ (**with**) essere a pensione (presso *or* da); (*bullet etc*) conficcarsi ♦ *vt* (*appeal etc*) presentare, fare; **to** ~ **a complaint** presentare un reclamo; ~**r** *n* affittuario/a; (*with room and meals*) pensionante *m/f*.

lodgings [ˈlɔdʒɪŋz] *npl* camera d'affitto; camera ammobiliata.

loft [lɔft] *n* solaio, soffitta.

lofty [ˈlɔftɪ] *adj* alto(a); (*haughty*) altezzoso(a).

log [lɔg] *n* (*of wood*) ceppo; (*book*) = **logbook** ♦ *vt* registrare.

logbook [ˈlɔgbuk] *n* (*NAUT, AVIAT*) diario di bordo; (*AUT*) libretto di circolazione.

loggerheads [ˈlɔgəhɛdz] *npl*: **at** ~ (**with**) ai ferri corti (con).

logic [ˈlɔdʒɪk] *n* logica; ~**al** *adj* logico(a).

loin [lɔɪn] *n* (*CULIN*) lombata.

loiter [ˈlɔɪtə*] *vi* attardarsi.

loll [lɔl] *vi* (*also*: ~ **about**) essere stravaccato(a).

lollipop [ˈlɔlɪpɔp] *n* lecca lecca *m inv*; ~ **man/lady** (*BRIT*) *n* impiegato/a che aiuta i bambini ad attraversare la strada in vicinanza di scuole.

London [ˈlʌndən] *n* Londra; ~**er** *n*

londinese *m/f*.

lone [ləun] *adj* solitario(a).

loneliness [ˈləunlɪnɪs] *n* solitudine *f*, isolamento.

lonely [ˈləunlɪ] *adj* solo(a); solitario(a), isolato(a).

long [lɔŋ] *adj* lungo(a) ♦ *adv* a lungo, per molto tempo ♦ *vi*: **to** ~ **for sth/to do** desiderare qc/di fare; non veder l'ora di aver qc/di fare; **so** *or* **as** ~ **as** (*while*) finché; (*provided that*) sempre che + *sub*; **don't be** ~! fai presto!; **how** ~ **is this river/course?** quanto è lungo questo fiume/corso?; **6 metres** ~ lungo 6 metri; **6 months** ~ che dura 6 mesi, di 6 mesi; **all night** ~ tutta la notte; **he no** ~**er comes** non viene più; ~ **before** molto tempo prima; **before** ~ (+*future*) presto, fra poco; (+*past*) poco tempo dopo; **at** ~ **last** finalmente; ~**-distance** *adj* (*race*) di fondo; (*call*) interurbano(a); ~**-haired** *adj* dai capelli lunghi; ~**hand** *n* scrittura normale; ~**ing** *n* desiderio, voglia, brama.

longitude [ˈlɔŋgɪtjuːd] *n* longitudine *f*.

long: ~ **jump** *n* salto in lungo; ~**-life** *adj* (*milk*) a lunga conservazione; (*batteries*) di lunga durata; ~**-lost** *adj* perduto(a) da tempo; ~**-playing record** *n* (disco) 33 giri *m inv*; ~**-range** *adj* a lunga portata; ~**-sighted** *adj* presbite; ~**-standing** *adj* di vecchia data; ~**-suffering** *adj* estremamente paziente, infinitamente tollerante; ~**-term** *adj* a lungo termine; ~ **wave** *n* onde *fpl* lunghe; ~**-winded** *adj* prolisso(a), interminabile.

loo [luː] (*BRIT: inf*) *n* W.C. *m inv*, cesso.

look [luk] *vi* guardare; (*seem*) sembrare, parere; (*building etc*): **to** ~ **south/on to the sea** dare a sud/sul mare ♦ *n* sguardo; (*appearance*) aspetto, aria; ~**s** *npl* (*good* ~**s**) bellezza; ~ **after** *vt fus* occuparsi di, prendere cura di; (*keep an eye on*) guardare, badare a; ~ **at** *vt fus* guardare; ~ **back** *vi*: **to** ~ **back on** (*event etc*) ripensare a; ~ **down on** *vt fus* (*fig*) guardare dall'alto, disprezzare; ~ **for** *vt fus* cercare; ~

forward to *vt fus* non veder l'ora di; (*in letters*): **we ~ forward to hearing from you** in attesa di una vostra gentile risposta; **~ into** *vt fus* esaminare; **~ on** *vi* fare da spettatore; **~ out** *vi* (*beware*): **to ~ out (for)** stare in guardia (per); **~ out for** *vt fus* cercare; **~ round** *vi* (*turn*) girarsi, voltarsi; (*in shop*) dare un'occhiata; **~ to** *vt fus* (*rely on*) contare su; **~ up** *vi* alzare gli occhi; (*improve*) migliorare ♦ *vt* (*word*) cercare; (*friend*) andare a trovare; **~ up to** *vt fus* avere rispetto per; **~-out** *n* posto d'osservazione; guardia; **to be on the ~-out (for)** stare in guardia (per).

loom [lu:m] *n* telaio ♦ *vi* (*also: ~ up*) apparire minaccioso(a); (*event*) essere imminente.

loony ['lu:nɪ] (*inf*) *n* pazzo/a.

loop [lu:p] *n* cappio ♦ *vt*: **to ~ sth round sth** passare qc intorno a qc; **~hole** *n* via d'uscita; scappatoia.

loose [lu:s] *adj* (*knot*) sciolto(a); (*screw*) allentato(a); (*stone*) cadente; (*clothes*) ampio(a), largo(a); (*animal*) in libertà, scappato(a); (*life, morals*) dissoluto(a) ♦ *n*: **to be on the ~** essere in libertà; **~ change** *n* spiccioli *mpl*, moneta; **~ chippings** *npl* (*on road*) ghiaino; **~ end** *n*: **to be at a ~ end** (*BRIT*) or **at ~ ends** (*US*) non saper che fare; **~ly** *adv* senza stringere; approssimativamente; **~n** *vt* sciogliere; (*belt etc*) allentare.

loot [lu:t] *n* bottino ♦ *vt* saccheggiare.

lop [lɔp] *vt* (*also: ~ off*) tagliare via, recidere.

lop-sided ['lɔp'saɪdɪd] *adj* non equilibrato(a), asimmetrico(a).

lord [lɔ:d] *n* signore *m*; **L~ Smith** lord Smith; **the L~** il Signore; **good L~!** buon Dio!; **the (House of) L~s** (*BRIT*) la Camera dei Lord; **~ship** *n*: **your L~ship** Sua Eccellenza.

lore [lɔ:*] *n* tradizioni *fpl*.

lorry ['lɔrɪ] (*BRIT*) *n* camion *m inv*; **~ driver** (*BRIT*) *n* camionista *m*.

lose [lu:z] (*pt, pp* **lost**) *vt* perdere ♦ *vi* perdere; **to ~** (*time*) (*clock*) ritardare;

~r *n* perdente *m/f*.

loss [lɔs] *n* perdita; **to be at a ~** essere perplesso(a).

lost [lɔst] *pt, pp of* **lose** ♦ *adj* perduto(a); **~ property** (*US* **~ and found**) *n* oggetti *mpl* smarriti.

lot [lɔt] *n* (*at auctions*) lotto; (*destiny*) destino, sorte *f*; **the ~** tutto(a) quanto(a); **tutti(e) quanti(e)**; **a ~** molto; **a ~ of** una gran quantità di, un sacco di; **~s of** molto(a); **to draw ~s (for sth)** tirare a sorte (per qc).

lotion ['ləʊʃən] *n* lozione *f*.

lottery ['lɔtərɪ] *n* lotteria.

loud [laʊd] *adj* forte, alto(a); (*gaudy*) vistoso(a), sgargiante ♦ *adv* (*speak etc*) forte; **out ~** (*read etc*) ad alta voce; **~hailer** (*BRIT*) *n* portavoce *m inv*; **~ly** *adv* fortemente, ad alta voce; **~speaker** *n* altoparlante *m*.

lounge [laʊndʒ] *n* salotto, soggiorno; (*at airport, station*) sala d'attesa; (*BRIT*: *also: ~ bar*) bar *m inv* con servizio a tavolino ♦ *vi* oziare; **~ about** or **around** *vi* starsene colle mani in mano; **~ suit** (*BRIT*) *n* completo da uomo.

louse [laʊs] (*pl* **lice**) *n* pidocchio.

lousy ['laʊzɪ] (*inf*) *adj* orrendo(a), schifoso(a); **to feel ~** stare da cani.

lout [laʊt] *n* zoticone *m*.

lovable ['lʌvəbl] *adj* simpatico(a), carino(a); amabile.

love [lʌv] *n* amore *m* ♦ *vt* amare; voler bene a; **to ~ to do: I ~ to do** mi piace fare; **to be/fall in ~ with** essere innamorato(a)/innamorarsi di; **to make ~** fare l'amore; **"15 ~"** (*TENNIS*) "15 a zero"; **~ affair** *n* relazione *f*; **~ life** *n* vita sentimentale.

lovely ['lʌvlɪ] *adj* bello(a); (*delicious: smell, meal*) buono(a).

lover ['lʌvə*] *n* amante *m/f*; (*person in love*) innamorato/a; (*amateur*): **a ~ of** un(un')amante di; un(un')appassionato(a) di.

loving ['lʌvɪŋ] *adj* affettuoso(a).

low [laʊ] *adj* basso(a) ♦ *adv* in basso ♦ *n* (*METEOR*) depressione *f*; **to be ~ on** (*supplies etc*) avere scarsità di; **to feel ~** sentirsi giù; **~-alcohol** *adj* a basso contenuto alcolico; **~-cut** *adj* (*dress*) scollato(a); **~er** *adj* (*bottom*: *of 2 things*) più basso; (*less important*) meno importante ♦ *vt* calare; (*prices, eyes, voice*) abbassare; **~-fat** *adj* magro(a); **~lands** *npl* (GEO) pianura; **~ly** *adj* umile, modesto(a).

loyal ['lɔɪəl] *adj* fedele, leale; **~ty** *n* fedeltà, lealtà.

lozenge ['lɔzɪndʒ] *n* (MED) pastiglia.

L.P. *n abbr* = **long-playing record**.

L-plates (BRIT) *npl* cartelli sui veicoli dei guidatori principianti.

Ltd *abbr* (= *limited*) ≈ S.r.l.

lubricate ['luːbrɪkeɪt] *vt* lubrificare.

luck [lʌk] *n* fortuna, sorte *f*; **bad ~** sfortuna, mala sorte; **good ~!** buona fortuna!; **~ily** *adv* fortunatamente, per fortuna; **~y** *adj* fortunato(a), (*number etc*) che porta fortuna.

ludicrous ['luːdɪkrəs] *adj* ridicolo(a).

lug [lʌg] (*inf*) *vt* trascinare.

luggage ['lʌgɪdʒ] *n* bagagli *mpl*; **~ rack** *n* portabagagli *m inv*.

lukewarm ['luːkwɔːm] *adj* tiepido(a).

lull [lʌl] *n* intervallo di calma ♦ *vt*: **to ~ sb to sleep** cullare qn finché si addormenta; **to be ~ed into a false sense of security** illudersi che tutto vada bene.

lullaby ['lʌləbaɪ] *n* ninnananna.

lumbago [lʌm'beɪgəu] *n* lombaggine *f*.

lumber ['lʌmbə*] *n* (*wood*) legname *m*; (*junk*) roba vecchia; **~ with** *vt*: **to be ~ed with sth** doversi sorbire qc; **~jack** *n* boscaiolo.

luminous ['luːmɪnəs] *adj* luminoso(a).

lump [lʌmp] *n* pezzo; (*in sauce*) grumo; (*swelling*) gonfiore *m*; (*also*: **sugar ~**) zolletta ♦ *vt* (*also*: **~ together**) riunire, mettere insieme; **a ~ sum** una somma globale; **~y** *adj* (*sauce*) pieno(a) di grumi; (*bed*) bitorzoluto(a).

lunatic ['luːnətɪk] *adj* pazzo(a), matto(a).

lunch [lʌntʃ] *n* pranzo, colazione *f*.

luncheon ['lʌntʃən] *n* pranzo; **~ meat** *n* ≈ mortadella; **~ voucher** (BRIT) *n* buono *m* pasto *inv*.

lunch time *n* ora di pranzo.

lung [lʌŋ] *n* polmone *m*.

lunge [lʌndʒ] *vi* (*also*: **~ forward**) fare un balzo in avanti; **to ~ at** balzare su.

lurch [ləːtʃ] *vi* vacillare, barcollare ♦ *n* scatto improvviso; **to leave sb in the ~** piantare in asso qn.

lure [luə*] *n* richiamo; lusinga ♦ *vt* attirare (con l'inganno).

lurid ['luərɪd] *adj* sgargiante; (*details etc*) impressionante.

lurk [ləːk] *vi* stare in agguato.

luscious ['lʌʃəs] *adj* succulento(a); delizioso(a).

lush [lʌʃ] *adj* lussureggiante.

lust [lʌst] *n* lussuria; cupidigia; desiderio; (*fig*): **~ for** sete *f* di; **~ after** *or* **for** *vt fus* bramare, desiderare.

lusty ['lʌstɪ] *adj* vigoroso(a), robusto(a).

Luxembourg ['lʌksəmbəːg] *n* (*state*) Lussemburgo *m*; (*city*) Lussemburgo *f*.

luxuriant [lʌg'zjuərɪənt] *adj* lussureggiante; (*hair*) folto(a).

luxurious [lʌg'zjuərɪəs] *adj* sontuoso(a), di lusso.

luxury ['lʌkʃərɪ] *n* lusso ♦ *cpd* di lusso.

lying ['laɪɪŋ] *n* bugie *fpl*, menzogne *fpl* ♦ *adj* bugiardo(a).

lynch [lɪntʃ] *vt* linciare.

lyrical ['lɪrɪkl] *adj* lirico(a); (*fig*) entusiasta.

lyrics ['lɪrɪks] *npl* (*of song*) parole *fpl*.

M

m. *abbr* = **metre**; **mile**; **million**.

M.A. *abbr* = **Master of Arts**.

mac [mæk] (BRIT) *n* impermeabile *m*.

macaroni [mækə'rəunɪ] *n* maccheroni *mpl*.

machine [mə'ʃiːn] *n* macchina ♦ *vt* (TECH) lavorare a macchina; (*dress etc*) cucire a macchina; **~ gun** *n* mitragliatrice *f*; **~ry** *n* macchinario, macchine *fpl*; (*fig*) macchina.

mackerel ['mækrl] *n inv* sgombro.

mackintosh ['mækɪntɔʃ] (BRIT) *n* impermeabile *m*.

mad [mæd] *adj* matto(a), pazzo(a); (*foolish*) sciocco(a); (*angry*) furioso(a); **to be ~ about** (*keen*) andare pazzo(a) per.

madam ['mædəm] *n* signora.

madden ['mædn] *vt* fare infuriare.

made [meɪd] *pt, pp of* **make**.

Madeira [mə'dɪərə] *n* (*GEO*) Madera; (*wine*) madera.

made-to-measure (*BRIT*) *adj* fatto(a) su misura.

madly ['mædlɪ] *adv* follemente.

madman ['mædmən] *n* pazzo, alienato.

madness ['mædnɪs] *n* pazzia.

magazine [mægə'ziːn] *n* (*PRESS*) rivista; (*RADIO, TV*) rubrica.

maggot ['mægət] *n* baco, verme *m*.

magic ['mædʒɪk] *n* magia ♦ *adj* magico(a); **~al** *adj* magico(a); **~ian** [mə'dʒɪʃən] *n* mago/a.

magistrate ['mædʒɪstreɪt] *n* magistrato; giudice *m/f*.

magnet ['mægnɪt] *n* magnete *m*, calamita; **~ic** [-'nɛtɪk] *adj* magnetico(a).

magnificent [mæg'nɪfɪsnt] *adj* magnifico(a).

magnify ['mægnɪfaɪ] *vt* ingrandire; **~ing glass** *n* lente *f* d'ingrandimento.

magnitude ['mægnɪtjuːd] *n* grandezza; importanza.

magpie ['mægpaɪ] *n* gazza.

mahogany [mə'hɔgənɪ] *n* mogano.

maid [meɪd] *n* domestica; (*in hotel*) cameriera; **old ~** (*pej*) vecchia zitella.

maiden ['meɪdn] *n* fanciulla ♦ *adj* (*aunt etc*) nubile; (*speech, voyage*) inaugurale; **~ name** *n* nome *m* da nubile *or* da ragazza.

mail [meɪl] *n* posta ♦ *vt* spedire (per posta); **~box** (*US*) *n* cassetta delle lettere; **~ing list** *n* elenco d'indirizzi; **~-order** *n* vendita (*or* acquisto) per corrispondenza.

maim [meɪm] *vt* mutilare.

main [meɪn] *adj* principale ♦ *n* (*pipe*) conduttura principale; **the ~s** *npl* (*ELEC*) la linea principale; **in the ~** nel complesso, nell'insieme; **~frame** *n* (*COMPUT*) mainframe *m inv*; **~land** *n* continente *m*; **~ly** *adv* principalmente, soprattutto; **~ road** *n* strada

principale; **~stay** *n* (*fig*) sostegno principale; **~stream** *n* (*fig*) corrente *f* principale.

maintain [meɪn'teɪn] *vt* mantenere; (*affirm*) sostenere; **maintenance** ['meɪntənəns] *n* manutenzione *f*; (*alimony*) alimenti *mpl*.

maize [meɪz] *n* granturco, mais *m*.

majestic [mə'dʒɛstɪk] *adj* maestoso(a).

majesty ['mædʒɪstɪ] *n* maestà *f inv*.

major ['meɪdʒə*] *n* (*MIL*) maggiore *m* ♦ *adj* (*greater, MUS*) maggiore; (*in importance*) principale, importante.

Majorca [mə'jɔːkə] *n* Maiorca.

majority [mə'dʒɔrɪtɪ] *n* maggioranza.

make [meɪk] (*pt, pp* **made**) *vt* fare; (*manufacture*) fare, fabbricare; (*cause to be*): **to ~ sb sad** *etc* rendere qn triste *etc*; (*force*): **to ~ sb do sth** costringere qn a fare qc, far fare qc a qn; (*equal*): **2 and 2 ~ 4** 2 più 2 fa 4 ♦ *n* fabbricazione *f*; (*brand*) marca; **to ~ a fool of sb** far fare a qn la figura dello scemo; **to ~ a profit** realizzare un profitto; **to ~ a loss** subire una perdita; **to ~ it** (*arrive*) arrivare; (*achieve sth*) farcela; **what time do you ~ it?** che ora fai?; **to ~ do with** arrangiarsi con; **~ for** *vt fus* (*place*) avviarsi verso; **~ out** *vt* (*write out*) scrivere; (: *cheque*) emettere; (*understand*) capire; (*see*) distinguere; (: *numbers*) decifrare; **~ up** *vt* (*constitute*) formare; (*invent*) inventare; (*parcel*) fare ♦ *vi* conciliarsi; (*with cosmetics*) truccarsi; **~ up for** *vt fus* compensare; ricuperare; **~-believe** *n*: **a world of ~-believe** un mondo di favole; **it's just ~-believe** è tutta un'invenzione; **~r** *n* (*of programme etc*) creatore/trice; (*manufacturer*) fabbricante *m*; **~shift** *adj* improvvisato(a); **~-up** *n* trucco; **~-up remover** *n* struccatore *m*.

making ['meɪkɪŋ] *n* (*fig*): **in the ~** in formazione; **to have the ~s of** (*actor, athlete etc*) avere la stoffa di.

maladjusted [mælə'dʒʌstɪd] *adj* disadattato(a).

malaise [mæ'leɪz] *n* malessere *m*.

malaria [mə'lɛərɪə] *n* malaria.

Malaya [mə'leɪə] n Malesia.
male [meɪl] n (BIOL) maschio ♦ adj maschile; maschio(a).
malfunction [mæl'fʌŋkʃən] n funzione f difettosa.
malice ['mælɪs] n malevolenza; **malicious** [mə'lɪʃəs] adj malevolo(a); (LAW) doloso(a).
malign [mə'laɪn] vt malignare su; calunniare.
malignant [mə'lɪgnənt] adj (MED) maligno(a).
mall [mɔːl] n (also: shopping ~) centro commerciale.
mallet ['mælɪt] n maglio.
malnutrition [mælnjuː'trɪʃən] n denutrizione f.
malpractice [mæl'præktɪs] n prevaricazione f; negligenza.
malt [mɔːlt] n malto.
Malta ['mɔːltə] n Malta.
mammal ['mæml] n mammifero.
mammoth ['mæməθ] n mammut m inv ♦ adj enorme, gigantesco(a).
man [mæn] (pl men) n uomo ♦ vt fornire d'uomini; stare a; **an old ~** un vecchio; **~ and wife** marito e moglie.
manage ['mænɪdʒ] vi farcela ♦ vt (be in charge of) occuparsi di; gestire; **to ~ to do sth** riuscire a far qc; **~able** adj maneggevole; fattibile; **~ment** n amministrazione f, direzione f; **~r** n direttore m; (of shop, restaurant) gerente m; (of artist, SPORT) manager m inv; **~ress** [-ə'res] n direttrice f; gerente f; **~rial** [-ə'dʒɪərɪəl] adj dirigenziale; **managing director** n amministratore m delegato.
mandarin ['mændərɪn] n (person, fruit) mandarino.
mandatory ['mændətərɪ] adj obbligatorio(a); ingiuntivo(a).
mane [meɪn] n criniera. •
maneuver etc [mə'nuːvə*] (US) = **manoeuvre** etc.
manfully ['mænfəlɪ] adv valorosamente.
mangle ['mæŋgl] vt straziare; mutilare.
mango ['mæŋgəu] (pl ~es) n mango.
mangy ['meɪndʒɪ] adj rognoso(a).
manhandle ['mænhændl] vt malmenare.

manhole ['mænhəul] n botola stradale.
manhood ['mænhud] n età virile; virilità.
man-hour n ora di lavoro.
manhunt ['mænhʌnt] n caccia all'uomo.
mania ['meɪnɪə] n mania; **~c** ['meɪnɪæk] n maniaco/a.
manic ['mænɪk] adj (behaviour, activity) maniacale.
manicure ['mænɪkjuə*] n manicure f inv; **~ set** n trousse f inv della manicure.
manifest ['mænɪfest] vt manifestare ♦ adj manifesto(a), palese.
manifesto [mænɪ'festəu] n manifesto.
manipulate [mə'nɪpjuleɪt] vt manipolare.
mankind [mæn'kaɪnd] n umanità, genere m umano.
manly ['mænlɪ] adj virile; coraggioso(a).
man-made adj sintetico(a); artificiale.
manner ['mænə*] n maniera, modo; (behaviour) modo di fare; (type, sort): **all ~ of things** ogni genere di cosa; **~s** npl (conduct) maniere fpl; **bad ~s** maleducazione f; **~ism** n vezzo, tic m inv.
manoeuvre [mə'nuːvə*] (US **maneuver**) vt manovrare ♦ vi far manovre ♦ n manovra.
manor ['mænə*] n (also: ~ house) maniero.
manpower ['mænpauə*] n manodopera.
mansion ['mænʃən] n casa signorile.
manslaughter ['mænslɔːtə*] n omicidio preterintenzionale.
mantelpiece ['mæntlpiːs] n mensola del caminetto.
manual ['mænjuəl] adj manuale ♦ n manuale m.
manufacture [mænju'fæktʃə*] vt fabbricare ♦ n fabbricazione f, manifattura; **~r** n fabbricante m.
manure [mə'njuə*] n concime m.
manuscript ['mænjuskrɪpt] n manoscritto.
many ['menɪ] adj molti(e) ♦ pron molti(e); **a great ~** moltissimi(e), un gran numero (di); **~ a time** molte

map 146 mass-production

volte.

map [mæp] *n* carta (geografica); ~ **out** *vt* tracciare un piano di.

maple ['meɪpl] *n* acero.

mar [mɑ:*] *vt* sciupare.

marathon ['mærəθən] *n* maratona.

marauder [mə'rɔ:də*] *n* saccheggiatore *m*.

marble ['mɑ:bl] *n* marmo; (*toy*) pallina, bilia.

March [mɑ:tʃ] *n* marzo.

march [mɑ:tʃ] *vi* marciare; sfilare ♦ *n* marcia.

mare [mɛə*] *n* giumenta.

margarine [mɑ:dʒə'ri:n] *n* margarina.

margin ['mɑ:dʒɪn] *n* margine *m*; ~**al (seat)** *n* (*POL*) *seggio elettorale ottenuto con una stretta maggioranza*.

marigold ['mærɪɡəʊld] *n* calendola.

marijuana [mærɪ'wɑ:nə] *n* marijuana.

marine [mə'ri:n] *adj* (*animal, plant*) marino(a); (*forces, engineering*) marittimo(a) ♦ *n* (*BRIT*) fante *m* di marina; (*US*) marine *m inv*.

marital ['mærɪtl] *adj* maritale, coniugale; ~ **status** stato coniugale.

mark [mɑ:k] *n* segno; (*stain*) macchia; (*of skid etc*) traccia; (*BRIT*: *SCOL*) voto; (*SPORT*) bersaglio; (*currency*) marco ♦ *vt* segnare; (*stain*) macchiare; (*indicate*) indicare; (*BRIT*: *SCOL*) dare un voto a; correggere; **to ~ time** segnare il passo; ~**ed** *adj* spiccato(a), chiaro(a); ~**er** *n* (*sign*) segno; (*bookmark*) segnalibro.

market ['mɑ:kɪt] *n* mercato ♦ *vt* (*COMM*) mettere in vendita; ~ **garden** (*BRIT*) *n* orto industriale; ~**ing** *n* marketing *m*; ~ **place** *n* piazza del mercato; (*COMM*) piazza, mercato; ~ **research** *n* indagine *f or* ricerca di mercato.

marksman ['mɑ:ksmən] *n* tiratore *m* scelto.

marmalade ['mɑ:məleɪd] *n* marmellata d'arance.

maroon [mə'ru:n] *vt* (*also fig*): **to be** ~**ed** (**in** *or* **at**) essere abbandonato(a) (in) ♦ *adj* bordeaux *inv*.

marquee [mɑ:'ki:] *n* padiglione *m*.

marquess ['mɑ:kwɪs] *n* = **marquis**.

marquis ['mɑ:kwɪs] *n* marchese *m*.

marriage ['mærɪdʒ] *n* matrimonio; ~ **bureau** *n* agenzia matrimoniale; ~ **certificate** *n* certificato di matrimonio.

married ['mærɪd] *adj* sposato(a); (*life, love*) coniugale, matrimoniale.

marrow ['mærəʊ] *n* midollo; (*vegetable*) zucca.

marry ['mærɪ] *vt* sposare, sposarsi con; (*subj: father, priest etc*) dare in matrimonio ♦ *vi* (*also: get married*) sposarsi.

Mars [mɑ:z] *n* (*planet*) Marte *m*.

marsh [mɑ:ʃ] *n* palude *f*.

marshal ['mɑ:ʃl] *n* maresciallo; (*US*: *fire*) capo; (: *police*) capitano ♦ *vt* (*thoughts, support*) ordinare; (*soldiers*) adunare.

martyr ['mɑ:tə*] *n* martire *m/f*; ~**dom** *n* martirio.

marvel ['mɑ:vl] *n* meraviglia ♦ *vi*: **to ~ (at)** meravigliarsi (di); ~**lous** (*US* ~**ous**) *adj* meraviglioso(a).

Marxist ['mɑ:ksɪst] *adj*, *n* marxista *m/f*.

marzipan ['mɑ:zɪpæn] *n* marzapane *m*.

mascara [mæs'kɑ:rə] *n* mascara *m*.

masculine ['mæskjulɪn] *adj* maschile; (*woman*) mascolino(a).

mash [mæʃ] *vt* passare, schiacciare; ~**ed potatoes** *npl* purè *m* di patate.

mask [mɑ:sk] *n* maschera ♦ *vt* mascherare.

mason ['meɪsn] *n* (*also*: *stone*~) scalpellino; (*also*: *free*~) massone *m*; ~**ry** *n* muratura.

masquerade [mæskə'reɪd] *vi*: **to ~ as** farsi passare per.

mass [mæs] *n* moltitudine *f*, massa; (*PHYSICS*) massa; (*REL*) messa ♦ *cpd* di massa ♦ *vi* ammassarsi; **the ~es** *npl* (*ordinary people*) le masse; ~**es of** (*inf*) una montagna di.

massacre ['mæsəkə*] *n* massacro.

massage ['mæsɑ:ʒ] *n* massaggio.

masseur [mæ'sə:*] *n* massaggiatore *m*; **masseuse** [-'sə:z] *n* massaggiatrice *f*.

massive ['mæsɪv] *adj* enorme, massiccio(a).

mass media *npl* mass media *mpl*.

mass-production *n* produzione *f* in

serie.

mast [mɑːst] n albero.

master ['mɑːstə*] n padrone m; (ART etc, teacher: in primary school) maestro; (: in secondary school) professore m; (title for boys): M~ X Signorino X ♦ vt domare; (learn) imparare a fondo; (understand) conoscere a fondo; ~ **key** n chiave f maestra; ~**ly** adj magistrale; ~**mind** n mente f superiore ♦ vt essere il cervello di; **M~ of Arts/ Science** n Master m inv in lettere/ scienze; ~**piece** n capolavoro; ~**y** n dominio; padronanza.

mat [mæt] n stuoia; (also: door~) stoino, zerbino; (also: table ~) sottopiatto ♦ adj = **matt**.

match [mætʃ] n fiammifero; (game) partita, incontro; (fig) uguale m/f; (matrimonio; partito ♦ vt intonare; (go well with) andare benissimo con; (equal) uguagliare; (correspond to) corrispondere a; (pair: also: ~ **up**) accoppiare ♦ vi combaciare; **to be a good** ~ andare bene; ~**box** n scatola per fiammiferi; ~**ing** adj ben assortito(a).

mate [meɪt] n compagno/a di lavoro; (inf: friend) amico/a; (animal) compagno/a; (in merchant navy) secondo ♦ vi accopplarsi.

material [məˈtɪərɪəl] n (substance) materiale m, materia; (cloth) stoffa ♦ adj materiale; ~**s** npl (equipment) materiali mpl.

maternal [məˈtəːnl] adj materno(a).

maternity [məˈtəːnɪtɪ] n maternità; ~ **dress** n vestito m pre-maman inv; ~ **hospital** n ≈ clinica ostetrica.

math [mæθ] (US) n = **maths**.

mathematical [mæθəˈmætɪkl] adj matematico(a).

mathematics [mæθəˈmætɪks] n matematica.

maths [mæθs] (US **math**) n matematica.

matinée ['mætɪneɪ] n matinée f inv.

mating call ['meɪtɪŋ-] n richiamo sessuale.

matriculation [mətrɪkjuˈleɪʃən] n immatricolazione f.

matrimonial [mætrɪˈməʊnɪəl] adj matrimoniale, coniugale.

matrimony ['mætrɪmənɪ] n matrimonio.

matron ['meɪtrən] n (in hospital) capoinfermiera; (in school) infermiera.

mat(t) [mæt] adj opaco(a).

matted ['mætɪd] adj ingarbugliato(a).

matter ['mætə*] n questione f; (PHYSICS) materia, sostanza; (content) contenuto; (MED: pus) pus m ♦ vi importare; **it doesn't** ~ non importa; (I don't mind) non fa niente; **what's the** ~? che cosa c'è?; **no** ~ **what** qualsiasi cosa accada; **as a** ~ **of course** come cosa naturale; **as a** ~ **of fact** in verità; ~-**of-fact** adj prosaico(a).

mattress ['mætrɪs] n materasso.

mature [məˈtjuə*] adj maturo(a); (cheese) stagionato(a) ♦ vi maturare; stagionare.

maul [mɔːl] vt lacerare.

mauve [məʊv] adj malva inv.

maverick ['mævərɪk] n chi sta fuori dal branco.

maxim ['mæksɪm] n massima.

maxima ['mæksɪmə] npl of **maximum**.

maximum ['mæksɪməm] (pl **maxima**) adj massimo(a) ♦ n massimo.

May [meɪ] n maggio.

may [meɪ] (conditional: **might**) vi (indicating possibility): **he** ~ **come** può darsi che venga; (be allowed to): ~ **I smoke?** posso fumare?; (wishes): ~ **God bless you!** Dio la benedica!; **you** ~ **as well go** tanto vale che tu te ne vada.

maybe ['meɪbiː] adv forse, può darsi; ~ **he'll** ... può darsi che lui ... + sub, forse lui ....

May Day n il primo maggio.

mayhem ['meɪhem] n cagnara.

mayonnaise [meɪəˈneɪz] n maionese f.

mayor [mɛə*] n sindaco; ~**ess** n sindaco (donna); moglie f del sindaco.

maze [meɪz] n labirinto, dedalo.

M.D. abbr = **Doctor of Medicine**.

me [miː] pron mi, m' + vowel or silent "h"; (stressed, after prep) me; **he heard** ~ mi ha or m'ha sentito; **give** ~ **a book** dammi (or mi dia) un libro; **it's** ~ sono io; **with** ~ con me; **without** ~

senza di me.

meadow ['mɛdəu] n prato.

meagre ['mi:gə*] (US **meager**) adj magro(a).

meal [mi:l] n pasto; (flour) farina; ~**time** n l'ora di mangiare.

mean [mi:n] (pt, pp **meant**) adj (with money) avaro(a), gretto(a); (unkind) meschino(a), maligno(a); (shabby) misero(a); (average) medio(a) ♦ vt (signify) significare, voler dire; (intend): **to ~ to do** aver l'intenzione di fare ♦ n mezzo; (MATH) media; ~**s** npl (way, money) mezzi mpl; **by ~s of** per mezzo di; **by all ~s** ma certo, prego; **to be meant for** essere destinato a; **do you ~ it?** dice sul serio?; **what do you ~?** che cosa vuol dire?

meander [mɪ'ændə*] vi far meandri.

meaning ['mi:nɪŋ] n significato, senso; ~**ful** adj significativo(a); ~**less** adj senza senso.

meant [mɛnt] pt, pp of **mean**.

meantime ['mi:ntaɪm] adv (also: **in the ~**) nel frattempo.

meanwhile ['mi:nwaɪl] adv nel frattempo.

measles ['mi:zlz] n morbillo.

measly ['mi:zlɪ] (inf) adj miserabile.

measure ['mɛʒə*] vt, vi misurare ♦ n misura; (also: tape ~) metro; ~**ments** npl (size) misure fpl.

meat [mi:t] n carne f; **cold ~** affettato; ~**ball** n polpetta di carne; **~ pie** n pasticcio di carne in crosta.

Mecca ['mɛkə] n (also fig) la Mecca.

mechanic [mɪ'kænɪk] n meccanico; ~**al** adj meccanico(a); ~**s** n meccanica ♦ npl meccanismo.

mechanism ['mɛkənɪzəm] n meccanismo.

medal ['mɛdl] n medaglia; ~**lion** [mɪ'dælɪən] n medaglione m; ~**list** (US ~**ist**) n (SPORT): **to be a gold ~list** essere medaglia d'oro.

meddle ['mɛdl] vi: **to ~ in** immischiarsi in, mettere le mani in; **to ~ with** toccare.

media ['mi:dɪə] npl media mpl.

mediaeval [mɛdɪ'i:vl] adj = **medieval**.

median ['mi:dɪən] (US) n (also: **~ strip**) banchina f spartitraffico.

mediate ['mi:dɪeɪt] vi fare da mediatore/trice.

Medicaid ['mɛdɪkeɪd] (US) n assistenza medica ai poveri.

medical ['mɛdɪkl] adj medico(a) ♦ n visita medica.

Medicare ['mɛdɪkeə*] (US) n assistenza medica agli anziani.

medication [mɛdɪ'keɪʃən] n medicinali mpl, farmaci mpl.

medicine ['mɛdsɪn] n medicina.

medieval [mɛdɪ'i:vl] adj medievale.

mediocre [mi:dɪ'əukə*] adj mediocre.

meditate ['mɛdɪteɪt] vi: **to ~ (on)** meditare (su).

Mediterranean [mɛdɪtə'reɪnɪən] adj mediterraneo(a); **the ~ (Sea)** il (mare) Mediterraneo.

medium ['mi:dɪəm] (pl **media**) adj medio(a) ♦ n (means) mezzo; (pl **mediums**: person) medium m inv; ~**wave** n onde fpl medie.

medley ['mɛdlɪ] n selezione f; (MUS) pot-pourri m inv.

meek [mi:k] adj dolce, umile.

meet [mi:t], (pt, pp **met**) vt incontrare; (for the first time) fare la conoscenza di; (go and fetch) andare a prendere; (fig) affrontare; soddisfare; raggiungere ♦ vi incontrarsi; (in session) riunirsi; (join: objects) unirsi; **~ with** vt fus incontrare; ~**ing** n incontro; (session: of club etc) riunione f; (interview) intervista; **she's at a ~ing** (COMM) è in riunione.

megabyte ['mɛgəbaɪt] n (COMPUT) megabyte m inv.

megaphone ['mɛgəfəun] n megafono.

melancholy ['mɛlənkəlɪ] n malinconia ♦ adj malinconico(a).

mellow ['mɛləu] adj (wine, sound) ricco(a); (light) dolce; (colour) caldo(a) ♦ vi (person) addolcirsi.

melody ['mɛlədɪ] n melodia.

melon ['mɛlən] n melone m.

melt [mɛlt] vi (gen) sciogliersi, struggersi; (metals) fondersi ♦ vt sciogliere, struggere; fondere; **~ down** vt fondere; ~ **down** vt fondere; ~**down** n (in nuclear reactor) fusione f (dovuta a surriscaldamento); ~**ing pot** n (fig) crogiolo.

member ['mɛmbə*] n membro; **M~ of the European Parliament** (BRIT) n eurodeputato; **M~ of Parliament** (BRIT) n deputato; ~**ship** n iscrizione f; (numero d')iscritti mpl, membri mpl; ~**ship card** n tessera (di iscrizione).

memento [mə'mɛntəu] n ricordo, souvenir m inv.

memo ['mɛməu] n appunto; (COMM etc) comunicazione f di servizio.

memoirs ['mɛmwɑ:z] npl memorie fpl, ricordi mpl.

memoranda [mɛmə'rændə] npl of **memorandum**.

memorandum [mɛmə'rændəm] (pl **memoranda**) n appunto; (COMM etc) comunicazione f di servizio.

memorial [mɪ'mɔ:rɪəl] n monumento commemorativo ♦ adj commemorativo(a).

memorize ['mɛməraɪz] vt memorizzare.

memory ['mɛmərɪ] n (also COMPUT) memoria; (recollection) ricordo.

men [mɛn] npl of **man**.

menace ['mɛnəs] n minaccia ♦ vt minacciare.

mend [mɛnd] vt aggiustare, riparare; (darn) rammendare ♦ n: **on the ~** in via di guarigione; **to ~ one's ways** correggersi.

menial ['mi:nɪəl] adj da servo, domestico(a); umile.

meningitis [mɛnɪn'dʒaɪtɪs] n meningite f.

menopause ['mɛnəupɔ:z] n menopausa.

menstruation [mɛnstru'eɪʃən] n mestruazione f.

mental ['mɛntl] adj mentale.

mentality [mɛn'tælɪtɪ] n mentalità f inv.

menthol ['mɛnθɔl] n mentolo.

mention ['mɛnʃən] n menzione f ♦ vt menzionare, far menzione di; **don't ~ it!** non c'è di che!, prego!

menu ['mɛnju:] n (set ~, COMPUT) menù m inv; (printed) carta.

MEP n abbr = **Member of the European Parliament**.

mercenary ['mə:sɪnərɪ] adj venale ♦ n mercenario.

merchandise ['mə:tʃəndaɪz] n merci fpl.

merchant ['mə:tʃənt] n mercante m, commerciante m; ~ **bank** (BRIT) n banca d'affari; ~ **navy** (US ~ **marine**) n marina mercantile.

merciful ['mə:sɪful] adj pietoso(a), clemente.

merciless ['mə:sɪlɪs] adj spietato(a).

mercury ['mə:kjurɪ] n mercurio.

mercy ['mə:sɪ] n pietà; (REL) misericordia; **at the ~ of** alla mercè di.

mere [mɪə*] adj semplice; **by a ~ chance** per mero caso; ~**ly** adv semplicemente, non ... che.

merge [mə:dʒ] vt unire ♦ vi fondersi, unirsi; (COMM) fondersi; ~**r** n (COMM) fusione f.

meringue [mə'ræŋ] n meringa.

merit ['mɛrɪt] n merito, valore m ♦ vt meritare.

mermaid ['mə:meɪd] n sirena.

merry ['mɛrɪ] adj gaio(a), allegro(a); **M~ Christmas!** Buon Natale!; ~**-go-round** n carosello.

mesh [mɛʃ] n maglia; rete f.

mesmerize ['mɛzməraɪz] vt ipnotizzare; affascinare.

mess [mɛs] n confusione f, disordine m; (fig) pasticcio; (dirt) sporcizia; (MIL) mensa; ~ **about** (inf) vi (also: ~ around) trastullarsi; ~ **about with** (inf) vt fus (also: ~ around with) gingillarsi con; (plans) fare un pasticcio di; ~ **up** vt sporcare; fare un pasticcio di; rovinare.

message ['mɛsɪdʒ] n messaggio.

messenger ['mɛsɪndʒə*] n messaggero/a.

Messrs ['mɛsəz] abbr (on letters) Spett.

messy ['mɛsɪ] adj sporco(a); disordinato(a).

met [mɛt] pt, pp of **meet**.

metal ['mɛtl] n metallo; ~**lic** [-'tælɪk] adj metallico(a).

metaphor ['mɛtəfə*] n metafora.

mete [mi:t] vt: **to ~ out** vt infliggere.

meteorology [mi:tɪə'rɔlədʒɪ] n meteorologia.

m; (*parking* ~) parchimetro; (*US: unit*) = metre.

method ['mɛθəd] *n* metodo; ~**ical** [mɪ'θɒdɪkl] *adj* metodico(a).

Methodist ['mɛθədɪst] *n* metodista *m/f*.

meths [mɛθs] (*BRIT*) *n* = **methylated spirit**.

methylated spirit ['mɛθɪleɪtɪd-] (*BRIT*) *n* alcool *m* denaturato.

metre ['miːtə*] (*US* **meter**) *n* metro.

metric ['mɛtrɪk] *adj* metrico(a).

metropolitan [mɛtrə'pɒlɪtən] *adj* metropolitano(a); **the M~ Police** (*BRIT*) *n* la polizia di Londra.

mettle ['mɛtl] *n*: **to be on one's ~** essere pronto(a) a dare il meglio di se stesso(a).

mew [mjuː] *vi* (*cat*) miagolare.

mews [mjuːz] (*BRIT*) *n*: ~ **flat** *appartamento ricavato da un'antica scuderia.*

Mexico ['mɛksɪkəu] *n* Messico.

miaow [miː'au] *vi* miagolare.

mice [maɪs] *npl of* **mouse**.

micro... ['maɪkrəu] *prefix* micro...; ~**chip** *n* microcircuito integrato; ~**(computer)** *n* microcomputer *m inv*; ~**film** *n* microfilm *m inv*; ~**phone** *n* microfono; ~**scope** *n* microscopio; ~**wave** *n* (*also*: ~*wave oven*) forno a microonde.

mid [mɪd] *adj*: ~ **May** metà maggio; ~ **afternoon** metà pomeriggio; **in ~ air** a mezz'aria; ~**day** *n* mezzogiorno.

middle ['mɪdl] *n* mezzo; centro; (*waist*) vita ♦ *adj* di mezzo; **in the ~ of the night** nel bel mezzo della notte; ~**-aged** *adj* di mezza età; **the M~ Ages** *npl* il Medioevo; ~**-class** *adj* ≈ borghese; **the ~ class(es)** *n(pl)* ≈ la borghesia; **M~ East** *n* Medio Oriente *m*; ~**man** *n* intermediario; agente *m* rivenditore; ~**name** *n* secondo nome *m*; ~**-of-the-road** *adj* moderato(a); ~**weight** *n* (*BOXING*) peso medio.

middling ['mɪdlɪŋ] *adj* medio(a).

midge [mɪdʒ] *n* moscerino.

midget ['mɪdʒɪt] *n* nano/a.

Midlands ['mɪdləndz] *npl contee del centro dell'Inghilterra.*

midnight ['mɪdnaɪt] *n* mezzanotte *f*.

midriff ['mɪdrɪf] *n* diaframma *m*.

midst [mɪdst] *n*: **in the ~ of** in mezzo a.

midsummer [mɪd'sʌmə*] *n* mezza *or* piena estate *f*.

midway [mɪd'weɪ] *adj, adv*: ~ **(between)** a mezza strada (fra); ~ **(through)** a metà (di).

midweek [mɪd'wiːk] *adv* a metà settimana.

midwife ['mɪdwaɪf] (*pl* **midwives**) *n* levatrice *f*.

midwinter [mɪd'wɪntə*] *n*: **in ~** in pieno inverno.

midwives ['mɪdwaɪvz] *npl of* **midwife**.

might [maɪt] *vb see* **may** ♦ *n* potere *m*, forza; ~**y** *adj* forte, potente.

migraine ['miːgreɪn] *n* emicrania.

migrant ['maɪgrənt] *adj* (*bird*) migratore(trice); (*worker*) emigrato(a).

migrate [maɪ'greɪt] *vi* (*bird*) migrare; (*person*) emigrare.

mike [maɪk] *n abbr* (= *microphone*) microfono.

Milan [mɪ'læn] *n* Milano *f*.

mild [maɪld] *adj* mite; (*person, voice*) dolce; (*flavour*) delicato(a); (*illness*) leggero(a); (*interest*) blando(a).

mildew ['mɪldjuː] *n* muffa.

mildly ['maɪldlɪ] *adv* mitemente; dolcemente; delicatamente; leggermente; blandamente; **to put it ~** a dire poco.

mile [maɪl] *n* miglio; ~**age** *n* distanza in miglia, ≈ chilometraggio.

mileometer [maɪ'lɒmɪtə*] *n* ≈ contachilometri *m inv*.

milestone ['maɪlstəun] *n* pietra miliare.

milieu ['miːljəː] *n* ambiente *m*.

militant ['mɪlɪtnt] *adj* militante.

military ['mɪlɪtərɪ] *adj* militare.

militate ['mɪlɪteɪt] *vi*: **to ~ against** essere d'ostacolo a.

milk [mɪlk] *n* latte *m* ♦ *vt* (*cow*) mungere; (*fig*) sfruttare; ~ **chocolate** *n* cioccolato al latte; ~**man** *n* lattaio; ~ **shake** *n* frappé *m inv*; ~**y** *adj* lattiginoso(a); (*colour*) latteo(a); **M~y Way** *n* Via Lattea.

mill [mɪl] *n* mulino; (*small: for coffee,*

pepper etc) macinino; (*factory*) fabbrica; (*spinning* ~) filatura ♦ *vt* macinare ♦ *vi* (*also*: ~ *about*) brulicare.

miller ['mɪlə*] *n* mugnaio.

milli... ['mɪlɪ] *prefix*: ~**gram(me)** *n* milligrammo; ~**metre** (*US* ~**meter**) *n* millimetro.

millinery ['mɪlɪnərɪ] *n* modisteria.

million ['mɪljən] *n* milione *m*; ~**aire** *n* milionario, ≈ miliardario.

milometer [maɪ'lɔmɪtə*] *n* = **mileometer.**

mime [maɪm] *n* mimo ♦ *vt, vi* mimare.

mimic ['mɪmɪk] *n* imitatore/trice ♦ *vt* fare la mimica di.

min. *abbr* = **minute(s)**; **minimum.**

mince [mɪns] *vt* tritare, macinare ♦ *vi* (*in walking*) camminare a passettini ♦ *n* (*BRIT: CULIN*) carne *f* tritata *or* macinata; ~**meat** *n frutta secca tritata per uso in pasticceria*; (*US*) carne *f* tritata *or* macinata; ~ **pie** *n specie di torta con frutta secca*; ~**r** *n* tritacarne *m inv.*

mind [maɪnd] *n* mente *f* ♦ *vt* (*attend to, look after*) badare a, occuparsi di; (*be careful*) fare attenzione a, stare attento(a) a; (*object to*): **I don't** ~ **the noise** il rumore non mi dà alcun fastidio; **I don't** ~ non m'importa; **it is on my** ~ mi preoccupa; **to my** ~ secondo me, a mio parere; **to be out of one's** ~ essere uscito(a) di mente; **to keep** *or* **bear sth in** ~ non dimenticare qn; **to make up one's** ~ decidersi; ~ **you, ...** sì, però va detto che ...; **never** ~ non importa, non fa niente; (*don't worry*) non preoccuparti; "~ **the step**" "attenzione allo scalino"; ~**er** *n* (*child* ~*er*) bambinaia; (*bodyguard*) guardia del corpo; ~**ful** *adj*: ~**ful of** attento(a) a; memore di; ~**less** *adj* idiota.

mine¹ [maɪn] *pron* il(la) mio(a), *pl* i(le) miei(mie); **that book is** ~ quel libro è mio; **yours is red,** ~ **is green** il tuo è rosso, il mio è verde; **a friend of** ~ un mio amico.

mine² [maɪn] *n* miniera; (*explosive*) mina ♦ *vt* (*coal*) estrarre; (*ship, beach*)

minare; ~**field** *n* (*also fig*) campo minato.

miner ['maɪnə*] *n* minatore *m*.

mineral ['mɪnərəl] *adj* minerale ♦ *n* minerale *m*; ~**s** *npl* (*BRIT: soft drinks*) bevande *fpl* gasate; ~ **water** *n* acqua minerale.

mingle ['mɪŋgl] *vi*: **to** ~ **with** mescolarsi a, mischiarsi con.

miniature ['mɪnətʃə*] *adj* in miniatura ♦ *n* miniatura.

minibus ['mɪnɪbʌs] *n* minibus *m inv.*

minim ['mɪnɪm] *n* (*MUS*) minima.

minima ['mɪnɪmə] *npl of* **minimum.**

minimum ['mɪnɪməm] (*pl* **minima**) *n* minimo ♦ *adj* minimo(a).

mining ['maɪnɪŋ] *n* industria mineraria.

miniskirt ['mɪnɪskə:t] *n* minigonna.

minister ['mɪnɪstə*] *n* (*BRIT. POL*) ministro; (*REL*) pastore *m* ♦ *vi*: **to** ~ **to sb** assistere qn; **to** ~ **to sb's needs** provvedere ai bisogni di qn; ~**ial** [-'tɪərɪəl] (*BRIT*) *adj* (*POL*) ministeriale.

ministry ['mɪnɪstrɪ] *n* (*BRIT: POL*) ministero; (*REL*): **to go into the** ~ diventare pastore.

mink [mɪŋk] *n* visone *m*.

minnow ['mɪnəu] *n* pesciolino d'acqua dolce.

minor ['maɪnə*] *adj* minore, di poca importanza; (*MUS*) minore ♦ *n* (*LAW*) minorenne *m/f*.

minority [maɪ'nɔrɪtɪ] *n* minoranza.

mint [mɪnt] *n* (*plant*) menta; (*sweet*) pasticca di menta ♦ *vt* (*coins*) battere; **the (Royal) M~** (*BRIT*), **the (US) M~** (*US*) la Zecca; **in** ~ **condition** come nuovo(a) di zecca.

minus ['maɪnəs] *n* (*also*: ~ *sign*) segno meno ♦ *prep* meno.

minute [*adj* maɪ'nju:t, *n* 'mɪnɪt] *adj* minuscolo(a); (*detail*) minuzioso(a) ♦ *n* minuto; ~**s** *npl* (*of meeting*) verbale *m*.

miracle ['mɪrəkl] *n* miracolo.

mirage ['mɪrɑ:ʒ] *n* miraggio.

mirror ['mɪrə*] *n* specchio; (*in car*) specchietto.

mirth [mə:θ] *n* ilarità.

misadventure [mɪsəd'ventʃə*] *n* disavventura; **death by** ~ morte *f* accidentale.

misapprehension ['mɪsæprɪ'hɛnʃən] *n* malinteso.

misappropriate [mɪsə'prəuprɪeɪt] *vt* appropriarsi indebitamente di.

misbehave [mɪsbɪ'heɪv] *vi* comportarsi male.

miscarriage ['mɪskærɪdʒ] *n* (*MED*) aborto spontaneo; ~ **of justice** errore *m* giudiziario.

miscellaneous [mɪsɪ'leɪnɪəs] *adj* (*items*) vario(a); (*selection*) misto(a).

mischance [mɪs'tʃɑ:ns] *n* sfortuna.

mischief ['mɪstʃɪf] *n* (*naughtiness*) birichineria; (*maliciousness*) malizia; **mischievous** *adj* birichino(a).

misconception ['mɪskən'sɛpʃən] *n* idea sbagliata.

misconduct [mɪs'kɔndʌkt] *n* cattiva condotta; **professional** ~ reato professionale.

misdemeanour [mɪsdɪ'mi:nə*] (*US* **misdemeanor**) *n* misfatto; infrazione *f*.

miser ['maɪzə*] *n* avaro.

miserable ['mɪzərəbl] *adj* infelice; (*wretched*) miserabile; (*weather*) deprimente; (*offer, failure*) misero(a).

miserly ['maɪzəlɪ] *adj* avaro(a).

misery ['mɪzərɪ] *n* (*unhappiness*) tristezza; (*wretchedness*) miseria.

misfire [mɪs'faɪə*] *vi* far cilecca; (*car engine*) perdere colpi.

misfit ['mɪsfɪt] *n* (*person*) spostato/a.

misfortune [mɪs'fɔ:tʃən] *n* sfortuna.

misgiving [mɪs'gɪvɪn] *n* apprensione *f*; **to have ~s about** avere dei dubbi per quanto riguarda.

misguided [mɪs'gaɪdɪd] *adj* sbagliato(a); poco giudizioso(a).

mishandle [mɪs'hændl] *vt* (*mismanage*) trattare male.

mishap ['mɪshæp] *n* disgrazia.

misinterpret [mɪsɪn'tə:prɪt] *vt* interpretare male.

misjudge [mɪs'dʒʌdʒ] *vt* giudicare male.

mislay [mɪs'leɪ] (*irreg*) *vt* smarrire.

mislead [mɪs'li:d] (*irreg*) *vt* sviare; **~ing** *adj* ingannevole.

mismanage [mɪs'mænɪdʒ] *vt* gestire male.

misnomer [mɪs'nəumə*] *n* termine *m* sbagliato *or* improprio.

misplace [mɪs'pleɪs] *vt* smarrire.

misprint ['mɪsprɪnt] *n* errore *m* di stampa.

Miss [mɪs] *n* Signorina. .

miss [mɪs] *vt* (*fail to get*) perdere; (*fail to hit*) mancare; (*fail to see*): **you can't ~ it** non puoi non vederlo; (*regret the absence of*): **I ~ him** sento la sua mancanza ♦ *vi* mancare ♦ *n* (*shot*) colpo mancato; ~ **out** (*BRIT*) *vt* omettere.

misshapen [mɪs'ʃeɪpən] *adj* deforme.

missile ['mɪsaɪl] *n* (*MIL*) missile *m*; (*object thrown*) proiettile *m*.

missing ['mɪsɪn] *adj* perso(a), smarrito(a); (*person*) scomparso(a); (: *after disaster*, *MIL*) disperso(a); (*removed*) mancante; **to be ~** mancare.

mission ['mɪʃən] *n* missione *f*; **~ary** *n* missionario/a.

misspent ['mɪs'spɛnt] *adj*: **his ~ youth** la sua gioventù sciupata.

mist [mɪst] *n* nebbia, foschia ♦ *vi* (*also*: ~ **over**, ~ **up**) annebbiarsi; (: *BRIT*: *windows*) appannarsi.

mistake [mɪs'teɪk] (*irreg*: *like* **take**) *n* sbaglio, errore *m* ♦ *vt* sbagliarsi di; fraintendere; **to make a ~** fare uno sbaglio, sbagliare; **by ~** per sbaglio; **to ~ for** prendere per; **mistaken** *pp* of **mistake** ♦ *adj* (*idea etc*) sbagliato(a); **to be mistaken** sbagliarsi. .

mister ['mɪstə*] (*inf*) *n* signore *m*; *see* **Mr.**

mistletoe ['mɪsltəu] *n* vischio.

mistook [mɪs'tuk] *pt of* **mistake**.

mistress ['mɪstrɪs] *n* padrona; (*lover*) amante *f*; (*BRIT*: *SCOL*) insegnante *f*.

mistrust [mɪs'trʌst] *vt* diffidare di.

misty ['mɪstɪ] *adj* nebbioso(a), brumoso(a).

misunderstand [mɪsʌndə'stænd] (*irreg*) *vt*, *vi* capire male, fraintendere; **~ing** *n* malinteso, equivoco.

misuse [*n* mɪs'ju:s, *vb* mɪs'ju:z] *n* cattivo uso; (*of power*) abuso ♦ *vt* far cattivo uso di; abusare di.

mitigate ['mɪtɪgeɪt] *vt* mitigare.

mitt(en) ['mɪt(n)] n mezzo guanto; manopola.

mix [mɪks] vt mescolare ♦ vi (people): **to ~ with** avere a che fare con ♦ n mescolanza; preparato; **~ up** vt mescolare; (confuse) confondere; **~ed** adj misto(a); **~ed-up** adj (confused) confuso(a); **~er** n (for food: electric) frullatore m; (: hand) frullino; (person): **he is a good ~er** è molto socievole; **~ture** n mescolanza; (blend: of tobacco etc) miscela; (MED) sciroppo; **~-up** n confusione f.

moan [məun] n gemito ♦ vi (inf: complain): **to ~ (about)** lamentarsi (di).

moat [məut] n fossato.

mob [mɔb] n calca ♦ vt accalcarsi intorno a.

mobile ['məubaɪl] adj mobile ♦ n (decoration) mobile m; **~ home** n grande roulotte f inv (utilizzata come domicilio).

mock [mɔk] vt deridere, burlarsi di ♦ adj falso(a); **~ery** n derisione f; **to make a ~ery of** burlarsi di; (exam, trial) rendere una farsa; **~-up** n modello.

mod [mɔd] adj see **convenience**.

mode [məud] n modo.

model ['mɔdl] n modello; (person: for fashion) indossatore/trice; (: for artist) modello/a ♦ adj (small-scale: railway etc) in miniatura; (child, factory) modello inv ♦ vt modellare ♦ vi fare l'indossatore (or l'indossatrice); **to ~ clothes** presentare degli abiti.

modem ['məudɛm] n modem m inv.

moderate [adj 'mɔdərət, vb 'mɔdəreɪt] adj moderato(a) ♦ vi moderarsi, placarsi ♦ vt moderare.

modern ['mɔdən] adj moderno(a); **~ize** vt modernizzare.

modest ['mɔdɪst] adj modesto(a); **~y** n modestia.

modicum ['mɔdɪkəm] n: **a ~ of** un minimo di.

modify ['mɔdɪfaɪ] vt modificare.

mogul ['məugl] n (fig) magnate m, pezzo grosso.

mohair ['məuhɛə*] n mohair m.

moist [mɔɪst] adj umido(a); **~en** ['mɔɪsn] vt inumidire; **~ure** ['mɔɪstʃə*] n umidità; (on glass) goccioline fpl di vapore; **~urizer** ['mɔɪstʃəraɪzə*] n idratante f.

molar ['məulə*] n molare m.

mold [məuld] (US) n, vt = **mould**.

mole [məul] n (animal, fig) talpa; (spot) neo.

molest [məu'lɛst] vt molestare.

mollycoddle ['mɔlɪkɔdl] vt coccolare, vezzeggiare.

molt [məult] (US) vi = **moult**.

molten ['məultən] adj fuso(a).

mom [mɔm] (US) n = **mum**.

moment ['məumənt] n momento, istante m; **at that ~** in quel momento; **at the ~** al momento, in questo momento; **~ary** adj momentaneo(a), passeggero(a), **~ous** [-'mɛntəs] adj di grande importanza.

momentum [məu'mɛntəm] n (PHYSICS) momento; (fig) impeto; **to gather ~** aumentare di velocità.

mommy ['mɔmɪ] (US) n = **mummy**.

Monaco ['mɔnəkəu] n Principato di Monaco.

monarch ['mɔnək] n monarca m; **~y** n monarchia.

monastery ['mɔnəstərɪ] n monastero.

Monday ['mʌndɪ] n lunedì m inv.

monetary ['mʌnɪtərɪ] adj monetario(a).

money ['mʌnɪ] n denaro, soldi mpl; **~ order** n vaglia m inv; **~-spinner** (inf) n miniera d'oro (fig).

mongol ['mɔŋgəl] adj, n (MED) mongoloide m/f.

mongrel ['mʌŋgrəl] n (dog) cane m bastardo.

monitor ['mɔnɪtə*] n (TV, COMPUT) monitor m inv ♦ vt controllare.

monk [mʌŋk] n monaco.

monkey ['mʌŋkɪ] n scimmia; **~ nut** (BRIT) n nocciolina americana; **~ wrench** n chiave f a rullino.

mono ['mɔnəu] adj (recording) (in) mono inv.

monopoly [mə'nɔpəlɪ] n monopolio.

monotone ['mɔnətəun] n pronunzia (or voce f) monotona.

monotonous [mə'nɔtənəs] *adj* monotono(a).

monsoon [mɔn'suːn] *n* monsone *m*.

monster ['mɔnstə*] *n* mostro.

monstrous ['mɔnstrəs] *adj* mostruoso(a); (*huge*) gigantesco(a).

montage [mɔn'tɑːʒ] *n* montaggio.

month [mʌnθ] *n* mese *m*; ~**ly** *adj* mensile ♦ *adv* al mese; ogni mese.

monument ['mɔnjumənt] *n* monumento.

moo [muː] *vi* muggire, mugghiare.

mood [muːd] *n* umore *m*; **to be in a good/bad** ~ essere di buon/cattivo umore; ~**y** *adj* (*variable*) capriccioso(a), lunatico(a); (*sullen*) imbronciato(a).

moon [muːn] *n* luna; ~**light** *n* chiaro di luna; ~**lighting** *n* lavoro nero; ~**lit** *adj*: **a** ~**lit night** una notte rischiarata dalla luna.

moor [muə*] *n* brughiera ♦ *vt* (*ship*) ormeggiare ♦ *vi* ormeggiarsi.

moorland ['muələnd] *n* brughiera.

moose [muːs] *n inv* alce *m*.

mop [mɔp] *n* lavapavimenti *m inv*; (*also*: ~ **of hair**) zazzera ♦ *vt* lavare con lo straccio; (*face*) asciugare; ~ **up** *vt* asciugare con uno straccio.

mope [məup] *vi* fare il broncio.

moped ['məuped] *n* ciclomotore *m*.

moral ['mɔrl] *adj* morale ♦ *n* morale *f*; ~**s** *npl* (*principles*) moralità.

morale [mɔ'rɑːl] *n* morale *m*.

morality [mə'rælıtı] *n* moralità.

morass [mə'ræs] *n* palude *f*, pantano.

morbid ['mɔːbɪd] *adj* morboso(a).

┌─────────────┐
│ *KEYWORD* │
└─────────────┘

more [mɔː*] *adj* **1** (*greater in number etc*) più; ~ **people/letters than we expected** più persone/lettere di quante ne aspettavamo; **I have** ~ **wine/money than you** ho più vino/soldi di te; **I have** ~ **wine than beer** ho più vino che birra

2 (*additional*) altro(a), ancora; **do you want (some)** ~ **tea?** vuole dell'altro tè?, vuole ancora del tè?; **I have no** *or* **I don't have any** ~ **money** non ho più soldi

♦ *pron* **1** (*greater amount*) più; ~ **than**

10 più di 10; **it cost** ~ **than we expected** ha costato più di quanto ci aspettavamo

2 (*further or additional amount*) ancora; **is there any** ~? ce n'è ancora?; **there's no** ~ non ce n'è più; **a little** ~ ancora un po'; **many/much** ~ molti(e)/molto(a) di più

♦ *adv*: ~ **dangerous/easily (than)** più pericoloso/facilmente (di); ~ **and** ~ sempre più di più; ~ **and** ~ **difficult** sempre più difficile; ~ **or less** più o meno; ~ **than ever** più che mai.

moreover [mɔː'rəuvə*] *adv* inoltre, di più.

morgue [mɔːg] *n* obitorio.

morning ['mɔːnɪŋ] *n* mattina, mattino; (*duration*) mattinata ♦ *cpd* del mattino; **in the** ~ la mattina; **7 o'clock in the** ~ le 7 di *or* della mattina; ~ **sickness** *n* nausee *fpl* mattutine.

Morocco [mə'rɔkəu] *n* Marocco.

moron ['mɔːrɔn] (*inf*) *n* deficiente *m/f*.

morose [mə'rəus] *adj* cupo(a), tetro(a).

Morse [mɔːs] *n* (*also*: ~ **code**) alfabeto Morse.

morsel ['mɔːsl] *n* boccone *m*.

mortal ['mɔːtl] *adj* mortale ♦ *n* mortale *m*.

mortar ['mɔːtə*] *n* mortaio; (*CONSTR*) malta.

mortgage ['mɔːgɪdʒ] *n* ipoteca; (*loan*) prestito ipotecario ♦ *vt* ipotecare; ~ **company** (*US*) *n* società *f inv* di credito immobiliare.

mortuary ['mɔːtjuərɪ] *n* camera mortuaria; obitorio.

mosaic [məu'zeɪɪk] *n* mosaico.

Moscow ['mɔskəu] *n* Mosca.

Moslem ['mɔzləm] *adj*, *n* = **Muslim**.

mosque [mɔsk] *n* moschea.

mosquito [mɔs'kiːtəu] (*pl* ~**es**) *n* zanzara.

moss [mɔs] *n* muschio.

most [məust] *adj* (*almost all*) la maggior parte di; (*largest, greatest*): **who has (the)** ~ **money?** chi ha più soldi di tutti? ♦ *pron* la maggior parte ♦ *adv* più; (*work, sleep etc*) di più; (*very*) molto, estremamente; **the** ~

(*also*: +*adjective*) il(la) più; ~ of la maggior parte di; ~ of them quasi tutti; **I** saw (the) ~ ho visto più io; **at the (very)** ~ al massimo; **to make the** ~ **of** trarre il massimo vantaggio da; **a** ~ **interesting book** un libro estremamente interessante; ~**ly** *adv* per lo più.

MOT (*BRIT*) *n abbr* (= *Ministry of Transport*): **the** ~ (**test**) *revisione annuale obbligatoria degli autoveicoli.*

motel (*BRIT*) *n* motel *m inv.*

moth [mɔθ] *n* farfalla notturna; tarma; ~**ball** *n* pallina di naftalina.

mother ['mʌðə*] *n* madre *f* ♦ *vt* (*care for*) fare da madre a; ~**hood** *n* maternità; ~**-in-law** *n* suocera; ~**ly** *adj* materno(a); ~**-of-pearl** *n* madreperla; ~**-to-be** *n* futura mamma; ~ **tongue** *n* madrelingua.

motion ['məuʃən] *n* movimento, moto; (*gesture*) gesto; (*at meeting*) mozione *f* ♦ *vt, vi*: **to** ~ (**to**) **sb to do** fare cenno a qn di fare; ~**less** *adj* immobile; ~ **picture** *n* film *m inv.*

motivated ['məutɪveɪtɪd] *adj* motivato(a).

motive ['məutɪv] *n* motivo.

motley ['mɔtlɪ] *adj* eterogeneo(a), molto vario(a).

motor ['məutə*] *n* motore *m*; (*BRIT*: *inf*: *vehicle*) macchina ♦ *cpd* automobilistico(a); ~**bike** *n* moto *f inv*; ~**boat** *n* motoscafo; ~**car** (*BRIT*) *n* automobile *f*; ~**cycle** *n* motocicletta; ~**cyclist** *n* motociclista *m/f*; ~**ing** (*BRIT*) *n* turismo automobilistico; ~**ist** *n* automobilista *m/f*; ~ **racing** (*BRIT*) *n* corse *fpl* automobilistiche; ~**way** (*BRIT*) *n* autostrada.

mottled ['mɔtld] *adj* chiazzato(a), marezzato(a).

motto ['mɔtəu] (*pl* ~**es**) *n* motto.

mould [məuld] (*US* **mold**) *n* forma, stampo; (*mildew*) muffa ♦ *vt* formare; (*fig*) foggiare; ~**y** *adj* ammuffito(a); (*smell*) di muffa.

moult [məult] (*US* **molt**) *vi* far la muta.

mound [maund] *n* rialzo, collinetta; (*heap*) mucchio.

mount [maunt] *n* (*GEO*) monte *m* ♦ *vt* montare; (*horse*) montare a ♦ *vi* (*increase*) aumentare; ~ **up** *vi* (*build up*) accumularsi.

mountain ['mauntɪn] *n* montagna ♦ *cpd* di montagna; ~**eer** [-'nɪə*] *n* alpinista *m/f*; ~**eering** [-'nɪərɪŋ] *n* alpinismo; ~**ous** *adj* montagnoso(a); ~ **rescue team** *n* squadra di soccorso alpino; ~**side** *n* fianco della montagna.

mourn [mɔ:n] *vt* piangere, lamentare ♦ *vi*: **to** ~ (**for sb**) piangere (la morte di qn); ~**er** *n* parente *m/f or* amico/a del defunto; ~**ful** *adj* triste, lugubre; ~**ing** *n* lutto; **in** ~**ing** in lutto.

mouse [maus] (*pl* **mice**) *n* topo; (*COMPUT*) mouse *m inv*; ~**trap** *n* trappola per i topi.

mousse [mu:s] *n* mousse *f inv.*

moustache [məs'tɑ:ʃ] (*US* **mustache**) *n* baffi *mpl.*

mousy ['mausɪ] *adj* (*hair*) né chiaro(a) né scuro(a).

mouth [mauθ, *pl* mauðz] *n* bocca; (*of river*) bocca, foce *f*; (*opening*) orifizio; ~**ful** *n* boccata; ~ **organ** *n* armonica; ~**piece** *n* (*of musical instrument*) imboccatura, bocchino; (*spokesman*) portavoce *m/f inv*; ~**wash** *n* collutorio; ~**-watering** *adj* che fa venire l'acquolina in bocca.

movable ['mu:vəbl] *adj* mobile.

move [mu:v] *n* (*movement*) movimento; (*in game*) mossa; (: *turn to play*) turno; (*change: of house*) trasloco; (: *of job*) cambiamento ♦ *vt* muovere, spostare; (*emotionally*) commuovere; (*POL: resolution etc*) proporre ♦ *vi* (*gen*) muoversi, spostarsi; (*also*: ~ *house*) cambiar casa, traslocare; **to get a** ~ **on** affrettarsi, sbrigarsi; **to** ~ **sb to do sth** indurre *or* spingere qn a fare qc; **to** ~ **towards** andare verso; ~ **about** *or* **around** *vi* spostarsi; ~ **along** *vi* muoversi avanti; ~ **away** *vi* allontanarsi, andarsene; ~ **back** *vi* (*return*) ritornare; ~ **forward** *vi* avanzare; ~ **in** *vi* (*to a house*) entrare (in una nuova casa); (*police etc*) intervenire; ~ **on** *vi* riprendere la strada; ~ **out** *vi* (*of house*) sgombrare; ~ **over** *vi* spostarsi; ~ **up** *vi* avanzare.

moveable ['mu:vəbl] *adj* = **movable**.

movement ['mu:vmənt] *n* (*gen*) movimento; (*gesture*) gesto; (*of stars, water, physical*) moto.

movie ['mu:vɪ] *n* film *m inv*; **the** ~**s** il cinema; ~ **camera** *n* cinepresa.

moving ['mu:vɪŋ] *adj* mobile; (*causing emotion*) commovente.

mow [məʊ] (*pt* **mowed**, *pp* **mowed** *or* **mown**) *vt* (*grass*) tagliare; (*corn*) mietere; ~ **down** *vt* falciare; ~**er** *n* (*also: lawnmower*) tagliaerba *m inv*; **mown** *pp* of **mow**.

MP *n abbr* = **Member of Parliament**.

m.p.h. *abbr* = **miles per hour** (60 *m.p.h.* = 96 *km/h*).

Mr ['mɪstə*] (*US* **Mr.**) *n*: ~ **X** Signor X, Sig. X.

Mrs ['mɪsɪz]`(*US* **Mrs.**) *n*: ~ **X** Signora X, Sig.ra X.

Ms [mɪz] (*US* **Ms.**) *n* (= *Miss or Mrs*): ~ **X** ≈ Signora X, Sig.ra X.

M.Sc. *abbr* = **Master of Science**.

───────────
KEYWORD
───────────

much [mʌtʃ] *adj, pron* molto(a); **he's done so ~ work** ha lavorato così tanto; **I have as ~ money as you** ho tanti soldi quanti ne hai tu; **how ~ is it?** quant'è?; **it costs too ~** costa troppo; **as ~ as you want** quanto vuoi
♦ *adv* **1** (*greatly*) molto, tanto; **thank you very ~** molte grazie; **he's very ~ the gentleman** è il vero gentiluomo; **I read as ~ as I can** leggo quanto posso; **as ~ as you** tanto quanto te
2 (*by far*) molto; **it's ~ the biggest company in Europe** è di gran lunga la più grossa società in Europa
3 (*almost*) grossomodo, praticamente; **they're ~ the same** sono praticamente uguali.

───────────────

muck [mʌk] *n* (*dirt*) sporcizia; ~ **about** *or* **around** (*inf*) *vi* fare lo stupido; (*waste time*) gingillarsi; ~ **up** (*inf*) *vt* (*ruin*) rovinare.

mud [mʌd] *n* fango.

muddle ['mʌdl] *n* confusione *f*, disordine *m*; pasticcio ♦ *vt* (*also*: ~ **up**) confondere; ~ **through** *vi* cavarsela alla meno peggio.

muddy ['mʌdɪ] *adj* fangoso(a).

mudguard ['mʌdgɑ:d] *n* parafango.

muesli ['mju:zlɪ] *n* muesli *m*.

muffin ['mʌfɪn] *n* specie di pasticcino soffice da tè.

muffle ['mʌfl] *vt* (*sound*) smorzare, attutire; (*against cold*) imbacuccare.

muffler ['mʌflə*] (*US*) *n* (*AUT*) marmitta; (: *on motorbike*) silenziatore *m*.

mug [mʌg] *n* (*cup*) tazzone *m*; (*for beer*) boccale *m*; (*inf*: *face*) muso; (: *fool*) scemo/a ♦ *vt* (*assault*) assalire; ~**ging** *n* assalto.

muggy ['mʌgɪ] *adj* afoso(a).

mule [mju:l] *n* mulo.

mull over [mʌl-] *vt* rimuginare.

multi-level ['mʌltɪ-] (*US*) *adj* = **multistorey**.

multiple ['mʌltɪpl] *adj* multiplo(a); molteplice ♦ *n* multiplo; ~ **sclerosis** *n* sclerosi *f* a placche.

multiplication [mʌltɪplɪ'keɪʃən] *n* moltiplicazione *f*.

multiply ['mʌltɪplaɪ] *vt* moltiplicare ♦ *vi* moltiplicarsi.

multistorey ['mʌltɪ'stɔ:rɪ] (*BRIT*) *adj* (*building, car park*) a più piani.

mum [mʌm] (*BRIT*: *inf*) *n* mamma ♦ *adj*: **to keep ~** non aprire bocca.

mumble ['mʌmbl] *vt, vi* borbottare.

mummy ['mʌmɪ] *n* (*BRIT*: *mother*) mamma; (*embalmed*) mummia.

mumps [mʌmps] *n* orecchioni *mpl*.

munch [mʌntʃ] *vt, vi* sgranocchiare.

mundane [mʌn'deɪn] *adj* terra a terra *inv*.

municipal [mju:'nɪsɪpl] *adj* municipale.

mural ['mjʊərl] *n* dipinto murale.

murder ['mɜ:də*] *n* assassinio, omicidio ♦ *vt* assassinare; ~**er** *n* omicida *m*, assassino; ~**ous** *adj* omicida.

murky ['mɜ:kɪ] *adj* tenebroso(a).

murmur ['mɜ:mə*] *n* mormorio ♦ *vt, vi* mormorare.

muscle ['mʌsl] *n* muscolo; (*fig*) forza;

~ **in** *vi* immischiarsi.
muscular ['mʌskjulə*] *adj* muscolare; (*person, arm*) muscoloso(a).
muse [mju:z] *vi* meditare, sognare ♦ *n* musa.
museum [mju:'zɪəm] *n* museo.
mushroom ['mʌʃrum] *n* fungo ♦ *vi* crescere in fretta.
music ['mju:zɪk] *n* musica; ~**al** *adj* musicale; (*person*) portato(a) per la musica ♦ *n* (*show*) commedia musicale; ~**al instrument** *n* strumento musicale; ~ **hall** *n* teatro di varietà; ~**ian** [-'zɪʃən] *n* musicista *m/f*.
musk [mʌsk] *n* muschio.
Muslim ['mʌzlɪm] *adj, n* musulmano(a).
muslin ['mʌzlɪn] *n* mussola.
mussel ['mʌsl] *n* cozza.
must [mʌst] *aux vb* (*obligation*): **I** ~ **do it** devo farlo; (*probability*): **he** ~ **be there by now** dovrebbe essere arrivato ormai; **I** ~ **have made a mistake** devo essermi sbagliato ♦ *n*: **it's a** ~ è d'obbligo.
mustache ['mʌstæʃ] (*US*) *n* = **moustache.**
mustard ['mʌstəd] *n* senape *f*, mostarda.
muster ['mʌstə*] *vt* radunare.
mustn't ['mʌsnt] = **must not.**
musty ['mʌstɪ] *adj* che sa di muffa *or* di rinchiuso.
mute [mju:t] *adj, n* muto(a).
muted ['mju:tɪd] *adj* smorzato(a).
mutiny ['mju:tɪnɪ] *n* ammutinamento.
mutter ['mʌtə*] *vt, vi* borbottare, brontolare.
mutton ['mʌtn] *n* carne *f* di montone.
mutual ['mju:tʃuəl] *adj* mutuo(a), reciproco(a); ~**ly** *adv* reciprocamente.
muzzle ['mʌzl] *n* muso; (*protective device*) museruola; (*of gun*) bocca ♦ *vt* mettere la museruola a.
my [maɪ] *adj* il(la) mio(a), *pl* i(le) miei(mie); ~ **house** la mia casa; ~ **books** i miei libri; ~ **brother** mio fratello; **I've washed** ~ **hair/cut** ~ **finger** mi sono lavato i capelli/tagliato il dito.
myself [maɪ'self] *pron* (*reflexive*) mi;

(*emphatic*) io stesso(a); (*after prep*) me; *see also* **oneself.**
mysterious [mɪs'tɪərɪəs] *adj* misterioso(a).
mystery ['mɪstərɪ] *n* mistero.
mystify ['mɪstɪfaɪ] *vt* mistificare; (*puzzle*) confondere.
mystique [mɪs'ti:k] *n* fascino.
myth [mɪθ] *n* mito; ~**ology** [mɪ'θɔlədʒɪ] *n* mitologia.

N

n/a *abbr* = **not applicable.**
nag [næg] *vt* tormentare ♦ *vi* brontolare in continuazione; ~**ging** *adj* (*doubt, pain*) persistente.
nail [neɪl] *n* (*human*) unghia; (*metal*) chiodo ♦ *vt* inchiodare; **to** ~ **sb down to** (**doing**) **sth** costringere qn a (fare) qc; ~**brush** *n* spazzolino da *or* per unghie; ~**file** *n* lima da *or* per unghie; ~ **polish** *n* smalto da *or* per unghie; ~ **polish remover** *n* acetone *m*, solvente *m*; ~ **scissors** *npl* forbici *fpl* da *or* per unghie; ~ **varnish** (*BRIT*) *n* = ~ **polish.**
naïve [naɪ'i:v] *adj* ingenuo(a).
naked ['neɪkɪd] *adj* nudo(a).
name [neɪm] *n* nome *m*; (*reputation*) nome, reputazione *f* ♦ *vt* (*baby etc*) chiamare; (*plant, illness*) nominare; (*person, object*) identificare; (*price, date*) fissare; **what's your** ~? come si chiama?; **by** ~ di nome; **she knows them all by** ~ li conosce tutti per nome; ~**less** *adj* senza nome; ~**ly** *adv* cioè; ~**sake** *n* omonimo.
nanny ['nænɪ] *n* bambinaia.
nap [næp] *n* (*sleep*) pisolino; (*of cloth*) peluria; **to be caught** ~**ping** essere preso alla sprovvista.
nape [neɪp] *n*: ~ **of the neck** nuca.
napkin ['næpkɪn] *n* (*also: table* ~) tovagliolo.
nappy ['næpɪ] (*BRIT*) *n* pannolino; ~ **rash** *n* arrossamento (causato dal pannolino).
narcissi [nɑ:'sɪsaɪ] *npl of* **narcissus.**
narcissus [nɑ:'sɪsəs] (*pl* **narcissi**) *n*

narciso.

narcotic [nɑːˈkɒtɪk] n narcotico ♦ adj narcotico(a).

narrative [ˈnærətɪv] n narrativa.

narrow [ˈnærəu] adj stretto(a); (fig) limitato(a), ristretto(a) ♦ vi restringersi; **to have a ~ escape** farcela per un pelo; **to ~ sth down to** ridurre qc a; **~ly** adv per un pelo; (time) per poco; **~-minded** adj meschino(a).

nasty [ˈnɑːstɪ] adj (person, remark: unpleasant) cattivo(a); (: rude) villano(a); (smell, wound, situation) brutto(a).

nation [ˈneɪʃən] n nazione f.

national [ˈnæʃənl] adj nazionale ♦ n cittadino/a; **~ dress** n costume m nazionale; **N~ Health Service** (BRIT) n servizio nazionale di assistenza sanitaria, ≈ S.A.U.B. f; **N~ Insurance** (BRIT) n ≈ Previdenza Sociale; **~ism** n nazionalismo; **~ity** [-ˈnælɪtɪ] n nazionalità f inv; **~ize** vt nazionalizzare; **~ly** adv a livello nazionale.

nationwide [ˈneɪʃənwaɪd] adj diffuso(a) in tutto il paese ♦ adv in tutto il paese.

native [ˈneɪtɪv] n abitante m/f del paese; (of tribe etc) indigeno/a ♦ adj indigeno(a); (country) natio(a); (ability) innato(a); **a ~ of Russia** un nativo della Russia; **a ~ speaker of French** una persona di madrelingua francese; **~ language** n madrelingua.

Nativity [nəˈtɪvɪtɪ] n: **the ~** la Natività.

NATO [ˈneɪtəu] n abbr (= North Atlantic Treaty Organization) N.A.T.O. f.

natural [ˈnætʃrəl] adj naturale; (ability) innato(a); (manner) semplice; **~ gas** n gas m metano; **~ize** vt naturalizzare; **to become ~ized** (person) naturalizzarsi; (plant) acclimatarsi; **~ly** adv naturalmente; (by nature: gifted) di natura.

nature [ˈneɪtʃə*] n natura; (character) natura, indole f; **by ~** di natura.

naught [nɔːt] n = nought.

naughty [ˈnɔːtɪ] adj (child) birichino(a), cattivello(a); (story, film) spinto(a).

nausea [ˈnɔːsɪə] n (MED) nausea; (fig: disgust) schifo; **~te** [ˈnɔːsɪeɪt] vt nauseare; far schifo a.

nautical [ˈnɔːtɪkl] adj nautico(a).

naval [ˈneɪvl] adj navale; **~ officer** n ufficiale m di marina.

nave [neɪv] n navata centrale.

navel [ˈneɪvl] n ombelico.

navigate [ˈnævɪɡeɪt] vt percorrere navigando ♦ vi navigare; (AUT) fare da navigatore; **navigation** [-ˈɡeɪʃən] n navigazione f; **navigator** n (NAUT, AVIAT) ufficiale m di rotta; (explorer) navigatore m; (AUT) copilota m/f.

navvy [ˈnævɪ] (BRIT) n manovale m.

navy [ˈneɪvɪ] n marina; **~(-blue)** adj blu scuro inv.

Nazi [ˈnɑːtsɪ] n nazista m/f.

NB abbr (= nota bene) N.B.

near [nɪə*] adj vicino(a); (relation) prossimo(a) ♦ adv vicino ♦ prep (also: ~ to) vicino a, presso; (: time) verso ♦ vt avvicinarsi a; **~by** [nɪəˈbaɪ] adj vicino(a) ♦ adv vicino; **~ly** adv quasi; **I ~ly fell** per poco non sono caduto; **~ miss** n: **that was a ~ miss** c'è mancato poco; **~side** n (AUT: in Britain) lato sinistro; (: in US, Europe etc) lato destro; **~-sighted** adj miope.

neat [niːt] adj (person, room) ordinato(a); (work) pulito(a); (solution, plan) ben indovinato(a), azzeccato(a); (spirits) liscio(a); **~ly** adv con ordine; (skilfully) abilmente.

necessarily [ˈnɛsɪsrɪlɪ] adv necessariamente.

necessary [ˈnɛsɪsrɪ] adj necessario(a).

necessity [nɪˈsɛsɪtɪ] n necessità f inv.

neck [nɛk] n collo; (of garment) colletto ♦ vi (inf) pomiciare, sbaciucchiarsi; **~ and ~** testa a testa.

necklace [ˈnɛklɪs] n collana.

neckline [ˈnɛklaɪn] n scollatura.

necktie [ˈnɛktaɪ] n cravatta.

née [neɪ] adj: **~ Scott** nata Scott.

need [niːd] n bisogno ♦ vt aver bisogno di; **to ~ to do** dover fare; aver bisogno di fare; **you don't ~ to go** non devi andare, non c'è bisogno che tu vada.

needle [ˈniːdl] n ago; (on record player)

puntina ♦ *vt* punzecchiare.
needless ['ni:dlɪs] *adj* inutile.
needlework ['ni:dlwə:k] *n* cucito.
needn't ['ni:dnt] = **need not.**
needy ['ni:dɪ] *adj* bisognoso(a).
negative ['negətɪv] *n* (*LING*) negazione *f*; (*PHOT*) negativo ♦ *adj* negativo(a).
neglect [nɪ'glɛkt] *vt* trascurare ♦ *n* (*of person, duty*) negligenza; (*of child, house etc*) scarsa cura; **state of ~** stato di abbandono.
negligee ['nɛglɪʒeɪ] *n* négligé *m inv*.
negligence ['nɛglɪdʒəns] *n* negligenza.
negligible ['nɛglɪdʒɪbl] *adj* insignificante, trascurabile.
negotiable [nɪ'gəuʃɪəbl] *adj* (*cheque*) trasferibile.
negotiate [nɪ'gəuʃɪeɪt] *vi*: **to ~ (with)** negoziare (con) ♦ *vt* (*COMM*) negoziare; (*obstacle*) superare; **negotiation** [-'eɪʃən] *n* negoziato, trattativa.
Negress ['ni:grɪs] *n* negra.
Negro ['ni:grəu] (*pl* ~**es**) *adj, n* negro(a).
neigh [neɪ] *vi* nitrire.
neighbour ['neɪbə*] (*US* **neighbor**) *n* vicino/a; ~**hood** *n* vicinato; ~**ing** *adj* vicino(a); ~**ly** *adj*: **he is a ~ly person** è un buon vicino.
neither ['naɪðə*] *adj, pron* né l'uno(a) né l'altro(a), nessuno(a) dei(delle) due ♦ *conj* neanche, nemmeno, neppure ♦ *adv*: **~ good nor bad** né buono né cattivo; **I didn't move and ~ did Claude** io non mi mossi e nemmeno Claude; ..., **~ did I refuse** ..., ma non ho nemmeno rifiutato.
neon ['ni:ɔn] *n* neon *m*; **~ light** *n* luce *f* al neon.
nephew ['nɛvju:] *n* nipote *m*.
nerve [nə:v] *n* nervo; (*fig*) coraggio; (*impudence*) faccia tosta; **a fit of ~s** una crisi di nervi; ~-**racking** *adj* che spezza i nervi.
nervous ['nə:vəs] *adj* nervoso(a); (*anxious*) agitato(a), in apprensione; ~ **breakdown** *n* esaurimento nervoso.
nest [nɛst] *n* nido ♦ *vi* fare il nido, nidificare; ~ **egg** *n* (*fig*) gruzzolo.
nestle ['nɛsl] *vi* accoccolarsi.

net [nɛt] *n* rete *f* ♦ *adj* netto(a) ♦ *vt* (*fish etc*) prendere con la rete; (*profit*) ricavare un utile netto di; ~**ball** *n* specie di pallacanestro; ~ **curtains** *npl* tende *fpl* di tulle.
Netherlands ['nɛðələndz] *npl*: **the ~ i** Paesi Bassi.
nett [nɛt] *adj* = **net.**
netting ['nɛtɪŋ] *n* (*for fence etc*) reticolato.
nettle ['nɛtl] *n* ortica.
network ['nɛtwə:k] *n* rete *f*.
neurotic [njuə'rɔtɪk] *adj, n* nevrotico(a).
neuter ['nju:tə*] *adj* neutro(a) ♦ *vt* (*cat etc*) castrare.
neutral ['nju:trəl] *adj* neutro(a); (*person, nation*) neutrale ♦ *n* (*AUT*): **in ~** in folle; ~**ize** *vt* neutralizzare.
never ['nɛvə*] *adv* (non...) mai; ~ **again** mai più; **I'll ~ go there again** non ci vado più; ~ **in my life** mai in vita mia; *see also* **mind**; ~-**ending** *adj* interminabile; ~**theless** [nɛvəðə'lɛs] *adv* tuttavia, ciò nonostante, ciò nondimeno.
new [nju:] *adj* nuovo(a); (*brand new*) nuovo di zecca; ~-**born** *adj* neonato(a); ~-**comer** ['nju:kʌmə*] *n* nuovo(a) venuto(a); ~-**fangled** ['nju:fæŋgld] (*pej*) *adj* stramoderno(a); ~-**found** *adj* nuovo(a); ~**ly** *adv* di recente; ~**ly-weds** *npl* sposini *mpl*, sposi *mpl* novelli.
news [nju:z] *n* notizie *fpl*; (*RADIO*) giornale *m* radio; (*TV*) telegiornale *m*; **a piece of ~** una notizia; ~ **agency** *n* agenzia di stampa; ~**agent** (*BRIT*) *n* giornalaio; ~**caster** *n* (*RADIO, TV*) annunciatore/trice; ~**dealer** (*US*) *n* = ~**agent**; ~ **flash** *n* notizia *f* lampo *inv*; ~**letter** *n* bollettino; ~**paper** *n* giornale *m*; ~**print** *n* carta da giornale; ~**reader** *n* = ~**caster**; ~**reel** *n* cinegiornale *m*; ~ **stand** *n* edicola.
newt [nju:t] *n* tritone *m*.
New Year *n* Anno Nuovo; ~'**s Day** *n* il Capodanno; ~'**s Eve** *n* la vigilia di Capodanno.
New York [-'jɔ:k] *n* New York *f*.
New Zealand [-'zi:lənd] *n* Nuova Zelanda; ~**er** *n* neozelandese *m/f*.

next [nɛkst] *adj* prossimo(a) ♦ *adv* accanto; (*in time*) dopo; **the ~ day** il giorno dopo, l'indomani; **~ time** la prossima volta; **~ year** l'anno prossimo; **when do we meet ~?** quando ci rincontriamo?; **~ to** accanto a; **~ to nothing** quasi niente; **~ please!** (avanti) il prossimo!; **~ door** *adv, adj* accanto *inv*; **~-of-kin** *n* parente *m/f* prossimo(a).

NHS *n abbr* = **National Health Service.**

nib [nɪb] *n* (*of pen*) pennino.

nibble [ˈnɪbl] *vt* mordicchiare.

Nicaragua [nɪkəˈrægjuə] *n* Nicaragua *m.*

nice [naɪs] *adj* (*holiday, trip*) piacevole; (*flat, picture*) bello/a; (*person*) simpatico/a, gentile; **~ly** *adv* bene.

niceties [ˈnaɪsɪtɪz] *npl* finezze *fpl.*

nick [nɪk] *n* taglietto; tacca ♦ *vt* (*inf*) rubare; **in the ~ of time** appena in tempo.

nickel [ˈnɪkl] *n* nichel *m*; (*US*) moneta da cinque centesimi di dollaro.

nickname [ˈnɪkneɪm] *n* soprannome *m* ♦ *vt* soprannominare.

niece [niːs] *n* nipote *f.*

Nigeria [naɪˈdʒɪərɪə] *n* Nigeria *f.*

nigger [ˈnɪgə*] (*inf!*) *n* (*highly offensive*) negro/a.

niggling [ˈnɪglɪŋ] *adj* insignificante; (*annoying*) irritante.

night [naɪt] *n* notte *f*; (*evening*) sera; **at ~** la sera; **by ~** di notte; **the ~ before last** l'altro ieri notte (*or* sera); **~cap** *n* bicchierino prima di andare a letto; **~ club** *n* locale *m* notturno; **~dress** *n* camicia da notte; **~fall** *n* crepuscolo; **~gown** *n* = **~dress**; **~ie** [ˈnaɪtɪ] *n* = **~dress.**

nightingale [ˈnaɪtɪŋgeɪl] *n* usignolo.

nightlife [ˈnaɪtlaɪf] *n* vita notturna.

nightly [ˈnaɪtlɪ] *adj* di ogni notte *or* sera; (*by night*) notturno(a) ♦ *adv* ogni notte *or* sera.

nightmare [ˈnaɪtmɛə*] *n* incubo.

night: ~ porter *n* portiere *m* di notte; **~ school** *n* scuola serale; **~ shift** *n* turno di notte; **~-time** *n* notte *f.*

nil [nɪl] *n* nulla *m*; (*BRIT: SPORT*) zero.

Nile [naɪl] *n*: **the ~** il Nilo.

nimble [ˈnɪmbl] *adj* agile.

nine [naɪn] *num* nove; **~teen** *num* diciannove; **~ty** *num* novanta.

ninth [naɪnθ] *adj* nono(a).

nip [nɪp] *vt* pizzicare; (*bite*) mordere.

nipple [ˈnɪpl] *n* (*ANAT*) capezzolo.

nitrogen [ˈnaɪtrədʒən] *n* azoto.

┌─ KEYWORD ─┐

no [nəʊ] (*pl* ~es) *adv* (*opposite of "yes"*) no; **are you coming? — ~ (I'm not)** viene? — no (non vengo); **would you like some more? — ~ thank you** ne vuole ancora un po'? — no, grazie
♦ *adj* (*not any*) nessuno(a); **I have ~ money/time/books** non ho soldi/tempo/libri; **~ student would have done it** nessuno studente lo avrebbe fatto; **"~ parking"** "divieto di sosta"; **"~ smoking"** "vietato fumare"
♦ *n* no *m inv.*

nobility [nəʊˈbɪlɪtɪ] *n* nobiltà.

noble [ˈnəʊbl] *adj* nobile.

nobody [ˈnəʊbədɪ] *pron* nessuno.

nod [nɒd] *vi* accennare col capo, fare un cenno; (*in agreement*) annuire con un cenno del capo; (*sleep*) sonnecchiare ♦ *vt*: **to ~ one's head** fare di sì col capo ♦ *n* cenno; **~ off** *vi* assopirsi.

noise [nɔɪz] *n* rumore *m*; (*din, racket*) chiasso; **noisy** *adj* (*street, car*) rumoroso(a); (*person*) chiassoso(a).

nominal [ˈnɒmɪnl] *adj* nominale; (*rent*) simbolico(a).

nominate [ˈnɒmɪneɪt] *vt* (*propose*) proporre come candidato; (*elect*) nominare.

nominee [nɒmɪˈniː] *n* persona nominata; candidato/a.

non... [nɒn] *prefix* non...; **~alcoholic** *adj* analcolico(a); **~-aligned** *adj* non allineato(a).

nonchalant [ˈnɒnʃələnt] *adj* disinvolto(a), noncurante.

non-committal [ˈnɒnkəˈmɪtl] *adj* evasivo(a).

nondescript [ˈnɒndɪskrɪpt] *adj* qualunque *inv.*

none [nʌn] *pron* (*not one thing*) niente;

(*not one person*) nessuno(a); ~ **of you** nessuno(a) di voi; **I've ~ left** non ne ho più; **he's ~ the worse for it** non ne ha risentito.

nonentity [nɔ'nɛntɪtɪ] *n* persona insignificante.

nonetheless [nʌnðə'lɛs] *adv* nondimeno.

non-existent [-ɪg'zɪstənt] *adj* inesistente.

non-fiction *n* saggistica.

nonplussed [nɔn'plʌst] *adj* sconcertato(a).

nonsense ['nɔnsəns] *n* sciocchezze *fpl*.

non: ~**-smoker** *n* non fumatore/trice; ~**-stick** *adj* antiaderente, antiadesivo(a); ~**-stop** *adj* continuo(a); (*train, bus*) direttissimo(a) ♦ *adv* senza sosta.

noodles ['nu:dlz] *npl* taglierini *mpl*.

nook [nuk] *n*: ~**s and crannies** angoli *mpl*.

noon [nu:n] *n* mezzogiorno.

no one ['nəuwʌn] *pron* = **nobody.**

noose [nu:s] *n* nodo scorsoio; (*hangman's*) cappio.

nor [nɔ:*] *conj* = **neither** ♦ *adv see* **neither.**

norm [nɔ:m] *n* norma.

normal ['nɔ:ml] *adj* normale; ~**ly** *adv* normalmente.

north [nɔ:θ] *n* nord *m*, settentrione *m* ♦ *adj* nord *inv*, del nord, settentrionale ♦ *adv* verso nord; **N~ America** *n* America del Nord; ~**-east** *n* nord-est *m*; ~**erly** ['nɔ:ðəlɪ] *adj* (*point, direction*) verso nord; ~**ern** ['nɔ:ðən] *adj* del nord, settentrionale; **N~ern Ireland** *n* Irlanda del Nord; **N~ Pole** *n* Polo Nord; **N~ Sea** *n* Mare *m* del Nord; ~**ward(s)** ['nɔ:θwəd(z)] *adv* verso nord; ~**-west** *n* nord-ovest *m*.

Norway ['nɔ:weɪ] *n* Norvegia.

Norwegian [nɔ:'wi:dʒən] *adj* norvegese ♦ *n* norvegese *m/f*; (*LING*) norvegese *m*.

nose [nəuz] *n* naso; *of* (*of animal*) muso ♦ *vi*: **to ~ about** aggirarsi; ~**bleed** *n* emorragia nasale; ~**-dive** *n* picchiata; ~**y** (*inf*) *adj* = **nosy.**

nostalgia [nɔs'tældʒɪə] *n* nostalgia.

nostril ['nɔstrɪl] *n* narice *f*; (*of horse*) frogia.

nosy ['nəuzɪ] (*inf*) *adj* curioso(a).

not [nɔt] *adv* non; **he is ~** *or* **isn't here** non è qui, non c'è; **you must ~** *or* **you mustn't do that** non devi fare quello; **it's too late, isn't it** *or* **is it ~?** è troppo tardi, vero?; ~ **that I don't like him** non che (lui) non mi piaccia; ~ **yet/now** non ancora/ora; *see also* **all; only.**

notably ['nəutəblɪ] *adv* (*markedly*) notevolmente; (*particularly*) in particolare.

notary ['nəutərɪ] *n* notaio.

notch [nɔtʃ] *n* tacca; (*in saw*) dente *m*.

note [nəut] *n* nota; (*letter, banknote*) biglietto ♦ *vt* (*also:* ~ **down**) prendere nota di; **to take ~s** prendere appunti; ~**book** *n* taccuino; ~**d** ['nəutɪd] *adj* celebre; ~**pad** *n* bloc-notes *m inv*; ~**paper** *n* carta da lettere.

nothing ['nʌθɪŋ] *n* nulla *m*, niente *m*; (*zero*) zero; **he does ~** non fa niente; ~ **new/much** *etc* niente di nuovo/speciale *etc*; **for ~** per niente.

notice ['nəutɪs] *n* avviso; (*of leaving*) preavviso ♦ *vt* notare, accorgersi di; **to take ~ of** fare attenzione a; **to bring sth to sb's ~** far notare qc a qn; **at short ~** con un breve preavviso; **until further ~** fino a nuovo avviso; **to hand in one's ~** licenziarsi; ~**able** *adj* evidente; ~**board** (*BRIT*) *n* tabellone *m* per affissi.

notify ['nəutɪfaɪ] *vt*: **to ~ sth to sb** far sapere qc a qn; **to ~ sb of sth** avvisare qn di qc.

notion ['nəuʃən] *n* idea; (*concept*) nozione *f*.

notorious [nəu'tɔ:rɪəs] *adj* famigerato(a).

notwithstanding [nɔtwɪθ'stændɪŋ] *adv* nondimeno ♦ *prep* nonostante, malgrado.

nougat ['nu:gɑ:] *n* torrone *m*.

nought [nɔ:t] *n* zero.

noun [naun] *n* nome *m*, sostantivo.

nourish ['nʌrɪʃ] *vt* nutrire.

novel ['nɔvl] *n* romanzo ♦ *adj* nuovo(a); ~**ist** *n* romanziere/a; ~**ty** *n* novità *f* *inv*.

November [nəu'vɛmbə*] *n* novembre *m*.

novice ['nɔvɪs] n principiante m/f; (REL) novizio/a.

now [nau] adv ora, adesso ♦ conj: ~ **(that)** adesso che, ora che; **by** ~ ormai; **just** ~ proprio ora; **right** ~ subito, immediatamente; ~ **and then,** ~ **and again** ogni tanto; **from** ~ **on** da ora in poi; ~**adays** ['nauədeɪz] adv oggidì.

nowhere ['nəuwɛə*] adv in nessun luogo, da nessuna parte.

nozzle ['nɔzl] n (of hose etc) boccaglio; (of fire extinguisher) lancia.

nuance ['njuːɑ̃ːns] n sfumatura.

nuclear ['njuːklɪə*] adj nucleare.

nuclei ['njuːklɪaɪ] npl of nucleus.

nucleus ['njuːklɪəs] (pl nuclei) n nucleo.

nude [njuːd] adj nudo(a) ♦ n (ART) nudo; **in the** ~ tutto(a) nudo(a).

nudge [nʌdʒ] vt dare una gomitata a.

nudist ['njuːdɪst] n nudista m/f.

nuisance ['njuːsns] n: **it's a** ~ è una seccatura; **he's a** ~ è uno scocciatore.

null [nʌl] adj: ~ **and void** nullo(a).

numb [nʌm] adj: ~ **(with)** intorpidito(a) (da); (with fear) impietrito(a) (da); ~ **with cold** intirizzito(a) (dal freddo).

number ['nʌmbə*] n numero ♦ vt numerare; (include) contare; **a** ~ **of** un certo numero di; **to be** ~**ed among** venire annoverato(a) tra; **they were 10 in** ~ erano in tutto 10; ~ **plate** (BRIT) (AUT) targa.

numeral ['njuːmərəl] n numero, cifra.

numerate ['njuːmərɪt] adj: **to be** ~ avere nozioni di aritmetica.

numerical [njuː'mɛrɪkl] adj numerico(a).

numerous ['njuːmərəs] adj numeroso(a).

nun [nʌn] n suora, monaca.

nurse [nəːs] n infermiere/a; (also: ~**maid**) bambinaia ♦ vt (patient, cold) curare; (baby: BRIT) cullare; (: US) allattare, dare il latte a.

nursery ['nəːsərɪ] n (room) camera dei bambini; (institution) asilo; (for plants) vivaio; ~ **rhyme** n filastrocca; ~ **school** n scuola materna; ~ **slope** (BRIT) n (SKI) pista per principianti.

nursing ['nəːsɪŋ] n (profession) professione f di infermiere (or di infermiera); (care) cura; ~ **home** n casa di cura.

nurture ['nəːtʃə*] vt allevare; nutrire.

nut [nʌt] n (of metal) dado; (fruit) noce f; ~**crackers** npl schiaccianoci m inv.

nutmeg ['nʌtmɛg] n noce f moscata.

nutritious [njuː'trɪʃəs] adj nutriente.

nuts [nʌts] (inf) adj matto(a).

nutshell ['nʌtʃɛl] n guscio di noce; **in a** ~ in poche parole.

nylon ['naɪlɔn] n nailon m ♦ adj di nailon.

O

oak [əuk] n quercia ♦ adj di quercia.

O.A.P. (BRIT) n abbr = **old age pensioner.**

oar [ɔː*] n remo.

oasis [əu'eɪsɪs] (pl oases) n oasi f inv.

oath [əuθ] n giuramento; (swear word) bestemmia.

oatmeal ['əutmiːl] n farina d'avena.

oats [əuts] npl avena.

obedience [ə'biːdɪəns] n ubbidienza.

obedient [ə'biːdɪənt] adj ubbidiente.

obey [ə'beɪ] vt ubbidire a; (instructions, regulations) osservare.

obituary [ə'bɪtjuərɪ] n necrologia.

object [n 'ɔbdʒɪkt, vb əb'dʒɛkt] n oggetto; (purpose) scopo, intento; (LING) complemento oggetto ♦ vi: **to** ~ **to** (attitude) disapprovare; (proposal) protestare contro, sollevare delle obiezioni contro; **expense is no** ~ non si bada a spese; **to** ~ **that** obiettare che; **I** ~! mi oppongo!; ~**ion** [əb'dʒɛkʃən] n obiezione f; ~**ionable** [əb'dʒɛkʃənəbl] adj antipatico(a); (language) scostumato(a); ~**ive** n obiettivo.

obligation [ɔblɪ'geɪʃən] n obbligo, dovere m; **without** ~ senza impegno.

oblige [ə'blaɪdʒ] vt (force): **to** ~ **sb to do** costringere qn a fare; (do a favour) fare una cortesia a; **to be** ~**d to sb for sth** essere grato a qn per qc; **obliging** adj servizievole, compiacente.

oblique [ə'bliːk] adj obliquo(a);

(*allusion*) indiretto(a).

obliterate [ə'blɪtəreɪt] *vt* cancellare.

oblivion [ə'blɪvɪən] *n* oblio.

oblivious [ə'blɪvɪəs] *adj*: ~ of incurante di; inconscio(a) di.

oblong ['ɒblɒŋ] *adj* oblungo(a) ♦ *n* rettangolo.

obnoxious [əb'nɒkʃəs] *adj* odioso(a); (*smell*) disgustoso(a), ripugnante.

oboe ['əubəu] *n* oboe *m*.

obscene [əb'si:n] *adj* osceno(a).

obscure [əb'skjuə*] *adj* oscuro(a) ♦ *vt* oscurare; (*hide: sun*) nascondere.

observant [əb'zɔ:vnt] *adj* attento(a).

observation [ɒbzə'veɪʃən] *n* osservazione *f*; (*by police etc*) sorveglianza.

observatory [əb'zɔ:vətrɪ] *n* osservatorio.

observe [əb'zɔ:v] *vt* osservare; (*remark*) fare osservare; ~**r** *n* osservatore/trice.

obsess [əb'sɛs] *vt* ossessionare; ~**ive** *adj* ossessivo(a).

obsolescence [ɒbsə'lɛsns] *n* obsolescenza.

obsolete ['ɒbsəli:t] *adj* obsoleto(a).

obstacle ['ɒbstəkl] *n* ostacolo.

obstinate ['ɒbstɪnɪt] *adj* ostinato(a).

obstruct [əb'strʌkt] *vt* (*block*) ostruire, ostacolare; (*halt*) fermare; (*hinder*) impedire.

obtain [əb'teɪn] *vt* ottenere; ~**able** *adj* ottenibile.

obvious ['ɒbvɪəs] *adj* ovvio(a), evidente; ~**ly** *adv* ovviamente; certo.

occasion [ə'keɪʒən] *n* occasione *f*; (*event*) avvenimento; ~**al** *adj* occasionale; ~**ally** *adv* ogni tanto.

occupation [ɒkju'peɪʃən] *n* occupazione *f*; (*job*) mestiere *m*, professione *f*; ~**al hazard** *n* rischio del mestiere.

occupier ['ɒkjupaɪə*] *n* occupante *m/f*.

occupy ['ɒkjupaɪ] *vt* occupare; **to** ~ **o.s. in doing** occuparsi a fare.

occur [ə'kə:*] *vi* accadere, capitare; **to** ~ **to sb** venire in mente a qn; ~**rence** *n* caso, fatto; presenza.

ocean ['əuʃən] *n* oceano; ~-**going** *adj* d'alto mare.

o'clock [ə'klɒk] *adv*: **it is 5** ~ sono le 5.

OCR *n abbr* (= *optical character recognition*) lettura ottica; (= *optical character reader*) lettore *m* ottico.

octave ['ɒktɪv] *n* ottavo.

October [ɒk'təubə*] *n* ottobre *m*.

octopus ['ɒktəpəs] *n* polpo, piovra.

odd [ɒd] *adj* (*strange*) strano(a), bizzarro(a); (*number*) dispari *inv*; (*not of a set*) spaiato(a); 60-~ 60 e oltre; **at** ~ **times** di tanto in tanto; **the** ~ **one out** l'eccezione *f*; ~**ity** *n* bizzarria; (*person*) originale *m*; ~-**job man** *n* tuttofare *m inv*; ~ **jobs** *npl* lavori *mpl* occasionali; ~**ly** *adv* stranamente; ~**ments** *npl* (*COMM*) rimanenze *fpl*; ~**s** *npl* (*in betting*) quota; ~**s and ends** *npl* avanzi *mpl*; **it makes no** ~**s** non importa; **at** ~**s** in contesa.

odometer [ə'dɒmɪtə*] *n* odometro.

odour ['əudə*] (*US* **odor**) *n* odore *m*; (*unpleasant*) cattivo odore.

of [ɒv, əv] *prep* **1** (*gen*) di; **a boy** ~ **10** un ragazzo di 10 anni; **a friend** ~ **ours** un nostro amico; **that was kind** ~ **you** è stato molto gentile da parte sua
2 (*expressing quantity, amount, dates etc*) di; **a kilo** ~ **flour** un chilo di farina; **how much** ~ **this do you need?** quanto gliene serve?; **there were 3** ~ **them** (*people*) erano in 3; (*objects*) ce n'erano 3; **3** ~ **us went** 3 di noi sono andati; **the 5th** ~ **July** il 5 luglio
3 (*from, out of*) di, in; **made** ~ **wood** (fatto) di *or* in legno.

off [ɒf] *adv* **1** (*distance, time*): **it's a long way** ~ è lontano; **the game is 3 days** ~ la partita è tra 3 giorni
2 (*departure, removal*) via; **to go** ~ **to Paris** andarsene a Parigi; **I must be** ~ devo andare via; **to take** ~ **one's coat** togliersi il cappotto; **the button came** ~ il bottone è venuto via *or* si è staccato; **10%** ~ con lo sconto del 10%
3 (*not at work*): **to have a day** ~ avere un giorno libero; **to be** ~ **sick** essere

assente per malattia

♦ adj (engine) spento(a); (tap) chiuso(a); (cancelled) sospeso(a); (BRIT: food) andato(a) a male; **on the ~ chance** nel caso; **to have an ~ day** non essere in forma

♦ prep **1** (motion, removal etc) da; (distant from) a poca distanza da; **a street ~ the square** una strada che parte dalla piazza

2: to be ~ meat non mangiare più la carne.

offal ['ɔfl] n (CULIN) frattaglie fpl.

off-colour (BRIT) adj (ill) malato(a), indisposto(a).

offence [ə'fɛns] (US **offense**) n (LAW) contravvenzione f; (: more serious) reato; **to take ~ at** offendersi per.

offend [ə'fɛnd] vt (person) offendere; **~er** n delinquente m/f; (against regulations) contravventore/trice.

offense [ə'fɛns] (US) n = offence.

offensive [ə'fɛnsɪv] adj offensivo(a); (smell etc) sgradevole, ripugnante ♦ n (MIL) offensiva.

offer ['ɔfə*] n offerta, proposta ♦ vt offrire; **"on ~"** (COMM) "in offerta speciale''; **~ing** n offerta.

offhand [ɔf'hænd] adj disinvolto(a), noncurante ♦ adv su due piedi.

office ['ɔfɪs] n (place) ufficio; (position) carica; **doctor's ~** (US) studio; **to take ~** entrare in carica; **~ automation** n automazione f dell'ufficio; burotica; **~ block** (US **~ building**) n complesso di uffici; **~ hours** npl orario d'ufficio; (US: MED) orario di visite.

officer ['ɔfɪsə*] n (MIL etc) ufficiale m; (also: **police ~**) agente m di polizia; (of organization) funzionario.

office worker n impiegato/a d'ufficio.

official [ə'fɪʃl] adj (authorized) ufficiale ♦ n ufficiale m; (civil servant) impiegato/a statale; funzionario; **~dom** (pej) n burocrazia.

officiate [ə'fɪʃɪeɪt] vi presenziare.

officious [ə'fɪʃəs] adj invadente.

offing ['ɔfɪŋ] n: **in the ~** (fig) in vista.

off: ~-licence (BRIT) n (shop) spaccio

di bevande alcoliche; **~-line** adj, adv (COMPUT) off-line inv, fuori linea; (: switched off) spento(a); **~-peak** adj (ticket, heating etc) a tariffa ridotta; (time) non di punta; **~-putting** (BRIT) adj sgradevole, antipatico(a); **~-season** adj, adv fuori stagione.

offset ['ɔfsɛt] (irreg) vt (counteract) controbilanciare, compensare.

offshoot ['ɔfʃuːt] n (fig) diramazione f.

offshore [ɔf'ʃɔː*] adj (breeze) di terra; (island) vicino alla costa; (fishing) costiero(a).

offside ['ɔf'saɪd] adj (SPORT) fuori gioco; (AUT: in Britain) destro(a); (: in Italy etc) sinistro(a).

offspring ['ɔfsprɪŋ] n inv prole f, discendenza.

off: ~stage adv dietro le quinte; **~-the-peg** (US **~-the-rack**) adv prêt-à-porter; **~-white** adj bianco sporco inv.

often ['ɔfn] adv spesso; **how ~ do you go?** quanto spesso ci vai?

ogle ['əugl] vt occhieggiare.

oh [əu] excl oh!

oil [ɔɪl] n olio; (petroleum) petrolio; (for central heating) nafta ♦ vt (machine) lubrificare; **~can** n oliatore m a mano; (for storing) latta da olio; **~field** n giacimento petrolifero; **~ filter** n (AUT) filtro dell'olio; **~ painting** n quadro a olio; **~ refinery** n raffineria di petrolio; **~ rig** n derrick m inv; (at sea) piattaforma per trivellazioni subacquee; **~skins** npl indumenti mpl di tela cerata; **~ tanker** n (ship) petroliera; (truck) autocisterna per petrolio; **~ well** n pozzo petrolifero; **~y** adj unto(a), oleoso(a); (food) grasso(a).

ointment ['ɔɪntmənt] n unguento.

O.K. ['əu'keɪ] excl d'accordo! ♦ adj non male inv ♦ vt approvare; **is it ~?, are you ~?** tutto bene?

okay ['əu'keɪ] excl, adj, vt = O.K.

old [əuld] adj vecchio(a); (ancient) antico(a), vecchio(a); (person) vecchio(a), anziano(a); **how ~ are you?** quanti anni ha?; **he's 10 years ~** ha 10 anni; **~er brother** fratello maggiore; **~**

age n vecchiaia; ~ **age pensioner** (BRIT) n pensionato/a; ~-**fashioned** adj antiquato(a), fuori moda; (person) all'antica.

olive ['ɔlɪv] n (fruit) oliva; (tree) olivo ♦ adj (also: ~-green) verde oliva inv; ~ **oil** n olio d'oliva.

Olympic [əu'lɪmpɪk] adj olimpico(a); the ~ **Games**, the ~s i giochi olimpici, le Olimpiadi.

omelet(te) ['ɔmlɪt] n omelette f inv.

omen ['əumən] n presagio, augurio.

ominous ['ɔmɪnəs] adj minaccioso(a); (event) di malaugurio.

omit [əu'mɪt] vt omettere.

KEYWORD
---

on [ɔn] prep 1 (indicating position) su; ~ **the wall** sulla parete; ~ **the left** a or sulla sinistra

2 (indicating means, method, condition etc): ~ **foot** a piedi; ~ **the train/plane** in treno/aereo; ~ **the telephone** al telefono; ~ **the radio/television** alla radio/televisione; **to be** ~ **drugs** drogarsi; ~ **holiday** in vacanza

3 (referring to time): ~ **Friday** venerdì; ~ **Fridays** il or di venerdì; ~ **June 20th** il 20 giugno; ~ **Friday, June 20th** venerdì, 20 giugno; **a week** ~ **Friday** venerdì a otto; ~ **his arrival** al suo arrivo; ~ **seeing this** vedendo ciò

4 (about, concerning) su, di; **information · train services** informazioni sui collegamenti ferroviari; **a book** ~ **Goldoni/physics** un libro su Goldoni/di or sulla fisica

♦ adv 1 (referring to dress, covering): **to have one's coat** ~ avere indosso il cappotto; **to put one's coat** ~ mettersi il cappotto; **what's she got** ~? cosa indossa?; **she put her boots/gloves/hat** ~ si mise gli stivali/i guanti/il cappello; **screw the lid** ~ **tightly** avvita bene il coperchio

2 (further, continuously): **to walk** ~, **go** ~ etc continuare, proseguire etc; **to read** ~ continuare a leggere; ~ **and off** ogni tanto

♦ adj 1 (in operation: machine, TV, light) acceso(a); (: tap) aperto(a); (: brake) inserito(a); **is the meeting still** ~? (in progress) la riunione è ancora in corso?; (not cancelled) è confermato l'incontro?; **there's a good film** ~ **at the cinema** danno un buon film al cinema

2 (inf): **that's not** ~! (not acceptable) non si fa così!; (not possible) non se ne parla neanche!

once [wʌns] adv una volta ♦ conj non appena, quando; ~ **he had left/it was done** dopo che se n'era andato/fu fatto; **at** ~ subito; (simultaneously) a un tempo; ~ **a week** una volta per settimana; ~ **more** ancora una volta; ~ **and for all** una volta per sempre; ~ **upon a time** c'era una volta.

oncoming ['ɔnkʌmɪŋ] adj (traffic) che viene in senso opposto.

KEYWORD
---

one [wʌn] num uno(a); ~ **hundred and fifty** centocinquanta; ~ **day** un giorno

♦ adj 1 (sole) unico(a); **the** ~ **book which** l'unico libro che; **the** ~ **man who** l'unico che

2 (same) stesso(a); **they came in the** ~ **car** sono venuti nella stessa macchina

♦ pron 1: **this** ~ questo/a; **that** ~ quello/a; **I've already got** ~/**a red** ~ ne ho già uno/uno rosso; ~ **by** ~ uno per uno

2: ~ **another** l'un l'altro; **to look at** ~ **another** guardarsi

3 (impersonal) si; ~ **never knows** non si sa mai; **to cut** ~'s **finger** tagliarsi un dito; ~ **needs to eat** bisogna mangiare.

one: ~-**day excursion** (US) n biglietto giornaliero di andata e ritorno; ~-**man** adj (business) diretto(a) etc da un solo uomo; ~-**man band** n suonatore ambulante con vari strumenti; ~-**off** (BRIT: inf) n fatto eccezionale.

oneself [wʌn'sɛlf] pron (reflexive) si; (after prep) se stesso(a), sé; **to do sth** (**by**) ~ fare qc da sé; **to hurt** ~ farsi male; **to keep sth for** ~ tenere qc per sé; **to talk to** ~ parlare da solo.

one: ~**-sided** *adj* (*argument*)
unilaterale; ~**-to-~** *adj* (*relationship*)
univoco(a); ~**-upmanship** [-ˈʌpmənʃɪp] *n*
l'arte di fare sempre meglio degli altri;
~**-way** *adj* (*street, traffic*) a senso
unico.

ongoing [ˈɔngəʊɪŋ] *adj* in corso; in
attuazione.

onion [ˈʌnjən] *n* cipolla.

on-line *adj, adv* (COMPUT) on-line *inv*.

onlooker [ˈɔnlʊkəʳ] *n* spettatore/trice.

only [ˈəʊnlɪ] *adv* solo, soltanto ♦ *adj*
solo(a), unico(a) ♦ *conj* solo che, ma;
an ~ child un figlio unico; **not ~ ... but
also** non solo ... ma anche.

onset [ˈɔnsɛt] *n* inizio.

onshore [ˈɔnʃɔ:ʳ] *adj* (*wind*) di mare.

onslaught [ˈɔnslɔ:t] *n* attacco, assalto.

onto [ˈɔntu] *prep* = on to.

onus [ˈəʊnəs] *n* onere *m*, peso.

onward(s) [ˈɔnwəd(z)] *adv* (*move*) in
avanti; **from that time ~** da quella
volta in poi.

onyx [ˈɔnɪks] *n* onice *f*.

ooze [u:z] *vi* stillare.

opaque [əʊˈpeɪk] *adj* opaco(a).

OPEC [ˈəʊpɛk] *n abbr* (= *Organization
of Petroleum-Exporting Countries*)
O.P.E.C. *f*.

open [ˈəʊpn] *adj* aperto(a); (*road*)
libero(a); (*meeting*) pubblico(a) ♦ *vt*
aprire ♦ *vi* (*eyes, door, debate*) aprirsi;
(*flower*) sbocciare; (*shop, bank,
museum*) aprire; (*book etc:
commence*) cominciare; **in the ~** (*air*)
all'aperto; ~ **on to** *vt fus* (*subj: room,
door*) dare su; ~ **up** *vt* aprire;
(*blocked road*) sgombrare ♦ *vi* (*shop,
business*) aprire; ~**ing** *adj* (*speech*) di
apertura ♦ *n* apertura; (*opportunity*)
occasione *f*, opportunità *f inv*; sbocco;
~**ly** *adv* apertamente; ~**-minded** *adj*
che ha la mente aperta; ~**-necked** *adj*
col collo slacciato; ~**-plan** *adj* senza
pareti divisorie.

opera [ˈɔpərə] *n* opera.

operate [ˈɔpəreɪt] *vt* (*machine*)
azionare, far funzionare; (*system*)
usare ♦ *vi* funzionare; (*drug*) essere
efficace; **to ~ on sb** (**for**) (MED)

operare qn (di).

operatic [ɔpəˈrætɪk] *adj* dell'opera,
lirico(a).

operating [ˈɔpəreɪtɪŋ] *adj*: ~ **table**
tavolo operatorio; ~ **theatre** sala
operatoria.

operation [ɔpəˈreɪʃən] *n* operazione *f*; **to
be in ~** (*machine*) essere in azione *or*
funzionamento; (*system*) essere in
vigore; **to have an ~** (MED) subire
un'operazione; ~**al** *adj* in funzione;
d'esercizio.

operative [ˈɔpərətɪv] *adj* (*measure*)
operativo(a).

operator [ˈɔpəreɪtəʳ] *n* (*of machine*)
operatore/trice; (TEL) centralinista *m/f*.

opinion [əˈpɪnɪən] *n* opinione *f*, parere
m; **in my ~** secondo me, a mio avviso;
~**ated** *adj* dogmatico(a); ~ **poll** *n*
sondaggio di opinioni.

opium [ˈəʊpɪəm] *n* oppio.

opponent [əˈpəʊnənt] *n* avversario/a.

opportunist [ɔpəˈtju:nɪst] *n* opportunista
m/f.

opportunity [ɔpəˈtju:nɪtɪ] *n* opportunità
f inv, occasione *f*; **to take the ~ of
doing** cogliere l'occasione per fare.

oppose [əˈpəʊz] *vt* opporsi a; ~**d to** con-
trario(a) a; **as ~d to** in contrasto con;
opposing *adj* opposto(a); (*team*)
avversario(a).

opposite [ˈɔpəzɪt] *adj* opposto(a);
(*house etc*) di fronte ♦ *adv* di fronte,
dirimpetto ♦ *prep* di fronte a ♦ *n*: **the ~**
il contrario, l'opposto; **the ~ sex** l'altro
sesso.

opposition [ɔpəˈzɪʃən] *n* opposizione *f*.

oppress [əˈprɛs] *vt* opprimere.

opt [ɔpt] *vi*: **to ~ for** optare per; **to ~ to
do** scegliere di fare; ~ **out** *vi*: **to ~ out
of** ritirarsi da.

optical [ˈɔptɪkl] *adj* ottico(a).

optician [ɔpˈtɪʃən] *n* ottico.

optimist [ˈɔptɪmɪst] *n* ottimista *m/f*; ~**ic**
[-ˈmɪstɪk] *adj* ottimistico(a).

optimum [ˈɔptɪməm] *adj* ottimale.

option [ˈɔpʃən] *n* scelta; (SCOL) materia
facoltativa; (COMM) opzione *f*; ~**al** *adj*
facoltativo(a); (COMM) a scelta.

or [ɔ:ʳ] *conj* o, oppure; (*with negative*):

oral 167 out

oral

he hasn't seen ~ heard anything non ha visto né sentito niente; ~ else se no, altrimenti; oppure.

oral ['ɔːrəl] *adj* orale ♦ *n* esame *m* orale.

orange ['ɒrɪndʒ] *n (fruit)* arancia ♦ *adj* arancione.

orator ['ɒrətə*] *n* oratore/trice.

orbit ['ɔːbɪt] *n* orbita ♦ *vt* orbitare intorno a.

orchard ['ɔːtʃəd] *n* frutteto.

orchestra ['ɔːkɪstrə] *n* orchestra; *(US: seating)* platea.

orchid ['ɔːkɪd] *n* orchidea.

ordain [ɔːˈdeɪn] *vt (REL)* ordinare; *(decide)* decretare.

ordeal [ɔːˈdiːl] *n* prova, travaglio.

order ['ɔːdə*] *n* ordine *m*; *(COMM)* ordinazione *f* ♦ *vt* ordinare; **in** ~ **in** ordine; *(of document)* in regola, in **(working)** ~ funzionante; **in** ~ **to do** per fare; **in** ~ **that** affinché +*sub*; **on** ~ *(COMM)* in ordinazione; **out of** ~ non in ordine; *(not working)* guasto; **to** ~ **sb to do** ordinare a qn di fare; ~ **form** *n* modulo d'ordinazione; ~**ly** *n (MIL)* attendente *m*; *(MED)* inserviente *m* ♦ *adj (room)* in ordine; *(mind)* metodico(a); *(person)* ordinato(a), metodico(a).

ordinary ['ɔːdnrɪ] *adj* normale, comune; *(pej)* mediocre; **out of the** ~ diverso dal solito, fuori dell'ordinario.

Ordnance Survey ['ɔːdnəns-] *(BRIT) n* istituto cartografico britannico.

ore [ɔː*] *n* minerale *m* grezzo.

organ ['ɔːgən] *n* organo; ~**ic** [ɔːˈgænɪk] *adj* organico(a).

organization [ɔːgənaɪˈzeɪʃən] *n* organizzazione *f*.

organize ['ɔːgənaɪz] *vt* organizzare; ~**r** *n* organizzatore/trice.

orgasm ['ɔːgæzəm] *n* orgasmo.

orgy ['ɔːdʒɪ] *n* orgia.

Orient ['ɔːrɪənt] *n*: **the** ~ l'Oriente *m*; **oriental** [-ˈɛntl] *adj, n* orientale *m/f*.

origin ['ɒrɪdʒɪn] *n* origine *f*.

original [əˈrɪdʒɪnl] *adj* originale; *(earliest)* originario(a) ♦ *n* originale *m*; ~**ly** *adv (at first)* all'inizio.

originate [əˈrɪdʒɪneɪt] *vi*: **to** ~ **from**

essere originario(a) di; *(suggestion)* provenire da; **to** ~ **in** avere origine in.

Orkneys ['ɔːknɪz] *npl*: **the** ~ *(also: the Orkney Islands)* le Orcadi.

ornament ['ɔːnəmənt] *n* ornamento; *(trinket)* ninnolo; ~**al** [-ˈmɛntl] *adj* ornamentale.

ornate [ɔːˈneɪt] *adj* molto ornato(a).

orphan ['ɔːfn] *n* orfano/a; ~**age** *n* orfanotrofio.

orthodox ['ɔːθədɒks] *adj* ortodosso(a).

orthopaedic [ɔːθəˈpiːdɪk] *(US* **orthopedic)** *adj* ortopedico(a).

ostensibly [ɒsˈtɛnsɪblɪ] *adv* all'apparenza.

ostentatious [ɒstɛnˈteɪʃəs] *adj* pretenzioso(a); ostentato(a).

ostrich ['ɒstrɪtʃ] *n* struzzo.

other ['ʌðə*] *adj* altro(a) ♦ *pron*: **the** ~ **(one)** l'altro(a); ~**s** *(~ people)* altri *mpl*; ~ **than** altro che; a parte; ~**wise** *adv, conj* altrimenti.

otter ['ɒtə*] *n* lontra.

ouch [autʃ] *excl* ohi!, ahi!

ought [ɔːt] *(pt* ought) *aux vb*: **I** ~ **to do it** dovrei farlo; **this** ~ **to have been corrected** questo avrebbe dovuto essere corretto; **he** ~ **to win** dovrebbe vincere.

ounce [auns] *n* oncia (= *28.35 g; 16 in a pound)*.

our ['auə*] *adj* il(la) nostro(a), *pl* i(le) nostri(e); *see also* **my**; ~**s** *pron* il(la) nostro(a), *pl* i(le) nostri(e); *see also* **mine**; ~**selves** *pron pl (reflexive)* ci; *(after preposition)* noi; *(emphatic)* noi stessi(e); *see also* **oneself**.

oust [aust] *vt* cacciare, espellere.

KEYWORD
---

out [aut] *adv (gen)* fuori; ~ **here/there** qui/là fuori; **to speak** ~ **loud** parlare forte; **to have a night** ~ uscire una sera; **the boat was 10 km** ~ la barca era a 10 km dalla costa; **3 days** ~ **from Plymouth** a 3 giorni da Plymouth ♦ *adj*: **to be** ~ *(gen)* essere fuori; *(unconscious)* aver perso i sensi; *(style, singer)* essere fuori moda; **before the week was** ~ prima che la settimana fosse finita; **to be** ~ **to do sth** avere

intenzione di fare qc; **to be ~ in one's calculations** aver sbagliato i calcoli
♦ **out of** *prep* **1** (*outside, beyond*) fuori di; **to go ~ of the house** uscire di casa; **to look ~ of the window** guardare fuori dalla finestra
2 (*because of*) per
3 (*origin*) da; **to drink ~ of a cup** bere da una tazza
4 (*from among*): **~ of 10** su 10
5 (*without*) senza; **~ of petrol** senza benzina.

out-and-out *adj* (*liar, thief etc*) vero(a) e proprio(a).
outback ['autbæk] *n* (*in Australia*) interno, entroterra.
outboard ['autbɔːd] *n*: **~ (motor)** (*motore m*) fuoribordo.
outbreak ['autbreik] *n* scoppio; epidemia.
outburst ['autbəːst] *n* scoppio.
outcast ['autkɑːst] *n* esule *m/f*; (*socially*) paria *m inv*.
outcome ['autkʌm] *n* esito, risultato.
outcrop ['autkrɔp] *n* (*of rock*) affioramento.
outcry ['autkrai] *n* protesta, clamore *m*.
outdated [aut'deitid] *adj* (*custom, clothes*) fuori moda; (*idea*) sorpassato(a).
outdo [aut'duː] (*irreg*) *vt* sorpassare.
outdoor [aut'dɔː*] *adj* all'aperto; **~s** *adv* fuori; all'aria aperta.
outer ['autə*] *adj* esteriore; **~ space** *n* spazio cosmico.
outfit ['autfit] *n* (*clothes*) completo; (: *for sport*) tenuta.
outgoing ['autɡəuiŋ] *adj* (*character*) socievole; **~s** (*BRIT*) *npl* (*expenses*) spese *fpl*, uscite *fpl*.
outgrow [aut'ɡrəu] (*irreg*) *vt*: **he has ~n his clothes** tutti i vestiti gli sono diventati piccoli.
outhouse ['authaus] *n* costruzione *f* annessa.
outing ['autiŋ] *n* gita; escursione *f*.
outlandish [aut'lændiʃ] *adj* strano(a).
outlaw ['autlɔː] *n* fuorilegge *m/f* ♦ *vt* bandire.

outlay ['autlei] *n* spese *fpl*; (*investment*) sborsa, spesa.
outlet ['autlet] *n* (*for liquid etc*) sbocco, scarico; (*US: ELEC*) presa di corrente; (*also: retail ~*) punto di vendita.
outline ['autlain] *n* contorno, profilo; (*summary*) abbozzo, grandi linee *fpl* ♦ *vt* (*fig*) descrivere a grandi linee.
outlive [aut'liv] *vt* sopravvivere a.
outlook ['autluk] *n* prospettiva, vista.
outlying ['autlaiiŋ] *adj* periferico(a).
outmoded [aut'məudid] *adj* passato(a) di moda; antiquato(a).
outnumber [aut'nʌmbə*] *vt* superare in numero.
out-of-date *adj* (*passport*) scaduto(a); (*clothes*) fuori moda *inv*.
out-of-the-way *adj* (*place*) fuori mano *inv*.
outpatient ['autpeiʃənt] *n* paziente *m/f* esterno(a).
outpost ['autpəust] *n* avamposto.
output ['autput] *n* produzione *f*; (*COMPUT*) output *m inv*.
outrage ['autreidʒ] *n* oltraggio; scandalo ♦ *vt* oltraggiare; **~ous** [-'reidʒəs] *adj* oltraggioso(a); scandaloso(a).
outright [*adv* aut'rait, *adj* 'autrait] *adv* completamente; schiettamente; apertamente; sul colpo ♦ *adj* completo(a); schietto(a) e netto(a).
outset ['autset] *n* inizio.
outside [aut'said] *n* esterno, esteriore *m* ♦ *adj* esterno(a), esteriore ♦ *adv* fuori, all'esterno ♦ *prep* fuori di, all'esterno di; **at the ~** (*fig*) al massimo; **~ lane** *n* (*AUT*) corsia di sorpasso; **~-left/-right** *n* (*FOOTBALL*) ala sinistra/destra; **~ line** *n* (*TEL*) linea esterna; **~r** *n* (*in race etc*) outsider *m inv*; (*stranger*) estraneo/a.
outsize ['autsaiz] *adj* (*clothes*) per taglie forti.
outskirts ['autskəːts] *npl* sobborghi *mpl*.
outspoken [aut'spəukən] *adj* molto franco(a).
outstanding [aut'stændiŋ] *adj* eccezionale, di rilievo; (*unfinished*) non completo(a); non evaso(a); non regolato(a).

outstay [aut'steɪ] vt: **to ~ one's wel-come** diventare un ospite sgradito.

outstretched [aut'strɛtʃt] adj (hand) teso(a); (body) disteso(a).

outstrip [aut'strɪp] vt (competitors, demand) superare.

out-tray n contenitore m per la corrispondenza in partenza.

outward ['autwəd] adj (sign, appearances) esteriore; (journey) d'andata; **~ly** adv esteriormente; in apparenza.

outweigh [aut'weɪ] vt avere maggior peso di.

outwit [aut'wɪt] vt superare in astuzia.

oval ['əuvl] adj ovale ♦ n ovale m.

ovary ['əuvərɪ] n ovaia.

oven ['ʌvn] n forno; **~proof** adj da forno.

over ['əuvə*] adv al di sopra ♦ adj (or adv) (finished) finito(a), terminato(a); (too) troppo; (remaining) che avanza ♦ prep su; sopra; (above) al di sopra di; (on the other side of) di là di; (more than) più di; (during) durante; **~ here** qui; **~ there** là; **all ~** (everywhere) dappertutto; (finished) tutto(a) finito(a); **~ and ~ (again)** più e più volte; **~ and above** oltre (a); **to ask sb ~** invitare qn (a passare).

overall [adj, n 'əuvərɔːl, adv əuvər'ɔːl] adj totale ♦ n (BRIT) grembiule m ♦ adv nell'insieme, complessivamente; **~s** npl (worker's • • 3) tuta (da lavoro).

overawe [əuvər'ɔː] vt intimidire.

overbalance [əuvə'bæləns] vi perdere l'equilibrio.

overbearing [əuvə'bɛərɪŋ] adj imperioso(a), prepotente.

overboard ['əuvəbɔːd] adv (NAUT) fuori bordo, in mare.

overbook [əuvə'buk] vt: **the hotel was ~ed** le prenotazioni all'albergo superavano i posti disponibili.

overcast ['əuvəkɑːst] adj coperto(a).

overcharge [əuvə'tʃɑːdʒ] vt: **to ~ sb for sth** far pagare troppo caro a qn per qc.

overcoat ['əuvəkəut] n soprabito, cappotto.

overcome [əuvə'kʌm] (irreg) vt superare; sopraffare.

overcrowded [əuvə'kraudɪd] adj sovraffollato(a).

overdo [əuvə'duː] (irreg) vt esagerare; (overcook) cuocere troppo.

overdose ['əuvədəus] n dose f eccessiva.

overdraft ['əuvədrɑːft] n scoperto (di conto).

overdrawn [əuvə'drɔːn] adj (account) scoperto(a).

overdue [əuvə'djuː] adj in ritardo.

overestimate [əuvər'ɛstɪmeɪt] vt sopravvalutare.

overflow [vb əuvə'fləu, n 'əuvəfləu] vi traboccare ♦ n (also: **~ pipe**) troppopieno.

overgrown [əuvə'grəun] adj (garden) ricoperto(a) di vegetazione.

overhaul [vb əuvə'hɔːl, n 'əuvəhɔːl] vt revisionare ♦ n revisione f.

overhead [adv əuvə'hɛd, adj, n 'əuvəhɛd] adv di sopra ♦ adj aereo(a); (lighting) verticale ♦ n (US) = **~s**; **~s** npl spese fpl generali.

overhear [əuvə'hɪə*] (irreg) vt sentire (per caso).

overheat [əuvə'hiːt] vi (engine) surriscaldare.

overjoyed [əuvə'dʒɔɪd] adj pazzo(a) di gioia.

overkill ['əuvəkɪl] n (fig) eccessi mpl.

overlap [əuvə'læp] vi sovrapporsi.

overleaf [əuvə'liːf] adv a tergo.

overload [əuvə'ləud] vt sovraccaricare.

overlook [əuvə'luk] vt (have view of) dare su; (miss) trascurare; (forgive) passare sopra a.

overnight [əuvə'naɪt] adv (happen) durante la notte; (fig) tutto ad un tratto ♦ adj di notte; **he stayed there ~** ci ha passato la notte.

overpass ['əuvəpɑːs] n cavalcavia m inv.

overpower [əuvə'pauə*] vt sopraffare; **~ing** adj irresistibile; (heat, stench) soffocante.

overrate [əuvə'reɪt] vt sopravvalutare.

override [əuvə'raɪd] (irreg: like **ride**) vt (order, objection) passar sopra a; (decision) annullare; **overriding** adj preponderante.

overrule [əuvəˈruːl] *vt* (*decision*) annullare; (*claim*) respingere.

overrun [əuvəˈrʌn] (*irreg: like* **run**) *vt* (*country*) invadere; (*time limit*) superare.

overseas [əuvəˈsiːz] *adv* oltremare; (*abroad*) all'estero ♦ *adj* (*trade*) estero(a); (*visitor*) straniero(a).

overshadow [əuvəˈʃædəu] *vt* far ombra su; (*fig*) eclissare.

overshoot [əuvəˈʃuːt] (*irreg*) *vt* superare.

oversight [ˈəuvəsaɪt] *n* omissione *f*, svista.

oversleep [əuvəˈsliːp] (*irreg*) *vt* dormire troppo a lungo.

overstate [əuvəˈsteɪt] *vt* esagerare.

overstep [əuvəˈstep] *vt*: **to ~ the mark** superare ogni limite.

overt [əuˈvəːt] *adj* palese.

overtake [əuvəˈteɪk] (*irreg*) *vt* sorpassare.

overthrow [əuvəˈθrəu] (*irreg*) *vt* (*government*) rovesciare.

overtime [ˈəuvətaɪm] *n* (lavoro) straordinario.

overtone [ˈəuvətəun] *n* sfumatura.

overture [ˈəuvətʃuə*] *n* (*MUS*) ouverture *f inv*; (*fig*) approccio.

overturn [əuvəˈtəːn] *vt* rovesciare ♦ *vi* rovesciarsi.

overweight [əuvəˈweɪt] *adj* (*person*) troppo grasso(a).

overwhelm [əuvəˈwelm] *vt* sopraffare; sommergere; schiacciare; **~ing** *adj* (*victory, defeat*) schiacciante; (*heat, desire*) intenso(a).

overwork [əuvəˈwəːk] *n* eccessivo lavoro.

overwrought [əuvəˈrɔːt] *adj* molto agitato(a).

owe [əu] *vt*: **to ~ sb sth, to ~ sth to sb** dovere qc a qn; **owing to** *prep* a causa di.

owl [aul] *n* gufo.

own [əun] *vt* possedere ♦ *adj* proprio(a); **a room of my ~** la mia propria camera; **to get one's ~ back** vendicarsi; **on one's ~** tutto(a) solo(a);

~ up *vi* confessare; **~er** *n* proprietario/a; **~ership** *n* possesso.

ox [ɔks] *pl* **oxen** *n* bue *m*.

oxen [ˈɔksn] *npl of* **ox**.

oxtail [ˈɔksteɪl] *n*: **~ soup** minestra di coda di bue.

oxygen [ˈɔksɪdʒən] *n* ossigeno; **~ mask/tent** *n* maschera/tenda ad ossigeno.

oyster [ˈɔɪstə*] *n* ostrica.

oz. *abbr* = **ounce(s)**.

ozone [ˈəuzəun] *n* ozono; **~ layer** *n* strato di ozono.

P

p [piː] *abbr* = **penny; pence**.

P.A. *n abbr* = **personal assistant; public address system**.

p.a. *abbr* = **per annum**.

pa [pɑː] (*inf*) *n* papà *m inv*, babbo.

pace [peɪs] *n* passo; (*speed*) passo; velocità ♦ *vi*: **to ~ up and down** camminare su e giù; **to keep ~ with** camminare di pari passo a; (*events*) tenersi al corrente di; **~maker** *n* (*MED*) segnapasso; (*SPORT: also:* **~ setter**) battistrada *m inv*.

pacific [pəˈsɪfɪk] *n*: **the P~** (**Ocean**) il Pacifico, l'Oceano Pacifico.

pacify [ˈpæsɪfaɪ] *vt* calmare, placare.

pack [pæk] *n* pacco; (*US: of cigarettes*) pacchetto; (*back~*) zaino; (*of hounds*) muta; (*of thieves etc*) banda; (*of cards*) mazzo ♦ *vt* (*in suitcase etc*) mettere; (*box*) riempire; (*cram*) stipare, pigiare; **to ~** (**one's bags**) fare la valigia; **to ~ sb off** spedire via qn; **~ it in!** (*inf*) dacci un taglio!

package [ˈpækɪdʒ] *n* pacco; balla; (*also:* **~ deal**) pacchetto; forfait *m inv*; **~ holiday** *n* vacanza organizzata; **~ tour** *n* viaggio organizzato.

packed lunch *n* pranzo al sacco.

packet [ˈpækɪt] *n* pacchetto.

packing [ˈpækɪŋ] *n* imballaggio; **~ case** *n* cassa da imballaggio.

pact [pækt] *n* patto, accordo; trattato.

pad [pæd] *n* blocco; (*to prevent friction*)

cuscinetto; (*inf: flat*) appartamentino ♦ *vt* imbottire; ~**ding** *n* imbottitura.

paddle ['pædl] *n* (*oar*) pagaia; (*US: for table tennis*) racchetta da ping-pong ♦ *vi* sguazzare ♦ *vt*: **to** ~ **a canoe** *etc* vogare con la pagaia; ~ **steamer** *n* battello a ruote; **paddling pool** (*BRIT*) *n* piscina per bambini.

paddock ['pædək] *n* prato recintato; (*at racecourse*) paddock *m inv*.

paddy field ['pædɪ-] *n* risaia.

padlock ['pædlɔk] *n* lucchetto.

paediatrics [pi:dɪ'ætrɪks] (*US* **pediatrics**) *n* pediatria.

pagan ['peɪgən] *adj*, *n* pagano(a).

page [peɪdʒ] *n* pagina; (*also*: ~ **boy**) paggio ♦ *vt* (*in hotel etc*) (far) chiamare.

pageant ['pædʒənt] *n* spettacolo storico; grande cerimonia; ~**ry** *n* pompa.

paid [peɪd] *pt, pp* of **pay** ♦ *adj* (*work, official*) rimunerato(a); **to put** ~ **to** (*BRIT*) mettere fine a.

pail [peɪl] *n* secchio.

pain [peɪn] *n* dolore *m*; **to be in** ~ soffrire, aver male; **to take** ~**s to do** mettercela tutta per fare; ~**ed** *adj* addolorato(a), afflitto(a); ~**ful** *adj* doloroso(a), che fa male; difficile, penoso(a); ~**fully** *adv* (*fig: very*) fin troppo; ~**killer** *n* antalgico, antidolorifico; ~**less** *adj* indolore.

painstaking ['peɪnzteɪkɪŋ] *adj* (*person*) sollecito(a); (*work*) accurato(a).

paint [peɪnt] *n* vernice *f*, colore *m* ♦ *vt* dipingere; (*walls, door etc*) verniciare; **to** ~ **the door blue** verniciare la porta di azzurro; ~**brush** *n* pennello; ~**er** *n* (*artist*) pittore *m*; (*decorator*) imbianchino; ~**ing** *n* pittura; verniciatura; (*picture*) dipinto, quadro; ~**work** *n* tinta; (*of car*) vernice *f*.

pair [pɛə*] *n* (*of shoes, gloves etc*) paio; (*of people*) coppia; duo *m inv*; **a** ~ **of scissors/trousers** un paio di forbici/pantaloni.

pajamas [pɪ'dʒɑ:məz] (*US*) *npl* pigiama *m*.

Pakistan [pɑ:kɪ'stɑ:n] *n* Pakistan *m*; ~**i** *adj, n* pakistano(a).

pal [pæl] (*inf*) *n* amico/a, compagno/a.

palace ['pæləs] *n* palazzo.

palatable ['pælɪtəbl] *adj* gustoso(a).

palate ['pælɪt] *n* palato.

palatial [pə'leɪʃəl] *adj* sontuoso(a), sfarzoso(a).

palaver [pə'lɑ:və*] (*inf*) *n* chiacchiere *fpl*; storie *fpl*.

pale [peɪl] *adj* pallido(a) ♦ *n*: **to be beyond the** ~ aver oltrepassato ogni limite.

Palestine ['pælɪstaɪn] *n* Palestina; **Palestinian** [-'tɪnɪən] *adj, n* palestinese *m/f*.

palette ['pælɪt] *n* tavolozza.

palings ['peɪlɪŋz] *npl* (*fence*) palizzata.

pall [pɔ:l] *n* (*of smoke*) cappa ♦ *vi*: **to** ~ (**on**) diventare noioso(a) (a).

pallet ['pælɪt] *n* (*for goods*) paletta.

pallid ['pælɪd] *adj* pallido(a), smorto(a).

pallor ['pælə*] *n* pallore *m*.

palm [pɑ:m] *n* (*ANAT*) palma, palmo; (*also*: ~ **tree**) palma ♦ *vt*: **to** ~ **sth off on sb** (*inf*) rifilare qc a qn; **P**~ **Sunday** *n* Domenica delle Palme.

palpable ['pælpəbl] *adj* palpabile.

paltry ['pɔ:ltrɪ] *adj* irrisorio(a); insignificante.

pamper ['pæmpə*] *vt* viziare, coccolare.

pamphlet ['pæmflət] *n* dépliant *m inv*.

pan [pæn] *n* (*also: sauce*~) casseruola; (*also: frying* ~) padella.

panache [pə'næʃ] *n* stile *m*.

pancake ['pænkeɪk] *n* frittella.

pancreas ['pæŋkrɪəs] *n* pancreas *m inv*.

panda ['pændə] *n* panda *m inv*; ~ **car** (*BRIT*) *n* auto *f* della polizia.

pandemonium [pændɪ'məʊnɪəm] *n* pandemonio.

pander ['pændə*] *vi*: **to** ~ **to** lusingare; concedere tutto a.

pane [peɪn] *n* vetro.

panel ['pænl] *n* (*of wood, cloth etc*) pannello; (*RADIO, TV*) giuria; ~**ling** (*US* ~**ing**) *n* rivestimento a pannelli.

pang [pæŋ] *n*: **a** ~ **of regret** un senso di rammarico; **hunger** ~**s** morsi *mpl* della fame.

panic ['pænɪk] *n* panico ♦ *vi* perdere il sangue freddo; ~**ky** *adj* (*person*) pauroso(a); **~-stricken** *adj* (*person*) preso(a) dal panico, in preda al panico; (*look*) terrorizzato(a).

pansy ['pænzı] *n* (*BOT*) viola del pensiero, pensée *f inv*; (*inf: pej*) femminuccia.

pant [pænt] *vi* ansare.

panther ['pænθə*] *n* pantera.

panties ['pæntız] *npl* slip *m*, mutandine *fpl*.

pantihose ['pæntıhəuz] (*US*) *n* collant *m inv*.

pantomime ['pæntəmaım] (*BRIT*) *n* pantomima.

pantry ['pæntrı] *n* dispensa.

pants [pænts] *npl* mutande *fpl*, slip *m*; (*US: trousers*) pantaloni *mpl*.

papal ['peıpəl] *adj* papale, pontificio(a).

paper ['peıpə*] *n* carta; (*also: wall~*) carta da parati, tappezzeria; (*also: news~*) giornale *m*; (*study, article*) saggio; (*exam*) prova scritta ♦ *adj* di carta ♦ *vt* tappezzare; **~s** *npl* (*also: identity ~s*) carte *fpl*, documenti *mpl*; **~back** *n* tascabile *m*; edizione *f* economica; ~ **bag** *n* sacchetto di carta; ~ **clip** *n* graffetta, clip *f inv*; ~ **hankie** *n* fazzolettino di carta; **~weight** *n* fermacarte *m inv*; **~work** *n* lavoro amministrativo.

papier-mâché ['pæpıeı'mæʃeı] *n* cartapesta.

par [pɑ:*] *n* parità, pari *f*; (*GOLF*) norma; **on a** ♦ **with** alla pari con.

parable ['pærəbl] *n* parabola.

parachute ['pærəʃu:t] *n* paracadute *m inv*.

parade [pə'reıd] *n* parata ♦ *vt* (*fig*) fare sfoggio di ♦ *vi* sfilare in parata.

paradise ['pærədaıs] *n* paradiso.

paradox ['pærədɔks] *n* paradosso; **~ically** [-'dɔksıklı] *adv* paradossalmente.

paraffin ['pærəfın] (*BRIT*) *n*: ~ (**oil**) paraffina.

paragon ['pærəgən] *n* modello di perfezione *or* di virtù.

paragraph ['pærəgrɑ:f] *n* paragrafo.

parallel ['pærəlel] *adj* parallelo(a); (*fig*) analogo(a) ♦ *n* (*line*) parallela; (*fig, GEO*) parallelo.

paralyse ['pærəlaız] (*US* **paralyze**) *vt* paralizzare.

paralysis [pə'rælısıs] *n* paralisi *f inv*.

paralyze ['pærəlaız] (*US*) *vt* = **paralyse**.

paramount ['pærəmaunt] *adj*: **of ~ importance** di capitale importanza.

paranoid ['pærənɔıd] *adj* paranoico(a).

paraphernalia [pærəfə'neılıə] *n* attrezzi *mpl*, roba.

parasol ['pærəsɔl] *n* parasole *m*.

paratrooper ['pærətru:pə*] *n* paracadutista *m* (*soldato*).

parcel ['pɑ:sl] *n* pacco, pacchetto ♦ *vt* (*also: ~ up*) impaccare.

parch [pɑ:tʃ] *vt* riardere; **~ed** *adj* (*person*) assetato(a).

parchment ['pɑ:tʃmənt] *n* pergamena.

pardon ['pɑ:dn] *n* perdono; grazia ♦ *vt* perdonare; (*LAW*) graziare; ~ **me!** mi scusi!; **I beg your ~!** scusi!; **I beg your ~?** (*BRIT*), ~ **me?** (*US*) prego?

parent ['peərənt] *n* genitore *m*; **~s** *npl* (*mother and father*) genitori *mpl*; **~al** [pə'rentl] *adj* dei genitori.

parentheses [pə'renθısi:z] *npl of* **parenthesis**.

parenthesis [pə'renθısıs] (*pl* **parentheses**) *n* parentesi *f inv*.

Paris ['pærıs] *n* Parigi *f*.

parish ['pærıʃ] *n* parrocchia; (*BRIT: civil*) ≈ municipio.

park [pɑ:k] *n* parco ♦ *vt, vi* parcheggiare.

parka ['pɑ:kə] *n* eskimo.

parking ['pɑ:kıŋ] *n* parcheggio; "**no ~**" "sosta vietata"; ~ **lot** (*US*) *n* posteggio, parcheggio; ~ **meter** *n* parchimetro; ~ **ticket** *n* multa per sosta vietata.

parlance ['pɑ:ləns] *n* gergo.

parliament ['pɑ:ləmənt] *n* parlamento; **~ary** [-'mentərı] *adj* parlamentare.

parlour ['pɑ:lə*] (*US* **parlor**) *n* salotto.

parochial [pə'rəukıəl] (*pej*) *adj* provinciale.

parody ['pærədı] *n* parodia.

parole [pə'rəul] *n*: **on ~** in libertà per buona condotta.

parrot ['pærət] *n* pappagallo.

parry ['pærı] *vt* parare.

parsley ['pɑ:slı] *n* prezzemolo.

parsnip ['pɑ:snɪp] n pastinaca.
parson ['pɑ:sn] n prete m; (Church of England) parroco.
part [pɑ:t] n parte f; (of machine) pezzo; (US: in hair) scriminatura ♦ adj in parte ♦ adv = **partly** ♦ vt separare ♦ vi (people) separarsi; **to take ~ in** prendere parte a; **for my ~** per parte mia; **to take sth in good ~** prendere bene qc; **to take sb's ~** parteggiare per or prendere le parti di qn; **for the most ~** in generale; nella maggior parte dei casi; **~ with** vt fus separarsi da; rinunciare a; **~ exchange** (BRIT) n: **in ~ exchange** in pagamento parziale.
partial ['pɑ:ʃl] adj parziale; **to be ~ to** avere un debole per.
participate [pɑ:'tɪsɪpeɪt] vi: **to ~ (in)** prendere parte a, partecipare (a); **participation** [-'peɪʃən] n partecipazione f.
participle ['pɑ:tɪsɪpl] n participio.
particle ['pɑ:tɪkl] n particella.
particular [pə'tɪkjulə*] adj particolare; speciale; (fussy) difficile; meticoloso(a); **in ~** in particolare, particolarmente; **~ly** adv particolarmente; in particolare; **~s** npl particolari mpl, dettagli mpl; (information) informazioni fpl.
parting ['pɑ:tɪŋ] n separazione f; (BRIT: in hair) scriminatura ♦ adj d'addio.
partisan [pɑ:tɪ'zæn] n partigiano/a ♦ adj partigiano(a); di parte.
partition [pɑ:'tɪʃən] n (POL) partizione f; (wall) tramezzo.
partly ['pɑ:tlɪ] adv parzialmente; in parte.
partner ['pɑ:tnə*] n (COMM) socio/a; (wife, husband etc, SPORT) compagno/a; (at dance) cavaliere/dama; **~ship** n associazione f; (COMM) società f inv.
partridge ['pɑ:trɪdʒ] n pernice f.
part-time adj, adv a orario ridotto.
party ['pɑ:tɪ] n (POL) partito; (group) gruppo; (LAW) parte f; (celebration) ricevimento; serata; festa ♦ cpd (POL) del partito, di partito; **~ dress** n vestito della festa; **~ line** n (TEL) duplex m inv.

pass [pɑ:s] vt (gen) passare; (place) passare davanti a; (exam) passare, superare; (candidate) promuovere; (overtake, surpass) sorpassare, superare; (approve) approvare ♦ vi passare ♦ n (permit) lasciapassare m inv; permesso; (in mountains) passo, gola; (SPORT) passaggio; (SCOL): **to get a ~** prendere la sufficienza; **to ~ sth through a hole** etc far passare qc attraverso un buco etc; **to make a ~ at sb** (inf) fare delle proposte or delle avances a qn; **~ away** vi morire; **~ by** vi passare ♦ vt trascurare; **~ on** vt passare; **~ out** vi svenire; **~ up** vt (opportunity) lasciarsi sfuggire, perdere; **~able** adj (road) praticabile; (work) accettabile.
passage ['pæsɪdʒ] n (gen) passaggio; (also: **~way**) corridoio; (in book) brano, passo; (by boat) traversata.
passbook ['pɑ:sbuk] n libretto di risparmio.
passenger ['pæsɪndʒə*] n passeggero/a.
passer-by [pɑ:sə'baɪ] n passante m/f.
passing ['pɑ:sɪŋ] adj (fig) fuggevole; **to mention sth in ~** accennare a qc di sfuggita; **~ place** n (AUT) piazzola di sosta.
passion ['pæʃən] n passione f; amore m; **~ate** adj appassionato(a).
passive ['pæsɪv] adj (also LING) passivo(a).
Passover ['pɑ:səuvə*] n Pasqua ebraica.
passport ['pɑ:spɔ:t] n passaporto; **~ control** n controllo m passaporti inv.
password ['pɑ:swɜ:d] n parola d'ordine.
past [pɑ:st] prep (further than) oltre, di là di; dopo; (later than) dopo ♦ adj passato(a); (president etc) ex inv ♦ n passato; **he's ~ forty** ha più di quarant'anni; **ten ~ eight** le otto e dieci; **for the ~ few days** da qualche giorno; in questi ultimi giorni; **to run ~** passare di corsa.
pasta ['pæstə] n pasta.
paste [peɪst] n (glue) colla; (CULIN) pâté m inv; pasta ♦ vt collare.
pastel ['pæstl] adj pastello inv.
pasteurized ['pæstəraɪzd] adj pa-

storizzato(a).

pastille ['pæstl] *n* pastiglia.

pastime ['pɑːstaɪm] *n* passatempo.

pastry ['peɪstrɪ] *n* pasta.

pasture ['pɑːstʃə*] *n* pascolo.

pasty[1] ['pæstɪ] *n* pasticcio di carne.

pasty[2] ['peɪstɪ] *adj (face etc)* smorto(a).

pat [pæt] *vt* accarezzare, dare un colpetto (affettuoso) a.

patch [pætʃ] *n (of material, on tyre)* toppa; *(eye ~)* benda; *(spot)* macchia ♦ *vt (clothes)* rattoppare; **(to go through) a bad ~** (attraversare) un brutto periodo; **~ up** *vt* rappezzare; *(quarrel)* appianare; **~y** *adj* irregolare.

pâté ['pæteɪ] *n* pâté *m inv*.

patent ['peɪtnt] *n* brevetto ♦ *vt* brevettare ♦ *adj* patente, manifesto(a); **~ leather** *n* cuoio verniciato.

paternal [pə'tɜːnl] *adj* paterno(a).

path [pɑːθ] *n* sentiero, viottolo; viale *m*; *(fig)* via, strada; *(of planet, missile)* traiettoria.

pathetic [pə'θetɪk] *adj (pitiful)* patetico(a); *(very bad)* penoso(a).

pathological [pæθə'lɒdʒɪkl] *adj* patologico(a).

pathway ['pɑːθweɪ] *n* sentiero.

patience ['peɪʃns] *n* pazienza; *(BRIT: CARDS)* solitario.

patient ['peɪʃnt] *n* paziente *m/f*; malato/a ♦ *adj* paziente.

patio ['pætɪəʊ] *n* terrazza.

patriot ['peɪtrɪət] *n* patriota *m/f*; **~ic** [pætrɪ'ɒtɪk] *adj* patriottico(a); **~ism** *n* patriottismo.

patrol [pə'trəʊl] *n* pattuglia ♦ *vt* pattugliare; **~ car** *n* autoradio *f inv* (della polizia); **~man** *(US)* *n* poliziotto.

patron ['peɪtrən] *n (in shop)* cliente *m/f*; *(of charity)* benefattore/trice; **~ of the arts** mecenate *m/f*; **~ize** ['pætrənaɪz] *vt* essere cliente abituale di; *(fig)* trattare dall'alto in basso.

patter ['pætə*] *n* picchiettio; *(sales talk)* propaganda di vendita ♦ *vi* picchiettare; **a ~ of footsteps** un rumore di passi.

pattern ['pætən] *n* modello, disegno, motivo.

paunch [pɔːntʃ] *n* pancione *m*.

pauper ['pɔːpə*] *n* indigente *m/f*.

pause [pɔːz] *n* pausa ♦ *vi* fare una pausa, arrestarsi.

pave [peɪv] *vt* pavimentare; **to ~ the way for** aprire la via a.

pavement ['peɪvmənt] *(BRIT)* *n* marciapiede *m*.

pavilion [pə'vɪlɪən] *n (SPORT)* edificio annesso a campo sportivo.

paving ['peɪvɪŋ] *n* pavimentazione *f*; **~ stone** *n* lastra di pietra.

paw [pɔː] *n* zampa.

pawn [pɔːn] *n (CHESS)* pedone *m*; *(fig)* pedina ♦ *vt* dare in pegno; **~broker** *n* prestatore *m* su pegno; **~shop** *n* monte *m* di pietà.

pay [peɪ] *(pt, pp paid) n* stipendio, paga ♦ *vt* pagare ♦ *vi (be profitable)* rendere; **to ~ attention (to)** fare attenzione (a); **to ~ sb a visit** far visita a qn; **to ~ one's respects to sb** porgere i propri rispetti a qn; **~ back** *vt* rimborsare; **~ for** *vt fus* pagare; **~ in** *vt* versare; **~ off** *vt (debt)* saldare; *(person)* pagare; *(employee)* pagare e licenziare ♦ *vi (scheme, decision)* dare dei frutti; **~ up** *vt* saldare; **~able** *adj* pagabile; **~ee** *n* beneficiario/a; **~ envelope** *(US) n* = **~ packet**; **~ment** *n* pagamento; versamento; saldo; **~ packet** *(BRIT)* *n* busta *f* paga *inv*; **~ phone** *n* cabina telefonica; **~roll** *n* ruolo (organico); **~ slip** *n* foglio *m* paga *inv*.

PC *n abbr* = **personal computer**.

p.c. *abbr* = **per cent**.

pea [piː] *n* pisello.

peace [piːs] *n* pace *f*; **~ful** *adj* pacifico(a), calmo(a).

peach [piːtʃ] *n* pesca.

peacock ['piːkɒk] *n* pavone *m*.

peak [piːk] *n (of mountain)* cima, vetta; *(mountain itself)* picco; *(of cap)* visiera; *(fig)* apice *m*, culmine *m*; **~ hours** *npl* ore *fpl* di punta; **~ period** *n* = **~ hours**.

peal [piːl] *n (of bells)* scampanio, carillon *m inv*; **~s of laughter** scoppi *mpl* di risa.

peanut ['piːnʌt] *n* arachide *f*, nocciolina americana; ~ **butter** *n* burro di arachidi.

pear [pɛə*] *n* pera.

pearl [pəːl] *n* perla.

peasant ['pɛznt] *n* contadino/a.

peat [piːt] *n* torba.

pebble ['pɛbl] *n* ciottolo.

peck [pɛk] *vt* (*also:* ~ *at*) beccare ♦ *n* colpo di becco; (*kiss*) bacetto; ~**ing order** *n* ordine *m* gerarchico; ~**ish** (*BRIT: inf*) *adj*: **I feel** ~**ish** ho un languorino.

peculiar [pɪ'kjuːlɪə*] *adj* strano(a), bizzarro(a); peculiare; ~ **to** peculiare di.

pedal ['pɛdl] *n* pedale *m* ♦ *vi* pedalare.

pedantic [pɪ'dæntɪk] *adj* pedantesco(a).

peddler ['pɛdlə*] *n* (*also: drugs* ~) spacciatore/trice.

pedestal ['pɛdəstl] *n* piedestallo.

pedestrian [pɪ'dɛstrɪən] *n* pedone/a ♦ *adj* pedonale; (*fig*) prosaico(a), pedestre; ~ **crossing** (*BRIT*) *n* passaggio pedonale.

pediatrics [piːdɪ'ætrɪks] (*US*) *n* = **paediatrics**.

pedigree ['pɛdɪgriː] *n* (*of animal*) pedigree *m inv*; (*fig*) background *m inv* ♦ *cpd* (*animal*) di razza.

pee [piː] (*inf*) *vi* pisciare.

peek [piːk] *vi* guardare furtivamente.

peel [piːl] *n* buccia; (*of orange, lemon*) scorza ♦ *vt* sbucciare ♦ *vi* (*paint etc*) staccarsi.

peep [piːp] *n* (*BRIT: look*) sguardo furtivo, sbirciata; (*sound*) pigolio ♦ *vi* (*BRIT*) guardare furtivamente; ~ **out** *vi* mostrarsi furtivamente; ~**hole** *n* spioncino.

peer [pɪə*] *vi*: **to** ~ **at** scrutare ♦ *n* (*noble*) pari *m inv*; (*equal*) pari *m/f inv*, uguale *m/f*; (*contemporary*) contemporaneo/a; ~**age** *n* dignità di pari; pari *mpl*.

peeved [piːvd] *adj* stizzito(a).

peevish ['piːvɪʃ] *adj* stizzoso(a).

peg [pɛg] *n* caviglia; (*for coat etc*) attaccapanni *m inv*; (*BRIT: also: clothes* ~) molletta.

Peking [piː'kɪŋ] *n* Pechino *f*.

pelican ['pɛlɪkən] *n* pellicano; ~ **crossing** (*BRIT*) *n* (*AUT*) attraversamento pedonale con semaforo a controllo manuale.

pellet ['pɛlɪt] *n* pallottola, pallina.

pelt [pɛlt] *vt*: **to** ~ **sb** (**with**) bombardare qn (con) ♦ *vi* (*rain*) piovere a dirotto; (*inf: run*) filare ♦ *n* pelle *f*.

pelvis ['pɛlvɪs] *n* pelvi *f inv*, bacino.

pen [pɛn] *n* penna; (*for sheep*) recinto.

penal ['piːnl] *adj* penale; ~**ize** *vt* punire; (*SPORT, fig*) penalizzare.

penalty ['pɛnltɪ] *n* penalità *f inv*; sanzione *f* penale; (*fine*) ammenda; (*SPORT*) penalizzazione *f*; ~ (**kick**) *n* (*SPORT*) calcio di rigore.

penance ['pɛnəns] *n* penitenza.

pence [pɛns] (*BRIT*) *npl of* **penny**.

pencil ['pɛnsl] *n* matita; ~ **case** *n* astuccio per matite; ~ **sharpener** *n* temperamatite *m inv*.

pendant ['pɛndnt] *n* pendaglio.

pending ['pɛndɪŋ] *prep* in attesa di ♦ *adj* in sospeso.

pendulum ['pɛndjuləm] *n* pendolo.

penetrate ['pɛnɪtreɪt] *vt* penetrare.

penfriend ['pɛnfrɛnd] (*BRIT*) *n* corrispondente *m/f*.

penguin ['pɛŋgwɪn] *n* pinguino.

penicillin [pɛnɪ'sɪlɪn] *n* penicillina.

peninsula [pə'nɪnsjulə] *n* penisola.

penis ['piːnɪs] *n* pene *m*.

penitent ['pɛnɪtnt] *adj* penitente.

penitentiary [pɛnɪ'tɛnʃərɪ] (*US*) *n* carcere *m*.

penknife ['pɛnnaɪf] *n* temperino.

pen name *n* pseudonimo.

penniless ['pɛnɪlɪs] *adj* senza un soldo.

penny ['pɛnɪ] (*pl* **pennies** *or* **pence** (*BRIT*)) *n* penny *m*; (*US*) centesimo.

penpal ['pɛnpæl] *n* corrispondente *m/f*.

pension ['pɛnʃən] *n* pensione *f*; ~**er** (*BRIT*) *n* pensionato/a.

pensive ['pɛnsɪv] *adj* pensoso(a).

penthouse ['pɛnthaus] *n* appartamento (di lusso) nell'attico.

pent-up ['pɛntʌp] *adj* (*feelings*) represso(a).

people ['pi:pl] npl gente f; persone fpl; (citizens) popolo ♦ n (nation, race) popolo; 4/several ~ came 4/parecchie persone sono venute; ~ say that ... si dice che ....

pep [pɛp] (inf) n dinamismo; ~ up vt vivacizzare; (food) rendere più gustoso(a).

pepper ['pɛpə*] n pepe m; (vegetable) peperone m ♦ vt (fig): to ~ with spruzzare di; ~mint n (sweet) pasticca di menta.

peptalk ['pɛptɔ:k] (inf) n discorso di incoraggiamento.

per [pə:*] prep per; a; ~ hour all'ora; ~ kilo etc il chilo etc; ~ day al giorno; ~ annum adv all'anno; ~ capita adj, adv pro capite inv.

perceive [pə'si:v] vt percepire; (notice) accorgersi di.

per cent [pə'sɛnt] adv per cento.

percentage [pə'sɛntɪdʒ] n percentuale f.

perception [pə'sɛpʃən] n percezione f; sensibilità; perspicacia.

perceptive [pə'sɛptɪv] adj percettivo(a); perspicace.

perch [pə:tʃ] n (fish) pesce m persico; (for bird) sostegno, ramo ♦ vi appollaiarsi.

percolator ['pə:kəleɪtə*] n (also: coffee ~) caffettiera a pressione; caffettiera elettrica.

percussion [pə'kʌʃən] n percussione f; (MUS) strumenti mpl a percussione.

peremptory [pə'rɛmptərɪ] adj perentorio(a).

perennial [pə'rɛnɪəl] adj perenne.

perfect [adj, n 'pə:fɪkt, vb pə'fɛkt] adj perfetto(a) ♦ n (also: ~ tense) perfetto, passato prossimo ♦ vt perfezionare; mettere a punto; ~ly adv perfettamente, alla perfezione.

perforate ['pə:fəreɪt] vt perforare; **perforation** [-'reɪʃən] n perforazione f.

perform [pə'fɔ:m] vt (carry out) eseguire, fare; (symphony etc) suonare; (play, ballet) dare; (opera) fare ♦ vi suonare; recitare; ~ance n esecuzione f; (at theatre etc) rappresentazione f, spettacolo; (of an artist) interpretazione f; (of player etc) performance f; (of car, engine) prestazione f; ~er n artista m/f.

perfume ['pə:fju:m] n profumo.

perfunctory [pə'fʌŋktərɪ] adj superficiale, per la forma.

perhaps [pə'hæps] adv forse.

peril ['pɛrɪl] n pericolo.

perimeter [pə'rɪmɪtə*] n perimetro.

period ['pɪərɪəd] n periodo; (HISTORY) epoca; (SCOL) lezione f; (full stop) punto; (MED) mestruazioni fpl ♦ adj (costume, furniture) d'epoca; ~ic(al) [-'ɔdɪk(l)] adj periodico(a); ~ical [-'ɔdɪkl] n periodico.

peripheral [pə'rɪfərəl] adj periferico(a) ♦ n (COMPUT) unità f inv periferica.

perish ['pɛrɪʃ] vi perire, morire; (decay) deteriorarsi; ~able adj deperibile.

perjury ['pə:dʒərɪ] n spergiuro.

perk [pə:k] (inf) n vantaggio; ~ up vi (cheer up) rianimarsi; ~y adj (cheerful) vivace, allegro(a).

perm [pə:m] n (for hair) permanente f.

permanent ['pə:mənənt] adj permanente.

permeate ['pə:mɪeɪt] vi penetrare ♦ vt permeare.

permissible [pə'mɪsɪbl] adj permissibile, ammissibile.

permission [pə'mɪʃən] n permesso.

permissive [pə'mɪsɪv] adj permissivo(a).

permit [n 'pə:mɪt, vb pə'mɪt] n permesso ♦ vt permettere; to ~ sb to do permettere a qn di fare.

perpendicular [pə:pən'dɪkjulə*] adj perpendicolare ♦ n perpendicolare f.

perplex [pə'plɛks] vt lasciare perplesso(a).

persecute ['pə:sɪkju:t] vt perseguitare.

persevere [pə:sɪ'vɪə*] vi perseverare.

Persian ['pə:ʃən] adj persiano(a) ♦ n (LING) persiano; the (~) Gulf n il Golfo Persico.

persist [pə'sɪst] vi: to ~ (in doing) persistere (nel fare); ostinarsi (a fare); ~ent adj persistente; ostinato(a).

person ['pə:sn] n persona; in ~ di or in

persona, personalmente; **~al** *adj* personale; individuale; **~al assistant** *n* segretaria personale; **~al column** *n* ≈ messaggi *mpl* personali; **~al computer** *n* personal computer *m inv*; **~ality** [-'nælɪtɪ] *n* personalità *f inv*; **~ally** *adv* personalmente; **to take** sth **~ally** prendere qc come una critica personale; **~al organizer** *n* agenda personale.

personnel [pə:sə'nɛl] *n* personale *m*.

perspective [pə'spɛktɪv] *n* prospettiva.

Perspex ['pə:spɛks] ® (*BRIT*) *n* tipo di *resina termoplastica*.

perspiration [pə:spɪ'reɪʃən] *n* traspirazione *f*, sudore *m*.

persuade [pə'sweɪd] *vt*: **to ~** sb **to do** sth persuadere qn a fare qc.

pertaining [pə:'teɪnɪŋ]: **~ to** *prep* che riguarda.

perturb [pə'tə:b] *vt* turbare.

peruse [pə'ru:z] *vt* leggere.

pervade [pə'veɪd] *vt* pervadere.

pervert [*n* 'pə:və:t, *vb* pə'və:t] *n* pervertito/a ♦ *vt* pervertire.

pessimism ['pɛsɪmɪzəm] *n* pessimismo.

pessimist ['pɛsɪmɪst] *n* pessimista *m/f*; **~ic** [-'mɪstɪk] *adj* pessimistico(a).

pest [pɛst] *n* animale *m* (*or* insetto) pestifero; (*fig*) peste *f*.

pester ['pɛstə*] *vt* tormentare, molestare.

pet [pɛt] *n* animale *m* domestico ♦ *cpd* favorito(a) ♦ *vt* accarezzare ♦ *vi* (*inf*) fare il petting; **teacher's ~** favorito/a del maestro.

petal ['pɛtl] *n* petalo.

peter ['pi:tə*]: **to ~ out** *vi* esaurirsi, estinguersi.

petite [pə'ti:t] *adj* piccolo(a) e aggraziato(a).

petition [pə'tɪʃən] *n* petizione *f*.

petrified ['pɛtrɪfaɪd] *adj* (*fig*) morto(a) di paura.

petrol ['pɛtrəl] (*BRIT*) *n* benzina; **two/ four-star ~** ≈ benzina normale/super; **~ can** *n* tanica per benzina.

petroleum [pə'trəʊlɪəm] *n* petrolio.

petrol: ~ pump (*BRIT*) *n* (*in car, at garage*) pompa di benzina; **~ station**

(*BRIT*) *n* stazione *f* di rifornimento; **~ tank** (*BRIT*) *n* serbatoio della benzina.

petticoat ['pɛtɪkəʊt] *n* sottana.

petty ['pɛtɪ] *adj* (*mean*) meschino(a); (*unimportant*) insignificante; **~ cash** *n* piccola cassa; **~ officer** *n* sottufficiale *m* di marina.

petulant ['pɛtjulənt] *adj* irritabile.

pew [pju:] *n* panca (di chiesa).

pewter ['pju:tə*] *n* peltro.

phallic ['fælɪk] *adj* fallico(a).

phantom ['fæntəm] *n* fantasma *m*.

pharmaceutical [fɑ:mə'sju:tɪkl] *adj* farmaceutico(a).

pharmacy ['fɑ:məsɪ] *n* farmacia.

phase [feɪz] *n* fase *f*, periodo ♦ *vt*: **to ~** sth **in/out** introdurre/eliminare qc progressivamente.

Ph.D. *n abbr* = **Doctor of Philosophy**.

pheasant ['fɛznt] *n* fagiano.

phenomena [fə'nɔmɪnə] *npl of* **phenomenon**.

phenomenon [fə'nɔmɪnən] (*pl* **phenomena**) *n* fenomeno.

Philippines ['fɪlɪpi:nz] *npl*: **the ~** le Filippine.

philosophical [fɪlə'sɔfɪkl] *adj* filosofico(a).

philosophy [fɪ'lɔsəfɪ] *n* filosofia.

phlegmatic [flɛg'mætɪk] *adj* flemmatico(a).

phobia ['fəʊbjə] *n* fobia.

phone [fəʊn] *n* telefono ♦ *vt* telefonare; **to be on the ~** avere il telefono; (*be calling*) essere al telefono; **~ back** *vt*, *vi* richiamare; **~ up** *vt* telefonare a ♦ *vi* telefonare; **~ book** *n* guida del telefono, elenco telefonico; **~ booth** *n* = **~ box**; **~ box** *n* cabina telefonica; **~ call** *n* telefonata; **~-in** *n* (*BRIT*: *RADIO, TV*) trasmissione *f* a filo diretto con gli ascoltatori.

phonetics [fə'nɛtɪks] *n* fonetica.

phoney ['fəʊnɪ] *adj* falso(a), fasullo(a).

phonograph ['fəʊnəgrɑ:f] (*US*) *n* giradischi *m inv*.

phosphorus ['fɔsfərəs] *n* fosforo.

photo ['fəʊtəʊ] *n* foto *f inv*.

photo... ['fəʊtəʊ] *prefix*: **~copier** *n* fotocopiatrice *f*; **~copy** *n* fotocopia ♦ *vt* fotocopiare; **~graph** n fotografia ♦ vt fotografare; **~grapher** [fə'tɔgrəfə*] n fotografo; **~graphy** [fə'tɔgrəfɪ] n fotografia.

phrase [freɪz] n espressione f; (LING) locuzione f; (MUS) frase f ♦ vt esprimere; **~ book** n vocabolarietto.

physical ['fɪzɪkl] adj fisico(a); **~ education** n educazione f fisica; **~ly** adv fisicamente.

physician [fɪ'zɪʃən] n medico.

physicist ['fɪzɪsɪst] n fisico.

physics ['fɪzɪks] n fisica.

physiology [fɪzɪ'ɔlədʒɪ] n fisiologia.

physique [fɪ'ziːk] n fisico; costituzione f.

pianist ['piːənɪst] n pianista m/f.

piano [pɪ'ænəu] n pianoforte m.

piccolo ['pɪkələu] n ottavino.

pick [pɪk] n (tool: also: **~-axe**) piccone m ♦ vt scegliere; (gather) cogliere; (remove) togliere; (lock) far scattare; **take your ~** scelga; **the ~ of** il fior fiore di; **to ~ one's nose** mettersi le dita nel naso; **to ~ one's teeth** pulirsi i denti con lo stuzzicadenti; **to ~ a quarrel** attaccar briga; **~ at** vt fus: **to ~ at one's food** piluccare; **~ on** vt fus (person) avercela con; **~ out** vt scegliere; (distinguish) distinguere; **~ up** vi (improve) migliorarsi ♦ vt raccogliere; (POLICE, RADIO) prendere; (collect) passare a prendere; (AUT: give lift to) far salire; (person: for sexual encounter) rimorchiare; (learn) imparare; **to ~ up speed** acquistare velocità; **to ~ o.s. up** rialzarsi.

picket ['pɪkɪt] n (in strike) scioperante m/f che fa parte di un picchetto; picchetto ♦ vt picchettare.

pickle ['pɪkl] n (also: **~s: as condiment**) sottaceti mpl; (fig: mess) pasticcio ♦ vt mettere sottaceto; mettere in salamoia.

pickpocket ['pɪkpɔkɪt] n borsaiolo.

pickup ['pɪkʌp] n (small truck) camioncino.

picnic ['pɪknɪk] n picnic m inv.

picture ['pɪktʃə*] n quadro; (painting) pittura; (photograph) foto(grafia); (drawing) disegno; (film) film m inv ♦ vt raffigurarsi; **~s** (BRIT) npl (cinema):

the **~s** il cinema; **~ book** n libro illustrato.

picturesque [pɪktʃə'rɛsk] adj pittoresco(a).

pie [paɪ] n torta; (of meat) pasticcio.

piece [piːs] n pezzo; (of land) appezzamento; (item): **a ~ of furniture/advice** un mobile/consiglio ♦ vt: **to ~ together** mettere insieme; **to take to ~s** smontare; **~meal** adv pezzo a pezzo, a spizzico; **~work** n (lavoro a) cottimo.

pie chart n grafico a torta.

pier [pɪə*] n molo; (of bridge etc) pila.

pierce [pɪəs] vt forare; (with arrow etc) trafiggere.

piercing ['pɪəsɪŋ] adj (cry) acuto(a); (eyes) penetrante; (wind) pungente.

pig [pɪg] n maiale m, porco.

pigeon ['pɪdʒən] n piccione m; **~hole** n casella.

piggy bank ['pɪgɪ-] n salvadanaro.

pigheaded ['pɪg'hɛdɪd] adj caparbio(a), cocciuto(a).

piglet ['pɪglɪt] n porcellino.

pigskin ['pɪgskɪn] n cinghiale m.

pigsty ['pɪgstaɪ] n porcile m.

pigtail ['pɪgteɪl] n treccina.

pike [paɪk] n (fish) luccio.

pilchard ['pɪltʃəd] n specie di sardina.

pile [paɪl] n (pillar, of books) pila; (heap) mucchio; (of carpet) pelo ♦ vt (also: **~ up**) ammucchiare ♦ vi (also: **~ up**) ammucchiarsi; **to ~ into** (car) stiparsi or ammucchiarsi in.

piles [paɪlz] npl emorroidi fpl.

pileup ['paɪlʌp] n (AUT) tamponamento a catena.

pilfering ['pɪlfərɪŋ] n rubacchiare m.

pilgrim ['pɪlgrɪm] n pellegrino/a; **~age** n pellegrinaggio.

pill [pɪl] n pillola; **the ~** la pillola.

pillage ['pɪlɪdʒ] vt saccheggiare.

pillar ['pɪlə*] n colonna; **~ box** (BRIT) n cassetta postale.

pillion ['pɪljən] n: **to ride ~** (on motor cycle) viaggiare dietro.

pillory ['pɪlərɪ] vt mettere alla berlina.

pillow ['pɪləu] n guanciale m; **~case** n federa.

pilot ['paɪlət] *n* pilota *m/f* ♦ *cpd* (*scheme etc*) pilota *inv* ♦ *vt* pilotare; ~ **light** *n* fiamma pilota.

pimp [pɪmp] *n* mezzano.

pimple ['pɪmpl] *n* foruncolo.

pin [pɪn] *n* spillo; (*TECH*) perno ♦ *vt* attaccare con uno spillo; ~**s and needles** formicolio; **to** ~ **sb down** (*fig*) obbligare qn a pronunziarsi; **to** ~ **sth on sb** (*fig*) addossare la colpa di qc a qn.

pinafore ['pɪnəfɔ:*] *n* (*also:* ~ **dress**) grembiule *m* (senza maniche).

pinball ['pɪnbɔ:l] *n* flipper *m inv*.

pincers ['pɪnsəz] *npl* pinzette *fpl*.

pinch [pɪntʃ] *n* pizzicotto, pizzico ♦ *vt* pizzicare; (*inf: steal*) grattare; **at a** ~ in caso di bisogno.

pincushion ['pɪnkuʃən] *n* puntaspilli *m inv*.

pine [paɪn] *n* (*also:* ~ **tree**) pino ♦ *vi*: **to** ~ **for** struggersi dal desiderio di; ~ **away** *vi* languire.

pineapple ['paɪnæpl] *n* ananas *m inv*.

ping [pɪŋ] *n* (*noise*) tintinnio; ~**-pong** ® *n* ping-pong *m* ®.

pink [pɪŋk] *adj* rosa *inv* ♦ *n* (*colour*) rosa *m inv*; (*BOT*) garofano.

pinpoint ['pɪnpɔɪnt] *vt* indicare con precisione.

pint [paɪnt] *n* pinta (*BRIT* = 0.57*l*; *US* = 0.47*l*); (*BRIT: inf*) ≈ birra da mezzo.

pioneer [paɪə'nɪə*] *n* pioniere/a.

pious ['paɪəs] *adj* pio(a).

pip [pɪp] *n* (*seed*) seme *m*; (*BRIT: time signal on radio*) segnale *m* orario.

pipe [paɪp] *n* tubo; (*for smoking*) pipa ♦ *vt* portare per mezzo di tubazione; ~**s** *npl* (*also:* bag~**s**) cornamusa (scozzese); ~ **down** (*inf*) *vi* calmarsi; ~ **cleaner** *n* scovolino; ~ **dream** *n* vana speranza; ~**line** *n* conduttura; (*for oil*) oleodotto; ~**r** *n* piffero; suonatore/trice di cornamusa.

piping ['paɪpɪŋ] *adv*: ~ **hot** caldo bollente.

pique [pi:k] *n* picca.

pirate ['paɪərət] *n* pirata *m* ♦ *vt* riprodurre abusivamente.

Pisces ['paɪsi:z] *n* Pesci *mpl*.

piss [pɪs] (*inf*) *vi* pisciare; ~**ed** (*inf*)

adj (*drunk*) ubriaco(a) fradicio(a).

pistol ['pɪstl] *n* pistola.

piston ['pɪstən] *n* pistone *m*.

pit [pɪt] *n* buca, fossa; (*also: coal* ~) miniera; (*quarry*) cava ♦ *vt*: **to** ~ **sb against sb** opporre qn a qn; ~**s** *npl* (*AUT*) box *m*.

pitch [pɪtʃ] *n* (*BRIT: SPORT*) campo; (*MUS*) tono; (*tar*) pece *f*; (*fig*) grado, punto ♦ *vt* (*throw*) lanciare ♦ *vi* (*fall*) cascare; **to** ~ **a tent** piantare una tenda; ~**ed battle** *n* battaglia campale.

pitchfork ['pɪtʃfɔ:k] *n* forcone *m*.

piteous ['pɪtɪəs] *adj* pietoso(a).

pitfall ['pɪtfɔ:l] *n* trappola.

pith [pɪθ] *n* (*of plant*) midollo; (*of orange*) parte *f* interna della scorza; (*fig*) essenza, succo; vigore *m*.

pithy ['pɪθɪ] *adj* conciso(a); vigoroso(a).

pitiful ['pɪtɪful] *adj* (*touching*) pietoso(a).

pitiless ['pɪtɪlɪs] *adj* spietato(a).

pittance ['pɪtns] *n* miseria, magro salario.

pity ['pɪtɪ] *n* pietà ♦ *vt* aver pietà di; **what a** ~! che peccato!

pivot ['pɪvət] *n* perno.

pizza ['pi:tsə] *n* pizza.

placard ['plækɑ:d] *n* affisso.

placate [plə'keɪt] *vt* placare, calmare.

place [pleɪs] *n* posto, luogo; (*proper position, rank, seat*) posto; (*house*) casa, alloggio; (*home*): **at/to his** ~ **a** casa sua ♦ *vt* (*object*) posare, mettere; (*identify*) riconoscere; individuare; **to take** ~ aver luogo; succedere; **to change** ~**s with sb** scambiare il posto con qn; **out of** ~ (*not suitable*) inopportuno(a); **in the first** ~ in primo luogo; **to** ~ **an order** dare un'ordinazione; **to be** ~**d** (*in race, exam*) classificarsi.

placid ['plæsɪd] *adj* placido(a), calmo(a).

plagiarism ['pleɪdʒərɪzəm] *n* plagio.

plague [pleɪg] *n* peste *f* ♦ *vt* tormentare.

plaice [pleɪs] *n inv* pianuzza.

plaid [plæd] *n* plaid *m inv*.

plain [pleɪn] *adj* (*clear*) chiaro(a), palese; (*simple*) semplice; (*frank*) franco(a), aperto(a); (not handsome) bruttino(a); (without seasoning etc) scondito(a); naturale; (in one colour) tinta unita inv ♦ adv francamente, chiaramente ♦ n pianura; ~ **chocolate** n cioccolato fondente; ~ **clothes** npl: in ~ **clothes** (police) in borghese; ~**ly** adv chiaramente; (frankly) francamente.

plaintiff ['pleɪntɪf] n attore/trice.

plaintive ['pleɪntɪv] adj (cry, voice) dolente, lamentoso(a).

plait [plæt] n treccia.

plan [plæn] n pianta; (scheme) progetto, piano ♦ vt (think in advance) progettare; (prepare) organizzare ♦ vi far piani or progetti; **to ~ to do** progettare di fare.

plane [pleɪn] n (AVIAT) aereo; (tree) platano; (tool) pialla; (ART, MATH etc) piano ♦ adj piano(a), piatto(a) ♦ vt (with tool) piallare.

planet ['plænɪt] n pianeta m.

plank [plæŋk] n tavola, asse f.

planner ['plænə*] n pianificatore/trice.

planning ['plænɪŋ] n progettazione f; **family ~** pianificazione f delle nascite; ~ **permission** n permesso di costruzione.

plant [plɑ:nt] n pianta; (machinery) impianto; (factory) fabbrica ♦ vt piantare; (bomb) mettere.

plantation [plæn'teɪʃən] n piantagione f.

plaque [plæk] n placca.

plaster ['plɑ:stə*] n intonaco; (also: ~ of Paris) gesso; (BRIT: also: sticking ~) cerotto ♦ vt intonacare; ingessare; (cover): **to ~ with** coprire di; ~**ed** (inf) adj ubriaco(a) fradicio(a).

plastic ['plæstɪk] n plastica ♦ adj (made of ~) di or in plastica; ~ **bag** n sacchetto di plastica.

Plasticine ['plæstɪsi:n] ® n plastilina ®.

plastic surgery n chirurgia plastica.

plate [pleɪt] n (dish) piatto; (in book) tavola, (PHOT) lastra; **gold/silver ~** vasellame m d'oro/d'argento.

plateau ['plætəu] (pl ~s or ~x) n altipiano.

plateaux ['plætəuz] npl of **plateau**.

plate glass n vetro piano.

platform ['plætfɔ:m] n (stage, at meeting) palco; (RAIL) marciapiede m; (BRIT: of bus) piattaforma.

platinum ['plætɪnəm] n platino.

platitude ['plætɪtju:d] n luogo comune.

platoon [plə'tu:n] n plotone m.

platter ['plætə*] n piatto.

plausible ['plɔ:zɪbl] adj plausibile, credibile; (person) convincente.

play [pleɪ] n gioco; (THEATRE) commedia ♦ vt (game) giocare a; (team, opponent) giocare contro; (instrument, piece of music) suonare; (record, tape) ascoltare; (role, part) interpretare ♦ vi giocare; suonare; recitare; **to ~ safe** giocare sul sicuro; ~ **down** vt minimizzare; ~ **up** vi (cause trouble) fare i capricci; ~**boy** n playboy m inv; ~**er** n giocatore/trice; (THEATRE) attore/trice; (MUS) musicista m/f; ~**ful** adj giocoso(a); ~**ground** n (in school) cortile m per la ricreazione; (in park) parco m giochi inv; ~**group** n giardino d'infanzia; ~**ing card** n carta da gioco; ~**ing field** n campo sportivo; ~**mate** n compagno/a di gioco; ~**-off** n (SPORT) bella; ~**pen** n box m inv; ~**thing** n giocattolo; ~**time** n (SCOL) ricreazione f; ~**wright** n drammaturgo/a.

plc abbr (= public limited company) società per azioni a responsabilità limitata quotata in borsa.

plea [pli:] n (request) preghiera, domanda; (LAW) (argomento di) difesa.

plead [pli:d] vt patrocinare; (give as excuse) addurre a pretesto ♦ vi (LAW) perorare la causa; (beg): **to ~ with sb** implorare qn.

pleasant ['plɛznt] adj piacevole, gradevole; ~**ries** npl (polite remarks): **to exchange ~ries** scambiarsi i convenevoli.

please [pli:z] excl per piacere!, per favore!; (acceptance): **yes, ~** sì, grazie ♦ vt piacere a ♦ vi piacere; (think fit): **do as you ~** faccia come le pare; ~ **yourself!** come ti (or le) pare!; ~**d** adj: ~**d (with)** contento(a) (di); ~**d to meet you!** piacere!; **pleasing** adj piacevole, che fa piacere.

pleasure ['plɛʒə*] n piacere m; "it's a ~" "prego"; ~ **boat** n imbarcazione f da diporto.

pleat [pliːt] n piega.

pledge [plɛdʒ] n pegno; (promise) promessa ♦ vt impegnare; promettere.

plentiful ['plɛntɪful] adj abbondante, copioso(a).

plenty ['plɛntɪ] n: ~ **of** tanto(a), molto(a); un'abbondanza di.

pleurisy ['pluərɪsɪ] n pleurite f.

pliable ['plaɪəbl] adj flessibile; (fig: person) malleabile.

pliant [plaɪənt] adj = **pliable**.

pliers ['plaɪəz] npl pinza.

plight [plaɪt] n situazione f critica.

plimsolls ['plɪmsəlz] (BRIT) npl scarpe fpl da tennis.

plinth [plɪnθ] n plinto; piedistallo.

plod [plɒd] vi camminare a stento; (fig) sgobbare.

plonk [plɒŋk] (inf) n (BRIT: wine) vino da poco ♦ vt: to ~ **sth down** buttare giù qc bruscamente.

plot [plɒt] n congiura, cospirazione f; (of story, play) trama; (of land) lotto ♦ vt (mark out) fare la pianta di; rilevare; (: diagram etc) tracciare; (conspire) congiurare, cospirare ♦ vi congiurare; ~ter n (instrument) plotter m inv.

plough [plau] (US **plow**) n aratro ♦ vt (earth) arare; to ~ **money into** (company etc) investire danaro in; ~ **through** vt fus (snow etc) procedere a fatica in; ~**man's lunch** (BRIT) n pasto a base di pane, formaggio e birra.

ploy [plɔɪ] n stratagemma m.

pluck [plʌk] vt (fruit) cogliere; (musical instrument) pizzicare; (bird) spennare; (hairs) togliere ♦ n coraggio, fegato; to ~ **up courage** farsi coraggio.

plug [plʌg] n tappo; (ELEC) spina; (AUT: also: spark(ing) ~) candela ♦ vt (hole) tappare; (inf: advertise) spingere; ~ **in** vt (ELEC) attaccare a una presa.

plum [plʌm] n (fruit) susina ♦ cpd: ~ **job** (inf) impiego ottimo or favoloso.

plumb [plʌm] vt: to ~ **the depths** (fig) toccare il fondo.

plumber ['plʌmə*] n idraulico.

plumbing ['plʌmɪŋ] n (trade) lavoro di idraulico; (piping) tubature fpl.

plume [pluːm] n piuma, penna; (decorative) pennacchio.

plummet ['plʌmɪt] vi: to ~ (**down**) cadere a piombo.

plump [plʌmp] adj grassoccio(a) ♦ vi: to ~ **for** (inf: choose) decidersi per; ~ **up** vt (cushion etc) sprimacciare.

plunder ['plʌndə*] n saccheggio ♦ vt saccheggiare.

plunge [plʌndʒ] n tuffo; (fig) caduta ♦ vt immergere ♦ vi (fall) cadere, precipitare; (dive) tuffarsi; to take the ~ saltare il fosso; ~**r** n sturalavandini m inv; **plunging** adj (neckline) profondo(a).

pluperfect [pluː'pəːfɪkt] n piuccheperfetto.

plural ['pluərl] adj plurale ♦ n plurale m.

plus [plʌs] n (also: ~ **sign**) segno più ♦ prep più; **ten/twenty** ~ più di dieci/venti.

plush [plʌʃ] adj lussuoso(a).

ply [plaɪ] vt (a trade) esercitare ♦ vi (ship) fare il servizio ♦ n (of wool, rope) capo; to ~ **sb with drink** dare di bere continuamente a qn; ~**wood** n legno compensato.

P.M. n abbr = **prime minister**.

p.m. adv abbr (= post meridiem) del pomeriggio.

pneumatic drill [njuː'mætɪk] n martello pneumatico.

pneumonia [njuː'məunɪə] n polmonite f.

poach [pəutʃ] vt (cook: egg) affogare; (: fish) cuocere in bianco; (steal) cacciare (or pescare) di frodo ♦ vi fare il bracconiere; ~**er** n bracconiere m.

P.O. Box n abbr = **Post Office Box**.

pocket ['pɒkɪt] n tasca ♦ vt intascare; to be out of ~ (BRIT) rimetterci; ~**book** (US) n (wallet) portafoglio; ~ **knife** n temperino; ~ **money** n paghetta, settimana.

pod [pɒd] n guscio.

podgy ['pɒdʒɪ] adj grassoccio(a).

podiatrist [pɒ'diːətrɪst] (US) n callista m/f, pedicure m/f.

poem ['pəʊɪm] n poesia.

poet ['pəʊɪt] n poeta/essa; ~**ic** [-'ɛtɪk] adj poetico(a); ~ **laureate** n poeta m laureato (nominato dalla Corte Reale); ~**ry** n poesia.

poignant ['pɔɪnjənt] adj struggente.

point [pɔɪnt] n (gen) punto; (tip: of needle etc) punta; (in time) punto, momento; (SCOL) voto; (main idea, important part) nocciolo; (ELEC) presa (di corrente); (also: decimal ~): 2 ~ 3 (2.3) 2 virgola 3 (2,3) ♦ vt (show) indicare; (gun etc): to ~ sth at puntare qc contro ♦ vi: to ~ at mostrare a dito; ~**s** npl (AUT) puntine fpl; (RAIL) scambio; to be on the ~ of doing sth essere sul punto di or stare per fare qc; to make a ~ fare un'osservazione; to get/miss the ~ capire/non capire; to come to the ~ venire al fatto; there's no ~ (in doing) è inutile (fare); ~ **out** vt far notare; ~ **to** vt fus indicare; (fig) dimostrare; ~-**blank** adv (also: at ~-blank range) a bruciapelo; (fig) categoricamente; ~**ed** adj (shape) aguzzo(a), appuntito(a); (remark) specifico(a); ~**edly** adv in maniera inequivocabile; ~**er** n (needle) lancetta; (fig) indicazione f, consiglio; ~**less** adj inutile, vano(a); ~ **of view** n punto di vista.

poise [pɔɪz] n (composure) portamento; ~**d** adj: to be ~d to do tenersi pronto(a) a fare.

poison ['pɔɪzn] n veleno ♦ vt avvelenare; ~**ous** adj velenoso(a).

poke [pəʊk] vt (fire) attizzare; (jab with finger, stick etc) punzecchiare; (put): to ~ sth in(to) spingere qc dentro; ~ **about** vi frugare.

poker ['pəʊkə*] n attizzatoio; (CARDS) poker m.

poky ['pəʊkɪ] adj piccolo(a) e stretto(a).

Poland ['pəʊlənd] n Polonia.

polar ['pəʊlə*] adj polare; ~ **bear** n orso bianco.

Pole [pəʊl] n polacco/a.

pole [pəʊl] n (of wood) palo; (ELEC, GEO) polo; ~ **bean** n (US) (runner bean) fagiolino; ~ **vault** n salto con l'asta.

police [pə'liːs] n polizia ♦ vt mantenere l'ordine in; ~ **car** n macchina della polizia; ~**man** n poliziotto, agente m di polizia; ~ **station** n posto di polizia; ~**woman** n donna f poliziotto inv.

policy ['pɔlɪsɪ] n politica; (also: insurance ~) polizza (d'assicurazione).

polio ['pəʊlɪəʊ] n polio f.

Polish ['pəʊlɪʃ] adj polacco(a) ♦ n (LING) polacco.

polish ['pɔlɪʃ] n (for shoes) lucido; (for floor) cera; (for nails) smalto; (shine) lucentezza, lustro; (fig: refinement) raffinatezza ♦ vt lucidare; (fig: improve) raffinare; ~ **off** vt (work) sbrigare; (food) mangiarsi; ~**ed** adj (fig) raffinato(a).

polite [pə'laɪt] adj cortese; ~**ness** n cortesia.

political [pə'lɪtɪkl] adj politico(a); ~**ly** adv politicamente.

politician [pɔlɪ'tɪʃən] n politico.

politics ['pɔlɪtɪks] n politica ♦ npl (views, policies) idee fpl politiche.

poll [pəʊl] n scrutinio; (votes cast) voti mpl; (also: opinion ~) sondaggio (d'opinioni) ♦ vt ottenere.

pollen ['pɔlən] n polline m.

polling day ['pəʊlɪŋ-] (BRIT) n giorno delle elezioni.

polling station ['pəʊlɪŋ-] (BRIT) n sezione f elettorale.

pollute [pə'luːt] vt inquinare.

pollution [pə'luːʃən] n inquinamento.

polo ['pəʊləʊ] n polo; ~-**necked** adj a collo alto risvoltato.

polyester [pɔlɪ'ɛstə*] n poliestere m.

polystyrene [pɔlɪ'staɪriːn] n polistirolo.

polytechnic [pɔlɪ'tɛknɪk] n (college) istituto superiore ad indirizzo tecnologico.

polythene ['pɔlɪθiːn] n politene m; ~ **bag** n sacco di plastica.

pomegranate ['pɔmɪɡrænɪt] n melagrana.

pomp [pɔmp] n pompa, fasto.

pompom ['pɔmpɔm] n pompon m inv.

pompon ['pɔmpɔn] n = **pompom**.

pompous ['pɔmpəs] adj pomposo(a).

pond [pɒnd] n pozza; stagno.

ponder ['pɒndə*] vt ponderare, riflettere su; ~ous adj ponderoso(a), pesante.

pong [pɒŋ] (BRIT: inf) n puzzo.

pony ['pəʊnɪ] n pony m inv; ~tail n coda di cavallo; ~ **trekking** (BRIT) n escursione f a cavallo.

poodle ['puːdl] n barboncino, barbone m.

pool [puːl] n (puddle) pozza; (pond) stagno; (also: swimming ~) piscina; (fig: of light) cerchio; (billiards) specie di biliardo a buca ♦ vt mettere in comune; ~s npl (football ~s) ≈ totocalcio; typing ~ servizio comune di dattilografia.

poor [puə*] adj povero(a); (mediocre) mediocre, cattivo(a) ♦ npl: the ~ i poveri; ~ in povero(a) di; ~ly adv poveramente; male ♦ adj indisposto(a), malato(a).

pop [pɒp] n (noise) schiocco; (MUS) musica pop; (drink) bibita gasata; (US: inf: father) babbo ♦ vt (put) mettere (in fretta) ♦ vi scoppiare; (cork) schioccare; ~ **in** vi passare; ~ **out** vi fare un salto fuori; ~ **up** vi apparire, sorgere; ~corn n pop-corn m.

pope [pəʊp] n papa m.

poplar ['pɒplə*] n pioppo.

popper ['pɒpə*] n bottone m a pressione.

poppy ['pɒpɪ] n papavero.

popsicle ['pɒpsɪkl] (US) n (ice lolly) ghiacciolo.

populace ['pɒpjʊlɪs] n popolino.

popular ['pɒpjʊlə*] adj popolare; (fashionable) in voga; ~ity [-'lærɪtɪ] n popolarità; ~ize vt divulgare; (science) volgarizzare.

population [pɒpjʊ'leɪʃən] n popolazione f.

porcelain ['pɔːslɪn] n porcellana.

porch [pɔːtʃ] n veranda.

porcupine ['pɔːkjʊpaɪn] n porcospino.

pore [pɔː*] n poro ♦ vi: to ~ over essere immerso(a) in.

pork [pɔːk] n carne f di maiale.

pornographic [pɔːnə'græfɪk] adj pornografico(a).

pornography [pɔː'nɒɡrəfɪ] n pornografia.

porpoise ['pɔːpəs] n focena.

porridge ['pɒrɪdʒ] n porridge m.

port [pɔːt] n (gen, wine) porto; (NAUT: left side) babordo; ~ **of call** (porto di) scalo.

portable ['pɔːtəbl] adj portatile.

porter ['pɔːtə*] n (for luggage) facchino, portabagagli m inv; (doorkeeper) portiere m, portinaio.

portfolio [pɔːt'fəʊlɪəʊ] n (case) cartella; (POL, FINANCE) portafoglio; (of artist) raccolta dei propri lavori.

porthole ['pɔːthəʊl] n oblò m inv.

portion ['pɔːʃən] n porzione f.

portly ['pɔːtlɪ] adj corpulento(a).

portrait ['pɔːtreɪt] n ritratto.

portray [pɔː'treɪ] vt fare il ritratto di; (character on stage) rappresentare; (in writing) ritrarre.

Portugal ['pɔːtjʊɡl] n Portogallo.

Portuguese [pɔːtjʊ'ɡiːz] adj portoghese ♦ n inv portoghese m/f; (LING) portoghese m.

pose [pəʊz] n posa ♦ vi posare; (pretend): to ~ **as** atteggiarsi a, posare a ♦ vt porre.

posh [pɒʃ] (inf) adj elegante; (family) per bene.

position [pə'zɪʃən] n posizione f; (job) posto ♦ vt sistemare.

positive ['pɒzɪtɪv] adj positivo(a); (certain) sicuro(a), certo(a); (definite) preciso(a); definitivo(a).

posse ['pɒsɪ] (US) n drappello.

possess [pə'zɛs] vt possedere; ~ion [pə'zɛʃən] n possesso; ~ions npl (belongings) beni mpl; ~ive adj possessivo(a).

possibility [pɒsɪ'bɪlɪtɪ] n possibilità f inv.

possible ['pɒsɪbl] adj possibile; as big as ~ il più grande possibile.

possibly ['pɒsɪblɪ] adv (perhaps) forse; if you ~ can se le è possibile; I cannot ~ come proprio non posso venire.

post [pəʊst] n (BRIT) posta; (: collection) levata; (job, situation) posto; (MIL) postazione f; (pole) palo ♦ vt (BRIT: send by post) impostare; (:

appoint): **to ~ to** assegnare a; **~age** *n* affrancatura; **~age stamp** *n* francobollo; **~al order** *n* vaglia *m inv* postale; **~box** (*BRIT*) *n* cassetta postale; **~card** *n* cartolina; **~ code** (*BRIT*) *n* codice *m* (di avviamento) postale.

poster ['pəustə*] *n* manifesto, affisso.

poste restante [pəust'rɛstã:nt] (*BRIT*) *n* fermo posta *m*.

postgraduate ['pəust'grædjuət] *n* laureato/a che continua gli studi.

posthumous ['pɔstjuməs] *adj* postumo(a).

postman ['pəustmən] *n* postino.

postmark ['pəustmɑ:k] *n* bollo *or* timbro postale.

post-mortem [-'mɔ:təm] *n* autopsia.

post office *n* (*building*) ufficio postale; (*organization*): **the Post Office** ≈ le Poste e Telecomunicazioni; **Post Office Box** *n* casella postale.

postpone [pəs'pəun] *vt* rinviare.

postscript ['pəustskrɪpt] *n* poscritto.

posture ['pɔstʃə*] *n* portamento, (*pose*) posa, atteggiamento.

postwar ['pəust'wɔ:*] *adj* del dopoguerra.

posy ['pəuzɪ] *n* mazzetto di fiori.

pot [pɔt] *n* (*for cooking*) pentola; casseruola; (*tea~*) teiera; (*coffee~*) caffettiera; (*for plants, jam*) vaso; (*inf: marijuana*) erba ♦ *vt* (*plant*) piantare in vaso; **a ~ of tea for two** tè per due; **to go to ~** (*inf: work, performance*) andare in malora.

potato [pə'teɪtəu] (*pl* **~es**) *n* patata; **~ peeler** *n* sbucciapatate *m inv*.

potent ['pəutnt] *adj* potente, forte.

potential [pə'tɛnʃl] *adj* potenziale ♦ *n* possibilità *fpl*.

pothole ['pɔthəul] *n* (*in road*) buca; (*BRIT*: *underground*) caverna; **potholing** (*BRIT*) *n*: **to go potholing** fare speleologia.

potluck [pɔt'lʌk] *n*: **to take ~** tentare la sorte.

potted ['pɔtɪd] *adj* (*food*) in conserva; (*plant*) in vaso; (*account etc*) condensato(a).

potter ['pɔtə*] *n* vasaio ♦ *vi*: **to ~ around, ~ about** (*BRIT*) lavoracchiare; **~y** *n* ceramiche *fpl*; (*factory*) fabbrica di ceramiche.

potty ['pɔtɪ] *adj* (*inf*: *mad*) tocco(a) ♦ *n* (*child's*) vasino.

pouch [pautʃ] *n* borsa; (*ZOOL*) marsupio.

poultry ['pəultrɪ] *n* pollame *m*.

pounce [pauns] *vi*: **to ~ (on)** piombare (su).

pound [paund] *n* (*weight*) libbra; (*money*) (lira) sterlina ♦ *vt* (*beat*) battere; (*crush*) pestare, polverizzare ♦ *vi* (*beat*) battere, martellare; **~ sterling** *n* sterlina (inglese).

pour [pɔ:*] *vt* versare ♦ *vi* riversarsi; (*rain*) piovere a dirotto; **~ away** *vt* vuotare; **~ in** *vi* affluire in gran quantità; **~ off** *vt* vuotare; **~ out** *vi* (*people*) uscire a fiumi ♦ *vt* vuotare; versare; (*fig*) sfogare; **~ing** *adj*: **~ing rain** pioggia torrenziale.

pout [paut] *vi* sporgere le labbra; fare il broncio.

poverty ['pɔvətɪ] *n* povertà, miseria; **~-stricken** *adj* molto povero(a), misero(a).

powder ['paudə*] *n* polvere *f* ♦ *vt*: **to ~ one's face** incipriarsi il viso; **~ compact** *n* portacipria *m inv*; **~ed milk** *n* latte *m* in polvere; **~ puff** *n* piumino della cipria; **~ room** *n* toilette *f inv* (per signore).

power ['pauə*] *n* (*strength*) potenza, forza; (*ability, POL: of party, leader*) potere *m*; (*ELEC*) corrente *f*; **to be in ~** (*POL etc*) essere al potere; **~ cut** (*BRIT*) *n* interruzione *f or* mancanza di corrente; **~ed** *adj*: **~ed by** azionato(a) da; **~ failure** *n* interruzione *f* della corrente elettrica; **~ful** *adj* potente, forte; **~less** *adj* impotente; **~less to do** impossibilitato(a) a fare; **~ point** (*BRIT*) *n* presa di corrente; **~ station** *n* centrale *f* elettrica.

p.p. *abbr* (= *per procurationem*): **~ J. Smith** per J. Smith; (= *pages*) p.p.

PR *abbr* = **public relations**.

practicable ['præktɪkəbl] *adj* (*scheme*)

praticabile.

practical ['præktɪkl] *adj* pratico(a); ~**ity** [-'kælɪtɪ] *(no pl) n (of situation etc)* lato pratico; ~ **joke** *n* beffa; ~**ly** *adv* praticamente.

practice ['præktɪs] *n* pratica; *(of profession)* esercizio; *(at football etc)* allenamento; *(business)* gabinetto; clientela ♦ *vt, vi (US)* = **practise**; **in** ~ *(in reality)* in pratica; **out of** ~ fuori esercizio.

practise ['præktɪs] *(US* **practice**) *vt (work at: piano, one's backhand etc)* esercitarsi a; *(train for: skiing, running etc)* allenarsi a; *(a sport, religion)* praticare; *(method)* usare; *(profession)* esercitare ♦ *vi* esercitarsi; *(train)* allenarsi; *(lawyer, doctor)* esercitare; **practising** *adj (Christian etc)* praticante; *(lawyer)* che esercita la professione.

practitioner [præk'tɪʃənə*] *n* professionista *m/f*.

pragmatic [præg'mætɪk] *adj* pragmatico(a).

prairie ['prɛərɪ] *n* prateria.

praise [preɪz] *n* elogio, lode *f* ♦ *vt* elogiare, lodare; ~**worthy** *adj* lodevole.

pram [præm] *(BRIT) n* carrozzina.

prance [prɑːns] *vi (person)* camminare pavoneggiandosi; *(horse)* caracollare.

prank [præŋk] *n* burla.

prawn [prɔːn] *n* gamberetto.

pray [preɪ] *vi* pregare.

prayer [prɛə*] *n* preghiera.

preach [priːtʃ] *vt, vi* predicare.

precarious [prɪ'kɛərɪəs] *adj* precario(a).

precaution [prɪ'kɔːʃən] *n* precauzione *f*.

precede [prɪ'siːd] *vt* precedere.

precedent ['prɛsɪdənt] *n* precedente *m*.

precept ['priːsɛpt] *n* precetto.

precinct ['priːsɪŋkt] *n (US)* circoscrizione *f*; ~**s** *npl (of building)* zona recintata; **pedestrian** ~ *(BRIT)* zona pedonale; **shopping** ~ *(BRIT)* centro commerciale (chiuso al traffico).

precious ['prɛʃəs] *adj* prezioso(a).

precipitate [prɪ'sɪpɪteɪt] *vt* precipitare.

precise [prɪ'saɪs] *adj* preciso(a); ~**ly** *adv* precisamente.

preclude [prɪ'kluːd] *vt* precludere, impedire.

precocious [prɪ'kəuʃəs] *adj* precoce.

precondition [priːkən'dɪʃən] *n* condizione *f* necessaria.

predecessor ['priːdɪsɛsə*] *n* predecessore/a.

predicament [prɪ'dɪkəmənt] *n* situazione *f* difficile.

predict [prɪ'dɪkt] *vt* predire; ~**able** *adj* prevedibile.

predominantly [prɪ'dɒmɪnəntlɪ] *adv* in maggior parte; soprattutto.

predominate [prɪ'dɒmɪneɪt] *vi* predominare.

pre-empt [priː'ɛmpt] *vt* pregiudicare.

preen [priːn] *vt:* **to** ~ **itself** *(bird)* lisciarsi le penne; **to** ~ **o.s.** agghindarsi.

prefab ['priːfæb] *n* casa prefabbricata.

preface ['prɛfəs] *n* prefazione *f*.

prefect ['priːfɛkt] *n (BRIT: in school)* studente/essa con funzioni disciplinari; *(in Italy)* prefetto.

prefer [prɪ'fɔː*] *vt* preferire; **to** ~ **doing** *or* **to do** preferire fare; ~**ably** ['prɛfrəblɪ] *adv* preferibilmente; ~**ence** ['prɛfrəns] *n* preferenza; ~**ential** [prɛfə'rɛnʃəl] *adj* preferenziale.

prefix ['priːfɪks] *n* prefisso.

pregnancy ['prɛgnənsɪ] *n* gravidanza.

pregnant ['prɛgnənt] *adj* incinta *af*.

prehistoric ['priːhɪs'tɒrɪk] *adj* preistorico(a).

prejudice ['prɛdʒudɪs] *n* pregiudizio; *(harm)* torto, danno; ~**d** *adj:* ~**d** **(against)** prevenuto(a) (contro); ~**d** **(in favour of)** ben disposto(a) (verso).

preliminary [prɪ'lɪmɪnərɪ] *adj* preliminare.

premarital ['priː'mærɪtl] *adj* prematrimoniale.

premature ['prɛmətʃuə*] *adj* prematuro(a).

premier ['prɛmɪə*] *adj* primo(a) ♦ *n (POL)* primo ministro.

première ['prɛmɪɛə*] *n* prima.

premise ['prɛmɪs] *n* premessa; ~**s** *npl (of business, institution)* locale *m*; **on the** ~**s** sul posto.

premium ['priːmɪəm] *n* premio; **to be at**

a ~ essere ricercatissimo; ~ **bond** (*BRIT*) *n* obbligazione *f* a premio.

premonition [prɛmə'nɪʃən] *n* premonizione *f*.

preoccupied [pri:'ɔkjupaɪd] *adj* preoccupato(a).

prep [prɛp] *n* (*SCOL*: *study*) studio.

prepaid [pri:'peɪd] *adj* pagato(a) in anticipo.

preparation [prɛpə'reɪʃən] *n* preparazione *f*; ~s *npl* (*for trip*, *war*) preparativi *mpl*.

preparatory [prɪ'pærətərɪ] *adj* preparatorio(a); ~ **school** *n* scuola elementare privata.

prepare [prɪ'pɛə*] *vt* preparare ♦ *vi*: to ~ **for** prepararsi a; ~**d** to pronto(a) a.

preposition [prɛpə'zɪʃən] *n* preposizione *f*.

preposterous [prɪ'pɔstərəs] *adj* assurdo(a).

prep school *n* = **preparatory school.**

prerequisite [pri:'rɛkwɪzɪt] *n* requisito indispensabile.

prescribe [prɪ'skraɪb] *vt* (*MED*) prescrivere.

prescription [prɪ'skrɪpʃən] *n* prescrizione *f*; (*MED*) ricetta.

presence ['prɛzns] *n* presenza; ~ **of mind** presenza di spirito.

present [*adj*, *n* 'prɛznt, *vb* prɪ'zɛnt] *adj* presente; (*wife*, *residence*, *job*) attuale ♦ *n* (*actuality*): the ~ il presente; (*gift*) regalo ♦ *vt* presentare; (*give*): to ~ **sb with sth** offrire qc a qn; to **give sb a** ~ fare un regalo a qn; at ~ al momento; ~**ation** [-'teɪʃən] *n* presentazione *f*; (*ceremony*) consegna ufficiale; ~-**day** *adj* attuale, d'oggigiorno; ~**er** *n* (*RADIO*, *TV*) presentatore/trice; ~**ly** *adv* (*soon*) fra poco, presto; (*at present*) al momento.

preservative [prɪ'zə:vətɪv] *n* conservante *m*.

preserve [prɪ'zə:v] *vt* (*keep safe*) preservare, proteggere; (*maintain*) conservare; (*food*) mettere in conserva ♦ *n* (*often pl*: *jam*) marmellata; (: *fruit*) frutta sciroppata.

preside [prɪ'zaɪd] *vi*: to ~ (**over**)

presiedere (a).

president ['prɛzɪdənt] *n* presidente *m*; ~**ial** [-'dɛnʃl] *adj* presidenziale.

press [prɛs] *n* (*newspapers etc*): the P~ la stampa; (*tool*, *machine*) pressa; (*for wine*) torchio ♦ *vt* (*push*) premere, pigiare; (*squeeze*) spremere; (: *hand*) stringere; (*clothes*: *iron*) stirare; (*pursue*) incalzare; (*insist*): to ~ **sth on sb** far accettare qc da qn ♦ *vi* premere; accalcare; **we are** ~**ed for time** ci manca il tempo; to ~ **for sth** insistere per avere qc; ~ **on** *vi* continuare; ~ **conference** *n* conferenza *f* stampa *inv*; ~**ing** *adj* urgente; ~ **stud** (*BRIT*) *n* bottone *m* a pressione; ~-**up** (*BRIT*) *n* flessione *f* sulle braccia.

pressure ['prɛʃə*] *n* pressione *f*; to **put** ~ **on sb** (**to do**) mettere qn sotto pressione (affinché faccia); ~ **cooker** *n* pentola a pressione; ~ **gauge** *n* manometro; ~ **group** *n* gruppo di pressione.

prestige [prɛs'ti:ʒ] *n* prestigio.

presumably [prɪ'zju:məblɪ] *adv* presumibilmente.

presume [prɪ'zju:m] *vt* supporre.

presumption [prɪ'zʌmpʃən] *n* presunzione *f*.

presumptuous [prɪ'zʌmpʃəs] *adj* presuntuoso(a).

pretence [prɪ'tɛns] (*US* **pretense**) *n* (*claim*) pretesa; to **make a** ~ **of doing** far finta di fare; **under false** ~**s** con l'inganno.

pretend [prɪ'tɛnd] *vt* (*feign*) fingere ♦ *vi* far finta; to ~ **to do** far finta di fare.

pretense [prɪ'tɛns] (*US*) *n* = **pretence.**

pretentious [prɪ'tɛnʃəs] *adj* pretenzioso(a).

pretext ['pri:tɛkst] *n* pretesto.

pretty ['prɪtɪ] *adj* grazioso(a), carino(a) ♦ *adv* abbastanza, assai.

prevail [prɪ'veɪl] *vi* (*win*, *be usual*) prevalere; (*persuade*): to ~ (**up**)**on sb to do** persuadere qn a fare; ~**ing** *adj* dominante.

prevalent ['prɛvələnt] *adj* (*belief*) predominante; (*customs*) diffuso(a); (*fashion*) corrente; (*disease*) comune.

prevent [prɪ'vɛnt] vt: to ~ sb from doing impedire a qn di fare; to ~ sth from happening impedire che qc succeda; ~**ative** adj = ~**ive**; ~**ion** [-'vɛnʃən] n prevenzione f; ~**ive** adj preventivo(a).

preview ['pri:vju:] n (of film) anteprima.

previous ['pri:vɪəs] adj precedente; anteriore; ~**ly** adv prima.

prewar ['pri:'wɔ:*] adj anteguerra inv.

prey [preɪ] n preda ♦ vi: to ~ on far preda di; it was ~ing on his mind lo stava ossessionando.

price [praɪs] n prezzo ♦ vt (goods) fissare il prezzo di; valutare; ~**less** adj inapprezzabile; ~ **list** n listino (dei) prezzi.

prick [prɪk] n puntura ♦ vt pungere; to ~ up one's ears drizzare gli orecchi.

prickle ['prɪkl] n (of plant) spina; (sensation) pizzicore m.

prickly ['prɪklɪ] adj spinoso(a); ~ **heat** n sudamina.

pride [praɪd] n orgoglio; superbia ♦ vt: to ~ o.s. on essere orgoglioso di; vantarsi di.

priest [pri:st] n prete m, sacerdote m; ~**hood** n sacerdozio.

prig [prɪg] n: he's a ~ è compiaciuto di se stesso.

prim [prɪm] adj pudico(a); contegnoso(a).

primarily ['praɪmərɪlɪ] adv principalmente, essenzialmente.

primary ['praɪmərɪ] adj primario(a); (first in importance) primo(a) ♦ n (US: election) primarie fpl; ~ **school** (BRIT) n scuola elementare.

prime [praɪm] adj primario(a), fondamentale; (excellent) di prima qualità ♦ vt (wood) preparare; (fig) mettere al corrente ♦ n: in the ~ of life nel fiore della vita; P~ **Minister** n primo ministro.

primeval [praɪ'mi:vl] adj primitivo(a).

primitive ['prɪmɪtɪv] adj primitivo(a).

primrose ['prɪmrəuz] n primavera.

primus (stove) ['praɪməs(-)] ® (BRIT) n fornello a petrolio.

prince [prɪns] n principe m.

princess [prɪn'sɛs] n principessa.

principal ['prɪnsɪpl] adj principale ♦ n (headmaster) preside m.

principle ['prɪnsɪpl] n principio; in ~ in linea di principio; on ~ per principio.

print [prɪnt] n (mark) impronta; (letters) caratteri mpl; (fabric) tessuto stampato; (ART, PHOT) stampa ♦ vt imprimere; (publish) stampare, pubblicare; (write in capitals) scrivere in stampatello; out of ~ esaurito(a); ~**ed matter** n stampe fpl; ~**er** n tipografo; (machine) stampante f; ~**ing** n stampa; ~**-out** n (COMPUT) tabulato.

prior ['praɪə*] adj precedente; (claim etc) più importante; ~ **to doing** prima di fare.

priority [praɪ'ɔrɪtɪ] n priorità f inv; precedenza.

prise [praɪz] vt: to ~ **open** forzare.

prison ['prɪzn] n prigione f ♦ cpd (system) carcerario(a); (conditions, food) nelle or delle prigioni; ~**er** n prigioniero/a.

pristine ['prɪsti:n] adj immacolato(a).

privacy ['prɪvəsɪ] n solitudine f, intimità.

private ['praɪvɪt] adj privato(a); personale ♦ n soldato semplice; "~" (on envelope) "riservata"; (on door) "privato"; in ~ in privato; ~ **enterprise** n iniziativa privata; ~ **eye** n investigatore m privato; ~**ly** adv in privato; (within oneself) dentro di sé; ~ **property** n proprietà privata; **privatize** vt privatizzare.

privet ['prɪvɪt] n ligustro.

privilege ['prɪvɪlɪdʒ] n privilegio.

privy ['prɪvɪ] adj: to be ~ to essere al corrente di.

prize [praɪz] n premio ♦ adj (example, idiot) perfetto(a); (bull, novel) premiato(a) ♦ vt apprezzare, pregiare; ~ **giving** n premiazione f; ~**winner** n premiato/a.

pro [prəu] n (SPORT) professionista m/f ♦ prep pro; the ~s and cons il pro e il contro.

probability [prɔbə'bɪlɪtɪ] n probabilità f inv; in all ~ con tutta probabilità.

probable ['prɔbəbl] *adj* probabile; **probably** *adv* probabilmente.
probation [prə'beɪʃən] *n*: **on ~** (*employee*) in prova; (*LAW*) in libertà vigilata.
probe [prəub] *n* (*MED, SPACE*) sonda; (*enquiry*) indagine *f*, investigazione *f* ♦ *vt* sondare, esplorare; indagare.
problem ['prɔbləm] *n* problema *m*.
procedure [prə'siːdʒə*] *n* (*ADMIN, LAW*) procedura; (*method*) metodo, procedimento.
proceed [prə'siːd] *vi* (*go forward*) avanzare, andare avanti; (*go about it*) procedere; (*continue*): **to ~ (with)** continuare; **to ~ to** andare a; passare a; **to ~ to do** mettersi a fare; **~ings** *npl* misure *fpl*; (*LAW*) procedimento; (*meeting*) riunione *f*; (*records*) rendiconti *mpl*; atti *mpl*; **~s** ['prəusiːdz] *npl* profitto, incasso.
process ['prəuses] *n* processo; (*method*) metodo, sistema *m* ♦ *vt* trattare; (*information*) elaborare; **~ing** *n* trattamento; elaborazione *f*.
procession [prə'seʃən] *n* processione *f*, corteo; **funeral ~** corteo funebre.
proclaim [prə'kleɪm] *vt* proclamare, dichiarare.
procrastinate [prəu'kræstɪneɪt] *vi* procrastinare.
prod [prɔd] *vt* dare un colpetto a; pungolare ♦ *n* colpetto.
prodigal ['prɔdɪgl] *adj* prodigo(a).
prodigy ['prɔdɪdʒɪ] *n* prodigio.
produce [*n* 'prɔdjuːs, *vb* prə'djuːs] *n* (*AGR*) prodotto, prodotti *mpl* ♦ *vt* produrre; (*to show*) esibire, mostrare; (*cause*) cagionare, causare; **~r** *n* (*THEATRE*) regista *m/f*; (*AGR, CINEMA*) produttore *m*.
product ['prɔdʌkt] *n* prodotto.
production [prə'dʌkʃən] *n* produzione *f*; **~ line** *n* catena di lavorazione.
productivity [prɔdʌk'tɪvɪtɪ] *n* produttività.
profane [prə'feɪn] *adj* profano(a); (*language*) empio(a).
profess [prə'fes] *vt* (*claim*) dichiarare; (*opinion etc*) professare.

profession [prə'feʃən] *n* professione *f*; **~al** *n* professionista *m/f* ♦ *adj* professionale; (*work*) da professionista.
professor [prə'fesə*] *n* professore *m* (*titolare di una cattedra*); (*US*) professore/essa.
proficiency [prə'fɪʃənsɪ] *n* competenza, abilità.
profile ['prəufaɪl] *n* profilo.
profit ['prɔfɪt] *n* profitto; beneficio ♦ *vi*: **to ~ (by** *or* **from)** approfittare (di); **~ability** [-'bɪlɪtɪ] *n* redditività; **~able** *adj* redditizio(a).
profound [prə'faund] *adj* profondo(a).
profusely [prə'fjuːslɪ] *adv* con grande effusione.
programme ['prəugræm] (*US* **program**) *n* programma *m* ♦ *vt* programmare; **~r** (*US* **programer**) *n* programmatore/trice.
progress [*n* 'prəugres, *vb* prə'gres] *n* progresso ♦ *vi* avanzare, procedere; **in ~** in corso; **to make ~** far progressi; **~ive** [-'gresɪv] *adj* progressivo(a); (*person*) progressista.
prohibit [prə'hɪbɪt] *vt* proibire, vietare; **~ion** [prəuɪ'bɪʃən] *n* proibizione *f*, divieto; (*US*): **P~** proibizionismo; **~ive** *adj* (*price etc*) proibitivo(a).
project [*n* 'prɔdʒekt, *vb* prə'dʒekt] *n* (*plan*) piano; (*venture*) progetto; (*SCOL*) studio ♦ *vt* proiettare ♦ *vi* (*stick out*) sporgere.
projectile [prə'dʒektaɪl] *n* proiettile *m*.
projector [prə'dʒektə*] *n* proiettore *m*.
prolific [prə'lɪfɪk] *adj* (*artist etc*) fecondo(a).
prolong [prə'lɔŋ] *vt* prolungare.
prom [prɔm] *n abbr* = **promenade**; (*US*: *ball*) ballo studentesco.
promenade [prɔmə'nɑːd] *n* (*by sea*) lungomare *m*; **~ concert** *n* concerto (*con posti in piedi*).
prominent ['prɔmɪnənt] *adj* (*standing out*) prominente; (*important*) importante.
promiscuous [prə'mɪskjuəs] *adj* (*sexually*) di facili costumi.
promise ['prɔmɪs] *n* promessa ♦ *vt*, *vi* promettere; **to ~ sb sth, ~ sth to sb** promettere qc a qn; **to ~ (sb) that/to do**

sth promettere (a qn) che/di fare qc; **promising** adj promettente.

promote [prə'məut] vt promuovere; (venture, event) organizzare; ~**r** n promotore/trice; (of sporting event) organizzatore/trice; **promotion** [-'məuʃən] n promozione f.

prompt [prɔmpt] adj rapido(a), svelto(a); puntuale; (reply) sollecito(a) ♦ adv (punctually) in punto ♦ n (COMPUT) prompt m ♦ vt incitare; provocare; (THEATRE) suggerire a; **to ~ sb to do** incitare qn a fare; ~**ly** adv prontamente; puntualmente.

prone [prəun] adj (lying) prono(a); ~ **to** propenso(a) a, incline a.

prong [prɔŋ] n rebbio, punta.

pronoun ['prəunaun] n pronome m.

pronounce [prə'nauns] vt pronunciare.

pronunciation [prənʌnsɪ'eɪʃən] n pronuncia.

proof [pruːf] n prova; (of book) bozza; (PHOT) provino ♦ adj: ~ **against** a prova di.

prop [prɔp] n sostegno, appoggio ♦ vt (also: ~ up) sostenere, appoggiare; (lean): **to ~ sth against** appoggiare qc contro or a.

propaganda [prɔpə'gændə] n propaganda.

propel [prə'pɛl] vt spingere (in avanti), muovere; ~**ler** n elica.

propensity [prə'pɛnsɪtɪ] n tendenza.

proper ['prɔpə*] adj (suited, right) adatto(a), appropriato(a); (seemly) decente; (authentic) vero(a); (inf: real) noun + vero(a) e proprio(a); ~**ly** adv (eat, study) bene; (behave) come si deve; ~ **noun** n nome m proprio.

property ['prɔpətɪ] n (things owned) beni mpl; (land, building) proprietà f inv; (CHEM etc: quality) proprietà; ~ **owner** n proprietario/a.

prophecy ['prɔfɪsɪ] n profezia.

prophesy ['prɔfɪsaɪ] vt predire.

prophet ['prɔfɪt] n profeta m.

proportion [prə'pɔːʃən] n proporzione f; (share) parte f; ~**al** adj proporzionale; ~**ate** adj proporzionato(a).

proposal [prə'pəuzl] n proposta; (plan)

progetto; (of marriage) proposta di matrimonio.

propose [prə'pəuz] vt proporre, suggerire ♦ vi fare una proposta di matrimonio; **to ~ to do** proporsi di fare, aver l'intenzione di fare.

proposition [prɔpə'zɪʃən] n proposizione f; (offer) proposta.

proprietor [prə'praɪətə*] n proprietario/a.

propriety [prə'praɪtɪ] n (seemliness) decoro, rispetto delle convenienze sociali.

pro rata ['prəu'rɑːtə] adv in proporzione.

prose [prəuz] n prosa.

prosecute ['prɔsɪkjuːt] vt processare; **prosecution** [-'kjuːʃən] n processo; (accusing side) accusa; **prosecutor** n (also: public prosecutor) ≈ procuratore m della Repubblica.

prospect [n 'prɔspɛkt, vb prə'spɛkt] n prospettiva; (hope) speranza ♦ vi: **to ~ for** cercare; ~**s** npl (for work etc) prospettive fpl; ~**ive** [-'spɛktɪv] adj possibile; futuro(a).

prospectus [prə'spɛktəs] n prospetto, programma m.

prosperity [prɔ'spɛrɪtɪ] n prosperità.

prostitute ['prɔstɪtjuːt] n prostituta; **male ~** uomo che si prostituisce.

prostrate ['prɔstreɪt] adj bocconi inv.

protect [prə'tɛkt] vt proteggere, salvaguardare; ~**ion** n protezione f; ~**ive** adj protettivo(a).

protégé ['prəutəʒeɪ] n protetto.

protein ['prəutiːn] n proteina.

protest [n 'prəutɛst, vb prə'tɛst] n protesta ♦ vt, vi protestare.

Protestant ['prɔtɪstənt] adj, n protestante m/f.

protester [prə'tɛstə*] n dimostrante m/f.

prototype ['prəutətaɪp] n prototipo.

protracted [prə'træktɪd] adj tirato(a) per le lunghe.

protrude [prə'truːd] vi sporgere.

proud [praud] adj fiero(a), orgoglioso(a); (pej) superbo(a).

prove [pruːv] vt provare, dimostrare ♦ vi: **to ~ (to be) correct** etc risultare vero(a) etc; **to ~ o.s.** mostrare le pro-

prie capacità.
proverb ['prɔvə:b] *n* proverbio.
provide [prə'vaɪd] *vt* fornire,
provvedere; **to ~ sb with sth** fornire *or*
provvedere qn di qc; **~ for** *vt fus*
provvedere a; *(future event)*
prevedere; **~d (that)** *conj* purché
+ *sub*, a condizione che + *sub*.
providing [prə'vaɪdɪŋ] *conj* purché
+ *sub*, a condizione che + *sub*.
province ['prɔvɪns] *n* provincia;
provincial [prə'vɪnʃəl] *adj* provinciale.
provision [prə'vɪʒən] *n* *(supply)* riserva;
(supplying) provvista; rifornimento;
(stipulation) condizione *f*; **~s** *npl* *(food)*
provviste *fpl*; **~al** *adj* provvisorio(a).
proviso [prə'vaɪzəu] *n* condizione *f*.
provocative [prə'vɔkətɪv] *adj* *(aggressive)* provocatorio(a); *(thought-provoking)* stimolante; *(seductive)*
provocante.
provoke [prə'vəuk] *vt* provocare;
incitare.
prow [prau] *n* prua.
prowess ['praus] *n* prodezza.
prowl [praul] *vi* *(also: ~ about, ~ around)* aggirarsi ♦ *n*: **to be on the ~**
aggirarsi; **~er** *n* tipo sospetto *(che
s'aggira con l'intenzione di rubare, aggredire etc)*.
proximity [prɔk'sɪmɪtɪ] *n* prossimità.
proxy ['prɔksɪ] *n*: **by ~** per procura.
prude [pru:d] *n* puritano/a.
prudent ['pru:dnt] *adj* prudente.
prudish ['pru:dɪʃ] *adj* puritano(a).
prune [pru:n] *n* prugna secca ♦ *vt*
potare.
pry [praɪ] *vi*: **to ~ into** ficcare il naso in.
PS *abbr* (= *postscript*) P.S.
psalm [sɑ:m] *n* salmo.
pseudo- ['sju:dəu] *prefix* pseudo....
pseudonym ['sju:dənɪm] *n* pseudonimo.
psyche ['saɪkɪ] *n* psiche *f*.
psychiatric [saɪkɪ'ætrɪk] *adj* psichiatrico(a).
psychiatrist [saɪ'kaɪətrɪst] *n* psichiatra
m/f.
psychic ['saɪkɪk] *adj* *(also: ~al)* psichico(a); *(person)* dotato(a) di qualità
telepatiche

psychoanalyst [saɪkəu'ænəlɪst] *n* psicanalista *m/f*.
psychological [saɪkə'lɔdʒɪkl] *adj* psicologico(a).
psychologist [saɪ'kɔlədʒɪst] *n* psicologo/
a.
psychology [saɪ'kɔlədʒɪ] *n* psicologia.
psychopath ['saɪkəupæθ] *n* psicopatico/
a.
P.T.O. *abbr* (= *please turn over*) v.r.
pub [pʌb] *n abbr* (= *public house*) pub
m inv.
pubic ['pju:bɪk] *adj* pubico(a), del pube.
public ['pʌblɪk] *adj* pubblico(a) ♦ *n* pubblico; **in ~** in pubblico; **~ address
system** *n* impianto di amplificazione.
publican ['pʌblɪkən] *n* proprietario di un
pub.
publication [pʌblɪ'keɪʃən] *n* pubblicazione *f*.
public: ~ company *n* società *f inv*
per azioni *(costituita tramite pubblica
sottoscrizione)*; **~ convenience** *(BRIT)* *n*
gabinetti *mpl*; **~ holiday** *n* giorno festivo, festa nazionale; **~ house** *(BRIT)*
n pub *m inv*.
publicity [pʌb'lɪsɪtɪ] *n* pubblicità.
publicize ['pʌblɪsaɪz] *vt* rendere pubblico(a).
publicly ['pʌblɪklɪ] *adv* pubblicamente.
public: ~ opinion *n* opinione *f* pubblica; **~ relations** *n* pubbliche relazioni
fpl; **~ school** *n* *(BRIT)* scuola privata;
(US) scuola statale; **~-spirited** *adj* che
ha senso civico; **~ transport** *n* mezzi
mpl pubblici.
publish ['pʌblɪʃ] *vt* pubblicare; **~er** *n*
editore *m*; **~ing** *n* *(industry)* editoria;
(of a book) pubblicazione *f*.
puce [pju:s] *adj* marroncino rosato *inv*.
pucker ['pʌkə*] *vt* corrugare.
pudding ['pudɪŋ] *n* budino; *(BRIT:
dessert)* dolce *m*; **black ~**
sanguinaccio.
puddle ['pʌdl] *n* pozza, pozzanghera.
puff [pʌf] *n* sbuffo ♦ *vt*: **to ~ one's pipe**
tirare sboccate di fumo ♦ *vi* *(pant)*
ansare; **~ out** *vt* *(cheeks etc)* gonfiare;
~ed *(inf)* *adj* *(out of breath)* senza
fiato; **~ pastry** *n* pasta sfoglia; **~y** *adj*

gonfio(a).

pull [pul] *n* (*tug*): **to give sth a ~** tirare su qc ♦ *vt* tirare; (*muscle*) strappare; (*trigger*) premere ♦ *vi* tirare; **to ~ to pieces** fare a pezzi; **to ~ one's punches** (*BOXING*) risparmiare l'avversario; **to ~ one's weight** dare il proprio contributo; **to ~ o.s. together** ricomporsi, riprendersi; **to ~ sb's leg** prendere in giro qn; **~ apart** *vt* (*break*) fare a pezzi; **~ down** *vt* (*house*) demolire; (*tree*) abbattere; **~ in** *vi* (*AUT: at the kerb*) accostarsi; (*RAIL*) entrare in stazione; **~ off** *vt* (*clothes*) togliere; (*deal etc*) portare a compimento; **~ out** *vi* partire; (*AUT: come out of line*) spostarsi sulla mezzeria ♦ *vt* staccare; far uscire; (*withdraw*) ritirare; **~ over** *vi* (*AUT*) accostare; **~ through** *vi* farcela; **~ up** *vi* (*stop*) fermarsi ♦ *vt* (*raise*) sollevare; (*uproot*) sradicare.

pulley ['puli] *n* puleggia, carrucola.

pullover ['puləuvə*] *n* pullover *m inv*.

pulp [pʌlp] *n* (*of fruit*) polpa.

pulpit ['pulpit] *n* pulpito.

pulsate [pʌl'seit] *vi* battere, palpitare.

pulse [pʌls] *n* polso; (*BOT*) legume *m*.

pummel ['pʌml] *vt* dare pugni a.

pump [pʌmp] *n* pompa; (*shoe*) scarpetta ♦ *vt* pompare; **~ up** *vt* gonfiare.

pumpkin ['pʌmpkin] *n* zucca.

pun [pʌn] *n* gioco di parole.

punch [pʌntʃ] *n* (*blow*) pugno; (*tool*) punzone *m*; (*drink*) ponce *m* ♦ *vt* (*hit*): **to ~ sb/sth** dare un pugno a qn/qc; **~ line** *n* (*of joke*) battuta finale; **~-up** (*BRIT: inf*) *n* rissa.

punctual ['pʌŋktjuəl] *adj* puntuale.

punctuation [pʌŋktju'eiʃən] *n* interpunzione *f*, punteggiatura.

puncture ['pʌŋktʃə*] *n* foratura ♦ *vt* forare.

pundit ['pʌndit] *n* sapientone/a.

pungent ['pʌndʒənt] *adj* pungente.

punish ['pʌniʃ] *vt* punire; **~ment** *n* punizione *f*.

punk [pʌŋk] *n* (*also*: **~ rocker**) punk *m/f inv*; (*also*: **~ rock**) musica punk, punk rock *m*; (*US: inf: hoodlum*) teppi-

sta *m*.

punt [pʌnt] *n* (*boat*) barchino.

punter ['pʌntə*] (*BRIT*) *n* (*gambler*) scommettitore/trice; (: *inf*) cliente *m/f*.

puny ['pju:ni] *adj* gracile.

pup [pʌp] *n* cucciolo/a.

pupil ['pju:pl] *n* allievo/a; (*ANAT*) pupilla.

puppet ['pʌpit] *n* burattino.

puppy ['pʌpi] *n* cucciolo/a, cagnolino/a.

purchase ['pə:tʃis] *n* acquisto, compera ♦ *vt* comprare; **~r** *n* compratore/trice.

pure [pjuə*] *adj* puro(a).

purée ['pjuərei] *n* (*of potatoes*) purè *m*; (*of tomatoes*) passato; (*of apples*) crema.

purely ['pjuəli] *adv* puramente.

purge [pə:dʒ] *n* (*MED*) purga; (*POL*) epurazione *f* ♦ *vt* purgare.

puritan ['pjuəritən] *adj*, *n* puritano(a).

purity ['pjuəriti] *n* purezza.

purple ['pə:pl] *adj* di porpora; viola *inv*.

purport [pə:'pɔ:t] *vi*: **to ~ to be/do** pretendere di essere/fare.

purpose ['pə:pəs] *n* intenzione *f*, scopo; **on ~** apposta; **~ful** *adj* deciso(a), risoluto(a).

purr [pə:*] *vi* fare le fusa.

purse [pə:s] *n* (*BRIT*) borsellino; (*US*) borsetta ♦ *vt* contrarre.

purser ['pə:sə*] *n* (*NAUT*) commissario di bordo.

pursue [pə'sju:] *vt* inseguire; (*fig: activity etc*) continuare con; (: *aim etc*) perseguire.

pursuit [pə'sju:t] *n* inseguimento; (*fig*) ricerca; (*pastime*) passatempo.

push [puʃ] *n* spinta; (*effort*) grande sforzo; (*drive*) energia ♦ *vt* spingere; (*button*) premere; (*thrust*): **to ~ sth (into)** ficcare qc (in); (*fig*) fare pubblicità a ♦ *vi* spingere; premere; **to ~ for** (*fig*) insistere per; **~ aside** *vt* scostare; **~ off** (*inf*) *vi* filare; **~ on** *vi* (*continue*) continuare; **~ through** *vi* farsi largo spingendo ♦ *vt* (*measure*) far approvare; **~ up** *vt* (*total, prices*) far salire; **~chair** (*BRIT*) *n* passeggino; **~er** *n* (*drug ~er*) spacciatore/trice; **~over** (*inf*) *n*: **it's a ~over** è un lavoro

da bambini; ~**-up** (US) n (press-up) flessione f sulle braccia; ~**y** (pej) adj opportunista.
puss [pus] (inf) n = **pussy**(-cat).
pussy(-cat) ['pusɪ(-)] (inf) n micio.
put [put] (pt, pp **put**) vt mettere, porre; (say) dire, esprimere; (a question) fare; (estimate) stimare; ~ **about** or **around** vt (rumour) diffondere; ~ **across** vt (ideas etc) comunicare; far capire; ~ **away** vt (return) mettere a posto; ~ **back** vt (replace) rimettere (a posto); (postpone) rinviare; (delay) ritardare; ~ **by** vt (money) mettere da parte; ~ **down** vt (parcel etc) posare, mettere giù; (pay) versare; (in writing) mettere per iscritto; (revolt, animal) sopprimere; (attribute) attribuire; ~ **forward** vt (ideas) avanzare, proporre; ~ **in** vt (application, complaint) presentare; (time, effort) mettere; ~ **off** vt (postpone) rimandare, rinviare; (discourage) dissuadere; ~ **on** vt (clothes, lipstick etc) mettere; (light etc) accendere; (play etc) mettere in scena; (food, meal) mettere su; (brake) mettere; **to** ~ **on weight** ingrassare; **to** ~ **on airs** darsi delle arie; ~ **out** vt mettere fuori; (one's hand) porgere; (light etc) spegnere; (person: inconvenience) scomodare; ~ **through** vt (TEL: call) passare; (: person) mettere in comunicazione; (plan) far approvare; ~ **up** vt (raise) sollevare, alzare; (: umbrella) aprire; (: tent) montare; (pin up) affiggere; (hang) appendere; (build) costruire, erigere; (increase) aumentare; (accommodate) alloggiare; ~ **up with** vt fus sopportare.
putt [pʌt] n colpo leggero; ~**ing green** n green m inv; campo da putting.
putty ['pʌtɪ] n stucco.
puzzle ['pʌzl] n enigma m, mistero; (jigsaw) puzzle m; (also: crossword ~) parole fpl incrociate, cruciverba m inv ♦ vt confondere, rendere perplesso(a) ♦ vi scervellarsi.
pyjamas [pɪ'dʒɑːməz] (BRIT) npl pigiama m.

pylon ['paɪlən] n pilone m.
pyramid ['pɪrəmɪd] n piramide f.
Pyrenees [pɪrɪ'niːz] npl: **the** ~ i Pirenei.

Q

quack [kwæk] n (of duck) qua qua m inv; (pej: doctor) dottoruccio/a.
quad [kwɒd] n abbr = **quadrangle**; **quadruplet**.
quadrangle ['kwɒdræŋgl] n (courtyard) cortile m.
quadruple [kwɔ'druːpl] vt quadruplicare ♦ vi quadruplicarsi.
quadruplets [kwɔ'druːplɪts] npl quattro gemelli mpl.
quagmire ['kwægmaɪə*] n pantano.
quail [kweɪl] n (ZOOL) quaglia ♦ vi (person): **to** ~ **at** or **before** perdersi d'animo davanti a.
quaint [kweɪnt] adj bizzarro(a); (old-fashioned) antiquato(a); grazioso(a), pittoresco(a).
quake [kweɪk] vi tremare ♦ n abbr = **earthquake**.
Quaker ['kweɪkə*] n quacchero/a.
qualification [kwɒlɪfɪ'keɪʃən] n (degree etc) qualifica, titolo; (ability) competenza, qualificazione f; (limitation) riserva, restrizione f.
qualified ['kwɒlɪfaɪd] adj qualificato(a); (able): ~ **to** competente in, qualificato(a) a; (limited) condizionato(a).
qualify ['kwɒlɪfaɪ] vt abilitare; (limit: statement) modificare, precisare ♦ vi: **to** ~ (**as**) qualificarsi (come); **to** ~ (**for**) acquistare i requisiti necessari (per); (SPORT) qualificarsi (per or a).
quality ['kwɒlɪtɪ] n qualità f inv.
qualm [kwɑːm] n dubbio; scrupolo.
quandary ['kwɒndrɪ] n: **in a** ~ in un dilemma.
quantity ['kwɒntɪtɪ] n quantità f inv; ~ **surveyor** n geometra m (specializzato nel calcolare la quantità e il costo del materiale da costruzione).
quarantine ['kwɒrntiːn] n quarantena.
quarrel ['kwɒrl] n lite f, disputa ♦ vi

litigare; ~**some** adj litigioso(a).

quarry ['kwɔrɪ] n (for stone) cava; (animal) preda.

quart [kwɔːt] n ≈ litro.

quarter ['kwɔːtə*] n quarto; (US: coin) quarto di dollaro; (of year) trimestre m; (district) quartiere m ♦ vt dividere in quattro; (MIL) alloggiare; ~s npl (living ~s) alloggio; (MIL) alloggi mpl, quadrato; **a ~ of an hour** un quarto d'ora; ~ **final** n quarto di finale; ~**ly** adj trimestrale ♦ adv trimestralmente.

quartet(te) [kwɔː'tɛt] n quartetto.

quartz [kwɔːts] n quarzo.

quash [kwɔʃ] vt (verdict) annullare.

quaver ['kweɪvə*] n (BRIT: MUS) croma ♦ vi tremolare.

quay [kiː] n (also: ~side) banchina.

queasy ['kwiːzɪ] adj (stomach) delicato(a); **to feel ~** aver la nausea.

queen [kwiːn] n (gen) regina; (CARDS etc) regina, donna; ~ **mother** n regina madre.

queer [kwɪə*] adj strano(a), curioso(a) ♦ n (inf) finocchio.

quell [kwɛl] vt domare.

quench [kwɛntʃ] vt: **to ~ one's thirst** dissetarsi.

querulous ['kwɛruləs] adj querulo(a).

query ['kwɪərɪ] n domanda, questione f ♦ vt mettere in questione.

quest [kwɛst] n cerca, ricerca.

question ['kwɛstʃən] n domanda, questione f ♦ vt (person) interrogare; (plan, idea) mettere in questione or in dubbio; **it's a ~ of doing** si tratta di fare; **beyond ~** fuori di dubbio; **out of the ~** fuori discussione, impossibile; ~**able** adj discutibile; ~ **mark** n punto interrogativo.

questionnaire [kwɛstʃə'nɛə*] n questionario.

queue [kjuː] n (BRIT) n coda, fila ♦ vi fare la coda.

quibble ['kwɪbl] vi cavillare.

quiche [kiːʃ] n torta salata a base di uova, formaggio, prosciutto o altro.

quick [kwɪk] adj rapido(a), veloce; (reply) pronto(a); (mind) pronto(a), acuto(a) ♦ n: **cut to the ~** (fig)

toccato(a) sul vivo; **be ~!** fa presto!; ~**en** vt accelerare, affrettare ♦ vi accelerare, affrettarsi; ~**ly** adv rapidamente, velocemente; ~**sand** n sabbie fpl mobili; ~**-witted** adj pronto(a) d'ingegno.

quid [kwɪd] (BRIT: inf) n inv sterlina.

quiet ['kwaɪət] adj tranquillo(a), quieto(a); (ceremony) semplice ♦ n tranquillità, calma ♦ vt, vi (US) = ~**en**; **keep ~!** sta zitto!; ~**en** (also: ~**en down**) vi calmarsi, chetarsi ♦ vt calmare, chetare; ~**ly** adv tranquillamente, calmamente; sommessamente.

quilt [kwɪlt] n trapunta; (continental ~) piumino.

quin [kwɪn] n abbr = **quintuplet**.

quinine [kwɪ'niːn] n chinino.

quintuplets [kwɪn'tjuːplɪts] npl cinque gemelli mpl.

quip [kwɪp] n frizzo.

quirk [kwəːk] n ghiribizzo.

quit [kwɪt] (pt, pp **quit** or **quitted**) vt mollare; (premises) lasciare, partire da ♦ vi (give up) mollare; (resign) dimettersi.

quite [kwaɪt] adv (rather) assai; (entirely) completamente, del tutto; **I ~ understand** capisco perfettamente; **that's not ~ big enough** non è proprio sufficiente; **~ a few of them** non pochi di loro; ~ (**so**)! esatto!

quits [kwɪts] adj: ~ (**with**) pari (con); **let's call it ~** adesso siamo pari.

quiver ['kwɪvə*] vi tremare, fremere.

quiz [kwɪz] n (game) quiz m inv, indovinello ♦ vt interrogare; ~**zical** adj enigmatico(a).

quota ['kwəʊtə] n quota.

quotation [kwəʊ'teɪʃən] n citazione f; (of shares etc) quotazione f; (estimate) preventivo; ~ **marks** npl virgolette fpl.

quote [kwəʊt] n citazione f ♦ vt (sentence) citare; (price) dare, fissare; (shares) quotare ♦ vi: **to ~ from** citare; ~**s** npl = **quotation marks**.

R

rabbi ['ræbaɪ] n rabbino.

rabbit ['ræbɪt] n coniglio; ~ **hutch** n conigliera.

rabble ['ræbl] (pej) n canaglia, plebaglia.

rabies ['reɪbiːz] n rabbia.

RAC (BRIT) n abbr = **Royal Automobile Club**.

raccoon [rə'kuːn] n procione m.

race [reɪs] n razza; (competition, rush) corsa ♦ vt (horse) far correre ♦ vi correre; (engine) imballarsi; ~ **car** (US) n = **racing car**; ~ **car driver** (US) n = **racing driver**; ~**course** n campo di corse, ippodromo; ~**horse** n cavallo da corsa; ~**track** n pista.

racial ['reɪʃl] adj razziale.

racing ['reɪsɪŋ] n corsa; ~ **car** (BRIT) n macchina da corsa; ~ **driver** (BRIT) n corridore m automobilista.

racism ['reɪsɪzəm] n razzismo; **racist** adj, n razzista m/f.

rack [ræk] n rastrelliera; (also: luggage ~) rete f, portabagagli m inv; (also: roof ~) portabagagli; (dish ~) scolapiatti m inv ♦ vt: ~**ed by** torturato(a) da; **to** ~ **one's brains** scervellarsi.

racket ['rækɪt] n (for tennis) racchetta; (noise) fracasso; baccano; (swindle) imbroglio, truffa; (organized crime) racket m inv.

racoon [rə'kuːn] n = **raccoon**.

racquet ['rækɪt] n racchetta.

racy ['reɪsɪ] adj brioso(a); piccante.

radar ['reɪdɑ:*] n radar m.

radial ['reɪdɪəl] adj (also: ~**ply**) radiale.

radiant ['reɪdɪənt] adj raggiante; (PHYSICS) radiante.

radiate ['reɪdɪeɪt] vt (heat) irraggiare, irradiare ♦ vi (lines) irradiarsi.

radiation [reɪdɪ'eɪʃən] n irradiamento; (radioactive) radiazione f.

radiator ['reɪdɪeɪtə*] n radiatore m.

radical ['rædɪkl] adj radicale.

radii ['reɪdɪaɪ] npl of **radius**.

radio ['reɪdɪəu] n radio f inv; **on the** ~ alla radio.

radioactive [reɪdɪəu'æktɪv] adj radioattivo(a).

radio station n stazione f radio inv.

radish ['rædɪʃ] n ravanello.

radius ['reɪdɪəs] (pl **radii**) n raggio.

RAF n abbr = **Royal Air Force**.

raffle ['ræfl] n lotteria.

raft [rɑ:ft] n zattera; (also: life ~) zattera di salvataggio.

rafter ['rɑ:ftə*] n trave f.

rag [ræg] n straccio, cencio; (pej: newspaper) giornalaccio, bandiera; (for charity) iniziativa studentesca a scopo benefico; ~**s** npl (torn clothes) stracci mpl, brandelli mpl; ~**-and-bone man** (BRIT) n = **ragman**; ~ **doll** n bambola di pezza.

rage [reɪdʒ] n (fury) collera, furia ♦ vi (person) andare su tutte le furie; (storm) infuriare; **it's all the** ~ fa furore.

ragged ['rægɪd] adj (edge) irregolare; (clothes) logoro(a); (appearance) pezzente.

ragman ['rægmæn] n straccivendolo.

raid [reɪd] n (MIL) incursione f; (criminal) rapina; (by police) irruzione f ♦ vt fare un'incursione in; rapinare; fare irruzione in.

rail [reɪl] n (on stair) ringhiera; (on bridge, balcony) parapetto; (of ship) battagliola; ~**s** npl (for train) binario, rotaie fpl; **by** ~ per ferrovia; ~**ing(s)** n(pl) ringhiere fpl; ~**road** (US) n = ~**way**; ~**way** (BRIT) n ferrovia; ~**way line** (BRIT) n linea ferroviaria; ~**way-man** (BRIT) n ferroviere m; ~**way station** (BRIT) n stazione f ferroviaria.

rain [reɪn] n pioggia ♦ vi piovere; **in the** ~ sotto la pioggia; **it's** ~**ing** piove; ~**bow** n arcobaleno; ~**coat** n impermeabile m; ~**drop** n goccia di pioggia; ~**fall** n pioggia; (measurement) piovosità; ~**y** adj piovoso(a).

raise [reɪz] n aumento ♦ vt (lift) alzare; sollevare; (increase) aumentare; (a protest, doubt, question) sollevare; (cattle, family) allevare; (crop) coltivare; (*army, funds*) raccogliere; (*loan*) ottenere; **to ~ one's voice** alzare la voce.

raisin ['reɪzn] *n* uva secca.

rake [reɪk] *n* (*tool*) rastrello ♦ *vt* (*garden*) rastrellare; (*with machine gun*) spazzare.

rally ['rælɪ] *n* (*POL etc*) riunione *f*; (*AUT*) rally *m inv*; (*TENNIS*) scambio ♦ *vt* riunire, radunare ♦ *vi* (*sick person, Stock Exchange*) riprendersi; **~ round** *vt fus* raggrupparsi intorno a; venire in aiuto di.

RAM [ræm] *n abbr* (= *random access memory*) memoria ad accesso casuale.

ram [ræm] *n* montone *m*, ariete *m* ♦ *vt* conficcare; (*crash into*) cozzare, sbattere contro; percuotere; speronare.

ramble ['ræmbl] *n* escursione *f* ♦ *vi* (*pej: also:* **~ on**) divagare; **~r** *n* escursionista *m/f*; (*BOT*) rosa rampicante; **rambling** *adj* (*speech*) sconnesso(a); (*house*) tutto(a) a nicchie e corridoi; (*BOT*) rampicante.

ramp [ræmp] *n* rampa; **on/off ~** (*US: AUT*) raccordo di entrata/uscita.

rampage [ræm'peɪdʒ] *n*: **to go on the ~** scatenarsi in modo violento.

rampant ['ræmpənt] *adj* (*disease etc*) che infierisce.

rampart ['ræmpɑːt] *n* bastione *m*.

ramshackle ['ræmʃækl] *adj* (*house*) cadente; (*car etc*) sgangherato(a).

ran [ræn] *pt of* **run**.

ranch [rɑːntʃ] *n* ranch *m inv*; **~er** *n* proprietario di un ranch; cowboy *m inv*.

rancid ['rænsɪd] *adj* rancido(a).

rancour ['ræŋkə*] (*US* **rancor**) *n* rancore *m*.

random ['rændəm] *adj* fatto(a) or detto(a) per caso; (*COMPUT, MATH*) casuale ♦ *n*: **at ~** a casaccio; **~ access** *n* (*COMPUT*) accesso casuale.

randy ['rændɪ] (*BRIT: inf*) *adj* arrapato(a); lascivo(a).

rang [ræŋ] *pt of* **ring**.

range [reɪndʒ] *n* (*of mountains*) catena; (*of missile, voice*) portata; (*of proposals, products*) gamma; (*MIL: also: shooting* **~**) campo di tiro; (*also:*

kitchen **~**) fornello, cucina economica ♦ *vt* disporre ♦ *vi*: **to ~ over** coprire; **to ~ from ... to** andare da ... a.

ranger ['reɪndʒə*] *n* guardia forestale.

rank [ræŋk] *n* fila; (*status, MIL*) grado; (*BRIT: also: taxi* **~**) posteggio di taxi ♦ *vi*: **to ~ among** essere tra ♦ *adj* puzzolente; vero(a) e proprio(a); **the ~ and file** (*fig*) la gran massa.

rankle ['ræŋkl] *vi* bruciare.

ransack ['rænsæk] *vt* rovistare; (*plunder*) saccheggiare.

ransom ['rænsəm] *n* riscatto; **to hold sb to ~** (*fig*) esercitare pressione su qn.

rant [rænt] *vi* vociare.

rap [ræp] *vt* bussare a; picchiare su.

rape [reɪp] *n* violenza carnale, stupro; (*BOT*) ravizzone *m* ♦ *vt* violentare; **~(seed) oil** *n* olio di ravizzone.

rapid ['ræpɪd] *adj* rapido(a); **~s** *npl* (*GEO*) rapida; **~ly** *adv* rapidamente.

rapist ['reɪpɪst] *n* violentatore *m*.

rapport [ræ'pɔː*] *n* rapporto.

rapture ['ræptʃə*] *n* estasi *f inv*.

rare [rɛə*] *adj* raro(a); (*CULIN: steak*) al sangue.

rarely ['rɛəlɪ] *adv* raramente.

raring ['rɛərɪŋ] *adj*: **to be ~ to go** (*inf*) non veder l'ora di cominciare.

rascal ['rɑːskl] *n* mascalzone *m*.

rash [ræʃ] *adj* imprudente, sconsiderato(a) ♦ *n* (*MED*) eruzione *f*; (*of events etc*) scoppio.

rasher ['ræʃə*] *n* fetta sottile (di lardo or prosciutto).

raspberry ['rɑːzbərɪ] *n* lampone *m*.

rasping ['rɑːspɪŋ] *adj* stridulo(a).

rat [ræt] *n* ratto.

rate [reɪt] *n* (*proportion*) tasso, percentuale *f*; (*speed*) velocità *f inv*; (*price*) tariffa ♦ *vt* giudicare; stimare; **~s** *npl* (*BRIT: property tax*) imposte *fpl* comunali; (*fees*) tariffe *fpl*; **to ~ sb/sth as** valutare qn/qc come; **~able value** (*BRIT*) *n* valore *m* imponibile or locativo (di una proprietà); **~payer** (*BRIT*) *n* contribuente *m/f* (che paga le imposte comunali).

rather ['rɑːðə*] *adv* piuttosto; **it's ~ expensive** è piuttosto caro; (*too*) è un po' caro; **there's ~ a lot** ce n'è parecchio; **I would** *or* **I'd ~ go** preferirei andare.

ratify ['rætɪfaɪ] *vt* ratificare.

rating ['reɪtɪŋ] *n* (*assessment*) valutazione *f*; (*score*) punteggio di merito; (*BRIT: NAUT: sailor*) marinaio semplice.

ratio ['reɪʃɪəu] *n* proporzione *f*, rapporto.

ration ['ræʃən] *n* (*gen pl*) razioni *fpl* ♦ *vt* razionare.

rational ['ræʃənl] *adj* razionale, ragionevole; (*solution, reasoning*) logico(a); **~e** [-'nɑ:l] *n* fondamento logico; giustificazione *f*; **~ize** *vt* razionalizzare.

rat race *n* carrierismo, corsa al successo.

rattle ['rætl] *n* tintinnio; (*louder*) strepito; (*for baby*) sonaglino ♦ *vi* risuonare, tintinnare; fare un rumore di ferraglia ♦ *vt* scuotere (con strepito); **~snake** *n* serpente *m* a sonagli.

raucous ['rɔːkəs] *adj* rumoroso(a), fragoroso(a).

ravage ['rævɪdʒ] *vt* devastare; **~s** *npl* danni *mpl*.

rave [reɪv] *vi* (*in anger*) infuriarsi; (*with enthusiasm*) andare in estasi; (*MED*) delirare.

raven ['reɪvən] *n* corvo.

ravenous ['rævənəs] *adj* affamato(a).

ravine [rə'viːn] *n* burrone *m*.

raving ['reɪvɪŋ] *adj*: **~ lunatic** pazzo(a) furioso(a).

ravishing ['rævɪʃɪŋ] *adj* incantevole.

raw [rɔː] *adj* (*uncooked*) crudo(a); (*not processed*) greggio(a); (*sore*) vivo(a); (*inexperienced*) inesperto(a); (*weather, day*) gelido(a); **~ deal** (*inf*) *n* bidonata; **~ material** *n* materia prima.

ray [reɪ] *n* raggio; **a ~ of hope** un barlume di speranza.

rayon ['reɪɔn] *n* raion *m*.

raze [reɪz] *vt* radere, distruggere.

razor ['reɪzə*] *n* rasoio; **~ blade** *n* lama di rasoio.

Rd *abbr* = **road**.

re [riː] *prep* con riferimento a.

reach [riːtʃ] *n* portata; (*of river etc*)

tratto ♦ *vt* raggiungere; arrivare a ♦ *vi* stendersi; **out of/within ~** fuori/a portata di mano; **within ~ of the shops/station** vicino ai negozi/alla stazione; **~ out** *vt* (*hand*) allungare ♦ *vi*: **to ~ out for** stendere la mano per prendere.

react [riːˈækt] *vi* reagire; **~ion** [-ˈækʃən] *n* reazione *f*.

reactor [riːˈæktə*] *n* reattore *m*.

read [riːd, *pt, pp* rɛd] (*pt, pp* read) *vi* leggere ♦ *vt* leggere; (*understand*) intendere, interpretare; (*study*) studiare; **~ out** *vt* leggere ad alta voce; **~able** *adj* (*writing*) leggibile; (*book etc*) che si legge volentieri; **~er** *n* lettore/trice; (*book*) libro di lettura; (*BRIT: at university*) professore con funzioni preminenti di ricerca; **~ership** *n* (*of paper etc*) numero di lettori.

readily ['rɛdɪlɪ] *adv* volentieri; (*easily*) facilmente; (*quickly*) prontamente.

readiness ['rɛdɪnɪs] *n* prontezza; **in ~** (*prepared*) pronto(a).

reading ['riːdɪŋ] *n* lettura; (*understanding*) interpretazione *f*; (*on instrument*) indicazione *f*.

readjust [riːəˈdʒʌst] *vt* riaggiustare ♦ *vi* (*person*): **to ~ (to)** riadattarsi (a).

ready ['rɛdɪ] *adj* pronto(a); (*willing*) pronto(a), disposto(a); (*available*) disponibile ♦ *n*: **at the ~** (*MIL*) pronto a sparare; **to get ~** *vi* prepararsi ♦ *vt* preparare; **~-made** *adj* prefabbricato(a); (*clothes*) confezionato(a); **~ money** *n* denaro contante, contanti *mpl*; **~ reckoner** *n* prontuario di calcolo; **~-to-wear** *adj* prêt-à-porter *inv*.

reaffirm [riːəˈfəːm] *vt* riaffermare.

real [rɪəl] *adj* reale; vero(a); **in ~ terms** in realtà; **~ estate** *n* beni *mpl* immobili; **~ism** *n* (*also ART*) realismo; **~ist** *n* realista *m/f*; **~istic** [-ˈlɪstɪk] *adj* realistico(a).

reality [riːˈælɪtɪ] *n* realtà *f inv*.

realization [rɪəlaɪˈzeɪʃən] *n* presa di coscienza; realizzazione *f*.

realize ['rɪəlaɪz] *vt* (*understand*) rendersi conto di; (*a project, COMM: asset*) realizzare.

really ['rɪəlɪ] *adv* veramente, davvero; ~! (*indicating annoyance*) oh, insomma!

realm [rɛlm] *n* reame *m*, regno.

realtor ['rɪəltɔ:*] (*US*) *n* agente *m* immobiliare.

reap [ri:p] *vt* mietere; (*fig*) raccogliere.

reappear [ri:ə'pɪə*] *vi* ricomparire, riapparire.

rear [rɪə*] *adj* di dietro; (*AUT: wheel etc*) posteriore ♦ *n* didietro, parte *f* posteriore ♦ *vt* (*cattle, family*) allevare ♦ *vi* (*also: ~ up: animal*) impennarsi.

rearmament [ri:'ɑ:məmənt] *n* riarmo.

rearrange [ri:ə'reɪndʒ] *vt* riordinare.

rear-view: ~ **mirror** *n* (*AUT*) specchio retrovisore.

reason ['ri:zn] *n* ragione *f*; (*cause, motive*) ragione, motivo ♦ *vi*: **to ~ with sb** far ragionare qn; **it stands to ~ that** è ovvio che; **~able** *adj* ragionevole; (*not bad*) accettabile; **~ably** *adv* ragionevolmente; **~ed** *adj*: **a well-~ed argument** una forte argomentazione; **~ing** *n* ragionamento.

reassurance [ri:ə'ʃuərəns] *n* rassicurazione *f*.

reassure [ri:ə'ʃuə*] *vt* rassicurare; **to ~ sb of** rassicurare qn di *or* su.

rebate ['ri:beɪt] *n* (*on tax etc*) sgravio.

rebel [*n* 'rɛbl, *vb* rɪ'bɛl] *n* ribelle *m/f* ♦ *vi* ribellarsi; **~lion** *n* ribellione *f*; **~lious** *adj* ribelle.

rebound [*vb* rɪ'baund, *n* 'ri:baund] *vi* (*ball*) rimbalzare ♦ *n*: **on the ~** di rimbalzo.

rebuff [rɪ'bʌf] *n* secco rifiuto.

rebuke [rɪ'bju:k] *vt* rimproverare.

rebut [rɪ'bʌt] *vt* rifiutare.

recall [rɪ'kɔ:l] *vt* richiamare; (*remember*) ricordare, richiamare alla mente ♦ *n* richiamo.

recant [rɪ'kænt] *vi* ritrattarsi; (*REL*) fare abiura.

recap ['ri:kæp] *vt* ricapitolare ♦ *vi* riassumere.

recapitulate [ri:kə'pɪtjuleɪt] *vt*, *vi* = **recap.**

rec'd *abbr* = **received.**

recede [rɪ'si:d] *vi* allontanarsi; ritirarsi;

calare; **receding** *adj* (*forehead, chin*) sfuggente; **he's got a receding hairline** sta stempiando.

receipt [rɪ'si:t] *n* (*document*) ricevuta; (*act of receiving*) ricevimento; **~s** *npl* (*COMM*) introiti *mpl*.

receive [rɪ'si:v] *vt* ricevere; (*guest*) ricevere, accogliere.

receiver [rɪ'si:və*] *n* (*TEL*) ricevitore *m*; (*RADIO, TV*) apparecchio ricevente; (*of stolen goods*) ricettatore/trice; (*COMM*) curatore *m* fallimentare.

recent ['ri:snt] *adj* recente; **~ly** *adv* recentemente.

receptacle [rɪ'sɛptɪkl] *n* recipiente *m*.

reception [rɪ'sɛpʃən] *n* ricevimento; (*welcome*) accoglienza; (*TV etc*) ricezione *f*; ~ **desk** *n* (*in hotel*) reception *f inv*; (*in hospital, at doctor's*) accettazione *f*; (*in offices etc*) portineria; **~ist** *n* receptionist *m/f inv*.

receptive [rɪ'sɛptɪv] *adj* ricettivo(a).

recess [rɪ'sɛs] *n* (*in room, secret place*) alcova; (*POL etc: holiday*) vacanze *fpl*; **~ion** [-'sɛʃən] *n* recessione *f*.

recharge [ri:'tʃɑ:dʒ] *vt* (*battery*) ricaricare.

recipe ['rɛsɪpɪ] *n* ricetta.

recipient [rɪ'sɪpɪənt] *n* beneficiario/a; (*of letter*) destinatario/a.

recital [rɪ'saɪtl] *n* recital *m inv*.

recite [rɪ'saɪt] *vt* (*poem*) recitare.

reckless ['rɛkləs] *adj* (*driver etc*) spericolato(a); (*spending*) folle.

reckon ['rɛkən] *vt* (*count*) calcolare; (*think*): **I ~ that ...** penso che ...; ~ **on** *vt fus* contare su; **~ing** *n* conto; stima.

reclaim [rɪ'kleɪm] *vt* (*demand back*) richiedere, reclamare; (*land*) bonificare; (*materials*) recuperare; **reclamation** [rɛklə'meɪʃən] *n* bonifica.

recline [rɪ'klaɪn] *vi* stare sdraiato(a); **reclining** *adj* (*seat*) ribaltabile.

recognition [rɛkəg'nɪʃən] *n* riconoscimento; **transformed beyond** ~ irriconoscibile.

recognize ['rɛkəgnaɪz] *vt*: **to ~ (by/as)** riconoscere (a *or* da/come).

recoil [rɪ'kɔɪl] *vi* (*person*): **to ~ from doing sth** rifuggire dal fare qc ♦ *n* (*of* *gun)* rinculo.

recollect [rekə'lekt] *vt* ricordare; ~**ion** [-'lekʃən] *n* ricordo.

recommend [rekə'mend] *vt* raccomandare; *(advise)* consigliare.

reconcile ['rekənsail] *vt (two people)* riconciliare; *(two facts)* conciliare, quadrare; **to ~ o.s. to** rassegnarsi a.

recondition [ri:kən'dɪʃən] *vt* rimettere a nuovo.

reconnaissance [rɪ'kɒnɪsns] *n (MIL)* ricognizione *f*.

reconnoitre [rekə'nɔɪtə*] *(US* **reconnoiter)** *vt (MIL)* fare una ricognizione di.

reconstruct [ri:kən'strʌkt] *vt* ricostruire.

record [*n* 'rekɔ:d, *vb* rɪ'kɔ:d] *n* ricordo, documento; *(of meeting etc)* nota, verbale *m*; *(register)* registro; *(file)* pratica, dossier *m inv*; *(COMPUT)* record *m inv*; *(also: criminal ~)* fedina penale sporca; *(MUS: disc)* disco; *(SPORT)* record *m inv*, primato ♦ *vt (set down)* prendere nota di, registrare; *(MUS: song etc)* registrare; **in ~ time** a tempo di record; **off the ~** *adj* ufficioso(a) ♦ *adv* ufficiosamente; ~ **card** *n (in file)* scheda; ~**ed delivery** *(BRIT) n (POST):* ~**ed delivery letter** *etc* lettera *etc* raccomandata; ~**er** *n (MUS)* flauto diritto; ~ **holder** *n (SPORT)* primatista *m/f*; ~**ing** *n (MUS)* registrazione *f*; ~ **player** *n* giradischi *m inv*.

recount [rɪ'kaunt] *vt* raccontare, narrare.

re-count [*n* 'ri:kaunt, *vb* ri:'kaunt] *n (POL: of votes)* nuovo computo ♦ *vt* ricontare.

recoup [rɪ'ku:p] *vt* ricuperare.

recourse [rɪ'kɔ:s] *n:* **to have ~ to** ricorrere a, far ricorso a.

recover [rɪ'kʌvə*] *vt* ricuperare ♦ *vi:* **to ~ (from)** riprendersi (da).

recovery [rɪ'kʌvərɪ] *n* ricupero; ristabilimento; ripresa.

recreation [rekrɪ'eɪʃən] *n* ricreazione *f*; svago; ~**al** *adj* ricreativo(a).

recrimination [rɪkrɪmɪ'neɪʃən] *n* recriminazione *f*.

recruit [rɪ'kru:t] *n* recluta; *(in company)* nuovo(a) assunto(a) ♦ *vt* reclutare.

rectangle ['rektæŋgl] *n* rettangolo; **rectangular** [-'tæŋgjulə*] *adj* rettangolare.

rectify ['rektɪfaɪ] *vt (error)* rettificare; *(omission)* riparare.

rector ['rektə*] *n (REL)* parroco *(anglicano)*; ~**y** *n* presbiterio.

recuperate [rɪ'kju:pəreɪt] *vi* ristabilirsi.

recur [rɪ'kə:*] *vi* riaccadere; *(symptoms)* ripresentarsi; ~**rent** *adj* ricorrente, periodico(a).

red [red] *n* rosso; *(POL: pej)* rosso/a ♦ *adj* rosso(a); **in the ~** *(account)* scoperto; *(business)* in deficit; ~ **carpet treatment** *n* cerimonia col gran pavese; **R~ Cross** *n* Croce *f* Rossa; ~**currant** *n* ribes *m inv*; ~**den** *vt* arrossare ♦ *vi* arrossire; ~**dish** *adj* rossiccio(a).

redeem [rɪ'di:m] *vt (debt)* riscattare; *(sth in pawn)* ritirare; *(fig, also REL)* redimere; ~**ing** *adj:* ~**ing feature** unico aspetto positivo.

redeploy [ri:dɪ'plɔɪ] *vt (resources)* riorganizzare.

red-haired [-'heəd] *adj* dai capelli rossi.

red-handed [-'hændɪd] *adj:* **to be caught ~** essere preso(a) in flagrante *or* con le mani nel sacco.

redhead ['redhed] *n* rosso/a.

red herring *n (fig)* falsa pista.

red-hot *adj* arroventato(a).

redirect [ri:daɪ'rekt] *vt (mail)* far seguire.

red light *n:* **to go through a ~** *(AUT)* passare col rosso; **red-light district** *n* quartiere *m* a luci rosse.

redo [ri:'du:] *(irreg) vt* rifare.

redolent ['redələnt] *adj:* ~ **of** che sa di; *(fig)* che ricorda.

redouble [ri:'dʌbl] *vt:* **to ~ one's efforts** raddoppiare gli sforzi.

redress [rɪ'dres] *n* riparazione *f* ♦ *vt* riparare.

Red Sea *n:* **the ~** il Mar Rosso.

redskin ['redskɪn] *n* pellerossa *m/f*.

red tape *n (fig)* burocrazia.

reduce [rɪ'dju:s] *vt* ridurre; *(lower)* ridurre, abbassare; **"~ speed now"**

(AUT) "rallentare"; **at a ~d price** scontato(a); **reduction** [rɪ'dʌkʃən] n riduzione f; (of price) ribasso; (discount) sconto.

redundancy [rɪ'dʌndənsɪ] n licenziamento.

redundant [rɪ'dʌndnt] adj (worker) licenziato(a); (detail, object) superfluo(a); **to be made ~** essere licenziato (per eccesso di personale).

reed [riːd] n (BOT) canna; (MUS: of clarinet etc) ancia.

reef [riːf] n (at sea) scogliera.

reek [riːk] vi: **to ~ (of)** puzzare (di).

reel [riːl] n bobina, rocchetto; (FISHING) mulinello; (CINEMA) rotolo; (dance) danza veloce scozzese ♦ vi (sway) barcollare; **~ in** vt tirare su.

ref [rɛf] (inf) n abbr (= referee) arbitro.

refectory [rɪ'fɛktərɪ] n refettorio.

refer [rɪ'fəː*] vt: **to ~ sth to** (dispute, decision) deferire qc a; **to ~ sb to** (inquirer, MED: patient) indirizzare qn a; (reader: to text) rimandare qn a ♦ vi: **~ to** (allude to) accennare a; (consult) rivolgersi a.

referee [rɛfə'riː] n arbitro; (BRIT: for job application) referenza ♦ vt arbitrare.

reference ['rɛfrəns] n riferimento; (mention) menzione f, allusione f; (for job application) referenza; **with ~ to** (COMM: in letter) in or con riferimento a; **~ book** n libro di consultazione; **~ number** n numero di riferimento.

referenda [rɛfə'rɛndə] npl of **referendum**.

referendum [rɛfə'rɛndəm] (pl referenda) n referendum m inv.

refill [vb riː'fɪl, n 'riːfɪl] vt riempire di nuovo; (pen, lighter etc) ricaricare ♦ n (for pen etc) ricambio.

refine [rɪ'faɪn] vt raffinare; **~d** adj (person, taste) raffinato(a).

reflect [rɪ'flɛkt] vt (light, image) riflettere; (fig) rispecchiare ♦ vi (think) riflettere, considerare; **it ~s badly/well on him** si ripercuote su di lui in senso negativo/positivo; **~ion** [-'flɛkʃən] n riflessione f; (image) riflesso; (criticism): **~ion on** giudizio su;

attacco a; **on ~ion** pensandoci sopra.

reflex ['riːflɛks] adj riflesso(a) ♦ n riflesso; **~ive** [rɪ'flɛksɪv] adj (LING) riflessivo(a).

reform [rɪ'fɔːm] n (of sinner etc) correzione f; (of law etc) riforma ♦ vt correggere; riformare; **the R~ation** [rɛfə'meɪʃən] n la Riforma; **~atory** (US) n riformatorio.

refrain [rɪ'freɪn] vi: **to ~ from doing** trattenersi dal fare ♦ n ritornello.

refresh [rɪ'frɛʃ] vt rinfrescare; (subj: food, sleep) ristorare; **~er course** (BRIT) n corso di aggiornamento; **~ing** adj (drink) rinfrescante; (sleep) riposante, ristoratore(trice); **~ments** npl rinfreschi mpl.

refrigerator [rɪ'frɪdʒəreɪtə*] n frigorifero.

refuel [riː'fjuəl] vi far rifornimento (di carburante).

refuge ['rɛfjuːdʒ] n rifugio; **to take ~ in** rifugiarsi in.

refugee [rɛfju'dʒiː] n rifugiato/a, profugo/a.

refund [n 'riːfʌnd, vb rɪ'fʌnd] n rimborso ♦ vt rimborsare.

refurbish [riː'fəːbɪʃ] vt rimettere a nuovo.

refusal [rɪ'fjuːzəl] n rifiuto; **to have first ~ on** avere il diritto d'opzione su.

refuse [n 'rɛfjuːs, vb rɪ'fjuːz] n rifiuti mpl ♦ vt, vi rifiutare; **to ~ to do** rifiutare di fare; **~ collection** n raccolta di rifiuti.

refute [rɪ'fjuːt] vt confutare.

regain [rɪ'geɪn] vt riguadagnare; riacquistare, ricuperare.

regal ['riːgl] adj regale; **~ia** [rɪ'geɪlɪə] n insegne fpl regie.

regard [rɪ'gɑːd] n riguardo, stima ♦ vt considerare, stimare; **to give one's ~s to** porgere i suoi saluti a; **"with kindest ~s"** "cordiali saluti"; **~ing, as ~s, with ~ to** riguardo a; **~less** adv lo stesso; **~less of** a dispetto di, nonostante.

regenerate [rɪ'dʒɛnəreɪt] vt rigenerare.

régime [reɪ'ʒiːm] n regime m.

regiment ['rɛdʒɪmənt] n reggimento; **~al** [-'mɛntl] adj reggimentale.

region ['riːdʒən] n regione f; **in the ~ of**

(*fig*) all'incirca di; ~al *adj* regionale.

register ['rɛdʒɪstə*] *n* registro; (*also: electoral* ~) lista elettorale ♦ *vt* registrare; (*vehicle*) immatricolare; (*letter*) assicurare; (*subj: instrument*) segnare ♦ *vi* iscriversi; (*at hotel*) firmare il registro; (*make impression*) entrare in testa; ~ed (*BRIT*) *adj* (*letter*) assicurato(a); ~ed trademark *n* marchio depositato.

registrar ['rɛdʒɪstrɑ:*] *n* ufficiale *m* di stato civile; segretario.

registration [rɛdʒɪs'treɪʃən] *n* (*act*) registrazione *f*; iscrizione *f*; (*AUT: also*: ~ *number*) numero di targa.

registry ['rɛdʒɪstrɪ] *n* ufficio del registro; ~ office (*BRIT*) *n* anagrafe *f*; to get married in a ~ office ≈ sposarsi in municipio.

regret [rɪ'grɛt] *n* rimpianto, rincrescimento ♦ *vt* rimpiangere; ~fully *adv* con rincrescimento; ~table *adj* deplorevole.

regular ['rɛgjulə*] *adj* regolare; (*usual*) abituale, normale; (*soldier*) dell'esercito regolare ♦ *n* (*client etc*) cliente *m/f* abituale; ~ly *adv* regolarmente.

regulate ['rɛgjuleɪt] *vt* regolare; regulation [-'leɪʃən] *n* regolazione *f*; (*rule*) regola, regolamento.

rehabilitation ['ri:həbɪlɪ'teɪʃən] *n* (*of offender*) riabilitazione *f*; (*of disabled*) riadattamento.

rehearsal [rɪ'hə:səl] *n* prova.

rehearse [rɪ'hə:s] *vt* provare.

reign [reɪn] *n* regno ♦ *vi* regnare.

reimburse [ri:ɪm'bə:s] *vt* rimborsare.

rein [reɪn] *n* (*for horse*) briglia.

reindeer ['reɪndɪə*] *n inv* renna.

reinforce [ri:ɪn'fɔ:s] *vt* rinforzare; ~d concrete *n* cemento armato; ~ment *n* rinforzo; ~ments *npl* (*MIL*) rinforzi *mpl*.

reinstate [ri:ɪn'steɪt] *vt* reintegrare.

reiterate [ri:'ɪtəreɪt] *vt* reiterare, ripetere.

reject [*n* 'ri:dʒɛkt, *vb* rɪ'dʒɛkt] *n* (*COMM*) scarto ♦ *vt* rifiutare, respingere; (*COMM: goods*) scartare; ~ion

[rɪ'dʒɛkʃən] *n* rifiuto.

rejoice [rɪ'dʒɔɪs] *vi*: to ~ (at *or* over) provare diletto in.

rejuvenate [rɪ'dʒu:vəneɪt] *vt* ringiovanire.

relapse [rɪ'læps] *n* (*MED*) ricaduta.

relate [rɪ'leɪt] *vt* (*tell*) raccontare; (*connect*) collegare ♦ *vi*: to ~ to (*connect*) riferirsi a; (*get on with*) stabilire un rapporto con; ~d *adj*: ~ (to) imparentato(a) (con); collegato(a) *or* connesso(a) (a); relating to che riguarda, rispetto a.

relation [rɪ'leɪʃən] *n* (*person*) parente *m/f*; (*link*) rapporto, relazione *f*; ~ship *n* rapporto; (*personal ties*) rapporti *mpl*, relazioni *fpl*; (*also: family* ~ship) legami *mpl* di parentela.

relative ['rɛlətɪv] *n* parente *m/f* ♦ *adj* relativo(a); (*respective*) rispettivo(a).

relax [rɪ'læks] *vi* rilassarsi; (*person: unwind*) rilassarsi ♦ *vt* rilasciare; (*mind, person*) rilassare; ~ation [ri:læk'seɪʃən] *n* rilasciamento; rilassamento; (*entertainment*) ricreazione *f*, svago; ~ed *adj* rilassato(a); ~ing *adj* rilassante.

relay [rɪ'leɪ] *n* (*SPORT*) corsa a staffetta ♦ *vt* (*message*) trasmettere.

release [rɪ'li:s] *n* (*from prison*) rilascio; (*from obligation*) liberazione *f*; (*of gas etc*) emissione *f*; (*of film etc*) distribuzione *f*; (*record*) disco; (*device*) disinnesto ♦ *vt* (*prisoner*) rilasciare; (*from obligation, wreckage etc*) liberare; (*book, film*) fare uscire; (*news*) rendere pubblico(a); (*gas etc*) emettere; (*TECH: catch, spring etc*) disinnestare.

relegate ['rɛləgeɪt] *vt* relegare; (*BRIT: SPORT*): to be ~d essere retrocesso(a).

relent [rɪ'lɛnt] *vi* cedere; ~less *adj* implacabile.

relevant ['rɛləvənt] *adj* pertinente; (*chapter*) in questione; ~ to pertinente a.

reliability [rɪlaɪə'bɪlɪtɪ] *n* (*of person*) serietà; (*of machine*) affidabilità.

reliable [rɪ'laɪəbl] *adj* (*person, firm*) fidato(a), che dà affidamento; (*method*) sicuro(a); (*machine*) affidabile; **reliably** *adv*: **to be reliably informed** sapere da fonti sicure.

reliance [rɪ'laɪəns] *n*: ~ **(on)** fiducia (in); bisogno (di).

relic ['rɛlɪk] *n* (*REL*) reliquia; (*of the past*) resto.

relief [rɪ'liːf] *n* (*from pain, anxiety*) sollievo; (*help, supplies*) soccorsi *mpl*; (*ART, GEO*) rilievo.

relieve [rɪ'liːv] *vt* (*pain, patient*) sollevare; (*bring help*) soccorrere; (*take over from: gen*) sostituire; (: *guard*) cambiare; **to ~ sb of sth** (*load*) alleggerire qn di qc; **to ~ o.s.** fare i propri bisogni.

religion [rɪ'lɪdʒən] *n* religione *f*; **religious** *adj* religioso(a).

relinquish [rɪ'lɪŋkwɪʃ] *vt* abbandonare; (*plan, habit*) rinunziare a.

relish ['rɛlɪʃ] *n* (*CULIN*) condimento; (*enjoyment*) gran piacere *m* ♦ *vt* (*food etc*) godere; **to ~ doing** adorare fare.

relocate ['riːləʊ'keɪt] *vt* trasferire ♦ *vi* trasferirsi.

reluctance [rɪ'lʌktəns] *n* riluttanza.

reluctant [rɪ'lʌktənt] *adj* riluttante, mal disposto(a); **~ly** *adv* di mala voglia, a malincuore.

rely [rɪ'laɪ]: **to ~ on** *vt fus* contare su; (*be dependent*) dipendere da.

remain [rɪ'meɪn] *vi* restare, rimanere; **~der** *n* resto; (*COMM*) rimanenza; **~ing** *adj* che rimane; **~s** *npl* resti *mpl*.

remand [rɪ'mɑːnd] *n*: **on ~** in detenzione preventiva ♦ *vt*: **to ~ in custody** rinviare in carcere; trattenere a disposizione della legge; **~ home** (*BRIT*) *n* riformatorio, casa di correzione.

remark [rɪ'mɑːk] *n* osservazione *f* ♦ *vt* osservare, dire; **~able** *adj* notevole; eccezionale.

remedial [rɪ'miːdɪəl] *adj* (*tuition, classes*) di riparazione; (*exercise*) correttivo(a).

remedy ['rɛmədɪ] *n*: ~ **(for)** rimedio (per) ♦ *vt* rimediare a.

remember [rɪ'mɛmbə*] *vt* ricordare, ricordarsi di; ~ **me to him** salutalo da parte mia; **remembrance** *n* memoria;

ricordo.

remind [rɪ'maɪnd] *vt*: **to ~ sb of sth** ricordare qc a qn; **to ~ sb to do** ricordare a qn di fare; **~er** *n* richiamo; (*note etc*) promemoria *m inv*.

reminisce [rɛmɪ'nɪs] *vi*: **to ~ (about)** abbandonarsi ai ricordi (di).

reminiscent [rɛmɪ'nɪsnt] *adj*: ~ **of** che fa pensare a, che richiama.

remiss [rɪ'mɪs] *adj* negligente.

remission [rɪ'mɪʃən] *n* remissione *f*.

remit [rɪ'mɪt] *vt* (*send: money*) rimettere; **~tance** *n* rimessa.

remnant ['rɛmnənt] *n* resto, avanzo; **~s** *npl* (*COMM*) scampoli *mpl*; fine *f* serie.

remorse [rɪ'mɔːs] *n* rimorso; **~ful** *adj* pieno(a) di rimorsi; **~less** *adj* (*fig*) spietato(a).

remote [rɪ'məʊt] *adj* remoto(a), lontano(a); (*person*) distaccato(a); ~ **control** *n* telecomando; **~ly** *adv* remotamente; (*slightly*) vagamente.

remould ['riːməʊld] (*BRIT*) *n* (*tyre*) gomma rivestita.

removable [rɪ'muːvəbl] *adj* (*detachable*) staccabile.

removal [rɪ'muːvəl] *n* (*taking away*) rimozione *f*; soppressione *f*; (*BRIT: from house*) trasloco; (*from office: dismissal*) destituzione *f*; (*MED*) ablazione *f*; **~ van** (*BRIT*) *n* furgone *m* per traslochi.

remove [rɪ'muːv] *vt* togliere, rimuovere; (*employee*) destituire; (*stain*) far sparire; (*doubt, abuse*) sopprimere, eliminare; **~rs** (*BRIT*) *npl* (*company*) ditta *or* impresa di traslochi.

Renaissance [rɪ'neɪsɑːns] *n*: **the ~** il Rinascimento.

render ['rɛndə*] *vt* rendere; **~ing** *n* (*MUS etc*) interpretazione *f*.

rendez-vous ['rɒndɪvuː] *n* appuntamento; (*place*) luogo d'incontro; (*meeting*) incontro.

renegade ['rɛnɪgeɪd] *n* rinnegato/a.

renew [rɪ'njuː] *vt* rinnovare; (*negotiations*) riprendere; **~al** *n* rinnovo; ripresa.

renounce [rɪ'naʊns] *vt* rinunziare a.

renovate ['rɛnəveɪt] *vt* rinnovare; (*art*

work) restaurare; **renovation** [-'veɪʃən] *n* rinnovamento; restauro.

renown [rɪ'naun] *n* rinomanza; ~**ed** *adj* rinomato(a).

rent [rɛnt] *n* affitto ♦ *vt* (*take for* ~) prendere in affitto; (*also:* ~ *out*) dare in affitto; ~**al** *n* (*for television, car*) fitto.

renunciation [rɪnʌnsɪ'eɪʃən] *n* rinunzia.

rep [rɛp] *n abbr* (*COMM:* = *representative*) rappresentante *m/f*; (*THEATRE:* = *repertory*) teatro di repertorio.

repair [rɪ'pɛə°] *n* riparazione *f* ♦ *vt* riparare; **in good/bad** ~ in buone/cattive condizioni; ~ **kit** *n* corredo per riparazioni.

repatriate [ri:'pætrieɪt] *vt* rimpatriare.

repay [ri:'peɪ] (*irreg*) *vt* (*money, creditor*) rimborsare, ripagare; (*sb's efforts*) ricompensare; (*favour*) ricambiare; ~**ment** *n* pagamento; rimborso.

repeal [rɪ'pi:l] *n* (*of law*) abrogazione *f* ♦ *vt* abrogare.

repeat [rɪ'pi:t] *n* (*RADIO, TV*) replica ♦ *vt* ripetere; (*pattern*) riprodurre; (*promise, attack, also COMM: order*) rinnovare ♦ *vi* ripetere; ~**edly** *adv* ripetutamente, spesso.

repel [rɪ'pɛl] *vt* respingere; (*disgust*) ripugnare a; ~**lent** *adj* repellente ♦ *n*: insect ~**lent** prodotto *m* anti-insetti *inv*.

repent [rɪ'pɛnt] *vi*: to ~ (of) pentirsi (di); ~**ance** *n* pentimento.

repertoire ['rɛpətwɑ:°] *n* repertorio.

repertory ['rɛpətəri] *n* (*also:* ~ *theatre*) teatro di repertorio.

repetition [rɛpɪ'tɪʃən] *n* ripetizione *f*.

repetitive [rɪ'pɛtɪtɪv] *adj* (*movement*) che si ripete; (*work*) monotono(a); (*speech*) pieno(a) di ripetizioni.

replace [rɪ'pleɪs] *vt* (*put back*) rimettere a posto; (*take the place of*) sostituire; ~**ment** *n* rimessa; sostituzione *f*; (*person*) sostituto/a.

replay ['ri:pleɪ] *n* (*of match*) partita ripetuta; (*of tape, film*) replay *m inv*.

replenish [rɪ'plɛnɪʃ] *vt* (*glass*) riempire; (*stock etc*) rifornire.

replete [rɪ'pli:t] *adj* (*well-fed*) sazio(a).

replica ['rɛplɪkə] *n* replica, copia.

reply [rɪ'plaɪ] *n* risposta ♦ *vi* rispondere; ~ **coupon** *n* buono di risposta.

report [rɪ'pɔ:t] *n* rapporto; (*PRESS etc*) cronaca; (*BRIT: also: school* ~) pagella; (*of gun*) sparo ♦ *vt* riportare; (*PRESS etc*) fare una cronaca su; (*bring to notice: occurrence*) segnalare; (: *person*) denunciare ♦ *vi* (*make a report*) fare un rapporto (*or* una cronaca); (*present o.s.*): **to** ~ (**to sb**) presentarsi (a qn); ~ **card** (*US, SCOTTISH*) *n* pagella; ~**edly** *adv* stando a quanto si dice; **he** ~**edly told them to ...** avrebbe detto loro di ...; ~**er** *n* reporter *m inv*.

repose [rɪ'pəuz] *n*: **in** ~ (*face, mouth*) in riposo.

reprehensible [rɛprɪ'hɛnsɪbl] *adj* riprovevole.

represent [rɛprɪ'zɛnt] *vt* rappresentare; ~**ation** [-'teɪʃən] *n* rappresentazione *f*; (*petition*) rappresentanza; ~**ations** *npl* (*protest*) protesta; ~**ative** *n* rappresentante *m/f*; (*US: POL*) deputato/a ♦ *adj* rappresentativo(a).

repress [rɪ'prɛs] *vt* reprimere; ~**ion** [-'prɛʃən] *n* repressione *f*.

reprieve [rɪ'pri:v] *n* (*LAW*) sospensione *f* dell'esecuzione della condanna; (*fig*) dilazione *f*.

reprimand ['rɛprɪmɑ:nd] *n* rimprovero ♦ *vt* rimproverare.

reprint ['ri:prɪnt] *n* ristampa.

reprisal [rɪ'praɪzl] *n* rappresaglia.

reproach [rɪ'prəutʃ] *n* rimprovero ♦ *vt*: **to** ~ **sb for sth** rimproverare qn di qc; ~**ful** *adj* di rimprovero.

reproduce [ri:prə'dju:s] *vt* riprodurre ♦ *vi* riprodursi; **reproduction** [-'dʌkʃən] *n* riproduzione *f*.

reproof [rɪ'pru:f] *n* riprovazione *f*.

reprove [rɪ'pru:v] *vt*: **to** ~ (**for**) biasimare (per).

reptile ['rɛptaɪl] *n* rettile *m*.

republic [rɪ'pʌblɪk] *n* repubblica; ~**an** *adj*, *n* repubblicano(a).

repudiate [rɪ'pju:dɪeɪt] *vt* (*accusation*) respingere.

repulse [rɪ'pʌls] *vt* respingere.

repulsive [rɪ'pʌlsɪv] *adj* ripugnante, ripulsivo(a).

reputable ['rɛpjutəbl] *adj* di buona reputazione; (*occupation*) rispettabile.

reputation [rɛpju'teɪʃən] *n* reputazione *f*.

reputed [rɪ'pju:tɪd] *adj* reputato(a); **~ly** *adv* secondo quanto si dice.

request [rɪ'kwɛst] *n* domanda; (*formal*) richiesta ♦ *vt*: **to ~ (of** *or* **from sb)** chiedere (a qn); **~ stop** (*BRIT*) *n* (*for bus*) fermata facoltativa *or* a richiesta.

require [rɪ'kwaɪə*] *vt* (*need: subj: person*) aver bisogno di; (*: thing, situation*) richiedere; (*want*) volere; esigere; (*order*): **to ~ sb to do sth** ordinare a qn di fare qc; **~ment** *n* esigenza; bisogno; requisito.

requisite ['rɛkwɪzɪt] *n* cosa necessaria ♦ *adj* necessario(a).

requisition [rɛkwɪ'zɪʃən] *n*: **~ (for)** richiesta (di) ♦ *vt* (*MIL*) requisire.

rescue ['rɛskju:] *n* salvataggio; (*help*) soccorso ♦ *vt* salvare; **~ party** *n* squadra di salvataggio; **~r** *n* salvatore/trice.

research [rɪ'sə:tʃ] *n* ricerca, ricerche *fpl* ♦ *vt* fare ricerche su; **~er** *n* ricercatore/trice.

resemblance [rɪ'zɛmbləns] *n* somiglianza.

resemble [rɪ'zɛmbl] *vt* assomigliare a.

resent [rɪ'zɛnt] *vt* risentirsi di; **~ful** *adj* pieno(a) di risentimento; **~ment** *n* risentimento.

reservation [rɛzə'veɪʃən] *n* (*booking*) prenotazione *f*; (*doubt*) dubbio; (*protected area*) riserva; (*BRIT: on road: also: central ~*) spartitraffico *m inv*.

reserve [rɪ'zə:v] *n* riserva ♦ *vt* (*seats etc*) prenotare; **~s** *npl* (*MIL*) riserve *fpl*; **in ~** in serbo; **~d** *adj* (*shy*) riservato(a).

reservoir ['rɛzəvwɑ:*] *n* serbatoio.

reshuffle [ri:'ʃʌfl] *n*: **Cabinet ~** (*POL*) rimpasto governativo.

reside [rɪ'zaɪd] *vi* risiedere.

residence ['rɛzɪdəns] *n* residenza; **~ permit** (*BRIT*) *n* permesso di soggiorno.

resident ['rɛzɪdənt] *n* residente *m/f*; (*in hotel*) cliente *m/f* fisso(a) ♦ *adj*

residente; (*doctor*) fisso(a); (*course, college*) a tempo pieno con pernottamento; **~ial** [-'dɛnʃəl] *adj* di residenza; (*area*) residenziale.

residue ['rɛzɪdju:] *n* resto; (*CHEM, PHYSICS*) residuo.

resign [rɪ'zaɪn] *vt* (*one's post*) dimettersi da ♦ *vi* dimettersi; **to ~ o.s.** to rassegnarsi a; **~ation** [rɛzɪg'neɪʃən] *n* dimissioni *fpl*; rassegnazione *f*; **~ed** *adj* rassegnato(a).

resilience [rɪ'zɪlɪəns] *n* (*of material*) elasticità, resilienza; (*of person*) capacità di recupero.

resilient [rɪ'zɪlɪənt] *adj* elastico(a); (*person*) che si riprende facilmente.

resin ['rɛzɪn] *n* resina.

resist [rɪ'zɪst] *vt* resistere a; **~ance** *n* resistenza.

resolution [rɛzə'lu:ʃən] *n* risoluzione *f*.

resolve [rɪ'zɔlv] *n* risoluzione *f* ♦ *vi* (*decide*): **to ~ to do** decidere di fare ♦ *vt* (*problem*) risolvere.

resort [rɪ'zɔ:t] *n* (*town*) stazione *f*; (*recourse*) ricorso ♦ *vi*: **to ~ to** aver ricorso a; **in the last ~** come ultima risorsa.

resound [rɪ'zaund] *vi*: **to ~ (with)** risonare (di); **~ing** *adj* risonante; (*fig*) clamoroso(a).

resource [rɪ'sɔ:s] *n* risorsa; **~s** *npl* (*coal, iron etc*) risorse *fpl*; **~ful** *adj* pieno(a) di risorse, intraprendente.

respect [rɪs'pɛkt] *n* rispetto ♦ *vt* rispettare; **~s** *npl* (*greetings*) ossequi *mpl*; **with ~ to** rispetto a, riguardo a; **in this ~** per questo riguardo; **~able** *adj* rispettabile; **~ful** *adj* rispettoso(a).

respective [rɪs'pɛktɪv] *adj* rispettivo(a).

respite ['rɛspaɪt] *n* respiro, tregua.

resplendent [rɪs'plɛndənt] *adj* risplendente.

respond [rɪs'pɔnd] *vi* rispondere.

response [rɪs'pɔns] *n* risposta.

responsibility [rɪspɔnsɪ'bɪlɪtɪ] *n* responsabilità *f inv*.

responsible [rɪs'pɔnsɪbl] *adj* (*trustworthy*) fidato(a); (*job*) di (grande) responsabilità; **~ (for)** responsabile (di).

responsive [rɪs'pɒnsɪv] *adj* che reagisce.

rest [rɛst] *n* riposo; *(stop)* sosta, pausa; *(MUS)* pausa; *(object: to support sth)* appoggio, sostegno; *(remainder)* resto, avanzi *mpl* ♦ *vi* riposarsi; *(remain)* rimanere, restare; *(be supported)*: **to ~ on** appoggiarsi su ♦ *vt* (far) riposare; *(lean)*: **to ~ sth on/against** appoggiare qc su/contro; **the ~ of them** gli altri; **it ~s with him to decide** sta a lui decidere.

restaurant ['rɛstərɔŋ] *n* ristorante *m*; ~ **car** *(BRIT)* *n* vagone *m* ristorante.

restful ['rɛstful] *adj* riposante.

rest home *n* casa di riposo.

restitution [rɛstɪ'tjuːʃən] *n*: **to make ~ to sb for sth** compensare qn di qc.

restive ['rɛstɪv] *adj* agitato(a), impaziente.

restless ['rɛstlɪs] *adj* agitato(a), irrequieto(a).

restoration [rɛstə'reɪʃən] *n* restauro; restituzione *f*.

restore [rɪ'stɔː*] *vt* *(building, to power)* restaurare; *(sth stolen)* restituire; *(peace, health)* ristorare.

restrain [rɪs'treɪn] *vt* *(feeling, growth)* contenere, frenare; *(person)*: **to ~ (from doing)** trattenere (dal fare); ~**ed** *adj* *(style)* contenuto(a), sobrio(a); *(person)* riservato(a); ~**t** *n* *(restriction)* limitazione *f*; *(moderation)* ritegno; *(of style)* contenutezza.

restrict [rɪs'trɪkt] *vt* restringere, limitare; ~**ion** [-kʃən] *n*: ~ **(on)** restrizione *f* (di), limitazione *f*.

rest room *(US)* *n* toletta.

restructure [riː'strʌktʃə*] *vt* ristrutturare.

result [rɪ'zʌlt] *n* risultato ♦ *vi*: **to ~ in** avere per risultato; **as a ~ of** in *or* di conseguenza a, in seguito a.

resume [rɪ'zjuːm] *vt, vi* *(work, journey)* riprendere.

résumé ['reɪzjuːmeɪ] *n* riassunto *m*; *(US)* curriculum *m inv* vitae.

resumption [rɪ'zʌmpʃən] *n* ripresa.

resurgence [rɪ'sɜːdʒəns] *n* rinascita.

resurrection [rɛzə'rɛkʃən] *n* risurrezione *f*.

resuscitate [rɪ'sʌsɪteɪt] *vt* *(MED)* risuscitare; **resuscitation** [-'teɪʃən] *n* rianimazione *f*.

retail ['riːteɪl] *adj, adv* al minuto ♦ *vt* vendere al minuto; ~**er** *n* commerciante *m/f* al minuto, dettagliante *m/f*; ~ **price** *n* prezzo al minuto.

retain [rɪ'teɪn] *vt* *(keep)* tenere, serbare; ~**er** *n* *(fee)* onorario.

retaliate [rɪ'tælɪeɪt] *vi*: **to ~ (against)** vendicarsi (di); **retaliation** [-'eɪʃən] *n* rappresaglie *fpl*.

retarded [rɪ'tɑːdɪd] *adj* ritardato(a).

retch [rɛtʃ] *vi* aver conati di vomito.

retire [rɪ'taɪə*] *vi* *(give up work)* andare in pensione; *(withdraw)* ritirarsi, andarsene; *(go to bed)* andare a letto, ritirarsi; ~**d** *adj* *(person)* pensionato(a); ~**ment** *n* pensione *f*; *(act)* pensionamento; **retiring** *adj* *(leaving)* uscente; *(shy)* riservato(a).

retort [rɪ'tɔːt] *vi* rimbeccare.

retrace [riː'treɪs] *vt*: **to ~ one's steps** tornare sui passi.

retract [rɪ'trækt] *vt* *(statement)* ritrattare; *(claws, undercarriage, aerial)* ritrarre, ritirare.

retrain [riː'treɪn] *vt* *(worker)* riaddestrare.

retread ['riːtrɛd] *n* *(tyre)* gomma rigenerata.

retreat [rɪ'triːt] *n* ritirata; *(place)* rifugio ♦ *vi* battere in ritirata.

retribution [rɛtrɪ'bjuːʃən] *n* castigo.

retrieval [rɪ'triːvəl] *n* *(see vb)* ricupero; riparazione *f*.

retrieve [rɪ'triːv] *vt* *(sth lost)* ricuperare, ritrovare; *(situation, honour)* salvare; *(error, loss)* rimediare a; ~**r** *n* cane *m* da riporto.

retrospect ['rɛtrəspɛkt] *n*: **in ~** guardando indietro; ~**ive** [-'spɛktɪv] *adj* retrospettivo(a); *(law)* retroattivo(a).

return [rɪ'tɜːn] *n* *(going or coming back)* ritorno; *(of sth stolen etc)* restituzione *f*; *(FINANCE: from land, shares)* profitto, reddito ♦ *cpd* *(journey, match)* di ritorno; *(BRIT: ticket)* di andata e ritorno ♦ *vi* tornare, ritornare ♦ *vt* rendere, restituire; *(bring back)* riportare; (*send back*) mandare indietro; (*put back*) rimettere; (*POL: candidate*) eleggere; ~s npl (*COMM*) incassi mpl; profitti mpl; in ~ (for) in cambio (di); by ~ of post a stretto giro di posta; **many happy** ~s (**of the day**)! cento di questi giorni!

reunion [ri:ˈjuːnɪən] n riunione f.

reunite [riːjuːˈnaɪt] vt riunire.

rev [rɛv] n abbr (*AUT: = revolution*) giro ♦ vt (*also*: ~ up) imballare.

revamp [ˈriːˈvæmp] vt (*firm*) riorganizzare.

reveal [rɪˈviːl] vt (*make known*) rivelare, svelare; (*display*) rivelare, mostrare; ~**ing** adj rivelatore(trice); (*dress*) scollato(a).

reveille [rɪˈvælɪ] n (*MIL*) sveglia.

revel [ˈrɛvl] vi: to ~ **in sth/in doing** dilettarsi di qc/a fare.

revelation [rɛvəˈleɪʃən] n rivelazione f.

revelry [ˈrɛvlrɪ] n baldoria.

revenge [rɪˈvɛndʒ] n vendetta ♦ vt vendicare; **to take** ~ **on** vendicarsi di.

revenue [ˈrɛvənjuː] n reddito.

reverberate [rɪˈvəːbəreɪt] vi (*sound*) rimbombare; (*light*) riverberarsi; (*fig*) ripercuotersi.

revere [rɪˈvɪə*] vt venerare.

reverence [ˈrɛvərəns] n venerazione f, riverenza.

Reverend [ˈrɛvərənd] adj (*in titles*) reverendo(a).

reverie [ˈrɛvərɪ] n fantasticheria.

reversal [rɪˈvəːsl] n capovolgimento.

reverse [rɪˈvəːs] n contrario, opposto; (*back, defeat*) rovescio; (*AUT: also*: ~ gear) marcia indietro ♦ adj (*order, direction*) contrario(a), opposto(a) ♦ vt (*turn*) invertire, rivoltare; (*change*) capovolgere, rovesciare; (*LAW: judgment*) cassare; (*car*) fare marcia indietro con ♦ vi (*BRIT: AUT, person etc*) fare marcia indietro; ~**d charge call** (*BRIT*) n (*TEL*) telefonata con addebito al ricevente; **reversing lights** (*BRIT*) npl (*AUT*) luci fpl per la retromarcia.

revert [rɪˈvəːt] vi: to ~ to tornare a.

review [rɪˈvjuː] n rivista; (*of book, film*) recensione f; (*of situation*) esame m ♦ vt passare in rivista; fare la recensione di; fare il punto di; ~**er** n recensore/a.

revile [rɪˈvaɪl] vt insultare.

revise [rɪˈvaɪz] vt (*manuscript*) rivedere, correggere; (*opinion*) emendare, modificare; (*study: subject, notes*) ripassare; **revision** [rɪˈvɪʒən] n revisione f; ripasso.

revitalize [riːˈvaɪtəlaɪz] vt ravvivare.

revival [rɪˈvaɪvəl] n ripresa; ristabilimento; (*of faith*) risveglio.

revive [rɪˈvaɪv] vt (*person*) rianimare; (*custom*) far rivivere; (*hope, courage, economy*) ravvivare; (*play, fashion*) riesumare ♦ vi (*person*) rianimarsi; (*hope*) ravvivarsi; (*activity*) riprendersi.

revolt [rɪˈvəult] n rivolta, ribellione f ♦ vi rivoltarsi, ribellarsi ♦ vt (*fai*) rivoltare; ~**ing** adj ripugnante.

revolution [rɛvəˈluːʃən] n rivoluzione f; (*of wheel, spin*) rivoluzione, giro; ~**ary** adj, n rivoluzionario(a).

revolve [rɪˈvɔlv] vi girare.

revolver [rɪˈvɔlvə*] n rivoltella.

revolving [rɪˈvɔlvɪŋ] adj girevole.

revue [rɪˈvjuː] n (*THEATRE*) rivista.

revulsion [rɪˈvʌlʃən] n ripugnanza.

reward [rɪˈwɔːd] n ricompensa, premio ♦ vt: to ~ (for) ricompensare (per); ~**ing** adj (*fig*) gratificante.

rewind [riːˈwaɪnd] vt (*irreg*) (*watch*) ricaricare; (*ribbon etc*) riavvolgere.

rewire [riːˈwaɪə*] vt (*house*) rifare l'impianto elettrico di.

reword [riːˈwəːd] vt formulare or esprimere con altre parole.

rheumatism [ˈruːmətɪzəm] n reumatismo.

Rhine [raɪn] n: the ~ il Reno.

rhinoceros [raɪˈnɔsərəs] n rinoceronte m.

rhododendron [rəudəˈdɛndrən] n rododendro.

Rhone [rəun] n: the ~ il Rodano.

rhubarb [ˈruːbɑːb] n rabarbaro.

rhyme [raɪm] n rima; (*verse*) poesia.

rhythm [ˈrɪðm] n ritmo.

rib [rɪb] n (*ANAT*) costola ♦ vt (*tease*) punzecchiare.

ribbon ['rɪbən] n nastro; **in ~s** (torn) a brandelli.

rice [raɪs] n riso; ~ **pudding** n budino di riso.

rich [rɪtʃ] adj ricco(a); (clothes) sontuoso(a); (abundant): ~ **in** ricco(a) di; **the** ~ npl (wealthy people) i ricchi; ~**es** npl ricchezze fpl; ~**ly** adv riccamente; (dressed) sontuosamente; (deserved) pienamente.

rickets ['rɪkɪts] n rachitismo.

rickety ['rɪkɪtɪ] adj traballante.

rickshaw ['rɪkʃɔː] n risciò m inv.

ricochet ['rɪkəʃeɪ] vi rimbalzare.

rid [rɪd] (pt, pp rid) vt: **to ~ sb of** sbarazzare or liberare qn di; **to get ~ of** sbarazzarsi di.

ridden ['rɪdn] pp of **ride**.

riddle ['rɪdl] n (puzzle) indovinello ♦ vt: **to be ~d with** (holes) essere crivellato(a) di; (doubts) essere pieno(a) di.

ride [raɪd] (pt rode, pp ridden) n (on horse) cavalcata; (outing) passeggiata; (distance covered) cavalcata; corsa ♦ vi (as sport) cavalcare; (go somewhere: on horse, bicycle) andare (a cavallo or in bicicletta etc); (journey: on bicycle, motorcycle, bus) andare, viaggiare ♦ vt (a horse) montare, cavalcare; **to take sb for a ~** (fig) prendere in giro qn; fregare qn; **to ~ a horse/bicycle/camel** montare a cavallo/in bicicletta/in groppa a un cammello; **to ~ at anchor** (NAUT) essere alla fonda; ~**r** n cavalcatore/trice; (in race) fantino; (on bicycle) ciclista m/f; (on motorcycle) motociclista m/f.

ridge [rɪdʒ] n (of hill) cresta; (of roof) colmo; (on object) riga (in rilievo).

ridicule ['rɪdɪkjuːl] n ridicolo; scherno ♦ vt mettere in ridicolo.

ridiculous [rɪ'dɪkjuləs] adj ridicolo(a).

riding ['raɪdɪŋ] n equitazione f; ~ **school** n scuola d'equitazione.

rife [raɪf] adj diffuso(a); **to be ~ with** abbondare di.

riffraff ['rɪfræf] n canaglia.

rifle ['raɪfl] n carabina ♦ vt vuotare; ~

through vt fus frugare tra; ~ **range** n campo di tiro; (at fair) tiro a segno.

rift [rɪft] n fessura, crepatura; (fig: disagreement) incrinatura, disaccordo.

rig [rɪg] n (also: oil ~: on land) derrick m inv; (: at sea) piattaforma di trivellazione ♦ vt (election etc) truccare; ~ **out** (BRIT) vt: **to ~ out as/in** vestire da/in; ~ **up** vt allestire; ~**ging** n (NAUT) attrezzatura.

right [raɪt] adj giusto(a); (suitable) appropriato(a); (not left) destro(a) ♦ n giusto; (title, claim) diritto; (not left) destra ♦ adv (answer) correttamente; (not on the left) a destra ♦ vt raddrizzare; (fig) riparare ♦ excl bene!; **to be ~** (person) aver ragione; (answer) essere giusto(a) or corretto(a); **by ~s** di diritto; **on the ~** a destra; **to be in the ~** aver ragione, essere nel giusto; ~ **now** proprio adesso; subito; ~ **away** subito; ~ **angle** n angolo retto; ~**eous** ['raɪtʃəs] adj retto(a), virtuoso(a); (anger) giusto(a), giustificato(a); ~**ful** adj (heir) legittimo(a); ~**-handed** adj (person) che adopera la mano destra; ~**-hand man** n braccio destro; ~**-hand side** n il lato destro; ~**ly** adv bene, correttamente; (with reason) a ragione; ~ **of way** n diritto di passaggio; (AUT) precedenza; ~**-wing** adj (POL) di destra.

rigid ['rɪdʒɪd] adj rigido(a); (principle) rigoroso(a).

rigmarole ['rɪgmərəul] n tiritera; commedia.

rile [raɪl] vt irritare, seccare.

rim [rɪm] n orlo; (of spectacles) montatura; (of wheel) cerchione m.

rind [raɪnd] n (of bacon) cotenna; (of lemon etc) scorza.

ring [rɪŋ] (pt rang, pp rung) n anello; (of people, objects) cerchio; (of spies) giro; (of smoke etc) spirale m; (arena) pista, arena; (for boxing) ring m inv; (sound of bell) scampanio ♦ vi (person, bell, telephone) suonare; (also: ~ out: voice, words) risuonare; (TEL) telefonare; (ears) fischiare ♦ vt (BRIT: TEL) telefonare a; (bell, doorbell) suonare; **to give sb a** ~ (BRIT: TEL) dare un colpo di telefono a qn; ~ **back** vt, vi (TEL) richiamare; ~ **off** (BRIT) vi (TEL) mettere giù, riattaccare; ~ **up** (BRIT) vt (TEL) telefonare a; ~**ing** n (of bell) scampanio; (of telephone) squillo; (in ears) ronzio; ~**ing tone** (BRIT) n (TEL) segnale m di libero; ~**leader** n (of gang) capobanda m.

ringlets ['rɪŋlɪts] npl boccoli mpl.

ring road (BRIT) n raccordo anulare.

rink [rɪŋk] n (also: ice ~) pista di pattinaggio.

rinse [rɪns] n risciacquatura; (hair tint) cachet m inv ♦ vt sciacquare.

riot ['raɪət] n sommossa, tumulto; (of colours) orgia ♦ vi tumultuare; **to run** ~ creare disordine; ~**ous** adj tumultuoso(a); (living) strenato(a); (party) scatenato(a).

rip [rɪp] n strappo ♦ vt strappare ♦ vi strapparsi; ~**cord** n cavo di sfilamento.

ripe [raɪp] adj (fruit, grain) maturo(a); (cheese) stagionato(a); ~**n** vt maturare ♦ vi maturarsi.

ripple ['rɪpl] n increspamento, ondulazione f; mormorio ♦ vi incresparsi.

rise [raɪz] (pt rose, pp risen) n (slope) salita, pendio; (hill) altura; (increase: in wages: BRIT) aumento; (: in prices, temperature) rialzo, aumento; (fig: to power etc) ascesa ♦ vi alzarsi, levarsi; (prices) aumentare; (waters, river) crescere; (sun, wind, person: from chair, bed) levarsi; (also: ~ up: building) ergersi; (: rebel) insorgere; ribellarsi; (in rank) salire; **to give** ~ **to** provocare, dare origine a; **to** ~ **to the occasion** essere all'altezza; **risen** ['rɪzn] pp of **rise**; **rising** adj (increasing: number) sempre crescente; (: prices) in aumento; (tide) montante; (sun, moon) nascente, che sorge.

risk [rɪsk] n rischio; pericolo ♦ vt rischiare; **to take** or **run the** ~ **of doing** correre il rischio di fare; **at** ~ in pericolo; **at one's own** ~ a proprio rischio e pericolo; ~**y** adj rischioso(a).

risqué ['riːskeɪ] adj (joke) spinto(a).

rissole ['rɪsəul] n crocchetta.

rite [raɪt] n rito; **last** ~s l'estrema unzione.

ritual ['rɪtjuəl] adj rituale ♦ n rituale m.

rival ['raɪvl] n rivale m/f; (in business) concorrente m/f ♦ adj rivale; che fa concorrenza ♦ vt essere in concorrenza con; **to** ~ **sb/sth in** competere con qn/qc in; ~**ry** n rivalità; concorrenza.

river ['rɪvə*] n fiume m ♦ cpd (port, traffic) fluviale; **up/down** ~ a monte/ valle; ~**bank** n argine m; ~**bed** n letto di fiume.

rivet ['rɪvɪt] n ribattino, rivetto ♦ vt (fig) concentrare, fissare.

Riviera [rɪvɪ'ɛərə] n: **the (French)** ~ la Costa Azzurra; **the Italian** ~ la Riviera.

road [rəud] n strada; (small) cammino; (in town) via ♦ cpd stradale; **major/ minor** ~ strada con/senza diritto di precedenza; ~**block** n blocco stradale; ~**hog** n guidatore m egoista e spericolato; ~ **map** n carta stradale; ~ **safety** n sicurezza sulle strade; ~**side** n margine m della strada; ~**sign** n cartello stradale; ~ **user** n chi usa la strada; ~**way** n carreggiata; ~**works** npl lavori mpl stradali; ~**worthy** adj in buono stato di marcia.

roam [rəum] vi errare, vagabondare.

roar [rɔː*] n ruggito; (of crowd) tumulto; (of thunder, storm) muggito; (of laughter) scoppio ♦ vi ruggire; tumultuare; muggire; **to** ~ **with laughter** scoppiare dalle risa; **to do a** ~**ing trade** fare affari d'oro.

roast [rəust] n arrosto ♦ vt arrostire; (coffee) tostare, torrefare; ~ **beef** n arrosto di manzo.

rob [rɔb] vt (person) rubare; (bank) svaligiare; **to** ~ **sb of sth** derubare qn di qc; (fig: deprive) privare qn di qc; ~**ber** n ladro; (armed) rapinatore m; ~**bery** n furto; rapina.

robe [rəub] n (for ceremony etc) abito; (also: bath ~) accappatoio; (US: also: lap ~) coperta.

robin ['rɔbɪn] n pettirosso.

robot ['rəubɔt] n robot m inv.

robust [rəu'bʌst] adj robusto(a);

(*economy*) solido(a).

rock [rɔk] n (*substance*) roccia; (*boulder*) masso; roccia; (*in sea*) scoglio; (*US: pebble*) ciottolo; (*BRIT: sweet*) zucchero candito ♦ vt (*swing gently: cradle*) dondolare; (: *child*) cullare; (*shake*) scrollare, far tremare ♦ vi dondolarsi; scrollarsi, tremare; **on the ~s** (*drink*) col ghiaccio; (*marriage etc*) in crisi; **~ and roll** n rock and roll m; **~-bottom** adj bassissimo(a); **~ery** n giardino roccioso.

rocket ['rɔkɪt] n razzo.

rock fall n parete f della roccia.

rocking ['rɔkɪŋ]: **~ chair** n sedia a dondolo; **~ horse** n cavallo a dondolo.

rocky ['rɔkɪ] adj (*hill*) roccioso(a); (*path*) sassoso(a); (*unsteady: table*) traballante; (: *marriage etc*) instabile.

rod [rɔd] n (*metallic, TECH*) asta; (*wooden*) bacchetta; (*also: fishing ~*) canna da pesca.

rode [rəud] pt of **ride**.

rodent ['rəudnt] n roditore m.

rodeo ['rəudiəu] n rodeo.

roe [rəu] n (*species: also: ~ deer*) capriolo; (*of fish, also: hard ~*) uova fpl di pesce; **soft ~** latte m di pesce.

rogue [rəug] n mascalzone m.

role [rəul] n ruolo.

roll [rəul] n rotolo; (*of banknotes*) mazzo; (*also: bread ~*) panino; (*register*) lista; (*sound: of drums etc*) rullo ♦ vt rotolare; (*also: ~ up: string*) aggomitolare; (*also: ~ up: sleeves*) rimboccare; (*cigarettes*) arrotolare; (*eyes*) roteare; (*also: ~ out: pastry*) stendere; (*lawn, road etc*) spianare ♦ vi rotolare; (*wheel*) girare; (*drum*) rullare; (*vehicle: also: ~ along*) avanzare; (*ship*) rollare; **~ about or around** vi rotolare qua e là; (*person*) rotolarsi; **~ by** vi (*time*) passare; **~ in** vi (*mail, cash*) arrivare a fiumi; **~ over** vi rivoltarsi; **~ up** (*inf*) vi (*arrive*) arrivare ♦ vt (*carpet*) arrotolare; **~ call** n appello; **~er** n rullo; (*wheel*) rotella; (*for hair*) bigodino; **~er coaster** n montagne fpl russe; **~er skates** npl pattini mpl a

rotelle.

rolling ['rəulɪŋ] adj (*landscape*) ondulato(a); **~ pin** n matterello; **~ stock** n (*RAIL*) materiale m rotabile.

ROM [rɔm] n abbr (= *read only memory*) memoria di sola lettura.

Roman ['rəumən] adj, n romano(a); **~ Catholic** adj, n cattolico(a).

romance [rə'mæns] n storia (or avventura or film m inv) romantico(a); (*charm*) poesia; (*love affair*) idillio.

Romania [rəu'meɪnɪə] n = **Rumania**.

Roman numeral n numero romano.

romantic [rə'mæntɪk] adj romantico(a); sentimentale.

Rome [rəum] n Roma.

romp [rɔmp] n gioco rumoroso ♦ vi (*also: ~ about*) far chiasso, giocare in un modo rumoroso.

rompers ['rɔmpəz] npl pagliaccetto.

roof [ruːf] n tetto; (*of tunnel, cave*) volta ♦ vt coprire (con un tetto); **~ of the mouth** palato; **~ing** n materiale m per copertura; **~ rack** n (*AUT*) portabagagli m inv.

rook [ruk] n (*bird*) corvo nero; (*CHESS*) torre f.

room [ruːm] n (*in house*) stanza; (*bed~, in hotel*) camera; (*in school etc*) sala; (*space*) posto, spazio; **~s** npl (*lodging*) alloggio; "**~s to let**" (*BRIT*), "**~s for rent**" (*US*) "si affittano camere"; **there is ~ for improvement** si potrebbe migliorare; **~ing house** (*US*) n casa in cui si affittano camere o appartamentini ammobiliati; **~mate** n compagno/a di stanza; **~ service** n servizio da camera; **~y** adj spazioso(a); (*garment*) ampio(a).

roost [ruːst] vi appollaiarsi.

rooster ['ruːstə*] n gallo.

root [ruːt] n radice f ♦ vi (*plant, belief*) attecchire; **~ about** vi (*fig*) frugare; **~ for** vt fus fare il tifo per; **~ out** vt estirpare.

rope [rəup] n corda, fune f; (*NAUT*) cavo ♦ vt (*box*) legare; (*climbers*) legare in cordata; (*area: also: ~ off*) isolare cingendo con cordoni; **to know the ~s** (*fig*) conoscere i trucchi del mestiere;

~ **in** vt (fig) coinvolgere; ~ **ladder** n scala a corda.

rosary ['rəʊzərɪ] n rosario; roseto.

rose [rəʊz] pt of **rise** ♦ n rosa; (also: ~ **bush**) rosaio; (on watering can) rosetta.

rosé ['rəʊzeɪ] n vino rosato.

rosebud ['rəʊzbʌd] n bocciolo di rosa.

rosebush ['rəʊzbʊʃ] n rosaio.

rosemary ['rəʊzmərɪ] n rosmarino.

rosette [rəʊ'zɛt] n coccarda.

roster ['rɒstə*] n: **duty** ~ ruolino di servizio.

rostrum ['rɒstrəm] n tribuna.

rosy ['rəʊzɪ] adj roseo(a).

rot [rɒt] n (decay) putrefazione f; (inf: nonsense) stupidaggini fpl ♦ vt, vi imputridire, marcire.

rota ['rəʊtə] n tabella dei turni.

rotary ['rəʊtərɪ] adj rotante.

rotate [rəʊ'teɪt] vt (revolve) far girare; (change round: jobs) fare a turno ♦ vi (revolve) girare; **rotating** adj (movement) rotante.

rote [rəʊt] n: **by** ~ (by heart) a memoria; (mechanically) meccanicamente.

rotten ['rɒtn] adj (decayed) putrido(a), marcio(a); (dishonest) corrotto(a); (inf: bad) brutto(a); (: action) vigliacco(a); **to feel** ~ (ill) sentirsi da cani.

rouble ['ru:bl] (US ruble) n rublo.

rouge [ru:ʒ] n belletto.

rough [rʌf] adj (skin, surface) ruvido(a); (terrain, road) accidentato(a); (voice) rauco(a); (person, manner: coarse) rozzo(a), aspro(a); (: violent) brutale; (district) malfamato(a); (weather) cattivo(a); (sea) mosso(a); (plan) abbozzato(a); (guess) approssimativo(a) ♦ n (GOLF) macchia; **to** ~ **it** far vita dura; **to sleep** ~ (BRIT) dormire all'addiaccio; ~**age** n alimenti mpl ricchi in cellulosa; ~**and-ready** adj rudimentale; ~**cast** n intonaco grezzo; ~ **copy** n brutta copia; ~**ly** adv (handle) rudemente, brutalmente; (make) grossolanamente; (speak) bruscamente; (approximately)

approssimativamente; ~**ness** n ruvidità; (of manner) rozzezza.

roulette [ru:'lɛt] n roulette f.

Roumania [ru:'meɪnɪə] n = **Rumania**.

round [raʊnd] adj rotondo(a); (figures) tondo(a) ♦ n (BRIT: of toast) fetta; (duty: of policeman, milkman etc) giro; (: of doctor) visite fpl; (game: of cards, golf, in competition) partita; (of ammunition) cartuccia; (BOXING) round m inv; (of talks) serie f inv ♦ vt (corner) girare; (bend) prendere ♦ prep intorno a ♦ adv: **all** ~ tutt'attorno; **to go the long way** ~ fare il giro più lungo; **all the year** ~ tutto l'anno; **it's just** ~ **the corner** (also fig) è dietro l'angolo; ~ **the clock** ininterrottamente; **to go** ~ **to sb's house** andare da qn; **go** ~ **the back** passi dietro; **to go** ~ **a house** visitare una casa; **enough to go** ~ abbastanza per tutti; ~ **of applause** applausi mpl; ~ **of drinks** giro di bibite; ~ **of sandwiches** sandwich m inv; ~ **off** vt (speech etc) finire; ~ **up** vt radunare; (criminals) fare una retata di; (prices) arrotondare; ~**about** n (BRIT: AUT) rotatoria; (: at fair) giostra ♦ adj (route, means) indiretto(a); ~**ers** npl (game) gioco simile al baseball; ~**ly** adv (fig) chiaro e tondo; ~**shouldered** adj dalle spalle tonde; ~ **trip** n (viaggio di) andata e ritorno; ~**up** n raduno; (of criminals) retata.

rouse [raʊz] vt (wake up) svegliare; (stir up) destare; provocare; risvegliare; **rousing** adj (speech, applause) entusiastico(a).

rout [raʊt] n (MIL) rotta ♦ vt (defeat) mettere in rotta.

route [ru:t] n itinerario; (of bus) percorso; ~ **map** (BRIT) n (for journey) cartina di itinerario.

routine [ru:'ti:n] adj (work) corrente, abituale; (procedure) solito(a) ♦ n (pej) routine f, tran tran m; (THEATRE) numero.

rove [rəʊv] vt vagabondare per.

row¹ [rəʊ] n (line) riga, fila; (KNITTING) ferro; (behind one another: of cars, people) fila; (in boat) remata ♦

vi (*in boat*) remare; (*as sport*) vogare ♦ *vt* (*boat*) manovrare a remi; **in a ~** (*fig*) di fila.

row² [rau] *n* (*racket*) baccano, chiasso; (*dispute*) lite *f*; (*scolding*) sgridata ♦ *vi* (*argue*) litigare.

rowboat ['rəubəut] (*US*) *n* barca a remi.

rowdy ['raudɪ] *adj* chiassoso(a); turbolento(a) ♦ *n* teppista *m/f*.

rowing ['rəuɪŋ] *n* canottaggio; **~ boat** (*BRIT*) *n* barca a remi.

royal ['rɔɪəl] *adj* reale; **R~ Air Force** *n* *aeronautica militare britannica*.

royalty ['rɔɪəltɪ] *n* (*royal persons*) (membri *mpl* della) famiglia reale; (*payment: to author*) diritti *mpl* d'autore.

r.p.m. *abbr* (= *revolutions per minute*) giri/min.

R.S.V.P. *abbr* (= *répondez s'il vous plaît*) R.S.V.P.

Rt Hon. (*BRIT*) *abbr* (= *Right Honourable*) ≈ Onorevole.

rub [rʌb] *n*: **to give sth a ~** strofinare qc; (*sore place*) massaggiare qc ♦ *vt* strofinare, massaggiare; (*hands: also:* **~ together**) sfregarsi; **to ~ sb up** (*BRIT*) *or* **~ sb the wrong way** (*US*) lisciare qn contro pelo; **~ off** *vi* andare via; **~ off on** *vt fus* lasciare una traccia su; **~ out** *vt* cancellare.

rubber ['rʌbə*] *n* gomma; **~ band** *n* elastico; **~ plant** *n* ficus *m inv*; **~y** *adj* gommoso(a).

rubbish ['rʌbɪʃ] *n* (*from household*) immondizie *fpl*, rifiuti *mpl*; (*fig: pej*) cose *fpl* senza valore; robaccia; sciocchezze *fpl*; **~ bin** (*BRIT*) *n* pattumiera; **~ dump** *n* (*in town*) immondezzaio.

rubble ['rʌbl] *n* macerie *fpl*; (*smaller*) pietrisco.

ruble ['ru:bl] (*US*) *n* = **rouble**.

ruby ['ru:bɪ] *n* rubino.

rucksack ['rʌksæk] *n* zaino.

rudder ['rʌdə*] *n* timone *m*.

ruddy ['rʌdɪ] *adj* (*face*) rubicondo(a); (*inf: damned*) maledetto(a).

rude [ru:d] *adj* (*impolite: person*) scortese, rozzo(a); (: *word, manners*) grossolano(a), rozzo(a); (*shocking*) indecente; **~ness** *n* scortesia; grossolanità.

rueful ['ru:ful] *adj* mesto(a), triste.

ruffian ['rʌfɪən] *n* briccone *m*, furfante *m*.

ruffle ['rʌfl] *vt* (*hair*) scompigliare; (*clothes, water*) increspare; (*fig: person*) turbare.

rug [rʌg] *n* tappeto; (*BRIT: for knees*) coperta.

rugby ['rʌgbɪ] *n* (*also:* **~ football**) rugby *m*.

rugged ['rʌgɪd] *adj* (*landscape*) aspro(a); (*features, determination*) duro(a); (*character*) brusco(a).

rugger ['rʌgə*] (*BRIT: inf*) *n* rugby *m*.

ruin ['ru:ɪn] *n* rovina ♦ *vt* rovinare; **~s** *npl* (*of building, castle etc*) rovine *fpl*, ruderi *mpl*; **~ous** *adj* rovinoso(a); (*expenditure*) inverosimile.

rule [ru:l] *n* regola; (*regulation*) regolamento, regola; (*government*) governo; (**~r**) riga ♦ *vt* (*country*) governare; (*person*) dominare ♦ *vi* regnare; decidere; (*LAW*) dichiarare; **as a ~** normalmente; **~ out** *vt* escludere; **~d** *adj* (*paper*) vergato(a); **~r** *n* (*sovereign*) sovrano/a; (*for measuring*) regolo, riga; **ruling** *adj* (*party*) al potere; (*class*) dirigente ♦ *n* (*LAW*) decisione *f*.

rum [rʌm] *n* rum *m*.

Rumania [ru:'meɪnɪə] *n* Romania.

rumble ['rʌmbl] *n* rimbombo; brontolio ♦ *vi* rimbombare; (*stomach, pipe*) brontolare.

rummage ['rʌmɪdʒ] *vi* frugare.

rumour ['ru:mə*] (*US* **rumor**) *n* voce *f* ♦ *vt*: **it is ~ed that** corre voce che.

rump [rʌmp] *n* groppa; **~ steak** *n* bistecca di girello.

rumpus ['rʌmpəs] (*inf*) *n* baccano; (*quarrel*) rissa.

run [rʌn] (*pt* **ran**, *pp* **run**) *n* corsa; (*outing*) gita (in macchina); (*distance travelled*) percorso, tragitto; (*SKI*) pista; (*CRICKET, BASEBALL*) meta; (*series*) serie *f*; (*THEATRE*) periodo di rappresentazione; (*in tights, stockings*) smagliatura ♦ *vt* (*distance*) correre;

(*operate: business*) gestire, dirigere; (: *competition, course*) organizzare; (: *hotel*) gestire; (: *house*) governare; (*COMPUT*) eseguire; (*water, bath*) far scorrere; (*force through: rope, pipe*): **to ~ sth through** far passare qc attraverso; (*pass: hand, finger*): **to ~ sth over** passare qc su; (*PRESS: feature*) presentare ♦ *vi* correre; (*flee*) scappare; (*pass: road etc*) passare; (*work: machine, factory*) funzionare, andare; (*bus, train: operate*) far servizio; (: *travel*) circolare; (*continue: play, contract*) durare; (*slide: drawer; flow: river, bath*) scorrere; (*colours, washing*) stemperarsi; (*in election*) presentarsi candidato; (*nose*) colare; **there was a ~ on** ... c'era una corsa a ...; **in the long ~** a lungo andare; **on the ~** in fuga; **to ~ a race** partecipare ad una gara; **I'll ~ you to the station** la porto alla stazione; **to ~ a risk** correre un rischio; **~ about** *or* **around** *vi* (*children*) correre qua e là; **~ across** *vt fus* (*find*) trovare per caso; **~ away** *vi* fuggire; **~ down** *vt* (*production*) ridurre gradualmente; (*factory*) rallentare l'attività di; (*AUT*) investire; (*criticize*) criticare; **to be ~ down** (*person: tired*) essere esausto(a); **~ in** (*BRIT*) *vt* (*car*) rodare, fare il rodaggio di; **~ into** *vt fus* (*meet: person*) incontrare per caso; (: *trouble*) incontrare, trovare; (*collide with*) andare a sbattere contro; **~ off** *vi* fuggire ♦ *vt* (*water*) far scolare; (*copies*) fare; **~ out** *vi* (*person*) uscire di corsa; (*liquid*) colare; (*lease*) scadere; (*money*) esaurirsi; **~ out of** *vt fus* rimanere a corto di; **~ over** *vt* (*AUT*) investire, mettere sotto ♦ *vt fus* (*revise*) rivedere; **~ through** *vt fus* (*instructions*) dare una scorsa a; (*rehearse: play*) riprovare, ripetere; **~ up** *vt* (*debt*) lasciar accumulare; **to ~ up against** (*difficulties*) incontrare; **~away** *adj* (*person*) fuggiasco(a); (*horse*) in libertà; (*truck*) fuori controllo.

rung [rʌŋ] *pp of* **ring** ♦ *n* (*of ladder*) piolo.

runner ['rʌnə*] *n* (*in race*) corridore *m*; (: *horse*) partente *m/f*; (*on sledge*) pattino; (*for drawer etc*) guida; **~ bean** (*BRIT*) *n* fagiolo rampicante; **~-up** *n* secondo(a) arrivato(a).

running ['rʌnɪŋ] *n* corsa; direzione *f*; organizzazione *f*; funzionamento ♦ *adj* (*water*) corrente; (*commentary*) simultaneo(a); **to be in/out of the ~ for sth** essere/non essere più in lizza per qc; **6 days ~** 6 giorni di seguito; **~ costs** *npl* costi *mpl* d'esercizio; (*of car*) spese *fpl* di mantenimento.

runny ['rʌnɪ] *adj* che cola.

run-of-the-mill *adj* solito(a), banale.

runt [rʌnt] *n* (*also pej*) omuncolo; (*ZOOL*) animale *m* più piccolo del normale.

run-through *n* prova.

run-up *n*: **~ to** (*election etc*) periodo che precede.

runway ['rʌnweɪ] *n* (*AVIAT*) pista (di decollo).

rupee [ru:'pi:] *n* rupia.

rupture ['rʌptʃə*] *n* (*MED*) ernia.

rural ['ruərl] *adj* rurale.

ruse [ru:z] *n* trucco.

rush [rʌʃ] *n* corsa precipitosa; (*hurry*) furia, fretta; (*sudden demand*): **~ for** corsa a; (*current*) flusso; (*of emotion*) impeto; (*BOT*) giunco ♦ *vt* mandare *or* spedire velocemente; (*attack: town etc*) prendere d'assalto ♦ *vi* precipitarsi; **~ hour** *n* ora di punta.

rusk [rʌsk] *n* biscotto.

Russia ['rʌʃə] *n* Russia; **~n** *adj* russo(a) ♦ *n* russo/a; (*LING*) russo.

rust [rʌst] *n* ruggine *f* ♦ *vi* arrugginirsi.

rustic ['rʌstɪk] *adj* rustico(a).

rustle ['rʌsl] *vi* frusciare ♦ *vt* (*paper*) far frusciare; (*US: cattle*) rubare.

rustproof ['rʌstpru:f] *adj* inossidabile.

rusty ['rʌstɪ] *adj* arrugginito(a).

rut [rʌt] *n* solco; (*ZOOL*) fregola; **to get into a ~** (*fig*) adagiarsi troppo.

ruthless ['ru:θlɪs] *adj* spietato(a).

rye [raɪ] *n* segale *f*; **~ bread** *n* pane *m* di segale.

S

Sabbath ['sæbǝθ] *n* (*Jewish*) sabato; (*Christian*) domenica.

sabotage ['sæbǝtɑːʒ] *n* sabotaggio ♦ *vt* sabotare.

saccharin(e) ['sækǝrɪn] *n* saccarina.

sachet ['sæʃeɪ] *n* bustina.

sack [sæk] *n* (*bag*) sacco ♦ *vt* (*dismiss*) licenziare, mandare a spasso; (*plunder*) saccheggiare; **to get the ~** essere mandato a spasso; ~**ing** *n* tela di sacco; (*dismissal*) licenziamento.

sacrament ['sækrǝmǝnt] *n* sacramento.

sacred ['seɪkrɪd] *adj* sacro(a).

sacrifice ['sækrɪfaɪs] *n* sacrificio ♦ *vt* sacrificare.

sad [sæd] *adj* triste.

saddle ['sædl] *n* sella ♦ *vt* (*horse*) 'sellare; **to be ~d with sth** (*inf*) avere qc sulle spalle; ~**bag** *n* (*on bicycle*) borsa.

sadistic [sǝ'dɪstɪk] *adj* sadico(a).

sadness ['sædnɪs] *n* tristezza.

s.a.e. *n abbr* = **stamped addressed envelope**.

safe [seɪf] *adj* sicuro(a); (*out of danger*) salvo(a), al sicuro; (*cautious*) prudente ♦ *n* cassaforte *f*; ~ **from** al sicuro da; ~ **and sound** sano(a) e salvo(a); (*just*) **to be on the ~ side** per non correre rischi; ~**-conduct** *n* salvacondotto; ~**-deposit** *n* (*vault*) caveau *m inv*; (*box*) cassetta di sicurezza; ~**guard** *n* salvaguardia ♦ *vt* salvaguardare; ~**keeping** *n* custodia; ~**ly** *adv* sicuramente; sano(a) e salvo(a); prudentemente.

safety ['seɪftɪ] *n* sicurezza; ~ **belt** *n* cintura di sicurezza; ~ **pin** *n* spilla di sicurezza; ~ **valve** *n* valvola di sicurezza.

saffron ['sæfrǝn] *n* zafferano.

sag [sæg] *vi* incurvarsi; afflosciarsi.

sage [seɪdʒ] *n* (*herb*) salvia; (*man*) saggio.

Sagittarius [sædʒɪ'tɛǝrɪǝs] *n* Sagittario.

Sahara [sǝ'hɑːrǝ] *n*: **the ~ (Desert)** il (deserto del) Sahara.

said [sɛd] *pt, pp of* **say**.

sail [seɪl] *n* (*on boat*) vela; (*trip*): **to go for a ~** fare un giro in barca a vela ♦ *vt* (*boat*) condurre, governare ♦ *vi* (*travel: ship*) navigare; (: *passenger*) viaggiare per mare; (*set off*) salpare; (*sport*) fare della vela; **they ~ed into Genoa** entrarono nel porto di Genova; ~ **through** *vt fus* (*fig*) superare senza difficoltà; ~**boat** (*US*) *n* barca a vela; ~**ing** *n* (*sport*) vela; **to go ~ing** fare della vela; ~**ing boat** *n* barca a vela; ~**ing ship** *n* veliero; ~**or** *n* marinaio.

saint [seɪnt] *n* santo/a; ~**ly** *adj* santo(a).

sake [seɪk] *n*: **for the ~ of** per, per amore di.

salad ['sælǝd] *n* insalata; ~ **bowl** *n* insalatiera; ~ **cream** (*BRIT*) *n* (tipo di) 'maionese *f*; ~ **dressing** *n* condimento per insalata.

salami [sǝ'lɑːmɪ] *n* salame *m*.

salary ['sælǝrɪ] *n* stipendio.

sale [seɪl] *n* vendita; (*at reduced prices*) svendita, liquidazione *f*; (*auction*) vendita all'asta; "**for ~**" "in vendita"; **on ~** in vendita; **on ~ or return** da vendere o rimandare; ~**room** *n* sala delle aste; ~**s assistant** (*US* ~**s clerk**) *n* commesso/a; ~**sman/swoman** *n* commesso/a; (*representative*) rappresentante *m/f*.

sallow ['sælǝu] *adj* giallastro(a).

salmon ['sæmǝn] *n inv* salmone *m*.

saloon [sǝ'luːn] *n* (*US*) saloon *m inv*, bar *m inv*; (*BRIT: AUT*) berlina; (*ship's lounge*) salone *m*.

salt [sɔlt] *n* sale *m* ♦ *vt* salare; ~ **cellar** *n* saliera; ~**water** *adj* di mare; ~**y** *adj* salato(a).

salute [sǝ'luːt] *n* saluto ♦ *vt* salutare.

salvage ['sælvɪdʒ] *n* (*saving*) salvataggio; (*things saved*) beni *mpl* salvati *or* recuperati ♦ *vt* salvare, mettere in salvo.

salvation [sæl'veɪʃǝn] *n* salvezza; **S~ Army** *n* Esercito della Salvezza.

same [seɪm] *adj* stesso(a), medesimo(a) ♦ *pron*: **the ~** lo(la) stesso(a), gli(le) stessi(e); **the ~ book as** lo stesso libro di (o che); **at the ~ time** allo stesso tempo; **all** or **just the ~** tuttavia; **to do the ~ as sb** fare come qn; **the ~ to you!** altrettanto a te!

sample ['sɑːmpl] n campione m ♦ vt (food) assaggiare; (wine) degustare.

sanctimonious [sæŋktɪ'məunɪəs] adj bigotto(a), bacchettone(a).

sanction ['sæŋkʃən] n sanzione f ♦ vt sancire, sanzionare.

sanctity ['sæŋktɪtɪ] n santità.

sanctuary ['sæŋktjuərɪ] n (holy place) santuario; (refuge) rifugio; (for wildlife) riserva.

sand [sænd] n sabbia ♦ vt (also: ~ down) cartavetrare.

sandal ['sændl] n sandalo.

sandbox ['sændbɔks] (US) n = sandpit.

sandcastle ['sændkɑːsl] n castello di sabbia.

sandpaper ['sændpeɪpə*] n carta vetrata.

sandpit ['sændpɪt] n (for children) buca di sabbia.

sandstone ['sændstəun] n arenaria.

sandwich ['sændwɪtʃ] n tramezzino, panino, sandwich m inv ♦ vt: **~ed between** incastrato(a) fra; **cheese/ham ~** sandwich al formaggio/prosciutto; **~ course** (BRIT) n corso di formazione professionale.

sandy ['sændɪ] adj sabbioso(a); (colour) color sabbia inv, biondo(a) rossiccio(a).

sane [seɪn] adj (person) sano(a) di mente; (outlook) sensato(a).

sang [sæŋ] pt of **sing**.

sanitary ['sænɪtərɪ] adj (system, arrangements) sanitario(a); (clean) igienico(a); **~ towel** (US **~ napkin**) n assorbente m (igienico).

sanitation [sænɪ'teɪʃən] n (in house) impianti mpl sanitari; (in town) fognature fpl; **~ department** (US) n nettezza urbana.

sanity ['sænɪtɪ] n sanità mentale; (common sense) buon senso.

sank [sæŋk] pt of **sink**.

Santa Claus [sæntə'klɔːz] n Babbo Natale.

sap [sæp] n (of plants) linfa ♦ vt (strength) fiaccare.

sapling ['sæplɪŋ] n alberello.

sapphire ['sæfaɪə*] n zaffiro.

sarcasm ['sɑːkæzm] n sarcasmo.

sardine [sɑː'diːn] n sardina.

Sardinia [sɑː'dɪnɪə] n Sardegna.

sash [sæʃ] n fascia.

sat [sæt] pt, pp of **sit**.

Satan ['seɪtən] n Satana m.

satchel ['sætʃl] n cartella.

satellite ['sætəlaɪt] adj satellite ♦ n satellite m; **~ dish** n antenna parabolica.

satin ['sætɪn] n raso ♦ adj di raso.

satire ['sætaɪə*] n satira.

satisfaction [sætɪs'fækʃən] n soddisfazione f.

satisfactory [sætɪs'fæktərɪ] adj soddisfacente.

satisfy ['sætɪsfaɪ] vt soddisfare; (convince) convincere; **~ing** adj soddisfacente.

Saturday ['sætədɪ] n sabato.

sauce [sɔːs] n salsa; (containing meat, fish) sugo; **~pan** n casseruola.

saucer ['sɔːsə*] n sottocoppa m, piattino.

saucy ['sɔːsɪ] adj impertinente.

Saudi ['saudɪ]: **~ Arabia** n Arabia Saudita; **~ (Arabian)** adj, n arabo(a) saudita.

sauna ['sɔːnə] n sauna.

saunter ['sɔːntə*] vi andare a zonzo, bighellonare.

sausage ['sɔsɪdʒ] n salsiccia; **~ roll** n rotolo di pasta sfoglia ripieno di salsiccia.

sauté ['səuteɪ] adj: **~ potatoes** patate fpl saltate in padella.

savage ['sævɪdʒ] adj (cruel, fierce) selvaggio(a), feroce; (primitive) primitivo(a) ♦ n selvaggio/a ♦ vt attaccare selvaggiamente.

save [seɪv] vt (person, belongings, COMPUT) salvare; (money) risparmiare, mettere da parte; (time) risparmiare; (food) conservare; (avoid: trouble) evitare; (SPORT) parare ♦ vi (also: ~ up) economizzare ♦ n (SPORT) parata ♦ prep salvo, a eccezione di.

saving ['seɪvɪŋ] n risparmio ♦ adj: **the ~**

grace of l'unica cosa buona di; ~s *npl* (*money*) risparmi *mpl*; ~s **account** *n* libretto di risparmio; ~s **bank** *n* cassa di risparmio.

saviour ['seɪvjə*] (*US* **savior**) *n* salvatore *m*.

savour ['seɪvə*] (*US* **savor**) *vt* gustare; ~y *adj* (*dish:_ not sweet*) salato(a).

saw [sɔː] (*pt* **sawed**, *pp* **sawed** *or* **sawn**) *pt of* **see** ♦ *n* (*tool*) sega ♦ *vt* segare; ~**dust** *n* segatura; ~**mill** *n* segheria; **sawn** *pp of* **saw**; ~**n-off shotgun** *n* fucile *m* a canne mozze.

saxophone ['sæksəfəun] *n* sassofono.

say [seɪ] (*pt, pp* **said**) *n*: **to have one's** ~ fare sentire il proprio parere; **to have a** *or* **some** ~ avere voce in capitolo ♦ *vt* dire; **could you** ~ **that again?** potrebbe ripeterlo?; **that goes without** ~**ing** va da sé; ~**ing** *n* proverbio, detto.

scab [skæb] *n* crosta; (*pej*) crumiro/a.

scaffold ['skæfəuld*] *n* (*gallows*) patibolo; ~**ing** *n* impalcatura.

scald [skɔːld] *n* scottatura ♦ *vt* scottare.

scale [skeɪl] *n* scala; (*of fish*) squama ♦ *vt* (*mountain*) scalare; ~s *npl* (*for weighing*) bilancia; **on a large** ~ su vasta scala; ~ **of charges** tariffa; ~ **down** *vt* ridurre (proporzionalmente).

scallop ['skɔləp] *n* (*ZOOL*) pettine *m*; (*SEWING*) smerlo.

scalp [skælp] *n* cuoio capelluto ♦ *vt* scotennare.

scalpel ['skælpl] *n* bisturi *m inv*.

scamper ['skæmpə*] *vi*: **to** ~ **away**, ~ **off** darsela a gambe.

scampi ['skæmpɪ] *npl* scampi *mpl*.

scan [skæn] *vt* scrutare; (*glance at quickly*) scorrere, dare un'occhiata a; (*TV*) analizzare; (*RADAR*) esplorare ♦ *n* (*MED*) ecografia.

scandal ['skændl] *n* scandalo; (*gossip*) pettegolezzi *mpl*.

Scandinavia [skændɪ'neɪvɪə] *n* Scandinavia; ~**n** *adj, n* scandinavo(a).

scant [skænt] *adj* scarso(a); ~**y** *adj* insufficiente; (*swimsuit*) ridotto(a).

scapegoat ['skeɪpgəut] *n* capro espiatorio.

scar [skɑː] *n* cicatrice *f* ♦ *vt* sfregiare.

scarce [skɛəs] *adj* scarso(a); (*copy, edition*) raro(a); **to make o.s.** ~ (*inf*) squagliarsela; ~**ly** *adv* appena; **scarcity** *n* scarsità, mancanza.

scare [skɛə*] *n* spavento; panico ♦ *vt* spaventare, atterrire; **there was a bomb** ~ **at the bank** hanno evacuato la banca per paura di un attentato dinamitardo; **to** ~ **sb stiff** spaventare a morte qn; ~ **off** *or* **away** *vt* mettere in fuga; ~**crow** *n* spaventapasseri *m inv*; ~**d** *adj*: **to be** ~**d** aver paura.

scarf [skɑːf] (*pl* **scarves** *or* ~**s**) *n* (*long*) sciarpa; (*square*) fazzoletto da testa, foulard *m inv*.

scarlet ['skɑːlɪt] *adj* scarlatto(a); ~ **fever** *n* scarlattina.

scarves [skɑːvz] *npl of* **scarf**.

scary ['skɛərɪ] *adj* che spaventa.

scathing ['skeɪðɪŋ] *adj* aspro(a).

scatter ['skætə*] *vt* spargere; (*crowd*) disperdere ♦ *vi* disperdersi; ~**brained** *adj* sbadato(a).

scavenger ['skævəndʒə*] *n* (*person*) accattone/a.

scenario [sɪ'nɑːrɪəu] *n* (*THEATRE, CINEMA*) copione *m*; (*fig*) situazione *f*.

scene [siːn] *n* (*THEATRE, fig etc*) scena; (*of crime, accident*) scena, luogo; (*sight, view*) vista, veduta; ~**ry** *n* (*THEATRE*) scenario; (*landscape*) panorama *m*, panoramico(a).

scent [sɛnt] *n* profumo; (*sense of smell*) olfatto, odorato; (*fig: track*) pista.

sceptical ['skɛptɪkəl] (*US* **skeptical**) *adj* scettico(a).

sceptre ['sɛptə*] (*US* **scepter**) *n* scettro.

schedule ['ʃɛdjuːl, (*US*) 'skɛdjuːl] *n* programma *m*, piano; (*of trains*) orario; (*of prices etc*) lista, tabella ♦ *vt* fissare; **on** ~ in orario; **to be ahead of/behind** ~ essere in anticipo/ritardo sul previsto; ~**d flight** *n* volo di linea.

scheme [skiːm] *n* piano, progetto; (*method*) sistema *m*; (*dishonest plan, plot*) intrigo, trama; (*arrangement*) disposizione *f*, sistemazione *f*; (*pension* ~ *etc*) programma *m* ♦ *vi* fare progetti; (*intrigue*) complottare; **scheming** *adj* intrigante ♦ n intrighi mpl, macchinazioni fpl.

schism ['skɪzəm] n scisma m.

scholar ['skɔlə*] n erudito/a; (pupil) scolaro/a; ~ly adj dotto(a), erudito(a); ~ship n erudizione f; (grant) borsa di studio.

school [sku:l] n (primary, secondary) scuola; (university: US) università f inv ♦ cpd scolare, scolastico(a) ♦ vt (animal) addestrare; ~ age n età scolare; ~book n libro scolastico; ~boy n scolaro; ~children npl scolari mpl; ~days npl giorni mpl di scuola; ~girl n scolara; ~ing n istruzione f; ~master n (primary) maestro; (secondary) insegnante m; ~mistress n maestra; insegnante f; ~teacher n insegnante m/f, docente m/f; (primary) maestro/a.

sciatica [saɪˈætɪkə] n sciatica.

science ['saɪəns] n scienza; ~ fiction n fantascienza; **scientific** [-'tɪfɪk] adj scientifico(a); **scientist** n scienziato/a.

scissors ['sɪzəz] npl forbici fpl.

scoff [skɔf] vt (BRIT: inf: eat) trangugiare, ingozzare ♦ vi: to ~ (at) (mock) farsi beffe (di).

scold [skəuld] vt rimproverare.

scone [skɔn] n focaccina da tè.

scoop [sku:p] n mestolo; (for ice cream) cucchiaio dosatore; (PRESS) colpo giornalistico, notizia (in) esclusiva; ~ out vt scavare; ~ up vt tirare su, sollevare.

scooter ['sku:tə*] n (motor cycle) motoretta, scooter m inv; (toy) monopattino.

scope [skəup] n (capacity: of plan, undertaking) portata; (: of person) capacità fpl; (opportunity) possibilità fpl.

scorch [skɔ:tʃ] vt (clothes) strinare, bruciacchiare; (earth, grass) seccare, bruciare.

score [skɔ:*] n punti mpl, punteggio; (MUS) partitura, spartito; (twenty) venti ♦ vt (goal, point) segnare, fare; (success) ottenere ♦ vi segnare; (FOOTBALL) fare un goal; (keep score) segnare i punti; ~s of (very many) un sacco di; **on that** ~ a questo riguardo; **to ~ 6 out of 10** prendere 6 su 10; ~ **out** vt cancellare con un segno; ~**board** n tabellone m segnapunti.

scorn [skɔ:n] n disprezzo ♦ vt disprezzare.

scornful ['skɔ:nful] adj sprezzante.

Scorpio ['skɔ:pɪəu] n Scorpione m.

scorpion ['skɔ:pɪən] n scorpione m.

Scot [skɔt] n scozzese m/f.

scotch [skɔtʃ] vt (rumour etc) soffocare; **S~** n whisky m scozzese, scotch m.

scot-free adv: **to get off** ~ farla franca.

Scotland ['skɔtlənd] n Scozia.

Scots [skɔts] adj scozzese; ~**man/woman** n scozzese m/f.

Scottish ['skɔtɪʃ] adj scozzese.

scoundrel ['skaundrl] n farabutto/a; (child) furfantello/a.

scour ['skauə*] vt (search) battere, perlustrare.

scourge [skə:dʒ] n flagello.

scout [skaut] n (MIL) esploratore m; (also: boy ~) giovane esploratore, scout m inv; ~ **around** vi cercare in giro; **girl** ~ (US) n giovane esploratrice f.

scowl [skaul] vi acciglarsi, aggrottare le sopracciglia; **to** ~ **at** guardare torvo.

scrabble ['skræbl] vi (claw): **to** ~ (at) graffiare, grattare; (also: ~ around: search) cercare a tentoni ♦ n: **S~** ® Scarabeo ®.

scraggy ['skrægɪ] adj scarno(a), molto magro(a).

scram [skræm] (inf) vi filare via.

scramble ['skræmbl] n arrampicata ♦ vi inerpicarsi; **to** ~ **out** etc uscire etc in fretta; **to** ~ **for** azzuffarsi per; ~**d eggs** npl uova fpl strapazzate.

scrap [skræp] n pezzo, pezzetto; (fight) zuffa; (also: ~ iron) rottami mpl di ferro, ferraglia ♦ vt demolire; (fig) scartare ♦ vi: **to** ~ (**with sb**) fare a botte (con qn); ~**s** npl (waste) scarti mpl; ~**book** n album m inv di ritagli; ~ **dealer** n commerciante m di ferraglia.

scrape [skreip] *vt, vi* raschiare, grattare ♦ *n*: **to get into a ~** cacciarsi in un guaio; **~ through** *vi* farcela per un pelo; **~ together** *vt* (*money*) raggranellare; **~r** *n* raschietto.

scrap: **~ heap** *n*: **on the ~ heap** (*fig*) nel dimenticatoio; **~ merchant** (*BRIT*) *n* commerciante *m* di ferraglia; **~ paper** *n* cartaccia.

scrappy ['skræpi] *adj* frammentario(a), sconnesso(a).

scratch [skrætʃ] *n* graffio ♦ *cpd*: **~ team** squadra raccogliticcia ♦ *vt* graffiare, rigare ♦ *vi* grattare; (*paint, car*) graffiare; **to start from ~** cominciare *or* partire da zero; **to be up to ~** essere all'altezza.

scrawl [skrɔ:l] *n* scarabocchio ♦ *vi* scarabocchiare.

scrawny ['skrɔ:ni] *adj* scarno(a), pelle e ossa *inv*.

scream [skri:m] *n* grido, urlo ♦ *vi* urlare, gridare.

scree [skri:] *n* ghiaione *m*.

screech [skri:tʃ] *vi* stridere.

screen [skri:n] *n* schermo; (*fig*) muro, cortina, velo ♦ *vt* schermare, fare schermo a; (*from the wind etc*) riparare; (*film*) proiettare; (*book*) adattare per lo schermo; (*candidates etc*) selezionare; **~ing** *n* (*MED*) dépistage *m inv*; **~play** *n* sceneggiatura.

screw [skru:] *n* vite *f* ♦ *vt* avvitare; **~ up** *vt* (*paper etc*) spiegazzare; (*inf: ruin*) rovinare; **to ~ up one's eyes** strizzare gli occhi; **~driver** *n* cacciavite *m*.

scribble ['skribl] *n* scarabocchio ♦ *vt* scribacchiare in fretta ♦ *vi* scarabocchiare.

script [skript] *n* (*CINEMA etc*) copione *m*; (*in exam*) elaborato *or* compito d'esame.

scripture(s) ['skriptʃə(z)] *n(pl)* sacre Scritture *fpl*.

scroll [skrəul] *n* rotolo di carta.

scrounge [skraundʒ] (*inf*) *vt*: **to ~ sth (off *or* from sb)** scroccare qc (a qn) ♦ *n*: **on the ~** a sbafo.

scrub [skrʌb] *n* (*land*) boscaglia ♦ *vt* pulire strofinando; (*reject*) annullare.

scruff [skrʌf] *n*: **by the ~ of the neck** per la collottola.

scruffy ['skrʌfi] *adj* sciatto(a).

scrum(mage) ['skrʌm(idʒ)] *n* mischia.

scruple ['skru:pl] *n* scrupolo.

scrutiny ['skru:tini] *n* esame *m* accurato.

scuff [skʌf] *vt* (*shoes*) consumare strascicando.

scuffle ['skʌfl] *n* baruffa, tafferuglio.

sculptor ['skʌlptə*] *n* scultore *m*.

sculpture ['skʌlptʃə*] *n* scultura.

scum [skʌm] *n* schiuma; (*pej: people*) feccia.

scupper ['skʌpə*] (*BRIT: inf*) *vt* far naufragare.

scurrilous ['skʌriləs] *adj* scurrile, volgare.

scurry ['skʌri] *vi* sgambare, affrettarsi; **~ off** *vi* andarsene a tutta velocità.

scuttle ['skʌtl] *n* (*also: coal ~*) secchio del carbone ♦ *vt* (*ship*) autoaffondare ♦ *vi* (*scamper*): **to ~ away, ~ off** darsela a gambe, scappare.

scythe [saið] *n* falce *f*.

SDP (*BRIT*) *n abbr* = **Social Democratic Party**.

sea [si:] *n* mare *m* ♦ *cpd* marino(a), del mare; (*bird, fish*) di mare; (*route, transport*) marittimo(a); **by ~** (*travel*) per mare; **on the ~** (*boat*) in mare; (*town*) di mare; **to be all at ~** (*fig*) non sapere che pesci pigliare; **out to ~** al largo; (*out*) **at ~** in mare; **~board** *n* costa; **~food** *n* frutti *mpl* di mare; **~ front** *n* lungomare *m*; **~gull** *n* gabbiano.

seal [si:l] *n* (*animal*) foca; (*stamp*) sigillo; (*impression*) impronta del sigillo ♦ *vt* sigillare; **~ off** *vt* (*close*) sigillare; (*forbid entry to*) bloccare l'accesso a.

sea level *n* livello del mare.

seam [si:m] *n* cucitura; (*of coal*) filone *m*.

seaman ['si:mən] *n* marinaio.

seamy ['si:mi] *adj* orribile.

seance ['seiɔns] *n* seduta spiritica.

seaplane ['si:pleɪn] n idrovolante m.

seaport ['si:pɔ:t] n porto di mare.

search [sə:tʃ] n ricerca; (LAW: at sb's home) perquisizione f ♦ vt frugare ♦ vi: **to** ~ **for** ricercare; **in** ~ **of** alla ricerca di; ~ **through** vt fus frugare; ~**ing** adj minuzioso(a); penetrante; ~**light** n proiettore m; ~ **party** n squadra di soccorso; ~ **warrant** n mandato di perquisizione.

seashore ['si:ʃɔ:*] n spiaggia.

seasick ['si:sɪk] adj che soffre il mal di mare.

seaside ['si:saɪd] n spiaggia; ~ **resort** n stazione f balneare.

season ['si:zn] n stagione f ♦ vt condire, insaporire; ~**al** adj stagionale; ~**ed** adj (fig) con esperienza; ~**ing** n condimento; ~ **ticket** n abbonamento.

seat [si:t] n sedile m; (in bus, train: place) posto; (PARLIAMENT) seggio; (buttocks) didietro; (of trousers) fondo ♦ vt far sedere; (have room for) avere or essere fornito(a) di posti a sedere per; **to be** ~**ed** essere seduto(a); ~ **belt** n cintura di sicurezza.

sea water n acqua di mare.

seaweed ['si:wi:d] n alghe fpl.

seaworthy ['si:wə:ðɪ] adj atto(a) alla navigazione.

sec. abbr = **second(s)**.

secluded [sɪ'klu:dɪd] adj isolato(a), appartato(a).

seclusion [sɪ'klu:ʒən] n isolamento.

second[1] [sɪ'kɔnd] (BRIT) vt (worker) distaccare.

second[2] ['sɛkənd] num secondo(a) ♦ adv (in race etc) al secondo posto ♦ n (unit of time) secondo; (AUT: also: ~ **gear**) seconda; (COMM: imperfect) scarto; (BRIT: SCOL: degree) laurea con punteggio discreto ♦ vt (motion) appoggiare; ~**ary** adj secondario(a); ~**ary school** n scuola secondaria; ~-**class** adj di seconda classe ♦ adv in seconda classe; ~**er** n sostenitore/trice; ~**hand** adj di seconda mano, usato(a); ~ **hand** n (on clock) lancetta dei secondi; ~**ly** adv in secondo luogo; ~-**rate** adj scadente; ~ **thoughts** npl

ripensamenti mpl; **on** ~ **thoughts** (BRIT) or **thought** (US) ripensandoci bene.

secrecy ['si:krəsɪ] n segretezza.

secret ['si:krɪt] adj segreto(a) ♦ n segreto; **in** ~ in segreto.

secretarial [sɛkrɪ'tɛərɪəl] adj di segretario(a).

secretariat [sɛkrɪ'tɛərɪət] n segretariato.

secretary ['sɛkrətərɪ] n segretario/a; S~ **of State (for)** (BRIT: POL) ministro (di).

secretive ['si:krətɪv] adj riservato(a).

sect [sɛkt] n setta; ~**arian** [-'tɛərɪən] adj settario(a).

section ['sɛkʃən] n sezione f.

sector ['sɛktə*] n settore m.

secure [sɪ'kjuə*] adj sicuro(a); (firmly fixed) assicurato(a), ben fermato(a); (in safe place) al sicuro ♦ vt (fix) fissare, assicurare; (get) ottenere, assicurarsi.

security [sɪ'kjuərɪtɪ] n sicurezza; (for loan) garanzia.

sedan [sɪ'dæn] (US) n (AUT) berlina.

sedate [sɪ'deɪt] adj posato(a); calmo(a) ♦ vt calmare.

sedation [sɪ'deɪʃən] n (MED) effetto dei sedativi.

sedative ['sɛdɪtɪv] n sedativo, calmante m.

seduce [sɪ'dju:s] vt sedurre; **seduction** [-'dʌkʃən] n seduzione f; **seductive** [-'dʌktɪv] adj seducente.

see [si:] (pt **saw**, pp **seen**) vt vedere; (accompany): **to** ~ **sb to the door** accompagnare qn alla porta ♦ vi vedere; (understand) capire ♦ n sede f vescovile; **to** ~ **that** (ensure) badare che +sub, fare in modo che +sub; ~ **you soon!** a presto!; ~ **about** vt fus occuparsi di; ~ **off** vt salutare alla partenza; ~ **through** vt portare a termine ♦ vt fus non lasciarsi ingannare da; ~ **to** vt fus occuparsi di.

seed [si:d] n seme m; (fig) germe m; (TENNIS) testa di serie; **to go to** ~ fare seme; (fig) scadere; ~**ling** n piantina di semenzaio; ~**y** adj (shabby: person) sciatto(a); (: place) squallido(a).

seeing ['si:ɪŋ] conj: ~ **(that)** visto che.

seek [si:k], (pt, pp **sought**) vt cercare.

seem [si:m] *vi* sembrare, parere; **there ~s to be** ... sembra che ci sia ...; **~ingly** *adv* apparentemente.

seen [si:n] *pp of* see.

seep [si:p] *vi* filtrare, trapelare.

seesaw ['si:sɔ:] *n* altalena a bilico.

seethe [si:ð] *vi* ribollire; **to ~ with anger** fremere di rabbia.

see-through *adj* trasparente.

segregate ['sɛɡrɪɡeɪt] *vt* segregare, isolare.

seize [si:z] *vt* (*grasp*) afferrare; (*take possession of*) impadronirsi di; (*LAW*) sequestrare; **~ (up)on** *vt fus* ricorrere a; **~ up** *vi* (*TECH*) grippare.

seizure ['si:ʒə*] *n* (*MED*) attacco; (*LAW*) confisca, sequestro.

seldom ['sɛldəm] *adv* raramente.

select [sɪ'lɛkt] *adj* scelto(a) ♦ *vt* scegliere, selezionare; **~ion** [-'lɛkʃən] *n* selezione *f*, scelta.

self [sɛlf] *n*: **the ~** l'io *m* ♦ *prefix* auto...; **~-assured** *adj* sicuro(a) di sé; **~-catering** (*BRIT*) *adj* in cui ci si cucina da sé; **~-centred** (*US* **~-centered**) *adj* egocentrico(a); **~-coloured** (*US* ~colored*) *adj* monocolore; **~-confidence** *n* sicurezza di sé; **~-conscious** *adj* timido(a); **~-contained** (*BRIT*) *adj* (*flat*) indipendente; **~-control** *n* autocontrollo; **~-defence** (*US* ~defense*) *n* autodifesa; (*LAW*) legittima difesa; **~-discipline** *n* autodisciplina; **~-employed** *adj* che lavora in proprio; **~-evident** *adj* evidente; **~-governing** *adj* autonomo(a); **~-indulgent** *adj* indulgente verso se stesso(a); **~-interest** *n* interesse *m* personale; **~-ish** *adj* egoista; **~-ishness** *n* egoismo; **~-less** *adj* dimentico(a) di sé, altruista; **~-pity** *n* autocommiserazione *f*; **~-portrait** *n* autoritratto; **~-possessed** *adj* controllato(a); **~-preservation** *n* istinto di conservazione; **~-respect** *n* rispetto di sé, amor proprio; **~-righteous** *adj* soddisfatto(a) di sé; **~-sacrifice** *n* abnegazione *f*; **~-satisfied** *adj* compiaciuto(a) di sé; **~-service** *n* autoservizio, self-service *m*; **~-sufficient** *adj* autosufficiente; **~-taught**

adj autodidatta.

sell [sɛl] (*pt, pp* sold) *vt* vendere ♦ *vi* vendersi; **to ~ at** *or* **for 1000 lire** essere in vendita a 1000 lire; **~ off** *vt* svendere, liquidare; **~ out** *vi*: **to ~ out (of sth)** esaurire (qc); **the tickets are all sold out** i biglietti sono esauriti; **~ by date** *n* data di scadenza; **~er** *n* venditore/trice; **~ing price** *n* prezzo di vendita.

sellotape ['sɛləuteɪp] ® (*BRIT*) *n* nastro adesivo, scotch *m* ®.

selves [sɛlvz] *npl of* self.

semaphore ['sɛməfɔ:*] *n* segnalazioni *fpl* con bandierine; (*RAIL*) semaforo (ferroviario).

semblance ['sɛmbləns] *n* parvenza, apparenza.

semen ['si:mən] *n* sperma *m*.

semester [sɪ'mɛstə*] (*US*) *n* semestre *m*.

semi... ['sɛmɪ] *prefix* semi...; **~circle** *n* semicerchio; **~colon** *n* punto e virgola; **~detached (house)** (*BRIT*) *n* casa gemella; **~final** *n* semifinale *f*.

seminar ['sɛminɑ:*] *n* seminario.

seminary ['sɛminəri] *n* (*REL*) seminario.

semiskilled ['sɛmɪ'skɪld] *adj* (*worker*) parzialmente qualificato(a); (*work*) che richiede una qualificazione parziale.

senate ['sɛnɪt] *n* senato; **senator** *n* senatore/trice.

send [sɛnd] (*pt, pp* sent) *vt* mandare; **~ away** *vt* (*letter, goods*) spedire; (*person*) mandare via; **~ away for** *vt fus* richiedere per posta, farsi spedire; **~ back** *vt* rimandare; **~ for** *vt fus* mandare a chiamare, far venire; **~ off** *vt* (*goods*) spedire; (*BRIT: SPORT: player*) espellere; **~ out** *vt* (*invitation*) diramare; **~ up** *vt* (*person, price*) far salire; (*BRIT: parody*) mettere in ridicolo; **~er** *n* mittente *m/f*; **~-off** *n*: **to give sb a good ~-off** festeggiare la partenza di qn.

senior ['si:nɪə*] *adj* (*older*) più vecchio(a); (*of higher rank*) di grado più elevato; **~ citizen** *n* persona anziana; **~ity** [-'ɔrɪtɪ] *n* anzianità.

sensation [sɛn'seɪʃən] *n* sensazione *f*; **~al** *adj* sensazionale; (*marvellous*) eccezionale.

sense [sɛns] n senso; *(feeling)* sensazione f, senso; *(meaning)* senso, significato; *(wisdom)* buonsenso ♦ vt sentire, percepire; **it makes ~** ha senso; **~less** adj sciocco(a); *(unconscious)* privo(a) di sensi.

sensible ['sɛnsɪbl] adj sensato(a), ragionevole.

sensitive ['sɛnsɪtɪv] adj sensibile; *(skin, question)* delicato(a).

sensual ['sɛnsjuəl] adj sensuale.

sensuous ['sɛnsjuəs] adj sensuale.

sent [sɛnt] pt, pp of **send**.

sentence ['sɛntns] n *(LING)* frase f; *(LAW: judgment)* sentenza; (: *punishment)* condanna ♦ vt: **to ~ sb to death/to 5 years** condannare qn a morte/a 5 anni.

sentiment ['sɛntɪmənt] n sentimento; *(opinion)* opinione f; **~al** [-'mɛntl] adj sentimentale.

sentry ['sɛntrɪ] n sentinella.

separate [adj 'sɛprɪt, vb 'sɛpəreɪt] adj separato(a) ♦ vt separare ♦ vi separarsi; **~ly** adv separatamente; **~s** npl *(clothes)* coordinati mpl; **separation** [-'reɪʃən] n separazione f.

September [sɛp'tɛmbə*] n settembre m.

septic ['sɛptɪk] adj settico(a); *(wound)* infettato(a); **~ tank** n fossa settica.

sequel ['si:kwl] n conseguenza; *(of story)* seguito; *(of film)* sequenza.

sequence ['si:kwəns] n *(series)* serie f, *(order)* ordine m.

sequin ['si:kwɪn] n lustrino, paillette f inv.

serene [sə'ri:n] adj sereno(a), calmo(a).

sergeant ['sɑ:dʒənt] n sergente m; *(POLICE)* brigadiere m.

serial ['sɪərɪəl] n *(PRESS)* romanzo a puntate; *(RADIO, TV)* trasmissione f a puntate, serial m inv; **~ize** vt pubblicare *(or trasmettere)* a puntate; **~ number** n numero di serie.

series ['sɪərɪːz] n inv serie f inv; *(PUBLISHING)* collana.

serious ['sɪərɪəs] adj serio(a), grave; **~ly** adv seriamente.

sermon ['sə:mən] n sermone m.

serrated [sɪ'reɪtɪd] adj seghettato(a).

serum ['sɪərəm] n siero.

servant ['sə:vənt] n domestico/a.

serve [sə:v] vt *(employer etc)* servire, essere a servizio di; *(purpose)* servire a; *(customer, food, meal)* servire; *(apprenticeship)* fare; *(prison term)* scontare ♦ vi *(also TENNIS)* servire; *(be useful)*: **to ~ as/for/to do** servire da/per/per fare ♦ n *(TENNIS)* servizio; **it ~s him right** ben gli sta, se l'è meritata; **~ out** vt *(food)* servire; **~ up** vt = **~ out**.

service ['sə:vɪs] n servizio; *(AUT: maintenance)* assistenza, revisione f ♦ vt *(car, washing machine)* revisionare; **the S~s** le forze armate; **to be of ~ to sb** essere d'aiuto a qn; **~able** adj pratico(a), utile; **~ charge** *(BRIT)* n servizio; **~man** n militare m; **~ station** n stazione f di servizio.

serviette [sə:vɪ'ɛt] *(BRIT)* n tovagliolo.

session ['sɛʃən] n *(sitting)* seduta, sessione f; *(SCOL)* anno scolastico *(or accademico)*.

set [sɛt] *(pt, pp set)* n serie f inv; *(of cutlery etc)* servizio; *(RADIO, TV)* apparecchio; *(TENNIS)* set m inv; *(group of people)* mondo, ambiente m; *(CINEMA)* scenario; *(THEATRE: stage)* scene fpl; (: *scenery)* scenario; *(MATH)* insieme m; *(HAIRDRESSING)* messa in piega ♦ adj *(fixed)* stabilito(a), determinato(a); *(ready)* pronto(a) ♦ vt *(place)* posare, mettere; *(arrange)* sistemare; *(fix)* fissare; *(adjust)* regolare; *(decide: rules etc)* stabilire, fissare ♦ vi *(sun)* tramontare; *(jam, jelly)* rapprendersi; *(concrete)* fare presa; **to be ~ on doing** essere deciso a fare; **to ~ to music** mettere in musica; **to ~ on fire** dare fuoco a; **to ~ free** liberare; **to ~ sth going** mettere in moto qc; **to ~ sail** prendere il mare; **~ about** vt fus *(task)* intraprendere, mettersi a; **~ aside** vt mettere da parte; **~ back** vt *(in time)*: **to ~ back (by)** mettere indietro (di); *(inf: cost)*: **it ~ me back £5** mi è costato la bellezza di 5 sterline; **~ off** vi partire ♦ vt *(bomb)* far scoppiare; *(cause to start)*

mettere in moto; (*show up well*) dare
risalto a; ~ **out** *vi* partire ♦ *vt*
(*arrange*) disporre; (*state*) esporre,
presentare; **to** ~ **out to do** proporsi di
fare; ~ **up** *vt* (*organization*) fondare,
costituire; ~**back** *n* (*hitch*) contrattempo, inconveniente *m*; ~ **menu** *n*
menù *m inv* fisso.

settee [sɛ'tiː] *n* divano, sofà *m inv*.

setting ['sɛtɪŋ] *n* (*background*)
ambiente *m*; (*of controls*) posizione *f*;
(*of sun*) tramonto; (*of jewel*)
montatura.

settle ['sɛtl] *vt* (*argument, matter*)
appianare; (*accounts*) regolare; (*MED*:
calm) calmare ♦ *vi* (*bird, dust etc*)
posarsi; (*sediment*) depositarsi; (*also*:
~ **down**) sistemarsi, stabilirsi;
calmarsi; **to** ~ **for sth** accontentarsi di
qc; **to** ~ **on sth** decidersi per qc; ~ **in**
vi sistemarsi; ~ **up** *vi*: **to** ~ **up with sb**
regolare i conti con qn; ~**ment** *n*
(*payment*) pagamento, saldo;
(*agreement*) accordo; (*colony*) colonia;
(*village etc*) villaggio, comunità *f inv*;
~**r** *n* colonizzatore/trice.

setup ['sɛtʌp] *n* (*arrangement*) sistemazione *f*; (*situation*) situazione *f*.

seven ['sɛvn] *num* sette; ~**teen** *num*
diciassette; ~**th** *num* settimo(a); ~**ty**
num settanta.

sever ['sɛvə*] *vt* recidere, tagliare;
(*relations*) troncare.

several ['sɛvərl] *adj, pron* alcuni(e),
diversi(e); ~ **of us** alcuni di noi.

severance ['sɛvərəns] *n* (*of relations*)
rottura; ~ **pay** *n* indennità di
licenziamento.

severe [sɪ'vɪə*] *adj* severo(a); (*serious*)
serio(a), grave; (*hard*) duro(a);
(*plain*) semplice, sobrio(a); **severity**
[sɪ'vɛrɪtɪ] *n* severità; gravità; (*of
weather*) rigore *m*.

sew [səu] (*pt* sewed, *pp* sewn) *vt, vi*
cucire; ~ **up** *vt* ricucire.

sewage ['suːɪdʒ] *n* acque *fpl* di scolo.

sewer ['suːə*] *n* fogna.

sewing ['səuɪŋ] *n* cucitura; cucito; ~
machine *n* macchina da cucire.

sewn [səun] *pp of* sew.

sex [sɛks] *n* sesso; **to have** ~ **with** avere
rapporti sessuali con; ~**ist** *adj, n* sessi-
sta *m/f*.

sexual ['sɛksjuəl] *adj* sessuale.

sexy ['sɛksɪ] *adj* provocante, sexy *inv*.

shabby ['ʃæbɪ] *adj* malandato(a);
(*behaviour*) vergognoso(a).

shack [ʃæk] *n* baracca, capanna.

shackles ['ʃæklz] *npl* ferri *mpl*, catene
fpl.

shade [ʃeɪd] *n* ombra; (*for lamp*)
paralume *m*; (*of colour*) tonalità *f inv*;
(*small quantity*): **a** ~ (**too large/more**)
un po' (troppo grande/di più) ♦ *vt* om-
breggiare, fare ombra a; **in the** ~
all'ombra.

shadow ['ʃædəu] *n* ombra ♦ *vt* (*follow*)
pedinare; ~ **cabinet** (*BRIT*) *n* (*POL*)
governo *m* ombra *inv*; ~**y** *adj* om-
breggiato(a), ombroso(a); (*dim*)
vago(a), indistinto(a).

shady ['ʃeɪdɪ] *adj* ombroso(a); (*fig*:
dishonest) losco(a), equivoco(a).

shaft [ʃɑːft] *n* (*of arrow, spear*) asta;
(*AUT, TECH*) albero; (*of mine*) pozzo;
(*of lift*) tromba; (*of light*) raggio.

shaggy ['ʃægɪ] *adj* ispido(a).

shake [ʃeɪk] (*pt* shook, *pp* shaken) *vt*
scuotere; (*bottle, cocktail*) agitare ♦ *vi*
tremare; **to** ~ **one's head** (*in refusal,
dismay*) scuotere la testa; **to** ~ **hands
with sb** stringere *or* dare la mano a qn;
~ **off** *vt* scrollare (via); (*fig*)
sbarazzarsi di; ~ **up** *vt* scuotere;
shaken *pp of* shake; **shaky** *adj* (*hand,
voice*) tremante; (*building*) traballante.

shall [ʃæl] *aux vb*: **I** ~ **go** andrò; ~ **I
open the door?** apro io la porta?; **I'll
get some,** ~ **I?** ne prendo un po', va
bene?

shallow ['ʃæləu] *adj* poco profondo(a);
(*fig*) superficiale.

sham [ʃæm] *n* finzione *f*, messinscena;
(*jewellery, furniture*) imitazione *f*.

shambles ['ʃæmblz] *n* confusione *f*,
baraonda, scompiglio.

shame [ʃeɪm] *n* vergogna ♦ *vt* far
vergognare; **it is a** ~ (**that/to do**) è un
peccato (che +*sub*/fare); **what a** ~!
che peccato!; ~**faced** *adj* vergo-

gnoso(a); ~**ful** *adj* vergognoso(a); ~**less** *adj* sfrontato(a); (*immodest*) spudorato(a).

shampoo [ʃæm'puː] *n* shampoo *m inv* ♦ *vt* fare lo shampoo a; ~ **and set** *n* shampoo e messa in piega.

shamrock ['ʃæmrɔk] *n* trifoglio (*simbolo nazionale dell'Irlanda*).

shandy ['ʃændɪ] *n* birra con gassosa.

shan't [ʃɑːnt] = **shall not**.

shanty town ['ʃæntɪ-] *n* bidonville *f inv*.

shape [ʃeɪp] *n* forma ♦ *vt* formare; (*statement*) formulare; (*sb's ideas*) condizionare; **to take** ~ prendere forma; ~ **up** *vi* (*events*) andare, mettersi; (*person*) cavarsela; **-shaped** *suffix*: **heart-shaped** a forma di cuore; ~**less** *adj* senza forma, informe; ~**ly** *adj* ben proporzionato(a).

share [ʃɛə*] *n* (*thing received, contribution*) parte *f*; (*COMM*) azione *f* ♦ *vt* dividere; (*have in common*) condividere, avere in comune; ~ **out** *vi* dividere; ~**holder** *n* azionista *m/f*.

shark [ʃɑːk] *n* squalo, pescecane *m*.

sharp [ʃɑːp] *adj* (*razor, knife*) affilato(a); (*point*) acuto(a), acuminato(a); (*nose, chin*) aguzzo(a); (*outline, contrast*) netto(a); (*cold, pain*) pungente; (*voice*) stridulo(a); (*person: quick-witted*) sveglio(a); (: *unscrupulous*) disonesto(a); (*MUS*): **C** ~ do diesis ♦ *n* (*MUS*) diesis *m inv* ♦ *adv*: **at 2 o'clock** ~ alle due in punto; ~**en** *vt* affilare; (*pencil*) fare la punta a; (*fig*) acuire; ~**ener** *n* (*also: pencil* ~**ener**) temperamatite *m inv*; ~**-eyed** *adj* dalla vista acuta; ~**ly** *adv* (*turn, stop*) bruscamente; (*stand out, contrast*) nettamente; (*criticize, retort*) duramente, aspramente.

shatter ['ʃætə*] *vt* mandare in frantumi, frantumare; (*fig: upset*) distruggere; (: *ruin*) rovinare ♦ *vi* frantumarsi, andare in pezzi.

shave [ʃeɪv] *vt* radere, rasare ♦ *vi* radersi, farsi la barba ♦ *n*: **to have a** ~ farsi la barba; ~**r** *n* (*also: electric* ~**r**) rasoio elettrico.

shaving ['ʃeɪvɪŋ] *n* (*action*) rasatura; ~**s** *npl* (*of wood etc*) trucioli *mpl*; ~ **brush** *n* pennello da barba; ~ **cream** *n* crema da barba; ~ **foam** *n* = ~ **cream**.

shawl [ʃɔːl] *n* scialle *m*.

she [ʃiː] *pron* ella, lei; ~**-cat** *n* gatta; ~**-elephant** *n* elefantessa.

sheaf [ʃiːf] (*pl* **sheaves**) *n* covone *m*; (*of papers*) fascio.

shear [ʃɪə*] (*pt* ~**ed**, *pp* ~**ed** *or* **shorn**) *vt* (*sheep*) tosare; ~ **off** *vi* spezzarsi; ~**s** *npl* (*for hedge*) cesoie *fpl*.

sheath [ʃiːθ] *n* fodero, guaina; (*contraceptive*) preservativo.

sheaves [ʃiːvz] *npl of* **sheaf**.

shed [ʃed] (*pt, pp* **shed**) *n* capannone *m* ♦ *vt* (*leaves, fur etc*) perdere; (*tears, blood*) versare; (*workers*) liberarsi di.

she'd [ʃiːd] = **she had**; **she would**.

sheen [ʃiːn] *n* lucentezza.

sheep [ʃiːp] *n inv* pecora; ~**dog** *n* cane *m* da pastore; ~**ish** *adj* vergognoso(a), timido(a); ~**skin** *n* pelle *f* di pecora.

sheer [ʃɪə*] *adj* (*utter*) vero(a) (e proprio(a)); (*steep*) a picco, perpendicolare; (*almost transparent*) sottile ♦ *adv* a picco.

sheet [ʃiːt] *n* (*on bed*) lenzuolo *m*; (*of paper*) foglio; (*of glass, ice*) lastra; (*of metal*) foglio, lamina; ~ **lightning** *n* lampo diffuso.

sheik(h) [ʃeɪk] *n* sceicco.

shelf [ʃelf] (*pl* **shelves**) *n* scaffale *m*, mensola.

shell [ʃel] *n* (*on beach*) conchiglia; (*of egg, nut etc*) guscio; (*explosive*) granata; (*of building*) scheletro ♦ *vt* (*peas*) sgranare; (*MIL*) bombardare.

she'll [ʃiːl] = **she will**; **she shall**.

shellfish ['ʃelfɪʃ] *n inv* (*crab etc*) crostaceo; (*scallop etc*) mollusco; (*pl: as food*) crostacei; molluschi.

shelter ['ʃeltə*] *n* riparo, rifugio ♦ *vt* riparare, proteggere; (*give lodging to*) dare rifugio or asilo a ♦ *vi* ripararsi, mettersi al riparo; ~**ed** *adj* riparato(a); ~**ed housing** (*BRIT*) *n* alloggi dotati di strutture per anziani o handicappati.

shelve [ʃelv] *vt* (*fig*) accantonare,

rimandare; **~s** *npl of* **shelf**.

shepherd ['ʃɛpəd] *n* pastore *m* ♦ *vt* (*guide*) guidare; **~'s pie** (*BRIT*) *n* timballo di carne macinata e purè di patate.

sheriff ['ʃɛrɪf] (*US*) *n* sceriffo.

sherry ['ʃɛrɪ] *n* sherry *m inv*.

she's [ʃiːz] = **she is**; **she has**.

Shetland ['ʃɛtlənd] *n* (*also: the ~s, the ~ Isles*) le isole Shetland, le Shetland.

shield [ʃiːld] *n* scudo; (*trophy*) scudetto; (*protection*) schermo ♦ *vt*: **to ~ (from)** riparare (da), proteggere (da or contro).

shift [ʃɪft] *n* (*change*) cambiamento; (*of workers*) turno ♦ *vt* spostare, muovere; (*remove*) rimuovere ♦ *vi* spostarsi, muoversi; **~less** *adj*: **a ~less person** un(a) fannullone(a); **~ work** *n* lavoro a squadre; **~y** *adj* ambiguo(a); (*eyes*) sfuggente.

shilling ['ʃɪlɪŋ] (*BRIT*) *n* scellino (= *12 old pence*; *20 in a pound*).

shilly-shally ['ʃɪlɪʃælɪ] *vi* tentennare, esitare.

shimmer ['ʃɪmə*] *vi* brillare, luccicare.

shin [ʃɪn] *n* tibia.

shine [ʃaɪn] (*pt, pp* **shone**) *n* splendore *m*, lucentezza ♦ *vi* (ri)splendere, brillare ♦ *vt* far brillare, far risplendere; (*torch*): **to ~ sth on** puntare qc verso.

shingle ['ʃɪŋgl] *n* (*on beach*) ciottoli *mpl*; **~s** *n* (*MED*) herpes zoster *m*.

shiny ['ʃaɪnɪ] *adj* lucente, lucido(a).

ship [ʃɪp] *n* nave *f* ♦ *vt* trasportare (via mare); (*send*) spedire (via mare); **~building** *n* costruzione *f* navale; **~ment** *n* carico; **~ping** *n* (*ships*) naviglio; (*traffic*) navigazione *f*; **~shape** *adj* in perfetto ordine; **~wreck** *n* relitto; (*event*) naufragio ♦ *vt*: **to be ~wrecked** naufragare, fare naufragio; **~yard** *n* cantiere *m* navale.

shire ['ʃaɪə*] (*BRIT*) *n* contea.

shirk [ʃəːk] *vt* sottrarsi a, evitare.

shirt [ʃəːt] *n* camicia; **in ~ sleeves** in maniche di camicia.

shit [ʃɪt] (*inf!*) *excl* merda (*!*).

shiver ['ʃɪvə*] *n* brivido ♦ *vi* rab-

brividire, tremare.

shoal [ʃəul] *n* (*of fish*) banco; (*fig*) massa.

shock [ʃɔk] *n* (*impact*) urto, colpo; (*ELEC*) scossa; (*emotional*) colpo, shock *m inv*; (*MED*) shock ♦ *vt* colpire, scioccare; scandalizzare; **~ absorber** *n* ammortizzatore *m*; **~ing** *adj* scioccante, traumatizzante; scandaloso(a).

shod [ʃɔd] *pt, pp of* **shoe**.

shoddy ['ʃɔdɪ] *adj* scadente.

shoe [ʃuː] (*pt, pp* **shod**) *n* scarpa; (*also: horse~*) ferro di cavallo ♦ *vt* (*horse*) ferrare; **~brush** *n* spazzola per scarpe; **~lace** *n* stringa; **~ polish** *n* lucido per scarpe; **~shop** *n* calzoleria; **~string** *n* (*fig*): **on a ~string** con quattro soldi.

shone [ʃɔn] *pt, pp of* **shine**.

shoo [ʃuː] *excl* sciò!, via!

shook [ʃuk] *pt of* **shake**.

shoot [ʃuːt] (*pt, pp* **shot**) *n* (*on branch, seedling*) germoglio ♦ *vt* (*game*) cacciare, andare a caccia di; (*person*) sparare a; (*execute*) fucilare; (*film*) girare ♦ *vi* (*with gun*): **to ~ (at)** sparare (a), fare fuoco (su); (*with bow*): **to ~ (at)** tirare (su); (*FOOTBALL*) sparare, tirare (forte); **~ down** *vt* (*plane*) abbattere; **~ in/out** *vi* entrare/uscire come una freccia; **~ up** *vi* (*fig*) salire alle stelle; **~ing** *n* (*shots*) sparatoria; (*HUNTING*) caccia; **~ing star** *n* stella cadente.

shop [ʃɔp] *n* negozio; (*workshop*) officina ♦ *vi* (*also: go ~ping*) fare spese; **~ assistant** (*BRIT*) *n* commesso/a; **~ floor** *n* officina; (*BRIT: fig*) operai *mpl*, maestranze *fpl*; **~keeper** *n* negoziante *m/f*, bottegaio/a; **~lifting** *n* taccheggio; **~per** *n* compratore/trice; **~ping** *n* (*goods*) spesa, acquisti *mpl*; **~ping bag** *n* borsa per la spesa; **~ping centre** (*US* **~ping center**) *n* centro commerciale; **~-soiled** *adj* sciupato(a) a forza di stare in vetrina; **~ steward** (*BRIT*) *n* (*INDUSTRY*) rappresentante *m* sindacale; **~ window** *n* vetrina.

shore [ʃɔː*] *n* (*of sea*) riva, spiaggia; (*of lake*) riva ♦ *vt*: **to ~ (up)**

puntellare; **on** ~ a riva.
shorn [ʃɔːn] pp of **shear**.
short [ʃɔːt] adj (not long) corto(a); (soon finished) breve; (person) basso(a); (curt) brusco(a), secco(a); (insufficient) insufficiente ♦ n (also: ~ film) cortometraggio; (a pair of) ~s (i) calzoncini; **to be** ~ **of sth** essere a corto di or mancare di qc; **in** ~ in breve; ~ **of doing** a meno che non si faccia; **everything** ~ **of** tutto fuorché; **it is** ~ **for** è l'abbreviazione or il diminutivo di; **to cut** ~ (speech, visit) accorciare, abbreviare; **to fall** ~ **of** venir meno a; non soddisfare; **to run** ~ **of** rimanere senza; **to stop** ~ fermarsi di colpo; **to stop** ~ **of** non arrivare fino a; ~**age** n scarsezza, carenza; ~**bread** n biscotto di pasta frolla; ~**-change** vt: **to** ~**-change sb** imbrogliare qn sul resto; ~**circuit** n cortocircuito; ~**coming** n difetto; ~**(crust) pastry** (BRIT) n pasta frolla; ~**cut** n scorciatoia; ~**en** vt accorciare, ridurre; ~**fall** n deficit m; ~**hand** (BRIT) n stenografia; ~**hand typist** (BRIT) n stenodattilografo/a; ~**list** (BRIT) n (for job) rosa dei candidati; ~**lived** adj di breve durata; ~**ly** adv fra poco; ~**-sighted** (BRIT) adj miope; ~**-staffed** adj a corto di personale; ~ **story** n racconto, novella; ~**-tempered** adj irascibile; ~**-term** adj (effect) di or a breve durata; (borrowing) a breve scadenza; ~**wave** n (RADIO) onde fpl corte.
shot [ʃɔt] pt, pp of **shoot** ♦ n sparo, colpo; (try) prova; (FOOTBALL) tiro; (injection) iniezione f; (PHOT) foto f inv; **like a** ~ come un razzo; (very readily) immediatamente; ~**gun** n fucile m da caccia.
should [ʃud] aux vb: **I** ~ **go now** dovrei andare ora; **he** ~ **be there now** dovrebbe essere arrivato ora; **I** ~ **go if I were you** se fossi in te andrei; **I** ~ **like to** mi piacerebbe.
shoulder [ʃəuldə*] n spalla; (BRIT: of road): **hard** ~ banchina ♦ vt (fig) addossarsi, prendere sulle proprie spalle; ~ **bag** n borsa a tracolla; ~

blade n scapola; ~ **strap** n bretella, spallina.
shouldn't [ʃudnt] = should not.
shout [ʃaut] n urlo, grido ♦ vt gridare ♦ vi (also: ~ **out**) urlare, gridare; ~ **down** vt zittire gridando; ~**ing** n urli mpl.
shove [ʃʌv] vt spingere; (inf: put): **to** ~ **sth in** ficcare qc in; ~ **off** (inf) vi sloggiare, smammare.
shovel [ˈʃʌvl] n pala ♦ vt spalare.
show [ʃəu] (pt ~**ed**, pp **shown**) n (of emotion) dimostrazione f, manifestazione f; (semblance) apparenza; (exhibition) mostra, esposizione f; (THEATRE, CINEMA) spettacolo ♦ vt far vedere, mostrare; (courage etc) dimostrare, dar prova di; (exhibit) esporre ♦ vi vedersi, essere visibile; **for** ~ per fare scena, **on** ~ (exhibits etc) esposto(a); ~ **in** vt (person) far entrare; ~ **off** vi (pej) esibirsi, mettersi in mostra ♦ vt (display) mettere in risalto; (pej) mettere in mostra; ~ **out** vt (person) accompagnare alla porta; ~ **up** vi (stand out) essere ben visibile; (inf: turn up) farsi vedere ♦ vt mettere in risalto; ~ **business** n industria dello spettacolo; ~**down** n prova di forza.
shower [ˈʃauə*] n (rain) acquazzone m; (of stones etc) pioggia; (also: ~**bath**) doccia ♦ vi fare la doccia ♦ vt: **to** ~ **sb with** (gifts, abuse etc) coprire qn di; (missiles) lanciare contro qn una pioggia di; **to have a** ~ fare la doccia; ~**proof** adj impermeabile.
showing [ˈʃəuɪŋ] n (of film) proiezione f.
show jumping n concorso ippico (di salto ad ostacoli).
shown [ʃəun] pp of **show**.
show-off (inf) n (person) esibizionista m/f.
showpiece [ˈʃəupiːs] n pezzo forte.
showroom [ˈʃəurum] n sala d'esposizione.
shrank [ʃræŋk] pt of **shrink**.
shrapnel [ˈʃræpnl] n shrapnel m.
shred [ʃred] n (gen pl) brandello ♦ vt fare a brandelli; (CULIN) sminuzzare,

tagliuzzare; ~**der** n (vegetable ~der) grattugia; (document ~der) distruttore m di documenti.

shrewd [ʃruːd] adj astuto(a), scaltro(a).

shriek [ʃriːk] n strillo ♦ vi strillare.

shrill [ʃrɪl] adj acuto(a), stridulo(a), stridente.

shrimp [ʃrɪmp] n gamberetto.

shrine [ʃraɪn] n reliquario; (place) santuario.

shrink [ʃrɪŋk] (pt **shrank**, pp **shrunk**) vi restringersi; (fig) ridursi; (also: ~ away) ritrarsi ♦ vt (wool) far restringere ♦ n (inf: pej) psicanalista m/f; **to** ~ **from doing sth** rifuggire dal fare qc; ~**age** n restringimento; ~**wrap** vt confezionare con pellicola di plastica.

shrivel [ʃrɪvl] (also: ~ up) vt raggrinzare, avvizzire ♦ vi raggrinzirsi, avvizzire.

shroud [ʃraud] n sudario ♦ vt: ~**ed in mystery** avvolto(a) nel mistero.

Shrove Tuesday [ʃrəuv-] n martedì m grasso.

shrub [ʃrʌb] n arbusto; ~**bery** n arbusti mpl.

shrug [ʃrʌg] n scrollata di spalle ♦ vt, vi: **to** ~ (**one's shoulders**) alzare le spalle, fare spallucce; ~ **off** vt passare sopra a.

shrunk [ʃrʌŋk] pp of **shrink**.

shudder [ʃʌdə*] n brivido ♦ vi rabbrividire.

shuffle [ʃʌfl] vt (cards) mescolare; **to** ~ (**one's feet**) strascicare i piedi.

shun [ʃʌn] vt sfuggire, evitare.

shunt [ʃʌnt] vt (RAIL: direct) smistare; (: divert) deviare; (object) spostare.

shut [ʃʌt] (pt, pp **shut**) vt chiudere ♦ vi chiudersi, chiudere; ~ **down** vt, vi chiudere definitivamente; ~ **off** vt fermare, bloccare; ~ **up** vi (inf: keep quiet) stare zitto(a), fare silenzio ♦ vt (close) chiudere; (silence) far tacere; ~**ter** n imposta; (PHOT) otturatore m.

shuttle [ʃʌtl] n spola, navetta; (space ~) navetta (spaziale); (also: ~ service) servizio m navetta inv.

shuttlecock [ʃʌtlkɔk] n volano.

shy [ʃaɪ] adj timido(a).

sibling [sɪblɪŋ] n fratello/sorella.

Sicily [sɪsɪlɪ] n Sicilia.

sick [sɪk] adj (ill) malato(a); (vomiting): **to be** ~ vomitare; (humour) macabro(a); **to feel** ~ avere la nausea; **to be** ~ **of** (fig) averne abbastanza di; ~ **bay** n infermeria; ~**en** vt nauseare ♦ vi: **to be** ~**ening for sth** (cold etc) covare qc.

sickle [sɪkl] n falcetto.

sick: ~ **leave** n congedo per malattia; ~**ly** adj malaticcio(a); (causing nausea) nauseante; ~**ness** n malattia; (vomiting) vomito; ~ **pay** n sussidio per malattia.

side [saɪd] n lato; (of lake) riva; (team) squadra ♦ cpd (door, entrance) laterale ♦ vi: **to** ~ **with sb** parteggiare per qn, prendere le parti di qn; **by the** ~ **of** a fianco di; (road) sul ciglio di; ~ **by** ~ fianco a fianco; **from** ~ **to** ~ da una parte all'altra; **to take** ~**s** (**with**) schierarsi (con); ~**board** n credenza; ~**burns** (BRIT ~**boards**) npl (whiskers) basette fpl; ~ **effect** n (MED) effetto collaterale; ~**light** n (AUT) luce f di posizione; ~**line** n (SPORT) linea laterale; (fig) attività secondaria; ~**long** adj obliquo(a); ~**saddle** adv all'amazzone; ~ **show** n attrazione f; ~**step** vt (question) eludere; (problem) scavalcare; ~ **street** n traversa; ~**track** vt (fig) distrarre; ~**walk** (US) n marciapiede m; ~**ways** adv (move) di lato, di fianco.

siding [saɪdɪŋ] n (RAIL) binario di raccordo.

sidle [saɪdl] vi: **to** ~ **up** (**to**) avvicinarsi furtivamente (a).

siege [siːdʒ] n assedio.

sieve [sɪv] n setaccio ♦ vt setacciare.

sift [sɪft] vt passare al crivello; (fig) vagliare.

sigh [saɪ] n sospiro ♦ vi sospirare.

sight [saɪt] n (faculty) vista; (spectacle) spettacolo; (on gun) mira ♦ vt avvistare; **in** ~ in vista; **on** ~ a vista; **out of** ~ non visibile; ~**seeing** n giro turistico; **to go ~seeing** visitare una località.

[saɪn] n segno; (with hand etc) segno, gesto; (notice) insegna, cartello ♦ vt firmare; (player) ingaggiare; ~ **on** vi (MIL) arruolarsi; (as unemployed) iscriversi sulla lista (dell'ufficio di collocamento) ♦ vt (MIL) arruolare; (employee) assumere; ~ **over** vt: **to ~ sth over to sb** cedere qc con scrittura legale a qn; ~ **up** vi (MIL) arruolarsi; (for course) iscriversi ♦ vt (player) ingaggiare; (recruits) reclutare.

signal ['sɪgnl] n segnale m ♦ vi (AUT) segnalare, mettere la freccia ♦ vt (person) fare segno a; (message) comunicare per mezzo di segnali; ~ **man** n (RAIL) deviatore m.

signature ['sɪgnətʃə*] n firma; ~ **tune** n sigla musicale.

signet ring ['sɪgnət-] n anello con sigillo.

significance [sɪg'nɪfɪkəns] n significato; importanza.

significant [sɪg'nɪfɪkənt] adj significativo(a).

sign language n linguaggio dei muti.

signpost ['saɪnpəust] n cartello indicatore.

silence ['saɪlns] n silenzio ♦ vt far tacere, ridurre al silenzio; ~**r** n (on gun, BRIT: AUT) silenziatore m.

silent ['saɪlnt] adj silenzioso(a); (film) muto(a); **to remain ~** tacere, stare zitto; ~ **partner** n (COMM) socio inattivo.

silhouette [sɪlu:'ɛt] n silhouette f inv.

silicon chip ['sɪlɪkən-] n piastrina di silicio.

silk [sɪlk] n seta ♦ adj di seta; ~**y** adj di seta.

silly ['sɪlɪ] adj stupido(a), sciocco(a).

silt [sɪlt] n limo.

silver ['sɪlvə*] n argento; (money) monete da 5, 10 or 50 pence; (also: ~ware) argenteria ♦ adj d'argento; ~ **paper** (BRIT) n carta argentata, (carta) stagnola; ~**-plated** adj argentato(a); ~**smith** n argentiere m; ~**y** adj (colour) argenteo(a); (sound)

argentino(a).

similar ['sɪmɪlə*] adj: ~ **(to)** simile (a); ~**ly** adv allo stesso modo; così pure.

simile ['sɪmɪlɪ] n similitudine f.

simmer ['sɪmə*] vi cuocere a fuoco lento.

simpering ['sɪmpərɪŋ] adj lezioso(a), smorfioso(a).

simple ['sɪmpl] adj semplice; **simplicity** [-'plɪsɪtɪ] n semplicità; **simply** adv semplicemente.

simultaneous [sɪməl'teɪnɪəs] adj simultaneo(a).

sin [sɪn] n peccato ♦ vi peccare.

since [sɪns] adv da allora ♦ prep da ♦ conj (time) da quando; (because) poiché, dato che; ~ **then, ever** ~ da allora.

sincere [sɪn'sɪə*] adj sincero(a); ~**ly** adv: **yours** ~**ly** (in letters) distinti saluti; **sincerity** [-'serɪtɪ] n sincerità.

sinew ['sɪnju:] n tendine m.

sinful ['sɪnful] adj peccaminoso(a).

sing [sɪŋ] (pt **sang**, pp **sung**) vt, vi cantare.

singe [sɪndʒ] vt bruciacchiare.

singer ['sɪŋə*] n cantante m/f.

singing ['sɪŋɪŋ] n canto.

single ['sɪŋgl] adj solo(a), unico(a); (unmarried: man) celibe; (: woman) nubile; (not double) semplice ♦ n (BRIT: also: ~ ticket) biglietto di (sola) andata; (record) 45 giri m; ~**s** n (TENNIS) singolo; ~ **out** vt scegliere; (distinguish) distinguere; ~ **breasted** adj a un petto; ~ **file** n: **in** ~ **file** in fila indiana; ~**-handed** adv senza aiuto, da solo(a); ~**-minded** adj tenace, risoluto(a); ~ **room** n camera singola.

singly ['sɪŋglɪ] adv separatamente.

singular ['sɪŋgjulə*] adj (exceptional, LING) singolare ♦ n (LING) singolare m.

sinister ['sɪnɪstə*] adj sinistro(a).

sink [sɪŋk] (pt **sank**, pp **sunk**) n lavandino, acquaio ♦ vt (ship) (fare) affondare, colare a picco; (foundations) scavare; (piles etc): **to ~ sth into** conficcare qc in ♦ vi affondare, andare a fondo; (ground etc) cedere, avvallarsi; **my heart sank** mi sentii venir meno; ~ **in** vi penetrare.

sinner ['sɪnə*] n peccatore/trice.
sinus ['saɪnəs] n (ANAT) seno.
sip [sɪp] n sorso ♦ vt sorseggiare.
siphon ['saɪfən] n sifone m; ~ **off** vt travasare (con un sifone).
sir [sə*] n signore m; S~ **John Smith** Sir John Smith; **yes** ~ sì, signore.
siren ['saɪərn] n sirena.
sirloin ['sə:lɔɪn] n controfiletto.
sissy ['sɪsɪ] (inf) n femminuccia.
sister ['sɪstə*] n sorella; (nun) suora; (BRIT: nurse) infermiera f caposala inv; ~**-in-law** n cognata.
sit [sɪt] (pt, pp **sat**) vi sedere, sedersi; (assembly) essere in seduta; (for painter) posare ♦ vt (exam) sostenere, dare; ~ **down** vi sedersi; ~ **in on** vt fus assistere a; ~ **up** vi tirarsi su a sedere; (not go to bed) stare alzato(a) fino a tardi.
sitcom ['sɪtkɔm] n abbr (= situation comedy) commedia di situazione; (TV) telefilm m inv comico d'interni.
site [saɪt] n posto; (also: building ~) cantiere m ♦ vt situare.
sit-in n (demonstration) sit-in m inv.
sitting ['sɪtɪŋ] n (of assembly etc) seduta; (in canteen) turno; ~ **room** n soggiorno.
situated ['sɪtjʊeɪtɪd] adj situato(a).
situation [sɪtjʊ'eɪʃən] n situazione f; (job) lavoro; (location) posizione f; "~**s vacant**" (BRIT) "offerte fpl di impiego".
six [sɪks] num sei; ~**teen** num sedici; ~**th** num sesto(a); ~**ty** num sessanta.
size [saɪz] n dimensioni fpl; (of clothing) taglia, misura; (of shoes) numero; (glue) colla; ~ **up** vt giudicare, farsi un'idea di; ~**able** adj considerevole.
sizzle ['sɪzl] vi sfrigolare.
skate [skeɪt] n pattino; (fish: pl inv) razza ♦ vi pattinare; ~**board** n skateboard m inv; ~**r** n pattinatore/trice; **skating** n pattinaggio; **skating rink** n pista di pattinaggio.
skeleton ['skelɪtn] n scheletro; ~ **staff** n personale m ridotto.
skeptical ['skeptɪkl] (US) adj = **sceptical.**

sketch [sketʃ] n (drawing) schizzo, abbozzo; (THEATRE) scenetta comica, sketch m inv ♦ vt abbozzare, schizzare; ~ **book** n album m inv per schizzi; ~**y** adj incompleto(a), lacunoso(a).
skewer ['skju:ə*] n spiedo.
ski [ski:] n sci m inv ♦ vi sciare; ~ **boot** n scarpone m da sci.
skid [skɪd] n slittamento ♦ vi slittare.
skier ['ski:ə*] n sciatore/trice.
skiing ['ski:ɪŋ] n sci m.
ski jump n (ramp) trampolino; (event) salto con gli sci.
skilful ['skɪlful] (US **skillful**) adj abile.
ski lift ['ski:lɪft] n sciovia.
skill [skɪl] n abilità f inv, capacità f inv; ~**ed** adj esperto(a); (worker) qualificato(a), specializzato(a); ~**ful** (US) adj = **skilful.**
skim [skɪm] vt (milk) scremare; (glide over) sfiorare ♦ vi: **to** ~ **through** (fig) scorrere, dare una scorsa a; ~**med milk** n latte m scremato.
skimp [skɪmp] vt (work: also: ~ **on**) fare alla carlona; (cloth etc) lesinare; ~**y** adj misero(a); striminzito(a); frugale.
skin [skɪn] n pelle f ♦ vt (fruit etc) sbucciare; (animal) scuoiare, spellare; ~**-deep** adj superficiale; ~ **diving** n nuoto subacqueo; ~**ny** adj molto magro(a), pelle e ossa inv; ~**tight** adj (dress etc) aderente.
skip [skɪp] n saltello, balzo; (BRIT: container) benna ♦ vi saltare; (with rope) saltare la corda ♦ vt saltare.
ski pants npl pantaloni mpl da sci.
ski pole n racchetta (da sci).
skipper ['skɪpə*] n (NAUT, SPORT) capitano.
skipping rope ['skɪpɪŋ-] (BRIT) n corda per saltare.
skirmish ['skə:mɪʃ] n scaramuccia.
skirt [skə:t] n gonna, sottana ♦ vt fiancheggiare, costeggiare; ~**ing board** (BRIT) n zoccolo.
ski slope n pista da sci.
ski suit n tuta da sci.
skit [skɪt] n parodia; scenetta satirica.
skittle ['skɪtl] n birillo; ~**s** n (game)

(gioco dei) birilli *mpl*.
skive [skaɪv] (*BRIT: inf*) *vi* fare il lavativo.
skulk [skʌlk] *vi* muoversi furtivamente.
skull [skʌl] *n* cranio, teschio.
skunk [skʌŋk] *n* moffetta.
sky [skaɪ] *n* cielo; ~**light** *n* lucernario; ~**scraper** *n* grattacielo.
slab [slæb] *n* lastra; (*of cake, cheese*) fetta.
slack [slæk] *adj* (*loose*) allentato(a); (*slow*) lento(a); (*careless*) negligente; ~**en** (*also:* ~**en off**) *vi* rallentare, diminuire ♦ *vt* allentare; (*speed*) diminuire; ~**s** *npl* (*trousers*) pantaloni *mpl*.
slag heap [slæg-] *n* ammasso di scorie.
slag off [slæg-] (*BRIT: inf*) *vt* sparlare di.
slain [sleɪn] *pp of* **slay**.
slam [slæm] *vt* (*door*) sbattere; (*throw*) scaraventare; (*criticize*) stroncare ♦ *vi* sbattere.
slander [ˈslɑːndə*] *n* calunnia; diffamazione *f*.
slang [slæŋ] *n* gergo, slang *m*.
slant [slɑːnt] *n* pendenza, inclinazione *f*; (*fig*) angolazione *f*, punto di vista; ~**ed** *adj* in pendenza, inclinato(a); (*eyes*) obliquo(a); ~**ing** *adj* = ~**ed**.
slap [slæp] *n* manata, pacca; (*on face*) schiaffo ♦ *vt* dare una manata a; schiaffeggiare ♦ *adv* (*directly*) in pieno; ~ **a coat of paint on it** dagli una mano di vernice; ~**dash** *adj* negligente; (*work*) raffazzonato(a); ~**stick** *n* (*comedy*) farsa grossolana; ~-**up** (*BRIT*) *adj*: **a** ~-**up meal** un pranzo (*or* una cena) coi fiocchi.
slash [slæʃ] *vt* tagliare; (*face*) sfregiare; (*fig: prices*) ridurre drasticamente, tagliare.
slat [slæt] *n* (*of wood*) stecca; (*of plastic*) lamina.
slate [sleɪt] *n* ardesia; (*piece*) lastra di ardesia ♦ *vt* (*fig: criticize*) stroncare, distruggere.
slaughter [ˈslɔːtə*] *n* strage *f*, massacro ♦ *vt* (*animal*) macellare; (*people*) trucidare, massacrare.

slave [sleɪv] *n* schiavo/a ♦ *vi* (*also:* ~ *away*) lavorare come uno schiavo; ~**ry** *n* schiavitù *f*; **slavish** *adj* servile; (*copy*) pedissequo(a).
slay [sleɪ] (*pt* **slew**, *pp* **slain**) *vt* (*formal*) uccidere.
sleazy [ˈsliːzɪ] *adj* trasandato(a).
sledge [sledʒ] *n* slitta; ~**hammer** *n* mazza, martello da fabbro.
sleek [sliːk] *adj* (*hair, fur*) lucido(a), lucente; (*car, boat*) slanciato(a), affusolato(a).
sleep [sliːp] (*pt, pp* **slept**) *n* sonno ♦ *vi* dormire; **to go to** ~ addormentarsi; ~ **around** *vi* andare a letto con tutti; ~ **in** *vi* (*oversleep*) dormire fino a tardi; ~**er** (*BRIT*) *n* (*RAIL: on track*) traversina; (: *train*) treno di vagoni letto; ~**ing bag** *n* sacco a pelo; ~**ing car** *n* vagone *m* letto *inv*, carrozza *f* letto *inv*; ~**ing partner** (*BRIT*) *n* (*COMM*) socio inattivo; ~**ing pill** *n* sonnifero; ~**less** *adj*: **a** ~**less night** una notte in bianco; ~**walker** *n* sonnambulo/a; ~**y** *adj* assonnato(a), sonnolento(a); (*fig*) addormentato(a).
sleet [sliːt] *n* nevischio.
sleeve [sliːv] *n* manica; (*of record*) copertina.
sleigh [sleɪ] *n* slitta.
sleight [slaɪt] *n*: ~ **of hand** gioco di destrezza.
slender [ˈslɛndə*] *adj* snello(a), sottile; (*not enough*) scarso(a), esiguo(a).
slept [slɛpt] *pt, pp of* **sleep**.
slew [sluː] *pt of* **slay** ♦ *vi* (*BRIT*) girare.
slice [slaɪs] *n* fetta ♦ *vt* affettare, tagliare a fette.
slick [slɪk] *adj* (*skilful*) brillante; (*clever*) furbo(a) ♦ *n* (*also: oil* ~) chiazza di petrolio.
slide [slaɪd] (*pt, pp* **slid**) *n* scivolone *m*; (*in playground*) scivolo; (*PHOT*) diapositiva; (*BRIT: also: hair* ~) fermaglio (per capelli) ♦ *vt* far scivolare ♦ *vi* scivolare; ~ **rule** *n* regolo calcolatore; **sliding** *adj* (*door*) scorrevole; **sliding scale** *n* scala mobile.
slight [slaɪt] *adj* (*slim*) snello(a), sottile; (*frail*) delicato(a), fragile;

(*trivial*) insignificante; (*small*) piccolo(a) ♦ *n* offesa, affronto; **not in the** ~**est** affatto, neppure per sogno; ~**ly** *adv* lievemente, un po'.

slim [slɪm] *adj* magro(a), snello(a) ♦ *vi* dimagrire; fare (*or* seguire) una dieta dimagrante.

slime [slaɪm] *n* limo, melma; viscidume *m*.

slimming ['slɪmɪŋ] *adj* (*diet*) dimagrante; (*food*) ipocalorico(a).

sling [slɪŋ] (*pt, pp* **slung**) *n* (*MED*) fascia al collo; (*for baby*) marsupio ♦ *vt* lanciare, tirare.

slip [slɪp] *n* scivolata, scivolone *m*; (*mistake*) errore *m*, sbaglio; (*underskirt*) sottoveste *f*; (*of paper*) striscia di carta; tagliando, scontrino ♦ *vt* (*slide*) far scivolare ♦ *vi* (*slide*) scivolare; (*move smoothly*): **to ~ into/out of** scivolare in/fuori da; (*decline*) declinare; **to ~ sth on/off** infilarsi/togliersi qc; **to give sb the ~** sfuggire qn; **a ~ of the tongue** un lapsus linguae; ~ **away** *vi* svignarsela; ~ **in** *vt* infilare ♦ *vi* (*error*) scivolare; ~ **out** *vi* scivolare fuori; ~ **up** *vi* sbagliarsi; ~**ped disc** *n* spostamento delle vertebre.

slipper ['slɪpə*] *n* pantofola.

slippery ['slɪpərɪ] *adj* scivoloso(a).

slip road (*BRIT*) *n* (*to motorway*) rampa di accesso.

slipshod ['slɪpʃɒd] *adj* sciatto(a), trasandato(a).

slip-up *n* granchio (*fig*).

slipway ['slɪpweɪ] *n* scalo di costruzione.

slit [slɪt] (*pt, pp* **slit**) *n* fessura, fenditura; (*cut*) taglio ♦ *vt* fendere; tagliare.

slither ['slɪðə*] *vi* scivolare, sdrucciolare.

sliver ['slɪvə*] *n* (*of glass, wood*) scheggia; (*of cheese etc*) fettina.

slob [slɒb] (*inf*) *n* sciattone/a.

slog [slɒg] (*BRIT*) *n* faticata ♦ *vi* lavorare con accanimento, sgobbare.

slogan ['sləʊgən] *n* motto, slogan *m inv*.

slop [slɒp] *vi* (*also*: ~ **over**) traboccare; versarsi ♦ *vt* versare.

slope [sləʊp] *n* pendio; (*side of mountain*) versante *m*; (*ski ~*) pista; (*of roof*) pendenza; (*of floor*) inclinazione *f* ♦ *vi*: **to ~ down** declinare; **to ~ up** essere in salita; **sloping** *adj* inclinato(a).

sloppy ['slɒpɪ] *adj* (*work*) tirato(a) via; (*appearance*) sciatto(a).

slot [slɒt] *n* fessura ♦ *vt*: **to ~ sth into** infilare qc in.

sloth [sləʊθ] *n* (*laziness*) pigrizia, accidia.

slot machine *n* (*BRIT*: *vending machine*) distributore *m* automatico; (*for gambling*) slot-machine *f inv*.

slouch [slautʃ] *vi* (*when walking*) camminare dinoccolato(a); **she was ~ing in a chair** era sprofondata in una poltrona.

slovenly ['slʌvənlɪ] *adj* sciatto(a), trasandato(a).

slow [sləʊ] *adj* lento(a); (*watch*): **to be ~** essere indietro ♦ *adv* lentamente ♦ *vt, vi* (*also*: ~ **down**, ~ **up**) rallentare; "**~**" (*road sign*) "rallentare"; ~**ly** *adv* lentamente; ~ **motion** *n*: **in ~ motion** al rallentatore.

sludge [slʌdʒ] *n* fanghiglia.

slue [sluː] (*US*) *vi* = **slew**.

slug [slʌg] *n* lumaca; (*bullet*) pallottola; ~**gish** *adj* lento(a); (*trading*) stagnante.

sluice [sluːs] *n* chiusa.

slum [slʌm] *n* catapecchia.

slumber ['slʌmbə*] *n* sonno.

slump [slʌmp] *n* crollo, caduta; (*economic*) depressione *f*, crisi *f inv* ♦ *vi* crollare.

slung [slʌŋ] *pt, pp of* **sling**.

slur [sləː*] *n* (*fig*): ~ (**on**) calunnia (su) ♦ *vt* pronunciare in modo indistinto.

slush [slʌʃ] *n* neve *f* mista a fango; ~ **fund** *n* fondi *mpl* neri.

slut [slʌt] *n* donna trasandata, sciattona.

sly [slaɪ] *adj* (*smile*, *remark*) sornione(a); (*person*) furbo(a).

smack [smæk] *n* (*slap*) pacca; (*on face*) schiaffo ♦ *vt* schiaffeggiare; (*child*) picchiare ♦ *vi*: **to ~ of** puzzare di.

small [smɔːl] *adj* piccolo(a); ~ **ads** (*BRIT*) *npl* piccola pubblicità; ~ **change**

n moneta, spiccioli *mpl*; ~ **fry** *npl* pesci *mpl* piccoli; ~-**holder** *n* piccolo proprietario; ~ **hours** *npl*: **in the** ~ **hours** alle ore piccole; ~**pox** *n* vaiolo; ~ **talk** *n* chiacchiere *fpl*.

smart [smɑːt] *adj* elegante; *(fashionable)* alla moda; *(clever)* intelligente; *(quick)* sveglio(a) ♦ *vi* bruciare; ~**en up** *vi* farsi bello(a) ♦ *vt (people)* fare bello(a); *(things)* abbellire.

smash [smæʃ] *n (also:* ~-**up)** scontro, collisione *f*; *(~ hit)* successone *m* ♦ *vt* frantumare, fracassare; *(SPORT: record)* battere ♦ *vi* frantumarsi, andare in pezzi; ~**ing** *(inf) adj* favoloso(a), formidabile.

smattering ['smætərɪŋ] *n*: **a** ~ **of** un'infarinatura di.

smear [smɪə*] *n* macchia; *(MED)* striscio ♦ *vt* spalmare; *(make dirty)* sporcare; ~ **campaign** *n* campagna diffamatoria.

smell [smɛl] *(pt, pp* **smelt** *or* **smelled)** *n* odore *m*; *(sense)* olfatto, odorato ♦ *vt* sentire (l')odore di ♦ *vi (food etc)*: **to** ~ **(of)** avere odore (di); *(pej)* puzzare, avere un cattivo odore; ~**y** *adj* puzzolente.

smile [smaɪl] *n* sorriso ♦ *vi* sorridere.

smirk [smɜːk] *n* sorriso furbo; sorriso compiaciuto.

smithy ['smɪðɪ] *n* fucina.

smock [smɔk] *n* grembiule *m*, camice *m*; *(US)* tuta.

smog [smɔg] *n* smog *m*.

smoke [sməuk] *n* fumo ♦ *vt, vi* fumare; ~**d** *adj (bacon, glass)* affumicato(a); ~**r** *n (person)* fumatore/trice; *(RAIL)* carrozza per fumatori; ~ **screen** *n (MIL)* cortina fumogena *or* di fumo; *(fig)* copertura; **smoking** *n* fumo; "**no smoking**" *(sign)* "vietato fumare"; **smoky** *adj* fumoso(a); *(taste)* affumicato(a).

smolder ['sməuldə*] *(US) vi =* **smoulder**.

smooth [smuːð] *adj* liscio(a); *(sauce)* omogeneo(a); *(flavour, whisky)* amabile; *(movement)* regolare; *(person)* mellifluo(a) ♦ *vt (also:* ~ **out)** lisciare, spianare; *(: difficulties)*

appianare.

smother ['smʌðə*] *vt* soffocare.

smoulder ['sməuldə*] *(US* **smolder)** *vi* covare sotto la cenere.

smudge [smʌdʒ] *n* macchia; sbavatura ♦ *vt* imbrattare, sporcare.

smug [smʌg] *adj* soddisfatto(a), compiaciuto(a).

smuggle ['smʌgl] *vt* contrabbandare; ~**r** *n* contrabbandiere/a; **smuggling** *n* contrabbando.

smutty ['smʌtɪ] *adj (fig)* osceno(a), indecente.

snack [snæk] *n* spuntino; ~ **bar** *n* tavola calda, snack bar *m inv*.

snag [snæg] *n* intoppo, ostacolo imprevisto.

snail [sneɪl] *n* chiocciola.

snake [sneɪk] *n* serpente *m*.

snap [snæp] *n (sound)* schianto, colpo secco; *(photograph)* istantanea ♦ *adj* improvviso(a) ♦ *vt (far)* schioccare; *(break)* spezzare di netto ♦ *vi* spezzarsi con un rumore secco; *(fig: person)* parlare con tono secco; **to** ~ **shut** chiudersi di scatto; ~ **at** *vt fus (subj: dog)* cercare di mordere; ~ **off** *vt (break)* schiantare; ~ **up** *vt* afferrare; ~**py** *(inf) adj (answer, slogan)* d'effetto; **make it** ~**py!** *(hurry up)* sbrigati!, svelto!; ~**shot** *n* istantanea.

snare [snɛə*] *n* trappola.

snarl [snɑːl] *vi* ringhiare.

snatch [snætʃ] *n (small amount)* frammento ♦ *vt* strappare (con violenza); *(fig)* rubare.

sneak [sniːk] *(pt (US)* **snuck)** *vi*: **to** ~ **in/out** entrare/uscire di nascosto ♦ *n* spione/a; **to** ~ **up on sb** avvicinarsi quatto quatto a qn; ~**ers** *npl* scarpe *fpl* da ginnastica.

sneer [snɪə*] *vi* sogghignare; **to** ~ **at** farsi beffe di.

sneeze [sniːz] *n* starnuto ♦ *vi* starnutire.

sniff [snɪf] *n* fiutata, annusata ♦ *vi* tirare su col naso ♦ *vt* fiutare, annusare.

snigger ['snɪgə*] *vi* ridacchiare, ridere sotto i baffi.

snip [snɪp] *n* pezzetto; *(bargain)* (buon) affare *m*, occasione *f* ♦ *vt* tagliare.

sniper ['snaɪpə*] n (marksman) franco tiratore m, cecchino.

snippet ['snɪpɪt] n frammento.

snivelling ['snɪvlɪŋ] adj (whimpering) piagnucoloso(a).

snob [snɔb] n snob m/f inv; **~bery** n snobismo; **~bish** adj snob inv.

snooker ['snuːkə*] n tipo di gioco del biliardo.

snoop ['snuːp] vi: **to ~ about** curiosare.

snooty ['snuːtɪ] adj borioso(a), snob inv.

snooze [snuːz] n sonnellino, pisolino ♦ vi fare un sonnellino.

snore [snɔː*] vi russare.

snorkel ['snɔːkl] n (of swimmer) respiratore m a tubo.

snort [snɔːt] n sbuffo ♦ vi sbuffare.

snout [snaut] n muso.

snow [snəu] n neve f ♦ vi nevicare; **~ball** n palla di neve ♦ vi (fig) crescere a vista d'occhio; **~bound** adj bloccato(a) dalla neve; **~drift** n cumulo di neve (ammucchiato dal vento); **~drop** n bucaneve m inv; **~fall** n nevicata; **~flake** n fiocco di neve; **~man** n pupazzo di neve; **~plough** (US **~plow**) n spazzaneve m inv; **~shoe** n racchetta da neve; **~storm** n tormenta.

snub [snʌb] vt snobbare ♦ n offesa, affronto; **~-nosed** adj dal naso camuso.

snuff [snʌf] n tabacco da fiuto.

snug [snʌg] adj comodo(a); (room, house) accogliente, comodo(a).

snuggle ['snʌgl] vi: **to ~ up to sb** stringersi a qn.

---KEYWORD---

so [səu] adv 1 (thus, likewise) così; **if ~** se è così, quand'è così; **I didn't do it — you did ~!** non l'ho fatto io — sì che l'hai fatto!; **~ do I, ~ am I** etc anch'io; **it's 5 o'clock — ~ it is!** sono le 5 — davvero!; **I hope ~** lo spero; **I think ~** penso di sì; **~ far** finora, fin qui; (in past) fino ad allora
2 (in comparisons etc: to such a degree) così; **~ big (that)** così grande (che); **she's not ~ clever as her brother** lei non è (così) intelligente come suo fratello

3: **~ much** adj tanto(a) ♦ adv tanto; **I've got ~ much work/money** ho tanto lavoro/tanti soldi; **I love you ~ much** ti amo tanto; **~ many** tanti(e)
4 (phrases): **10 or ~** circa 10; **~ long!** (inf: goodbye) ciao!, ci vediamo!
♦ conj 1 (expressing purpose): **~ as to do** in modo or così da fare; **we hurried ~ as not to be late** ci affrettammo per non fare tardi; **~ (that)** affinché + sub, perché + sub
2 (expressing result): **he didn't arrive ~ I left** non è venuto così me ne sono andata; **~ you see, I could have gone** vedi, sarei potuto andare.

soak [səuk] vt inzuppare; (clothes) mettere a mollo ♦ vi (clothes etc) essere a mollo; **~ in** vi penetrare; **~ up** vt assorbire.

soap [səup] n sapone m; **~flakes** npl sapone m in scaglie; **~ opera** n opera f inv; **~ powder** n detersivo; **~y** adj insaponato(a).

soar [sɔː*] vi volare in alto; (price etc) salire alle stelle; (building) ergersi.

sob [sɔb] n singhiozzo ♦ vi singhiozzare.

sober ['səubə*] adj sobrio(a); (not drunk) non ubriaco(a); (moderate) moderato(a); **~ up** vt far passare la sbornia a ♦ vi farsi passare la sbornia.

so-called ['səu'kɔːld] adj cosiddetto(a).

soccer ['sɔkə*] n calcio.

sociable ['səuʃəbl] adj socievole.

social ['səuʃl] adj sociale ♦ n festa, serata; **~ club** n club m inv sociale; **~ism** n socialismo; **~ist** adj, n socialista m/f; **~ize** vi: **to ~ize (with)** socializzare (con); **~ security** n (BRIT) previdenza sociale; **~ work** n servizio sociale; **~ worker** n assistente m/f sociale.

society [sə'saɪətɪ] n società f inv; (club) società, associazione f; (also: high ~) alta società.

sociology [səusɪ'ɔlədʒɪ] n sociologia.

sock [sɔk] n calzino.

socket ['sɔkɪt] n cavità f inv; (of eye) orbita; (BRIT: ELEC: also: wall ~) presa di corrente.

sod [sɔd] *n* (*of earth*) zolla erbosa; (*BRIT*: *inf!*) bastardo/a (*!*).

soda ['səudə] *n* (*CHEM*) soda; (*also*: ~ *water*) acqua di seltz; (*US*: *also*: ~ *pop*) gassosa.

sodden ['sɔdn] *adj* fradicio(a).

sodium ['səudɪəm] *n* sodio.

sofa ['səufə] *n* sofà *m inv*.

soft [sɔft] *adj* (*not rough*) morbido(a); (*not hard*) soffice; (*not loud*) sommesso(a); (*not bright*) tenue; (*kind*) gentile; ~ **drink** *n* analcolico; **~en** ['sɔfn] *vt* ammorbidire; addolcire; attenuare ♦ *vi* ammorbidirsi; addolcirsi; attenuarsi; **~ly** *adv* dolcemente; morbidamente; **~ness** *n* dolcezza; morbidezza; ~ **spot** *n*: **to have a ~ spot for sb** avere un debole per qn.

software ['sɔftwɛə*] *n* (*COMPUT*) software *m*.

soggy ['sɔgɪ] *adj* inzuppato(a).

soil [sɔɪl] *n* terreno ♦ *vt* sporcare.

solace ['sɔlɪs] *n* consolazione *f*.

solar ['səulə*] *adj* solare.

sold [səuld] *pt*, *pp of* sell; ~ **out** *adj* (*COMM*) esaurito(a).

solder ['səuldə*] *vt* saldare ♦ *n* saldatura.

soldier ['səuldʒə*] *n* soldato, militare *m*.

sole [səul] *n* (*of foot*) pianta (del piede); (*of shoe*) suola; (*fish*: *pl inv*) sogliola ♦ *adj* solo(a), unico(a).

solemn ['sɔləm] *adj* solenne.

sole trader *n* (*COMM*) commerciante *m* in proprio.

solicit [sə'lɪsɪt] *vt* (*request*) richiedere, sollecitare ♦ *vi* (*prostitute*) adescare i passanti.

solicitor [sə'lɪsɪtə*] (*BRIT*) *n* (*for wills etc*) ≈ notaio; (*in court*) ≈ avvocato.

solid ['sɔlɪd] *adj* solido(a); (*not hollow*) pieno(a); (*meal*) sostanzioso(a) ♦ *n* solido.

solidarity [sɔlɪ'dærɪtɪ] *n* solidarietà.

solitaire [sɔlɪ'tɛə*] *n* (*games*, *gem*) solitario.

solitary ['sɔlɪtərɪ] *adj* solitario(a); ~ **confinement** *n* (*LAW*) isolamento.

solo ['səuləu] *n* assolo; **~ist** *n* solista *m/ f*.

soluble ['sɔljubl] *adj* solubile.

solution [sə'lu:ʃən] *n* soluzione *f*.

solve [sɔlv] *vt* risolvere.

solvent ['sɔlvənt] *adj* (*COMM*) solvibile ♦ *n* (*CHEM*) solvente *m*.

sombre ['sɔmbə*] (*US* **somber**) *adj* scuro(a); (*mood*, *person*) triste.

KEYWORD

some [sʌm] *adj* **1** (*a certain amount or number of*): ~ **tea/water/cream** del tè/ dell'acqua/della panna; ~ **children/ apples** dei bambini/delle mele

2 (*certain*: *in contrasts*) certo(a); ~ **people say that ...** alcuni dicono che ..., certa gente dice che ...

3 (*unspecified*) un(a) certo(a), qualche; ~ **woman was asking for you** una tale chiedeva di lei; ~ **day** un giorno; ~ **day next week** un giorno della prossima settimana

♦ *pron* **1** (*a certain number*) alcuni(e), certi(e); **I've got ~** (*books etc*) ne ho alcuni; ~ (*of them*) **have been sold** alcuni sono stati venduti

2 (*a certain amount*) un po'; **I've got ~** (*money*, *milk*) ne ho un po'; **I've read ~ of the book** ho letto parte del libro

♦ *adv*: ~ **10 people** circa 10 persone.

---

somebody ['sʌmbədɪ] *pron* = someone.

somehow ['sʌmhau] *adv* in un modo o nell'altro, in qualche modo; (*for some reason*) per qualche ragione.

someone ['sʌmwʌn] *pron* qualcuno.

someplace ['sʌmpleɪs] (*US*) *adv* = somewhere.

somersault ['sʌməsɔːlt] *n* capriola; salto mortale ♦ *vi* fare una capriola (*or* un salto mortale); (*car*) cappottare.

something ['sʌmθɪŋ] *pron* qualcosa, qualche cosa; ~ **nice** qualcosa di bello; ~ **to do** qualcosa da fare.

sometime ['sʌmtaɪm] *adv* (*in future*) una volta o l'altra; (*in past*): ~ **last month** durante il mese scorso.

sometimes ['sʌmtaɪmz] *adv* qualche volta.

somewhat ['sʌmwɔt] *adv* piuttosto.

somewhere ['sʌmwɛə*] *adv* in *or* da qualche parte.

son [sʌn] *n* figlio.

song [sɒŋ] *n* canzone *f*.

sonic ['sɒnɪk] *adj* (*boom*) sonico(a).

son-in-law *n* genero.

sonnet ['sɒnɪt] *n* sonetto.

sonny ['sʌnɪ] (*inf*) *n* ragazzo mio.

soon [su:n] *adv* presto, fra poco; (*early, a short time after*) presto; ~ **afterwards** poco dopo; *see also* **as**; ~**er** *adv* (*time*) prima; (*preference*): **I would** ~**er do** preferirei fare; ~**er or later** prima o poi.

soot [sut] *n* fuliggine *f*.

soothe [su:ð] *vt* calmare.

sophisticated [sə'fɪstɪkeɪtɪd] *adj* sofisticato(a); raffinato(a); complesso(a).

sophomore ['sɒfəmɔ:*] (*US*) *n* studente/ essa del secondo anno.

sopping ['sɒpɪŋ] *adj* (*also*: ~ *wet*) bagnato(a) fradicio(a).

soppy ['sɒpɪ] (*pej*) *adj* sentimentale.

soprano [sə'prɑ:nəu] *n* (*voice*) soprano *m*; (*singer*) soprano *m/f*.

sorcerer ['sɔ:sərə*] *n* stregone *m*, mago.

sore [sɔ:*] *adj* (*painful*) dolorante ♦ *n* piaga; ~**ly** *adv* (*tempted*) fortemente.

sorrow ['sɒrəu] *n* dolore *m*; ~**ful** *adj* doloroso(a).

sorry ['sɒrɪ] *adj* spiacente; (*condition, excuse*) misero(a); ~**!** scusa! (*or* scusi! *or* scusate!); **to feel** ~ **for sb** rincrescersi per qn.

sort [sɔ:t] *n* specie *f*, genere *m* ♦ *vt* (*also*: ~ *out*: *papers*) classificare; ordinare; (: *letters etc*) smistare; (: *problems*) risolvere; ~**ing office** *n* ufficio *m* smistamento *inv*.

SOS *n abbr* (= *save our souls*) S.O.S. *m inv*.

so-so *adv* così così.

sought [sɔ:t] *pt, pp of* **seek**.

soul [səul] *n* anima; ~**-destroying** *adj* demoralizzante; ~**ful** *adj* pieno(a) di sentimento.

sound [saund] *adj* (*healthy*) sano(a); (*safe, not damaged*) solido(a), in buono stato; (*reliable, not superficial*) solido(a); (*sensible*) giudizioso(a), di

buon senso ♦ *adv*: ~ **asleep** profondamente addormentato ♦ *n* suono; (*noise*) rumore *m*; (*GEO*) stretto ♦ *vt* (*alarm*) suonare ♦ *vi* suonare; (*fig*: *seem*) sembrare; **to** ~ **like** rassomigliare a; ~ **out** *vt* sondare; ~ **barrier** *n* muro del suono; ~ **effects** *npl* effetti sonori; ~**ly** *adv* (*sleep*) profondamente; (*beat*) duramente; ~**proof** *adj* insonorizzato(a), isolato(a) acusticamente; ~**track** *n* (*of film*) colonna sonora.

soup [su:p] *n* minestra; brodo; zuppa; **in the** ~ (*fig*) nei guai; ~ **plate** *n* piatto fondo; ~**spoon** *n* cucchiaio da minestra.

sour ['sauə*] *adj* aspro(a); (*fruit*) acerbo(a); (*milk*) acido(a); (*fig*) arcigno(a); acido(a); **it's** ~ **grapes** è soltanto invidia.

source [sɔ:s] *n* fonte *f*, sorgente *f*; (*fig*) fonte.

south [sauθ] *n* sud *m*, meridione *m*, mezzogiorno ♦ *adj* del sud, sud *inv*, meridionale ♦ *adv* verso sud; **S~ Africa** *n* Sudafrica *m*; **S~ African** *adj, n* sudafricano(a); **S~ America** *n* Sudamerica *m*, America del sud; **S~ American** *adj, n* sudamericano(a); ~**-east** *n* sud-est *m*; ~**erly** ['sʌðəlɪ] *adj* del sud; ~**ern** ['sʌðən] *adj* del sud, meridionale; esposto(a) a sud; **S~ Pole** *n* Polo Sud; ~**ward(s)** *adv* verso sud; ~**-west** *n* sud-ovest *m*.

souvenir [su:və'nɪə*] *n* ricordo, souvenir *m inv*.

sovereign ['sɒvrɪn] *adj, n* sovrano(a).

soviet ['səuvɪət] *adj* sovietico(a); **the S~ Union** l'Unione *f* Sovietica.

sow[1] [səu] (*pt* ~**ed**, *pp* **sown**) *vt* seminare.

sow[2] [sau] *n* scrofa.

sown [səun] *pp of* **sow**.

soy [sɔɪ] (*US*) *n* = **soya**.

soya ['sɔɪə] (*US* **soy**) *n*: ~ **bean** *n* seme *m* di soia; ~ **sauce** *n* salsa di soia.

spa [spɑ:] *n* (*resort*) stazione *f* termale; (*US*: *also*: *health* ~) centro di cure estetiche.

space [speɪs] *n* spazio; (*room*) posto;

spazio; (*length of time*) intervallo ♦ *cpd* spaziale ♦ *vt* (*also*: ~ **out**) distanziare; ~**craft** *n inv* veicolo spaziale; ~**man/woman** *n* astronauta *m/f*, cosmonauta *m/f*; ~**ship** *n* = ~**craft**; **spacing** *n* spaziatura.

spacious ['speɪʃəs] *adj* spazioso(a), ampio(a).

spade [speɪd] *n* (*tool*) vanga; pala; (*child's*) paletta; ~**s** *npl* (*CARDS*) picche *fpl*.

Spain [speɪn] *n* Spagna.

span [spæn] *n* (*of bird, plane*) apertura alare; (*of arch*) campata; (*in time*) periodo; durata ♦ *vt* attraversare; (*fig*) abbracciare.

Spaniard ['spænjəd] *n* spagnolo/a.

spaniel ['spænjəl] *n* spaniel *m inv*.

Spanish ['spænɪʃ] *adj* spagnolo(a) ♦ *n* (*LING*) spagnolo; **the ~** *npl* gli Spagnoli.

spank [spæŋk] *vt* sculacciare.

spanner ['spænə*] (*BRIT*) *n* chiave *f* inglese.

spar [spɑ:*] *n* asta, palo ♦ *vi* (*BOXING*) allenarsi.

spare [spɛə*] *adj* di riserva, di scorta; (*surplus*) in più, d'avanzo ♦ *n* (*part*) pezzo di ricambio ♦ *vt* (*do without*) fare a meno di; (*afford to give*) concedere; (*refrain from hurting, using*) risparmiare; **to ~** (*surplus*) d'avanzo; ~ **part** *n* pezzo di ricambio; ~ **time** *n* tempo libero; ~ **wheel** *n* (*AUT*) ruota di scorta.

sparing ['spɛərɪŋ] *adj*: **to be ~ with sth** risparmiare qc; ~**ly** *adv* moderatamente.

spark [spɑ:k] *n* scintilla; ~**(ing) plug** *n* candela.

sparkle ['spɑ:kl] *n* scintillio, sfavillio ♦ *vi* scintillare, sfavillare; **sparkling** *adj* scintillante, sfavillante; (*conversation, wine*) frizzante.

sparrow ['spærəu] *n* passero.

sparse [spɑ:s] *adj* sparso(a), rado(a).

spartan ['spɑ:tən] *adj* (*fig*) spartano(a).

spasm ['spæzəm] *n* (*MED*) spasmo; (*fig*) accesso, attacco; ~**odic** [spæz'mɔdɪk] *adj* spasmodico(a); (*fig*) intermittente.

spastic ['spæstɪk] *n* spastico/a.

spat [spæt] *pt, pp of* **spit**.

spate [speɪt] *n* (*fig*): ~ **of** diluvio *or* fiume *m* di.

spatter ['spætə*] *vt, vi* schizzare.

spawn [spɔ:n] *vi* deporre le uova ♦ *n* uova *fpl*.

speak [spi:k] (*pt* **spoke**, *pp* **spoken**) *vt* (*language*) parlare; (*truth*) dire ♦ *vi* parlare; **to ~ to sb/of** *or* **about sth** parlare a qn/di qc; ~ **up!** parla più forte!; ~**er** *n* (*in public*) oratore/trice; (*also*: *loud*~**er**) altoparlante *m*; (*POL*): **the S~er** il presidente della Camera dei Comuni (*BRIT*) *or* dei Rappresentanti (*US*).

spear [spɪə*] *n* lancia ♦ *vt* infilzare; ~**head** *vt* (*attack etc*) condurre.

spec [spɛk] (*inf*) *n*: **on ~** sperando bene.

special ['spɛʃl] *adj* speciale; ~**ist** *n* specialista *m/f*; ~**ity** [spɛʃɪ'ælɪtɪ] *n* specialità *f inv*; ~**ize** *vi*: **to ~ize (in)** specializzarsi (in); ~**ly** *adv* specialmente, particolarmente; ~**ty** *n* = **speciality**.

species ['spi:ʃi:z] *n inv* specie *f inv*.

specific [spə'sɪfɪk] *adj* specifico(a); preciso(a); ~**ally** *adv* esplicitamente; (*especially*) appositamente.

specimen ['spɛsɪmən] *n* esemplare *m*, modello; (*MED*) campione *m*.

speck [spɛk] *n* puntino, macchiolina; (*particle*) granello.

speckled ['spɛkld] *adj* macchiettato(a).

specs [spɛks] (*inf*) *npl* occhiali *mpl*

spectacle ['spɛktəkl] *n* spettacolo; ~**s** *npl* (*glasses*) occhiali *mpl*; **spectacular** [-'tækjulə*] *adj* spettacolare.

spectator [spɛk'teɪtə*] *n* spettatore *m*.

spectra ['spɛktrə] *npl of* **spectrum**.

spectre ['spɛktə*] (*US* **specter**) *n* spettro.

spectrum ['spɛktrəm] (*pl* **spectra**) *n* spettro.

speculation [spɛkju'leɪʃən] *n* speculazione *f*; congettura *fpl*.

speech [spi:tʃ] *n* (*faculty*) parola; (*talk, THEATRE*) discorso; (*manner of speaking*) parlata; ~**less** *adj* ammutolito(a), muto(a).

speed [spi:d] *n* velocità *f inv*; (*promptness*) prontezza; **at full** *or* **top**

~ a tutta velocità; ~ **up** *vi, vt* accelerare; ~**boat** *n* motoscafo; ~**ily** *adv* velocemente; prontamente; ~**ing** *n* (*AUT*) eccesso di velocità; ~ **limit** *n* limite *m* di velocità; ~**ometer** [spɪ'dɔmɪtə*] *n* tachimetro; ~**way** *n* (*sport*) corsa motociclistica (su pista); ~**y** *adj* veloce, rapido(a); pronto(a).

spell [spɛl] (*pt, pp* **spelt** (*BRIT*) *or* ~**ed**) *n* (*also: magic* ~) incantesimo; (*period of time*) (*breve*) periodo ♦ *vt* (*in writing*) scrivere (lettera per lettera); (*aloud*) dire lettera per lettera; (*fig*) significare; **to cast a** ~ **on sb** fare un incantesimo a qn; **he can't** ~ fa errori di ortografia; ~**bound** *adj* incantato(a); affascinato(a); ~**ing** *n* ortografia; **spelt** (*BRIT*) *pt, pp of* **spell**.

spend [spɛnd] (*pt, pp* **spent**) *vt* (*money*) spendere; (*time, life*) passare; ~**thrift** *n* spendaccione/a; **spent** *pt, pp of* **spend**.

sperm [spə:m] *n* sperma *m*.

spew [spju:] *vt* vomitare.

sphere [sfɪə*] *n* sfera.

spice [spaɪs] *n* spezia ♦ *vt* aromatizzare.

spick-and-span ['spɪkən'spæn] *adj* impeccabile.

spicy ['spaɪsɪ] *adj* piccante.

spider ['spaɪdə*] *n* ragno.

spike [spaɪk] *n* punta.

spill [spɪl] (*pt, pp* **spilt** *or* ~**ed**) *vt* versare, rovesciare ♦ *vi* versarsi, rovesciarsi; ~ **over** *vi* (*liquid*) versarsi; (*crowd*) riversarsi; **spilt** *pt, pp of* **spill**.

spin [spɪn] (*pt, pp* **spun**) *n* (*revolution of wheel*) rotazione *f*; (*AVIAT*) avvitamento; (*trip in car*) giretto ♦ *vt* (*wool etc*) filare; (*wheel*) far girare ♦ *vi* girare; ~ **out** *vt* far durare.

spinach ['spɪnɪtʃ] *n* spinacio; (*as food*) spinaci *mpl*.

spinal ['spaɪnl] *adj* spinale; ~ **cord** *n* midollo spinale.

spindly ['spɪndlɪ] *adj* lungo(a) e sottile, filiforme.

spin-dryer (*BRIT*) *n* centrifuga.

spine [spaɪn] *n* spina dorsale; (*thorn*) spina.

spinning ['spɪnɪŋ] *n* filatura; ~ **top** *n* trottola; ~ **wheel** *n* filatoio.

spin-off *n* (*product*) prodotto secondario.

spinster ['spɪnstə*] *n* nubile *f*; zitella.

spiral ['spaɪərl] *n* spirale *f* ♦ *vi* (*fig*) salire a spirale; ~ **staircase** *n* scala a chiocciola.

spire ['spaɪə*] *n* guglia.

spirit ['spɪrɪt] *n* spirito; (*ghost*) spirito, fantasma *m*; (*mood*) stato d'animo, umore *m*; (*courage*) coraggio; ~**s** *npl* (*drink*) alcolici *mpl*; **in good** ~**s** di buon umore; ~**ed** *adj* vivace, vigoroso(a); (*horse*) focoso(a); ~ **level** *n* livella a bolla (d'aria).

spiritual ['spɪrɪtjuəl] *adj* spirituale.

spit [spɪt] (*pt, pp* **spat**) *n* (*for roasting*) spiedo; (*saliva*) sputo; saliva ♦ *vi* sputare; (*fire, fat*) scoppiettare.

spite [spaɪt] *n* dispetto ♦ *vt* contrariare, far dispetto a; **in** ~ **of** nonostante, malgrado; ~**ful** *adj* dispettoso(a).

spittle ['spɪtl] *n* saliva; sputo.

splash [splæʃ] *n* spruzzo; (*sound*) splash *m* *inv*; (*of colour*) schizzo ♦ *vt* spruzzare ♦ *vi* (*also: ~ about*) sguazzare.

spleen [spli:n] *n* (*ANAT*) milza.

splendid ['splendɪd] *adj* splendido(a), magnifico(a).

splint [splɪnt] *n* (*MED*) stecca.

splinter ['splɪntə*] *n* scheggia ♦ *vi* scheggiarsi.

split [splɪt] (*pt, pp* **split**) *n* spaccatura; (*fig: division, quarrel*) scissione *f* ♦ *vt* spaccare; (*party*) dividere; (*work, profits*) spartire, ripartire ♦ *vi* (*divide*) dividersi; ~ **up** *vi* (*couple*) separarsi, rompere; (*meeting*) sciogliersi.

splutter ['splʌtə*] *vi* farfugliare; sputacchiare.

spoil [spɔɪl] (*pt, pp* **spoilt** *or* ~**ed**) *vt* (*damage*) rovinare, guastare; (*mar*) sciupare; (*child*) viziare; ~**s** *npl* bottino; ~**sport** *n* guastafeste *m/f inv*; **spoilt** *pt, pp of* **spoil**.

spoke [spəʊk] *pt of* **speak** ♦ *n* raggio.

spoken ['spəʊkn] *pp of* **speak**.

spokesman ['spəʊksmən] *n* portavoce *m inv*.

spokeswoman ['spəʊkswʊmən] *n* portavoce *f inv*.

sponge [spʌndʒ] *n* spugna; (*also*: ~ *cake*) pan *m* di spagna ♦ *vt* spugnare, pulire con una spugna ♦ *vi*: **to ~ off** *or* **on** scroccare a; **~ bag** (*BRIT*) *n* nécessaire *m inv*.

sponsor ['spɒnsə*] *n* (*RADIO, TV, SPORT etc*) sponsor *m inv*; (*POL: of bill*) promotore/trice ♦ *vt* sponsorizzare; (*bill*) presentare; **~ship** *n* sponsorizzazione *f*.

spontaneous [spɒn'teɪnɪəs] *adj* spontaneo(a).

spooky ['spuːkɪ] (*inf*) *adj* che fa accappanare la pelle.

spool [spuːl] *n* bobina.

spoon [spuːn] *n* cucchiaio; **~-feed** *vt* nutrire con il cucchiaio; (*fig*) imboccare; **~ful** *n* cucchiaiata.

sport [spɔːt] *n* sport *m inv*; (*person*) persona di spirito ♦ *vt* sfoggiare; **~ing** *adj* sportivo(a); **to give sb a ~ing chance** dare a qn una possibilità (di vincere); **~ jacket** (*US*) *n* = **~s jacket**; **~s car** *n* automobile *f* sportiva; **~s jacket** (*BRIT*) *n* giacca sportiva; **~sman** *n* sportivo; **~smanship** *n* spirito sportivo; **~swear** *n* abiti *mpl* sportivi; **~swoman** *n* sportiva; **~y** *adj* sportivo(a).

spot [spɒt] *n* punto; (*mark*) macchia; (*dot: on pattern*) pallino; (*pimple*) foruncolo; (*place*) posto; (*RADIO, TV*) spot *m inv*; (*small amount*): **a ~ of** un po' di ♦ *vt* (*notice*) individuare, distinguere; **on the ~** sul posto; (*immediately*) su due piedi; (*in difficulty*) nei guai; **~ check** *n* controllo senza preavviso; **~less** *adj* immacolato(a); **~light** *n* proiettore *m*; (*AUT*) faro ausiliario; **~ted** *adj* macchiato(a); a puntini, a pallini; **~ty** *adj* (*face*) foruncoloso(a).

spouse [spauz] *n* sposo/a.

spout [spaut] *n* (*of jug*) beccuccio; (*of pipe*) scarico ♦ *vi* zampillare.

sprain [spreɪn] *n* storta, distorsione *f* ♦ *vt*: **to ~ one's ankle** storcersi una caviglia.

sprang [spræŋ] *pt of* **spring**.

sprawl [sprɔːl] *vi* sdraiarsi (in modo scomposto); (*place*) estendersi (disordinatamente).

spray [spreɪ] *n* spruzzo; (*container*) nebulizzatore *m*, spray *m inv*; (*of flowers*) mazzetto ♦ *vt* spruzzare; (*crops*) irrorare.

spread [spred] (*pt, pp* **spread**) *n* diffusione *f*; (*distribution*) distribuzione *f*; (*CULIN*) pasta (da spalmare); (*inf: food*) banchetto ♦ *vt* (*cloth*) stendere, distendere; (*butter etc*) spalmare; (*disease, knowledge*) propagare, diffondere ♦ *vi* stendersi, distendersi; spalmarsi; propagarsi, diffondersi; **~ out** *vi* (*move apart*) separarsi; **~-eagled** ['spredɪːgld] *adj* a gambe e braccia aperte; **~sheet** *n* (*COMPUT*) foglio elettronico ad espansione.

spree [spriː] *n*: **to go on a ~** fare baldoria.

sprightly ['spraɪtlɪ] *adj* vivace.

spring [sprɪŋ] (*pt* **sprang**, *pp* **sprung**) *n* (*leap*) salto, balzo; (*coiled metal*) molla; (*season*) primavera; (*of water*) sorgente *f* ♦ *vi* saltare, balzare; **~ up** *vi* (*problem*) presentarsi; **~board** *n* trampolino; **~-clean(ing)** *n* grandi pulizie *fpl* di primavera; **~time** *n* primavera.

sprinkle ['sprɪŋkl] *vt* spruzzare; spargere; **to ~ water** *etc* **on**, **~ with water** *etc* spruzzare dell'acqua *etc* su; **~r** *n* (*for lawn*) irrigatore *m*; (*to put out fire*) sprinkler *m inv*.

sprint [sprɪnt] *n* scatto ♦ *vi* scattare; **~er** *n* (*SPORT*) velocista *m/f*.

sprout [spraut] *vi* germogliare; **~s** *npl* (*also: Brussels* **~s**) cavolini *mpl* di Bruxelles.

spruce [spruːs] *n inv* abete *m* rosso ♦ *adj* lindo(a); azzimato(a).

sprung [sprʌŋ] *pp of* **spring**.

spry [spraɪ] *adj* arzillo(a), sveglio(a).

spun [spʌn] *pt, pp of* **spin**.

spur [spəː*] *n* sperone *m*; (*fig*) sprone *m*, incentivo ♦ *vt* (*also*: ~ *on*) spronare; **on the ~ of the moment** lì per lì.

spurious ['spjuərıəs] *adj* falso(a).

spurn [spə:n] *vt* rifiutare con disprezzo, sdegnare.

spurt [spə:t] *n* (*of water*) getto; (*of energy*) scatto ♦ *vi* sgorgare.

spy [spaı] *n* spia ♦ *vi*: to ~ on spiare ♦ *vt* (*see*) scorgere; ~ing *n* spionaggio.

sq. *abbr* = **square**.

squabble ['skwɔbl] *vi* bisticciarsi.

squad [skwɔd] *n* (*MIL*) plotone *m*; (*POLICE*) squadra.

squadron ['skwɔdrn] *n* (*MIL*) squadrone *m*; (*AVIAT, NAUT*) squadriglia.

squalid ['skwɔlıd] *adj* squallido(a).

squall [skwɔ:l] *n* raffica; burrasca.

squalor ['skwɔlə*] *n* squallore *m*.

squander ['skwɔndə*] *vt* dissipare.

square [skwɛə*] *n* quadrato; (*in town*) piazza ♦ *adj* quadrato(a); (*inf*: *ideas, person*) di vecchio stampo ♦ *vt* (*arrange*) regolare; (*reconcile*) conciliare; **all** ~ pari; **a** ~ **meal** un pasto abbondante; **2 metres** ~ di 2 metri per 2; **1** ~ **metre** 1 metro quadrato; ~**ly** *adv* diritto; fermamente.

squash [skwɔʃ] *n* (*SPORT*) squash *m*; (*BRIT*: *drink*): **lemon/orange** ~ sciroppo di limone/arancia; (*US*) zucca; (*SPORT*) squash *m* ♦ *vt* schiacciare.

squat [skwɔt] *adj* tarchiato(a), tozzo(a) ♦ *vi* (*also*: ~ **down**) accovacciarsi; ~**ter** *n* occupante *m/f* abusivo(a).

squawk [skwɔ:k] *vi* emettere strida rauche.

squeak [skwi:k] *vi* squittire.

squeal [skwi:l] *vi* strillare.

squeamish ['skwi:mıʃ] *adj* schizzinoso(a); disgustato(a).

squeeze [skwi:z] *n* pressione *f*; (*also ECON*) stretta ♦ *vt* premere; (*hand, arm*) stringere; ~ **out** *vt* spremere.

squelch [skwɛltʃ] *vi* fare ciac; sguazzare.

squid [skwıd] *n* calamaro.

squiggle ['skwıgl] *n* ghirigoro.

squint [skwınt] *vi* essere strabico(a) ♦ *n*: **he has a** ~ è strabico.

squire ['skwaıə*] (*BRIT*) *n* proprietario terriero.

squirm [skwə:m] *vi* contorcersi.

squirrel ['skwırəl] *n* scoiattolo.

squirt [skwə:t] *vi* schizzare; zampillare ♦ *vt* spruzzare.

Sr *abbr* = **senior**.

St *abbr* = **saint**; **street**.

stab [stæb] *n* (*with knife etc*) pugnalata; (*of pain*) fitta; (*inf*: *try*): **to have a** ~ **at (doing) sth** provare (a fare) qc ♦ *vt* pugnalare.

stable ['steıbl] *n* (*for horses*) scuderia; (*for cattle*) stalla ♦ *adj* stabile.

stack [stæk] *n* catasta, pila ♦ *vt* accatastare, ammucchiare.

stadium ['steıdıəm] *n* stadio.

staff [stɑ:f] *n* (*work force*: *gen*) personale *m*; (: *BRIT*: *SCOL*) personale insegnante ♦ *vt* fornire di personale.

stag [stæg] *n* cervo.

stage [steıdʒ] *n* palcoscenico; (*profession*): **the** ~ il teatro, la scena; (*point*) punto; (*platform*) palco ♦ *vt* (*play*) allestire, mettere in scena; (*demonstration*) organizzare; **in** ~**s** per gradi; **a tappe**; ~**coach** *n* diligenza; ~ **manager** *n* direttore *m* di scena.

stagger ['stægə*] *vi* barcollare ♦ *vt* (*person*) sbalordire; (*hours, holidays*) scaglionare; ~**ing** *adj* (*amazing*) sbalorditivo(a).

stagnate [stæg'neıt] *vi* stagnare.

stag party *n* festa di addio al celibato.

staid [steıd] *adj* posato(a), serio(a).

stain [steın] *n* macchia; (*colouring*) colorante *m* ♦ *vt* macchiare; (*wood*) tingere; ~**ed glass window** *n* vetrata; ~**less** *adj* (*steel*) inossidabile; ~ **remover** *n* smacchiatore *m*.

stair [stɛə*] *n* (*step*) gradino; ~**s** *npl* (*flight of* ~**s**) scale *fpl*, scala; ~**case** *n* scale *fpl*, scala; ~**way** *n* = ~**case**.

stake [steık] *n* palo, piolo; (*COMM*) interesse *m*; (*BETTING*) puntata, scommessa ♦ *vt* (*bet*) scommettere; (*risk*) rischiare; **to be at** ~ essere in gioco.

stale [steıl] *adj* (*bread*) raffermo(a); (*food*) stantio(a); (*air*) viziato(a); (*beer*) svaporato(a); (*smell*) di chiuso.

stalemate ['steılmeıt] *n* stallo; (*fig*)

punto morto.

stalk [stɔ:k] *n* gambo, stelo ♦ *vt* inseguire; ~ **off** *vi* andarsene impettito(a).

stall [stɔ:l] *n* bancarella; (*in stable*) box *m inv* di stalla ♦ *vt* (*AUT*) far spegnere; (*fig*) bloccare ♦ *vi* (*AUT*) spegnersi, fermarsi; (*fig*) temporeggiare; ~s *npl* (*BRIT: in cinema, theatre*) platea.

stallion ['stæljən] *n* stallone *m*.

stalwart ['stɔ:lwət] *adj* fidato(a); risoluto(a).

stamina ['stæmɪnə] *n* vigore *m*, resistenza.

stammer ['stæmə*] *n* balbuzie *f* ♦ *vi* balbettare.

stamp [stæmp] *n* (*postage* ~) francobollo; (*implement*) timbro; (*mark, also fig*) marchio, impronta; (*on document*) bollo; timbro ♦ *vi* (*also:* ~ *one's foot*) battere il piede ♦ *vt* battere; (*letter*) affrancare; (*mark with a* ~) timbrare; ~ **album** *n* album *m inv* per francobolli; ~ **collecting** *n* filatelia.

stampede [stæm'pi:d] *n* fuggi fuggi *m inv*.

stance [stæns] *n* posizione *f*.

stand [stænd] (*pt, pp* **stood**) *n* (*position*) posizione *f*; (*for taxis*) posteggio; (*structure*) supporto, sostegno; (*at exhibition*) stand *m inv*; (*in shop*) banco; (*at market*) bancarella; (*booth*) chiosco; (*SPORT*) tribuna ♦ *vi* stare in piedi; (*rise*) alzarsi in piedi; (*be placed*) trovarsi ♦ *vt* (*place*) mettere, porre; (*tolerate, withstand*) resistere, sopportare; (*treat*) offrire; **to make a** ~ **prendere posizione; to** ~ **for parliament** (*BRIT*) presentarsi come candidato (per il parlamento); ~ **by** *vi* (*be ready*) tenersi pronto(a) ♦ *vt fus* (*opinion*) sostenere; ~ **down** *vi* (*withdraw*) ritirarsi; ~ **for** *vt fus* (*signify*) rappresentare, significare; (*tolerate*) sopportare, tollerare; ~ **in for** *vt fus* sostituire; ~ **out** *vi* (*be prominent*) spiccare; ~ **up** *vi* (*rise*) alzarsi in piedi; ~ **up for** *vt fus* difendere; ~ **up to** *vt fus* tener testa a, resistere a.

standard ['stændəd] *n* modello, standard *m inv*; (*level*) livello; (*flag*) stendardo ♦ *adj* (*size etc*) normale, standard *inv*; ~s *npl* (*morals*) principi *mpl*, valori *mpl*; ~ **lamp** (*BRIT*) *n* lampada a stelo; ~ **of living** *n* livello di vita.

stand-by *n* riserva, sostituto; **to be on** ~ (*gen*) tenersi pronto(a); (*doctor*) essere di guardia; ~ **ticket** *n* (*AVIAT*) biglietto senza garanzia.

stand-in *n* sostituto/a.

standing ['stændɪŋ] *adj* diritto(a), in piedi; (*permanent*) permanente ♦ *n* rango, condizione *f*, posizione *f*; **of many years'** ~ che esiste da molti anni; ~ **joke** *n* barzelletta; ~ **order** (*BRIT*) *n* (*at bank*) ordine *m* di pagamento (permanente); ~ **room** *n* posto all'impiedi.

standoffish [stænd'ɔfɪʃ] *adj* scostante, freddo(a).

standpoint ['stændpɔɪnt] *n* punto di vista.

standstill ['stændstɪl] *n*: **at a** ~ fermo(a); (*fig*) a un punto morto; **to come to a** ~ fermarsi; giungere a un punto morto.

stank [stæŋk] *pt of* **stink**.

staple ['steɪpl] *n* (*for papers*) graffetta ♦ *adj* (*food etc*) di base ♦ *vt* cucire; ~**r** *n* cucitrice *f*.

star [stɑ:*] *n* stella; (*celebrity*) divo/a ♦ *vi*: **to** ~ (**in**) essere il (*or* la) protagonista (di) ♦ *vt* (*CINEMA*) essere interpretato(a) da.

starboard ['stɑ:bəd] *n* dritta.

starch [stɑ:tʃ] *n* amido.

stardom ['stɑ:dəm] *n* celebrità.

stare [stɛə*] *n* sguardo fisso ♦ *vi*: **to** ~ **at** fissare.

starfish ['stɑ:fɪʃ] *n* stella di mare.

stark [stɑ:k] *adj* (*bleak*) desolato(a) ♦ *adv*: ~ **naked** completamente nudo(a).

starling ['stɑ:lɪŋ] *n* storno.

starry ['stɑ:rɪ] *adj* stellato(a); ~-**eyed** *adj* (*innocent*) ingenuo(a).

start [stɑ:t] *n* inizio; (*of race*) partenza; (*sudden movement*) sobbalzo; (*advantage*) vantaggio ♦ *vt* cominciare, iniziare; (*car*) mettere in moto ♦ *vi* cominciare; (*on journey*) partire, mettersi in viaggio; (*jump*) sobbalzare; **to ~ doing** *or* **to do sth** (in)cominciare a fare qc; **~ off** *vi* cominciare; (*leave*) partire; **~ up** *vi* cominciare; (*car*) avviarsi ♦ *vt* iniziare; (*car*) avviare; **~er** *n* (*AUT*) motorino d'avviamento; (*SPORT*: *official*) starter *m inv*; (*BRIT*: *CULIN*) primo piatto; **~ing point** *n* punto di partenza.

startle ['stɑːtl] *vt* far trasalire; **startling** *adj* sorprendente.

starvation [stɑːˈveɪʃən] *n* fame *f*, inedia.

starve [stɑːv] *vi* morire di fame; soffrire la fame ♦ *vt* far morire di fame, affamare.

state [steɪt] *n* stato ♦ *vt* dichiarare, affermare; annunciare; **the S~s** (*USA*) gli Stati Uniti; **to be in a ~** essere agitato(a); **~ly** *adj* maestoso(a), imponente; **~ment** *n* dichiarazione *f*; **~sman** *n* statista *m*.

static ['stætɪk] *n* (*RADIO*) scariche *fpl* ♦ *adj* statico(a).

station ['steɪʃən] *n* stazione *f* ♦ *vt* collocare, disporre.

stationary ['steɪʃənərɪ] *adj* fermo(a), immobile.

stationer ['steɪʃənə*] *n* cartolaio/a; **~'s (shop)** *n* cartoleria; **~y** *n* articoli *mpl* di cancelleria.

station master *n* (*RAIL*) capostazione *m*.

station wagon (*US*) *n* giardinetta.

statistic [stəˈtɪstɪk] *n* statistica; **~s** *n* (*science*) statistica.

statue ['stætjuː] *n* statua.

status ['steɪtəs] *n* posizione *f*, condizione *f* sociale; prestigio; stato; **~ symbol** *n* simbolo di prestigio.

statute ['stætjuːt] *n* legge *f*; **statutory** *adj* stabilito(a) dalla legge, statutario(a).

staunch [stɔːntʃ] *adj* fidato(a), leale.

stave [steɪv] *vt*: **to ~ off** (*attack*) respingere; (*threat*) evitare.

stay [steɪ] *n* (*period of time*) soggiorno, permanenza ♦ *vi* rimanere; (*reside*) alloggiare, stare; (*spend some time*) trattenersi, soggiornare; **to ~ put** non muoversi; **to ~ the night** fermarsi per la notte; **~ behind** *vi* restare indietro; **~ in** *vi* (*at home*) stare in casa; **~ on** *vi* restare, rimanere; **~ out** *vi* (*of house*) rimanere fuori (di casa); **~ up** *vi* (*at night*) rimanere alzato(a); **~ing power** *n* capacità di resistenza.

stead [stɛd] *n*: **in sb's ~** al posto di qn; **to stand sb in good ~** essere utile a qn.

steadfast ['stɛdfɑːst] *adj* fermo(a), risoluto(a).

steadily ['stɛdɪlɪ] *adv* (*firmly*) saldamente; (*constantly*) continuamente; (*fixedly*) fisso; (*walk*) con passo sicuro.

steady ['stɛdɪ] *adj* (*not wobbling*) fermo(a); (*regular*) costante; (*person, character*) serio(a); (: *calm*) calmo(a), tranquillo(a) ♦ *vt* stabilizzare; calmare.

steak [steɪk] *n* (*meat*) bistecca; (*fish*) trancia.

steal [stiːl] (*pt* **stole**, *pp* **stolen**) *vt* rubare ♦ *vi* rubare; (*move*) muoversi furtivamente.

stealth [stɛlθ] *n*: **by ~** furtivamente; **~y** *adj* furtivo(a).

steam [stiːm] *n* vapore *m* ♦ *vt* (*CULIN*) cuocere a vapore ♦ *vi* fumare; **~ engine** *n* macchina a vapore; (*RAIL*) locomotiva a vapore; **~er** *n* piroscafo, vapore *m*; **~roller** *n* rullo compressore; **~ship** *n* = **~er**; **~y** *adj* (*room*) pieno(a) di vapore; (*window*) appannato(a).

steel [stiːl] *n* acciaio ♦ *adj* di acciaio; **~works** *n* acciaieria.

steep [stiːp] *adj* ripido(a), scosceso(a); (*price*) eccessivo(a) ♦ *vt* inzuppare; (*washing*) mettere a mollo.

steeple ['stiːpl] *n* campanile *m*.

steer [stɪə*] *vt* guidare ♦ *vi* (*NAUT*: *person*) governare; (*car*) guidarsi; **~ing** *n* (*AUT*) sterzo; **~ing wheel** *n* volante *m*.

stem [stɛm] *n* (*of flower, plant*) stelo; (*of tree*) fusto; (*of glass*) gambo; (*of fruit, leaf*) picciolo ♦ *vt* contenere, arginare; **~ from** *vt fus* provenire da, derivare da.

stench [stɛntʃ] *n* puzzo, fetore *m*.

stencil ['stɛnsl] *n* (*of metal, cardboard*)

stampino, mascherina; (in typing) matrice f ♦ vt disegnare con stampino.

stenographer [stɛˈnɔgrəfə*] (US) n stenografo/a.

step [stɛp] n passo; (stair) gradino, scalino; (action) mossa, azione f ♦ vi: **to ~ forward/back** fare un passo avanti/indietro; **~s** npl (BRIT) = **stepladder**; **to be in/out of ~ (with)** stare/ non stare al passo (con); **~ down** vi (fig) ritirarsi; **~ on** vt fus calpestare; **~ up** vt aumentare; intensificare; **~brother** n fratellastro; **~daughter** n figliastra; **~father** n patrigno; **~ladder** n scala a libretto; **~mother** n matrigna; **~ping stone** n pietra di un guado; **~sister** n sorellastra; **~son** n figliastro.

stereo [ˈstɛrɪəu] n (system) sistema m stereofonico; (record player) stereo m inv ♦ adj (also: **~phonic**) stereofonico (a).

sterile [ˈstɛraɪl] adj sterile; **sterilize** [ˈstɛrɪlaɪz] vt sterilizzare.

sterling [ˈstəːlɪŋ] adj (gold, silver) di buona lega ♦ n (ECON) (lira) sterlina; **a pound ~** una lira sterlina.

stern [stəːn] adj severo(a) ♦ n (NAUT) poppa.

stew [stjuː] n stufato ♦ vt cuocere in umido.

steward [ˈstjuːəd] n (AVIAT, NAUT, RAIL) steward m inv; (in club etc) dispensiere m; **~ess** n assistente f di volo, hostess f inv.

stick [stɪk] n (pt, pp stuck) n bastone m; (of rhubarb, celery) gambo; (of dynamite) candelotto ♦ vt (glue) attaccare; (thrust): **to ~ sth into** conficcare or piantare or infiggere qc in; (inf: put) ficcare; (inf: tolerate) sopportare ♦ vi attaccarsi; (remain) restare, rimanere; **~ out** vi sporgere, spuntare; **~ up** vi sporgere, spuntare; **~ up for** vt fus difendere; **~er** n cartellino adesivo; **~ing plaster** n cerotto adesivo.

stickler [ˈstɪklə*] n: **to be a ~ for** essere pignolo(a) su, tenere molto a.

stick-up (inf) n rapina a mano armata.

sticky [ˈstɪkɪ] adj attaccaticcio(a), vi-

schioso(a); (label) adesivo(a); (fig: situation) difficile.

stiff [stɪf] adj rigido(a), duro(a); (muscle) legato(a), indolenzito(a); (difficult) difficile, arduo(a); (cold) freddo(a), formale; (strong) forte; (high: price) molto alto(a) ♦ adv: **bored ~** annoiato(a) a morte; **~en** vt irrigidire; rinforzare ♦ vi irrigidirsi; indurirsi; **~ neck** n torcicollo.

stifle [ˈstaɪfl] vt soffocare.

stigma [ˈstɪgmə] n (fig) stigma m.

stile [staɪl] n cavalcasiepe m; cavalcasteccato.

stiletto [stɪˈlɛtəu] (BRIT) n (also: **~ heel**) tacco a spillo.

still [stɪl] adj fermo(a); silenzioso(a) ♦ adv (up to this time, even) ancora; (nonetheless) tuttavia, ciò nonostante; **~born** adj nato(a) morto(a); **~ life** n natura morta.

stilt [stɪlt] n trampolo; (pile) palo.

stilted [ˈstɪltɪd] adj freddo(a), formale; artificiale.

stimulate [ˈstɪmjuleɪt] vt stimolare.

stimuli [ˈstɪmjulaɪ] npl of **stimulus**.

stimulus [ˈstɪmjuləs] (pl **stimuli**) n stimolo.

sting [stɪŋ] (pt, pp stung) n puntura; (organ) pungiglione m ♦ vt pungere.

stingy [ˈstɪndʒɪ] adj spilorcio(a), tirchio(a).

stink [stɪŋk] (pt stank, pp stunk) n fetore m, puzzo ♦ vi puzzare; **~ing** (inf) adj (fig): **a ~ing ...** uno schifo di ..., un(a) maledetto(a) ....

stint [stɪnt] n lavoro, compito ♦ vi: **to ~ on** lesinare su.

stir [stəː*] n agitazione f, clamore m ♦ vt mescolare; (fig) risvegliare ♦ vi muoversi; **~ up** vt provocare, suscitare.

stirrup [ˈstɪrəp] n staffa.

stitch [stɪtʃ] n (SEWING) punto; (KNITTING) maglia; (MED) punto (di sutura); (pain) fitta ♦ vt cucire, attaccare; suturare.

stoat [stəut] n ermellino.

stock [stɔk] n riserva, provvista; (COMM) giacenza, stock m inv; (AGR) bestiame *m*; (*CULIN*) brodo; (*descent*) stirpe *f*; (*FINANCE*) titoli *mpl*, azioni *fpl* ♦ *adj* (*fig: reply etc*) consueto(a); classico(a) ♦ *vt* (*have in stock*) avere, vendere; ~**s and shares** valori *mpl* di borsa; **in** ~ in magazzino; **out of** ~ esaurito(a); ~ **up** *vi*: **to** ~ **up** (**with**) fare provvista (di).

stockbroker ['stɔkbrəukə*] *n* agente *m* di cambio.

stock cube (*BRIT*) *n* dado.

stock exchange *n* Borsa (valori).

stocking ['stɔkɪŋ] *n* calza.

stockist ['stɔkɪst] (*BRIT*) *n* fornitore *m*.

stock: ~ **market** *n* Borsa, mercato finanziario; ~ **phrase** *n* cliché *m inv*; ~**pile** *n* riserva ♦ *vt* accumulare riserve di; ~**taking** (*BRIT*) *n* (*COMM*) inventario.

stocky ['stɔkɪ] *adj* tarchiato(a), tozzo(a).

stodgy ['stɔdʒɪ] *adj* pesante, indigesto(a).

stoke [stəuk] *vt* alimentare.

stole [stəul] *pt of* **steal** ♦ *n* stola.

stolen ['stəuln] *pp of* **steal**.

stolid ['stɔlɪd] *adj* impassibile.

stomach ['stʌmək] *n* stomaco; (*belly*) pancia ♦ *vt* sopportare, digerire; ~**ache** *n* mal *m* di stomaco.

stone [stəun] *n* pietra; (*pebble*) sasso, ciottolo; (*in fruit*) nocciolo; (*MED*) calcolo; (*BRIT: weight*) = 6.348 kg.; *14 libbre* ♦ *adj* di pietra ♦ *vt* lapidare; (*fruit*) togliere il nocciolo a; ~-**cold** *adj* gelido(a); ~-**deaf** *adj* sordo(a) come una campana; ~**work** *n* muratura; **stony** *adj* sassoso(a); (*fig*) di pietra.

stood [stud] *pt, pp of* **stand**.

stool [stu:l] *n* sgabello.

stoop [stu:p] *vi* (*also: have a* ~) avere una curvatura; (*also:* ~ *down*) chinarsi, curvarsi.

stop [stɔp] *n* arresto; (*stopping place*) fermata; (*in punctuation*) punto ♦ *vt* arrestare, fermare; (*break off*) interrompere; (*also: put a* ~ *to*) porre fine a ♦ *vi* fermarsi; (*rain, noise etc*) cessare, finire; **to** ~ **doing sth** cessare *or* finire di fare qc; **to** ~ **dead** fermarsi

di colpo; ~ **off** *vi* sostare brevemente; ~ **up** *vt* (*hole*) chiudere, turare; ~**gap** *n* tappabuchi *m inv*; ~**over** *n* breve sosta; (*AVIAT*) scalo.

stoppage ['stɔpɪdʒ] *n* arresto, fermata; (*of pay*) trattenuta; (*strike*) interruzione *f* del lavoro.

stopper ['stɔpə*] *n* tappo.

stop press *n* ultimissime *fpl*.

stopwatch ['stɔpwɔtʃ] *n* cronometro.

storage ['stɔ:rɪdʒ] *n* immagazzinamento; ~ **heater** *n* radiatore *m* elettrico che accumula calore.

store [stɔ:*] *n* provvista, riserva; (*depot*) deposito; (*BRIT: department* ~) grande magazzino; (*US: shop*) negozio ♦ *vt* immagazzinare; ~**s** *npl* (*provisions*) rifornimenti *mpl*, scorte *fpl*; **in** ~ di riserva; in serbo; ~ **up** *vt* conservare; mettere in serbo; ~**room** *n* dispensa.

storey ['stɔ:rɪ] (*US* **story**) *n* piano.

stork [stɔ:k] *n* cicogna.

storm [stɔ:m] *n* tempesta, temporale *m*, burrasca; uragano ♦ *vi* (*fig*) infuriarsi ♦ *vt* prendere d'assalto; ~**y** *adj* tempestoso(a), burrascoso(a).

story ['stɔ:rɪ] *n* storia; favola; racconto; (*US*) = **storey**; ~**book** *n* libro di racconti.

stout [staut] *adj* solido(a), robusto(a); (*friend, supporter*) tenace; (*fat*) corpulento(a), grasso(a) ♦ *n* birra scura.

stove [stəuv] *n* (*for cooking*) fornello; (: *small*) fornelletto; (*for heating*) stufa.

stow [stəu] *vt* (*also:* ~ *away*) mettere via; ~**away** *n* passeggero(a) clandestino(a).

straddle ['strædl] *vt* stare a cavalcioni di; (*fig*) essere a cavallo di.

straggle ['strægl] *vi* crescere (*or* estendersi) disordinatamente; trascinarsi; rimanere indietro; **straggly** *adj* (*hair*) in disordine.

straight [streɪt] *adj* dritto(a); (*frank*) onesto(a), franco(a); (*simple*) semplice ♦ *adv* diritto; (*drink*) liscio; **to put** *or* **get** ~ mettere in ordine, mettere ordine in; ~ **away,** ~ **off** (*at once*) immediatamente; ~**en** *vt* (*also:* ~**en**

out) raddrizzare; **~-faced** *adj* impassibile, imperturbabile; **~forward** *adj* semplice; onesto(a), franco(a).

strain [streɪn] *n* (*TECH*) sollecitazione *f*; (*physical*) sforzo; (*mental*) tensione *f*; (*MED*) strappo; distorsione *f*; (*streak, trace*) tendenza; elemento ♦ *vt* tendere; (*muscle*) sforzare; (*ankle*) storcere; (*resources*) pesare su; (*food*) colare; passare; **~s** *npl* (*MUS*) note *fpl*; **~ed** *adj* (*muscle*) stirato(a); (*laugh etc*) forzato(a); (*relations*) teso(a); **~er** *n* passino, colino.

strait [streɪt] *n* (*GEO*) stretto; **~s** *npl*: **to be in dire ~s** (*fig*) essere nei guai; **~jacket** *n* camicia di forza; **~-laced** *adj* bacchettone(a).

strand [strænd] *n* (*of thread*) filo; **~ed** *adj* nei guai; senza mezzi di trasporto.

strange [streɪndʒ] *adj* (*not known*) sconosciuto(a); (*odd*) strano(a), bizzarro(a); **~ly** *adv* stranamente; **~r** *n* sconosciuto/a; estraneo/a.

strangle ['stræŋgl] *vt* strangolare; **~hold** *n* (*fig*) stretta (mortale).

strap [stræp] *n* cinghia; (*of slip, dress*) spallina, bretella.

strapping ['stræpɪŋ] *adj* ben piantato(a).

strategic [strə'tiːdʒɪk] *adj* strategico(a).

strategy ['strætɪdʒɪ] *n* strategia.

straw [strɔː] *n* paglia; (*drinking ~*) cannuccia; **that's the last ~!** è la goccia che fa traboccare il vaso!

strawberry ['strɔːbərɪ] *n* fragola.

stray [streɪ] *adj* (*animal*) randagio(a); (*bullet*) vagante; (*scattered*) sparso(a) ♦ *vi* perdersi.

streak [striːk] *n* striscia; (*of hair*) mèche *f inv* ♦ *vt* striare, screziare ♦ *vi*: **to ~ past** passare come un fulmine.

stream [striːm] *n* ruscello; corrente *f*; (*of people, smoke etc*) fiume *m* ♦ *vt* (*SCOL*) dividere in livelli di rendimento ♦ *vi* scorrere; **to ~ in/out** entrare/uscire a fiotti.

streamer ['striːmə*] *n* (*of paper*) stella filante.

streamlined ['striːmlaɪnd] *adj* aerodinamico(a), affusolato(a).

street [striːt] *n* strada, via; **~car** (*US*) *n*

tram *m inv*; **~ lamp** *n* lampione *m*; **~ plan** *n* pianta (di una città); **~wise** (*inf*) *adj* esperto(a) dei bassifondi.

strength [streŋθ] *n* forza; **~en** *vt* rinforzare; fortificare; consolidare.

strenuous ['strɛnjuəs] *adj* vigoroso(a), energico(a); (*tiring*) duro(a), pesante.

stress [strɛs] *n* (*force, pressure*) pressione *f*; (*mental strain*) tensione *f*; (*accent*) accento ♦ *vt* insistere su, sottolineare; accentare.

stretch [strɛtʃ] *n* (*of sand etc*) distesa ♦ *vi* stirarsi; (*extend*): **to ~ to** *or* **as far as** estendersi fino a ♦ *vt* tendere, allungare; (*spread*) distendere; (*fig*) spingere (al massimo); **~ out** *vi* allungarsi, estendersi ♦ *vt* (*arm etc*) allungare, tendere; (*to spread*) distendere.

stretcher ['strɛtʃə*] *n* barella, lettiga.

strewn [struːn] *adj*: **~ with** cosparso(a) di.

stricken ['strɪkən] *adj* (*person*) provato(a); (*city, industry etc*) colpito(a); **~ with** (*disease etc*) colpito(a) da.

strict [strɪkt] *adj* (*severe*) rigido(a), severo(a); (*precise*) preciso(a), stretto(a).

stridden ['strɪdn] *pp of* **stride**.

stride [straɪd] (*pt* **strode**, *pp* **stridden**) *n* passo lungo ♦ *vi* camminare a grandi passi.

strife [straɪf] *n* conflitto; litigi *mpl*.

strike [straɪk] (*pt*, *pp* **struck**) *n* sciopero; (*of oil etc*) scoperta; (*attack*) attacco ♦ *vt* colpire; (*oil etc*) scoprire, trovare; (*bargain*) fare; (*fig*): **the thought** *or* **it ~s me that ...** mi viene in mente che ... ♦ *vi* scioperare; (*attack*) attaccare; (*clock*) suonare; **on ~** (*workers*) in sciopero; **to ~ a match** accendere un fiammifero; **~ down** *vt* (*fig*) atterrare; **~ up** *vt* (*MUS, conversation*) attaccare; **to ~ up a friendship with** fare amicizia con; **~r** *n* scioperante *m/f*; (*SPORT*) attaccante *m*; **striking** *adj* che colpisce.

string [strɪŋ] (*pt*, *pp* **strung**) *n* spago; (*row*) fila; sequenza; catena; (*MUS*) corda ♦ *vt*: **to ~ out** disporre di fianco;

to ~ **together** (*words, ideas*) mettere insieme; the ~s *npl* (*MUS*) gli archi; to **pull** ~s **for** sb (*fig*) raccomandare qn; ~ **bean** *n* fagiolino; ~**(ed) instrument** *n* (*MUS*) strumento a corda.

stringent ['strɪndʒənt] *adj* rigoroso(a).

strip [strɪp] *n* striscia ♦ *vt* spogliare; (*paint*) togliere; (*also*: ~ *down*: *machine*) smontare ♦ *vi* spogliarsi; ~ **cartoon** *n* fumetto.

stripe [straɪp] *n* striscia, riga; (*MIL, POLICE*) gallone *m*; ~**d** *adj* a strisce *or* righe.

strip lighting *n* illuminazione *f* al neon.

stripper ['strɪpə*] *n* spogliarellista *m/f*.

striptease ['strɪptiːz] *n* spogliarello.

strive [straɪv] (*pt* **strove**, *pp* **striven**) *vi*: to ~ to do sforzarsi di fare; **striven** ['strɪvn] *pp* of **strive**.

strode [strəud] *pt* of **stride**.

stroke [strəuk] *n* colpo; (*SWIMMING*) bracciata; (: *style*) stile *m*; (*MED*) colpo apoplettico ♦ *vt* accarezzare; **at a** ~ in un attimo.

stroll [strəul] *n* giretto, passeggiatina ♦ *vi* andare a spasso; ~**er** (*US*) *n* passeggino.

strong [strɒŋ] *adj* (*gen*) forte; (*sturdy*: *table, fabric etc*) robusto(a); **they are 50** ~ sono in 50; ~**box** *n* cassaforte *f*; ~**hold** *n* (*also fig*) roccaforte *f*; ~**ly** *adv* fortemente, con forza; energicamente; vivamente; ~**room** *n* camera di sicurezza.

strove [strəuv] *pt* of **strive**.

struck [strʌk] *pt, pp* of **strike**.

structural ['strʌktʃərəl] *adj* strutturale.

structure ['strʌktʃə*] *n* struttura; (*building*) costruzione *f*, fabbricato.

struggle ['strʌgl] *n* lotta ♦ *vi* lottare.

strum [strʌm] *vt* (*guitar*) strimpellare.

strung [strʌŋ] *pt, pp* of **string**.

strut [strʌt] *n* sostegno, supporto ♦ *vi* pavoneggiarsi.

stub [stʌb] *n* mozzicone *m*; (*of ticket etc*) matrice *f*, talloncino ♦ *vt*: to ~ **one's toe** urtare *or* sbattere il dito del piede; ~ **out** *vt* schiacciare.

stubble ['stʌbl] *n* stoppia; (*on chin*) barba ispida.

stubborn ['stʌbən] *adj* testardo(a), ostinato(a).

stuck [stʌk] *pt, pp* of **stick** ♦ *adj* (*jammed*) bloccato(a); ~**-up** *adj* presuntuoso(a).

stud [stʌd] *n* bottoncino; borchia; (*also*: ~ *earring*) orecchino a pressione; (*also*: ~ *farm*) scuderia, allevamento di cavalli; (*also*: ~ *horse*) stallone *m* ♦ *vt* (*fig*): ~**ded with** tempestato(a) di.

student ['stjuːdənt] *n* studente/essa ♦ *cpd* studentesco(a); universitario(a); degli studenti; ~ **driver** (*US*) *n* conducente *m/f* principiante.

studio ['stjuːdɪəu] *n* studio; ~ **flat** (*US* ~ **apartment**) *n* monolocale *m*.

studious ['stjuːdɪəs] *adj* studioso(a); (*studied*) studiato(a), voluto(a); ~**ly** *adv* (*carefully*) deliberatamente, di proposito.

study ['stʌdɪ] *n* studio ♦ *vt* studiare; esaminare ♦ *vi* studiare.

stuff [stʌf] *n* roba; (*substance*) sostanza, materiale *m* ♦ *vt* imbottire; (*CULIN*) farcire; (*dead animal*) impagliare; (*inf*: *push*) ficcare; ~**ing** *n* imbottitura; (*CULIN*) ripieno; ~**y** *adj* (*room*) mal ventilato(a), senz'aria; (*ideas*) antiquato(a).

stumble ['stʌmbl] *vi* inciampare; to ~ **across** (*fig*) imbattersi in; **stumbling block** *n* ostacolo, scoglio.

stump [stʌmp] *n* ceppo; (*of limb*) moncone *m* ♦ *vt*: to be ~**ed** essere sconcertato(a).

stun [stʌn] *vt* stordire; (*amaze*) sbalordire.

stung [stʌŋ] *pt, pp* of **sting**.

stunk [stʌŋk] *pp* of **stink**.

stunning ['stʌnɪŋ] *adj* sbalorditivo(a); (*girl etc*) fantastico(a).

stunt [stʌnt] *n* bravata; trucco pubblicitario; ~**ed** *adj* stentato(a), rachitico(a); ~**man** *n* cascatore *m*.

stupefy ['stjuːpɪfaɪ] *vt* stordire; intontire; (*fig*) stupire.

stupendous [stjuː'pɛndəs] *adj* stupendo(a), meraviglioso(a).

stupid ['stjuːpɪd] *adj* stupido(a); ~**ity**

[-'pɪdɪti] n stupidità f inv, stupidaggine f.

stupor ['stju:pə*] n torpore m.

sturdy ['stə:dɪ] adj robusto(a), vigoroso(a); solido(a).

stutter ['stʌtə*] n balbuzie f ♦ vi balbettare.

sty [staɪ] n (of pigs) porcile m.

stye [staɪ] n (MED) orzaiolo.

style [staɪl] n stile m; (distinction) eleganza, classe f; **stylish** adj elegante.

stylus ['staɪləs] n (of record player) puntina.

suave [swɑ:v] adj untuoso(a).

sub... [sʌb] prefix sub..., sotto...; **~conscious** adj subcosciente ♦ n subcosciente m; **~contract** vt subappaltare.

subdue [səb'dju:] vt sottomettere, soggiogare; **~d** adj pacato(a); (light) attenuato(a).

subject [n 'sʌbdʒɪkt, vb səb'dʒɛkt] n soggetto; (citizen etc) cittadino/a; (SCOL) materia ♦ vt: **to ~ to** sottomettere a; esporre a; **to be ~ to** (law) essere sottomesso(a) a; (disease) essere soggetto(a) a; **~ive** [-'dʒɛktɪv] adj soggettivo(a); **~ matter** n argomento; contenuto.

subjunctive [səb'dʒʌŋktɪv] n congiuntivo.

sublet [sʌb'lɛt] vt subaffittare.

submachine gun ['sʌbmə'ʃi:n-] n mitra m inv.

submarine [sʌbmə'ri:n] n sommergibile m.

submerge [səb'mə:dʒ] vt sommergere; immergere ♦ vi immergersi.

submission [səb'mɪʃən] n sottomissione f; (claim) richiesta.

submissive [səb'mɪsɪv] adj remissivo(a).

submit [səb'mɪt] vt sottomettere ♦ vi sottomettersi.

subnormal [sʌb'nɔ:məl] adj subnormale.

subordinate [sə'bɔ:dɪnət] adj, n subordinato(a).

subpoena [səb'pi:nə] n (LAW) citazione f, mandato di comparizione.

subscribe [səb'skraɪb] vi contribuire; **to ~ to** (opinion) approvare, condividere; (fund) sottoscrivere a; (newspaper) abbonarsi a; essere abbonato(a) a; **~r** n (to periodical, telephone) abbonato/a.

subscription [səb'skrɪpʃən] n sottoscrizione f; abbonamento.

subsequent ['sʌbsɪkwənt] adj successivo(a), seguente; conseguente; **~ly** adv in seguito, successivamente.

subside [səb'saɪd] vi cedere, abbassarsi; (flood) decrescere; (wind) calmarsi; **~nce** [-'saɪdns] n cedimento, abbassamento.

subsidiary [səb'sɪdɪərɪ] adj sussidiario(a); accessorio(a) ♦ n (also: **~ company**) filiale f.

subsidize ['sʌbsɪdaɪz] vt sovvenzionare.

subsidy ['sʌbsɪdɪ] n sovvenzione f.

subsistence [səb'sɪstəns] n esistenza; mezzi mpl di sostentamento; **~ allowance** n indennità f inv di trasferta.

substance ['sʌbstəns] n sostanza.

substantial [səb'stænʃl] adj solido(a); (amount, progress etc) notevole; (meal) sostanzioso(a).

substantiate [səb'stænʃɪeɪt] vt comprovare.

substitute ['sʌbstɪtju:t] n (person) sostituto/a; (thing) succedaneo, surrogato ♦ vt: **to ~ sth/sb for** sostituire qc/qn a.

subterfuge ['sʌbtəfju:dʒ] n sotterfugio.

subterranean [sʌbtə'reɪnɪən] adj sotterraneo(a).

subtitle ['sʌbtaɪtl] n (CINEMA) sottotitolo.

subtle ['sʌtl] adj sottile; **~ty** n sottigliezza.

subtotal [sʌb'təutl] n somma parziale.

subtract [səb'trækt] vt sottrarre; **~ion** [-'trækʃən] n sottrazione f.

suburb ['sʌbə:b] n sobborgo; **the ~s** la periferia; **~an** [sə'bə:bən] adj suburbano(a); **~ia** n periferia, sobborghi mpl.

subversive [səb'və:sɪv] adj sovversivo(a).

subway ['sʌbweɪ] n (US: underground) metropolitana; (BRIT: underpass) sottopassaggio.

succeed [sək'si:d] vi riuscire; avere successo ♦ vt succedere a; **to ~ in**

doing riuscire a fare; ~**ing** adj (following) successivo(a).

success [sək'sɛs] n successo; ~**ful** adj (venture) coronato(a) da successo, riuscito(a); **to be** ~**ful (in doing)** riuscire (a fare); ~**fully** adv con successo.

succession [sək'sɛʃən] n successione f.

successive [sək'sɛsɪv] adj successivo(a); consecutivo(a).

succumb [sə'kʌm] vi soccombere.

such [sʌtʃ] adj tale; (of that kind): ~ **a book** un tale libro, un libro del genere; ~ **books** tali libri, libri del genere; (so much): ~ **courage** tanto coraggio ♦ adv talmente, così; ~ **a long trip** un viaggio così lungo; ~ **a lot of** talmente o così tanto(a); ~ **as** (like) come; **as** ~ come or in quanto tale; ~-**and**-~ adj tale (after noun).

suck [sʌk] vt succhiare; (breast, bottle) poppare; ~**er** n (ZOOL, TECH) ventosa; (inf) gonzo/a, babbeo/a.

suction ['sʌkʃən] n succhiamento; (TECH) aspirazione f.

sudden ['sʌdn] adj improvviso(a); **all of a** ~ improvvisamente, all'improvviso; ~**ly** adv bruscamente, improvvisamente, di colpo.

suds [sʌdz] npl schiuma (di sapone).

sue [su:] vt citare in giudizio.

suede [sweɪd] n pelle f scamosciata.

suet ['suɪt] n grasso di rognone.

suffer ['sʌfə*] vt soffrire, patire; (bear) sopportare, tollerare ♦ vi soffrire; **to ~ from** soffrire di; ~**er** n malato/a; ~**ing** n sofferenza.

suffice [sə'faɪs] vi essere sufficiente, bastare.

sufficient [sə'fɪʃənt] adj sufficiente; ~ **money** abbastanza soldi; ~**ly** adv sufficientemente, abbastanza.

suffocate ['sʌfəkeɪt] vi (have difficulty breathing) soffocare; (die through lack of air) asfissiare.

suffused [sə'fju:zd] adj: ~ **with** (colour) tinto(a) di; **the room was** ~ **with light** nella stanza c'era una luce soffusa.

sugar ['ʃugə*] n zucchero ♦ vt zuccherare; ~ **beet** n barbabietola da zucchero; ~ **cane** n canna da zucchero.

suggest [sə'dʒɛst] vt proporre, suggerire; indicare; ~**ion** [-'dʒɛstʃən] n suggerimento, proposta; indicazione f; ~**ive** (pej) adj indecente.

suicide ['suɪsaɪd] n (person) suicida m/f; (act) suicidio; see also **commit**.

suit [su:t] n (man's) vestito; (woman's) completo, tailleur m inv; (LAW) causa; (CARDS) seme m, colore m ♦ vt andar bene a or per; essere adatto(a) a or per; (adapt): **to ~ sth to** adattare qc a; **well** ~**ed** ben assortito(a); ~**able** adj adatto(a); appropriato(a); ~**ably** adv (dress) in modo adatto; (impressed) favorevolmente.

suitcase ['su:tkeɪs] n valigia.

suite [swi:t] n (of rooms) appartamento; (MUS) suite f inv; (furniture): **bedroom/dining room** ~ arredo or mobilia per la camera da letto/sala da pranzo.

suitor ['su:tə*] n corteggiatore m, spasimante m.

sulfur ['sʌlfə*] (US) n = **sulphur**.

sulk [sʌlk] vi fare il broncio; ~**y** adj imbronciato(a).

sullen ['sʌlən] adj scontroso(a); cupo(a).

sulphur ['sʌlfə*] (US **sulfur**) n zolfo.

sultana [sʌl'tɑ:nə] n (fruit) uva (secca) sultanina.

sultry ['sʌltrɪ] adj afoso(a).

sum [sʌm] n somma; (SCOL etc) addizione f; ~ **up** vt, vi riassumere.

summarize ['sʌməraɪz] vt riassumere, riepilogare.

summary ['sʌmərɪ] n riassunto.

summer ['sʌmə*] n estate f ♦ cpd d'estate, estivo(a); ~ **holidays** npl vacanze fpl estive; ~**house** n (in garden) padiglione m; ~**time** n (season) estate f; ~ **time** n (by clock) ora legale (estiva).

summit ['sʌmɪt] n cima, sommità; (POL) vertice m.

summon ['sʌmən] vt chiamare, convocare; ~ **up** vt raccogliere, fare appello a; ~**s** n ordine m di comparizione ♦ vt citare.

sump [sʌmp] n (BRIT) (AUT) coppa

dell'olio.

sumptuous ['sʌmptjuəs] adj sontuoso(a).

sun [sʌn] n sole m; ~**bathe** vi prendere un bagno di sole; ~**burn** n (painful) scottatura; ~**burnt** adj abbronzato(a); (painfully) scottato(a).

Sunday ['sʌndɪ] n domenica; ~ **school** n ≈ scuola di catechismo.

sundial ['sʌndaɪəl] n meridiana.

sundown ['sʌndaun] n tramonto.

sundry ['sʌndrɪ] adj vari(e), diversi(e); **all and** ~ tutti quanti; **sundries** npl articoli diversi, cose diverse.

sunflower ['sʌnflauə*] n girasole m.

sung [sʌŋ] pp of **sing**.

sunglasses ['sʌŋglɑːsɪz] npl occhiali mpl da sole.

sunk [sʌŋk] pp of **sink**.

sun: ~**light** n (luce f del) sole m; ~**lit** adj soleggiato(a); ~**ny** adj assolato(a), soleggiato(a); (fig) allegro(a), felice; ~**rise** n levata del sole, alba; ~ **roof** n (AUT) tetto apribile; ~**set** n tramonto; ~**shade** n parasole m; ~**shine** n (luce f del) sole m; ~**stroke** n insolazione f, colpo di sole; ~**tan** n abbronzatura; ~**tan lotion** n lozione f solare; ~**tan oil** n olio solare.

super ['suːpə*] (inf) adj fantastico(a).

superannuation [suːpərænjuˈeɪʃən] n contributi mpl pensionistici; pensione f.

superb [suːˈpəːb] adj magnifico(a).

supercilious [suːpəˈsɪlɪəs] adj sprezzante, sdegnoso(a).

superficial [suːpəˈfɪʃəl] adj superficiale.

superhuman [suːpəˈhjuːmən] adj sovrumano(a).

superimpose ['suːpərɪmˈpəuz] vt sovrapporre.

superintendent [suːpərɪnˈtɛndənt] n direttore/trice; (POLICE) ≈ commissario (capo).

superior [suˈpɪərɪə*] adj, n superiore m/f; ~**ity** [-ˈɔrɪtɪ] n superiorità.

superlative [suˈpəːlətɪv] adj superlativo(a), supremo(a) ♦ n (LING) superlativo.

superman ['suːpəmæn] n superuomo.

supermarket ['suːpəmɑːkɪt] n supermercato.

supernatural [suːpəˈnætʃərəl] adj soprannaturale ♦ n soprannaturale m.

superpower ['suːpəpauə*] n (POL) superpotenza.

supersede [suːpəˈsiːd] vt sostituire, soppiantare.

superstitious [suːpəˈstɪʃəs] adj superstizioso(a).

supertanker ['suːpətæŋkə*] n superpetroliera.

supervise ['suːpəvaɪz] vt (person etc) sorvegliare; (organization) soprintendere a; **supervision** [-ˈvɪʒən] n sorveglianza; supervisione f; **supervisor** n sorvegliante m/f; soprintendente m/f; (in shop) capocommesso/a.

supine ['suːpaɪn] adj supino(a).

supper ['sʌpə*] n cena.

supplant [səˈplɑːnt] vt (person, thing) soppiantare.

supple ['sʌpl] adj flessibile; agile.

supplement [n 'sʌplɪmənt, vb sʌplɪˈmɛnt] n supplemento ♦ vt completare, integrare; ~**ary** [-ˈmɛntərɪ] adj supplementare.

supplier [səˈplaɪə*] n fornitore m.

supply [səˈplaɪ] vt (provide) fornire; (equip): **to** ~ (**with**) approvvigionare (di); attrezzare (con) ♦ n riserva, provvista; (supplying) approvvigionamento; (TECH) alimentazione f; **supplies** npl (food) viveri mpl; (MIL) sussistenza; ~ **teacher** (BRIT) n supplente m/f.

support [səˈpɔːt] n (moral, financial etc) sostegno, appoggio; (TECH) supporto ♦ vt sostenere; (financially) mantenere; (uphold) sostenere, difendere; ~**er** n (POL etc) sostenitore/trice, fautore/trice; (SPORT) tifoso/a.

suppose [səˈpəuz] vt supporre, immaginare; **to be** ~**d to do** essere tenuto(a) a fare; ~**dly** [səˈpəuzɪdlɪ] adv presumibilmente; **supposing** conj se, ammesso che + sub.

suppress [səˈprɛs] vt reprimere; sopprimere; occultare.

supreme [suˈpriːm] adj supremo(a).

surcharge ['səːtʃɑːdʒ] n supplemento.

sure [ʃuə*] *adj* sicuro(a); (*definite, convinced*) sicuro(a), certo(a); ~! (*of course*) senz'altro!, certo!; ~ **enough** infatti; **to make** ~ **of** sth/that assicurarsi di qc/che; ~**-footed** *adj* dal passo sicuro; ~**ly** *adv* sicuramente; certamente.

surety ['ʃuərətɪ] *n* garanzia.

surf [sə:f] *n* (*waves*) cavalloni *mpl*; (*foam*) spuma.

surface ['sə:fɪs] *n* superficie *f* ♦ *vt* (*road*) asfaltare ♦ *vi* risalire alla superficie; (*fig: news, feeling*) venire a galla; ~ **mail** *n* posta ordinaria.

surfboard ['sə:fbɔ:d] *n* tavola per surfing.

surfeit ['sə:fɪt] *n*: **a** ~ **of** un eccesso di; un'indigestione di.

surfing ['sə:fɪŋ] *n* surfing *m*.

surge [sə:dʒ] *n* (*strong movement*) ondata; (*of feeling*) impeto ♦ *vi* gonfiarsi; (*people*) riversarsi.

surgeon ['sə:dʒən] *n* chirurgo.

surgery ['sə:dʒərɪ] *n* chirurgia; (*BRIT: room*) studio *or* gabinetto medico, ambulatorio; (: *also:* ~ **hours**) orario delle visite *or* di consultazione; **to undergo** ~ subire un intervento chirurgico.

surgical ['sə:dʒɪkl] *adj* chirurgico(a); ~ **spirit** (*BRIT*) *n* alcool *m* denaturato.

surly ['sə:lɪ] *adj* scontroso(a), burbero(a).

surname ['sə:neɪm] *n* cognome *m*.

surpass [sə:'pɑ:s] *vt* superare.

surplus ['sə:pləs] *n* eccedenza; (*ECON*) surplus *m inv* ♦ *adj* eccedente, d'avanzo.

surprise [sə'praɪz] *n* sorpresa; (*astonishment*) stupore *m* ♦ *vt* sorprendere; stupire; **surprising** *adj* sorprendente, stupefacente; **surprisingly** *adv* (*easy, helpful*) sorprendentemente.

surrender [sə'rɛndə*] *n* resa, capitolazione *f* ♦ *vi* arrendersi.

surreptitious [sʌrəp'tɪʃəs] *adj* furtivo(a).

surrogate ['sʌrəgɪt] *n* surrogato; ~ **mother** *n* madre *f* provetta.

surround [sə'raund] *vt* circondare; (*MIL*

etc) accerchiare; ~**ing** *adj* circostante; ~**ings** *npl* dintorni *mpl*; (*fig*) ambiente *m*.

surveillance [sə:'veɪləns] *n* sorveglianza, controllo.

survey [*n* 'sə:veɪ, *vb* sə:'veɪ] *n* quadro generale; (*study*) esame *m*; (*in housebuying etc*) perizia; (*of land*) rilevamento, rilievo topografico ♦ *vt* osservare; esaminare; valutare; rilevare; ~**or** *n* perito; geometra *m*; (*of land*) agrimensore *m*.

survival [sə'vaɪvl] *n* sopravvivenza; (*relic*) reliquia, vestigio.

survive [sə'vaɪv] *vi* sopravvivere ♦ *vt* sopravvivere a; **survivor** *n* superstite *m/f*, sopravvissuto/a.

susceptible [sə'sɛptəbl] *adj*: ~ (**to**) sensibile (a); (*disease*) predisposto(a) (a).

suspect [*adj, n* 'sʌspɛkt, *vb* səs'pɛkt] *adj* sospetto(a) ♦ *n* persona sospetta ♦ *vt* sospettare; (*think likely*) supporre; (*doubt*) dubitare.

suspend [səs'pɛnd] *vt* sospendere; ~**ed sentence** *n* condanna con la condizionale; ~**er belt** *n* reggicalze *m inv*; ~**ers** *npl* (*BRIT*) giarrettiere *fpl*; (*US*) bretelle *fpl*.

suspense [səs'pɛns] *n* apprensione *f*; (*in film etc*) suspense *m*; **to keep sb in** ~ tenere qn in sospeso.

suspension [səs'pɛnʃən] *n* (*gen AUT*) sospensione *f*; (*of driving licence*) ritiro temporaneo; ~ **bridge** *n* ponte *m* sospeso.

suspicion [səs'pɪʃən] *n* sospetto.

suspicious [səs'pɪʃəs] *adj* (*suspecting*) sospettoso(a); (*causing suspicion*) sospetto(a).

sustain [səs'teɪn] *vt* sostenere; sopportare; (*LAW: charge*) confermare; (*suffer*) subire; ~**ed** *adj* (*effort*) prolungato(a).

sustenance ['sʌstɪnəns] *n* nutrimento; mezzi *mpl* di sostentamento.

swab [swɔb] *n* (*MED*) tampone *m*.

swagger ['swægə*] *vi* pavoneggiarsi.

swallow ['swɔləu] *n* (*bird*) rondine *f* ♦ *vt* inghiottire; (*fig: story*) bere; ~ **up**

vt inghiottire.

swam [swæm] *pt of* swim.

swamp [swɔmp] *n* palude *f* ♦ *vt* sommergere.

swan [swɔn] *n* cigno.

swap [swɔp] *vt*: **to ~ (for)** scambiare (con).

swarm [swɔ:m] *n* sciame *m* ♦ *vi* (*bees*) sciamare; (*people*) brulicare; (*place*): **to be ~ing with** brulicare di.

swarthy ['swɔ:ðɪ] *adj* di carnagione scura.

swastika ['swɔstɪkə] *n* croce *f* uncinata, svastica.

swat [swɔt] *vt* schiacciare.

sway [sweɪ] *vi* (*tree*) ondeggiare; (*person*) barcollare ♦ *vt* (*influence*) influenzare, dominare.

swear [sweə*] (*pt* swore, *pp* sworn) *vi* (*curse*) bestemmiare, imprecare ♦ *vt* (*promise*) giurare; **~word** *n* parolaccia.

sweat [swet] *n* sudore *m*, traspirazione *f* ♦ *vi* sudare.

sweater ['swetə*] *n* maglione *m*.

sweatshirt ['swetʃə:t] *n* felpa.

sweaty ['swetɪ] *adj* sudato(a); bagnato(a) di sudore.

Swede [swi:d] *n* svedese *m/f*.

swede [swi:d] (*BRIT*) *n* rapa svedese.

Sweden ['swi:dn] *n* Svezia.

Swedish ['swi:dɪʃ] *adj* svedese ♦ *n* (*LING*) svedese *m*.

sweep [swi:p] (*pt*, *pp* swept) *n* spazzata; (*also*: *chimney* ~) spazzacamino ♦ *vt* spazzare, scopare; (*current*) spazzare ♦ *vi* (*hand*) muoversi con gesto ampio; (*wind*) infuriare; ~ **away** *vt* spazzare via; trascinare via; ~ **past** *vi* sfrecciare accanto; passare accanto maestosamente; ~ **up** *vt*, *vi* spazzare; **~ing** *adj* (*gesture*) ampio(a); circolare; **a ~ing statement** un'affermazione generica.

sweet [swi:t] *n* (*BRIT*: *pudding*) dolce *m*; (*candy*) caramella ♦ *adj* dolce; (*fresh*) fresco(a); (*fig*) piacevole; delicato(a), grazioso(a); gentile; **~corn** *n* granturco dolce; **~en** *vt* addolcire;

zuccherare; **~heart** *n* innamorato/a; **~ness** *n* sapore *m* dolce; dolcezza; **~ pea** *n* pisello odoroso.

swell [swel] (*pt* ~ed, *pp* swollen, ~ed) *n* (*of sea*) mare *m* lungo ♦ *adj* (*US*: *inf*: *excellent*) favoloso(a) ♦ *vt* gonfiare, ingrossare; aumentare ♦ *vi* gonfiarsi, ingrossarsi; (*sound*) crescere; (*also*: ~ *up*) gonfiarsi; **~ing** *n* (*MED*) tumefazione *f*, gonfiore *m*.

sweltering ['sweltərɪŋ] *adj* soffocante.

swept [swept] *pt*, *pp of* sweep.

swerve [swə:v] *vi* deviare; (*driver*) sterzare; (*boxer*) scartare.

swift [swɪft] *n* (*bird*) rondone *m* ♦ *adj* rapido(a), veloce.

swig [swɪg] (*inf*) *n* (*drink*) sorsata.

swill [swɪl] *vt* (*also*: ~ *out*, ~ *down*) risciacquare.

swim [swɪm] (*pt* swam, *pp* swum) *n*: **to go for a ~** andare a fare una nuotata ♦ *vi* nuotare; (*SPORT*) fare del nuoto; (*head*, *room*) girare ♦ *vt* (*river*, *channel*) attraversare *or* percorrere a nuoto; (*length*) nuotare; **~mer** *n* nuotatore/trice; **~ming** *n* nuoto; **~ming cap** *n* cuffia; **~ming costume** (*BRIT*) *n* costume *m* da bagno; **~ming pool** *n* piscina; **~ming trunks** *npl* costume *m* da bagno (da uomo); **~suit** *n* costume *m* da bagno.

swindle ['swɪndl] *n* truffa ♦ *vt* truffare.

swine [swaɪn] (*inf!*) *n inv* porco (!).

swing [swɪŋ] (*pt*, *pp* swung) *n* altalena; (*movement*) oscillazione *f*; (*MUS*) ritmo; swing *m* ♦ *vt* dondolare, far oscillare; (*also*: ~ *round*) far girare ♦ *vi* oscillare, dondolare; (*also*: ~ *round*: *object*) roteare; (: *person*) girarsi, voltarsi; **to be in full ~** (*activity*) essere in piena attività; (*party etc*) essere nel pieno; **~ door** (*US* **~ing door**) *n* porta battente.

swingeing ['swɪndʒɪŋ] *adj* (*BRIT*: *defeat*) violento(a); (: *cuts*) enorme.

swipe [swaɪp] *vt* (*hit*) colpire con forza; dare uno schiaffo a; (*inf*: *steal*) sgraffignare.

swirl [swə:l] *vi* turbinare, far mulinello.

swish [swɪʃ] *vi* sibilare.

Swiss [swɪs] *adj*, *n inv* svizzero(a).

switch [swɪtʃ] *n* (*for light, radio etc*) interruttore *m*; (*change*) cambiamento ♦ *vt* (*change*) cambiare; scambiare; ~ **off** *vt* spegnere; ~ **on** *vt* accendere; (*engine, machine*) mettere in moto, avviare; ~**board** *n* (*TEL*) centralino.

Switzerland ['swɪtsələnd] *n* Svizzera.

swivel ['swɪvl] *vi* (*also*: ~ *round*) girare.

swollen ['swəulən] *pp of* **swell**.

swoon [swu:n] *vi* svenire.

swoop [swu:p] *n* incursione *f* ♦ *vi* (*also*: ~ *down*) scendere in picchiata, piombare.

swop [swɔp] *n*, *vt* = **swap**.

sword [sɔ:d] *n* spada; ~**fish** *n* pesce *m* spada *inv*.

swore [swɔ:*] *pt of* **swear**.

sworn [swɔ:n] *pp of* **swear** ♦ *adj* giurato(a).

swot [swɔt] *vi* sgobbare.

swum [swʌm] *pp of* **swim**.

swung [swʌŋ] *pt*, *pp of* **swing**.

syllable ['sɪləbl] *n* sillaba.

syllabus ['sɪləbəs] *n* programma *m*.

symbol ['sɪmbl] *n* simbolo.

symmetry ['sɪmɪtrɪ] *n* simmetria.

sympathetic [sɪmpə'θɛtɪk] *adj* (*showing pity*) compassionevole; (*kind*) comprensivo(a); ~ **towards** ben disposto(a) verso.

sympathize ['sɪmpəθaɪz] *vi*: **to** ~ **with** (*person*) compatire; partecipare al dolore di; (*cause*) simpatizzare per; ~**r** *n* (*POL*) simpatizzante *m/f*.

sympathy ['sɪmpəθɪ] *n* compassione *f*; **sympathies** *npl* (*support, tendencies*) simpatie *fpl*; **in** ~ **with** (*strike*) per solidarietà con; **with our deepest** ~ con le nostre più sincere condoglianze.

symphony ['sɪmfənɪ] *n* sinfonia.

symptom ['sɪmptəm] *n* sintomo; indizio.

synagogue ['sɪnəgɔg] *n* sinagoga.

syndicate ['sɪndɪkɪt] *n* sindacato.

synonym ['sɪnənɪm] *n* sinonimo.

synopses [sɪ'nɔpsi:z] *npl of* **synopsis**.

synopsis [sɪ'nɔpsɪs] (*pl* **synopses**) *n* sommario, sinossi *f inv*.

syntax ['sɪntæks] *n* sintassi *f inv*.

syntheses ['sɪnθəsi:z] *npl of* **synthesis**.

synthesis ['sɪnθəsɪs] (*pl* **syntheses**) *n* sintesi *f inv*.

synthetic [sɪn'θɛtɪk] *adj* sintetico(a).

syphilis ['sɪfɪlɪs] *n* sifilide *f*.

syphon ['saɪfən] *n*, *vb* = **siphon**.

Syria ['sɪrɪə] *n* Siria.

syringe [sɪ'rɪndʒ] *n* siringa.

syrup ['sɪrəp] *n* sciroppo; (*also*: *golden* ~) melassa raffinata.

system ['sɪstəm] *n* sistema *m*; (*order*) metodo; (*ANAT*) organismo; ~**atic** [-'mætɪk] *adj* sistematico(a); metodico(a); ~ **disk** *n* (*COMPUT*) disco del sistema; ~**s analyst** *n* analista *m* di sistemi.

T

ta [tɑ:] (*BRIT*: *inf*) *excl* grazie!

tab [tæb] *n* (*loop on coat etc*) laccetto; (*label*) etichetta; **to keep** ~**s on** (*fig*) tenere d'occhio.

tabby ['tæbɪ] *n* (*also*: ~ *cat*) (gatto) soriano, gatto tigrato.

table ['teɪbl] *n* tavolo, tavola; (*MATH, CHEM etc*) tavola ♦ *vt* (*BRIT*: *motion etc*) presentare; **to lay** *or* **set the** ~ apparecchiare *or* preparare la tavola; ~**cloth** *n* tovaglia; ~ **of contents** *n* indice *m*; ~ **d'hôte** [ta:bl'dəut] *adj* (*meal*) a prezzo fisso; ~ **lamp** *n* lampada da tavolo; ~**mat** *n* sottopiatto; ~**spoon** *n* cucchiaio da tavola; (*also*: ~**spoonful**: *as measurement*) cucchiaiata.

tablet ['tæblɪt] *n* (*MED*) compressa; (*of stone*) targa.

table: ~ **tennis** *n* tennis *m* da tavolo, ping-pong *m* ®; ~ **wine** *n* vino da tavola.

tabulate ['tæbjuleɪt] *vt* (*data, figures*) tabulare, disporre in tabelle.

tacit ['tæsɪt] *adj* tacito(a).

tack [tæk] *n* (*nail*) bulletta; (*fig*) approccio ♦ *vt* imbullettare; imbastire ♦ *vi* bordeggiare.

tackle ['tækl] *n* attrezzatura, equipaggiamento; (*for lifting*) paranco;

(*FOOTBALL*) contrasto; (*RUGBY*) placcaggio ♦ *vt* (*difficulty*) affrontare; (*FOOTBALL*) contrastare; (*RUGBY*) placcare.

tacky ['tækɪ] *adj* appiccicaticcio(a); (*pej*) scadente.

tact [tækt] *n* tatto; **~ful** *adj* delicato(a), discreto(a).

tactical ['tæktɪkl] *adj* tattico(a).

tactics ['tæktɪks] *n, npl* tattica.

tactless ['tæktlɪs] *adj* che manca di tatto.

tadpole ['tædpəul] *n* girino.

taffy ['tæfɪ] (*US*) *n* caramella *f* mou *inv*.

tag [tæg] *n* etichetta; **~ along** *vi* seguire.

tail [teɪl] *n* coda; (*of shirt*) falda ♦ *vt* (*follow*) seguire, pedinare; **~ away** *vi* = **~ off**; **~ off** *vi* (*in size, quality etc*) diminuire gradatamente; **~back** (*BRIT*) *n* (*AUT*) ingorgo; **~ end** *n* (*of train, procession etc*) coda; (*of meeting etc*) fine *f*; **~gate** *n* (*AUT*) portellone *m* posteriore.

tailor ['teɪlə*] *n* sarto; **~ing** *n* (*cut*) stile *m*; (*craft*) sartoria; **~-made** *adj* (*also fig*) fatto(a) su misura.

tailwind ['teɪlwɪnd] *n* vento di coda.

tainted ['teɪntɪd] *adj* (*food*) guasto(a); (*water, air*) infetto(a); (*fig*) corrotto(a).

take [teɪk] (*pt* **took**, *pp* **taken**) *vt* prendere; (*gain: prize*) ottenere, vincere; (*require: effort, courage*) occorrere, volerci; (*tolerate*) accettare, sopportare; (*hold: passengers etc*) contenere; (*accompany*) accompagnare; (*bring, carry*) portare; (*exam*) sostenere, presentarsi a; **to ~ a photo/a shower** fare una fotografia/una doccia; **I ~ it that** suppongo che; **~ after** *vt fus* assomigliare a; **~ apart** *vt* smontare; **~ away** *vt* portare via; togliere; **~ back** *vt* (*return*) restituire; riportare; (*one's words*) ritirare; **~ down** *vt* (*building*) demolire; (*letter etc*) scrivere; **~ in** *vt* (*deceive*) imbrogliare, abbindolare; (*understand*) capire; (*include*) comprendere, includere; (*lodger*) prendere, ospitare; **~**

off *vi* (*AVIAT*) decollare; (*go away*) andarsene ♦ *vt* (*remove*) togliere; **~ on** *vt* (*work*) accettare, intraprendere; (*employee*) assumere; (*opponent*) sfidare, affrontare; **~ out** *vt* portare fuori; (*remove*) togliere; (*licence*) prendere, ottenere; **to ~ sth out of sth** (*drawer, pocket etc*) tirare qc fuori da qc; estrarre qc da qc; **~ over** *vt* (*business*) rilevare ♦ *vi*: **to ~ over from** sb prendere le consegne *or* il controllo da qn; **~ to** *vt fus* (*person*) prendere in simpatia; (*activity*) prendere gusto a; **~ up** *vt* (*dress*) accorciare; (*occupy: time, space*) occupare; (*engage in: hobby etc*) mettersi a; **to ~ sb up on sth** accettare qc da qn; **~away** (*BRIT*) *n* (*shop etc*) ≈ rosticceria; (*food*) pasto per asporto; **~off** *n* (*AVIAT*) decollo; **~out** (*US*) *n* = **~away**; **~over** *n* (*COMM*) assorbimento.

takings ['teɪkɪŋz] *npl* (*COMM*) incasso.

talc [tælk] *n* (*also*: **~um powder**) talco.

tale [teɪl] *n* racconto, storia; **to tell ~s** (*fig: to teacher, parent etc*) fare la spia.

talent ['tælnt] *n* talento; **~ed** *adj* di talento.

talk [tɔːk] *n* discorso; (*gossip*) chiacchiere *fpl*; (*conversation*) conversazione *f*; (*interview*) discussione *f* ♦ *vi* parlare; **~s** *npl* (*POL etc*) colloqui *mpl*; **to ~ about** parlare di; **to ~ sb out of/into doing** dissuadere qn da/convincere qn a fare; **to ~ shop** parlare di lavoro *or* di affari; **~ over** *vt* discutere; **~ative** *adj* loquace, ciarliero(a); **~ show** *n* conversazione *f* televisiva, talk show *m inv*.

tall [tɔːl] *adj* alto(a); **to be 6 feet ~** ≈ essere alto 1 metro e 80; **~ story** *n* panzana, frottola.

tally ['tælɪ] *n* conto, conteggio ♦ *vi*: **to ~ (with)** corrispondere (a).

talon ['tælən] *n* artiglio.

tambourine [tæmbə'riːn] *n* tamburello.

tame [teɪm] *adj* addomesticato(a); (*fig: story, style*) insipido(a), scialbo(a).

tamper ['tæmpə*] *vi*: **to ~ with** manomettere.

tampon ['tæmpɔn] *n* tampone *m*.

tan [tæn] *n* (*also*: sun~) abbronzatura ♦ *vi* abbronzarsi ♦ *adj* (*colour*) marrone rossiccio *inv*.

tang [tæŋ] *n* odore *m* penetrante; sapore *m* piccante.

tangent ['tændʒənt] *n* (MATH) tangente *f*; **to go off at a ~** (*fig*) partire per la tangente.

tangerine [tændʒə'ri:n] *n* mandarino.

tangle ['tæŋgl] *n* groviglio; **to get into a ~** aggrovigliarsi; (*fig*) combinare un pasticcio.

tank [tæŋk] *n* serbatoio; (*for fish*) acquario; (MIL) carro armato.

tanker ['tæŋkə*] *n* (*ship*) nave *f* cisterna *inv*; (*truck*) autobotte *f*, autocisterna.

tanned [tænd] *adj* abbronzato(a).

tantalizing ['tæntəlaizɪŋ] *adj* allettante.

tantamount ['tæntəmaunt] *adj*: **~ to** equivalente a.

tantrum ['tæntrəm] *n* accesso di collera.

tap [tæp] *n* (*on sink etc*) rubinetto; (*gentle blow*) colpetto ♦ *vt* dare un colpetto a; (*resources*) sfruttare, utilizzare; (*telephone*) mettere sotto controllo; **on ~** (*fig: resources*) a disposizione; **~ dancing** *n* tip tap *m*.

tape [teɪp] *n* nastro; (*also: magnetic ~*) nastro (magnetico); (*sticky ~*) nastro adesivo ♦ *vt* (*record*) registrare (su nastro); (*stick*) attaccare con nastro adesivo; **~ deck** *n* piastra; **~ measure** *n* metro a nastro.

taper ['teɪpə*] *n* candelina ♦ *vi* assottigliarsi.

tape recorder *n* registratore *m* (a nastro).

tapestry ['tæpɪstrɪ] *n* arazzo; tappezzeria.

tar [tɑ:*] *n* catrame *m*.

target ['tɑ:gɪt] *n* bersaglio; (*fig: objective*) obiettivo.

tariff ['tærɪf] *n* tariffa.

tarmac ['tɑ:mæk] *n* (BRIT: *on road*) macadam *m* al catrame; (AVIAT) pista di decollo.

tarnish ['tɑ:nɪʃ] *vt* offuscare, annerire; (*fig*) macchiare.

tarpaulin [tɑ:'pɔ:lɪn] *n* tela incatramata.

tarragon ['tærəgən] *n* dragoncello.

tart [tɑ:t] *n* (CULIN) crostata; (BRIT: *inf: pej: woman*) sgualdrina ♦ *adj* (*flavour*) aspro(a), agro(a); **~ up** (*inf*) *vt* agghindare.

tartan ['tɑ:tn] *n* tartan *m inv*.

tartar ['tɑ:tə*] *n* (*on teeth*) tartaro; **~(e) sauce** *n* salsa tartara.

task [tɑ:sk] *n* compito; **to take to ~** rimproverare; **~ force** *n* (MIL, POLICE) unità operativa.

tassel ['tæsl] *n* fiocco.

taste [teɪst] *n* gusto; (*flavour*) sapore *m*, gusto; (*sample*) assaggio; (*fig: glimpse, idea*) idea ♦ *vt* gustare; (*sample*) assaggiare ♦ *vi*: **~ of** or **like** (*fish etc*) sapere or avere sapore di; **you can ~ the garlic (in it)** (ci) si sente il sapore dell'aglio; **in good/bad ~** di buon/cattivo gusto; **~ful** *adj* di buon gusto; **~less** *adj* (*food*) insipido(a); (*remark*) di cattivo gusto; **tasty** *adj* saporito(a), gustoso(a).

tatters ['tætəz] *npl*: **in ~** a brandelli.

tattoo [tə'tu:] *n* tatuaggio; (*spectacle*) parata militare ♦ *vt* tatuare.

tatty ['tætɪ] *adj* malridotto(a).

taught [tɔ:t] *pt, pp of* **teach**.

taunt [tɔ:nt] *n* scherno ♦ *vt* schernire.

Taurus ['tɔ:rəs] *n* Toro.

taut [tɔ:t] *adj* teso(a).

tax [tæks] *n* (*on goods*) imposta; (*on services*) tassa; (*on income*) imposte *fpl*, tasse *fpl* ♦ *vt* tassare; (*fig: strain: patience etc*) mettere alla prova; **~able** *adj* (*income*) imponibile; **~ation** [-'seɪʃən] *n* tassazione *f*; tasse *fpl*, imposte *fpl*; **~ avoidance** *n* elusione *f* fiscale; **~ disc** (BRIT) *n* (AUT) ≈ bollo; **~ evasion** *n* evasione *f* fiscale; **~-free** *adj* esente da imposte.

taxi ['tæksɪ] *n* taxi *m inv* ♦ *vi* (AVIAT) rullare; **~ driver** *n* tassista *m/f*; **~ rank** (BRIT) *n* = **~ stand**; **~ stand** *n* posteggio dei taxi.

tax: ~ payer *n* contribuente *m/f*; **~ relief** *n* agevolazioni *fpl* fiscali; **~ return** *n* dichiarazione *f* dei redditi.

TB *n abbr* = **tuberculosis**.

tea [ti:] *n* tè *m inv*; (BRIT: *snack: for*

children) merenda; **high** ~ (*BRIT*) cena leggera (*presa nel tardo pomeriggio*); ~ **bag** n bustina di tè; ~ **break** (*BRIT*) n intervallo per il tè.

teach [tiːtʃ] (*pt, pp* **taught**) vt: **to ~ sb sth, ~ sth to sb** insegnare qc a qn ♦ vi insegnare; ~**er** n insegnante m/f; (*in secondary school*) professore/essa; (*in primary school*) maestro/a; ~**ing** n insegnamento.

tea cosy n copriteiera m inv.

teacup [ˈtiːkʌp] n tazza da tè.

teak [tiːk] n teak m.

tea leaves npl foglie fpl di tè.

team [tiːm] n squadra; (*of animals*) tiro; ~**work** n lavoro di squadra.

teapot [ˈtiːpɔt] n teiera.

tear[1] [tɛə*] (*pt* **tore**, *pp* **torn**) n strappo ♦ vt strappare ♦ vi strapparsi; ~ **along** vi (*rush*) correre all'impazzata; ~ **up** vt (*sheet of paper etc*) strappare.

tear[2] [tɪə*] n lacrima; **in** ~**s** in lacrime; ~**ful** adj piangente, lacrimoso(a); ~ **gas** n gas m lacrimogeno.

tearoom [ˈtiːruːm] n sala da tè.

tease [tiːz] vt canzonare; (*unkindly*) tormentare.

tea set n servizio da tè.

teaspoon [ˈtiːspuːn] n cucchiaino da tè; (*also:* ~**ful:** *as measurement*) cucchiaino.

teat [tiːt] n capezzolo.

teatime [ˈtiːtaɪm] n ora del tè.

tea towel (*BRIT*) n strofinaccio (per i piatti).

technical [ˈtɛknɪkl] adj tecnico(a); ~ **college** (*BRIT*) n ≈ istituto tecnico; ~**ity** [-ˈkælɪtɪ] n tecnicità; (*detail*) dettaglio tecnico; (*legal*) cavillo.

technician [tɛkˈnɪʃən] n tecnico/a.

technique [tɛkˈniːk] n tecnica.

technological [tɛknəˈlɔdʒɪkl] adj tecnologico(a).

technology [tɛkˈnɔlədʒɪ] n tecnologia.

teddy (bear) [ˈtɛdɪ-] n orsacchiotto.

tedious [ˈtiːdɪəs] adj noioso(a), tedioso(a).

tee [tiː] n (*GOLF*) tee m inv.

teem [tiːm] vi: **to ~ with** brulicare di; **it is** ~**ing (with rain)** piove a dirotto.

teenage [ˈtiːneɪdʒ] adj (*fashions etc*) per giovani, per adolescenti; ~**r** n adolescente m/f.

teens [tiːnz] npl: **to be in one's** ~ essere adolescente.

tee-shirt [ˈtiːʃəːt] n = T-shirt.

teeter [ˈtiːtə*] vi barcollare, vacillare.

teeth [tiːθ] npl of **tooth**.

teethe [tiːð] vi mettere i denti.

teething ring [ˈtiːðɪŋ-] n dentaruolo.

teething troubles [ˈtiːðɪŋ-] npl (*fig*) difficoltà fpl iniziali.

teetotal [ˈtiːˈtəutl] adj astemio(a).

telegram [ˈtɛlɪɡræm] n telegramma m.

telegraph [ˈtɛlɪɡrɑːf] n telegrafo.

telepathy [təˈlɛpəθɪ] n telepatia.

telephone [ˈtɛlɪfəun] n telefono ♦ vt (*person*) telefonare a; (*message*) comunicare per telefono; ~ **booth** (*BRIT* ~ **box**) n cabina telefonica; ~ **call** n telefonata; ~ **directory** n elenco telefonico; ~ **number** n numero di telefono; **telephonist** [təˈlɛfənɪst] (*BRIT*) n telefonista m/f.

telescope [ˈtɛlɪskəup] n telescopio.

television [ˈtɛlɪvɪʒən] n televisione f; **on** ~ alla televisione; ~ **set** n televisore m.

telex [ˈtɛlɛks] n telex m inv ♦ vt trasmettere per telex; **to ~ sb** contattare qn via telex.

tell [tɛl] (*pt, pp* **told**) vt dire; (*relate: story*) raccontare; (*distinguish*): **to ~ sth from** distinguere qc da ♦ vi (*talk*): **to ~ (of)** parlare (di); (*have effect*) farsi sentire, avere effetto; **to ~ sb to do** dire a qn di fare; ~ **off** vt rimproverare, sgridare; ~**er** n (*in bank*) cassiere/a; ~**ing** adj (*remark, detail*) rivelatore(trice); ~**tale** adj (*sign*) rivelatore(trice).

telly [ˈtɛlɪ] (*BRIT*: *inf*) n abbr (= *television*) tivù f inv.

temerity [təˈmɛrɪtɪ] n temerarietà.

temp [tɛmp] n abbr (= *temporary*) segretaria temporanea.

temper [ˈtɛmpə*] n (*nature*) carattere m; (*mood*) umore m; (*fit of anger*) collera ♦ vt (*moderate*) temperare, moderare; **to be in a** ~ essere in collera; **to lose one's ~** andare in collera.

temperament ['tempramant] n (nature) temperamento; **~al** [-'mentl] adj capriccioso(a).

temperate ['temprət] adj moderato(a); (climate) temperato(a).

temperature ['temprətʃə*] n temperatura; **to have** or **run a ~** avere la febbre.

tempest ['tempɪst] n tempesta.

template ['templɪt] n sagoma.

temple ['templ] n (building) tempio; (ANAT) tempia.

temporary ['tempərərɪ] adj temporaneo(a); (job, worker) avventizio(a), temporaneo(a).

tempt [tempt] vt tentare; **to ~ sb into doing** indurre qn a fare; **~ation** [-'teɪʃən] n tentazione f; **~ing** adj allettante.

ten [ten] num dieci.

tenacity [tə'næsɪtɪ] n tenacia.

tenancy ['tenənsɪ] n affitto; condizione f di inquilino.

tenant ['tenənt] n inquilino/a.

tend [tend] vt badare a, occuparsi di ♦ vi: **to ~ to do** tendere a fare.

tendency ['tendənsɪ] n tendenza.

tender ['tendə*] adj tenero(a); (sore) dolorante ♦ n (COMM: offer) offerta; (money): **legal ~** moneta in corso legale ♦ vt offrire.

tendon ['tendən] n tendine m.

tenement ['tenəmənt] n casamento.

tenet ['tenət] n principio.

tennis ['tenɪs] n tennis m; **~ ball** n palla da tennis; **~ court** n campo da tennis; **~ player** n tennista m/f; **~ racket** n racchetta da tennis; **~ shoes** npl scarpe fpl da tennis.

tenor ['tenə*] n (MUS) tenore m.

tenpin bowling ['tenpɪn-] n bowling m.

tense [tens] adj teso(a) ♦ n (LING) tempo.

tension ['tenʃən] n tensione f.

tent [tent] n tenda.

tentative ['tentətɪv] adj esitante, incerto(a); (conclusion) provvisorio(a).

tenterhooks ['tentəhuks] npl: **on ~** sulle spine.

tenth [tenθ] num decimo(a).

tent: ~ peg n picchetto da tenda; **~ pole** n palo da tenda, montante m.

tenuous ['tenjuəs] adj tenue.

tenure ['tenjuə*] n (of property) possesso; (of job) permanenza; titolarità.

tepid ['tepɪd] adj tiepido(a).

term [tə:m] n termine m; (SCOL) trimestre m; (LAW) sessione f ♦ vt chiamare, definire; **~s** npl (conditions) condizioni fpl; (COMM) prezzi mpl, tariffe fpl; **in the short/long ~** a breve/lunga scadenza; **to be on good ~s with sb** essere in buoni rapporti con qn; **to come to ~s with** (problem) affrontare.

terminal ['tə:mɪnl] adj finale, terminale; (disease) terminale ♦ n (ELEC) morsetto; (COMPUT) terminale m; (AVIAT, for oil, ore etc) terminal m inv; (BRIT: also: coach ~) capolinea m.

terminate ['tə:mɪneɪt] vt mettere fine a.

termini ['tə:mɪnaɪ] npl of **terminus**.

terminus ['tə:mɪnəs] (pl **termini**) n (for buses) capolinea m; (for trains) stazione f terminale.

terrace ['terəs] n terrazza; (BRIT: row of houses) fila di case a schiera; **the ~s** npl (BRIT: SPORT) le gradinate; **~d** adj (garden) a terrazze.

terracotta ['terə'kɔtə] n terracotta.

terrain [tɛ'reɪn] n terreno.

terrible ['terɪbl] adj terribile; **terribly** adv terribilmente; (very badly) malissimo.

terrier ['terɪə*] n terrier m inv.

terrific [tə'rɪfɪk] adj incredibile, fantastico(a); (wonderful) formidabile, eccezionale.

terrify ['terɪfaɪ] vt terrorizzare.

territory ['terɪtərɪ] n territorio.

terror ['terə*] n terrore m; **~ism** n terrorismo; **~ist** n terrorista m/f.

terse [tə:s] adj (style) conciso(a); (reply) laconico(a).

Terylene ['terəli:n] ® n terital m ®, terilene m ®.

test [test] n (trial, check, of courage etc) prova; (MED) esame m; (CHEM) analisi *f inv*; (*exam: of intelligence etc*) test *m inv*; (: *in school*) compito in classe; (*also: driving ~*) esame *m* di guida ♦ *vt* provare; esaminare; analizzare; sottoporre ad esame; **to ~ sb in history** esaminare qn in storia.

testament ['tɛstəmənt] *n* testamento; **the Old/New T~** il Vecchio/Nuovo testamento.

testicle ['tɛstɪkl] *n* testicolo.

testify ['tɛstɪfaɪ] *vi* (*LAW*) testimoniare, deporre; **to ~ to sth** (*LAW*) testimoniare qc; (*gen*) comprovare *or* dimostrare qc.

testimony ['tɛstɪmənɪ] *n* (*LAW*) testimonianza, deposizione *f*.

test: ~ match *n* (*CRICKET, RUGBY*) partita internazionale; **~ pilot** *n* pilota *m* collaudatore; **~ tube** *n* provetta.

tetanus ['tɛtənəs] *n* tetano.

tether ['tɛðə*] *vt* legare ♦ *n*: **at the end of one's ~** al limite (della pazienza).

text [tɛkst] *n* testo; **~book** *n* libro di testo.

textiles ['tɛkstaɪlz] *npl* tessuti *mpl*; (*industry*) industria tessile.

texture ['tɛkstʃə*] *n* tessitura; (*of skin, paper etc*) struttura.

Thames [tɛmz] *n*: **the ~** il Tamigi.

than [ðæn, ðən] *conj* (*in comparisons*) che; (*with numerals, pronouns, proper names*) di; **more ~ 10/once** più di 10/una volta; **I have more/less ~ you** ne ho più/meno di te; **I have more pens ~ pencils** ho più penne che matite; **she is older ~ you think** è più vecchia di quanto tu (non) pensi.

thank [θæŋk] *vt* ringraziare; **~ you (very much)** grazie (tante); **~s** *npl* ringraziamenti *mpl*, grazie *fpl* ♦ *excl* grazie!; **~s to** grazie a; **~ful** *adj*: **~ful (for)** riconoscente (per); **~less** *adj* ingrato(a); **T~sgiving (Day)** *n* giorno del ringraziamento.

that [ðæt] (*pl* **those**) *adj* (*demonstrative*) quel(quell', quello) *m*; quella(quell') *f*; **~ man/woman/book** quell'uomo/quella donna/quel libro; (*not*

"this") quell'uomo/quella donna/quel libro là; **~ one** quello(a) là
♦ *pron* **1** (*demonstrative*) ciò; (*not "this one"*) quello(a); **who's ~?** chi è?; **what's ~?** cos'è quello?; **is ~ you?** sei tu?; **I prefer this to ~** preferisco questo a quello; **~'s what he said** questo è ciò che ha detto; **what happened after ~?** che è successo dopo?; **~ is (to say)** cioè
2 (*relative: direct*) che; (: *indirect*) cui; **the book (~) I read** il libro che ho letto; **the box (~) I put it in** la scatola in cui l'ho messo; **the people (~) I spoke to** le persone con cui *or* con le quali ho parlato
3 (*relative: of time*) in cui; **the day (~) he came** il giorno in cui è venuto
♦ *conj* che; **he thought ~ I was ill** pensava che io fossi malato
♦ *adv* (*demonstrative*) così; **I can't work ~ much** non posso lavorare (così) tanto; **~ high** così alto; **the wall's about ~ high and ~ thick** il muro è alto circa così e spesso circa così.

thatched [θætʃt] *adj* (*roof*) di paglia; **~ cottage** *n* cottage *m inv* col tetto di paglia.

thaw [θɔ:] *n* disgelo ♦ *vi* (*ice*) sciogliersi; (*food*) scongelarsi ♦ *vt* (*food: also: ~ out*) (fare) scongelare.

the [ði:, ðə] *def art* **1** (*gen*) il(lo, l') *m*; la(l') *f*; i(gli) *mpl*; le *fpl*; **~ boy/girl/ink** il ragazzo/la ragazza/l'inchiostro; **~ books/pencils** i libri/le matite; **~ history of ~ world** la storia del mondo; **give it to ~ postman** dallo al postino; **I haven't ~ time/money** non ho tempo/soldi; **~ rich and ~ poor** i ricchi e i poveri
2 (*in titles*): **Elizabeth ~ First** Elisabetta prima; **Peter ~ Great** Pietro il grande
3 (*in comparisons*): **~ more he works, ~ more he earns** più lavora più guadagna.

theatre ['θɪətə*] (*US* **theater**) *n* teatro; (*also: lecture ~*) aula magna; (*also:*

operating ~) sala operatoria; ~-**goer** *n* frequentatore/trice di teatri.

theatrical [θɪ'ætrɪkl] *adj* teatrale.

theft [θɛft] *n* furto.

their [ðɛə*] *adj* il(la) loro, *pl* i(le) loro; ~**s** *pron* il(la) loro, *pl* i(le) loro; *see also* **my**; **mine**.

them [ðɛm, ðəm] *pron* (*direct*) li(le); (*indirect*) gli, loro (*after vb*); (*stressed, after prep: people*) loro; (: *people, things*) essi(e); *see also* **me**.

theme [θi:m] *n* tema *m*; ~ **park** *n* parco di divertimenti (*intorno a un tema centrale*); ~ **song** *n* tema musicale.

themselves [ðəm'sɛlvz] *pl pron* (*reflexive*) si; (*emphatic*) loro stessi(e); (*after prep*) se stessi(e).

then [ðɛn] *adv* (*at that time*) allora; (*next*) poi, dopo; (*and also*) e poi ♦ *conj* (*therefore*) perciò, dunque, quindi ♦ *adj*: **the** ~ **president** il presidente di allora; **by** ~ allora; **from** ~ **on** da allora in poi.

theology [θɪ'ɔlədʒɪ] *n* teologia.

theorem ['θɪərəm] *n* teorema *m*.

theoretical [θɪə'rɛtɪkl] *adj* teorico(a).

theory ['θɪərɪ] *n* teoria.

therapy ['θɛrəpɪ] *n* terapia.

KEYWORD
---

there [ðɛə*] *adv* **1**: ~ **is**, ~ **are** c'è, ci sono; ~ **are 3 of them** (*people*) sono in 3; (*things*) ce ne sono 3; ~ **is no-one here** non c'è nessuno qui; ~ **has been an accident** c'è stato un incidente

2 (*referring to place*) là, lì; **up/in/down** ~ lassù/là dentro/laggiù; **he went** ~ **on Friday** ci è andato venerdì; **I want that book** ~ voglio quel libro là *or* lì; ~ **he is!** eccolo!

3: ~, ~ (*esp to child*) su, su.

---

thereabouts [ðɛərə'bauts] *adv* (*place*) nei pressi, da quelle parti; (*amount*) giù di lì, all'incirca.

thereafter [ðɛər'ɑ:ftə*] *adv* da allora in poi.

thereby [ðɛə'baɪ] *adv* con ciò.

therefore ['ðɛəfɔ:*] *adv* perciò, quindi.

there's [ðɛəz] = **there is**; **there has**.

thermal ['θə:ml] *adj* termico(a).

thermometer [θə'mɔmɪtə*] *n* termometro.

Thermos ['θə:məs] ® *n* (*also:* ~ *flask*) thermos *m inv* ®.

thesaurus [θɪ'sɔ:rəs] *n* dizionario dei sinonimi.

these [ði:z] *pl pron, adj* questi(e).

theses ['θi:si:z] *npl of* **thesis**.

thesis ['θi:sɪs] (*pl* **theses**) *n* tesi *f inv*.

they [ðeɪ] *pl pron* essi(esse); (*people only*) loro; ~ **say that ...** (*it is said that*) si dice che ...; ~'**d** = **they had**; **they would**; ~'**ll** = **they shall**; **they will**; ~'**re** = **they are**; ~'**ve** = **they have**.

thick [θɪk] *adj* spesso(a); (*crowd*) compatto(a); (*stupid*) ottuso(a), lento(a) ♦ *n*: **in the** ~ **of** nel folto di; **it's 20 cm** ~ ha uno spessore di 20 cm; ~**en** *vi* ispessire ♦ *vt* (*sauce etc*) ispessire, rendere più denso(a); ~**ly** *adv* (*spread*) a strati spessi; (*cut*) a fette grosse; (*populated*) densamente; ~**ness** *n* spessore *m*; ~**set** *adj* tarchiato(a), tozzo(a); ~**skinned** *adj* (*fig*) insensibile.

thief [θi:f] (*pl* **thieves**) *n* ladro/a.

thieves [θi:vz] *npl of* **thief**.

thigh [θaɪ] *n* coscia.

thimble ['θɪmbl] *n* ditale *m*.

thin [θɪn] *adj* sottile; (*person*) magro(a); (*soup*) poco denso(a) ♦ *vt*: **to** ~ (**down**) (*sauce, paint*) diluire.

thing [θɪŋ] *n* cosa; (*object*) oggetto; (*mania*): **to have a** ~ **about** essere fissato(a) con; ~**s** *npl* (*belongings*) cose *fpl*; **poor** ~ poverino(a); **the best** ~ **would be to** la cosa migliore sarebbe di; **how are** ~**s?** come va?

think [θɪŋk] (*pt, pp* **thought**) *vi* pensare, riflettere ♦ *vt* pensare, credere; (*imagine*) immaginare; **to** ~ **of** pensare a; **what did you** ~ **of them?** cosa ne ha pensato?; **to** ~ **about sth/sb** pensare a qc/qn; **I'll** ~ **about it** ci penserò; **to** ~ **of doing** pensare di fare; **I** ~ **so/not** penso di sì/no; **to** ~ **well of** avere una buona opinione di; ~ **out** *vt* (*plan*) elaborare;

(*solution*) trovare; ~ **over** *vt* riflettere su; ~ **through** *vt* riflettere a fondo su; ~ **up** *vt* ideare; ~ **tank** *n* commissione *f* di esperti.

third [θə:d] *num* terzo(a) ♦ *n* terzo/a; (*fraction*) terzo, terza parte *f*; (*AUT*) terza; (*BRIT: SCOL: degree*) laurea col minimo dei voti; ~**ly** *adv* in terzo luogo; ~ **party insurance** (*BRIT*) *n* assicurazione *f* contro terzi; ~-**rate** *adj* di qualità scadente; **the T~ World** *n* il Terzo Mondo.

thirst [θə:st] *n* sete *f*; ~**y** *adj* (*person*) assetato(a), che ha sete.

thirteen [θə:'ti:n] *num* tredici.

thirty ['θə:tɪ] *num* trenta.

┌─────────────┐
│ _KEYWORD_ │
└─────────────┘

this [ðɪs] (*pl* **these**) *adj* (*demonstrative*) questo(a); ~ **man/woman/book** quest'uomo/questa donna/questo libro; (*not "that"*) quest'uomo/questa donna/questo libro qui; ~ **one** questo(a) qui ♦ *pron* (*demonstrative*) questo(a); (*not "that one"*) questo(a) qui; **who/what is ~?** chi è/che cos'è questo?; **I prefer ~ to that** preferisco questo a quello; ~ **is where I live** io abito qui; ~ **is what he said** questo è ciò che ha detto; ~ **is Mr Brown** (*in introductions, photo*) questo è il signor Brown; (*on telephone*) sono il signor Brown ♦ *adv* (*demonstrative*): ~ **high/long** *etc* alto/lungo *etc* così; **I didn't know things were ~ bad** non sapevo andasse così male.

└─────────────────────────────┘

thistle ['θɪsl] *n* cardo.

thong [θɒŋ] *n* cinghia.

thorn [θɔ:n] *n* spina; ~**y** *adj* spinoso(a).

thorough ['θʌrə] *adj* (*search*) minuzioso(a); (*knowledge, research*) approfondito(a), profondo(a); (*person*) coscienzioso(a); (*cleaning*) a fondo; ~**bred** *n* (*horse*) purosangue *m/f inv*; ~**fare** *n* strada transitabile; "**no ~fare**" "divieto di transito"; ~**ly** *adv* (*search*) minuziosamente; (*wash, study*) a fondo; (*very*) assolutamente.

those [ðəuz] *pl pron* quelli(e) ♦ *pl a*

quei(quegli) *mpl*; quelle *fpl*.

though [ðəu] *conj* benché, sebbene ♦ *adv* comunque.

thought [θɔ:t] *pt, pp of* **think** ♦ *n* pensiero; (*opinion*) opinione *f*; ~**ful** *adj* pensieroso(a), pensoso(a); (*considerate*) premuroso(a); ~**less** *adj* sconsiderato(a); (*behaviour*) scortese.

thousand ['θauzənd] *num* mille; **one** ~ mille; ~**s of** migliaia di; ~**th** *num* millesimo(a).

thrash [θræʃ] *vt* picchiare; bastonare; (*defeat*) battere; ~ **about** *vi* dibattersi; ~ **out** *vt* dibattere.

thread [θrɛd] *n* filo; (*of screw*) filetto ♦ *vt* (*needle*) infilare; ~**bare** *adj* consumato(a)', logoro(a).

threat [θrɛt] *n* minaccia; ~**en** *vi* (*storm*) minacciare ♦ *vt*: **to ~en sb with/to do** minacciare qn con/di fare.

three [θri:] *num* tre; ~-**dimensional** *adj* tridimensionale; (*film*) stereoscopico(a); ~-**piece suit** *n* completo (con gilè); ~-**piece suite** *n* salotto comprendente un divano e due poltrone; ~-**ply** *adj* (*wool*) a tre fili.

thresh [θrɛʃ] *vt* (*AGR*) trebbiare.

threshold ['θrɛʃhəuld] *n* soglia.

threw [θru:] *pt of* **throw**.

thrifty ['θrɪftɪ] *adj* economico(a).

thrill [θrɪl] *n* brivido ♦ *vt* (*audience*) elettrizzare; **to be ~ed** (*with gift etc*) essere elettrizzato(a); ~**er** *n* thriller *m inv*; ~**ing** *adj* (*book*) pieno(a) di suspense; (*news, discovery*) elettrizzante.

thrive [θraɪv] (*pt* **thrived** *or* **throve**, *pp* **thrived** *or* **thriven**) *vi* crescere *or* svilupparsi bene; (*business*) prosperare; **he ~s on it** gli fa bene, ne gode; **thriven** ['θrɪvn] *pp of* **thrive**; **thriving** *adj* fiorente.

throat [θrəut] *n* gola; **to have a sore** ~ avere (un *or* il) mal di gola.

throb [θrɒb] *n* (*of heart*) palpito; (*of wound*) pulsazione *f*; (*of engine*) vibrazione *f* ♦ *vi* palpitare; pulsare; vibrare.

throes [θrəuz] *npl*: **in the ~ of** alle prese con; in preda a.

thrombosis [θrɔm'bəusɪs] *n* trombosi *f*.

throne [θrəʊn] *n* trono.

throng [θrɔŋ] *n* moltitudine *f* ♦ *vt* affollare.

throttle ['θrɔtl] *n* (*AUT*) valvola a farfalla ♦ *vt* strangolare.

through [θru:] *prep* attraverso; (*time*) per, durante; (*by means of*) per mezzo di; (*owing to*) a causa di ♦ *adj* (*ticket, train, passage*) diretto(a) ♦ *adv* attraverso; **to put sb ~ to sb** (*TEL*) passare qn a qn; **to be ~** (*TEL*) ottenere la comunicazione; (*have finished*) essere finito(a); **"no ~ road"** (*BRIT*) ''strada senza sbocco''; **~out** *prep* (*place*) dappertutto in; (*time*) per o durante tutto(a) ♦ *adv* dappertutto; sempre.

throve [θrəʊv] *pt of* **thrive**.

throw [θrəʊ] (*pt* **threw**, *pp* **thrown**) *n* (*SPORT*) lancio, tiro ♦ *vt* tirare, gettare; (*SPORT*) lanciare, tirare; (*rider*) disarcionare; (*fig*) confondere; **to ~ a party** dare una festa; **~ away** *vt* gettare *or* buttare via; **~ off** *vt* sbarazzarsi di; **~ out** *vt* buttare fuori; (*reject*) respingere; **~ up** *vi* vomitare; **~away** *adj* da buttare; **~-in** *n* (*SPORT*) rimessa in gioco; **thrown** *pp of* **throw**.

thru [θru:] (*US*) *prep, adj, adv* = **through**.

thrush [θrʌʃ] *n* tordo.

thrust [θrʌst] (*pt, pp* **thrust**) *n* (*TECH*) spinta ♦ *vt* spingere con forza; (*push in*) conficcare.

thud [θʌd] *n* tonfo.

thug [θʌg] *n* delinquente *m*.

thumb [θʌm] *n* (*ANAT*) pollice *m*; **to ~ a lift** fare' l'autostop; **~ through** *vt fus* (*book*) sfogliare; **~tack** (*US*) *n* puntina da disegno.

thump [θʌmp] *n* colpo forte; (*sound*) tonfo ♦ *vt* (*person*) picchiare; (*object*) battere su ♦ *vi* picchiare; battere.

thunder ['θʌndə*] *n* tuono ♦ *vi* tuonare; (*train etc*): **to ~ past** passare con un rombo; **~bolt** *n* fulmine *m*; **~clap** *n* rombo di tuono; **~storm** *n* temporale *m*; **~y** *adj* temporalesco(a).

Thursday ['θə:zdɪ] *n* giovedì *m inv*.

thus [ðʌs] *adv* così.

thwart [θwɔ:t] *vt* contrastare.

thyme [taɪm] *n* timo.

thyroid ['θaɪrɔɪd] *n* (*also*: **~ gland**) tiroide *f*.

tiara [tɪ'ɑ:rə] *n* (*woman's*) diadema *m*.

Tiber ['taɪbə*] *n*: **the ~** il Tevere.

tick [tɪk] *n* (*sound: of clock*) tic tac *m inv*; (*mark*) segno; spunta; (*ZOOL*) zecca; (*BRIT: inf*): **in a ~** in un attimo ♦ *vi* fare tic tac ♦ *vt* spuntare; **~ off** *vt* spuntare; (*person*) sgridare; **~ over** *vi* (*engine*) andare al minimo; (*fig*) andare avanti come al solito.

ticket ['tɪkɪt] *n* biglietto; (*in shop: on goods*) etichetta; (*parking* ~) multa; (*for library*) scheda; **~ collector** *n* bigliettaio; **~ office** *n* biglietteria.

tickle ['tɪkl] *vt* fare il solletico a; (*fig*) solleticare ♦ *vi*: **it ~s** mi (*or* gli *etc*) fa il solletico; **ticklish** [-lɪʃ] *adj* che soffre il solletico; (*problem*) delicato(a).

tidal ['taɪdl] *adj* di marea; (*estuary*) soggetto(a) alla marea; **~ wave** *n* onda anomala.

tidbit ['tɪdbɪt] (*US*) *n* (*food*) leccornia; (*news*) notizia ghiotta.

tiddlywinks ['tɪdlɪwɪŋks] *n* gioco della pulce.

tide [taɪd] *n* marea; (*fig: of events*) corso; **high/low ~** alta/bassa marea; **~ over** *vt* dare una mano a.

tidy ['taɪdɪ] *adj* (*room*) ordinato(a), lindo(a); (*dress, work*) curato(a), in ordine; (*person*) ordinato(a) ♦ *vt* (*also*: **~ up**) riordinare, mettere in ordine.

tie [taɪ] *n* (*string etc*) legaccio; (*BRIT: also: neck~*) cravatta; (*fig: link*) legame *m*; (*SPORT: draw*) pareggio ♦ *vt* (*parcel*) legare; (*ribbon*) annodare ♦ *vi* (*SPORT*) pareggiare; **to ~ sth in a bow** annodare qc; **to ~ a knot in sth** fare un nodo a qc; **~ down** *vt* legare; (*to price etc*) costringere ad accettare; **~ up** *vt* (*parcel, dog*) legare; (*boat*) ormeggiare; (*arrangements*) concludere; **to be ~d up** (*busy*) essere occupato(a) *or* preso(a).

tier [tɪə*] *n* fila; (*of cake*) piano, strato.

tiger ['taɪgə*] *n* tigre *f*.

tight [taɪt] *adj* (*rope*) teso(a), tirato(a);

(*money*) poco(a); (*clothes, budget, bend etc*) stretto(a); (*control*) severo(a), fermo(a); (*inf: drunk*) sbronzo(a) ♦ *adv* (*squeeze*) fortemente; (*shut*) ermeticamente; ~s (*BRIT*) *npl* collant *m inv*; ~en *vt* (*rope*) tendere; (*screw*) stringere; (*control*) rinforzare ♦ *vi* tendersi; stringersi; ~-fisted *adj* avaro(a); ~ly *adv* (*grasp*) bene, saldamente; ~rope *n* corda (da acrobata).

tile [taɪl] *n* (*on roof*) tegola; (*on wall or floor*) piastrella, mattonella; ~d *adj* di tegole; a piastrelle, a mattonelle.

till [tɪl] *n* registratore *m* di cassa ♦ *vt* (*land*) coltivare ♦ *prep, conj* = until.

tiller ['tɪlə*] *n* (*NAUT*) barra del timone.

tilt [tɪlt] *vt* inclinare, far pendere ♦ *vi* inclinarsi, pendere.

timber ['tɪmbə*] *n* (*material*) legname *m*; (*trees*) alberi *mpl* da legname.

time [taɪm] *n* tempo; (*epoch: often pl*) epoca, tempo; (*by clock*) ora; (*moment*) momento; (*occasion*) volta; (*MUS*) tempo ♦ *vt* (*race*) cronometrare; (*programme*) calcolare la durata di; (*fix moment for*) programmare; (*remark etc*) dire (*or* fare) al momento giusto; **a long ~** molto tempo; **for the ~ being** per il momento; **4 at a ~** 4 per *or* alla volta; **from ~ to ~** ogni tanto; **at ~s** a volte; **in ~** (*soon enough*) in tempo; (*after some ~*) col tempo; (*MUS*) a tempo; **in a week's ~** fra una settimana; **in no ~** in un attimo; **any ~** in qualsiasi momento; **on ~** puntualmente; **5 ~s 5** 5 volte 5, 5 per 5; **what ~ is it?** che ora è?, che ore sono?; **to have a good ~** divertirsi; ~ **bomb** *n* bomba a orologeria; ~ **lag** *n* intervallo, ritardo; (*in travel*) differenza di fuso orario; ~**less** *adj* eterno(a); ~**ly** *adj* opportuno(a); ~ **off** *n* tempo libero; ~**r** *n* (~ **switch**) temporizzatore *m*; (*in kitchen*) contaminuti *m inv*; ~ **scale** *n* periodo; ~ **switch** (*BRIT*) *n* temporizzatore *m*; ~**table** *n* orario; ~ **zone** *n* fuso orario.

timid ['tɪmɪd] *adj* timido(a); (*easily scared*) pauroso(a).

timing ['taɪmɪŋ] *n* (*SPORT*) cronometraggio; (*fig*) scelta del momento opportuno.

timpani ['tɪmpənɪ] *npl* timpani *mpl*.

tin [tɪn] *n* stagno; (*also:* ~ **plate**) latta; (*container*) scatola; (*BRIT: can*) barattolo (di latta), lattina; ~**foil** *n* stagnola.

tinge [tɪndʒ] *n* sfumatura ♦ *vt:* ~**d with** tinto(a) di.

tingle ['tɪŋgl] *vi* pizzicare.

tinker ['tɪŋkə*]: ~ **with** *vt fus* armeggiare intorno a; cercare di riparare.

tinned [tɪnd] (*BRIT*) *adj* (*food*) in scatola.

tin opener ['-əupnə*] (*BRIT*) *n* apriscatole *m inv*.

tinsel ['tɪnsl] *n* decorazioni *fpl* natalizie (argentate).

tint [tɪnt] *n* tinta; ~**ed** *adj* (*hair*) tinto(a); (*spectacles, glass*) colorato(a).

tiny ['taɪnɪ] *adj* minuscolo(a).

tip [tɪp] *n* (*end*) punta; (*gratuity*) mancia; (*BRIT: for rubbish*) immondezzaio; (*advice*) suggerimento ♦ *vt* (*waiter*) dare la mancia a; (*tilt*) inclinare; (*overturn: also:* ~ **over**) capovolgere; (*empty: also:* ~ **out**) scaricare; ~-**off** *n* (*hint*) soffiata; ~**ped** (*BRIT*) *adj* (*cigarette*) col filtro.

Tipp-Ex ['tɪpɛks] ® *n* correttore *m*.

tipsy ['tɪpsɪ] *adj* brillo(a).

tiptoe ['tɪptəu] *n:* **on ~** in punta di piedi.

tiptop ['tɪp'tɔp] *adj:* **in ~ condition** in ottime condizioni.

tire ['taɪə*] *n* (*US*) = **tyre** ♦ *vt* stancare ♦ *vi* stancarsi; ~**d** *adj* stanco(a); **to be ~d of** essere stanco *or* stufo di; ~**less** *adj* instancabile; ~**some** *adj* noioso(a); **tiring** *adj* faticoso(a).

tissue ['tɪʃuː] *n* tessuto; (*paper handkerchief*) fazzoletto di carta; ~ **paper** *n* carta velina.

tit [tɪt] *n* (*bird*) cinciallegra; **to give ~ for tat** rendere pan per focaccia.

titbit ['tɪtbɪt] (*BRIT*) *n* (*food*) leccornia; (*news*) notizia ghiotta.

title ['taɪtl] *n* titolo; ~ **deed** *n* (*LAW*)

titolo di proprietà; **~ role** *n* ruolo *or* parte *f* principale.

titter ['tɪtə*] *vi* ridere sciocamente.

TM *abbr* = trademark.

KEYWORD

to [tuː, tə] *prep* **1** (*direction*) a; **to go ~ France/London/school** andare in Francia/a Londra/a scuola; **to go ~ Paul's/the doctor's** andare da Paul/dal dottore; **the road ~ Edinburgh** la strada per Edimburgo; **~ the left/right** a sinistra/destra

2 (*as far as*) (fino) a; **from here ~ London** da qui a Londra; **to count ~ 10** contare fino a 10; **from 40 ~ 50 people** da 40 a 50 persone

3 (*with expressions of time*): **a quarter ~ 5** le 5 meno un quarto; **it's twenty ~ 3** sono le 3 meno venti

4 (*for, of*): **the key ~ the front door** la chiave della porta d'ingresso; **a letter ~ his wife** una lettera per la moglie

5 (*expressing indirect object*) a; **to give sth ~ sb** dare qc a qn; **to talk ~ sb** parlare a qn; **to be a danger ~ sb/sth** rappresentare un pericolo per qn/qc

6 (*in relation to*) a; **3 goals ~ 2** 3 goal a 2; **30 miles ~ the gallon** ≈ 11 chilometri con un litro

7 (*purpose, result*): **to come ~ sb's aid** venire in aiuto a qn; **to sentence sb ~ death** condannare a morte qn; **~ my surprise** con mia sorpresa

♦ *with vb* **1** (*simple infinitive*): **~ go/eat etc** andare/mangiare etc

2 (*following another vb*): **to want/try/start ~ do** volere/cercare di/cominciare a fare

3 (*with vb omitted*): **I don't want ~** non voglio (farlo); **you ought ~** devi (farlo)

4 (*purpose, result*) per; **I did it ~ help you** l'ho fatto per aiutarti

5 (*equivalent to relative clause*): **I have things ~ do** ho da fare; **the main thing is ~ try** la cosa più importante è provare

6 (*after adjective etc*): **ready ~ go** pronto a partire; **too old/young ~ ...**

troppo vecchio/giovane per ...

♦ *adv*: **to push the door ~** accostare la porta.

toad [təud] *n* rospo; **~stool** *n* fungo (velenoso).

toast [təust] *n* (CULIN) pane *m* tostato; (*drink, speech*) brindisi *m inv* ♦ *vt* (CULIN) tostare; (*drink to*) brindare a; **a piece** *or* **slice of ~** una fetta di pane tostato; **~er** *n* tostapane *m inv*.

tobacco [tə'bækəu] *n* tabacco; **~nist** *n* tabaccaio/a; **~nist's (shop)** *n* tabaccheria.

toboggan [tə'bɔgən] *n* toboga *m inv*.

today [tə'deɪ] *adv* oggi ♦ *n* (*also fig*) oggi *m*.

toddler ['tɔdlə*] *n* bambino/a che impara a camminare.

to-do *n* (*fuss*) storie *fpl*.

toe [təu] *n* dito del piede; (*of shoe*) punta; **to ~ the line** (*fig*) stare in riga, conformarsi; **~nail** *n* unghia del piede.

toffee ['tɔfɪ] *n* caramella; **~ apple** *n* mela caramellata.

toga ['təugə] *n* toga.

together [tə'gɛðə*] *adv* insieme; (*at same time*) allo stesso tempo; **~ with** insieme a.

toil [tɔɪl] *n* travaglio, fatica ♦ *vi* affannarsi; sgobbare.

toilet ['tɔɪlət] *n* (BRIT: *lavatory*) gabinetto ♦ *cpd* (*bag, soap etc*) da toletta; **~ paper** *n* carta igienica; **~ries** *npl* articoli *mpl* da toletta; **~ roll** *n* rotolo di carta igienica; **~ water** *n* acqua di colonia.

token ['təukən] *n* (*sign*) segno; (*substitute coin*) gettone *m*; **book/record/gift ~** (BRIT) buono-libro/disco/regalo.

told [təuld] *pt, pp of* tell.

tolerable ['tɔlərəbl] *adj* (*bearable*) tollerabile; (*fairly good*) passabile.

tolerant ['tɔlərnt] *adj*: **~ (of)** tollerante (nei confronti di).

tolerate ['tɔləreɪt] *vt* sopportare; (MED, TECH) tollerare.

toll [təul] *n* (*tax, charge*) pedaggio ♦ *vi* (*bell*) suonare; **the accident ~ on the roads** il numero delle vittime della

strada.
tomato [təˈmɑːtəʊ] (pl ~es) n pomodoro.
tomb [tuːm] n tomba.
tomboy [ˈtɒmbɔɪ] n maschiaccio.
tombstone [ˈtuːmstəʊn] n pietra tombale.
tomcat [ˈtɒmkæt] n gatto.
tomorrow [təˈmɒrəʊ] adv domani ♦ n (also fig) domani m inv; **the day after ~** dopodomani; **~ morning** domani mattina.
ton [tʌn] n tonnellata (BRIT = 1016 kg; US = 907 kg; metric = 1000 kg); **~s of** (inf) un mucchio or sacco di.
tone [təʊn] n tono ♦ vi (also: ~ in) intonarsi; **~ down** vt (colour, criticism, sound) attenuare; **~ up** vt (muscles) tonificare; **~-deaf** adj che non ha orecchio (musicale).
tongs [tɒŋz] npl tenaglie fpl; (for coal) molle fpl; (for hair) arricciacapelli m inv.
tongue [tʌŋ] n lingua; **~ in cheek** (say, speak) ironicamente; **~-tied** adj (fig) muto(a); **~-twister** n scioglilingua m inv.
tonic [ˈtɒnɪk] n (MED) tonico; (also: ~ water) acqua tonica.
tonight [təˈnaɪt] adv stanotte; (this evening) stasera ♦ n questa notte; questa sera.
tonnage [ˈtʌnɪdʒ] n (NAUT) tonnellaggio, stazza.
tonsil [ˈtɒnsl] n tonsilla; **~litis** [-ˈlaɪtɪs] n tonsillite f.
too [tuː] adv (excessively) troppo; (also) anche; **~ much** adv troppo ♦ adj troppo(a); **~ many** troppi(e).
took [tʊk] pt of take.
tool [tuːl] n utensile m, attrezzo; **~ box** n cassetta f portautensili.
toot [tuːt] n (of horn) colpo di clacson; (of whistle) fischio ♦ vi suonare; (with car horn) suonare il clacson.
tooth [tuːθ] (pl teeth) n (ANAT, TECH) dente m; **~ache** n mal m di denti; **~brush** n spazzolino da denti; **~paste** n dentifricio; **~pick** n stuzzicadenti m inv.

top [tɒp] n (of mountain, page, ladder) cima; (of box, cupboard, table) sopra m inv, parte f superiore; (lid: of box, jar) coperchio; (: of bottle) tappo; (blouse etc) sopra m inv; (toy) trottola ♦ adj più alto(a); (in rank) primo(a); (best) migliore ♦ vt (exceed) superare; (be first in) essere in testa a; **on ~ of** sopra, in cima a; (in addition to) oltre a; **from ~ to bottom** da cima a fondo; **~ up** (US ~ off) vt riempire; (salary) integrare; **~ floor** n ultimo piano; **~ hat** n cilindro; **~-heavy** adj (object) con la parte superiore troppo pesante.
topic [ˈtɒpɪk] n argomento; **~al** adj d'attualità.
top: ~less adj (bather etc) col seno scoperto; **~-level** adj (talks) ad alto livello; **~most** adj il(la) più alto(a).
topple [ˈtɒpl] vt rovesciare, far cadere ♦ vi cadere; traballare.
top-secret adj segretissimo(a).
topsy-turvy [ˈtɒpsɪˈtɜːvɪ] adj, adv sottosopra inv.
torch [tɔːtʃ] n torcia; (BRIT: electric) lampadina tascabile.
tore [tɔː*] pt of tear.
torment [n ˈtɔːmɛnt, vb tɔːˈmɛnt] n tormento ♦ vt tormentare.
torn [tɔːn] pp of tear.
torpedo [tɔːˈpiːdəʊ] (pl ~es) n siluro.
torrent [ˈtɒrnt] n torrente m.
torrid [ˈtɒrɪd] adj torrido(a); (love affair) infuocato(a).
tortoise [ˈtɔːtəs] n tartaruga; **~shell** [ˈtɔːtəʃɛl] adj di tartaruga.
torture [ˈtɔːtʃə*] n tortura ♦ vt torturare.
Tory [ˈtɔːrɪ] (BRIT: POL) adj dei tories, conservatore(trice) ♦ n tory m/f inv, conservatore/trice.
toss [tɒs] vt gettare, lanciare; (one's head) scuotere; **to ~ a coin** fare a testa o croce; **to ~ up for sth** fare a testa o croce per qc; **to ~ and turn** (in bed) girarsi e rigirarsi.
tot [tɒt] n (BRIT: drink) bicchierino; (child) bimbo/a.
total [ˈtəʊtl] adj totale ♦ n totale m ♦ vt (add up) sommare; (amount to)

ammontare a.

totally ['təutəlɪ] adv completamente.

totter ['tɔtə*] vi barcollare.

touch [tʌtʃ] n tocco; (sense) tatto; (contact) contatto ♦ vt toccare; **a ~ of** (fig) un tocco di; un pizzico di; **to get in ~ with** mettersi in contatto con; **to lose ~** (friends) perdersi di vista; **~ on** vt fus (topic) sfiorare, accennare a; **~ up** vt (paint) ritoccare; **~-and-go** adj incerto(a); **~down** n atterraggio; (on sea) ammaraggio; (US: FOOTBALL) meta; **~ed** adj commosso(a); **~ing** adj commovente; **~line** n (SPORT) linea laterale; **~y** adj (person) suscettibile.

tough [tʌf] adj duro(a); (resistant) resistente; **~en** vt rinforzare.

toupee ['tu:peɪ] n parrucchino.

tour ['tuə*] n viaggio; (also: package ~) viaggio organizzato or tutto compreso; (of town, museum) visita; (by artist) tournée f inv ♦ vt visitare; **~ing** n turismo.

tourism ['tuərɪzəm] n turismo.

tourist ['tuərɪst] n turista m/f ♦ adv (travel) in classe turistica ♦ cpd turistico(a); **~ office** n pro loco f inv.

tournament ['tuənəmənt] n torneo.

tousled ['tauzld] adj (hair) arruffato(a).

tout [taut] vi: **to ~ for** procacciare, raccogliere; cercare clienti per ♦ n (also: ticket ~) bagarino.

tow [təu] vt rimorchiare; **"on ~"** (BRIT), **"in ~"** (US) "veicolo rimorchiato".

toward(s) [tə'wɔ:d(z)] prep verso; (of attitude) nei confronti di; (of purpose) per.

towel ['tauəl] n asciugamano; (also: tea ~) strofinaccio; **~ling** n (fabric) spugna; **~ rail** (US **~ rack**) n portasciugamano.

tower ['tauə*] n torre f; **~ block** (BRIT) n palazzone m; **~ing** adj altissimo(a), imponente.

town [taun] n città f inv; **to go to ~** andare in città; (fig) mettercela tutta; **~ centre** n centro (città); **~ council** n consiglio comunale; **~ hall** n ≈ municipio; **~ plan** n pianta della città;

~ planning n urbanistica.

towrope ['təurəup] n (cavo da) rimorchio.

tow truck (US) n carro m attrezzi inv.

toxic ['tɔksɪk] adj tossico(a).

toy [tɔɪ] n giocattolo; **~ with** vt fus giocare con; (idea) accarezzare, trastullarsi con; **~ shop** n negozio di giocattoli.

trace [treɪs] n traccia ♦ vt (draw) tracciare; (follow) seguire; (locate) rintracciare; **tracing paper** n carta da ricalco.

track [træk] n (of person, animal) traccia; (on tape, SPORT, path: gen) pista; (: of bullet etc) traiettoria; (: of suspect, animal) pista, tracce fpl; (RAIL) binario, rotaie fpl ♦ vt seguire le tracce di; **to keep ~ of** seguire; **~ down** vt (prey) scovare; snidare; (sth lost) rintracciare; **~suit** n tuta sportiva.

tract [trækt] n (GEO) tratto, estensione f; (pamphlet) opuscolo, libretto.

tractor ['træktə*] n trattore m.

trade [treɪd] n commercio; (skill, job) mestiere m ♦ vi commerciare ♦ vt: **to ~ sth (for sth)** barattare qc (con qc); **to ~ with/in** commerciare con/in; **~ in** vt (old car etc) dare come pagamento parziale; **~ fair** n fiera commerciale; **~mark** n marchio di fabbrica; **~ name** n marca, nome m depositato; **~r** n commerciante m/f; **~sman** n fornitore m; (shopkeeper) negoziante m; **~ union** n sindacato; **~ unionist** n sindacalista m/f.

tradition [trə'dɪʃən] n tradizione f; **~al** adj tradizionale.

traffic ['træfɪk] n traffico ♦ vi: **to ~ in** (pej: liquor, drugs) trafficare in; **~ circle** (US) n isola rotatoria; **~ jam** n ingorgo (del traffico); **~ lights** npl semaforo; **~ warden** n addetto/a al controllo del traffico e del parcheggio.

tragedy ['trædʒədɪ] n tragedia.

tragic ['trædʒɪk] adj tragico(a).

trail [treɪl] n (tracks) tracce fpl, pista; (path) sentiero; (of smoke etc) scia ♦ vt trascinare, strascicare; (follow) seguire ♦ *vi* essere al traino; (*dress etc*) strusciare; (*plant*) arrampicarsi; strisciare; (*in game*) essere in svantaggio; ~ **behind** *vi* essere al traino; ~**er** *n* (*AUT*) rimorchio; (*US*) roulotte *f inv*; (*CINEMA*) prossimamente *m inv*; ~**er truck** (*US*) *n* (*articulated lorry*) autoarticolato.

train [treɪn] *n* treno; (*of dress*) coda, strascico ♦ *vt* (*apprentice, doctor etc*) formare; (*sportsman*) allenare; (*dog*) addestrare; (*memory*) esercitare; (*point: gun etc*): **to ~ sth on** puntare qc contro ♦ *vi* formarsi; allenarsi; **one's ~ of thought** il filo dei propri pensieri; ~**ed** *adj* qualificato(a); allenato(a); addestrato(a); ~**ee** [treɪ'niː] *n* (*in trade*) apprendista *m/f*; ~**er** *n* (*SPORT*) allenatore/trice; (: *shoe*) scarpa da ginnastica; (*of dogs etc*) addestratore/trice; ~**ing** *n* formazione *f*; allenamento; addestramento; **in** ~**ing** (*SPORT*) in allenamento; ~**ing college** *n* istituto professionale; (*for teachers*) ≈ istituto magistrale; ~**ing shoes** *npl* scarpe *fpl* da ginnastica.

traipse [treɪps] *vi* girovagare, andare a zonzo.

trait [treɪt] *n* tratto.

traitor ['treɪtə*] *n* traditore *m*.

tram [træm] (*BRIT*) *n* (*also*: ~*car*) tram *m inv*.

tramp [træmp] *n* (*person*) vagabondo/a; (*inf: pej: woman*) sgualdrina ♦ *vi* camminare con passo pesante.

trample ['træmpl] *vt*: **to ~ (underfoot)** calpestare.

trampoline ['træmpəliːn] *n* trampolino.

tranquil ['træŋkwɪl] *adj* tranquillo(a); ~**lizer** *n* (*MED*) tranquillante *m*.

transact [træn'zækt] *vt* (*business*) trattare; ~**ion** [-'zækʃən] *n* transazione *f*.

transatlantic ['trænzət'læntɪk] *adj* transatlantico(a).

transcript ['trænskrɪpt] *n* trascrizione *f*.

transfer [*n* 'trænsfə*, *vb* træns'fə*] *n* (*gen, also SPORT*) trasferimento; (*POL: of power*) passaggio; (*picture, design*) decalcomania; (: *stick-on*) autoadesivo ♦ *vt* trasferire; passare; **to ~ the**

charges (*BRIT: TEL*) fare una chiamata a carico del destinatario.

transform [træns'fɔːm] *vt* trasformare.

transfusion [træns'fjuːʒən] *n* trasfusione *f*.

transient ['trænzɪənt] *adj* transitorio(a), fugace.

transistor [træn'zɪstə*] *n* (*ELEC*) transistor *m inv*; (*also*: ~ *radio*) radio *f inv* a transistor.

transit ['trænzɪt] *n*: **in ~** in transito.

transitive ['trænzɪtɪv] *adj* (*LING*) transitivo(a).

translate [trænz'leɪt] *vt* tradurre; **translation** [-'leɪʃən] *n* traduzione *f*; **translator** *n* traduttore/trice.

transmission [trænz'mɪʃən] *n* trasmissione *f*.

transmit [trænz'mɪt] *vt* trasmettere; ~**ter** *n* trasmettitore *m*.

transparency [træns'pɛərnsɪ] *n* trasparenza; (*BRIT: PHOT*) diapositiva.

transparent [træns'pærnt] *adj* trasparente.

transpire [træn'spaɪə*] *vi* (*happen*) succedere; (*turn out*): **it ~d that** si venne a sapere che.

transplant [*vb* træns'plɑːnt, *n* 'trænsplɑːnt] *vt* trapiantare ♦ *n* (*MED*) trapianto.

transport [*n* 'trænspɔːt, *vb* træns'pɔːt] *n* trasporto ♦ *vt* trasportare; ~**ation** [-'teɪʃən] *n* (*mezzo di*) trasporto; ~ **café** (*BRIT*) *n* trattoria per camionisti.

trap [træp] *n* (*snare, trick*) trappola; (*carriage*) calesse *m* ♦ *vt* prendere in trappola, intrappolare; ~ **door** *n* botola.

trapeze [trə'piːz] *n* trapezio.

trappings ['træpɪŋz] *npl* ornamenti *mpl*; indoratura, sfarzo.

trash [træʃ] (*pej*) *n* (*goods*) ciarpame *m*; (*nonsense*) sciocchezze *fpl*; ~ **can** (*US*) *n* secchio della spazzatura.

trauma ['trɔːmə] *n* trauma *m*; ~**tic** [-'mætɪk] *adj* traumatico(a).

travel ['trævl] *n* viaggio; viaggi *mpl* ♦ *vi* viaggiare ♦ *vt* (*distance*) percorrere; ~ **agency** *n* agenzia (di) viaggi; ~ **agent** *n* agente *m* di viaggio; ~**ler** (*US* ~**er**) *n* viaggiatore/trice; ~**ler's cheque** (*US*

~er's check) *n* assegno turistico; ~ling
(*US* ~ing) *n* viaggi *mpl*; ~ sickness *n*
mal *m* d'auto (*or* di mare *or* d'aria).

travesty ['trævəstɪ] *n* parodia.

trawler ['trɔːlə*] *n* peschereccio (a strascico).

tray [treɪ] *n* (*for carrying*) vassoio; (*on
desk*) vaschetta.

treacherous ['trɛtʃərəs] *adj* infido(a).

treachery ['trɛtʃərɪ] *n* tradimento.

treacle ['triːkl] *n* melassa.

tread [trɛd] (*pt* trod, *pp* trodden) *n*
passo; (*sound*) rumore *m* di passi; (*of
stairs*) pedata; (*of tyre*) battistrada *m
inv* ♦ *vi* camminare; ~ on *vt fus* calpestare.

treason ['triːzn] *n* tradimento.

treasure ['trɛʒə*] *n* tesoro ♦ *vt* (*value*)
tenere in gran conto, apprezzare molto;
(*store*) custodire gelosamente.

treasurer ['trɛʒərə*] *n* tesoriere/a.

treasury ['trɛʒərɪ] *n*: **the T~** (*BRIT*), **the
T~ Department** (*US*) il ministero del
Tesoro.

treat [triːt] *n* regalo ♦ *vt* trattare; (*MED*)
curare; **to ~ sb to sth** offrire qc a qn.

treatment ['triːtmənt] *n* trattamento.

treaty ['triːtɪ] *n* patto, trattato.

treble ['trɛbl] *adj* triplo(a), triplice ♦ *vt*
triplicare ♦ *vi* triplicarsi; ~ **clef** *n*
chiave *f* di violino.

tree [triː] *n* albero; ~ **trunk** *n* tronco
d'albero.

trek [trɛk] *n* escursione *f* a piedi;
escursione *f* in macchina; (*tiring walk*)
camminata sfiancante ♦ *vi* (*as holiday*)
fare dell'escursionismo.

trellis ['trɛlɪs] *n* graticcio.

tremble ['trɛmbl] *vi* tremare.

tremendous [trɪ'mɛndəs] *adj*
(*enormous*) enorme; (*excellent*)
meraviglioso(a), formidabile.

tremor ['trɛmə*] *n* tremore *m*, tremito;
(*also: earth* ~) scossa sismica.

trench [trɛntʃ] *n* trincea.

trend [trɛnd] *n* (*tendency*) tendenza; (*of
events*) corso; (*fashion*) moda; ~y *adj*
(*idea*) di moda; (*clothes*) all'ultima
moda.

trepidation [trɛpɪ'deɪʃən] *n* trepidazione

f, agitazione *f*.

trespass ['trɛspəs] *vi*: **to ~ on** entrare
abusivamente in; "**no ~ing**" "proprietà
privata", "vietato l'accesso".

trestle ['trɛsl] *n* cavalletto.

trial ['traɪəl] *n* (*LAW*) processo; (*test: of
machine etc*) collaudo; ~s *npl* (*unpleasant experiences*) dure prove *fpl*;
on ~ (*LAW*) sotto processo; **by ~ and
error** a tentoni; ~ **period** periodo di
prova.

triangle ['traɪæŋgl] *n* (*MATH, MUS*)
triangolo.

tribe [traɪb] *n* tribù *f inv*; ~sman *n*
membro di tribù.

tribunal [traɪ'bjuːnl] *n* tribunale *m*.

tributary ['trɪbjutərɪ] *n* (*river*)
tributario, affluente *m*.

tribute ['trɪbjuːt] *n* tributo, omaggio; **to
pay ~ to** rendere omaggio a.

trice [traɪs] *n*: **in a ~** in un attimo.

trick [trɪk] *n* trucco; (*joke*) tiro;
(*CARDS*) presa ♦ *vt* imbrogliare,
ingannare; **to play a ~ on sb** giocare un
tiro a qn; **that should do the** ~ vedrai
che funziona; ~ery *n* inganno.

trickle ['trɪkl] *n* (*of water etc*) rivolo;
gocciolio ♦ *vi* gocciolare.

tricky ['trɪkɪ] *adj* difficile, delicato(a).

tricycle ['traɪsɪkl] *n* triciclo.

trifle ['traɪfl] *n* sciocchezza; (*BRIT:
CULIN*) ≈ zuppa inglese ♦ *adv*: **a ~ long**
un po' lungo; **trifling** *adj* insignificante.

trigger ['trɪgə*] *n* (*of gun*) grilletto; ~
off *vt* dare l'avvio a.

trim [trɪm] *adj* (*house, garden*) ben
tenuto(a); (*figure*) snello(a) ♦ *n*
(*haircut etc*) spuntata, regolata;
(*embellishment*) finiture *fpl*; (*on car*)
guarnizioni *fpl* ♦ *vt* spuntare;
(*decorate*): **to ~ (with)** decorare (con);
(*NAUT: a sail*) orientare; ~mings *npl*
decorazioni *fpl*; (*extras: gen CULIN*)
guarnizione *f*.

trinket ['trɪŋkɪt] *n* gingillo; (*piece of
jewellery*) ciondolo.

trip [trɪp] *n* viaggio; (*excursion*) gita,
escursione *f*; (*stumble*) passo falso ♦ *vi*
inciampare; (*go lightly*) camminare
con passo leggero; **on a ~** in viaggio; ~

up *vi* inciampare ♦ *vt* fare lo sgambetto a.
tripe [traɪp] *n* (*CULIN*) trippa; (*pej: rubbish*) sciocchezze *fpl*, fesserie *fpl*.
triple ['trɪpl] *adj* triplo(a).
triplets ['trɪplɪts] *npl* bambini(e) trigemini(e).
triplicate ['trɪplɪkət] *n*: **in ~** in triplice copia.
tripod ['traɪpɔd] *n* treppiede *m*.
trite [traɪt] *adj* banale, trito(a).
triumph ['traɪʌmf] *n* trionfo ♦ *vi*: **to ~ (over)** trionfare (su).
trivia ['trɪvɪə] *npl* banalità *fpl*.
trivial ['trɪvɪəl] *adj* insignificante; (*commonplace*) banale.
trod [trɔd] *pt of* **tread**; **~den** *pp of* **tread**.
trolley ['trɔlɪ] *n* carrello; **~ bus** ·*n* filobus *m inv*.
trombone [trɔm'bəun] *n* trombone *m*.
troop [tru:p] *n* gruppo; (*MIL*) squadrone *m*; **~s** *npl* (*MIL*) truppe *fpl*; **~ in/out** *vi* entrare/uscire a frotte; **~ing the colour** *n* (*ceremony*) sfilata della bandiera.
trophy ['trəufɪ] *n* trofeo.
tropic ['trɔpɪk] *n* tropico; **~al** *adj* tropicale.
trot [trɔt] *n* trotto ♦ *vi* trottare; **on the ~** (*BRIT: fig*) di fila, uno(a) dopo l'altro(a).
trouble ['trʌbl] *n* difficoltà *f inv*, problema *m*; difficoltà *fpl*, problemi; (*worry*) preoccupazione *f*; (*bother, effort*) sforzo; (*POL*) conflitti *mpl*, disordine *m*; (*MED*): **stomach** *etc* **~** disturbi *mpl* gastrici *etc* ♦ *vt* disturbare; (*worry*) preoccupare ♦ *vi*: **to ~ to do** disturbarsi a fare; **~s** *npl* (*POL etc*) disordini *mpl*; **to be in ~** avere dei problemi; **it's no ~!** di niente!; **what's the ~?** cosa c'è che non va?; **~d** *adj* (*person*) preoccupato(a), inquieto(a); (*epoch, life*) agitato(a), difficile; **~maker** *n* elemento disturbatore, agitatore/trice; (*child*) disloco/a; **~shooter** *n* (*in conflict*) conciliatore *m*; **~some** *adj* fastidioso(a), seccante.
trough [trɔf] *n* (*also: drinking ~*) abbeveratoio; (*also: feeding ~*) trogolo,

mangiatoia; (*channel*) canale *m*.
trousers ['trauzəz] *npl* pantaloni *mpl*, calzoni *mpl*; **short ~** calzoncini *mpl*.
trousseau ['tru:səu] (*pl* **~x** *or* **~s**) *n* corredo da sposa.
trousseaux ['tru:səuz] *npl of* **trousseau**.
trout [traut] *n inv* trota.
trowel ['trauəl] *n* cazzuola.
truant ['truənt] (*BRIT*) *n*: **to play ~** marinare la scuola.
truce [tru:s] *n* tregua.
truck [trʌk] *n* autocarro, camion *m inv*; (*RAIL*) carro merci aperto; (*for luggage*) carrello *m* portabagagli *inv*; **~ driver** *n* camionista *m/f*; **~ farm** (*US*) *n* orto industriale.
trudge [trʌdʒ] *vi* (*also: ~ along*) trascinarsi pesantemente.
true [tru:] *adj* vero(a); (*accurate*) accurato(a), esatto(a); (*genuine*) reale; (*faithful*) fedele; **to come ~** avverarsi.
truffle ['trʌfl] *n* tartufo.
truly ['tru:lɪ] *adv* veramente; (*truthfully*) sinceramente; (*faithfully*): **yours ~** (*in letter*) distinti saluti.
trump [trʌmp] *n* (*also: ~ card*) atout *m inv*; **~ed-up** *adj* inventato(a).
trumpet ['trʌmpɪt] *n* tromba.
truncheon ['trʌntʃən] *n* sfollagente *m inv*.
trundle ['trʌndl] *vt* far rotolare rumorosamente ♦ *vi*: **to ~ along** rotolare rumorosamente.
trunk [trʌŋk] *n* (*of tree, person*) tronco; (*of elephant*) proboscide *f*; (*case*) baule *m*; (*US: AUT*) bagagliaio; **~s** *npl* (*also: swimming ~s*) calzoncini *mpl* da bagno.
truss [trʌs] *n* (*MED*) cinto erniario; **~ (up)** *vt* (*CULIN*) legare.
trust [trʌst] *n* fiducia; (*LAW*) amministrazione *f* fiduciaria; (*COMM*) trust *m inv* ♦ *vt* (*rely on*) contare su; (*hope*) sperare; (*entrust*): **to ~ sth to sb** affidare qc a qn; **~ed** *adj* fidato(a); **~ee** [trʌs'ti:] *n* (*LAW*) amministratore(trice) fiduciario(a); (*of school etc*) amministratore/trice; **~ful** *adj* fiducioso(a); **~ing** *adj* = **~ful**; **~worthy** *adj* fidato(a), degno(a) di

fiducia.

truth [truːθ, *pl* truːðz] *n* verità *f inv*;
~**ful** *adj* (*person*) sincero(a); (*description*) veritiero(a), esatto(a).

try [traɪ] *n* prova, tentativo; (*RUGBY*)
meta ♦ *vt* (*LAW*) giudicare; (*test: also:*
~ *out*) provare; (*strain*) mettere alla
prova ♦ *vi* provare; **to have a** ~ fare un
tentativo; **to** ~ **to do** (*seek*) cercare di
fare; ~ **on** *vt* (*clothes*) provare; ~**ing**
adj (*day, experience*) logorante,
pesante; (*child*) difficile, insopportabile.

tsar [zɑː*] *n* zar *m inv*.

T-shirt ['tiː-] *n* maglietta.

T-square ['tiː-] *n* riga a T.

tub [tʌb] *n* tinozza; mastello; (*bath*) bagno.

tuba ['tjuːbə] *n* tuba.

tubby ['tʌbɪ] *adj* grassoccio(a).

tube [tjuːb] *n* tubo; (*BRIT: underground*)
metropolitana, metrò *m inv*; (*for tyre*)
camera d'aria; ~ **station** (*BRIT*) *n*
stazione *f* della metropolitana.

tubular ['tjuːbjulə*] *adj* tubolare.

TUC (*BRIT*) *n abbr* (= *Trades Union
Congress*) confederazione *f* dei
sindacati britannici.

tuck [tʌk] *vt* (*put*) mettere; ~ **away** *vt*
riporre; (*building*): **to be ~ed away**
essere in un luogo isolato; ~ **in** *vt*
mettere dentro; (*child*) rimboccare ♦ *vi*
(*eat*) mangiare di buon appetito;
abbuffarsi; ~ **up** *vt* (*child*) rimboccare
le coperte a; ~ **shop** *n* negozio di pasticceria (*in una scuola*).

Tuesday ['tjuːzdɪ] *n* martedì *m inv*.

tuft [tʌft] *n* ciuffo.

tug [tʌg] *n* (*ship*) rimorchiatore *m* ♦ *vt*
tirare con forza; ~**-of-war** *n* tiro alla
fune.

tuition [tjuːˈɪʃən] *n* (*BRIT*) lezioni *fpl* ♦ (*:
private ~*) lezioni *fpl* private; (*US:
school fees*) tasse *fpl* scolastiche.

tulip ['tjuːlɪp] *n* tulipano.

tumble ['tʌmbl] *n* (*fall*) capitombolo ♦
vi capitombolare, ruzzolare; **to** ~ **to sth**
(*inf*) realizzare qc; ~**down** *adj*
cadente, diroccato(a); ~ **dryer** (*BRIT*) *n*
asciugatrice *f*.

tumbler ['tʌmblə*] *n* bicchiere *m* (*senza*

stelo).

tummy ['tʌmɪ] (*inf*) *n* pancia.

tumour ['tjuːmə*] (*US* **tumor**) *n* tumore
m.

tuna ['tjuːnə] *n inv* (*also:* ~ *fish*) tonno.

tune [tjuːn] *n* (*melody*) melodia, aria ♦
vt (*MUS*) accordare; (*RADIO, TV, AUT*)
regolare, mettere a punto; **to be in/out
of** ~ (*instrument*) essere accordato(a)/
scordato(a); (*singer*) essere
intonato(a)/ stonato(a); ~ **in** *vi*: **to** ~ **in
(to)** (*RADIO, TV*) sintonizzarsi (su); ~
up *vi* (*musician*) accordare lo
strumento; ~**ful** *adj* melodioso(a); ~**r**
n: **piano** ~**r** accordatore *m*.

tunic ['tjuːnɪk] *n* tunica.

Tunisia [tjuːˈnɪzɪə] *n* Tunisia.

tunnel ['tʌnl] *n* galleria ♦ *vi* scavare
una galleria.

turban ['təːbən] *n* turbante *m*.

turbulence ['təːbjuləns] *n* (*AVIAT*)
turbolenza.

tureen [təˈriːn] *n* zuppiera.

turf [təːf] *n* terreno erboso; (*clod*) zolla
♦ *vt* coprire di zolle erbose; ~ **out** (*inf*)
vt buttar fuori.

turgid ['təːdʒɪd] *adj* (*speech*)
ampolloso(a), pomposo(a).

Turin [tjuəˈrɪn] *n* Torino *f*.

Turk [təːk] *n* turco/a.

Turkey ['təːkɪ] *n* Turchia.

turkey ['təːkɪ] *n* tacchino.

Turkish ['təːkɪʃ] *adj* turco(a) ♦ *n* (*LING*)
turco.

turmoil ['təːmɔɪl] *n* confusione *f*,
tumulto.

turn [təːn] *n* giro; (*change*)
cambiamento; (*in road*) curva;
(*tendency: of mind, events*) tendenza;
(*performance*) numero; (*chance*)
turno; (*MED*) crisi *f inv*, attacco ♦ *vt*
girare, voltare; (*change*): **to** ~ **sth into**
trasformare qc in ♦ *vi* girare; (*person:
look back*) girarsi, voltarsi; (*reverse
direction*) girare; (*change*) cambiare;
(*milk*) andare a male; (*become*)
diventare; **a good** ~ un buon servizio; **it
gave me quite a** ~ mi ha fatto prendere
un bello spavento; **"no left** ~**"** (*AUT*)
"divieto di svolta a sinistra"; **it's your**

~ tocca a lei; **in** ~ a sua volta; a turno; **to take** ~**s (at sth)** fare (qc) a turno; ~ **away** *vi* girarsi (dall'altra parte) ♦ *vt* mandare via; ~ **back** *vi* ritornare, tornare indietro ♦ *vt* far tornare indietro; (*clock*) spostare indietro; ~ **down** *vt* (*refuse*) rifiutare; (*reduce*) abbassare; (*fold*) ripiegare; ~ **in** *vi* (*inf: go to bed*) andare a letto ♦ *vt* (*fold*) voltare in dentro; ~ **off** *vi* (*from road*) girare, voltare ♦ *vt* (*light, radio, engine etc*) spegnere; ~ **on** *vt* (*light, radio etc*) accendere; ~ **out** *vt* (*light, gas*) chiudere; spegnere ♦ *vi* (*voters*) presentarsi; **to** ~ **out to be ...** rivelarsi ..., risultare ...; ~ **over** *vi* (*person*) girarsi ♦ *vt* girare; ~ **round** *vi* girare; (*person*) girarsi; ~ **up** *vi* (*person*) arrivare, presentarsi; (*lost object*) saltar fuori ♦ *vt* (*collar, sound*) alzare; ~**ing** *n* (*in road*) curva; ~**ing point** *n* (*fig*) svolta decisiva.

turnip ['tə:nɪp] *n* rapa.

turnout ['tə:naut] *n* presenza, affluenza.

turnover ['tə:nəuvə*] *n* (COMM) turnover *m inv*.

turnpike ['tə:npaɪk] (US) *n* autostrada a pedaggio.

turnstile ['tə:nstaɪl] *n* tornella.

turntable ['tə:nteɪbl] *n* (*on record player*) piatto.

turn-up (BRIT) *n* (*on trousers*) risvolto.

turpentine ['tə:pəntaɪn] *n* (*also: turps*) acqua ragia.

turquoise ['tə:kwɔɪz] *n* turchese *m* ♦ *adj* turchese.

turret ['tʌrɪt] *n* torretta.

turtle ['tə:tl] *n* testuggine *f*; ~**neck (sweater)** *n* maglione *m* con il collo alto.

tusk [tʌsk] *n* zanna.

tussle ['tʌsl] *n* baruffa, mischia.

tutor ['tju:tə*] *n* (*in college*) docente *m/f* (*responsabile di un gruppo di studenti*); (*private teacher*) precettore *m*; ~**ial** [-'tɔ:rɪəl] *n* (SCOL) lezione *f* con discussione (*a un gruppo limitato*).

tuxedo [tʌk'si:dəu] (US) *n* smoking *m inv*.

TV [ti:'vi:] *n abbr* (= television) tivù *f*

inv.

twang [twæŋ] *n* (*of instrument*) suono vibrante; (*of voice*) accento nasale.

tweed [twi:d] *n* tweed *m inv*.

tweezers ['twi:zəz] *npl* pinzette *fpl*.

twelfth [twelfθ] *num* dodicesimo(a).

twelve [twelv] *num* dodici; **at** ~ (*o'clock*) alle dodici, a mezzogiorno; (*midnight*) a mezzanotte.

twentieth ['twentɪθ] *num* ventesimo(a).

twenty ['twentɪ] *num* venti.

twice [twaɪs] *adv* due volte; ~ **as much** due volte tanto.

twiddle ['twɪdl] *vt, vi*: **to** ~ (**with**) **sth** giocherellare con qc; **to** ~ **one's thumbs** (*fig*) girarsi i pollici.

twig [twɪg] *n* ramoscello ♦ *vt, vi* (*inf*) capire.

twilight ['twaɪlaɪt] *n* crepuscolo.

twin [twɪn] *adj, n* gemello(a) ♦ *vt*: **to** ~ **one town with another** far il gemellaggio di una città con un'altra; ~**-bedded room** *n* stanza con letti gemelli.

twine [twaɪn] *n* spago, cordicella ♦ *vi* attorcigliarsi.

twinge [twɪndʒ] *n* (*of pain*) fitta; **a** ~ **of conscience/regret** un rimorso/rimpianto.

twinkle ['twɪŋkl] *vi* scintillare; (*eyes*) brillare.

twirl [twə:l] *vt* far roteare ♦ *vi* roteare.

twist [twɪst] *n* torsione *f*; (*in wire, flex*) piega; (*in road*) curva; (*in story*) colpo di scena ♦ *vt* attorcigliare; (*ankle*) slogare; (*weave*) intrecciare; (*roll around*) arrotolare; (*fig*) distorcere ♦ *vi* (*road*) serpeggiare.

twit [twɪt] (*inf*) *n* cretino(a).

twitch [twɪtʃ] *n* tiratina; (*nervous*) tic *m inv* ♦ *vi* contrarsi.

two [tu:] *num* due; **to put** ~ **and** ~ **together** (*fig*) fare uno più uno; ~**-door** *adj* (AUT) a due porte; ~**-faced** (*pej*) *adj* (*person*) falso(a); ~**-fold** *adv*: **to increase** ~**fold** aumentare del doppio; ~**-piece (suit)** *n* due pezzi *m inv*; ~**-piece (swimsuit)** *n* (*costume m da bagno a*) due pezzi *m inv*; ~**some** *n* (*people*) coppia; ~**-way** *adj* (*traffic*) a due sensi.

tycoon [taɪ'ku:n] *n*: (**business**) ~ magnate m.

type [taɪp] n (category) genere m; (model) modello; (example) tipo; (TYP) tipo, carattere m ♦ vt (letter etc) battere (a macchina), dattilografare; **~-cast** adj (actor) a ruolo fisso; **~face** n carattere m tipografico; **~script** n dattiloscritto; **~writer** n macchina da scrivere; **~written** adj dattiloscritto(a), battuto(a) a macchina.

typhoid ['taɪfɔɪd] n tifoidea.

typhoon [taɪ'fuːn] n tifone m.

typical ['tɪpɪkl] adj tipico(a).

typify ['tɪpɪfaɪ] vt caratterizzare; (person) impersonare.

typing ['taɪpɪŋ] n dattilografia.

typist ['taɪpɪst] n dattilografo/a.

tyrant ['taɪərnt] n tiranno.

tyre ['taɪə*] (US tire) n pneumatico, gomma; **~ pressure** n pressione f (delle gomme).

tzar [zɑː*] n = tsar.

U

U-bend ['juː'-] n (in pipe) sifone m.

ubiquitous [juː'bɪkwɪtəs] adj onnipresente.

udder ['ʌdə*] n mammella.

UFO ['juːfəu] n abbr (= unidentified flying object) UFO m inv.

ugh [əːh] excl puah!

ugly ['ʌglɪ] adj brutto(a).

UK n abbr = United Kingdom.

ulcer ['ʌlsə*] n ulcera; (also: mouth ~) afta.

Ulster ['ʌlstə*] n Ulster m.

ulterior [ʌl'tɪərɪə*] adj ulteriore; **~ motive** n secondo fine m.

ultimate ['ʌltɪmət] adj ultimo(a), finale; (authority) massimo(a), supremo(a); **~ly** adv alla fine; in definitiva, in fin dei conti.

ultrasound [ʌltrə'saund] n (MED) ultrasuono.

umbilical cord [ʌmbɪ'laɪkl-] n cordone m ombelicale.

umbrella [ʌm'brelə] n ombrello.

umpire ['ʌmpaɪə*] n arbitro.

umpteen [ʌmp'tiːn] adj non so quanti(e); **for the ~th time** per l'ennesima volta.

UN n abbr (= United Nations) ONU f.

unable [ʌn'eɪbl] adj: **to be ~ to** non potere, essere nell'impossibilità di; essere incapace di.

unaccompanied [ʌnə'kʌmpənɪd] adj (child, lady) non accompagnato(a).

unaccountably [ʌnə'kauntəblɪ] adv inesplicabilmente.

unaccustomed [ʌnə'kʌstəmd] adj: **to be ~ to sth** non essere abituato a qc.

unanimous [juː'nænɪməs] adj unanime; **~ly** adv all'unanimità.

unarmed [ʌn'ɑːmd] adj (without a weapon) disarmato(a); (combat) senz'armi.

unashamed [ʌnə'ʃeɪmd] adj sfacciato(a).

unassuming [ʌnə'sjuːmɪŋ] adj modesto(a), senza pretese.

unattached [ʌnə'tætʃt] adj senza legami, libero(a).

unattended [ʌnə'tendɪd] adj (car, child, luggage) incustodito(a).

unattractive [ʌnə'træktɪv] adj poco attraente.

unauthorized [ʌn'ɔːθəraɪzd] adj non autorizzato(a).

unavoidable [ʌnə'vɔɪdəbl] adj inevitabile.

unaware [ʌnə'weə*] adj: **to be ~ of** non sapere, ignorare; **~s** adv di sorpresa, alla sprovvista.

unbalanced [ʌn'bælənst] adj squilibrato(a).

unbearable [ʌn'bɛərəbl] adj insopportabile.

unbeknown(st) [ʌnbɪ'nəun(st)] adv: **~ to** all'insaputa di.

unbelievable [ʌnbɪ'liːvəbl] adj incredibile.

unbend [ʌn'bend] (irreg: like bend)) vi distendersi ♦ vt (wire) raddrizzare.

unbias(s)ed [ʌn'baɪəst] adj (person, report) obiettivo(a), imparziale.

unborn [ʌn'bɔːn] adj non ancora nato(a).

unbreakable [ʌn'breɪkəbl] adj infrangibile.

unbroken [ʌn'brəukən] *adj* intero(a); (*series*) continuo(a); (*record*) imbattuto(a).

unbutton [ʌn'bʌtn] *vt* sbottonare.

uncalled-for [ʌn'kɔːld-] *adj* (*remark*) fuori luogo *inv*; (*action*) ingiustificato(a).

uncanny [ʌn'kænɪ] *adj* misterioso(a), strano(a).

unceasing [ʌn'siːsɪŋ] *adj* incessante.

unceremonious ['ʌnsɛrɪ'məunɪəs] *adj* (*abrupt, rude*) senza tante cerimonie.

uncertain [ʌn'səːtn] *adj* incerto(a); dubbio(a); ~**ty** *n* incertezza.

unchanged [ʌn'tʃeɪndʒd] *adj* invariato(a).

unchecked [ʌn'tʃɛkt] *adj* incontrollato(a).

uncivilized [ʌn'sɪvɪlaɪzd] *adj* (*gen*) selvaggio(a); (*fig*) incivile, barbaro(a).

uncle ['ʌŋkl] *n* zio.

uncomfortable [ʌn'kʌmfətəbl] *adj* scomodo(a); (*uneasy*) a disagio, agitato(a); (*unpleasant*) fastidioso(a).

uncommon [ʌn'kɔmən] *adj* raro(a), insolito(a), non comune.

uncompromising [ʌn'kɔmprəmaɪzɪŋ] *adj* intransigente, inflessibile.

unconcerned [ʌnkən'səːnd] *adj*: **to be ~ (about)** non preoccuparsi (di *or* per).

unconditional [ʌnkən'dɪʃənl] *adj* incondizionato(a), senza condizioni.

unconscious [ʌn'kɔnʃəs] *adj* privo(a) di sensi, svenuto(a); (*unaware*) inconsapevole, inconscio(a) ♦ *n*: **the ~** l'inconscio; ~**ly** *adv* inconsciamente.

uncontrollable [ʌnkən'trəuləbl] *adj* incontrollabile; indisciplinato(a).

unconventional [ʌnkən'vɛnʃənl] *adj* poco convenzionale.

uncouth [ʌn'kuːθ] *adj* maleducato(a), grossolano(a).

uncover [ʌn'kʌvə*] *vt* scoprire.

undecided [ʌndɪ'saɪdɪd] *adj* indeciso(a).

under ['ʌndə*] *prep* sotto; (*less than*) meno di; al disotto di; (*according to*) secondo, in conformità a ♦ *adv* (al) disotto; ~ **there** là sotto; ~ **repair** in riparazione.

under... ['ʌndə*] *prefix* sotto..., sub...; ~ **age** *adj* minorenne; ~**carriage** (*BRIT*) *n* carrello (d'atterraggio); ~**charge** *vt* far pagare di meno a; ~**clothes** *npl* biancheria (intima); ~**coat** *n* (*paint*) mano *f* di fondo; ~**cover** *adj* segreto(a), clandestino(a); ~**current** *n* corrente *f* sottomarina; ~**cut** *vt irreg* vendere a prezzo minore di; ~**developed** *adj* sottosviluppato(a); ~**dog** *n* oppresso/a; ~**done** *adj* (*CULIN*) al sangue; (*pej*) poco cotto(a); ~**estimate** *vt* sottovalutare; ~**fed** *adj* denutrito(a); ~**foot** *adv* sotto i piedi; ~**go** *vt irreg* subire; (*treatment*) sottoporsi a; ~**graduate** *n* studente(essa) universitario(a); ~**ground** *n* (*BRIT*: *railway*) metropolitana; (*POL*) movimento clandestino ♦ *adj* sotterraneo(a); (*fig*) clandestino(a) ♦ *adv* sottoterra; **to go** ~**ground** (*fig*) darsi alla macchia; ~**growth** *n* sottobosco; ~**hand(ed)** *adj* (*fig*) furtivo(a), subdolo(a); ~**lie** *vt irreg* essere alla base di; ~**line** *vt* sottolineare; ~**ling** ['ʌndəlɪŋ] (*pej*) *n* subalterno/a, tirapiedi *m/f inv*; ~**mine** *vt* minare; ~**neath** [ʌndə'niːθ] *adv* sotto, disotto ♦ *prep* sotto, al di sotto di; ~**paid** *adj* sottopagato(a); ~**pants** *npl* mutande *fpl*, slip *m inv*; ~**pass** (*BRIT*) *n* sottopassaggio; ~**privileged** *adj* non abbiente; meno favorito(a); ~**rate** *vt* sottovalutare; ~**shirt** (*US*) *n* maglietta; ~**shorts** (*US*) *npl* mutande *fpl*, slip *m inv*; ~**side** *n* disotto; ~**skirt** (*BRIT*) *n* sottoveste *f*.

understand [ʌndə'stænd] (*irreg: like* stand) *vt, vi* capire, comprendere; **I ~ that ...** sento che ...; credo di capire che ...; ~**able** *adj* comprensibile; ~**ing** *adj* comprensivo(a) ♦ *n* comprensione *f*; (*agreement*) accordo.

understatement [ʌndə'steɪtmənt] *n*: **that's an ~!** a dire poco!

understood [ʌndə'stud] *pt, pp of* **understand** ♦ *adj* inteso(a); (*implied*) sottinteso(a).

understudy ['ʌndəstʌdɪ] *n* sostituto/a, attore/trice supplente.

undertake [ʌndə'teɪk] (*irreg: like* **take**) *vt* intraprendere; **to ~ to do sth** impegnarsi a fare qc.

undertaker ['ʌndəteɪkə*] *n* impresario di pompe funebri.

undertaking [ʌndə'teɪkɪŋ] *n* impresa; (*promise*) promessa.

undertone ['ʌndətəun] *n*: **in an ~** a mezza voce, a voce bassa.

underwater [ʌndə'wɔːtə*] *adv* sott'acqua ♦ *adj* subacqueo(a).

underwear ['ʌndəwɛə*] *n* biancheria (intima).

underworld ['ʌndəwəːld] *n* (*of crime*) malavita.

underwriter ['ʌndəraɪtə*] *n* (*INSURANCE*) sottoscrittore/trice.

undesirable [ʌndɪ'zaɪərəbl] *adj* sgradevole.

undies ['ʌndɪz] (*inf*) *npl* biancheria intima da donna.

undo [ʌn'duː] *vt irreg* disfare; **~ing** *n* rovina, perdita.

undoubted [ʌn'dautɪd] *adj* sicuro(a), certo(a); **~ly** *adv* senza alcun dubbio.

undress [ʌn'dres] *vi* spogliarsi.

undue [ʌn'djuː] *adj* eccessivo(a).

undulating ['ʌndjuleɪtɪŋ] *adj* ondeggiante; ondulato(a).

unduly [ʌn'djuːlɪ] *adv* eccessivamente.

unearth [ʌn'əːθ] *vt* dissotterrare; (*fig*) scoprire.

unearthly [ʌn'əːθlɪ] *adj* (*hour*) impossibile.

uneasy [ʌn'iːzɪ] *adj* a disagio; (*worried*) preoccupato(a); (*peace*) precario(a).

uneconomic(al) ['ʌniːkə'nɔmɪk(l)] *adj* antieconomico(a).

unemployed [ʌnɪm'plɔɪd] disoccupato(a) ♦ *npl*: **the ~** i disoccupati.

unemployment [ʌnɪm'plɔɪmənt] *n* disoccupazione *f*.

unending [ʌn'endɪŋ] *adj* senza fine.

unerring [ʌn'əːrɪŋ] *adj* infallibile.

uneven [ʌn'iːvn] *adj* ineguale; irregolare.

unexpected [ʌnɪk'spektɪd] *adj* inatteso(a), imprevisto(a); **~ly** *adv* inaspettatamente.

unfailing [ʌn'feɪlɪŋ] *adj* (*supply, energy*) inesauribile; (*remedy*) infallibile.

unfair [ʌn'fɛə*] *adj*: **~ (to)** ingiusto(a) (nei confronti di).

unfaithful [ʌn'feɪθful] *adj* infedele.

unfamiliar [ʌnfə'mɪlɪə*] *adj* sconosciuto(a), strano(a); **to be ~ with** non avere familiarità con.

unfashionable [ʌn'fæʃnəbl] *adj* (*clothes*) fuori moda; (*district*) non alla moda.

unfasten [ʌn'fɑːsn] *vt* slacciare; sciogliere.

unfavourable [ʌn'feɪvərəbl] (*US* **unfavorable**) *adj* sfavorevole.

unfeeling [ʌn'fiːlɪŋ] *adj* insensibile, duro(a).

unfinished [ʌn'fɪnɪʃt] *adj* incompleto(a).

unfit [ʌn'fɪt] *adj* (*ill*) malato(a), in cattiva salute; (*incompetent*): **~ (for)** incompetente (in); (: *work*, *MIL*) inabile (a).

unfold [ʌn'fəuld] *vt* spiegare ♦ *vi* (*story, plot*) svelarsi.

unforeseen ['ʌnfɔː'siːn] *adj* imprevisto(a).

unforgettable [ʌnfə'getəbl] *adj* indimenticabile.

unfortunate [ʌn'fɔːtʃnət] *adj* sfortunato(a); (*event, remark*) infelice; **~ly** *adv* sfortunatamente, purtroppo.

unfounded [ʌn'faundɪd] *adj* infondato(a).

unfriendly [ʌn'frendlɪ] *adj* poco amichevole, freddo(a).

ungainly [ʌn'geɪnlɪ] *adj* goffo(a), impacciato(a).

ungodly [ʌn'gɔdlɪ] *adj*: **at an ~ hour** a un'ora impossibile.

ungrateful [ʌn'greɪtful] *adj* ingrato(a).

unhappiness [ʌn'hæpɪnɪs] *n* infelicità.

unhappy [ʌn'hæpɪ] *adj* infelice; **~ about/with** (*arrangements etc*) insoddisfatto(a) di.

unharmed [ʌn'hɑːmd] *adj* incolume, sano(a) e salvo(a).

unhealthy [ʌn'helθɪ] *adj* (*gen*) malsano(a); (*person*) malaticcio(a).

unheard-of [ʌn'həːdɔv] *adj* inaudito(a), senza precedenti.

unhurt [ʌn'hə:t] *adj* illeso(a).
uniform ['ju:nifɔ:m] *n* uniforme *f*, divisa
♦ *adj* uniforme.
uninhabited [ʌnin'hæbitid] *adj*
disabitato(a).
unintentional [ʌnin'tenʃənəl] *adj*
involontario(a).
union ['ju:njən] *n* unione *f*; (*also: trade*
~) sindacato ♦ *cpd* sindacale, dei
sindacati; **U~ Jack** *n* bandiera
nazionale britannica.
unique [ju:'ni:k] *adj* unico(a).
unit ['ju:nit] *n* unità *f inv*; (*section: of
furniture etc*) elemento; (*team, squad*)
reparto, squadra.
unite [ju:'nait] *vt* unire ♦ *vi* unirsi; ~**d**
adj unito(a); unificato(a); (*efforts*)
congiunto(a); **U~d Kingdom** *n* Regno
Unito; **U~d Nations (Organization)** *n*
(Organizzazione *f* delle) Nazioni Unite;
U~d States (of America) *n* Stati *mpl*
Uniti (d'America).
unit trust (*BRIT*) *n* fondo d'investi-
mento.
unity ['ju:niti] *n* unità.
universal [ju:ni'və:sl] *adj* universale.
universe ['ju:nivə:s] *n* universo.
university [ju:ni'və:siti] *n* università *f
inv*.
unjust [ʌn'dʒʌst] *adj* ingiusto(a).
unkempt [ʌn'kempt] *adj* trasandato(a);
spettinato(a).
unkind [ʌn'kaind] *adj* scortese; crudele.
unknown [ʌn'nəun] *adj* sconosciuto(a).
unlawful [ʌn'lɔ:ful] *adj* illecito(a),
illegale.
unleash [ʌn'li:ʃ] *vt* (*fig*) scatenare.
unless [ʌn'les] *conj* a meno che (non)
+ *sub*.
unlike [ʌn'laik] *adj* diverso(a) ♦ *prep* a
differenza di, contrariamente a.
unlikely [ʌn'laikli] *adj* improbabile.
unlisted [ʌn'listid] (*US*) *adj* (*TEL*): **to be**
~ non essere sull'elenco.
unload [ʌn'ləud] *vt* scaricare.
unlock [ʌn'lɔk] *vt* aprire.
unlucky [ʌn'lʌki] *adj* sfortunato(a);
(*object, number*) che porta sfortuna.
unmarried [ʌn'mærid] *adj* non
sposato(a); (*man only*) scapolo, celibe;

(*woman only*) nubile.
unmistakable [ʌnmis'teikəbl] *adj*
inconfondibile.
unmitigated [ʌn'mitigeitid] *adj* non
mitigato(a), assoluto(a), vero(a) e pro-
prio(a).
unnatural [ʌn'nætʃrəl] *adj* innaturale;
contro natura.
unnecessary [ʌn'nesəsəri] *adj* inutile,
superfluo(a).
unnoticed [ʌn'nəutist] *adj*: (**to go**) ~
(passare) inosservato(a).
UNO ['ju:nəu] *n abbr* (= *United Nations
Organization*) ONU *f*.
unobtainable [ʌnəb'teinəbl] *adj* (*TEL*)
non ottenibile.
unobtrusive [ʌnəb'tru:siv] *adj* di-
screto(a).
unofficial [ʌnə'fiʃl] *adj* non ufficiale;
(*strike*) non dichiarato(a) dal
sindacato.
unpack [ʌn'pæk] *vi* disfare la valigia (*or
le valigie*) ♦ *vt* disfare.
unpalatable [ʌn'pælətəbl] *adj*
sgradevole.
unparalleled [ʌn'pærəleld] *adj*
incomparabile, impareggiabile.
unpleasant [ʌn'pleznt] *adj* spiacevole.
unplug [ʌn'plʌg] *vt* staccare.
unpopular [ʌn'pɔpjulə*] *adj* impopolare.
unprecedented [ʌn'presidəntid] *adj*
senza precedenti.
unpredictable [ʌnpri'diktəbl] *adj* imprevedibile.
unprofessional [ʌnprə'feʃənl] *adj* poco
professionale.
unqualified [ʌn'kwɔlifaid] *adj* (*teacher*)
non abilitato(a); (*success*) assoluto(a),
senza riserve.
unquestionably [ʌn'kwestʃənəbli] *adv*
indiscutibilmente.
unravel [ʌn'rævl] *vt* dipanare, districare.
unreal [ʌn'riəl] *adj* irreale.
unrealistic [ʌnriə'listik] *adj* non reali-
stico(a).
unreasonable [ʌn'ri:znəbl] *adj*
irragionevole.
unrelated [ʌnri'leitid] *adj*: ~ (**to**) senza
rapporto (con); non imparentato(a)
(con).

unrelenting [ʌnrɪˈlɛntɪŋ] *adj* senza tregua.

unreliable [ʌnrɪˈlaɪəbl] *adj* (*person, machine*) che non dà affidamento; (*news, source of information*) inattendibile.

unremitting [ʌnrɪˈmɪtɪŋ] *adj* incessante.

unreservedly [ʌnrɪˈzɜːvɪdlɪ] *adv* senza riserve.

unrest [ʌnˈrɛst] *n* agitazione *f*.

unroll [ʌnˈrəul] *vt* srotolare.

unruly [ʌnˈruːlɪ] *adj* indisciplinato(a).

unsafe [ʌnˈseɪf] *adj* pericoloso(a), rischioso(a).

unsaid [ʌnˈsɛd] *adj*: **to leave sth ~** passare qc sotto silenzio.

unsatisfactory [ˈʌnsætɪsˈfæktərɪ] *adj* che lascia a desiderare, insufficiente.

unsavoury [ʌnˈseɪvərɪ] (*US* **unsavory**) *adj* (*fig: person, place*) losco(a).

unscathed [ʌnˈskeɪðd] *adj* incolume.

unscrew [ʌnˈskruː] *vt* svitare.

unscrupulous [ʌnˈskruːpjuləs] *adj* senza scrupoli.

unsettled [ʌnˈsɛtld] *adj* (*person*) turbato(a); indeciso(a); (*weather*) instabile.

unshaven [ʌnˈʃeɪvn] *adj* non rasato(a).

unsightly [ʌnˈsaɪtlɪ] *adj* brutto(a), sgradevole a vedersi.

unskilled [ʌnˈskɪld] *adj* non specializzato(a).

unspeakable [ʌnˈspiːkəbl] *adj* (*indescribable*) indicibile; (*awful*) abominevole.

unstable [ʌnˈsteɪbl] *adj* (*gen*) instabile; (*mentally*) squilibrato(a).

unsteady [ʌnˈstɛdɪ] *adj* instabile, malsicuro(a).

unstuck [ʌnˈstʌk] *adj*: **to come ~** scollarsi; (*fig*) fare fiasco.

unsuccessful [ʌnsəkˈsɛsful] *adj* (*writer, proposal*) che non ha successo; (*marriage, attempt*) mal riuscito(a), fallito(a); **to be ~** (*in attempting sth*) non avere successo.

unsuitable [ʌnˈsuːtəbl] *adj* inadatto(a); inopportuno(a); sconveniente.

unsure [ʌnˈʃuə*] *adj* incerto(a); **to be ~ of o.s.** essere insicuro(a).

unsuspecting [ʌnsəˈspɛktɪŋ] *adj* che non

sospetta nulla.

unsympathetic [ʌnsɪmpəˈθɛtɪk] *adj* (*person*) antipatico(a); (*attitude*) poco incoraggiante.

untapped [ʌnˈtæpt] *adj* (*resources*) non sfruttato(a).

unthinkable [ʌnˈθɪŋkəbl] *adj* impensabile, inconcepibile.

untidy [ʌnˈtaɪdɪ] *adj* (*room*) in disordine; (*appearance*) trascurato(a); (*person*) disordinato(a).

untie [ʌnˈtaɪ] *vt* (*knot, parcel*) disfare; (*prisoner, dog*) slegare.

until [ʌnˈtɪl] *prep* fino a; (*after negative*) prima di ♦ *conj* finché, fino a quando; (*in past, after negative*) prima che + *sub*, prima di + *infinitive*; **~ he comes** finché *or* fino a quando non arriva; **~ now** finora; **~ then** fino ad allora.

untimely [ʌnˈtaɪmlɪ] *adj* intempestivo(a), inopportuno(a); (*death*) prematuro(a).

untold [ʌnˈtəuld] *adj* (*story*) mai rivelato(a); (*wealth*) incalcolabile; (*joy, suffering*) indescrivibile. ˙

untoward [ʌntəˈwɔːd] *adj* sfortunato(a), sconveniente.

unused [ʌnˈjuːzd] *adj* nuovo(a).

unusual [ʌnˈjuːʒuəl] *adj* insolito(a), eccezionale, raro(a).

unveil [ʌnˈveɪl] *vt* scoprire; svelare.

unwanted [ʌnˈwɒntɪd] *adj* (*clothing*) smesso(a); (*child*) non desiderato(a).

unwavering [ʌnˈweɪvərɪŋ] *adj* fermo(a), incrollabile.

unwelcome [ʌnˈwɛlkəm] *adj* non gradito(a).

unwell [ʌnˈwɛl] *adj* indisposto(a); **to feel ~** non sentirsi bene.

unwieldy [ʌnˈwiːldɪ] *adj* poco maneggevole.

unwilling [ʌnˈwɪlɪŋ] *adj*: **to be ~ to do** non voler fare; **~ly** *adv* malvolentieri.

unwind [ʌnˈwaɪnd] (*irreg: like* **wind**) *vt* svolgere, srotolare ♦ *vi* (*relax*) rilassarsi.

unwise [ʌnˈwaɪz] *adj* poco saggio(a).

unwitting [ʌnˈwɪtɪŋ] *adj* involontario(a).

unworkable [ʌnˈwəːkəbl] *adj* (*plan*)

inattuabile.
unworthy [ʌn'wɜːðɪ] *adj* indegno(a).
unwrap [ʌn'ræp] *vt* disfare; aprire.
unwritten [ʌn'rɪtn] *adj* (*agreement*) tacito(a); (*law*) non scritto(a).

KEYWORD

up [ʌp] *prep*: he went ~ the stairs/the hill è salito su per le scale/sulla collina; the cat was ~ a tree il gatto era su un albero; they live further ~ the street vivono un po' più su nella stessa strada
♦ *adv* **1** (*upwards, higher*) su, in alto; ~ in the sky/the mountains su nel cielo/in montagna; ~ there lassù; ~ above su in alto
2: to be ~ (*out of bed*) essere alzato(a); (*prices, level*) essere salito(a)
3: ~ to (*as far as*) fino a; ~ to now finora
4: to be ~ to (*depending on*): it's ~ to you sta a lei, dipende da lei; (*equal to*): he's not ~ to it (*job, task etc*) non ne è all'altezza; (*inf: be doing*): what is he ~ to? cosa sta combinando?
♦ *n*: ~s and downs alti e bassi *mpl*.

---

upbringing ['ʌpbrɪŋɪŋ] *n* educazione *f*.
update [ʌp'deɪt] *vt* aggiornare.
upgrade [ʌp'greɪd] *vt* (*house, job*) migliorare; (*employee*) avanzare di grado.
upheaval [ʌp'hiːvl] *n* sconvolgimento; tumulto.
uphill [ʌp'hɪl] *adj* in salita; (*fig: task*) difficile ♦ *adv*: to go ~ andare in salita, salire.
uphold [ʌp'həʊld] (*irreg: like hold*) *vt* approvare; sostenere.
upholstery [ʌp'həʊlstərɪ] *n* tappezzeria.
upkeep ['ʌpkiːp] *n* manutenzione *f*.
upon [ə'pɒn] *prep* su.
upper ['ʌpə*] *adj* superiore ♦ *n* (*of shoe*) tomaia; ~-class *adj* dell'alta borghesia; ~ hand *n*: to have the ~ hand avere il coltello dalla parte del manico; ~most *adj* il(la) più alto(a); predominante.
upright ['ʌpraɪt] *adj* diritto(a);

verticale; (*fig*) diritto(a), onesto(a).
uprising ['ʌpraɪzɪŋ] *n* insurrezione *f*, rivolta.
uproar ['ʌprɔː*] *n* tumulto, clamore *m*.
uproot [ʌp'ruːt] *vt* sradicare.
upset [*n* 'ʌpset, *vb, adj* ʌp'set] (*irreg: like set*) *n* (*to plan etc*) contrattempo; (*stomach* ~) disturbo ♦ *vt* (*glass etc*) rovesciare; (*plan, stomach*) scombussolare; (*person: offend*) contrariare; (: *grieve*) addolorare; sconvolgere ♦ *adj* contrariato(a); addolorato(a); (*stomach*) scombussolato(a).
upshot ['ʌpʃɒt] *n* risultato.
upside down ['ʌpsaɪd-] *adv* sottosopra.
upstairs [ʌp'stɛəz] *adv, adj* di sopra, al piano superiore ♦ *n* piano di sopra.
upstart ['ʌpstɑːt] *n* parvenu *m inv*.
upstream [ʌp'striːm] *adv* a monte.
uptake ['ʌpteɪk] *n*: he is quick/slow on the ~ è pronto/lento di comprendonio.
uptight [ʌp'taɪt] (*inf*) *adj* teso(a).
up-to-date *adj* moderno(a); aggiornato(a).
upturn ['ʌptɜːn] *n* (*in luck*) svolta favorevole; (*COMM: in market*) rialzo.
upward ['ʌpwəd] *adj* ascendente; verso l'alto; ~(s) *adv* in su, verso l'alto.
urban ['ɜːbən] *adj* urbano(a).
urbane [ɜː'beɪn] *adj* civile, urbano(a), educato(a).
urchin ['ɜːtʃɪn] *n* monello.
urge [ɜːdʒ] *n* impulso; stimolo; forte desiderio ♦ *vt*: to ~ sb to do sth esortare qn a fare, spingere qn a fare; raccomandare a qn di fare.
urgency ['ɜːdʒənsɪ] *n* urgenza; (*of tone*) insistenza.
urgent ['ɜːdʒənt] *adj* urgente; (*voice*) insistente.
urinate ['jʊərɪneɪt] *vi* orinare.
urine ['jʊərɪn] *n* orina.
urn [ɜːn] *n* urna; (*also: tea* ~) bollitore *m* per il tè.
us [ʌs] *pron* ci; (*stressed, after prep*) noi; *see also* **me**.
US(A) *n abbr* (= United States (of America)) USA *mpl*.
usage ['juːzɪdʒ] *n* uso.

use [n ju:s, vb ju:z] n uso; impiego, utilizzazione f ♦ vt usare, utilizzare, servirsi di; **in ~** in uso; **out of ~** fuori uso; **to be of ~** essere utile, servire; **it's no ~** non serve, è inutile; **she ~d to do it** lo faceva (una volta), era solita farlo; **to be ~d to** avere l'abitudine di; **~ up** vt consumare; esaurire; **~d** adj (object, car) usato(a); **~ful** adj utile; **~fulness** n utilità; **~less** adj inutile; (person) inetto(a); **~r** n utente m/f; **~r-friendly** adj (computer) di facile uso.

usher ['ʌʃə*] n usciere m; **~ette** [-'rɛt] n (in cinema) maschera.

USSR n: **the ~** l'URSS f.

usual ['ju:ʒuəl] adj solito(a); **as ~** come al solito, come d'abitudine; **~ly** adv di solito.

utensil [ju:'tɛnsl] n utensile m; **kitchen ~s** utensili da cucina.

uterus ['ju:tərəs] n utero.

utility [ju:'tɪlɪtɪ] n utilità; (also: public ~) servizio pubblico; **~ room** n locale adibito alla stiratura dei panni etc.

utmost ['ʌtməust] adj estremo(a) ♦ n: **to do one's ~** fare il possibile or di tutto.

utter ['ʌtə*] adj assoluto(a), totale ♦ vt pronunciare, proferire; emettere; **~ance** n espressione f; parole fpl; **~ly** adv completamente, del tutto.

U-turn ['ju:'tɜ:n] n inversione f a U.

V

v. abbr = **verse**; **versus**; **volt**; (= vide) vedi, vedere.

vacancy ['veɪkənsɪ] n (BRIT: job) posto libero; (room) stanza libera.

vacant ['veɪkənt] adj (job, seat etc) libero(a); (expression) assente; **~ lot** (US) n terreno non occupato; (for sale) terreno in vendita.

vacate [və'keɪt] vt lasciare libero(a).

vacation [və'keɪʃən] n (esp US) vacanze fpl.

vaccinate ['væksɪneɪt] vt vaccinare.

vacuum ['vækjum] n vuoto; **~ cleaner** n

aspirapolvere m inv; **~-packed** adj confezionato(a) sottovuoto.

vagina [və'dʒaɪnə] n vagina.

vagrant ['veɪgrnt] n vagabondo/a.

vague [veɪg] adj vago(a); (blurred: photo, memory) sfocato(a); **~ly** adv vagamente.

vain [veɪn] adj (useless) inutile, vano(a); (conceited) vanitoso(a); **in ~** inutilmente, invano.

valentine ['væləntaɪn] n (also: ~ card) cartolina or biglietto di San Valentino; (person) innamorato/a.

valet ['væleɪ] n cameriere m personale.

valiant ['vælɪənt] adj valoroso(a), coraggioso(a).

valid ['vælɪd] adj valido(a), valevole; (excuse) valido(a).

valley ['vælɪ] n valle f.

valour ['vælə*] (US valor) n valore m.

valuable ['væljuəbl] adj (jewel) di (grande) valore; (time, help) prezioso(a); **~s** npl oggetti mpl di valore.

valuation [vælju'eɪʃən] n valutazione f, stima.

value ['vælju:] n valore m ♦ vt (fix price) valutare, dare un prezzo a; (cherish) apprezzare, tenere a; **~ added tax** (BRIT) n imposta sul valore aggiunto; **~d** adj (appreciated) stimato(a), apprezzato(a).

valve [vælv] n valvola.

van [væn] n (AUT) furgone m; (BRIT: RAIL) vagone m.

vandal ['vændl] n vandalo/a; **~ism** n vandalismo.

vanilla [və'nɪlə] n vaniglia ♦ cpd (ice cream) alla vaniglia.

vanish ['vænɪʃ] vi svanire, scomparire.

vanity ['vænɪtɪ] n vanità.

vantage ['vɑ:ntɪdʒ] n: **~ point** posizione f or punto di osservazione; (fig) posizione vantaggiosa.

vapour ['veɪpə*] (US vapor) n vapore m.

variable ['vɛərɪəbl] adj variabile; (mood) mutevole.

variance ['vɛərɪəns] n: **to be at ~ (with)** essere in disaccordo (con); (facts) essere in contraddizione (con).

varicose ['værɪkəus] *adj*: ~ **veins** vene *fpl* varicose.

varied ['vɛərɪd] *adj* vario(a), diverso(a).

variety [və'raɪətɪ] *n* varietà *f inv*; (*quantity*) quantità, numero; ~ **show** *n* varietà *m inv*.

various ['vɛərɪəs] *adj* vario(a), diverso(a); (*several*) parecchi(e), molti(e).

varnish ['vɑːnɪʃ] *n* vernice *f*; (*nail* ~) smalto ♦ *vt* verniciare; mettere lo smalto su.

vary ['vɛərɪ] *vt, vi* variare, mutare.

vase [vɑːz] *n* vaso.

Vaseline ['væsɪliːn] ® *n* vaselina.

vast [vɑːst] *adj* vasto(a); (*amount, success*) enorme.

VAT [væt] *n abbr* (= *value added tax*) I.V.A. *f*.

vat [væt] *n* tino.

Vatican ['vætɪkən] *n*: **the** ~ il Vaticano.

vault [vɔːlt] *n* (*of roof*) volta; (*tomb*) tomba; (*in bank*) camera blindata ♦ *vt* (*also*: ~ *over*) saltare (d'un balzo).

vaunted ['vɔːntɪd] *adj*: **much-**~ tanto celebrato(a).

VCR *n abbr* = video cassette recorder.

VD *n abbr* = venereal disease.

VDU *n abbr* = visual display unit.

veal [viːl] *n* vitello.

veer [vɪə*] *vi* girare, virare.

vegetable ['vɛdʒtəbl] *n* verdura, ortaggio ♦ *adj* vegetale.

vegetarian [vɛdʒɪ'tɛərɪən] *adj, n* vegetariano(a).

vehement ['viːɪmənt] *adj* veemente, violento(a).

vehicle ['viːɪkl] *n* veicolo.

veil [veɪl] *n* velo; ~**ed** *adj* (*fig: threat*) velato(a).

vein [veɪn] *n* vena; (*on leaf*) nervatura.

velvet ['vɛlvɪt] *n* velluto ♦ *adj* di velluto.

vending machine ['vɛndɪŋ-] *n* distributore *m* automatico.

vendor ['vɛndə*] *n* venditore/trice.

veneer [və'nɪə*] *n* impiallacciatura; (*fig*) vernice *f*.

venereal [vɪ'nɪərɪəl] *adj*: ~ **disease** malattia venerea.

Venetian [vɪ'niːʃən] *adj* veneziano(a);

~ **blind** *n* (tenda alla) veneziana.

vengeance ['vɛndʒəns] *n* vendetta; **with a** ~ (*fig*) davvero; furiosamente.

Venice ['vɛnɪs] *n* Venezia.

venison ['vɛnɪsn] *n* carne *f* di cervo.

venom ['vɛnəm] *n* veleno.

vent [vɛnt] *n* foro, apertura; (*in dress, jacket*) spacco ♦ *vt* (*fig: one's feelings*) sfogare, dare sfogo a.

ventilate ['vɛntɪleɪt] *vt* (*room*) dare aria a, arieggiare; **ventilator** *n* ventilatore *m*.

ventriloquist [vɛn'trɪləkwɪst] *n* ventriloquo/a.

venture ['vɛntʃə*] *n* impresa (rischiosa) ♦ *vt* rischiare, azzardare ♦ *vi* avventurarsi; **business** ~ iniziativa commerciale.

venue ['vɛnjuː] *n* luogo (designato) per l'incontro.

verb [vəːb] *n* verbo; ~**al** *adj* verbale; (*translation*) orale.

verbatim [vəː'beɪtɪm] *adj, adv* parola per parola.

verdict ['vəːdɪkt] *n* verdetto.

verge [vəːdʒ] (*BRIT*) *n* bordo, orlo; "**soft** ~**s**" (*BRIT: AUT*) banchine *fpl* cedevoli; **on the** ~ **of doing** sul punto di fare; ~ **on** *vt fus* rasentare.

veritable ['vɛrɪtəbl] *adj* vero(a).

vermin ['vəːmɪn] *npl* animali *mpl* nocivi; (*insects*) insetti *mpl* parassiti.

vermouth ['vəːməθ] *n* vermut *m inv*.

versatile ['vəːsətaɪl] *adj* (*person*) versatile; (*machine, tool etc*) (che si presta) a molti usi.

verse [vəːs] *n* versi *mpl*; (*stanza*) stanza, strofa; (*in bible*) versetto.

versed [vəːst] *adj*: (**well-**)~ **in** pratico(a) di.

version ['vəːʃən] *n* versione *f*.

versus ['vəːsəs] *prep* contro.

vertical ['vəːtɪkl] *adj* verticale ♦ *n* verticale *m*; ~**ly** *adv* verticalmente.

vertigo ['vəːtɪgəu] *n* vertigine *f*.

verve [vəːv] *n* brio; entusiasmo.

very ['vɛrɪ] *adv* molto ♦ *adj*: **the** ~ **book which** proprio il libro che; **the** ~ **last** proprio l'ultimo; **at the** ~ **least** almeno; ~ **much** moltissimo.

vessel ['vɛsl] n (ANAT) vaso; (NAUT) nave f; (container) recipiente m.

vest [vɛst] n (BRIT) maglia; (: sleeveless) canottiera; (US: waistcoat) gilè m inv.

vested interests ['vɛstɪd-] npl (COMM) diritti mpl acquisiti.

vet [vɛt] n abbr (BRIT: = veterinary surgeon) veterinario ♦ vt esaminare minuziosamente.

veteran ['vɛtərn] n (also: war ~) veterano.

veterinary ['vɛtrɪnəri] adj veterinario(a); ~ **surgeon** (US **veterinarian**) n veterinario.

veto ['viːtəu] (pl ~es) n veto ♦ vt opporre il veto a.

vex [vɛks] vt irritare, contrariare; ~**ed** adj (question) controverso(a), dibattuto(a).

via ['vaɪə] prep (by way of) via; (by means of) tramite.

viable ['vaɪəbl] adj attuabile; vitale.

viaduct ['vaɪədʌkt] n viadotto.

vibrant ['vaɪbrənt] adj (lively, bright) vivace; (voice) vibrante.

vibrate [vaɪ'breɪt] vi: to ~ (with) vibrare (di); (resound) risonare (di).

vicar ['vɪkə*] n pastore m; ~**age** n presbiterio.

vicarious [vɪ'kɛərɪəs] adj indiretto(a).

vice [vaɪs] n (evil) vizio; (TECH) morsa.

vice- [vaɪs] prefix vice....

vice squad n (squadra del) buon costume f.

vice versa ['vaɪsɪ'vəːsə] adv viceversa.

vicinity [vɪ'sɪnɪtɪ] n vicinanze fpl.

vicious ['vɪʃəs] adj (remark, dog) cattivo(a); (blow) violento(a); ~ **circle** n circolo vizioso.

victim ['vɪktɪm] n vittima.

victor ['vɪktə*] n vincitore m.

Victorian [vɪk'tɔːrɪən] adj vittoriano(a).

victory ['vɪktərɪ] n vittoria.

video ['vɪdɪəu] cpd video... ♦ n (~ film) video m inv; (also: ~ cassette) videocassetta; (also: ~ cassette recorder) videoregistratore m; ~ **tape** n videotape m inv.

vie [vaɪ] vi: to ~ with competere con,

rivaleggiare con.

Vienna [vɪ'ɛnə] n Vienna.

Vietnam [vjɛt'næm] n Vietnam m; ~**ese** adj, n inv vietnamita m/f.

view [vjuː] n vista, veduta; (opinion) opinione f ♦ vt (look at: also fig) considerare; (house) visitare; **on** ~ (in museum etc) esposto(a); **in full** ~ **of** sotto gli occhi di; **in** ~ **of the weather/ the fact that** considerato il tempo/che; **in my** ~ a mio parere; ~**er** n spettatore/trice; ~**finder** n mirino; ~**point** n punto di vista; (place) posizione f.

vigil ['vɪdʒɪl] n veglia.

vigorous ['vɪgərəs] adj vigoroso(a).

vile [vaɪl] adj (action) vile; (smell) disgustoso(a), nauseante; (temper) pessimo(a).

villa ['vɪlə] n villa.

village ['vɪlɪdʒ] n villaggio; ~**r** n abitante m/f di villaggio.

villain ['vɪlən] n (scoundrel) canaglia; (BRIT: criminal) criminale m; (in novel etc) cattivo.

vindicate ['vɪndɪkeɪt] vt comprovare; giustificare.

vindictive [vɪn'dɪktɪv] adj vendicativo(a).

vine [vaɪn] n vite f; (climbing plant) rampicante m.

vinegar ['vɪnɪgə*] n aceto.

vineyard ['vɪnjɑːd] n vigna, vigneto.

vintage ['vɪntɪdʒ] n (year) annata, produzione f ♦ cpd d'annata; ~ **car** n auto f inv d'epoca; ~ **wine** n vino d'annata.

vinyl ['vaɪnl] n vinile m.

violate ['vaɪəleɪt] vt violare.

violence ['vaɪələns] n violenza.

violent ['vaɪələnt] adj violento(a).

violet ['vaɪələt] adj (colour) viola inv, violetto(a) ♦ n (plant) violetta; (colour) violetto.

violin [vaɪə'lɪn] n violino; ~**ist** n violinista m/f.

VIP n abbr (= very important person) V.I.P. m/f inv.

virgin ['vəːdʒɪn] n vergine f ♦ adj vergine inv.

Virgo ['və:gəʊ] n (sign) Vergine f.
virile ['vɪraɪl] adj virile.
virtually ['və:tjʊəlɪ] adv (almost) praticamente.
virtue ['və:tju:] n virtù f inv; (advantage) pregio, vantaggio; **by ~ of** grazie a.
virtuous ['və:tjʊəs] adj virtuoso(a).
virus ['vaɪərəs] n virus m inv.
visa ['vi:zə] n visto.
vis-à-vis [vi:zə'vi:] prep rispetto a, nei riguardi di.
visibility [vɪzɪ'bɪlɪtɪ] n visibilità.
visible ['vɪzəbl] adj visibile.
vision ['vɪʒən] n (sight) vista; (foresight, in dream) visione f.
visit ['vɪzɪt] n visita; (stay) soggiorno ♦ vt (person: US also: ~ **with**) andare a trovare; (place) visitare; ~**ing hours** npl (in hospital etc) orario delle visite; ~**or** n visitatore/trice; (guest) ospite m/f.
visor ['vaɪzə*] n visiera.
vista ['vɪstə] n vista, prospettiva.
visual ['vɪzjʊəl] adj visivo(a); visuale; ottico(a); ~ **aid** n sussidio visivo; ~ **display unit** n visualizzatore m.
visualize ['vɪzjʊəlaɪz] vt immaginare, figurarsi; (foresee) prevedere.
vital ['vaɪtl] adj vitale; ~**ly** adv estremamente; ~ **statistics** npl (fig) misure fpl.
vitamin ['vɪtəmɪn] n vitamina.
vivacious [vɪ'veɪʃəs] adj vivace.
vivid ['vɪvɪd] adj vivido(a); ~**ly** adv (describe) vividamente; (remember) con precisione.
V-neck ['vi:nɛk] n maglione m con lo scollo a V.
vocabulary [vəʊ'kæbjʊlərɪ] n vocabolario.
vocal ['vəʊkl] adj (MUS) vocale; (communication) verbale; ~ **chords** npl corde fpl vocali.
vocation [vəʊ'keɪʃən] n vocazione f; ~**al** adj professionale.
vociferous [və'sɪfərəs] adj rumoroso(a).
vodka ['vɒdkə] n vodka f inv.
vogue [vəʊg] n moda, (popularity) popolarità, voga.

voice [vɔɪs] n voce f ♦ vt (opinion) esprimere.
void [vɔɪd] n vuoto ♦ adj (invalid) nullo(a); (empty): ~ **of** privo(a) di.
volatile ['vɒlətaɪl] adj volatile; (fig) volubile.
volcano [vɒl'keɪnəʊ] (pl ~**es**) n vulcano.
volition [və'lɪʃən] n: **of one's own** ~ di sua volontà.
volley ['vɒlɪ] n (of gunfire) salva; (of stones, questions etc) raffica; (TENNIS etc) volata; ~**ball** n pallavolo f.
volt [vəʊlt] n volt m inv; ~**age** n tensione f, voltaggio.
voluble ['vɒljʊbl] adj loquace, ciarliero(a).
volume ['vɒlju:m] n volume m.
voluntarily ['vɒləntrɪlɪ] adv volontariamente; gratuitamente.
voluntary ['vɒləntərɪ] adj volontario(a); (unpaid) gratuito(a), non retribuito(a).
volunteer [vɒlən'tɪə*] n volontario/a ♦ vt offrire volontariamente ♦ vi (MIL) arruolarsi volontario; **to** ~ **to do** offrire (volontariamente) di fare.
voluptuous [və'lʌptjʊəs] adj voluttuoso(a).
vomit ['vɒmɪt] n vomito ♦ vt, vi vomitare.
vote [vəʊt] n voto, suffragio; (cast) voto; (franchise) diritto di voto ♦ vt: **to be** ~**d chairman** etc venir eletto presidente etc; (propose): **to** ~ **that** approvare la proposta che ♦ vi votare; ~ **of thanks** discorso di ringraziamento; ~**r** n elettore/trice; **voting** n scrutinio.
vouch [vaʊtʃ]: **to** ~ **for** vt fus farsi garante di.
voucher ['vaʊtʃə*] n (for meal, petrol etc) buono.
vow [vaʊ] n voto, promessa solenne ♦ vt: **to** ~ **to do/that** giurare di fare/che.
vowel ['vaʊəl] n vocale f.
voyage ['vɔɪɪdʒ] n viaggio per mare, traversata.
V-sign ['vi:-] (BRIT) n gesto volgare con le dita.
vulgar ['vʌlgə*] adj volgare.
vulnerable ['vʌlnərəbl] adj vulnerabile.
vulture ['vʌltʃə*] n avvoltoio.

W

wad [wɔd] *n* (*of cotton wool, paper*) tampone *m*; (*of banknotes etc*) fascio.

waddle ['wɔdl] *vi* camminare come una papera.

wade [weɪd] *vi*: **to ~ through** camminare a stento in; (*fig: book*) leggere con fatica.

wafer ['weɪfə*] *n* (*CULIN*) cialda.

waffle ['wɔfl] *n* (*CULIN*) cialda; (*inf*) ciance *fpl* ♦ *vi* cianciare.

waft [wɔft] *vt* portare ♦ *vi* diffondersi.

wag [wæg] *vt* agitare, muovere ♦ *vi* agitarsi.

wage [weɪdʒ] *n* (*also*: ~s) salario, paga ♦ *vt*: **to ~ war** fare la guerra; **~ earner** *n* salariato/a; **~ packet** *n* busta *f* paga *inv*.

wager ['weɪdʒə*] *n* scommessa.

waggle ['wægl] *vt* dimenare, agitare.

wag(g)on ['wægən] *n* (*horse-drawn*) carro; (*BRIT: RAIL*) vagone *m* (merci).

wail [weɪl] *n* gemito; (*of siren*) urlo ♦ *vi* gemere; urlare.

waist [weɪst] *n* vita, cintola; **~coat** (*BRIT*) *n* panciotto, gilè *m inv*; **~line** *n* (giro di) vita.

wait [weɪt] *n* attesa ♦ *vi* aspettare, attendere; **to lie in ~ for** stare in agguato a; **to ~ for** aspettare; **I can't ~ to** (*fig*) non vedo l'ora di; **~ behind** *vi* rimanere (ad aspettare); **~ on** *vt fus* servire; **~er** *n* cameriere *m*; **~ing** *n*: "**no ~ing**" (*BRIT: AUT*) "divieto di sosta"; **~ing list** *n* lista di attesa; **~ing room** *n* sala d'aspetto *or* d'attesa; **~ress** *n* cameriera.

waive [weɪv] *vt* rinunciare a, abbandonare.

wake [weɪk] (*pt* **woke**, **~d**, *pp* **woken**, **~d**) *vt* (*also*: ~ **up**) svegliare ♦ *vi* (*also*: ~ **up**) svegliarsi ♦ *n* (*for dead person*) veglia funebre; (*NAUT*) scia; **waken** *vt*, *vi* = **wake**.

Wales [weɪlz] *n* Galles *m*.

walk [wɔːk] *n* passeggiata; (*short*) giretto; (*gait*) passo, andatura; (*path*) sentiero; (*in park etc*) sentiero, vialetto ♦ *vi* camminare; (*for pleasure, exercise*) passeggiare ♦ *vt* (*distance*) fare *or* percorrere a piedi; (*dog*) accompagnare, portare a passeggiare; **10 minutes' ~ from** 10 minuti di cammino *or* a piedi da; **from all ~s of life** di tutte le condizioni sociali; **~ out** *vi* (*audience*) andarsene; (*workers*) scendere in sciopero; **~ out on** (*inf*) *vt fus* piantare in asso; **~er** *n* (*person*) camminatore/trice; **~ie-talkie** ['wɔːkɪ-'tɔːkɪ] *n* walkie-talkie *m inv*; **~ing** *n* camminare *m*; **~ing shoes** *npl* pedule *fpl*; **~ing stick** *n* bastone *m* da passeggio; **~out** *n* (*of workers*) sciopero senza preavviso *or* a sorpresa; **~over** (*inf*) *n* vittoria facile, gioco da ragazzi; **~way** *n* passaggio pedonale.

wall [wɔːl] *n* muro; (*internal, of tunnel, cave*) parete *f*; **~ed** *adj* (*city*) fortificato(a); (*garden*) cintato(a).

wallet ['wɔlɪt] *n* portafoglio.

wallflower ['wɔːlflaʊə*] *n* violacciocca; **to be a ~** (*fig*) fare da tappezzeria.

wallop ['wɔləp] (*inf*) *vt* pestare.

wallow ['wɔləʊ] *vi* sguazzare.

wallpaper ['wɔːlpeɪpə*] *n* carta da parati ♦ *vt* (*room*) mettere la carta da parati in.

wally ['wɔlɪ] (*inf*) *n* imbecille *m/f*.

walnut ['wɔːlnʌt] *n* noce *f*; (*tree, wood*) noce *m*.

walrus ['wɔːlrəs] (*pl* ~ *or* ~**es**) *n* tricheco.

waltz [wɔːlts] *n* valzer *m inv* ♦ *vi* ballare il valzer.

wan [wɔn] *adj* pallido(a), smorto(a); triste.

wand [wɔnd] *n* (*also*: *magic* ~) bacchetta (magica).

wander ['wɔndə*] *vi* (*person*) girare senza meta, girovagare; (*thoughts*) vagare ♦ *vt* girovagare per.

wane [weɪn] *vi* calare.

wangle [wæŋgl] (*BRIT: inf*) *vt* procurare con l'astuzia.

want [wɔnt] *vt* volere; (*need*) aver bisogno di ♦ *n*: **for ~ of** per mancanza di; **~s** *npl* (*needs*) bisogni *mpl*; **to ~ to do**

volere fare; **to ~ sb to do** volere che qn faccia; **~ed** adj (criminal) ricercato(a); "~ed" (in adverts) "cercasi"; **~ing** adj: **to be found ~ing** non risultare all'altezza.

wanton ['wɒntn] adj sfrenato(a); senza motivo.

war [wɔ:*] n guerra; **to make ~ (on)** far guerra (a).

ward [wɔ:d] n (in hospital: room) corsia; (: section) reparto; (POL) circoscrizione f; (LAW: child: also: **~ of court**) pupillo/a; **~ off** vt parare, schivare.

warden ['wɔ:dn] n (of park, game reserve, youth hostel) guardiano/a; (BRIT: of institution) direttore/trice; (BRIT: also: traffic ~) addetto/a al controllo del traffico e del parcheggio.

warder ['wɔ:də*] (BRIT) n guardia carceraria.

wardrobe ['wɔ:drəub] n (cupboard) guardaroba m inv, armadio; (clothes) guardaroba; (CINEMA, THEATRE) costumi mpl.

warehouse ['wɛəhaus] n magazzino.

wares [wɛəz] npl merci fpl.

warfare ['wɔ:feə*] n guerra.

warhead ['wɔ:hɛd] n (MIL) testata.

warily ['wɛərɪlɪ] adv cautamente, con prudenza.

warlike ['wɔ:laɪk] adj bellicoso(a).

warm [wɔ:m] adj caldo(a); (thanks, welcome, applause) caloroso(a); (person) cordiale; **it's ~** fa caldo; **I'm ~** ho caldo; **~ up** vi scaldarsi, riscaldarsi ♦ vt scaldare, riscaldare; (engine) far scaldare; **~-hearted** adj affettuoso(a); **~ly** adv (applaud, welcome) calorosamente; (dress) con abiti pesanti; **~th** n calore m.

warn [wɔ:n] vt: **to ~ sb that/(not) to do/ of** avvertire or avvisare qn che/di (non) fare/di; **~ing** n avvertimento; (notice) avviso; (signal) segnalazione f; **~ing light** n spia luminosa; **~ing triangle** n (AUT) triangolo.

warp [wɔ:p] vi deformarsi ♦ vt (fig) corrompere.

warrant ['wɔrnt] n (voucher) buono;

(LAW: to arrest) mandato di cattura; (: to search) mandato di perquisizione.

warranty ['wɔrəntɪ] n garanzia.

warren ['wɔrən] n (of rabbits) tana; (fig: of streets etc) dedalo.

warrior ['wɔrɪə*] n guerriero/a.

Warsaw ['wɔ:sɔ:] n Varsavia.

warship ['wɔ:ʃɪp] n nave f da guerra.

wart [wɔ:t] n verruca.

wartime ['wɔ:taɪm] n: **in ~** in tempo di guerra.

wary ['wɛərɪ] adj prudente.

was [wɒz] pt of **be**.

wash [wɒʃ] vt lavare ♦ vi lavarsi; (sea etc): **to ~ over/against sth** infrangersi su/contro qc ♦ n lavaggio; (of ship) scia; **to give sth a ~** lavare qc, dare una lavata a qc; **to have a ~** lavarsi; **~ away** vt (stain) togliere lavando; (subj: river etc) trascinare via; **~ off** vi andare via con il lavaggio; **~ up** vi (BRIT) lavare i piatti; (US) darsi una lavata; **~able** adj lavabile; **~basin** (US **~bowl**) n lavabo; **~cloth** (US) n (face cloth) pezzuola (per lavarsi); **~er** n (TECH) rondella; **~ing** n (linen etc) bucato; **~ing machine** n lavatrice f; **~ing powder** (BRIT) n detersivo (in polvere); **~ing-up** n rigovernatura, lavatura dei piatti; **~ing-up liquid** n detersivo liquido (per stoviglie); **~-out** (inf) n disastro; **~room** n gabinetto.

wasn't ['wɒznt] = **was not**.

wasp [wɒsp] n vespa.

wastage ['weɪstɪdʒ] n spreco; (in manufacturing) scarti mpl; **natural ~** diminuzione f di manodopera (per pensionamento, decesso etc).

waste [weɪst] n spreco; (of time) perdita; (rubbish) rifiuti mpl; (also: household ~) immondizie fpl ♦ adj (material) di scarto; (food) avanzato(a); (land) incolto(a) ♦ vt sprecare; **~s** npl (area of land) distesa desolata; **to lay ~** (destroy) devastare; **~ away** vi deperire; **~ disposal unit** (BRIT) n eliminatore m di rifiuti; **~ful** adj sprecone(a); (process) dispendioso(a); **~ ground** (BRIT) n terreno incolto or abbandonato; **~paper**

basket *n* cestino per la carta straccia; ~**pipe** *n* tubo di scarico.

watch [wɔtʃ] *n* (*also: wrist* ~) orologio (da polso); (*act of watching, vigilance*) sorveglianza; (*guard*: MIL, NAUT) guardia; (NAUT: *spell of duty*) quarto ♦ *vt* (*look at*) osservare; (: *match, programme*) guardare; (*spy on, guard*) sorvegliare, tenere d'occhio; (*be careful of*) fare attenzione a ♦ *vi* osservare, guardare; (*keep guard*) fare or montare la guardia; ~ **out** *vi* fare attenzione; ~**dog** *n* (*also fig*) cane *m* da guardia; ~**ful** *adj* attento(a), vigile; ~**maker** *n* orologiaio/a; ~**man** *n see* **night**; ~ **strap** *n* cinturino da orologio.

water ['wɔ:tə*] *n* acqua ♦ *vt* (*plant*) annaffiare ♦ *vi* (*eyes*) lacrimare; (*mouth*): **to make sb's mouth** ~ far venire l'acquolina in bocca a qn; **in British** ~**s** nelle acque territoriali britanniche; ~ **down** *vt* (*milk*) diluire; (*fig: story*) edulcorare; ~ **cannon** *n* idrante *m*; ~ **closet** (BRIT) *n* water *m inv*; ~**colour** *n* acquerello; ~**cress** *n* crescione *m*; ~**fall** *n* cascata; ~ **heater** *n* scaldabagno; ~**ing can** *n* annaffiatoio; ~ **lily** *n* ninfea; ~**line** *n* (NAUT) linea di galleggiamento; ~**logged** *adj* saturo(a) d'acqua; imbevuto(a) d'acqua; (*football pitch etc*) allagato(a); ~ **main** *n* conduttura dell'acqua; ~**melon** *n* anguria, cocomero; ~**proof** *adj* impermeabile; ~**shed** *n* (GEO, *fig*) spartiacque *m*; ~**skiing** *n* sci *m* acquatico; ~**tight** *adj* stagno(a); ~**way** *n* corso d'acqua navigabile; ~**works** *npl* impianto idrico; ~**y** *adj* (*colour*) slavato(a); (*coffee*) acquoso(a); (*eyes*) umido(a).

watt [wɔt] *n* watt *m inv*.

wave [weɪv] *n* onda; (*of hand*) gesto, segno; (*in hair*) ondulazione *f*; (*fig: surge*) ondata ♦ *vi* fare un cenno con la mano; (*branches, grass*) ondeggiare; (*flag*) sventolare ♦ *vt* (*hand*) fare un gesto con; (*handkerchief*) sventolare; (*stick*) brandire; ~**length** *n* lunghezza d'onda.

waver ['weɪvə*] *vi* esitare; (*voice*) tremolare.

wavy ['weɪvɪ] *adj* ondulato(a); ondeggiante.

wax [wæks] *n* cera ♦ *vt* dare la cera a; (*car*) lucidare ♦ *vi* (*moon*) crescere; ~**works** *npl* cere *fpl* ♦ *n* museo delle cere.

way [weɪ] *n* via, strada; (*path, access*) passaggio; (*distance*) distanza; (*direction*) parte *f*, direzione *f*; (*manner*) modo, stile *m*; (*habit*) abitudine *f*; **which** ~? – **this** – da che parte or in quale direzione? – da questa parte or per di qua; **on the** ~ (*en route*) per strada; **to be on one's** ~ essere in cammino or sulla strada; **to be in the** ~ bloccare il passaggio; (*fig*) essere tra i piedi or d'impiccio; **to go out of one's** ~ **to do** (*fig*) mettercela tutta or fare di tutto per fare; **under** ~ (*project*) in corso; **to lose one's** ~ perdere la strada; **in a** ~ in un certo senso; **in some** ~**s** sotto certi aspetti; **no** ~! (*inf*) neanche per idea!; **by the** ~ ... a proposito ...; "~ **in**" (BRIT) "entrata", "ingresso"; "~ **out**" (BRIT) "uscita"; **the** ~ **back** la strada del ritorno; "**give** ~" (BRIT: AUT) "dare la precedenza".

waylay [weɪ'leɪ] (*irreg: like* **lay**) *vt* tendere un agguato a; attendere al passaggio.

wayward ['weɪwəd] *adj* capriccioso(a); testardo(a).

W.C. ['dʌblju'si:] (BRIT) *n* W.C. *m inv*, gabinetto.

we [wi:] *pl pron* noi.

weak [wi:k] *adj* debole; (*health*) precario(a); (*beam etc*) fragile; (*tea*) leggero(a); ~**en** *vi* indebolirsi ♦ *vt* indebolire; ~**ling** ['wi:klɪŋ] *n* smidollato/a; debole *m/f*; ~**ness** *n* debolezza; (*fault*) punto debole, difetto; **to have a** ~**ness for** avere un debole per.

wealth [wɛlθ] *n* (*money, resources*) ricchezza, ricchezze *fpl*; (*of details*) abbondanza, profusione *f*; ~**y** *adj* ricco(a).

wean [wi:n] *vt* svezzare.

weapon ['wɛpən] *n* arma.

wear [wɛə*] (*pt* **wore**, *pp* **worn**) *n* (*use*)

uso; (*damage through use*) logorio, usura; (*clothing*): **sports/baby** ~ abbigliamento sportivo/per neonati ♦ *vt* (*clothes*) portare; (*put on*) mettersi; (*damage: through use*) consumare ♦ *vi* (*last*) durare; (*rub etc through*) consumarsi; **evening** ~ abiti *mpl or* tenuta da sera; ~ **away** *vt* consumare; erodere ♦ *vi* consumarsi; essere eroso(a); ~ **down** *vt* consumare; (*strength*) esaurire; ~ **off** *vi* sparire lentamente; ~ **out** *vt* consumare; (*person, strength*) esaurire; ~ **and tear** *n* usura, consumo.

weary ['wɪərɪ] *adj* stanco(a) ♦ *vi*: to ~ **of** stancarsi di.

weasel ['wiːzl] *n* (*ZOOL*) donnola.

weather ['wɛðə°] *n* tempo ♦ *vt* (*storm, crisis*) superare; **under the** ~ (*fig: ill*) poco bene; ~**-beaten** *adj* (*face, skin*) segnato(a) dalle intemperie; (*building*) logorato(a) dalle intemperie; ~**cock** *n* banderuola; ~ **forecast** *n* previsioni *fpl* del tempo, bollettino meteorologico; ~**man** (*inf*) *n* meteorologo; ~ **vane** *n* = ~**cock**.

weave [wiːv] (*pt* **wove**, *pp* **woven**) *vt* (*cloth*) tessere; (*basket*) intrecciare; ~**r** *n* tessitore/trice; **weaving** *n* tessitura.

web [wɛb] *n* (*of spider*) ragnatela; (*on foot*) palma; (*fabric, also fig*) tessuto.

wed [wɛd] (*pt, pp* **wedded**) *vt* sposare ♦ *vi* sposarsi.

we'd [wiːd] = **we had**; **we would**.

wedding ['wɛdɪŋ] *n* matrimonio; **silver/golden** ~ (**anniversary**) *n* nozze *fpl* d'argento/d'oro; ~ **day** *n* giorno delle nozze *or* del matrimonio; ~ **dress** *n* abito nuziale; ~ **ring** *n* fede *f*.

wedge [wɛdʒ] *n* (*of wood etc*) zeppa; (*of cake*) fetta ♦ *vt* (*fix*) fissare con zeppe; (*pack tightly*) incastrare.

Wednesday ['wɛdnzdɪ] *n* mercoledì *m inv*.

wee [wiː] (*SCOTTISH*) *adj* piccolo(a).

weed [wiːd] *n* erbaccia ♦ *vt* diserbare; ~**killer** *n* diserbante *m*; ~**y** *adj* (*person*) allampanato(a).

week [wiːk] *n* settimana; **a** ~ **today/on**

Friday oggi/venerdì a otto; ~**day** *n* giorno feriale; (*COMM*) giornata lavorativa; ~**end** *n* fine settimana *m or f inv*, weekend *m inv*; ~**ly** *adv* ogni settimana, settimanalmente ♦ *adj* settimanale ♦ *n* settimanale *m*.

weep [wiːp] (*pt, pp* **wept**) *vi* (*person*) piangere; ~**ing willow** *n* salice *m* piangente.

weigh [weɪ] *vt, vi* pesare; to ~ **anchor** salpare l'ancora; ~ **down** *vt* (*branch*) piegare; (*fig: with worry*) opprimere, caricare; ~ **up** *vt* valutare.

weight [weɪt] *n* peso; to **lose/put on** ~ dimagrire/ingrassare; ~-**ing** *n* (*allowance*) indennità; ~ **lifter** *n* pesista *m*; ~**y** *adj* pesante; (*fig*) importante, grave.

weir [wɪə°] *n* diga.

weird [wɪəd] *adj* strano(a), bizzarro(a); (*eerie*) soprannaturale.

welcome ['wɛlkəm] *adj* benvenuto(a) ♦ *n* accoglienza, benvenuto ♦ *vt* dare il benvenuto a; (*be glad of*) rallegrarsi di; **thank you – you're** ~! grazie – prego!

weld [wɛld] *n* saldatura ♦ *vt* saldare.

welfare ['wɛlfɛə°] *n* benessere *m*; ~ **state** *n* stato assistenziale; ~ **work** *n* assistenza sociale.

well [wɛl] *n* pozzo ♦ *adv* bene ♦ *adj*: to **be** ~ (*person*) stare bene ♦ *excl* allora!; ma!; ebbene!; **as** ~ anche; **as** ~ **as** così come; oltre a; ~ **done!** bravo(a)!; **get** ~ **soon!** guarisci presto!; to **do** ~ andare bene; ~ **up** *vi* sgorgare.

we'll [wiːl] = **we will**; **we shall**.

well: ~-**behaved** *adj* ubbidiente; ~-**being** *n* benessere *m*; ~-**built** *adj* (*person*) ben fatto(a); ~-**deserved** *adj* meritato(a); ~-**dressed** *adj* ben vestito(a), vestito(a) bene; ~-**heeled** (*inf*) *adj* (*wealthy*) agiato(a), facoltoso(a).

wellingtons ['wɛlɪŋtənz] *npl* (*also: wellington boots*) stivali *mpl* di gomma.

well: ~-**known** *adj* noto(a), famoso(a); ~-**mannered** *adj* ben educato(a); ~-**meaning** *adj* ben intenzionato(a); ~-**off** adj benestante, danaroso(a); ~-**read** adj colto(a); ~-**to-do** adj abbiente, benestante; ~-**wisher** n ammiratore/trice.

Welsh [welʃ] adj gallese ♦ n (LING) gallese m; **the** ~ npl i Gallesi; ~**man/woman** n gallese m/f; ~ **rarebit** n crostino al formaggio.

went [went] pt of go.

wept [wept] pt, pp of weep.

were [wəː*] pt of be.

we're [wɪə*] = we are.

weren't [wəːnt] = were not.

west [west] n ovest m, occidente m, ponente m ♦ adj (a) ovest inv, occidentale ♦ adv verso ovest; **the W**~ l'Occidente m; **the W**~ **Country** (BRIT) n il sud-ovest dell'Inghilterra; ~**erly** adj (point) a ovest; (wind) occidentale, da ovest; ~**ern** adj occidentale, dell'ovest ♦ n (CINEMA) western m inv; **W**~ **Germany** n Germania Occidentale; **W**~ **Indian** adj delle Indie Occidentali ♦ n abitante m/f delle Indie Occidentali; **W**~ **Indies** npl Indie fpl Occidentali; ~**ward(s)** adv verso ovest.

wet [wet] adj umido(a), bagnato(a); (soaked) fradicio(a); (rainy) piovoso(a) ♦ n (BRIT: POL) politico moderato; **to get** ~ bagnarsi; "~ **paint**" "vernice fresca"; ~ **blanket** n (fig) guastafeste m/f; ~ **suit** n tuta da sub.

we've [wiːv] = we have.

whack [wæk] vt picchiare, battere.

whale [weɪl] n (ZOOL) balena.

wharf [wɔːf] (pl **wharves**) n banchina.

wharves [wɔːvz] npl of wharf.

───────────
KEYWORD
───────────

what [wɔt] adv **1** (in direct/indirect questions) che; quale; ~ **size is it?** che taglia è?; ~ **colour is it?** di che colore è?; ~ **books do you want?** quali or che libri vuole?

2 (in exclamations) che; ~ **a mess!** che disordine!

♦ pron **1** (interrogative) che cosa, cosa, che; ~ **are you doing?** che or (cha) cosa fai?; ~ **are you talking about?** di

che cosa parli?; ~ **is it called?** come si chiama?; ~ **about me?** e io?; ~ **about doing ...?** e se facessimo ...?

2 (relative) ciò che, quello che; **I saw** ~ **you did/was on the table** ho visto quello che hai fatto/quello che era sul tavolo

3 (indirect use) (che) cosa; **he asked me** ~ **she had said** mi ha chiesto che cosa avesse detto; **tell me** ~ **you're thinking about** dimmi a cosa stai pensando

♦ excl (disbelieving) cosa!, come!

───────────

whatever [wɔt'evə*] adj: ~ **book** qualunque or qualsiasi libro + sub ♦ pron: **do** ~ **is necessary/you want** faccia qualunque or qualsiasi cosa sia necessaria/lei voglia; ~ **happens** qualunque cosa accada; **no reason** ~ or **whatsoever** nessuna ragione affatto or al mondo; **nothing** ~ proprio niente.

whatsoever [wɔtsəu'evə*] adj = whatever.

wheat [wiːt] n grano, frumento.

wheedle ['wiːdl] vt: **to** ~ **sb into doing sth** convincere qn a fare qc (con lusinghe); **to** ~ **sth out of sb** ottenere qc da qn (con lusinghe).

wheel [wiːl] n ruota; (AUT: also: steering ~) volante m; (NAUT) (ruota del) timone m ♦ vt spingere ♦ vi (birds) roteare; (also: ~ round) girare; ~**barrow** n carriola; ~**chair** n sedia a rotelle; ~ **clamp** n (AUT) morsa che blocca la ruota di una vettura in sosta vietata.

wheeze [wiːz] vi ansimare.

───────────
KEYWORD
───────────

when [wen] adv quando; ~ **did it happen?** quando è successo?

♦ conj **1** (at, during, after the time that) quando; **she was reading** ~ **I came in** quando sono entrato lei leggeva; **that was** ~ **I needed you** era allora che avevo bisogno di te

2 (on, at which): **on the day** ~ **I met him** il giorno in cui l'ho incontrato; **one day** ~ **it was raining** un giorno che

pioveva
3 (*whereas*) quando, mentre; **you said
I was wrong ~ in fact I was right** mi
hai detto che avevo torto, quando in
realtà avevo ragione.

whenever [wɛn'ɛvə*] *adv* quando mai ♦
conj quando; (*every time that*) ogni
volta che.

where [wɛə*] *adv, conj* dove; **this is ~**
è qui che; **~abouts** *adv* dove ♦ *n*: sb's
~abouts luogo dove qn si trova; **~as**
conj mentre; **~by** *pron* per cui; **~upon**
conj al ché; **wherever** [-'ɛvə*] *conj*
dovunque +*sub*; (*interrogative*) dove
mai; **~withal** *n* mezzi *mpl*.

whet [wɛt] *vt* (*appetite etc*) stimolare.

whether ['wɛðə*] *conj* se; **I don't know
~ to accept or not** non so se accettare o
no; **it's doubtful ~** è poco probabile
che; **~ you go or not** che lei vada o no.

⎯⎯⎯⎯⎯⎯
│ *KEYWORD* │
⎯⎯⎯⎯⎯⎯

which [wɪtʃ] *adj* **1** (*interrogative:
direct, indirect*) quale; **~ picture do
you want?** quale quadro vuole?; **~ one?**
quale?; **~ one of you did it?** chi di voi
lo ha fatto?

2: in ~ case nel qual caso

♦ *pron* **1** (*interrogative*) quale; **~ (of
these) are yours?** quali di questi sono
suoi?; **~ of you are coming?** chi di voi
viene?

2 (*relative*) che; (: *indirect*) cui, il (la)
quale; **the apple ~ you ate/~ is on the
table** la mela che hai mangiato/che è
sul tavolo; **the chair on ~ you are
sitting** la sedia sulla quale *or* su cui sei
seduto; **he said he knew, ~ is true** ha
detto che lo sapeva, il che è vero; **after
~** dopo di che.

whichever [wɪtʃ'ɛvə*] *adj*: **take ~ book
you prefer** prenda qualsiasi libro che
preferisce; **~ book you take** qualsiasi libro prenda.

whiff [wɪf] *n* soffio; sbuffo; odore
m.

while [waɪl] *n* momento ♦ *conj* mentre;
(*as long as*) finché; (*although*) sebbene

+*sub*; per quanto +*sub*; **for a ~** per un
po'; **~ away** *vt* (*time*) far passare.

whim [wɪm] *n* capriccio.

whimper ['wɪmpə*] *n* piagnucolio ♦ *vi*
piagnucolare.

whimsical ['wɪmzɪkl] *adj* (*person*) ca-
priccioso(a); (*look*) strano(a).

whine [waɪn] *n* gemito ♦ *vi* gemere;
uggiolare; piagnucolare.

whip [wɪp] *n* frusta; (*for riding*) frustino; (*POL: person*) capogruppo (*che
sovrintende alla disciplina dei colleghi
di partito*) ♦ *vt* frustare; (*cream, eggs*)
sbattere; **~ped cream** *n* panna
montata; **~-round** (*BRIT*) *n* colletta.

whirl [wə:l] *vt* (*far*) girare
rapidamente; (*far*) turbinare ♦ *vi*
(*dancers*) volteggiare; (*leaves, water*)
sollevarsi in vortice; **~pool** *n*
mulinello; **~wind** *n* turbine *m*.

whirr [wə:*] *vi* ronzare; rombare;
frullare.

whisk [wɪsk] *n* (*CULIN*) frusta; frullino ♦
vt sbattere, frullare; **to ~ sb away** *or*
off portar via qn a tutta velocità.

whiskers ['wɪskəz] *npl* (*of animal*) baffi
mpl; (*of man*) favoriti *mpl*.

whisky ['wɪskɪ] (*US, IRELAND* **whiskey**) *n*
whisky *m inv*.

whisper ['wɪspə*] *n* sussurro ♦ *vt, vi*
sussurrare.

whist [wɪst] *n* whist *m*.

whistle ['wɪsl] *n* (*sound*) fischio;
(*object*) fischietto ♦ *vi* fischiare.

white [waɪt] *adj* bianco(a); (*with fear*)
pallido(a) ♦ *n* bianco; (*person*) bianco/
a; **~ coffee** (*BRIT*) *n* caffellatte *m inv*;
~-collar worker *n* impiegato; **~
elephant** *n* (*fig*) oggetto (*or* progetto)
costoso ma inutile; **~ lie** *n* bugia
pietosa; **~ness** *n* bianchezza; **~ paper**
n (*POL*) libro bianco; **~wash** (*paint*)
bianco di calce ♦ *vt* imbiancare; (*fig*)
coprire.

whiting ['waɪtɪŋ] *n inv* (*fish*) merlango.

Whitsun ['wɪtsn] *n* Pentecoste *f*.

whittle ['wɪtl] *vt*: **to ~ away**, **~ down**
ridurre, tagliare.

whizz [wɪz] *vi*: **to ~ past** *or* **by** passare
sfrecciando; **~ kid** (*inf*) *n* prodigio.

KEYWORD

who [hu:] pron **1** (interrogative) chi; ~ is it?, ~'s there? chi è?
2 (relative) che; **the man ~ spoke to me** l'uomo che ha parlato con me; **those ~ can swim** quelli che sanno nuotare.

whodunit [hu:'dʌnɪt] (inf) n giallo.
whoever [hu:'ɛvə*] pron: ~ **finds it** chiunque lo trovi; **ask ~ you like** lo chieda a chiunque vuole; ~ **she marries** chiunque sposerà, non importa chi sposerà; ~ **told you that?** chi mai gliel'ha detto?
whole [həʊl] adj (complete) tutto(a), completo(a); (not broken) intero(a), intatto(a) ♦ n (all): **the ~ of** tutto(a) il(la); (entire unit) tutto; (not broken) tutto; **the ~ of the town** tutta la città, la città intera; **on the ~, as a ~** nel complesso, nell'insieme; ~ **food(s)** n(pl) cibo integrale; ~**hearted** adj sincero(a); ~**meal** adj (bread, flour) integrale; ~**sale** n commercio or vendita all'ingrosso ♦ adj all'ingrosso; (destruction) totale; ~**saler** n grossista m/f; ~**some** adj sano(a); salutare; ~**wheat** adj = ~**meal**; **wholly** adv completamente, del tutto.

KEYWORD

whom [hu:m] pron **1** (interrogative) chi; ~ **did you see?** chi hai visto?; **to ~ did you give it?** a chi lo hai dato?
2 (relative) che, prep +il (la) quale (check syntax of Italian verb used); **the man ~ I saw/to ~ I spoke** l'uomo che ho visto/al quale ho parlato.

whooping cough ['hu:pɪŋ-] n pertosse f.
whore [hɔ:*] (inf: pej) n puttana.

KEYWORD

whose [hu:z] adj **1** (possessive: interrogative) di chi; ~ **book is this?**, ~ **is this book?** di chi è questo libro?; ~ **daughter are you?** di chi sei figlia?

2 (possessive: relative): **the man ~ son you rescued** l'uomo il cui figlio hai salvato; **the girl ~ sister you were speaking to** la ragazza alla cui sorella stavi parlando
♦ pron di chi; ~ **is this?** di chi è questo?; **I know ~ it is** so di chi è.

why [waɪ] adv, conj perché ♦ excl (surprise) ma guarda un po'!; (remonstrating) ma (via)!; (explaining) ebbene!; ~ **not?** perché no?; ~ **not do it now?** perché non farlo adesso?; **that's not ~ I'm here** non è questo il motivo per cui sono qui; **the reason ~** il motivo per cui; ~**ever** adv perché mai.
wicked ['wɪkɪd]. adj cattivo(a), malvagio(a); maligno(a); perfido(a).
wickerwork ['wɪkəwə:k] adj di vimini ♦ n articoli mpl di vimini.
wicket ['wɪkɪt] n (CRICKET) porta; area tra le due porte.
wide [waɪd] adj largo(a); (area, knowledge) vasto(a); (choice) ampio(a) ♦ adv: **to open ~** spalancare; **to shoot ~** tirare a vuoto or fuori bersaglio; ~**-angle lens** n grandangolare m; ~**-awake** adj completamente sveglio(a); ~**ly** adv (differing) molto, completamente; (travelled, spaced) molto; (believed) generalmente; ~**n** vt allargare, ampliare; ~ **open** adj spalancato(a); ~**spread** adj (belief etc) molto or assai diffuso(a).
widow ['wɪdəʊ] n vedova; ~**ed** adj: **to be ~ed** restare vedovo(a); ~**er** n vedovo.
width [wɪdθ] n larghezza.
wield [wi:ld] vt (sword) maneggiare; (power) esercitare.
wife [waɪf] (pl **wives**) n moglie f.
wig [wɪg] n parrucca.
wiggle ['wɪgl] vt dimenare, agitare.
wild [waɪld] adj selvatico(a); selvaggio(a); (sea, weather) tempestoso(a); (idea, life) folle; stravagante; (applause) frenetico(a); ~**s** npl regione f selvaggia; ~**erness** ['wɪldənɪs] n deserto; ~ **goose chase** n (fig) pista falsa; ~**life** n natura; ~**ly** adv

selvaggiamente; (*applaud*) frenetica-
mente; (*hit*, *guess*) a casaccio; (*happy*)
follemente.
wilful ['wɪlful] (*US* **willful**) *adj* (*person*)
testardo(a), ostinato(a); (*action*)
intenzionale; (*crime*) premeditato(a).

KEYWORD

will [wɪl] (*pt*, *pp* ~**ed**) *aux vb* **1**
(*forming future tense*): **I ~ finish it
tomorrow** lo finirò domani; **I ~ have
finished it by tomorrow** lo finirò entro
domani; ~ **you do it?** – **yes I ~/no I
won't** lo farai? – sì (lo farò)/no (non lo
farò)
2 (*in conjectures, predictions*): **he ~** or
he'll be there by now dovrebbe essere
arrivato ora; **that ~ be the postman**
sarà il postino
3 (*in commands, requests, offers*): ~
you be quiet! vuoi stare zitto?; ~ **you
come?** vieni anche tu?; ~ **you help me?**
mi aiuti?, mi puoi aiutare?; ~ **you have
a cup of tea?** vorrebbe una tazza di
tè?; **I won't put up with it!** non lo
accetterò!
♦ *vt*: **to ~ sb to do** volere che qn
faccia; **he ~ed himself to go on**
continuò grazie a un grande sforzo di
volontà
♦ *n* volontà; testamento.

---

willful ['wɪlful] (*US*) *adj* = **wilful**.
willing ['wɪlɪŋ] *adj* volonteroso(a); ~ **to
do** disposto(a) a fare; ~**ly** *adv*
volentieri; ~**ness** *n* buona volontà.
willow ['wɪləu] *n* salice *m*.
will power *n* forza di volontà.
willy-nilly ['wɪlɪ'nɪlɪ] *adv* volente o
nolente.
wilt [wɪlt] *vi* appassire.
wily ['waɪlɪ] *adj* furbo(a).
win [wɪn] (*pt*, *pp* **won**) *n* (*in sports etc*)
vittoria ♦ *vt* (*battle*, *prize*, *money*)
vincere; (*popularity*) conquistare ♦ *vi*
vincere; ~ **over** *vt* convincere; ~
round (*BRIT*) *vt* convincere.
wince [wɪns] *vi* trasalire.
winch [wɪntʃ] *n* verricello, argano.
wind[1] [waɪnd] (*pt*, *pp* **wound**) *vt* attorci-

gliare; (*wrap*) avvolgere; (*clock*, *toy*)
caricare ♦ *vi* (*road*, *river*) serpeggiare;
~ **up** *vt* (*clock*) caricare; (*debate*) concludere.
wind[2] [wɪnd] *n* vento; (*MED*)
flatulenza; (*breath*) respiro, fiato ♦ *vt*
(*take breath away*) far restare senza
fiato; ~**fall** *n* (*money*) guadagno in-
sperato.
winding ['waɪndɪŋ] *adj* (*road*)
serpeggiante; (*staircase*) a chiocciola.
wind instrument *n* (*MUS*) strumento a
fiato.
windmill ['wɪndmɪl] *n* mulino a vento.
window ['wɪndəu] *n* finestra; (*in car*,
train) finestrino; (*in shop etc*) vetrina;
(*also*: ~ **pane**) vetro; ~ **box** *n* cassetta
da fiori; ~ **cleaner** *n* (*person*) pulitore
m di finestre; ~ **envelope** *n* busta a
finestra; ~ **ledge** *n* davanzale *m*; ~
pane *n* vetro; ~**-shopping** *n*: **to go** ~**-
shopping** andare a vedere le vetrine;
~**sill** *n* davanzale *m*.
windpipe ['wɪndpaɪp] *n* trachea.
windscreen ['wɪndskriːn] *n* parabrezza
m inv; ~ **washer** *n* lavacristallo; ~
wiper *n* tergicristallo.
windshield ['wɪndʃiːld] (*US*) *n* = **windscreen**.
windswept ['wɪndswept] *adj*
spazzato(a) dal vento.
windy ['wɪndɪ] *adj* ventoso(a); **it's ~** c'è
vento.
wine [waɪn] *n* vino; ~ **bar** *n* bar *m inv*
(*con licenza per alcolici*); ~ **cellar** *n*
cantina; ~ **glass** *n* bicchiere *m* da
vino; ~ **list** *n* lista dei vini; ~
merchant *n* commerciante *m* di vini; ~
tasting *n* degustazione *f* dei vini; ~
waiter *n* sommelier *m inv*.
wing [wɪŋ] *n* ala; (*AUT*) fiancata; ~**s** *npl*
(*THEATRE*) quinte *fpl*; ~**er** *n* (*SPORT*)
ala.
wink [wɪŋk] *n* ammiccamento ♦ *vi*
ammiccare, fare l'occhiolino; (*light*)
baluginare.
winner ['wɪnə*] *n* vincitore/trice.
winning ['wɪnɪŋ] *adj* (*team*, *goal*)
vincente; (*smile*) affascinante; ~**s** *npl*
vincite *fpl*.

winter ['wɪntə*] n inverno; ~ **sports** npl sport mpl invernali.

wintry ['wɪntrɪ] adj invernale.

wipe [waɪp] n pulita, passata ♦ vt pulire (strofinando); (erase: tape) cancellare; ~ **off** vt cancellare; (stains) togliere strofinando; ~ **out** vt (debt) pagare, liquidare; (memory) cancellare; (destroy) annientare; ~ **up** vt asciugare.

wire ['waɪə*] n filo; (ELEC) filo elettrico; (TEL) telegramma m ♦ vt (house) fare l'impianto elettrico di; (also: ~ **up**) collegare, allacciare; (person) telegrafare a.

wireless ['waɪəlɪs] (BRIT) n (set) (apparecchio m) radio f inv.

wiring ['waɪərɪŋ] n impianto elettrico.

wiry ['waɪərɪ] adj magro(a) e nerboruto(a); (hair) ispido(a).

wisdom ['wɪzdəm] n saggezza; (of action) prudenza; ~ **tooth** n dente m del giudizio.

wise [waɪz] adj saggio(a); prudente; giudizioso(a).

...wise [waɪz] suffix: **time~** per quanto riguarda il tempo, in termini di tempo.

wisecrack ['waɪzkræk] n battuta di spirito.

wish [wɪʃ] n (desire) desiderio; (specific desire) richiesta ♦ vt desiderare, volere; best ~**es** (on birthday etc) i migliori auguri; **with best ~es** (in letter) cordiali saluti, con i migliori saluti; **to ~ sb goodbye** dire arrivederci a qn; **he ~ed me well** mi augurò di riuscire; **to ~ to do/sb to do** desiderare or volere fare/che qn faccia; **to ~ for** desiderare; ~**ful** adj: **it's ~ful thinking** è prendere i desideri per realtà.

wishy-washy [wɪʃɪ'wɔʃɪ] (inf) adj (colour) slavato(a); (ideas, argument) insulso(a).

wisp [wɪsp] n ciuffo, ciocca; (of smoke) filo.

wistful ['wɪstful] adj malinconico(a).

wit [wɪt] n (also: ~**s**) intelligenza; presenza di spirito; (wittiness) spirito, arguzia; (person) bello spirito.

witch [wɪtʃ] n strega.

with [wɪð, wɪθ] prep **1** (in the company of) con; **I was ~ him** ero con lui; **we stayed ~ friends** siamo stati da amici; **I'll be ~ you in a minute** vengo subito **2** (descriptive) con; **a room ~ a view** una stanza con vista sul mare (or sulle montagne etc); **the man ~ the grey hat/blue eyes** l'uomo con il cappello grigio/gli occhi blu **3** (indicating manner, means, cause): ~ **tears in her eyes** con le lacrime agli occhi; **red ~ anger** rosso dalla rabbia; **to shake ~ fear** tremare di paura **4**: **I'm ~ you** (I understand) la seguo; **to be ~ it** (inf: up-to-date) essere alla moda; (: alert) essere sveglio(a).

withdraw [wɪθ'drɔ:] (irreg: like draw) vt ritirare; (money from bank) ritirare; prelevare ♦ vi ritirarsi; ~**al** n ritiro; prelievo; (of army) ritirata; ~**al symptoms** (MED) crisi f di astinenza; ~**n** adj (person) distaccato(a).

wither ['wɪðə*] vi appassire.

withhold [wɪθ'həuld] (irreg: like hold) vt (money) trattenere; (permission): **to ~ (from)** rifiutare (a); (information): **to ~ (from)** nascondere (a).

within [wɪð'ɪn] prep all'interno di; (in time, distances) entro ♦ adv all'interno, dentro; ~ **reach (of)** alla portata (di); ~ **sight (of)** in vista (di); ~ **a mile of** entro un miglio da; ~ **the week** prima della fine della settimana.

without [wɪð'aut] prep senza; **to go ~ sth** fare a meno di qc.

withstand [wɪθ'stænd] (irreg: like stand) vt resistere a.

witness ['wɪtnɪs] n (person, also LAW) testimone m/f ♦ vt (event) essere testimone di; (document) attestare l'autenticità di; ~ **box** (US ~ **stand**) n banco dei testimoni.

witticism ['wɪtɪsɪzm] n spiritosaggine f.

witty ['wɪtɪ] adj spiritoso(a).

wives [waɪvz] npl of **wife**.

wizard ['wɪzəd] n mago.

wk abbr = **week**.

wobble ['wɔbl] *vi* tremare; *(chair)* traballare.

woe [wəu] *n* dolore *m*; disgrazia.

woke [wəuk] *pt of* **wake**; **woken** *pp of* **wake**.

wolf [wulf] *(pl* **wolves**) *n* lupo.

wolves [wulvz] *npl of* **wolf**.

woman ['wumən] *(pl* **women**) *n* donna; ~ **doctor** *n* dottoressa; **women's lib** *(inf) n* movimento femminista.

womb [wu:m] *n (ANAT)* utero.

women ['wimin] *npl of* **woman**.

won [wʌn] *pt, pp of* **win**.

wonder ['wʌndə*] *n* meraviglia ♦ *vi*: **to ~ whether/why** domandarsi se/perché; **to ~ at** essere sorpreso(a) di; meravigliarsi di; **to ~ about** domandarsi di; pensare a; **it's no ~ that** c'è poco *or* non c'è da meravigliarsi che + *sub*; **~ful** *adj* meraviglioso(a).

won't [wəunt] = **will not**.

woo [wu:] *vt (woman, audience)* cercare di conquistare.

wood [wud] *n* legno; *(timber)* legname *m*; *(forest)* bosco; ~ **carving** *n* scultura in legno, intaglio; **~ed** *adj* boschivo(a); boscoso(a); **~en** *adj* di legno; *(fig)* rigido(a); inespressivo(a); **~pecker** *n* picchio; **~wind** *npl (MUS):* **the ~wind** i legni; **~work** *n (craft, subject)* falegnameria; **~worm** *n* tarlo del legno.

wool [wul] *n* lana; **to pull the ~ over sb's eyes** *(fig)* imbrogliare qn; **~len** *(US* **~en)** *adj* di lana; *(industry)* laniero(a); **~lens** *npl* indumenti *mpl* di lana; **~ly** *(US* **~y)** *adj* di lana; *(fig: ideas)* confuso(a).

word [wə:d] *n* parola; *(news)* notizie *fpl* ♦ *vt* esprimere, formulare; **in other ~s** in altre parole; **to break/keep one's ~** non mantenere/mantenere la propria parola; **to have ~s with sb** avere un diverbio con qn; **~ing** *n* formulazione *f*; ~ **processing** *n* elaborazione *f* di testi, word processing *m*; ~ **processor** *n* word processor *m inv*.

wore [wɔ:*] *pt of* **wear**.

work [wə:k] *n* lavoro; *(ART, LITERATURE)* opera ♦ *vi* lavorare; *(mechanism, plan etc)* funzionare; *(medicine)* essere efficace ♦ *vt (clay, wood etc)* lavorare; *(mine etc)* sfruttare; *(machine)* far funzionare; *(cause: effect, miracle)* fare; **to be out of ~** essere disoccupato(a); **~s** *n (BRIT: factory)* fabbrica ♦ *npl (of clock, machine)* meccanismo; **to ~ loose** allentarsi; ~ **on** *vt fus* lavorare a; *(person)* lavorarsi; *(principle)* basarsi su; ~ **out** *vi (plans etc)* riuscire, andare bene ♦ *vt (problem)* risolvere; *(plan)* elaborare; **it ~s out at £100 fa** 100 sterline; ~ **up** *vt*: **to get ~ed up** andare su tutte le furie; eccitarsi; **~able** *adj (solution)* realizzabile; **~aholic** *n* maniaco/a del lavoro; **~er** *n* lavoratore/trice, operaio/a; **~force** *n* forza lavoro; **~ing class** *n* classe *f* operaia; **~ing-class** *adj* operaio(a); **~ing order** *n*: **in ~ing order** funzionante; **~man** *n* operaio; **~manship** *n* abilità; **~sheet** *n* foglio col programma di lavoro; **~shop** *n* officina; *(practical session)* gruppo di lavoro; ~ **station** *n* stazione *f* di lavoro; **~-to-rule** *(BRIT)* *n* sciopero bianco.

world [wə:ld] *n* mondo ♦ *cpd (champion)* del mondo; *(power, war)* mondiale; **to think the ~ of sb** *(fig)* pensare un gran bene di qn; **~ly** *adj* di questo mondo; *(knowledgeable)* di mondo; **~-wide** *adj* universale.

worm [wə:m] *n (also: earth~)* verme *m*.

worn [wɔ:n] *pp of* **wear** ♦ *adj* usato(a); **~-out** *adj (object)* consumato(a), logoro(a); *(person)* sfinito(a).

worried ['wʌrid] *adj* preoccupato(a).

worry ['wʌri] *n* preoccupazione *f* ♦ *vt* preoccupare ♦ *vi* preoccuparsi.

worse [wə:s] *adj* peggiore ♦ *adv*, peggio; **a change for the ~** un peggioramento; **~n** *vt*, *vi* peggiorare; ~ **off** *adj* in condizioni (economiche) peggiori.

worship ['wə:ʃip] *n* culto ♦ *vt (God)* adorare, venerare; *(person)* adorare; **Your W~** *(BRIT: to mayor)* signor sindaco; *(: to judge)* signor giudice.

worst [wəːst] *adj* il(la) peggiore ♦ *adv, n* peggio; **at** ~ al peggio, per male che vada.

worth [wəːθ] *n* valore *m* ♦ *adj*: **to be** ~ valere; **it's** ~ **it** ne vale la pena; **it is** ~ **one's while (to do)** vale la pena (fare); ~**less** *adj* di nessun valore; ~**while** *adj* (*activity*) utile; (*cause*) lodevole.

worthy [ˈwəːðɪ] *adj* (*person*) degno(a); (*motive*) lodevole; ~ **of** degno di.

<hr>

KEYWORD

would [wud] *aux vb* **1** (*conditional tense*): **if you asked him he** ~ **do it** se glielo chiedesse lo farebbe; **if you had asked him he** ~ **have done it** se glielo avesse chiesto lo avrebbe fatto
2 (*in offers, invitations, requests*): ~ **you like a biscuit?** vorrebbe *or* vuole un biscotto?; ~ **you ask him to come in?** lo faccia entrare, per cortesia; ~ **you open the window please?** apra la finestra, per favore
3 (*in indirect speech*): **I said I** ~ **do it** ho detto che l'avrei fatto
4 (*emphatic*): **it** WOULD **have to snow today!** doveva proprio nevicare oggi!
5 (*insistence*): **she** ~**n't do it** non ha voluto farlo
6 (*conjecture*): **it** ~ **have been midnight** sarà stato mezzanotte; **it** ~ **seem so** sembrerebbe proprio di sì
7 (*indicating habit*): **he** ~ **go there on Mondays** andava lì ogni lunedì.

<hr>

would-be (*pej*) *adj* sedicente.
wouldn't [ˈwudnt] = **would not**.
wound¹ [waund] *pt, pp of* **wind**.
wound² [wuːnd] *n* ferita ♦ *vt* ferire.
wove [wəuv] *pt of* **weave**; **woven** *pp of* **weave**.
wrangle [ˈræŋgl] *n* litigio.
wrap [ræp] *n* (*stole*) scialle *m*; (*cape*) mantellina ♦ *vt* avvolgere; (*pack*: *also*: ~ **up**) incartare; ~**per** *n* (*on chocolate*) carta; (*BRIT*: *of book*) copertina; ~**ping paper** *n* carta da pacchi; (*for gift*) carta da regali.
wrath [rɔθ] *n* collera, ira.
wreak [riːk] *vt* (*havoc*) portare,

causare; **to** ~ **vengeance on** vendicarsi su.
wreath [riːθ, *pl* riːðz] *n* corona.
wreck [rɛk] *n* (*sea disaster*) naufragio; (*ship*) relitto; (*pej*: *person*) rottame *m* ♦ *vt* demolire; (*ship*) far naufragare; (*fig*) rovinare; ~**age** *n* rottami *mpl*; (*of building*) macerie *fpl*; (*of ship*) relitti *mpl*.
wren [rɛn] *n* (*ZOOL*) scricciolo.
wrench [rɛntʃ] *n* (*TECH*) chiave *f*; (*tug*) torsione *f* brusca; (*fig*) strazio ♦ *vt* strappare; storcere; **to** ~ **sth from** strappare qc a *or* da.
wrestle [ˈrɛsl] *vi*: **to** ~ **(with sb)** lottare (con qn); ~**r** *n* lottatore/trice; **wrestling** *n* lotta.
wretched [ˈrɛtʃɪd] *adj* disgraziato(a); (*inf*: *weather, holiday*) orrendo(a), orribile; (: *child, dog*) pestifero(a).
wriggle [ˈrɪgl] *vi* (*also*: ~ **about**) dimenarsi; (: *snake, worm*) serpeggiare, muoversi serpeggiando.
wring [rɪŋ] (*pt, pp* **wrung**) *vt* torcere; (*wet clothes*) strizzare; (*fig*): **to** ~ **sth out of** strappare qc a.
wrinkle [ˈrɪŋkl] *n* (*on skin*) ruga; (*on paper etc*) grinza ♦ *vt* (*nose*) torcere; (*forehead*) corrugare ♦ *vi* (*skin, paint*) raggrinzirsi.
wrist [rɪst] *n* polso; ~**watch** *n* orologio da polso.
writ [rɪt] *n* ordine *m*; mandato.
write [raɪt] (*pt* **wrote**, *pp* **written**) *vt, vi* scrivere; ~ **down** *vt* annotare; (*put in writing*) mettere per iscritto; ~ **off** *vt* (*debt, plan*) cancellare; ~ **out** *vt* mettere per iscritto; (*cheque, receipt*) scrivere; ~ **up** *vt* redigere; ~**-off** *n* perdita completa; ~**r** *n* autore/trice, scrittore/trice.
writhe [raɪð] *vi* contorcersi.
writing [ˈraɪtɪŋ] *n* scrittura; (*of author*) scritto, opera; **in** ~ per iscritto; ~ **paper** *n* carta da lettere.
written [ˈrɪtn] *pp of* **write**.
wrong [rɔŋ] *adj* sbagliato(a); (*not suitable*) inadatto(a); (*wicked*) cattivo(a); (*unfair*) ingiusto(a) ♦ *adv* in modo sbagliato, erroneamente ♦ *n*

(*injustice*) torto ♦ *vt* fare torto a; **you are ~ to do it** ha torto a farlo; **you are ~ about that, you've got it ~** si sbaglia; **to be in the ~** avere torto; **what's ~?** cosa c'è che non va?; **to go ~** (*person*) sbagliarsi; (*plan*) fallire, non riuscire; (*machine*) guastarsi; **~ful** *adj* illegittimo(a); ingiusto(a); **~ly** *adv* (*incorrectly, by mistake*) in modo sbagliato.

wrote [rəut] *pt of* write.

wrought [rɔːt] *adj*: **~ iron** ferro battuto.

wrung [rʌŋ] *pt, pp of* wring.

wry [raɪ] *adj* storto(a).

X

Xmas ['ɛksməs] *n abbr* = Christmas.

X-ray ['ɛks'reɪ] *n* raggio X; (*photograph*) radiografia ♦ *vt* radiografare.

xylophone ['zaɪləfəun] *n* xilofono.

Y

yacht [jɔt] *n* panfilo, yacht *m inv*; **~ing** *n* yachting *m*, sport *m* della vela.

Yank [jæŋk] (*pej*) *n* yankee *m/f inv*.

Yankee ['jæŋkɪ] (*pej*) *n* = Yank.

yap [jæp] *vi* (*dog*) guaire.

yard [jɑːd] *n* (*of house etc*) cortile *m*; (*measure*) iarda (= *914 mm; 3 feet*); **~stick** *n* (*fig*) misura, criterio.

yarn [jɑːn] *n* filato; (*tale*) lunga storia.

yawn [jɔːn] *n* sbadiglio ♦ *vi* sbadigliare; **~ing** *adj* (*gap*) spalancato(a).

yd. *abbr* = yard(s).

yeah [jɛə] (*inf*) *adv* sì.

year [jɪə*] *n* anno; (*referring to harvest, wine etc*) annata; **he is 8 ~s old** ha 8 anni; **an eight-~-old child** un(a) bambino(a) di otto anni; **~ly** *adj* annuale ♦ *adv* annualmente.

yearn [jɔːn] *vi*: **to ~ for sth/to do** desiderare ardentemente qc/di fare.

yeast [jiːst] *n* lievito.

yell [jɛl] *n* urlo ♦ *vi* urlare.

yellow ['jɛləu] *adj* giallo(a).

yelp [jɛlp] *vi* guaire, uggiolare.

yeoman ['jəumən] *n*: **~ of the guard** guardiano della Torre di Londra.

yes [jɛs] *adv* sì ♦ *n* sì *m inv*; **to say/ answer ~** dire/rispondere di sì.

yesterday ['jɛstədɪ] *adv* ieri ♦ *n* ieri *m inv*; **~ morning/evening** ieri mattina/ sera; **all day ~** ieri per tutta la giornata.

yet [jɛt] *adv* ancora; già ♦ *conj* ma, tuttavia; **it is not finished ~** non è ancora finito; **the best ~** finora il migliore; **as ~** finora.

yew [juː] *n* tasso (*albero*).

yield [jiːld] *n* produzione *f*, resa; reddito ♦ *vt* produrre, rendere; (*surrender*) cedere ♦ *vi* cedere; (*US: AUT*) dare la precedenza.

YMCA *n abbr* (= *Young Men's Christian Association*) Y.M.C.A. *m*.

yog(h)ourt ['jəugət] *n* = yog(h)urt.

yog(h)urt ['jəugət] *n* iogurt *m inv*.

yoke [jəuk] *n* (*also fig*) giogo.

yolk [jəuk] *n* tuorlo, rosso d'uovo.

KEYWORD

you [juː] *pron* **1** (*subject*) tu; (*: polite form*) lei; (*: pl*) voi; (*: very formal*) loro; **~ Italians enjoy your food** a voi Italiani piace mangiare bene; **~ and I will go** tu ed io *or* lei ed io andiamo

2 (*object: direct*) ti; la; vi; loro (*after vb*); (*: indirect*) ti; le; vi; loro (*after vb*); **I know ~** ti *or* la *or* vi conosco; **I gave it to ~** te l'ho dato; glie l'ho dato; ve l'ho dato; l'ho dato loro

3 (*stressed, after prep, in comparisons*) te; lei; voi; loro; **I told you** to do it ho detto a TE (*or* a LEI *etc*) di farlo; **she's younger than ~** è più giovane di te (*or* lei *etc*)

4 (*impers: one*) si; **fresh air does ~ good** l'aria fresca fa bene; **~ never know** non si sa mai.

you'd [juːd] = you had; you would.

you'll [juːl] = you will; you shall.

young [jʌŋ] *adj* giovane ♦ *npl* (*of animal*) piccoli *mpl*; (*people*): **the ~** i giovani, la gioventù; **~er** *adj* più

giovane; (*brother*) minore, più giovane;
~**ster** *n* giovanotto, ragazzo; (*child*)
bambino/a.

your [jɔː*] *adj* il(la) tuo(a), *pl* i(le)
tuoi(tue); il(la) suo(a), *pl* i(le)
suoi(sue); il(la) vostro(a), *pl* i(le) vo-
stri(e); il(la) loro, *pl* i(le) loro; *see
also* **my**.

you're [juə*] = **you are**.

yours [jɔːz] *pron* il(la) tuo(a), *pl* i(le)
tuoi(tue); (*polite form*) il(la) suo(a), *pl*
i(le) suoi(sue); (*pl*) il(la) vostro(a), *pl*
i(le) vostri(e); (: *very formal*) il(la)
loro, *pl* i(le) loro; *see also* **mine**;
faithfully; **sincerely**.

yourself [jɔːˈsɛlf] *pron* (*reflexive*) ti; si;
(*after prep*) te; sé; (*emphatic*) tu
stesso(a); lei stesso(a); **yourselves** *pl*
pron (*reflexive*) vi; si; (*after prep*) voi;
loro; (*emphatic*) voi stessi(e); loro
stessi(e); *see also* **oneself**.

youth [juːθ, *pl* juːðz] *n* gioventù *f*;
(*young man*) giovane *m*, ragazzo; ~
club *n* centro giovanile; ~**ful** *adj*
giovane; da giovane; giovanile; ~
hostel *n* ostello della gioventù.

you've [juːv] = **you have**.

Yugoslav [ˈjuːɡəuˈslɑːv] *adj*, *n* jugo-
slavo(a).

Yugoslavia [ˈjuːɡəuˈslɑːvɪə] *n* Jugoslavia.

yuppie [ˈjʌpɪ] (*inf*) *n*, *adj* yuppie *m/f*
inv.

YWCA *n abbr* (= *Young Women's Christian Association*) Y.W.C.A. *m*.

Z

zany [ˈzeɪnɪ] *adj* un po' pazzo(a).

zap [zæp] *vt* (*COMPUT*) cancellare.

zeal [ziːl] *n* zelo; entusiasmo.

zebra [ˈziːbrə] *n* zebra; ~ **crossing**
(*BRIT*) *n* (passaggio pedonale a) strisce
fpl, zebre *fpl*.

zero [ˈzɪərəu] *n* zero.

zest [zɛst] *n* gusto; (*CULIN*) buccia.

zigzag [ˈzɪɡzæɡ] *n* zigzag *m inv* ♦ *vi*
zigzagare.

Zimbabwe [zɪmˈbɑːbwɪ] *n* Zimbabwe *m*.

zinc [zɪŋk] *n* zinco.

zip [zɪp] *n* (*also*: ~ *fastener*, (*US*) ~*per*)
chiusura *f* or cerniera *f* lampo *inv* ♦ *vt*
(*also*: ~ *up*) chiudere con una cerniera
lampo; ~ **code** (*US*) *n* codice *m* di
avviamento postale.

zodiac [ˈzəudɪæk] *n* zodiaco.

zombie [ˈzɒmbɪ] *n* (*fig*): **like a** ~ come
un morto che cammina.

zone [zəun] *n* (*also MIL*) zona.

zoo [zuː] *n* zoo *m inv*.

zoology [zuːˈɒlədʒɪ] *n* zoologia.

zoom [zuːm] *vi*: **to** ~ **past** sfrecciare; ~
lens *n* zoom *m inv*, obiettivo a focale
variabile.

zucchini [zuːˈkiːnɪ] (*US*) *npl* (*courgettes*)
zucchine *fpl*.

USING YOUR COLLINS POCKET DICTIONARY

Introduction

We are delighted that you have decided to invest in this Collins Pocket Dictionary! Whether you intend to use it in school, at home, on holiday or at work, we are sure that you will find it very useful.

The purpose of this supplement is to help you become aware of the wealth of vocabulary and grammatical information your dictionary contains, to explain how this information is presented and also to point out some of the traps one can fall into when using an Italian-English English-Italian dictionary.

In the pages which follow you will find explanations and wordgames (not too difficult!) designed to give you practice in exploring the dictionary's contents and in retrieving information for a variety of purposes. Answers are provided at the end. If you spend a little time on these pages you should be able to use your dictionary more efficiently and effectively. Have fun!

Contents

HOW INFORMATION IS PRESENTED IN YOUR DICTIONARY

A great deal of information is packed into your Collins Pocket Dictionary using colour, various typefaces, sizes of type, symbols, abbreviations and brackets. The purpose of this section is to acquaint you with the conventions used in presenting information.

Headwords

A headword is the word you look up in a dictionary. Headwords are listed in alphabetical order throughout the dictionary. They are printed in colour so that they stand out clearly from all the other words on the dictionary page.

Note that at the top of each page two headwords appear. These tell you which is the first and last word dealt with on the page in question. They are there to help you scan through the dictionary more quickly.

The Italian alphabet consists in practice of the same 26 letters as the English alphabet but j, k, w, x and y are found only in words of foreign origin. Where words are distinguished only by an accent, the unaccented form precedes the accented — e.g. te, tè.

A dictionary entry

An entry is made up of a headword and all the information about that headword. Entries will be short or long depending on how frequently a word is used in either English or Italian and how many meanings it has. Inevitably, the fuller the dictionary entry the more care is needed in sifting through it to find the information you require.

Meanings

The translations of a headword are given in ordinary type. Where there is more than one meaning or usage, a semi-colon separates one from the other.

cannocchi'ale [kannok'kjale] *sm* telescope.

can'none *sm* (*MIL*) gun; (*: STORIA*) cannon; (*tubo*) pipe, tube; (*piega*) box pleat; (*fig*) ace.

can'nuccia, ce [kan'nuttʃa] *sf* (drinking) straw.

ca'noa *sf* canoe.

---

profes'sare *vt* to profess; (*medicina etc*) to practise.

te *pron* (*soggetto: in forme comparative, oggetto*) you.
tè *sm inv* tea; (*trattenimento*) tea party.

pro'gresso *sm* progress *no pl*; **fare ~i** to make progress.

'fragola *sf* strawberry.

---

fu'ori *av* outside; (*all'aperto*) outdoors, outside; (*fuori di casa, SPORT*) out; (*esclamativo*) get out! ♦ *prep*: ~ **(di)** out of, outside ♦ *sm* outside; **lasciar ~ qc/qn** to leave sth/sb out; **far ~ qn** (*fam*) to kill sb, do sb in; **essere ~ di sé** to be beside o.s.; ~ **luogo** (*inopportuno*) out of place, uncalled for; ~ **mano** out of the way, remote; ~ **pericolo** out of danger; ~ **uso** oldfashioned; obsolete.

'grande (*qualche volta* **gran** +*C*, **grand'** +*V*) *ag* (*grosso, largo, vasto*) big, large; (*alto*) tall; (*lungo*) long; (*in sensi astratti*) great ♦ *sm/f* (*persona adulta*) adult, grown-up; (*chi ha ingegno e potenza*) great man/woman; **fare le cose in ~** to do things in style; **una gran bella donna** a very beautiful woman; **non è una gran cosa** *o* **un gran che** it's nothing special; **non ne so gran che** I don't know very much about it.

291

In addition, you will often find other words appearing in *italics* in brackets before the translations. These either give some notion of the contexts in which the headword might appear (as with 'alto' opposite — 'una persona alta', 'un suono alto', etc.) or else they provide synonyms (as with 'reggere' opposite — 'tenere', 'sostenere', etc.).

Phonetic spellings

Where an Italian word contains a sound which is difficult for the English-speaker, the phonetic spelling of the word — i.e. its pronunciation — is given in square brackets immediately after it. The phonetic transcription of Italian and English vowels and consonants is given on pages vii to viii at the front of your dictionary.

Additional information about headwords

Information about the form or usage of certain headwords is given in brackets between the headword and the translation or translations. Have a look at the entries for 'A.C.I.', 'camerino', 'materia' and 'leccapiedi' opposite. This information is usually given in abbreviated form. A helpful list of abbreviations is given on pages iv to vi at the front of your dictionary.

You should be particularly careful with colloquial words or phrases. Words labelled (*fam*) would not normally be used in formal speech, while those labelled (*fam!*) would be considered offensive. Careful consideration of such style labels will help you avoid many an embarrassing situation when using Italian!

Expressions in which the headword appears

An entry will often feature certain common expressions in which the head-word appears. These expressions are in **bold** type but in black as opposed to colour. A swung dash (~) is used instead of repeating a headword in an entry. 'Freno' and 'idea' opposite illustrate this point. Sometimes the swung dash is used with the appropriate ending shown after it; e.g. 'mano', where '~i' is used to indicate the plural form, 'mani'.

Related words

In the Pocket Dictionary words related to certain headwords are sometimes given at the end of an entry, as with 'finestra' and 'accept' opposite. These are easily picked out as they are also in colour. These words are placed in alphabetical order after the headword to which they belong: cf. 'acceptable', 'acceptance' opposite.

'alto, a *ag* high; *(persona)* tall; *(tessuto)* wide, broad; *(sonno, acque)* deep; *(suono)* high(-pitched); *(GEO)* upper; *(: settentrionale)* northern ♦ *sm* top (part) ♦ *av* high; *(parlare)* aloud, loudly; **il palazzo è ~ 20 metri** the building is 20 metres high;

pron'tezza [pron'tettsa] *sf* readiness; quickness, promptness.

A.C.I. ['atʃi] *sigla m* (= *Automobile Club d'Italia*) ≈ A.A.

came'rino *sm* *(TEATRO)* dressing room.

scocci'are [skot'tʃare] *(fam) vt* to bother, annoy; **~rsi** *vr* to be bothered *o* annoyed.

fre'gare *vt* to rub; *(fam: truffare)* to take in, cheat; *(: rubare)* to swipe, pinch; **fregarsene** *(fam!)*: **chi se ne frega?** who gives a damn (about it)?

'freno *sm* brake; *(morso)* bit; **~ a disco** disc brake; **~ a mano** handbrake; **tenere a ~** to restrain.

i'dea *sf* idea; *(opinione)* opinion, view; *(ideale)* ideal; **dare l'~ di** to seem, look like; **~ fissa** obsession; **neanche** *o* **neppure per ~!** certainly not!

fi'nestra *sf* window; **fines'trino** *sm* (di

reggere ['reddʒere] *vt* *(tenere)* to hold; *(sostenere)* to support, bear, hold up; *(portare)* to carry, bear; *(resistere)* to withstand; *(dirigere: impresa)* to manage, run; *(governare)* to rule,

reci'tare [retʃi'tare] *vt* *(poesia, lezione)* to recite; *(dramma)* to perform; *(ruolo)* to play *o* act (the part of); **recitazi'one** *sf* recitation; *(di attore)* acting.

ma'teria *sf* *(FISICA)* matter; *(TECN, COMM)* material, matter *no pl*; *(disciplina)* subject; *(argomento)* subject

leccapi'edi *(peg) sm/f inv* toady, bootlicker.

'rompere *vt* to break; *(conversazione, fidanzamento)* to break off ♦ *vi* to break; **~rsi** *vr* to break; **mi rompe le scatole** *(fam)* he (*o* she) is a pain in the neck; **~rsi un braccio** to break an arm;

mano, i *sf* hand; *(strato: di vernice etc)* coat; **di prima ~** *(notizia)* first-hand; **di seconda ~** second-hand; **man ~ little by little, gradually; **man ~ che** as; **darsi** *o* **stringersi la ~** to shake hands; **mettere le ~i avanti** *(fig)* to safeguard o.s.; **restare a ~i vuote** to be left empty-handed; **venire alle ~i** to come to blows; **a ~** by hand; **~i in alto!** hands up!

accept [ək'sɛpt] *vt* accettare; **~able** *adj* accettabile; **~ance** *n* accettazione *f*.

'Key' words

Your Collins Pocket Dictionary gives special status to certain Italian and English words which can be looked on as 'key' words in each language. These are words which have many different usages. 'Molto', 'volere' and 'così' opposite are typical examples in Italian. You are likely to become familiar with them in your day-to-day language studies.

There will be occasions, however, when you want to check on a particular usage. Your dictionary can be very helpful here. Note how with 'volere', for example, different parts of speech and different usages are clearly indicated by a combination of lozenges - ♦ - and numbers. Additionally, further guides to usage are given in the language of the user who needs them. These are bracketed and in italics.

PAROLA CHIAVE

vo'lere *sm* will, wish(es); **contro il ~ di** against the wishes of; **per ~ di qn** in obedience to sb's will *o* wishes

♦ *vt* **1** (*esigere, desiderare*) to want; **voler fare/che qn faccia** to want to do/sb to do; **volete del caffè?** would you like *o* do you want some coffee?; **vorrei questo/fare** I would *o* I'd like this/to do; **come vuoi** as you like; **senza ~** (*inavvertitamente*) without meaning to, unintentionally

2 (*consentire*): **vogliate attendere, per piacere** please wait; **vogliamo andare?** shall we go?; **vuole essere così gentile da ...?** would you be so kind as to ...?; **non ha voluto ricevermi** he wouldn't see me

3: **volerci** (*essere necessario: materiale, attenzione*) to need; (: *tempo*) to take; **quanta farina ci vuole per questa torta?** how much flour do you need for this cake?; **ci vuole un'ora per arrivare a Venezia** it takes an hour to get to Venice

4: **voler bene a qn** (*amore*) to love sb; (*affetto*) to be fond of sb, like sb very much; **voler male a qn** to dislike sb; **volerne a qn** to bear sb a grudge; **voler dire** to mean.

PAROLA CHIAVE

'molto, a *det* (*quantità*) a lot of, much; (*numero*) a lot of, many; **~ pane/carbone** a lot of bread/coal; **~a gente** a lot of people, many people; **~i libri** a lot of books, many books; **non ho ~ tempo** I haven't got much time; **per ~ (tempo)** for a long time

♦ *av* **1** a lot, (very) much; **viaggia ~** he travels a lot; **non viaggia ~** he doesn't travel much *o* a lot

2 (*intensivo: con aggettivi, avverbi*) very; (: *con participio passato*) (very) much; **~ buono** very good; **~ migliore, ~ meglio** much *o* a lot better

♦ *pron* much, a lot; **~i, e** *pron pl* many, a lot; **~i pensano che ...** many (people) think ...,

PAROLA CHIAVE

così *av* **1** (*in questo modo*) like this, (in) this way; (*in tal modo*) so; **le cose stanno ~** this is the way things stand; **non ho detto ~!** I didn't say that!; **come stai? — (e) ~ ~** how are you? — so-so; **e ~ via** and so on; **per ~ dire** so to speak

2 (*tanto*) so; **~ lontano** so far away; **un ragazzo ~ intelligente** such an intelligent boy

♦ *ag inv* (*tale*): **non ho mai visto un film ~** I've never seen such a film

♦ *cong* **1** (*perciò*) so, therefore

2: **~ ... come** as ... as; **non è ~ bravo come te** he's not as good as you; **~ ... che** so ... that.

WORDGAME 1

HEADWORDS

Study the following sentences. In each sentence a wrong word spelt very similarly to the correct word has deliberately been put in and the sentence doesn't make sense. This word is shaded each time. Write out each sentence again, putting in the <u>correct</u> word which you will find in your dictionary near the wrong word.

Example   Vietato l'ingrosso agli estranei

['ingrosso' ('all 'ingrosso' = 'wholesale') is the wrong word and should be replaced by 'ingresso' (= 'entry')]

1. Ha agito contro il volare della maggioranza.
2. Inserire la moneta e pigliare il pulsante.
3. Non dobbiamo molare proprio adesso.
4. Ho dovuto impanare la lezione a memoria.
5. Il prato era circondato da uno stecchito.
6. Vorrei sentire il tuo parare.
7. Vorrei un po' di panno sulle fragole.
8. Qual'è l'oratorio d'apertura dell'ufficio?
9. Quel negoziante mi ha imbrigliato!
10. Sedevano fiasco a fiasco.

WORDGAME 2
DICTIONARY ENTRIES

Complete the crossword below by looking up the English words in the list and finding the correct Italian translations. There is a slight catch, however! All the English words can be translated several ways into Italian, but only one translation will fit correctly into each part of the crossword.

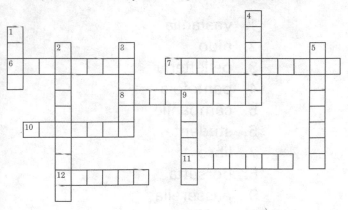

1. THREAD	7. COLD
2. PERMIT	8. WAIT
3. PRESENT	9. NOTICE
4. WANT	10. RETURN
5. JOURNEY	11. CUT
6. FREE	12. REST

WORDGAME 3

FINDING MEANINGS

In this list there are eight pairs of words that have some sort of connection with each other. For example, **'laurea'** (= 'degree') and **'studente'** (= 'student') are linked. Find the other pairs.

1. vestaglia
2. nido
3. pelletteria
4. pantofola
5. campanile
6. studente
7. libro
8. borsetta
9. passerella
10. pinna
11. laurea
12. scaffale
13. gazza
14. nave
15. campana
16. squalo

WORDGAME 4

SYNONYMS

Complete the crossword by supplying SYNONYMS of the words below. You will sometimes find the synonym you are looking for in italics and bracketed at the entries for the words listed below. Sometimes you will have to turn to the English-Italian section for help.

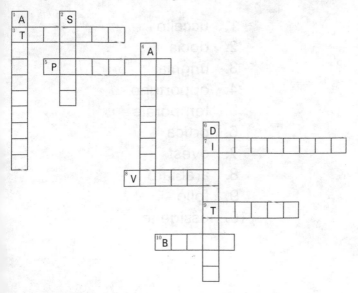

1. RIGUARDO
2. GALA
3. GALLERIA
4. CANCELLARE
5. GALERA

6. BUFFO
7. GIOCARE
8. RAPIDO
9. PAURA
10. MARRONE

WORDGAME 5

SPELLING

You will often use your dictionary to check spellings. The person who has compiled this list of ten Italian words has made <u>three</u> spelling mistakes. Find the three words which have been misspelt and write them out correctly.

1. uccello
2. docia
3. unghia
4. opportuno
5. temporale
6. ortica
7. ovest
8. arabiato
9. folio
10. ossigeno

WORDGAME 6
ANTONYMS

Complete the crossword by supplying ANTONYMS (i.e. opposites) in Italian of the words below. Use your dictionary to help you.

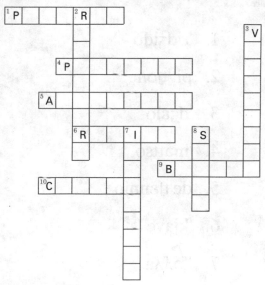

1. ricchezza
2. accettare
3. coraggioso
4. ridere
5. difendere

6. liscio
7. colpevole
8. chiaro
9. bello
10. aperto

WORDGAME 7

PHONETIC SPELLINGS

The phonetic transcriptions of ten Italian words are given below. If you study pages vii to viii near the front of your dictionary you should be able to work out what the words are.

1. 'ridʒido

2. pit'tʃone

3. 'dʒɛlo

4. 'mattso

5. de'tʃɛnnjo

6. 'kjave

7. 'fɔʎʎa

8. 'soɲɲo

9. 'aʃʃa

10. 'gjanda

EXPRESSIONS IN WHICH THE HEADWORD APPEARS

If you look up the headword 'colpo' in the Italian-English section of your dictionary you will find that the word can have many meanings. Study the entry carefully and translate the following sentences into English.

1. La sua sconfitta è stata un duro colpo per tutti.

2. Ha preso un brutto colpo in testa.

3. Dammi un colpo di telefono domani mattina.

4. Sparò quattro colpi di pistola.

5. Il rumore cessò di colpo.

6. La sua fuga è stata un colpo di testa.

7. Un colpo di vento fece sbattere le persiane.

8. Gli è preso un colpo ed è morto.

9. Hai fatto colpo col tuo discorso, ieri.

10. Gli ho dato un colpo senza volere ed è caduto.

11. Con questo caldo è facile prendere un colpo di sole.

12. Hanno arrestato gli autori del fallito colpo di stato.

WORDGAME 9

RELATED WORDS

Fill in the blanks in the pairs of sentences below. The missing words are related to the words on the left. Choose the correct 'relative' each time. You will find it in your dictionary near the headword provided.

HEADWORD	RELATED WORDS
impiegare	1. Fa l'_____ di banca. 2. Ha appena lasciato il suo _____.
studiare	3. Ha vissuto a Firenze quand'era _____. 4. Ha uno _____ in centro.
usare	5. Si raccomanda l'_____ delle cinture di sicurezza. 6. La tua macchina è nuova o _____?
unità	7. È una famiglia molto _____. 8. Vi potete _____ a noi, se volete.
rifiuto	9. È un'offerta che non potrete _____. 10. Dov'è il bidone dei _____?
festeggiare	11. Il negozio è chiuso nei giorni _____. 12. Ha organizzato una _____ di compleanno.

WORDGAME 10

'KEY' WORDS

Study carefully the entry **'fare'** in your dictionary and find translations for the following:

1. the weather is fine

2. to do psychology

3. go ahead!

4. let me see

5. to get one's hair cut

6. this is the way it's done

7. to do the shopping

8. to be quick

9. to start up the engine

10. he made as if to leave

THE DICTIONARY AND GRAMMAR

While it is true that a dictionary can never be a substitute for a detailed grammar reference book, the dictionary nevertheless provides a great deal of grammatical information. If you know how to extract this information you will be able to use Italian more accurately both in speech and in writing.

The Collins Pocket Dictionary presents grammatical information as follows.

Parts of speech

Parts of speech are given in italics immediately after the phonetic spellings of headwords. Abbreviated forms are used. Abbreviations can be checked on pages iv to vi.

Changes in parts of speech within an entry — for example, from adjective to adverb to noun — are indicated by means of lozenges - ♦ - as with the Italian 'forte' and the English 'act' opposite.

Genders of Italian nouns

The gender of each noun in the Italian-English section of the dictionary is indicated in the following way:

sm = sostantivo maschile

sf = sostantivo femminile

You will occasionally see 'sm/f' beside an entry. This indicates that a noun — 'insegnante', for example — can be either masculine or feminine.

Feminine and *irregular* plural forms of nouns are shown, as with 'bambino', 'autore' and 'bruco' opposite.

So many things depend on your knowing the correct gender of an Italian noun — whether you use 'il' or 'la' etc. to translate 'the'; the way you spell and pronounce certain adjectives; the changes you make to past participles, etc. If you are in any doubt as to the gender of a noun, it is always best to check it in your dictionary.

ono'rare *vt* to honour; (*far onore a*) to do credit to; **~rsi** *vr*: **~rsi di** to feel honoured at, be proud of.

quassù *av* up here.

perciò [per'tʃɔ] *cong* so, for this (*o* that) reason.

'pranzo ['prandzo] *sm* dinner; (*a mezzogiorno*) lunch.

'cena ['tʃena] *sf* dinner; (*leggera*) supper.

bam'bino, a *sm/f* child.

au'tore, 'trice *sm/f* author.

'bruco, chi *sm* caterpillar; grub.

'forte *ag* strong; (*suono*) loud; (*spesa*) considerable, great; (*passione, dolore*) great, deep ♦ *av* strongly; (*velocemente*) fast; (*a voce alta*) loud(ly); (*violentemente*) hard ♦ *sm* (*edificio*) fort; (*specialità*) forte, strong point; **essere ~ in qc** to be good at sth.

act [ækt] *n* atto; (*in music-hall etc*) numero; (*LAW*) decreto ♦ *vi* agire; (*THEATRE*) recitare; (*pretend*) fingere ♦ *vt* (*part*) recitare; **to ~ as** agire da; **~ing** *adj* che fa le funzioni di ♦ *n* (*of actor*) recitazione *f*; (*activity*): **to do some ~ing** fare del teatro (*or* del cinema).

inse'gnante [inseɲ'ɲante] *ag* teaching ♦ *sm/f* teacher.

307

Adjectives

Adjectives are given in both their masculine and feminine forms, where these are different. The usual rule is to drop the 'o' of the masculine form and add an 'a' to make an adjective feminine, as with 'nero' opposite.

Some adjectives have identical masculine and feminine forms, as with 'verde' opposite.

Many Italian adjectives, however, do not follow the regular pattern. Where an adjective has irregular plural forms, this information is clearly provided in your dictionary, usually with the irregular endings, being given. Consider the entries for 'bianco' and 'lungo' opposite.

Adverbs

Adverbs are not always listed in your dictionary. The normal rule for forming adverbs in Italian is to add '-mente' to the feminine form of the adjective. Thus:

> vero > vera > veramente

The '-mente' ending is often the equivalent of the English '-ly':

> veramente — really
> certamente — certainly

Adjectives ending in '-e' and '-le' are slightly different:

> recente > recentemente
> reale > realmente

Where an adverb is very common in Italian, or where its translation(s) cannot be derived from translations for the adjective, it will be listed in alphabetical order, either as a headword or as a subentry. Compare 'solamente' and 'attualmente' opposite.

In many cases, however, Italian adverbs are not given, since the English translation can easily be derived from the relevant translation of the adjective headword: e.g. 'cortese' opposite.

Information about verbs

A major problem facing language learners is that the form of a verb will change according to the subject and/or the tense being used. A typical Italian verb can take on many different forms — too many to list in a dictionary entry.

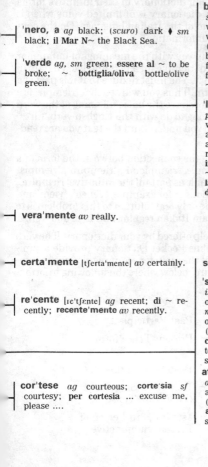

'nero, a ag black; (scuro) dark ♦ sm black; **il Mar N~** the Black Sea.

'verde ag, sm green; **essere al ~** to be broke; **~ bottiglia/oliva** bottle/olive green.

vera'mente av really.

certa'mente [tʃerta'mente] av certainly.

re'cente [re'tʃɛnte] ag recent; **di ~** recently; **recente'mente** av recently.

cor'tese ag courteous; **corte·sia** sf courtesy; **per cortesia** ... excuse me, please ....

bi'anco, a, chi, che ag white; (non scritto) blank ♦ sm white; (intonaco) whitewash ♦ sm/f white, white man/woman; **in ~** (foglio, assegno) blank; (notte) sleepless; **in ~ e nero** (TV, FOT) black and white; **mangiare in ~** to follow a bland diet; **pesce in ~** boiled fish; **andare in ~** (non riuscire) to fail; **~ dell'uovo** egg-white.

'lungo, a, ghi, ghe ag long; (lento: persona) slow; (diluito: caffè, brodo) weak, watery, thin ♦ sm length ♦ prep along; **~ 3 metri** 3 metres long; **a ~** for a long time; **a ~ andare** in the long run; **di gran ~a** (molto) by far; **andare in ~ o per le lunghe** to drag on; **saperla ~a** to know what's what; **in ~ e in largo** far and wide, all over; **~ il corso dei secoli** throughout the centuries.

sola'mente av only, just.

'solo, a ag alone; (in senso spirituale: isolato) lonely; (unico): **un ~ libro** only one book, a single book; (con ag numerale): **veniamo noi tre ~i** just o only the three of us are coming ♦ av (soltanto) only, just; **non ~ ... ma anche** not only .., but also; **fare qc da ~** to do sth (all) by oneself; **da me ~** single-handed, on my own.

attu'ale ag (presente) present; (di attualità) topical; (che è in atto) actual; **attualità** sf inv topicality; (avvenimento) current event; **attual'mente** av at the moment, at present.

309

Yet, although verbs are listed in your dictionary in their infinitive forms only, this does not mean that the dictionary is of limited value when it comes to handling the verb system of the Italian language. On the contrary, it contains much valuable information.

First of all, your dictionary will help you with the meanings of unfamiliar verbs. If you came across the word 'riempie' in a text and looked it up in your dictionary you wouldn't find it. You must deduce that it is part of a verb and look for the infinitive form. Thus you will see that 'riempie' is a form of the verb 'riempire'. You now have the basic meaning of the word you are concerned with — something to do with the English verb 'fill' — and this should be enough to help you understand the text you are reading.

It is usually an easy task to make the connection between the form of a verb and the infinitive. For example, 'riempiono', 'riempirò', 'riempissero' and 'riempii' are all recognisable as parts of the infinitive 'riempire'. However, sometimes it is less obvious — for example, 'vengo', 'vieni' and 'verrò' are all parts of 'venire'. The only real solution to this problem is to learn the various forms of the main Italian regular and irregular verbs.

And this is the second source of help offered by your dictionary. The verb tables on pages ix to x of the Collins Pocket Dictionary provide a summary of some of the main forms of the main tenses of regular and irregular verbs. Consider the verb 'venire' below where the following information is given:

2	venuto	— Past Participle
3	vengo, vieni, viene, vengono	— Present Tense forms
5	venni, venisti	— Past Tense forms
6	verrò *etc.*	— 1st Person Singular of the Future Tense
8	venga	— 1st, 2nd, 3rd Person of Present Subjunctive

The regular '-are' verb 'parlare' is presented in greater detail, as are the regular '-ire' and '-ere' verbs. The main tenses and the different endings are given in full. This information can be transferred and applied to all verbs in the list. In addition, the main parts of the most common irregular verbs are listed in the body of the dictionary.

PARLARE

1 parlando
2 parlato
3 parlo, parli, parla, parliamo, parlate, parlano
4 parlavo, parlavi, parlava, parlavamo, parlavate, parlavano
5 parlai, parlasti, parlò, parlammo, parlaste, parlarono
6 parlerò, parlerai, parlerà, parleremo, parlerete, parleranno
7 parlerei, parleresti, parlerebbe, parleremmo, parlereste, parlerebbero
8 parli, parli, parli, parliamo, parliate, parlino
9 parlassi, parlassi, parlasse, parlassimo, parlaste, parlassero
10 parla!, parli!, parlate!, parlino!

In order to make maximum use of the information contained in these pages, a good working knowledge of the various rules affecting Italian verbs is required. You will acquire this in the course of your Italian studies and your Collins dictionary will serve as a useful reminder. If you happen to forget how to form the second person singular form of the Future Tense of 'venire' there will be no need to panic — your dictionary contains the information!

WORDGAME 11
PARTS OF SPEECH

In each sentence below a word has been shaded. Put a tick in the appropriate box to indicate the **part of speech** each time. Remember, different parts of speech are indicated by lozenges within entries.

SENTENCE	Noun	Adj	Adv	Verb
1. Studia diritto a Roma.				
2. Parla più piano! Il bambino dorme.				
3. Ho già versato la minestra nel piatto.				
4. Ho spento il televisore prima della fine del film.				
5. Ha finto di andarsene ed è rimasto ad ascoltare.				
6. Non gli ho permesso di venire.				
7. Vuoi una fetta di dolce?				
8. Abbassi il volume, per favore? Così è troppo forte.				
9. Dopo la notizia sembrava molto scossa.				
10. Hanno assunto un capo del personale per la nostra sezione.				

WORDGAME 12
NOUNS

This list contains the feminine form of some Italian nouns. Use your dictionary to find the **masculine** form.

MASCULINE	FEMININE
	amica
	cantante
	direttrice
	straniera
	regista
	studentessa
	cugina
	lettrice
	professoressa
	collaboratrice

WORDGAME 13

MEANING CHANGES WITH GENDER

There are some pairs of Italian nouns which are distinguished only by their ending and gender, e.g. 'il partito' and 'la partita'. Fill in the blanks below with the appropriate member of each pair and the correct article — **'il, la, un'** etc — where an article is required.

1. L'ho scritto su _____ da qualche parte   foglio *or*
   Guarda! Sulla pianta è spuntata _____   foglia?

2. Non è questo _____ di fare le cose!   moda *or*
   È un colore che non va più di _____   modo?

3. È arrivato di _____   corso *or*
   Credo che mi iscriverò ad _____   corsa?
   di spagnolo

4. In questa zona ci sono tanti _____   castagne o.
   Ho comprato un sacchetto di _____   castagni?

5. Fammi vedere _____ della mano!   palma *or*
   Sedevano sulla spiaggia all'ombra   palmo?
   di _____

6. Ti va di fare _____ a tennis?   partito *or*
   _____ si sta preparando alle elezioni   partita?

7. Devo mettere _____ su questi pantaloni   pezzo *or*
   Vuoi _____ di torta?   pezza?

8. Per oggi basta lavorare! Vado a _____   caso *or*
   Ci siamo conosciuti per _____   casa?

314

WORDGAME 14

NOUN AND ADJECTIVE FORMS

Use your dictionary to find the following forms of these words.

MASCULINE	FEMININE
1. bianco	
2. fresco	
3. largo	
4. verde	
5. grave	

SINGULAR	PLURAL
6. poca	
7. giovane	
8. grande	
9. veloce	
10. poeta	
11. diadema	
12. triste	
13. tronco	
14. tromba	
15. dialogo	

WORDGAME 15

ADVERBS

Translate the following Italian adverbs into English. Put an asterisk next to those that don't appear in the Italian-English section of the Collins dictionary.

1. recentemente

2. redditiziamente

3. costantemente

4. gentilmente

5. mensilmente

6. naturalmente

7. aggressivamente

8. semplicemente

9. tenacemente

10. esattamente

WORDGAME 16

VERB TENSES

Use your dictionary to help you fill in the blanks in the table below. (Remember the important pages at the front of your dictionary.)

INFINITIVE	PRESENT TENSE	PAST PARTICIPLE	FUTURE
venire			io
rimanere			
vedere			io
avere	io		
offrire			
muovere			
finire	io		
uscire	io		
dovere			io
dormire			io
vivere			
potere	io		

PAST PARTICIPLES

Use the verb tables at the front of your dictionary to work out the past participle of these verbs. Check that you have found the correct form by looking in the main text.

INFINITIVE	PAST PARTICIPLE
venire	
contrarre	
coprire	
vivere	
offrire	
sorridere	
prendere	
mettere	
sorprendere	
percorrere	
accogliere	
dipingere	
condurre	
scendere	

WORDGAME 18

IDENTIFYING INFINITIVES

In the sentences below you will see various Italian verbs shaded. Use your dictionary to help you find the **infinitive** form of each verb.

1. Quand'ero a Londra dividevo un'appartamento con degli amici.

2. I miei amici mi raggiunsero in discoteca.

3. Sua madre lo accompagnava a scuola in macchina.

4. Domani mi alzerò alle nove.

5. Questo fine settimana andremo tutti in campagna.

6. Hanno già venduto la casa.

7. Entrò e si mise a sedere.

8. È nato in Germania.

9. Gli piacerebbe vivere negli Stati Uniti.

10. Faranno una partita a tennis.

11. Ha ricominciato a piovere.

12. Non so cosa gli sia successo.

13. Vorremmo visitare il castello.

14. I bambini avevano freddo.

15. Non so cosa sia meglio fare.

MORE ABOUT MEANING

In this section we will consider some of the problems associated with using a bilingual dictionary.

Overdependence on your dictionary

That the dictionary is an invaluable tool for the language learner is beyond dispute. Nevertheless, it is possible to become overdependent on your dictionary, turning to it in an almost automatic fashion every time you come up against a new Italian word or phrase. Tackling an unfamiliar text in this way will turn reading in Italian into an extremely tedious activity. If you stop to look up every new word you may actually be *hindering* your ability to read in Italian — you are so concerned with the individual words that you pay no attention to the text as a whole and to the context which gives them meaning. It is therefore important to develop appropriate reading skills — using clues such as titles, headlines, illustrations, etc, understanding relations within a sentence, etc to predict or infer what a text is about.

A detailed study of the development of reading skills is not within the scope of this supplement; we are concerned with knowing how to use a dictionary, which is only one of several important skills involved in reading. Nevertheless, it may be instructive to look at one example. You see the following text in an Italian newspaper and are interested in working out what it is about.

Contextual clues here include the words in large type which you would probably recognise as an Italian name, something that looks like a date in the middle, and the name and address in the bottom right-hand corner. The Italian words 'annunciare' and 'clinica' resemble closely the words 'announce' and 'clinic' in English, so you would not

> *Siamo lieti di annunciare*
> *la nascita di*
>
> # Mario, Francesco
>
> il 29 marzo 1988
>
> *Monica e Franco ROSSI*
> *Clinica*   corso Italia n° 18
> *del Sole*   34142 Padova

have to look them up in your dictionary. Other 'form' words such as 'siamo', 'la', 'il', and 'di' will be familiar to you from your general studies in Italian. Given that we are dealing with a newspaper, you will probably have worked ... by now that this could be an announcement placed in the 'Personal ... umn'.

So you have used a series of cultural, contextual and word-formation clues to get you to the point where you have understood that Monica and Franco Rossi have placed this notice in the 'Personal Column' of the newspaper and that something happened to Francesco on 29 March 1988, something connected with a hospital. And you have reached this point *without* opening your dictionary once. Common sense and your knowledge of newspaper contents in this country might suggest that this must be an announcement of someone's birth or death. Thus 'lieti' ('happy') and 'nascita' ('birth') become the only words that you might have to look up in order to confirm that this is indeed a birth announcement.

When learning Italian we are helped considerably by the fact that many Italian and English words look and sound alike and have exactly the same meaning. Such words are called 'COGNATES'. Many words which look similar in Italian and English come from a common Latin root. Other words are the same or nearly the same in both languages because Italian has borrowed a word from English or vice versa. The dictionary will often not be necessary where cognates are concerned — provided you know the English word that the Italian word resembles!

Words with more than one meaning

The need to examine with care *all* the information contained in a dictionary entry must be stressed. This is particularly important with the many Italian words which have more than one meaning. For example, the Italian 'giornale' can mean 'personal diary' as well as 'newspaper'. How you translated the word would depend on the context in which you found it.

Similarly, if you were trying to translate a phrase such as 'era in corso . . .', you would have to look through the whole entry for 'corso' to get the right translation. If you restricted your search to the first lines of the entry and saw that the meanings given are 'course' and 'main street', you might be tempted to assume that the phrase meant 'it was in the main street'. But if you examined the entry closely you would see that 'in corso' means 'in progress, under way'. So 'era in corso' means 'it was in progress', as in the phrase 'lavori in corso'.

The same need for care applies when you are using the English-Italian section of your dictionary to translate a word from English into Italian. Watch out in particular for the lozenges indicating changes in parts of speech.

The noun 'sink' is 'lavandino, acquaio', while the verb is 'affondare'. If you don't watch what you are doing, you could end up with ridiculous non-Italian e.g. 'Ha messo i piatti sporchi nell'affondare.'

Phrasal verbs

Another potential source of difficulty is English phrasal verbs. These consist of a common verb ('go', 'make', etc.) plus an adverb and/or a preposition to give English expressions such as 'to make out', 'to take after', etc. Entries for such verbs tend to be fairly full, so close examination of the contents is required. Note how these verbs appear in colour within the entry.

False friends

make [meɪk] (*pt, pp* **made**) *vt* fare; (*manufacture*) fare, fabbricare; (*cause to be*): **to ~ sb sad** *etc* rendere qn triste *etc*; (*force*): **to ~ sb do sth** costringere qn a fare qc, far fare qc a qn; (*equal*): **2 and 2 ~ 4** 2 più 2 fa 4 ♦ *n* fabbricazione *f*; (*brand*) marca; **to ~ a fool of sb** far fare a qn la figura dello scemo; **to ~ a profit** realizzare un profitto; **to ~ a loss** subire una perdita; **~ for** *vt fus* (*place*) avviarsi verso; **~ out** *vt* (*write out*) scrivere; (: *cheque*) emettere; (*understand*) capire; (*see*) distinguere; (: *numbers*) decifrare; **~ up** *vt* (*constitute*) formare; (*invent*) inventare; (*parcel*) fare ♦ *vi* conciliarsi; (*with cosmetics*) truccarsi; **~ up for** *vt fus* compensare; ricuperare; **~-believe** *n*: **a world of ~-**

Many Italian and English words have similar forms *and* meanings. Many Italian words, however, *look* like English words but have a completely *different* meaning. For example, 'attualmente' means 'at present'; 'eventuale' means 'possible'. This can easily lead to serious mistranslations.

Sometimes the meaning of the Italian word is *close* to the English. For example, 'la moneta' means 'small change' rather than 'money'; 'il soprannome' means 'nickname' not 'surname'. But some Italian words have two meanings, one the same as the English, the other completely different! 'L'editore' can mean 'publisher' as well as 'editor'; 'la marcia' can mean 'march/running/walking' but also 'the gear (of a car)'.

Such words are often referred to as 'false friends'. You will have to look at the context in which they appear to arrive at the correct meaning. If they seem to fit with the sense of the passage as a whole, you will probably not need to look them up. If they don't make sense, however, you may be dealing with 'false friends'.

WORDGAME 19

WORDS IN CONTEXT

Study the sentences below. Translations of the shaded words are given at the bottom. Match the number of the sentence and the letter of the translation correctly each time.

1. In questa zona è proibito cacciare.
2. L'ho visto cacciare i soldi in tasca.
3. È il ritratto di una dama del Settecento.
4. Facciamo una partita a dama?
5. Ha versato il vino nei bicchieri.
6. Hanno versato tutti i soldi sul loro conto.
7. Ti presento il mio fratello maggiore.
8. Aveva il grado di maggiore nell'esercito.
9. Ho finito i dadi per brodo.
10. In un angolo due uomini giocavano a dadi.
11. Sua madre è già partita per il mare.
12. Ti va di fare una partita a carte?
13. Il ladro è stato visto da un passante.
14. Devi infilare la cintura nel passante.
15. È corso verso di me.
16. Leggete ad alta voce il primo verso della poesia.

a. poured	e. loop	i. dice	m. passer-by
b. hunt	f. towards	j. major	n. draughts
c. left	g. paid	k. stock cubes	o. older
d. game	h. line	l. stick	p. lady

WORDGAME 20

WORDS WITH MORE THAN ONE MEANING

Look at the advertisements below. The words which are shaded can have more than one meaning. Use your dictionary to help you work out the correct translation in the context.

1

Desidero ricevere maggiori informazioni per un soggiorno al Lago di Garda

Nome e cognome: _____

Indirizzo: _____

2

Con il patrocinio della

REGIONE TOSCANA e CAMERA DI

COMMERCIO DELLA TOSCANA

3

TRILLO
LA SVEGLIA ELETTRONICA
CHE NON TI TRADISCE
4 funzioni: ore, minuti, secondi,
sveglia
Funzionamento a pile

4

ECONOMIA E
FINANZA
ORSA E FONDI

5

Albergo Ristorante

"La Cantina"

cucina casalinga

a 500 metri dalla piazza

6

SI PREGA DI RITIRARE LO SCONTRINO ALLA CASSA

7

Visite guidate al paese di Alassio

8

CASSA
rurale ed artigiana
Via Basovizza 2
Trieste

9

Una casa in riva al mare
"CALA DEI TEMPLARI"

Soggiorno, una camera da letto, bagno, balcone

10

PRATOLINI
la cucina su misura per te
Pratolini S.p.A. — 57480 Frascati — Roma
(0733) 5581 (10 linee) —
Telex 478192 PRATO I

WORDGAME 21
FALSE FRIENDS

Look at the advertisements below. The words which are shaded resemble English words but have different meanings here. Find a correct translation for each word in the context.

1

Boutique "La Moda"
Liquidazione di tutti gli articoli

2

Pensione Miramonti

camere con bagno/doccia
parcheggio privato
bar, ristorante

3

ACCENDERE LE LUCI IN GALLERIA

4

LIBRERIA
Il Gabbiano

Libri — Giornali — Articoli
spiaggia — Guide turistiche
— Cartoline

SASSARI
Via Mazzini 46

5

ITALMODA CRAVATTE

LE GRANDI FIRME
Divisione della BST,
Bergamo S.p.A

6

La direzione di questo albergo
declina ogni responsabilità per lo
smarrimento di oggetti lasciati
incustoditi

7

Questo esercizio resterà
chiuso nei giorni festivi
e il lunedì

8

"Le bollicine"
Locale notturno
— pianobar
— discoteca

9

Lago di Garda
camping, sport acquatici,
gite in battello

10

Attenzione: per l'uso leggere
attentamente l'istruzione
interna.
Da vendersi dietro
presentazione di ricetta medica.

HAVE FUN WITH YOUR DICTIONARY

Here are some word games for you to try. You will find your dictionary helpful as you attempt the activities.

WORDGAME 22

In the boxes below, the letters of eight Italian words have been replaced by numbers. A number represents the same letter each time.

Try to crack the code and find the eight words. If you need help, use your dictionary.

Here is a clue: all the words you are looking for have something to do with TRANSPORT.

1 | T¹ | R² | E³ | 4 | 5 |

2 | 6 | 7 | 8 | 9 | 5 | 4 |

3 | 4 | 7 | 10 | 3 |

4 | 7 | 11 | 1 | 5 | 12 | 11 | 16 |

5 | 1 | 2 | 7 | 13 | 14 | 3 | 1 | 1 | 5 |

6 | 8 | 5 | 1 | 5 | 6 | 9 | 6 | 15 | 3 | 1 | 1 | 7 |

7 | 12 | 7 | 2 | 6 | 7 |

8 | 7 | 11 | 1 | 5 | 8 | 5 | 12 | 9 | 15 | 3 |

WORDGAME 23

PAROLE DECAPITATE

If you 'behead' certain Italian words, i.e. take away their first letter, you are left with another Italian word. For example, if you behead **'maglio'** (= 'mallet'), you get **'aglio'** (= 'garlic').

The following words have their heads chopped off, i.e. the first letter has been removed. Use your dictionary to help you form a new Italian word by adding one letter to the start of each word below. Write down the new Italian word and its meaning. There may be more than one new word you can form.

1. arto (= limb)
2. alto (= high)
3. esca (= bait)
4. unto (= greasy)
5. ora (= hour)
6. acca (= letter H)
7. orale (= oral)
8. otto (= eight)
9. orda (= horde)
10. alone (= halo)
11. oca (= goose)
12. anca (= hip)
13. ascia (= axe)
14. anno (= year)
15. rete (= net)

WORDGAME 24

PAROLE INCROCIATE

Complete this crossword by looking up the words listed below in the English-Italian section of your dictionary. Remember to read through the entry carefully to find the word that will fit.

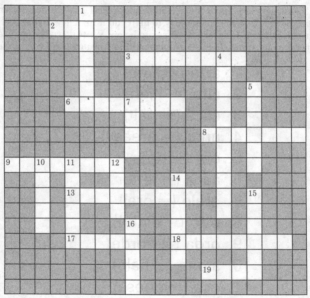

1 (a piece of) news	5 story	10 rough	15 adder
2 to dirty	6 relationship	11 swarm	16 harbour
3 to admire	7 porthole	12 air	17 ebony
4 to reassure	8 deposit	13 employ	18 to take off
	9 strip	14 sad	19 night